lonely planet

Thailand

Chiang Mai Province p309

Northern Thailand p203

Northeastern Thailand p367

Central Thailand p165

Bangkok & Around p67

Ko Chang & the Eastern Seaboard p449

Hua Hin & the Upper Gulf p491

Phuket & the Andaman Coast p595

Ko Samui & the Lower Gulf p525

David Eimer, Anirban Mahapatra, Daniel McCrohan, Tim Bewer,
Paul Harding, Ashley Harrell, Tharik Hussain, Michael Kohn,
Olivia Pozzan, Barbara Woolsey

Contents

INCENSE STICKS

GABRIEL PEREZ / GETTY IMAGES ©

DAMNOEN SADUAK
FLOATING MARKET P154

TUUL & BRUNO MORANDI / GETTY IMAGES ©

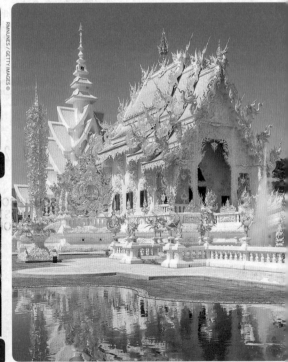

RM.NUNES / GETTY IMAGES ©

Contents

WAT RONG KHUN P214

COVID-19

We have re-checked every business in this book before publication to ensure that it is still open after the COVID-19 outbreak. However, the economic and social impacts of COVID-19 will continue to be felt long after the outbreak has been contained, and many businesses, services and events referenced in this guide may experience ongoing restrictions. Some businesses may be temporarily closed, have changed their opening hours and services, or require bookings; some unfortunately could have closed permanently. We suggest you check with venues before visiting for the latest information.

ON THE ROAD

SÔM.ĐAM (THAI PAPAYA
SALAD) P52

SONGKRAN RITUALS P333,
CHIANG MAI

Contents

RICE PADDIES, CHIANG MAI
PROVINCE P309

Right: Ao Phang-Nga
Marine National Park
(p616)

BENTO FOTOGRAPHY/GETTY IMAGES ©

WELCOME TO
Thailand

Thailand inspires insatiable obsessions with travel. There's something for every stripe of explorer in the dynamic capital or across remote mountaintops and

seascapes. Adventures here are intense but visceral and euphoric; whether temple-hopping around ancient ruins, embarking on sweaty jungle treks, squeezing through night markets or into Bangkok's underground parties. Intertwined are ample opportunities for true relaxation or retrospection: white-sand beaches, pulverising massages and Buddhist rituals. And you can eat well here! Thailand's street food and restaurants are renowned for satisfaction, flavour and prices for every pocketbook – plus service with a smile.

By Barbara Woolsey, Writer
🐦 @barbarawoolsey 📷 @barbara.woolsey
For more about our writers, see p800.

Thailand

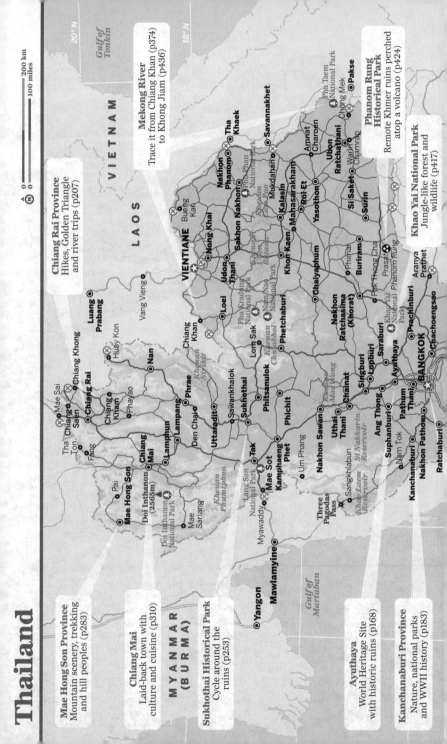

Mae Hong Son Province
Mountain scenery, trekking and hill peoples (p283)

Chiang Mai
Laid-back town with culture and cuisine (p310)

MYANMAR (BURMA)

Sukhothai Historical Park
Cycle around the ruins (p253)

Chiang Rai Province
Hikes, Golden Triangle and river trips (p207)

Mekong River
Trace it from Chiang Khan (p374) to Khong Jiam (p436)

Phanom Rung Historical Park
Remote Khmer ruins perched atop a volcano (p424)

Khao Yai National Park
Jungle-like forest and wildlife (p417)

Ayutthaya
World Heritage Site with historic ruins (p168)

Kanchanaburi Province
Nature, national parks and WWII history (p183)

VIETNAM

LAOS

0   100 miles
0   200 km

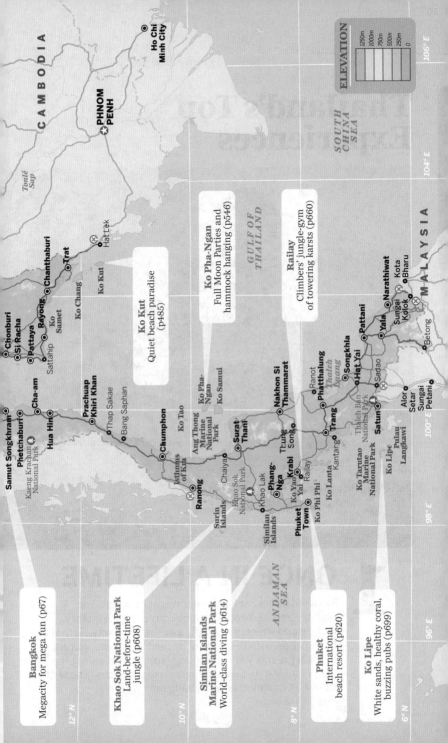

ELEVATION

1250m
1000m
750m
500m
250m
0

CAMBODIA

★ PHNOM PENH

Tonlé Sap

⊚ Ho Chi Minh City

SOUTH CHINA SEA

GULF OF THAILAND

ANDAMAN SEA

MALAYSIA

Bangkok
Megacity for mega fun (p67)

Khao Sok National Park
Land-before-time jungle (p608)

Similan Islands Marine National Park
World-class diving (p614)

Phuket
International beach resort (p620)

Ko Lipe
White sands, healthy coral, buzzing pubs (p699)

Ko Kut
Quiet beach paradise (p485)

Ko Pha-Ngan
Full Moon Parties and hammock hanging (p546)

Railay
Climbers' jungle-gym of towering karsts (p660)

Hat Lek ⊗

Trat
Chanthaburi
Rayong
Ko Chang
Ko Kut
Ko Samet
Chonburi
Si Racha
Pattaya
Sattahip

Samut Songkhram
Phetchaburi
Cha-am
Hua Hin
Kaeng Krachan National Park
Prachuap Khiri Khan
Thap Sakae
Bang Saphan

Chumphon
Isthmus of Kra
Ko Tao

Ranong ⊗
Chaiya
Khao Sok National Park
Khao Lak
Surin Islands
Simlan Islands

Ang Thong Marine National Park
Ko Pha-Ngan
Ko Samui
Surat Thani
Ttung Song
Nakhon Si Thammarat

Phang-Nga
Ko Yao Yai
Phuket Town
Railay
Ko Phi Phi
Krabi
Ko Lanta
Kantang
Trang
Thaleh Ban National Park
Ko Tarutao Marine National Park
Ko Lipe
Pulau Langkawi
Satun ⊗
Alor Setar
Sungai Petani

Ranot
Phatthalung
Thaleh Luang
Songkhla
Hat Yai
Sadao ⊗

Pattani
Yala
Betong
Narathiwat
Sungai Kolok ⊗
Kota Bharu

106° E
104° E
100° E
98° E
96° E

12° N
10° N
8° N
6° N

Thailand's Top Experiences

1 ONCE IN A LIFETIME

Thailand offers aspirational travel at its finest. The country and its diverse destinations combine history, culture and scenery in a truly awe-inspiring way. Sprawling landscapes, with the ruins of ancient kingdoms, vibrant tropical greenery and charming remote villages, set the stage for life-changing, immersive experiences. These are the kind of memories you'll hang onto forever.

Above: Phang-Nga (p605)

Follow the Mekong River

Northeastern Thailand's glorious arc of the Mekong River offers an smorgasbord of culture and beauty. Chase the meandering river aboard a rickety bus, long-tail boat or even a bicycle. Those who follow this little-visited trail are rewarded with true tales to tell.

Right: Amphawa Floating Market (p154), Mekong River

Sukhothai

Step back some 800 years in time at one of Thailand's most impressive and formative historical parks. Exploring the ruins of this former capital by bicycle is a leisurely way to wind through the crumbling temples, graceful Buddha statues and fish-filled ponds. p253

Above left: Sukhothai Historical Park

Trekking in Chiang Rai

Chiang Rai is arguably Thailand's most beautiful province. Formerly the Thai extension of the notorious Golden Triangle region, and once home to opium fields aplenty, Chiang Rai now draws visitors for wholesome fresh-air fun. Hiking and treks to minority villages is a wonderful experience, plus it's a convenient gateway to Myanmar and Laos. p207

Above right: Doi Mae Salong (p218), Chang Rai Province

2 NATURE'S TREASURES

Thailand is home to 127 national parks, including 22 marine parks. The options for outdoor adventures from peak to coast are endless: wildlife spotting, rafting, ziplining and canoeing, always accompanied by the backdrop of lush tropical jungle interiors. Hiking past silvery waterfalls and clambering into caves build stamina and a sense of wonder. Accommodation ranges from pitching a tent to tree-top bungalows, traditional homestays and lavish resorts.

Khao Yai National Park

Khao Yai is home to elephants, monkeys, gibbons, hornbills, pythons, bears, a million bats and even a few wily tigers. Your odds of a wildlife sighting are excellent at this reserve just a few hours from Bangkok. The orchids, birds and waterfalls round out the adventure. p417

Below: Nam Tok Haew Suwat waterfall

Khao Sok National Park

This ancient rainforest (pictured above left) is filled with long hiking routes up dramatic limestone formations that pay off with breath-taking views. Birds and bats call this forest home, as does the rare *Rafflesia kerrii*, one of the world's largest and stinkiest flowers. p608

Above left: Kayaking, Chiaw Lan Lake

Mae Hong Son Province

This province has more in common with Myanmar than anywhere else in Thailand. With its remote location, soaring mountains and unique culture, Mae Hong Son seems like a different country. Tramp through one of four national parks, explore on your motorcycle or do a self-guided trek. p283

Above right: Pai Canyon

BEACH BLISS

Southern Thailand has the celebrity beaches, but the eastern seaboard also has a couple of coastal spots worth checking out. Both regions encompass a mix of beach-party action and remote beaches with a more tranquil, low-key vibe – duplicity that's hard to beat. As if lounging on velvety sands isn't enough, top-class spas, beachside massages and yoga and meditation retreats add an extra layer of de-stressing.

TUUL & BRUNO MORANDI/GETTY IMAGES ©

RAZVAN CIUCA/GETTY IMAGES ©

RONEMMONS/SHUTTERSTOCK ©

Railay

At the tip of the Krabi peninsula are some of Thailand's most famous beachy features: the soaring limestone karsts of Railay, anchored in the ocean. Visitors arrive by long-tail boat to lounge, swim, dive or rock-climb. Some get good enough to climb rope-free then fall harmlessly into the cobalt sea. p660

Above left: Hat Tham Phra Nang

Ko Lanta

A beach bum's best friend, Ko Lanta (pictured top right) sports a mellow island vibe and a parade of peachy sand. Social butterflies alight on the northern beaches for the party scene. Solitude-seekers migrate southwards to low-key beach huts and a sleepy village ambience. p674

Ko Chang

This island (pictured bottom right) offers top-notch resorts and spas, several escape-from-it-all guesthouses where the only facility is a hammock, and jaw-droppingly good sunsets. A long line of enticing beaches ranges from backpacker focused to family-friendly. p474

4 SIZZLING STREET FOOD

The intense, multidimensional flavours of Thai food are reason to fall in love. Eating well is super delicious, remarkably convenient and well-priced. Dishes (and doses of chilli heat) range according to the region; every auntie has her own curry recipe that is rich and pungent. Savour the luscious tropical fruits in vendors' glass cases, sliced and diced for just a few baht, plus all the grilled seafood delights.

Discovering Isan Food

The northeast's triumvirate of dishes – *gài yâhng* (grilled chicken; pictured below left), *sôm·đam* (spicy green papaya salad) and *kôw něe·o* (sticky rice) – are among Thailand's spiciest and most delicious. p379

YAOWALAK RAHUNG/SHUTTERSTOCK ©

Feeding Frenzy in Chinatown

Yaowarat Road (pictured top right), Bangkok's modern Chinatown, is perfect for a foodie crawl: visit the Thanon Phadungdao Seafood Stalls and Jek Pui, famous for its Thai-Chinese curries. p125

Gourmet Street Food

Jay Fai (pictured bottom right) cooks Bangkok's tastiest crab omelettes – she even has a Michelin star. Look for the crowds outside her little kitchen, and the chef herself wearing ski goggles and red lipstick. p120

5 TEMPLE-HOPPING

BAMGRAPHY/SHUTTERSTOCK ©

IPHOTO-THAILAND/SHUTTERSTOCK ©

DEVIN TOLLESON/SHUTTERSTOCK ©

Exploring glittering Buddhist temples, golden shrines and ancient Khmer sanctuaries is an important part of discovering Thailand's past, but also its present and future. Buddhist traditions are interwoven into everyday life, from daily almsgiving to politics. At temples, you'll see Thais building karma with offerings of gold leaf and candles plus earnest prayer – and while these places of worship are architecturally stunning, it's these moments that make the experience.

Chiang Mai

The cultural capital of the north, Chiang Mai is jam-packed with temples from the once independent Lanna kingdom. These and the area's winding side roads are best explored by bicycle. p310

Above: Wat Phra That Doi Suthep (p325)

Ayuthaya

Ayuthaya, the second capital of Siam from the 14th to the 18th century, now holds a certain mystique. Cycle around the brick-and-stucco temple ruins forming part of a Unesco World Heritage Site. p168

Phanom Rung Historical Park

Perched high atop an extinct volcano, Thailand's most impressive Khmer ruin is something special. While not as awesome as Cambodia's Angkor Wat, it's unique enough to consider visiting both. p424

6 DREAM DIVES

Thailand is among the world's top dive sites with warm and clear seas. Opportunities abound to see manta rays, whale sharks and other large pelagic fish. Above the waterline, the islands are an attraction in their own right, with jungle-filled interiors, limestone cliffs and crags, and smooth white beaches surrounded by coral reefs. Here you can truly get off the beaten track.

METHASIT9/SHUTTERSTOCK ©

RAINAN DENBEN/SHUTTERSTOCK ©

Surin & Similan Islands National Marine Parks

Surin (p606) and Similan (pictured top left) have dramatic rocky gorges, hard and soft coral reefs and plenty of marine life. p614

Ko Lipe

Dive sites with healthy coral, a deep pinnacle and good visibility in the early rainy season. Ko Lipe (pictured below left) takes work to reach but a burgeoning band of devotees agree it's worth it. p699

Ko Tao

With abundant dive schools, shallow waters and year-round conditions, Ko Tao (pictured above right) remains the country's dive-training headquarters. p564

7 PARTY HEARTY

Ko Pha-Ngan

Famous for its techno-fuelled Full Moon Parties, Ko Pha-Ngan has graduated from a sleepy bohemian island to Asia's Ibiza.

Top left: Hat Rin (p546)

Pai

Pai's party scene combines an old-school hippie vibe and beautiful mountain scenery. Backpackers love the reggae shows at open-air bars and VW vans. p283

Bangkok's Rooftop Bars

The City of Angels lives up to its name thanks to rooftop bars overlooking the street chaos with calm. It tends to stay chill up here but can escalate quickly with a pool or good DJ involved.

Bottom left: Park Society bar (p138)

If you're looking to drink, dance and be merry, you've come to the right place. Thailand's party circuit is well-varied; from fancy nightclubs and sky bars in Bangkok and resort towns to down-home backpacker bars and sand-covered dancefloors. Live music is especially big here – look out for acoustic guitar seshes, reggae gigs and DJ extravaganzas. Sips range from serious cocktails to buckets of Red Bull and vodka liable for almighty hangovers.

8 MARKET MADNESS

Shopping sprees at Thai markets are thrilling. The experience can be exhilarating and atmospheric; from the buzzy crowds to buskers and sheer purchase power: street food, drinks, clothing, antiques and all kinds of curio for fabulous prices. You mostly can't try garments on, but some finds are worth the risk. Besides, haggling itself is an art form and an adrenaline rush!

Chatuchak Weekend Market

Among the world's largest open-air markets, Chatuchak (also referred to as 'Jatujak' or 'JJ'; pictured below left) in Bangkok is a labyrinth of eclectic what-nots. Buy now – you may not find the stand again! p150

Cicada

One of Thailand's most unique, non-traditional markets, Cicada (pictured top right) on Hua Hin's outskirts is full of young artisans selling handmade wares. Live entertainment and a good food court up the ante. p501

Khon Kaen Walking Street Market

Khon Kaen's weekend bazaar (pictured bottom right) isn't touristy at all. Hundreds of vendors take over, buskers abound and Chinese-style lanterns create a charming ambience. p439

9 FAR OUT FESTIVALS

TAKE PHOTO/SHUTTERSTOCK ©

You can't go too far in Thailand without finding a festival that involves eating, partying or parading. The biggest, most widely-celebrated festivals are Buddhist holidays like the five-day Thai New Year, but Thailand is also known for excellent jazz and electronic music blowouts. On the quirkier side, rural towns hold fruit festivals – in Chiang Rai, the lychee is revered, while Chanthaburi celebrates the world's stinkiest fruit, the durian.

Songkran

Thailand's New Year festival in April is about using water to cleanse and show respect in temples. Once that's done, water fights erupt on the streets! p30

Loi Krathong

Every November, Thais pray for forgiveness by setting lanterns afloat on waterways. The tradition is especially beloved by families and young Thai lovebirds. p32

Above: Loi Krathong festival, Chiang Mai (p333)

Vegetarian Festivals

Vegetarian festivals are marked across Thailand in October; Phuket's is famous (p623). Locals of Chinese ancestry celebrate the start of a meat-free diet for 10 days of spiritual cleansing. p32

Need to Know

For more information, see Survival Guide (p751)

Currency
Thai baht (B)

Language
Thai

Visas
For visitors from 64 countries, visas are not required for stays of up to 30 days.

Money
Most places in Thailand only accept cash. Foreign credit cards are accepted by some travel agents, and in some upmarket hotels, restaurants, shopping malls and stores.

Mobile Phones
The easiest option for making calls in Thailand is to buy a local SIM card. Make sure that your mobile phone is unlocked before travelling.

Time
GMT plus seven hours

When to Go

Mae Hong Son
GO Nov–Mar

Chiang Mai
GO Nov–Feb

BANGKOK
GO Nov–Feb

Ko Samui
GO Dec–Aug

Phuket
GO Oct–Apr

■ Tropical climate, rain year-round

■ Tropical climate, wet & dry seasons

High Season
(Nov–Mar)

➡ A cool and dry season follows the monsoons, meaning the landscape is lush and temperatures are comfortable.

➡ Christmas and the western New Year holidays bring crowds and inflated rates.

Shoulder Season (Apr–Jun, Sep & Oct)

➡ April to June is generally very hot and dry, with an average Bangkok temperature of 30°C. Sea breezes cool coastal areas.

➡ In September and October, the gulf coast islands are your best bet for avoiding rain.

Low Season
(Jul–Oct)

➡ Monsoon season ranges from afternoon showers to major flooding. Rain is usually in short, intense bursts.

➡ Some islands shut down; boat service is limited during stormy weather. Be flexible with travel plans.

Useful Websites

Thaivisa (www.thaivisa.com) Expat site for news and discussions.

Richard Barrow (www.richard barrow.com) Prolific blogger and tweeter focusing on Thai travel.

Tourism Authority of Thailand (TAT; www.tourismthailand.org) National tourism department covering info and special events.

Thai Language (www.thai language.com) Online dictionary and Thai tutorials.

Lonely Planet (lonely planet.com/thailand) Destination information, hotel bookings, traveller forum and more.

Important Numbers

Thailand's country code	☏66
Emergency	☏191
International access codes	☏001, ☏007, ☏008, ☏009 (& other promotional codes)
Operator-assisted international calls	☏100
Tourist police	☏1155

Exchange Rates

Australia	A$1	20B
Canada	C$1	23B
China	Y10	42B
Euro	€1	33B
Japan	¥100	27B
New Zealand	NZ$1	19B
South Korea	1000W	25B
UK	£1	38B
US	US$1	30B

For current exchange rates see www.xe.com.

Daily Costs

Budget: Less than 1000B

➡ Basic guesthouse room: 500–1000B

➡ Market/street stall meal: 40–100B

➡ Small bottle of beer: 100B

➡ Public transport around town: 20–50B

Midrange: 1000–4000B

➡ Flashpacker guesthouse or midrange hotel room: 1000–4000B

➡ Western lunches and seafood dinner: 150–350B

➡ Organised tour or activity: 1000–1500B

➡ Motorbike hire: 150–250B

Top end: More than 4000B

➡ Boutique hotel room: 4000B

➡ Meal at fine-dining restaurant: 350–1000B

➡ Private tours: 2000B

➡ Car hire: from 900B per day

Opening Hours

Banks and government offices close for national holidays. Some bars and clubs close during elections and certain religious holidays when alcohol sales are banned. Shopping centres have banks that open late.

Banks 8.30am–4.30pm Monday to Friday; ATMs 24hr

Bars 6pm–midnight or 1am

Clubs 8pm–2am

Government offices 8.30am–4.30pm Monday to Friday; some close for lunch

Restaurants 8am–10pm

Shops 10am–7pm

Arriving in Thailand

Suvarnabhumi International Airport (Bangkok) The Airport Rail Link (45B, 30 minutes) runs to Phaya Thai station, buses run to Th Khao San (60B, 1 hour) and metered taxis (250B to 400B, 1 hour) run 24 hours.

Don Mueang International Airport (Bangkok) Four bus lines run into Bangkok, including one to Th Khao San (50B, 1 hour), metered taxis (250B to 400B, 1 hour) run 24 hours, and a free shuttle bus (1 hour) runs to Suvarnabhumi.

Chiang Mai International Airport Taxis (150B, 15 minutes) to the city centre run 24 hours.

Phuket International Airport Buses (100B, 1 hour) run to Phuket Town, metered taxis (500B to 700B, 30 minutes to 1 hour) and minivans (200B to 300B, up to 2 hours) run to the beaches and Phuket Town.

Safe Travel

Thailand is generally a safe country to visit, but it's smart to exercise caution, especially when it comes to dealing with strangers (both Thais and foreigners) and travelling alone.

Assault of travellers is relatively rare in Thailand, but it does happen.

Possession of drugs can result in a year or more of prison time. Drug smuggling carries considerably higher penalties, including execution.

Disregard all offers of free shopping or sightseeing help from strangers. These are scams that invariably take a commission from your purchases.

For much more on **getting around**, see p769

First Time Thailand

For more information, see Survival Guide (p751)

Checklist

➡ Ensure your passport is valid for at least six months.

➡ Apply for a tourist visa from a Thai consulate for visits longer than 30 days.

➡ Organise travel insurance, diver's insurance and international driving permit (IDP).

➡ Visit your doctor for a check-up and medical clearance if intending to dive.

➡ Inform your bank and credit-card company of your travel plans.

What to Pack

➡ Driving licence and international driving permit (IDP)

➡ Thai phrasebook

➡ GSM mobile phone and charger

➡ Hat and sunglasses

➡ Sandals

➡ Earplugs

➡ Rain-gear and dry bag if travelling in the rainy season

Top Tips for Your Trip

➡ Eat at markets or street stalls for true Thai flavour.

➡ Hop aboard local transport – it's cheap and a great way to hang out with the locals.

➡ Hire a bicycle to tour towns and neighbourhoods.

➡ Memorise a few Thai phrases and always smile.

➡ Dodge the first-timer scams: one-day gem sales in Bangkok, insanely low (or high) transport prices, pushy tailors etc.

➡ Learn how to bargain without being a jerk.

➡ Avoid touching Thai people on the head.

➡ Don't point with your feet.

➡ Dress conservatively (don't expose your shoulders or too much leg) and remove your shoes when visiting Buddhist temples.

➡ Steer clear of politics and don't make disparaging remarks about any member of Thailand's royal family; it's illegal.

What to Wear

In general, light, loose-fitting clothes will prove the most comfortable in the tropical heat. It's worth bringing one jacket that can double as a raincoat and keep you warm in higher elevations. When you visit temples, wear clothes that cover to your elbows and knees. Bring something smart if you plan on fine dining or clubbing in Bangkok or Phuket.

Sleeping

Finding a place to stay in Thailand is easy. For peace of mind, book a room for your first few nights; after that, you can wing it unless you're heading to popular destinations.

Guesthouses Family-run options are the best. Rooms run from basic (bed and fan) to plush (private bathroom and air-con).

Hotels From boutique to business, hotels offer mostly modern rooms and sometimes a swimming pool.

Hostels Just as the standard of guesthouses has improved, hostels have become more modern and stylish.

Money

Most places in Thailand only accept cash. Foreign credit cards are accepted by some travel agents and in some upmarket hotels, restaurants, shopping malls and stores.

For more information, see p759.

Bargaining

Thais respect a good haggler. Always let the vendor make the first offer, then ask 'Can you lower the price?'. This usually results in a discount. Now it's your turn to make a counteroffer. Always start low, but don't bargain unless you're serious about buying. If you're buying several of an item, you have much more leverage to request and receive a lower price. It helps immeasurably to keep the negotiations relaxed and friendly.

Tipping

Tipping is not generally expected in Thailand, though it is appreciated. The exception is loose change from a large restaurant bill – if a meal costs 488B and you pay with a 500B note, some Thais will leave the change. It's a way of saying 'I'm not so money grubbing as to grab every last baht'. At many hotel restaurants and more upmarket eateries, a 10% service charge will be added to your bill.

Language

Tourist towns are well stocked with English speakers, though bus drivers, market vendors and taxi drivers are less fluent, so it helps to know how to order food and count in Thai.

Thailand has its own script. Street signs are transliterated into English, but there is no standard system so spellings vary widely. Not all letters are pronounced as they appear ('Ph' is an aspirated 'p' not an 'f').

Etiquette

Thais are generally very understanding and hospitable, but there are some important taboos and social conventions.

Monarchy It is a criminal offence to disrespect the royal family; treat objects depicting the king (like money) with respect.

Temples Wear clothing that covers to your knees and elbows. Remove all footwear before entering. Sit with your feet tucked behind you, so they are not facing the Buddha image. Women should never touch a monk or a monk's belongings; step out of the way on footpaths and don't sit next to them on public transport.

Modesty At the beach, avoid public nudity or topless sunbathing. Cover-up going to and from the beach.

Body language Avoid touching anyone on the head and be careful where you point your feet; they're the lowest part of the body literally and metaphorically.

Saving face The best way to win over Thais is to smile – visible anger or arguing is seen as embarrassing.

Eating

Thailand's eateries span the entire spectrum. Booking is only necessary at a handful of the country's most acclaimed restaurants.

Street stalls The most ubiquitous source of prepared food in Thailand, street stalls can be found just about anywhere, at any time of day or night.

Shophouse restaurants A step up, in terms of comfort and price, from the street stalls, these semi-outdoor eateries serve some of the best food in the country.

Restaurants Thailand's restaurant scene is vast and varied, in terms of cuisine, amenities and price..

What's New

Here's the lowdown on what's new and happening in Thailand. Visitors now have the chance to experience an elephant-friendly reserve, as well as Thailand's first beachfront shopping mall, while new trains and buses will make getting around the country even easier

Ethical Elephant Experience

ChangChill (p324) is the only elephant reserve in Northern Thailand to be designated elephant-friendly by World Animal Protection. Guests spend their time watching the elephants from an observation deck, learning about their behaviour, gathering food for them and chatting with mahouts.

Beachfront Shopping Mall

Thailand's first beachfront shopping mall has opened in Hua Hin and is proving a hit with both locals and visitors. Seenspace (p508) features a trendy layout of concrete walls and open-air areas, all home to restaurants, shops, a beach club and a boutique hotel.

Beach Cleanups

Trash Heroes (https://trashhero.org) is a growing initiative around Thailand's beaches, with volunteers picking up rubbish across Phuket, Ko Samui, Ko Chang and most other major beaches and islands.

LOCAL KNOWLEDGE

WHAT'S HAPPENING IN THAILAND

Barbara Woolsey and David Eimer, Lonely Planet Writers

Throughout 2020 and into 2021, Bangkok was the site of frequent political protests largely organised and led by students. The so-called pro-democracy movement has seen thousands of Thais taking to the capital's streets and social media, many symbolically holding up the three-finger salute from *The Hunger Games* film as a show of unity.

The protesters are calling for a new constitution and monarchy reform. In 2019 a much-delayed election saw prime minister Prayut Chan-o-cha, the former junta leader, confirmed as the head of a coalition government, while King Maha Vajiralongkorn, also known as Rama X, was crowned in a three-day ceremony in Bangkok.

The protests have mostly been peaceful, but reveal a country that remains politically polarised with people in the north and northeast of Thailand remaining loyal to the party of the exiled former prime minister Thaksin Shinawatra, while Prayut's supporters can be found among the traditional elite, the urban middle classes and voters in the south of the country.

A massive gap between the rich and poor – in 2018 Thailand was officially ranked as the world's most unequal country – is the principal reason for that political divide. There is also an increasing awareness of the environmental challenges facing Thailand, with rising levels of air pollution in the big cities and the impact of tourism on beaches and coastlines a particular concern.

Visa Exemption Program Expanded

Thailand's Visa Exemption Rule has expanded to cover 64 countries. If you hold a passport from one of those countries you can now stay for up to 30 days, whether you arrive by air, land or sea.

Singha Nakhon

It's not new but it's worth making tracks for tracks for Singha Nakhon. It's a history buff's dream, with ancient walls, forgotten tombs and decaying, jungle-covered military forts scattered across the shores of Songkhla Lake.

Bangkok SkyWalk

Perched atop Thailand's tallest building, SkyWalk at King Power Mahanakhon (p85) offers an unparalleled and nerve-jangling 360-degree view of the Bangkok cityscape. The glass-floored balcony hangs 78 floors above the earth.

Better Train Travel

The State Railway of Thailand (p771) is slated to open Southeast Asia's largest railway station in 2021. The shiny new Bang Sue Grand Station in northern Bangkok is expected to cure some of the capital's traffic congestion and make cross-country travel even easier with new trains. With 26 platforms across four storeys, Bang Sue will accommodate up to 600,000 passengers daily – retiring its century-old predecessor, the grand dame station Hua Lamphong (p156), into a museum.

Phuket Smart Bus

The Phuket Smart Bus (p625) travels from Phuket's airport down the west coast to Rawai, making stops at the beaches. A three-day unlimited pass is available for 500B.

Paddleboarding in Kanchanaburi

It is now possible to travel Mae Nam Kwae Yai and other rivers in Kanchanaburi by

standup paddleboard (p187), a new way to see some of the most stunning scenery in Thailand.

Bangkok Duty Free

There's no need to wait until your flight home to do your duty-free shopping – just head to King Power Mahanakhon (p147), four floors of excise-free goodies. You can even claim VAT refunds here.

LISTEN, WATCH AND FOLLOW

For inspiration and up-to-date news, visit www.lonelyplanet.com/thailand/travel-tips-and-articles.

twitter.com/thailandfanclub Official Twitter account for Tourism Authority of Thailand (@ThailandFanClub).

twitter.com/bangkokpostnews Official Twitter account for the English-language *Bangkok Post* newspaper (@BangkokPostNews).

instagram@thailandluxe Stunning images from across Thailand.

The Bangkok Podcast (www.bangkokpodcast.com) Podcast in English covering all that is weird and wonderful about Thailand's capital.

FAST FACTS

Food Trend High-end regional Thai restaurants

Number of islands in Thailand 1430

Number of languages spoken in Thailand 74

Pop 69.3 million

THAILAND   USA

≈ 35 people per sq km

Accommodation

Find more accommodation reviews throughout the On the Road chapters (from p65)

Accommodation Types

➡ **Guesthouses** Family-run options are the best. In smaller destinations some guesthouses can be old-school and basic, with shared bathrooms and ancient fans, but private en-suite facilities, air-con and a TV are now the norm in most places.

➡ **Hotels** Thailand has a wide choice of hotels, most offering modern rooms. Budget and mid-range chain hotels are available across the country, while boutique places congregate in Bangkok and Chiang Mai especially. International-class four- and five-star hotels can be found in the big cities and the high-end beach destinations.

➡ **Hostels** European-style hostels are often the best budget option in big cities and on expensive islands. Many of the newer ones share a common design theme of smooth concrete walls and floors and a vague industrial-chic look. Communal activities are normally on offer.

➡ **Homestays** A less-commercial budget option, mostly found in rural areas, where you stay in a family home with food included in the price.

➡ **National Parks Accommodation** Most national parks have bungalows and/or campsites to stay in. Bungalows are often basic – no wi-fi. Tents and camping gear can often be hired.

Price Ranges
Big Cities & Beach Resorts

The following price ranges refer to a double room with private bathroom and are the high-season walk-in rates.

$ less than 1000B

$$ 1000–4000B

$$$ more than 4000B

Elsewhere

The following price ranges refer to a double room with private bathroom and are the high-season walk-in rates.

$ less than 600B

$$ 600–1500B

$$$ more than 1500B

Best Places to Stay
Best on a Budget

Thailand has a huge range of budget accommodation, from hostels to guesthouses via old-school hotels. Hostels can be found everywhere, but are especially prevalent in the most popular city destinations. Budget guesthouses are spread across the country, too. You're most likely to find bargain-rate hotels in towns off the tourist trail.

➡ Infinity Beach Hostel (p554) Great-value hostel metres from the beach on Ko Pha-Ngan.

➡ Chern (p103) Big dorms and the private rooms are a steal for Bangkok.

➡ Pak-Up Hostel (p657) Krabi Town's most popular hostel features comfortable dorms.

➡ Paradise Cottage (p481) Well-run and relaxing retreat on Ko Chang's Lonely Beach.

➡ Riverside Guest House (p249) Charming traditional wooden house on the river in Lampang.

➡ Nok Chan Mee Na (p365) Pristine and comfortable bungalows set in a photogenic rice paddy.

Best for Families

Thailand is a supremely child-friendly destination and families are welcomed everywhere. But the best family-orientated places are located on the islands – Phuket, Ko Samui, Ko Lanta, Ko Chang especially – or along the mainland's beaches. The region south of Hua Hin is very popular with families. Swimming pools and other entertainment options are less available in more remote areas.

➡ Samui Jasmine Resort (p535) Kiddies pool, babysitting and creche services at this beachfront place on Ko Samui.

➡ The Sands (p613) Khao Lak resort with a terrific water park, multiple pools and playgrounds.

➡ Dolphin Bay Resort (p512) This Pranburi place has holiday-camp ambience, and the beach is across the road.

➡ Phi-Phi Island Village (p671) A self-contained world of its own, by a blissful white-sand beach on Ko Phi-Phi.

➡ Fern Resort (p298) Long-standing Mae Hong Son favourite with swimming pools, nature trails and a huge garden to play in.

➡ Awana House (p335) The staff at this Chiang Mai guesthouse go the extra mile for kids.

Best for Solo Travellers

So many visitors are passing through Thailand at any one time that solo travellers who want to stay solitary may find it difficult to do so. Hostels on the islands and in key mainland destinations like Bangkok, Chiang Mai and Pai arrange tours and daily events, while some guesthouses organise nightly dinners where people can meet and socialise.

➡ Common Grounds (p285) Pai's most social and party-friendly hostel.

➡ The Chic Lipe (p701) Boutique hostel on Ko Lipe with a restaurant, bar and library.

➡ Sri Pat Guest House (p334) Stand-out flashpacker place in Chiang Mai.

➡ BB Lonely Beach (p481) Backpacker hangout on Ko Chang's party beach.

➡ Lub d (p113) A bar and plenty of games to play at this fun Bangkok hostel.

➡ King's Home (p505) Family-run Hua Hin guesthouse with a warm and welcoming vibe.

Best Nature Retreats

Thailand has many accommodation options located in areas far from the hustle of the cities and the most-visited destinations. They range from digs alongside the Mekong River, to eco-friendly resorts hidden away on islands and in the forests and mountains of northern Thailand. Families travelling away from the beaches will find that big gardens and plenty of animal-spotting opportunities help keep kids amused.

➡ Sang Tong Huts (p298) Individually-designed bamboo and wood bungalows set amidst woods outside Mae Hong Son.

➡ Bann Makok (p485) Boutique eco-resort tucked into the mangroves on idyllic Ko Kut.

➡ Bulunburi (p288) Eleven bungalows nestling in a secluded valley of rice fields and streams near Pai.

➡ Viking Natures Resort (p671) Monkeys in the jungly garden, a beach and driftwood-decorated digs in Ko Phi-Phi.

➡ Rai Saeng Arun (p230) Laid-back eco-friendly resort that sits right by the Mekong River outside Chiang Khong.

➡ Railay Great View Resort (p663) Tropical-chic thatch-roofed bungalows in a forested garden on Railay that leads to a private beach.

Booking

Finding a place to stay in Thailand is easy. For peace of mind, book a room for your first few nights; after that, you can wing it unless you're heading to the most popular destinations. Bear in mind that vacancies can be scarce during certain holidays and peak travel periods.

Lonely Planet (www.lonelyplanet.com/thailand/hotels) Find independent reviews, as well as recommendations on the best places to stay – and then book them online.

Agoda (www.agoda.com/country/thailand.html) Asia-based booking site that covers the full range of accommodation, from hostels to luxury resorts.
Travelfish (www.travelfish.org/country/thailand) Independent reviews with lots of reader feedback.

Month by Month

January

The weather is cool and dry, ushering in the peak tourist season.

✳ Chinese New Year

Thais with Chinese ancestry celebrate the Chinese lunar new year (*drùt jeen*) with a week of house-cleaning and fireworks.

February

Still in the high season, but less crowded than December and January, Thailand is sun and fun for anyone escaping colder weather elsewhere.

✳ Flower Festival

Chiang Mai displays its floral beauty during a three-day period. The festival highlight is the flower-decorated floats that parade through town.

✳ Makha Bucha

Makha Bucha *(mah·ká boo·chah)* commemorates the day when 1250 *arahant* (Buddhists who had achieved enlightenment) assembled to visit Buddha and received the principles of Buddhism; the festival falls on the full moon of the third lunar month. It is a public holiday.

March

The hot and dry season approaches and the beaches start to empty out, coinciding with Thailand's semester break ('mid-term'), when students head out on sightseeing trips.

✳ Mango Season

Luscious ripe mangoes come into season from March to June and are sliced before your eyes, packed in a container with sticky rice and accompanied with a coconut-milk-based dressing.

✳ Kite-Flying Festivals

During the windy season, colourful kites battle it out over the skies of Sanam Luang in Bangkok and elsewhere in the country.

April

Hot, dry weather sweeps across the land. Though the main tourist season is winding down, make reservations well in advance – the whole country is on the move for Songkran.

✳ Poy Sang Long

This colourful Buddhist novice ordination festival held in late March/early April in Mae Hong Son and Chiang Mai sees young Shan (Tai Yai) boys between the ages of seven and 14 parading in festive costumes, headdresses and make-up.

✳ Songkran

Thailand's traditional new year (13–15 April) begins as a respectful affair then degenerates into a water war. Morning visits to the temple involve water-sprinkling ceremonies of sacred Buddha images. Afterwards, Thais load up their water guns and head out to the streets for combat.

May

Leading up to the rainy season, festivals believed to encourage plentiful rains and bountiful harvests take place. Prices are low and tourists are few but it is still remorselessly hot.

✸ Rocket Festival

In the northeast, where rain can be scarce, villagers craft painted bamboo rockets *(bâng fai)* that are fired into the sky to encourage precipitation. This festival is celebrated in Yasothon, Ubon Ratchathani and Nong Khai.

✸ Royal Ploughing Ceremony

This royal ceremony employs astrology and ancient Brahman rituals to kick off the rice-planting season. Sacred oxen are hitched to a wooden plough and part the ground of Sanam Luang in Bangkok.

✸ Visakha Bucha

The holy day of Visakha Bucha *(wí·săh·kà boo·chah)* falls on the 15th day of the waxing moon in the sixth lunar month and commemorates the date of the Buddha's birth, enlightenment and *parinibbana* (passing away).

June

In some parts of the country, the rainy season is merely an afternoon shower, leaving the rest of the day for music and merriment. This month is a shoulder season.

✕ Chanthaburi Fruit Festival

Held at the end of May or the start of June, this festival in Chanthaburi is an opportunity to enjoy an abundance of fruit: mangosteen, rambutan, longkong, longan, salak and the pungent durian.

☆ Hua Hin Jazz Festival

Jazz groups descend on this royal retreat in mid-June for a musical homage to the late king, an accomplished jazz saxophonist and composer.

✸ Phi Ta Khon

The Buddhist holy day of Bun Phra Wet is given a carnival makeover in Dan Sai village in northeast Thailand. Revellers disguise themselves in garish 'spirit' costumes and parade through the streets wielding wooden phalluses and downing rice whisky. Dates vary between June and July.

☆ Pattaya International Music Festival

Pattaya showcases pop and rock bands from across Asia at this free music event, attracting bus-loads of Bangkok university students.

July

The start of the rainy season ushers in Buddhist Lent, a period of reflection and meditation. Summer holidays bring an upsurge in tourists.

✸ Asahna Bucha

The full moon of the eighth lunar month commemorates Buddha's first sermon, in which he described the religion's four noble truths. It is considered one of Buddhism's holiest days.

✸ Khao Phansaa

The day after Asahna Bucha marks the beginning of Buddhist Lent (the first day of the waning moon in the eighth lunar month), the traditional time for men to enter monasteries. In Ubon Ratchathani, traditional candle offerings have grown into a festival of elaborately carved wax sculptures.

✸ HM the King's Birthday

The king's birthday is celebrated as a public holiday on 28 July.

August

Overcast skies and daily showers mark the middle of the rainy season and, in theory, mean fewer visitors.

✸ HM the Queen's Birthday

The Queen Mother's birthday (12 August) is a public holiday and also marks national Mother's Day.

October

Religious preparations for the end of the rainy season and Buddhist Lent begin. The monsoons are reaching the finish line (in most of the country).

✸ King Chulalongkorn Day

Rama V is honoured on the anniversary of his death at the Royal Plaza in Bangkok's

Dusit neighbourhood. Held on 23 October.

Ork Phansaa

The end of Buddhist Lent (three lunar months after Khao Phansaa) is marked by the *gà·tĭn* ceremony, in which new robes are given to the monks by merit-makers.

Vegetarian Festival

A holiday from meat is taken for nine days in adherence with Chinese beliefs of mind and body purification. In Phuket the festival gets extreme, with entranced marchers turning themselves into human shish kebabs. Generally held late September/early October.

Bangkok Biennale

Running from October to February in alternate years, the Bangkok Biennale is a new mega-festival that started in 2018–19, showcasing the works of some of Asia's biggest and trendiest artists at public spaces across the metropolis. The next edition is scheduled for 2020–21.

November

The cool, dry season has arrived, and if you get here early enough, you'll beat the tourist crowds. The beaches are inviting and the landscape is lush.

Loi Krathong

One of Thailand's most beloved festivals, Loi Krathong is celebrated on the first full moon of the 12th lunar month. Small origami-like boats (called *kràthong* or *grà·tong*) festooned with flowers and candles are sent adrift in the waterways.

Lopburi Monkey Festival

On the last Sunday in November, the town's troublesome macaques get pampered with their very own banquet, while merit-makers watch on.

December

The peak of the tourist season has returned with fair skies, busy beach resorts and a holiday mood.

Chiang Mai Red Cross & Winter Fair

A 10-day festival in late December that displays Chiang Mai's cultural heritage with a country-fair atmosphere; expect food (lots of it) and traditional performances.

Rama IX's Birthday

Honouring the late king's birthday on 5 December, this public holiday hosts parades and merit-making events, and is combined with Father's Day.

Itineraries

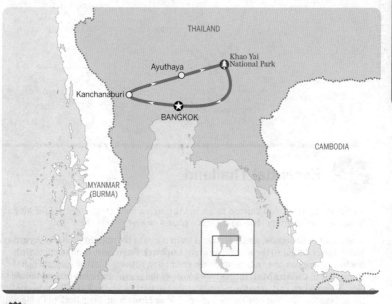

Bangkok & Around

If time is not on your side, you can still explore jungles, temples and Thai culture – all of which are within easy reach of Bangkok.

After a quick look around the major temples and markets in the **capital**, and hitting its top restaurants, embark on the wonderfully scenic train ride to **Kanchanaburi**. Here, enjoy a dip in the seven-tiered Erawan waterfall before visiting the Hellfire Pass Memorial, a poignant tribute to the thousands of prisoners of war who died making the Death Railway during WWII. The nearby forests are ideal for adventure activities or outdoor excursions, such as ziplining over the forest canopies or cruising along the River Kwai.

Next, jump in a minivan bound for **Ayuthaya** and cycle around the impressive ruins of this erstwhile capital. Finally, head over to **Khao Yai National Park**, transiting through Pak Chong. Spend a day hiking through the jungle in search of elephants and tigers, and a night camping under the stars before making your way back to Bangkok.

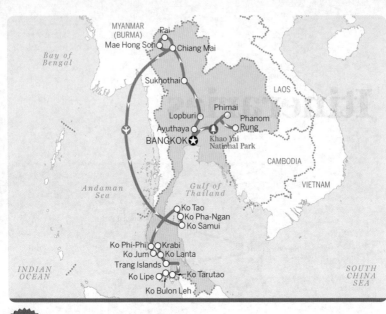

4 WEEKS Essential Thailand

A fully rounded trip to Thailand meanders through almost every corner of the kingdom. If you need to save time, hop on a flight – planes go everywhere these days.

Start off in **Bangkok**, and then take a train north to the ancient capital of **Ayuthaya**. Make a brief detour to the monkey town of **Lopburi**. From here, head north to **Sukhothai**, where you can cycle through the crumbling ruins of another ancient capital. Hightail it to **Chiang Mai**, the laid-back 'rose of the north', and cycle around the old temples. Then switch back into the mountains for the party scene in **Pai**. Climb deeper into the hills to the Myanmar-influenced town of **Mae Hong Son**. Loop back to Chiang Mai.

Fly to the Gulf of Thailand and stop at **Ko Samui** for its resort-island trappings, **Ko Pha-Ngan** for beach bumming and partying, and **Ko Tao** for diving and snorkelling.

Next, get over to the Andaman Coast and its limestone mountains jutting out of the sea. **Ko Phi-Phi** is the prettiest and most party-fuelled of them all. Little **Ko Jum** holds tight to a fast-disappearing beach-shack, hippie vibe. **Ko Lanta** has gentrified into a package-tour destination, but the dive scene is the real attraction. Rock-climbers opt for mainland **Krabi** and nearby Railay.

If you've got the itch for more sand then continue down the peninsula to the **Trang Islands**, another collection of limestone sea mountains lapped by clear waters. Or opt for the idyllic islands offshore from Satun. There's also emerging and midrange **Ko Bulon Leh**, rustic **Ko Tarutao** and laid-back but hip **Ko Lipe**.

Alternatively, skip the beaches south of Krabi and instead try a cultural tour of the northeast, Thailand's agricultural heartland. Transit through Bangkok and then crawl through the jungles of **Khao Yai National Park**. From here, head to Nakhon Ratchasima (Khorat), a transit point for trips to the Angkor ruins at **Phimai**. Follow the Khmer trail east to **Phanom Rung**, the most important and visually impressive of the Angkor temples in Thailand. Surrounding Phanom Rung are a handful of smaller, more remote and forgotten temples with regal ambience.

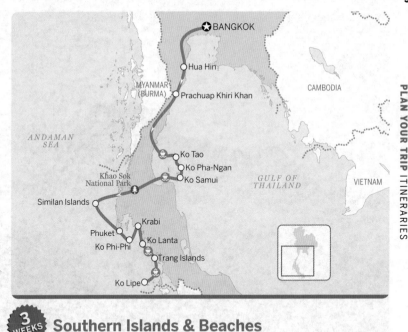

3 WEEKS Southern Islands & Beaches

Hitting all of Thailand's top beaches requires some serious island-hopping, but it can be done. This trip takes you there by land and sea, but if you need to hurry up, hop on a flight along the way.

From **Bangkok**, dip south into **Hua Hin**, an upmarket resort town where all the top hotel chains have a spot on the beach. Then on to **Prachuap Khiri Khan**, where you can hire a bike and check out the undulating coast, bays and laid-back beach scene.

Now for some island time, first stop **Ko Tao** (via Chumphon). Sign up for a dive course or enjoy a few days of snorkelling before island-hopping to **Ko Pha-Ngan** for Full Moon Party fun or an other-side-of-the-island escape. Retire to the resort island of **Ko Samui** for some pampering (or, if you have the energy, more partying), from here it's a short ferry ride to transport hub Surat Thani. Buses leave hourly for **Khao Sok National Park**, where you can enjoy some jungle time in one of the world's oldest rainforests before making the short transfer to Khao Lak, a mainland beach resort that serves as the perfect base for dive trips to the world-famous **Similan Islands** and, to the north, the Surin Islands. Consider spending a few days on a live-aboard to linger in the underwater world full of rays, sharks and seahorses. Once you surface, go south to **Phuket** – Thailand's largest island – and gulp down the numerous attractions and activities on offer here (don't miss a day trip to Ao Phang-Nga).

From Phuket, jump on a boat bound for **Ko Phi-Phi**, a party island that stays up all night and still looks fantastic in the morning. From here you can head back to the mainland and explore the gorgeous coastline of **Krabi** (be sure to take a long-boat to Railay beach, regarded as one of the finest in Thailand) or ferry straight to **Ko Lanta** to collapse in a hammock and drink in the bucolic island life. Continue south by ferry past the beautiful **Trang Islands** to popular but still stunning **Ko Lipe**. Catch a speedboat back to the mainland when you're ready to begin your journey home.

Top: Hikers, Doi Chiang Dao (p359)

Bottom: Wat Phra That Phanom (p402)

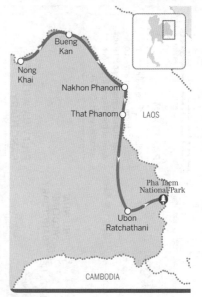

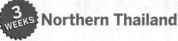

Northern Thailand
3 WEEKS

Hike in a region of lush mountains and ethnic-minority villages that cling to the border between Thailand, Myanmar and Laos.

Chiang Mai is an ideal base, with meditation, language and massage courses on offer. Follow the northwestern spur to **Pai**, a mountain retreat with daytime hikes and night-time carousing. Next is **Soppong**, a mecca for caving. Continue to **Mae Hong Son**, a remote region more akin to Myanmar than Bangkok. The last stop is **Mae Sariang**, a small riverside town with a good reputation for sustainable trekking.

Return to civilisation in Chiang Mai and plot your move towards Chiang Rai. More mountains await in **Chiang Dao**. Next, head for Chiang Rai via the charming riverside village of **Tha Ton** before zigzagging up the mountain ridge to **Doi Mae Salong**, a Yunnanese-Chinese tea settlement. Slide into **Chiang Rai** for a hill-people homestay and culturally sensitive treks, before continuing on to **Chiang Saen** and **Sop Ruak**, formerly part of the infamous Golden Triangle. Bypass the crowds with a stop in **Phayao**, a pleasant northern town for temple-spotting, before returning to Chiang Mai.

Mekong River
2 WEEKS

The most scenic route through Thailand's rural northeast (known as Isan) is along the Mekong River, which divides Thailand and Laos. There aren't a lot of big-ticket attractions but those who venture here will find plenty of culture, an old-fashioned way of life, easygoing people and interesting homestays.

Start in the charming town of **Nong Khai**, a rock-skipping throw from Laos and an easy border-crossing point. If the pace here is too fast, follow the river road east to **Bueng Kan**, a dusty speck of a town with a nearby temple built on a rocky outcrop and several neighbouring homestays with forays into wild-elephant territory. Pass through **Nakhon Phanom** for its picturesque river promenade and tiny **That Phanom**, with its famous Lao-style temple, honoured with a vibrant 10-day festival early in the year.

For a little urban Isan, check out **Ubon Ratchathani**, surrounded by the **Pha Taem National Park**, river rapids and handicraft villages. From here you can exit into Laos at Pakse or catch an overnight train to Bangkok.

Off the Beaten Track: Thailand

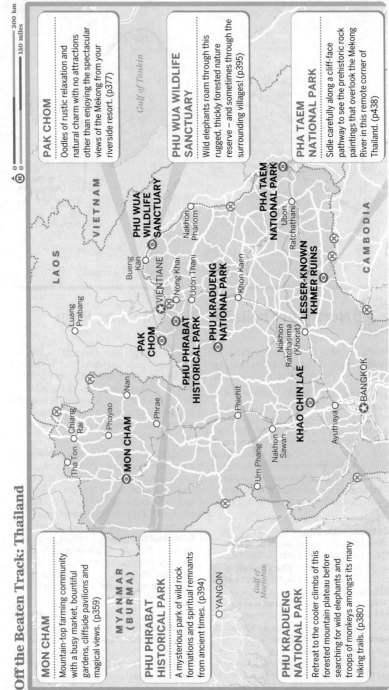

PAK CHOM

Oodles of rustic relaxation and natural charm with no attractions other than enjoying the spectacular views of the Mekong from your riverside resort. (p377)

PHU WUA WILDLIFE SANCTUARY

Wild elephants roam through this rugged, thickly forested nature reserve – and sometimes through the surrounding villages! (p395)

PHA TAEM NATIONAL PARK

Sidle carefully along a cliff-face pathway to see the prehistoric rock paintings that overlook the Mekong River in this remote corner of Thailand. (p438)

MON CHAM

Mountain-top farming community with a busy market, bountiful gardens, cliffside pavilions and magical views. (p359)

PHU PHRABAT HISTORICAL PARK

A mysterious park of wild rock formations and spiritual remnants from ancient times. (p394)

PHU KRADUENG NATIONAL PARK

Retreat to the cooler climbs of this forested mountain plateau before searching for wild elephants and troops of monkeys amongst its many hiking trails. (p380)

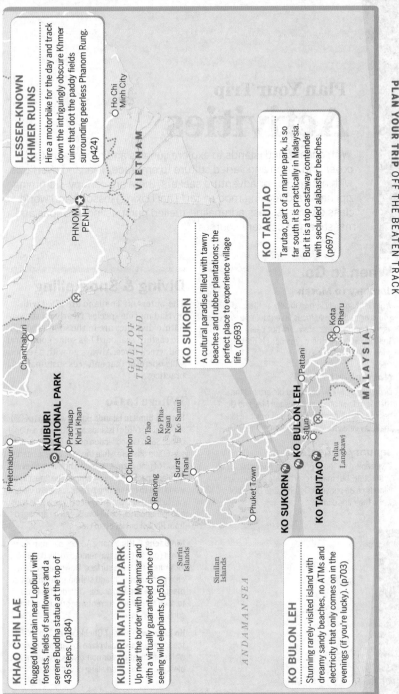

LESSER-KNOWN KHMER RUINS

Hire a motorbike for the day and track down the intriguingly obscure Khmer ruins that dot the paddy fields surrounding peerless Phanom Rung. (p424)

KO TARUTAO

Ko Tarutao, part of a marine park, is so far south it is practically in Malaysia. But it is a top castaway contender with secluded alabaster beaches. (p697)

KO SUKORN

A cultural paradise filled with tawny beaches and rubber plantations; the perfect place to experience village life. (p693)

KHAO CHIN LAE

Rugged Mountain near Lopburi with forests, fields of sunflowers and a serene Buddha statue at the top of 436 steps. (p184)

KUIBURI NATIONAL PARK

Up near the border with Myanmar and with a virtually guaranteed chance of seeing wild elephants. (p510)

KO BULON LEH

Stunning rarely-visited island with dreamy sandy beaches, no ATMs and electricity that only comes on in the evenings (if you're lucky). (p703)

Plan Your Trip
Activities

With oceans and islands to explore, jungles and mountains to discover and a rich and varied culture to embrace, Thailand overflows with activities. For adventure seekers, there are canopy-skimming ziplines, hard-kicking moo·ay tai (Thai boxing) lessons and world-class dive sites. Less adrenaline-fuelled pursuits include spas and massage and cookery courses.

When to Go

January to March

What is laughingly known locally as the cold season is a great time to focus on outdoor pursuits, as the temperatures are warm but bearable. Trekking in the northern provinces is particularly good around this time.

November to April

Diving visibility can be incredible around the islands in the Andaman. Between May and October resorts tend to grind to a halt or close due to the rainy season.

January to September

Dive capital Ko Tao is primed for diving nearly all year round, but many resorts here and on nearby islands close between October and December when the rains come.

Diving & Snorkelling

The waters off Thailand are filled with myriad marine species. Nearly all the signature dive sites are in the south, though the eastern seaboard has some good coral and wreck dives. Always go with a responsible operator that enforces sustainable practices.

Where to Go

Surin & Similan Islands Both the Surin (p606) and Similan (p614) Islands are stunning national parks. Surin is a collection of five islands that sits 60km offshore while the Similan is a nearby group of nine granite islands. Their dive sites are regularly named as being among the finest in the world due to the visiting pelagics, superb visibility (up to 35m) and the array of canyons. Dive trips and live-aboards, for all levels, can be arranged from Phuket or Hat Khao Lak.

Hin Daeng & Hin Muang Accessible from Ko Lanta (p674), these two remote rocks don't look much from the surface. Down below things change dramatically and sightings often include manta rays and barracuda. With depths of up to 40m and strong currents, divers should have some experience.

Ko Tao New to diving? Check out Ko Tao (p564), the cheapest and best place to get your open-water certification. For non-divers, there are plenty of simple snorkelling coves.

Top: Scuba divers in the Andaman Sea (p595)

Bottom: Thai cooking class, Chiang Mai (p310)

ANNA EWA BIENIEK / SHUTTERSTOCK ©

Hiking & Trekking

Northern Thailand has excellent hiking routes filled with cascading waterfalls, dense jungle and soaring mountain ranges. Stay overnight in minority villages or pitch a tent with nature as your only neighbour. Along with treks, guides can arrange cycling, kayaking and rafting excursions. Choose operators who promote sustainability.

Where to Go

Chiang Mai (p310) Northern capital Chiang Mai is the main jumping-off point for treks, such as day trips to Doi Inthanon (p364), Thailand's highest mountain. Hardcore trekkers head to more remote spots such as Um Phang Wildlife Sanctuary (p280), home to the kingdom's largest waterfall, or learn survival skills from guides who grew up near the jungles.

Loei (p370) There are some spectacular trekking options in Loei. Among them is Phu Kradueng National Park (p380), where you can take the 5.5km trail to the plateau, or experience the relatively cooler climes of the pine forests and savannah.

Spas & Yoga

Supreme pampering is available at any number of world-class spas. Yoga, too, is huge and there are teachers, classes and retreats all around the country.

Where to Go

Phuket (p620) probably has the greatest concentration of superior spas in Thailand, but Bangkok (p67), Chiang Mai (p310) and Ko Samui (p528) are all spa-central, too.

Bangkok has numerous yoga studios, but the best retreats are on the islands in the south, especially Ko Pha-Ngan (p546) and Ko Samui, or in Chiang Mai and Pai (p285) in northern Thailand.

Thai Cooking

Learning how to cook authentic Thai food is high on many visitors' to-do lists. Many Thai chefs are happy to share their secrets and take foodies on trips to local markets to teach them about specific ingredients.

Where to Go

Bangkok Thailand's capital is home to the biggest spread of Thai-cooking schools (p96).

Chiang Mai To master Thailand's northern cuisine, pick one of the numerous cookery schools in Chiang Mai (p331). Some focus on vegetarian or organic options.

Thai Boxing

Ever dreamed of becoming a Thai boxing champ? *Moo·ay tai* (also spelt *muay thai*) training camps put you through your paces with packages that involve general fitness and ring work.

Where to Go

Bangkok Thailand's capital is home to a number of schools spanning every level. Beginners are particularly well catered for at gyms such as Jaroenthong Muay Thai Gym (p93).

Pattaya Fairtex Sports Club (Map p457; ☎038 253888; www.fairtexpattaya.com; 179/185-212 Mu 5, Th Pattaya Neua; sessions 800B) has excellent facilities aimed at training foreign visitors with any level of fitness or fighting experience. National champions and MMA (mixed martial arts) fighters also drop in to spar.

Chiang Mai The northern capital has several top *moo·ay tai* gyms, including Lanna Muay Thai Boxing Camp (p333), where everyone – from national champions to total beginners – comes to train.

Damnoen Saduak Floating Market (p154), Ratchaburi

Plan Your Trip

Eat & Drink Like a Local

Incendiary curries, oodles of noodles, fresh seafood and the tropical fruit you've been dreaming about – Thailand has it all. To experience the country's full gastronomic glory, you need to familiarise yourself with the dishes of its various regions and ethnic groups.

The Year in Food

Summer (March to June)

Thailand's hot season is the best time of year for fruit. Durian, mangoes, mangosteen and lychees are all at their juicy peak during these months.

Rainy Season (July to October)

One event to look out for during the rainy season is Thailand's annual Vegetarian Festival, typically held in late September or early October. The festival is celebrated particularly in places with large Chinese populations, such as Bangkok, Phuket Town and Trang.

Winter (November to January)

During Thailand's brief cool season, open-air beer halls, many serving spicy Thai drinking snacks, spring up in the larger cities.

Food Experiences

Meals of a Lifetime

➡ **Saawaan** (p124) This Michelin-starred Bangkok restaurant is one of the finest Thai eateries in the world.

➡ **Gaa** (p127) 10- to 12-course tasting menus of exquisite Indian and Thai dishes in Bangkok.

➡ **Dining on the Rocks** (p540) Ko Samui's ultimate dining experience: you eat on verandas seemingly suspended over the waves.

➡ **Khao Soi Lam Duan Fah Ham** (p344) Chiang Mai's top bowl of *kôw soy* (wheat-and-egg noodles in curry broth).

➡ **Jek Pia** (p506) Family-run joint in Hua Hin that has been serving supreme seafood for over 50 years.

➡ **Blue Rice** (p192) Masterful spice blends add to the creative menu at this riverside Kanchanaburi favourite.

Cheap Treats

➡ **MBK Food Island** (p129) A cheap, clean and tasty Bangkok introduction to Thai and Thai-Chinese staples.

➡ **Paa Suk** (p214) Some of the north's best noodles – at a pocket-change price tag in Chiang Rai.

➡ **Bang Ian Night Market** (p175) Feast on mouthwatering barbecued fish or colourful *roh·dee săi măi* (candyfloss in a crêpe) at this lively Ayuthaya market.

➡ **Talat Pratu Chang Pheuak** (p342) Come hungry to this bustling Chiang Mai food market to dine on an array of local fare including the famous and sublime *kôw kăh mŏo* (braised pork leg with rice) prepared by the hard-to-miss 'Cowboy Hat Lady'.

➡ **Jek Pia** (p506) Some of Hua Hin's best cooks work together at this culinary gem.

➡ **Krua Talay** (p586) Simply superb Thai seafood in an alluring garden setting in Nakhon Si Thammarat.

➡ **Sai Ngam** (p416) In Phimai, where eating *pàt mèe pímai* (local-style fried noodles) from one of the restaurants is almost obligatory.

Local Specialities

Curries & Soups

In Thai, *gaang* (it sounds somewhat similar to the English 'gang') is often translated as 'curry', but it actually describes any dish with a lot of liquid and can thus refer to soups (such as *gaang jèut*) as well as the classic chilli-paste-based curries for which Thai cuisine is famous. The preparation of the latter begins with a *krêu·ang gaang,* created by mashing, pounding and grinding an array of fresh ingredients with a stone mortar and pestle to form an aromatic, extremely pungent-tasting and rather thick paste. Typical ingredients in a *krêu·ang gaang* include chilli, galangal, lemongrass, kaffir lime zest, shallots, garlic, shrimp paste and salt.

Another food celebrity that falls into the soupy category is *đôm yam,* the famous Thai spicy-and-sour soup. Fuelling the fire beneath *đôm yam's* often velvety surface are fresh *prík kêe nŏo* (tiny chillies) or, alternatively, half a teaspoonful of *nám prík pŏw* (roasted chilli paste). Lemongrass, kaffir lime leaves and lime juice give *đôm yam* its characteristic tang.

Salads

Standing right alongside curries in terms of Thai-ness is the ubiquitous *yam,* a hot and tangy 'salad' typically based around seafood, meat or vegetables. Lime juice provides the tang, while abundant use of chilli generates the heat. Most *yam* are served at room temperature, or just slightly warmed by any cooked ingredients. The dish functions equally well as part of a meal or on its own as *gàp glâam,* snack food to accompany a night of boozing.

Rice

In Thailand, to eat is to eat rice, and throughout most of the country a meal is not acceptable without this staple. Thailand maintains the world's fifth-largest area of land dedicated to growing rice, an industry that employs more than half the country's arable land and a significant portion of its population. Rice is so central to Thai food culture that the most common term for 'eat' is *gin kôw* (literally, 'consume rice') and one of the most common greetings is *Gin kôw rěu yang?* (Have you consumed rice yet?).

CATHERINE SUTHERLAND / LONELY PLANET ©

Gaang kĕe-o wăhn (Thai green curry; p52)

PLAN YOUR TRIP EAT & DRINK LIKE A LOCAL

THAI NOODLE DISHES

Some Thai noodle dishes can be ordered *hâang,* meaning 'dry', in which the noodles are served with just enough broth to keep them moist.

➡ **Bà·mèe** Wheat-and-egg noodles that are usually served with barbecued pork slices, greens and, if you like, wontons.

➡ **Gŏo·ay jáp** Rice noodles and pork offal served in a fragrant, peppery broth; a dish popular among the Thai-Chinese.

➡ **Gŏo·ay dĕe·o kaang** A Thai-Muslim dish of rice noodles served with a curry broth, often including garnishes such as tofu, hard-boiled egg and peanuts.

➡ **Gŏo·ay dĕe·o lôok chín** This dish combines rice noodles in a generally clear broth with pork- or fish-based balls (or less commonly, beef or chicken); one of the most common types of noodles across the country. When ordering *gŏo·ay dĕe·o,* the cook will ask which type of noodle you would like, from *sên lék* (thin noodles) to *sên yài* (wide noodles).

➡ **Gŏo·ay dĕe·o reu·a** Pork- or beef-based bowls of noodles with a full flavour that comes from the pig's or cow's blood they are prepared in.

➡ **Kà·nŏm jeen** This dish, named after its noodle, combines thin rice threads and a typically mild, curry-like broth, served with a self-selection of fresh and pickled vegetables and herbs. *Kà·nŏm jeen* varies immensely from region to region, and also tends to be one of the cheapest noodle dishes in the country.

➡ **Kôw soy** Associated with northern Thailand, this dish combines wheat-and-egg noodles and a rich, fragrant, curry-based broth.

➡ **Yen đah foh** Meatballs, cubes of boiled blood and crispy greens are combined with a distinctive crimson broth. It's particularly popular in Bangkok.

Thai pancakes known as *kà·nŏm buang*

Stir-Fries & Deep Fries

Pàt (stir-fries) were introduced to Thailand by the Chinese, and many cling to their Chinese roots, such as the ubiquitous *pàt pàk bûng fai daang* (morning glory flash-fried with garlic and chilli). Others are Thai-Chinese hybrids, such as *pàt pèt* (literally 'spicy stir-fry').

Tôrt (deep-frying in oil) is mainly reserved for snacks such as *glôo·ay tôrt* (deep-fried bananas) or *pò·pée·a* (egg rolls). An exception is *plah tôrt* (deep-fried fish), which is a common way to prepare fish.

Nám Prík

Although more home than restaurant food, *nám prík* are spicy chilli-based dips. Typically eaten with rice, vegetables and herbs, they're also among the most regional of Thai dishes – you could probably pinpoint the province you're in by simply looking at the *nám prík* on offer.

Fruits

Thailand excels in the fruit department. *Má·môo·ang* (mangoes) alone come in a dozen varieties that are eaten at different stages of ripeness. Other common fruit include *sàp·bà·rót* (pineapple), *má·lá·gor* (papaya) and *daang moh* (watermelon), all of which are sold from ubiquitous vendor carts and accompanied by a dipping mix of salt, sugar and ground chilli.

Here is a list of other lesser-known tropical fruits:

➡ **Custard apple** Known in Thai as *nóy nàh,* the knobbly green skin of this fruit conceals hard black seeds and sweet, gloopy flesh with a granular texture.

➡ **Durian** Known in Thai as *tú·ree·an,* the king of fruit is also Thailand's most infamous, due to its intense flavour and odour, which can suggest everything from custard to onions.

➡ **Guava** A native of South America, *fa·ràng* – the same as the word for Westerner – is a green, apple-like ball containing pink or white flesh that's sweet and crispy.

➡ **Jackfruit** The gigantic green pod of *kà·nŭn* – it's considered the world's largest fruit – conceals dozens of waxy yellow sections that taste like a blend of pineapple and bananas (it reminds us of Juicy Fruit chewing gum).

➡ **Langsat** Strip away the yellowish peel of this fruit, known in Thai as *long·gong,* to find a

Rambutan

PLAN YOUR TRIP EAT & DRINK LIKE A LOCAL

segmented, perfumed pearlescent flesh with a lychee-like flavour.

⇒ **Longan** *Lam yai* takes the form of a tiny hard ball; it's like a mini lychee with sweet, perfumed flesh. Peel it, eat the flesh and spit out the hard seed.

⇒ **Lychee** The pink skin of *lín·jèe* conceals an addictive translucent flesh similar in flavour to a grape. It's generally only available between April and June.

⇒ **Mangosteen** The hard purple shell of *mang·kút,* the queen of Thai fruit, conceals delightfully fragrant white segments, some containing a hard seed.

⇒ **Pomelo** Like a grapefruit on steroids, *sôm oh* takes the form of a thick pithy green skin hiding sweet, tangy segments. Cut into the skin, peel off the pith and then break open the segments and munch on the flesh inside.

⇒ **Rambutan** People have different theories about what *ngó* look like, not all repeatable in polite company. Regardless, the hairy shell contains sweet translucent flesh that you scrape off the seed with your teeth.

⇒ **Rose apple** Known in Thai as *chom·pôo,* rose apple is an elongated pink or red fruit with a smooth, shiny skin and pale, watery flesh. It's a good thirst-quencher on a hot day.

⇒ **Salak** Also known as snake fruit because of its scaly skin. The exterior of *sàlà* looks like a mutant strawberry and the soft flesh tastes like unripe bananas.

⇒ **Starfruit** The star-shaped cross-section of *má·feu·ang* is the giveaway. The yellow flesh is sweet and tangy and believed by many to lower blood pressure.

Sweets

Thai-style sweets are generally consumed as breakfast or as a sweet snack, not directly following a meal. *Kŏrng wăhn,* which translates as 'sweet things', are small, rich sweets that often boast a slightly salty flavour. Prime ingredients for *kŏrng wăhn* include grated coconut, coconut milk, rice flour (from white rice or sticky rice), cooked sticky rice, tapioca, mung-bean starch, boiled taro and various fruits.

Closer to the European concept of pastries are *kà·nŏm.* Probably the most popular type are the bite-sized items wrapped in banana leaves, especially *kôw đôm gà·tí* and *kôw đôm mát.* Both consist of sticky rice grains steamed with *gà·tí* (coconut milk) inside a banana-leaf wrapper.

THE FOUR FLAVOURS

Simply put, sweet, sour, salty and spicy are the parameters that define Thai food, and although many associate the cuisine with fiery heat, virtually every dish is an exercise in balancing these four tastes. This balance might be obtained by a squeeze of lime juice, a spoonful of sugar and a glug of fish sauce, or a tablespoon of fermented soybeans and a strategic splash of vinegar. Bitter also factors into many Thai dishes, and often comes from the addition of a vegetable or herb. Regardless of the source, the goal is the same: a favourable balance of four clear, vibrant flavours.

Top: *Bà ·mèe* (wheat-and-egg noodles) with pork

Bottom: Thai iced tea

Regional Variations

Southern Thai Cuisine

Don't say we didn't warn you: southern Thai cooking is undoubtedly the spiciest regional cooking style in a land of spicy regional cuisines. The food of Thailand's southern provinces also tends to be very salty, and seafood, not surprisingly, plays an important role.

Central Thai Cuisine

The people of central Thailand are fond of sweet/savoury flavours, and many dishes include freshwater fish, pork, coconut milk and palm sugar – common ingredients in the central Thai plains.

Northern Thai Cuisine

Probably the least spicy of all Thailand's regional cuisines, the food of northern Thailand is more reliant on bitter flavours and dried spices. Northern Thai food is also very seasonal, reflecting the locals' love of vegetables. Pork is the most commonly used meat, although chicken is widely available, and *kôw něe·o* (sticky rice) is the traditional accompaniment.

Fusion Specialities

Thai-Chinese Cuisine

It was most likely Chinese labourers and vendors who introduced the wok and several varieties of noodle dishes to Thailand. Look out for the following dishes:

➡ **Kôw kǎh mǒo** Braised pork leg served over rice, often with a side of greens and a hard-boiled egg, is the epitome of the Thai-Chinese one-dish meal. It's available at the **Soi 10 Food Centres** (Map p100 Soi 10, Th Silom; mains 50-100B; ⊘8am-3pm Mon-Fri; ⓂSi Lom exit 2, ⓈSala Daeng exit 1) and other street markets.

➡ **Kôw man gài** Chicken rice, originally from the Chinese island of Hainan, is now found in just about every corner of Bangkok. We particularly like the version served at **Boon Tong Kiat Singapore Chicken Rice** (Map p110; 440/5 Soi 55/Thong Lor, Th Sukhumvit; mains 80-300B; ⊘10am-10pm; ⊛; ⓈThong Lo exit 1/3 & taxi).

HOW TO EAT THE THAI WAY

➡ To achieve a balance of flavours and textures, traditionally a party orders a curry, a steamed or fried fish, a stir-fried vegetable dish and a soup, taking care to balance cool and hot, sour and sweet, salty and plain.

➡ Whether at home or in a restaurant, Thai meals are always served 'family style' – that is, from common serving platters. Put no more than one spoonful onto your plate at a time. Heaping your plate will look greedy to Thais.

➡ To dine the Thai way, use a serving spoon, or alternatively your own, to take a single mouthful of food from a central dish and ladle it over a portion of your rice. A fork is then used to push the now-food-soaked portion of rice back onto the spoon before entering the mouth.

➡ Chopsticks are reserved for eating Chinese-style food from bowls, or for eating in all-Chinese restaurants (you will be supplied with chopsticks without having to ask)

➡ **Bà·mèe** Chinese-style wheat-and-egg noodles typically served with slices of barbecued pork, a handful of greens and/or wontons. Mangkorn Khǎo (p121), a street stall in Chinatown, does one of Bangkok's better bowls.

➡ **Săh·lah bow** Chinese-style steamed buns, served with sweet or savoury fillings, are a favourite snack in Bangkok.

➡ **Gǒo·ay děe·o kôoa gài** Wide rice noodles fried with little more than egg, chicken, salted squid and garlic oil is a popular Thai-Chinese dish.

Thai-Muslim Cuisine

When Muslims first visited Thailand during the late 14th century, they brought with them a meat- and dried-spice-based cuisine from their homelands in India and the Middle East. Nearly 700 years later, the impact of this culinary commerce can still be felt in Bangkok.

Amita Thai Cooking Class (p97)

Common Thai-Muslim dishes include the following:

➡ **Gaang mát·sà·màn** 'Muslim curry' is a rich coconut-milk-based dish, which, unlike most Thai curries, gets much of its flavour from dried spices. As with many Thai-Muslim dishes, there is an emphasis on the sweet. A non-halal version is often served at upmarket restaurants such as nahm (p126) in Bangkok.

➡ **Kôw mòk** Biryani, a dish found across the Muslim world, also has a foothold in Bangkok. Here the dish is typically made with chicken and is served with a sweet-and-sour dipping sauce and a bowl of chicken broth.

COOKING COURSES

A standard one-day course usually features a shopping trip to a local market to choose ingredients, followed by preparation of curry pastes, soups, curries, salads and desserts.

➡ **Amita Thai Cooking Class** (p97) Learn to make Thai dishes at this Bangkok canalside family compound.

➡ **Small House Chiang Mai Thai Cooking School** (p331) Northern Thai–style dishes are taught at this Chiang Mai home school.

➡ **Apple & Noi Thai Cooking** (p187) Cooking lessons in a rural setting near Kanchanaburi.

➡ **Borderline Shop cookery course** (p274) Dip into the dishes of Thailand's neighbour, Myanmar, at Mae Sot.

➡ **Samui Institute of Thai Culinary Arts** (p532) Courses in fruit-carving are also available at this Ko Samui school.

➡ **Phuket Thai Cookery School** (p623) A menu of dishes that changes on a daily basis is taught at this Ko Sireh school.

restaurants) where inexpensive food is served buffet-style. Dishes are almost always 100% vegan (ie no meat, poultry, fish or fish sauce, dairy or egg products).

The phrase 'I'm vegetarian' in Thai is *pŏm gin jair* (for men) or *dì·chăn gin jair* (for women). Loosely translated this means 'I eat only vegetarian food', which includes no eggs and no dairy products – in other words, total vegan.

Chicken *sà·đé* (satay)

➡ **Sà·đé** (satay) These grilled skewers of meat probably came to Thailand via Malaysia. The savoury peanut-based dipping sauce is often mistakenly associated with Thai cooking.

➡ **Má·đà·bà** Known as murtabak in Malaysia and Indonesia, these are *roh·đee* that have been stuffed with a savoury or sometimes sweet filling and fried until crispy. It's available at Karim Roti-Mataba (p120) in Bangkok.

➡ **Sà·làt kàak** Literally 'Muslim salad' (*kàak* is a somewhat derogatory word used to describe people or things of Indian and/or Muslim origin), this dish combines iceberg lettuce, chunks of firm tofu, cucumber, hard-boiled egg and tomato, all topped with a sweet peanut sauce.

Vegetarians & Vegans

Vegetarianism isn't widespread, but many tourist-oriented restaurants cater to vegetarians, and there are also a handful of *ráhn ah·hăhn mang·sà·wí·rát* (vegetarian

MENU DECODER

a·ròy – the Thai word for delicious

bà·mèe – wheat-and-egg noodles

đôm yam – Thailand's famous sour and spicy soup

gaang – curry

gài – chicken

gŏo·ay đĕe·o – the generic term for noodle soup

kà·nŏm – Thai-style sweet snacks

kôw – rice

kôw nĕe·o – sticky rice

lâhp – a 'salad' of minced meat

mŏo – pork

nám dèum – drinking water

nám þlah – fish sauce

nám prík – chilli-based dips

pàk – vegetables

pàt – fried

pàt see·éw – wide rice noodles fried with pork and greens

pàt tai – thin rice noodles fried with egg and seasonings

pèt – spicy

þèt – duck

þlah – fish

pŏn·lá·mái – fruit

prík – chilli

ráhn ah·hăhn – restaurant

tôrt – deep-fried

yam – a Thai-style salad

Food Spotter's Guide

Spanning four distinct regions, influences from China to the Middle East, a multitude of ingredients and a reputation for spice, Thai food can be more than a bit over-whelming. So to point you in the direction of the good stuff, we've put together a short-list of the country's must-eat dishes.

1. Đôm yam
The 'sour Thai soup' moniker featured on many menus is a feeble description of this mouth-puckeringly tart and intensely spicy herbal broth.

2. Pàt tai
Thin rice noodles fried with egg, tofu and shrimp, and seasoned with fish sauce, tamarind and dried chilli, have emerged as the poster child for Thai food.

3. Gaang kěe·o wǎhn
Known outside of Thailand as green curry, this intersection of a piquant, herbal spice paste and rich coconut milk is single-handedly emblematic of Thai cuisine's unique flavours and ingredients.

4. Yam
This family of Thai 'salads' combines meat or sea-food with a tart and spicy dressing and fresh herbs.

5. Lâhp
Minced meat seasoned with roasted rice powder, lime, fish sauce and fresh herbs is a one-dish crash course in the rustic flavours of Thailand's northeast.

6. Bà·mèe
Although Chinese in origin, these wheat-and-egg noodles, typically served with roast pork and/or crab, have become a Thai hawker-stall staple.

7. Kôw mòk
The Thai version of biryani couples golden rice and tender chicken with a sweet and sour dip and a savoury broth.

8. Sôm·đam
'Papaya salad' hardly does justice to this tear-inducingly spicy dish of strips of crunchy unripe papaya pounded in a mortar and pestle with tomato, long beans, chilli, lime and fish sauce.

9. Kôw soy
Even outside of its home in Thailand's north, there's a cult following for this soup that combines flat egg-and-wheat noodles in a rich, spice-laden, coconut-milk-based broth.

10. Pàt pàk bûng fai daang
Crunchy green vegetables, flash-fried with heaps of chilli and garlic, is Thai comfort food.

NARIN NONTHAMAND / SHUTTERSTOCK ©

NENEULTIMATE / SHUTTERSTOCK ©

CHOOKEE ROMKAEW / SHUTTERSTOCK ©

PAUL BRIGHTON / SHUTTERSTOCK ©

MOXUMBIC / SHUTTERSTOCK ©

CBENJASUWAN / SHUTTERSTOCK ©

PIYATO / SHUTTERSTOCK ©

Plan Your Trip

Choose Your Beach

It's a terrible dilemma: Thailand has too many beaches to choose from. Choices can be daunting even for those visiting a second time, and development is so rapid that where you went five years ago may now be completely different. Here, we break it down for you so you can find your dream beach.

Best Beaches For....

Relaxation and Activities

Ko Mak Beach-bar scene, explorably flat and expanses of deserted sand.

Ko Phayam Bike back roads to empty beaches or to parties.

Hat Mae Nam Quiet Ko Samui beach close to lots of action.

Ko Bulon Leh Chilled-out vibe but lots to do.

Local Culture

Ko Yao Noi Thai-Muslim fishing island with beautiful karst scenery.

Ko Sukorn Agricultural and fishing gem filled with mangroves and water buffalo.

Ko Phra Thong Look for rare orchids with a *chow lair* (a Moken 'sea gypsy') guide.

Hua Hin Mingle with middle-class Thais in this urban beach getaway.

The Price of Paradise

The personality of a Thai resort town depends a lot on the prices. In places where midrange options dominate, you'll usually find package tourists, rows of beach loungers and umbrellas along the sand, and plenty of big boats full of snorkelling tours.

At upmarket places things settle down. The ritzier beaches of Phuket, like Surin and Ao Bang Thao, are among the quieter on the island yet still have some dining and cocktail options. Ko Kut, off the eastern seaboard, has lovely resorts on some of the country's most unspoiled beaches, while the more secluded beaches of northeastern Ko Samui have some of the most luxurious resorts in Thailand. Once you go very high-end, privacy and seclusion become a bigger part of the picture.

There are a few remaining beach huts that are mostly found on some of the country's most secluded beaches, such as Ko Mak, Ko Wai, Ko Lanta and Ko Pha-Ngan.

Easy Access from Bangkok

Nowadays the closest beaches to Bangkok aren't necessarily the quickest and easiest to get to. There are international flights direct to Phuket and Ko Samui that allow you to skip the big city altogether, and flights from Bangkok (and some other Southeast Asian countries) can shuttle you to several southern towns with ease.

If you don't want to fly but are still short on time, the nearest beach island to Bangkok is Ko Samet (count on around four hours' total travel time), while the closest beach resorts are Bang Saen (one hour by bus) and Pattaya (1½ hours). The next-closest stops by land are the beach towns of Cha-am (2½ hours) and Hua Hin (three hours). It takes around six hours to get to Ko Chang, which beats the minimum of 10 hours to reach the Lower Gulf islands. If you're in a hurry and want to take the bus, the Andaman Coast is not your best choice.

> ### NIGHTLIFE IN PARADISE
>
> **Your Party Level**
>
> **1: Dead Calm** Surin and Similan Islands, Laem Son National Park, Hat Pak Meng, Hat Chang Lang, Ko Phra Thong
>
> **2: A Flicker of Light** Ko Tarutao, Ko Libong, Prachuap Khiri Khan, Ko Wai
>
> **3: There's a Bar** Ko Yao, Ao Khanom
>
> **4: Maybe a Few Bars** Hat Khao Lak, Ao Thong Nai Pan (Ko Pha-Ngan), Ko Kut, Ko Mak
>
> **5: Easy to Find a Drink** Hua Hin, Bo Phut (Ko Samui), Ao Nang
>
> **6: There's a Beach-Bar Scene** Ko Phayam, Railay
>
> **7: Still Going Past Midnight** Ko Lanta, Ko Chang, Ban Tai (Ko Pha-Ngan), Ton Sai
>
> **8: Now We're Rocking** Hat Lamai (Ko Samui), Ko Lipe, Ko Samet
>
> **9: What Happened Last Night?** Hat Chaweng (Ko Samui), Pattaya, Ko Tao
>
> **10: Don't Tell Me What Happened Last Night** Patong (Phuket), Ko Phi-Phi, Hat Rin (Ko Pha-Ngan)

Activities

Diving & Snorkelling

Thailand is a diving and snorkelling paradise. The Andaman Coast and Ko Tao in the Lower Gulf have the best undersea views in the country. Islands like Ko Samui and Ko Lanta don't have great snorkelling from the beach, but snorkelling tours can take you to nearby sites where you'll see some corals and fish, and a turtle or shark if you're lucky. On the eastern seaboard, Ko Chang and Ko Kut offer an improving dive scene, including wreck dives.

Culture

For a taste of authentic Thai culture, head out of the main tourist zones to coastal towns like Trang, Surat Thani or Nakhon Si Thammarat, to lesser-known islands like Ko Si Chang or Ko Sukorn, or to the less-visited parts of islands like the south coast of Ko Samui or the east coast of Ko Lanta. But even tourist-central Patong or Ko Phi-Phi can give you a taste of what's beyond resort-land, just by eating at food stalls and talking to the owners, smiling a lot and being open to interactions with locals.

Climbing

Railay is the best-known place to climb in southern Thailand; it's ideal for both beginners and experienced climbers, and a fun scene. The main climbing centres are Railay and nearby Tonsai, and there are less busy and more off-the-beaten-path climbing options around the appealing town of Krabi. The Ko Yao islands are slowly getting bolted and offer horizons to more seasoned climbers. Ko Tao also attracts rock-climbers.

Hiking

The mainland national parks like Khao Sok have the most jungle-trekking opportunities, but more forested islands such as Ko Chang, Ko Pha-Ngan and even Phuket have great hiking, often to waterfalls or vistas across the blue sea.

Staying Safe

If renting a scooter or motorbike, you may not be insured. Insurance is not included in most rentals and your own insurance

JIRAPHOTO/SHUTTERSTOCK ©

Top: Ang Thong Marine
National Park (p578)

Bottom: Surin Islands
Marine National Park
(p606)

may not cover the cost of any accident. It is likely that you will be liable for medical expenses and repair or replacement costs for any damaged vehicle. If you don't have a Thai driving licence or an international driving licence, you will also be driving illegally (many rental outfits don't check). If you do rent, watch out for sand or grit on the road (especially if braking), drive slowly (under 40km/h), particularly after rain, avoid overtaking vehicles unless you have clear sight ahead and avoid alcohol. Above all, wear a helmet.

Drownings are common. Pay attention to red- and yellow-flag warnings and be aware that many beaches do not have life guards. Also beware of rip tides, which can carry you out to sea. If caught in a rip tide in deep water, do not fight against it as you may rapidly, and dangerously, tire. It is more advisable to try to call for help, but go with the flow and conserve energy; the rip tide will take you further out to sea, but once it releases you, you should be able to swim back. Rip tide channels are quite narrow, so another technique is to gradually swim parallel to the shore when caught in a rip tide and you should escape it.

Signs on some beaches warn of box jellyfish, so check before swimming. Stings from box jellyfish can be fatal, and although there are few deaths, there were three fatalities in Ko Pha-Ngan and Ko Samui waters in a 12-month period between 2014 and 2015.

Watch out for jet skis and long-tail boats coming in to the shore when swimming. Do not expect them to see you.

The Impact of Tourism

Thailand's islands and beaches are among the most popular destinations in Southeast Asia. This has led to rampant development, filling the most popular beaches of the gulf and Andaman Coast with rows of sunbeds, jet-skis and luxurious all-inclusive resorts.

The result is that tourist infrastructure is stretched to the limit, especially during the peak winter tourist season (December to February). Ecosystems are threatened as larger hotels and all-inclusive mega resorts are built, replacing small family guest-houses and beach huts.

On small but busy islands it is increasingly difficult to adequately maintain fresh water supplies and dispose of waste without having a negative impact on the environment. Water pollution and large numbers of visitors can in turn cause damage to coral reefs. Visitors can play their part in reducing the effects of overtourism:

➡ Opt for lesser-known islands or beaches such as Ko Kut, Ko Mak and Ko Wai on the eastern seaboard, or Ko Yao Noi, Ko Chang (Ranong) or Ko Phayam on the Andaman Coast.

➡ Travel out of high season – the quietest (and cheapest) period is June to October.

➡ Check the eco-credentials and safety records of tour operators and dive outfits.

➡ Dispose of rubbish carefully.

➡ Take care when diving and snorkelling. Remember that it is an offence to damage or remove coral in marine parks and make sure that no equipment touches the reef.

WHEN TO GO

REGION	JAN-MAR	APR-JUN	JUL-SEP	OCT-DEC
Bangkok	hotter towards Mar	hot & humid	rainy season	cooler towards Dec
Eastern Seaboard	peak season; thins towards Mar	rainy season begins in May	smaller islands close for the monsoon	cooler weather; low hotel rates
Upper Gulf	hot & dry	hot & dry	occasional rains & strong winds	occasional rains & strong winds
Lower Gulf	clear & sunny	hot & dry	clear & sunny; increasing wind & rain on Ko Tao	monsoon & rough waters
Northern Andaman	high season; high prices	fringe season with variable weather	rainy season & surf season	high season picks up again
Southern Andaman	high season	monsoons usually begin in May	some resorts close for rainy season	crowds return with the sun

OVERVIEW OF THAILAND'S ISLANDS & BEACHES

BEACHES	PACKAGE, TOURISTS	BACK-PACKERS	FAMILIES	PARTIES	DIVE/SNORKEL	PERSONALITY
Ko Chang & Eastern Seaboard						
Ko Samet	✓	✓	✓	✓		pretty beaches, easy getaway from Bangkok
Ko Chang	✓	✓	✓	✓	✓	international resort, mediocre beaches, jungle
Ko Wai		✓	✓		✓	basic; day-trippers, deserted in the evening
Ko Mak	✓	✓	✓			mediocre beaches, great island vibe
Ko Kut	✓	✓	✓			lovely semi-developed island, great for solitude
Hua Hin & the Upper Gulf						
Hua Hin	✓	✓	✓			international resort, easy access to Bangkok
Pranburi area	✓		✓			quiet & close to Bangkok
Ban Krut			✓			low-key, popular with Thais
Bang Saphan Yai		✓	✓			cheap mainland beach
Ko Samui & the Lower Gulf						
Ko Samui	✓	✓	✓	✓		international resort for social beach-goers
Ko Pha-Ngan	✓	✓	✓	✓	✓	popular beaches, some secluded; boozy Hat Rin
Ko Tao	✓	✓	✓	✓	✓	dive schools galore
Ang Thong		✓	✓			karst scenery, rustic
Ao Khanom		✓	✓			quiet, little-known
Phuket & the Andaman Coast						
Ko Chang (Ranong)		✓	✓		✓	rustic and secluded
Ko Phayam		✓	✓			quiet, getting more popular
Surin & Similan Islands		✓			✓	dive sites accessed by live-aboards
Ko Yao	✓	✓	✓			poor beaches but nice vibe, great scenery
Phuket	✓	✓	✓	✓	✓	international resort for social beach-goers
Ao Nang	✓	✓	✓		✓	touristy, close to Railay
Railay	✓	✓	✓			rock-climbing centre with some superb beaches
Ko Phi-Phi	✓	✓		✓	✓	pretty party island
Ko Jum	✓	✓	✓			mediocre beach, nice vibe
Ko Lanta	✓	✓	✓		✓	reasonable beaches
Trang Islands	✓	✓	✓		✓	Ko Ngai is good for kids
Ko Bulon Leh		✓	✓		✓	pretty, little-known
Ko Tarutao		✓	✓			developing national park
Ko Lipe	✓	✓	✓	✓	✓	hotspot, good beaches, handy for visa runs
Ko Adang		✓			✓	popular with day-trippers

Plan Your Trip
Family Travel

Looking for an exotic destination that the kids can handle? Thailand has it all: beaches, mountains, wildlife, sparkling temples and bustling markets; there's something for each age range here.

Children Will Love...

Beaches

Hua Hin (p500) Arguably the country's most family-friendly beach.

Pattaya (p456) Despite the bad rap, this seaside town has lots of activities to appeal to families.

Hat Chaweng (p531) Ko Samui's most popular beach has something for kids of every age.

Ko Chang (p474) An easy ocean entry point.

Outdoor Activities

Ancient City (p162) Open-air museum outside Bangkok that brings together scale models of the country's most famous monuments.

River Kwai Canoe Travel Services (Map p188; ☑087 001 9137, 086 168 5995; riverkwaicanoe@ yahoo.com; 11 Th Mae Nam Khwae; ⊗hours vary) Entry-level kayaking experiences in Kanchanaburi, Central Thailand.

Lumphini Park (p85) Central Bangkok's largest park has paddle boats, play areas and giant monitor lizards.

Chiang Mai (p309) This province is home to a variety of trekking options, some of which are appropriate for families.

Indoor Activities

Bangkok's malls are magnets for teens, both domestic and foreign, but there are plenty of other indoor distractions besides.

Keeping Costs Down

Sleeping

Many hotels and guesthouses offer family rooms that can sleep four comfortably. Some hotels will provide baby cots on request, although not always for free.

Eating Out

Families are always welcomed in restaurants but few offer discounted meals for children.

Transport

Children under three and up to 100cm in height travel free on the State Railway of Thailand (p771) network and on Bangkok's skytrain and subway network. Discounted tickets are available for children under 12 and less than 150cm tall.

On buses and boats, toddlers and babies are not charged. Some ferry operators offer discounted tickets for children up to 150cm in height.

Activities

Some attractions and museums offer half-price tickets for children under 12. Kids under three usually enter for free.

Art in Paradise (p323) Kids enjoy posing for photos against the wacky backdrops at this Chiang Mai gallery.

Children's Discovery Museum (p103)Learning is disguised as fun at this recently renovated Bangkok museum.

KidZania (Map p94; ☎02 683 1888; www.bangkok.kidzania.com; 991/1 Rama I, 5th fl, Siam Paragon; adult 640-800B, child 700-1350B; 🕘10am-5pm Mon-Fri, 10.30am-8pm Sat & Sun; [S]Siam exit 3/5) Hyper-sophisticated play park in Siam Paragon (p148) in the Bangkok city centre.

Museum of Siam (p76) An introduction to Thai culture with a kid-forward feel in the capital.

Transport

BTS, Bangkok The Thai capital's above-ground Skytrain system is a hit with young kids.

Chao Phraya Express Boat (p157) River taxis are the most fun way to get around Bangkok.

Cycling There are many bicycle-tour outfits with suitable bikes and helmets for children.

State Railway of Thailand (p771) Lots of kids like overnight train journeys, where they can be assigned lower sleeping berths with views of the stations and scenery.

Region by Region

Bangkok & Around

Museums and activities galore – kids love the sharks and penguins at Sea Life Ocean World (p89) – as well as parks, markets and many air-conditioned shopping malls with cinemas and restaurants.

Central Thailand

Mischievous monkeys rule the roost in Lopburi (p178) and provide endless fascination for kids. Children of all ages love animal-spotting and splashing around in the waterfalls at Erawan National Park (p194) in Kanchanburi Province.

Northern Thailand

Thailand's most amazing caves and waterfalls are here, including Nam Tok Thilawsu (p279), and there's rafting and wildlife sanctuaries, too.

Chiang Mai Province

The overnight train journey from Bangkok to Chiang Mai (p355) is a hit with children, as is the chance to see elephants at the Burm and Emily's Elephant Sanctuary (p361).

Northeastern Thailand

Foreign children are treated as celebrities in this little-visited region. Khao Yai National Park (p417) has elephants and gibbons and Nong Khai has a fun Rocket Festival (p383).

Ko Chang & Eastern Seaboard

Thailand's second-biggest island Ko Chang (p474) has shallow and gentle seas that are ideal for kids. Children over seven can swing through the trees like Tarzan at the **Tree Top Adventure Park** (www.treetopadventurepark.com; Ao Bailan; 1250B; 🕘9am-5pm).

Hua Hin & the Upper Gulf

The long sandy beaches at Hua Hin (p500) are perhaps the most child-friendly of all Thailand's strips of sand. Kuiburi National Park (p510) and Kaeng Krachan National Park (p493) tempt with the opportunity to spot wild elephants and gibbons.

Ko Samui & the Lower Gulf

Super beaches and snorkellng off-shore on the islands here, while there are tons of eating options and outdoor activities on Ko Samui (p528) itself.

Phuket & the Andaman Coast

The most stunning beaches in Thailand and some of the most family-orientated islands, like Ko Lanta (p674), Phuket has it all – beaches, national parks, aquariums, adventure parks and wildlife sanctuaries.

Good to Know

Look out for the 👪 icon for family-friendly suggestions throughout this guide.

Animals While kids love seeing Thailand's many monkeys in action, remember they are wild animals and they do bite. Be careful around stray dogs, as some are aggressive and carry diseases such as rabies.

Attention Magnets Thais love kids and shower them with affection, but that can be overwhelming for some young children. To deflect attention, just say he or she is 'shy' ('*kîi ai*').

Cities Thai cities can be loud, chaotic and claustrophobic. Air-conditioned shopping malls make a good escape from the heat and streets, as do hotels with swimming pools.

Dining Out Thai food is known for its spiciness but there are always a handful of child-friendly dishes that staff can recommend. High chairs for toddlers are rarely available.

Prams & Strollers Pavements in Thailand are often uneven, narrow or just non-existent. A back carrier to transport tots is a good idea.

Transport Thailand's roads are dangerous. If you're hiring a car, bear in mind that car seats for kids are not always available. Increasing numbers of cycle shops rent bikes and helmets for kids.

When to Go If you're worried about your children coping with the heat, time your visit for the low season (Jul-Oct); it will rain, but usually only in short bursts.

Useful Resources

Lonely Planet Kids (www.lonelyplanetkids.com) Loads of activities and great blog content.

Family Fun Thailand (www.familyfun.tourismthailand.org) Discount deals for families on hotels, activities and restaurants throughout Thailand.

Thailand for Children (www.thailandforchildren.com) Tips on the best destinations for kids.

Tourism Thailand (www.tourismthailand.org) Official website of the Tourism Authority of Thailand.

Kids' Corner

Say What?

Hello.	sà-wàt-dee
Goodbye.	lah gòrn
Thank you.	kòrp kun
My name is ...	pŏm/dì-chăn chêu ... (m/f)...

Did You Know? ℹ

- Siamese cats come from Thailand.
- In Thailand it's unlucky to get your hair cut on a Wednesday.

Have You Tried?

Deep-fried grasshoppers – Tak-ka-tæn

KRIANGKRAI THITIMAKORN/GETTY IMAGES ©

Regions at a Glance

Bangkok & Around

Culture
Food
Nightlife

Pilgrimage Sites

The great temples along Mae Nam Chao Phraya (Chao Phraya River) are national pilgrimage sites cradling revered religious symbols and the country's greatest displays of classical art and architecture.

Global Fare

This city loves to eat. Food can be found in every nook and cranny, from noodle pushcarts and wok shops to fine dining and fashion-minded cafes. All of Bangkok's expat communities have their culinary outposts, providing exotic flavours from almost every corner of the globe.

Beer & Cocktails

The quintessential night out in Bangkok is still a plastic table filled with sweating Chang beers, but rooftop bars, with cool breezes and fizzy cocktails, may make for better Instagram pictures. Hip university students are always out on the town, filling indie clubs or pop discos.

p67

Central Thailand

Culture/History
Mountains
Getaways

Monumental Ruins

The ruins of Ayu-thaya, Thailand's greatest empire, are a Unesco World Heritage Site. Lop-buri and its ancient ruins are ruled by troops of monkeys. Kanchanaburi has poignant memorials to the POWs who worked on the Death Railway during WWII.

National Parks

Kanchanaburi is the gateway to the misty mountains of western Thailand. Rivers and waterfalls carve the contours, and a collection of national parks makes this one of Thailand's wildest corners.

Enchanting Escapes

Sangkhlaburi and Thong Pha Phum are intoxicating end-of-the-road getaways that are easy to reach, but hard to leave.

p165

Northern Thailand

Culture/History
Mountains
Food

Ancient City-States

The remains of ancient city-states, with their fortressed walls and sandstone Buddhist monuments, are dotted throughout northern Thailand.

Dramatic Scenery

The hills and mountains here form some of the country's most dramatic scenery. High-altitude villages of ethnic minorities, are the highlights of provinces such as Chiang Rai and Mae Hong Son.

Sour & Bitter

The north's cooler climate has shaped a menu of dishes characterised by sour and bitter notes, many influenced by Thai, Shan, Burmese and Yunnanese cuisine. The region's most famous dish is *kôw soy*, a mild curry served over noodles.

p203

Chiang Mai Province

Culture/History
Food
Outdoor
Adventures

Fortified City

A refreshing counterpoint to Bangkok's mayhem, Chiang Mai showcases northern Thailand's history and culture in its antique-fortified city. Culture geeks come for sightseeing or courses in cooking, language and massage.

Vegetarian Food

Northern Thailand has its own unique cuisine, reflecting its cooler climate and proximity to China's Yúnnán province and Myanmar. Chiang Mai converts carnivores with its vegetarian health food.

Nature Escapes

Just beyond the city limits is a lush and mountainous landscape that can be explored on muddy hikes, river paddle tours or via zipline.

p309

Northeastern Thailand

Culture/History
Outdoors
Festivals

Ancient Khmer

The Lower Isan region is the site of the Ancient Khmer Hwy. Remnants of the mighty Khmer empire can still be seen in Phanom Rung and Phimai, as well as many other imposing temples.

Wild Scenery

The region's national parks include the evergreen forests of Khao Yai and the eerie rock formations of Phu Phrabat. The Mekong River draws visitors for its stunning scenery and riverside resorts.

Fun Festivities

In the hot season northeasterners busy themselves with having fun. The Rocket Festivals and Phi Ta Khon festival are wild and spectacular affairs.

p367

Ko Chang & the Eastern Seaboard

Beaches
Diving/ Snorkelling
Small Towns

Coastal Views

Jungle-covered Ko Chang is loved for its tropical ambience and thriving party scene. Quiet Ko Kut excels in seaside seclusion, Ko Mak boasts a laid-back island vibe, and little Ko Wai has the prettiest views.

Underwater Worlds

Surrounding Ko Chang is a national marine park filled with beginner-friendly dive sites. Seamounts and rock pinnacles serve as shelter for schooling fish and turtles.

Rural Charm

Often-overlooked Chanthaburi is famous for its weekend gem market and restored waterfront community, while Trat, a transit link to Ko Chang, has a simple charm.

p449

Hua Hin & the Upper Gulf

Culture/History
Beaches
Food

Royal Retreats

Successive Bangkok kings escaped to this coastal getaway, which includes Phetchaburi and its historic hilltop palace, and Hua Hin, which served as Rama IX's seaside retreat.

Beaches

Beach-lovers looking for a sense of place will find it in Prachuap Khiri Khan, a mellow town with karst-studded bays, and Hua Hin, a mod-con seaside resort ideal for families and honeymooners.

Local Seafood

With its proximity to Bangkok and popularity with domestic tourists, this region excels in local-style seafood, served in the raucous Hua Hin night market, by roaming vendors in Cha-am and at oceanfront restaurants.

p491

Ko Samui & the Lower Gulf

Beaches
Diving/
Snorkelling
Nightlife

Island-Hopping

The three sister islands of the Lower Gulf have enticed island-hoppers for decades. Professional Ko Samui caters to resort-style vacations with stunning sugar-white beaches, while Ko Pha-Ngan is more bohemian with cosy coves.

Dive Schools

The warm, gentle seas and wallet-friendly prices keep Ko Tao beloved for dive training, but Ko Pha-Ngan is close behind.

Beach Parties

Ko Pha-Ngan becomes a giant rave during its Full Moon Parties, when revellers storm the beach to dance under the moon. Booze buckets, Day-Glo paint and drunken shenanigans abound.

p525

Phuket & the Andaman Coast

Scenery
Beaches
Diving/
Snorkelling

Outdoor Wonderland

Limestone mountains jut out of jewel-coloured waters with monumental stature. A variety of activities, based out of Krabi, Trang and Ko Yao, turn the pinnacles into a breathtaking outdoor playground.

Beaches

Andaman beaches come in every shape and flavour. Phuket excels in comfort for the masses and top-end luxury. Laid-back Ko Lanta and the increasingly popular Ko Phayam are worth a look.

Marine Parks

Big fish, coral gardens, sunken wrecks – diving and snorkelling sites here include the famous Similan Islands and Surin Islands Marine National Parks.

p595

On the Road

AT A GLANCE

POPULATION
9,600,000

NUMBER OF SKYSCRAPERS
92

BEST OUTDOOR MARKET
Chatuchak Weekend Market (p150)

BEST GREEN LUNG
Lumphini Park (p85)

BEST SUNDOWNER SPOT
Wat Arun (p73)

WHEN TO GO
Nov–Feb Best time to visit for relatively cool and dry weather. Expect crowds and inflated rates.

Mar–Jun City living gets sticky and uncomfortable. Rooftops and pools provide relief – and without crowds, are quite enjoyable.

Jul–Oct Rainy season and flash floods aren't for everyone. Accommodation is cheaper, though.

Lumphini Park (p85) and Bangkok skyline
ANEK.SOOWANNAPHOOM/SHUTTERSTOCK ©

Bangkok & Around

Same same, but different. This T-shirt line epitomises Bangkok, where the familiar and exotic come together like the robust flavours on a plate of *pàt tai* (fried noodles).

Climate-controlled megamalls sit side by side with 200-year-old village homes; gold-spired temples share space with neon-lit strips of sleaze; slow-moving traffic is bypassed by long-tail boats plying the royal river. For adventurous foodies who don't need white tablecloths, there's probably no better dining destination.

Daily life is conducted largely on the streets. Cap off a boat trip with a visit to a hidden market. Get lost in Chinatown's lanes and stumble upon a Chinese opera performance. Or, after dark, let the Skytrain escort you to Sukhumvit, where the nightlife reveals a dynamic city.

INCLUDES

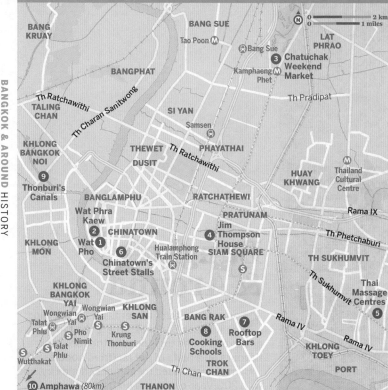

Bangkok Highlights

❶ Wat Pho (p69)
Encountering the jaw-dropping sculpture of an enormous reclining Buddha.

❷ Wat Phra Kaew (p72)
Basking in the glow of the Emerald Buddha within the majestic Grand Palace complex.

❸ Chatuchak Weekend Market (p150) Burning your baht on colourful souvenirs and vintage gear.

❹ Jim Thompson House (p86) Admiring the best of Thai architecture.

❺ Thai Massage (p91)
Being blissfully pounded into submission at a terrific-value massage centre.

❻ Chinatown (p125)
Eating yourself into a stupor at Chinatown's street stalls.

❼ Rooftop Bars (p138)
Toasting the stars and twinkling skyscraper lights from a lofty bar.

❽ Cooking Schools (p96) Mastering spices and learning authentic recipes in a Thai cookery class.

❾ Thonburi's Canals (p108) Gliding between sightseeing spots on a leisurely cruise.

❿ Amphawa (p161)
Exploring quaint wooden buildings in this canalside town outside Bangkok.

History

Since the late 18th century, the history of Bangkok has essentially been the history of Thailand. Many of the country's defining events have unfolded here, and today the language and culture of the city have come to represent those of the entire country. This situation may once have seemed impossible, given the city's origins as little more than an obscure Chinese trading port, but, today with a population of close to 10 million, Bangkok will continue to shape Thailand's history.

Modern Times

In 1855 Rama IV (King Mongkut; r 1851–68) signed the Bowring Treaty with Britain. This agreement marked Siam's break from exclusive economic involvement with China, and the subsequent ascension of Rama V (King Chulalongkorn; r 1868–1910) led to the largest period of European influence on Siam.

Rama V gave Bangkok 120 new roads during his reign. In 1893 Bangkok opened its first railway line, and a 20km electric tramway opened the following year. By 1900 Bangkok had three daily English-language newspapers.

In 1924 a handful of Siamese students in Paris formed the Promoters of Political Change, a group that met to discuss ideas for a future Siamese government modelled on Western democracy. A bloodless revolution in 1932, initiated by the group and a willing Rama VII (King Prajadhipok; r 1925–35), transformed Siam from an absolute monarchy into a constitutional one. Bangkok thus found itself the nerve centre of a vast new civil service, which, coupled with its growing success as a world port, transformed the city into a mecca for Siamese seeking economic opportunities.

Recent Past

In January 2001 billionaire and former police colonel Thaksin Shinawatra became prime minister after winning a landslide victory in nationwide elections – the first in Thailand under the strict guidelines established in the 1997 constitution. Despite numerous controversies, during the February 2005 general elections Thaksin became the first Thai leader in history to be re-elected to a consecutive second term. But in 2006, Thaksin is accused of abusing his powers and of conflicts of interest.

Parliamentary elections in 2011 saw the election of Yingluck Shinawatra, the younger sister of Thaksin (then in exile). In May 2014, Thailand's Constitutional Court found Yingluck and nine members of her cabinet guilty of abuse of power, forcing them to stand down. The military quickly filled the vacuum after Yingluck's ousting, declaring martial law on 20 May and, two days later, officially announcing that it had seized power of the country. In August 2014, former Commander in Chief of the Royal Thai Army Prayut Chan-o-cha shed his uniform to become Thailand's prime minister.

On 13 October 2016, at the age of 89, King Bhumibol, Thailand's – and the world's – longest-serving monarch, passed away. The occasion was marked by a year of mourning culminating in a funeral at Bangkok's Grand Palace that cost US$90 million. Power was passed to his son, Maha Vajiralongkorn, who had assumed many of the royal duties during his father's illness.

Three years after the passing of Thailand's much-adored King Rama IX, his son Maha Vajiralongkorn was formally crowned the country's new emperor in May 2019. With his coronation, Maha Vajiralongkorn assumed the title of Rama X in keeping with the dynastic tradition.

Elections were conducted in March 2019 in a bid to restore democracy in Thailand. However, preliminary results were not clear-cut, and in the lack of a decisive mandate, the Thai Parliament appointed former army chief Prayut Chan-o-cha as the country's prime minister.

◉ Sights

◉ Ko Ratanakosin & Thonburi

Nearly all of Bangkok's big-hitter sights are found in the two linked neighbourhoods of Ko Ratanakosin and Thonburi. Combined, they cover a relatively small area, and it's possible to tackle most if not all sights in one (hot and sweaty) day.

★**Wat Pho**   BUDDHIST TEMPLE
(วัดโพธิ์/วัดพระเชตุพน, Wat Phra Chetuphon; Map p78; www.watpho.com; Th Sanam Chai; 200B; ⊙8.30am-6.30pm; ⊠Tien Pier) You'll find (slightly) fewer tourists here than at neighbouring Wat Phra Kaew (p72), but Wat Pho is our absolute favourite among Bangkok's biggest sights. In fact, the compound incorporates a host of superlatives: the city's largest reclining Buddha, the largest collection of Buddha images in Thailand and the country's earliest centre for public education. Almost too big for its shelter is Wat Pho's highlight, the genuinely impressive **Reclining Buddha**, housed in a pavilion on the western edge of the temple complex.

The rambling grounds of Wat Pho cover 8 hectares, with the major tourist sites occupying the northern side of Th Chetuphon and the monastic facilities found on the southern side. The temple compound is

Greater Bangkok

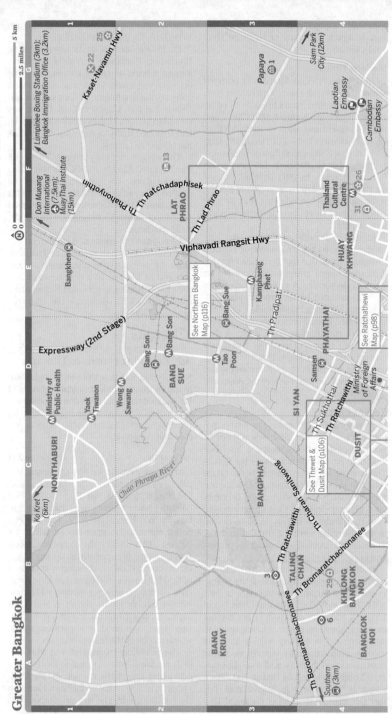

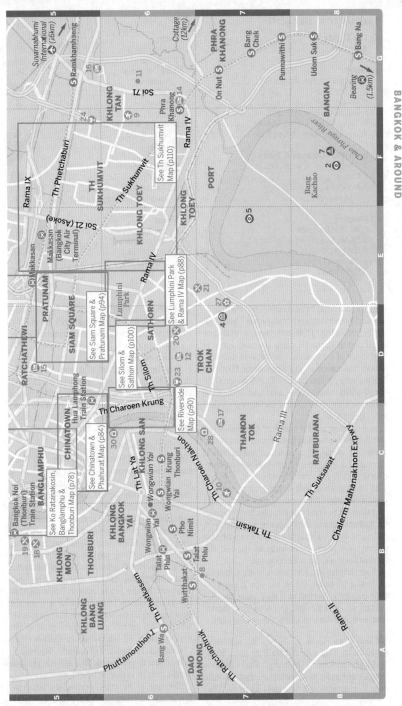

Suvarnabhumi International (16km)
Ramkhamhaeng
16
24
11
Soi 71
KHLONG TAN
9
14
Phra Khanong
Rama IV
Cottage (12km)
PHRA KHANONG
On Nut
Bang Chak
Punnawithi
Udom Suk
Bang Na
BANGNA
Bearing (1.5km)
Chao Phraya River
7
2
Bang Kachao
5
PORT
KHLONG TOEY
See Th Sukhumvit Map (p110)
Rama IX
Th Phetchaburi
TH SUKHUMVIT
Th Sukhumvit
KHLONG TOEY
Soi 21 (Asoke)
Makkasan (Bangkok City Air Terminal)
Makkasan
Rama IV
PRATUNAM
15
RATCHATHEWI
SIAM SQUARE
See Siam Square & Pratunam Map (p94)
Lumphini Park
See Lumphini Park & Rama IV Map (p88)
21
27
4
SATHORN
See Silom & Sathon Map (p100)
20
12
TROK CHAN
23
Th Silom
CHINATOWN
Hua Lamphong Train Station
See Chinatown & Phahurat Map (p84)
Th Charoen Krung
30
KHLONG SAN
See Riverside Map (p90)
17
28
THANON TOK
Rama III
RATBURANA
Th Suksawat
Chalerm Mahanakhon Expwy
Bangkok Noi (Thonburi) Train Station
BANGLAMPHU
See Ko Ratanakosin, Banglamphu & Thonburi Map (p78)
19
18
KHLONG MON
KHLONG BANGKOK YAI
THONBURI
Th Lat Ya
Wongwian Yai
Wongwian Yai
Pho Nimit
Th Charoen Nakhon
10
Th Taksin
KHLONG BANG LUANG
Wutthakat
Talat Phlu
Talat Phlu
8
DAO KHANONG
Bang Wa
Th Ratchaphruk
Phuttamonthon 1
Th Phetkasem
Rama II

Greater Bangkok

also the national headquarters for the teaching and preservation of traditional Thai medicine, including Thai massage, a mandate legislated by Rama III when the tradition was in danger of extinction. The famous massage school has two **massage pavilions** (Map p78; Thai massage per hour from 540B; ⊙9am-4pm;) located within the temple area and additional rooms within the training facility (p97) outside the temple.

A common public ritual at the temple of the Reclining Buddha is to donate coins (representing alms) in a series of metal bowls placed in a long row to the rear of the Buddha statue. If you don't have enough coins on you, an attendant will oblige you with loose change for bigger denominations. Shoes must be taken off to enter the temple. You'll be given a plastic bag at the entrance, in which you can wrap your shoes and carry them with you during your visit. Once outside, deposit the (reusable) bags in a collection vat.

Your admission includes a complimentary bottle of water (trust us: you'll need it) that can be collected at a stall near the Reclining Buddha temple. Dress in long skirts/trousers and sleeved shirts when you visit.

★**Wat Phra Kaew**   BUDDHIST TEMPLE
(วัดพระแก้ว; Map p78; Th Na Phra Lan; 500B; ⊙8.30am-3.30pm; ⊠Chang Pier, Maharaj Pier) Architecturally fantastic, this temple complex is also the spiritual core of Thai

Buddhism and the monarchy, symbolically united in what is the country's most holy image, the Emerald Buddha. Attached to the temple complex is the Grand Palace (p73), the former royal residence, once a sealed city of intricate ritual and social stratification. The ground was consecrated in 1782, the first year of Bangkok rule, and is today Bangkok's biggest tourist attraction and a pilgrimage destination for devout Buddhists. See p74 for more information.

➡ **Emerald Buddha**

Upon entering Wat Phra Kaew you'll meet the *yaksha*, brawny guardian giants from the *Ramakian* (the Thai version of the Indian epic, *Ramayana*). Beyond them is a courtyard where the central *bòht* (ordination hall) houses the Emerald Buddha. The spectacular ornamentation inside and out does an excellent job of distracting first-time visitors from paying their respects to the image. Here's why: the Emerald Buddha is only 66cm tall and sits so high above worshippers in the main temple building that the gilded shrine is more striking than the small figure it cradles. No one knows exactly where it comes from or who sculpted it, but it first appeared on record in 15th-century Chiang Rai in northern Thailand. Stylistically it seems to belong to Thai artistic periods of the 13th to 14th centuries.

Because of its royal status, the Emerald Buddha is ceremoniously draped in monastic robes. There are now three royal robes: for the hot, rainy and cool seasons. The three robes are still solemnly changed by the king at the beginning of each season.

➡ Ramakian Murals

Outside the main *bòht* is a stone statue of the Chinese goddess of mercy, Kuan Im, and nearby are two cow figures, representing the year of Rama I's birth. In the 2km-long cloister that defines the perimeter of the complex are 178 murals depicting the *Ramakian* in its entirety, beginning at the north gate and moving clockwise around the compound.

The story begins with the hero, Rama (the green-faced character), and his bride, Sita (the beautiful topless maiden). The young couple is banished to the forest, along with Rama's brother. In this pastoral setting, the evil king Ravana (the character with many arms and faces) disguises himself as a hermit in order to kidnap Sita.

Rama joins forces with Hanuman, the monkey king (depicted as the white monkey), to attack Ravana and rescue Sita. Although Rama has the pedigree, Hanuman is the unsung hero. He is loyal, fierce and clever. En route to the final fairy-tale ending, great battles and schemes of trickery ensue until Ravana is finally killed. After withstanding a loyalty test of fire, Sita and Rama are triumphantly reunited.

If the temple grounds seem overrun by tourists, the mural area is usually mercifully quiet and shady. Admission to the temple is included in the ticket for the Grand Palace.

★ Grand Palace PALACE

(พระบรมมหาราชวัง; Map p78; Th Na Phra Lan; 500B; ⊙ 8.30am-3.30pm; 🚢 Chang Pier, Maharaj Pier) Part of the greater complex that also encompasses the hallowed Wat Phra Kaew (p72) temple, the Grand Palace (Phra Borom Maharatchawang) is a former royal residence that is today only used on ceremonial occasions. Visitors are allowed to survey the Grand Palace grounds and four of the remaining palace buildings, which are interesting for their royal bombast. Remember to dress in long skirts/trousers and sleeved shirts. Guides can be hired at the ticket kiosk; audio guides can be rented for 200B.

The 94.5-hectare grounds encompass more than 100 buildings that represent 200 years of royal history and architectural experimentation. Most of the architecture, royal or sacred, can be classified as Ratanakosin (old-Bangkok style).

At the eastern end of the palace complex, **Borombhiman Hall** is a French-inspired structure that served as a residence for Rama VI (King Vajiravudh; r 1910–25). Today it can only be viewed through its iron gates. In April 1981 General San Chitpatima used it as the headquarters for an attempted coup. **Amarindra Hall**, to the west, was originally a hall of justice but is used (very rarely indeed) for coronation ceremonies.

The largest of the palace buildings is the triple-winged **Chakri Mahaprasat** (Grand Palace Hall). Completed in 1882 following a plan by British architects, the exterior shows a peculiar blend of Italian Renaissance and traditional Thai architecture. It's a style often referred to as *fa·ràng sài chá·dah* (Westerner wearing a Thai classical dancer's headdress), because each wing is topped by a *mon·dòp* (a layered, heavily ornamented spire). It is believed the original plan called for the palace to be topped with a dome, but Rama V (King Chulalongkorn; r 1868–1910) was persuaded to go for a Thai-style roof instead. The tallest of the *mon·dòp,* in the centre, contains the ashes of Chakri dynasty kings; the flanking *mon·dòp* enshrine the ashes of the many Chakri princes who failed to inherit the throne. The last building to the west is the Ratanakosin-style **Dusit Hall**, which initially served as a venue for royal audiences and later as a royal funerary hall.

Until Rama VI decided one wife was enough for any man, even a king, Thai kings housed their huge harems in the inner palace area (not open to the public), which was guarded by combat-trained female sentries. The intrigue and rituals that occurred within the walls of this cloistered community live on in the fictionalised epic *Four Reigns,* by Kukrit Pramoj, which follows a young girl named Phloi growing up within the Royal City. See p74 for more information.

★ Wat Arun BUDDHIST TEMPLE

(วัดอรุณฯ; Map p78; www.watarun.net; off Th Arun Amarin; 50B; ⊙ 8am-6pm; 🚢 river-crossing ferry from Tien Pier, 🚢 Chao Phraya Express Boat) After the fall of Ayuthaya, King Taksin ceremoniously clinched control here on the site of a local shrine and established a royal palace and a temple to house the Emerald Buddha. The temple was renamed after Arun – the Indian god of dawn – and in honour of the literal and symbolic founding of a new Ayuthaya. Today the temple is one of Bangkok's most iconic structures – not to mention one

BANGKOK & AROUND SIGHTS

Wat Phra Kaew & Grand Palace

EXPLORE BANGKOK'S PREMIER MONUMENTS TO RELIGION & REGENCY

The first area tourists enter is the Buddhist temple compound generally referred to as Wat Phra Kaew. A covered walkway surrounds the area, the inner walls of which are decorated with the ❶ ❷ **murals of the Ramakian**. Originally painted during the reign of Rama I (r 1782–1809), the murals, which depict the Hindu epic the *Ramayana*, span 178 panels that describe the struggles of Rama to rescue his kidnapped wife, Sita.

After taking in the story, pass through one of the gateways guarded by ❸ **yaksha** to the inner compound. The most important structure here is the ❹ **bòht (ordination hall)**, which houses the ❺ **Emerald Buddha**.

Kinaree
These graceful half-swan, half-women creatures from Hindu-Buddhist mythology stand outside Prasat Phra Thep Bidon.

Prasat Phra Thep Bidon

Borombhiman Hall

Amarindra Hall

Phra Si Ratana

Murals of the Ramakian
These wall paintings, which begin at the eastern side of Wat Phra Kaew, often depict scenes more reminiscent of 19th-century Thailand than of ancient India.

Hanuman
Rows of these mischievous monkey deities from Hindu mythology appear to support the lower levels of two small *chedi* near Prasat Phra Thep Bidon.

Head east to the so-called Upper Terrace, an elevated area home to the **6 spires of the three primary chedi**. The middle structure, Phra Mondop, is used to house Buddhist manuscripts. This area is also home to several of Wat Phra Kaew's noteworthy mythical beings, including beckoning **7 kinaree** and several grimacing **8 Hanuman**.

Proceed through the western gate to the compound known as the Grand Palace. Few of the buildings here are open to the public. The most noteworthy structure is **9 Chakri Mahaprasat**. Built in 1882, the exterior of the hall is a unique blend of Western and traditional Thai architecture.

The Three Spires
The elaborate seven-tiered roof of Phra Mondop, the Khmer-style peak of Prasat Phra Thep Bidon, and the gilded Phra Si Ratana *chedi* are the tallest structures in the compound.

LEPNEVA IRINA / SHUTTERSTOCK ©

Emerald Buddha
Despite the name, this diminutive statue (it's only 66cm tall) is actually carved from nephrite, a type of jade.

ALEXEY STOP / GETTY IMAGES ©

The Death of Thotsakan
The panels progress clockwise, culminating at the western edge of the compound with the death of Thotsakan, Sita's kidnapper, and his elaborate funeral procession.

Chakri Mahaprasat
This structure is sometimes referred to as *fa·ràng sài chá·dah* (Westerner in a Thai crown) because each wing is topped by a *mon·dòp:* a spire representing a Thai adaptation of a Hindu shrine.

DESIGN PICS / BLAKE KENT / GETTY IMAGES ©

Dusit Hall

Yaksha
Each entrance to the Wat Phra Kaew compound is watched over by a pair of vigilant and enormous *yaksha*, ogres or giants from Hindu mythology.

ZZVET / GETTY IMAGES ©

Bòht (Ordination Hall)
This structure is an early example of the Ratanakosin school of architecture, which combines traditional stylistic holdovers from Ayuthaya along with more modern touches from China and the West.

of the few Buddhist temples you are encouraged to climb on.

It wasn't until the capital and the Emerald Buddha were moved to Bangkok that Wat Arun received its most prominent characteristic: the 82m-high *prahng* (Khmer-style tower). The tower's construction was started during the first half of the 19th century by Rama II (King Phraphutthaloetla Naphalai; r 1809–24) and later completed by Rama III (King Phranangklao; r 1824–51). Steep stairs lead to the top, from where there's amazing views of the Chao Phraya River. Not apparent from a distance are the fabulously ornate floral mosaics made from broken, multihued Chinese porcelain, a common temple ornamentation in the early Ratanakosin period, when Chinese ships calling at the port of Bangkok discarded tonnes of old porcelain as ballast.

The main Buddha image at the temple is said to have been designed by Rama II himself. The murals date from the reign of Rama V (King Chulalongkorn; r 1868–1910); particularly impressive is one that depicts Prince Siddhartha encountering examples of birth, old age, sickness and death outside his palace walls, an experience that led him to abandon the worldly life. The ashes of Rama II are interred in the base of the presiding Buddha image.

Frequent cross-river ferries run over to Wat Arun from Tien Pier. The Chao Phraya Express Boat also calls at the temple pier.

National Museum

MUSEUM

(พิพิธภัณฑสถานแห่งชาติ; Map p78; 4 Th Na Phra That; 200B; ⊙9am-4pm Wed-Sun; 🛥Chang Pier, Maharaj Pier) Thailand's National Museum is home to an impressive collection of items dating from throughout the country's glittering past. Most of the museum's structures were built in 1782 as the palace of Rama I's viceroy, Prince Wang Na. Rama V turned it into a museum in 1874, and today there are three permanent exhibitions spread out over several buildings. The principal exhibition, Gallery of Thai History, is home to some of the country's most beautiful Buddha images and sculptures of Hindu gods.

Siriraj Medical Museum

MUSEUM

(พิพิธภัณฑ์นิติเวชศาสตร์สงกรานต์นิยมเสน; Map p78; 2nd fl, Adulyadejvikrom Bldg, Siriraj Hospital; 200B; ⊙10am-4pm Wed-Mon; 🛥Wang Lang/Siriraj Pier, Thonburi Railway Station Pier) Collectively dedicated to anatomy, pathology and forensic sciences, this museum has a somewhat atypical (bordering on macabre) array of exhibits ranging from mummified cadavers, two-headed foetuses and cancer-riddled human organs to various appendages, murder weapons and grisly crime-scene evidence. Although the intent is ostensibly to educate rather than nauseate, exhibits such as the preserved body of Si Ouey, a serial killer who murdered – and then ate – several children in the 1950s before being executed, often do the latter.

Museum of Siam

MUSEUM

(สถาบันพิพิธภัณฑ์การเรียนรู้แห่งชาติ; Map p78; Th Maha Rat; 200B; ⊙10am-6pm Tue-Sun; 🚻; 🛥Tien Pier) This fun museum's collection employs a variety of media to explore the origins of the Thai people and their culture. Housed in a European-style 19th-century building that was once the Ministry of Commerce, the exhibits are presented in a contemporary, engaging and interactive fashion not typically found in Thailand's museums. They are also refreshingly balanced and entertaining, with galleries dealing with a range of questions about the origins of the nation and its people.

Amulet Market

MARKET

(ตลาดพระเครื่องวัดมหาธาตุ; Map p78; Th Maha Rat; ⊙7am-5pm; 🛥Chang Pier, Maharaj Pier) This arcane and fascinating market claims both the footpaths along Th Maha Rat and Th Phra Chan, as well as a dense network of covered market stalls that runs south from Phra Chan Pier. The easiest entry point is clearly marked 'Trok Maha That'. The trade is based around small talismans highly prized by collectors, monks, taxi drivers and people in dangerous professions.

Potential buyers, often already sporting many amulets, can be seen bargaining and flipping through magazines dedicated to the amulets, some of which command astronomical prices. It's a great place to just wander and watch men (because it's rarely women) looking through magnifying glasses at the tiny amulets, seeking hidden meaning and, if they're lucky, hidden value.

Royal Barges National Museum

MUSEUM

(พิพิธภัณฑสถานแห่งชาติเรือพระราชพิธี; Map p78; Khlong Bangkok Noi or 80/1 Th Arun Amarin; admission 100B, camera 100B; ⊙9am-5pm; 🛥Phra Pin Klao Bridge Pier) The royal barges are slender, fantastically ornamented vessels used in ceremonial processions. The tradition of using them dates back to the Ayuthaya era,

BANGKOK TONGUE TWISTER

Upon completion of the royal district of Ko Ratanakosin in 1785, at a three-day consecration ceremony attended by tens of thousands of Siamese, the capital of Siam was given a new name: 'Krungthep Mahanakhon Amonratanakosin Mahintara Ayuthaya Mahadilok Pop-nopparat Ratchathani Burirom Udomratchaniwet Mahasathan Amonpiman Avatansathit Sakkathattiya Witsanukamprasit'. This lexical gymnastic feat translates roughly as: 'Great City of Angels, the Repository of Divine Gems, the Great Land Unconquerable, the Grand and Prominent Realm, the Royal and Delightful Capital City full of Nine Noble Gems, the Highest Royal Dwelling and Grand Palace, the Divine Shelter and Living Place of Reincarnated Spirits'.

Understandably, foreign traders continued to call the capital Bang Makok, which eventually truncated itself to 'Bangkok', the name most commonly known to the outside world. These days all Thais understand 'Bangkok' but use a shortened version of the official name, Krung Thep (City of Angels). When referring to greater Bangkok, they talk about Krung Thep Mahanakhon (Metropolis of the City of Angels).

when travel (for commoners and royals) was by boat. When not in use, the barges are on display at this Thonburi museum. The most convenient way to get here is by motorcycle taxi from Phra Pin Klao Bridge Pier (ask the driver to go to *reu·a prá têe nâng*) – you can also walk if you wish.

Saranrom Royal Garden   PARK

(สวนสราญรมย์; Map p78; bounded by Th Ratchini, Th Charoen Krung & Th Sanam Chai; ⊘ 5am-9pm; ⊠ Tien Pier) Easily mistaken for a European public garden, this Victorian-era green space was originally designed as a royal residence in the time of Rama IV. After Rama VII abdicated in 1935, the palace served as the headquarters of the People's Party, the political organisation that orchestrated the handover of the government. The open space remained and in 1960 was opened to the public.

⊙ Banglamphu

The sights are relatively few and generally low-key in this part of Bangkok, and are largely made up of Buddhist temples. Most could be hit in a half-day of wandering.

★ Wat Suthat   BUDDHIST TEMPLE

(วัดสุทัศน์; Map p78; Th Bamrung Meuang; 100B; ⊘ 8.30am-9pm; ⊠ klorng boat Phanfa Leelard Pier) Other than being just plain huge and impressive, Wat Suthat also holds the highest royal temple grade. Inside the *wí·hǎhn* (sanctuary for a Buddha sculpture) are intricate *Jataka* (stories of the Buddha) murals and the 8m-high Phra Si Sakayamuni, Thailand's largest surviving Sukhothai-period bronze, cast in the former capital of Sukhothai in the

14th century. The ashes of Rama VIII (King Ananda Mahidol; r 1935–46) are contained in the base of the image.

★ Golden Mount   BUDDHIST TEMPLE

(ภูเขาทอง, Phu Khao Thong; Map p78; off Th Boriphat; summit admission 50B; ⊘ 7.30am-5.30pm; ⊠ klorng boat Phanfa Leelard Pier) Even if you're wát-ed out, you should tackle the brisk ascent to the Golden Mount. Serpentine steps wind through an artificial hill shaded by gnarled trees, some of which are signed in English, and past graves and pictures of wealthy benefactors. At the peak, you'll find a breezy 360-degree view of Bangkok's most photogenic side.

The hill was created when a large stupa, under construction by Rama III (King Phranangklao; r 1824–51), collapsed because the soft soil beneath would not support it. The resulting mud-and-brick hill was left to sprout weeds until Rama IV (King Mongkut; r 1851–68) built a small stupa on its crest. Rama V (King Chulalongkorn; r 1868–1910) later added to the structure and housed a Buddha relic from India (given to him by the British government) in the stupa. The concrete walls were added during WWII to prevent the hill from eroding.

In November there's a festival in the grounds that includes an enchanting candle-light procession up the Golden Mount.

Thanon Khao San   AREA

(Map p78; Th Khao San, Banglamphu; ⊠ Phra Athit/ Banglamphu Pier) From seedy backpacker ghetto of the 1980s to atmospheric flash-packer central of the current times, Th Khao San has undergone a considerable image makeover through the years. However, the

Ko Ratanakosin, Banglamphu & Thonburi

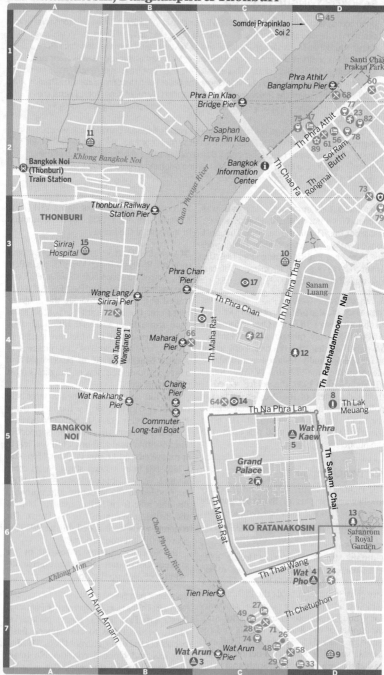

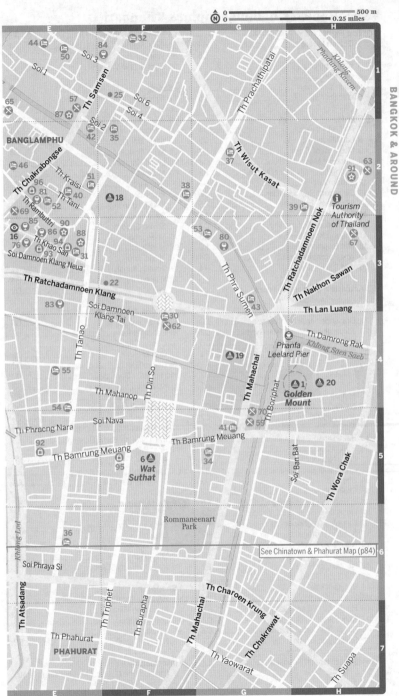

Ko Ratanakosin, Banglamphu & Thonburi

undying energy and charm of the pedestrianised road remains quite intact, and a network of cheerful side streets complement the iconic thoroughfare to constitute a unique tourist ecosystem featuring some excellent sleeping, eating and drinking options for every traveller.

Wat Ratchanatdaram
BUDDHIST TEMPLE

(วัดราชนัดดาราม; Loha Prasat; Map p78; Th Mahachai; ⏰8am-5pm; 🚤klorng boat Phanfa Leelard Pier) This temple was built for Rama III (King Phranangklao; r 1824–51) in the 1840s, and its design is said to derive from metal temples built in India and Sri Lanka more than 2000 years ago. Unsurprisingly, the temple is colloquially referred to by the moniker *loha prasat,* which translates as 'iron palace' in Sanskrit. At the back of the compound, behind the formal gardens, is a well-known market selling *prá krêu·ang* (Buddhist amulets) in all sizes, shapes and styles.

Wat Bowonniwet
BUDDHIST TEMPLE

(วัดบวรนิเวศวิหาร; Map p78; www.watbowon.org; Th Phra Sumen; ⏰8.30am-5pm; 🚤Phra Athit/Banglamphu Pier) Founded in 1826, Wat Bowonniwet (known colloquially as Wat Bowon) is the national headquarters for the Thammayut monastic sect, a reformed version of Thai Buddhism. Travellers visit the temple for the noteworthy murals in its *bòht* (ordination hall), which include Thai depictions of Western life (possibly copied from magazine illustrations) during the early 19th century. The former emperor Rama IX's ashes are enshrined here. Because of its high royal status, visitors should be particularly careful to dress properly for admittance.

Rama IV (King Mongkut; r 1851–68), who set out to be a scholar, not a king, founded the Thammayut sect and began the royal tradition of ordination at this temple. In fact, Mongkut was the abbot of Wat Bowon for several years. Rama IX (King Bhumibol Adulyadej; r 1946–2016) and Rama X (King Maha Vajiralongkorn; r 2016–), as well as several other males in the royal family, have been ordained as monks here.

Wat Saket
BUDDHIST TEMPLE

(วัดสระเกศ; Map p78; off Th Boriphat; ⏰daylight hours; 🚤klorng boat Phanfa Leelard Pier) Wat Saket contains murals that are among the most beautiful in the country. Proceed directly to the pillar behind the Buddha statue, however, for some rather explicit depictions of Buddhist hell. Wat Saket stands to the immediate east of Golden Mount (p77), within the same compound.

👁 Chinatown

Chinatown's most touted sights are its temples, but if you're willing to do some self-guided exploration, its winding streets and frenetic fresh markets are additional reasons to visit.

★Wat Traimit (Golden Buddha)
BUDDHIST TEMPLE

(วัดไตรมิตร, Temple of the Golden Buddha; Map p84; Th Mittaphap Thai-China; 40B; ⏰8am-5pm; 🚤Marine Department Pier, Ⓜ Hua Lamphong exit 1) The attraction at Wat Traimit is undoubtedly the impressive 3m-tall, 5.5-tonne, solid-gold Buddha image, which gleams like, well, gold. Sculpted in the graceful Sukhothai style, the image was 'discovered' some 65 years ago beneath a stucco/plaster exterior, when it fell from a crane while being moved within the temple compound. It's speculated that the covering was added to protect it from marauding Burmese invaders, during a siege either in the late Sukhothai period or the Ayuthaya period.

The temple itself is said to date from the early 13th century. Donations and a constant flow of tourists have proven profitable, and the statue is now housed in an imposing four-storey marble structure called Phra Maha Mandop. The 2nd floor of the building is home to the Yaowarat Chinatown Heritage Center (ศูนย์ประวัติศาสตร์เยาวราช; Map p84; 100B; ⏰8am-5pm Tue-Sun;), a small but engaging museum with multimedia exhibits on the history of Bangkok's Chinatown and its residents, while the 3rd floor is home to the Phra Buddha Maha Suwanna Patimakorn Exhibition (นิทรรศการพระพุทธมหาสุวรรณปฏิมากร; Map p84; 100B; ⏰8am-5pm Tue-Sun), which has exhibits on how the statue was made.

★Talat Mai
MARKET

(ตลาดใหม่, New Market; Map p84; Soi Yaowarat 6/Charoen Krung 16; ⏰6am-6pm; 🚤Ratchawong Pier, Ⓜ Hua Lamphong exit 1 & taxi) With some two centuries of commerce under its belt, New Market is no longer an entirely accurate name for this strip of commerce. Regardless, this is Bangkok's quintessential Chinese market, and the dried goods, seasonings, spices and sauces will be familiar to anyone who's ever spent time in China. Even if you're not interested in food, the hectic atmosphere (watch out for motorcycles squeezing between shoppers) and exotic sights and smells create a somewhat surreal sensory experience for curious wanderers.

★ **Talat Noi** AREA

(ตลาดน้อย; Map p90; off Th Charoen Krung; ⊙7am-7pm; 🚢Marine Department Pier) This microcosm of soi (lane) life is named after a small *(nói)* market *(dà·làht)* that sets up between Soi 22 and Soi 20, along the atmospheric Soi Wanit 2 that runs parallel to Th Charoen Krung. Wandering here you'll find maze-like tentacular soi turning in on themselves, weaving through innumerable grease-stained machinery shops, grocery outlets, warehouses and people's living rooms. The crumbling buildings, vivid wall art and tree-boughed alleyways make it a fantastic area for casual ambling and candid street photography.

Flower Market MARKET

(ปากคลองตลาด; Pak Khlong Talat; Map p84; Th Chakkaraphet; ⊙24hr; 🚢Flower Market Pier) In 2016, as part of a cleaning drive, Bangkok's famous and formerly streetside flower market – also called Pak Khlong Talat – was moved indoors. Within the giant warehouse-like market that now houses the resettled stalls, you'll find piles of delicate orchids, rows of roses and stacks of button carnations. The best time to come is late at night, when the fresh blossoms arrive from upcountry for sale the following day.

DRESS FOR SUCCESS
....

Most of Bangkok's biggest tourist attractions are in fact sacred places, and visitors should dress and behave appropriately. In particular, at Wat Phra Kaew and the Grand Palace, you won't be allowed to enter unless you're well covered. Shorts, sleeveless shirts, spaghetti-strap tops, cropped pants – basically anything that reveals more than your lower arms and head – are not allowed. Those who aren't dressed appropriately can expect to be shown into a dressing room and issued with a sarong before being allowed in – this adds to queuing and unnecessary delays.

Wat Mangkon Kamalawat BUDDHIST TEMPLE

(วัดมังกรกมลาวาส; Map p84; cnr Th Charoen Krung & Th Mangkon; ⊙6am-6pm; 🚢Ratchawong Pier, Ⓜ Hua Lamphong exit 1 & taxi) Clouds of incense and the sounds of chanting form the backdrop at this Chinese-style Mahayana Buddhist temple. Surrounding the temple are vendors selling food for the gods – steamed lotus-shaped dumplings and oranges – which are donated to the temple in exchange for merit. Dating back to 1871, it's the largest and most important religious structure in the area, and during the annual Vegetarian Festival (p101), religious and culinary activities are particularly active here.

Holy Rosary Church CHURCH

(วัดแม่พระลูกประคำกาลหว่าร์; Map p90; cnr Th Yotha & Soi Wanit 2; ⊙Thai-language Mass 7.30pm Mon-Sat, 8am, 10am & 7.30pm Sun; 🚢Marine Department Pier) When a Portuguese contingent moved across the river to the present-day Talat Noi (p82) area of Chinatown in 1787, they were given this piece of land and built the Holy Rosary Church. It's known in Thai as Wat Kalawar, from the Portuguese 'Calvario' (Calvary). Over the years the Portuguese community dispersed and the church fell into disrepair. However, Vietnamese and Cambodian Catholics displaced by the Indochina wars adopted it, and together with Chinese speakers now constitute much of the parish.

Sampeng Lane MARKET

(สำเพ็ง; Map p84; Soi Wanit 1; ⊙8am-6pm; 🚢Ratchawong Pier, Ⓜ Hua Lamphong exit 1 & taxi) Soi Wanit 1 – colloquially known as Sampeng Lane – is a narrow artery running parallel to Th Yaowarat and bisecting the commercial areas of Chinatown and Phahurat. The Chinatown portion of Sampeng Lane is lined with wholesale shops of hair accessories, pens, stickers, household wares and beeping, flashing knick-knacks. Near Th Chakrawat, gem and jewellery shops abound. Weekends are horribly crowded, and it takes a gymnast's flexibility to squeeze past the pushcarts, motorcycles and other roadblocks.

◉ Riverside, Silom & Lumphini

These three contiguous 'hoods are less about big-hitter, must-see attractions and more about casual exploration. That said, there are a couple of sights along the way that make the wander worth its while.

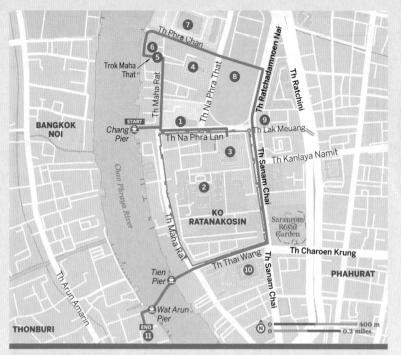

🏃 City Walk
Ko Ratanakosin Stroll

START CHANG PIER
END WAT ARUN
LENGTH 4KM; THREE TO FIVE HOURS

The bulk of Bangkok's 'must-see' destinations are in the former royal district, Ko Ratanakosin. Start early and dress modestly to meet temple dress codes.

Start at Chang Pier and follow Th Na Phra Lan east, with a quick diversion to ❶ **Silpakorn University** (มหาวิทยาลัยศิลปากร; Map p78; 31 Th Na Phra Lan; 🚢 Chang Pier, Maharaj Pier), Thailand's premier fine-arts university. Continue east to the main gate into the ❷ **Grand Palace** (p73), home to the hallowed ❸ **Wat Phra Kaew** (p72) temple, consecrated to the Emerald Buddha.

Return to Th Maha Rat and proceed north, through an enclave of herbal apothecaries and footpath amulet sellers. On your right you'll see ❹ **Wat Mahathat**, one of Thailand's most reputed Buddhist universities.

Turn left into narrow ❺ **Trok Maha That** to discover the ❻ **Amulet Market** (p76).

Winding north through the market, amulets turn to food vendors before you reach ❼ **Thammasat University** (มหาวิทยาลัย ธรรมศาสตร์; Map p78; www.tu.ac.th; 2 Th Phra Chan; 🚢 Chang Pier, Maharaj Pier), known for its law and political science departments.

Exiting at Phra Chan Pier, cross Th Na Phra That and continue east to ❽ **Sanam Luang** (สนามหลวง; Map p78; bounded by Th Na Phra That, Th Ratchadamnoen Nai & Th Na Phra Lan; ⊙ daylight hours; 🚢 Chang Pier, Maharaj Pier), the 'Royal Field'. Cross the field and continue south along Th Ratchadamnoen Nai to the pillar-shrine home of Bangkok's city spirit, ❾ **Lak Meuang** (ศาลหลักเมือง; Map p78; cnr Th Sanam Chai & Th Lak Meuang; ⊙ 6.30am-6.30pm; 🚢 Chang Pier, Maharaj Pier). Then head south along Th Sanam Chai and turn right onto Th Thai Wang to reach the entrance of ❿ **Wat Pho** (p69), home of the giant Reclining Buddha. Finally, catch the cross-river ferry from adjacent Tien Pier to ⓫ **Wat Arun** (p73).

Chinatown & Phahurat

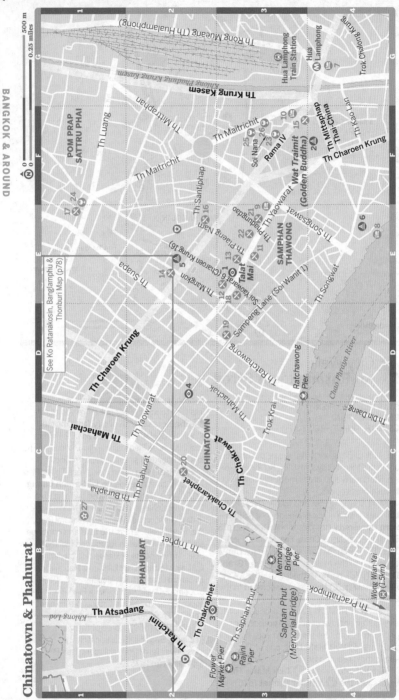

0 --- 500 m
0 --- 0.25 miles

Th Rong Mueang (Th Hualamphong)

Hua Lamphong Train Station

Hua Lamphong

Khlong Phadung Krung Kasem

Th Krung Kasem

POM PRAP
SATTRU PHAI

Th Luang

Th Mittaphan

Th Maitrichit

Th Maitrichit

Th Maitrichit

Th Santiphap

Th Maitrichit

Soi Nana

Rama IV

Th Mittaphap Thai-China

Th Charoen Krung

Th Charoen Krung

Th Plaeng Nam

Th Phadungdao

Wat Traimit (Golden Buddha)

SAMPHAN THAWONG

Th Songsawat

Th Songwat

Th Plaeng Nam

See Ko Ratanakosin, Banglamphu & Thonburi Map (p78)

Th Suapa

Th Mangkon

Th Yaowarat & 6 (Charoen Krung 16)

Talat Mai

Soi Yaowarat 6 (Soi Wanit 1)

Sampeng Lane (Soi Wanit 1)

Ratchawong Pier

Chao Phraya River

Th Din Daeng

Th Charoen Krung

Th Mahachai

Th Yaowarat

Th Ratchawong

CHINATOWN

Th Chakrawat

Th Chakrawat

Th Mahachak

Th Chakkaraphet

Trok Krai

Th Chakkaraphet

Th Phahurat

PHAHURAT

Th Burapha

Th Triphet

Memorial Bridge Pier

Th Prachathipok

Th Atsadang

Th Ratchini

Th Chakraphet

Flower Market Pier

Rajini Pier

Saphan Phut Pier

Th Saphan Phut

Saphan Phut (Memorial Bridge)

Wong Wian Yai (1.5km)

Khlong Lod

Chinatown & Phahurat

Top Sights
1 Talat Mai E3
2 Wat Traimit (Golden Buddha) F4

Sights
3 Flower Market A2
Phra Buddha Maha Suwanna Patimakorn Exhibition .... (see 2)
4 Sampeng Lane D2
5 Wat Mangkon Kamalawat E2
6 Wat Pathum Khongka Ratchaworawihan E4
Yaowarat Chinatown Heritage Center .... (see 2)

Sleeping
7 @Hua Lamphong G4
8 Loy La Long E4
9 Shanghai Mansion E3
10 Wanderlust BKK F3

Eating
11 Boo·a loy nám kĭng E3
12 Gŏo·ay đĕe·o kôo·a gài E3
13 Hoon Kuang E3
Hua Seng Hong .... (see 13)
14 Jék Pûi E2
15 Khun Yah Cuisine F3
Mangkorn Khăo .... (see 11)
16 Nai Mong Hoi Thod E2
17 Nay Hong E1
18 Nay Lék Ûan E3
19 Pat Tai Ratchawong D3
20 Royal India C2
21 Thanon Phadungdao Seafood Stalls E3
22 Yoo Fishball E3

Drinking & Nightlife
23 El Chiringuito F3
24 Let the Boy Die F1
25 Pijiu Bar F3
Teens of Thailand .... (see 25)
26 Tep Bar F3

Entertainment
27 Sala Chalermkrung B1

★SkyWalk at King Power Mahanakhon — VIEWPOINT

(Map p100; ☎02 677 8721; www.kingpowermahanakhon.co.th/skywalk; 114 Th Naradhiwas Rajanagarindra; observatory/rooftop 850/1050B; ⏲10am-midnight; [S] Chong Nonsi exit 3) Offering an unparalleled 360-degree view of Bangkok's cityscape, this two-tiered viewpoint is perched atop King Power Mahanakhon, currently Thailand's tallest building. Stepping onto the dizzying SkyWalk – a glass-floored balcony dangling 78 floors above the earth at 310m – is a spine-chilling experience, but you can soothe your nerves afterwards with a stiff sundowner at the open-air bar one flight up on the skyscraper's pinnacle at 314m. An indoor 74th-floor observatory offers a less adrenalised experience, and comes 200B cheaper.

★Lumphini Park — PARK

(สวนลุมพินี; Map p88; bounded by Th Sarasin, Rama IV, Th Witthayu/Wireless Rd & Th Ratchadamri; ⏲4.30am-9pm; 👪; [M] Lumphini exit 3, Si Lom exit 1, [S] Sala Daeng exit 3/4, Ratchadamri exit 2) Named after the Buddha's birthplace in Nepal (Lumbini), Lumphini Park is central Bangkok's largest and most popular park. Its 58 hectares are home to an artificial lake surrounded by broad, well-tended lawns, wooded areas, walking paths and startlingly large resident monitor lizards to complement the shuffling citizens. It's the best outdoor escape from Bangkok without actually leaving town. The park was originally a royal reserve, but in 1925 Rama VI (King Vajiravudh; r 1910–25) declared it a public space.

★Bangkokian Museum — MUSEUM

(พิพิธภัณฑ์ชาวบางกอก; Map p90; 273 Soi 43, Th Charoen Krung; ⏲9am-4pm Tue-Sun; ⛴Si Phraya/River City Pier) [FREE] Comprising three early 20th-century wooden bungalows, the charming Bangkokian Museum illustrates an often-overlooked period of Bangkok's history. The main residential building was constructed in 1937 for the Surawadee family – it is filled with beautiful wooden furniture, porcelain and other detritus of pre- and postwar family life. An adjacent two-storey shophouse contains themed displays of similar items. The third building, to the rear, was built in 1929 as a British doctor's clinic (he died soon after arriving in Thailand).

A visit takes the form of an informal guided tour in halting English, and photography is encouraged.

MR Kukrit Pramoj House — HISTORIC BUILDING

(บ้านหม่อมราชวงศ์คึกฤทธิ์ปราโมช; Map p100; ☎02 286 8185; Soi 7, Th Naradhiwas Rajanagarindra; adult/child 50/20B; ⏲10am-4pm; [S] Chong Nonsi exit 5) Author and statesman Mom Ratchawong Kukrit Pramoj (1911–95) once

KHAO SAN: A LONG AND WINDING ROAD

Th Khao San (*kôw sǎhn,* meaning 'uncooked rice') is perhaps the most high-profile product of the age of independent travel. Of course, it hasn't always been this way. In its earlier life it was just another unremarkable road in old Bangkok. The first guesthouses appeared around 1982, and as more backpackers arrived through the '80s the old wooden homes were converted one by one into low-rent dosshouses. By the time Alex Garland's novel *The Beach* was published in 1996, with its opening scenes set in the seedier side of Khao San, staying here had become a rite of passage for backpackers coming to Southeast Asia.

The publicity from Garland's book and the movie that followed pushed Khao San into the mainstream, romanticising the seedy, and stereotyping the backpackers it attracted as unwashed and counterculturalist. It also brought the long-simmering debate about the relative merits of Th Khao San to the top of backpacker conversations across the region. With the help of all that publicity, Khao San continued to evolve, with bedbug-infested guesthouses replaced by boutique hotels, and downmarket TV bars showing pirated movies transformed into hip design bars peopled by flashpackers in designer threads.

But the most interesting change has been in the way Thais see Khao San. Once written off as home to cheap, dirty *fa·ràng kêe ngók* (stingy foreigners), Banglamphu has become just about the coolest district in Bangkok. Attracted in part by the long-derided independent traveller and their modern ideas, the city's own counterculture kids have moved in and brought with them a tasty selection of small bars, organic cafes and shops. Indeed, Bangkok's indie crowd has proved to be the Thai spice this melting pot always lacked.

resided in this charming complex now open to the public. Surrounded by a manicured garden, the five teak buildings introduce visitors to traditional Thai architecture and arts, and the former resident, who served as prime minister of Thailand in 1974 and '75, wrote more than 150 books and spent 20 years decorating the house.

Queen Saovabha
Memorial Institute   ZOO
(สถานเสาวภา, Snake Farm; Map p100; cnr Rama IV & Th Henri Dunant; ⊗9.30am-3.30pm Mon-Fri, to 1pm Sat & Sun; ⊕; Ⓜ Si Lom exit 2, Ⓢ Sala Daeng exit 1/3) FREE Founded in 1923, Asia's oldest snake farm gathers antivenom by milking snakes, injecting it into horses, and then harvesting and purifying the antigens the equines produce. Milking sessions (11am Monday to Friday) and snake-handling performances (2.30pm Monday to Friday and 11am weekends) are held at the outdoor amphitheatre. The latter is quite a spectacle – picture a 3m king cobra furiously lashing at a handler as he deftly demonstrates his handling capabilities. Leave a donation for the snakes at the office.

The compound houses several varieties of snakes in glass/metal cages, mostly pythons of varying sizes.

⊙ Siam Square, Pratunam, Phloen Chit & Ratchathewi

Emerge from the malls and there's relatively little in terms of visit-worthy sights in this part of town, the exceptions being Jim Thompson House (p86) and a couple of art galleries.

★ **Jim Thompson House**   HISTORIC BUILDING
(เรือนไทยจิมทอมป์สัน; Map p94; ☑02 218 7368; www.jimthompsonhouse.com; 6 Soi Kasem San 2; adult/student 200/100B; ⊗9am-6pm, compulsory tours every 30min; ⊕klorng boat Sapan Hua Chang Pier, Ⓢ National Stadium exit 1) This jungly compound is the former home of the eponymous American silk entrepreneur and art collector. Born in Delaware in 1906, Thompson briefly served in the Office of Strategic Services (the forerunner of the CIA) in Thailand during WWII. He settled in Bangkok after the war, when his neighbours' handmade silk caught his eye and piqued his business sense. He sent samples to fashion houses in Milan, London and Paris, gradually building a steady worldwide clientele.

In addition to textiles, Thompson also collected parts of various derelict Thai homes and had them reassembled in their current location in 1959. Some of the homes were brought from the old capital of Ayuthaya;

others were pulled down and floated across the *klorng* (canal; also spelt *khlong*) from Baan Khrua (p89), including the first building you enter on the tour. One striking departure from tradition is the way each wall has its exterior side facing the house's interior, thus exposing the wall's bracing system. His small but splendid Asian art collection and his personal belongings are also on display in the main house.

Thompson's story doesn't end with his informal reign as Bangkok's best-adapted foreigner, however. While out for an afternoon walk in the Cameron Highlands of western Malaysia in 1967, Thompson mysteriously disappeared. That same year his sister was murdered in the USA, fuelling various conspiracy theories. Was it communist spies? Business rivals? Or a hungry tiger? Although the mystery has never been solved, evidence revealed by American journalist Joshua Kurlantzick in his profile of Thompson, *The Ideal Man,* suggests that the vocal anti-American stance Thompson took later in his life may have made him a potential target of suppression by the CIA.

Beware of well-dressed touts in soi (lanes) near the Thompson house who will tell you it is closed and try to haul you off on a dodgy buying spree.

★ **Bangkok Art & Culture Centre** GALLERY
(BACC; หอศิลปวัฒนธรรมแห่งกรุงเทพมหานคร; Map p94; www.bacc.or.th; cnr Th Phayathai & Rama I; ⏲10am-9pm Tue-Sat; [S] National Stadium exit 3) [FREE] This large, modern building in the centre of Bangkok has become one of the more significant players in the city's contemporary arts scene. As well as its three floors and 3000 sq metres of gallery space, the centre also contains shops, private galleries, cafes and an art library. Visit the website to see what exhibitions are on when you're in town.

★ **Suan Pakkad Palace Museum** MUSEUM
(วังสวนผักกาด; Map p98; www.suanpakkad.com; Th Si Ayuthaya; 100B; ⏲9am-4pm; [S] Phaya Thai exit 4) An overlooked treasure, Suan Pakkad (literally 'lettuce farm') is a collection of eight traditional wooden Thai houses that was once the residence of Princess Chumbon of Nakhon Sawan and before that a lettuce farm. Within the stilt buildings are displays of art, antiques and furnishings, and the landscaped grounds are a peaceful oasis complete with ducks, swans and a semi-enclosed garden.

YELO House GALLERY
(Map p94; www.yelohouse.com; 20/2 Soi Kasem San 1; ⏲11am-8pm Wed-Mon; [S] National Stadium exit 1) An art gallery? Vintage-clothing market?

SILOM'S ART GALLERIES

Upper Silom and the contiguous area of Sathorn are home to some of Bangkok's nicer contemporary art galleries, where you can step in to gain a good overview of the Thai contemporary art scene.

Kathmandu Photo Gallery (Map p100; ☎02 234 6700; www.kathmanduphotobkk.com; 87 Th Pan; ⏲11am-6pm Tue-Sat; [S] Surasak exit 1/3) [FREE] Bangkok's only gallery wholly dedicated to photography is housed in a charmingly restored Sino-Portuguese shophouse.

Bangkok CityCity Gallery (Map p88; ☎083 087 2725; www.bangkokcitycity.com; 13/3 Soi Attakarn Prasit; ⏲1-7pm Wed-Sun; [M] Lumphini exit 2) [FREE] This small, modern-feeling gallery hosts changing exhibitions featuring the work of domestic, often pop-inspired artists, as well as the occasional performance.

Number 1 Gallery (Map p90; ☎02 630 2523; www.number1gallery.com; 19 Soi 21, Th Silom; ⏲11am-7pm Mon-Sat; [S] Surasak exit 1) [FREE] This gallery has established itself by featuring the often attention-grabbing contemporary work of Thai artists such as Vasan Sitthiket, Sutee Kunavichayanont and Thaweesak Srithongdee.

Gallery VER (Map p70; ☎02 103 4067; www.galleryver.com; 10 Soi 22, Th Naradhiwas Rajanagarindra; ⏲noon-6pm Wed-Sun; [S] Chong Nonsi exit 5 & taxi) [FREE] A vast art space that has hosted a variety of work by both established and emerging domestic artists.

H Gallery (Map p100; ☎085 021 5508; www.hgallerybkk.com; 201 Soi 12, Th Sathon Neua/North; ⏲10am-6pm Wed-Mon; [S] Surasak exit 1/3) [FREE] Housed in a refurbished wooden building, H is generally considered among the city's leading private galleries.

Lumphini Park & Rama IV

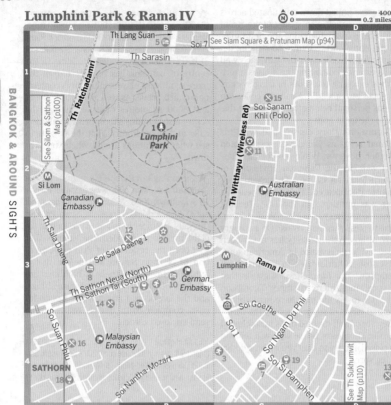

Lumphini Park & Rama IV

Co-working space? Cafe/restaurant? YELO House is so cool, it's hard to pin down what it actually is. So we'll go with the website's claim that it's a multifunction space for creative people. In practical terms, this means it's a place to dig through vintage clothes and ceramics, check out the latest exhibition, or enjoy an espresso in the canalside cafe.

Erawan Shrine
MONUMENT

(ศาลพระพรหม; Map p94; cnr Th Ratchadamri & Th Phloen Chit; ⊙6am-11pm; ⓈChit Lom exit 8, Siam exit 6) FREE Erawan Shrine was originally built in 1956 as something of a last-ditch effort to end a string of misfortunes that occurred during the construction of a hotel, at that time known as the Erawan Hotel. It is consecrated to the Hindu Lord Brahma, creator of the universe. A bomb exploded near the shrine in August 2015, killing 20 and slightly damaging the shrine. It was repaired and reopened just two days later.

Baan Khrua
AREA

(บ้านครัว; Map p94; ☷klorng boat Sapan Hua Chang Pier, ⓈNational Stadium exit 1) This canalside neighbourhood dates back to the turbulent years at the end of the 18th century, when Cham Muslims from Cambodia and Vietnam fought on the side of the new Thai king and were rewarded with this plot of land east of the new capital. The immigrants brought their silk-weaving traditions with them, and the community grew when the residents built Khlong Saen Saeb to better connect them to the river.

Sea Life Ocean World
AQUARIUM

(Map p94; www.sealifebangkok.com; 991/1 Rama I, basement, Siam Paragon; adult/child from 1090/890B; ⊙10am-9pm; ⓈSiam exit 3/5) More than 400 species of fish, crustaceans and even penguins populate this vast underground facility. Diving with sharks (for a fee) is also an option if you have your diving licence, and there are shark and penguin feedings, although note that animal-welfare groups suggest interaction with animals held in captivity creates stress for these creatures.

⊙ Thanon Sukhumvit

There's very little in the way of sights along Th Sukhumvit. Instead, the street is a go-to destination for dining, drinking and shopping.

★Siam Society & Kamthieng House
MUSEUM

(สยามสมาคม & บ้านคำเที่ยง; Map p110; www.siam-society.org; 131 Soi 21/Asoke, Th Sukhumvit; adult/child 100B/free; ⊙9am-5pm Tue-Sat; ⓂSukhumvit exit 1, ⓈAsok exit 3 or 6) Kamthieng House transports visitors to a northern Thai village complete with informative displays on daily rituals, folk beliefs and everyday household chores, all within the setting of a traditional wooden house. This museum is operated by – and shares space with – the Siam Society, publisher of the renowned *Journal of the Siam Society* and a valiant preserver of traditional Thai culture.

Subhashok The Arts Centre
GALLERY

(SAC; Map p110; www.sac.gallery; 160/3 Soi 33, Th Sukhumvit; ⊙10am-6pm Tue-Sun; ⓈPhrom Phong exit 6 & taxi) Tucked deep in a residential Th Sukhumvit side street is this vast gallery, one of the city's most ambitious art spaces. A collaboration with Paris' Galerie Adler, its featured artists largely stem from the big-name, and often politically motivated, Thai art world.

Khlong Toey Market
MARKET

(ตลาดคลองเตย; Map p110; cnr Th Ratchadaphisek & Rama IV; ⊙5-10am; ⓂKhlong Toei exit 1) This wholesale market, one of the city's largest, is the origin of many of the meals you'll eat during your stay in Bangkok. Get there early, and bring a camera. Although some corners of the market can't exactly be described as photogenic, the cheery fishmongers and stacks of durians make great happy snaps. By 10am, most vendors have already packed up and left.

⊙ Thewet & Dusit

Most of Dusit's royal buildings and parks were closed to visitors at different times in recent years, with no definite dates set for their reopening. Note that traffic and pedestrian movement in the area may be restricted during state festivals or regal ceremonies.

★Wat Benchamabophit
BUDDHIST TEMPLE

(วัดเบญจมบพิตร/วัดเบญจะฯ; Map p106; cnr Th Si Ayutthaya & Rama V; 50B; ⊙8am-5pm; ☷Thewet Pier, ⓈPhaya Thai exit 2/4 & taxi) You might recognise this iconic temple from its impression on the back of the ubiquitous Thai 5B coin. Also referred to as the Marble Temple, it was fashioned out of white marble imported from Italy. The distinctive *bòht* (ordination hall) of Wat Ben, as it is colloquially known, was built in the late 19th century under Rama V. The base of the central Buddha image, a copy of the revered Phra Phuttha Chinnarat in Phitsanulok, northern Thailand, contains his ashes.

Wat Thevarat Kunchorn
BUDDHIST TEMPLE

(วัดเทวราชกุญชร; Map p106; Th Si Ayutthaya; ⊙8am-5pm; ☷Thewet Pier) The origins of this riverside Buddhist temple located near

Riverside

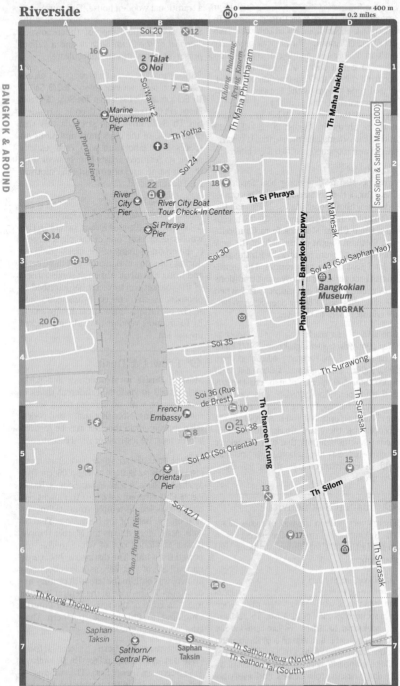

Riverside

Thewet Pier date back to pre-Ratanakosin days, but it was successively built upon and renovated by later kings. The interiors have some interesting murals depicting stories from Buddhist lore. It's hardly ever visited by tourists, and is thus a great place to admire Thai temple architecture in relative peace and silence.

⊙ Northern Bangkok

The main sights in Bangkok's northern suburbs are its popular markets, catering in equal measures to residents and tourists.

★Papaya MUSEUM
(Map p70; www.papaya55.com; Soi 55/2 Lat Phrao; ◷9am-6.30pm; Ⓜ Lat Phrao exit 2 & taxi) **FREE** What began as a private hobby for Papaya's reticent owner has snowballed over the years into a mindboggling collection of 19th- and 20th-century artefacts that occupy every inch within a warehouse-size exhibition space. Art-deco furniture, 1960s beer signage, superhero statues, Piaggio scooters, typewriters, movie projectors, love seats, TV sets, VHS players, wall clocks, storefront mannequins, lampshades – the list goes on. Many objects are technically for sale, but the owner prices them astronomically just to keep his collection from depleting.

Chang Chui MARKET
(ช้างชุ่ย; Map p70; www.changchuibangkok.com; 460/8 Th Sirindhorn; ◷11am-11pm Thu-Tue) An abandoned areoplane, craft-beer bars, a hipster barber shop, performance spaces, a skull-shaped florist, an insect-themed restaurant... This tough-to-pin-down marketplace is one of the most eclectic and exciting openings Bangkok has seen in years. Spanning 18 different structures (all of which are made from discarded objects), a handful of the outlets are open during the day, but the best time to go is during weekend evenings, when the place has the vibe of an artsy, more sophisticated Chatuchak Weekend Market.

🏃 Activities

Spas & Massage

According to the teachings of traditional Thai healing, the use of herbs and massage should be part of a regular health-and-beauty regimen, not just an excuse for pampering. In other words, you need no excuse to get a massage in Bangkok, and it's just as well, because the city could mount a strong claim to being the massage capital of the world. Exactly what type of massage you're after is another question. Variations range from store-front traditional Thai massage to an indulgent 'spa experience' with service and style. And even within the enormous spa category there are many options: there's plenty of pampering going around, but some spas now focus more on the medical than the sensory, while plush resort-style spas offer a menu of appealing beauty treatments.

★ Oriental Spa SPA

(Map p90; ☑ 02 659 9000; www.mandarinoriental. com; Mandarin Oriental; massage & spa packages from 2900B; ⊙ 9am-10pm; ⊠ Oriental Pier & hotel shuttle boat) Regarded as among the premier spas in the world, the Oriental Spa is located in a charming villa on the western bank of the Chao Phraya River, and pretty much sets the standard for Asian-style spa treatment among its peers. Depending on where you flew in from, the jet-lag massage might be a good option. All treatments require advance booking.

Banyan Tree Spa SPA

(Map p88; ☑ 02 679 1052; www.banyantreespa. com; 21st fl, Banyan Tree Hotel, 21/100 Th Sathon Tai/South; massage/spa packages from 2800/6000B; ⊙ 10am-10pm; Ⓜ Lumphini exit 2) A combination of highly trained staff and high-tech facilities has provided this hotel spa with a glowing reputation. Come for pampering regimens based on Thai traditions, or unique signature treatments.

Divana Massage & Spa SPA

(Map p110; ☑ 02 261 6784; www.divanaspa.com; 7 Soi 25, Th Sukhumvit; massage from 1200B, spa packages from 3000B; ⊙ 11am-11pm Mon-Fri, 10am-11pm Sat & Sun; Ⓜ Sukhumvit exit 2, Ⓢ Asok exit 6) Classy Divana retains a unique Thai touch with a private and soothing setting in a garden house, and an array of signature spa and massage treatments. It's one of the chain's many branches across Bangkok.

THAI MASSAGE 101

The most common variety is traditional Thai massage (*nôo·at păan boh·rahn*). Although it sounds relaxing, at times it can seem more closely related to Thai boxing than to shiatsu. Thai massage is based on yogic techniques for general health, which involve pulling, stretching, bending and manipulating pressure points. If done well, a traditional massage will leave you sore but revitalised. Full-body massages usually include camphor-scented balms or herbal compresses. Note that 'oil massage' is sometimes taken as code for 'sexy massage'. A foot massage is arguably (and it's a strong argument) the best way to treat the leg-weariness of sightseeing.

Spa 1930 SPA

(Map p94; ☑ 02 254 8606; www.spa1930.com; 42 Th Ton Son; Thai massage from 1000B, spa packages from 3500B; ⊙ 9.30am-9.30pm; Ⓢ Chit Lom exit 4) Discreet and sophisticated, Spa 1930 rescues relaxers from the contrived spa ambience of New Age music and ingredients you'd rather see at a dinner party. The menu is simple (face, body care and body massage) and the scrubs and massage oils are meant to soothe and rejuvenate.

Babylon SPA

(Map p88; ☑ 02 679 7984; www.babylonbangkok. com; 34 Soi Nantha; sauna 230-350B; ⊙ 10.30am-10.30pm; Ⓜ Lumphini exit 2) Bangkok's most famous gay sauna remains extremely popular with visitors, many from neighbouring Singapore and Hong Kong. B&B-style accommodation is also available.

Yunomori Onsen & Spa ONSEN

(Map p110; www.yunomorionsen.com; 120/5 Soi 26 (Soi Ari), Th Sukhumvit; onsen 450B, massage from 450B; ⊙ 10.30am-11pm; Ⓢ Phrom Phong exit 4 & taxi) Bangkok as a whole can often seem like a sauna, but for a more refined approach to sweating, consider this *onsen* (Japanese-style hot-spring bath). The thermal water is trucked up from southern Thailand and employed in the gender-divided, open pools. In addition to sauna, steam bath and soak pools, massage and other spa treatments are also available.

Health Land MASSAGE

(Map p100; ☑ 02 637 8883; www.healthlandspa. com; 120 Th Sathon Neua/North; massage from 600B; ⊙ 9am-11pm; Ⓢ Surasak exit 1/3) This main branch of a long-standing Thai massage mini-empire is located in Sathorn, and offers a range of great-value massage and spa treatments in a tidy environment. The staff are excellently trained, and it's so popular with locals and tourists that you must call and book in advance, especially if you're planning a weekend visit.

Baan Dalah MASSAGE

(Map p110; ☑ 02 653 3358; www.baandalahmind bodyspa.com; 2 Soi 8, Th Sukhumvit; Thai massage from 500B; ⊙ 10am-midnight; Ⓢ Nana exit 4) A small, conveniently located spa with services ranging from foot massage to full-body Thai massage.

Asia Herb Association MASSAGE

(Map p110; ☑ 02 392 3631; www.asiaherb association.com; 58/19-25 Soi 55/Thong Lor, Th

Sukhumvit; Thai massage from 500B, with herbal compress 1½hr 1100B; ⏰9am-midnight; [S] Thong Lo exit 3) With multiple branches along Th Sukhumvit, this Japanese-owned chain specialises in massage using *prà·kóp* (traditional Thai herbal compresses) filled with 18 different herbs.

Coran MASSAGE

(Map p70; ☎02 726 9978; www.coranbangkok.com; 94-96/1 Soi Ekamai 10, Soi 63/Ekamai, Th Sukhumvit; Thai massage per hr from 600B; ⏰11am-10pm; [S] Ekkamai exit 3 & taxi) A classy, low-key spa housed in a Thai villa. Aroma and Thai-style massage are available.

Yoga, Pilates & Meditation

Yoga studios – and enormous accompanying billboards of smiling gurus – have popped up faster than mushrooms at a Full Moon Party. Expect to pay about 500B for a one-off class.

Absolute You YOGA

(Map p94; ☎02 252 4400; www.absoluteyou.com; Th Phloen Chit, 4th fl, Amarin Plaza; classes from 750B; [S] Chit Lom exit 6) This is the largest of Bangkok's yoga studios, teaching Bikram yoga plus a host of other styles. Package rates for certain courses are available.

The Pilates Studio HEALTH & FITNESS

(Map p94; ☎02 650 7797; www.pilates.co.th; 888/58-59 Mahatun Plaza, Th Phloen Chit; classes from 550B; ⏰8am-7pm; [S] Phloen Chit exit 2) A prominent choice of instruction for those in Bangkok looking for Pilates classes and training.

Center Meditation Wat Mahadhatu MEDITATION

(Map p78; ☎02 222 6011; Section 5, Th Maha Rat, Wat Mahathat; donations accepted; ⏰classes 1pm & 6pm; ⛴Chang Pier, Maharaj Pier) Located within Wat Mahathat, this small centre offers informal daily meditation classes. Taught by English-speaking teachers, classes last between two and three hours. Longer periods of study, which include accommodation and food, can be arranged, but students are expected to follow a strict regimen of conduct.

Moo·ay tai (Thai Boxing)

Jaroenthong Muay Thai Gym MARTIAL ARTS

(Map p78; ☎02 629 2313; www.jaroenthongmuaythaikhaosan.com; Th Phra Athit; lessons from 600B; ⏰drop-in hours 10-11.30am & 2-8pm; ⛴Phra Athit/Banglamphu Pier) With branches around the country, this lauded martial-arts gym has a training centre a short walk from Th Khao San. Beginners can drop in and train in air conditioned comfort, while the more experienced can opt for longer training regimens.

Dinner Cruises

A dinner cruise on the Chao Phraya River is one of the quintessential experiences of a Bangkok vacation. A slew of yachts and catamarans ply the river in the evening, slowly shuttling back and forth on a stretch of the waterway while guests sit onboard and enjoy a dinner experience that can range from fine to tacky and elegant to raucous, depending on one's budget and style preferences.

★**Supanniga Cruise** CRUISE

(Map p90; ☎02 714 7608; www.supannigacruise.com; River City; cocktail/dinner cruises 1250/3250B; ⏰cruises 4.45-5.45pm & 6.15-8.30pm; ⛴Si Phraya/River City Pier) Breathing life into the somewhat tired Bangkok dinner-cruise genre is this outfit, linked with the Thai restaurant of the same name (p123). Options include a sunset cocktail cruise or a dinner cruise, the latter revolving around the same regional Thai dishes that have made the restaurant a city favourite.

Manohra Cruises BOATING

(Map p70; ☎02 476 0022; www.manohracruises.com; Anantara Riverside Resort & Spa; cruises 2300B; ⛴Sathorn/Central Pier & hotel shuttle boat) This cruise takes place aboard a restored teak rice barge, and probably has the best food and ambience of Bangkok's various dinner cruises. It departs from Anantara Riverside Resort & Spa, accessible via hotel shuttle boat from Sathorn/Central Pier.

Sport

National Stadium SWIMMING

(Map p94; Rama I; 100B; ⏰8am-5pm Mon-Sat; [S] National Stadium exit 2) This state-run sports complex has a championship-size pool. It's a good place to swim – or practise your dives – especially if your choice of accommodation in town doesn't come with a pool.

Noah Tennis Club TENNIS

(Map p110; ☎02 259 8425; www.noahbkk26.com; 12/74 Atthakawee, Th Rama 4; per hour outdoor/indoor courts 650/1200B; ⏰7am-10pm; [S] Phrom Phong exit 4 & taxi) Noah is one of Bangkok's nicest tennis clubs, where you can drop in for an invigorating session on one of the

Siam Square & Pratunam

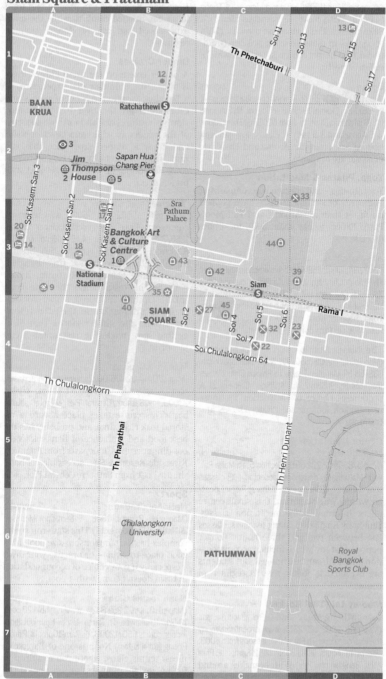

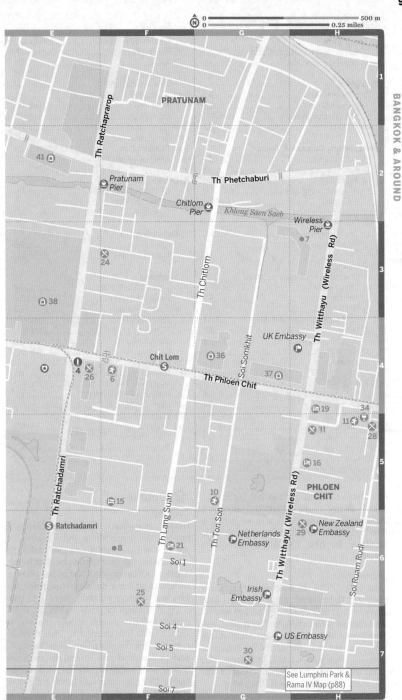

0   500 m
0   0.25 miles

PRATUNAM

Th Ratchaprarop

41

Pratunam Pier

Th Phetchaburi

Chitlom Pier

Khlong Saen Saeb

Wireless Pier

7

24

Th Chitlom

38

Soi Somkhit

UK Embassy

Chit Lom

36

37

Th Phloen Chit

4

26

6

19

34

11

31

28

16

PHLOEN CHIT

15

Th Ratchadamri

Ratchadamri

10

Th Lang Suan

Th Tron Son

Netherlands Embassy

Th Witthayu (Wireless Rd)

29

New Zealand Embassy

8

21

Soi 1

Soi Ruam Rudi

25

Irish Embassy

Soi 4

Soi 5

30

US Embassy

See Lumphini Park & Rama IV Map (p88)

Soi 7

Siam Square & Pratunam

Top Sights
1 Bangkok Art & Culture Centre B3
2 Jim Thompson House A2

Sights
3 Baan Khrua A2
4 Erawan Shrine E4
Sea Life Ocean World .... (see 44)
5 YELO House B2

Activities, Courses & Tours
6 Absolute You F4
7 Asian Oasis H3
8 Asian Trails F6
Issaya Cooking Studio .... (see 37)
KidZania .... (see 44)
9 National Stadium A3
10 Spa 1930 .... G5
11 The Pilates Studio H5
12 Union Language School B1

Sleeping
13 Boxpackers Hostel D1
14 Chao Hostel A3
15 Hansar F5
16 Hotel Indigo H5
17 Lit Bangkok Hotel & Residence B3
18 Lub d A3
19 Okura Prestige H4
20 Siam@Siam A3
21 Urbana F6

Eating
22 Ban Khun Mae C4
23 Coca Suki D4
Eathai .... (see 37)
Food Loft .... (see 36)
Food Republic .... (see 42)
24 FoodPark F3
25 Gaa F6
26 Ginza Sushi-Ichi E4
Gourmet Paradise .... (see 44)
Hong Bao .... (see 37)
27 Koko C4
28 La Monita H5
MBK Food Island .... (see 40)
29 Nonna Nella H6
Nuer Koo .... (see 44)
Open House .... (see 37)
30 Saneh Jaan G7
31 Sanguan Sri H5
32 Somtam Nua C4
33 Sra Bua by Kiin Kiin D2

Drinking & Nightlife
CRU Champagne Bar .... (see 38)
34 Hair of the Dog H5
Red Sky .... (see 38)

Entertainment
35 Apex Scala B3
Major Cineplex .... (see 44)

Shopping
36 Central Chidlom G4
37 Central Embassy G4
38 CentralWorld E3
Elephant Parade .... (see 43)
Flynow .... (see 42)
Gin & Milk .... (see 42)
Karmakamet .... (see 38)
39 Kinokuniya D3
40 MBK Center B4
Objects of Desire Store .... (see 43)
41 Platinum Fashion Mall E2
42 Siam Center C3
43 Siam Discovery B3
44 Siam Paragon C3
45 Siam Square C4
Tango .... (see 42)
Thann .... (see 38)

four hardcourts. If it's too hot (or rainy), simply switch to the air-con indoor courts. Solo players have the option of hiring a marker (350B) to hit balls with. Rackets available for hire. Call ahead to book a court.

Aspire Club GYM

(Map p110; ☎080 118 4114; www.theaspireclub.com; 725 Th Sukhumvit, 8th fl, Metropolis Bldg; day/week pass 650/2500B; 🕒6am-9pm Mon-Fri, 8am-6pm Sat & Sun; [S] Phrom Phong exit 3) Aspire is one of Bangkok's many state-of-the-art gyms, but with the added advantage of day and week passes aimed at tourists who want to flex their muscles or squeeze a cardio session into their travel itineraries.

Courses

Cooking

Having consumed everything Bangkok has to offer is one thing, but imagine the points you'll rack up if you can make the same dishes for your friends back at home. A visit to a Thai cooking school has become a must-do on many Bangkok itineraries and for some visitors it's a highlight of their trip.

Courses range in price and value, but a typical half-day course should include at least a basic introduction to Thai ingredients and flavours and a hands-on chance to both prepare and cook several dishes. Nearly all lessons include a set of printed recipes and end with a communal lunch consisting of your handiwork.

★**Cooking with Poo & Friends** COOKING
(☎080 434 8686; www.cookingwithpoo.com; classes 1500B; ⌚8.30am-1pm; 👪) This popular cooking course was started by a native of Khlong Toey's slums and is held in her neighbourhood. Courses, which must be booked in advance, span three dishes and include a visit to Khlong Toey Market (p89) and transport to and from Emporium Shopping Centre.

★**Amita Thai Cooking Class** COOKING
(Map p70; ☎02 466 8966; www.amitathaicooking.com; 162/17 Soi 14, Th Wutthakat, Thonburi; classes 3000B; ⌚9.30am-1pm Thu-Tue; ⛴klorng boat from Maharaj Pier) One of Bangkok's most charming cooking schools is held in this canalside house in Thonburi. Taught by the delightfully enthusiastic Piyawadi 'Tam' Jantrupon, a course here includes a romp through the garden and instruction in four dishes. The fee also covers transport, which in this case takes the form of a boat ride from Maharaj Pier.

Blue Elephant Thai Cooking School COOKING
(Map p100; ☎02 673 9353; www.blueelephant.com; 233 Th Sathon Tai/South; classes from 3295B; ⌚8.45am-1pm & 1.30-4.30pm Mon-Sat; [S] Surasak exit 2/4) Bangkok's most internationally renowned Thai cooking school offers two lessons Monday to Saturday. The morning class squeezes in a visit to a local market, while the afternoon session includes a detailed introduction to Thai ingredients.

Issaya Cooking Studio COOKING
(Map p94; ☎02 160 5636; www.issayastudio.com; 1031 Th Phloen Chit, Eatthai, level LG, Central Embassy; classes from 1200B; ⌚11am-9pm; [S] Phloen Chit exit 5) Started by home-grown celebrity chef Pongtawat 'Ian' Chalermkittichai, lessons here include instructions in dishes from his linked restaurant Issaya Siamese Club (p123), along with baking, dessert making and mixology. Check the calendar on the website to see what's coming up (along with respective timings and fees). Specialised and private lessons with the master chef can also be arranged.

Thai Massage

Wat Pho Thai Traditional Massage School HEALTH & WELLBEING
(Map p78; ☎02 622 3551; www.watpomassage.com; 392/32-33 Soi Phen Phat; lessons from 2500B, Thai massage per hour from 540B; ⌚lessons 9am-4pm, massage 9am-8pm; ⛴Tien Pier) Associated with the nearby temple (p69) of the same name, this institute offers basic and advanced courses in traditional massage. Basic courses offer 30 hours spread over five days and cover either general massage or foot massage. Thai massage services are also available for nonstudents. The school is outside the temple compound in a restored Bangkok shophouse in Soi Phen Phat.

Phussapa Thai Massage School HEALTH & WELLBEING
(Map p110; ☎02 204 2922; www.facebook.com/phussapa; 25/8 Soi 26 (Soi Ari), Th Sukhumvit; tuition

IS BANGKOK SINKING?

Anybody who has been to Bangkok during the rainy season has probably witnessed it first-hand: floods that make the city's streets seem more like rivers than roads. While traditionally these occurrences were seasonal, some predict that a perfect storm of factors means that in the future the city will be encountering such scenarios – and potentially much worse – on a more frequent basis.

Much of Bangkok was built on soft clay, and scientists suspect that the weight of all those tall buildings is effectively compressing the soil. Some estimate that the city is sinking at a rate of between 10mm and 20mm per year, a phenomenon exacerbated by unregulated use of ground water. And located only 2m above sea level and a scant 50km from the Gulf of Thailand, Bangkok is also threatened by rising sea levels. Indeed, the head of Thailand's National Disaster Warning Center has predicted that by the year 2030, the city will be under 1.5m of water, and by 2100, a virtual Atlantis.

Solutions posed include building a massive sea wall in the Gulf of Thailand, but at an estimated cost of nearly US$3 billion, it's a hard sell. Some have even proposed moving the capital to another location altogether. For the time being, it's most likely that Bangkok will forget about its imminent fate until the next rainy season, when the floods will serve as a watery reminder.

Ratchathewi

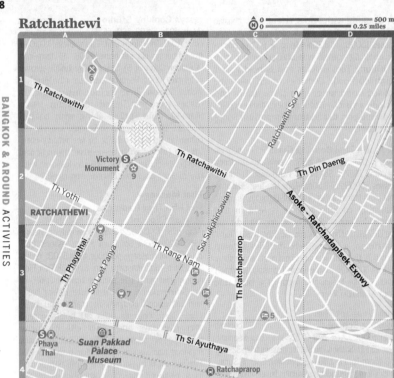

Ratchathewi

from 6000B, Thai massage per hour 250B; ⊘ lessons 9am-4pm, massage 11am-11pm; Ⓢ Phrom Phong exit 4) Run by a long-time Japanese resident of Bangkok, the basic course in Thai massage here spans 30 hours over five days.

Phussapa Thai Massage School also offers shorter courses in foot massage and self massage.

Language

Union Language School   LANGUAGE
(Map p94; ☑ 02 214 6033; www.unionthailanguage. com; 7th fl, 328 CCT Office Bldg, Th Phayathai; courses from 7000B; Ⓢ Ratchathewi exit 1) Generally recognised as having the best and most rigorous Thai-language courses (many missionaries study here), Union employs a balance of structure- and communication-

oriented methodologies beginning with 80-hour, four-week modules.

AAA LANGUAGE
(Advance Alliance Academy Thai Language School; Map p98; ☎ 02 045 1427; www.aaathai.school; 35 Th Phaya Thai, 10th fl, Wannasorn Tower; tuition per hr 700B; [S] Phaya Thai exit 4) Opened by a group of experienced Thai-language teachers from various schools, good-value AAA has a loyal following.

Moo·ay tai (Thai Boxing)

MuayThai Institute MARTIAL ARTS
(☎ 082 985 1115; www.muaythai-institute.net; Rangsit Stadium, 336/932 Th Prachatipat, Pathum Thani; 10-day course from 8000B; [M] Chatuchak Park exit 2 & taxi, [S] Mo Chit exit 3 & taxi) Associated with the respected World Muay Thai Council, the institute offers a fundamental course in Thai boxing (consisting of three levels of expertise), as well as courses for instructors, referees and judges.

Tours

Walking & Speciality Tours

Chili Paste Tours TOURS
(☎ 094 552 2361, 085 143 6779; www.foodtoursbangkok.com; tours from 2000B) This outfit organises culinary tours of Bangkok's older neighbourhoods.

Asian Trails TOURS
(Map p94; ☎ 02 626 2000; www.asiantrails.travel; 9th fl, SG Tower, 161/1 Soi Mahadlek Luang 3) Tour operator that runs programs for overseas brokers. Trips include a mix of on- and off-the-beaten-path destinations.

Bicycle Tours

Grasshopper Adventures CYCLING
(Map p78; ☎ 02 280 0832; www.grasshopperadventures.com; 57 Th Ratchadamnoen Klang; half-/full-day tours from 1350/2400B; 🕒 8.30am-6.30pm; ⛴ klorng boat Phanfa Leelard Pier) This reputable global outfit runs a variety of unique bicycle tours in and around Bangkok, including a night tour and a tour of the city's historic zone.

Velo Thailand CYCLING
(Map p78; ☎ 089 201 7782, 02 628 8628; www.velothailand.com; 29 Soi 4, Th Samsen; tours 1100B; 🕒 tours 9am & 1pm; ⛴ Phra Athit/Banglamphu Pier) Velo is a small and personal bike tour outfit based out of Banglamphu. Tours range from three to four hours, and feature routes in Bangkok, including some on the Thonburi side. Tours are also available further afield in Hua Hin.

Co van Kessel Bangkok Tours CYCLING
(Map p90; ☎ 02 639 7351; www.covankessel.com; Soi 24, Th Charoen Krung, River City; tours from 950B; 🕒 6am-7pm; ⛴ River City Pier) This originally Dutch-run outfit offers a variety of tours in Chinatown, Thonburi and Bangkok's green zones. Most are cycling tours, but some also involve walking and boat rides. Tours depart from the company's office in the River City shopping centre.

ABC Amazing Bangkok Cyclists CYCLING
(Map p110; ☎ 081 812 9641; www.realasia.net; 10/5-7 Soi Aree, Soi 26, Th Sukhumvit; tours from 1300B; 🕒 daily tours at 8am, 10am, 1pm & 6pm; 👪; [S] Phrom Phong exit 4) This is a long-running operation offering morning,

THE ORIGINAL WHITE ELEPHANTS

Think 'white elephant' and something like Howard Hughes' Spruce Goose comes to mind. But why is it that this and other supposedly valuable but hugely expensive and basically useless items are known as white elephants? The answer lies in the sacred status once given to albino elephants by the kings of Thailand, Cambodia, Laos and Myanmar.

The tradition derives from the story in which the Buddha's mother is said to have dreamt of a white elephant presenting her with a lotus flower – a symbol of purity and wisdom – just before she gave birth. Extrapolating from this, a monarch possessing a white elephant was regarded as a just and benign ruler. Across the region any genuinely albino elephant automatically became crown property. Laws prevented sacred white elephants from working, so despite being highly regarded, they were of no practical value and cost a fortune to keep.

In contemporary Thailand, the white elephant has retained its sacred status. The animal was prominently featured on the flag of Siam from 1855 to 1916, and the late King Bhumibol Adulyadej possessed 11 of them, more than any previous monarch. The elephants were once kept at Chitlada Palace in Bangkok, but now reside at three different locations upcountry.

Silom & Sathon

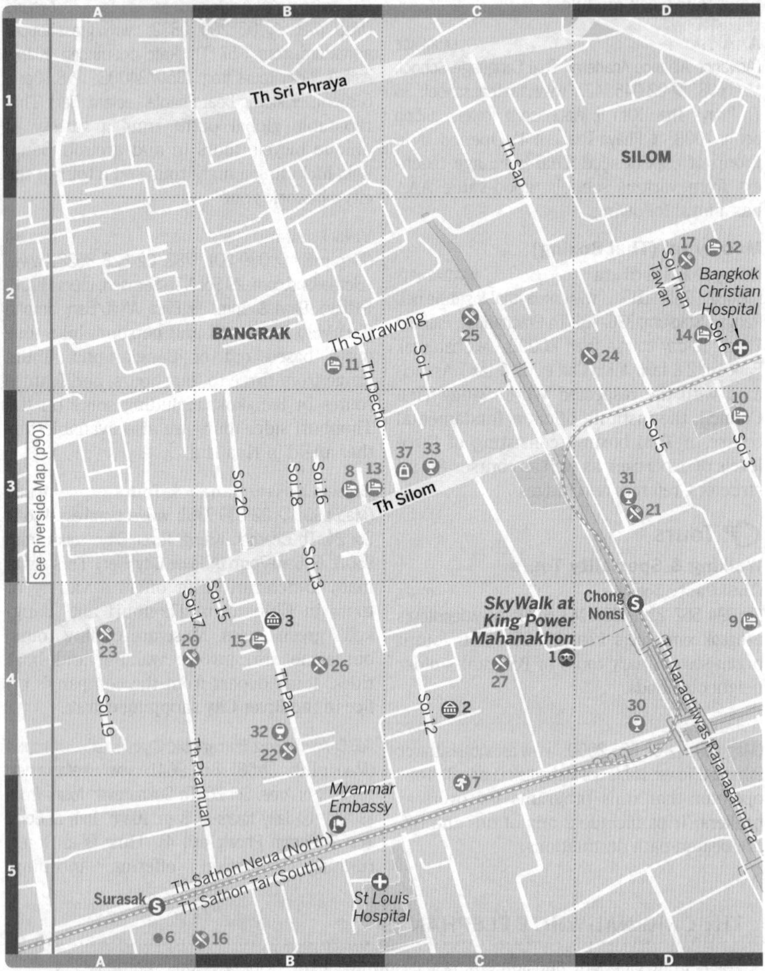

afternoon and all-day bike tours of Bangkok and its suburbs.

SpiceRoads CYCLING

(Map p70; ☎02 381 7490; www.spiceroads.com; 45 Soi Phanni, Soi Pridi Banomyong 26; ⏰9am-6pm Mon-Fri, 10am-3pm Sat) Offers a variety of regional cycling programmes, from day or night trips in Bangkok, central Thailand and Chiang Mai to week-long journeys linking Thailand and neighbouring countries.

River & Canal Trips

The cheapest and most obvious way to commute between riverside attractions is on the commuter boats run by Chao Phraya Express Boat (p158). The terminus for most northbound boats is Nonthaburi Pier, while for most southbound boats it's Sathorn Pier (also called Central Pier), near the Saphan Taksin BTS station (although some boats run as far south as Wat Ratchasingkhon). For a more personal view, you might consider chartering a long-tail boat along the city's canals.

Asian Oasis BOATING

(Map p94; ☎088 809 7047; www.asian-oasis.com; 7th fl, Nai Lert Tower, 2/4 Th Witthayu/Wireless Rd; [S]Phloen Chit exit 1) Cruise the Chao Phraya River aboard a fleet of restored rice barges

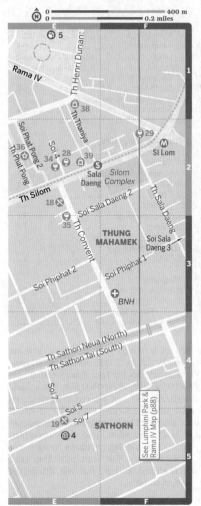

with old-world charm and modern conveniences. Trips include either an upstream or downstream journey to/from Ayuthaya with bus transfer in the opposite direction. Costs vary according to season and direction.

🎎 Festivals & Events

Many Thai festivals follow the lunar calendar, and their dates therefore change annually relative to the Gregorian calendar. Contact local tourist offices for exact festival dates.

Chinese New Year   CULTURAL
(🕑 Jan or Feb) Thai-Chinese celebrate the Lunar New Year with a week of house cleaning,

lion dances and fireworks. Most festivities centre on Chinatown. Dates vary.

Songkran   CULTURAL
(🕑 mid-Apr) The celebration of the Thai New Year has morphed into a water war with high-powered water guns and water balloons being launched at suspecting and unsuspecting participants. The most intense water battles take place on Th Silom and Th Khao San, and festivities continue for three days.

Bangkok Biennale   ART
(🕑 Oct-Feb) The inaugural Bangkok Biennale in 2018–19 created ripples by showcasing the works of some of Asia's biggest artists at public spaces across the metropolis. Featured installations and artworks were exhibited in several temples, shopping malls, buildings and piazzas throughout the city, and were free for the public to view. The next edition is scheduled for 2020–21.

Vegetarian Festival   FOOD & DRINK
(🕑 Sep or Oct) This nine-day Chinese-Buddhist festival wheels out yellow-bannered streetside vendors serving meatless meals. The greatest concentration of vendors is found in Chinatown. Dates vary.

Loi Krathong   CULTURAL
(🕑 Nov) A beautiful festival where, on the night of the full moon, small lotus-shaped boats made of banana leaf and containing a lit candle are set adrift on the Chao Phraya River. One of the best locations for watching the festivities is from the promenade at Asiatique (p146). The lake within Lumphini Park (p85) is an alternative venue for the ritual.

🛏 Sleeping

If your idea of the typical Bangkok hotel was influenced by *The Hangover Part II,* you'll be relieved to learn that the city is home to a variety of modern hostels, guesthouses and hotels. Much of Bangkok's accommodation offers excellent value, and competition is so intense that discounts are almost always available. Thanks to the abundance of options, booking ahead isn't generally required apart from at some of the smaller boutique places.

🛏 Ko Ratanakosin & Thonburi

If you've opted to rest your head in Ko Ratanakosin or Thonburi, you've got the bulk of Bangkok's most famous sights at

Silom & Sathon

your door. Riverside views and a glut of charming midrange places along Th Maha Rat are reasons enough to stay here; a lack of drinking and dining options and the schlep to the newer parts of Bangkok aren't.

Arom D   HOSTEL $$
(Map p78; ☑ 02 622 1055; www.aromdhostel.com; 336 Th Maha Rat; dm/r incl breakfast 800/2250B; ❋ @ ⧄; ⊜ Tien Pier) The rooms here are united by a cutesy design theme and a host of inviting communal areas, including a rooftop deck, computers and a ground-floor cafe. They don't have much space and could use a bit of TLC, but they do have style. Also, you're right in the heart of the hipster Tien village area.

Royal ThaTien Village   HOTEL $$
(Map p78; ☑ 095 151 5545; www.theroyalthatien. com; 392/29 Soi Phen Phat; s & d from 900B; ❋ @ ⧄; ⊜ Tien Pier) These 12 rooms spread over two converted shophouses are relatively unassuming, but TV, fridge, air-con, lots of space and shiny wood floors, not to mention a cosy homestay atmosphere, edge this place into the recommendable category. It's popular, so be sure to book ahead.

★ Sala Ratanakosin   HOTEL $$$
(Map p78; ☑ 02 622 1388; www.salaresorts.com/ rattanakosin; Soi Tha Tian; d incl breakfast from 4000B; ❋ @ ⧄; ⊜ Tien Pier) Sala has a sleek, modernist feel – a somewhat jarring contrast with the former warehouse in which it's located. The 15 rooms are decked out in black and white, and have open-plan bathrooms and big windows looking out on the river and Wat Arun (p73). They can't be described as vast, but will satisfy the fashion-conscious.

★ Arun Residence   HOTEL $$$
(Map p78; ☑ 02 221 9158; www.arunresidence. com; 36-38 Soi Pratu Nokyung; d incl breakfast from 4200B; ❋ @ ⧄; ⊜ Tien Pier) Although strategically located on the river directly across from Wat Arun (p73), this multilevel wooden house has much more than just great views. The seven rooms here manage to feel both homey and stylish (the best are the top-floor, balcony-equipped suites). There are also inviting communal areas, including a library, rooftop bar and restaurant. Advance reservations absolutely essential.

Chakrabongse Villas   HOTEL $$$
(Map p78; ☑ 02 222 1290; www.chakrabongse villas.com; 396 Th Maha Rat; d incl breakfast from

6000B; ✳@🛜☃; 🚲Tien Pier) This almost fairy-tale-like compound incorporates three sumptuous but cramped rooms and four larger suites and villas, some with great river views, all surrounding a still-functioning royal palace dating back to 1908. There's a pool, jungle-like gardens and an elevated deck for romantic riverside dining. No walk-ins.

Aurum: The River Place HOTEL $$$
(Map p78; ☎02 622 2248; www.aurum-bangkok. com; 394/27-29 Soi Pansuk; d incl breakfast from 3700B; ✳@🛜; 🚲Tien Pier) The 12 rooms here don't necessarily reflect the grand European exterior of this refurbished shophouse. Nonetheless they're comfortable, modern and well appointed, and most offer fleeting views of the Chao Phraya River. The quiet location away from the din of Th Maha Rat is a plus.

🛏 Banglamphu

Banglamphu still holds the bulk of Bangkok's budget places, although nowadays it's also home to nearly the entire spectrum of accommodation. Lots of eating, drinking and shopping options are other clever reasons to stay in Banglamphu, although it can feel somewhat isolated from the rest of Bangkok.

★Chern HOSTEL $
(Map p78; ☎02 621 1133; www.chernbangkok.com; 17 Soi Ratchasak; dm/r 350/900B; ✳@🛜; 🚲klorng boat Phanfa Leelard Pier) The vast, open spaces and white, overexposed tones of this hostel converge in an almost afterlife-like feel. The eight-bed dorms are above average,

but the private rooms are particularly impressive, with attractively minimalist touches, a large desk, TV, safe, fridge and heaps of space, and are a steal at this price.

Niras Bankoc HOSTEL $
(Map p78; ☎02 221 4442; www.nirasbankoc.com; 204-206 Th Mahachai; dm/d incl breakfast from 400/1300B; ✳🛜; 🚲klorng boat Phanfa Leelard Pier) A counterpart to Bangkok's predominately modern hostels, Niras takes advantage of its location in an antique shophouse to arrive at a charmingly old-school feel. Both the four- and six-bed dorms and private rooms (some of which share bathrooms) feature dark woods and vintage furniture, with access to friendly staff, a cosy ground-floor cafe and an atmospheric location.

NapPark Hostel HOSTEL $
(Map p78; ☎02 282 2324; www.nappark.com; 5 Th Tani; dm 440-550B; ✳@🛜; 🚲Phra Athit/Banglamphu Pier) This popular hostel features dorm rooms of various sizes, the smallest and most expensive of which has six pod-like beds outfitted with power points, mini-TV, reading lamp and wi-fi. Cultural-based activities and inviting communal areas ensure you may not actually get the chance to plug in. A busy street market peddling travel souvenirs and accessories is located out front.

Wild Orchid Villa HOTEL $
(Map p78; ☎02 629 4378; www.wildorchidvilla. com; 8 Soi Chana Songkhram; s/d incl breakfast 450/1000B; ✳🛜☃; 🚲Phra Athit/Banglamphu Pier) The cheapies here (fan-cooled and with shared bathrooms) are some of the tiniest we've seen anywhere, but like most of the rooms at Wild Orchid are clean and neat, and come in a bright, friendly package. The

---

BIG ADVENTURES FOR LITTLE ONES

The suburbs north of Bangkok are home to a handful of kid-oriented museums and theme parks. All of the following are accessible via taxi from Mo Chit BTS station or Chatuchak Park MRT station.

Children's Discovery Museum (พิพิธภัณฑ์เด็ก; Map p116; Th Kamphaeng Phet 4, Queen Sirikit Park; ⊙10am-4pm Tue-Sun; 🚼; Ⓜ Chatuchak Park exit 1, Ⓢ Mo Chit exit 1) **FREE** Learning is disguised as fun at this museum, with exhibits ranging from construction to culture.

Siam Park City (☎02 919 7200; www.siamparkcity.com; 203 Th Suansiam; adult/child US$25/20; ⊙10am-6pm; Ⓜ Chatuchak Park exit 2 & taxi, Ⓢ Mo Chit exit 1 & taxi) Features more than 30 rides and a water park with the largest wave pool in the world.

Dream World (☎02 577 8666; www.dreamworld.co.th; 62 Mu 1, Th Rangsit-Nakornnayok, Pathum Thani; from 1200B; ⊙10am-5pm Mon-Fri, to 7pm Sat & Sun; Ⓜ Chatuchak Park exit 2 & taxi, Ⓢ Mo Chit exit 1 & taxi) An expansive amusement park that also has a (predictably popular) snow room.

popular multicuisine restaurant and the on-site swimming pool are fabulous dealmakers. It's extremely popular, so be sure to book ahead.

Suneta Hostel Khaosan
HOSTEL $

(Map p78; ☑ 02 629 0150; www.sunetahostel. com; 209-211 Th Kraisi; dm/r incl breakfast from 470/1200B; ❄ @ ☞; ☑ Phra Athit/Banglamphu Pier) A pleasant, low-key atmosphere, a unique, retro-themed design (some of the dorm rooms resemble sleeping-car carriages), a location just off the main drag and friendly service are what make Suneta stand out among the tight competition.

Vivit Hostel
HOSTEL $

(Map p78; ☑ 02 224 5888; www.vivithostel.com; 510 Th Tanao; dm/r incl breakfast 450/1000B; ❄ ☞; ☑ klorng boat Phanfa Leelard Pier) Flower-patterned curtains, framed portraits of flowers and grandfather clocks provide this hostel with an overwhelmingly mature feel, despite it having opened only in 2017. Nonetheless the dorms represent excellent – if slightly bland – value.

★ Nouvo City Hotel
HOTEL $$

(Map p78; ☑ 02 282 7500; www.nouvocityhotel. com; 2 Soi 2, Th Samsen; s & d incl breakfast from 1600B; ❄ ☞ ☒; ☑ Phra Athit/Banglamphu Pier) A modern and luxurious hotel in the Samsen area, Nouvo prides itself as a halal-certified establishment oriented towards Muslim travellers. Rooms aren't the most spacious for the price, but are well appointed and adorned in pleasant colour schemes and upholstery. A terrace pool and on-site spa are added bonuses, as is the quiet canalside location. Praying facilities are available on-site.

★ Lamphu Treehouse
HOTEL $$

(Map p78; ☑ 02 282 0991; www.lamphutreehotel. com; 155 Wanchat Bridge, off Th Prachathipatai; d incl breakfast from 1650B; ❄ @ ☞ ☒; ☑ klorng boat Phanfa Leelard Pier) Despite the name, this attractive midranger has its feet firmly on land, and represents brilliant value. The wood-panelled rooms are attractive, inviting and well maintained, and the rooftop sun lounge, pool, internet cafe, restaurant and quiet canalside location ensure you may never feel the need to leave. A nearby annexe increases the odds of snagging an elusive reservation.

Warehouse
HOTEL $$

(Map p78; ☑ 02 622 2935; www.thewarehouse bangkok.com; 120 Th Bunsiri; d incl breakfast from 2000B; ❄ @ ☞; ☑ klorng boat Phanfa Leelard

Pier) Wooden pallets as furniture, yellow-and-black wall art, and exposed fittings and other industrial elements contribute to the factory theme at this midrange option. Against all odds, the Warehouse pulls it off, and what you get are 36 rooms that are fun, functional and relatively spacious, if not stupendous value.

Chillax Resort
HOTEL $$

(Map p78; ☑ 083 099 0638; www.chillaxresort.com; 272 Soi 2, Th Samsen; d incl breakfast from 2700B; ❄ @ ☞ ☒; ☑ Phra Athit/Banglamphu Pier) If the name isn't a giveaway, this giant operation vies for traveller attention with a curious aesthetic style that's halfway between period and bling. Purple neon-inspired lighting matches pink-and-beige upholstery in its comfortable and well-kept rooms. It's located at the end of a quiet lane by the canal.

Nanda Heritage
HOTEL $$

(Map p78; ☑ 02 282 2900; www.nandaheritage.com; 632 Th Wisut Kasat; d incl breakfast from 2000B; ❄ ☞; ☑ klorng boat Phanfa Leelard Pier) Taking cues from the teak home that used to reside here and the wooden buildings that still surround it is this contemporary design-forward hotel. Rooms are well equipped, and come decked out in subtle, earthy colours, with spacious en suite bathrooms. It's a clever choice for the sophisticated but still-want-to-be-near-Th-Khao-San crowd.

Villa Cha-Cha
HOTEL $$

(Map p78; ☑ 02 280 1025; www.villachacha.com; 36 Th Tani; d 1300B; ❄ ☞ ☒; ☑ Phra Athit/Banglamphu Pier) Wind your way between Balinese statues, lounging residents, a rambling restaurant and a tiny pool to emerge at this seemingly hidden but popular hotel. Rooms are adequate – bar the frequently clumsy stabs made at interior design (like art-school nude portraits) – but the real draw is the hyper-social, resort-like atmosphere.

Baan Dinso 2
HOTEL $$

(Map p78; ☑ 096 556 9795; www.baandinso.com; 78/3 Th Ratchadamnoen Klang; s/d incl breakfast from 1250B; ❄ ☞; ☑ klorng boat Phanfa Leelard Pier) Overlooking what may arguably be the most famous visual-reference intersection for travellers in Bangkok, the 27 modern rooms at this establishment range from tiny singles with shared bathrooms to the more spacious grand rooms, many of which offer fleeting views of the Democracy Monument. The buzzing traveller ghetto of Th Khao San is only about 400m away.

KNOW YOUR BEDS

Hostels

Those counting every baht can get a dorm bed (or a closet-like room) with a shared bathroom for as little as 300B. The latest trend in Bangkok is slick 'flashpacker' hostels that blur the line between budget and midrange. A bed at these will cost between around 400B and 800B.

If you're on a shoestring budget, Bangkok has plenty of options for you, ranging from high-tech, pod-like dorm beds in a brand-new hostel to cosy bunk beds in a refurbished Chinatown shophouse. (If you decide that you need a bit more privacy, nearly all of Bangkok's hostels also offer private rooms.)

Guesthouses

Guesthouses mentioned in this book are essentially budget places featuring rooms in family homes. Guesthouses and similar budget hotels are generally found in somewhat inconveniently located corners of old Bangkok (Banglamphu, Chinatown and Thewet), which means that the money you're saving in rent will probably go on taxi fares. Rates begin at about 500B.

Hotels

The cheapest places often share bathrooms and may not even supply a towel. Some remain fan-cooled or will only run the air-con between certain hours. Wi-fi, if available, is typically free.

'Midrange' has come to mean a private room with air-con, fridge, hot water, TV and free wi-fi. However, it's not uncommon for a room to have all of these but lack a view (or windows). Breakfast can be 'buffets' based around toast and oily fried eggs to healthier meals with yoghurt or fruit.

Top-end hotels supply all the facilities you'd expect at this level. Swimming pools are standard, as are fitness and business centres, restaurants and bars. Breakfast is often buffet-style.

Buddy Lodge   HOTEL $$
(Map p78; ☑02 629 4477; www.buddylodge.com; 256 Th Khao San; s & d from 1200B; ﹡@☎☀; ☀Phra Athit/Banglamphu Pier) This huge complex, which includes a pool, fitness room and (ahem) a branch of McDonald's, features 70 rooms that are comfortable, well equipped and evocative of a breezy, tropical manor house. Prices usually drop if you stay five days or longer. The property also features a popular bar and a cool boutique for handicrafts.

Hotel Dé Moc   HOTEL $$
(Map p78; ☑02 629 2100; www.hoteldemoc.com; 78 Th Prachathipatai; s & d incl breakfast from 1300B; ﹡@☎☀; ☀klorng boat Phanfa Leelard Pier) With high ceilings and generous windows, the rooms at this 1960s-era hotel feel spacious, although the furnishings, like the exterior, are still stuck sometime in the previous century. The grounds include an inviting and retro-feeling pool and cafe, while complimentary transport to Th Khao San and free use of bikes are thoughtful perks.

Rambuttri Village Plaza   HOSTEL $$
(Map p78; ☑02 282 9162; www.rambuttrivillage. com; 95 Soi Ram Buttri; s/d from 700/900B; ﹡☎☀; ☀Phra Athit/Banglamphu Pier) Located off the main Soi Ram Buttri drag, this mid-sized hotel has a decades-long reputation for delivering unbeatable value for money. With an abundance of compact yet clean and well-appointed rooms, a ground-floor courtyard with restaurants and shops and a pretty terrace pool, this is both a convenient and comfortable place to stay.

Old Capital Bike Inn   HOTEL $$
(Map p78; ☑02 629 1787; www.oldcapitalbkk.com; 609 Th Phra Sumen; d incl breakfast from 3200B; ﹡@☎; ☀klorng boat Phanfa Leelard Pier) The dictionary definition of a honeymoon hotel, this antique shophouse has 10 rooms that are decadent and sumptuous, blending rich colours and heavy wood furnishings. True to its name, the bicycle theme runs throughout, and bikes can be borrowed free of charge.

Thewet & Dusit

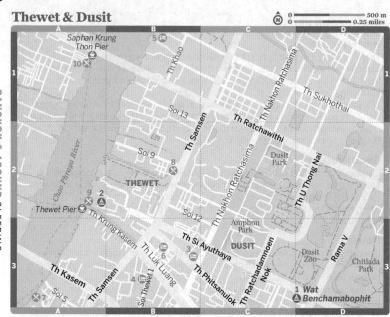

Thewet & Dusit

Villa Phra Sumen　　　　　　　　　HOTEL **$$**

(Map p78; ☑ 080 085 0085; www.villaphrasumen.
com; 457 Th Phra Sumen; d incl breakfast from
2000B; ✳@🔊; 🛥klorng boat Phanfa Leelard
Pier) Surrounding a garden and edging the
canal, Villa Phra Sumen boasts a secluded,
secret feel. Gain access to the compound and
inside you'll find 24 somewhat tight (and
somewhat overpriced) rooms, all of which
come equipped with balconies and contem-
porary amenities, and are looked after by
service-minded staff.

★**Praya Palazzo**　　　　　　　　　HOTEL **$$$**

(Map p78; ☑ 02 883 2998; www.prayapalazzo.com;
757/1 Somdej Prapinklao Soi 2; d incl breakfast from
3600B; ✳🔊✉; 🛥hotel shuttle boat from Phra
Athit/Banglamphu Pier) After lying dormant
for over 30 years, this elegant 19th-century
mansion in Thonburi was reborn as an attractive riverside boutique hotel in 2011. The
17 rooms can seem rather tight, and river
views can be elusive, but the meticulous renovation, handsome antique furnishings and
bucolic atmosphere deliver a boutique hotel
with authentic old-world charm.

The fact that the hotel is located on a
canal-bound islet and can only be accessed
by the riverway makes it an unwise choice
for night owls, but an excellent hideaway
for honeymooners, sleep-deprived souls and
solitude seekers.

Riva Surya　　　　　　　　　　　HOTEL **$$$**

(Map p78; ☑ 02 633 5000; www.nexthotels.com;
23 Th Phra Athit; d incl breakfast from 4300B;
✳@✉; 🛥Phra Athit/Banglamphu Pier) A for-
mer condo has been transformed into one
of the more design-conscious hotels in this
part of town. The 68 rooms are decked out
in greys and blacks, with contemporary fur-
nishings, and in the case of the Deluxe and
Riva rooms, great river views, although not

always tonnes of space. The undersized pool can feel a bit crammed at times.

🛏 Chinatown

Chinatown is home to some good-value budget and midrange accommodation options. It's also close to Bangkok's main train station for out of town trips. Downsides include noise, pollution and the neighbourhood's relative distance from the BTS Skytrain network and 'new' Bangkok.

Wanderlust BKK   HOSTEL $
(Map p84; ☑089 757 7770; 149-151 Rama IV; dm 350B, d from 700B; ❄🛜; Ⓜ Hua Lamphong exit 1) An almost clinical-feeling industrial vibe rules at this hip hostel. The dorms span four to eight beds, and the private rooms are on the tight side, with the cheapest sharing bathrooms. These are united by a hyper-chic ground-floor cafe-restaurant. Not the greatest value accommodation in Chinatown, but quite possibly the most image-conscious.

Loftel 22   HOSTEL $
(Map p90; ☑086 807 1144; 952 Soi 22, Th Charoen Krung; dm 250-400B, r with shared bathroom 700-1300B; ❄@🛜; 🚢 Marine Department Pier, Ⓜ Hua Lamphong exit 1) Stylish, inviting dorms and private rooms (all with shared bathrooms) have been coaxed out of these two adjoining shophouses. Friendly service and a location in one of Chinatown's atmospheric neighbourhoods round out the package.

@Hua Lamphong   HOSTEL $
(Map p84; ☑02 639 1925; www.hualamphong hostel.com; 326/1 Rama IV; dm 350B, r 900-1100B; ❄@🛜; Ⓜ Hua Lamphong exit 1) Not only does this hostel provide the most handy access to Bangkok's main train terminal, it's also clean and very well run. The private rooms, some of which are huge and feature balconies, are particularly good value. Factoring in convenience, comfort and amenities in equal measures, this place easily features among the city's best hostels.

★ Shanghai Mansion   HOTEL $$
(Map p84; ☑02 221 2121; www.shanghaimansion. com; 479-481 Th Yaowarat; r/ste incl breakfast from 2100/3500B; ❄@🛜; 🚢 Ratchawong Pier, Ⓜ Hua Lamphong exit 1 & taxi) Easily the most consciously stylish place to stay in Chinatown, this award-winning boutique hotel screams Shanghai c 1935 with stained glass, an abundance of lamps, bold colours and cheeky kitsch. If you're willing to splurge, ask for

one of the bigger streetside rooms with tall windows that allow more light. It's located smack in Chinatown's atmospheric centre.

★ Loy La Long   HOTEL $$$
(Map p84; ☑02 639 1390; www.loylalong. com; 1620/2 Th Songwat, Wat Pathum Khongka Ratchaworawihan; s/d incl breakfast 2700/4900B; ❄🛜; 🚢 Ratchawong Pier, Ⓜ Hua Lamphong exit 1 & taxi) Rustic, retro, charming: the six rooms in this teak house lay claim to more than their share of personality. Occupying a prestigious location stilted over the Chao Phraya's waters, it also has a hidden, almost secret, feel. The only hitch is in finding it; proceed to Th Songwat and cut through Wat Pathum Khongka Ratchaworawihan (วัดปทุมคงคาราชวรวิหาร; Map p84; off Th Songwat; ⊙daylight hours; 🚢 Marine Department Pier, Ⓜ Hua Lamphong exit 1 & taxi) to the riverside.

Feung Nakorn Balcony   HOTEL $$$
(Map p78; ☑02 622 1100; www.feungnakorn. com; 20 Soi Fuang Thong, Th Fuang Nakhon; s/d incl breakfast 2500/4000B; ❄@🛜; 🚢 Memorial Bridge Pier) Located in a former school, the 42 rooms here surround an inviting garden courtyard and are generally large, bright and cheery. Amenities such as a free minibar, safe and flat-screen TV are standard, and the hotel has a quiet and secluded location away from the main road. A charming and inviting (if not somewhat great-value) place to stay.

🛏 Riverside, Silom & Lumphini

You will find some fantastic budget and luxury accommodation in these co-joined 'hoods, but there's relatively little in-between.

★ Warm Window   HOSTEL $
(Map p100; ☑02 235 8759; www.warmwindow silom.com; 50/18-19 Th Pan; dm/d incl breakfast from 360/1200B; ❄@🛜; Ⓢ Surasak exit 1/3) A fairly recent addition to Silom's ever-evolving hostel scene, this sleek address has two fantastic 10-bed dorms, both of which feature comfy, curtain-lined bunk beds fitted with elegant wood panelling. The private rooms are an absolute steal for the price, and the downstairs cafe is a superb place to lounge in if you feel like some me-time amid your citywide explorations.

Smile Society   HOSTEL $
(Map p100; ☑095 228 2415; www.smilesociety hostel.com; 130/3-4 Soi 6, Th Silom; dm/r from 260/950B; ❄@🛜; Ⓜ Si Lom exit 2, Ⓢ Sala Daeng

ROLLIN' ON THE CANAL

Bangkok was formerly known as the Venice of the East, as the city used to be criss-crossed by an advanced network of *klorng* (also spelt *khlong*), artificial canals that inhabitants used both for transport and to ship goods. A peek into the watery Bangkok of yesteryear can still be had west of the Chao Phraya River, in Thonburi.

Thonburi's network of canals and river tributaries still carries a motley fleet of water-craft, from paddle canoes to rice barges. Homes, trading houses and temples are built on stilts with front doors opening out to the water. According to residents, these waterways protect them from the seasonal flooding that plagues the capital. **Khlong Bangkok Noi** is lined with greenery and historic temples; smaller **Khlong Mon** is largely residential. **Khlong Bangkok Yai** was in fact the original course of the river until a canal was built to expedite transits. Today long-tail boats that ply these and other Thonburi canals are available for charter at Chang Pier and Tien Pier, both on Ko Ratanakosin. Prices at these piers are slightly higher than elsewhere and allow little room for negotiation, but you stand the least chance of being conned or hit up for tips and other unexpected fees.

Trips generally traverse Khlong Bangkok Noi and Khlong Mon, taking in the Royal Barges National Museum (p76), Wat Arun (p73) and a riverside temple with fish feeding. Longer trips diverge into Khlong Bangkok Yai, and can include a visit to an orchid farm. On weekends, you have the option of visiting the Taling Chan Floating Market (p154). Most operators have set tour routes, but if you have a specific destination in mind, you can request it. Tours are generally conducted from 8am to 5pm.

If you'd prefer something longer or more personalised, **Pandan Tour** (📞096 937 8803; www.thaicanaltour.com; tours from 2400B) conducts a variety of mostly full-day tours. A budget alternative is to take the one-way-only **commuter long-tail boat** (Map p78; Chang Pier; ⏰4.30am-7.30pm; 🚤Chang Pier) from Chang Pier to Bang Yai, at the distant northern end of Khlong Bangkok Noi, although foreigners are sometimes discouraged from doing so.

exit 1) Part boutique hotel, part hostel, this four-storey operation combines small but comfortable and well-equipped rooms, and dorms with spotless shared bathrooms. A central location, overwhelmingly positive guest feedback, and helpful, English-speaking staff are other perks. A virtually identical annexe next door helps with spillover as Smile Society gains more fans.

All That Bangkok   HOSTEL $
(Map p70; 📞094 493 6637; www.allthatbangkok hostel.com; 4 Soi 11, Yaek 5, Th Sathon Tai/South; dm 450-550B; ❄@🛜; 🚆Chong Nonsi exit 5) This boutique hostel is tucked down a residential side street. Upstairs are three mixed-bed dorms with 19 comfortable beds, plus one room with private shower (1900B). On the ground floor, an industrial-styled cafe has Nitro coffee on tap and whips up a decent eggs Benedict for only 95B. Walking distance to the BTS means easy transport around town.

Silom Art Hostel   HOSTEL $
(Map p100; 📞02 635 8070; www.silomarthostel. com; 198/19-22 Soi 14, Th Silom; dm/r 450/950B; ❄@🛜; 🚆Chong Nonsi exit 3) Quirky, artsy, bright and fun, Silom Art Hostel combines

recycled materials, unconventional furnishings and colourful wall paintings to culminate in a hostel that's quite unlike anywhere else in town. It's not all about style though: beds and rooms are functional and comfortable, with lots of appealing communal areas.

S1 Hostel   HOSTEL $
(Map p88; 📞02 679 7777; 35/1-4 Soi Ngam Du Phli; dm/r from 330/900B; ❄@🛜; Ⓜ️Lumphini exit 1) This huge hostel has dorm beds and private rooms decked out in a simple yet attractive primary-colour scheme. A host of facilities – laundry, kitchen, rooftop garden – and a convenient location within walking distance of the MRT make it great value.

HQ Hostel   HOSTEL $
(Map p100; 📞02 233 1598; www.hqhostel.com; 5/3-4 Soi 3, Th Silom; dm/r 480/1750B; ❄@🛜; Ⓜ️Si Lom exit 2, 🚆Sala Daeng exit 2) HQ is a flashpacker hostel in the polished-concrete-and-industrial-style mould. It includes four- to six-bed dorms, a few private double and triple rooms (some with en suite bathrooms) and inviting communal areas in a narrow multistorey building in the middle of Bangkok's financial district.

★**kokotel**　　　　　　　HOTEL **$$**
(Map p100; ☏02 235 7555, 02 026 3218; www.
kokotel.com; 181/1-5 Th Surawong; s/d incl break-
fast 1600/2600B; ✱@🛜; ⓢChong Nonsi exit 3)
Quite possibly one of Bangkok's most fami-
ly-friendly accommodations, kokotel unites
big, sun-filled rooms with puffy beds, an ex-
pansive children's play area and a downstairs
cafe (with, appropriately, a slide). Friendly
rates – including super sales conducted from
time to time – also make it great value, espe-
cially considering its central location.

★**Siam Heritage**　　　BOUTIQUE HOTEL **$$**
(Map p100; ☏02 353 6166; www.thesiamheritage.
com; 115/1 Th Surawong; d incl breakfast from
1800B; ✱@🛜🏊; Ⓜ️Si Lom exit 2, ⓢSala Daeng
exit 1) Tucked off busy Th Surawong, this hotel overflows with homey Thai charm – and
is a total steal at its competitive midrange
price point. The 73 rooms are decked out
in silk and dark woods with classy design
touches and thoughtful amenities. There's
an inviting rooftop garden/pool/spa, and
it's all cared for by a team of professional,
accommodating staff. Highly recommended.

Amber　　　　　　　　HOTEL **$$**
(Map p100; ☏02 635 7272; www.amberboutique
silom.com; 200 Soi 14, Th Silom; d incl breakfast
1500-1800B; ✱@🛜; ⓢChong Nonsi exit 3)
Spanning design themes such as Moroccan,
Sino-Portuguese and Modern, it's easy to
assume that Amber might emphasise style
over comfort. But nothing here is flashy or
overwrought, and what you'll get are 19 ex-
cellent-value, spacious rooms with lots of
amenities and natural light in a quiet loca-
tion. Frequent promotions often bring the
rates down, making it terrific value.

Café Ice Residence　　GUESTHOUSE **$$**
(Map p100; ☏02 636 7373; cafeiceresidences@
gmail.com; 44/2 Soi 8, Th Sathon Neua/North;
d incl breakfast from 2400B; ✱@🛜; ⓢChong
Nonsi exit 2) This spotless, classy villa is more
home than hotel, with nine inviting, spacious and comfortable rooms. Outfitted with
subtle yet attractive furnishings, they also
share a location with a Thai restaurant on
a quiet street branching north off the main
Sathon thoroughfare.

W Home　　　　　　　GUESTHOUSE **$$**
(Map p70; ☏02 291 5622; www.whomebangkok.
com; Yaek 8, Soi 79, Th Charoen Krung; s/d incl
breakfast 1200/1500B; ✱@🛜; ⓢSaphan Taksin
exit 2 & taxi) It's admittedly off the grid, but
that's part of the charm at this 60-year-old

renovated house. Welcoming hosts, four
small but attractive and thoughtfully fur-
nished rooms (one with en suite bathroom),
inviting communal areas and an authen-
tic homestay atmosphere round out the
package.

Soi 79 branches off Th Charoen Krung
about 1km south of Saphan Taksin. W Home
is 250m east of the main road.

Swan Hotel　　　　　HOTEL **$$**
(Map p90; ☏02 235 9271; www.swanhotelbkk.
com; 31 Soi 36/Rue de Brest, Th Charoen Krung;
s/d 1000/1500B; ✱@🛜🏊; ⓔOriental Pier) The
1960s-era furnishings somewhat date this
classic Bangkok hotel, but the rooms are
airy and virtually spotless, and the antiquated vibe provides the Swan, particularly its
pool area, with a fun, hip vibe.

LUXX XL　　　　　　　HOTEL **$$**
(Map p88; ☏02 684 1111; www.staywithluxx.com;
82/8 Th Langsuan; r 1700-2400B; ste from 2500B;
✱@🛜🏊; ⓢRatchadamri exit 2) LUXX XL
oozes with a contemporary, minimalist hip-
ness that wouldn't be out of place in Lon-
don or New York. Floor-to-ceiling windows
allow heaps of natural light, suites have an
added kitchenette, and all rooms are decked
out with appropriately stylish furnishings.
There's another slightly cheaper (and small-
er) branch on Th Decho, off Th Silom.

★**Peninsula Hotel**　　　HOTEL **$$$**
(Map p90; ☏02 020 2888; www.peninsula.com;
333 Th Charoen Nakhon; d incl breakfast from
8800B; ✱@🛜🏊; ⓔhotel shuttle boat from
Sathorn/Central Pier) The matchless and age-
less Pen has it all: the location (towering
over the river); the reputation (it's consistently among the world's top-ranking luxury
hotels); and one of the highest levels of service in town. Its stately rooms are an absolute delight to stay in, and a lavish breakfast
at the riverside open-air restaurant provides
the perfect start to your day.

★**Metropolitan by COMO**　HOTEL **$$$**
(Map p88; ☏02 625 3333; www.comohotels.com;
27 Th Sathon Tai/South; r/ste incl breakfast from
5100/8700B; ✱@🛜🏊; Ⓜ️Lumphini exit 2) The
exterior of Bangkok's former YMCA has
changed relatively little, but a peek inside
reveals one of the city's sleekest, sexiest ho-
tels. The 171 rooms come in striking tones
of black, white and yellow, though it's worth
noting that the City rooms tend to feel a bit
tight, while in contrast the two-storey pent-
house suites are like small homes.

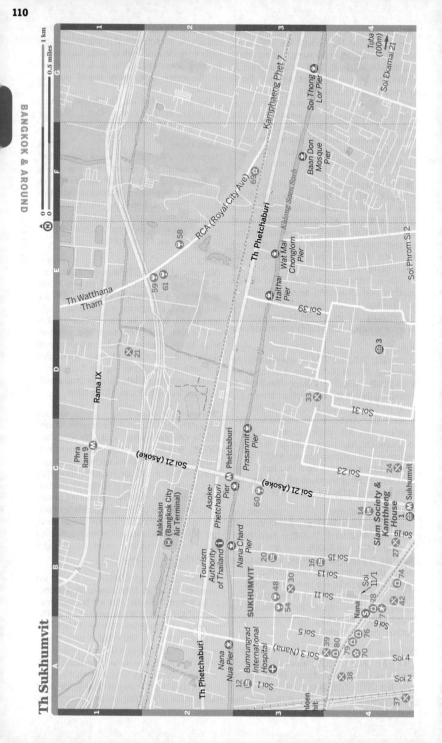

Th Sukhumvit

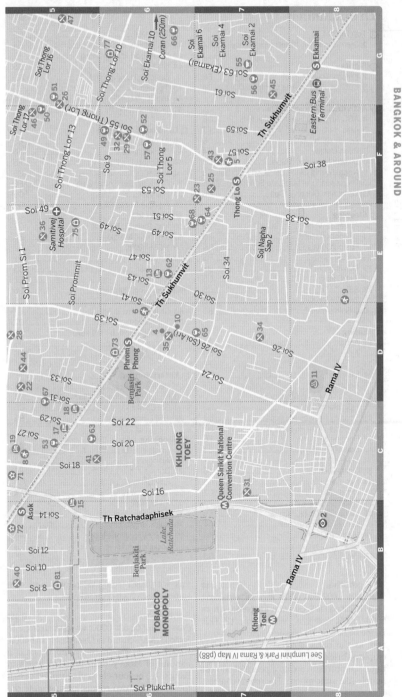

Th Sukhumvit

Top Sights

1 Siam Society & Kamthieng House........C4

Sights

2 Khlong Toey Market........B8
3 Subhashok The Arts Centre........D4

Activities, Courses & Tours

4 ABC Amazing Bangkok Cyclists........D6
5 Asia Herb Association........F7
6 Aspire Club........D6
7 Baan Dalah........B4
8 Divana Massage & Spa........C5
9 Noah Tennis Club........E8
10 Phussapa Thai Massage School........D6
11 Yunomori Onsen & Spa........D8

Sleeping

12 AriyasomVilla........A3
13 Cabochon Hotel........E6
14 Fusion Suites........C4
15 Ma Du Zi........B5
16 Mövenpick........B3
17 RetrOasis........C5
18 S31........C5
19 Tints of Blue........C5
20 U Sukhumvit........B3

Eating

21 Anotai........D1
22 Appia........D5
23 Bacco........F7
24 Bharani........C4
25 Bo.lan........F7
26 Boon Tong Kiat Singapore Chicken Rice........G5
27 Charley Browns Mexicana........B4
28 Cocotte Farm Roast & Winery........D5
29 Congee & Curry........F6
30 Daniel Thaiger........B3
31 El Mercado........C7
32 Gokfayuen........F6
33 Haoma........D3
34 Indus........D7
35 Jidori Cuisine Ken........D6
36 Klang Soi Restaurant........E5
37 Lenzi Tuscan Kitchen........A4
38 Marriott Café........A4
39 Nasir Al-Masri........A4
40 Prai Raya........B5
41 Rang Mahal........C5
42 Scandinavian Smorgaasbuffet........B4
43 Soul Food Mahanakorn........F7
44 Sri Trat........D5
Sunday Jazzy Brunch........(see 72)
45 Teppen........G7
46 theCOMMONS........F5
47 Wattana Panich........G5

Drinking & Nightlife

48 Above 11........B3
49 Backstage Bar........F6
50 Badmotel........F5
51 Beam........G5
52 Black Amber Social Club........F6
53 Brewski........C5
54 Havana Social Club........B3
55 Ink & Lion........G7
56 Iron Balls Distillery & Bar........G7
57 J Boroski Mixology........F6
58 NOMA BKK........E2
59 Onyx........E2
60 Q&A Bar........C3
61 Route 66........E2
62 Sing Sing Theater........E6
63 Sky on 20........C5
64 Studio Lam........E7
65 Taproom........D7
66 Tasting Room by Mikkeller........G6
67 Walden........D5
68 WTF........E6

Entertainment

69 House........F3
70 Nana Entertainment Plaza........A4
71 Soi Cowboy........C5
72 The Living Room........B5

Shopping

73 Another Story........D6
74 Artbox........B4
75 Duly........E5
Emquartier........(see 73)
76 Nickermann's........A4
77 Paya Shop........G6
78 Raja's Fashions........B4
79 Rajawongse........A4
80 Ricky's Fashion House........A4
Sop Moei Arts........(see 36)
81 Tailor on Ten........B5

★ Sukhothai HOTEL $$$

(Map p88; ☎02 344 8888; www.sukhothai.com; 13/3 Th Sathon Tai/South; r/ste incl breakfast from 5000/7300B; ❄@☜≋; Ⓜ Lumphini exit 2) This is one of Bangkok's classiest luxury options, and, as the name suggests, the Sukhothai employs brick stupas, courtyards and antique sculptures to create a peaceful, almost temple-like atmosphere. The rooms contrast this with high-tech TVs, phones and – in some cases – high-tech toilets.

Sofitel So HOTEL $$$

(Map p88; ☎02 624 0000; www.sofitel.com; 2 Th Sathon Neua/North; d incl breakfast from 6400B; ❄@☜≋; Ⓜ Lumphini exit 2) This is one of a handful of large-yet-hip branded hotels in Bangkok. The four-elements-inspired design theme has no two rooms looking quite the same, but all are spacious and stylish, contemporary and young. The infinity pool has a fabulous view of Bangkok's skyline, fronted by the Lumphini Park greens.

🛏 Siam Square, Pratunam, Phloen Chit & Ratchathewi

These co-joined 'hoods offer a good selection of budget and midrange accommodation. Added benefits include a central location and easy access to food, shopping and public transport.

★ Lub d   HOSTEL $

(Map p94; ☑ 02 612 4999; www.lubd.com/siamsquare; 925/9 Rama I; dm/r incl breakfast from 900/1400B; ❄ @ 🛜; Ⓢ National Stadium exit 1) The title is a play on the Thai làp dee, meaning 'sleep well', but the fun atmosphere at this modern hostel might make you want to stay up all night. Diversions include an inviting communal area stocked with games and a bar, and facilities range from washing machines to a theatre room.

Chao Hostel   HOSTEL $

(Map p94; ☑ 02 217 3083; www.chaohostel.com; 8th fl, 865 Rama I, Siam@Siam Bldg; dm/r 550/1400B; ❄ @ 🛜; Ⓢ National Stadium exit 1) Blending modern minimalist and Thai design elements, not to mention tonnes of open space, the Chao is one of the most sophisticated hostels in Bangkok. Dorms are roomy, with six beds and en suite bathrooms, and include access to several inviting communal areas.

Boxpackers Hostel   HOSTEL $

(Map p94; ☑ 02 656 2828; www.boxpackers hostel.com; 39/3 Soi 15, Th Phetchaburi; dm/q from 420/1800B; ❄ 🛜; Ⓢ Ratchathewi exit 1 & taxi) A contemporary, sparse hostel with dorms ranging in size from four to 12 double-decker pods – some of which are double beds. Communal areas are inviting, and include a ground-floor cafe and a lounge with pool table. A linked hotel also offers 14 small but similarly attractive private rooms.

K Maison   BOUTIQUE HOTEL $$

(Map p98; ☑ 02 245 1953; www.kmaisonboutique. com; Soi Ruam Chit; d incl breakfast from 2200B; ❄ 🛜; Ⓢ Victory Monument exit 4) The lobby, with its pure white, swirling marble and streaks of blue, sets the tone of this boutique hotel. The 21 rooms follow suit, and are handsome in a delicate and attractively sparse way. Lest you think it's all about image, fear not: K Maison is also functional and comfortable.

The Bangkokians   HOMESTAY $$

(Map p98; ☑ 02 642 5497; www.thebangkokians. com; 335/1 Soi 12, Th Ratchaprarop; d incl breakfast 1500B; ❄ 🛜; Ⓢ Victory Monument exit 1/3 & taxi) Weary of the standard hotel experience? Then consider a stay at this residential-feeling, homestay-like hotel. Housed in four bungalows dotting an inviting garden, the rooms offer space, lots of natural light and old-school Thai charm. Check-in is at the nearby Hotel de Bangkok.

Cacha Art Hotel   HOTEL $$

(Map p70; ☑ 02 216 8950; www.cachahotel. com; 156/5-9 Th Phetchaburi; s/d incl breakfast 1200/1600B; ❄ 🛜; Ⓢ Ratchathewi exit 3) The ubiquitous industrial-chic look is given a breath of fresh air via Thai/elephant touches at this charming, if somewhat inconveniently located, small hotel. The 35 rooms are decked out in stylish, functional furniture and colourful wall paintings, although some of the cheapest lack windows. Thoughtful amenities, including a laundry room and a ground-floor cafe, are pluses.

Bizotel   HOTEL $$

(Map p98; ☑ 02 245 2424; www.bizotelbkk.com; 104/40 Th Rang Nam; d incl breakfast from 1900B; ❄ @ 🛜; Ⓢ Victory Monument exit 4) Attractive, bright and stuffed with useful amenities, you could be fooled into believing that the rooms at this hotel cost twice this much. A location in a relatively quiet part of town is another bonus, while helpful, friendly staff seal the deal.

★ Siam@Siam   HOTEL $$$

(Map p94; ☑ 02 217 3000; www.siamatsiam. com; 865 Rama I; d incl breakfast from 3300B; ❄ @ 🛜 ⊠; Ⓢ National Stadium exit 1) A seemingly random mishmash of colours and industrial/recycled materials here result in a style one could describe as 'junkyard chic' – in a good way. The rooms are found between the 14th and 24th floors, and offer terrific city views. There's a rooftop restaurant and an excellently maintained 11th-floor pool.

★ Hansar   HOTEL $$$

(Map p94; ☑ 02 209 1234; www.hansarbangkok. com; 3 Soi Mahadlekluang 2; ste incl breakfast from 6000B; ❄ @ 🛜 ⊠; Ⓢ Ratchadamri exit 4) The Hansar can claim that elusive amalgam of style and value. All 94 rooms here are handsome and feature huge bathrooms and giant desks, but the smallest (and cheapest) studios are probably the best deal, as they have a kitchenette, washing machine, stand-alone tub and, in most, a balcony.

Lit Bangkok Hotel & Residence HOTEL $$$

(Map p94; ☑ 02 612 3456; www.litbangkok.com; 36/1 Soi Kasem San 1; d incl breakfast from 3400B; ✸@☞☲; Ⓢ National Stadium exit 1) This modern, architecturally striking hotel has a variety of room styles united by a theme based on dramatic accent lighting. Check out a few, as they vary significantly, and some features, such as a shower that can be seen from the living room, aren't necessarily for everybody.

Hotel Indigo HOTEL $$$

(Map p94; ☑ 02 207 4999; www.ihg.com; 81 Th Witthayu/Wireless Rd; d incl breakfast from 4900B; ✸@☞☲; Ⓢ Phloen Chit exit 5) An international chain with local flavour, the Indigo has borrowed from the history and culture of Bangkok to arrive at a hotel that is retro, modern, Thai and artsy all at the same time. Many of the 192 rooms overlook some of the greener areas of Bangkok's embassy district, and all are decked out with colourful furnishings and functional amenities.

Okura Prestige HOTEL $$$

(Map p94; ☑ 02 687 9000; www.okurabangkok. com; 57 Th Witthayu/Wireless Rd; d incl breakfast from 7700B; Ⓟ✸@☞☲; Ⓢ Phloen Chit exit 5) The Bangkok venture of this Japanese chain is – unlike many other big-name operations in Bangkok – distinctly unflashy. But we like the minimalist, almost contemplative feel of the lobby and the 240 rooms, and the subtle but thoughtful, often distinctly Japanese, touches. Significant online discounts are available from time to time.

🛏 Thanon Sukhumvit

Th Sukhumvit is home to a significant slice of Bangkok's hotels, though it excels in the top-end luxury chain variety. Many of the hotels located deep in the side streets offer complimentary shuttles to the nearest BTS station every 30 minutes through the day.

Refill Now! HOSTEL $

(Map p70; ☑ 02 713 2044; www.refillnow.co.th; 191 Yaek 5, Soi Pridi Bhanom Yong 42, Soi 71, Th Sukhumvit; dm/r 365/1450B; ✸@☞☲; Ⓢ Phra Khanong exit 3 & taxi) This is the kind of place that might make you feel quite comfy about sleeping in a dorm. Rooms and dorms are stylishly minimalist and the latter have flirtatious pull screens between each double-bunk; women-only dorms are also available. There's a hip chill-out area and, upstairs, a massage centre.

★ Tints of Blue HOTEL $$

(Map p110; ☑ 099 289 7744; www.tintsofblue.com; 47 Soi 27, Th Sukhumvit; d incl breakfast 2000-2200B; ✸☞☲; Ⓢ Sukhumvit exit 2, Ⓢ Asok exit 6) The location in a leafy, quiet street is reflected in the rooms here, which manage to feel secluded, homey and warm. Equipped with kitchenettes, lots of space and natural light, and balconies, they're also great value for this price. There's a pleasantly stretched out – if tiny – swimming pool on the terrace, and a mini gym for a quick cardio session.

★ Mövenpick HOTEL $$

(Map p110; ☑ 02 119 3100; www.movenpick. com/en/asia/thailand/bangkok/bangkok; 47 Soi 15, Th Sukhumvit; d incl breakfast from 3000B; ✸@☞☲; Ⓢ Nana exit 3) A pleasant surprise awaits you at this fantastic hotel, which amazingly manages to offer top-end luxuries and amenities at prices that just about skirt the top of the midrange bracket. Rooms are thoughtfully appointed and have plenty of light and air, and the rooftop pool (though somewhat smallish) is a great place for a relaxing swim.

S31 HOTEL $$

(Map p110; ☑ 02 260 1111; www.s31hotel.com; 545 Soi 31, Th Sukhumvit; d incl breakfast from 3500B; ✸☞☲; Ⓢ Phrom Phong exit 5) The bold patterns and graphics of its interior and exterior make the S31 a fun, youthful choice. Thoughtful touches like kitchenettes with large fridge, super-huge beds, and courses (Thai boxing and yoga) prove that the style also has substance. Significant discounts can be found online, and additional branches are located on Soi 15 and Soi 33.

U Sukhumvit HOTEL $$

(Map p110; ☑ 02 651 3355; www.uhotelsresorts. com/usukhumvitbangkok; 81 Soi 15, Th Sukhumvit; d incl breakfast from 2100B; ✸☞☲; Ⓜ Sukhumvit exit 3, Ⓢ Asok exit 5) This modern hotel features the Thai regions as a design theme across its accommodation units. Rooms are colourful, with lively rustic touches, not to mention being spacious and well equipped. It's a midrange keeper, and quite a steal given its competitive tariffs.

Beat Hotel HOTEL $$

(Map p70; ☑ 02 178 0077; www.beathotelbangkok. com; Soi 71, Th Sukhumvit; d from 1500B; ✸@☞☲; Ⓢ Phra Khanong exit 3) This art-themed hotel has a youthful vibe that kicks off in the lobby. The 54 rooms continue this feeling, ranging in design from those with colourful floor-to-ceiling wall art to others painted in a monochromatic bold hue. It's worth shelling out a few hundred baht more for the super-huge deluxe rooms.

RetroOasis   HOTEL $$
(Map p110; ☑ 02 665 2922; www.retroasishotel. com; 503 Th Sukhumvit; d 1300-1900B; ✳ ⱳ ✻; Ⓜ Sukhumvit exit 2, Ⓢ Asok exit 6) This former tryst hotel dating back to the '60s has been converted to a fun midranger. Bright paint and an inviting central pool give the hotel a young, fresh vibe, while vintage furniture and architecture serve as reminders of its real age.

Fusion Suites   HOTEL $$
(Map p110; ☑ 02 665 2778; www.fusionbangkok. com; 143/61-62 Soi 21/Asoke, Th Sukhumvit; s/d incl breakfast 1600/2800B; ✳ @ ⱳ; Ⓜ Sukhumvit exit 1, Ⓢ Asok exit 1) Fusion is a disproportionately hip hotel for this price range. The unconventional furnishings provide the rooms here with heaps of style, although the cheapest can be a bit dark. The priciest rooms come with Jacuzzi-style baths.

★ AriyasomVilla   HOTEL $$$
(Map p110; ☑ 02 254 8880; www.ariyasom.com; 65 Soi 1, Th Sukhumvit; d incl breakfast from 6400B; ✳ @ ⱳ ✻; Ⓢ Phloen Chit exit 3) Located at the end of Soi 1 behind a wall of tropical greenery, this beautifully renovated 1940s-era villa is one of the worst-kept accommodation secrets in Bangkok. The 24 rooms are spacious and meticulously outfitted with thoughtful Thai design touches and sumptuous, beautiful antique furniture. There's also a spa and an inviting tropical pool. Book well in advance.

Breakfast comprises a vegetarian set menu served in the villa's stunning glass-encased dining room.

Cabochon Hotel   BOUTIQUE HOTEL $$$
(Map p110; ☑ 02 259 2871; www.cabochonhotel. com; 14/29 Soi 45, Th Sukhumvit; d incl breakfast from 5800B; Ⓟ ⱳ ✳ ⱳ ✻; Ⓢ Phrom Phong exit 3) The Cabochon, which means polished gem, is indeed a diamond in rowdy Bangkok. Rooms are light-filled and unfussy, and packed with thoughtful curiosities such as antique telephones, typewriters, tortoise shells, model aeroplanes and vintage tea sets. Venture to the rooftop pool or nosh street-food-style on mouth-watering Thai and Laotian dishes at the cosy Thai Lao Yeh Restaurant.

The hotel is hidden down tranquil Soi 45.

Ma Du Zi   HOTEL $$$
(Map p110; ☑ 02 615 6400; www.maduzihotel.com; cnr Th Ratchadaphisek & Soi 16, Th Sukhumvit; d incl breakfast from 5700B; ✳ @ ⱳ; Ⓜ Queen Sirikit National Convention Centre exit 4) The name is Thai for 'come take a look', somewhat of a misnomer for this reservations-only,

BANGKOK & AROUND SLEEPING

APARTMENT RENTALS

If you're planning on staying longer than a few days, there are ample alternatives to the traditional hotel in Bangkok, such as Airbnb and serviced apartments. While Airbnb (www.airbnb.com) has many listings in the city, these were determined to be illegal in Thailand a few years ago, due to many private properties operating without commercial licenses. Despite the official decree, several private properties still continue to do their share of business.

The ubiquitous serviced apartments in the city offer a long-stay option with the benefits of a hotel (door attendants, housekeeping, room service), as well as extra facilities (kitchen, washing machine etc) for a similar price to, or less expensive than, a hotel. And most are happy to take short-term guests, too. Recommended places include:

Siri Sathorn (Map p88; ☑ 02 266 2345; www.sirisathorn.com; 27 Soi Sala Daeng 1; ste incl breakfast from 3500B; ✳ @ ⱳ ✻; Ⓜ Lumphini exit 2, Ⓢ Sala Daeng exit 2) Chic modern apartments starting at 60 sq metres; also includes shuttle bus, spa and professional service.

Centre Point (Map p90; ☑ 02 266 0521; www.centrepoint.com; 1522/2 Soi Kaysorn 1, Th Charoen Krung; d incl breakfast from 2400B; ✳ @ ⱳ ✻; ⛴ Sathorn/Central Pier, Ⓢ Saphan Taksin exit 3) One of Bangkok's biggest managers of serviced apartments, with five properties across the city.

Urbana (Map p94; ☑ 02 250 6666; www.urbanahospitality.com; 55 Th Langsuan; ste incl breakfast from 3700B; ✳ ⱳ ✻; Ⓢ Chit Lom exit 4) Reputable serviced-apartment provider with two properties in Bangkok.

Northern Bangkok

Northern Bangkok

◎ **Sights**

1 Children's Discovery	
Museum	B2
2 Or Tor Kor Market	B2

🛏 **Sleeping**

3 Capital Mansion	B3
4 Siamaze	D3
5 The Yard	A4
6 Yim Bangkok	D4

🍽 **Eating**

7 Baan Pueng Chom	A3
8 Cantina Wine Bar & Italian Kitchen	A4
9 Kaobahn	B4
10 Khua Kling Pak Sod	A4
11 Puritan	A4
12 Yang Gao Gorn	B3

🍸 **Drinking & Nightlife**

13 Aree	A3
14 Fake Club The Next Gen	D3
15 O'glee	A4

no-walk-ins hotel. If you've gained access, behind the gate you'll find a modern, sophisticated mid-sized hotel steeped in dark, chic tones and designs. We particularly like the immense bathrooms, equipped with a walk-in tub and minimalist shower.

🛏 **Thewet & Dusit**

Thewet and Dusit are home to a handful of decent budget options set in a vibrant riverside neighbourhood, which can appeal to those seeking a less touristy experience compared to nearby Banglamphu.

Hi Baan Thewet
HOSTEL **$**

(Map p106; ☑ 02 281 0361; www.hi-baanthewet. com; 25/2 Th Phitsanulok; s/d/tr 500/850/1200B; ✳@☎; ⊡Thewet Pier) This somewhat institutional place is part of the global Hostelling International youth hostel network, and has 14 well-appointed, pastel-shaded rooms that keep the retro feel alive. The inviting communal areas with cheerful stained-glass panelling and the leafy, quiet, off-the-beaten-track location make a stay here rather pleasant and comfortable.

Samsen Sam Place
GUESTHOUSE **$**

(Map p78; ☑ 02 628 7067; www.samsensam.com; 48 Soi 3, Th Samsen; r without/with air-con from 430/770B; ✳@☎; ⊡Thewet Pier) One of the homiest budget places in the Samsen area (if not all of Bangkok), this colourful, refurbished antique villa gets glowing reports about its friendly service and quiet location. The rooms here are extremely tidy and thoughtfully appointed. If you're on a severely restricted budget, grab one of the few fan-cooled shared-bathroom options.

★Phra-Nakorn Norn-Len
HOTEL **$$**

(Map p106; ☑ 02 628 8188; www.phranakorn nornlen.com; 46 Soi Thewet 1; d incl breakfast 2200-4200B; ✳@☎; ⊡Thewet Pier) Set in an enclosed garden compound decorated like a Bangkok neighbourhood of yesteryear, this bright and cheery hotel is fun and atmospheric, and stupendous value. Although the 31 rooms are attractively furnished with antiques and paintings, it's worth noting that they don't include TV, a fact made up for by daily activities, massage and endless opportunities for peaceful relaxing.

Casa Nithra
HOTEL **$$**

(Map p78; ☑ 02 628 6228; www.casanithra.com; 176 Th Samsen; d incl breakfast from 2300B; ✳@☎✷; ⊡Thewet Pier) The 74 rooms in this modern hotel come in earthy shades of brown, with subtle furnishings and flourishes that intertwine contemporary and Thai design themes. Deluxe rooms throw in a bit more space, as well as an inviting, free-standing bathtub. Online discounts often chip away at the tariff.

SSIP Boutique
BOUTIQUE HOTEL **$$**

(Map p106; ☑ 02 282 1899; www.ssiphotelthailand. com; 42 Th Phitsanulok; d incl breakfast from 2200B; ✳@☎; ⊡Thewet Pier) Handsome tiles, heavy wood furniture, antique furnishings: the 20 rooms at this stylish midrange hotel have been meticulously designed to emulate an old-school Bangkok feel. Modern amenities (TV, fridge, safe) and a team of thoughtful and efficient staff ensure a thoroughly contemporary stay. Prices without breakfast are about 500B cheaper.

Penpark Place
HOTEL **$$**

(Map p78; ☑ 02 628 8896; www.penparkplace.com; 22 Soi 3, Th Samsen; s/d 700/1200B; ✳@☎; ⊡Thewet Pier) This former factory has been turned into a good-value budget hotel with a wide selection of rooms at different price points. A room in the original building is little more than a bed and a fan, but an adjacent add-on sees a handful of well-equipped apartment-like rooms and suites (1900B). Pretty lawns and abundant greenery add to the overall feel.

★Siam
HOTEL **$$$**

(Map p106; ☑ 02 206 6999; www.thesiamhotel. com; 3/2 Th Khao; d incl breakfast from 18,900B; ✳@☎✷; ⊡hotel shuttle boat from Sathorn/ Central Pier) Zoom back to the 1930s in this retro-chic riverside heritage hotel, where art deco influences, marbled floorings, plantain-lined aqua courtyards and beautiful antiques set the standard for a classy experience. The rooms are a splurge, while villas up the ante with rooftop balconies and plunge pools. The main swimming pool by the riverside is an absolute delight to flop about in.

🛏 Northern Bangkok

Staying outside of Bangkok's centre can offer great value, especially when it comes to budget and midrange accommodation. Despite improving public transport, however, it still feels like a compromise staying here rather than closer to the centre.

Siamaze
HOSTEL **$**

(Map p116; ☑ 02 693 6336; www.siamaze.com; 90 Soi 17, Th Ratchadaphisek; d incl breakfast from 700B; ✳@☎; Ⓜ Sutthisan exit 4) Siamaze is an unflashy, casual budget hotel with spacious private rooms. The cheaper units share bathrooms but like their pricier counterparts (with attached loos) have access to thoughtful, convenient facilities. If you're OK with staying away from the main tourist drag, it's an excellent deal.

The Yard
HOSTEL **$**

(Map p116; ☑ 089 677 4050; www.theyardhostel. com; 51 Soi 5, Th Phahonyothin; dm/r incl breakfast from 500/1350B; ✳☎; Ⓢ Ari exit 1) This fun

MANDARIN ORIENTAL

Now a famous grande dame, the Mandarin Oriental (Map p90; ☑ 02 659 9000; www.mandarinoriental.com; 48 Soi 40/Oriental, Th Charoen Krung; d/ste incl breakfast from 20,000/46,000B; ✴ @ ☜ ☒; ☐ Oriental Pier) started its career as the seafarers' version of a Th Khao San guesthouse. The original owners, two Danish sea captains, traded the nest to Hans Niels Andersen, the founder of the formidable East Asiatic Company. Andersen transformed the hotel into a civilised palace of grand architecture and luxurious standards. He hired an Italian architect, S Cardu, to design what is now the Authors' Wing, which was the city's most fantastic building not commissioned by the king.

The rest of the hotel's history relies on its famous guests. A Polish-born sailor named Joseph Conrad stayed here in 1888. The hotel brought him good luck: he got his first command on the ship *Otago*, from Bangkok to Port Adelaide, Australia, which in turn gave him ideas for several early stories. W Somerset Maugham stumbled into the hotel with an advanced case of malaria. In his feverish state, he heard the German manager arguing with the doctor about how a death in the hotel would hurt business. Maugham's overland Southeast Asian journey is recorded in *The Gentleman in the Parlour: A Record of a Journey from Rangoon to Haiphong*, which gave literary appeal to the hotel. Other notable guests have included Noël Coward, Graham Greene, John le Carré, James Michener, Gore Vidal and Barbara Cartland. Some modern-day writers claim that a stay here will help overcome writer's block – though we suspect any writer booking in these days would need a very generous advance indeed.

hostel is comprised of 10 converted shipping containers. Predictably, neither the dorm nor private rooms are huge, but are attractive and cosy, and have access to inviting communal areas ranging from the eponymous lawn (which also functions as a bar) to a kitchen.

Yim Bangkok
HOSTEL **$**

(Map p116; ☑ 080 965 9994; www.yimbangkok.com; 70 Th Pracha Rat Bamphen; dm/r incl breakfast from 450/1450B; ✴ ☜; Ⓜ Huay Khwang exit 1) A suburban hostel decked out in an eclectic, colourful fashion, with dorm rooms ranging in size from four to six comfortable, high-tech bunk beds and some well-appointed private double rooms. Yes, it's far from any sights, but it is very close to the MRT.

Be My Guest Bed & Breakfast
GUESTHOUSE **$**

(Map p70; ☑ 080 999 5560; 35/189 Soi 36, Th Ratchadaphisek; d 700B; ✴ ☜; Ⓜ Lat Phrao exit 4 & taxi) This is a cheap, but comfortable, guesthouse with clean, spacious rooms located in a residential neighbourhood. The price is unbeatable, but do consider its distance from the city centre before you decide to make a booking. The nearest MRT station is about 2km away.

Capital Mansion
HOTEL **$$**

(Map p116; ☑ 02 278 7979; 1371 Th Phahonyothin; d incl breakfast from 1800B; ✴ ☜ ☒; Ⓢ Saphan Khwai exit 1) After previous lives as a base for US soldiers during the Vietnam War and the

embassy of the People's Republic of China, the former Capital Hotel was reincarnated as a hotel for travellers. A significant renovation hasn't erased all of 1962 from the hotel, but the rooms are spacious and tidy, if somewhat plain. The pool is an added bonus.

✖ Eating

Nowhere else is the Thai reverence for food more evident than in Bangkok. To the outsider, the life of a Bangkokian appears to be a string of meals and snacks punctuated by the odd stab at work, not the other way around. If you can adjust your mental clock – and palate – to this schedule, your visit will be a delicious one indeed.

✖ Ko Ratanakosin & Thonburi

In stark contrast to the rest of Bangkok, there aren't many restaurants or stalls in Ko Ratanakosin (even fewer in Thonburi), and those that are here predominantly serve Thai cuisine. The best of the lot are in Tien village, a tiny hipster 'hood along Th Maha Rat. For something more international, consider heading to nearby Banglamphu.

Ming Lee
THAI, CHINESE **$**

(Map p78; 28-30 Th Na Phra Lan; mains 70-100B; ◷ 11.30am-4pm; ☐ Chang Pier, Maharaj Pier) Hidden in plain sight across from Wat Phra Kaew (p72) is this decades-old shophouse restaurant. The menu spans Western/

Chinese dishes (eg stewed tongue) and Thai standards (such as 'beef spicy salad'). There's no English sign; it's the first shophouse in the lime-washed commercial building across the road from Wat Phra Kaew's northern wall as you walk in from Chang Pier.

Wang Lang Market THAI $
(Map p78; Trok Wang Lang; mains 40-80B; ⊙10am-3pm Mon-Fri; 🚢 Wang Lang/Siriraj Pier) Running south from Siriraj Hospital is this busy market bringing together takeaway stalls and basic restaurants. Options range from noodles to curries ladled over rice, and come lunch, the area is positively mobbed by the area's office staff.

⭐**Tonkin Annam** VIETNAMESE $$
(Map p78; ☑ 093 469 2969; 69 Soi Tha Tien; mains 150-300B; ⊙11am-10pm Wed-Mon; ❄; 🚢 Tien Pier) The retro-minimalist interior here might be a red flag for hipster ethnic cuisine, but Tonkin Annam serves some of the best Vietnamese food in Bangkok. Come for the *phở* (noodle soup), deliciously tart and peppery banana blossom salad, or dishes you won't find elsewhere, such as *bánh bèo* (steamed cups of rice flour topped with pork), a speciality of Hue.

Savoey THAI $$
(Map p78; ☑ 02 024 1317; www.savoey.co.th; 1st fl, Maharaj Pier, Th Maha Rat; mains 160-400B; ⊙11am-9.30pm; ❄; 🚢 Maharaj Pier) At this chain with other branches across town, you're not going to find heaps of character, but you will get consistency, river views, aircon and a seafood-heavy menu. Come cool evenings, take advantage of the open-air, riverside deck.

Err THAI $$
(Map p78; ☑ 02 622 2292; off Th Maha Rat; mains 100-350B; ⊙11am-4pm & 5-9pm Tue-Sun; ❄; 🚢 Tien Pier) Think of all those different smoky, spicy, crispy, meaty bites you've encountered on the street. Now imagine them assembled in one hip, retro-themed locale, and coupled with tasty Thai-themed cocktails and domestic microbrews. If Err (a Thai colloquialism for agreement) seems too good to be true, allow us to insist that it's indeed true.

Sala Rattanakosin THAI $$$
(Map p78; ☑ 02 622 1388; www.salaresorts.com/rattanakosin; Soi Tha Tian; mains 250-700B; ⊙11am-3.30pm & 5.30-11pm; ❄ 🛜; 🚢 Tien Pier) With fabulous cross-river views of Wat Arun (p73) through floor-to-ceiling windows, this

excellent in-house Thai restaurant of the eponymous hotel has nailed both its location and food. Delicious central and northern Thai dishes with occasional Western twists are served up on white-clothed tables in an elegant setting by smiling staff. Call ahead to reserve a table on weekends.

🍴 Banglamphu

Banglamphu is famous for its old-school central Thai food – the predominant cuisine in this part of town. For something more international, head to Th Khao San, where you'll find a few international fast-food franchises as well as foreign and vegetarian restaurants.

⭐**Thip Samai** THAI $
(Map p78; 313 Th Mahachai; mains 50-250B; ⊙5pm-2am, closed alternate Wed; 🚢 klorng boat to Phanfa Leelard Pier) This institution reputedly serves the definitive version of *pàt tai* – period. Every evening, scores of eager diners queue on the pavement for a table (the queue moves fast, so don't walk away in despair if you see 50-odd people ahead of you). Your patience is duly rewarded in the end with a delicious platter of the iconic dish.

Khun Daeng THAI $
(Map p78; Th Phra Athit; mains 50-100B; ⊙11am-9.30pm Mon-Sat; 🚢 Phra Athit/Banglamphu Pier) This popular place does *gŏo·ay jáp yoo·an*, identified on the menu as 'Vietnamese noodle'. Introduced to northeastern Thailand via Vietnamese immigrants, the dish combines peppery pork sausage, a quail egg, thin rice noodles and a garnish of crispy fried shallots in a slightly viscous broth. There's no English-language sign here; look for the white-and-green shopfront and scores of local diners.

STREET SENSE

Bangkok street names often seem unpronounceable, and the inconsistency of romanised names and spellings really doesn't help. For example, the street Th Ratchadamri is sometimes spelt 'Rajdamri'. And one of the most popular locations for foreign embassies is known both as Wireless Rd and Th Witthayu (*wí·tá·yú* is Thai for 'radio').

THONBURI'S SOUTHERN RESTAURANTS

The area around Thonburi's Siriraj Hospital is one of the best places in Bangkok for southern Thai food, the theory being that the cuisine took root here because of the nearby train station that served southern destinations. In particular, between Soi 8 and Soi 13 of Th Wang Lang, there is a knot of authentic, southern Thai-style curry shops: Dao Tai (Map p70; 508/26 Th Wang Lang; mains from 30B; ⏰7am-8.30pm; 🚤Wang Lang/Siriraj Pier), Ruam Tai (Map p70; 376/4 Th Wang Lang; mains from 40B; ⏰7am-8pm; 🚤Wang Lang/Siriraj Pier) and Chawang (Map p70; 375/5-6 Th Wang Lang; mains from 40B; ⏰7am-7pm; 🚤Wang Lang/Siriraj Pier). A menu isn't necessary as all feature bowls and trays of prepared curries, soups, stir-fries and relishes; simply point to whatever looks tasty.

Pua-Kee   THAI $

(Map p78; Th Phra Sumen; mains 50-90B; ⏰9am-4pm; 🚤Phra Athit/Banglamphu Pier) Come here for the central Thai classic, *gǒo·ay děe·o dôm yam* ('rice noodle soup hotspicy with mixed fishball' on the menu), fishball noodles preseasoned with sugar, lime and dried chilli, and served with a crispy deep-fried wonton. There's no English-language sign, but it's located next door to the clearly labelled Makalin Clinic.

Karim Roti-Mataba   THAI $

(Map p78; 136 Th Phra Athit; mains 50-140B; ⏰9am-10pm Tue-Sun; ❄; 🚤Phra Athit/Banglamphu Pier) This classic Bangkok eatery serves tasty Thai-Muslim dishes such as roti, *gaang mát·sà·màn* ('Muslim curry'), *biryani*, tart fish curry and *má·dà·bà* (deep-fried pancakes stuffed with a meat and egg filling). An upstairs air-con dining area and a couple of outdoor tables provide barely enough seating for loyal fans and curious tourists alike.

★ Krua Apsorn   THAI $$

(Map p78; www.kruaapsorn.com; Th Din So; mains 100-350B; ⏰10.30am-8pm Mon-Sat; ❄; 🚤klorng boat Phanfa Leelard Pier) This cafeteria-like dining room is a favourite of members of the Thai royal family and restaurant critics alike. Just about all of the central and southern Thai dishes are tasty, but regulars never miss the chance to order the decadent stir-fried crab with yellow-pepper chilli or the *tortilla Española*–like fluffy crab omelette.

There's another branch (p131) on Th Samsen in the Thewet and Dusit area.

Shoshana   ISRAELI $$

(Map p78; 88 Th Chakrabongse; mains 80-300B; ⏰10am-11.30pm; ❄🍴; 🚤Phra Athit/Banglamphu Pier) One of Khao San's longest-running Israeli restaurants, Shoshana might resemble your grandparents' living room right down to the tacky wall art and plastic placemats. Feel safe ordering anything deepfried – the kitchen staff do an excellent job of it – and don't miss the deliciously garlicky eggplant dip.

ZeZe   ISRAELI $$

(Map p78; 📞02 282 2774; 45 Th Chakrabongse; mains 100-300B; ⏰8am-midnight; ❄🍴; 🚤Phra Athit/Banglamphu Pier) Fabulous platters of homestyle Israeli food are served up by cheerful staff who divide their time between a travel agency desk and a dining area at this convivial shophouse. The stir-fried chicken liver and gizzard with onion, red wine and balsamic vinegar is a great choice. A good selection of vegetarian options is also available.

Nopparat   THAI $$

(Map p78; 132 Th Phra Athit; mains 100-300B; ⏰10.30am-9.30pm Wed-Mon; ❄; 🚤Phra Athit/Banglamphu Pier) Featuring floral murals and portraits of royals on its bare concrete walls, this stylish restaurant serves some of the best Thai food in this part of town. No fancy departures from conventional recipes; no going easy on spice levels; no convenient adaptations to suit Western palates – everything here comes to your table just the way it was meant to be.

Bangkok Poutine   INTERNATIONAL $$

(Map p78; www.facebook.com/bangkokpoutine; Th Samsen; mains 100-200B; ⏰11am-11pm; ❄🍴; 🚤Phra Athit/Banglamphu Pier) You've conquered the deep-fried scorpion, now wrangle with poutine: French fries topped with cheese curds and gravy. Run by guys from Québec, this is the place to go for Francophone pop and the latest hockey game, as well as dishes ranging in cuisine from Thai to Lebanese, including lots of meat-free items.

★ Jay Fai   THAI $$$

(Raan Jay Fai; Map p78; 327 Th Mahachai; mains 200-1000B; ⏰2pm-2am Tue-Sat; 🚤klorng boat

Phanfa Leelard Pier) Wearing ski goggles and furiously cooking over a charcoal fire, septuagenarian Jay Fai is renowned for serving Bangkok's tastiest (and priciest) crab omelettes and *pàt kêe mow* (wide rice noodles fried with seafood and Thai herbs). The price, however, is justified by copious fresh seafood, plus a distinct frying style resulting in an almost oil-free finished dish.

✗ Chinatown

When you mention Chinatown, most Bangkokians immediately dream of street food, the bulk of which is found just off Th Yaowarat.

On the western side of the neighbourhood is Phahurat, Bangkok's Little India, filled with small Indian and other subcontinental restaurants tucked into the tiny soi (lane) off Th Chakkaraphet.

Yoo Fishball   CHINESE $
(Map p84; 433 Th Yaowarat; mains 100-120B; ⊘10am-11pm; ⛴Ratchawong Pier, Ⓜ Hua Lamphong exit 1) Yoo easily serves some of the best fishballs in town. We can also vouch for the shrimp wontons, deep-fried taro balls and fish cakes, all of which are extremely tasty. If you feel spoilt for choice, just have them all in a bowl by ordering the signature mixed ball soup.

Nay Hong   STREET FOOD $
(Map p84; Th Yukol 2; mains 50-100B; ⊘5-10pm; ⛴Ratchawong Pier, Ⓜ Hua Lamphong exit 1) The reward for locating this hole-in-the-wall is a delicious plate of *gŏo·ay dĕe·o kôo·a gài* (flat rice noodles fried with garlic oil, chicken and egg). No English menu, no English signage. To find it, proceed north from the corner of Th Suapa and Th Luang, then turn right into the first side street; it's at the end of the alleyway.

Khun Yah Cuisine   THAI $
(Map p84; off Th Mittaphap Thai-China; mains from 50B; ⊘6am-1.30pm Mon-Fri; ⛴Ratchawong Pier, Ⓜ Hua Lamphong exit 1) Strategically located for a lunch break after visiting Wat Traimit (Golden Buddha) (p81), Khun Yah specialises in the full-flavoured curries, relishes, stir-fries and noodle dishes of central Thailand. Many dishes are already sold out by noon. Khun Yah has no English-language sign (nor an English-language menu), but is located east of the Golden Buddha temple, in the same compound.

Nai Mong Hoi Thod   CHINESE $
(Map p84; 539 Th Phlap Phla Chai; mains 100-200B; ⊘11am-9pm Tue-Sun; ⛴Ratchawong Pier, Ⓜ Hua Lamphong exit 1) This restaurant is renowned for its delicious *hŏy tôrt* – oyster omelettes featuring deep-fried eggs and molluscs in a sticky batter. Order your omelette in small, medium or large servings, and swap oysters with mussels if you wish. There's also a decent crab fried rice on offer, but nothing much else.

Mangkorn Khǎo   STREET FOOD $
(Map p84; cnr Th Yaowarat & Th Yaowaphanit; mains from 50B; ⊘6pm-midnight Tue-Sun; ⛴Ratchawong Pier, Ⓜ Hua Lamphong exit 1) Delicious wontons and – if your stomach can manage it – *bà·mèe* (Chinese-style wheat noodles) are the order of the evening at this respected vendor. There's no English-language menu, but most diners stick to the two signature dishes, so it's an easy pick.

Jék Pûi   STREET FOOD $
(Map p84; Th Mangkon; mains from 50B; ⊘3-8pm Tue-Sun; ⛴Ratchawong Pier, Ⓜ Hua Lamphong exit 1) Jék Pûi is a table-less food stall incredibly popular for its Chinese-style Thai curries. Try the *gaang kĕe·o wăhn lôok chín plah grai,* a mild green curry with freshwater fish dumplings. There's no English-language menu.

80/20   INTERNATIONAL $$
(Map p90; ☑099 118 2200; 1052-1054 Th Charoen Krung; mains 250-450B; ⊘6-11pm Tue-Sun; ✸🛜; ⛴Si Phraya/River City Pier, Ⓜ Hua Lamphong exit 1) Freshly renovated in 2019, 80/20 continues to excel at what it has always done with perfection – blending Thai and Western ingredients and dishes to arrive at something altogether unique. The often savoury-leaning desserts are especially worth the trip. It's a progressive breath of air in an otherwise conservative Chinatown dining scene.

Fou de Joie   FRENCH $$
(Map p90; 831 Soi 31, Th Charoen Krung; mains from 200B; ⊘6pm-midnight Wed-Sun; ✸; ⛴Marine Department Pier, Ⓜ Hua Lamphong exit 1) Dining at the retro Hong Kong–themed Fou de Joie is like being an extra in a Wong Kar-wai film. Better yet, the French-style crêpes and cheese platters – not to mention the upstairs barbecue – are more than just set pieces, and also offer terrific value.

Hoon Kuang   CHINESE $$
(Map p84; 381 Th Yaowarat; mains 100-250B; ⊘noon-7.30pm Mon-Sat; ✸; ⛴Ratchawong Pier,

A SOUPY ISSUE

Many of the ostentatious, neon-signed restaurants you'll see along Th Yaowarat – Chinatown's main drag – advertise soups made from two obscure but valued commodities: birds' nests and shark fins.

The birds' nests in question don't consist of twigs or grass, but rather are the hardened saliva of a type of swiftlet. Pried from the walls of island-bound caves in southern Thailand, the nests are rehydrated and cleaned of impurities before being combined with broth and served in the form of a soup. Despite consisting of jellylike, tasteless strands (the soup is often supplemented with honey and egg to provide it with some flavour), the dish is considered a delicacy by the Chinese, who also believe it benefits the skin. Depending on the colour and purity of the bird's nest, a bowl of the soup can cost as much as 2000B or more. The nests can be harvested sustainably, but overexploitation does occur.

Many of the same restaurants that sell bird's-nest soup also serve shark-fin soup. Yet another Chinese delicacy that is believed to have healing properties, shark-fin soup has become highly stigmatised in recent years, as many animal welfare experts have pointed out that the fins are gathered via a process that is unsustainable and unethical – the sharks are often caught and stripped of their fins, then dumped in the water to die. Despite the bad press, the dish continues to feature prominently in Bangkok's Chinatown menus.

Ⓜ Hua Lamphong exit 1) Serving the food of Chinatown's streets in air-con comfort is this low-key, long-standing staple. The must-eat dishes are pictured on the door. It'd be a pity to miss the 'prawn curry flat rice noodle', a unique mash-up of two Chinese-Thai dishes – crab in curry powder and flash-fried noodles – that will make you wonder why they were ever served apart.

Thanon Phadungdao Seafood Stalls
STREET FOOD $$

(Map p84; cnr Th Phadungdao & Th Yaowarat; mains 100-400B; ⊙4pm-midnight Tue-Sun; 🚢 Ratchawong Pier, Ⓜ Hua Lamphong exit 1) After sunset, this line of open-air restaurants – each claiming to be better than its neighbour – becomes a culinary supernova of outdoor barbecues, screaming staff, iced seafood trays and messy pavement seating. True, the vast majority of diners are foreign tourists, but this has little impact on the cheerful setting, the fun experience and the cheap bills.

Hua Seng Hong
CHINESE $$

(Map p84; 371-373 Th Yaowarat; mains 80-350B; ⊙9am-9pm; 🌶; 🚢 Ratchawong Pier, Ⓜ Hua Lamphong exit 1) 🍴 Hua Seng Hong's varied menu, including braised goose feet, seafood hotpot, soft-shell crab in curry powder, crab fried rice and a variety of noodles, makes it a handy destination for anybody craving good Chinese food. Order a lavish dim sum spread for lunch, choosing from the wide range of dumplings on offer.

Royal India
INDIAN $$

(Map p84; 392/1 Th Chakkaraphet; mains 150-300B; ⊙10am-10pm; 🌶🖊; 🚢 Memorial Bridge Pier) This hole-in-the-wall restaurant has long been the most reliable place to eat in Bangkok's Indian neighbourhood. The kebabs and naans (oven-baked flatbreads) here give stiff competition to Delhi's *dhabas* (local eateries). Vegetarians will love the creamy *palak paneer* (cottage-cheese cubes in spinach sauce) to go with their bread of choice.

🍴 Riverside, Silom & Lumphini

Silom and Lumphini are home to some of Bangkok's most popular restaurants, many of which are located on quiet alleys far from the mayhem. They span everything from no-frills street dining to high-end fusion experiences – there's something here to suit every pocket and palate. The Riverside area is ideal for classy dining at restaurants in luxury hotels.

Hai
THAI $

(Somtam Convent; Map p100; 2/4-5 Th Convent; mains 60-150B; ⊙11am-9pm Mon-Fri, to 5pm Sat; Ⓜ Si Lom exit 2, Ⓢ Sala Daeng exit 2) An excellent introduction to the wonders of *lâhp* (spicy, herbal mince-meat 'salad'), *sôm·đam* (spicy green papaya salad) and other Isan (northeastern) delights can be had at this affordable, popular and long-standing restaurant. The soupy chicken with lemongrass and coconut milk, and the delicately grilled pork neck, are menu winners. You'll have to share tables with strangers during lunch.

Saravana Bhavan SOUTH INDIAN $

(Map p100; ☎02 635 4556; 663 Th Silom; mains 100-250B; 🕐9.30am-10.30pm; ❄🌱; [S] Surasak exit 1) This well-reputed overseas branch of a legendary Indian eating house makes a fabulous range of southern Indian vegetarian dishes. We love the *dosai* (crispy rice-flour crepes), *ghee pongal* (savoury pudding made from stone-ground rice and lentils) and *vada* (deep-fried savoury doughnuts made of lentil batter). Highly recommended for vegetarians with a palate for subcontinental flavours.

Though the restaurant technically looks onto Th Silom, the entrance and staircase leading up to the 1st-floor dining area is on the building's western side, on Soi 19.

Muslim Restaurant THAI $

(Map p90; 1354-6 Th Charoen Krung; mains 50-170B; 🕐7am-5.30pm; ⛴Sathorn/Central Pier, [S] Saphan Taksin exit 3) Plant yourself in this blue-walled ancient eatery for a glimpse into what restaurants in Bangkok once used to be like. The menu, much like the interior design, doesn't appear to have changed much in the restaurant's decades-long history, and the *biryani,* curries and samosas remain more Indian-influenced than Thai. Try the beef brain curry for its unique flavour and texture.

★ **Supanniga Eating Room** THAI $$

(Map p100; www.supannigaeatingroom.com; 28 Soi 10, Th Sathon Neua/North; mains 150-350B; 🕐11.30am-2.30pm & 5.30-11.30pm; ❄📶; [S] Chong Nonsi exit 1/5) Supanniga has three outlets across Bangkok (plus a superpopular dinner cruise), but this branch in Sathorn is a favourite in terms of ambience and service. A brilliant selection of northern Thai dishes is on offer, with specials such as grilled Isan sausages, stir-fried sun-dried beef jerky, and baby squid stuffed with ground pork. Ask for an upstairs (quieter) table.

Chef Man CHINESE $$

(Map p100; ☎02 212 3789; 33/1 Th Sathon Tai/South, Hotel Eastin Grand Sathon; mains 150-350B; 🕐11am-2.30pm & 6-10pm; ❄; [S] Surasak exit 4) If you're a dumpling fan, drop into this elegant restaurant during lunchtime, when its open kitchen serves some of the nicest dim sum and *siu mai* (open-face Chinese dumplings) you can bite into. Other Sichuan-style dishes, including delicious duck, fish and vegetarian preparations, are also on offer. Dinner is largely the preserve of local patrons, who converge with their families.

Bitterman INTERNATIONAL $$

(Map p88; ☎02 636 3256; www.bittermanbkk.com; 120/1 Soi 1/1, Th Sala Daeng; mains 240-420B; 🕐11am-11pm; ❄📶; [M] Lumphini exit 2, [S] Sala Daeng exit 4) This leafy greenhouse is the antithesis of the steel structures in central Silom and a welcome respite from the heat for daytime dining. Dishes include comfort food at its finest with pulled pork toast, baked mac and cheese, and British style fish and chips. Sunday brunch with live DJ sets runs from 12.30pm until 4.30pm.

Issaya Siamese Club THAI $$

(Map p88; ☎02 672 9040; www.issaya.com; 4 Soi Sri Aksorn; mains 250-500B; 🕐11.30am-2.30pm & 6-10.30pm; ❄; [M] Khlong Toei exit 1 & taxi) Housed in a charming 1920s-era villa, Issaya is a top-of-the-line outpost serving Thai food. Dishes alternate between somewhat saucy, meaty items and lighter dishes using produce from the restaurant's organic garden. Sample the soft shell crab in egg sauce or the creamy and spicy lamb massaman curry, and you'll know why it's regarded as one of Bangkok's best Thai eateries.

The restaurant can be a bit tricky to find, and is best approached in a taxi via Soi Ngam Du Phli.

Baan THAI $$

(Map p88; ☎02 655 8995; www.baanbkk.com; 139/5 Th Witthayu/Wireless Rd; mains 250-400B; 🕐11am-2.30pm & 6-10.30pm Wed-Mon; ❄; [M] Lumphini exit 3) The slick, modern interior here belies the fact that Baan is a family-run restaurant. The menu is inspired by full-bodied recipes and ingredients that are integral to Thai cuisine, and the occasionally obscure dishes with roots in home kitchens, such as the signature spicy five-spiced egg soup, reflect its dedication to the nation's culinary heritage.

Never Ending Summer THAI $$

(Map p90; ☎02 861 0953; 41/5 Th Charoen Nakhon; mains 250-450B; 🕐11am-11pm; ❄📶; ⛴River City Pier & shuttle ferry) The cheesy name doesn't do justice to this sophisticated Thai restaurant located in a former warehouse by the river. Join Bangkok's beautiful crowd for antiquated Thai dishes such as cubes of watermelon served with a dry 'dressing' of fish, sugar and deep-fried shallots, or fragrant green curry with pork and fresh bird's-eye chilli.

Daimasu
JAPANESE $$

(Map p100; 9/3 Soi Than Tawan; mains 100-300B; ⊙5.30pm-1am; ❄🛜; M Si Lom exit 2, S Sala Daeng exit 1) The emphasis at this cosy, retro-themed Japanese restaurant is *yakiniku* (DIY grilled meat), which as a culinary style is an absolute craze among Thai millennials. The tiny, tasty sides range from crispy spears of cucumber in a savoury marinade to a slightly bitter salad of paper-thin slices of eggplant.

Luka
CAFE $$

(Map p100; 📞02 637 8558; www.lukabangkok.format.com; 64/3 Th Pan; mains 190-350B; ⊙9am-6pm; ❄🛜; S Surasak exit 3) This extremely popular Silom cafe serves all-day brunch and comfort food such as truffle mushroom omelettes, shakshuka, and honey-glazed duck with burnt orange salad. Coffee comes from northern Thailand, while some artisanal tea blends are also available. Tables are set in a space coshared with homewares store Casa Pagoda, which is ideal for some take-home bric-a-brac post-meal.

The cafe is pet-friendly, and also doubles as a workspace for a dedicated group of digital nomads.

Polo Fried Chicken
THAI $$

(Kai Thort Jay Kee; Map p88; 137/1-3 Soi Sanam Khli/Polo; mains 50-200B; ⊙11am-9pm; ❄; M Lumphini exit 3) Although the *sôm-đam* (spicy green papaya salad), sticky rice and *lâhp* (a spicy salad of minced meat) of this former street stall give the impression of a northeastern-Thai-style eatery, the restaurant's namesake deep-fried bird is more southern in origin. Regardless, smothered in a thick layer of crispy, deep-fried garlic, it is none other than a true Bangkok culinary experience.

Kalapapruek
THAI $$

(Map p100; 📞02 236 4335; 27 Th Pramuan; mains 150-300B; ⊙8am-6pm Mon-Sat, to 3pm Sun; ❄; S Surasak exit 1/3) This venerable Thai eatery has numerous branches and mall spin-offs around town, but we still fancy the original branch on Th Pramuan, where local families gather to tuck into massive orders of delicious food over lunch. The diverse menu spans Thai specialities from just about every region, daily specials and, occasionally, seasonal treats as well.

Somboon Seafood
CHINESE $$

(Map p100; 📞02 233 3104; www.somboonseafood.com; cnr Th Surawong & Th Naradhiwas Rajanagarindra; mains 200-450B; ⊙4-11pm; ❄; S Chong Nonsi exit 1) Somboon, a hectic old-school seafood hall with a solid reputation, is known for doing the best curry-powder crab in town. Soy-steamed sea bass *(plah grà·pong nêung see-éw)* is also a speciality and, like all good Thai seafood, should be enjoyed with an immense platter of *kôw pàt boo* (fried rice with crab) and as many friends as you can gather together.

Suananda
INDIAN $$

(Map p100; 109 Th Pan; mains 120-250B; ⊙10am-9.30pm Mon-Sat; ❄📞; S Surasak exit 1/3) Down a quiet residential alleyway, this tiny yoga-themed health cafe does a wonderful range of inventive vegetarian Indian cuisine. Favourites are the spinach millet crepe and the paneer (cottage cheese) in creamy yoghurt sauce. Several platter-style meal combos are also on offer. Ask about yoga classes, which take place on the premises from time to time.

★ Saawaan
THAI $$$

(Map p88; 📞02 679 3775; www.saawaan.com; 39/19 Soi Suan Phlu; set menu 2450B; ⊙6pm-midnight; ❄; S Chong Nonsi exit 5) Two exceptionally talented chefs run what can easily be called one of the finest Thai restaurants in the world. Its name meaning 'heaven', this chic address has a seven-course tasting menu themed on cooking methods, featuring dishes that are inherently Thai but are executed with the fanciness, finesse and flair worthy of a Michelin-starred restaurant (which it is).

Expect dishes conjured from sea urchins, wild betel leaves or rice-paddy crabs, and wacky desserts (such as bitter chocolate with a hint of the stinky durian fruit). Advance bookings – and smart attire – essential.

★ Le Du
INTERNATIONAL $$$

(Map p100; 📞092 919 9969; www.ledubkk.com; 399/3 Soi 7, Th Silom; mains 600-1200B; ⊙6-10pm Mon-Sat; ❄🛜; S Chong Nonsi exit 4) A play on the Thai word for 'season', Le Du intertwines Thai dishes with Western flavours, and applies 21st-century deconstructionist cooking techniques with an emphasis on fresh, seasonal ingredients (including some rather unusual stuff, such as sea grape algae in spring).

For the full dinner experience, featuring inventive desserts, opt for the brilliantly conceptualised and presented tasting menus (four/six course 2990/3590B). Advance bookings are absolutely essential.

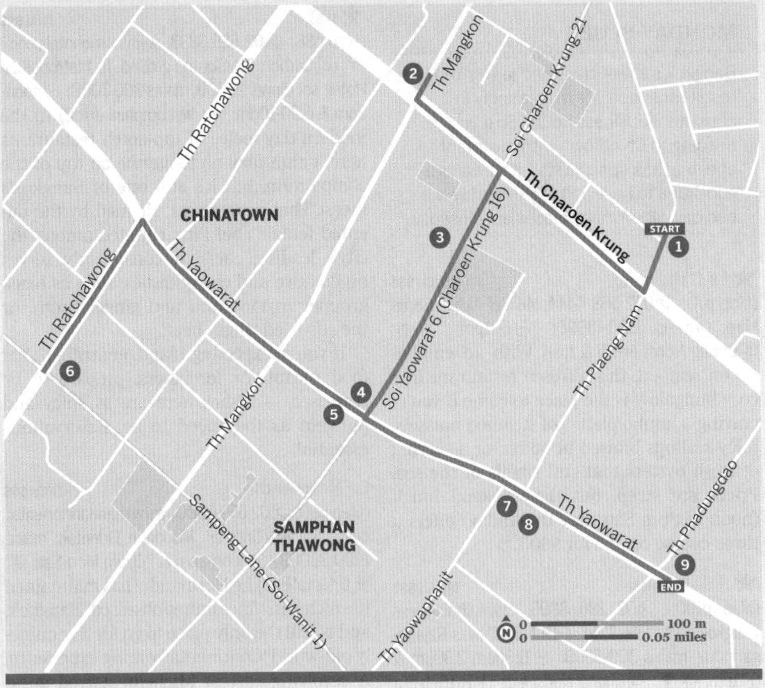

City Walk
Chinatown Evening Bites

START CNR TH PLAENG NAM & TH CHAROEN KRUNG
END CNR TH YAOWARAT & TH PHADUNGDAO
LENGTH 1.5KM; TWO TO THREE HOURS

Start near the Th Plaeng Nam/Th Charoen Krung crossing. Head north along Th Phlap Phla Chai to **1 Nai Mong Hoi Thod** (p121), renowned for its *hŏy tôrt* (oyster omelettes).

Return to Th Charoen Krung and turn right. Turn right at Th Mangkon; on your left is **2 Jék Pûi** (p121), famous for its curries. Return to Th Charoen Krung, turn left, and walk to **3 Talat Mai** market. Turn right, and walk to the Th Yaowarat crossing to reach a stall selling **4 gŏo·ay đĕe·o kôo·a gài** (Map p84; Soi 6, Th Yaowarat; mains from 40B; ⏰5-10pm Tue-Sun; ⛴Ratchawong Pier, [M]Hua Lamphong exit 1), rice noodles fried with chicken, egg and garlic oil.

Emerging at Th Yaowarat, cross to the market area across the street. The first vendor on the right, **5 Nay Lék Ûan** (Map p84; Soi Yaowarat 11; mains from 50B; ⏰5pm-midnight; ⛴Ratchawong Pier, [M]Hua Lamphong exit 1), sells *gŏo·ay jáp nám săi*, a peppery broth with noodles and pork offal. Walk west along Th Yaowarat to Th Ratchawong, then turn left. To your left is **6 Pat Tai Ratchawong** (Map p84; Th Ratchawong; mains from 40B; ⏰7-11pm Tue-Sun; ⛴Tha Ratchawong, [M]Hua Lamphong exit 1 & taxi), making the eponymous dish.

Returning to Th Yaowarat, turn right and go past the Soi Yaowarat 6 crossing. To your right is **7 Mangkorn Khăo** (p121), selling *bà·mèe* (Chinese-style wheat noodles), barbecued pork, and wontons. Further east along Th Yaowarat is **8 Boo·a loy nám kĭng** (Map p84; cnr Th Yaowarat & Th Yaowaphanit; mains from 40B; ⏰5-11pm Tue-Sun; 🌿; ⛴Ratchawong Pier, [M]Hua Lamphong exit 1), selling dough balls filled with black sesame in spicy ginger broth. Finally, at the next crossing, turn left into the busy **9 Seafood Stalls** (p122) on Th Phadungdao.

MONDAY BLUES

Bangkok's street stalls and family-run restaurants operate frustratingly inconsistent business hours. So if you're heading to Chinatown with the intent of eating at a specific stall, it's always a good idea to have a Plan B. Monday is a bad day, when many places are closed.

★Le Cabanon FRENCH $$$
(Map p70; ☎092 568 4444; 44 Soi Akhan Sangkhro; mains 1100-1800B; ⏲6-11pm; ❄📶; [S]Chong Nonsi exit 5 & taxi) With an emphasis on seafood, this alfresco restaurant in a cosy bungalow is the place to come if you're craving a jumbo platter of steamed mussels, juicy scallops braised in butter, or a serving of fresh oysters that still smells of the sea. Prices are steep, but the weekend lunch (noon to 3pm Saturday to Sunday) offers a three-course combo for 950B.

★Il Bolognese ITALIAN $$$
(Map p100; ☎02 286 8805; www.ilbolognesebangkok.com; 139/3 Soi 7, Th Naradhiwas Rajanagarindra; mains 300-550B; ⏲11.30am-2.30pm & 6-11pm; ❄📶; [S]Chong Nonsi exit 5) Run by a passionate, hands-on Italian chef, this fabulous restaurant serves a sturdy range of northern Italian goodies in its casual yet stylish premises. Try the grilled eggplant balls with tomato sauce and stracciatella, followed by the hearty grilled chicken, or any of the fluffy pizzas (vegetarian options available). Pair your food with a lovely Italian wine or beer.

The restaurant has its main entrance opening northward onto an alley called Soi Thian Siang, but in practice, the rear gate on Soi 7 is more easily accessible by either taxi or foot.

★Sühring GERMAN $$$
(Map p70; ☎02 287 1799; www.restaurantsuhring.com; 10 Soi 3, Th Yen Akat; mains 1800-2500B; ⏲5.30-9.30pm; ❄; [M]Khlong Toei exit 1 & taxi) Twin chefs Mathias and Thomas Sühring from Germany present a mix of family recipes in explosive renditions that could be framed and hung in a modern art museum. Service is warm and impeccable and, despite the creative gourmet execution and fancy presentation, you'll feel like you're dining at a friend's home. Totally worth the splurge, but book well in advance.

★nahm THAI $$$
(Map p88; ☎02 625 3333; www.comohotels.com; 27 Th Sathon Tai/South, ground fl, Metropolitan Hotel; set dinner 2500B, mains 300-700B; ⏲noon-2pm & 6.30-10pm; ❄; [M]Lumphini exit 2) In the modern-day melee of top-notch restaurants here, nahm may no longer be on top of the competition, but it's still one of Bangkok's nicest Thai restaurants. Helmed by the talented female chef Pim, counted among the city's leading chefs, it consistently serves up creative and classy dishes, such as black grouper in tamarind and ginger broth, or the stir-fried 'angry beef'.

If you're expecting bland, gentrified Thai food meant for foreigners, prepare to be surprised – dishes here are as spicy and pungent as they need to be. Reservations essential.

Le Normandie FRENCH $$$
(Map p90; ☎02 659 9000; www.mandarinoriental.com; Soi 40/Oriental, Mandarin Oriental; mains 2100-3300B; ⏲noon-2pm & 7-10pm Mon-Sat; ❄; ⛴Oriental Pier) Le Normandie has maintained its niche in fine-dining-obsessed Bangkok, and is still the only place to go for a genuinely old-world 'Continental' dining experience. A revolving cast of Michelin-starred guest chefs and some of the world's most lavish ingredients keep up the standard. An appropriately formal attire (including jacket) is required. Book well ahead.

🍴 Siam Square, Pratunam, Phloen Chit & Ratchathewi

Eating options in central Bangkok mostly comprise shopping-mall food courts, in-house hotel restaurants and chain food stores. However, this is still Thailand, and if you can ignore the prefabricated atmosphere, good eating options can be found and savoured.

Doy Kuay THAI $
(Map p98; Soi 18, Th Ratchawithi; mains from 40B; ⏲8am-5pm; [S]Victory Monument exit 3) The area surrounding Victory Monument is home to heaps of simple restaurants selling spicy, rich 'boat noodles' – so-called because they were once sold from boats plying central Thailand's rivers and canals. Our pick of the lot is Doy Kuay, located at the edge of the canal at the northern end of Soi 18, Th Ratchawithi. No English-language menu or sign.

Somtam Nua THAI $
(Map p94; 392/14 Soi 5, Siam Sq; mains 80-120B; ⏲11am-9.30pm; ❄; [S]Siam exit 4) It can't

compete with the street stalls for flavour and authenticity, but if you desire a good serving of thc iconic raw papaya salad, particularly while in air-con and hip surroundings, this is a good place to sample it, along with other northeastern Thai specialities. Expect a queue at dinner.

Sanguan Sri THAI $

(Map p94; 59/1 Th Witthayu/Wireless Rd; mains 80-200B; ⏲10am-3pm Mon-Sat; ❄; [S] Phloen Chit exit 2) The English-language menu is limited at this old-school Thai eatery, but simply pointing to the delicious dishes being consumed around you is almost certainly a wiser ordering strategy. There's no English-language signage outside; look for the bunker-like concrete structure crammed with office workers lunchtime dining.

★Hong Bao CHINESE $$

(Map p94; ☎092 667 2992; 5th fl, Central Embassy, Th Phloen Chit; dim sum 100-300B, mains 250-450B; ⏲11am-10pm; ❄; [S] Phloen Chit exit 5) The popular verdict is that this Cantonese restaurant makes some of the best dumplings in Bangkok, so make a point to drop in if you happen to be a fan. The extended menu includes some delicious items such as steamed radish cakes and a fiery fish soup in a broth featuring a million red chillies. No reservations.

Ban Khun Mae THAI $$

(Map p94; ☎02 250 1952; www.bankhunmae.com; 458/6-9 Soi 8, Siam Sq; mains 150-350B; ⏲11am-11pm; ❄✍; [S] Siam exit 2/4) More than two decades into its existence, this popular restaurant continues to serve top-notch Thai classics to an endless stream of locals and travellers day after day. The steamed snapper with lime in a lemon-chilli broth remains an absolute favourite, but do also order a smattering of other starters and entrees to make a great meal of it.

Open House CAFE $$

(Map p94; ☎02 119 7777; www.centralembassy.com/anchor/open-house; 1031 Th Phloen Chit, 6th fl, Central Embassy; mains 100-200B; ⏲10am-10pm; ❄📶👪; [S] Phloen Chit exit 5) Housed in posh Central Embassy (p149) mall, Open House is a chic, light-filled multi-use space from the same team who designed the Tokyo headquarters of YouTube and Google. The open floor plan incorporates restaurants, galleries, a bookshop, a breezy balcony for lounging and 180-degree views of buzzy Th Sukhumvit. Pop in to recharge with an iced latte and to connect to the fast wi-fi.

La Monita MEXICAN $$

(Map p94; ☎02 651 5605; www.lamonita.com; 888/26 Mahatun Plaza, Th Phloen Chit; mains 150-400B; ⏲11.30am-10pm; ❄✍; [S] Phloen Chit exit 2) Admittedly, the menu here is more Texas than Tijuana, but you can always drop in for an inviting, pleasant atmosphere and a repertoire of hearty dishes such as *queso fundido* (a skillet of melted cheese) and burritos. Ten years into its operation, the quality hasn't wavered and loyal customers keep coming back for more.

Nuer Koo CHINESE $$

(Map p94; 991/1 Rama I, 4th fl, Siam Paragon; mains 100-650B; ⏲11.30am-10pm; ❄; [S] Siam exit 3/5) Is this the future of the noodle stall? Mall-bound Nuer Koo does a luxe version of the formerly humble bowl of beef noodles. Choose your cut of beef (including Kobe beef from Japan), enjoy the rich broth and cool air-con, and quickly forget about the good old days.

Koko THAI $$

(Map p94; 262/2 Soi 3, Siam Sq; mains 100-250B; ⏲11am-9.30pm; ❄✍; [S] Siam exit 2) Perfect for omnivores and vegetarians alike, this casual cafe-like restaurant offers a lengthy vegetarian menu, not to mention a short but solid repertoire of meat-based Thai dishes, such as a Penang curry served with tender pork, or fish deep-fried and served with Thai herbs.

Coca Suki THAI $$

(Map p94; ☎02 251 6337; 416/3-8 Th Henri Dunant; mains 100-400B; ⏲11am-11pm; ❄✍; [S] Siam exit 6) Immensely popular with Thai families, *sù·gêe* takes the form of a bubbling hotpot of broth and the raw ingredients to dip therein. Coca is one of the oldest purveyors of the dish, and this branch reflects the brand's efforts to appear more modern. Insider tip for fans of spice: be sure to request the tangy *đôm yam* broth.

★Gaa INTERNATIONAL $$$

(Map p94; ☎091 419 2424; www.gaabkk.com; 68/4 Soi Langsuan; set menu 3200B; ⏲6-9.30pm Wed-Mon; ❄✍; [S] Ratchadamri exit 2) This uber-acclaimed restaurant is run by Michelin-starred chef Garima Arora (a protégé of former Bangkok chef Gaggan Anand) who also honed her craft at Copenhagen's famed Noma. Classic Indian and Thai dishes are the specialities here, upgraded with modern cooking techniques and presented in artful 10- to 12-course tasting menus. Wine pairing (if opted for) doubles the bill. Reservations absolutely essential.

★ Lenzi Tuscan Kitchen ITALIAN $$$

(Map p110; ☑ 02 001 0116; www.lenzibangkok. com; 69/1-2 Soi Ruam Rudi 2; mains 600-1200B; ◷ noon-2pm & 6-10.30pm; ❋; Ⓢ Phloen Chit exit 4) Stylish Lenzi embodies the basic tenets of Italian dining: using the best ingredients and producing a complex melange of flavours and tastes through simple and straightforward cooking. The prices are steep, but once you dig into the slow-cooked ravioli with taleggio cheese and truffle sauce or the roasted wild Sardinian sea bass, you'll know exactly what you paid for.

Nonna Nella ITALIAN $$$

(Map p94; ☑ 02 038 2184; www.nonna-nella. com; 87/2 Th Witthayu/Wireless Rd, ground fl, All Seasons Pl; mains 300-500B; ◷ 11.30am-10pm; ❋ ☑; Ⓢ Phloen Chit exit 2) We've heard many an Italian expat in Bangkok say this, and we concur: Nonna Nella makes the best pizzas in town. True to its name, invoking the spirit of an Italian grandmother's cooking, this restaurant is a great place to tuck into some fabulous comfort food – a breezy Caprese salad, a full-bodied Margherita pizza, or a spit-roasted porchetta.

Saneh Jaan THAI $$$

(Map p94; ☑ 02 650 9880; 130-132 Th Witthayu/ Wireless Rd, Glasshouse at Sindhorn; set menus 1600-2500B, mains 390-680B; ◷ 11.30am-2pm & 6-10pm; ❋; Ⓢ Phloen Chit exit 2 & taxi) A fabulous restaurant with an old-school feel, Saneh Jaan features a menu of intriguing, unusual – and delicious – Thai dishes, many with a southern Thai accent. The prices reflect the semiformal vibe of the dining room, but serves are generous. The set menus for lunch and dinner offer a good sampling of dishes. No shorts, flip-flops or sandals.

Sra Bua by Kiin Kiin THAI $$$

(Map p94; ☑ 02 162 9000; www.srabuabykiinkiin. com; 991/9 off Rama I, ground fl, Siam Kempinski Hotel; set menus 1850-3200B, mains 480-900B; ◷ noon-3pm & 6-10.30pm; ❋ ☑; Ⓢ Siam exit 3/5) Helmed by a Thai and a Dane whose Copenhagen restaurant, Kiin Kiin, snagged a Michelin star, Sra Bua takes a correspondingly international approach to Thai food. Putting local ingredients through the wringer of molecular gastronomy, the couple have created unconventional Thai dishes such as 'tom kha snow, mushrooms and pickled lemon'.

Ginza Sushi-Ichi SUSHI $$$

(Map p94; ☑ 02 250 0014; www.ginza-sushiichi.jp/ english/shop/bangkok.html; 494 Th Phloen Chit, ground fl, Erawan Bangkok; set lunch from 1800B, set dinner from 5000B; ◷ noon-2.30pm & 6-11pm Tue-Sat, noon-2.30pm & 6-10pm Sun; ❋; Ⓢ Chit Lom exit 8) This closet-sized restaurant – the Bangkok branch of a Tokyo-based recipient of a Michelin star – is arguably the city's premier place for sushi. The set menus depend on what was purchased at Tokyo's markets the previous day, which means that Ginza Sushi-Ichi does not open immediately following public holidays in Japan. Check the website calendar for details.

✗ Thanon Sukhumvit

Home to the city's largest selection of international restaurants, this seemingly endless ribbon of a road is where to go if – for the duration of a meal – you wish to forget that you're in Thailand.

Wattana Panich CHINESE $

(Map p110; 336-338, Soi 63/Ekamai; noodle soup 100B; ◷ 9.30am-8pm Tue-Sun; ❋; Ⓢ Ekkamai exit 3 & taxi) This mom-and-pop restaurant is highly revered for its signature beef stew, made of assorted meat cuts and a broth that has been constantly cooking for 45 years. Each day's leftover broth is cooled overnight and then added to the cauldron with fresh ingredients next morning. Years of slow cooking imparts subtleties in flavour and taste that are hardly imitable.

The ground-floor dining area is a throwback to earlier decades, while a more comfortable air-conditioned room upstairs draws in stylish millennial diners.

Congee & Curry THAI $

(Jok Bangkok; Map p110; ☑ 095 896 6692; 159/1 Soi 55/Thong Lor, Th Sukhumvit; mains 50-250B; ◷ 7am-midnight; ❋; Ⓢ Thong Lo exit 3) Despite its bright yellow signage, Congee & Curry is easy to miss among the massage parlours and high-end restaurants packed along Soi 55 (Thong Lor). Popular among locals and foreigners for its range of Thai dishes, the restaurant's affordable all-day curry sets (your choice of curry with roti or rice, tom yum soup, chicken sausage, and stir-fried greens) are a must-try.

Klang Soi Restaurant THAI $

(Map p110; Soi 49/9, Th Sukhumvit; mains 100-250B; ◷ 11am-2.30pm & 5-10pm Tue-Sun; ❋; Ⓢ Phrom Phong exit 3 & taxi) If you had a Thai grandma who lived in the Sukhumvit area, this is where she'd eat. The mimeographed menu spans old-school specialities from central and southern Thailand, as well as a few Western dishes. Located at the end of Soi 49/9, in the Racquet Club complex.

Gokfayuen · CHINESE $
(Map p110; www.gokfayuen.com; 161/7 Soi Thong Lor 9; mains 80-150B; ⏰11am-11.30pm; ❄; Ⓢ Thong Lo exit 1/3 & taxi) Gokfayuen has gone to great lengths to re-create classic Hong Kong noodle dishes in Bangkok. Couple your house-made wheat-and-egg noodles with roasted pork, steamed vegetables with oyster sauce, or the Hong Kong–style milk tea.

★ Soul Food Mahanakorn · THAI $$
(Map p110; ☏02 714 7708; www.soulfood mahanakorn.com; 56/10 Soi 55/Thong Lor, Th Sukhumvit; mains 150-350B; ⏰5.30pm-midnight; ❄✎; Ⓢ Thong Lo exit 1/3) This contemporary Thai diner is a favourite go-to place for a comfort meal. The menu – incorporating tasty interpretations of rustic Thai dishes – has not changed over several years, but the top quality of the food hasn't wavered either. The bar serves deliciously boozy, Thai-

influenced drinks, as well as cocktails and a few craft beers. Reservations recommended.

★ Sri Trat · THAI $$
(Map p110; ☏02 088 0968; www.facebook.com/ sritrat; 90 Soi 33, Th Sukhumvit; mains 200-450B; ⏰noon-11pm Wed-Mon; ❄; Ⓢ Phrom Phong exit 5) This fabulous restaurant specialises in the unique fare of Thailand's eastern provinces, Trat and Chanthaburi. What this means is lots of rich, slightly sweet, herbal flavours, fresh seafood and dishes you won't find anywhere else in town. That's also because it's a family operation, and most of the recipes originate in the family kitchen.

★ Indus · INDIAN $$
(Map p110; ☏086 339 8582; www.indusbangkok. com; 71 Soi 26/Soi Ari, Th Sukhumvit; mains 150-400B; ⏰11.30am-2.30pm & 6-10.30pm; ❄✎; Ⓢ Phrom Phong exit 4) Unless someone conclusively proves otherwise, Indus will reign as Bangkok's finest traditional Indian restaurant. Its North Indian staples such as *biryani,* kebab, dhal (spicy lentil soup)

BANGKOK & AROUND EATING

FOOD COURT FRENZY

The Siam Sq area is home to some of Bangkok's biggest malls, which means it also has more than its share of mall-based food courts. They're a great way to dip your toe in the sea of Thai food as they're generally cheap, clean, air-conditioned and have English-language menus. At most, paying is done by exchanging cash for vouchers or a temporary credit card at one of several counters; your change is refunded at the same desk after the meal.

MBK Food Island (Map p94; 6th fl, MBK Center, cnr Rama I & Th Phayathai; mains 50-150B; ⏰10am-9pm; ❄✎; Ⓢ National Stadium exit 4) The grandaddy of the genre offers dozens of vendors selling Thai-Chinese, regional Thai and international dishes.

Food Republic (Map p94; cnr Rama I & Th Phayathai, 4th fl, Siam Center; mains 50-200B; ⏰10am-10pm; ❄✎; Ⓢ Siam exit 1) The city's handsomest food court has a good mix of Thai and international (mostly Asian) outlets in an open, modern-feeling locale.

Eathai (Map p94; 1031 Th Phloen Chit, basement, Central Embassy; mains 60-350B; ⏰10am-10pm; ❄✎; Ⓢ Phloen Chit exit 5) This expansive food court spans Thai – and only Thai – dishes from just about every corner of the country, including those from several lauded Bangkok restaurants and stalls.

Gourmet Paradise (Map p94; 991/1 Rama I, ground fl, Siam Paragon; mains 50-200B; ⏰10am-10pm; ❄✎; Ⓢ Siam exit 3/5) The perpetually busy Gourmet Paradise unites international fast-food chains, domestic restaurants and food-court-style stalls, with a particular emphasis on the sweet stuff.

Food Loft (Map p94; 6th fl, Central Chidlom, 1027 Th Phloen Chit; mains 80-400B; ⏰10am-10pm; ❄✎; Ⓢ Chit Lom exit 5) This department-store-bound food court pioneered the concept of the upscale food court, and mock-ups of the Indian, Italian, Japanese and other international cuisines aid in the decision-making process.

FoodPark (Map p94; 97/11 Th Ratchadamri, 4th fl, Big C; mains 30-90B; ⏰9am-9pm; ❄; Ⓢ Sky Walk via Chit Lom exit 9) The selection may not inspire you to move here, but dishes are abundant and cheap, and are representative of the kind of 'fast food' Thais enjoy eating.

and myriad vegetarian dishes in tomato- or yoghurt-based curries are as good as those served at the best New Delhi restaurants. To make the most of it, go for the 990B all-you-can-eat buffet.

Charley Browns Mexicana
MEXICAN $$

(Map p110; ☑02 244 2553; www.facebook.com/charleybrownsmexicana; 19/9 Soi 19, Th Sukhumvit; mains 150-350B; ⊙noon-11pm; ☀; ⓢAsok exit 1) Chef Primo's flair for living it large reflects in the menu at this fun and irreverent restaurant serving authentic provincial Mexican dishes. Go beyond the usual taco-burrito drill and try the *albondigas* (meatballs) or the *pescadilla* – deep-fried corn tortilla stuffed with sea bass. Brave drinkers can try pairing their meal with a jalapeño margarita. Dancing sessions held on select days.

theCOMMONS
MARKET $$

(Map p110; www.thecommonsbkk.com; 335 Soi 17, Soi 55/Thong Lor, Th Sukhumvit; mains 200-500B; ⊙8am-midnight; ☀ ☑; ⓢThong Lo exit 1/3 & taxi) Hip Thong Lor gets even cooler with this marketplace-style alfresco dining complex that is packed with reliable names such as Soul Food 555, Peppina and Meat & Bones, along with a coffee roaster, a craft-beer bar and wine vendor. It's an ideal place to idle away an evening listening to Jack Johnson wannabes strum acoustic sets.

Daniel Thaiger
AMERICAN $$

(Map p110; ☑084 549 0995; www.facebook.com/danielthaiger; Soi 11, Th Sukhumvit; burgers from 260B; ⊙11am-8pm; ☀; ⓢNana exit 3) Bangkok's most-loved burgers – read ultrajuicy beef or lamb patties served in a brioche bun – are served from this American-run, food-truck-turned-restaurant that now operates out of a tiny shophouse on Soi 11. Sides include crunchy fries and the insanely crispy (and popular) onion rings. There's an exhaustive list of imported beers to go with your choice of food.

Daniel still continues to operate its food truck; check the Facebook page for location details.

Prai Raya
THAI $$

(Map p110; Soi 8, Th Sukhumvit; mains 150-600B; ⊙10.30am-10.30pm; ☀; ⓢNana exit 4) This Phuket institution's Bangkok branch – housed in a charming lime-washed villa – brings to the city the southern Thai island's uniquely spicy, occasionally Chinese-influenced cuisine. The menu descriptions may not always make sense, but you can't go wrong

choosing from the 'popular dishes', which include the signature deep-fried fish in tamarind sauce and crab meat in yellow curry and coconut milk.

Teppen
JAPANESE $$

(Map p110; www.facebook.com/TeppenThailand; 14/2 Soi 61, Th Sukhumvit; dishes 150-700B; ⊙6pm-midnight; ☀; ⓢEkkamai exit 1) This is one of our favourite Bangkok *izakaya* (Japanese tavern-style restaurants), and the menu here has a bit of everything that could comprise a hearty Japanese spread, from edamame starters to beef offal stew. There's good Japanese beer to go with your food.

Jidori Cuisine Ken
JAPANESE $$

(Map p110; ☑02 661 3457; www.facebook.com/jidoriken; off Soi 26 (Soi Ari), Th Sukhumvit; mains 80-350B; ⊙5-11pm; ☀; ⓢPhrom Phong exit 4) This cosy Japanese restaurant does tasty tofu dishes, delicious salads and even excellent desserts. Basically everything here is above average, but the highlight is the smoky, perfectly seasoned chicken skewers. Reservations recommended.

Bharani
THAI $$

(Map p110; ☑02 644 4454; 96/14 Soi 23, Th Sukhumvit; mains 150-300B; ⊙11am-10pm; ☀; ⓜSukhumvit exit 2, ⓢAsok exit 3) This cosy family-run Thai restaurant dabbles in a bit of everything, from ox-tongue stew to rice fried with shrimp paste. But the real reason to come is for the rich 'boat noodles' – so called because they used to be sold from boats plying the *klorng* (canals) of central Thailand. The decor is a nostalgic throwback to the restaurant's familial traditions.

Nasir Al-Masri
MIDDLE EASTERN $$

(Map p110; 4/6 Soi 3/1, Th Sukhumvit; mains 160-350B; ⊙24hr; ☀ ☑; ⓢNana exit 1) One of several Middle Eastern restaurants on Soi 3/1, Nasir Al-Masri is easily recognisable by its floor-to-ceiling stainless-steel 'theme'. Middle Eastern food often means meat, meat and more meat, but the menu here also includes several delicious vegie-based mezze (small dishes).

★ Cocotte Farm Roast & Winery
ITALIAN $$$

(Map p110; ☑092 664 6777; www.cocotte-bangkok.com; Soi 39, Th Sukhumvit; mains 390-790B; ⊙11am-2.30pm & 6pm-midnight; ☀; ⓢPhrom Phong exit 1) Cocotte brings a fine selection of organic farm products – sourced from Bangkok and Chiang Mai – to the table and pairs them with a classy selection of wines. The slow roasted duck confit, beef tartare with pickles and grilled bone marrow with beef cheek marmalade are just some of its many house specialities. Reservations essential, especially on weekends.

★Bacco ITALIAN $$$
(Osteria da Sergio; Map p110; www.bacco-bkk.com; 35/1 Soi 53, Th Sukhumvit; antipasti 200-400B, mains 350-700B; ⏰11.30am-2.30pm & 5.30pm-midnight Mon-Fri, 11am-midnight Sat & Sun; ❄📝; [S]Thong Lo exit 1) The slightly cheesy interior of this *osteria* (Italian-style wine bar) serves as a cover for a fabulous Italian menu. There's an abundance of delicious antipasti, but the emphasis here is on breads, from pizza to *piada* flatbread (try the *piada* stuffed with rocket and cheese). Meaty classics such as osso buco, braised brisket and saltimbocca are exceptional. Reservations essential at dinnertime.

★Bo.lan THAI $$$
(Map p110; ☎02 260 2962; www.bolan.co.th; 24 Soi 53, Th Sukhumvit; set meals 3280-3680B; ⏰6-10.30pm Tue-Fri, noon-2.30pm & 6-10.30pm Sat & Sun; ❄📝; [S]Thong Lo exit 1) Upscale Thai is often more garnish than flavour, but Bo.lan has proved to be the exception. Bo and Dylan (Bo.lan is a play on words that means 'ancient') take a scholarly approach to Thai cuisine, and generous set meals featuring full-flavoured Thai dishes are the results of this tuition (à la carte is not available; meat-free meals are). Reservations recommended.

El Mercado EUROPEAN $$$
(Map p110; ☎099 078 3444; www.elmercadobangkok.com; 490 Phai Singto Alley; mains 500-800B; ⏰noon-3pm & 6-10.30pm Tue-Fri, noon-10pm Sat & Sun; ❄📝; [M]Queen Sirikit National Convention Centre exit 1) A restaurant, charcuterie, fromagerie, boulangerie, winery and grocery store all rolled into one pleasant alfresco commercial complex, this popular food station does hearty platters of comfort food such as grilled chicken, tuna steak and beef tartare. The cheeseboards and cold platters (from 2090B) are good for sharing with a glass of prosecco while the kitchen plates up your main orders.

Appia ITALIAN $$$
(Map p110; ☎02 261 2056; www.appia-bangkok.com; 20/4 Soi 31, Th Sukhumvit; mains 400-1000B; ⏰6-11pm Mon-Sat, 11.30am-2.30pm & 6-11pm Sun; ❄📝; [S]Phrom Phong exit 5) Handmade pastas, slow-roasted meats and a carefully curated and relatively affordable wine list are the selling points of this restaurant serving Lazio-style Roman cuisine. If you don't mind the steep prices, it's easily among the most stylish places in town for an Italian dinner. Reservations recommended.

Haoma INDIAN $$$
(Map p110; ☎02 258 4744; www.haoma.dk; 231/3 Sukhumvit Rd; set menu 2390-2890B; ⏰6-11pm Tue-Fri, 11.30am-3pm & 6-11pm Sat & Sun; ❄📝; [M]Phetchaburi exit 1) 🌿 Innovative dishes at Bangkok's first 'urban farm' are complemented by cocktails using almost 40 edible herbs from the on-site garden. Chef Deepanker Khosla grows most of his produce on his Chiang Mai farm to create Neo Indian cuisine, a nod to his heritage, served as a set menu from nine to 13 dishes. A vegetarian dinner menu is also available.

🍴 Thewet & Dusit

What Thewet lacks in culinary diversity, it makes up for in riverfront views. There's little in terms of dining in Dusit, however.

★Likhit Kai Yang THAI $
(Map p78; off Th Ratchadamnoen Nok; mains 50-200B; ⏰10am-8.30pm; ❄📶; ⛴Thewet Pier, [S]Phaya Thai exit 3 & taxi) Located just behind Rajadamnern Stadium (p142), this decades-old restaurant is where locals come for a northeastern-style meal before a Thai boxing match. The friendly English-speaking owner will steer you through the ordering, but don't miss the deliciously herbal, eponymous 'charcoal roasted chicken'. There's no English-language sign; look for the bright pink shopfront and an overwhelming grilled-garlic smell emanating from inside.

Seven Spoons INTERNATIONAL $$
(Map p78; ☎02 629 9214; 22-24 Th Chakraphatdi Phong; mains 250-450B; ⏰11am-3pm & 6-11.30pm; ❄📝; ⛴Thewet Pier, [S]Phaya Thai exit 1/3 & taxi) Dark woods, old maps and prints on the smooth concrete walls, a menu including lots of vegetarian options – one doesn't expect a place this cosmopolitan in such an antiquated corner of Bangkok. Check out the many salads of the day, or relish an ox tongue pasta with creamy mushroom sauce. There's a good range of wines and craft beers, too.

★Krua Apsorn THAI $$
(Map p106; www.kruaapsorn.com; 503-505 Th Samsen; mains 150-400B; ⏰10.30am-8pm Mon-Sat; ❄📶; ⛴Thewet Pier) This is the original

SUNDAY BRUNCH

Sunday brunch has become a modern Bangkok tradition, particularly among members of the city's expat community, and the hotels along Th Sukhumvit offer some of the city's best – and most diverse – spreads. Here are some of our favourites.

Rang Mahal (Map p110; ✆ 02 261 7100; www.facebook.com/Rangmahal; 26th fl, Rembrandt Hotel, 19 Soi 18, Th Sukhumvit; mains 300-650B; ☺ 5pm-midnight Mon-Sat, noon-3pm & 5pm-midnight Sun; ❄ ✐; Ⓜ Sukhumvit exit 2, Ⓢ Asok exit 6) Combine views from this restaurant's 26th floor with an all-Indian buffet and a live band, and you have one of the most popular Sunday destinations for Bangkok's South Asian expat community.

Sunday Jazzy Brunch (Map p110; ✆ 02 649 8888; www.sheratongrandesukhumvit.com/sundayjazzybrunch; 1st fl, Sheraton Grande Sukhumvit, 250 Th Sukhumvit; buffet adult 2500-3700B, child 1250B; ☺ noon-3pm Sun; ❄ ✐; Ⓜ Sukhumvit exit 3, Ⓢ Asok exit 2) If you require more than just victuals, then consider the Sheraton's Sunday brunch, which unites all the hotel's dining outlets to a live jazz theme.

Marriott Café (Map p110; ✆ 02 656 7700; 4 Soi 2, Th Sukhumvit, ground fl, JW Marriott; buffet 2500B; ☺ noon-3pm Sun; ❄ ✐; Ⓢ Nana exit 2) The feast-like Sunday brunch at this American hotel chain is likened to Thanksgiving year-round.

Scandinavian Smorgaasbuffet (Map p110; Stable Lodge, 39 Soi 8, Th Sukhumvit; buffet 600B; ☺ noon-3pm Sat & Sun; ❄ ✐; Ⓢ Nana exit 4) Swap out the usual seafood station for pickled fish, and the roast beef for Swedish meatballs, and you'll get an idea of this unique, excellent-value weekend buffet option.

branch of this homey, award-winning and royally patronised restaurant. Expect a clientele of large families and middle-aged ladies, and a cuisine revolving around full-flavoured, largely seafood- and vegetable-heavy central and southern Thai dishes. The crab meat in curry powder remains a public favourite, as does the green curry with fish-balls. No reservations. Last orders at 7.30pm.

Water Front THAI $$
(Map p106; Th Ratchawithi, Saphan Krung Thon Pier; mains 150-220B; ☺ 5pm-midnight; ➍; ⛴ Saphan Krung Thon Pier) Located across the river from Thewet's touristy area, this pleasant riverside restaurant is largely the preserve of local patrons who gather here in the evenings to socialise over sumptuous dinners. The delicious fare is mostly Thai, there's a spot of live music on most evenings, and the beautiful riverside seating is ideal for a quiet but special dining experience.

Most dishes here can be tempered down in terms of spice to suit children. To get here, take the ferry one stop from Thewet to Saphan Krung Thon. Post dinner, stroll back to Thewet along Krung Thon bridge, spanning the dark waters of the Chao Phraya River.

Steve Café & Cuisine THAI $$
(Map p106; ✆ 02 281 0915; www.stevecafeandcuisine.com; 68 Soi 21, Th Si Ayuthaya; mains 150-450B; ☺ 11am-10.30pm; ⛴ Thewet Pier) This

sophisticated, house-bound, riverside Thai restaurant has its antique walls adorned with photos of royals and celebrities, and the dining area is thrown along a fabulous balcony overlooking the Chao Phraya River. The menu spans a great selection of Thai dishes, and service is friendly and efficient, even when the place is mobbed with local and expat patrons.

To get here, enter Th Si Ayuthaya and walk through Wat Thevarat Kunchorn (p89) until you reach the river. Locals will help point the way as you go.

Khinlom Chom Saphan THAI $$
(Map p106; ✆ 02 628 8382; www.khinlomchomsaphan.com; 11/6 Soi 3, Th Samsen; mains 150-450B; ☺ 11.30am-midnight; ⛴ Thewet Pier) Patrons come to this open-air restaurant for the combination of riverfront views and tasty, seafood-based eats. It also doubles quite neatly as a pub. It's popular with locals, especially large families, so be sure to call ahead to book a riverfront table.

✖ Northern Bangkok

Although a bit of a trek, an excursion to Bangkok's suburbs can be a profoundly tasty experience, with plenty of local restaurants that don't tone down their flavours for foreigners. The city's outskirts are also a great place to sample regional Thai cuisine.

Yusup THAI $
(Map p70; 531/12 Kaset-Navamin Hwy; mains 50-150B; ⏰8.30am 3pm; [S] Mo Chit exit 3 & taxi) The Thai-language sign in front of this restaurant boldly says *rah·chah kôw mòk* (King of Biryani) and Yusup backs it up with flawless *biryani,* not to mention sour oxtail soup and decadent *gaang mát·sà·màn* ('Muslim curry'). For dessert try *roh·đee wăhn,* a paratha-like crispy pancake with sweetened condensed milk and sugar – a dish that will send most carb-fearing Westerners fleeing.

To get here, take a taxi heading north from BTS Mo Chit and tell the driver to take you to the Kaset intersection and turn right on Th Kaset-Navamin. Yusup is on the left-hand side, about 1km past the first stoplight.

Kaobahn THAI $
(Map p116; ☎081 442 7777; www.facebook.com/kaobahn; Aran Bicicletta, 128/10 Soi, Th Phahonyothin; mains 50-120B; ⏰11am-9pm Fri-Wed; ❄; [S] Ari exit 2) Kaobahn means, roughly, home cooking, which is an accurate description of the no-frills-yet-full-flavoured central Thai dishes here. There's an iPad with images of the dishes, which range from a rich, spicy red curry with pork and pumpkin to a dip of grilled mackerel. You won't see an English-language sign; look for a steel-black gate with the number 128/10.

Baan Pueng Chom THAI $$
(Map p116; ☎02 279 4204; Soi Chua Chit, off Soi 7/Ari, Th Phahonyothin; mains 150-350B; ⏰11am-2pm & 4-10pm Mon-Sat; ❄; [S] Ari exit 1) These days, it takes venturing to Bangkok's northern 'burbs to find an old-school Thai restaurant like this. Ensconced in a watery jungle of a garden, Baan Pueng Chom has a fat, illustrated menu of typically full-flavoured, fragrant Thai dishes you're unlikely to find elsewhere. Call ahead if you wish to sit indoors.

Khua Kling Pak Sod THAI $$
(Map p116; ☎02 617 2553; 24 Soi 5, Th Phahonyothin; mains 150-400B; ⏰11am-2.30pm & 5.30-9.30pm; ❄; [S] Ari exit 1) Southern Thai is probably the country's spiciest regional cuisine, so if you're going to sweat over dinner, why not do so in white-tablecloth comfort. Recommended dishes at this elegant place include the eponymous *khua kling,* minced meat fried in an incendiary curry paste, or *mŏo hong,* a fragrant, almost candy-like braised pork belly, a Chinese-Thai speciality of Phuket.

Puritan DESSERTS $$
(Map p116; 46/1 Soi Ari 5, Th Phahonyothin; desserts from 120B; ⏰1-10pm Tue-Fri, 11am-10pm Sat & Sun; ❄; [S] Ari exit 1) A knight wearing a tiara: this might just be a pretty accurate summary of Puritan. The chandeliers, taxidermy exhibits, cherubs and antiquated Europhile touches need to be seen in person, while digging into its excellent selection of cakes and pies.

Yang Gao Gorn THAI $$
(Map p116; ☎099 024 2021; www.facebook.com/YangGaoGorn; 3/2 Soi 14, Th Phahonyothin; mains 80-250B; ⏰11.30am-10pm; ❄; [S] Ari exit 3 & taxi) Located in a cosy home in a suburban-feeling street, Yang Gao Gorn does appropriately homestyle Thai dishes such as sweet/savoury salads, rich curries and spicy stir-fries. The offerings definitely aren't those of your typical Thai place, but there's an English-language menu and the friendly, English-speaking owners can assist in the ordering process.

Anotai VEGETARIAN $$
(Map p110; ☎02 641 5366; www.facebook.com/anotaigo; 976/17 Soi Rama 9 Hospital, Rama IX; mains 150-300B; ⏰10am-9.30pm Thu-Tue; ❄🌿; [M] Phra Ram 9 exit 3 & taxi) An expansive range of Thai- and Italian-style veggie eats can be found at this upscale, long-standing and extremely popular restaurant. The establishment also has its own vegetable market and organic farm, where much of its fresh produce is sourced from.

Cantina Wine Bar & Italian Kitchen ITALIAN $$$
(Map p116; ☎02 038 5114; www.cantinabkk.com; 4 Soi Ari Samphan 3; mains 400-600B; ⏰5pm-midnight; ❄; [S] Ari exit 3) The popularity boom of the Ari neighbourhood brought in must-visit restaurants, which are mostly Asian, but this casual pizza and pasta joint is changing the landscape in terms of Western-style fine dining. Locally sourced ingredients top the Neapolitan pizzas, fresh oysters lead the menu seasonally, and a multipage wine list of New and Old World varietals are very reasonably priced.

🍷 Drinking & Nightlife

Shame on you if you think Bangkok's only nightlife options include the word 'go-go'. As in any big international metropolis, the drinking and partying scene in Bangkok ranges from trashy to classy and touches on just about everything in between.

🍷 Ko Ratanakosin & Thonburi

As with restaurants, bars are a rare sight in Ko Ratanakosin, although there is a growing number of hotel-based bars along the riverfront. Fortunately, the nightlife of Banglamphu is only a short taxi ride away. Thonburi has virtually nothing in terms of nightlife.

Rooftop
BAR

(Map p78; www.salaresorts.com/rattanakosin; Soi Tha Tian, 5th fl, Sala Rattanakosin; ⊙5-11pm; 🚤Tien Pier) The open-air bar atop Sala Rattanakosin hotel has upped the stakes for sunset views of Wat Arun across the river. If you can see the structure at all through the wall of selfie-snapping tourists, try clicking a photo at the magic hour, when the temple lights are switched on even as the sky retains some of the afterglow.

Amorosa
BAR

(Map p78; www.arunresidence.com; 36-38 Soi Pratu Nokyung, Arun Residence; ⊙5pm-midnight; 🚤Tien Pier) Perched above Arun Residence hotel, Amorosa takes advantage of a location directly above the river and opposite Wat Arun (p73). The cocktails aren't going to blow you away, but watching boats ply their way along the royal river as Wat Arun glows is a beautiful way to absorb Bangkok's dramatic riverside scenery at dusk.

🍷 Banglamphu

Vibrant Th Khao San is one of the city's best areas for a night out. Although Banglamphu used to be an almost exclusively foreign scene, locals have joined the mix in recent years, especially along Th Phra Athit. For those who find the main drag too intense, consider the quieter places along Soi Ram Buttri and Th Samsen.

★ Mitramit
TEAHOUSE

(Map p78; 32 Th Phra Sumen; ⊙2-11pm Sat-Thu; 🚤Phra Athit/Banglamphu Pier) A superb modern interpretation of a classic Bangkok teahouse, this tiny, atmospheric shophouse serves delectable blends of premium tea sourced from China and other regional tea-growing centres. Sit at one of its jade-green marble-topped tables and order a flask of your preferred brew, which comes with a complimentary serving of desserts. The owner is a trove of Thai cultural information.

★ Ku Bar
BAR

(Map p78; www.facebook.com/ku.bangkok; 3rd fl, 469 Th Phra Sumen; ⊙7pm-midnight Wed-Mon; 🚤klorng boat Phanfa Leelard Pier) Tired of buckets and cocktails that revolve around Red Bull? Head to Ku Bar, the polar opposite of the Khao San party scene. Climb three floors of stairs (look for the tiny sign) to emerge at an almost comically minimalist interior where sophisticated fruit- and food-heavy cocktails (sample names: Lychee, Tomato, Pineapple/Red Pepper) and obscure music augment the underground vibe.

Commé
BAR

(Map p78; 100/4-5 Th Phra Athit; ⊙6pm-1am; 🚤Phra Athit/Banglamphu Pier) The knot of vintage motorcycles is your visual cue, but most likely you'll hear Commé before you see it. A staple nightlife option for local hipsters, this classic Th Phra Athit semi-open-air bar is the place to go for a loud, boozy, Thai-style night out.

Babble & Rum
BAR

(Map p78; www.nexthotels.com; 23 Th Phra Athit, Riva Surya hotel; ⊙5-10pm; 🚤Phra Athit/Banglamphu Pier) This is one of the few riverside bars along this stretch of the Chao Phraya River. Come for the sunset views and breezes – or for the generous happy-hour drinks.

Macaroni Club
BAR

(Map p78; 36 Th Rambuttri; ⊙24hr; 🚤Phra Athit/Banglamphu Pier) There seems to be a current (and inexplicable) trend for beach-themed, almost tiki-bar-style pubs in Banglamphu. If this aesthetic appeals, hunker down with a fruity cocktail among the Easter Island heads and bamboo decor of this bizarrely named bar.

Madame Musur
BAR

(Map p78; www.facebook.com/madamemusur; 41 Soi Ram Buttri; ⊙8am-midnight; 🚤Phra Athit/Banglamphu Pier) Madame Musur pulls off that elusive combination of northern Thailand meets *The Beach* meets Th Khao San. It's a fun place to chat, drink and people-watch, and it's also not a bad place to eat, with a short menu of northern Thai dishes priced from 100B to 250B.

The Club
CLUB

(Map p78; www.facebook.com/theclubkhaosanbkk; 123 Th Khao San; admission Fri & Sat 120B; ⊙9pm-3am; 🚤Phra Athit/Banglamphu Pier) Located right in the middle of Th Khao San, this cavern-like dance hall hosts a good mix of locals and backpackers. Check the Facebook page for upcoming events and guest DJs.

Center Khao Sarn
BAR

(Map p78; Th Khao San; ☺10am-2am; 🚢Phra Athit/Banglamphu Pier) The open-air terrace here offers ringside seats for the ceaseless human parade that is Th Khao San. The upstairs bar hosts late-night bands.

Phra Nakorn Bar & Gallery
BAR

(Map p78; www.facebook.com/Phranakornbarand gallery; 58/2 Soi Damnoen Klang Tai; ☺6pm-midnight; 🚢klorng boat Phanfa Leelard Pier) Located an ambivalent arm's length from the hype of Th Khao San, Phra Nakorn Bar and Gallery is a home away from hovel for Thai students and arty types, with eclectic decor and changing gallery exhibits. Our tip: head directly for the breezy rooftop and order some of the bar's cheap and tasty Thai food.

Hippie de Bar
BAR

(Map p78; 46 Th Khao San; ☺3pm-2am; 🚢Phra Athit/Banglamphu Pier) Hippie has a cool, retro vibe and indoor and outdoor seating, all set to the type of indie-pop soundtrack that you're unlikely to hear elsewhere in town. Despite being located on Th Khao San, there are few foreign faces here, and it's a great place to make some Thai friends.

🍸 Chinatown

A handful of artsy and hipster bars on Soi Nana and along Th Charoen Krung has finally made Chinatown an interesting nightlife destination. However, it's still mostly for the quiet and conversational types; revellers will still have to go elsewhere.

★ Let the Boy Die
MICROBREWERY

(Map p84; 425 Th Luang; ☺5pm-midnight; Ⓜ Hua Lamphong exit 1) Quirky name aside, this watering hole originally opened in 2015 as Bangkok's first craft-beer bar. Given Thailand's liquor laws (heavily tilted against craft brewing at the time), it subsequently went on a two-year hiatus, but then came back as a microbrewery with 12 locally brewed beers on tap. Try the nutty stout or the American-style IPA, and mingle with fellow hopheads.

★ Tep Bar
BAR

(Map p84; 69-71 Soi Nana; ☺7pm-midnight Tue-Sun; Ⓜ Hua Lamphong exit 1) No one ever expects to find a bar this sophisticated – yet this fun – in Chinatown. Tep hits the spot with Thai-tinged, contemporary interiors and boozy signature cocktails; it also stocks a few delicious local rice-based brews. There are tasty drinking snacks on the side, and raucous live folk-music performances from Thursday to Sunday.

Tropic City
BAR

(Map p90; www.tropiccitybkk.com; Soi 28, Th Charoen Krung; ☺7pm-2am Tue-Sun; 🚢Si Phraya/ River City Pier) A hidden spot of happiness tucked in a quiet alley, this cool LGBTIQ-friendly bar is a superb place to end the night. The music is trippy, the pisco sour is eminently enjoyable, and the cheerful crowd mostly comprises a mix of hipsters and long-time expats. There's a tiny outdoor area where the party spills over once the place fills up.

Pijiu Bar
CRAFT BEER

(Map p84; www.facebook.com/pijiubar; 16 Soi Nana; ☺6pm-midnight Tue-Sun; 🚢Ratchawong Pier, Ⓜ Hua Lamphong exit 1) Old West meets old Shanghai at this classic retro bar. The emphasis here is on beer ('pijiu' is Chinese for beer), with four revolving craft brews on tap, but perhaps even more enticing are the charcuterie platters (300B) that unite a variety of smoked and preserved meats from some of the best vendors in Chinatown.

Teens of Thailand
BAR

(TOT; Map p84; 76 Soi Nana; ☺7pm-midnight Tue-Sun; ☎; Ⓜ Hua Lamphong exit 1) TOT is probably the edgiest of all bars in Chinatown's Soi Nana. Squeeze through the tiny handcarved wooden door of this refurbished shophouse to emerge in an artsy warehouse-like interior, with hipster barkeeps serving creative gin-based drinks, complemented by an endless supply of roasted chestnuts served by the bowlful. Try the jasmine rice brew punched with port — simply delicious.

El Chiringuito
BAR

(Map p84; www.facebook.com/elchiringuitobangkok; 221 Soi Nana; ☺6pm-midnight Thu-Sun; ☎; Ⓜ Hua Lamphong exit 1) Come to this retrofeeling bar for sangria, Spanish gin and bar snacks, or the revolving art exhibitions from time to time. If the name isn't a giveaway already, this is indeed a Spanish-themed establishment, so expect some tasty side dishes such as tortillas, tapas platters and deep-fried *patatas* (potato cubes) to go with your drinks.

River Vibe BAR

(Map p90; 8th fl, River View Guesthouse, off Soi Charoen Phanit; ⊙5.30-11pm; ☎; 🚤Marine Department Pier, ⓜHua Lamphong exit 1) Can't afford the overpriced cocktails at Bangkok's upscale rooftop bars? The excellent river views from the top of this guesthouse will hardly feel like a compromise – especially given its vantage location on a sweeping bend of the Chao Phraya River. Beers start at a mere 80B, and you're welcome to linger over a simple Thai dinner (mains 130B to 250B).

🍸 Riverside, Silom & Lumphini

Silom has a robust supply of fun pubs, sophisticated bars and hip nightclubs, many of which are LGBT-friendly. A sundowner at one of the trending rooftop bars in the area is not to be missed. Both the Riverside and Lumphini areas have some stylish terrace bars.

★Smalls BAR

(Map p88; www.facebook.com/smallsbkk; 186/3 Soi Suan Phlu; ⊙7pm-2am; ⓢChong Nonsi exit 5) Smalls aptly resembles a quintessential New York jazz bar. Fixtures include a revolving main door, a cheekily decadent interior, an inviting rooftop, food-themed nights (check the Facebook page) and live jazz on Wednesdays and Fridays. The eclectic cocktails are strong, and the absinthe servings are both generous and recommended.

★Vesper BAR

(Map p100; www.vesperbar.co; 10/15 Th Convent; ⊙5.30pm-1am; ☎; ⓜSi Lom exit 2, ⓢSala Daeng exit 2) This deceptively classic-feeling bar-restaurant is one of the most popular watering holes in Bangkok's business district. As the name unequivocally suggests, the emphasis here is on cocktails, including several revived classics and mixed drinks mellowed by ageing for six weeks in white-oak barrels. Call ahead for a table if you're planning to visit over the weekend.

Opus WINE BAR

(Map p100; 64 Th Pan; ⊙6pm-midnight; ☎; ⓢSurasak exit 1/3) This upscale wine-bar-cum-Italian-restaurant has one of the best cellars in Bangkok. Located to the rear of an uncharacteristic office building, this elegant establishment caters to (well-heeled) lovers of fine wine, and there's some excellent Italian fare on offer, to be paired with the label of your choice. No shorts, tees or flip-flops.

House on Sathorn BAR

(Map p100; W Bangkok, 106 Th Sathon Neua/North; ⊙noon-midnight; ☎; ⓢChong Nonsi exit 1/5) This classy bar is located in one of Bangkok's most charming heritage buildings – a registered historical landmark that in previous lives was a mansion, a hotel and, most recently, the Cold War–era Russian Embassy. The signature drinks are creative and pricey, yet worth it to gain access to the splendidly atmospheric surroundings.

The mansion is part of the W hotel, and shares compound space with the luxury address.

Namsaah Bottling Trust BAR

(Map p100; www.namsaah.com; 401 Soi 7, Th Silom; ⊙5pm-1am; ☎; ⓜSi Lom exit 2, ⓢChong Nonsi exit 4) Namsaah is a curveball of a place. Housed in a restored mansion incongruously painted hot pink and with a wacky interior comprised of samurai armours and neon lighting, this resto-bar is known for its tweak on classic cocktails (try mojitos with a mango and chilli garnish) and a menu featuring robust favourites such as Andaman tuna steaks in yellow curry.

Maggie Choo's BAR

(Map p90; www.maggiechoos.com; Fenix Silom, basement, Novotel Bangkok, 320 Th Silom; ⊙7.30pm-2am; ⓢSurasak exit 1) A former bank vault with a Chinatown-opium-den vibe, secret passageways and lounging women in silk dresses. With all this going on, it's easy to forget that Maggie Choo's is actually a bar, although you'll be reminded by the creative and somewhat sweet cocktails. Drag-queen shows and jazz concerts take place on select days – check the website for more details.

DJ Station GAY

(Map p100; www.dj-station.com; Soi 2, Silom; admission from 150B; ⊙9pm-2am; ⓜSi Lom exit 2, ⓢSala Daeng exit 3) One of Bangkok's – and indeed Asia's – most legendary gay dance clubs. The crowd here is a mix of Thai guppies (gay professionals) and a few Westerners. If it has already filled up by the time you get here, try any of the other similar clubs on and around the street.

Scarlett WINE BAR

(Map p100; 188 Th Silom, 37th fl, Hotel Pullman Bangkok; ⊙6pm-1am; ☎) This classy wine bar and restaurant sits on the 37th floor of the luxury Hotel Pullman and pairs lovely vistas of the city's skyline with your wine of choice. The dinner menu is largely French, with a

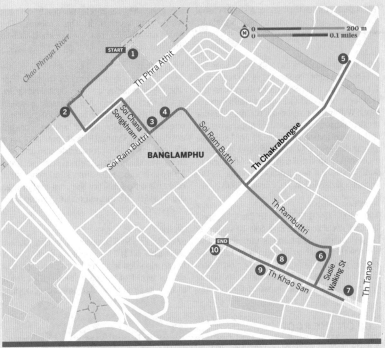

City Walk
Banglamphu Pub Crawl

START SHEEPSHANK
END HIPPIE DE BAR
LENGTH 1.5KM; THREE TO SIX HOURS

This pub crawl spans river views, people-watching, live music and late-night shenanigans. Start off at ❶ **Sheepshank** (Map p78; www.sheepshankpublichouse.com; 47 Th Phra Athit; mains 300-650B; ⏰6pm-midnight Tue-Sat; ❄; ⚓Phra Athit/Banglamphu Pier), a riverside gastropub known for its classic cocktails. If you have space for tapas, head west along the riverfront promenade to ❷ **Babble & Rum** (p134), the Riva Surya hotel's stylish open-air restaurant-bar.

From Th Phra Athit, enter Soi Chana Songkhram and take a left on Soi Ram Buttri. ❸ **Gecko Bar** (Map p78; cnr Soi Chana Songkhram & Soi Ram Buttri; ⏰10am-1am; ⚓Phra Athit/Banglamphu Pier) here is a fun and frugal place to gawk at other patrons and passers-by. A few doors down, ❹ **Madame**

Musur (p134) offers the same perks alongside tasty northern-style eats.

To add some music to the mix, head north on Th Chakrabongse (the continuation of Th Samsen) to the long-standing blues bar ❺ **Adhere the 13th** (p144), or to ❻ **Molly Bar** (Map p78; 108 Th Rambuttri; ⏰5pm-2am; ⚓Phra Athit/Banglamphu Pier) along Th Rambuttri.

Finally, crossing via Susie Walking St, proceed to Th Khao San. Make a pit stop at ❼ **Mulligans** (Map p78; www.mulligansthailand. com; 256 Th Khao San, Buddy Lodge; ⏰3pm-4am; ⚓Phra Athit/Banglamphu Pier), an Irish-themed bar in the Buddy Lodge. Alternatively, get a bird's-eye view of the human parade from elevated ❽ **The Roof Bar** (Map p78; Th Khao San; ⏰5pm-midnight; ⚓Phra Athit/Banglamphu Pier), or ringside at the noisy and buzzy ❾ **Center Khao Sarn** (p135). End the night on a good note at ❿ **Hippie de Bar** (p135).

few Italian staples thrown in. A smart casual dress code applies, much like Bangkok's other upscale bars.

JAM BAR

(Map p70; www.jambkk.com; 41 Soi Charoen Rat 1; ⏲6pm-midnight Tue-Sat; 📶; [S] Surasak exit 2) Take a break from Silom's rooftop bars and visit one of Bangkok's nicest indie-hipster dives. With walls plastered with fliers, regular musical performances, and an impressive calendar of exhibitions and events, JAM successfully mixes lowbrow and highbrow to offer a night of cheap drinks and art. After you're done catching a performance, try one of the kitchen's satisfying *katsu* curries (180B).

Telephone Pub BAR

(Map p100; 114/11-13 Soi 4, Th Silom; ⏲6pm-1am; 📶; [M] Si Lom exit 2, [S] Sala Daeng exit 1) Long-standing Telephone is famous for the phones that used to sit on every table, allowing you to phone up that person who's caught your eye across the room. Its popularity remains, even if most of the phones are gone. The clientele is mostly 30-plus white men with their Thai 'friends'. The beers are chilled, but the cocktails fail to impress.

Viva & Aviv BAR

(Map p90; www.vivaaviv.com; 23 Th Yotha, River City; ⏲noon-midnight; 📶; ⛴Si Phraya/River City Pier) An enviable riverside location makes this restaurant-bar a contender for one of Bangkok's better sunset cocktail destinations. Seating is both outdoors on a pleasant riverside promenade and indoors in a wood-and-iron-themed dining area. There are some refreshing sundowner-style cocktails on offer – try the rum-and-orange diplo (345B). It's located on the ground floor of River City.

Wong's Place BAR

(Map p88; 27/3 Soi Si Bamphen; ⏲9pm-late Tue-Sun; [M] Lumphini exit 1) This cramped, dusty (and a tad smelly) den is a time warp into the backpacker world of the early 1980s. It's known to be a last resort on Bangkok's bar-hopping

UP ON THE ROOF

In Bangkok, it's almost an unwritten architectural rule to slap the odd bar on top of a skyscraper. Indeed, the city has become associated with fabulous rooftop bars, and the area around Th Sathon and Th Silom is home to some of the best addresses, offering gorgeous views that are a permutation of the Chao Phraya riverline, hyper-urban building profiles and the odd spot of greenery.

Note that nearly all of Bangkok's hotel-based rooftop bars have strictly enforced dress codes, and will bar access to those wearing shorts and/or sandals.

Moon Bar (Vertigo; Map p88; www.banyantree.com; 21/100 Th Sathon Tai/South, 61st fl, Banyan Tree Hotel; ⏲5pm-1am; [M] Lumphini exit 2) An alarmingly low barrier at this rooftop bar is all that separates patrons from the street, 61 floors down. Located on top of the Banyan Tree Hotel, Moon Bar claims to be among the highest alfresco bars in the world. It's also a great place from which to see the Phrapradaeng Peninsula, the vast green area that's colloquially known as Bangkok's green lung.

Park Society (Map p88; 2 Th Sathon Neua/North, 29th fl, Sofitel So; ⏲6-11pm; [M] Lumphini exit 2) Gazing down at the green expanse of Lumphini Park, abruptly bordered by tall buildings on most sides, you can be excused for thinking that Bangkok almost, kinda, sorta feels like Manhattan. The drink prices at Park Society, 29 floors above the ground, may also remind you of New York City, although there are monthly promotions.

Sky Bar (Map p90; www.lebua.com; 1055 Th Silom, 63rd fl, State Tower; ⏲6pm-1am; ⛴Sathorn/Central Pier, [S] Saphan Taksin exit 3) Descend the Hollywood-like staircase to emerge at this bar that juts out over the city's skyline and the Chao Phraya River. This is the classic Bangkok rooftop bar – scenes from *The Hangover Part II* were filmed here – and the views are breathtaking, although the excessive drink prices and photo-snapping crowds have made it an increasingly hectic destination.

Three Sixty (Map p90; ☎02 442 2000; 123 Th Charoen Nakhorn, Millennium Hilton; ⏲5pm-1am; ⛴Sathorn/Central Pier & hotel shuttle boat) While technically being a jazz club, this terrace venue comes with a sweeping aerial panorama of Bangkok from across the Chao Phraya, affording a very different perspective of the city's skyline.

map, so expect functionality over finesse, and don't bother knocking until 1am. Drinks are cheap, and the place pretty much stays open until the last person crawls out.

Balcony   GAY
(Map p100; www.balconypub.com; Soi 4, Th Silom; ⏲5.30pm-2am; 🛜; Ⓜ Si Lom exit 2, Ⓢ Sala Daeng exit 1) Balcony is a long-standing Soi 4 gay pub that features the occasional drag-queen performance. The massive 3L jugs of beer make it a great place to visit with friends, and there are several themed events ranging from cheese evenings to pub quizzes that add to the variety of entertainment. Check the website for updates.

🍸 Siam Square, Pratunam, Phloen Chit & Ratchathewi

Bangkok's most central zone is home to a scant handful of bars.

Mitr Bar   MICROBREWERY
(Map p98; cnr Th Rang Nam & Th Phayathai, 2nd fl; ⏲5pm-midnight; Ⓢ Victory Monument exit 2) Run by a team of dedicated brewsters, Mitr is a low-key but top-notch pub patronised by a loyal group of hopheads with a palate for its fine offerings. Among the few places in town to brew its own crafts, Mitr ups the micro-brewing ante with two superb home-brewed meads. A basic selection of snacks is available on the side.

Hair of the Dog   CRAFT BEER
(Map p94; www.hairofthedogbkk.com; 888/26 Th Phloen Chit, 1st fl, Mahathun Plaza; ⏲5pm-midnight Mon-Sat; Ⓢ Phloen Chit exit 2) The craft-beer craze that has swept Bangkok over the last few years is epitomised at this semicon-cealed bar. With a morgue theme, dozens of bottles and 13 rotating taps, it's a great place for a hoppy night out. There's usually a unique 'tap of the month' selection, served and consumed with great vigour.

CRU Champagne Bar   ROOFTOP BAR
(Map p94; 📞02 100 6255; www.centarahotels resorts.com; 999/99 Rama I, 59th fl, Centara Grand, CentralWorld; ⏲5pm-1am; Ⓢ Sky Walk via Chit Lom exit 1) Bangkok is teeming with glitzy roof-top bars, and CRU Champagne happens to be one of the taller places for a tipple. From the 59th floor, soak up uninterrupted, 360-degree views while you sip a glass of bubbly or a fresh fruit cocktail. There's a dress code of long trousers for men and no flip-flops or tank tops.

Red Sky   BAR
(Map p94; www.centarahotelsresorts.com; 999/99 Rama I, 55th fl, Centara Grand, CentralWorld; ⏲6pm-1am; Ⓢ Sky Walk via Chit Lom exit 9) Perched on the 55th floor of a skyscraper smack-dab in the modern centre of Bang-kok, Red Sky provides one of Bangkok's most stunning rooftop views. The dramatic arch and all that glass provide the bar with a more upscale feel than many of Bangkok's other rooftoppers.

Sky Train Jazz Club   BAR
(Map p98; cnr Th Rang Nam & Th Phayathai, terrace fl; ⏲5pm-2am; Ⓢ Victory Monument exit 2) An evening at this comically misnamed bar is more like chilling at a stoner buddy's terrace flat than a jazz club. There are indeed views of the BTS, jazz on occasion and a scrappy speakeasy atmosphere. To find it, look for the sign and proceed up the graffiti-strewn stairway past Mitr Bar until you reach the roof.

Glen Bar   BAR
(Map p98; 8/2 Th Rang Nam, 1st fl, Pullman Bang-kok King Power; ⏲6pm-1am; Ⓢ Victory Monument exit 2) If the upmarket but chilled setting and spinning DJ aren't compelling enough reasons to venture from your Sukhumvit comfort zone, consider that this is probably the least expensive place in town to drink a premium-label wine. Frequent nibbles promotions span everything from imported cheeses and cold cuts to tapas.

🍸 Thanon Sukhumvit

Th Sukhumvit is home to many of Bangkok's most sophisticated bars and clubs. It also has a large number of microbreweries and craft beer pubs.

★Studio Lam   BAR, CLUB
(Map p110; www.facebook.com/studiolambangkok; 3/1 Soi 51, Th Sukhumvit; ⏲6pm-1am Tue-Sun; Ⓢ Thong Lo exit 3) Studio Lam is an exten-sion of uberhip record label ZudRangMa, and has a Jamaican-style sound system custom-built for world and retro-Thai DJ sets and the occasional live show. The bar stocks some fabulous house-made infusions (ginger and rhubarb, to name a couple) that lend inimitable flavours and aromas to its signature cocktails. It's packed to the gills on weekends.

NIGHTLIFE ON ROYAL CITY AVE (RCA)

By day a bland-looking strip of offices, come Friday and Saturday nights, Royal City Ave – known by everybody as RCA – transforms into one of Bangkok's most popular nightlife zones. Although some of the bigger clubs can draw thousands, keep in mind that they often require an ID check and also maintain a dress code (no shorts or sandals).

Onyx (Map p110; www.facebook.com/onyxbkk; RCA/Royal City Ave; admission 500B; ☺9pm-2am; Ⓜ Phra Ram 9 exit 3 & taxi) Probably the most sophisticated club along RCA – evidenced by the hefty entry fee and the coiffed and coddled clientele. Check the Facebook page for upcoming DJ events.

Route 66 (Map p110; www.route66club.com; 29/33-48 RCA/Royal City Ave; admission 300B; ☺9pm-2am; Ⓜ Phra Ram 9 exit 3 & taxi) This vast club has been around just about as long as RCA has, but frequent facelifts and expansions have kept it relevant. Top 40 hip-hop rules the main space here, although there are several different themed 'levels', featuring anything from Thai pop to live music.

NOMA BKK (Now Our Mother's Angry; Map p110; www.facebook.com/NOMABKK; 21/66 RCA/Royal City Ave; ☺7pm-2am; Ⓜ Phra Ram 9 exit 3 & taxi) This cool and casual bar has cheap beer and organises live music and freestyle hip-hop jams from time to time. It's immensely popular with Bangkok's young creative minds.

★ WTF   BAR

(Map p110; www.wtfbangkok.com; 7 Soi 51, Th Sukhumvit; ☺6pm-1am Tue-Sun; 🛜; Ⓢ Thong Lo exit 3) This cool and friendly neighbourhood bar also packs in a gallery space. Arty locals and resident foreigners come for the old-school cocktails, live music, DJ events, poetry readings, art exhibitions and tasty bar snacks. And we, like them, give WTF our top rating. The negroni here comes with a dash of spice, and is easily the best in Bangkok.

★ Tuba   BAR

(Map p70; www.facebook.com/tubabkk; 34 Room 11-12 A, Soi Thong Lor 20/Soi Ekamai 21; ☺11am-2am; Ⓢ Ekkamai exit 1/3 & taxi) Part storage room for over-the-top vintage furniture, part restaurant and part friendly local boozer, this quirky bar certainly doesn't lack diversity – nor fun. Indulge in a whole bottle (they'll hold onto it for your next visit if you don't finish it) and don't miss the chicken wings or the delicious deep-fried *lâhp* (spicy, herbal mincemeat salad).

Tasting Room by Mikkeller   MICROBREWERY

(Map p110; www.tastingroombkk.com; 26 Yaek 2, Soi Ekamai 10; ☺5pm-midnight; Ⓢ Ekkamai exit 1/3 & taxi) These buzz-generating Danish 'gypsy' brewers have set up shop in Bangkok, granting us more than 30 beers on tap. Expect brews ranging from the local (Sukhumvit Brown Ale) to the insane (Beer Geek, a 13%-alcohol oatmeal stout), as well as an inviting atmosphere and good bar snacks.

Havana Social Club   CLUB

(Map p110; www.facebook.com/pg/havanasocial bkk; Soi 11, Th Sukhumvit; ☺6pm-2am) Locate the phone booth, dial the secret code (the doorman will help you out here) and cross the threshold to pre-revolution Havana. Part bar, part dance club, Havana combines live music, great drinks and an expat-heavy crowd who all seem to know the right dance steps. No shorts, sandals, flip-flops or backpacks – in other words, look sharp to enter.

Q&A Bar   BAR

(Map p110; ☎02 664 1445; www.qnabar.com; 235/13 Soi 21/Asoke, Th Sukhumvit; ☺7pm-2am; Ⓜ Phetchaburi exit 1) Imagine a mid-century modern dining car or airport lounge, and you're close to picturing the interior of Q&A. The short list of featured cocktails can appear to be a divergence from the classic vibe, but an old-world dress code and manners are encouraged. Booking a table in advance often works to your advantage.

Sky on 20   ROOFTOP BAR

(Map p110; ☎02 009 4999; www.novotelbangkok sukhumvit20.com; 26th fl, Novotel, 19/9 Soi Sukhumvit 20; ☺5pm-1am; 🛜; Ⓢ Phrom Phong exit 2) With drinks averaging 250B, Sky on 20 has a reputation as a laid-back place for bargain sundowners. Electro house beats fill the open-air bar that has circular couches and lounge chairs overlooking Sirikit Lake and Benjasiri Park. Drinks made with local fruit juices rule the menu, and there is a retractable roof to keep the rainy season downpours at bay.

Brewski
ROOFTOP BAR

(Map p110; ☑ 02 302 3333; 489 Th Sukhumvit, Soi 27, 30/F Radisson Blu Plaza; ⏲ 5pm-1am; ☢; Ⓢ Asok exit 3) Rooftop bars are synonymous with a big bill, which is why Brewski is a breath of fresh air. With drinks starting at 90B, this beer-centric rooftop is a chilled-out spot to while away an evening 30 storeys above bustling Sukhumvit. The well-stocked bar includes 100 craft brews and ciders plus 12 on tap, such as Vedett Extra White and Wild Turkey Bourbon Stout.

Grab a balcony bar stool and order the Wagyu beef burger or Thai-style Isan sausage if hunger strikes. Check the website for a current list of specials and promotions.

Ink & Lion
COFFEE

(Map p110; www.facebook.com/inkandlioncafe; 1/7 Soi Ekamai 2, Th Sukhumvit; ⏲ 9am-6pm; Ⓢ Ekkamai exit 1/3) Intimate Ink & Lion in the charming Ekkamai neighbourhood blends strong hand-brewed coffees and sweet soy-and-honey drinks behind the bar with a mix of rotating art galleries from local artists on the wall. They roast small-batch beans (take home a bag) and offer sweet concoctions, such as slices of coconut cake, from the nearby Size S Bakery.

Taproom
CRAFT BEER

(Map p110; www.taproombkk.com; 51 Soi 26 (Soi Ari), Th Sukhumvit; ⏲ 5pm-midnight; Ⓢ Phrom Phong exit 4) If there was any doubt that craft beer is officially Bangkok's 'it' drink, this place puts those doubts to rest. Twenty-six taps rotate through beer lovers' favourites, including BrewDog, Flying Dog, Stone and Hitachino. Weekday acoustic sets and weekend DJs keep the party going.

Backstage Bar
BAR

(Map p110; www.facebook.com/backstagecocktail barbkk; 205/22-23 Soi 55, Th Sukhumvit; ⏲ 7pm-1am; Ⓢ Thong Lo exit 1/3 & taxi) Belonging to the theatre-themed Playhaus boutique hotel, Backstage keeps the performance vibe going. It's designed to look like a dressing room with the bar hiding behind thick velvety curtains and drinks of the day scribbled on mirrors. Excellent staff serve classic cocktails with a twist, such as the innovative and woody Earthbeet, made with beetroot-infused tequila, Campari and mezcal.

Sing Sing Theater
BAR

(Map p110; www.singsingbangkok.com; Soi 45, Th Sukhumvit; ⏲ 9pm-late Tue-Sun; Ⓢ Thong Lo exit 1) Dancers dressed in cheongsams or neon spacesuits (depending on the night) float through secret rooms, across towering platforms and onto the tiny dance floor at this wonderfully surreal and endlessly energetic bar-slash-nightclub. The strong drinks only help to heighten the feeling that you've fallen into a Chinese opium den.

Beam
CLUB

(Map p110; www.beamclub.com; 72 Courtyard, 72 Soi 55/Thong Lor, Th Sukhumvit; ⏲ 8pm-2am Wed-Sat; Ⓢ Thong Lo exit 1/3 & taxi) High-profile guest DJs spinning deep house and techno, a diverse crowd and a dance floor that literally vibrates have combined to make Beam Bangkok's club of the moment. Check the website for special events.

Black Amber Social Club
BAR

(Map p110; www.facebook.com/blackambersocial club; Soi 55/Thong Lor 6; ⏲ noon-2am; Ⓢ Thong Lo exit 1/3 & taxi) We're happy to tell you about Black Amber if you promise to keep it to yourself. A dark, sumptuous ambience (furnishings include an entire ostrich skeleton), moustached and/or coiffed staff (Black Amber is linked to a barber shop of the same name), and a drinks list that doesn't stray far from Scotch give Black Amber an authentically retro speakeasy vibe.

Iron Balls
Distillery & Bar
BAR

(Map p110; Parklane, Soi 63/Ekamai, Th Sukhumvit; ⏲ 6pm-2am; Ⓢ Ekkamai exit 1/3) Skeins of copper tubing, haphazardly placed one-of-a-kind antiques, zinc ceiling panels, and rows of glass vials and baubles culminate in one of the most fantastically decorated bars in Bangkok. An adjacent distillery provides fuel for the bar's largely gin-based cocktails.

J Boroski Mixology
BAR

(Map p110; www.josephboroski.com; off Soi 55/ Thong Lor, Th Sukhumvit; ⏲ 7pm-2am; ☢; Ⓢ Thong Lo exit 1/3 & taxi) The eponymous mixologist here has done away with both addresses and cocktail menus to arrive at the modern equivalent of the speakeasy. Tell the staff behind the bar what flavours you fancy, and using top-shelf liquor and unique ingredients they'll create something memorable. Located in an unmarked lane near Soi Thong Lor 6.

Walden
BAR

(Map p110; 7/1 Soi 31, Th Sukhumvit; ⏲ 7pm-1am Tue-Sat; Ⓢ Phrom Phong exit 5) Get past the hyper-minimalist vibe, and the thoughtful

Japanese touches of this bar make it one of the more welcoming places in town. The brief menu of drinks spans Japanese-style 'highballs', craft beers from the USA, and simple, delicious bar snacks.

Badmotel BAR
(Map p110; www.facebook.com/badmotel; 331/4-5 Soi 55/Thong Lor, Th Sukhumvit; ⏲5pm-1am; [S] Thong Lo exit 1/3 & taxi) Badmotel blends the modern and the kitschy, the cosmopolitan and the Thai, in a way that has struck a chord with Bangkok trendsetters. This is manifested in drinks that combine rum with Hale's Blue Boy, a Thai childhood drink staple, and bar snacks such as *nám prík òng* (a northern-style dip), served with pappadams.

Above 11 BAR
(Map p110; www.aboveeleven.com; Soi 11, Th Sukhumvit, 33rd fl, Fraser Suites Sukhumvit; ⏲6pm-2am; [S] Nana exit 3) This sophisticated rooftopper combines downward glances of Bangkok's most cosmopolitan neighbourhood with DJ sets and tasty Latin American snacks and mains. The pisco sours have a loyal following among Bangkok's resident expats.

🍷 Thewet & Dusit

Apart from the riverside restaurants that double as open-air bars, there's very little in terms of nightlife in this part of town. Luckily, Banglamphu and Th Khao San are a brief walk or taxi ride away.

Post Bar BAR
(Map p78; 161 Th Samsen; ⏲7pm-1am; ⛴ Thewet Pier) If 'Chinese pawn shop' can be considered a legitimate design theme, then Post Bar has nailed it. The dark wood walls of this narrow, shophouse-bound bar are decked with retro Thai kitsch, the soundtrack appropriately classic rock, the finger food deliciously tangy, and the clientele overwhelmingly Thai.

🍷 Northern Bangkok

Northern Bangkok spans a lot of real estate, but for years, the epicentre of entertainment has been the strip known as Royal City Ave. The area broadly known as Ari is also home to an increasingly sophisticated spread of restaurants that function equally well as bars.

O'glee BAR
(Map p116; www.facebook.com/ogleeari1; Soi Ari 1, Soi 7/Ari, Th Phahonyothin; ⏲5.30pm-midnight; [S] Ari exit 3) The name and decor of this bar vaguely call to mind an Irish pub. But rather than shamrocks and clichés, you get an astonishing selection of imported microbrews – both in bottles and on tap – served by a charming Thai family. There are some delicious snacks and light bites on offer as well.

Aree BAR
(Map p116; cnr Soi Ari 4/Nua & Soi 7/Ari, Th Phahonyothin; ⏲6pm-1am; [S] Ari exit 3) Exposed brick, chunky carpets and warm lighting give Aree a cosier feel than your average Bangkok bar. It also offers live music (from 8pm Tuesday to Sunday), contemporary Thai drinking snacks and a relatively sophisticated drinks list.

Fake Club The Next Gen CLUB
(Map p116; www.facebook.com/fakeclubthenextgen; 222/32 Th Ratchadaphisek; ⏲8pm-2am; [M] Sutthisan exit 3) A long-standing popular gay staple far away from the gaybourhood of Th Silom. Expect live music, cheesy choreography and lots of lasers.

☆ Entertainment

Moo·ay tai (Thai Boxing)

★ **Rajadamnern Stadium** SPECTATOR SPORT
(สนามมวยราชดำเนิน; Map p78; www.rajadamnern.com; off Th Ratchadamnoen Nok; tickets 3rd class/2nd class/club class/ringside 1000/1500/1800/2000B; ⏲matches 6.30pm Mon, Wed & Thu, 3pm & 6.30pm Sun; ⛴ Thewet Pier, [S] Phaya Thai exit 3 & taxi) Rajadamnern Stadium is Bangkok's oldest and most venerable venue for *moo·ay tai* (Thai boxing; also spelt *muay Thai*). Be sure to buy tickets from the official ticket counter or online, not from touts and scalpers who hang around outside the entrance.

Children under 120cm are allowed free entry (fights often get bloody, so it's probably best to not bring young kids along). There's a souvenir shop to the right of the ticket counters, where you can buy sundry accessories and paraphernalia associated with the sport, such as gloves and colourful shorts worn by contestants. The store is open during bouts.

Lumpinee Boxing Stadium SPECTATOR SPORT
(สนามมวยลุมพินี; ☎02 282 3141; www.lumpineemuaythai.com; 6 Th Ramintra; tickets 3rd class/2nd class/ringside 1000/1500/2000B; ⏲matches Tue & Fri 6pm, Sat 4pm & 8pm; [M] Chatuchak Park exit 2 & taxi, [S] Mo Chit exit 3

AGE OF CRAFT BEER

Sometime around 2016, Bangkok took an obsessive liking to brewing and consuming craft beers. In a beer industry largely dominated by mass-produced lager giants such as Singha, Chang and Leo, craft brewers steadily began to carve out their niche by producing small batch ales and stouts directed at the city's discerning beer lovers. The craze has only grown over time – more than 100 brewpubs and microbreweries are currently estimated to be operational in Thailand, most of them in Bangkok.

Strictly speaking, however, brewing small batch beer is still technically illegal in the country. Recent interpretations of the law have made room for some craft brews to be sold at specific microbreweries, as long as they are pulled from taps and not bottled. However, drop into any major supermarket in town, and you'll be bowled over by the sheer number of bottled crafts that are on sale. Chalawan, Chatri, Liger, Red Truck, Whale, Bussaba – the brands are as diverse as their flavours, ranging from mild *weizens* (wheat beer) and nutty stouts to deliciously hoppy IPAs. Ingeniously, these crafters have gotten around the law by simply moving their brewing and bottling operations to a nearby country, and then shipping the product back into Thailand as a legal import. This has obviously increased prices thanks to excise duties, but going by their astounding popularity across Bangkok's pubs, no one seems to be complaining.

Of course, this is all at a micro level, and has no substantial bearing on the mass market. But along with the hope that small-batch brewing would be legalised sooner than later, Bangkok's indie brewers are passionately invested in their art, and continue to extend the horizons of the city's artisanal beerscape with each passing day.

& taxi) The other of Bangkok's two premier Thai boxing rings is located in a modern venue far north of town.

Live Music

⭐ **Brick Bar**   LIVE MUSIC

(Map p78; www.brickbarkhaosan.com; basement, Buddy Lodge, 265 Th Khao San; admission Sat & Sun 150B; ⏲8pm-2am; 🚢Phra Athit/Banglamphu Pier) This basement pub, a favourite destination in Bangkok for live music, hosts a nightly revolving cast of bands for an almost exclusively Thai crowd – many of whom will end the night dancing on the tables. Brick Bar can get infamously packed, so be sure to arrive there early.

⭐ **Bamboo Bar**   LIVE MUSIC

(Map p90; ☑02 659 9000; www.mandarinoriental. com; 48 Soi 40/Oriental, Mandarin Oriental; ⏲5pm-12.30am Sun-Thu, to 1.30am Fri & Sat; 🚢Oriental Pier) After more than 65 years of service, the Mandarin Oriental's Bamboo Bar remains one of the city's premier locales for live jazz. Guest vocalists are flown in from across the globe – check the website to see who's in town – and the music starts at 9pm nightly.

⭐ **The Living Room**   LIVE MUSIC

(Map p110; ☑02 649 8888; www.thelivingroomat bangkok.com; 250 Th Sukhumvit, level 1, Sheraton Grande Sukhumvit; ⏲6pm-midnight; Ⓜ Sukhumvit exit 3, Ⓢ Asok exit 2) Don't let looks deceive you:

every night this bland hotel lounge transforms into the city's best venue for live jazz. True to the name, there's comfy, sofa-based seating, all of it within earshot of the music. Enquire ahead of time to see which sax master or hide-hitter is in town. An entry fee of 300B is charged after 8.30pm.

Saxophone Pub & Restaurant   LIVE MUSIC

(Map p98; ☑02 246 5472; www.saxophonepub. com; 3/8 Th Phayathai; ⏲6pm-2am; Ⓢ Victory Monument exit 2) After 30 years, Saxophone remains Bangkok's premier live-music venue – a dark, intimate space where you can pull up a chair just a few metres away from the band and see their every bead of sweat. If you prefer some mystique surrounding your musicians, watch the blues, jazz, reggae or rock from the balcony.

Tawandang German Brewery   LIVE MUSIC

(Map p70; www.tawandang.com; cnr Rama III & Th Naradhiwas Rajanagarindra; ⏲5pm-1am; Ⓢ Chong Nonsi exit 5 & taxi) It's Oktoberfest all year round at this hangar-sized musichall-cum-microbrewery. The Thai–German food is tasty, the house-brewed ales are eminently potable, and the nightly stage shows make singing along a necessity. Music starts at 8.30pm.

Parking Toys   LIVE MUSIC

(Map p70; ☑02 907 2228; 17/22 Soi Mayalap, off Kaset-Navamin Hwy; ⏲7pm-2am; Ⓜ Chatuchak

Park exit 2 & taxi, S Mo Chit exit 3 & taxi) One of northern Bangkok's best venues for live music, Parking Toys hosts an eclectic revolving cast of bands ranging in genre from rockabilly to electro-funk jam acts. Take a taxi north from BTS Mo Chit (or MRT Chatuchak Park) and go to Kaset intersection, then turn right on Th Kaset-Navamin. Parking Toys is past the second traffic light.

jazz happens!   LIVE MUSIC

(Map p78; 62 Th Phra Athit; ⊙5pm-midnight Fri-Wed; 🛜; ⛴Phra Athit/Banglamphu Pier) Linked with Silpakorn University, Thailand's most famous arts university, jazz happens! is a stage for aspiring musical talent. With four acts playing most nights and a huge selection of bar snacks, you'll be thoroughly entertained at this cubicle-sized watering hole.

Brown Sugar   LIVE MUSIC

(Map p78; www.brownsugarbangkok.com; 469 Th Phra Sumen; ⊙5pm-1am Tue-Thu & Sun, to 2am Fri & Sat; ⛴klorng boat Phanfa Leelard Pier) Located in a cavernous shophouse is this long-standing live-music staple. The music, which spans from funk to jazz, starts at 8pm most nights and, on weekends in particular, draws heaps of locals.

Adhere the 13th   LIVE MUSIC

(Map p78; www.facebook.com/adhere13thbluesbar; 13 Th Samsen; ⊙6pm-midnight; ⛴Phra Athit/ Banglamphu Pier) This closet-sized blues bar is everything a neighbourhood joint should be: lots of regulars, cold beer and heart-warming tunes delivered by a masterful house band (starting at 10pm). Everyone knows each other, so don't be shy about mingling.

Theatre

Sala Chalermkrung   THEATRE

(Map p84; ☑02 224 4499; www.salachalermkrung. com; 66 Th Charoen Krung; tickets 800-1200B; ⊙shows 7.30pm Fri; Ⓜ Memorial Bridge Pier, Ⓜ Hua Lamphong exit 1 & taxi) This art-deco Bangkok landmark, a former cinema dating to 1933, is one of the few remaining places *kŏhn* (masked dance-drama based on stories from the *Ramakian*, the Thai version of the Indian epic *Ramayana*) can be witnessed. The weekly traditional dance-drama is enhanced here by laser graphics, high-tech audio and English subtitles. Concerts and other events are also held; check the website for details.

Sala Rim Naam   THEATRE

(Map p90; ☑02 659 9000; www.mandarinoriental. com; Mandarin Oriental; tickets incl dinner adult/ child 2900/2300B; ⊙dinner 7-10.30pm, dance show 7.45pm; ⛴Oriental Pier & hotel shuttle boat) The historic Mandarin Oriental hosts a traditional dance theatre in a sumptuous Thai pavilion located across the river in Thonburi

---

KICKING & PUNCHING

More formally known as Phahuyut (from the Pali-Sanskrit *bahu* or 'arm' and *yudh* or 'combat'), Thailand's ancient martial art of *moo·ay tai* (or *muay Thai*) is one of the kingdom's most striking national icons. Many martial-arts aficionados agree that *moo·ay tai* is the most efficient, effective and generally unbeatable form of ring-centred, hand-to-hand combat ever practised.

After the Siamese were defeated at Ayuthaya in 1767, several expert *moo·ay boh·rahn* (from which *moo·ay tai* is derived) fighters were among the prisoners hauled off to Burma. A few years later a festival was held, and one of the Thai fighters, Nai Khanom Tom, was ordered to take on prominent Burmese boxers for the entertainment of the king and to determine which martial art was most effective. He promptly dispatched nine opponents in a row and, as legend has it, was offered money or beautiful women as a reward. Today a *moo·ay tai* festival in Ayuthaya is named after Nai Khanom Tom.

In the early days, combatants' fists were wrapped in thick horsehide for maximum impact with minimum knuckle damage. Tree bark and seashells were used to protect the groin. But the high incidence of death and physical injury led the Thai government to ban *moo·ay tai* in the 1920s. In the 1930s, the sport was revived under a modern set of regulations. Bouts were limited to five three-minute rounds separated by two-minute breaks. Contestants had to wear international-style gloves and trunks, and their feet were taped (no shoes are worn). However, all surfaces of the body remain fair targets, and any part of the body except the head may be used to strike an opponent. Common blows include high kicks to the neck, elbow thrusts to the face and head, knee hooks to the ribs and low kicks to the calf.

GO-GO BARS
....

Although technically illegal, sex work is fully 'out' in Bangkok, and the influence of organised crime and lucrative kickbacks means that it will be a long while before existing laws are ever enforced. Yet despite the image presented by much of the Western media, the underlying atmosphere of Bangkok's red-light districts is not one of illicitness and exploitation (although these do inevitably exist), but rather a trail of tackiness and boredom.

Patpong (Map p100; Th Phat Phong & Soi Phat Phong 2; ⊙6pm-2am; Ⓜ Si Lom exit 2, Ⓢ Sala Daeng exit 1) earned notoriety during the 1980s for its wild sex shows. Today it is more of a circus for curious spectators than sexual deviants. Soi Cowboy (Map p110; Soi Cowboy; ⊙4pm-2am; Ⓜ Sukhumvit exit 2, Ⓢ Asok exit 3) and Nana Entertainment Plaza (Map p110; Soi 4, Th Sukhumvit; ⊙4pm-2am; Ⓢ Nana exit 2) are the real scenes of sex for hire. Not all of the sex business is geared towards Westerners: Th Thaniya, off Th Silom, is filled with massage parlours for Japanese expats and visitors, while the immense massage parlours outside central Bangkok service almost exclusively Thai customers.

to complement a luxury dinner experience. Prices are well above average, but the performance gets positive reviews, as does the high-profile set menu served during the performance.

Siam Niramit
THEATRE

(Map p70; ☑02 649 9222; www.siamniramit.com; 19 Th Thiam Ruammit; tickets from 1500B; ⊙shows 8pm; Ⓜ Thailand Cultural Centre exit 1 & access by shuttle bus) A cultural theme park, this enchanted kingdom transports visitors to a Disneyesque version of ancient Siam with a brightly coloured stage show of traditional performance depicting the Lanna Kingdom, the Buddhist heaven and Thai festivals. A free shuttle-bus service is available at Thailand Cultural Centre MRT station, running every 15 minutes from 6pm to 7.45pm.

Cinema

⭐ Major Cineplex
CINEMA

(Map p94; ☑02 129 4635; www.majorcineplex. com; Th Rama I, 5th fl, Siam Paragon; Ⓢ Siam exits 3/5) In addition to housing Thailand's largest IMAX screen, Major Cineplex's options include the Blue Ribbon Screen, a cinema with a maximum of 72 seats, where you're plied with pillows, blankets, complimentary snacks and drinks and a 15-minute massage; and Enigma, where, in addition to a sofa-like love seat designed for couples, you'll be served cocktails and food.

Apex Scala
CINEMA

(Map p94; ☑02 251 2861; Soi 1, Siam Sq; Ⓢ Siam exit 2) A flagrantly 1960s-era cinema in central Bangkok, the Scala's one screen shows a mix of contemporary Hollywood and films from the past.

Bangkok Screening Room
CINEMA

(Map p88; www.bkksr.com; 1/3-7 Soi 1, Sala Daeng; ⊙screenings 4.15-8.30pm Tue-Thu, 11.15am-8.30pm Fri & Sat; Ⓜ Si Lom exit 2) Bangkok has heaps of attractions that draw tourists in – great weather, fantastic bars, unbeatable food, low prices – but it's not known for being a cinema haven. This theatre is trying to change that, one indie film at a time. Check the website for the revolving list of films; expect the roster to showcase budding Thai filmmakers.

Book tickets a day in advance to score one of the 50 seats in the single screen theatre and grab a craft beer before settling in.

The annual Bangkok LGBT Film Festival is organised here, usually in July.

House
CINEMA

(Map p110; www.facebook.com/houseRCA; 3rd fl, RCA Plaza, RCA/Royal City Ave; Ⓜ Phetchaburi exit 1 & taxi) Bangkok's first and biggest art-house cinema, House shows lots of foreign flicks of the non-Hollywood type. For updated screening information, check the Facebook page.

🔒 Shopping

Prime your credit card and shine your baht – shopping is serious business in Bangkok. Hardly a street corner in this city is free from a vendor, hawker or impromptu stall, and it doesn't stop there: Bangkok is also home to one of the world's largest outdoor markets, not to mention some of Southeast Asia's largest malls.

🔒 Banglamphu

Shopping in Banglamphu means street markets and a handful of shops that sell traditional items.

Heritage Craft
ARTS & CRAFTS

(Map p78; www.heritagecraft.org; 35 Th Bamrung Meuang; ⊘11am-6pm Mon-Fri; ⊒klorng boat Phanfa Leelard Pier) Handicrafts with a conscience: this boutique is an atmospheric showcase for quality domestic wares, some of which are produced via fair-trade practices. Items include silks from Thailand's northeast, baskets from the south and jewellery from the north, and there's also an inviting on-site cafe.

★Khao San Market
GIFTS & SOUVENIRS

(Map p78; Th Khao San; ⊘10am-midnight; ⊒Phra Athit/Banglamphu Pier) The main guesthouse strip in Banglamphu is a day-and-night shopping bazaar peddling all the backpacker 'essentials': profane T-shirts, bootleg DVDs of popular films and TV series, hemp clothing, knock-off designer wear, selfie sticks, orange juice and – of course – those wooden frogs that croak when you rub a stick down their spine. Cheap shopping thrills couldn't be better defined.

Mowaan
HEALTH & WELLNESS

(Map p78; 9 Soi Thesa; ⊘9am-5pm; ⊒klorng boat to Phanfa Leelard Pier) With nearly a century under its belt, this brand makes lozenges, inhalers, oils and balms rooted in Thai herbal medicine. Even if you are in satisfactory health, a visit to the immaculately preserved showroom is akin to a trip back in time.

Lofty Bamboo
ARTS & CRAFTS

(Map p78; ground fl, Buddy Lodge, 265 Th Khao San; ⊘10.30am-8pm; ⊒Phra Athit/Banglamphu Pier) No time to make it to northern Thailand? No problem. At this shop you can get the type of colourful, hill-tribe-inspired clothes, cloth items and other handicrafts you'd find at the markets in Chiang Mai and Chiang Rai. Best of all, a purchase supports economic self-sufficiency in upcountry villages.

Nittaya Thai Curry
FOOD & DRINKS

(Map p78; 136-40 Th Chakrabongse; ⊘9am-7pm Mon-Sat; ⊒Phra Athit/Banglamphu Pier) Follow your nose: Nittaya is famous throughout Thailand for her pungent, high-quality curry pastes. Pick up a couple of takeaway canisters for prospective dinner parties back home, or peruse the snack and gift sections, where visitors to Bangkok load up on local specialities for friends and family back in the provinces.

⌂ Chinatown

Chinatown might be the city's most commerce-heavy neighbourhood, although it must be said that the bulk of wares are utilitarian, and will hold little interest for most travellers.

★Lhong 1919
SHOPPING CENTRE

(Map p70; 248 Th Chiangmai, Khlong San; ⊘10am-10pm; ⊒mall shuttle boat from Sathorn/Central Pier, ⓈKrung Thonburi exit 1/3 & taxi) Spanning a group of restored defunct Chinese warehouses on the western bank of the Chao Phraya River, this concept shopping complex combines the old-world charm of its 19th-century premises with an artsy shopping experience promised by a line of designer stores and boutiques housed within the buildings. A few good restaurants thrown along the property's riverside promenade complete the evening-out experience.

⌂ Riverside, Silom & Lumphini

The Riverside and Silom areas are great places to shop for high-quality art, crafts and antiques. The vast buying options in the upscale riverside malls also add to the shopping quotient.

★ICONSIAM
MALL

(Map p90; www.iconsiam.com; 299 Charoen Nakhon Rd; ⊘10am-10pm; ⊒Sathorn/Central Pier & mall shuttle boat) This megamall on the Chao Phraya River has six floors dedicated to luxury shopping, encompassing everything from high-end to high street. It also rolls in two food courts to suit all palates and budgets. Adding to its diversity are speciality restaurants, a conjoined multilevel Japanese department store, the much-touted River Museum on the 8th floor, and a 12-theatre cinema.

To get here, hop onto the free shuttle boat that operates from Sathorn/Central Pier during the mall's business hours.

★Asiatique
MARKET

(Map p70; Soi 72-76, Th Charoen Krung; ⊘4pm-midnight; ⊒Sathorn/Central Pier & mall shuttle boat) Considered one of Bangkok's most popular night markets, Asiatique is housed within restored warehouses next to the Chao Phraya River. Expect clothing, handicrafts, souvenirs, several dining and drinking venues, and a 60m-high Ferris wheel. To get here, take one of the frequent, free shuttle boats from Sathorn (Central) Pier that run from 4pm to 11.30pm.

King Power Mahanakhon MALL
(Map p100; 114 Th Naradhiwas Rajanagarindra; ⊙10am-midnight; S Chong Nonsi exit 3) Occupying the first four floors of the Mahanakhon skyscraper, this vast duty-free outlet is run by King Power, a Thai duty-free company that also owns Leicester City, the English Premier League club. No more having to wait until your return flight home to splurge on some excise-free goodies – you can even claim VAT refunds on pricey buys at a ground-floor counter.

OP Place ANTIQUES
(Map p90; Soi 36, Th Charoen Krung; ⊙11am-7pm; ⛴ Oriental Pier) Significantly more understated than many other city malls in Bangkok, this is a good place to shop for authentic curios, antiques and rare collectibles. You're likely to pay steep prices here, but consider it a premium for the quality and authenticity of the purchase.

River City ANTIQUES
(Map p90; www.rivercity.co.th; 23 Th Yotha; ⊙10am-10pm; ⛴ Si Phraya/River City Pier) Several

upscale art and antique shops occupy the 3rd and 4th floors of this riverside mall. The vast majority of pieces appear to come from Myanmar and – to a lesser extent – Cambodia and Nepal. The 2nd floor has a mix of exhibition spaces where well-curated art, sculpture and multimedia exhibitions are organised from time to time.

Jim Thompson FASHION & ACCESSORIES
(Map p100; www.jimthompson.com; 9 Th Surawong; ⊙10am-9pm; M Si Lom exit 2, S Sala Daeng exit 3) The largest Jim Thompson outlet in town sells colourful silk handkerchiefs, place mats, wraps, cushions and a whole range of fashionable shirts and dresses that make for excellent self-indulging purchases as well as gifts.

Tamnan Mingmuang ARTS & CRAFTS
(Map p100; 2nd fl, Thaniya Plaza, Th Thaniya; ⊙10am-7pm; M Si Lom exit 2, S Sala Daeng exit 1) As soon as you step through the doors of this museum-like shop, the earthy smell of dried grass and stained wood rushes to meet you. Rattan, *yahn lí-pow* (a fern-like vine) and water hyacinth woven into patterns, and coconut shells carved into delicate bowls are

---

CHINATOWN'S SHOPPING STREETS

Chinatown is the neighbourhood version of a megastore divided up into categories of commerce, with streets as aisles; here's your in-store guide:

Th Charoen Krung Starting on the western end of the street, near the intersection of Th Mahachai, is a collection of old record stores. Talat Khlong Ong Ang consumes the next block, selling all sorts of used and new electronic gadgets. Further east, near Th Mahachak, is Talat Khlong Thom, a hardware centre. West of Th Ratchawong is everything you'd need to give a Chinese funeral.

Th Yaowarat A hundred years ago this was a poultry farm; now it's gold street, the biggest trading centre of the precious metal in the country. Along Th Yaowarat, gold is sold by the *bàht* (a unit of weight equivalent to 15g) from neon-lit storefronts that look more like shrines than shops. Near the intersection of Th Ratchawong, stores shift to Chinese and Singaporean tourists' tastes: dried fruit and nuts, chintzy talismans and accoutrements for Chinese festivals. The area also retains a few Chinese apothecaries, smelling of wood bark and ancient secrets.

Sampeng Lane (p82) Plastic cuteness in bulk, from pencil cases to pens, stuffed animals, hair flotsam and enough bling to kit out a rap video – it all hangs out near the eastern end of the alley.

Talat Mai (p81) This ancient produce market splays along the cramped alley between Th Yaowarat and Th Charoen Krung. It's Bangkok's quintessential Chinese market, and the dried goods, seasonings, spices and sauces will be familiar to anyone who's ever spent time in China.

Talat Noi (p82) Literally 'small market', this charming microcosm of everyday street life still harks back to bygone decades, where lanes turn on themselves like snakes gobbling their own tails, making for fantastic ambling and some candid street photography.

among the exquisite pieces that will outlast flashier souvenirs available on the streets.

House of Chao ANTIQUES

(Map p100; 9/1 Th Decho; ⏲10am-7pm; [S] Chong Nonsi exit 3) This three-storey antique shop, appropriately located in an antique shophouse, has everything necessary to deck out your fantasy colonial-era mansion. Particularly interesting are the various weather-worn doors, doorways, gateways and trellises that can be found in the covered area behind the showroom.

🛍 Siam Square, Pratunam, Phloen Chit & Ratchathewi

The area around Siam Sq is home to the city's greatest concentration of malls – if name brands are your thing, this is your place. Cheap unbranded clothing is found just north, in the Pratunam area.

★ **Siam Discovery** SHOPPING CENTRE

(Map p94; www.siamdiscovery.co.th; cnr Rama I & Th Phayathai; ⏲10am-10pm; [S] Siam exit 1) With an open, almost market-like feel and an impressive variety of unique goods ranging from housewares to clothing (including lots of items by Thai designers), the fashionable Siam Discovery is hands down the most design-conscious mall in town. Alongside established stores, don't forget to check out the kiosks, which often display some excellent locally designed merchandise.

★ **MBK Center** SHOPPING CENTRE

(Map p94; cnr Rama I & Th Phayathai; ⏲10am-10pm; [S] National Stadium exit 4) This eight-storey market in a mall has emerged as one of Bangkok's top attractions. On any given weekend half of Bangkok's residents (and most of its tourists) can be found here combing through a seemingly inexhaustible range of small stalls, shops and merchandise.

MBK is Bangkok's cheapest place to buy mobile phones and accessories (4th floor). It's also one of the better places to stock up on camera gear (ground floor and 5th floor), and the expansive food court (6th floor) is one of the best in town.

Kinokuniya BOOKS

(Map p94; Rama I, 4th fl, Siam Paragon Mall; ⏲10am-9pm; [S] Siam exit 4) Managed by one of Asia's best-known bookstore chains, this is Thailand's largest English-language bookshop. There's a vast catalogue of bestsellers, classics and critically acclaimed titles; translations of well-known foreign-language books; and an excellent selection of local and international magazines.

Siam Paragon SHOPPING CENTRE

(Map p94; www.siamparagon.co.th; 991/1 Rama I; ⏲10am-10pm; [S] Siam exit 3/5) As much an air-conditioned urban park as it is a shopping centre, Siam Paragon is home to Sea Life Ocean World (p89), Major Cineplex (p145) and Gourmet Paradise (p129), a huge basement-level food court. Then there are stores and more stores, selling clothes, souvenirs, accessories, electronics, and even Rolls-Royce and McLaren cars! On the 3rd floor is Kinokuniya, Thailand's largest English-language bookshop.

CentralWorld SHOPPING CENTRE

(Map p94; www.centralworld.co.th; Th Ratchadamri; ⏲10am-10pm; [S] Sky Walk via Chit Lom exit 9/ Siam exit 6) Spanning eight storeys of more than 500 shops and 100 restaurants, CentralWorld is one of Southeast Asia's largest shopping centres.

★ **Siam Square** SHOPPING CENTRE

(Map p94; Rama I; ⏲11am-9pm; [S] Siam exit 2/4) This open-air shopping zone is ground zero for teenage culture in Bangkok. Pop music blares out of tinny speakers, and gangs of youngsters in various costumes ricochet between fast-food restaurants and closet-sized

WHAT'S YOUR NUMBER?

The 4th floor of MBK Center resembles something of a digital produce market. A confusing maze of stalls sells all the components to send you into the land of cellular: a new phone, a new number and a SIM card. Even if you'd rather keep yourself out of reach, do a walk-through to observe the chaos and the mania over phone numbers. Computer printouts displaying all the available numbers for sale turn the phone numbers game into a commodities market. The luckier the phone number, the higher the price; the equivalent of thousands of dollars have been paid for numbers composed mostly of nines, considered lucky in honour of the former king, Rama IX (King Bhumibol Adulyadej; r 1946–2016), and because the Thai word for 'nine' is similar to the word for 'progress'.

boutiques. It's a great place to pick up labels and designs you're guaranteed not to find anywhere else, though most outfits require a barely there waistline.

Elephant Parade GIFTS & SOUVENIRS
(Map p94; www.elephantparade.com; cnr Rama I & Th Phayathai, 4th fl, Siam Discovery; ⌚10am-10pm; [S] Siam exit 1) Instead of visiting that elephant show – which animal-welfare activists claim can harm the animals – consider a purchase at this stall. The elephant-themed toys and knick-knacks are attractive and fun, and 20% of the proceeds goes towards helping elephant causes.

Objects of Desire Store HOMEWARES
(ODS; Map p94; www.facebook.com/objectsofdesirestore; cnr Rama I & Th Phayathai, 3rd fl, Siam Discovery; ⌚10am-10pm; [S] Siam exit 1) This pop-up-like boutique specialises in design-focused contemporary ceramics, paper products, furniture and other homewares, most of which are made by Thai artisans. The shop also hosts handicraft-themed workshops; see the Facebook page to see what's next.

Central Embassy SHOPPING CENTRE
(Map p94; www.centralembassy.com; Th Phloen Chit; ⌚10am-10pm; [S] Phloen Chit exit 5) This is one of the most premium shopping centres in central Bangkok, with countless designer stores and fine restaurants lining its five floors of commercial space.

Platinum Fashion Mall CLOTHING
(Map p94; www.platinumfashionmall.com; 644/3 Th Phetchaburi; ⌚9am-8pm; ⛴ klorng boat Pratunam Pier, [S] Ratchathewi exit 4) Linked with Bangkok's garment district, which lies just north across Th Phetchaburi, is this five-storey mall stocked with a seemingly never-ending selection of cheap, no-name couture.

Gin & Milk CLOTHING
(Map p94; www.facebook.com/ginandmilkstore; Rama I, 3rd fl, Siam Center; ⌚10am-9pm; [S] Siam exit 1) A one-stop shop for domestic menswear, with items ranging from leather shoes to accessories, in looks ranging from traditional to edgy.

Karmakamet HOMEWARES
(Map p94; www.karmakamet.co.th; Th Ratchadamri, 3rd fl, CentralWorld; ⌚10am-9.30pm; [S] Sky Walk via Chit Lom exit 9/Siam exit 6) This brand's scented candles, incense, essential oils and other fragrant and nonfragrant items double both as classy housewares and unique souvenirs.

Flynow CLOTHING
(Map p94; www.flynowbangkok.com; Rama I, 3rd fl, Siam Center; ⌚10am-9pm; [S] Siam exit 1) A long-standing leader in Bangkok's home-grown fashion scene, Flynow creates feminine couture that has appeared in several international shows.

Thann COSMETICS
(Map p94; www.thann.info; Th Ratchadamri, ground fl & 2nd fl, CentralWorld; ⌚10am-10pm; [S] Sky Walk via Chit Lom exit 9/Siam exit 6) Smell like a wisp of fresh spring breeze with these botanical-based spa products. The soaps, shampoos and lotions are all natural, rooted in Thai traditional medicine, and stylish enough to share space with brand-name beauty.

Tango FASHION & ACCESSORIES
(Map p94; www.tangothailand.com; 3rd fl, Siam Center, Rama I; ⌚10am-9pm; [S] Siam exit 1) This home-grown brand specialises in cool leather goods, but you may not even recognise the medium under the layers of bright embroidery and chunky jewels.

Siam Center SHOPPING CENTRE
(Map p94; www.siamcenter.co.th; Rama I; ⌚10am-9pm; [S] Siam exit 1) Siam Center, Thailand's first shopping centre, was built in 1976 but thanks to a nip and tuck that gave it a grungy overhaul, it hardly shows its age. Its 3rd floor is one of the best locations to check out established local labels.

Central Chidlom SHOPPING CENTRE
(Map p94; www.central.co.th; 1027 Th Phloen Chit; ⌚10am-10pm; [S] Chit Lom exit 5) Generally regarded as the country's best department store for quality and selection, Central has 13 branches across Bangkok, in addition to this address.

🛍 Thanon Sukhumvit

Th Sukhumvit can lay claim to nearly the entire spectrum of Bangkok-style shopping: upscale malls, street markets, quirky handicrafts and local fashion.

Emquartier SHOPPING CENTRE
(Map p110; www.theemdistrict.com; 693-695 Th Sukhumvit; ⌚10am-10pm; [S] Phrom Phong exit 1) Arguably one of Bangkok's flashiest malls. Come for brands you're not likely to find elsewhere, or get lost in the Helix, a seemingly never-ending spiral of innumerable restaurants and stores.

Artbox MARKET

(Map p110; Soi 10, Th Sukhumvit, Chuvit Garden; 🕒 3pm-1am; [S] Nana exit 4) This hipster market featuring stalls housed in refurbished shipping containers attracts hordes of young Bangkokians in the evening. Comprising a smattering of stalls selling garments, accessories, food and beverages, it's particularly busy on weekends.

Paya Shop HOMEWARES

(Map p110; ☎ 02 711 4457; www.payashop.net; 203 Soi Ekamai 5; 🕒 10am-6pm Mon-Sat; [S] Thong Lo exit 1 & taxi) Shop for flat-weave rugs, pottery, reclaimed wood furniture, woven baskets and trinkets sourced by a husband-and-wife duo from Chiang Mai. Most of the colourful textiles, such as pillows, placemats and napkins, are handmade by hill-tribe people, and the staff can relay the origin story of the pieces, making this a go-to stop for memorable keepsakes.

Another Story HOMEWARES

(Map p110; 4th fl, Emquartier, Th Sukhumvit; 🕒 10am-10pm; [S] Phrom Phong exit 1) A self-proclaimed 'lifestyle concept store', Another Story is probably more accurately described as an engaging assemblage of cool stuff. Even if you're not planning to buy, it's fun to flip through the unique, domestically made items such as ceramics from Prempacha in Chiang Mai, leather goods from brands such as Labrador, and fragrant soaps, oils and candles from BsaB.

Duly CLOTHING

(Map p110; ☎ 02 662 6647; www.laladuly.co.th; Soi 49, Th Sukhumvit; 🕒 10am-7pm; [S] Phrom Phong exit 1) High-quality Italian fabrics and experienced tailors make Duly one of the best places in Bangkok to commission a sharp shirt.

Sop Moei Arts ARTS & CRAFTS

(Map p110; www.sopmoeiarts.com; Soi 49/9, Th Sukhumvit; 🕒 9.30am-5pm Tue-Sat; [S] Phrom Phong exit 3 & taxi) The Bangkok showroom of this nonprofit organisation features the vibrant cloth creations of Karen weavers from Mae Hong Son, in northern Thailand. It's located at the end of Soi 49/9, in the Racquet Club complex.

🛍 Northern Bangkok

Vacation splurging is what draws most visitors to Bangkok's northern suburbs. Even if you're not buying, the area's markets offer a colourful and hectic taste of the many diverse facets of Thai life – from stacks of produce and hill-tribe wares through to pet outfits and cut-rate clothes.

★ **Chatuchak Weekend Market** MARKET

(ตลาดนัดจตุจักร, Talat Nat Jatujak; Map p151; www.chatuchakmarket.org; 587/10 Th Phahonyothin; 🕒 9am-6pm Sat & Sun, plants 7am-6pm Wed & Thu, wholesale 6pm-midnight Fri; [M] Chatuchak Park exit 1, Kamphaeng Phet exits 1 & 2, [S] Mo Chit exit 1) Among the largest open-air markets in the world, Chatuchak (also referred to as 'Jatujak' or simply 'JJ Market') seems to unite everything buyable, from used vintage sneakers to baby squirrels. Plan to spend a full day here, as there's plenty to see, do and buy. But come early, ideally around 10am, to beat the crowds and the heat. There is an information centre and bank with ATMs and foreign-exchange booths at the **Chatuchak Park Office** (Map p151; 🕒 9am-6pm Sat & Sun), near the northern end of the market's Soi 1, Soi 2 and Soi 3.

Schematic maps and toilets are located throughout the market.

Friday nights from around 8pm to midnight, several vendors, largely those selling clothing, accessories and food, open up shop in Chatuchak. There are a few vendors on weekday mornings, and a daily vegetable, plant and flower market opposite the market's southern side. One section of the latter, known as the **Or Tor Kor Market** (องค์กรตลาดเพื่อเกษตรกร; Map p116; Th Kamphaeng Phet 1; 🕒 8am-6pm; [M] Kamphaeng Phet exit 3), sells fantastically gargantuan fruit and seafood, and has a decent food court as well.

Once you're deep in the bowels of Chatuchak, it will seem like there is no order and no escape, but the market is arranged into relatively coherent sections. Use the clock tower as a handy landmark.

➡ Antiques, Handicrafts & Souvenirs

Section 1 is the place to go for bronze religious statues, old LPs and other random antiques with religious motifs. Arts and crafts, such as musical instruments and hill-tribe items, can be found in Sections 25 and 26. **Baan Sin Thai** (Map p151; Section 24, Stall 130, Soi 1; 🕒 9am-6pm Sat & Sun) sells a mixture of *kŏhn* masks and old-school Thai toys, all of which make fun souvenirs, and Kitcharoen Dountri (p153) specialises in Thai musical instruments, including flutes, whistles, drums

Chatuchak Market

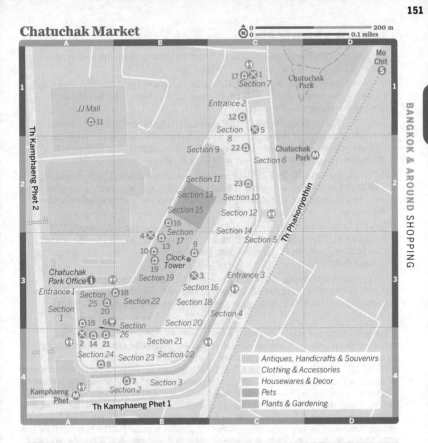

Chatuchak Market

Eating
1 Café Ice	C1
2 Foontalop	A4
3 Saman Islam	B3
4 Toh-Plue	B3
5 Viva 8	C1

Drinking & Nightlife
6 Viva's	A3

Shopping
7 AnyaDharu Scent Library	B4
8 Baan Sin Thai	A4
9 Chatuchak Weekend Market	B3
10 D-narn	B3
11 JJ Mall	A1
12 Kitcharoen Dountri	C1
13 Marché	B3
14 Meng	A4
15 Orange Karen Silver	A3
16 Papachu	B2
17 Pariwat A-nantachina	C1
18 PL Bronze	B3
19 Preecha Ceramic	B3
20 Roi	A3
21 Spice Boom	A4
22 Ton-Tan	C2
23 Tuptim Shop	C2

and CDs of classical Thai music. Other quirky gifts include the lifelike plastic Thai fruit and vegetables at **Marché** (Map p151; Section 17, Stall 254, Soi 1; ⊙ 9am-6pm Sat & Sun),

or their scaled-down miniature counterparts nearby at **Papachu** (Map p151; Section 17, Stall 23; ⊙ 9am-6pm Sat & Sun).

BANGKOK'S SAVILLE ROW

The strip of Th Sukhumvit (p149) between BTS stops at Nana and Asoke is home to tonnes of tailors – both reputable and otherwise. Some of the former:

Tailor on Ten (Map p110; ☎ 084 877 1543; 93 Soi 8, Th Sukhumvit; 🕒 9.30am-7pm Mon-Sat) It's not the cheapest in town, but set prices and good tailoring have earned this outfit heaps of praise and repeat customers.

Raja's Fashions (Map p110; ☎ 02 253 8379; www.rajasfashions.com; 160/1 Th Sukhumvit; 🕒 10.30am-8pm Mon-Sat; [S] Nana exit 4) With his photographic memory for names, Bobby will make you feel as important as the long list of ambassadors, foreign politicians and officers he's fitted over his family's decades in the business.

Rajawongse (Map p110; ☎ 02 255 3714; www.dress-for-success.com; 130 Th Sukhumvit; 🕒 10.30am-8pm Mon-Sat; [S] Nana exit 2) Another legendary and long-standing Bangkok tailor; Jesse's and Victor's creations are particularly renowned among American visitors and residents.

Ricky's Fashion House (Map p110; ☎ 02 254 6887; www.rickysfashionhouse.com; 73/5 Th Sukhumvit; 🕒 11am-10pm Mon-Sat, 1-5pm Sun; [S] Nana exit 1) Ricky gets positive reviews from locals and resident foreigners alike for his more casual styles of custom-made trousers and shirts.

Nickermann's (Map p110; ☎ 02 252 6682; basement, Landmark Hotel, 138 Th Sukhumvit; 🕒 11am-8pm Mon-Sat; [S] Nana exit 2) Corporate ladies rave about Nickermann's tailor-made power suits. Formal ball gowns are another area of expertise.

For less utilitarian goods, Section 7 is a virtual open-air gallery - we particularly liked **Pariwat A-nantachina** (Map p151; Section 7, Stall 117, Soi 63/3; 🕒 9am-6pm Sat & Sun;) for Bangkok-themed murals.

Several shops in Section 10, including **Tuptim Shop** (Map p151; Section 10, Stall 261, Soi 19; 🕒 9am-6pm Sat & Sun), sell new and antique Burmese lacquerware. **Meng** (Map p151; Section 26, Stall 195, Soi 8; 🕒 9am-6pm Sat & Sun) features a dusty mishmash of quirky antiques from both Thailand and Myanmar.

➡ Clothing & Accessories

Clothing dominates most of Chatuchak, starting in Section 8 and continuing through the even-numbered sections to 24. Sections 5 and 6 deal in used clothing for every Thai youth subculture, from punks to cowboys, while Soi 7, where it transects Sections 12 and 14, is heavy on the more underground hip-hop and skate fashions.

Somewhat more sophisticated independent labels can be found in Sections 2 and 3, while tourist-sized clothes and textiles are in Sections 8 and 10.

For accessories, several shops in Sections 24 and 26, such as Orange Karen Silver (p153), specialise in chunky silver jewellery and semiprecious uncut stones.

➡ Eating & Drinking

Lots of Thai-style eating and snacking will stave off Chatuchak rage (cranky behaviour brought on by dehydration or hunger), and numerous food stalls set up shop between Sections 6 and 8. Long-standing standouts include **Foontalop** (Map p151; Section 26, Stall 319,; mains 50-80B; 🕒 10am-6pm Sat & Sun), an incredibly popular Isan restaurant; **Café Ice** (Map p151; Section 7, Stall 267; mains 200-400B; 🕒 10am-6pm Sat & Sun), a Western-Thai fusion joint that does good, if overpriced, *pàt tai* and tasty fruit shakes; **Toh-Plue** (Map p151; opposite Section 17; mains 150-400B; 🕒 noon-8pm Sat & Sun), which does all the Thai standards; and **Saman Islam** (Map p151; Section 16, Stall 34, Soi 24; mains 40-100B; 🕒 10am-6pm Sat & Sun), a Thai-Muslim restaurant that serves a tasty chicken biryani. **Viva 8** (Map p151; www.facebook.com/Viva8JJ; Section 8, Stall 371; mains 150-300B; 🕒 9am-10pm Sat & Sun) features a DJ and a chef making huge platters of paella. And as evening draws near, down a beer at **Viva's** (Map p151; Section 26, Stall 161; 🕒 10am-10pm Sat & Su), a cafe-bar that features live music.

➡ Housewares & Decor

The western edge of the market, particularly Sections 8 to 26, specialises in all manner of housewares, from cheap plastic buckets to expensive brass woks. This area is a particularly good place to stock up on inexpensive Thai ceramics, ranging from celadon to the traditional rooster-themed bowls from Lampang.

PL Bronze (Map p151; Section 25, Stall 185, Soi 4; ⊘9am-6pm Sat & Sun) has a huge variety of stainless-steel flatware, and Ton-Tan (p155) deals in coconut- and sugar-palm-derived plates, bowls and other utensils.

Those looking to spice up the house should stop by Spice Boom (p154), were you can find dried herbs and spices for both consumption and decoration. Other notable olfactory indulgences include the handmade soaps, lotions, salts and scrubs at D-narn (p153), and the fragrant perfumes and essential oils at AnyaDharu Scent Library (p154).

➡ **Pets**

Possibly the most fun you'll ever have window-shopping will be petting puppies and cuddling kittens in Sections 13 and 15. Soi 9 of the former features several shops that deal solely in clothing for pets. It's also worth noting that this section has, in the past, been associated with the sale of illegal wildlife, although much of this trade has been driven underground.

➡ **Plants & Gardening**

The interior perimeter of Sections 2 to 4 features a huge variety of potted plants, flowers, herbs, fruits, and the accessories needed to maintain them. Many of these shops are also open on Wednesdays and Thursdays.

Talat Rot Fai   MARKET
(Rot Fai Night Market; Map p70; Esplanade Complex, 99 Th Ratchadaphisek; ⊘5pm-1am; ⓜThailand Cultural Centre exit 4) For a fun and light-hearted evening featuring copious amounts of food, booze and cheap shopping, consider a visit to Talat Rot Fai, one of Bangkok's most popular night markets featuring rows of tented stalls and wooden shacks in an open compound behind the Esplanade shopping centre on Th Ratchadaphisek. Weekends can be particularly crowded, but also more fun.

Preecha Ceramic   ARTS & CRAFTS
(Map p151; Section 19, Stall 196, Chatuchak Weekend Market, Th Phahonyothin; ⊘10am-6pm Sat & Sun; ⓜChatuchak Park exit 1, Kamphaeng Phet exits 1 & 2, ⓢMo Chit exits 1 & 3) Stocks a variety

of Thai ceramics, including the emblematic chicken bowls from Lampang.

JJ Mall   SHOPPING CENTRE
(Map p151; Th Kamphaeng Phet 2; ⊘10am-7pm; ⓜKamphaeng Phet exits 1 & 2, Chatuchak Park exit 1, ⓢMo Chit exit 1) A modern shopping centre located adjacent to Chatuchak Weekend Market, where you can find some fine souvenirs, handcrafted items and micro-furniture.

Note that the name JJ Mall specifically refers to this subsection of the greater Chatuchak Weekend Market, which is often colloquially referred to as 'JJ Market' in its entirety.

Orange
Karen Silver   FASHION & ACCESSORIES
(Map p151; Section 26, Stall 229, Soi 34/8, Chatuchak Weekend Market, Th Phahonyothin; ⊘9am-6pm Sat & Sun; ⓜChatuchak Park exit 1, Kamphaeng Phet exits 1 & 2, ⓢMo Chit exit 1) A stall at Chatuchak Weekend Market that specialises in chunky silver jewellery and uncut semiprecious stones.

Kitcharoen
Dountri   MUSIC
(Map p151; Section 8, Stall 464, Chatuchak Weekend Market, Th Phahonyothin; ⊘9am-6pm Sat & Sun; ⓜChatuchak Park exit 1, Kamphaeng Phet exits 1 & 2, ⓢMo Chit exit 1) A stall at Chatuchak Weekend Market that specialises in Thai musical instruments, including flutes, whistles and drums, and CDs of classical Thai music.

D-narn   COSMETICS
(Map p151; Section 19, Stall 203, Soi 1, Chatuchak Weekend Market, Th Phahonyothin; ⊘9am-6pm Sat & Sun; ⓜKamphaeng Phet exits 1 & 2, Chatuchak Park exit 1, ⓢMo Chit exit 1) For notable olfactory indulgences including handmade soaps, lotions, salts and scrubs, stop at D-narn, a stall in Chatuchak Weekend Market.

Roi   CLOTHING
(Map p151; Section 25, Stall 268, Soi 4, Chatuchak Weekend Market, Th Phahonyothin; ⊘9am-6pm Sat & Sun; ⓜKamphaeng Phet exits 1 & 2, Chatuchak exit 1, ⓢMo Chit exit 1) A stall in the market that sells hand-woven cotton scarves, clothes and other accessories from Thailand's north.

AnyaDharu Scent Library
PERFUME

(Map p151; Section 3, Stall 3, Soi 43/2, Chatuchak Weekend Market, Th Phahonyothin; ⊙9am-6pm Sat & Sun; Ⓜ Kamphaeng Phet exits 1 & 2, Chatuchak Park exit 1, Ⓢ Mo Chit exit 1) For fragrant perfumes and essential oils, stop at AnyaDharu Scent Library, a stall at Chatuchak Weekend Market.

Spice Boom
FOOD

(Map p151; Section 26, Stall 246, Soi 8, Chatuchak Weekend Market, Th Phahonyothin; ⊙9am-6pm Sat & Sun; Ⓜ Kamphaeng Phet exits 1 & 2, Chatuchak Park exit 1, Ⓢ Mo Chit exit 1) A stall in the market that sells dried herbs and spices for both consumption and decoration.

Ton-Tan
ARTS & CRAFTS

(Map p151; Section 8, Stall 460, Soi 15/1, Chatuchak Weekend Market, Th Phahonyothin; ⊙9am-6pm Sat & Sun; Ⓜ Kamphaeng Phet exits 1 & 2, Chatuchak Park exit 1, Ⓢ Mo Chit exit 1) A stall in Chatuchak Weekend Market that specialises in coconut- and sugar-palm-derived plates, bowls and other utensils.

FLOATING MARKETS

Pictures of đà·làht nám (floating markets) jammed full of wooden canoes pregnant with colourful exotic fruits have defined the official tourist profile of Thailand for decades. However, remember that roads moved Thais' daily market errands onto dry ground long ago, and today's floating markets are almost completely contrived for – and dependent upon – tourists. That said, if you can see them for what they are, a few of these floating markets are within reach.

Tha Kha Floating Market (ตลาดน้ำท่าคา; Tha Kha, Samut Songkhram; ⊙7am-noon Sat & Sun plus 2nd, 7th & 12th day of waxing & waning moons) This is the most real-feeling floating market, where a handful of vendors coalesce along an open rural klorng (canal; also spelt khlong) lined with coconut palms and old wooden houses. Boat rides (per person 50B, 45 minutes) can be arranged along the canal, and there are lots of tasty snacks and fruits for sale. To get here, take a morning sŏrng·tăa·ou (20B, 45 minutes) from Samut Songkhram's market area.

Amphawa Floating Market (ตลาดน้ำอัมพวา; Amphawa; dishes 30-80B; ⊙4-9pm Fri-Sun) The Amphawa Floating Market, located in Samut Songkhram Province, convenes near Wat Amphawa. The emphasis is on edibles and tourist knick-knacks; because the market is only there on weekends and popular with tourists from Bangkok, things can get pretty hectic.

Taling Chan Floating Market (ตลาดน้ำตลิ่งชัน; Map p70; Khlong Bangkok Noi, Thonburi; ⊙7am-4pm Sat & Sun; Ⓢ Wongwian Yai exit 3 & taxi) Located just outside Bangkok on the access road to Khlong Bangkok Noi, Taling Chan looks like any other fresh-food market busy with produce vendors from nearby farms. But the twist emerges at the canal where several floating docks serve as informal dining rooms and the kitchens are canoes tethered to the docks. Taling Chan is in Thonburi and can be reached via taxi from Wongwian Yai BTS station or via air-con bus 79 (16B, 25 minutes), which makes stops on Th Ratchadamnoen Klang.

Damnoen Saduak Floating Market (ตลาดน้ำดำเนินสะดวก; Damnoen Saduak, Ratchaburi; ⊙7am-noon) This 100-year-old floating market – once one of Thailand's prestige tourist attractions – is now essentially a floating souvenir stand filled with hordes of package tourists. It's an unapologetically commercial affair: a tour of the market requires you to hire a boat (per person/boat 800/3000B) that takes you through a network of canals, calling at virtually every stall flogging cheap knick-knacks at steep prices (including the boat operator's commission). Buses for Damnoen Saduak village depart from the Southern Bus Terminal in Thonburi (100B, two hours, frequent from 6am to 9pm).

Don Wai Market (ตลาดดอนหวาย; Don Wai, Nakhon Pathom; ⊙7am-6pm) Not technically a swimmer, this market claims a riverbank location in Nakhon Pathom Province, having originally started out in the early 20th century as a floating market for pomelo and jackfruit growers and traders. The easiest way to reach Don Wai Market is to take a minibus (50B, 40 minutes) from beside Central Pinklao in Thonburi.

❶ Information

EMERGENCY

The police contact number also functions as the de facto universal emergency number in Thailand and can also be used to call an ambulance or report a fire.

Bangkok area code	☑ 02
Country code	☑ 66
Directory assistance (free)	☑ 1133
International access code	☑ 001, ☑ 007
Police	☑ 191

INTERNET & TELEPHONE

It's hard to go 100 metres in Bangkok without potentially picking up a wireless signal. Wi-fi is standard in guesthouses, cafes and many restaurants. Cellular data networks continue to expand and increase in capability. If you acquire a local tourist SIM, you can access your network provider's free wi-fi network in shopping malls, BTS stations and public spaces across the city.

LGBTIQ+ TRAVELLERS

Bangkok has plenty of nightlife and entertainment spots catering to gay men, but there are fewer places that identify themselves as exclusive establishments for lesbian women.

MEDICAL SERVICES

The following hospitals have English-speaking doctors and staff, and world-class facilities:

Bangkok Christian Hospital (Map p100; ☑ 02 625 9000; 124 Th Silom; Ⓜ Si Lom exit 2, Ⓢ Sala Daeng exit 1) Modern hospital in central Bangkok.

BNH (Map p100; ☑ 02 022 0700; www.bnhhospital.com; 9/1 Soi Convent; Ⓜ Si Lom exit 2, Ⓢ Sala Daeng exit 2/4) Modern, centrally located hospital.

Bumrungrad International Hospital (Map p110; ☑ 02 066 8888; www.bumrungrad.com; 33 Soi 3, Th Sukhumvit; ⊗24hr; Ⓢ Nana exit 1) An internationally accredited hospital.

Samitivej Hospital (Map p110; ☑ 02 022 2222; www.samitivejhospitals.com; 133 Soi 49, Th Sukhumvit; ⊗24hr; Ⓢ Phrom Phong exit 3 & taxi) Acclaimed modern hospital.

St Louis Hospital (Map p100; ☑ 02 838 5555; www.saintlouis.or.th; 215 Th Sathon Tai/South; Ⓢ Surasak exit 4) Modern hospital preferred by locals.

CHANGE: THE ONLY CONSTANT

Bangkok's tourism landscape changes faster than water flowing down the Chao Phraya River. Restaurants here sometimes down shutters at the peak of their success or relocate to new addresses over mere weeks. Bars change names and overhaul their menus overnight, while hotels and shophouses are constantly caught up in a cycle of renovations. Moral of the story: expect surprises, go with the flow and be ever ready to embrace change.

MONEY

Most shops, restaurants, cafes and hotels deal in both cash or card; Visa and MasterCard are the most widely accepted. Cash only for street vendors.

POST

Thailand has a very efficient postal service and local postage is inexpensive. Post offices open from 8.30am to 4.30pm weekdays and 9am to noon on Saturday.

Central Post Office (Map p90; ☑ 02 105 7400; Th Charoen Krung; ⊗9.30am-5.30pm Mon-Fri; 🚢 Oriental Pier)

SAFE TRAVEL

Generally, Bangkok is a safe city, but it's good to keep the following in mind to avoid joining the list of tourists sucked in by Bangkok's numerous scam artists:

Gem scam We're literally begging you – if you aren't a gem trader do not buy unset stones in Thailand. Period.

Closed today Ignore any 'friendly' local who tells you that an attraction is closed for a Buddhist holiday or for cleaning.

Túk-túk rides for 20B These alleged 'tours' bypass the sights and instead cruise to all the fly-by-night gem and tailor shops that pay commissions.

Flat-fare taxi ride Flatly refuse any driver who quotes a flat fare, which will usually be three times more expensive than the reasonable meter rate.

Friendly strangers Be wary of smartly dressed men who approach you asking where you're from and where you're going.

TOURIST INFORMATION

Bangkok Information Center (Map p78; ☑ 02 225 7612-4; 17/1 Th Phra Athit; ⊗8am-7pm

MEDIA

→ Bangkok's predominant English-language newspapers are the *Bangkok Post* (www.bangkokpost.com) and the business-heavy *Nation* (www.nationmultimedia.com).

→ *Bangkok 101* (www.bangkok101.com) is a tourist-friendly listings magazine; *BK* (http://bk.asia-city.com) is a slightly more in-depth listings mag; and *Coconuts Bangkok* (https://coconuts.co/bangkok) is where to go for listings and offbeat local 'news'.

→ On Twitter, Richard Barrow (@RichardBarrow) is a great source of tourist information.

Mon-Fri, 9am-5pm Sat & Sun; ⛴ Phra Athit Pier) Handles city-specific tourism information.

Tourism Authority of Thailand (TAT; ☏ 02 134 0040, call centre 1672; www.tourismthailand.org; 2nd fl, btwn Gates 2 & 5, Suvarnabhumi International Airport; ⊗ 24hr) TAT runs a counter at Suvarnabhumi International Airport.

Tourism Authority of Thailand (TAT; Map p78; ☏ 02 283 1500, nationwide 1672; www.tourismthailand.org; cnr Th Ratchadamnoen Nok & Th Chakraphatdi Phong; ⊗ 8.30am-4.30pm; ⛴ klorng boat Phanfa Leelard Pier) Banglamphu branch.

ⓘ Getting There & Away

AIR

Suvarnabhumi International Airport (☏ 02 132 1888; www.airportthai.co.th; Samut Prakan), 30km east of central Bangkok, began commercial international and domestic service in 2006. Meaning 'golden land' in Sanskrit, the airport's name is pronounced *sù·wan·ná·poom*, and it inherited the airport code (BKK) previously held by the old airport at Don Mueang. The airport website has real-time details of arrivals and departures.

Bangkok's other airport, **Don Mueang International Airport** (☏ 02 535 1192; www.airportthai.co.th; Don Mueang), 25km north of central Bangkok, was formerly the city's principal air hub. It was retired from service in 2006 – after Suvarnabhumi was inaugurated – only to reopen later as the city's de facto budget hub with a new airport code (DMK). Terminal 1 handles international flights, while Terminal 2 is for domestic destinations.

BUS

Buses using government bus stations are far more reliable and less prone to incidents of theft than private connections departing from Th Khao San or other popular tourist centres.

The **Suvarnabhumi Public Transport Centre** (☏ 02 132 1888; Suvarnabhumi International Airport), located 3km from Suvarnabhumi International Airport, has frequent departures to Aranya Prathet (for the Cambodian border), Chanthaburi, Ko Chang, Nong Khai (for the Laos border), Pattaya, Rayong, Trat and Udon Thani. It can be reached by a free airport shuttle bus.

The **Eastern Bus Terminal** (Map p110; ☏ 02 391 2504; Soi 40, Th Sukhumvit; ⓢ Ekkamai exit 2) is the departure point for buses to Pattaya, Rayong, Chanthaburi and other points east, except for the border crossing at Aranya Prathet. Most people call it *sà·tăh·nee èk·gà·mai* (Ekamai station). It's near the Ekkamai BTS station.

The **Northern & Northeastern Bus Terminal** (Mo Chit; Map p116; ☏ northeastern routes 02 936 2852, ext 602/605, northern routes 02 936 2841, ext 325/614; Th Kamphaeng Phet; Ⓜ Kamphaeng Phet exit 1 & taxi, ⓢ Mo Chit exit 3 & taxi) is located just north of Chatuchak Park. This hectic bus station is also commonly called *kŏn sòng mŏr chít* (Mo Chit station) – not to be confused with Mo Chit BTS station. Buses depart from here for all northern and northeastern destinations, as well as regional international destinations including Pakse (Laos), Phnom Penh (Cambodia), Siem Reap (Cambodia) and Vientiane (Laos). To reach the bus station, take BTS (Skytrain) to Mo Chit or MRT (Metro) to Kamphaeng Phet and transfer onto city bus 3, 77 or 509, or hop on a taxi or motorcycle taxi.

TRAIN

The city's main train terminus is known as **Hua Lamphong** (☏ call centre 1690; www.railway.co.th; off Rama IV; Ⓜ Hua Lamphong exit 2). Ignore all touts here and avoid the travel agencies. To check timetables, destinations and fares, visit the official website of the State Railway of Thailand (www.railway.co.th/main/index_en.html).

Also known as Thonburi, **Bangkok Noi** (☏ call centre 1690; www.railway.co.th/main/index_en.html; off Th Itsaraphap; ⛴ Thonburi Railway Station) is a minuscule train station with departures for Kanchanaburi, Nakhon Pathom and Nam Tok.

Wongwian Yai (Map p70; ☏ 02 465 2017, call centre 1690; www.railway.co.th/main/index_en.html; off Th Phra Jao Taksin; ⓢ Wongwian Yai exit 4 & taxi) is a tiny station and the jumping-off point for the commuter line to Samut Sakhon (also known as Mahachai).

ⓘ Getting Around

Bangkok may seem chaotic and impenetrable at first, but its transport system is gradually improving. No matter how much you ride the BTS, MRT or ferry systems, you'll almost certainly find yourself stuck in road traffic at some point during your visit, but the traffic jams aren't as bad as they used to be.

BTS The elevated Skytrain runs from 6am to midnight. Tickets 16B to 52B.

MRT The Metro runs from 6am to midnight. Tickets 16B to 42B.

Taxi Outside of rush hours, Bangkok taxis are a great bargain. Flagfall 35B.

Chao Phraya Express Boat Runs 6am to 8pm, charging a flat 15B (orange, green or yellow flag). A tourist boat ride costs 60B.

Klorng boat Bangkok's canal boats run from 5.30am to 8pm most days. Tickets 9B to 19B.

Bus Cheap but a slow and confusing way to get around Bangkok. Tickets 10B to 25B.

TO/FROM THE AIRPORTS

Suvarnabhumi International Airport Airport Rail Link: BTS Phaya Thai to Suvarnabhumi (45B, 30 minutes, 6am to midnight). AC bus from Suvarnabhumi to Th Khao San (60B, 6am to 8pm). Meter taxis (300B to 400B plus 50B airport surcharge and optional expressway tolls).

Don Mueang International Airport Four bus lines: A1 to BTS Mo Chit (50B, 7.30am to 11.30pm); A2 to BTS Victory Monument (50B, 7.30am to 11.30pm); A3 to Lumphini Park (50B, 7.30am to 11.30pm); A4 to Sanam Luang (50B, 7.30am to 11.30pm). Meter taxis (300B to 350B plus 50B airport surcharge).

BICYCLE

Over the past few years, cycling has exploded in popularity in Bangkok. Bike sales are booming and a 23km bicycle track that circles Suvarnabhumi International Airport is steadily gaining popularity as a weekend activity among the city's cyclists. There's even a bike-share initiative (www.punpunbikeshare.com) – look for the pavement-side stands on the city's major thoroughfares branded 'Pun Pun'. Despite all this, however, dangerous roads, traffic, heat, pollution and lack of adequate bike lanes mean that Bangkok is still far from a safe or convenient place to use a bicycle as a means of transportation.

BOAT
Canal Boats

Canal taxi boats run along Khlong Saen Saep (Banglamphu to Ramkhamhaeng) and are an easy way to get between Banglamphu and Jim Thompson House, the Siam Sq shopping centres (get off at Sapan Hua Chang Pier for both) and other points further east along Th Sukhumvit – after a mandatory change of boat at Pratunam Pier.

➡ These boats are mostly used by daily commuters and pull into the piers for just a few seconds – jump straight on or you'll be left behind.

➡ Fares range from 12B to 15B and boats run from 5.30am to 7.15pm from Monday to Friday,

---

AIRPORT ACCOMMODATION

Those worried about a super-early departure or late arrival may consider a stay at one of the following airport hotels:

Novotel Suvarnabhumi Airport Hotel (☑ 02 131 1111; www.novotelairportbkk.com; Suvarnabhumi International Airport; r incl breakfast from 5300B; ❋ @ 🛜; 🚇 Suvarnabhumi Airport & hotel shuttle bus, Ⓢ Phra Khanong exit 3 & taxi) Has 600-plus luxurious rooms; located within the Suvarnabhumi International Airport compound.

The Cottage (☑ 02 727 5858; www.thecottagebangkokairport.com; 888/8 Th Lad Krabang; r incl breakfast 900-1700B; ❋ @ 🛜 🏊; 🚇 Suvarnabhumi Airport & hotel shuttle bus, Ⓢ Phra Khanong exit 3 & taxi) This solid midranger is near the Suvarnabhumi International Airport compound and within walking distance of food and shopping; has an airport shuttle.

Sleep Box (☑ 02 535 7555; www.sleepboxmiracle.com; Terminal 2, Don Mueang International Airport; s & d 500B; ❋ 🛜) Finally, an alternative to snoozing on the chairs at Don Mueang International Airport. Rooms may induce claustrophobia, but include en suite bathrooms, water, wi-fi and even food coupons. Short stays (1000B for three hours) and showers (300B) are also available.

Amari Don Mueang Airport Hotel (☑ 02 566 1020; www.amari.com/donmuang; 333 Th Choet Wutthakat; d incl breakfast from 2400B; ❋ @ 🛜 🏊; Ⓜ Chatuchak Park exit 2 & taxi, Ⓢ Mo Chit exit 3 & taxi) International-standard hotel located directly opposite Don Mueang International Airport.

from 6am to 6.30pm on Saturday and from 6am to 6pm on Sunday.

River Ferries

The **Chao Phraya Express Boat** (☑ 02 445 8888; www.chaophrayaexpressboat.com) operates the main ferry service along the Chao Phraya River. The central pier is known as Sathorn/Central Pier or Saphan Taksin, and connects to the BTS at Saphan Taksin station.

➤ Boats run from 6am to 7pm. Hold on to your ticket as proof of purchase (an occasional formality).

➤ The most common boats are the orange-flag vessels. These run from Wat Rajsingkorn in the south to Nonthaburi in the north, stopping at all major piers. Fares are a flat 15B, and boats run frequently from 6am to 7pm.

➤ Green-flag and yellow-flag boats skip a few piers along the way and are thus slightly quicker than the orange-flag vessels. They are fewer in number, though.

➤ A blue-flagged tourist boat (60B, every 30 minutes from 9.30am to 5.30pm) runs from Sathorn/Central Pier to Phra Athit/Banglamphu Pier, with stops at major sightseeing piers. A 200B all-day pass is also available, but unless you plan on doing a lot of boat travel, it's not great value.

➤ There are also dozens of cross-river ferries, which charge 3B and run every few minutes until late at night.

➤ Private long-tail boats can be hired for sightseeing trips at Phra Athit/Banglamphu Pier, Chang Pier, Tien Pier and Oriental Pier.

BTS & MRT

The elevated **BTS** (Skytrain; ☑ call centre 02 617 6000, tourist information 02 617 7341; www.bts.co.th), also known as the Skytrain (rót fai fáa), whisks you through 'new' Bangkok (Silom, Sukhumvit and Siam Sq). The interchange between the two lines is at Siam station and trains run frequently from 6am to midnight. Fares range from 16B to 52B or 140B for a one-day pass. Most ticket machines only accept coins, but change is available at the information booths.

Bangkok's Metro, the **MRT** (☑ 02 354 2000; www.transitbangkok.com), is most helpful for people staying in the Sukhumvit or Silom area to reach the train station at Hua Lamphong. Fares cost from 16B to 42B. The trains run frequently from 6am to midnight.

At the time of research, both networks were being extended in several directions to meet increasing commuter traffic, with completion deadlines staggered over 2020–21.

BUS

Bangkok's public buses are run by the **Bangkok Mass Transit Authority** (☑ 02 246 0973, call centre 1348; www.bmta.co.th).

➤ As the routes are not always clear, and with Bangkok taxis being such a good deal, you'd really have to be pinching pennies to rely on buses as a way to get around Bangkok.

➤ Air-con bus fares range from 12B to 25B; fares for fan-cooled buses start at 10B.

➤ Most of the bus lines run between 5am and 10pm or 11pm, except for the 'all-night' buses, which run from 3am or 4am to midmorning.

BANGKOK TAXI TIPS

➤ Never agree to take a taxi that won't use the meter; usually these drivers park outside hotels and in tourist areas. Simply get one that's passing by instead.

➤ Once they've agreed to plying a route, Bangkok taxi drivers will usually not 'take you for a ride' as happens in some other countries; they make more money from passenger turnover.

➤ It's worth keeping in mind that many Bangkok taxi drivers are in fact seasonal labourers fresh from the countryside and may not know their way around.

➤ If a driver refuses to take you somewhere, it's probably because they need to return the hired cab before a certain time, not because they don't like how you look.

➤ Very few Bangkok taxi drivers speak much English, so an address written in Thai can help immensely. Many hotels have business cards with the address printed in Thai.

➤ Older cabs may be less comfortable but typically have more experienced drivers because they are driver-owned, as opposed to the new cabs, which are usually hired. In general, yellow-green or white-pink cabs tend to be driven by experienced self-owned drivers, while taxis of other colours tend to be driven by hired hands of varying experience.

MOTORCYCLE TAXIS

➤ Motorcycle taxis (known as *motorsai*) serve two purposes in traffic congested Bangkok. Most commonly and popularly, they form an integral part of the public-transport network, running from the corner of a main thorough-fare, such as Th Sukhumvit, to the far ends of soi (streets) that run off that thoroughfare. Riders wear coloured, numbered vests and gather at either end of their soi, usually charging 10B to 20B for the trip. Helmets are available for pillion riders, but their hygiene is questionable.

➤ The other obvious purpose of *motorsai* is to beat the traffic, given their ability to slide through piled-up traffic. Just tell your rider where you want to go, negotiate a price (from 20B for a short trip up to about 150B going across town), strap on the helmet and say a prayer to any god you're into.

TAXI

➤ Although many first-time visitors are hesitant to use them, Bangkok's taxis are – in general – new and comfortable and the drivers are courteous and helpful, making them an excellent way to get around.

➤ All taxis are required to use their meters, which start at 35B, and fares to most places within central Bangkok cost 60B to 100B. Freeway tolls – 25B to 120B depending on where you start or end – must be paid by the passenger.

➤ App-based yellow-green taxis through Grab are available for 20B above the metered fare.

➤ If you leave something in a taxi your best chance of getting it back (still pretty slim) is to call 1644.

Ride-share Apps

App-based alternatives to the traditional taxis that operate in Bangkok:

All Thai Taxi (www.allthaitaxi.com; 02 018 9799)

GrabTaxi (www.grab.com/th)

Note that owner-driven private cars operating under Grab are technically not legal; only the commercially licensed yellow-green taxis are. However, a large number of private vehicles operate as Grab cars, and it's not uncommon for a stylish SUV or cool sedan to show up when you book a ride through Grab – unless you specifically ask for a taxi.

TÚK-TÚK

➤ Bangkok's iconic túk-túk (pronounced *đúk đúk*; motorised three-wheel taxis) are used by Thais for short hops. For foreigners, however, these emphysema-inducing machines are part of the Bangkok experience, so despite the fact that they overcharge outrageously and you can't see anything due to the low roof, pretty much everyone takes a túk-túk at least once.

➤ Túk-túk are notorious for taking little 'detours' to commission-paying gem and silk shops and massage parlours. En route to 'free' temples, you'll meet 'helpful' locals who will steer you to even more rip-off opportunities. Ignore anyone offering too-good-to-be-true 20B trips on 'special days'.

➤ The vast majority of túk-túk drivers ask too much from tourists (expat *fa·ràng* never use them). Expect to be quoted a 100B fare, if not more, for even the shortest trip. Try bargaining them down to about 50B for a short trip, preferably at night when the pollution (hopefully) won't be quite so bad. Once you've done it, you'll find that taxis are cheaper, cleaner, cooler and quieter.

AROUND BANGKOK

The Bangkok Metropolitan Region, as it is officially known, includes six provinces bordering the city of Bangkok, which add up to an area spanning more than 7500 sq km and have a population of around 10 million people. Because of their relative proximity and easy access, we have opted to include a few places in these neighbouring provinces in this designation, which can be visited as day trips from the city.

Ko Kret

An easy rural getaway from Bangkok, Ko Kret is an artificial island – the result of a canal having been dug nearly 300 years ago to shorten an oxbow bend in the Chao Phraya River's course. The area is one of Thailand's oldest settlements of Mon people, who were a dominant people of central Thailand between the 6th and 10th centuries AD. Today, Ko Kret is a popular weekend getaway, known for its hand-thrown terracotta pots and its busy weekend market.

◉ Sights

There are a couple of temples worth peeking into at Ko Kret, such as the leaning stupa at **Wat Poramai Yikawat** (วัดปรมัยยิกาวาส; Ko Kret, Nonthaburi; ⏰9am-5pm; 🚌166 & river-crossing ferry from Wat Sanam Neua), but the real highlight is taking in the bucolic riverside atmosphere. A 6km paved path circles the island and can be easily completed on foot or by bicycle, the latter available for rent from the pier (50B per day). Alternatively, it's possible to charter a boat for up to 10 people for 500B; the typical island tour stops at

Around Bangkok

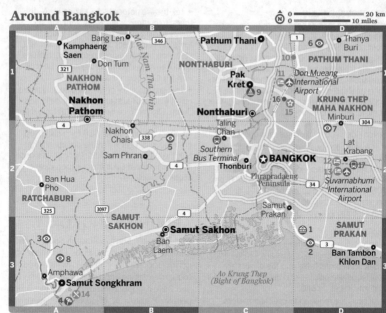

Around Bangkok

a batik workshop, a sweets factory and, on weekends, a floating market.

Ko Kret is known for its **hand-thrown terracotta pots**, sold at markets throughout Bangkok. Order an iced coffee from just about any vendor on the island and you'll get a small pot as a souvenir. From Wat Poramai Yikawat, go in either direction to find both abandoned kilns and working pottery centres on the east and north coasts. You'll find lots of souvenir stalls along the way, as well as restaurants.

If you come to Ko Kret on a weekday, you'll likely be the only visitor. On weekends, things change drastically as Ko Kret is an extremely popular destination for urban Thais. There's heaps more food, drink and things for sale, but with this come the crowds.

🍴 Eating

On weekends, droves of Thai visitors flock to Ko Kret to eat deep-fried snacks and Thai-style sweets, all of which are sold in food stalls lining the busy market lanes. One snack to look for is *khâw châa,* an unusual but delicious Mon dish of savoury titbits served with chilled fragrant rice.

Pa Ka Lung
THAI $

(Restaurant River Side; Ko Kret; mains 50-80B; ☺8am-4pm Mon-Fri, to 6pm Sat & Sun; ☒166 & river-crossing ferry from Wat Sanam Neua) An open-air food court with an English-language menu, this is a good place for trying *khâw châa* (an unusual but delicious Mon dish of savoury titbits served with chilled fragrant rice) and other local dishes. You'll find it on the busy northern edge of the island, not far from Wat Poramai Yikawat.

De Pala
THAI $$

(Ko Kret; mains 100-200B; ☺10am-9pm Sat & Sun; ☒166 & river-crossing ferry from Wat Sanam Neua) Located on a pretty canalside plot shaded by ferns, this relaxed restaurant is perhaps the nicest place on Ko Kret to end your explorations with a chilled beer and some delicious rustic Thai preparations. It's rather busy during lunch hours on weekends, and you might have to queue for a table.

ℹ Getting There & Away

Ko Kret is in Nonthaburi, about 15km north of central Bangkok. The coolest way of getting here is by chartering a four-seater speedboat from Nonthaburi Pier, the northern terminal of the Chao Phraya Express Boat service. The thrilling 20-minute ride along the Chao Phraya River in a narrow boat literally skimming over the water is vastly enjoyable, and costs 1000B for a two-way journey – bargain if required. The boat driver will pick you up from Ko Kret at an agreed time after you've finished sightseeing there.

Nonadrenalin junkies can alternatively take bus 166 from the Victory Monument or a taxi to Pak Kret before boarding the cross-river ferry (2B, 5am to 9pm) that leaves from Wat Sanam Neua.

Amphawa

📖 034 / POP 5000

Most people visit Amphawa (อัมพวา), a sleepy canalside village, to get a feel for its semirural setting and relaxed pace of life. While it bears some signs of gentrification, the village's canals, wooden buildings, atmospheric cafes and quaint water-borne traffic still retain heaps of charm. There's a floating market (p154) here on weekends; on a weekday you'll probably be the only tourist.

◉ Sights & Activities

Steps from Amphawa's central footbridge is Wat Amphawan Chetiyaram (วัดอัมพวันเจติยาราม; off Rte 6006, Amphawa, Samut Songkhram; ☺daylight hours), a graceful temple featuring accomplished murals believed to be located at the place of the family home of Rama II. A short walk from the temple is King Buddhalertla (Phuttha Loet La) Naphalai Memorial Park (อุทยานพระบรมราชานุสรณ์พระบาทสมเด็จพระพุทธเลิศหล้านภาลัย; off Rte 6006, Amphawa, Samut Songkhram; 20B; ☺8.30am-5pm), a museum housed in a collection of traditional central Thai houses set on 1½ landscaped hectares. Dedicated to Rama II, the museum contains a library of antiques from early-19th-century Siam.

At night, long-tail boats zip through Amphawa's sleeping waters to watch the Christmas-light-like dance of the *hìng hôy* (fireflies), most populous during the wet season. From Friday to Sunday, operators from several piers lead tours, charging 100B for a seat. Outside of these days, it costs 600B for a one-hour charter.

Don Hoi Lot
BEACH

(ดอนหอยหลอด; Samut Songkhram) Amphawa's second-most-famous tourist attraction (after the eponymous village) is a bank of fossilised shells at the mouth of Mae Nam Mae Klong, not far from Samut Songkhram. These shells come from *hŏy lòrt* (clams with a tube-like shell). The shell bank is best seen during April and May, when the river surface has receded to its lowest level.

To get here, hop into a *sŏrng·tăa·ou* in front of Samut Songkhram's Somdet Phra Phuttalertla Hospital at the intersection of Th Prasitpattana and Th Tamnimit (10B, about 15 minutes). Or charter a boat from Mae Klong Market pier *(tâh đà·làht mâa glorng),* a scenic journey of around 45 minutes (about 1000B).

🛏 Sleeping & Eating

Amphawa is exceedingly popular with Bangkok's weekend warriors and it seems like virtually every other house has opened its doors to tourists as a homestay. These can range from little more than a mattress on the floor and a mosquito net to upscale guesthouse-style accommodation. Rooms with fan start at about 400B, while rooms with air-con (many share bathrooms) begin at about 1500B. Prices halve on weekdays.

WORTH A TRIP

SAMUT PRAKAN

One of the six provinces that comprise the Bangkok Metropolitan Region, Samut Prakan is a sprawling suburb that makes for a rather interesting day trip from the city. Start your exploration by taking the BTS to Bang Na, then grab a taxi to the ferry pier at Wat Bang Na Nork. A short ferry ride from here takes you to **Bang Kachao**, an artificial island also known as Bangkok's 'green lung'. Here, you can explore **Si Nakhon Kheun Khan Park** (สวนศรีนครเขื่อนขันธ์; Map p70; 🕒6am-7pm; [S]Bang Na exit 2 & taxi) [FREE], a vast botanical garden that appeals to hikers, birdwatchers and cyclists. The island is also home to the atmospheric and rural **Bang Nam Pheung Market** (ตลาดบางน้ำผึ้ง; Map p70; 🕒8am-3pm Sat & Sun; [S]Bang Na exit 2 & taxi), and **Wat Bang Nam Pheung Nok** (วัดบางน้ำผึ้งนอก; Map p70; 🕒daylight hours; [S]Bang Na exit 2 & taxi), a 250-year-old Buddhist temple.

Bang Kachao can easily take the entire morning to explore – you'll find food stalls along the way, as well as several stalls in Bang Nam Pheung Market selling interesting rural-style food items. Post-lunch, backtrack to the BTS line and take a train to the southern terminus at Kheha. From here, a 10-minute taxi ride will take you to **Bang Pu Beach** (บางปู; Th Sukhumvit, Bang Pu; 🕒daylight hours; [S]Kheha exit 3/4 & taxi), Bangkok's de facto seaside promenade. You can spend the late afternoon and early evening here feeding resident seagulls and snapping sunset pictures, before taking the skytrain back into town.

Ancient City (เมืองโบราณ, Muang Boran; www.muangboranmuseum.com; 296/1 Th Sukhumvit; adult/child 700/350B; 🕒9am-7pm; [S]Bearing exit 1) comprises scaled-down versions of them in what claims to be the largest open-air museum in the world. It's an excellent place to explore by bicycle (included in entry fee) as it's usually quiet and rarely crowded. Ancient City lies east of Bangkok in neighbouring Samut Prakan province, which is most conveniently accessed via the park's shuttle bus from BTS Bearing station (see website for departure times).

ChababaanCham Resort HOTEL $$$
(☎081 984 1000; www.chababaancham.com; Th Rim Khlong; r incl breakfast 1500-2400B; ❄📶) Located just off the canal, this place has attractive, modern and spacious duplex-style rooms, the more expensive of which come equipped with a rooftop lounge area.

Baan Ku Pu HOTEL $$$
(☎081 941 1249; Th Rim Khlong; bungalows incl breakfast 1600-2000B; ❄📶) This is a Thai-style 'resort' featuring wooden bungalows in a relatively peaceful, canalside enclave. Room rates include a sumptuous breakfast comprising local dishes.

Seafood Restaurants SEAFOOD $
(Don Hoi Lot, Samut Songkhram; mains 80-200B; 🕒10am-10pm) The road leading to Don Hoi Lot is lined with seafood restaurants, nearly all serving delicious dishes made with *hŏy lòrt,* the area's eponymous shellfish. English is hardly spoken; don't expect English-language menus or English signage either.

ℹ Getting There & Away

From Bangkok's **Southern Bus Terminal** (Sai Tai Mai; ☎02 422 4444, call centre 1490; Th Boromaratchachonanee) in Thonburi, board any bus bound for Damnoen Saduak and ask to get off at Amphawa (80B, two hours, frequent 6am to 9pm). Alternatively, there are also frequent minivans to Samut Songkhram (also known as Mae Klong; 80B, 1½ hours, frequent from 6am to 9pm). From there, you can hop in a *sŏrng·tăa·ou* (passenger pick-up truck; 10B) near the market for the 10-minute ride to Amphawa.

Nakhon Pathom

☎034 / POP 120,000

Nakhon Pathom (นครปฐม) is a typical central Thai city, with Phra Pathom Chedi as a visible link to its claim as the country's oldest settlement. The town's name, which derives from the Pali 'Nagara Pathama' meaning 'First City' in Sanskrit, appears to lend some legitimacy to this boast.

The modern town is quite sleepy, but it is an easy destination in which to see everyday Thai ways and practise your newly acquired language skills with a community genuinely appreciative of such efforts.

◉ Sights

Phra Pathom Chedi   BUDDHIST TEMPLE
(พระปฐมเจดีย์; 60B; ☺temple daylight hours, museum 9am-4pm Wed-Sun) This massive stupa, rising more than 120m, is one of the tallest Buddhist monuments in the world. Its name in Sanskrit roughly translates to 'first monument', an indication of its ancient status among Thailand's religious structures. Exploring the site is a pleasant and calming experience; you can easily spend a couple of hours within the complex admiring the massive dome, visiting smaller shrines and watching devotees immersed in rituals and worship. The stupa is just south of the railway station.

The original structure was erected in the early 6th century by the Theravada Buddhists of Dvaravati. But, in the early 11th century the Khmer king, Suriyavarman I of Angkor, conquered the city and built a Brahman *prang* (Hindu/Khmer-style stupa) over the sanctuary. The Burmese of Bagan, under King Anawrahta, sacked the city in 1057 and the *prang* lay in ruins until Rama IV (King Mongkut) had it restored in 1860.

On the eastern side of the monument, in the *bòht* (ordination hall), is a Dvaravati-style Buddha seated in a European pose similar to the one in Wat Phra Meru in Ayuthaya. It may, in fact, have come from there.

Also of interest are the many examples of Chinese sculpture carved from a greenish stone that came to Thailand as ballast in the bottom of 19th-century Chinese junks. Opposite the *bòht* is a museum, with some interesting Dvaravati sculpture and lots of old junk. Within the *chedi* complex is Lablae Cave, an artificial tunnel containing the shrine of several Buddha figures.

The wát surrounding the stupa enjoys the kingdom's highest temple rank, Rachavoramahavihan; it's one of only six temples so honoured in Thailand. King Rama VI's ashes are interred in the base of the Sukhothai-era Phra Ruang Rochanarit, a large standing Buddha image in the wát's northern *wí·hăhn* (sanctuary).

✖ Eating

Nakhon Pathom has the excellent Don Wai Market (p154) along the road between the train station and Phra Pathom Chedi. There are many good, inexpensive food vendors and restaurants in the area.

❶ Getting There & Away

Nakhon Pathom is 64km west of Bangkok. The city doesn't have a central bus station, but most transport arrives and departs from near the market and train station.

The most convenient and fastest way to get to Nakhon Pathom from Bangkok is via minivan, which depart from the Southern Bus Terminal (70B, one hour, frequent 6am to 6pm).

There are also frequent trains from Bangkok's Hua Lamphong station throughout the day (20B to 60B, one hour).

POPULATION
20,000,000

LENGTH OF DEATH RAILWAY
415km (p190)

BEST STUPA VIEWS
Wat Phra Si Sanphet
(p168)

BEST HISTORY MUSEUM
Thailand-Burma Railway Centre (p184)

BEST TEMPLE CAVE
Wat Ban Tham
(p185)

WHEN TO GO
Oct–Jan The coolest months (relatively speaking).

Feb–Jun The hottest period. Because of altitude, Sangkhlaburi and its surrounding national parks make for a refreshing break.

Jun–Oct Welcome to the rainy season. Ayuthaya and Lopburi sit in wide, open plains that get wet and humid like Bangkok.

Wat Tham Seua (p187), Kanchanaburi
BANJONGSEAL324/SHUTTERSTOCK ©

Central Thailand

The past is never far behind in Central Thailand. Ayuthaya, Siam's former royal capital, is practically an open-air museum, with dozens of temple ruins, while Kanchanaburi's WWII memorials pay tribute to the thousands of lives lost building the Death Railway.

Nature is a key player here. The jagged mountain ranges that dominate Kanchanaburi's horizons host spectacular waterfalls and deep caves. In the far north, you'll be within touching distance of Myanmar and amid a vibrant ethnic mix. Laze away the day lakeside in lovely Sangkhlaburi or sleep among the treetops at Thong Pha Phum National Park.

Lopburi combines both nature and history, as hundreds of monkeys scamper among Khmer-era temples in what was once Siam's second capital.

Central Thailand Highlights

❶ Ayuthaya (p168) Cycling between enigmatic ruins and colossal Buddhas.

❷ Kanchanaburi (p184) Being rendered speechless by the harrowing history of the Death Railway.

❸ Erawan National Park (p194) Clambering up seven levels of waterfall to splash in aquamarine pools.

❹ Prang Sam Yot (p178) Admiring Lopburi's most famous 13th-century temple while dodging myriad monkeys.

❺ River Resorts (p198) Escaping to the wilderness at Nam Tok's floating resorts.

❻ Saphan Mon (p199) Striding across Thailand's longest wooden bridge for views of Sangkhlaburi's glassy lake.

❼ E-Thong (p197) Snaking up the mountainous, potholed road to this picturesque border village.

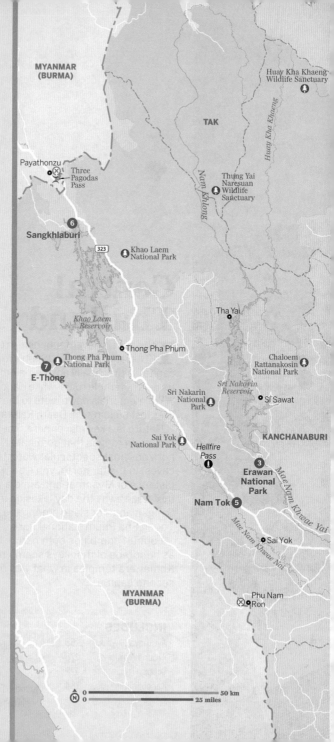

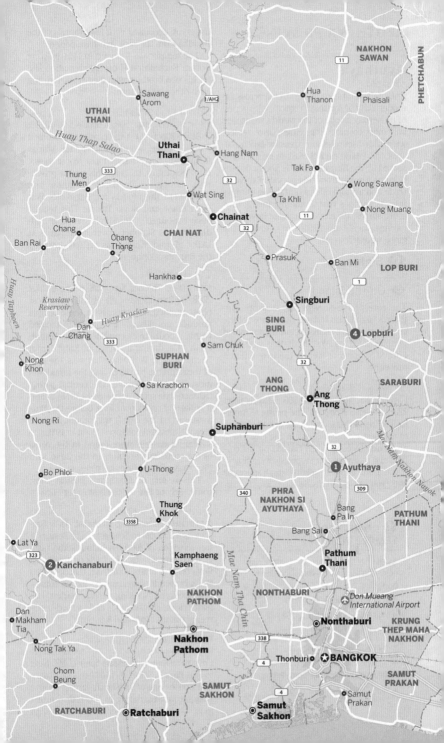

AYUTHAYA PROVINCE

Ayuthaya

POP 53,000

Enigmatic temple ruins are strewn across the modern city of Ayuthaya (อยุธยา), whispering of its heyday as one of the world's wealthiest and most cosmopolitan cities. Once replete with gilded temples and treasure-laden palaces, this island capital of Siam was brutally sacked by the Burmese in 1767. Today, dozens of ruins remain from this period of thriving trade and art and offer a tantalising glimpse into its glorious past. Standing among towering stupas, it's easy to imagine how international merchants visiting from around the globe were left in awe.

⊙ Sights

⊙ On the Island

The core of the ancient city was on Ayuthaya's island, and today it hosts most of the city's best-known sights including renowned temples such as Wat Mahathat and Wat Phra Si Sanphet as well as the two national museums.

★ **Wat Ratchaburana** RUINS
(วัดราชบูรณะ; Th Chee Kun; 50B, 6-temple ticket 220B; ⊗ 8am-6.30pm; P) The *prang* (Khmer-style spire) in this large temple complex is one of the best extant versions in the city. There are giant stucco-sculpted Garuda on the corners and many smaller stupas surrounding it. If you aren't afraid of heights, small spaces or bats, you can climb inside the *prang* to visit

---

ⓘ **COMBINED TEMPLE TICKET**

A pass for these six major temple ruins costs 220B, lasts 30 days and can be bought at each site:

➡ Wat Ratchaburana (p168)

➡ Wat Phra Si Sanphet (p168)

➡ Wat Phra Ram (p169)

➡ Wat Mahathat (p168)

➡ Wat Maheyong (วัดมเหยงคณ์; Soi Wat Maheyong; 50B; ⊗ 8am-6pm; P)

➡ Wat Chai Wattanaram (p171)

---

the crypt, decorated with faint murals of the Buddha from the early Ayuthaya period.

The temple was founded in 1424 by King Borom Rachathirat II on the cremation site for his two brothers who died while fighting each other for the throne.

★ **Wat Phra Si Sanphet** RUINS
(วัดพระศรีสรรเพชญ์; 50B, 6-temple ticket 220B; ⊗ 8am-6.30pm) At this captivating ruined temple, three wonderfully intact stupas form one of Ayuthaya's most iconic views. Built beginning in 1448, this was a private royal temple inside palace grounds, and these were the models for Bangkok's Wat Phra Kaew and Royal Palace. This temple once contained a 16m-high standing Buddha (Phra Si Sanphet) covered with at least 143kg of gold, which was melted down by the Burmese conquerers.

Wat Mahathat RUINS
(วัดมหาธาตุ; Th Chee Kun; 50B, 6-temple ticket 220B; ⊗ 8am-6.30pm; P) Ayuthaya's most photographed attraction is in these temple grounds: a sandstone Buddha head tangled within a bodhi tree's entwined roots. Founded in 1374, during the reign of King Borom Rachathirat I, Wat Mahathat was the seat of the supreme patriarch and the kingdom's most important temple. The central *prang* (Khmer-style spire) once stood 43m high and it collapsed on its own long before the Burmese sacked the city. It was rebuilt in more recent times, but collapsed again in 1911.

Many treasures were found in the ruins of the stupa and are now in the Chao Sam Phraya National Museum (p169).

This is one of Ayuthaya's busiest sites; come early or late for the best experience.

Ayutthaya Night Market MARKET
(อยุธยาไนท์มาร์เก็ต; Krung Sri Market; Th Si Sanphet; ⊗ 4.30-10pm Fri-Sun; P) FREE Besides a fun selection of food (including some rather uncommon ones, like fried butterfly pea flowers) and crafts sold from thatch-roofed stalls by vendors wearing period costumes, this weekend walking street market has boat rides, musicians, and sword-battle reenactments (7pm and 8.30pm).

Wihan Phra Mongkhon Bophit BUDDHIST TEMPLE
(วิหารพระมงคลบพิตร; ⊗ 8am-5pm) FREE Next to Wat Phra Si Sanphet (p168), this sanctuary hall houses one of Thailand's largest bronze Buddha images, dating to the 15th century, most likely. Coated in gold, the 12.5m-high

figure (17m with the base) was badly damaged by a lightning-induced fire around 1700, and again when the Burmese sacked the city. The Buddha and the building were repaired at various points in the 20th century and it's now one of Ayuthaya's must-sees.

In 1956, the Burmese Prime Minister donated 200,000B to restore the building, an act of belated atonement for his country's sacking of the city two centuries before.

Wat Lokayasutharam   RUINS, BUDDHIST STATUE
(วัดโลกยสุธาราม; off Th Khlong Thaw; ☉ daylight hours; 🅿) **FREE** This early-Ayuthaya temple ruin features an impressive 42m-long reclining Buddha in front of a precariously leaning *prang* (Khmer-style spire). The Buddha was restored in 1954 and is an important place of pilgrimage for Thais.

Touts selling lotuses for offering to the Buddha can be persistent here.

Million Toy Museum   MUSEUM
(พิพิธภัณฑ์ล้านของเล่นเกริกยุ้นพันธ์; 📞 081 890 5782; www.milliontoymuseum.com; Th U Thong; 50B; ☉ 9.30am-4pm Tue-Fri, 9.30am-5pm Sat & Sun; 🅿) Thousands of toys from across the decades are amassed in this jam-packed private museum. Rare porcelain elephants, wooden Japanese *kokeshi* dolls, wind-up robots and retro racing cars are filed alongside mass-produced Santa Claus and Shrek figurines. It isn't just toys; the impressively large and diverse collection includes the likes of ancient pottery and old coconut scrapers.

**Chao Sam Phraya
National Museum**   MUSEUM
(พิพิธภัณฑสถานแห่งชาติเจ้าสามพระยา; 📞 035 241587; Th Rotchana; 150B; ☉ 9am-4pm Tue-Sun; 🅿) The most impressive treasure of Ayuthaya's premier museum is the haul of royal gold (jewellery, utensils, votive tablets, spittoons) unearthed from the crypts of Wat Mahathat (p168) and Wat Ratchaburana (p168). Beautifully carved teak temple doors and numerous Buddha statues (some sculpted as far back as the 7th century) are also on display. Building 2 in the back holds a history of Thai pottery, from ancient figurines to gorgeous glazed dinnerware.

Temporary displays are held in the wooden building between the two main buildings and an expansion of the museum will soon bring many more of Ayuthaya's treasures to the public.

Lots of giant water monitors live in the surrounding ponds.

TEMPLE ETIQUETTE

Ayuthaya's ruins are symbols of both royalty and religion, two fundamental elements of Thai society, so visit respectfully. That means no posing for photos with your head positioned above Buddhas or taking the place of the statues' missing heads. Unless it's abundantly clear that you are permitted to ascend a stupa, do not climb on the ruins.

Wat Phra Ram   RUINS
(วัดพระราม; off Th Naresuan; 50B, 6-temple ticket 220B; ☉ 8am-6.30pm; 🅿) Wat Phra Ram's tall main *prang* (Khmer-style spire) isn't in the best condition, but it's definitely worth a visit. The temple was constructed on the cremation site of King U Thong (the Ayuthaya kingdom's first sovereign), perhaps in 1369, though details are unclear. The site attracts only a trickle of tourists.

Thai Boat Museum   MUSEUM
(พิพิธภัณฑ์เรือไทย; 📞 035 241195; www.thaiboatmuseum.com; Th Ho Rattanachai; by donation; ☉ 9.30am-noon & 1-4.30pm Tue-Sun) Think you can tell a spice boat from a *sam pan*? This interesting little private museum is full of wooden boats, both real and artistic miniatures, many of which still ply Thailand's rivers today. Ring the doorbell; you may have to wait for access.

Ayutthaya Tourist Center   MUSEUM
(ศูนย์ท่องเที่ยวอยุธยา; 📞 035 246076; Th Si Sanphet; ☉ 8.30am-4.30pm; 🅿) **FREE** A good first stop in Ayuthaya, the historical exhibitions in the former city hall contextualise the kingdom's history and culture from ancient times to present-day. One small room is designated the Ayutthaya National Art Museum and it hosts rotating exhibitions.

Downstairs is the tourist information centre (p176).

Pom Phet Fort   RUINS
(ป้อมเพชร; Th U Thong) **FREE** The 6.5m-high, 14m-thick weathered walls of this 1580 fortress once served as Ayuthaya island's primary line of defence. Besides making a good photo-op, it's a prime boat-watching spot.

◉ Off the Island

Though they receive fewer foreign visitors than those on the island, several of the

CENTRAL THAILAND

Ayuthaya

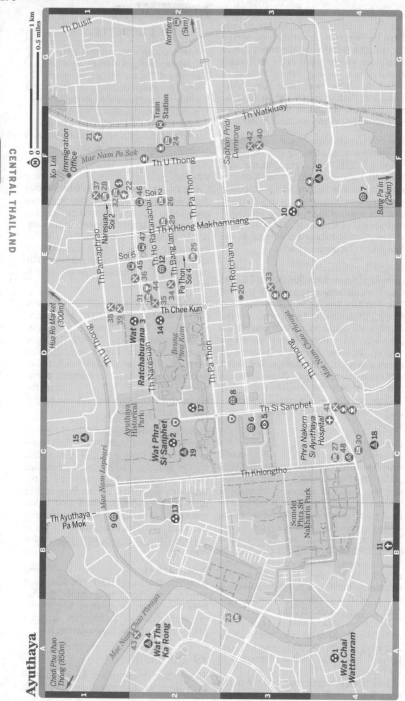

Chedi Phu Khao Thong (850m)

Th Dusit

Northern (5km)

Train Station

Th Watkluay

Ko Loi

Immigration Office

Mae Nam Pa Sak

Th U Thong

Saphan Phid Damrong

42
40

16

21

24

37 28
32 22
46
Soi 2
26

Th Pa Thon

7

Bang Pa In (25km)

10

Th Pamaphrao

Naresuan Soi 2

47
45
29
Th Ho Rattanachai

Th Khlong Makhamriang

Soi 6

36
12
Th Bang Ian

44

25

Pa Thon Soi 4

Th Rotchana

20

33

31
35
34

Th Chee Kun

38
39

Wat Ratchaburana

14

Beung Phra Ram

Th Naresuan

Th Pa Thon

Th U Thong

Mae Nam Chao Phraya

Th U Thong

Hua Ro Market (300m)

Ayuthaya Historical Park

8

17

Th Si Sanphet

41

Wat Phra Si Sanphet

2

6
5

Phra Nakorn Si Ayuthaya Hospital

Mae Nam Lopburi

15

19

27
48

30
18

Th Khlongtho

Th Ayuthaya – Pa Mok

9

13

Somdet Phra Sri Nakharin Park

11

23

43
4

Wat Tha Ka Rong

Mae Nam Chao Phraya

1

Wat Chai Wattanaram

Ayuthaya

CENTRAL THAILAND AYUTHAYA

temples on the opposite sides of the rivers, such as Wat Yai Chai Mongkhon and Wat Chai Wattanaram, are among Ayuthaya's best. All can be reached by bicycle.

Evening boat tours (p174) around the island are another way to see some of these temples.

★**Wat Chai Wattanaram** RUINS
(วัดไชยวัฒนาราม; Rte 3469; 50B, 6-temple ticket 220B; ⊘8am-6.30pm; **P**) Glorious in the early morning light and also at sunset, this temple is Ayuthaya's most impressive off-island site thanks to its 35m-high central *prang* (Khmer-style spire) and fine state of preservation. Heavily eroded relief panels on the backs of the surrounding stupas show scenes from the Buddha's life.

The temple was built by King Prasat Thong to honour his mother, and the design's resemblance to Cambodia's Angkor Wat is intentional. Construction began in 1630 and it took around 20 years to complete.

It's across the river from the southwestern corner of Ayuthaya island.

★**Wat Yai Chai Mongkhon** BUDDHIST TEMPLE
(วัดใหญ่ชัยมงคล; Rte 3477; 20B; ⊘6am-6pm; **P**) Visitors to this photogenic ruin 2km southeast of the island can climb stairs up into the crypt of the stunning 60m-tall, bell-shaped *chedi* (stupa). There you can drop coins into a bucket in hope of good luck and walk around the outside for a view of sculpted gardens and dozens of smaller stupas and stone Buddhas.

Founded by King U Thong in 1357, it housed monks returning from ordination in Sri Lanka. In 1593, King Naresuan added its fantastic *chedi* after a victory over the Burmese, and it thus became known as the 'temple of auspicious victory'.

Wat Na Phra Men BUDDHIST TEMPLE
(วัดหน้าพระเมรุ; Tambon Lum Phli; 20B; ⊘daylight hours, buildings 8am-5pm; **P**) Featuring a gorgeous 6m-high Buddha flanked by maroon columns, this active temple was one of the

> ℹ️ **ELEPHANT WARNING**
>
> Short elephant rides near Ayuthaya's main temples are available, but for the elephants' well-being we strongly advise these should be avoided.

few to escape the wrath of Burma's invading army in 1767; it survived by serving as the army's main base and weapons storehouse. The *bòht* (ordination hall) is massive, larger than most modern ones, and the Buddha image wears 'royal attire', which was common in the late Ayuthaya era. Despite what the English sign inside says, the Buddha is made of bronze, not gold.

⭐ **Wat Tha Ka Rong**　　BUDDHIST TEMPLE

(วัดท่าการ้อง; ⏲ 5am-6pm; 🅿️) FREE With animatronic ghosts, supersized crows and glowing Buddhas, Wat Tha Ka Rong is eerie and playful in equal measure and feels more like a carnival than a Buddhist temple. There are dozens of things to do and buy to make merit and hundreds of Buddhist, Hindu, animist and just-for-fun statues to see; the skeletons doing the *wâi* (palms-together Thai greeting) catch passers-by with motion sensors. It's just northwest of the island.

There's a weekend floating market (p175) nearby.

Wat Phutthai Sawan　　BUDDHIST TEMPLE

(วัดพุทไธศวรรย์; Rte 3469; ⏲ temple daylight hours, prang 8am-5.30pm; 🅿️) FREE Atmospheric ruins and lively temple worship can both be experienced at Wat Phutthai Sawan. King U Thong founded this temple in 1353 on the south bank of the Chao Phraya River at the spot where he and his followers lived before moving onto the island to create their great city. It's one of the few places spared by Burmese invaders and its bone-white, late-Ayuthaya-period *prang* (Khmer-style spire) still rises high above the old half of this temple complex. It's beautifully illuminated at night.

You can climb up inside the *prang* to see the massive relic vault, a reclining Buddha and lots of bats – because of the later, you do not need to remove your shoes.

Gold Buddhas on mosaicked pedestals surround the *prang* and east of this cloister is a stately stone Buddha reclining in a ruined building.

West of the cloister, the upper floor of the stark white and brown abbot's residence

(between the modern *prang* and the king statues) has faded 17th-century murals.

Wat Phanan Choeng　　BUDDHIST TEMPLE

(วัดพนัญเชิง; Rte 3477; 20B; ⏲ daylight hours, buildings 8am-5pm; 🅿️) This lively temple, believed to date to 1324 (26 years before the founding of Ayuthaya), revolves around the 19m-high Phra Phanan Choeng Buddha, aka 'Luang Po To'. This enormous statue sits within a soaring *wí·hǎhn* (assembly hall) surrounded by 10,800 small Buddha images lining the walls.

The buildings in front of the big Buddha have historical murals and along the river are three colourful Chinese shrines and a fish-feeding pier.

St Joseph Church　　CHURCH

(วัดนักบุญยอแซฟ; www.jsyutya.com; Rte 3469; ⏲ 8am-5pm; 🅿️) FREE In 1665, King Narai gave the French land next to the Christian Vietnamese settlement and donated money towards building the first St Joseph Church, which was made of wood. A brick church went up soon after, but it was destroyed in the Burmese invasion. The attractive, mustard-coloured Romanesque church standing now was completed in 1891.

Many of the families living around the church today are Catholic.

🎊 Festivals & Events

Wai Kru Muay Thai Ceremony　　CULTURAL

(⏲ mid-Mar) Thai boxers and their fans flock to Ayuthaya to show respect to the masters. Attendees can watch *moo·ay tai* matches, take lessons, observe sword making and witness the sacred Wai Kru Ceremony in which boxers pay respect to their teachers.

Ayutthaya World Heritage Fair　　LIGHT SHOW

(⏲ Dec or Jan) The sound-and-light shows (200B to 500B) at Wat Mahathat (p168) are the highlight of this event, usually happening in mid-December, but other places also get special illumination.

🛏️ Sleeping

Ayuthaya's accommodation scene satisfies all budgets. Most backpackers head for Naresuan Soi 2 (known as 'Soi Farang'), though there are good hostels and budget guesthouses all around the island. Staying along the river on the west side of the island is less convenient, but can be a very pleasant experience if you don't mind sporadic loud boat noise.

★ **Ayothaya Riverside House** GUESTHOUSE $
(☑ 081 644 5328; www.facebook.com/ayothaya riversidehouse; 17/2 Mu 7, Tambon Danpom; d/f without bathroom 400/1200B, d on boat 1500B; P ✲ 🛜) Across the Chao Phraya River on the west side of Ayuthaya, this wonderful guesthouse offers a choice between pleasant rooms with fans, mosquito nets and shared bathrooms in an old wooden house, or satin-and-wood-decorated air-con rooms on a classic wooden boat.

The untouristed neighbourhood setting off the island (but still in biking distance of the main sights) offers a low-key experience, and the owners are as friendly as can be.

Nakara Hostel HOSTEL $
(☑ 086 428 9246; www.facebook.com/nakarahostel ayutthaya; Th Bang Ian; dm 200-230B, d with shared bath 550B; ✲ 🛜) This new hostel has a great central location (between the historical park and Soi Farang) and impeccable cleanliness, but its greatest asset is an eager-to-please owner behind the counter. Dorms come in six- and 10-bed varieties with lockers available. The private rooms are fine, but overpriced.

Baan Are Gong GUESTHOUSE $
(☑ 081 595 3018, 087 107 0745; siriratsantitr@ yahoo.co.th; Soi Tambon Kramang; air-con d/tr/f 600/750/1400B, d/tr with shared bathroom & fan 400/600B; ✲ 🛜) Two minutes from the train station on the east bank of the Pasak River, Baan Are Gong's creaky but characterful rooms inhabit a century-old teak building. The soundproofing isn't great in either the shared-bath original rooms upstairs or the modern ones below, but it's run by a welcoming, reliable family who keep everything clean, and the wooden deck is a great place to relax.

Chantana House GUESTHOUSE $
(☑ 089 885 0257, 035 323200; chantanahouse@ yahoo.com; 12/22 Naresuan Soi 2; d with fan 400B, with air-con 500-550B; P ✲ 🛜) Rooms in this converted wooden home are plain but spotless and Chantana House arguably offers the best value on the backpacker strip. Staff are friendly, though English is limited.

★ **Ban Boonchu** GUESTHOUSE $$
(☑ 095 548 4662; 19/5 Pa Thon Soi 4; tw/tr incl breakfast 1000/1400B; P ✲ 🛜) Charming

---

AYUTHAYA'S FOREIGN QUARTER

One reason Ayuthaya's rulers thrived was their adroit diplomacy and tolerance towards other cultures and religions. At its peak, more than 40 ethnic groups resided here. People from nearby, such as the Mon, Lao and Khmer, as well as the Chinese, lived more or less freely among the locals. Those from further away, such as Indians, Persians, Javanese, Malay and Europeans, were given land, mostly to the south of the island, by the king to create their own settlements.

Baan Hollanda (บ้านฮอลันดา; ☑ 035 245683; www.baanhollanda.org; Soi Khan Rua, Mu 4; ⊙ 9am-4pm Wed-Sun; P) The little 'Dutch House' features a concise but informative exhibition of Dutch history in Thailand from 1604, when the Dutch East India Company (VOC) arrived in Ayuthaya, up to the present. Out the back are the excavated foundations of the second trading office, built in 1634. Just as interesting is the adjacent boatyard with many classic wooden craft.

The English village was just to the south and there was a Chinese village nearby, but nothing remains of either.

Japanese Village (หมู่บ้านญี่ปุ่น; ☑ 035 259867; 25/3 Mu 7, Tambon Kohrian; adult/student 50/20B; ⊙ 9.30am-6pm Mon-Fri, 8.30am-6pm Sat & Sun; P) Set within manicured, frangipani-fringed gardens, this small museum complex details the lives of the estimated 1500 Japanese who came to settle in Ayuthaya in the early 17th century. Some came to trade, but many were Christians fleeing persecution in their homeland. Both exhibition halls feature a video presentation.

Portuguese Village (หมู่บ้านโปรตุเกส; Rte 3469; ⊙ 9am-4pm; P) Arriving in the 16th century, the Portuguese were the first European settlers in Ayuthaya. Several of their skeletal remains are on view at this excavated burial site. More than 200 Portuguese and Christian converts were interred here. Behind the burial ground is the foundation of the 1540 **San Petro Church**, the first church built in Thailand.

Out the back, note the Thai-style spirit house with figures of St Joseph and St Paul.

GUIDED TOURS

Most guesthouses can arrange tours, though you'll usually get more options and flexibility by talking to a travel agency such as **Tour with Thai** (☑ 086 982 6265, 035 958226; http://tour-with-thai.business.site; Naresuan Soi 2; ☉ 8.30am-7pm).

The most promoted trip is a two-hour afternoon boat tour (200B per person) circling the island and stopping at Wat Phanan Choeng (p172), Wat Phutthai Sawan (p172) and Wat Chai Wattanaram (p171); it's a convenient, though rushed, way to see these three great off-island sites. You can also hire a boat on your own starting around 700B per hour: head up to the northeast corner of the island and look for one of the 'boat trip' signs near the immigration office (p176).

Ayutthaya Boat & Travel (☑ 081 733 5687; www.ayutthaya-boat.com; cnr Th Chee Kun & Th Rotchana; ☉ 9am-5pm Mon-Sat) offers lunch and dinner cruises on a teak rice barge, as well as longer cycling and boat tours, some with homestay accommodation.

Recreational Ayutthaya Biking (☑ 021 072500; www.ayutthayabiking.com; 141 Mu 1, Rte 3053; ☉ 8am-5pm) also has a few bike tours.

For a personal guided visit to the ruins, **Mr Pok** (☑ 081 253 9037; per hour 300B) comes highly recommended.

owner Kittiya has converted her wooden home into a three-room guesthouse that manages to be comfortable and cozy without covering up the historic feel. It's one of the friendliest places to stay in the city and is very convenient to the ruins.

★ The Treehouse
GUESTHOUSE $$

(☑ 081 627 6455; https://the-tree-house-organic-farm.business.site/; Mu 6, Ban Koh; r incl breakfast 900-1200B; ⓟ ⓢ) 🢅 Adventurous travellers will love this special countryside retreat 4km north of the island. The three guest rooms, giant deck and the bridge between them are built of wood – much of it reclaimed, giving it a castaway vibe – and one of the guest rooms is an actual tree house. Quarters are small and simple with bunk beds or mattresses on the floor and bathrooms require stepping outside.

The friendly owner makes breakfast from her organic garden and when you're back from roaming the ruins in the city you can swim or kayak in the Mae Lam Lopburi.

Reservations are required and minimum stay is two nights.

★ Tamarind Guesthouse
GUESTHOUSE $$

(☑ 089 010 0196, 081 655 7937; www.facebook.com/tamarindthai; off Th Chee Kun; d & tw 650-900B, f 1200B; ⓧ ⓢ) Service couldn't be friendlier at this guesthouse within an attractively and creatively modified wooden building. Hidden in a backstreet across from Wat Mahathat (p168), Tamarind feels like a retreat despite being close to major attractions. As in many wooden guesthouses,

creaky floors and thin walls aren't ideal for light sleepers; we think the traditional decor (colourful glass, repurposed painted wood) amply compensates.

★ Baifern
GUESTHOUSE $$

(☑ 035 242051; www.baifernhomestay.com; Th Khlongtho; d & tw incl breakfast 1200-1750B; ⓟ ⓧ ⓢ) One of the classiest guesthouses in Ayutthaya, Baifern's rooms are priced by size (sleeping up to four people) and attired with traditional fabrics and antique-effect furniture. There's an inviting lounge, a garden stalked by cats (and, unfortunately, plenty of mosquitoes) and an on-site restaurant serving tasty Thai food (mains around 120B).

Baan Bussara
GUESTHOUSE $$

(☑ 081 655 6379, 086 344 6186; www.facebook.com/Baanbussara; Th Bang Ian; r 650B; ⓧ ⓢ) Caring, attentive owners and a good, generally quiet location between Soi Farang and the Bang Ian Night Market (p175) make this one of the best guesthouses in this price range. The clean and comfortable rooms are large and equipped with desks and refrigerators.

Tony's Place
GUESTHOUSE $$

(☑ 035 252578; www.facebook.com/TonysPlace BedBreakfast; Naresuan Soi 2; d with air-con 600-850B, f with air-con 1200-1500B, d with fan and shared/private bath 200/400B; ⓧ ⓢ ⓢ) Tony's remains a prime destination for flashpackers and families thanks to its large outdoor **restaurant** (Naresuan Soi 2; mains 70-590B; ☉ 8am-10pm; ⓢ ⓢ) area (ideal for mingling), mini-pool and spacious, characterful rooms. Lodgings on the upper floor are the most attractive. The cheapest rooms are in an annexe and are quite basic.

Proximity to local bars makes Tony's a superb choice for night owls.

Sala Ayutthaya   BOUTIQUE HOTEL $$$
(☏035 242588; www.salaayutthaya.com; 9/2 Th U Thong, Mu 4; d incl breakfast 5870-11,680B; P✳🛜🏊) Stepping inside Sala Ayutthaya is reminiscent of entering one of the city's ruins, thanks to maze-like brick alcoves that lead to pure-white and wood-accented rooms and an equally minimalist pool and spa zone. The excellent (though pricey) restaurant, and some rooms, enjoy views across the river to Wat Phutthai Sawan (p172), especially magical when illuminated at night.

✕ Eating

Centuries of mingling with foreign traders has resulted in a wealth of food options in Ayuthaya. Defining dishes include river prawns, *roti săi măi* (sugary floss wrapped in a crepe) and boat noodles (*gŏo·ay đĕe·o reu·a;* pork noodle soup with a complex soy and pig's blood broth). Riverside restaurants tend to be expensive but usually worth it for quality and views.

Earl Restaurant   THAI $
(Th Naresuan; mains 45-80B; ⊙8am-10pm; 🖉) Fresh, flavourful food, low prices and a location near Wat Mahathat make this a great choice for lunch or dinner. And while you eat *gaeng gù·tí* (red curry) or *lâhp* (spicy, herbal mincemeat salad) you can also fill up on Ayuthaya info from Earl (pronounced Earn) himself.

Sainam Pomphet   THAI $
(Th U Thong; mains 70-400B; ⊙10am-10pm; P🛜) Spider crab – either steamed or fried with curry powder *(pàt pŏng gà·rèe)* – is the house speciality at this small riverside restaurant. Fish 'steamboat' dishes (in a simmering tureen) are also immensely popular. Those who aren't fans of seafood can tuck into a range of other Thai fare: try pineapple spare ribs or the spicy frog salad.

Outdoor seats gaze across the water and are kept cool by fans, and the live dinner music makes it a fully Thai experience.

Malakor   THAI $
(www.facebook.com/papayaoda; Th Chee Kun; mains 70-380B; ⊙restaurant 10.30am-10pm, coffee shop 8am-8pm; 🛜🖉) Targeting tourists but serving authentic flavours (unless you

ask them to make it milder), Malakor serves up southern catfish curry, *pàd gàprow gài* (chicken with basil) and a few Western dishes in a relaxing wooden hut. You will need to be patient with the service.

The downstairs coffee shop serves quality lattes and ice-blended drinks, best enjoyed with a brownie or slice of blueberry cake.

Bang Ian Night Market   MARKET $
(Th Bang Ian; mains from 30B; ⊙4.30-10pm; P) From fried fish to grilled bananas, this big, busy night market on its namesake street is a great destination for noshing. Sit-down dining is available at the east end.

Lung Lek   NOODLES $
(Th Chee Kun; mains 20-50B; ⊙8am-4pm Mon-Fri, 8am-4.30pm Sat & Sun) This locally adored hole-in-the-wall serves some of the most notable *gŏoay đĕeo reua* (boat noodles: a pork noodle soup with a complex soy and pig's-blood broth) in town. Uncle Lek has been filling bowls for more than four decades.

Gai Yang Mae Pong Sri   THAI $
(Th Pamaphrao; mains 40-80B; ⊙8.30am-5pm) This hole-in-the-wall Isan (northeastern Thai) joint around the corner from Soi Farang is in its fourth decade of serving spicy *sôm·đam* (papaya salad) and succulent *gài yâhng* (marinated grilled chicken).

The English-language menu includes a few central Thai dishes.

Coffee Old City   CAFE $
(Th Chee Kun; mains 59-129B; ⊙8am-5.30pm Mon-Sat; 🛜🖉) The location across from Wat Mahathat (p168) and air-con turned up to 11 make this a good place to recharge during a day of temple-hopping. There's shrimp noodle soup, croissant sandwiches, spicy spaghetti *kêe mow* and, of course, various forms of caffeine. It's all served amid cabinets full of traditional Thai art.

Talat Nam Wat Tha Ka Rong   MARKET $
(mains from 20B; ⊙8am-5pm Sat & Sun; P) Buying your food at this floating market, where vendors serve from boats tied to large rafts, is a great experience, though finding space at a table is less fun. It's on the Chao Phraya River behind its namesake temple (p172).

Roti Săi Măi Stalls   DESSERTS $
(Th U Thong; from 35B; ⊙6am-11pm) The dessert *roti săi măi* (silk thread roti) was invented in Ayuthaya and is sold all over town, though these stalls fronting the hospital are the most famous.

Buy a bag, then make your own by rolling together thin strands of melted palm sugar and wrapping them inside the sweet flatbread.

⭐ **Pae Krung Gao**   THAI **$$**
(Th U Thong; mains 60-700B; ☺10am-8pm; **P** 🛜) A wonderfully cluttered restaurant serving top-notch Thai food. Seemingly half the punters are here for grilled river prawns, though the *gaang kěe·o wǎhn* (green curry) and lotus stem salad are just as tasty.

Ban U-Thong   THAI **$$**
(Th U Thong; mains 80-390B; ☺10am-9.30pm; 🛜) One of many restaurants with riverside decks along this stretch of Mae Nam Chao Phraya, Ban U-Thong focuses on seafood, with grilled river prawns and fried fish with *sôm·đam* (spicy papaya salad) being popular picks, though the spicy *gaang ъàh* (forest curry) and banana blossom salad are pretty good, too.

🍸 Drinking & Nightlife

Most travellers limit their nightlife to the pack of street-side bars on Naresuan Soi 2 (Soi Farang). For a wholly Thai night out, there's the oddly named Coffee House (Th Naresuan; ☺6pm-midnight; 🛜) bar with live music nightly.

ℹ Information

EMERGENCIES
There is a **tourist police booth** (Th Si Sanphet; ☺7am-6pm) near the entrance to Wat Phra Si Sanphet, and a bit south is the main **tourist police station** (☏1155, 035 241446; Th Si Sanphet).

IMMIGRATION
Immigration Office (☏035 328411; Th U Thong; ☺8.30am-noon & 1-4.30pm Mon-Fri)

MEDICAL SERVICES
Phra Nakorn Si Ayuthaya Hospital (☏035 211888; www.ayhosp.go.th/ayh; Th U Thong) Near the historical park, this public hospital has an emergency centre.

Rajthanee Hospital (☏035 335555; www.rajthanee.com; Hwy 309) Private hospital with some English-speaking doctors, 4km east of the island.

MONEY
On the island, several banks have branches on Th Naresuan, and **Krungthai Bank** (KTB; ground fl, Amporn Department Store, Th Naresuan; ☺10am-1pm & 2-5.30pm) has an exchange booth open weekends in the Amporn Department Store. There are no full-service banks open evenings or weekends on or near the island, for that you need to go to **Ayutthaya City Park** (www.ayutthayacitypark.com; Hwy 32; ☺10am-9pm Sun-Thu, 10am-10pm Fri-Sat; 🛜) mall.

SAFE TRAVEL
When cycling, put bags around your body, not in baskets where they could be snatched. At night many packs of dogs roam the streets – keep your distance and avoid eye contact.

TOURIST INFORMATION
Tourism Authority of Thailand (TAT; ☏035 246076; tatyutya@tat.or.th; Th Si Sanphet; ☺8.30am-4.30pm) Has an information counter with maps and good advice at the Ayutthaya Tourist Center (p169).

ℹ Getting There & Away

BOAT
There are no public boats between Bangkok and Ayutthaya and the one-day 'cruises' available through travel agencies in Bangkok are really half-day Ayuthaya and Bang Pa In Palace bus tours with a three-hour boat ride through Bangkok at the start or end.

BUS & MINIVAN
Ayutthaya has two minivan stations on the island. The one just south of the backpacker strip is called **đà-làht tâh rót jôw prom** (Naresuan Soi 2) and it serves Suphanburi (transfer here for Kanchanaburi), Saraburi (for Pak Chong and Khorat) and Lopburi. A block and a half west is the **station** (Th Naresuan) for all destinations in Bangkok. Remember that in minivans you'll have to buy a second seat if you have a very big bag.

For Chiang Mai, Sukhothai and all destinations to the north, you'll need to go out to the **sai něua terminal** (☏035 335413; Hwy 32), 5km east of the island, though you can buy fee-free tickets from a town-centre **bus ticket office** (Th Naresuan; ☺7am-5pm). For a túk-túk/motorcycle taxi between the terminal and the island, expect to pay 150/70B.

Many people pay premium prices to book tickets at their hotel. The markup (usually about 150B per seat) includes transport to the station and sometimes a shower before departure. Many guesthouses also sell seats in private minivans to Kanchanaburi (350B, 2½ to three hours; 9am) and Aranya Prathet (at the Cambodian border; 500B; four to 4½ hours; five daily). The private minivans pickup at your hotel, but only go if there are enough passengers.

CAR
For a private sedan transfer between Bangkok and Ayutthaya, expect to pay about 1000B to

1500B (a few hundred less for a taxi) depending on your bartering power and the exact departure point. For a full day to and around Ayuthaya you're looking at about 2000B in a taxi and 3000B in a proper sedan. All prices include petrol and tolls.

TRAIN

Ayuthaya's **train station** (☎ 035 241521; Rte 3053) is conveniently located just across the river from the island. Trains are usually slower than buses and minibuses, except for those to Khao Yai National Park (Pak Chong station). For Bangkok, all trains stop at Bang Sue and Don Muang (for the airport) stations before arriving at Hua Lamphong.

If you're visiting Ayuthaya as a day trip before boarding an overnight train, there's luggage storage at the train station (6am to 11pm; per bag 10B); most guesthouses offer showers for 30B.

ⓘ Getting Around

BICYCLE & MOTORCYCLE

Cycling is the ideal way to see the city. Many guesthouses hire bicycles (per day 50B) and motorcycles (200B) and there are also rental

shops opposite Wat Ratchaburana (p168) and by both of the ferry piers by the train station. If you're staying in the southwest of the island, **Pak Khlong Tho** (☎ 087 668 7238; cnr Th U Thong and Th Khlongtho; ☉ 6.30am-8pm) has you covered.

Note that some shops hire for 24 hours and others for just the day, so be sure you know what you're getting.

BOAT

There are four river-ferry crossings, each different from the other. The most useful are the ferry between the **train station** (per person 5B, per bike 5B; ☉ 5am-8pm) and **Chao Phrom Market** (per person 5B, per bike 5B; ☉ 5am-8pm) (per person/bicycle 5/5B; 5am to 8pm) and the ferry between **Wat Khun Phrom** (per person 3B, per bike or motorcycle 5B; ☉ 24hrs) and **Sampao Lom** (per person 3B, per bike or motorcycle 5B; ☉ 24hrs) (person/bike or motorcycle 3/5B; 24 hours): both ferries run frequently and you pay at a table on the off-island side of the river.

An infrequent ferry runs between **Pom Phet** (per person 10B, per bike 10B; ☉ 7am-6pm), **Wat Bang Kracha** (per person 10B, per bike 10B; ☉ 7am-6pm) and **Wat Phanan Choeng** (per person 10B, per bike 10B; ☉ 7am-6pm)

BUSES FROM AYUTHAYA

DESTINATION	FARE (B)	DURATION (HR)	FREQUENCY
Bangkok (Don Mueang)	60	1	frequent (minivan)
Bangkok Northern (Mo Chit) bus terminal	60	1½	frequent (minivan)
Bangkok (Pinklao – nearest destination to Khao San Rd)	70	1½	every 30min (minivan)
BANGKOK (SOUTHERN BUS TERMINAL)	70	1½	every 30min (minivan)
Chiang Mai	412-823	8½-10	12 daily
Lopburi	60	1½	every 30min (minivan)
Saraburi	45	2	frequent
Sukhothai	263-338	6-7	6 daily
Suphanburi	80	1-1½	frequent (minivan)

TRAINS FROM AYUTHAYA

DESTINATION	FARE (B)	DURATION (HR)	FREQUENCY
Bang Pa In	3-20	¼	16 daily
Bangkok Hua Lamphong station	15-345	1½-2	frequent
Chiang Mai	221-1898	10-13	5 daily
Nong Khai	202-2302	8-10½	4 daily
Pak Chong	23-363	2-3	10 daily
Ubon Ratchathani	195-2268	7-10½	8 daily

(person/bicycle 10/10B ; 7am to 6pm); you may have to stand on the pier waiting awhile. To the west, the ferry (3B; 24 hours) near **Phra Nakorn Si Ayuthaya Hospital** (tâh reua nâh rohng pá·yah·bahn; per person 3B; ⊙24hr) on one side and **Wat Phutthai Sawan** (tâh reua nâh rohng pá·yah·bahn; per person 3B; ⊙24hr) on the other only carries people, no bikes. For these two ferries, you pay the driver.

CAR & TÚK-TÚK

Túk-túks are readily available (and in Ayuthaya are different from the classic Thai design thanks to their dome-shaped fronts, resembling Darth Vader's iconic mask). The drivers' initial offer is certain to be high, but for most one-way trips on the island the rate will be 50B to 100B. The going rate per hour visiting the sites is 200B, but half- and full-day hires should get discounts. For a túk-túk between the Northern bus terminal and the old city, expect to pay 150B. If rates sound cheap, check that driver isn't giving you the rate per person, rather than the total price. Motorcycle taxis are also easy to find and charge half what túk-túks do.

The standard rate for a sedan with driver is 300B per hour or 2000B per day including petrol. Arrange through your hotel or call **Nong Car Rental** (☑084 775 3409; www.facebook.com/CarRentCarNong).

Around Ayuthaya

Most day trip tours from Bangkok to Ayuthaya include dazzling Bang Pa In Palace, and it's really worth the time.

★**Bang Pa In Palace**　　　　PALACE
(พระราชวังบางปะอิน; 100B; ⊙8am-5pm, last entrance 4pm; P) Ornate buildings are sprinkled across Bang Pa In Palace's 19-hectare gardens. First established in the 17th century, the palace was revived in the 19th century by kings Rama IV and V, the latter adding most of its European styling. Today an eclectic assortment of architectural styles is arranged around manicured lawns, including the intricate Chinese-style Wehart Chamrun, the orange-and-red-striped observatory Ho Withun Thasana (1881) and a Thai pavilion that appears to float on the water. Dress modestly.

The palace grounds are ideal for strolling but renting an electric buggy (400B for one hour, 100B per hour thereafter) is a handy way to stay in the shade.

To reach the palace, take the train from Ayuthaya (3B to 20B, 15 minutes, 16 daily) to Bang Pa In station and then jump on a motorcycle taxi (around 20B) or túk-túk (50B) to the palace, which is 1.7km away. If you're driving, there's a large car park nearby (20B per vehicle).

Round-trip taxi transfers from Ayuthaya should cost around 800B.

Wat Niwet Thamaprawat　　BUDDHIST TEMPLE
(วัดนิเวศธรรมประวัติราชวรวิหาร; Bang Pa In; ⊙daylight hours; P) FREE On an island across the Chao Phraya River from Bang Pa In Palace (p178), this unique buttercup-yellow *ubosot* (ordination hall) was designed to resemble a European Gothic cathedral. And since its spire holds a Buddha relic, it's actually a one-of-a-kind stupa. Inside you can admire stained-glass windows and gilded filigree that wouldn't look out of place in a European church.

Take a free, monk-operated cable car across the river from the palace parking lot (leave a donation in the boxes).

LOPBURI PROVINCE

Lopburi

POP 161,000

In Thailand's 'Monkey City', imposing Khmer-era temples are assailed by an army of furry menaces. These adorable mischief-makers have the run of the town and are the headline attraction of Lopburi (ลพบุรี).

One of Thailand's oldest cities, Lopburi developed during the Dvaravati period (6th to 10th centuries), when it was known as Lavo. The palaces and temples that remain today, in various states of decay, are from the subsequent Khmer and Ayuthaya empires. King Narai (r 1657–88) made Lopburi a second capital, hosting many foreign dignitaries.

The 'old town' spreads northwest from the train station and encompasses Lopburi's temples and ruins. The 'new town' to the east has some of the best accommodation options.

The main sights can be seen in a day, but it's worth staying one more to venture out of the city for rock climbing, sunflower fields (November to January) and bat caves.

⦿ Sights

★**Prang Sam Yot**　　　　RUINS
(ปรางค์สามยอด; cnr Th Wichayen & Th Prang Sam Yot; 50B, combo ticket 150B; ⊙8.30am-6pm) As well known for its resident monkeys as its

looming towers, this is Lopburi's most famous attraction. The three linked towers were built from laterite and sandstone by the Khmer in the 13th century as a Mahayana Buddhist temple. It was converted to Theravada Buddhism by King Narai in the 17th century (there may have been a period of Shiva worship in between). Two ruined, headless Buddha images are inside; a third, more complete Buddha sits photogenically in front of the central tower.

Visitors can enter through a heavy metal door that keeps the monkeys out. The monkeys here are especially playful and while many people enjoy it, you can also borrow a stick from the ticket office to keep them away.

This is one of the combined ticket sites.

★ Phra Narai Ratchaniwet   MUSEUM

(วังนารายณ์ราชนิเวศน์, Somdet Phra Narai National Museum; ☎ 036 414372; entrance Th Sorasak; 150B; ◷ museum 8.30am-4.30pm Wed-Sun, grounds 7.30am-5pm daily) Plan to spend a few hours at this former royal palace, now the Somdet Phra Narai National Museum, which houses excellent displays of local history. Built from 1665 with help from French and Italian engineers, the palace was abandoned after King Narai's death, but reclaimed by King Rama IV (r 1851–68), and the main displays, including prehistoric jewellery and Khmer-era statues, are in his residence. Many of his personal belongings are displayed on the 3rd floor.

Next door are displays in memory of King Narai, out back are the Phra Pratiap Buildings (used primarily by queens, consorts and other women who travelled with the king), used for temporary exhibitions and storage.

After seeing the museum displays, take some time to roam the manicured palace grounds full of trees and ruins, including King Narai's elephant stables and a banquet room for receiving foreign visitors.

Enter through Pratu Phayakkha gate on Th Sorasak.

San Phra Kan   SHRINE

(ศาลพระกาฬ; Th Wichayen; ◷ 5.30am-5.30pm) **FREE** Lopburi's holiest place sits in the old town's roundabout. It has a modern (1951) shrine in front of a Khmer-era laterite base from a toppled *prang* (Khmer-style spire) that was previously known as the 'supreme shrine'. The principal statue inside is a four-armed Vishnu body in Lopburi-Khmer style with an Ayuthaya-era Buddha head attached.

ⓘ TICKETS

A single ticket (150B), valid for one day, covers Prang Sam Yot, Wat Phra Si Ratana Mahathat, Ban Wichayen and the distant, seldom-visited **Kraison Siharat Palace** (พระที่นั่งไกรสรสีหราช; Yen Palace; Soi Bun Pradit; 50B; ◷ 8.30am-4pm; 🅿).

People feed the monkeys milk, biscuits, fruit and other things throughout the day (and as a result they are unafraid of humans, so be wary of them), and a *lam* dance troupe performs from 8am to 1pm. Both are done as thanks to the 'black god' (the city's guardian spirit) after wishes are granted.

Wat Phra Si Ratana Mahathat   RUINS

(วัดพระศรีรัตนมหาธาตุ; Th Na Phra Kan; 50B, combo ticket 150B; ◷ 8.30am-4.30pm) Although almost every building at this large temple complex across from the train station dates from the Ayuthaya era; the 31m-tall *prang* (Khmer-style spire) at its heart was built by the Khmer in the late 13th century and it's still the tallest in Lopburi. It's a beautiful structure built mostly of laterite and stucco. The temple is one of the combined ticket (p179) sites.

Wat Phra Phutthabat   BUDDHIST TEMPLE

(วัดพระพุทธบาท; off Hwy 1, Saraburi; ◷ daylight hours; 🅿) **FREE** One of Thai Buddhism's holiest sites, this temple was founded in 1624 after the discovery of a natural depression in the rock resembling a footprint, which fit with local legend about the Buddha visiting what is now Thailand. The footprint now sits under a dazzling *mondap* (square, spired building) and merit-makers come from all corners of Thailand to put a piece of gold leaf on it.

Ban Wichayen   RUINS

(บ้านวิชาเยนทร์; Th Wichayen; 50B, combo ticket 150B; ◷ 8.30am-4pm) This compound, built in European style by King Narai, served as the residence of foreign ambassadors. It got its present name from the mistaken belief that it was the residence of infamous Greek trader Constantine Phaulkon (whose official Thai title was Chao Phraya Wichayen), who became a key adviser to the king. The middle of the three buildings was a Catholic church, but decorated with Thai-style trim around the doors and windows. It's one of the combined ticket sites.

Lopburi

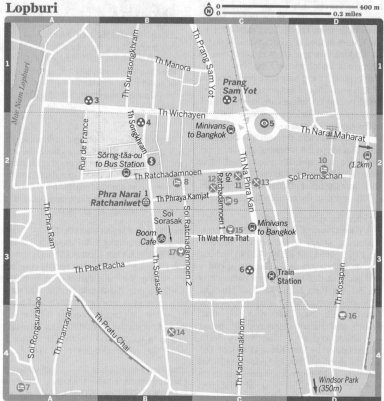

Lopburi

◎ Top Sights
1	Phra Narai Ratchaniwet	B2
2	Prang Sam Yot	C1

◎ Sights
3	Ban Wichayen	A1
4	Prang Khaek	B2
5	San Phra Kan	C2
6	Wat Phra Si Ratana Mahathat	C3

◎ Sleeping
7	Little Lopburi Village	A4
8	Nett Hotel	B2

9	Noom Guesthouse	C2
10	Pee Homestay	D2

◎ Eating
11	Khao Tom Hor	C2
12	Matini	C2
13	Night Market	C2
	Noom Restaurant	(see 9)
14	Vietnamese Restaurant by Khun Dai	B4

◎ Drinking & Nightlife
15	Come On Bar	C3
16	Lopburi Art Gallery	D4
17	Sahai Phanta	B3

Prang Khaek　　　　　　　　　　RUINS
(ปรางค์แขก; Th Songkhram; ⊘24hr) **FREE** The oldest monument in Lopburi, this 10th-century trio of brick towers was built by the Khmer, probably for the Hindu god Shiva. King Narai had it rebuilt after it collapsed and added the two other buildings.

It looks rather forlorn, pincered between two roads in the heart of the city.

✻ Festivals & Events

King Narai Fair　　　　　　　　CULTURAL
(⊘mid-Feb) Held annually at Phra Narai Ratchaniwet (p179), this weeklong fair

celebrates Ayuthaya's most revered monarch, who transformed Lopburi into a cultural and diplomatic centre. The festival features re-enactments of period ceremonies and other cultural activities, including a 'retro market' using shells as a historic currency.

There's also a sound-and-light show with battle re-enactments. Note that elephant processions feature in this festival.

Monkey Festival CULTURAL
(⊙late Nov) For Lopburi's thousands of simian inhabitants, this is the best day of the year. Beautiful buffet tables laden with fruits and sweets are set out several times during the day for the monkeys to devour. There's also a street fair and dance shows around town.

It's usually held the last Sunday in November.

🛏 Sleeping

Budget rooms are pretty much the only choice in the old town. The new town has a better range of hotels – mostly very far to the east – but there's surprisingly still a lack of genuinely good choices.

Pee Homestay HOMESTAY $
(☑086 164 2184; www.lopburimassage.com; Soi Promachan; d with fan 280-360B, with air-con 340-500B; ❄️🛜) This homestay northeast of the train station is run by the superfriendly Kanaree, a beautician and massage therapist. It's a laid-back local experience. The spick-and-span rooms, priced by size, have private, cold-water baths.

Kanaree has bikes for hire for her guests. Stay three nights, get one free.

Noom Guesthouse GUESTHOUSE $
(☑036 427693; Th Phraya Kamjat; dm 180B, d/tr without bathroom & fan 350/600, d with air-con 550B; ❄️🛜) Easily the most *fa·ràng*-friendly spot in town, family-run Noom has dorms in its wooden house and cozy little bungalows in back. Even if you aren't staying here, it's worth swinging by to rent a motorbike (from 300B), book a climbing tour or swap travel stories with backpackers in the restaurant (p182).

Nett Hotel HOTEL $
(☑036 411738; netthotel@hotmail.com; Soi Ratchadamnoen 2; d/tw with fan 350/450B, d/tw/tr with air-con 500/550/590B; P❄️🛜) New paint, tiles, and owners (the same as Noom Guesthouse) have breathed new life into this

old-school concrete box of a hotel. The main reason to stay here is for up-close monkey viewing from the caged rooftop. But know that resident monkeys can mean monkey odour, so give the room a sniff test before taking it. The cheapest rooms have cold-water showers.

Little Lopburi Village GUESTHOUSE $$
(☑085 484 2691, 061 475 2384; www.homestayin thai.com; Mu 2, Soi Rongsurakao; d/f 1300/1500B, d with fan and shared bath 500B; P❄️🛜) Large wooden bungalows sit at the back of a quiet garden in a very local neighbourhood just a short walk from Lopburi's main attractions. The price is a tad high, but these are among the best rooms in town, and the friendly English-speaking owners provide great hospitality. Reservations are required.

Note that the family room is just mattresses on the floor.

Windsor Park HOTEL $$
(☑036 411689; off Hwy 3196; d/tw/tr incl breakfast 650/680/800B; P❄️🛜) Sitting 1km south of the train station, this peach-coloured place doesn't have the best rooms in Lopburi, but it has the best combination of quality and location of any regular hotel in town. Next door are bungalows of a similar quality. Both suffer train noise, though there aren't many trains.

It has bikes for guests and will pick you up when you arrive in town.

🍴 Eating

The modest **night market** (Th Na Phra Kan; mains from 30B; ⊙4-10pm) has plenty of cheap eats and there's a good variety of restaurants on Th Phraya Kamjat and Th Sorasak. Overall, the dining scene isn't one of the town's strong points.

Vietnamese Restaurant by Khun Dai VIETNAMESE $
(☑036 411220; 43 Th Sorasak; mains 40-100B; ⊙11am-7.30pm; 🛜) Excellent spicy pork, pho, and mint-stuffed spring rolls cooked and served by a friendly Thai woman who fell in love with food from the east.

Khao Tom Hor THAI, CHINESE $
(☑036 411672; www.facebook.com/khaotomhor. lopburi; Th Na Phra Kan; mains 40-150B; ⊙5pm-3am; 🅿️) Constantly busy Khao Tom Hor offers Thai-Chinese dishes, including *plaa salid tôrd* (deep-fried salted fish) and fried tofu with chilli. Service is speedy and the food is delicious.

LOCAL KNOWLEDGE

MONKEY MAYHEM

Grown men arm their catapults, old women wield 2m-long poles and tourists alternately shriek and pose for photos. Welcome to Lopburi, a town that fights a losing battle to keep its iconic monkeys at bay. Hundreds of rhesus and crab-eating macaques (and cross-breeds of the two species) roam a wide swathe of the old city via its rooftops and power cables. They climb on cars, slide down sunshades and squabble over scraps, putting on a nonstop show that has put 'Monkey City' on the travel map.

Monkeys may be cute, but they are wild animals. Don't carry food (or anything that could be mistaken for food) within the monkey zone; otherwise, expect a dash-and-grab robbery. If you do suffer a mugging, don't resist – monkeys bite, and if this happens you'll need medical attention for potential diseases. It's also prudent to avoid walking below them (unless you're carrying an umbrella).

Seating in the one air-conditioned room costs 10B per person.

Matini INTERNATIONAL $
(18 Th Phraya Kamjat; mains 50-350B; ⊘9am-late; ☎🌐) Free pool, a Blues Brothers motif on the wall and good food (both Thai and Western) plant Matini firmly in the sights of backpackers. With indoor and outdoor areas, this is a great spot to tuck into sizeable portions of richly spiced curries (including veggie options), sip on smoothies or kick back late with a few beers.

It closes up during the hot season.

Noom Restaurant INTERNATIONAL $
(☎036 427693; Th Phraya Kamjat; mains 40-205B; ⊘8am-9.30pm; ☎🌐) Part of the backpacker-magnet guesthouse (p181), Noom is best at breakfast with options spanning muesli to *jóhk* (soupy boiled rice). There's also *pàt tai*, massaman curry and spaghetti.

Bua Luang THAI, CHINESE $$
(☎036 413009; www.facebook.com/bualuang.1980; Hwy 1; mains 65-380B; ⊘9.30am-10pm; 🅿☎🌐) This large Lopburi landmark in the far east end of town has a leafy outdoor dining area and white-linen indoor rooms. It serves a typical Thai-Chinese menu including *pàt pŏng gà·rèe* (crab in yellow curry), steamed white snapper and local favourite: stir-fried sunflower sprouts.

🍷 Drinking & Nightlife

Most locals head out in the new town, but the old town does have a handful of places for a beer-steeped evening. Traveller havens Noom (p181) and Matini (p182) both attract foreigners keen to shoot the breeze over pool and cocktails, while locals head to Come On (Th Wat Phra That; ⊘hours vary) for beers and Sahai

Phanta (Soi Sorasak; ⊘8pm-late) for whisky and live music.

The **Lopburi Art Gallery** (☎083 009 6175; www.facebook.com/Lopburi-Art-Gallery 209314409929805/; Th Kosapan; ⊘10am-9pm; ☎) is a good place to sit and relax with green tea, Ovaltine, longan juice and French fries. There are three floors of gallery and studio space with work from local artists on the walls.

ℹ Information

EMERGENCY

Lopburi's **tourist police** (☎036 424515; Th Narai Maharat) office is in the new town.

IMMIGRATION

Visa extensions are available at **Lopburi Immigration** (☎036 424686; Rte 1036; ⊘8.30am-noon & 1pm-4.30pm Mon-Fri).

MEDICAL SERVICES

Mueang Narai Hospital (โรงพยาบาลเมือง นารายณ์; ☎036 420666; www.mueangnarai. com; Hwy 1; ⊘24hr) For monkey bites or more serious health needs. It's in the far east end of town.

MONEY

There are several banks in the northern half of old Lopburi along Th Songkhram, including **Siam Commercial Bank** (Th Songkhram; ⊘8.30am-3.30pm Mon-Fri), though none are open evenings or weekends. For this you'll need to go to one of the shopping malls along Hwy 1 in the new town.

TOURIST INFORMATION

The **Tourism Authority of Thailand** (TAT; ☎036 770096; tatlobri@tat.or.th; Th Narai Maharat; ⊘8.30am-4.30pm) has helpful staff, but an inconvenient new town location. Noom Guesthouse (p181) can answer most questions about Lopburi.

ℹ Getting There & Away

Transport is quick and frequent to Ayuthaya and Bangkok, 70km and 150km away, respectively, but bus service to elsewhere is quite limited.

BUS & MINIVAN

Lopburi lies well off the main north–south highway, which means direct bus routes are limited. For Kanchanaburi you'll need to make a connection in Ayuthaya or Bangkok. Lopburi's **bus station** (☑036 411888; Sa Kaew Circle) is 2.5km east of the old town.

Besides the bus station, minivans to Bangkok depart from the **north** (Th Na Phra Kan by San Phra Kan shrine) and **south** (Th Na Phra Kan) ends of Th Na Phra Kan; the latter has an air-con waiting room.

TRAIN

Lopburi is on the northern train line, so many people visit as a day trip before continuing to Chiang Mai. The **train station** (☑036 411022; Th Na Phra Kan) is in the old town and has luggage storage for 15B per bag and showers for 10B.

ℹ Getting Around

Sŏrng·tăa·ou (Th Ratchadamnoen; 8B) run from Th Ratchadamnoen then down Th Wichayen and past San Phra Kan to the bus station (p183). *Săhm·lór* (three-wheel pedicabs) and motorcycle taxis will go anywhere in the old town for around 20B and to the bus station for 40B. Noom Guesthouse (p181) and **Boom Cafe** (www.facebook.com/BOOMCAFELopburi;

Th Sorasak; bike/motorcycle per day 60/300B; ⊙10am-8pm) both hire motorcycles (per day 300B) and the latter also has bicycles (60B).

KANCHANABURI PROVINCE

Given the jaw-dropping natural beauty of Kanchanaburi Province (กาญจนบุรี), it seems paradoxical that the region is best known for the horrors of WWII's Death Railway. The provincial capital's war memorials are a mandatory stop before heading deeper into the parks and preserves that comprise the southern end of the Western Forest Complex, one of Asia's largest protected areas. Numerous waterfalls and caves can be reached with minimal effort, but hiking trails plunging into thick jungle also lure hardened adventurers to this wild terrain.

In the far north, relaxed Sangkhlaburi is one of Thailand's most ethnically diverse towns. Many residents arrived to escape violence in Myanmar, and they've been joined by communities of foreign volunteers.

And if Sangkhlaburi isn't far-flung enough for you, the little border outpost of E-Thong, which improbably managed to avoid becoming a ghost town, should be on your itinerary.

BUSES FROM LOPBURI

DESTINATION	FARE (B)	DURATION (HR)	FREQUENCY
Ayuthaya	60	1½	every 30min (minivan)
Bangkok	110-120	2½	frequent (minivan)
Nakhon Ratchasima (Khorat)	148	3½-4	every 30min (minivan)
Nakhon Ratchasima (Khorat)	164	4-4½	6 daily (bus)
Pak Chong	80	2	every 30min (minivan)
Pak Chong	95	2½	6 daily (bus)
Saraburi	38	1	frequent (minivan)

TRAINS FROM LOPBURI

DESTINATION	FARE (B)	DURATION (HR)	FREQUENCY
Ayuthaya	13-340	½-1½	16 daily
Bangkok Hualamphong	28-374	2-3½	16 daily
Chiang Mai	252-2353	9-12	5 daily
Phitsanulok	49-1546	3-5	11 daily

KHAO CHIN LAE

The rugged mountains visible in the distance from Lopburi make a worthwhile day trip for outdoor enthusiasts and temple-hoppers.

For a serene excursion, head to Wat Khao Chin Lae (วัดเขาจีนแล, Peacock Temple; ☺ daylight hours; P) FREE, perched on the southeastern edge of the range 15km from Lopburi. It's home to hundreds of peacocks and fantastic views of the forest-clad mountains and nearby sunflower fields (blooming November to January). The latter are Lopburi's second claim to fame after its monkeys. Just 5km east of the temple by road is Ang Sap Lek (อ่างเก็บน้ำซับเหล็ก; ☺ daylight hours) FREE, a reservoir lined by restaurants with rafts and piers for eating lunch and dinner out over the water.

Want something more adrenaline drenched? Plan a rock climbing excursion with Noom Guesthouse (p181). The main point for rock-climbing is the 240m sheer peak soaring behind Wat Pa Suwannahong (northeast of Wat Khao Chin Lae). Another thrill is the large bat cave at Kao Ta Kra Thong (วัดเขาตะกร้าทอง, Wat Kao Ta Kra Thong; ☺ daylight hours; P) FREE mountain where hundreds of thousands of bats emerge for their nocturnal hunt just before sunset. Noom offers afternoon tours (800B to 1250B for groups of one to five people) to these sites plus Wat Phra Phutthabat (p179), the famous Buddha footprint temple in nearby Saraburi Province.

If you just want to see the sunflowers, take the bus heading to Wang Muang and get off around the turnoff (15B, 30 to 45 minutes, departures about every hour) north to Wat Khao Chin Lae where you will see some of the yellow fields unfurling.

Kanchanaburi

POP 94,600

Beyond its hectic modern centre and river views, Kanchanaburi has a dark history, paid tribute to at excellent memorials and museums. During WWII, Japanese forces used Allied prisoners of war (POWs) and conscripted Asian labourers to build a rail route from Thailand to Burma (Myanmar). The harrowing story became famous after the publication of Pierre Boulle's book *The Bridge Over the River Kwai*, based very loosely on real events, and the 1957 movie that followed. War cemeteries, museums and the chance to ride a section of the so-called 'Death Railway' draw numerous visitors to Kanchanaburi.

Kanchanaburi is also an ideal gateway to Thailand's wild west. There are some excellent national parks and an array of lush riverside resorts to the north, and many of them are accessible by public transport.

◉ Sights

◉ In Town

★ Death Railway Bridge   HISTORIC SITE
(สะพานข้ามแม่น้ำแคว, Bridge Over the River Kwai; ☺ 24hr) FREE Constructed by POW labour, this 300m-long bridge is heavy with the history of the Thailand–Burma Railway. Its

centre was destroyed by Allied bombs in 1945, so only the curved spans are original. You're free to roam over the bridge; stand in a safety point if a train appears. Food and souvenir hawkers surround the bridge, so the site can have a jarring, funfair-like atmosphere; come early or late to avoid the scrum.

The three old trains in the park near the station were used during WWII. Across the river, pop in to the colourful Kuan-Im Shrine on the right and view the bridge from its tranquil garden. On the south side of the shrine is the unique Chinese Soldier Tomb, with sad eyes peering out from under a giant helmet. Nothing remains of a second (wooden) bridge the Japanese built 100m downstream.

During late November or early December, a sound-and-light show (p189) tells the history of the Death Railway (p190).

★ Thailand–Burma
Railway Centre   MUSEUM
(ศูนย์รถไฟไทย-พม่า; ☑ 034 512721; www.tbrconline.com; 73 Th Jaokannun; adult/child 150/70B; ☺ 9am-5pm) This excellent museum balances statistics and historical context with personal accounts of the conditions endured by POWs and other imprisoned labourers forced to build the Thailand–Burma Railway. Kanchanaburi's role in WWII is thoroughly explained, but most of the museum

traces the journey of railway workers from transport in cramped boxcars to disease-ridden labour camps in the jungle, as well as survivors' fates after the war. Allow time for the poignant video with testimony from both POWs and Japanese soldiers.

Galleries upstairs display wartime artefacts, and there's a 3m-deep diorama showing how Hellfire Pass got its name.

You'll need at least an hour for your visit. For in-depth wartime and railway history, the centre can organise half-day (per two people 4100B) to multiday tours in and around Kanchanaburi. Advanced booking is required; enquire via its website (under 'Railway Pilgrimages').

Heritage Walking Street   AREA
(ถนนปากแพรก; Th Pakprak) A stroll along this city centre street offers a glimpse of a bygone Kanchanaburi. Many buildings date to the 1920s and '30s and their Sino-Portuguese, Thai, Vietnamese and Chinese styles have been preserved; faded yellow signs reveal the history, architecture and present owners of about 20 of them. WWII buffs should include this on their pilgrimage because some of the structures are connected to the construction of the Death Railway (p190).

The walk begins at the restored City Gate (ประตูเมือง; Th Lak Meuang).

JEATH War Museum   MUSEUM
(พิพิธภัณฑ์สงคราม; cnr Th Wisuttharangsi & Th Pak Phraek; 50B; ⏰8am-5pm) This small museum, opened in 1977, mostly focuses on the terrible ordeals of the POWs who built the Death Railway. Their harsh living conditions are shown in many original photos, letters and drawings from that time as well as personal effects and war relics, including an unexploded Allied bomb dropped to destroy the bridge. One of the three galleries is built from bamboo in the style of the shelters (called *attap*) the POWs lived in.

JEATH is an acronym of the warring countries involved in the railway: Japan, England, Australia/America, Thailand and Holland. This acronym is also used on signs outside the WWII Museum (พิพิธภัณฑ์สงครามโลกครั้งที่สอง; Art Gallery & War Museum; Th Mae Nam Khwae; 40B; ⏰8am-6pm), which causes some confusion – the two museums are not connected.

Kanchanaburi War Cemetery   CEMETERY
(สุสานทหารพันธมิตรดอนรัก, Allied War Cemetery; Th Saengchuto; ⏰daylight hours) FREE Immaculately maintained by the Commonwealth War Graves Commission, this is the larger of Kanchanaburi's two war cemeteries, and is right in town. Of the 6982 soldiers buried here, nearly half were British; the rest came mainly from Australia and the Netherlands. As you stand at the cemetery entrance, the entire right-hand side contains British victims, the front-left area contains Australian graves and the rear left the Dutch. The remains of unknown soldiers and 300 who were cremated due to dying of cholera are honoured all the way to the far left at the front.

All remains of American POWs were returned to the USA. If you're looking for the resting place of a loved one, a register is kept at the entrance.

👁 Outside Town

⭐ Wat Ban Tham   BUDDHIST TEMPLE
(วัดบ้านถ้ำ; Tambon Khao Noi; ⏰temple daylight hours, stairway 8am-5pm; P) FREE In the countryside around Kanchanaburi, cave temples are almost as common as convenience stores are inside the city, but this is one of the most interesting, in part because you walk up steps and into a dragon's mouth to reach the large main cave.

Wat Ban Tham is 10km southeast of town (4km before Wat Tham Seua (p187)) on the south bank of the river .

A section of one big rock is said to resemble Thai folklore figure Mae Nang Bua Kli, an innocent woman killed by her husband, and is regularly 'dressed' throughout the year. Above her is a Phra Siwali (an important disciple of the Buddha) statue illuminated by a single shaft of sunlight each cloudless morning. Continuing up the mountain on the metal spiral staircase at the cave entrance takes you to some minor shrines and major views. Tham Man Wichit cave, near the top, has steps, lights and some lovely rock formations.

Wat Tham Khao Pun   BUDDHIST TEMPLE
(วัดถ้ำเขาปูน; Rte 3228; 30B; ⏰6am-6pm; P) The nearest cave temple to Kanchanaburi town is a fun labyrinth of illuminated passageways. The marked trail is a bit of a squeeze in some places (and can be slippery), but ducking beneath limestone protrusions to discover these subterranean shrines is a special experience. It's a stop on the standard boat tour, but still rarely busy, so it might just be you and some fluttering bats. The temple is 4km southwest of town, beyond Chungkai War Cemetery (p186).

Kanchanaburi Province

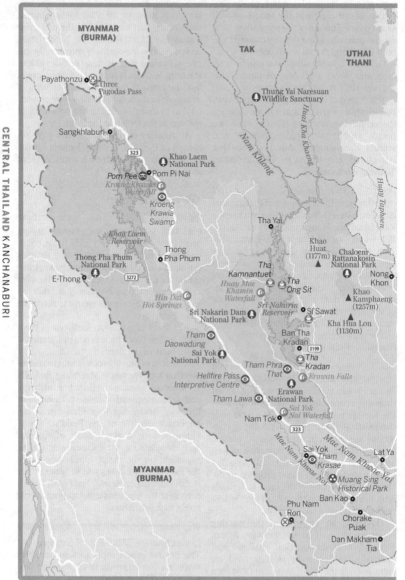

Chungkai War Cemetery   CEMETERY
(สุสานทหารพันธมิตรช่องไก่; Rte 3228; ☉ daylight
hours; 🅿) **FREE** The site of one of the biggest Allied POW camps, Chungkai honours
1426 Commonwealth and 313 Dutch soldiers. Prisoners built their own hospital and
church close by and the majority of those

buried here died at the hospital. The cemetery is near the river, 2.5km southwest of
the Wat Thewa Sangkharam bridge, and is
easily reached by bicycle. It's smaller and
less visited than the Kanchanaburi War
Cemetery (p185) in town, but just as well
maintained.

donations into a central bowl with a resounding clang. It's fun to ride the steep cable car (20B per person) to the top of the temple, but you can also climb the stairs.

Surrounding the main Buddha image are several styles of stupa. The biggest, nine stories (69m) high, is full of murals (mostly about war with Burma) and Buddha images, many in seldom seen postures. The namesake **Tiger Cave**, flanked by brightly painted tiger statues, is at the base of the hill, to the right (west) of the cable car. A former abbot's mummified body is on display in the big hall next to the cave.

The Chinese-style temple next door is **Wat Tham Khao Noi**, which is more interesting outside than in.

Wat Tham Seua is 14km southeast of central Kanchanaburi. After crossing the city's southernmost bridge, make the first left and follow the river. There's no public transport.

🏃 Activities

⭐ SUP Hire Thailand
WATER SPORTS
(☑ 090 975 9718; www.supkanchanaburi.com; Hwy 323, Tambon Kaeng Sian; ☉ hours vary) This responsible outfit has standup paddleboarding (SUP) lessons, trips and rentals with good instructors and equipment. Short and long trips are available, and for the uninitiated there's a two-hour 'taster session' (per person 450B, private lesson 800B) on a beautiful stretch of Mae Nam Kwae Yai just outside town. Also offers guided bike rides with high-quality hybrids, which can be combined with paddling.

🎒 Courses

⭐ Apple & Noi Thai Cooking
COOKING
(☑ 062 324 5879, 034 512017; www.applenoi kanchanaburi.com/apple-noi-cooking; Blue Rice restaurant, Mu 4, Ban Tamakham; per person 1950B; ☉ Tue, Wed, Fri & Sat) If you don't know your *sôm-đam* from your *đôm yam*, Khun Noi can assist. Her very popular one-day course has an emphasis on local recipes and seasonal produce, beginning at the local market and ending, four dishes later, at the dining table. Book well ahead.

Multiday courses are also available.

👉 Tours

Since there are many good sights outside the city, tours are a welcome option; though if you have a small group it is usually cheaper to hire a driver and plan your movements independently. Day trips generally cost around

Wat Tham Seua
BUDDHIST TEMPLE
(วัดถ้ำเสือ; Tambon Muang Chum; ☉ daylight hours; 🅿) **FREE** The centrepiece of this hilltop temple is a striking 18m-high Buddha covered in golden mosaic. One of the merit-making ceremonies for devotees is to place coins in small trays on a conveyor belt that drops

Kanchanaburi

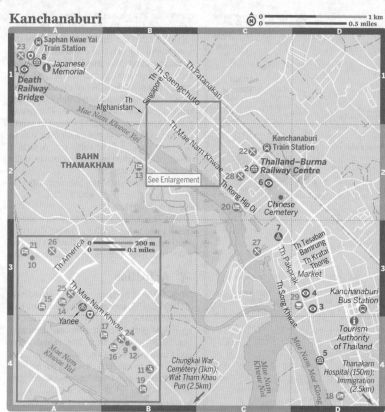

CENTRAL THAILAND KANCHANABURI

Kanchanaburi

800B to 1200B per person (prices are sometimes negotiable), including admission fees, lunch and bamboo rafting. Note that many of the trips also include tiger encounters and elephant riding, which we strongly discourage; they are harmful to the animals and not good in any way for conservation efforts.

Most companies, including long-standing reputable choices such as (but not limited to) Good Times Travel ($\boxed{\mathcal{J}}$081 913 7758, 034 624441; www.good-times-travel.com; Th Mae Nam Khwae; day tour per person from 800B; ⊙9am-9pm) and Toi's Tours ($\boxed{\mathcal{J}}$034 514209, 081 856 5523; Th Mae Nam Khwae; day tour per person from 790B; ⊙7am-10pm), do similar group-tour itineraries. One popular programme is a day to Erawan Falls (p194), Hellfire Pass (พิพิธภัณฑ์ช่องเขาขาด; $\boxed{\mathcal{J}}$034 919605; Hwy 323; ⊙museum 9am-4pm, grounds daylight hours; $\boxed{P}$) FREE and the Death Railway's 'wooden bridge' at Tham Krasae (p190). There's usually not enough interest in longer and more adventurous options, such as Huay Mae Khamin waterfall in Sri Nakarin Dam National Park (p194) or jungle trekking, but they can be done as private trips, which is the speciality of the animal-friendly Mellow Adventures ($\boxed{\mathcal{J}}$084 727 1959; www.mellowadventures.com; 295/5 Th Mae Nam Khwae; ⊙9am-5pm) ✦. For something different, enjoy beautiful river scenery from a standup paddleboard (p187).

The Thailand–Burma Railway Centre (p184) can organise tours in and around Kanchanaburi.

🎋 Festivals & Events

River Kwai Bridge Week   LIGHT SHOW
(Death Railway Bridge; 100-500B; ⊙late Nov/early Dec) The main event of this 10-day festival is a sound-and-light show retelling the sobering history of Kanchanaburi's Death Railway (p190), built by prisoners of war and Asian labourers in appalling conditions. Less solemn are the accompanying fireworks display, concerts and food fair.

🛏 Sleeping

Most travellers flock to the plentiful (and mostly ageing) accommodation along Th Mae Nam Khwae; it's centrally located and within walking distance from the bridge and main train station (p193). Many digs sit alongside (or literally on) the river. A few high-end resorts exist in town but the best are in the surrounding countryside where you'll need a car. Many Bangkokians weekend here; reserve well ahead.

🛏 In Town

★ Blue Star Guesthouse   GUESTHOUSE $
($\boxed{\mathcal{J}}$034 512161, 064 984 4329; www.bluestar-guesthouse.com; 241 Th Mae Nam Khwae; d & tw with fan 450B, with air-con 450-750B, d & tw bungalow with fan 300B, with air-con 550-650B, tr bungalow with air-con 650B; $\boxed{P}$✱🛜) Nature wraps itself around this family-run guesthouse's waterside lodgings. It has two parts: regular rooms up above and stilted bungalows in a jungly backwater bit of the river. The latter have limited or no wi-fi, but you trade this for a constant chorus of crickets and birds. Add helpful staff and this is one of the best budget choices in town.

T&T Hostel   GUESTHOUSE, HOSTEL $
($\boxed{\mathcal{J}}$034 514846; www.facebook.com/Hostel kanchanaburi; Th Mae Nam Khwae; dm 250B, r with shared bath & fan 200-300B, d & tw 500-800B; $\boxed{P}$✱🛜) The family that owns this little riverside spot lives here, making it almost as much a homestay as a guesthouse, with all the good (friendliness) and bad (occasional noise) this can bring. A big renovation has spruced things up very nicely making it one of the better choices in its class, though the raft rooms are just a mattress on the floor and a fan.

PY Guesthouse   GUESTHOUSE $$
($\boxed{\mathcal{J}}$081 208 4937; witaya1962@gmail.com; Soi Chai Chumpon 3; tw 750B; $\boxed{P}$✱🛜) This private garden oasis sits down a small street in the middle of a thoroughly local neighbourhood. Rooms lack the character of the common areas, but are very clean, and the owners go out of their way to look after guests.

Breakfast is available for purchase and bikes for hire.

Tara Raft   GUESTHOUSE $$
($\boxed{\mathcal{J}}$092 829 9419; www.tararoom.com/raft.html; Th Rong Hip Oi; d & tw 700-900B; $\boxed{P}$✱🛜) Though it's just 350m from the bustle of Th Mae Nam Khwae, there's an entirely different atmosphere along Rong Hip Oi road; it's peaceful and very local. We aren't enamoured with Tara Raft's landlocked rooms, but the floating versions are the best of their kind in town – they're bright, nicely decorated and have good mattresses, TVs, mini-fridges and in-room safes.

Ploy Resort   GUESTHOUSE $$
($\boxed{\mathcal{J}}$090 964 2653; www.ployresorts.com; 79/2 Th Mae Nam Khwae; d 1000-1900B, tr 1500B, f 2200-3000B; $\boxed{P}$✱🛜🏊) This stylish guesthouse-

resort has rooms in a sophisticated style, all cream walls and dark-wood furnishings, and a little garden outside the window. The best accommodation is cottage-style, but the 2nd-floor rooms, the cheapest, are just as comfortable and offer good value. Its multi-level backyard is one of the prettiest places in town to relax along the river.

U Dee Room & Coffee   GUESTHOUSE $$
(☏099 365 5449; www.facebook.com/udeecoffee; 295/9 Th Mae Nam Khwae; d & tw 700B; ✹🛜) Above a small cafe, these bright and sparkling clean rooms are just out of reach of the busier end of the tourist drag, practically guaranteeing a good night's sleep. Service is only available when the coffee shop is open, generally 9am to 6pm, unless you make other arrangements. As a (literal) perk, the coffee is excellent.

Apple's Retreat   GUESTHOUSE $$
(☏034 512017, 062 324 5879; www.applenoi-kanchanaburi.com; Mu 4, Ban Tamakham; d & tw incl breakfast 1090B; P✹🛜) Akin to a chic homestay, Apple and Noi, owners of Blue Rice (p192) restaurant, offer 16 simple rooms in a quiet part of town. The rooms are small and quite bare (ie not great value) and not everyone will like having the mattresses on a big platform instead of beds, but the friendly welcome, the location and bags of local knowledge give this place many repeat visitors.

Natee the Riverfront   HOTEL $$$
(☏034 518777; www.nateetheriverfront.com; Th Mae Nam Khwae; d & tw incl breakfast 2150-3750B; P✹🛜⛱) This beautiful, newly built hotel rises high over the river and the views are great, though not equal – a design flaw sets many of the balconies so far back the views are obstructed. The standard rooms are fairly tight, but all have Jacuzzis, wood trim and river views. Down below on the riverfront, the beanbag lounge and restaurant are reached by a tunnel under the pool.

Good Times Resort   HOTEL $$$
(☏090 143 4925; www.goodtimesriverkwai.com; 265/5 Th Mae Nam Khwae; incl breakfast d & tw 1500-2500B, tr 1850-2400B; P✹🛜⛱) The road here doesn't inspire confidence, but get past the car park and you'll find a palm-lined, riverside oasis. Ample rooms flooded with natural light and attractively flecked with colour surround the pool and garden and the good restaurant (mains 100B to 350B) is right at the river. Beaming staff are always around to assist. The 1500B rooms are a little overpriced.

🛏 Outside Town

Ban Sabai Sabai   GUESTHOUSE $$
(☏089 040 5268; www.bansabaisabai.com; 102/3 Mu 4, Nong Bua; d 400-800B, f 1600-2150B; P✹🛜) This place lives up to its name: Relaxation House. The various rooms around

---

BUILDING THE DEATH RAILWAY
···

The so-called 'Death Railway' was an astonishing feat of engineering constructed at immense human cost. Japan's Allied prisoners of war (POWs) and conscripted workers were armed only with basic tools and dynamite as they toiled. Well over 12,000 POWs and as many as 90,000 recruited and forced labourers (many of them ethnic Malay, Chinese and Indian) died due to disease, poor hygiene, lack of medical equipment and brutal treatment by camp guards. Many Thais risked their lives to aid the POWs, most of whom were Australian, American, British and Dutch, but they could offer only limited help.

The 415km railway was built during the WWII Japanese occupation of Thailand (1941–45). Its objective was to secure an overland supply route to Burma (Myanmar) for the Japanese conquest of other west Asian countries.

Because of the mountainous landscape, 688 bridges were built along the route. Most were wooden trestle bridges, such as those at the oft-visited Tham Krasae (ถ้ำ กระแซ; Tambon Lum Sum; ⊙24hrs; P) FREE. The bridge that spans the 'River Kwai' near Kanchanaburi city (now referred to as the Death Railway Bridge (p184)) was the only steel bridge built in Thailand. It was bombed several times by the Allies, but the POWs were sent to rebuild it. When the war's tide turned, the railway became an escape path for Japanese troops.

The northern end of the line is gone, but the State Railway of Thailand (SRT) still operates trains on 130km of the original route between Nong Pladuk, southeast of Kanchanaburi, and Nam Tok.

the florid garden are simple but well maintained, and guests are made to feel at home. It's located out in the countryside, some 7km west of town along Hwy 323 (down the road next to the giant Esso sign).

Buses pass nearby and you can ask ahead for a free pickup from town. Motorcycles are available for rent.

★ **Oriental Kwai Resort**　　　RESORT $$$
(☎ 061 673 0670; www.orientalkwai.com; 194/5 Mu 1, Tambon Lat Ya; cottages incl breakfast 2900-6200B; P❋☎☲) This Thai/Dutch-run spot has an exclusive feel. Set in a semiwild garden, all 12 cottages are sumptuously decorated with Thai sculpture and fabrics and brooding oxblood walls. Amenities include fridges and flat-screen TVs. Two are designed for families and sleep up to six people. It's 13km northwest of town, 1.5km off the road to Erawan National Park (p194).

X2 River Kwai　　　RESORT $$$
(☎ 034 552124; www.x2resorts.com/resorts/river-kwai; Tambon Nong Ya; ste incl breakfast 4700-9300B; P❋☎☲) Mannerly staff and water features immediately establish the tone of this sleek riverside resort, 10km southwest of the city. X2 has gorgeously designed rooms with slate feature walls, floor-to-ceiling windows and tasteful modern art, all facing an idyllic stretch of the river. The private rooftop sundecks are a fantastic feature and the XFloat Luxe rooms have their own private kayak docks.

You'll need your own transport. Book well ahead on weekends.

✖ Eating

Rahn Pa Kit　　　THAI $
(Th Mae Nam Khwae; mains 30-80B; ☺7am-8pm) To escape the mediocrity of guesthouse Thai food, look for the yellow 'Thai Food' sign at the entrance to Blue Star Guesthouse. The pair of women running this tiny street-side shop do all the standard foods very well.

Royal Nine Restaurant　　　INTERNATIONAL $
(Th Mae Nam Khwae; mains 50-400B, pizzas from 200B; ☺2-11pm; ☎) The menu at this little roadside restaurant is split between Thai and Western food, from green curry to grilled Norwegian salmon to wood-fired pizza that's pretty good for Thailand. Plus, owner Kay is a fount of knowledge about Kanchanaburi: if you're headed out to the hinterlands a stop here beforehand could be rewarding.

ELEPHANT INTERACTIONS

Tours around Kanchanburi often include elephant trekking. For the well-being of the elephants (p753) we strongly advise against this, no matter how good the tour company tells you the elephant camp is. If you do join one of these tours, you always have the option to walk alongside the elephant or go down to the river to bathe it instead of riding it.

The only place in Kanchanaburi that we can recommend for elephant interaction is **Elephant Haven** (☎ 053 272855; www.elephantnaturepark.org; Sai Yok; one-day adult/child 2500/1250B, 2 days 5800/2900B) ✐, a genuine sanctuary where the elephants' welfare is the primary concern.

Suk Jai Floating Market　　　MARKET $
(ตลาดน้ำสุขใจ; www.facebook.com/market71000; Wat Thewa Sangkharam; ☺5.30-8.30pm Fri; P) Despite its name, this is not a floating market, though it does take place along the river. Food is the focus and it's mostly snacks, like fried mushrooms and grilled sausages. There's also live music. It takes place every Friday night next to the big stupa at **Wat Thewa Sangkharam** (วัดเทวสังฆาราม; Wat Neua; Th Song Khwae; ☺daylight hours, murals 9am-3pm; P) FREE.

Zap Zap　　　THAI $
(Th Mae Nam Khwae; mains 40-150B; ☺11am-9.30pm; ☎) Though it has a broad menu, including pàt tai and panang curry, it's the spicy Isan-style sôm·đam that keep the tables full from open to close. For a blend of Thai and Isan try the fried papaya salad.

On's Thai-Issan　　　VEGETARIAN $
(☎ 087 364 2264; www.onsthaiissan.com; Th Mae Nam Khwae; mains 70-80B; ☺10am-9pm; ❋✐) Not your typical Thai-style vegan ('jay') restaurant, here On and her daughter make their Thai (and a few Isan) dishes not only healthy, but fully flavourful and as spicy as you want it. Big plates of ginger tofu and massaman curry are served with brown rice.

Friendly On will even teach you how to make your favourite dishes: a casual two-hour, three-dish cooking course costs 600B.

JJ Market　　　MARKET $
(Kanchanaburi Plaza; Th Saengchuto; mains from 30B; ☺5.30-10pm) Kanchanaburi's most

popular night market for dinner and shopping (Wednesday is secondhand day). Graze on barbecued cuttlefish, mango sticky rice and lots of stuff on a stick.

★ **Blue Rice** THAI $$

(www.applenoikanchanaburi.com/our-apples-restaurants; Mu 4, Ban Tamakham; mains from 135B; ⊘10.30am-3pm & 5-10pm, evenings only in low season; P 🤖 🥢) Masterful spice blends, a creative menu and peaceful river views make this one of the most irresistible restaurants in Kanchanaburi. The signature massaman curry is perfectly balanced, and Chef Apple puts a gourmet spin on Thai classics such as *yam sôm oh* (pomelo salad) and chicken-coconut soup with banana plant.

★ **Keeree Tara** THAI $$

(📞034 513855; www.facebook.com/keereeTara; 431/1 Th Mae Nam Khwae; mains 75-450B; ⊘10am-midnight, last order 9.30pm; P) This refined riverside eatery is ever so slightly upriver from the melee around the bridge, and has a pretty good view of it, especially from the raft seating that opens in the evening. It serves upmarket Thai dishes, both standards and some regionally popular dishes like giant freshwater prawns in tamarind sauce and river snail red curry.

Still hungry? Choose from Thai desserts including *da·go peu·ak* (taro pearls in coconut milk) and French-inspired gateaux and white chocolate mousse.

🍷 Drinking & Nightlife

There are bars for all tastes along the southern end of Th Mae Nam Khwae. Many venues have pool tables and screen sports matches (particularly the numerous Australian- and British-themed bars). For the brave, streetside bars here offer shots for 10B.

In Kanchanaburi the backpacker bars are interspersed with sex-tourism bars.

★ **Baan Sitthisang** CAFE

(Th Pakprak; ⊘8am-6pm; 🛜) Hunker down with a bit of history – plus great coffee and dainty baked goods – in this primrose-yellow building on the Heritage Walking Street (p185). This house (built in 1920) has been owned by the same family for generations; it's one of the best-preserved buildings along this storied street.

Ave CRAFT BEER

(Th Mae Nam Khwae; ⊘noon-midnight; 🛜) This little spot with great people-watching seats eschews the cheap-drinks, loud-music standard for this area and instead provides dozens of craft beers, most from Thai brewers. Staff greet you with a smile and there's a food menu with all the Thai standards.

ℹ️ Information

EMERGENCY

The **Tourist Police** (📞034 512795; Th Mae Nam Khwae) station is centrally located on Th Mae Nam Khwae and there is a small, helpful **booth** (⊘9am-6pm) at the Death Railway Bridge.

IMMIGRATION

The **immigration** (📞034 564279; www.kan-immigration.com; Hwy 3429; ⊘8.30am-noon & 1-4.30pm Mon-Fri) office for visa extensions is inconveniently south of town.

MEDICAL SERVICES

Thanakarn Hospital (📞034 540601; off Th Saengchuto) is the best-equipped hospital to deal with foreign visitors.

MONEY

Most major Thai banks can be found on Th Saengchuto near the bus terminal (p192). Two exchange booths in front of the WWII Museum (p185) open daily during normal business hours.

TOURIST INFORMATION

The **Tourism Authority of Thailand** (TAT; 📞034 511200; tatkan@tat.or.th; Th Saengchuto; ⊘8.30am-4.30pm) has a helpful, but not-very-central office out near the bus station.

ℹ️ Getting There & Away

BUS & MINIVAN

Kanchanaburi's **bus station** (📞034 515907; Th Lak Meuang) is in the centre of town by the clocktower, and minivans outnumber buses. (Remember with a minivan you need to buy an extra seat for very large bags.)

For Ayuthaya, you'll need to go to Suphanburi first. If heading south, it's quickest to transfer at Ratchaburi rather than Bangkok, but mostly old, non-air-con buses go there. Minivans to Bangkok depart until around 7pm.

A private minivan booked through (and picking up at) guesthouses serves Ayuthaya (350B, 2½ to three hours, 1.30pm) once daily.

TRAIN

Kanchanaburi is on the Thonburi–Nam Tok rail line (trains don't use Bangkok's Hualamphong station), which includes a portion of the Death Railway (p190). The State Railway of Thailand (SRT) promotes this as a historic route and charges foreigners 100B for any one-way journey along the line, regardless of the distance. The trains (leaving Thonburi at 7.50am and 1.55pm; 2½ hours) are 3rd class, meaning no air-con and mostly wooden benches, and you should not expect them to run on time. If you're planning a day trip to Kanchanaburi and time is tight, take a bus. Trains to Thonburi (three hours) depart **Kanchanaburi** (☑ 034 511285; Th Saengchuto) at 7.19am and 2.48pm.

The most interesting part of the journey begins after Kanchanaburi as the train crosses the Death Railway Bridge (p184) and terminates at Nam Tok station (two hours, leaving Kanchanaburi's main station at 6.07am, 10.35am and 4.26pm), which is near Hellfire Pass (p189). Most people headed from Kanchanaburi to Nam Tok board the train at the little **station** next to the Death Railway Bridge, so to be sure you get a seat (the left side of the train has the best views) board at the main station in town instead. Another option is a 'special car': the 300B tickets include a guaranteed seat (no standing), snacks and a 'certificate of pride'. The special tickets are sold next to the little tourist police booth close to the bridge.

Besides the regular trains, the SRT has special day-trip excursion trains (depart 6.30am, fan/air-con 120/240B) from Hualamphong Station on Saturdays and Sundays that stop at Phra Pathom Chedi (p163) in Nakhon Phatom Province, the Death Railway Bridge, Tham Krasae (p190) and Nam Tok with a bit of time to explore at each.

ⓘ Getting Around

BOAT

Long-tail boats can be hired at the Death Railway Bridge (p184) and JEATH War Museum (p185). The standard programme is a 1½-hour trip to Chungkai War Cemetery (p186), Wat Tham Khao Pun (p185) and either the bridge or the museum, depending on where you begin. The set price for up to six people is 800B, but this is sometimes negotiable.

BIKE & MOTORCYCLE

Kanchanaburi is quite spread out, so while walking between the sites is possible, bikes are the best way to go. Bikes (per day 50B) and motorcycles (200B) can be hired at dozens of guesthouses and shops along Th Mae Nam Khwae. **Yanee** (☑ 081 586 8428; Th Mae Nam Khwae; ◷ 6.30am-9pm), near the tourist police office, does regular maintenance and keeps long hours. SUP Hire Thailand (p187) has high quality hybrids (per day 150B) available.

PUBLIC TRANSPORT

Motorcycle taxis, many with sidecars that can carry several people and large luggage, are much more common than túk-túks. A trip from the bus station to the guesthouse area will probably cost you 60B.

Yellow and blue sŏrng·tăa·ou (passenger pickup trucks) run up and down Th Saengchuto (get off at the cemetery if you want the guesthouse area) for 10B per passenger. You can board them in the row of buses on the west edge of the bus station (p192). Orange sŏrng·tăa·ou do work as taxis rather than running regular routes.

Around Kanchanaburi

Kanchanaburi Province is lush, mountainous and teeming with natural beauty. The most easily accessible adventure is swimming beneath the waterfalls at Erawan National Park (p194) and/or Sri Nakarin Dam National Park (p194). Sai Yok National Park (p195) is another worthy choice, with long-tail boat rides, waterfalls and walking trails.

BUSES FROM KANCHANABURI

DESTINATION	FARE (B)	DURATION (HR)	FREQUENCY
Bangkok Northern (Mo Chit) bus terminal	120	3	frequent (minivan)
Bangkok Southern (Sai Tai Mai) bus terminal	110	3	frequent (minivan)
Chiang Mai	555-865	10-12	3 daily (8.30am, 6pm, 7pm)
Hua Hin	220	3½	hourly
Nong Khai	495	12	1 daily (7pm)
Ratchaburi	55-65	3	hourly
Sangkhlaburi (via Thong Pha Phum)	130-192	4-5	4 daily
Suphanburi	55-70	2	every 30min
Thong Pha Phum	80-115	2½-3	every 30-45min

⭐ **Erawan National Park** NATIONAL PARK
(อุทยานแห่งชาติเอราวัณ; ☑034 574222; adult/child 300/200B, car/motorbike 30/20B; ⊗park gate 8am-4pm; waterfall levels 1-3 8.30am-5pm, levels 4-7 8.30am-4pm; ℗) Splashing in emerald-green pools under **Erawan Falls** is the highlight of this very popular 550-sq-km park. Seven tiers of waterfall tumble through the forest, and bathing beneath these crystalline cascades is equally popular with locals and visitors. Reaching the first three tiers is easy; beyond here, walking shoes and some endurance are needed to complete the steep 2km hike but it's undoubtedly worth it.

Bring a swimming costume (and a cover-up T-shirt if you don't want to be stared at by more modest Thai visitors), but be aware you're sharing the bathing area with large, nibbling fish, and monkeys have been known to snatch swimmers' belongings. Level four has a natural rock slide and level six usually has the fewest swimmers. If you hit the trail early you can briefly have the place mostly to yourself. You can't take food beyond level two and though bottles of water are permitted, to prevent littering, you have to register them and leave a 20B returnable deposit. Buggies (adult/child 30/15B) can transport people to the first level.

You can escape the crowds near the waterfall by taking a ranger-led walk (arranged at the visitor centre: you must pay, but there's no set fee) on the 5km **Khao Hin Lan Pee Trail** that takes you through the forest to the falls' fifth tier. Elsewhere in the park, **Tham Phra That** (ถ้ำพระธาตุ; Erawan National Park; ⊗8am-4pm; ℗) is a seldom-visited cave full of shimmering limestone formations. There are some other fantastic caves in the park, but they've been closed to the public for years and may never reopen.

The park was named for Erawan, the three-headed elephant of Hindu mythology, whom the top tier is thought to resemble. Mixed deciduous forest covers over 80% of the park, but there's also dry evergreen and dry dipterocarp forest and big swathes of bamboo. Tigers, elephants, sambar deer, gibbons, red giant flying squirrels, king cobras and hornbills call the park home, but they don't frequent the waterfall area and the only large animal you might spot other than monkeys is wild boar.

Park **bungalows** (☑02 562 0760; http://nps. dnp.go.th/reservation.php?option=home; Erawan National Park; bungalows 800-2400B, 2-/4-person tent hire 120/300B, per person with own tent 30B; ℗✳)

sleep between two and eight people and there is a campground. Tent hire available.

Erawan is 65km north of Kanchanaburi. Buses (50B, 1½ hours) run hourly from 8am to 5.50pm and go right to the **visitor centre**, which is staffed 24 hours. The last bus back to town is at 5pm, and on weekends it will be packed. Touts at the bus station will try to talk you into hiring a private driver instead of taking the bus, but this isn't necessary.

⭐ **Sri Nakarin Dam National Park** NATIONAL PARK
(อุทยานแห่งชาติเขื่อนศรีนครินทร์; Khuean Srinagarindra National Park; ☑082 290 2466; adult/child 300/200B, car/motorbike 30/20B; ⊗waterfall trail 6.30am-5pm; ℗) Visitors to Erawan often find themselves wondering what the waterfall would be like without the hordes. The answer is **Namtok Huay Mae Khamin**.

Despite access on a good sealed road just 45km northwest of Erawan, this stunning cerulean waterfall at the heart of the 1532-sq-km park is usually peaceful and private. While Erawan might win a straight-out beauty contest, when you add atmosphere to the equation, Huay Mae Khamin unquestionably comes out on top.

Like Erawan, Huay Mae Khamin has seven named falls (though others between them are just as large and beautiful) along its forested course and swimming is permitted. The trailhead is at level four where a boardwalk leads down to level one, arguably the most beautiful of them all. It's a 1100m return trip and, if time is limited, this is the better half. Upstream, a gravel path, 2350m return, passes levels five to seven, though a sinkhole has robbed level five of its water. Additional trails branch off this path, but they're unmarked and seldom used. Allow at least three hours for a leisurely visit to all seven levels.

In the rainy season (particularly September and October) it would be wise to call ahead or check with the tourist office (p192) in Kanchanaburi before driving out here because sometimes floods force trail closures.

There are good **bungalows and a campground** (bungalows 900-1800B, 3-person tent hire 300B, per person with own tent 30B; ℗), both with lake views.

The waterfall is 110km from Kanchanaburi city. There's no public transport. Hiring a car from Kanchanaburi is at least 2000B a day.

Muang Sing Historical Park RUINS
(อุทยานประวัติศาสตร์เมืองสิงห์; ☑034 670264; Rte 3455; 100B, car/motorcycle 50/20B; ⊗8am-

ⓘ GETTING TO MYANMAR: PHU NAM RON TO HTEE KHEE

This crossing is still something of an adventure. Myanmar visas are not available at the border and e-visas are not accepted; the nearest place to get a visa is the embassy (Map p100; ☑ 02 233 7250; www.mfa.go.th; 132 Th Sathon Neua/North, Bangkok; ⊙ 9am-noon & 1-3pm Mon-Fri; Ⓢ Surasak exit 1/3) in Bangkok.

Getting to the border There are around six daily buses (70B to 80B, two hours) and minivans (100B, 1½ hours) from Kanchanaburi's bus station (p192) right to the border starting at 9am. If you leave early you can make it to Dawei, Myanmar, in a day, though there are guesthouses on both sides of the border if you need them.

At the border After getting stamped out of Thailand, take a motorcycle taxi (100B) to Myanmar immigration, 6km away. The border is open 6am to 6pm (5.30am to 5.30pm Myanmar time). Formalities are hassle-free, though in the early morning expect it to be busy with visa-run vans.

Moving on At Thai immigration, you'll be introduced to minivan drivers who will take you to Dawei for 800B per person, though this may be negotiable. You can also arrange this in advance through Hello Dawei Travel & Tours (☑ 09 44362 7636; www.hellodawei. com; 661 Pakaukukyaung St; ⊙ 8am-8pm). On the Myanmar side, you'll find minibuses for 20,000 kyat going when full: in the afternoon they may not have enough passengers. It's about five hours through the beautiful mountains to Dawei on a partly sealed – and sometimes rough – road, though improvements are planned.

5pm; Ⓟ) The ruins of 'Lion City', the westernmost-known Khmer outpost, are spread around a 102-hectare compound girded by 4.5km of walls. Serving most likely as both a military post and a relay point for trade along the Mae Nam Khwae Noi, the restored ruins, built almost entirely of laterite, feature Bayon form, which would place it in the late 12th- or 13th-century under the Buddhist king Jayavarman VII.

There are two large main monuments and the remnants of two others. The principal shrine, Prasat Muang Sing (labelled Monument #1 on the site signs and maps), is in the centre and faces east (the cardinal direction of most Angkor temples). Inside are replica statues of the eight-armed Bodhisattva Avalokitesvara and the goddess Prajnaparamita; the latter was probably originally installed in the other large shrine behind this one. The ponds were probably used for religious purposes.

Outside the city wall are seven additional layers of ramparts and moats, which are visible at the main entrance. And right next to the river is a prehistoric burial site that shows two skeletons, pottery and jewellery thought to date back 2000 years.

Muang Sing is 33km west of Kanchanaburi. Tha Kilen train station (100B) is a 1.5km walk away, but it's best to come with your own transport since trains are infrequent and the grounds are large.

Sai Yok National Park NATIONAL PARK
(อุทยานแห่งชาติไทรโยก; ☑ 034 686024; adult/child 300/200B, car/motorcycle 30/20B; ⊙ daylight hours) Caves, waterfalls and forest trails draw walkers to Sai Yok National Park (958 sq km), which never gets too crowded. The main sights are easily reached from the visitor centre (⊙ 8am-4.30pm), including the park's best known attraction, Nam Tok Sai Yok Yai (น้ำตกไทรโยกใหญ่, Sai Yok Yai Waterfall), where a stream makes a short, graceful drop into Mae Nam Khwae Noi. More impressive than the waterfalls are the soaring shoreline cliffs that can be seen on a boat trip (400B, 45 minutes) from the suspension bridge.

Also here are a good nature trail; a bat cave with the very rare Kitti's hog-nosed bat, the world's smallest mammal at no more than 3cm; and some WWII Death Railway (p190) relics – the rail line passed through what is now the park.

You can stay within the park in old bungalows (☑ 02 562 0760; http://nps.dnp.go.th/reservation.php?option=home; Sai Yok National Park; bungalows 800-2100B; Ⓟ), at a campground (tent hire 225B, per person with own tent)30B or in basic – but fun – raft resorts (☑ 081 805 6467; www.facebook.com/atRAFT saiyok; d & tw/tr incl breakfast 1000/2000B; Ⓟ).

Sai Yok National Park lies along the highway between Kanchanaburi and Thong Pha Phum and buses (fan/AC 55/75B, 1½ hours, every 30 to 45 minutes) between these destinations will stop at the park turnoff. A túk-túk driver can take you the last 3.5km for 30B per person, or 50B for one person. The visitor centre will call for a túk-túk when you're leaving the park.

Nam Tok

For travellers riding the heritage Death Railway (p190) route from Kanchanaburi, Nam Tok (น้ำตก) is the final destination. But it can also be a starting point for tramping into caves, placid river rowing and luxuriating in water's-edge resorts.

Though the trains stop at Nam Tok station, the track continues for another 1.5km and you can follow it to Nam Tok Sai Yok Noi. It's quite beautiful (when it has water) though gets crowded with Thai families swimming and picnicking. Above the falls is little Tham Sai Yok cave and 20km away is Tham Lawa, a lovely, large cave.

◉ Sights

Tham Lawa
CAVE
(ถ้ำละว้า, Lawa Cave; Sai Yok National Park, Tambon Wang Krachae; ⊗8am-4.30pm; ℗) Walking along the dimly lit 280m trail through Lawa Cave you'll pass several large chambers with imposing stalactites, stalagmites and other odd rock formations. Bring a torch (or try to borrow one from the rangers) for the full experience. Sai Yok National Park admission fees apply (show your ticket if you've been to other sights the same day). It's signed along country roads 20km from Nam Tok Sai Yok Noi.

The cave is a short way from the river, and you can reach it by boat from Pak Saeng Pier, next to Boutique Raft Resort. It takes one hour and around 1200B to go there and back.

Nam Tok Sai Yok Noi
WATERFALL
(น้ำตกไทรโยคน้อย, Sai Yok Noi Waterfall; Hwy 323; ⊗daylight hours; ℗) **FREE** This lovely waterfall, also known as Nam Tok Khao Pang, is a very popular place for Thais, who flock here at the weekends to have a swim and roll out their sitting mats for a picnic in the tree-shaded grounds. You can also see a WWII-era Japanese steam train parked here.

It's 1.5km northwest of Nam Tok's train station,, signposted north of Hwy 323, or you can just walk along the train tracks.

Up above the falls, 100m straight back from the dam, is little Tham Sai Yok Cave

(8am to 5pm). Two Buddha images are lit up by natural light while at the back is a holy snake-shaped rock you can only see if you bring a torch.

Although this is part of Sai Yok National Park, no fees are collected.

🍴 Sleeping & Eating

Enjoying some peace and quiet at a river resort – either on shore or on a raft – is reason enough to stay near Nam Tok. There are options for different budgets, though all are in the countryside around the village so you'll need private transport or to hire a driver to reach them. In town are several basic places that are fine for a night.

Tourists staying in Nam Tok tend to dine at their resort. The dining scene in the village isn't very exciting, though there's no shortage of choice along the highway both at and away from the waterfall.

Yayei Homestay
GUESTHOUSE $$
(☑081 008 2121; www.facebook.com/yayei-homestay; d & tw 700-790B, with shared bath 500B; ℗✱⊛⊜) A simple, but comfortable guesthouse on a small road between the train station and the waterfall (700m to each). The staff are friendly, the mattresses good and there's a beautiful limestone peak out the back door. The best rooms are set around a 2nd-floor terrace.

Bikes and motorcycles can be hired (p197), but we suggest you inform them in advance if you want to use them.

Boutique Raft Resort
RESORT $$$
(☑064 137 6909, 081 353 1056; www.boutiqueraft-riverkwai.com; Mu 3 Tambon Tha Sao; d & tw incl breakfast 2600-6000B; ℗✱⊜) Bamboo and wood floating rooms open straight onto the river at this small resort 3km south of Nam Tok train station. It's not to the deluxe standard of the more expensive raft resorts in this area, but it's good for the price and most people are pleased with their stay. You can relax on your private terrace watching bamboo rafts float by or take a dip in the 'river swimming pool' deck.

❶ Getting There & Away

Trains to Kanchanaburi (100B, two hours) depart **Nam Tok station** (☑034 565181) at 5.20am, 12.55pm and 3.30pm, while buses between Kanchanaburi (fan/air-con 40/50B, 1½ hours) and Thong Pha Phum (fan/air-con 50/70B, one hour) pass through at least every 30 minutes. Four of these buses go all the way to Sangkhlaburi (fan/air-con 100/150B, four hours), the last leaving at about 2.30pm.

ℹ Getting Around

Yayei Homestay (p196), between the train station and the waterfall, and a few other hotels in town rent motorcycles for around 350B per day. Yayei also has bikes (two hours/one day 50/150B), though they are really old.

E-Thong

POP 300

Guarded on all sides by jungle and mist, E-Thong (อีต่อง; pronounced E-Dong), the 'Mountain of the Gods', has a fairy-tale setting and a unique small-town ambience. A frontier village on the Myanmar border, from the 1940s to the 1980s E-Thong thrived as a multicultural outpost for tin and tungsten mining. The region gained the name *mĕuang pĕe·lôrk* (Ghost Mine) as a result of many mining-related deaths. Only traces of its heyday remain, but the village reinvented itself in the 2000s when intrepid Bangkokians began seeking a far-flung weekend getaway here. Foreign travellers have been slow to follow and spoken English is very rare.

◉ Sights

A trip to E-Thong is as much about the journey as the destination: the '399' shirts and stickers refer to the number of curves in the thickly forested road to get here from Thong Pha Phum.

There are retired **mining relics** (เหมือง ปีล๊อก; ⊘ daylight hours; **P**) **FREE** and, of course, a **temple** (วัดอีต่อง; Wat E-Thong; ⊘ daylight hours) **FREE** on the edge of the village, but the frequent fog blowing in between April and January is the most famous attraction. Thus it's a bit ironic that the two main places people visit are mountain viewpoints. Soaring **Noen Chang Suek** (เนินช้าง ศึก; ⊘ dawn-dusk; **P**) **FREE**, 2.7km (1.2km by foot) to the south, has fantastic views from its peak (when not engulfed in fog) while **Noen Sao Thong** (เนินเสาธง; ⊘ dawn-dusk; **P**) **FREE**, 750m to the west, is far inferior, but much easier to reach.

🛏 Sleeping & Eating

Despite its diminutive size, E-Thong has over two dozen guesthouses and homestays in and around it. Some are no-frills, but many meet big-city standards for design, comfort and amenities. They all call themselves homestays, but very few are actually in a family's home. Note that none have air-con because the village tends to be cool year-round.

E-Thong's unique tourism status means that there are all sorts of restaurants and coffee shops that would never be found in a normal village. Another oddity is the abundance of fresh seafood – E-Thong is just 50km as the crow flies from the Andaman Sea and gets regular deliveries from Myanmar.

Pilok Hill House GUESTHOUSE $$

(☏ 080 781 5702; www.pilokhillhouse.com; d & tw 1000-1500B, q loft incl breakfast 2500B; **P** 🛜) This welcoming and well-managed guesthouse, tucked into a leafy hillside garden on the village's east fringe, is arguably the best lodging in E-Thong. Tile-floored rooms are large and airy, although having a view of the football pitch isn't a highlight.

It's at the end of the village's main street; check in at the little wooden building.

Ban Mahat Geeratee GUESTHOUSE $$

(☏ 082 293 7747; d/fm 1100/2500B; 🛜) This newly built, large-by-local-standards guesthouse is at the west end of town facing the pond. The regular rooms are pretty good (although the mattresses could be better) and the roof-top deck is a great place to spend some time. Note that the family rooms are just mattresses on the floor.

★ Nong Noi Restaurant THAI $

(⊘ 7am-7.30pm) E-Thong's oldest restaurant (opened in 1999) has just a sheet-metal roof and plastic chairs, but the food – mostly Thai standards, though also Burmese *gaang hang lay* curry – is truly excellent. And friendly owner Nong Noi speaks a little English.

Krua Je Ni THAI $

(mains 40-500B; ⊘ 7am-8pm; 🛜) This easygoing restaurant, halfway along the village's main pedestrian-only street (look for cartoon-style animals and red Chinese lanterns), serves an array of Thai dishes, but it's the seafood, such as *boo pàt pŏng gà·rèe* (crab with yellow curry), that keeps the seats full.

ℹ Getting There & Away

E-Thong village is reached by 70km of winding road west from Thong Pha Phum. The border with neighbouring Myanmar isn't open.

BUS

Depending on demand, there's from one to four daily *sŏrng·tăa·ou* between E-Thong and

---

RIVERSIDE LUXURY

Central Thailand has countless raft resorts and waterside hotels, but Nam Tok (p196) does riverbank chic especially well. Guests at River Kwai Resotel (☑hotel 081 734 5238, reservations 02 642 5497; www.riverkwairesotel.net; Mu 5 Tambon Wang Krajae; incl breakfast d & tw 1500-3000B; tr 2850B; Ⓟ⊛🌐🏊) unwind in thatched-roof chalets set amid lush gardens; chalet interiors are beautifully modern with stone-effect bathrooms. Over at sister resort FloatHouse (☑hotel 084 725 8686, reservations 02 642 5497; www.thefloathouse-riverkwai.com; Mu 5 Tambon Wang Krachae; d & tw incl breakfast 5950B; Ⓟ⊛🌐), luxurious raft rooms roll with the movement of the river.

Both are accessed by long-tail boat (included in the room rate) from Phutakien Pier, 2km west of Hwy 323, where you can park your car. .

Thong Pha Phum (pickup minibus; 70B, two to 2½ hours). They're scheduled to leave E-Thong at 6.30am, 7am, 7.30am and 8am and return at 10.30am, 11.30am, 12.30pm and 1pm, but sometimes only one of them takes passengers, so check before you plan to leave. They will drop you at and pick you up from Thong Pha Phum National Park (p198); from Thong Pha Phum town you pay the full E-Thong fare while the 8km between the park and E-Thong costs 20B.

CAR

If driving yourself, allow extra time and drive defensively. The road is overall in decent condition, but potholed patches come out of nowhere – as can local drivers who take wild chances on this unforgiving, zigzagging road.

Nonresident vehicles mostly aren't allowed inside the village's tiny nucleus, so park in the lots near the ponds.

Around E-Thong

Thong Pha Phum National Park

NATIONAL PARK

(อุทยานแห่งชาติทองผาภูมิ; ☑034 510979; adult/child 200/100B, car/motorbike 30/20B; Ⓟ) This seldom-explored park sprawls across a serrated mountain range along the Myanmar border. Billing itself as the 'land of fog and freezing rainforest', mornings at the park have a brooding beauty, particularly when cold-season mist fills the valleys. Most of the park is inaccessible, but visitors can enjoy waterfalls, trekking and the 'Tarzan' treetop accommodation (☑national park service 02 562 0760, park visitor centre 034 510979; http://nps.dnp.go.th/reservation.php?option=home; Thong Pha Phum National Park; r 1500B, camping per person 30B, 4-person tent hire 225B; Ⓟ) near the end of one of Thailand's most remote and winding roads.

The park teems with wildlife, including elephants, tigers, bears, serow (Asian mountain goats), marbled cats and palm civets, though most animals are shy. That said, barking deer and kalij pheasant often wander through the visitor centre (8am to 4.30pm) and lodging area.

Thais know the park for its challenging ranger-led overnight treks (16km round trip) to 1249m Khao Chang Pheuk, which offers 360-degree views. The season is up to the weather, but trekking can begin as early as late November and lasts through January. The trek starts at E-Thong village, but registration is done at or before 7am at the visitor centre, 8km away. The cost is 2500B for up to 10 people (the park puts groups together) and porters are available for an extra fee. Numbers are limited so reservations are wise. Be prepared for leeches.

For a less-challenging bit of walking through healthy rainforest, let a ranger lead you (for a small tip) on a 4km two-hour walk from the visitor centre to Doi Tong Pala. Five kilometres southwest of the visitor centre, down a steep side road, Jokkadin Waterfall plummets 34m with force.

The serpentine 62km drive west from Thong Pha Phum town is along a paved but often potholed road. Yellow *sŏrng·tăa·ou* (passenger pickup trucks) to E-Thong pass the visitor centre (70B; 2¼ hours).

Sangkhlaburi

POP 8000

Few places in Thailand are as multicultural as Sangkhlaburi (สังขละบุรี), with Karen, Mon and Burmese, plus a few Lao, together outnumbering the Thai. Most were born here, but many came across the Myanmar border looking for a safer, more stable life. There's also a small but prominent community of foreign NGO workers and volunteers.

As with many places at the end of the road, this is a great place to just hang out. Though it's a fairly remote, sleepy place, Sankhlaburi's recent popularity with Thai tourists means it's full of resorts and restaurants, the best of which look out over the mountain-girded Khao Laem Reservoir and the massive, enchanting wooden bridge that spans it.

Sights

★ Saphan Mon BRIDGE
(สะพานมอญ; 24hr) FREE Sangkhlaburi's iconic, 447m-long wooden bridge, the largest in Thailand, connects the main town, home mostly to Thai and Karen, with the Mon settlement. This village (officially it's Ban Wang Ka, but even residents just call it Ban Mon: 'Mon Village') is a striking place to explore, peopled by cheroot-smoking women, sarong-wearing men and faces covered in *thanaka* (a yellow paste made from tree bark, used both as sunblock and decoration).

At the Mon end of the bridge is a souvenir market selling Karen shirts and dresses among other things. Follow the street uphill from the bridge and turn left on the main road to visit the Mon market (Talat Wat Wang; 6am-noon; P).

Giving morning alms to monks (at 6.30am) is a big event on the Mon side of the bridge. Tourists (mostly from Bangkok) donate from fancy trays alongside locals who stick to the Mon tradition of giving just a scoop of rice. .

Chedi Phuttakhaya BUDDHIST TEMPLE
(เจดีย์พุทธคยา; Chedi Luang Phaw Uttama; Rte 3024; daylight hours; P) FREE This striking stupa on a little peninsula on the Mon (south) side of the lake stands 59m high and is constructed in the style of the Mahabodhi stupa in Bodhgaya, India. Its gold-painted, art deco-like surface is full of niches holding little Buddha images.

Khao Laem Reservoir LAKE
(เขื่อนเขาแหลม) Backed by fuzzy green hills, the gigantic lake wrapped around Sangkhlaburi was formed in the 1980s by the Vajiralongkorn Dam (Khao Laem Dam, เขื่อนวชิรลงกรณ์; 6am-6pm; P) FREE. Two of the many villages submerged under the new lake were moved up to their present location and Saphan Mon was built to connect them. About all that remains of these original villages are ruined buildings from three temples. A boat ride allows you to see them up close, as well as feel the pace of life on the lake.

Wat Si Suwannaram BUDDHIST TEMPLE
(วัดศรีสุวรรณาราม; Th Si Suwankhiri; daylight hours; P) FREE Karen women and men come to this prominent temple, near the main lodging zone, most days (no set hours) to weave cotton fabric. The building they work in, behind the exercise equipment, also has a small dusty display of old baskets and bowls.

Wat Wang Wiwekaram BUDDHIST TEMPLE
(วัดวังก์วิเวการาม; Rte 3024; daylight hours; P) FREE Poking out of the forest on the south side of Saphan Mon (p199), this temple is the spiritual centre of Thailand's Mon people. The temple was established by Luang Phaw Uttama (1910–2006) and the *wí-hǎhn* (assembly hall) with three richly decorated green-and-yellow towers is a memorial to this highly respected monk, whose body lies in rest inside a giant shrine.

Born in Myanmar, Luang Phaw Uttama fled to Thailand in 1949 to escape the civil war and became a cornerstone of the Mon community in both countries, as well as a noted Buddhist leader in Thailand.

Activities

Boat Rides BOATING
(per boat 300-500B) Local operators approach tourists at both ends of the Mon bridge offering boat trips to the temple ruins in the Khao Laem Reservoir. It takes a about an hour to see all three abandoned temples (500B), or you can go for a shorter trip (300B) just to Wat Wang Wiwekaram Gao. The boats can carry up to six people.

The calm of early morning is the best time to go, though late afternoon before sunset is also good.

Baan Unrak VOLUNTEERING
(บ้านอุ่นรัก; 034 510778; www.baanunrak.org) Baan Unrak runs this charity caring for around 150 orphaned or abandoned children, including young Mon and Karen people. Volunteers (particularly English teachers, but officework and other skills are helpful as well) are always welcome. Accommodation and food are provided for those staying six months or longer; for shorter periods helpers are asked to donate US$150 per week (to a maximum US$900) for expenses.

Many of the children at Baan Unrak come from families who fled persecution in neighbouring Myanmar, while others were born in border areas and lack identity papers. As well as running the children's home, Baan Unrak helps single mothers, does medical outreach, has an animal shelter and runs a bakery and souvenir shop to provide an income for local women.

Courses

Villa Scenns Cookery COOKING
(☎080 602 3184; www.scenns.com; Th Ton Phueng; per person from 680B) Charming Scenn runs expert Thai cooking classes, catering with ease for vegetarians and those with other dietary requirements. Scenn imparts the secrets of seasonal food and offers a choice of menus for guests to prepare.

Uniquely decorated rooms are available at her small guesthouse (p200).

Tours

Sangkhlaburi Jungle Trekking TREKKING
(☎085 425 4434; jarunsaksri1@gmail.com) The forest around Sangkhlaburi is wilder and less visited than most trekking destinations in northern Thailand. 'Jack', who has years of experience as a guide, can tailor trips for different fitness levels and for family groups, but the most adventurous option is a week hiking the Myanmar border from Sangkhlaburi to Um Phang, staying in Karen villages along the way.

Prices depend on group size and trip length, but expect 2000B per person per day for three people or more. You'll need to bring your own tent and sleeping bag, or pay extra to hire one.

Lake Explorer BOATING
(☎02 821 5503; https://gobeyond.asia/thailand/kanchanaburi/the-lake-explorer-4-days; per person from 46,800B) Bangkok-based firm Go Beyond Asia runs four-day, three-night houseboat excursions on the Khao Laem Reservoir (p199), with various activities and trips like kayaking, cooking classes and village visits.

Sleeping

Reserve a few days ahead for Saturday nights, or any time around a public holiday. Better still, come between Monday and Friday, when the town is free from weekenders.

★ **J Family Homestay** HOMESTAY $
(☎081 763 2667, 034 595511; Th Ton Phueng; s/tw with shared bathroom 200/300B; [P] [wi-fi]) Rooms are just mattresses on the floor with shared cold-water bathrooms, but this welcoming homestay is very clean and offers a pleasant local experience. And English-speaking Kamsai, whose home you are sharing, is a friendly host. It's signed down the little road east of Wat Si Suwannaram (p199).

Sweetville Home GUESTHOUSE $
(☎063 232 9101; Th Ton Phueng; d 450-600B; [P] [wi-fi]) A good location and very good value, this newly built three-room guesthouse is at the north end of Th Ton Phueng, fairly near the bridge and away from most traffic. The mattresses are hard and there's no wi-fi (it may come later), but you get clean air-con rooms for the same price that many older places charge for shared-bath fan rooms.

★ **P Guesthouse** GUESTHOUSE $$
(☎081 450 2783, 034 595061; www.p-guesthouse.com; Th Si Suwankhiri; d with fan/air-con 400/950B, towel 30B; [P] [air-con] [wi-fi]) You don't often get views like this on a budget. Stone and log-built rooms gaze upon tranquil waters at this family-run spot, one of the few in Sangkhlaburi where English is spoken. Fan rooms share cold-water bathrooms, while air-conditioned rooms have en suites and the best views. The restaurant (mains 50B to 150B) is a fantastic place to lounge. You can rent a canoe almost from your door.

The owners can arrange a short trekking/rafting day trip into the surrounding forest.

Phu Than Resort GUESTHOUSE $$
(☎084 750 1648; Th Ton Phueng; bungalow 1000-1600B; [P] [air-con] [wi-fi]) Though these cute wooden bungalows, engulfed in greenery, are away from the river – hence no view – and starting to age (some of the bathrooms have gone slightly musty) this little resort remains good value for Sangkhlaburi and has more character than most of the resorts.

★ **Villa Scenns** GUESTHOUSE $$$
(☎080 602 3184; www.scenns.com; Th Ton Phueng; incl breakfast d 1500-1800B, tw 1600B; [P] [air-con] [wi-fi]) Not your ordinary guesthouse, each quirky and unique room here has wooden furnishings and comfy beds and you have access to a shared kitchen, common room and backyard garden. Bathrooms are all private, but two are located outside the guest rooms. You'll get good conversation and local advice with your kind hosts Scenn and Charlie.

Book ahead for excellent cooking classes.

Eating & Drinking

Sangkhlaburi has many good restaurants catering to tourists, so you can eat everything from pizza to *pàt tai*. The markets on both sides of the bridge, especially Sangkhlaburi's night market, are the best places to try local foods including the signature Mon dish of *kà·nŏm jeen nám yah yùak* (fresh rice noodles with fish sauce).

★ **Sangkhlaburi Night Market** MARKET $
(Th Thetsaban 5; ⊙3.30-8.30pm) There's as much Mon and Burmese food as Thai at Sangkhlaburi's small but popular night market. Keep an eye out for Myanmar *yam kôw soy*, a noodle and tofu salad in a tomato-based sauce, served as spicy as you like it.

Baan Unrak Bakery BAKERY $
(✐034 595 006; www.baanunrak.org; Th Si Suwankhiri; snacks 5-55B, mains 45-165B; ⊙8am-8pm; ☂⊚🖉) 🖋 This mostly vegan cafe, part of the nonprofit Baan Unrak (p199) organisation, makes meat-free *pàt tai*, green curry, pizza by the slice (it tastes better than it looks) and chocolate doughnuts. You can also inquire here about trekking trips.

★ **Ahahn Puen Mueang 7 Yang** THAI $
(Th Thetsaban 5; mains 20B; ⊙2.30-8.30pm) The friendly family behind the '7 Local Foods' shop in the southeast corner of Sangkhlaburi's night market (look for the big red picture menu) does Burmese, Karen and Mon dishes.

Toy's Restaurant THAI $
(Th Sangkhlaburi; mains 35-80B; ⊙8am-8pm Sat-Thu; 🕾) Toy, a transplant from Nong Khai, makes simple but delicious dishes from all corners of Thailand including massaman curry, *pàt tai*, Isan-style *lâhp* (spicy, herbal mincemeat salad) and fried chicken.

Rahn Nai Bon THAI $
(Th Uttama Nuson Soi 7; mains 30-40B; ⊙5am-7pm) For Mon cuisine, every local we talked to advised us to head up the hill to this simple restaurant across from the Mon Market (p199). The speciality is *gaang hang lay* curry with either *mǔu* (pork), *ɓlah* (fish) or *gài* (chicken). No English is spoken, but you can just look in the pots to choose.

Samprasob Restaurant THAI $$
(www.samprasob.com; Th Samprasob; mains 80-340B; ⊙4.30-9pm; ☂🕾) Our favourite scenic dining in Sangkhlaburi, this resort restaurant is perched above the Mon bridge with a view stretching deep back over the lake. Luckily, it's not all about the setting; the food – from the local speciality fern and oyster sauce salad to fried prawns with tamarind sauce – is delicious.

The Dog House BAR
(www.facebook.com/thedoghousebarsangkla; Th Si Suwankhiri; ⊙5-11pm Thu-Tue; 🕾) Volunteers, travellers and locals gather at this low-key watering hole. Between beers or games of pool (free on Sundays), have a look at the dogs on the sponsor wall – proceeds from the bar go to the animal shelter at Baan Unrak (p199).

Blend Cafe COFFEE
(www.facebook.com/BlendCafe.Thai; Th Thetsaban 1; ⊙8am-6pm; 🕾) Refreshing coffee spot with mix-and-match furniture. Besides the usual cakes, coffees and fruity Italian sodas, there's premium Doi Chang coffee from northern Thailand.

❶ Information

The tiny town centre has a few banks and ATMs, including **Krungthai** (Th Thetsaban 2; ⊙8.30am-4.30pm Mon-Fri).
Sangkhlaburi Hospital (✐034 595030; Th Sangkhlaburi; ⊙24hr) Some of the doctors here speak English. For anything serious, you should get to Kanchanaburi or Bangkok.

❶ Getting There & Away

Sangkhlaburi is around 210km north of Kanchanaburi via a picturesque, good-quality tarmac road.

BUS

From a **parking lot** (cnr Th Si Suwankhiri & Th Thetsaban) on the west side of the town centre, red buses depart for Kanchanaburi (fan/air-con 130/160B, four to five hours, 6.45am, 8.15am, 9.30am and 1.15pm) and a daily 1st-class air-con bus goes to Bangkok's Mo Chit terminal (304B, seven to eight hours, 8.30am). Tickets for the latter are not sold at the lot; rather you buy them from a small **office** (✐065 561 9962; Th Thetsaban 1; ⊙7am-7pm) just to the east of the bus stop next to Blend Cafe. **Minivans** (Th Sangkhlaburi at Th Thetsaban 1) to Kanchanaburi (175B, four hours, hourly 6am to 4pm) depart from the other side of the market, two blocks east of the bus stop.

The minivans' only regular stop between Sangkhlaburi and Kanchanaburi is Thong Pha Phum (fan/AC 70/80B, 1½ hours), so if you want to stop anywhere else, such as Sai Yok National Park (p195), you need to pay the full Thong Pha Phum or Kanchanaburi fare.

❶ Getting Around

J Family Homestay (p200) and P Guesthouse (p200) offer rental motorcycles (per day 200B) and the latter also has bicycles (100B) and canoes (per hour/day 60/250B).

A motorbike taxi between most guesthouses and the town centre or the bridge costs 20B.

AT A GLANCE

POPULATION
6 million

**NUMBER OF
NATIONAL PARKS**
31

BEST LAKE
Kwan Phayao (p232)

**BEST TREKKING
TOUR**
Rai Pian Karuna
(p210)

**BEST NORTHERN
CURRY SOUP**
Khao Soi Pa Orn
(p231)

WHEN TO GO

Nov–Jan Daytime
temps at the higher
elevations are rela-
tively comfortable,
but nights can dip
close to freezing in
some places.

Mar–May Daytime
temperatures can
exceed 40°C; smoke
from slash-and-burn
agriculture can fill
the skies.

Jun–Oct Avoid hik-
ing in rainy season.
Otherwise, showers
are strong but brief.

Cave, Mae Hong Son (p294)
GUITAR PHOTOGRAPHER/SHUTTERSTOCK ©

Northern Thailand

Northern Thailand's beautiful, rugged geography is the region's great temptation. Hidden among the forested mountains are Thailand's most iconic waterfalls and caves, as well as white-water rapids and jungle trails. The area is a playground for outdoor pursuits, too.

Northern Thailand's proximity to Laos and Myanmar gives the region a unique multicultural feel, and the Burmese, Chinese and Shan influences in towns such as Doi Mae Salong and Mae Hong Son might make you wonder which country you are in.

Conversely, the region's south is regarded as the birthplace of much of Thai culture. History buffs will love the Sukhothai and Kamphaeng Phet Historical Parks. And when you're not trekking or temple-hopping, Pai's party scene will keep you busy.

Northern Thailand Highlights

1 Nam Tok Thilawsu (p279)
Hiking and rafting to Thailand's most beautiful waterfall.

2 Doi Mae Salong (p218) Investigating the unique culture of the region's remote Chinese outposts.

3 Sukhothai Historical Park (p253) Time travelling back to Thailand's golden age.

4 Tham Lot (p291) Exploring one of the country's biggest caves, plus some of the 200 or so others in the area.

5 Mae Hong Son (p294) Kicking back in this laid-back town, with its palpable Burmese and Shan feel.

6 Pai (p283) Outdoor adventuring

7 Lampang (p246)
Taking in the cool cafes, designer hotels and great markets of Northern Thailand's hipster outpost.

8 Chiang Khong to Phayao (p232) Hiring a vehicle and driving one of the country's most stunning routes.

9 Nan (p234)
Living like a local in this little-visited city close to Laos.

by day and bar-hopping by night in the north's most popular backpacker destination.

History

Northern Thailand's history has been characterised by the shifting powers of a number of independent principalities. One of the most significant early cultural influences in the north was the Mon kingdom of Hariphunchai (based in contemporary Lamphun), which held sway from the late 8th century until the 13th century. Hariphunchai art and Buddha images are particularly distinctive, and many good examples can be found at the Hariphunchai National Museum (p245) in Lamphun.

The Thais, who are thought to have migrated south from China around the 7th century, united various principalities in the 13th century – this resulted in the creation of Sukhothai and the taking of Hariphunchai from the Mon. In 1238 Sukhothai declared itself an independent kingdom under King Si Intharathit and quickly expanded its sphere of influence. Because of this, and the significant influence the kingdom had on Thai art and culture, Sukhothai is considered by Thais to be the first true Thai kingdom.

In 1296 King Mengrai established Chiang Mai after conquering Hariphunchai. Later, in the 14th and 15th centuries, Chiang Mai, in an alliance with Sukhothai, became a part of the larger kingdom of Lan Na Thai (Million Thai Rice Fields), popularly referred to as Lanna. This empire extended as far south as Kamphaeng Phet and as far north as Luang Prabang in Laos. The golden age of Lanna was in the 15th century and, for a short time during this period, the Sukhothai capital was moved to Phitsanulok, and Chiang Mai increased in influence as a religious and cultural centre. However, during the 16th century, many of Lan Na Thai's important alliances weakened or fell apart, ultimately leading to the Burmese capturing Chiang Mai in 1556. Burmese control of Lanna lasted for the next two centuries. The Northern Thais regrouped after the Burmese took Ayuthaya in 1767 and, under King Kawila, Chiang Mai was recaptured in 1774 and the Burmese were pushed north.

In the late 19th century, Rama V of Bangkok made efforts to integrate the northern region with the centre to ward off the colonial threat. The completion of the northern railway to Chiang Mai in 1921 strengthened those links until the northern provinces finally became part of the kingdom of Siam in the early part of the 20th century.

NORTHERN THAILAND CHEAT SHEET

Northern Thailand covers a relatively big area, spanning lots of places, people and culture. It can all be a bit overwhelming, so to help you plan your trip, we've offered a few thematic leads.

Best for handicrafts Nan (p234)

Most exotic fresh market Mae Sot (p274)

Best for local food Chiang Rai (p213)

Best for noodles Sukhothai (p258)

Best for friendly locals Phrae (p240)

Best for cultural hiking Chiang Rai Province

Best for nature hiking Mae Hong Son Province (p283)

Best for ancient architecture Lampang (p246)

Best for ancient ruins nobody knows about Kamphaeng Phet (p270)

Best backpacker party scene Pai (p283)

Best off-the-beaten-track town Phayao (p232)

ⓘ Getting There & Away

AIR

For those in a hurry, Northern Thailand's air links are surprisingly good. At research time, Nok Air (p244), a subsidiary of Thai, had the most expansive network, with flights connecting several provincial capitals in the region with Bangkok or Chiang Mai. Other domestic airlines that cover the north include:

AirAsia (www.airasia.com) Within Northern Thailand, AirAsia flies between Bangkok's Don Mueang International Airport and Chiang Rai, Nan and Phitsanulok.

Bangkok Airways (www.bangkokair.com) Destinations in Northern Thailand include Chiang Rai, Lampang, Mae Hong Son and Sukhothai.

Thai Lion Air (www.lionairthai.com) Northern Thailand destinations include Chiang Rai and Phitsanulok.

Thai Smile (www.thaismileair.com) Flights to/from Chiang Rai and Mae Hong Son.

LAND

Just about everywhere in the region is accessible by bus and, increasingly, minivan, except among the communities along the Myanmar border,

SPEAKING NORTHERN THAI

Thailand's regional dialects vary greatly and can even be unintelligible to native speakers of Thai not familiar with the vernacular being spoken. Northerners used to take offence when outsiders tried speaking *găm méuang* (the colloquial name for the northern dialect) to them, an attitude that dates back to a time when central Thais considered northerners to be very backward and made fun of their dialect. Nowadays, most northerners are proud of their native language, and speaking a few words of the local lingo will go a long way in getting them to open up. The following are words and phrases that will help you talk to, flirt with, or perhaps just win some smiles from the locals.

Ôo găm méuang bòr jâhng I can't speak Northern Thai.

A yăng gór? What did you say?

An née tôw dai? How much is this?

Mee kôw nêung bòr? Do you have sticky rice?

Lám đáa đáa Delicious

Mâan lâ Yes/That's right

Yin dee nôe Thank you

Bòr mâan No

Gàht Market

Jôw (A polite word used by women; equivalent to the central Thai *ka*.)

where the *sŏrng·tăa·ou* (passenger pick-up truck, also spelt *songthaew*) is the transport of choice.

Train is the most comfortable way to get up north, although there's only one main northern line and it is comparatively slow.

ℹ️ Getting Around

An increasingly popular way of exploring Northern Thailand is with a hired vehicle. Despite the obvious risks of driving in Thailand, hiring is the best way to explore the countryside at your own pace and provides the opportunity to leave the beaten track at any moment. Car and motorcycle hire are available at most urban centres.

CHIANG RAI PROVINCE

Chiang Rai Province (จังหวัดเชียงราย), Thailand's northernmost province, is a geographical mishmash. The mountains in the far east are among the most dramatic in the country, the lowland Mekong River floodplains to the northeast are not unlike those one would find much further south in Isan, while the province shares borders with Myanmar and Laos. Those nearby frontiers help ensure that Chiang Rai is one of the most ethnically diverse provinces in Thailand, home to a significant minority of hill peoples, Shan and other Tai groups, as well as immigrants from China.

Chiang Rai

📞 053 / POP 77,000

This small, amiable city is worth getting to know, with its relaxed atmosphere, fine local food and good-value accommodation. This is despite the fact that Chiang Rai Province has such a diversity of attractions that its capital is often overlooked. It's also the logical base from which to plan excursions to the more remote corners of the province.

Founded by Phaya Mengrai in 1262 as part of the Lao–Thai Lanna kingdom, Chiang Rai (เชียงราย) didn't become a Siamese territory until 1786.

◉ Sights

⭐ **Mae Fah Luang**
Art & Culture Park MUSEUM
(ไร่แม่ฟ้าหลวง; www.maefahluang.org; 313 Mu 7, Ban Pa Ngiw; adult/child 200B/free; ⊙8.30am-5.30pm Tue-Sun) In addition to a museum that houses one of Thailand's biggest collections of Lanna artefacts, this vast, meticulously landscaped compound includes antique and contemporary art, Buddhist temples and other structures. It's located about 4km west of the centre of Chiang Rai; a túk-túk or taxi here will run to around 100B.

Haw Kaew, the park's museum, has a collection of mostly teak-based artefacts and art

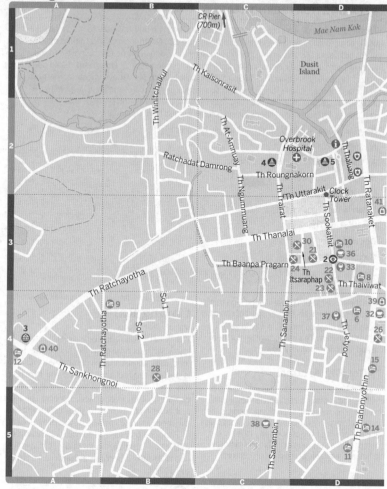

from across the former Lanna region, as well as a temporary exhibition room.

Haw Kham, a temple-like tower built in 1984 from the remains of 32 wooden houses, is arguably the park's centrepiece. The immense size of the structure – allegedly influenced by Lanna-era Wat Pongsanuk in Lampang – with its Buddha image seemingly hovering over white sand and its sacred, candlelit aura culminate in a vibe not unlike an indigenous place of worship.

You'll probably have to ask staff to open up Haw Kham Noi, a structure housing folksy but beautiful Buddhist murals taken from a dismantled teak temple in Phrae.

★ Hilltribe Museum
& Education Center   MUSEUM
(พิพิธภัณฑ์และศูนย์การศึกษาชาวเขา; www.pdacr. org; 3rd fl, 620/25 Th Thanalai; 50B; ⊙9am-6pm Mon-Fri, 10am-6pm Sat & Sun) This museum and cultural centre is a good place to visit before undertaking any hill-tribe trek. Run by a nonprofit, the venue has displays that are visually underwhelming but contain a wealth of information on Thailand's various tribes and the issues that surround them.

Wat Phra Kaew   BUDDHIST TEMPLE
(วัดพระแก้ว; Th Trairat; donations appreciated; ⊙temple 7am-7pm, museum 9am-5pm) Originally

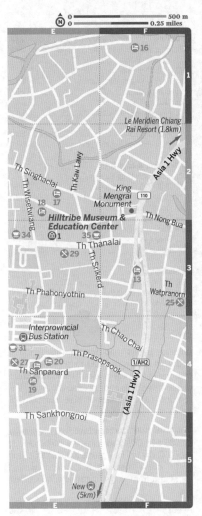

paraphernalia from virtually every corner of the former Lanna kingdom. The items, some of which truly are one of a kind, range from a monkey-bone food taster used by Lanna royalty to an impressive carved throne from Chiang Tung, Myanmar. The museum is located 2km west of the town centre and can be a bit tricky to find; túk-túk will go here for about 60B.

Wat Phra Singh BUDDHIST TEMPLE

(วัดพระสิงห์; Th Singhaclai; ☺ donations appreciated; ☺ daylight hours) This temple dates back to the late 14th century, and its oldest surviving original buildings are typical Northern Thai–style wooden structures with low, sweeping roofs. The main *wí·hǎhn* (sanctuary) houses impressive wooden doors thought to have been carved by local artists, as well as a copy of Chiang Mai's sacred Phra Singh Buddha.

Tham Tu Pu & Buddha Cave BUDDHIST TEMPLE

(ถ้ำตุ๊ปู่/ถ้ำพระ; Th Ka Salong; ☺ daylight hours) **FREE** Cross the Mae Fah Luang Bridge (located just northwest of the city centre) to the northern side of Mae Nam Kok and you'll come to a turn-off for both Tham Tu Pu and the Buddha Cave. Neither attraction is particularly amazing on its own, but the surrounding country is beautiful and makes an ideal destination for a lazy bike or motorcycle ride.

Follow the road for 1km, then turn off onto a dirt path for 200m to the base of a limestone cliff, where there is a steep set of stairs leading to a main chamber holding a dusty Buddha statue; this is **Tham Tu Pu**.

Continue along the same road for 3km more (the sign says 'Buddha Images Cave') and you'll reach **Buddha Cave**, a cavern by Mae Nam Kok containing a tiny but active Buddhist temple, a lone monk and numerous cats. The temple was one of several destinations on a visit to the region by King Rama V in the early 20th century.

Clock Tower LANDMARK

(หอนาฬิกา; Th Phahonyothin) Chiang Rai's 'main' clock tower lights up at night and is a popular photo opportunity.

👉 Tours

Nearly every guesthouse, hotel and travel agency in Chiang Rai offers hiking excursions in hill country, some of which have a grassroots, sustainable or nonprofit emphasis.

called Wat Pa Yia (Bamboo Forest Monastery) in the local dialect, this is the city's most revered Buddhist temple. The main prayer hall is a medium-sized, well-preserved wooden structure. The octagonal *chedi* (stupa) behind it dates from the late 14th century and is in typical Lanna style. The adjacent two-storey teak building is a museum housing various Lanna artefacts.

Oub Kham Museum MUSEUM

(พิพิธภัณฑ์อูบคำ; www.oubkhammuseum. com; Th Nakhai; adult/child incl tour 300/200B; ☺ 8am-5pm) This slightly zany private museum houses an impressive collection of

Chiang Rai

⊙ Top Sights
1 Hilltribe Museum & Education Center	E3

⊙ Sights
2 Clock Tower	D3
3 Oub Kham Museum	A4
4 Wat Phra Kaew	C2
5 Wat Phra Singh	D2

⊙ Activities, Courses & Tours
PDA Tours & Travel	(see 1)

⊜ Sleeping
6 Baan Bua Guest House	D4
7 Baan Warabordee	E4
8 Bed & Bike Poshtel	D3
9 Ben Guesthouse	B4
10 Chiangrai Hotel	D3
11 Connect Hostel	D5
12 De Hug	A4
13 FUN-D Hostel	F3
14 Happy Nest Hostel	D5
15 Hi Chiangrai	D4
16 Legend of Chiang Rai	F1
17 Moon & Sun Hotel	E2
18 Nak Nakara Hotel	E2
19 Na-Rak-O Resort	E4
20 Sleepy House	E4

⊗ Eating
21 Four Stars Restaurant	D3
22 Heaven Burger	D3
23 Khao Soi Phor Jai	D3
24 Kunda Vegan Vegetarian	D3
25 Lung Eed	F3
26 Muang Thong	D4
27 Namnigew Pa Nuan	E4
28 Paa Suk	B4
29 Phu Lae	E3
30 Rosprasert Muslim Food	D3

⊝ Drinking & Nightlife
31 BaanChivitMai Bakery	E4
32 Cat 'N' A Cup	D4
33 Chiang Rai Ramluek	D3
34 Doi Chaang	E3
35 Palamer Cafe	E3
36 Pangkhon Coffee	D3
37 Peace House Bar	D4
38 Roast	C5

⊝ Shopping
39 Night Bazaar	D4
40 Thanon Khon Muan	A4
41 Walking Street	D3

Trek pricing depends on the types of activities and the number of days and participants. A one-day trek for four people should start at around 1300B per person. For a three-night trek for four people, rates start at around 3500B per person. Everything from accommodation to transport and food is normally included in the price.

★ **Rai Pian Karuna**   TREKKING
(📞 062 246 1897; www.facebook.com/raipiankaruna; treks 2000-5000B) This community-based social enterprise conducts one-day and multiday treks and homestays at Akha, Lahu and Lua villages in Mae Chan, north of Chiang Rai. Other activities, from weeklong volunteering stints to cooking courses, are also on offer.

Chiang Rai Bicycle Tours   CYCLING
(📞 053 774506, 085 662 4347; www.chiangraibicycletour.com; half-/full-day tours from 1250/1850B) Recommended two-wheeled excursions in the area surrounding Chiang Rai. The office is 7km south of town: call or email to book a tour.

Mirror Foundation   TREKKING
(📞 053 719554; www.thailandecotour.org; 1-/2-/3-day treks from 2800/4300/5650B) Although its

rates are higher than other outfits, trekking with this nonprofit NGO helps support the training of its local guides. Treks range from one to three days and traverse the Akha, Karen and Lahu villages of Mae Yao District, north of Chiang Rai.

Thailand Hilltribe Holidays   TREKKING
(📞 085 548 0884; www.thailandhilltribeholidays.com; 1-/2-day trek for 4 people 1600/3200B) This outfit offers sustainably minded guided tours and homestays in and around Chiang Rai.

PDA Tours & Travel   TREKKING
(📞 053 740088; Hilltribe Museum & Education Center, 3rd fl, 620/25 Th Thanalai; treks 1200-3900B; ☻9am-6pm Mon-Fri, 10am-6pm Sat & Sun) One- to three-day treks are available through this NGO. Profits go back into community projects that include HIV/AIDS education, mobile health clinics, education scholarships and the establishment of village-owned banks.

Courses

Cook Thai Yourself   COOKING
(📞 081 844 9913; www.facebook.com/CTYchiangrai; lessons from 1000B; ☻lessons 9am-3pm) This outfit gets good feedback for its full-day

'food adventures', including the visits to the market for ingredients, and cookery lessons in a semi-rural location 20 minutes from Chiang Rai. Transportation is included in the fee.

Suwannee Thai Cooking Class COOKING
(☑084 740 7119; www.thaicookingclasschiangrai. com; lessons 1250B; ☉courses 9.30am-2pm) Suwannee's cooking courses involve a visit to a local market and instruction in cooking four dishes. Her house is about 3km outside the city centre, but she can pick you up at most centrally located hotels and guesthouses.

🛏 Sleeping

Chiang Rai has a great selection of lodgings, most of them reasonable value. Budget places cluster in the town centre around Th Jetyod; while the majority of midrange places are a brief walk from downtown. Chiang Rai's upscale accommodation is generally located outside the town centre.

🛏 Town Centre

Bed & Bike Poshtel HOSTEL $
(☑064 848 6566; bedandbikechiangrai@gmail. com; 869/53-54 Th Thaiviwat; 4-/8-bed dm 240/220B; r incl breakfast 500-700B; ☀🔊) There's an industrial theme – metal, wood and stone floors – to the design at this well-kept place. Dorms are windowless but comfortable, with curtains, reading lights and lockers. The private rooms share clean bathrooms. The downstairs cafe-bar features a pool table, and bikes can be hired.

FUN-D Hostel HOSTEL $
(☑053 716777; www.facebook.com/FunD HostelChiangRai; 753 Th Phahonyothin; incl breakfast dm 230B; r 650B; ☀🔊) This tidy hostel is located above a restaurant-bar-cafe. Dorms are spacious and bright, ranging from six to eight beds, and share clean bathrooms. The two private rooms here are big and comfortable and a decent deal. Free bicycles and motorbikes can be hired.

Connect Hostel HOSTEL $
(☑053 711672; www.facebook.com/connect hostel; 935/20 Th Phahonyothin; incl breakfast 6-/4-bed dm 200/250B, r 650B; ☀🔊) This newish place gets good feedback. Dorms are clean and have their own bathrooms; there's decent locker space and beds are curtained off. Free bicycles and treks can be organised. The hostel is about 600m south of the town centre.

Moon & Sun Hotel HOTEL $
(☑053 719279; 632 Th Singhaclai; r 399-699B; ☀🔊) It doesn't look like much from the outside, but this place has rooms that are good value, if a little dated. The cheapest rooms don't get a lot of natural light, but the more expensive ones are large and bright and have four-poster beds and sofas. The hotel sees more local travellers than foreigners.

Baan Bua Guest House GUESTHOUSE $
(☑053 718880; baanbua@yahoo.com; 879/2 Th Jetyod; r 350-600B; ☀🔊) Set around a peaceful garden, this quiet, friendly guesthouse is a decent budget option. The 17 rooms, the cheapest of which are fan-only, are a little dated (no TVs) but are clean and have small porches. There's also a wood-floored traditional house with four bedrooms for rent (2100B).

Sleepy House GUESTHOUSE $$
(☑064 114 9919; www.facebook.com/sleepy housecr; 90/5 Th Sanpanard; r incl breakfast 1100-1500B; ☀🔊) This new place on a residential street is walking distance from the interprovincial bus station. The 12 rooms aren't huge but are spotless, modern and comfortable, with beds raised off the floor on platforms. There's a small communal area outside, too.

Na-Rak-O Resort HOTEL $$
(☑081 951 7801; www.facebook.com/narako resort; off Th Sanpanard; r incl breakfast 900-1300B; 🅿☀🔊) *Nâh·rák* is Thai for 'cute', a spot-on description of this tucked-away hotel that has bright rooms decked out in pastel colours and strewn with beanbags. Beds are raised off the floor Chinese-style, the bathrooms are big and the staff smiley.

Happy Nest Hostel HOSTEL $$
(☑053 715031; www.happynesthostel.com; 931 Phahonyothin Rd; 6-/8-bed dm 370/320B, r 800-1400B; ☀🔊) It's a little more expensive than other hostels in town, but this bright and fresh place compensates with efficient staff, a downstairs cafe and a couple of chill-out areas spread over its three floors. Dorms come with proper beds and lockers; private rooms are on the small side. Bicycles can be hired and tours and treks arranged.

Chiangrai Hotel HOTEL $$
(☑053 711266; www.thechiangraihotel.com; 519 Th Sookathit; r 790-1220B; ☀🔊) Slap in the centre of town, the Chiang Rai is an efficient budget to midrange option with rooms on three floors set around a breezy atrium. The white-

NORTHERN THAI CUISINE

The cuisine of Thailand's northern provinces is indicative of the region's seasonal and relatively cool climate, not to mention a love for pork, veggies and all things deep fried. Northern Thai cuisine is probably the most seasonal and least spicy of Thailand's regional schools of cooking, often relying on bitter or other dried spice flavours.

Paradoxically (and unfortunately), it can be difficult to find authentic local food in Northern Thailand. Outside of Chiang Mai and the other large cities in Northern Thailand, there are relatively few restaurants serving northern-style dishes, and the vast majority of authentic local food is sold from stalls in 'to go' bags. Some must-try dishes include:

Đam sôm oh The Northern Thai version of *sôm·đam* substitutes pomelo for green papaya.

Đôm yam The Northern Thai version of this Thai soup staple is flavoured with some of the same dried spices that feature in *lâhp kôo·a*.

Gaang hang·lair Burmese in origin (*hang* is a corruption of the Burmese *hin*, meaning curry), this rich pork curry is often seen at festivals and ceremonies. Try a bowl at Phu Lae (673/1 Th Thanalai; mains 120-250B; ⊙11am-3pm & 5-10pm), in Chiang Rai.

Kà·nŏm jeen nám ngée·o Fresh rice noodles served with a meaty and tart pork- and tomato-based broth. An excellent bowl can be got at Paa Suk (p214), in Chiang Rai.

Kâap mŏo Deep-fried pork crackling is a common, delicious side dish in Northern Thailand.

Kôw gân jîn Banana leaf packets of rice mixed with blood, steamed and served with garlic oil. Available at Paa Suk (p214), in Chiang Rai.

Kôw soy This popular curry-based noodle dish is possibly Burmese in origin and was probably introduced to Northern Thailand by travelling Chinese merchants. A mild but tasty version is available at Khao Soi Phor Jai (p214), in Chiang Rai.

Lâhp kôo·a Literally 'fried *lâhp*', this dish takes the famous Thai minced-meat 'salad' and fries it with a mixture of unique dried spices. Try the version at Pu Som Restaurant (203/1 Th Khamyot; mains 35-95B; ⊙9am-9pm), in Nan.

Lôo Raw blood mixed with curry paste and served over deep-fried intestines and crispy noodles – the most hardcore northern dish of all and one often associated with Phrae Province.

Năam Fermented raw pork, a sour delicacy that tastes much better than it sounds.

Nám prík nùm Green chillies, shallots and garlic that are grilled then mashed into a stringy and spicy paste served with sticky rice, parboiled veggies and deep-fried pork crackling. Available at just about every evening market in Northern Thailand.

Nám prík òrng A chilli dip of Shan origin made from tomatoes and minced pork – a Northern Thai bolognese of sorts.

Sâi òo·a A grilled pork sausage seasoned with copious fresh herbs. Available at Muu Thup (p306), in Mae Sariang.

washed rooms are compact but clean and light with good beds. There are self-service laundry facilities plus bicycles and motorbikes for hire.

Baan Warabordee HOTEL $$
(☑053 754488; warabordee59@hotmail.com; 59/1 Th Sanpanard; r incl breakfast 800-1100B; ❄️🛜) A quiet, good-value hotel has been created from this three-storey Thai villa. Rooms are decked out in dark woods and light fabrics and there's an inviting garden. Expect a 30% discount in the low season (May to October).

Hi Chiangrai HOTEL $$$
(☑053 716699; www.hichiangrai.com; 902/3 Th Phahonyothin; r incl breakfast 1700-2700B; ❄️🛜🏊) A well-kept hotel that's popular with Chinese travellers, with modern and compact rooms set around an atrium featuring a mini indoor swimming pool, a unique touch in Chiang Rai. Some rooms have balconies, and all feature decent beds and safety boxes.

Nak Nakara Hotel HOTEL $$$
(☑053 717700; www.naknakara.com; 661 Th Uttarakit; r incl breakfast 2800-3800B; ste 5400B;

⊞ 🗟 🕮) A hit-and-miss Lanna theme pervades at this modern and expansive-feeling hotel. Rooms are set around a pleasant pool and shady garden, but have smallish bathrooms and are rather characterless. They are comfortable, though, and the staff are solicitous.

🛏 Outside Town

Ben Guesthouse   GUESTHOUSE **$$**
(☑ 053 716775; www.benguesthousechiangrai.com; 351/10 Soi 4, Th Sankhongnoi; r 400-600B, ste 1200B; ⊞ 🗟 🕮) This spotless compound has a bit of everything, from fan-cooled cheap rooms to immense suites, not to mention a pool. Rooms are plain and simple but reasonably sized and share long balconies.

It's 1.2km from the town centre, at the end of Soi 4 on Th Sankhongnoi (the street is called Th Sathanpayabarn where it intersects with Th Phahonyothin).

De Hug   HOTEL **$$$**
(☑ 053 711789; www.dehughotel.com; Rte 1211; r incl breakfast 1400-2500B; ⊞ 🗟 🕮) De Hug is a four-storey hotel complex with vast rooms outfitted with modern amenities and furniture. Bathrooms are a little plain for the price, but there's a pool and restaurant. It's comfortable without being flash and the staff are nice. The hotel is located 2km west of the town centre (a 60B túk-túk ride), across from the Oub Kham Museum.

⭐**Le Meridien Chiang Rai Resort** HOTEL **$$$**
(☑ 053 603333; www.lemeridien.com; 221/2 Th Kwaewai; incl breakfast r 7000-9000B, ste 20,000B; ⊞ 🗟 🕮) Chiang Rai's grandest upscale resort is about 2km outside the city centre on a beautiful stretch of the Mae Nam Kok. Rooms are immense and decked out in greys, whites and blacks, and are as comfortable as the prices suggest. The compound includes two restaurants, an infinity pool and a gym and spa.

Legend of Chiang Rai   HOTEL **$$$**
(☑ 053 910400; www.TheLegend-ChiangRai.com; 124/15 Th Kohloy; incl breakfast r 9900-17,500B, villas 27,500-38,000B; ⊞ 🗟 🕮) Boasting a tranquil riverside location, this resort is styled like a traditional Lanna village. Rooms are large and luxuriously understated, with furniture in calming creams and rattan, and feature rain showers and terraces or balconies. The riverside infinity pool and spa are the icing on the comfort-filled cake. Significant online discounts are available.

🍴 Eating

Come dinner time, you'll inevitably be pointed in the direction of Chiang Rai's night bazaar, but the food there is generally average – you've been warned. Instead, if

---

DON'T MISS

CAFE CULTURE IN CHIANG RAI

For a small city, Chiang Rai has an enviable spread of high-quality, Western-style cafes. That's mainly because some of Thailand's finest coffee beans are grown in the more remote corners of Chiang Rai Province.

BaanChivitMai Bakery (www.bcmthai.com; Th Prasopsook; ⊘ 8am-6pm Mon-Fri, to 5pm Sat & Sun; 🗟) In addition to a proper cup of coffee made from local beans, there are surprisingly authentic Swedish-style sweets and Western-style meals and sandwiches at this popular bakery. Profits go to BaanChivitMai, an organisation that runs homes and education projects for vulnerable, orphaned or AIDS-affected children.

Palamer Cafe (881/8 Th Nongsrijang; ⊘ 10am-8pm Tue-Fri, 10am-10pm Sat & Sun; 🗟) A stylish but relaxed place that offers both local and foreign beans in a refined atmosphere. There's a good bakery here, too.

Doi Chaang (Th Thanalai; ⊘ 6.30am-7.30pm; 🗟) Doi Chaang is the leading brand among Chiang Rai coffees, and its beans are now sold as far afield as Canada and Europe.

Pangkhon Coffee (Th Sookathit; ⊘ 7am-6pm; 🗟) Combine coffee brewed from local beans with views of Chiang Rai's gilded clock tower.

Roast (Th Sankhongluang; ⊘ 7.30am-5pm) This 'drip bar' treats local beans with the utmost respect. Th Sankhongluang is a block south of Chiang Rai Technical College, about 1.2km from the centre of town.

DON'T MISS

HEAVEN & HELL: TEMPLES OUTSIDE CHIANG RAI

Just outside Chiang Rai are Wat Rong Khun and Baandam, two of the province's most touted, bizarre and worthwhile destinations.

Whereas many of Thailand's Buddhist temples have centuries of history, Wat Rong Khun's (วัดร่องขุ่น; White Temple; off Rte 1/AH2; 50B; ☺8am-5.30pm) construction began in 1997 by noted Thai painter turned architect Chalermchai Kositpipat. It's a striking structure that, from a distance, seems to be made of glittering porcelain.

To enter the temple, you walk over a bridge and pool of reaching arms (symbolising desire). Inside, instead of the traditional Buddha life depictions, the artist has painted contemporary scenes representing samsara (the realm of rebirth and delusion). Images such as a plane smashing into the Twin Towers sit alongside reproductions of Keanu Reeves as Neo from The Matrix, Elvis, Hello Kitty and Superman, among many others.

The temple is located about 13km south of Chiang Rai. To get here, catch any bus from Chiang Rai's interprovincial bus station with 'White Temple' written on it in English (20B, 40 minutes, frequent services from 6.15am to 6.10pm).

A rather sinister counterpoint to Wat Rong Khun and the bizarre brainchild of Thai National Artist Thawan Duchanee, Baandam (บ้านดำ, Black House; off Rte 1/AH2; adult/child 80B/free; ☺9am-5pm) unites several structures, most of which are stained black and ominously decked out with animal pelts, antlers, skulls and bones.

The centrepiece is a black, cavernous, temple-like building holding a long wooden dining table and chairs made from deer antlers – a virtual Satan's dining room. Other buildings include white, breast-shaped bedrooms, dark phallus-decked bathrooms, and a bone- and fur-lined 'chapel'.

It's located 13km north of Chiang Rai in Nang Lae; any Mae Sai–bound bus will drop you off here for 20B.

---

you're in town on a weekend, hit the vendors at Chiang Rai's open-air markets, Thanon Khon Muan and the Walking Street, which feature a good selection of local dishes.

★ Heaven Burger   BURGERS $

(1025/5 Th Jetyod; mains 99-129B; ☺8am-9pm; 🖉) Owned and run by the whip-smart Jane, a member of the Akha minority, this place has a rustic setting with random garden furniture and sawn-off doors as tables. The food is great – all-day breakfasts and, above all, superb burgers, including a fine veggie option; all burgers come with home-made buns and gratinéed potato-skin fries.

★ Lung Eed   THAI $

(Th Watpranorn; mains 40-60B; ☺11am-9pm Mon-Sat) One of Chiang Rai's most delicious dishes is available at this simple, friendly shophouse restaurant. There's an English-language menu on the wall, but don't miss the sublime *lâhp gài* (minced chicken fried with local spices and topped with crispy deep-fried chicken skin, shallots and garlic). The restaurant is about 150m east of Rte 1/AH2.

★ Khao Soi Phor Jai   THAI $

(Th Jetyod; mains 40-50B; ☺8am-4pm) Phor Jai serves mild but delicious bowls of the eponymous curry noodle dish, as well as a few other northern Thai staples. There's no Roman-script sign, but look for the open-air shophouse with the white-and-blue interior.

Namnigew Pa Nuan   MULTICUISINE $

(Th Sanpanard; mains 35-220B; ☺9am-5pm) This semi-concealed gem (there's no Roman-script sign: look for the bamboo doorway) serves a unique mix of Vietnamese and Northern Thai dishes. Tasty food, friendly service and a fun atmosphere make us wish it was open for dinner as well.

Paa Suk   THAI $

(Th Sankhongnoi; mains 35-45B; ☺9am-3pm) Popular with locals, Paa Suk does big, rich bowls of *kà·nŏm jeen nám ngée·o* (a broth of pork or beef and tomatoes served over fresh rice noodles). The restaurant is between Soi 4 and Soi 5 of Th Sankhongnoi. There's no Roman-script sign; look for the yellow sign.

Rosprasert Muslim Food   THAI $

(Th Itsaraphap; mains 50-100B; ☺7am-8pm) This shophouse restaurant next to the mosque on Th Itsaraphap dishes up tasty Thai-Muslim favourites, including a fine *kôw mòk gài* (the Thai version of chicken biryani). It also does a decent beef oxtail soup and *kôw soy* (noodles in a curry broth). The English-language sign says 'Muslim Food'.

★**Kunda Vegan Vegetarian**   VEGETARIAN $$
(www.kundacafe.com; 372 Trairat Rd; mains 150-360B; ☺9am-5pm; ⚡) There's no tofu, no wi-fi and no reservations at this delightful addition to the Chiang Rai dining scene set over two floors of a former shophouse. Lounge on cushions and enjoy the old-school wood-panelled decor while tucking into vegan or veggie breakfasts, crêpes, salads and super smoothies. Everything – the bread, pesto, yoghurt and hummus – is made fresh daily.

Four Stars Restaurant   THAI $$
(423/3 Th Baanpa Pragarn; mains 45-240B; ☺10am-9pm Sun-Fri; 🛜) Popular with both Thais and foreign tourists thanks to a consistently tasty *kôw soy,* a noodle and meat dish served with a curry broth, though the *sâi òo·a* (Northern Thai sausage with herbs) is equally good. It also does a selection of classic rice and noodle dishes.

Muang Thong   MULTICUISINE $$
(cnr Th Sanpanard & Th Phahonyothin; mains 50-300B; ☺24hr) Comfort food for Thais and foreign travellers alike: this long-standing, semi-open-air place is always busy at night and serves the usual repertoire of satisfyingly salty and spicy Chinese-Thai dishes.

🍷 Drinking & Nightlife

Th Jetyod is Chiang Rai's rather tacky drinking strip. The streets close to Th Jetyod are also home to a growing number of Thai-style bars, a few with live music.

Cat 'N' A Cup   CAFE
(cnr Th Phahonyothin & Th Prasopsook; ☺11am-10pm; 🛜) The coffee and cakes here are good enough, but it's the presence of 25 cats – all different breeds – that have made this place wildly popular with both locals and visitors. Some cats are happy to be petted, others treat the customers with lofty disdain. After a hard day's lounging, the felines retire upstairs to their own luxury cat dormitory.

Peace House Bar   BAR
(Th Jetyod; ☺6pm-midnight; 🛜) Flying the Rasta flag in Chiang Rai, the Peace House has a pool table, live music a few nights a week, a mellow vibe and a shady garden that's popular with people who like to roll their own cigarettes.

Chiang Rai Ramluek   BAR
(Th Phahonyothin; ☺4pm-midnight) For a Thai-style night out on the town, consider this lively place. There's no English-language sign, but follow the live music and look for the knot of outdoor tables. Food is also available.

🛍 Shopping

Thanon Khon Muan   MARKET
(Th Sankhongnoi; ☺6-9pm Sun) Come Sunday evening, the stretch of Th Sankhongnoi from Soi 2 heading west is closed to traffic and in its place are vendors selling clothes, handicrafts and local food. Th Sankhongnoi is called Th Sathanpayabarn where it intersects with the southern end of Th Phahonyothin.

Walking Street   MARKET
(Th Thanalai; ☺4-10pm Sat) If you're in town on a Saturday evening, don't miss the open-air Walking Street, an expansive street market focusing on all things Chiang Rai, from handicrafts to local dishes. The market spans Th Thanalai from the Hilltribe Museum to the main fresh-produce market.

Night Bazaar   MARKET
(off Th Phahonyothin; ☺6-11pm) Adjacent to the bus station off Th Phahonyothin is Chiang Rai's night market. On a much smaller scale than the one in Chiang Mai, it is nevertheless an OK place to find an assortment of handicrafts and touristy souvenirs.

ℹ Information

There are many banks with ATMs and foreign-exchange services on both Th Phahonyothin and Th Thanalai.

ℹ Getting There & Away

AIR

Chiang Rai International Airport (Mae Fah Luang International Airport; ☎053 798000; www.chiangraiairportthai.com) is approximately 8km north of the city. The terminal has airline offices, restaurants, currency exchange, a post office and several car-rental booths. A new bus connects the airport with Chiang Rai's two bus stations (6am to 6pm, every 40 minutes, 20B). Taxis run into town from the airport for 160B. From town, a metered trip with **Chiang Rai Taxi** (☎053 773477) will cost around 130B.

There are 15 daily flights to Bangkok's Don Mueang International Airport and 14 to Bangkok's Suvarnabhumi International Airport. At the time of research the only direct international flight was to Kunming, China, with **China Eastern** (☑ 089 850 5889, nationwide 02 636 6980; www.ceair.com; King's Romans, Chiang Rai International Airport; ☺ 8.30am-5pm).

BOAT

Passenger boats ply Mae Nam Kok between Chiang Rai and Tha Ton (in Chiang Mai), stopping at Ban Ruam Mit along the way. Boats depart from the **CR Pier** (☑ 053 750009; ☺ 7am-4pm), 2km northwest of town. A túk-túk (motorised transport; pronounced đúk đúk') to the pier should cost about 80B.

Passenger boats depart from CR Pier at 10.30am daily; the trip to Tha Ton takes about three hours (400B), to Ban Ruam Mit around an hour (100B). Alternatively, you can charter a boat for 800B for around three hours. If water levels are low, boats may not be able to reach Tha Ton.

BUS & MINIVAN

Buses bound for destinations within Chiang Rai Province, as well as some minivans and mostly slow, fan-cooled buses bound for a handful of Northern Thailand destinations, depart from the **interprovincial bus station** (☑ 053 715952; Th Prasopsook) in the centre of town. If you're heading beyond Chiang Rai, you'll have to go to the **new bus station** (☑ 053 773989; Rte 1/ AH2), 5km south of town.

BUSES FROM CHIANG RAI

DESTINATION	FARE (B)	DURATION (HR)	FREQUENCY
Bangkok	544-890	11-12	frequent 8.30am-7.50pm (new bus station)
Bokeo (Laos)	220	3	10am & 4.30pm (new bus station)
Chiang Khong	65	2	frequent 6am-5pm (interprovincial bus station)
Chiang Mai	129-258	3-7	frequent 6.15am-7.30pm (interprovincial bus station)
Chiang Saen	37	1½	frequent 6am-5pm (interprovincial bus station)
Huay Xai (Laos)	220	3	10am (new bus station)
Lampang	137-274	4-5	8.40am, 10am, 1.20pm (interprovincial bus station)
Luang Prabang (Laos)	950	18	12.30pm Mon, Wed, Fri, Sun (new bus station)
Mae Chan (for Mae Salong/Santikhiri)	25	45min	frequent 6am-5pm (interprovincial bus station)
Mae Sai	39	1½	frequent 6am-5pm (interprovincial bus station)
Mae Sot	416	12	8.40am (new bus station)
Nakhon Ratchasima (Khorat)	569-664	12-13	4 departures 6.30am-7.20pm (new bus station)
Phayao	60-120	1½-2	8.40am, 10am, 1.20pm (interprovincial bus station)
Phitsanulok	304-355	6-7	hourly 6.30am-7.30pm (new bus station)
Phrae	185-216	4	frequent 6am-6pm (new bus station)
Sukhothai	231	8	hourly 7.30-10.30am (new bus station)
Ubon Ratchathani	884	12	2pm (new bus station)

MOTORCYCLE TOURING

A good introduction to motorcycle touring in Northern Thailand is the 100km Samoeng loop, which can be tackled in half a day. The route extends north from Chiang Mai and follows Rtes 107, 1096 and 1269, passing through excellent scenery and ample curves and providing a taste of what a longer ride up north will be like. The 470km Chiang Rai loop, which passes through scenic Fang and Tha Ton along Rtes 107, 1089 and 118, is another popular ride that can be broken up with a stay in Chiang Rai.

The classic northern route is the Mae Hong Son loop, a 600km ride that begins in Chiang Mai and takes in Rte 1095's 1864 curves, with possible stays in Pai, Mae Hong Son and Mae Sariang, before looping back to Chiang Mai via Rte 108. A lesser known but equally fun option is to follow Rtes 1155 and 1093 from Chiang Khong in Chiang Rai Province to the little-visited city of Phayao, a day trip that passes through some of the most dramatic mountain scenery in the country.

The best source of information on motorcycle touring in the north is Golden Triangle Rider (GT Rider; www.gt-rider.com). It publishes a series of terrific motorcycle-touring-based maps, with its website including heaps of information on hiring bikes (including recommended hire shops in Chiang Mai and Chiang Rai) and bike insurance, plus a variety of suggested tours with maps and an interactive forum.

Frequent *sŏrng·tǎa·ou* (passenger pick-up trucks) linking the new bus station and the interprovincial station run from 6am to 5.30pm (20B, 15 minutes). Or you can catch the purple-coloured bus that links the airport to the bus stations (6am to 6pm, every 40 minutes, 20B).

There's a direct international bus from Chiang Rai to Luang Prabang (Laos). There are also buses to Bokeo and Huay Xai (both in Laos), where it's possible to connect to Kunming (China), Luang Nam Tha (Laos) and Vientiane (Laos).

ⓘ Getting Around

Central Chiang Rai is easy enough to tackle on foot or bicycle. Bicycles (from 50B per day) and motorbikes (from 200B per day) can be hired from your accommodation or at travel agencies and shops around town. Otherwise, túk-túk congregate around the interprovincial bus station and charge approximately 30B to 50B per person for destinations in town.

Chiang Rai Taxi (p215) operates inexpensive metered taxis in and around town. Taxis can be found at the bus stations as well.

Ban Ruam Mit

☏ 053 / POP 3000

Ban Ruam Mit (บ้านร่วมมิตร) means 'mixed village', an accurate description of this riverside community that's home to ethnic groups including Thai, Karen, Lisu and Akha. Only 20km from Chiang Rai and accessed either by boat or road, Ban Ruam Mit makes a convenient base for exploration in the surrounding hills.

◉ Sights & Activities

Many visitors come to Ban Ruam Mit to ride elephants (which we don't recommend as it's been proven to be harmful to the animals). Better options include hikes to the surrounding area's numerous hill villages, as well as the local hot springs and national park.

Pha Soet Hot Spring HOT SPRINGS
(บ่อน้ำร้อนผาเสริฐ; Ban Pha Soet; adult/child 30/10B; ⊙ 8.30am-6pm) The hot water from this natural spring has been redirected into a communal pool; for a more private experience, rooms are also available (50B to 80B). Ban Pha Soet is located about 3km west of Ban Ruam Mit.

Lamnamkok National Park NATIONAL PARK
(อุทยานแห่งชาติลำน้ำกก; ⊙ 8am-4.30pm) Dating to 2002, this is one of Thailand's youngest national parks. The area is home to waterfalls and, most notably, a hot spring. The latter is a short walk from the park headquarters, while longer excursions require a guide. The headquarters are about 3km west of Ban Ruam Mit.

🛌 Sleeping & Eating

There are a few basic eateries in Ban Ruam Mit, and each of the hotels has its own restaurant.

Akha Hill House HOTEL $
(☏ 089 997 5505; www.akhahill.com; r 300-500B, bungalows 600-2000B; ❄ �ⓢ) On a steep hillside approaching an Akha village is

this beautifully situated yet underwhelming hotel. Accommodation ranges from shared-bathroom, fan-cooled rooms to spacious, air-con bungalows. Most visitors stay as part of trekking packages, which get mixed reviews. It's located about 5km south of Ban Pha Soet.

★ **Bamboo Nest de Chiang Rai**   GUESTHOUSE $$

(☎ 089 953 2330, 095 686 4755; www.bamboo nest-chiangrai.com; bungalows incl breakfast & dinner 1100-1400B) The Lahu village that's home to this unique place is only an hour's drive from Chiang Rai but feels very remote. Accommodation consists of simple but spacious bamboo huts perched on a steep hill overlooking tiered rice fields. Electricity is provided by solar panels, so give your devices a rest and instead take part in activities ranging from birdwatching to hiking.

Bamboo Nest is located about 2km from the headquarters of Lamnamkok National Park; free transport to/from Chiang Rai is available for those staying for two nights or more.

ⓘ Getting There & Away

Most travellers visit Ban Ruam Mit on day tours from Chiang Rai, as there is no public transport from the village to the surrounding area. Alternatively, the scenic way to get here from Chiang Rai is by long-tail boat. A daily passenger boat departs from CR Pier, 2km northwest of Chiang Rai, at 10.30am (100B, one hour); a charter will run to 800B. In the opposite direction, boats return from Ban Ruam Mit at around 2pm. If you miss the boat from Ban Ruam Mit, or if they aren't running, a taxi to Chiang Rai will cost 500B; ask at the restaurants and shops by the jetty.

Doi Mae Salong (Santikhiri)

☎ 053 / POP 20,000

For a taste of China without crossing any international borders, head to this atmospheric village perched among the back hills of Chiang Rai.

Doi Mae Salong (ดอยแม่สลอง) was originally settled by Chinese soldiers from Yunnan Province who fled communist rule in 1949. Generations later, the culture of this unique community persists. The Yunnanese dialect of Chinese remains the predominant language among the older residents; people tend to watch Chinese, rather than Thai, TV, and you'll find more Chinese than Thai food. And although Doi Mae Salong is now thoroughly on the beaten track, the Chinese vibe, mountain setting and abundance of hill peoples and tea plantations converge in a destination quite unlike anywhere else in Thailand. It's a great place to kick back for a couple of days, and the surrounding area is exceptional for self-guided exploration.

◉ Sights & Activities

Shin Sane Guest House and Little Home Guesthouse have free maps showing approximate trekking routes to Akha, Lisu, Mien, Lahu and Shan villages in the area. Nearby Akha and Lisu villages are less than half a day's walk away.

The best hikes are north of Mae Salong between Ban Thoet Thai and the Myanmar border. Check local travel conditions before heading off in this direction, as the trafficking of drugs across this section of the Thai-Myanmar border is rife.

Shin Sane Guest House also leads pony treks to four nearby villages for 600B for about three or four hours, although the ponies won't carry anyone over 60kg.

Wat Santikhiri   VIEWPOINT

(วัดสันติคีรี) To soak up the great views from Wat Santikhiri, go past the market and ascend 718 steps (or take the road if you have a motorbike or car). The wát is of the Mahayana tradition and Chinese in style.

Morning Market   MARKET

(ตลาดเช้าดอยแม่สลอง; off Rte 1130; ⊙ 6-8am) A tiny but busy and vibrant morning market convenes at the T-intersection near Shin Sane Guest House. The market attracts town residents and hill peoples from the surrounding districts and is worth waking up early for.

Chinese Martyr's Memorial Museum   MUSEUM

(พิพิธภัณฑ์วีรชนอดีตทหารจีนคณะชาติภาคเหนือ; off Rte 1130; 20B; ⊙ 8am-5pm) South of the turn-off to the KMT general's tomb is the Chinese Martyr's Memorial Museum, a Chinese-style building that houses some underwhelming displays on the KMT experience – battles, migration, culture – in Thailand.

🛏 Sleeping

There are many budget and midrange places to choose from in Doi Mae Salong. Prices are often negotiable, except during the high season (November to January). The cool weather means that few places have air-con.

🛏 In Town

Shin Sane Guest House GUESTHOUSE $
(☎053 765026; www.shinsaneguesthouse.com; Rte 1130; r 400B, bungalows 800B; 🛜) The older rooms in the original building of Mae Salong's oldest hotel are bare, with shared bathrooms, while those in the newer annexe and the bungalows are much more comfortable, with en-suite bathrooms and comfy beds. Located near the morning-market intersection.

Sabaidee Maesalong HOTEL $
(☎085 705 5570; Rte 1130; r 600B; 🛜) The budget rooms here are no great shakes – tiled floors and dated fixtures – but they come with balconies and good views over the village and the surrounding hills. Little English is spoken but the owner is pleasant.

★Baan Hom Muen Li HOTEL $$
(Osmanthus; ☎053 765455; osmanhouse@hotmail.com; Rte 1130; r incl breakfast 1200-1500B; ❄🛜) Slap in the middle of town, this stylish place consists of 22 rooms artfully decked out in modern and classical Chinese themes. Go for the more expensive upstairs rooms, which have big balconies offering fine views over the surrounding tea plantations. There's no Roman-script sign.

Little Home Guesthouse GUESTHOUSE $$
(☎053 765389; www.maesalonglittlehome.com; Rte 1130; r & bungalows 800-1000B; ❄🛜) Located near the morning-market intersection is this large yellow building backed by a handful of attractive bungalows. Rooms are a reasonable size – the more expensive ones come with air-con – and are tidy and sunny, while the good-value bungalows have balconies. The owners are friendly and helpful.

🛏 Outside Town

Maesalong Flower Hills Resort RESORT $$
(☎053 765496; www.maesalongflowerhills.com; Rte 1130; incl breakfast r & bungalows 800-2800B; ❄🛜🛝) Set amid lovingly manicured gardens – a monument to flower-based landscaping – the bungalows here come in a variety of sizes, and all have balconies and views. The cheaper rooms can be dark and don't enjoy vistas. There's a big pool and the place is a good choice for families.

Phumektawan Resort HOTEL $$
(☎052 029832; www.phumaketawanresort.com; Rte 1130; r 900-1500B, VIP r 2500B; ❄🛜) Phumektawan is not really a resort but the rooms here are perched on a hillside, allowing for spectacular views. There are even better vistas from the vast communal terrace. Rooms come in a variety of sizes but all are modern and comfortable and have balconies. Located east of the entrance to town; it's best if you have your own transport.

★Phu Chaisai Resort & Spa RESORT $$$
(☎053 910500; www.phu-chaisai.com; off Rte 1130; bungalows incl breakfast 4200-11,200B; ❄🛜🛝) On a remote hilltop, this resort is the most unique place to stay in the Mae Salong area. The more you pay, the bigger your bungalow and the better the views, but all the bungalows feature bamboo furniture, comfy beds and balconies. It's a lovely setting and the spa gets rave reviews.

Maesalong Mountain Home HOTEL $$$
(☎084 611 9508; www.maesalongmountainhome.com; off Rte 1130; r & bungalows 1000-3300B; ❄🛜) Down a steep dirt road 1km east of Mae Salong's town centre (look for the orange sign), this peaceful place is a great choice if you've got your own wheels or don't mind walking. The 15 simple but comfortable and bright bungalows sit in the middle of a working fruit farm and feature wide balconies and big bathrooms.

🍴 Eating & Drinking

Sweet Maesalong CAFE $
(Rte 1130; mains 50-150B; ⊙8.30am-5pm; 🛜) If you require more caffeine than the local tea leaves can provide, stop by this modern cafe with an extensive menu of coffee drinks made from local beans. Surprisingly sophisticated baked goods and one-plate dishes are also available. Located more or less in the middle of town.

★Salima Restaurant CHINESE $$
(Rte 1130; mains 50-250B; ⊙9am-8pm) One of the friendliest restaurants in town also happens to be the one serving the tastiest food. Salima does tasty Muslim-Chinese dishes, including a rich Yunnan-style beef curry and a deliciously tart, spicy tuna and tea-leaf salad. The noodle dishes are equally worthwhile and include a beef *kôw soy* (wheat-and-egg noodles in a curry broth). No alcohol is served. Salima is located five minutes' walk south of the 7-Eleven.

★Sue Hai CHINESE $$
(Rte 1130; mains 40-300B; ⊙8am-9pm; 🖉) East of the town centre, this is the most authentic

Yunnanese restaurant in Mae Salong. Specialities include local mushrooms fried with soy sauce, delicious air-dried pork fried with green peppers, and oolong-tea salad. There's an attached tea shop.

Cafe Yes I Do CAFE
(Rte 1130; ⊙8am-7pm; ⊛) A pleasant cafe that offers coffees, teas, smoothies and simple Thai dishes. The big draw is the breezy terrace with fine views over the countryside south of Mae Salong.

ℹ Information

There are a couple of ATMs that accept foreign cards on the main road through Mae Salong.

ℹ Getting There & Away

If you don't have your own wheels, the easiest way to get to Doi Mae Salong from Chiang Rai is to take a bus to Mae Chan, from where *sŏrng·tăa·ou* (passenger pick-up trucks) run to Doi Mae Salong from the market area when full (50B, one hour). It's best to get to Mae Chan in the morning as transport dries up later in the day. You can also charter your own *sŏrng·tăa·ou* for 500B. Alternatively, it's also possible to take a Mae Sai–bound bus to Ban Pasang, from where *sŏrng·tăa·ou* can be chartered for around 400B. In the reverse direction, you can flag down *sŏrng·tăa·ou* near Doi Mae Salong's 7-Eleven.

You can also reach Doi Mae Salong by road from Tha Ton in Chiang Mai. Yellow *sŏrng·tăa·ou* bound for Tha Ton stop near Little Home Guesthouse four times daily (60B, one hour).

ℹ Getting Around

Much of Doi Mae Salong is approachable on foot. If you want to go further (or are struggling with the hills), motorcycle taxis congregate by the 7-Eleven. A few places rent motorbikes (200B per day).

Mae Sai

📞 053 / POP 28,000
Mae Sai (แม่สาย), Thailand's northernmost town, appears to be little more than a large open-air market at first glance, with stalls and shops running west and south of the border crossing with Myanmar. But while there is little of intrinsic interest in Mae Sai itself, the town can serve as a base for exploring the Golden Triangle and Doi Mae Salong. Most travellers who visit, though, are en route to or from Myanmar's Shan State, which lies just across the frontier.

⊙ Sights

Wat Phra That Doi Wao BUDDHIST TEMPLE
(วัดพระธาตุดอยเวา; Soi 1, Th Phahonyothin; ⊙daylight hours) 𝐅𝐑𝐄𝐄 Take the steps up the hill near the border to Wat Phra That Doi Wao for superb views over the Myanmar border town of Tachileik. The wát was reportedly constructed in memory of soldiers from Myanmar who died fighting the KMT here in 1965 (you'll hear differing stories around town, including a version describing the KMT as the heroes).

🛏 Sleeping

Maesai Guest House HOTEL $
(☑053 732021; 688 Th Wiengpangkam; bungalows 400-800B; ⊛⊛) This long-standing collection of mostly fan-cooled, rustic, bamboo bungalows sits by the dirty Mae Nam Sai, just across from Myanmar. The bungalows vary in size – the more you pay, the more room you get – but all come with OK beds and balconies. The staff are pleasant and there's a riverside restaurant/bar area.

Baan Sabai Maesai GUESTHOUSE $$
(☑062 031 2233; www.facebook.com/BaanSabaiMaesai; Soi 8, Th Phahonyothin; r incl breakfast 900B; ⊛⊛) Tucked down an alley off Soi 8, Baan Sabai Maesai has individually decorated rooms that are big, bright and modern, with furniture designed by the helpful English-speaking owner. There's a downstairs communal area, motorbikes can be rented (200B to 300B per day) and tours to outlying villages arranged.

Afterglow Hostel HOSTEL $$
(☑053 734188; www.afterglowhostel.com; 139/5 Th Phahonyothin; r 600-800B, bungalows 500B; ⊛⊛) Boasting a ground-floor cafe and comfortable rooms with a stone-walled, minimalist feel, Afterglow is probably the hippest place to stay in Mae Sai. There are no dorms but there are some stylish bungalows out back. The downside is that it's located about 4km away from the border.

Maekhong Delta Boutique Hotel HOTEL $$
(☑053 642517; www.maekhonghotel.com; 230/5-6 Th Phahonyothin; incl breakfast r 1000-1200B, ste 1500-2600B; ⊛⊛) It's an odd name, considering that the Mekong Delta is way down in Vietnam. Odder still that, with their light-wood panelling, the rooms here are somehow reminiscent of a ski lodge. Regardless, they're attractive, albeit located nearly 4km

Mae Sai

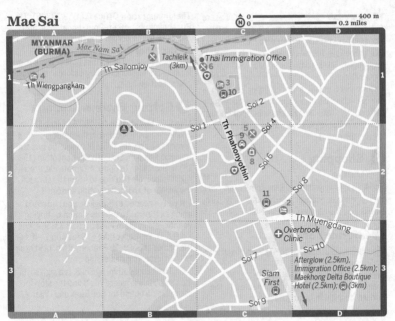

Mae Sai

◎ Sights
1 Wat Phra That Doi Wao B2

◎ Sleeping
2 Baan Sabai Maesai................................C2
3 Khanthongkham Hotel C1
4 Maesai Guest House A1

◎ Eating
5 Bismillah Halal Food C2
  Kangyuan ....(see 5)

6 Night Market...C1
7 Sukhothai Cuisine..................................B1

◎ Shopping
8 Gem Market.. C2

◎ Transport
9 Motorcycle Taxis to Bus Station C2
10 Sŏrng·tǎa·ou to Bus Station...................C1
11 Sŏrng·tǎa·ou to Sop Ruak &
   Chiang Saen C2

from the border. The hotel sees mainly Thai and other Asian tour groups.

Khanthongkham Hotel   HOTEL **$$**
(☑053 734222; www.ktkhotel.com; 7 Th Phahonyothin; r incl breakfast 1200B; 🏵🛜) Steps from the border, this Chinese-owned hotel features spacious rooms decorated in light woods. Many of the rooms don't have windows though, so check what you're getting first.

🍴 Eating

An expansive **night market** (Th Phahonyothin; mains 30-60B; ⊘5-11pm) unfolds every evening along Th Phahonyothin. During the day, several snack and drink vendors can be found in front of the police station on Th Phahonyothin.

Bismillah Halal Food   INTERNATIONAL **$**
(Soi 4, Th Phahonyothin; mains 40-100B; ⊘7am-4pm) This homey and popular restaurant does an excellent biryani, not to mention virtually everything else Muslim, from masala to roti and samosas, as well as a few Malaysian-inspired dishes. Get here early: the biryani goes quickly.

Sukhothai Cuisine   THAI **$**
(399/9 Th Sailomjoy; mains 40-60B; ⊘7am-5pm) This semi-open-air restaurant serves the namesake noodles from Sukhothai, as well as satay and a few Thai classics. There's no English-language sign, but look for the busy place right on the corner.

NORTHERN THAILAND MAE SAI

★ **Kangyuan** CHINESE $$

(Soi 4, Th Phahonyothin; mains 60-220B; ⊙9am-10pm; 🛜) If you like authentic Chinese food this place is a lifesaver, not least because it stays open later than most Mae Sai eating spots. Dishes are vaguely Sichuan-inspired – spicy beef noodles and hotpot (best in a group) – but it does dumplings and veggie options as well. No English is spoken but there's a reliable picture menu with prices in Roman numerals.

🛍 Shopping

Gem Market MARKET

(Soi 4, Th Phahonyothin; ⊙8am-4pm) Mae Sai's open-air gem market. Don't buy anything unless you know your precious stones.

ℹ️ Information

There are several banks with ATMs and exchange facilities near the border.

Overbrook Clinic (☑ 053 734422; 20/7 Th Phahonyothin; ⊙8am-8pm) Connected to the modern hospital in Chiang Rai.

Thai Immigration Office (☑ 053 733261; Th Phahonyothin; ⊙6am-9pm) Located at the entrance to the border bridge.

Tourist Police (☑ 115; Th Phahonyothin; ⊙8.30am-6pm) The tourist police booth is in front of the border crossing before the immigration office.

ℹ️ Getting There & Around

Mae Sai's **bus station** (☑ 053 646403; Th Phahonyothin) is 4km from the border; shared *sŏrng·tăa·ou* ply the route between the bus station and a stop on Soi 2, Th Phahonyothin (15B, 15 minutes, 6am to 6pm). Alternatively, it's a 40B motorcycle taxi ride to/from the stand at the corner of Th Phahonyothin and Soi 4.

If you're headed to Bangkok, you can avoid going all the way to the bus station by buying your tickets at **Siam First** (☑ 053 731504; cnr Soi 9 & Th Phahonyothin; ⊙8am-4pm) – it's on the corner of Soi 9, Th Phahonyothin, next door to the motorcycle dealership.

On Th Phahonyothin, by Soi 8, is a sign saying 'bus stop'; this is where you'll find the stop for *sŏrng·tăa·ou* bound for Sop Ruak and Chiang Saen.

TRANSPORT FROM MAE SAI
Buses

DESTINATION	FARE (B)	DURATION (HR)	FREQUENCY
Bangkok	581-904	12-13	5.30am & 6.15am & frequent 4.30-7.45pm
Chiang Mai	160-319	5	9 departures 6.15am-6pm
Chiang Rai	39	1½	frequent 5.45am-6pm
Mae Sot	416	12	6.45am
Phayao	122	3	6 departures 5.15am-6pm
Phitsanulok	344	8	5am
Phrae	225	5	5am

Minivan & Sŏrng·tăa·ou

DESTINATION	FARE (B)	DURATION (HR)	FREQUENCY
Chiang Rai	50	1	frequent minivans 6am-4pm
Chiang Saen	50	1	hourly *sŏrng·tăa·ou* 9am-noon
Fang	120	3	minivans 8am & 2pm
Sop Ruak (Golden Triangle)	40	45min	hourly *sŏrng·tăa·ou* 9am-noon
Tha Ton	140	2	minivans 7am, 8am & 2pm

BAN THOET THAI: VILLAGE OF THE OPIUM KING

Located in a narrow river valley about 20km north of Mae Salong, Ban Thoet Thai (บ้าน เทอดไทย) is a multiethnic village – home to Shan and Chinese, as well as Akha, Tai Lü, Lahu, Hmong, Lua and Lisu – with a remote, border-town vibe and an infamous recent past.

The village is best known for having served as one of the bases of Khun Sa, the most notorious of the Golden Triangle's narco-warlords. Between the 1960s and 1980s, the half-Shan, half-Chinese Khun Sa commanded a 20,000-strong army and dominated the opium and heroin trade in the Golden Triangle, a largely lawless region straddling the borders of Thailand, Myanmar, China and Laos. At that time, Ban Thoet Thai was essentially cut off from the rest of Thailand by the rough, mountainous terrain and a lack of sealed roads.

Find displays on the Opium King, as well as Shan culture and history, at the Khunsa Museum (พิพิธภัณฑ์ขุนส่า; ⊙8am-5pm) FREE, located in his former headquarters (about 500m north of the market area). Don't miss the VIP Living Room that boasts a creepy life-sized model of Khun Sa.

The best place to stay in Ban Thoet Thai is Rim Taan Guest House (☑053 730209; rimtaan_guesthouse@hotmail.co.th; 15 Mu 1, Thoet Thai; r & bungalows 500-1200B; ❄☎), located roughly in the middle of town with fan bungalows and air-con rooms set in an attractive stream-side garden. The nearby Restaurant Ting Ting (mains 40-150B; ⊙7am-9pm) stays open later than other places in the village and has an English-language menu of tasty Chinese dishes.

To reach Ban Thoet Thai from Chiang Rai, take any bus from the interprovincial bus station (p216) heading north to Mae Sai or Chiang Saen and get off in Mae Chan at the market (20B, 45 minutes, frequent services 6am to 6.30pm). Blue sŏrng·tăa·ou (passenger pick-up trucks) depart from Mae Chan's market to Ban Thoet Thai when full (50B, one hour). Motorcycle taxi drivers in Mae Salong will do the return trip to Ban Thoet Thai for 500B, including waiting time.

Sŏrng·tăa·ou around town cost 15B. Motorcycle taxis congregate by the market and cost 20B to 40B per trip.

Chiang Saen

☑053 / POP 11,000

A sleepy riverine town, Chiang Saen (เชียงแสน) is the site of a former Thai kingdom thought to date back to the 7th century. Scattered throughout Chiang Saen are the ruins of this empire – surviving architecture includes several chedi, Buddha images, wí·hăhn pillars and earthen city ramparts. Chiang Saen later became loosely affiliated with various Northern Thai kingdoms, as well as 18th-century Myanmar, but didn't become a Siamese possession until the 1880s.

Today, huge river barges from Yunnan Province in China moor at Chiang Saen, carrying fruit, engine parts and all manner of other imports, keeping the old China–Siam trade route open. But the commerce hasn't resulted in many changes to the town and Chiang Saen makes a much more pleasant base than the comparatively hectic and touristy Sop Ruak, the so-called 'Golden Triangle', 9km to the east.

◉ Sights & Activities

Wat Pa Sak   HISTORIC SITE

(วัดป่าสัก; off Rte 1290; historical park 50B; ⊙8.30am-4.30pm Wed-Sun) FREE About 200m from the Pratu Chiang Saen (the historic main gateway to the town's western flank) are the remains of Wat Pa Sak, where the ruins of seven monuments are visible in a historical park. The main mid-14th-century chedi combines elements of the Hariphunchai and Sukhothai styles with a possible Bagan influence, and still holds a great deal of attractive stucco relief work.

Chiang Saen National Museum   MUSEUM

(พิพิธภัณฑสถานแห่งชาติเชียงแสน; 702 Th Phahonyothin; 100B; ⊙9am-4pm Wed-Sun) Housing archaeological artefacts from the area, Buddha imagery and exhibitions about the local hill peoples, this is an impressive museum despite its relatively small size.

Wat Phra That Pha Ngao BUDDHIST TEMPLE

(วัดพระธาตุผางาว; off Rte 1129; ⊙daylight hours)
FREE Located 3km south of town in the
village of Sop Kham, this Buddhist temple
complex contains a large prayer hall built to
cover a partially excavated Chiang Saen–era
Buddha statue. There is a beautiful golden
teak *hŏr drai* (manuscript depository) and
a steep road leads to a hilltop pagoda and
temple with views over the area and the Mekong River.

Wat Pha Khao Pan BUDDHIST TEMPLE

(วัดผ้าขาวป้าน; Th Rimkhong; ⊙daylight hours)
Inside the grounds of this active *wát* near
the river stands a magnificent Lanna-period
chedi. The large square base contains Lanna-style walking Buddhas in niches on all
four sides. The Buddha facing east is sculpted in the *mudra* (calling for rain) pose,
with both hands held pointing down at the
image's sides – a pose common in Laos but
less so in Thailand.

Mekong River Trips BOATING

(☑085 392 4701; Th Rimkhong; ⊙8am-5pm)
Passenger speedboats leave from the waterfront jetty to Sop Ruak (per boat one way/
return 700/800B, one hour), or all the way
to Chiang Khong (per boat one way/return
3500/4000B, 1½ hours).

🛏 Sleeping

Tararin HOTEL $

(☑053 777445; off Th Phahonyothin; r 600B;
❈🛜) Anonymous Tararin is reminiscent
of a 1980s American motel, with rooms
grouped around a large car park. The rooms
are a tad old-fashioned but the location is
fine and it's a reasonable budget option in a
town that lacks hostels.

ⓘ GETTING TO MYANMAR: MAE SAI TO TACHILEIK

The Mae Sai–Tachileik border is a popular visa-run destination, but there are a few cave-
ats about crossing here for those who want to go further abroad. Border-crossing information is liable to change, so be sure to check the situation locally before you travel.

Getting to the border The border and Thai immigration office (p222) are a short walk
from most accommodation in Mae Sai.

At the border After taking care of the usual formalities at the Thai immigration office,
cross the bridge and head to the Myanmar immigration office. If you've already procured
a Myanmar visa, you'll be allowed to proceed by land to Kyaingtong (also known as
Kengtung) or via air to other points in Myanmar.

If you haven't already obtained a Myanmar visa, it's straightforward to cross to
Tachileik for the day and slightly more complicated to get a two-week border pass to visit
Kyaingtong.

Day trippers must pay a fee of 500B for a temporary ID card; your passport will be
kept at the border. There is little to do in Tachileik apart from sample the food and shop –
the prices are about the same as on the Thai side and everyone accepts baht. There's an
interesting morning market and it can be fun to hang about in the tea shops.

If you'd like to visit Kyaingtong but haven't already received a Myanmar visa, proceed
directly to the Myanmar Travels & Tours (MTT) office. There you'll need to inform the
authorities exactly where you're headed and you'll need three photos and US$10 or 500B
to process a border pass valid for 14 days. Your passport will be kept at the border, ensuring that you return the way you came. It's also obligatory to hire a guide for the duration of
your stay. Guides cost 1000B per day (plus a 400B 'guiding tax'), and if you haven't already arranged for a Kyaingtong-based guide to meet you at the border you'll be assigned
one by MTT and will also have to pay for your guide's food and accommodation during
your stay. Recommended Kyaingtong-based guides include Freddie (Sai Yot; ☑+95 9490
31934; yotkham@gmail.com) and Leng (☑+95 9490 31470; sairoctor.htunleng@gmail.com).

Moving on Buses bound for Kyaingtong (K10,000, five hours, 8am to 8.30am and
11.30am to 12.30pm) depart from Tachileik's bus station, a 2km *sŏrng·tăa·ou* (20B) or
motorcycle-taxi (50B) ride from the border. Alternatively, you can charter a taxi from the
same station from K60,000 or, if you're willing to wait until it's full, a seat in a share taxi
for K15,000.

Chiang Saen

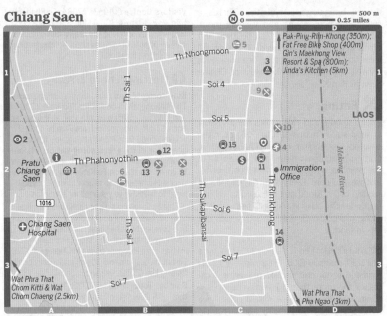

Chiang Saen

◎ Sights

1 Chiang Saen National Museum	A2
2 Wat Pa Sak	A2
3 Wat Pha Khao Pan	C1

Activities, Courses & Tours

4 Mekong River Trips	C2

Sleeping

5 Amphai Hotel	C1
6 Tararin	B2

⊗ Eating

7 108 Pun Pun	B2
8 Evening Food Vendors	B2
9 Kiaw Siang Hai	C1
10 Walking Street	C2

ⓘ Transport

11 Buses to Chiang Rai & Chiang Mai	C2
12 Motorcycle Hire Shop	B2
13 Sombat Tour	B2
14 Sŏrng·tăa·ou to Hat Bai	C3
15 Sŏrng·tăa·ou to Sop Ruak & Mae Sai	C2

Pak-Ping-Rim-Khong   GUESTHOUSE $$
(☏053 650151; www.facebook.com/PakPing
RimKhong; 484 Th Rimkhong; r incl breakfast
1200B; ❋🛜) There are clean, comfortable
and decent-sized rooms, some with balco-
nies, at this tidy villa compound just across
the road from the Mekong River. A new ex-
tension was under construction at the time
of research.

Amphai Hotel   GUESTHOUSE $$
(☏092 892 9561; Th Nhongmoon; r 400-800B;
❋🛜) Formerly known as Jay Nay, the Am-
phai has plain but modern and clean rooms
set around a forecourt. The more expensive
rooms have better beds. It's in a quiet location with friendly staff.

**Gin's Maekhong View
Resort & Spa**   HOTEL $$$
(☏053 650847; www.ginmaekhongview.com; 225
Th Rimkhong; incl breakfast r 1500B, bungalows
2000B; ❋🛜🏊) There's a choice here of
spacious, comfortable and attractive rooms
or three rather tight riverside bungalows.
There's a pool and vast sunflower field, as
well as a massage spa and cafe. Gin's is locat-
ed about 1km north of Chiang Saen's centre,
near the reconstructed city walls.

Viang Yonok   GUESTHOUSE $$$
(☏053 650444; www.viangyonok.com; off Rte 1016;
bungalows incl breakfast 2100-2450B; ❋🛜🏊)
The emphasis at this well-manicured
compound of seven comfortable, wood-

floored bungalows is activities. There's a swimming pool, sauna and weights room, while bicycles and kayaks can be hired and birdwatching trips arranged. The tranquil location by Chiang Saen Lake is a bonus. It's located approximately 5km west of Chiang Saen in Ban Khu Tao.

✕ Eating

Cheap noodle and rice dishes are available at food stalls (mains 30B to 60B) near the covered bus shelter on Th Phahonyothin. Come nightfall, evening food vendors (Th Phahonyothin; mains 30-60B; ⊗4-10pm) set up just west of here. Every Saturday evening, a section of Th Rimkhong is closed to vehicle traffic for the busy Walking Street (Th Rimkhong; mains 30-60B; ⊗4-9pm Sat), which has lots of food.

★ Jinda's Kitchen   THAI $
(Rte 1290; mains 30-100B; ⊗8am-4pm; 🎅) This roadside restaurant has been serving local dishes for more than 50 years and does a mean *kà·nŏm jeen nám ngée·o* (fresh rice noodles served with a meaty and tart pork- and tomato-based broth). It's located roughly halfway between Chiang Saen and Sop Ruak.

Kiaw Siang Hai   CHINESE $
(44 Th Rimkhong; mains 50-120B; ⊗8am-9pm) This reasonably authentic Chinese restaurant draws in the crews of the Chinese boats that dock at Chiang Saen. Try the decent dumplings, the spicy Sichuan-style fried tofu or one of the herbal soups. There's no English-language sign; look for the giant ceramic jars out front.

108 Pun Pun   THAI $
(Th Phahonyothin; mains 40-150B; ⊗8am-5pm) With its shaded outside area and a menu of simple but tasty rice and noodle dishes, as well as coffee, smoothies and ice cream, this place makes a decent lunch stop.

ℹ Information

Chiang Saen Hospital (☑053 777017; Rte 1016; ⊗24hr) This government hospital is just south of Wat Pa Sak.

Immigration Office (☑053 777118; Th Rimkhong; ⊗8.30am-4.30pm Mon-Fri) Chiang Saen's immigration office.

Police (Th Phahonyothin; ⊗24hr) Chiang Saen's main police station.

Siam Commercial Bank (Th Phahonyothin; ⊗8.30am-4.30pm Mon-Fri) Bank with foreign exchange and ATM.

Visitors Centre (☑053 777084; Th Phahonyothin; ⊗8.30am-4.30pm Mon-Sat) Has a good relief display showing the major ruin sites, as well as photos of various *chedi* before, during and after restoration.

ℹ Getting There & Away

Blue sŏrng·tăa·ou (passenger pick-up trucks; Th Phahonyothin) bound for Sop Ruak (20B) and Mae Sai (50B) wait at a stall at the eastern end of Th Phahonyothin from 7am to 3pm. If you're bound for Chiang Khong, you'll need to board one of the **green sŏrng·tăa·ou** (Th Rimkhong) bound for Hat Bai (50B, one hour, 9am to 2pm) at a stall on Th Rimkhong, south of the riverside immigration office; at Hat Bai you'll need to transfer to yet another *sŏrng·tăa·ou.*

Chiang Saen has no dedicated bus terminal. Instead, buses pick up and drop off passengers at a covered bus shelter at the eastern end of Th Phahonyothin. From this **stop** (Th Phahonyothin) there are frequent buses to Chiang Rai (37B, 1½ hours, 5.30am to 5.30pm) and a daily bus to Chiang Mai (205B, five hours, 9am).

Sombat Tour (☑053 650788; Th Phahonyothin; ⊗8.20am-4pm) operates two daily VIP buses to Bangkok (958B, 12 hours, 4pm and 5pm), departing from its small office on Th Phahonyothin.

ℹ Getting Around

Motorbike taxis will do short trips in town for 20B. They congregate near and across from the bus stop.

A good way to see the Chiang Saen area is on two wheels. Mountain bikes and motorcycles can be rented at the **motorcycle hire shop** (☑089 429 5798; 247/1 Th Phahonyothin; per 24hr bike 80B, motorcycle 200-300B; ⊗8am-7pm) linked with a barber shop or at the **Fat Free Bike Shop** (www.fatfreebike.com; Th Rimkhong; ⊗9am-5pm).

Sop Ruak

☑053 / POP 2000

The borders of Myanmar, Thailand and Laos meet at Sop Ruak (สบรวก), the so-called centre of the Golden Triangle, at the confluence of Nam Ruak and the Mekong River. The town's two opium-related museums are both worth a visit, and a boat trip is an enjoyable way to pass an hour. But the only reason to overnight here is if you've already booked a room in one of the area's outstanding luxury hotels.

◎ Sights & Activities

Long-tail boat trips on the Mekong River can be arranged at one of various piers

Golden Triangle & Around

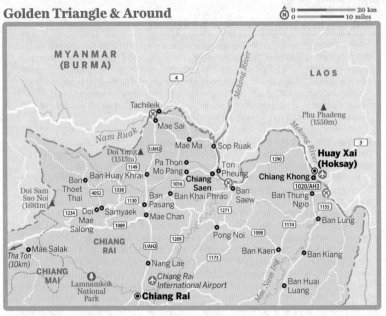

throughout the day. One-hour cruises for a maximum of five people per boat cost 500B; if you stop in Laos, a 40B tax is collected from each visitor.

★ Hall of Opium MUSEUM

(หอฝิ่น; Rte 1290; adult/child 200B/free; ⏰8.30am-4pm Tue-Sun) One kilometre north of Sop Ruak on a 40-hectare plot opposite the Anantara Golden Triangle Resort & Spa, the Mae Fah Luang Foundation has established the 5600-sq-metre Hall of Opium. The multimedia exhibitions include a fascinating history of opium, as well as engaging and informative displays on the effects of opium abuse on individuals and society. Well balanced and worth investigating.

House of Opium MUSEUM

(บ้านฝิ่น; Rte 1290; 50B; ⏰7am-7pm) This small but informative museum features historical displays pertaining to opium culture. Exhibits include the various implements used in the planting, harvesting, use and trade of the *Papaver somniferum* resin, including pipes, weights and scales.

The museum is at the southeastern end of Sop Ruak, roughly across from the huge Buddha statue at Phra Chiang Saen Si Phaendin.

🛏 Sleeping & Eating

Elephant rides and other pachyderm-related 'experiences' are on offer at the upscale resorts. As these activities have been proven to be harmful to the animals we don't recommend taking part in them.

Several tourist-oriented restaurants overlook the Mekong River.

★ Four Seasons Tented Camp HOTEL $$$

(📞053 910200; www.fourseasons.com; tent per night all-inclusive 95,000-115,000B; ❄️🛜🏊) If you can fit it into your schedule (and budget), this safari-inspired resort is among the most unusual accommodation experiences in Thailand. The 'tents' are appropriately luxurious and are decked out in colonial-era safari paraphernalia. A minimum stay of at least two nights is required, and guests take part in daily activities ranging from longboat river excursions to spa treatments.

Anantara Golden Triangle Resort & Spa HOTEL $$$

(📞053 784084; www.anantara.com; Rte 1290; per night all inclusive r/ste 42,700/58,700B; ❄️🛜🏊) This award-winning resort takes up a large patch of beautifully landscaped ground directly opposite the Hall of Opium. The rooms combine Thai and international

LOCAL KNOWLEDGE

THE GOLDEN TRIANGLE, PAST & PRESENT

In historical terms, the Golden Triangle refers to an area, stretching thousands of square kilometres into Myanmar, Laos, Thailand and China's Yunnan Province, within which the opium trade was once prevalent. From the early 20th century to the 1980s, this region was the world's biggest grower of *Papaver somniferum*, the poppy that produces opium. Poverty and lack of infrastructure and governance in the largely rebel-controlled areas meant that growing poppies and transporting opium proceeded virtually unchecked, eventually making its way around the world as refined heroin.

The most infamous player in the Golden Triangle drug trade was Khun Sa, a Shan-Chinese warlord dubbed the 'Opium King' by the press. From the late 1960s, Khun Sa's private army, ex-KMT fighters in Doi Mae Salong and other warlords in the region formed a partnership that would eventually claim a virtual monopoly of the world's opium trade.

In 1988, after having been the victim of two unsuccessful assassination attempts, Khun Sa offered to sell his entire crop of opium to the Australian government for A$50 million a year, claiming that this would essentially end the world's entire illegal trade in heroin. He made a similar offer to the US, but he was dismissed by both. With a US DEA bounty of US$2 million on his head, in 1996 Khun Sa gave himself up to Burmese officials. They refused to extradite him to the US and Khun Sa died a free man in Yangon in 2007.

Khun Sa's surrender seemed to signal the end of the Golden Triangle's domination of the global opium trade. And since the early 21st century, Afghanistan's Golden Crescent has replaced the region as the world's pre-eminent producer of opium. But Myanmar remains the second-biggest producer of opium – with much of it now heading to refineries in China to be turned into heroin. Laos, too, continues to grow opium, albeit in much smaller quantities than Myanmar.

Only tiny quantities of poppy are grown now in Thailand, but hoteliers and tour operators in Chiang Rai have been quick to cash in on the Golden Triangle's notoriety by rebranding the tiny village of Sop Ruak as the 'Golden Triangle'. From a tourism point of view it has been a success, with Sop Ruak a compulsory stop on package tours, although the only opium visitors are likely to encounter is on display in museums. The Golden Triangle's exotic reputation lives on elsewhere in Chiang Rai Province, too, with Khun Sa's former headquarters in Ban Thoet Thai opened as a low-key tourist attraction.

themes, and all have balconies looking over the Mekong River. Jacuzzi, squash and tennis courts, a gym, sauna and spa round out the luxury amenities, and activities such as cooking courses are included in most packages.

❶ Getting There & Away

There are frequent *sŏrng·tăa·ou* (passenger pick-up trucks) to Chiang Saen (20B, 15 minutes, 7am to noon) and Mae Sai (40B, 30 minutes, every 40 minutes from 8am to 1pm), both of which can be flagged down along the main strip. It's a flat and easy 9km bicycle ride from Chiang Saen to Sop Ruak.

Chiang Khong

☑ 053 / POP 14,500

Chiang Khong (เชียงของ) was historically an important market town for local hill peoples and for trade with northern Laos. Travellers have long passed through this riverine set-tlement en route to and from Laos. But since 2013, when a bridge over the Mekong River connecting Chiang Khong to Huay Xai in Laos was opened, fewer people are spending the night here. Nevertheless, there's still a small backpacker scene with quite a number of guesthouses and a few restaurants and bars. From Huay Xai, it's a two-day slow boat or a 14-hour bus trip to Luang Prabang. It's also possible to travel quickly and easily to Yunnan Province in China from Huay Xai.

⌂ Sleeping

There are around 45 accommodation options in Chiang Khong, most geared towards the budget market.

Namkhong Resort HOTEL $
(☑ 053 791055; tigerkriang911@hotmail.com; 94/2 Th Sai Klang; r incl breakfast 200-800B; ❋ ❈ ❋)
Just off the main drag is this semisecluded compound of tropical plants and handsome wooden structures. It's a popular spot: even

the fan-cooled, shared-bathroom cheapies go quickly. The most expensive rooms come with air-con and private bathrooms. There's an attached restaurant and the swimming pool is a bonus.

Rim Nam House   HOTEL $
(☑081 884 4586, 053 655680; abu_bumpbump@ sanook.com; off Th Sai Klang; r 500B; ❄️🛜) Rooms at this riverside place are a decent deal. They are plain but clean and reasonably sized with good beds, wood floors and balconies with river views. The location is on a quiet street and there are free bicycles for guests.

Baanrimtaling   GUESTHOUSE $
(☑053 791613, 084 615 5490; maleewan_th@ yahoo.com; 99/4 Soi 19, Th Sai Klang; dm 100B, r 150-450B; @🛜) There are a variety of simple, mostly fan-cooled rooms at this long-standing, rustic, riverside guesthouse. The rooms are basic, but there's a family feel, with a big garden and discounts for long-term stays or

if the eccentric owner likes you. It's located south of the markets on a quiet, residential street. Bicycles and motorbikes can be hired.

Baan-Fai Guest House   GUESTHOUSE $
(☑053 791394; baanfai-chiangkhong@hotmail. com; 108 Th Sai Klang; r 200-650B; ❄️🛜) This inviting wooden house has six rooms in the main structure with air-con and en-suite bathrooms, while the cheaper rooms are fan-only and share bathrooms. Some come with small balconies. The soundproofing isn't great, but there's an attached cafe and bicycles and motorbikes can be hired.

Funky Box   HOSTEL $
(☑093 278 2928; thehubchiangkhong@gmail.com; Soi 2, Th Sai Klang; dm 100B, d/tw 250-350B; 🛜) Pretty much what the label says: a box-like structure holding 16 fan-cooled dorm beds. There are also five fan-only private rooms that share bathrooms. Mattresses are a bit springy but both the dorm and private rooms are comfortable enough for a night or

> **ⓘ GETTING TO LAOS: CHIANG KHONG TO HUAY XAI**
>
> Since the completion of the Fourth Thai–Lao Friendship Bridge over the Mekong River in 2013, foreigners are no longer allowed to cross to Huay Xai by boat. This has made getting to Laos both less convenient and more expensive for most tourists.
>
> **Getting to the border** The jumping-off point is the Friendship Bridge, around 10km south of Chiang Khong, via a 140B chartered sǎhm·lór (three-wheeled pedicab) ride or a 50B white passenger truck ride running the route from downtown or the bus-stop market area.
>
> **At the border** After completing border formalities at the Thai immigration office, you'll board a shuttle bus (from 20B, 8am to 6pm) across the 630m span. On the Lao side, foreigners can purchase a 30-day visa for Laos upon arrival in Huay Xai for US$30 to US$42, depending on nationality. On your return to Thailand, unless you've already received a Thai visa, immigration will grant you permission to stay in the country for 30 days if you hold a passport from one of the 64 countries that has a visa exemption arrangement with Thailand (or 15 days if you don't).
>
> **Moving on** From the Lao side of the bridge, it's an exorbitant 100B/30,000K per person sǎhm·lór ride to the boat pier or Huay Xai's bus terminal. Bus destinations from Huay Xai include Luang Nam Tha (60,000K, four hours, 9am and 12.30pm), Luang Prabang (120,000K, 14 hours, 10am and 4pm), Udomxai (90,000K, eight hours, 9.30am and 1pm) and Vientiane (230,000K, 25 hours, 11.30am).
>
> If time is on your side, the daily slowboat (200,000K, 11.30am) to Luang Prabang takes two days, including a night in the village of Pak Beng. Note that the ticket price does not include accommodation in Pak Beng. Avoid the noisy fast boats (350,000K, six to hours, from 9am to 11am) as they are both dangerous and uncomfortable. Booking tickets through a Chiang Khong–based agent such as Easy Trip (p231) costs slightly more, but they arrange tickets for you and provide transport and a boxed lunch for the boat ride.
>
> If you already hold a Chinese visa, it's also possible to head to China from Huay Xai. Catch the bus to Luang Nam Tha, where there are daily buses bound for Jinghong (100,000K, six hours, 8am) in Yunnan Province.

NORTHERN THAILAND CHIANG KHONG

Chiang Khong

N 0 — 200 m
0 — 0.1 miles

two. Mountain bikes can be hired and kayaking and hiking trips arranged. There's an attached bar, the Hub.

★ **Sleeping Well Hostel**   HOSTEL $$
(☑097 280 4040; info.sleepingwell@gmail.com; 10/8 Th Sai Klang; dm 190B, r 490-1090B; ✳🛜) Housed in a stylish four-storey building connected by a winding staircase, the eight-bed dorm and rooms here are spotless and fresh, with white and wood finishes. A variety of rooms are available: the cheapest with shared bathrooms, the most expensive rooftop options with private terraces. There are communal spaces throughout and a downstairs cafe-restaurant.

Namkhong Riverside Hotel   HOTEL $$
(☑053 791801; www.namkhongriverside.com; 174-176 Th Sai Klang; r incl breakfast 1200-1500B; ✳🛜) This efficient three-storey hotel holds heaps of clean, neat rooms, most with private balconies overlooking the river. The

rooms aren't huge, but they're modern and comfortable and there are decent river views. The attached restaurant is OK, too.

★ **Rai Saeng Arun**   RESORT $$$
(☑096 565 9495; www.raisaengarun.com; Rte 4007; bungalows incl breakfast 4200-5000B; ✳🛜) 🍃 Located 22km from Chiang Khong on Rte 4007, this ecofriendly resort brings together 14 wooden bungalows in a breathtaking plot of land adjacent to the Mekong River. The bungalows are stylish and comfortable, feature balconies and open-air showers, and are connected by bridged walkways over rice fields. The restaurant sources its ingredients from the resort's own organic garden.

Chiangkhong Teak Garden Riverfront Hotel   HOTEL $$$
(☑053 792008; www.chiangkhongteakgarden. com; 666 Th Sai Klang; r incl breakfast 2500-3000B; ✳🛜🏊) Formerly known as the Ibis Styles, this is Chiang Khong's poshest hotel. The rooms are decent-sized, comfortable and come with balconies – the most expensive have river views, mini-jacuzzis and safety boxes. There's a riverside pool and a shaded bar and restaurant area. The rooms are still overpriced for this town, though.

✖ Eating & Drinking

On Wednesday and Saturday during the tourist season (from around November to May), Chiang Khong's main drag hosts a **Walking Street market** (Th Sai Klang; ⊙6-10pm Wed & Sat Nov-May), which has a decent selection of local eats.

★ Khao Soi Pa Orn   THAI $
(Soi 6, Th Sai Klang; mains 30-60B; ⊙8am-4pm) The Chiang Khong version of *kôw soy* – the famous northern curry noodle soup – forgoes the curry broth and replaces it with clear soup topped with a rich, spicy minced-pork mixture. It's still delicious, and this place is a compulsory stop for Thai tourists passing through town. A few rice dishes are also available.

There's no Roman-script sign, but it's located next to the giant highway-distance marker.

Nangnuan   THAI $
(mains 100-200B; ⊙8am-9pm) Freshwater fish from the Mekong River is the emphasis here and it's prepared in a variety of ways, as the extensive menu describes. There's a pleasant riverside terrace to dine on. The restaurant is located at the end of the road that leads to Ban Hat Khrai, about 1km south of town.

Bamboo
Mexican House   INTERNATIONAL $$
(Th Sai Klang; mains 160-280B; ⊙8am-8.30pm; 🐾📶) Run by a guitar-playing hippy with a love of Mexican dishes, this chilled, long-standing spot offers burritos, enchiladas and tacos, as well as pasta and a few Thai dishes. Fine coffee and tasty homemade breads and cakes are also on offer. It opens early and can provide boxed lunches for the boat ride to Luang Prabang.

Cafe de Lao   CAFE
(58 Th Sai Klang; ⊙9am-5.30pm; 📶) Chiang Khong's coolest cafe is tucked away in a shaded wood-framed building strewn with sofas. There's excellent coffee and smoothies, as well as a small selection of Northern Thai and Lao dishes. It's a pleasant spot to while away a few hours.

Hub   BAR
(thehubchiangkhong@gmail.com; Soi 2, Th Sai Klang; ⊙4-11pm; 📶) The Hub is attached to the next-door Funky Box hostel: the Belgian and Thai owners serve Belgian beers and reasonable cocktails (from 140B). There's

also a pool table and a lounging area with cushions. It's where you'll find Chiang Khong's tiny community of expats.

Rin Bar   BAR
(Th Sai Klang; ⊙4pm-midnight; 📶) The most lively of the bars on Chiang Khong's main drag, Rin has a pool table, live sport on TV and, if you really want it, karaoke. There's also a menu of Thai and western classics.

ℹ Information

A number of banks along Th Sai Klang, such as **Siam Commercial Bank** (Th Sai Klang; ⊙8.30am-3.30pm) and **Government Savings Bank** (Th Sai Klang; ⊙8.30am-3.30pm), have ATMs and/or foreign-exchange services.

Easy Trip (📱086 997 7246; www.discovery-laos.com; 183 Th Sai Klang; ⊙9am-7pm) This professional travel agency can help you arrange boat or bus transport in Laos.

Police Station (Th Sai Klang) Chiang Khong's main police station.

ℹ Getting There & Away

Chiang Khong has a **bus station** (📱053 792000; Rte 1020) located 3km south of town, which is exclusively for buses to Bangkok, but there is no need to go there as buses departing from there also stop in town, close to the market or at the **Sombat Tour** (📱053 791644; Rte 1020; ⊙6am-5pm) office, both south of the centre of town. Buses for other destinations (such as **Chiang Rai** (Rte 1020), **Chiang Mai and Phayao** (Rte 1020)) also pick up and drop off passengers at various points near the markets. There are daily minivans to Chiang Mai (350B, five to six hours, 10am and 5pm), which will pick you up at your guesthouse. If you're bound for Chiang Saen, you'll first need to take a **sörng·tǎa·ou to Hat Bai** (Th Sai Klang) from a stall on Th Sai Klang (50B, one hour, around 8am), where you'll need to transfer to another Chiang Saen–bound *sörng·tǎa·ou*.

TO	FARE (B)	DURATION (HR)	FREQUENCY
Bangkok	592-921	13	7.25am & frequent departures 3-4.30pm
Chiang Mai	202-395	6-7	7.30am, 9.45am & 10.30am
Chiang Rai	65	2½	every 30 mins 4.30am-4pm
Phayao	108-139	3	7.30am & 10.30am

NORTHERN THAILAND PHAYAO

ROAD TRIP: CHIANG KHONG TO PHAYAO

Start Chiang Khong

End Phayao

Length 225km; six hours

If you're in Chiang Khong and happen to have your own wheels, we have an excellent suggestion for a drive. Routes 1155 and 1093 are among Thailand's most dramatic roads, hugging steep mountainsides along the Thai–Lao border and passing waterfalls, incredible vistas and national parks. If you need a destination, you can continue all the way to Phayao, a little-visited town with ample accommodation and good food.

From Chiang Khong, the trip is as straightforward as heading south on Rte 1020 and following the signs to Phu Chi Fa, a national park near the Lao border. For Thailand, the signs are unusually clear, but a good companion nevertheless is the *Golden Triangle* map from Golden Triangle Rider (www.gt-rider.com). At the mountaintop village of Doi Pha Tang, consider a quick detour to Pratu Siam (1653m), one of Thailand's most impressive viewpoints. Basic lodging and food is available here.

Rte 1093 narrows and the roadside becomes markedly less populated as you approach Phu Chi Fa, a mountaintop that offers high-altitude views into Laos. There are a few different ways to approach the peak, the most popular being via Ban Rom Fah Thai. There is a variety of accommodation and some basic restaurants on either side of Phu Chi Fa.

Upon passing Phu Chi Fa, stay on Rte 1093 and follow the signs to Ban Huak. This is a picturesque village in Phayao Province, 2km from the Lao border. There's a border market on the 10th and 30th of every month, homestay-style accommodation in the town, and nearby Nam Tok Phu Sang, a unique waterfall of thermally heated water.

From Ban Huak, follow signs to Chiang Kham, then take Rte 1021 to Chun, from where it's a straight shot to Phayao (via Dok Kham Tai).

If you do the drive in one go, allow at least six hours, including stops for taking photos, coffee and a meal.

ⓘ Getting Around

A number of guesthouses around town rent out bicycles (from 100B per day) and motorbikes (from 200B per day).

Phayao

♩ 054 / POP 20,000

Little-visited Phayao (พะเยา) is one of the more pleasant and attractive towns in Northern Thailand. Its setting on Kwan Phayao, a vast wetland, is unusual and gives the town a back-to-nature feel that's utterly lacking in most Thai cities. Beyond the wetland, the tree-lined streets, temples and traditional wooden houses of 'downtown' Phayao provide a pleasing old-school Thai touch, while the locals seem genuinely pleased that visitors have taken the trouble to stop by.

All of this makes quiet Phayao the perfect place to break up your journey to/from Chiang Rai. The town can also serve as the bookend to a drive from Chiang Khong.

◉ Sights & Activities

★ Kwan Phayao   LAKE

(กว๊านพะเยา) This vast body of water is the largest swamp in Northern Thailand and a symbol of Phayao. Although it's naturally occurring, its water level is artificially controlled – otherwise the wetlands would go dry outside of the wet season. Framed by mountains, the swamp is in fact more scenic than the name suggests and is the setting for what must be among the most beautiful sunsets in Northern Thailand.

Rowing crews can be seen practising in the evenings, and there's a pier at the southern end of Th Chaykawan, where there are boat rides to what remains of Wat Tiloke Aram, a submerged 500-year-old temple.

In addition to lost Buddhist artefacts, there are at least 50 types of fish native to these waters, and there's a small fish breeding area, where for 5B you can feed the fish.

Wat Sri Khom Kham   BUDDHIST TEMPLE

(วัดศรีโคมคำ; Th Chaykawan; ⊙ daylight hours) FREE Phayao's most important temple is thought to date back to 1491, but its present structure was finished in 1923. The immense prayer hall holds the Phra Jao Ton Luang, the largest Chiang Saen–era Buddha statue in the country. It stands 18m high and legend has it that the construction of the statue took more than 30 years. It's not the most beautiful or well-proportioned Buddha image in Thailand, but it certainly is impressive.

Phayao Cultural Exhibition Hall
MUSEUM

(หอวัฒนธรรมนิทัศน์; Th Chaykawan; 40B; ⊙8.30am-4.30pm) This two-storey museum is packed with artefacts. Standout items include a unique 'black' Buddha statue and a fossil of two embracing crabs labelled 'Wonder Lover'. A few more English captions would be nice. It's next door to Wat Sri Khom Kham, about 2km from the northern end of Th Chaykawan.

Boat Rides
BOATING

(Th Chaykawan; per person 30B; ⊙8am-6pm) A pier at the southern end of Th Chaykawan offers boat rides to Wat Tiloke Aram.

🛏 Sleeping & Eating

Cozy Nest Boutique Hotel
HOTEL $$

(📋054 071222; www.cozynestroom.com; 59 Th Ratchawong; r incl breakfast 800-1000B; ste 2000B; ❀🐾) This is a sleek and modern hotel with spotless and sizeable rooms that come with decent bathrooms, comfy beds and small balconies. The staff are efficient and there are free bicycles for guests to use. It's steps away from the lake and popular, so book ahead.

Huanpak Jumjai
GUESTHOUSE $$

(📋054 482659; 37/5-6 Th Prasat; r 800B; ❀🐾) Rooms at this quiet, family-run place are spacious, clean and decked out in handsome wood, but only the top-floor ones with balconies offer lake views. It's located just off Th Chaykawan, a short walk from the waterfront. There's free bicycle use for guests.

Gateway Hotel
HOTEL $$

(📋054 484333; www.phayaogateway.com; 7/36 Soi 2, Th Pratu Khlong; incl breakfast r 900-1100B, ste 2000-2300B; ❀🐾🏊) Gateway is ostensibly Phayao's grandest hotel, with big rooms that boast a slightly faded midrange/business feel, while including all the amenities you'd expect from such a place. There's also a pool and a basic gym. It's next to the bus station.

★ Khao Soi Saeng Phian
THAI $

(Th Thakawan; mains 30-50B; ⊙8.30am-5pm) One of the better bowls of *kôw soy* (northern-style curry noodle soup) in this neck of the north is available at this family-run restaurant, a block back from Phayao's waterfront. The thick and delicious broth is available with chicken or beef. There's no English-language menu but some is spoken.

Night Market
THAI $

(Th Rob Wiang; mains 30-60B; ⊙6-10pm) An extensive night market convenes along the north side of Th Rob Wiang every evening.

Chue Chan
THAI $$

(Th Chaykawan; mains 80-240B; ⊙10am-10.30pm) Of all Phayao's waterfront restaurants, this place has received the most acclaim from various Thai food authorities. The lengthy menu, which has both pictures and English, spans tasty dishes you won't find elsewhere, such as stuffed pig leg or sour fish fried with egg.

ⓘ Information

There are several banks along Th Donsanam, near the town's morning market, with ATMs and exchange services.

ⓘ Getting There & Away

Phayao's **bus station** (📋054 431488; Th Pratu Khlong) is quite busy, primarily because the city lies on Thailand's main north–south highway.

In addition to buses, there are also minivans to Chiang Rai (63B, one hour, every 30 minutes from 7am to 7.30pm) and Phrae (102B, two hours, every 30 minutes from 7am to 7.30pm).

TO	FARE (B)	DURATION (HR)	FREQUENCY
Bangkok	484-753	11	18 departures 8.30am-9pm
Chiang Khong	108-139	3½	12.45pm & 4.30pm
Chiang Mai	111-221	5	10 departures 8am-5.45pm
Chiang Rai	60	2	frequent 7.30am-7pm
Lampang	87	3	10.20am & noon
Mae Sai	122-190	3	2.15pm
Mae Sot	315	5	10.10am
Nan	119	4	1.45pm
Sukhothai	183	6	9am & noon

NAN PROVINCE

The principal draw of remote Nan Province (จังหวัดน่าน), tucked into Thailand's northeastern corner, is its natural beauty. Nan's ethnic groups are another highlight and differ significantly from those in other northern provinces. Outside the Mae Nam Nan Valley, the predominant hill peoples are Mien, with smaller numbers of Hmong, while dispersed throughout Nan are four lesser-known groups seldom seen outside this province: the Tai Lü, Mabri, Htin and Khamu.

Nan

📞 054 / POP 20,000

Nan (น่าน) is not the kind of destination most travellers are going to stumble upon, as it's remote by Thai standards. But if you take the time to get here, you'll be rewarded with a relaxed city rich in both culture and history.

Many of Nan's residents are Tai Lü, the ancestors of immigrants from Xishuangbanna in southwestern China's Yunnan Province. Their cultural legacy can be seen in the city's art and architecture, particularly in its exquisite temples. But there's also a strong Lanna influence here, as revealed in the remains of the old city wall and several early wát.

◎ Sights

★ Wat Phumin   BUDDHIST TEMPLE
(วัดภูมินทร์; cnr Th Suriyaphong & Th Pha Kong; donations appreciated; ⊙daylight hours) Nan's most famous Buddhist temple is celebrated for its exquisite murals, executed during the late 19th century by a Thai Lü artist named Thit Buaphan. The exterior of the temple takes the form of a cruciform bòht (ordination hall) that was constructed in 1596 and restored during the reign of Chao Anantavorapitthidet (1867–74). The ornate altar in the centre of the bòht has four sides, with four Sukhothai-style sitting Buddhas facing in each direction.

★ Nan National Museum   MUSEUM
(พิพิธภัณฑสถานแห่งชาติน่าน; Th Pha Kong; ⊙9am-4pm Wed-Sun) FREE Housed in the 1903 vintage palace of Nan's last two feudal lords, this museum first opened its doors in 1973. It's one of the country's better provincial museums, featuring exhibits on Nan's ethnic minorities, local history and Buddhism, and there are English labels for most items.

The ground floor has ethnological exhibits covering the various ethnic groups found in the province. Among the items on display are textiles, silverwork, folk utensils and tribal costumes.

On the 2nd floor are exhibits on Nan history, archaeology, local architecture, royal regalia, weapons, ceramics and religious art. The museum's collection of Buddha images includes some rare Lanna styles as well as the floppy-eared local styles. Also on display on the 2nd floor is a rare 'black' elephant tusk said to have been presented to a Nan lord more than 300 years ago by the Khün ruler of Chiang Tung (Kyaingtong).

Wat Phra That Chae Haeng   BUDDHIST TEMPLE
(วัดพระธาตุแช่แห้ง; off Rte 1168; ⊙daylight hours) Located 2km past the bridge that spans Mae Nam Nan, heading southeast out of town, this Buddhist temple dating from 1355 is the most sacred wát in Nan Province. It's set in a square walled enclosure on top of a hill with a view of Nan and the valley. A round-trip motorcycle taxi here from the centre of Nan will run to about 100B.

The Tai Lü–influenced bòht (ordination hall) features a triple-tiered roof with carved wooden eaves and dragon reliefs over the doors. A gilded Lanna-style chedi sits on a large square base next to the bòht; visit late in the day and the structure practically glows in the afternoon light.

Wat Phra That Chang Kham   BUDDHIST TEMPLE
(วัดพระธาตุช้างค้ำ; cnr Th Suriyaphong & Th Pha Kong; ⊙daylight hours) The founding date of this wát, the second-most important temple in the city after Wat Phra That Chae Haeng, is unknown, but the main wí·hăhn, reconstructed in 1458, has a huge seated Buddha image and faint murals that have been partially recovered. The chedi behind the wí·hăhn is thought to date to around the same time as the temple was founded, and features elephant supports similar to those seen in Sukhothai and Si Satchanalai.

Next to the chedi is a small, undistinguished bòht (ordination hall) from the same era. Wat Phra That Chang Kham's current abbot tells an interesting story involving the bòht and a Buddha image that was once kept inside. According to the abbot, in 1955 art historian AB Griswold offered to purchase the 145cm-tall Buddha inside the small bòht. The image appeared to be

Nan

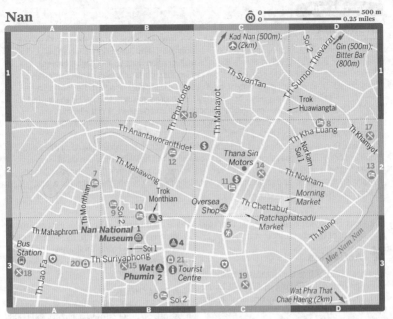

0   500 m
0   0.25 miles

Nan

a crude Sukhothai-style walking Buddha moulded of plaster. After agreeing to pay the abbot 25,000B for the image, Griswold began removing the image – but as he did it fell and the plaster around the statue broke away to reveal an original Sukhothai Buddha of pure gold underneath. Needless to say, the abbot made Griswold give it back, much to the latter's chagrin. Did Griswold suspect what lay beneath the plaster? The abbot refuses to say.

The image is now kept behind a glass partition in the *hŏr đrai* (manuscript library) adjacent to the *wí·hăhn*, the largest of its type in Thailand.

Wat Hua Khuang   BUDDHIST TEMPLE
(วัดหัวข่วง; cnr Th Mahaphrom & Th Pha Kong; ⊙daylight hours) This temple features a distinctive Lanna/Lan Xang–style *chedi* with four Buddha niches, a wooden *hŏr đrai* (manuscript library) and a noteworthy *bòht* (ordination hall) with a Luang Prabang–style carved wooden veranda. Inside is a carved ceiling and a huge *naga* (semi-divine part-human, part-serpent creature) altar. The temple's founding date is

WORTH A TRIP

NONG BUA

The neat and tidy Tai Lü village of Nong Bua, approximately 30km north of Nan, is famous for the Lü-style Wat Nong Bua (วัดหนองบัว; Ban Nong Bua; ⊙daylight hours). Featuring a typical two-tiered roof and carved wooden portico, the *wí·hăhn* (sanctuary) design is simple yet striking – note the carved *naga* (serpent) heads at the roof corners. Inside the *wí·hăhn* are rustic but beautiful *Jataka* murals thought to have been painted by Thit Buaphan, the same mural artist whose work can be seen at Wat Phumin.

There is a model Thai Lü house directly behind the *wát* where weaving is done – you can buy attractive local textiles here.

Nong Bua is near the town of Tha Wang Pha. To get to the temple, take a northbound bus or *sŏrng·tăa·ou* (passenger pick-up truck; 35B) to Tha Wang Pha. Get off at Samy-aek Longbom, walk west to a bridge over Mae Nam Nan and turn left. Continue until you reach another small bridge, after which Wat Nong Bua will be on your right. It's a long 3km from the highway to the *wát*.

unknown, but stylistic clues suggest that this may be one of the city's oldest *wát*.

🏃 Activities

Nan has nothing like the organised trekking industry found in Chiang Rai and Chiang Mai, and many visitors, particularly Thais, opt to float rather than walk. White-water rafting along Mae Nam Wa, in northern Nan, is only possible when the water level is high (from September to December), and is said to be best during the early part of the rainy season. The rapids span Classes I to IV and pass through intact jungle and remote villages.

Fhu Travel TREKKING
(☑054 710636, 081 287 7209; www.facebook.com/fhutravel; 453/4 Th Sumon Thevarat; trekking per person 1800B; ⊙9am-5pm) This long-standing outfit offers one-day treks around Nan. It can also organise kayaking (from 1500B) and rafting (from 2500B).

🛏 Sleeping

Ban Himwat Hostel HOSTEL $
(☑091 858 6516; www.facebook.com/BanHimwat Hostel; 31 Soi 1, Th Pha Kong; dm 400B; 🛜) Everything is spotless at this newish hostel that mostly sees Thai travellers. The six- and 10-bed dorms come with decent mattresses and their own bathrooms. The hostel is in a peaceful location with a shaded outside area and there are free bicycles for guests to use.

Banban Nannan Library GUESTHOUSE $
(☑089 859 5898; www.facebook.com/Banban Nannan; 14/1 Th Monthian; r 350-550B, f & air-con r 1000-1500B; ❄🛜) This rambling wooden house with an inviting garden has five rooms: the cheapest are fan-cooled and share bathrooms. The sole air-con room is very comfortable, with its own terrace. There are many communal areas for lounging, as well as a downstairs cafe and the eponymous library.

Nan Guest House HOTEL $
(☑081 288 8484, 054 771849; www.nanguest house.net; 57/15 Soi 2, Th Mahaphrom; r 350-600B; ❄🛜) In a quiet residential area a short stroll from Nan's most famous temples, this long-standing and well-maintained place has 10 old-fashioned but reasonably sized rooms. The cheapest are fan-cooled and share bathrooms. There's an attractive roof terrace for relaxing after visiting the temples.

Yindee Traveller's Lodge HOSTEL $
(☑081 806 0347; www.yindeetravellerslodge.com; 200/17 Th Mano; dm 350B; r 900-1000B; ❄🛜) Right by the river, and with a roof terrace for sunset views and beers, this new place has dorms that are well set up with lockers, private lights, curtains and OK mattresses. There are two compact private rooms and free bicycles to use.

Nan Lanna Hotel HOTEL $$
(☑054 772720; Trok Monthian; r 790B, f 1090B; ❄🛜) This place has cool rooms with little natural light, but lots of space, big bathrooms and attractive retro-themed design touches. The location – near Nan's most famous temples – is another bonus.

Sukkasem Hotel HOTEL $$
(☑054 772555; sukkasemhotel@hotmail.com; 119-121 Th Anantaworarittidet; r 450-1400B; ❄🛜) The Sukkasem Hotel is located on a busy street (by Nan standards, anyway), with modern, minimalist-feeling rooms that have wood

floors and white walls. The cheapest rooms aren't huge, but remain good value. Bicycles and motorbikes can be hired.

⭐**Pukha Nanfa Hotel**   HOTEL **$$$**
(☏054 771111; www.pukhananfahotel.co.th; 369 Th Sumon Thevarat; r incl breakfast 2600-3900B, ste 4700B; ❄🤶) The former and forgettable Nan Fah Hotel has been transformed into this charming boutique lodging. Its 14 rooms are cosy and classy, with aged wood accentuated by touches such as local cloth, handicrafts and art. Antique adverts and pictures add to the old-world feel and, to top it off, the place is conveniently located and has pleasant staff.

⭐**Nan Boutique Hotel**   HOTEL **$$$**
(☏054 775532; www.facebook.com/nanboutique hotel; 1/11 Th Kha Luang; r incl breakfast 2200-3400B; ❄🤶) This supertidy, hushed compound lacks the old-school character of some of Nan's other choices, but makes up for this with some of the city's most comfortable, modern and well-equipped rooms. There's also free airport and bus-station pick-up and drop-off, free bicycle use and an on-site spa.

🍴 Eating & Drinking

The town's **night market** (Th Pha Kong; mains 30-60B; ⊙4-10pm) provides a few decent food-stall offerings. Better yet is Nan's Saturday Walking Street (p239), where dishes and tables are provided for Northern Thai–style food.

Crazy Noodle   THAI **$**
(Th Kha Luang; mains 30-60B; ⊙8.30am-8.30pm; 🤶) The locals think the owner here is *tingtong* (crazy), so his shop is named accordingly. But he's friendly and seems sane to us. His noodles are fine as well, topped with tender pork and served with a spicy broth.

Khao Soi Ton Nam   THAI **$**
(38/1-2 Th Suriyaphong; mains 40-55B; ⊙8am-4pm) Come to this place, an offshoot of the next-door Hot Bread (p238), for fine *kôw soy* (northern-style curry noodle soup served with either chicken or beef).

Wan Da   THAI **$**
(Th Kha Luang; mains 30-50B; ⊙7am-4pm) This local legend serves just about everything from curries ladled over rice to satay, but those in the know come for the *kà·nŏm jeen* (fresh rice noodles served with various toppings).

NORTHERN THAILAND NAN

DON'T MISS

WAT PHUMIN'S MAGNIFICENT MURALS

Wat Phumin (p234) is Northern Thailand's Sistine Chapel, and the images on its walls are now found on everything from knick-knacks at Chiang Mai's night bazaar to postcards sold in Bangkok. Yet despite the seemingly happy scenes depicted, the murals were executed during a period that saw the end of Nan as a semi-independent kingdom. This resulted in several examples of political and social commentary manifesting themselves in the murals, a rarity in Thai religious art.

The murals commissioned by Jao Suliyaphong, the last king of Nan, include the *Khaddhana Jataka,* a relatively obscure story of one of the Buddha's lives that, according to Thai historian David K Wyatt in his excellent book, *Reading Thai Murals,* has never been illustrated elsewhere in the Buddhist world. The story, which is on the left side of the temple's northern wall, depicts an orphan in search of his parents. Wyatt argues that this particular tale was chosen as a metaphor for the kingdom of Nan, which also had been abandoned by a succession of 'parents': the Thai kingdoms of Sukhothai, Chiang Mai and Ayuthaya.

The murals are also valuable purely for their artistic beauty, something that is even more remarkable if you step back and consider the limited palette of colours that the artist, Thit Buaphan, had to work with. The paintings are also fascinating for their fly-on-the-wall depictions of local life in Nan during the end of the 19th century. A portrayal of three members of a hill tribe on the western wall includes such details as a man's immense goitre and a barking dog, suggesting this group's place as outsiders. Multiple depictions of a man wearing a feminine shawl, often seen performing traditionally female-only duties, are among the earliest depictions of *gà·teu·i* (also spelt *kàthoey;* Thai transgender people and cross dressers).

BAN BO LUANG: SALT WELL VILLAGE

Ban Bo Luang (บ้านบ่อหลวง; also known as Ban Bo Kleua or Salt Well Village) is a picturesque Htin village southeast of Doi Phu Kha National Park where the long-standing occupation has been the extraction of salt from local salt wells. It's easy to find the main community salt wells, which are more or less in the centre of the village.

If you have your own transport, the village is a good base for exploring the caves, waterfalls and minority villages of nearby Doi Phu Kha National Park (อุทยานแห่งชาติดอย ภูคา; ☑ 082 194 1349, accommodation 02 562 0760; www.dnp.go.th; 200B). A few kilometres north of Ban Bo Luang is Khun Nan National Park (อุทยานแห่งชาติขุนน่าน; ☑ 084 483 7240; www.dnp.go.th; adult/child 100/50B; ⊘ 8am-4.30pm), which has a 2km walk from the visitor centre that ends in a viewpoint looking over local villages and nearby Laos. Both parks have basic bungalows to stay in and two-person tents are also available for hire for 400B per night.

By far the best place to stay in Ban Bo Luang is Boklua View (☑ 054 778140, 081 809 6392; www.bokluaview.com; r & bungalows incl breakfast 1950B; ✳ 🛜), an attractive and well-run hillside resort overlooking the village and the river that runs through it. There are 11 brick and bamboo bungalows (more were under construction at the time of research) and a decent restaurant. There are a few simple restaurants in the village itself, including Hua Saphan (mains 70-120B; ⊘ 9am-9pm). There's no Roman-script sign, but it's located at the foot of the bridge.

There is a sole ATM in Ban Bo Luang. We recommend bringing cash.

To reach Ban Bo Luang from Nan, take a bus to Pua (50B, two hours, hourly from 6am to 5pm). Get off at the 7-Eleven and cross the highway to take the sŏrng·tăa·ou (passenger pick-up truck) that terminates in Ban Bo Luang (80B, one hour, 8.30am and 9.30am). To Pua, sŏrng·tăa·ou leave from near Ban Bo Luang's T-intersection at 9am and 10.30am.

A taxi from Nan to Ban Bo Luang costs 1500B.

Rak Khun
THAI $

(off Th Jao Fa; mains 60-210B; ⊘ 11am-10pm Mon-Sat) In new digs by the bus station (there's no Roman-script sign), this veteran place is a hit with the locals. Don't miss the gaì tôrt má·kwàan (chicken fried with local spices) or yam pàk gòot (a salad of ferns). The English-language menu is less comprehensive than the Thai one (which has photos).

Hot Bread
MULTICUISINE $

(38/1-2 Th Suriyaphong; mains 40-140B; ⊘ 8am-4pm; 🛜✎) This charming, retro-themed cafe and restaurant has a generous menu of Western-style breakfast dishes – including the eponymous and delicious homemade bread – and other Western and Thai items.

★ Gin
INTERNATIONAL $$

(www.facebook.com/ginrestaurant; 83/3 Th Sumon Thevarat; dishes 100-250B; ⊘ 11am-10pm) This cosy place doesn't look like much, but its menu mixes Thai and international cuisine to impressive effect. There are tart, colourful Thai salads and imaginative mains, such as soft-shell crab with mango, and white snapper with tomato puree and pepper garnish. It also serves pasta and the best steaks in Nan.

★ Bitter Bar
COCKTAIL BAR

(56 Th Sumon Thevarat; ⊘ 6pm-midnight; 🛜) What an unexpected pleasure to find this sophisticated but snug bar in remote Nan. Enter speakeasy-style up the unmarked staircase to the 2nd floor of a traditional wooden house: there's a proper bar counter to sit at as well as a few tables. The barman knows his drinks, and the floor vibrates when he's wielding his cocktail shaker.

🛍 Shopping

Nan is one of the best places in northern Thailand to pick up souvenirs. Good buys include local textiles, especially the Tai Lü weaving styles, which typically feature red-and-black thread on white cotton in floral, geometric and animal designs. Local Hmong appliqué and Mien embroidery are of excellent quality. Htin grass-and-bamboo baskets and mats are worth a look, too.

Walking Street   MARKET
(Th Pha Kong; ⊘5-10pm Fri-Sun) Every Friday, Saturday and Sunday evening, the stretch of Th Pha Kong in front of Wat Phumin is closed and vendors set up shop to sell food, textiles, clothing and local handicrafts.

Ngennan   ARTS & CRAFTS
(Nan Silver; 430/1 Th Sumon Thevarat; ⊘7am-6pm) This small but classy shop sells a huge variety of locally designed and produced silver items, including Hmong and Yao jewellery such as bracelets, necklaces and earrings.

Peera   CLOTHING
(26 Th Suriyaphong; ⊘8am-6pm) A short walk from Wat Phumin, Peera offers high-quality local textiles, mostly comprising women's skirts and blouses, as well as some men's shirts. Look for the tiny English-language sign.

ℹ Information

Bangkok Bank (Th Sumon Thewarat; ⊘8.30am-4.30pm Mon-Sat) Operates foreign-exchange services and has ATMs.
Police Station (☑24hr emergency 191; cnr Th Suriyaphong & Th Sumon Thevarat; ⊘24hr) Nan's main police station.
Siam Commercial Bank (Th Anantaworarit-tidet; ⊘8.30am-4.30pm Mon-Fri) ATM and foreign exchange.
Tourist Centre (☑054 751169; Th Pha Kong; ⊘8.30am-noon & 1-4.30pm) This helpful information centre is opposite Wat Phumin and hidden behind vendors and coffee shops.
Tourist Police (☑nationwide 1155; Th Suriyaphong; ⊘24hr) Nan's tourist police outpost.

ℹ Getting There & Away

Nan Nakhon Airport is located about 3km north of town. **AirAsia** (☑054 772635, nationwide 02 515 9999; www.airasia.com; Nan Nakhon Airport; ⊘7am-4.30pm) has three daily flights to/from Bangkok's Don Mueang International Airport (from 1000B, 1½ hours).
Klay Airport Taxi (☑086 188 0079; Nan Nakhon Airport) offers airport transfers for 100B per person.

From Nan, all buses, minivans and *sŏrng·tǎa·ou* (passenger pick-up trucks) leave from the **bus station** (☑054 711662; Th Jao Fa) at the southwestern edge of town. A motorcycle taxi between the station and the centre of town costs 30B.

There's a twice-weekly bus to Luang Prabang in Laos, as well as daily minivans to Ban Huay Kon, where there's a border crossing to Laos.

If you're connecting to the train station at Den Chai in Phrae, you can hop on any bus bound for Chiang Mai or Bangkok.

ℹ Getting Around

Avis (☑061 386 9646, nationwide 02 251 1131; www.avisthailand.com; Nan Nakhon Airport; ⊘8am-7pm) and **Thai Rent A Car** (☑054 059649, nationwide 1647; www.thairentacar.com; Nan Nakhon Airport; ⊘8am-6pm) have booths at Nan's airport.

NORTHERN THAILAND NAN

BUSES & MINIVANS FROM NAN

In addition to buses, there are also daily minivans to Ban Huay Kon (on the border with Laos; 95B, three hours, five departures from 5am to noon) and Phrae (83B, two hours, every 40 minutes from 5.30am to 6pm).

DESTINATION	FARE (B)	DURATION (HR)	FREQUENCY
Bangkok	464-790	10-11	frequent 8-10am & 6.15-7.45pm
Chiang Mai	197-395	6	frequent 7.30am-5pm & 10.30pm
Chiang Rai	181	6	9am
Lampang	203	4	frequent 8.30am-10.30pm
Luang Prabang (Laos)	660	9	8am Tue & Fri
Phayao	190	4	7.30am & 1.30pm
Phitsanulok	181	4	5 departures 7.45am-5.15pm
Phrae	110	2½	8 departures 8.30am-10.30pm
Pua (for Doi Phu Kha National Park)	50	2	hourly 6am-5pm

ⓘ GETTING TO LAOS: BAN HUAY KON TO MUANG NGEUN

Located 140km north of Nan, Ban Huay Kon is a sleepy village in the mountains near the Lao border. There's a border market on Saturday morning, but most people come here because of the town's status as an international border crossing into Laos.

Getting to the border To Ban Huay Kon, there are five daily minivans originating in Phrae and stopping in Nan between 5am and noon (95B, three hours). In the opposite direction, minivans bound for Nan (95B, three hours), Phrae (172B, five hours) and Den Chai (for the train; 200B) leave Ban Huay Kon at 9.15am, 10am, 11am, noon and 3pm.

At the border After passing the Thai immigration booth, foreigners can purchase a 30-day visa for Laos for US$30 to US$42, depending on nationality. There is an extra US$1 or 50B charge after 4pm and on weekends.

Moving on You can then proceed 2.5km to the Lao village of Muang Ngeun, where you could stay at the Phouxay Guesthouse or, if you're heading onward, go to the tiny Passenger Car Station beside the market, from where sŏrng·tăa·ou leave for Hongsa (40,000K, 1½ hours) between 2pm and 4pm.

Motorbike taxis can be found at the bus station and charge 20B and up for rides around town. **Nan Taxi** (☑ 084 610 7777, 054 773555) has metered taxis.

Some guesthouses offer free bicycle use or have motorbikes for rent. **Oversea Shop** (☑ 054 710258; 488 Th Sumon Thevarat; ⊙ 8.30am-5.30pm) and **Thana Sin Motors** (TS; ☑ 089 953 0896; 1-7 Th Sumon Thevarat; ⊙ 8am-5pm Mon-Sat) hire out motorcycles (from 250B).

PHRAE PROVINCE

Phrae (จังหวัดแพร่) is a rural, mountainous province most often associated with teak. Despite a nationwide ban on logging, there's not a whole lot of the hardwood left, and the little that does exist is under threat.

Phrae

☑ 054 / POP 20,000

Historic Phrae (แพร่) was once a key hub in the teak trade. The legacy of those days is an impressive collection of antique wooden mansions. Given this, along with ample greenery, scenic temples and a pleasant riverside location, you'd expect this small city to be well-established on the tourist trail. In fact, Phrae is a little-visited destination, which is all the better for those who do stop by.

It's a great place if you're looking to kick back for a few days by wandering the low-key attractions and enjoying the tasty local food. Phrae's residents – who include many monks – must be among the friendliest folks

in Thailand, too, which makes staying here all the more pleasurable.

⊙ Sights

Wat Luang BUDDHIST TEMPLE
(วัดหลวง; Soi 1, Th Kham Leu; ⊙ daylight hours)
This is the oldest wát in Phrae, probably dating from the founding of the city in the 12th or 13th century. There's also a museum here displaying some fine artefacts from the Lanna, Nan, Bago and Mon periods.

The veranda of the main wí·hăhn is in the classic Luang Prabang–Lan Xang style but has unfortunately been bricked in with laterite. Opposite the front of the wí·hăhn is Pratu Khong, part of the city's original entrance gate. No longer used as a gate, it now contains a statue of Chao Pu, an early Lanna ruler.

Phra That Luang Chang Kham, the large octagonal Lanna-style chedi, sits on a square base with elephants supporting it on all four sides. As is sometimes seen in Phrae and Nan, the chedi is occasionally swathed in Thai Lü fabric.

The museum displays temple antiques, ceramics and religious art. The 16th-century, Phrae-made sitting Buddha on the 2nd floor is particularly exquisite. There are also some 19th-century photos with English labels on display, including some gruesome shots of a beheading. The museum is usually open weekends only, but the monks will sometimes open it on weekdays on request.

Wat Phra Non BUDDHIST TEMPLE
(วัดพระนอน; Th Phra Non Neua; ⊙ daylight hours)
Located west of Wat Luang is this 300-year-old wát named after its highly revered

reclining Buddha image. The *bòht* (ordination hall) was built around 200 years ago and has an impressive roof with a separate, two-tiered portico and gilded, carved, wooden facade with *Ramayana* scenes. The adjacent *wí·hǎhn* contains the Buddha image, swathed in Thai Lü cloth with bead and foil decoration.

Wat Phra That Cho Hae   BUDDHIST TEMPLE

(วัดพระธาตุช่อแฮ; off Rte 1022; ☉daylight hours) **FREE** Named for the cloth that worshippers wrap around it, this hilltop *wát* is famous for its 33m-high gilded *chedi*. Like Chiang Mai's Wat Doi Suthep, it is an important pilgrimage site for Thais living in the north.

Tiered *naga* stairs lead to the temple compound. The interior of the *bòht* (chapel) is rather tackily decorated with a gilded wooden ceiling, rococo pillars and walls with lotus-bud mosaics. The Phra Jao Than Jai Buddha image here, which resembles the Phra Phuttha Chinnarat in Phitsanulok, is reputed to impart fertility to women who make offerings to it.

The temple is 9km southeast of Phrae off Rte 1022. *Sŏrng·tǎa·ou* between Phrae and Phra That Cho Hae (20B) depart from a stop near Talat Phrae Preeda, on Th Chaw Hae, from 6am to 4.30pm; outside these hours *sŏrng·tǎa·ou* can be chartered for 400B.

Wat Jom Sawan   BUDDHIST TEMPLE

(วัดจอมสวรรค์; Th Ban Mai; ☉daylight hours) Outside the old city, this temple was built by local Shan in the late 19th and early 20th centuries, and shows Shan and Burmese influences throughout. An adjacent copper-crowned *chedi* has lost most of its stucco to reveal the artful brickwork beneath. Since a recent renovation, Wat Jom Sawan is more of a museum piece than a functioning temple.

🛏 Sleeping

★ Phoomthai Garden   HOTEL $$

(☎054 627359; www.phoomthaigarden.com; 31 Th Sasiboot; r incl breakfast 1200-1500B, ste 2000B; ❈ ⎈ ⊠) Although it's a bit of a hike from the old town – 300m south of the former town wall – this is probably the best all-around choice in Phrae. Rooms are little more than functional, but sizeable, with big, comfy beds. Most rooms have balconies looking out on the attractive pool and garden. It's popular with tour groups.

Hug Inn   HOTEL $$

(☎062 572 0077; www.huginnphraehotel.com; 6/1 Teesaban Rd 2; r incl breakfast 1000B, f 1700-2200B; ❈ ⎈) There are 12 compact but comfortable rooms – some with exposed brick walls – in this industrial-chic block, one of the few contemporary hotels in central Phrae. There's an attached cafe and a pleasant garden. The hotel is down a lane opposite Phrae's small prison, in a quiet location.

Taris Art Hotel   HOTEL $$

(☎054 511122; www.tarisarthotel.com; 69 Th Rasdamnern; r incl breakfast 1100-1500B; ❈ ⎈) This '60s-era hotel has been rebooted in sultry shades of black and grey. The rooms, which feel more sombre than artsy, are nonetheless spacious and comfortable. The staff are pleasant and there's free bicycle use for guests.

Mee Bed & Breakfast   HOTEL $$

(☎054 061073; www.facebook.com/meebedandbreakfast; 16/5 Th Rasdamnern; ☉r incl breakfast 690B; ❈ ⎈) At this industrial-themed cube holding 12 rooms there's little natural light, although a few rooms have small balconies. There's lots of space, wall paintings, a friendly vibe and free bicycle use.

Gingerbread B & B   B&B $$

(☎054 523671; wimonmat_p@hotmail.com; 94/1 Th Charoen Meuang; r incl breakfast 800-1200B; ❈ ⎈) Five tidy and comfortable rooms are located here above the cafe of the same name. The pick are the three upstairs rooms that share a balcony. All come with decent beds and good bathrooms, as well as TVs and fridges.

★ Huern na na   HOTEL $$$

(☎054 524800; www.huernnana.com; 7/9 Th Sasiboot; incl breakfast r 2600, ste 5500B; ❈ ⎈ ⊠)

NORTHERN THAILAND PHRAE

> ## GHOST-LAND NATURE RESERVE
>
> The name **Phae Meuang Phi** (แพะเมือง ผี; off Rte 101; ☉6am-6pm) means 'Ghost Land', a reference to the bizarre pillars of soil and rock here that look like giant fungi, most likely the result of erosion, not the paranormal. The park, which has a few walking trails and viewpoints, is located approximately 18km northeast of Phrae off Rte 101; getting here by public transport is not an option. You can charter a *sŏrng·tǎa·ou* for about 600B.

Phrae

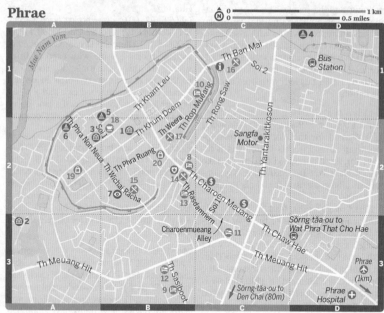

NORTHERN THAILAND PHRAE

Phrae

Rooms at Phrae's most sophisticated hotel are spacious, decked out in contemporary and Northern Thai–style themes and come with thoughtful amenities. Suites include a jacuzzi or kitchenette. There's also a spa, restaurant and pool. You'll find the hotel off Th Sasiboot, about 250m south of Th Meuang Hit.

✗ Eating & Drinking

Phrae's restaurants and **night market** (Th Rop Mueang; mains 30-60B; ⊙6-10pm) offer both Thai and Northern Thai dishes.

Gingerbread House Café & Gallery THAI $
(94/1 Th Charoen Meuang; mains 60-150B; ⊙8am-5pm; 🛜) This brick and wood cafe is a nice, air-conditioned retreat from the sun, and offers Western breakfasts as well as simple rice and noodle dishes. There's good coffee and smoothies, too, and there's a small handicrafts shop here as well.

Khao Soi Klang Wiang THAI $
(Th Wichai Racha; mains 40-99B; ⊙10am-2pm) There's just one dish here: fat bowls of top-notch *kôw soy* (noodle soup with a

curry broth). Order a regular or jumbo bowl supplemented with beef, pork or chicken. There's no Roman-script sign.

Pan Jai THAI $
(2 Th Weera; mains 35-80B; ☺8am-4pm) Popular with the locals for its pleasant, semi-open-air garden setting, come here for *kôw soy* (noodle soup with a curry broth), as well as *kà·nŏm jeen* (fresh rice noodles served with various curries and herbs) and rice dishes. There's also tasty chicken and pork satay. Look for the yellow sign.

My Vietnamese VIETNAMESE $$
(Th Ban Mai; mains 90-280B; ☺11am-9pm; 🐾) This fresh, bright place offers a local take on Vietnamese classics – *pho* (noodles), *banh xeo* (pancakes stuffed with meat or veggies) and *bun cha* (grilled pork and noodles) – as well as some Northern Thai dishes. There's a covered outdoor terrace, too.

Je Bar CAFE
(Th Kham Leu; ☺9am-6pm Tue-Fri, to 5pm Sat & Sun; 🐾) This isn't a bar, but a cafe on the ground floor of a traditional wooden house in the heart of Phrae's most historic neighbourhood. It makes a good hideaway from the heat while you're temple- and mansion-hopping.

🛍 Shopping

Phrae is known for the distinctive *sêua môr hôrm*, the indigo-dyed cotton farmer's shirt seen all over Northern Thailand. The cloth is made in Ban Thung Hong, just outside the city, but you can pick it up in town at **Maw Hawm Anian** (36 Th Charoen Meuang; ☺8am-8pm).

Kat Korng Kow MARKET
(Th Kham Leu; ☺2-8pm Sat) Every Saturday afternoon Phrae hosts Kat Korng Kow, an open-air market held at the western end of Th Kham Leu. It's mostly food on offer, but there's also a few souvenirs and handicrafts.

ℹ Information

Bangkok Bank (Th Charoen Meuang; ☺8.30am-4.30pm Mon-Fri) A bank with an ATM in Phrae.
Krung Thai Bank (Th Charoen Meuang; ☺8.30am-4.30pm Mon-Fri) A bank with an ATM in Phrae.

NORTHERN THAILAND PHRAE

DON'T MISS

PHRAE'S TEAK MANSIONS

The lucrative teak trade led to Phrae being home to more than its fair share of beautiful old mansions, some of which are open for visitors to peek inside.

Vongburi House (บ้านวงศ์บุรี; 50 Th Kham Leu; 30B; ☺9am-5pm) The two-storey teak house of the last prince of Phrae has been converted into a private museum. It was constructed between 1897 and 1907 for Luang Phongphibun and his wife Chao Sunantha, who once held a profitable teak concession in the city. Inside, many of the house's 20 rooms display late-19th-century teak antiques, documents (including early-20th-century slave concessions), photos and other artefacts from the bygone teak-dynasty era.

Khum Jao Luang (คุ้มเจ้าหลวง; Th Khum Doem; ☺8.30am-4.30pm) FREE Built in 1892, this imposing building, sporting a mixture of Thai and European architectural styles, was the home of the final Lord, or Chao Luang, of Phrae. The structure subsequently served as a governor's residence, and is today a museum on local history (no English signage). Ask to see the basement, which was used to punish and house slaves and prisoners.

Wichairacha House (คุ้มวิไชยราชา; 8 Th Wichai Racha; ☺daylight hours) This beautiful teak mansion is thought to have been built in 1898 by Cantonese artisans. Efforts are being made to turn the house into a museum, though at the time of research the work was far from complete.

Pratubjai House (บ้านประทับใจ; 100B; ☺8am-5pm) Known in Thai as Baan Pratubjai (Impressive House), this is a large Northern Thai–style teak house that was built using more than 130 teak logs, each over 300 years old. It's rather tackily decorated, so don't take the moniker 'impressive' too seriously. It's somewhat difficult to find; your best bet is to exit at the west gate of the former city wall and follow the signs, turning right after the school. A sǎhm·lór (three-wheel pedicab) here should cost about 60B.

Phrae Hospital (☎ 054 522444; Th Chaw Hae) Phrae's main hospital is southeast of town.

Police Station (Th Charoen Meuang; ☻24hr) Phrae's main police station.

Tourism Authority of Thailand (TAT; ☎ 054 521127, nationwide 1627; tatphrae@tat.or.th; Th Ban Mai; ☻8.30am-4.30pm) Just east of the centre of town. English-speaking staff and volunteers are keen to lend a hand.

ⓘ Getting There & Away

At the time of research, the only airline operating out of tiny **Phrae Airport** was **Nok Air** (☎ 054 522189, nationwide 1318; www.nokair. com; Phrae Airport; ☻8am-5pm), with two daily flights (from 1800B, 80 minutes) to/from Bangkok's Don Mueang International Airport. From the airport, 2.5km east of the city centre, **Fly Smile** (☎ 094 629 5151; Phrae Airport; ☻8am-5pm Mon-Sat) can provide transport to your hotel (100B).

Unlike those in most cities in Thailand, Phrae's **bus station** (☎ 054 511800; off Th Yantarakit-koson) is located within walking distance of a few accommodation options.

Phrae's closest rail link, **Den Chai train station** (☎ 054 613260, nationwide 1690; www. railway.co.th; Den Chai), is 23km south of town. There are frequent **blue sŏrng·tăa·ou** (Th Yantarakitkoson) (passenger pick-up trucks) to

TRANSPORT FROM PHRAE

Bus

DESTINATION	FARE (B)	DURATION (HR)	FREQUENCY
Bangkok	418-650	8	frequent 4.30am-9pm
Chiang Khong	197	4½	12.30pm
Chiang Mai	146-293	4	frequent 6am-12.20am
Chiang Rai	157	4	frequent 5am-6pm
Lampang	83	2	frequent 6am-12.20am
Mae Sai	190-381	5	10.30am, 11.30am & 3.30pm
Nan	101-157	2	8 departures 2.10am-10.10pm
Phayao	102-204	2	5 departures 10.30am-4pm
Phitsanulok	122-244	3	10 departures 8am-10.15pm
Sukhothai	132	3	11.30am & 2.30pm

Minivan

DESTINATION	FARE (B)	DURATION (HR)	FREQUENCY
Ban Huay Kon (border with Laos)	202	5	5 departures 3am-noon
Chiang Rai	189	4½	hourly 5am-6.30pm
Lampang	90	2	hourly 6am-5.20pm
Nan	94	2	frequent 3am-6.50pm
Phayao	118	2	hourly 5am-6pm

Train

DESTINATION	FARE (B)	DURATION (HR)	FREQUENCY
Bangkok	200-967	9-11	8 daily
Chiang Mai	93-598	4-6	6 daily
Lampang	23-603	2	6 daily
Phitsanulok	30-600	3½	8 daily

Den Chai (40B, 40 minutes, 6.30am to 5.30pm), departing from a stop in front of Phrae Vocational College, or you can charter one for 400B.

Sŏrng·tăa·ou to Wat Phra That Cho Hae (Th Chaw Hae) (20B) depart from a stop near Talat Phrae Preeda, on Th Chaw Hae, from 6am to 4.30pm; outside these hours sŏrng·tăa·ou can be chartered for 400B.

ℹ Getting Around

A săhm·lór (three-wheel pedicab) within the old town costs around 40B. Motorcycle taxis are available at the bus terminal and charge 20B to 40B for a trip around town.

Sangfa Motor (📞 054 521598; 163/8 Th Yantarakitkoson; per 24hr 200B; ⊙8am-4.30pm) is a motorcycle dealership that also hires out motorbikes. Many guesthouses and hotels offer free bicycle use for guests.

LAMPHUN

🎵 053 / POP 14,000

A convenient cultural stop for Chiang Mai sightseers, Lamphun (ลำพูน) slumbers quietly along the banks of the Mae Kuang, a tributary of the Mae Ping.

There's not much fanfare regarding Lamphun's status as one of Thailand's oldest settlements. The old fortress wall and ancient temples are surviving examples of the city's former life as the northernmost outpost of the ancient Mon Dvaravati kingdom, then known as Hariphunchai (AD 750–1281). During part of this period, the area was ruled by Chama Thewi, a Mon queen who has earned legendary status among Thailand's constellation of historic rulers.

The 26km voyage along a former highway between Chiang Mai and Lamphun makes a pleasant journey, with the road canopied in places by tall dipterocarp trees.

◉ Sights

Wat Phra That Hariphunchai BUDDHIST TEMPLE
(วัดพระธาตุหริภุญชัย; Th Inthayongyot; ⊙daylight hours) This temple, Lamphun's most famous, spans back to the Mon period, having originally been built on the site of Queen Chama Thewi's palace in 1044 (or 1108 or 1157 according to some datings). The temple boasts some interesting architecture, a couple of fine Buddha images and two old chedi in the original Hariphunchai style. The compound lay derelict until Khru Ba Sriwichai, a famous Northern Thai monk, ordered renovations in the 1930s.

Hariphunchai National Museum MUSEUM
(พิพิธภัณฑสถานแห่งชาติหริภุญไชย; Th Inthayongyot; ⊙8am-4pm Wed-Sun) FREE Across the street from Wat Phra That Hariphunchai is the informative Hariphunchai National Museum. Inside is a collection of Mon and Lanna artefacts and Buddhas from the Dvaravati kingdom, as well as a stone-inscription gallery with Mon and Thai Lanna scripts. There is a small bookshop with some English titles. Renovations were ongoing at the time of research.

Wat Chama Thewi BUDDHIST TEMPLE
(วัดจามเทวี; Th Chamadevi; ⊙daylight hours) An unusual Hariphunchai chedi can be seen at Wat Chama Thewi. The structure dates to around the 13th century, although two chedi go back to the 8th century. It has been restored many times since then and is now a mixture of several schools of architecture. Each side of the chedi has five rows of three Buddha figures. The standing Buddhas, although recently sculpted, are in Dvaravati style.

It's located about 1.5km from Wat Phra That Hariphunchai; you can take a motorcycle taxi (20B) from in front of the Hariphunchai National Museum.

✯ Festivals & Events

Lam Yai Festival FOOD & DRINK
(⊙mid-Aug) During the second week of August, Lamphun hosts an annual festival spotlighting the namesake agricultural product, also known as longan fruit. The festival features floats made of fruit and, of course, a Miss Lam Yai contest.

Songkran CULTURAL
(⊙mid-Apr) Should Chiang Mai's Songkran water fight be too wet and wild for your taste, Lamphun hosts a milder, more traditional affair in mid-April.

🛏 Sleeping & Eating

With Chiang Mai so close there is no reason to stay overnight in Lamphun. There is a string of decent noodle and rice shops on Lamphun's main street, just south of Wat Phra That Hariphunchai.

Dao Kanong THAI $
(340 Th Charoen Rat; mains 60-100B; ⊙10am-9pm) Long-standing Dao Kanong has a big selection of Northern Thai dishes. It's 1.5km east of Wat Phra That Hariphunchai on Th Charoen Rat (Th Chiang Mai-Lamphun).

WORTH A TRIP

DOI KHUN TAN NATIONAL PARK

This 225-sq-km national park straddles the mountains between Lamphun and Lampang Provinces. It ranges in elevation from 350m in the bamboo-forest lowlands to 1363m at the pine-studded summit of Doi Khun Tan. Wildflowers, including orchids, ginger and lilies, are abundant. At the park headquarters there are maps of well-marked trails that range from short walks around the headquarter's vicinity to hikes covering the mountain's four peaks; there's also a trail to a waterfall, Nam Tok Tat Moei (7km round trip).

The park is very popular on cool-season weekends. Intersecting the mountain slopes is Thailand's longest train tunnel (1352m), which opened in 1921 after six years of manual labour by thousands of Lao workers (several of whom are said to have been killed by tigers).

Bungalows (500B to 2700B) sleeping between two and nine people are available near the park headquarters, where there's also a restaurant.

The main access to the park is from the Khun Tan train station. To check timetables and prices from various destinations, call the State Railway of Thailand (p771) or check its website. Once at the Khun Tan station, cross the tracks and follow a steep, marked path 1.3km to the park headquarters. By car, take the Chiang Mai–Lampang highway to the Mae Tha turn-off then follow the signs along a steep unpaved road for 18km.

Shopping

Kad Khua Moong Tha Sing   MARKET
(Th Rop Mueang Nai; ⊗8am-5pm) Located just east of Wat Phra That Hariphunchai, Kad Khua Moong Tha Sing is a souvenir market selling local items such as dried *lam yai* (longan fruit) and silk.

ⓘ Getting There & Away

Frequent white minivans bound for Lamphun leave from Chiang Mai's Chang Pheuak terminal, a stop on Th Praisani in front of Talat Warorot, and from another stop on the eastern side of the river on Th Chiang Mai-Lamphun, just south of the Tourist Authority of Thailand (TAT) office (25B, 30 minutes, 6.30am to 6.10pm). Both can drop you off on Th Inthayongyot, at the stop in front of the Hariphunchai National Museum and Wat Phra That Hariphunchai.

Minivans (25B, 30 minutes, 6am to 7.30pm) return to Chiang Mai from the stop in front of the national museum or from the city's bus terminal on Th Sanam.

LAMPANG PROVINCE

Lampang Province (จังหวัดลำปาง) is a vast, mountainous area known for its natural beauty, a pleasant provincial capital and for some of Northern Thailand's most emblematic Buddhist temples. Formerly associated with the logging trade, today the province is more closely linked to industries such as mining and ceramics.

History

Although Lampang Province was inhabited as far back as the 7th century in the Dvaravati period, legend has it that Lampang city was founded by the son of Hariphunchai's (modern-day Lamphun's) Queen Chama Thewi and that the city played an important part in the history of the Hariphunchai Kingdom.

Like Chiang Mai, Phrae and other older northern cities, modern Lampang was built as a walled rectangle alongside a river (in this case, Mae Wang). At the end of the 19th and beginning of the 20th century, Lampang, along with nearby Phrae, became an important centre for the domestic and international teak trade. A large British-owned timber company brought in supervisors familiar with the teak industry in Myanmar to train loggers from Thailand and Myanmar in the area. These well-paid supervisors, along with independent teak merchants from Myanmar who plied their trade in Lampang, sponsored the construction of more than a dozen temples in the city, a legacy that lives on in several of Lampang's most impressive wát and the beautiful antique homes along Th Talad Gao.

Lampang

📱 054 / POP 53,000

Given the town's laid-back riverside charm, generous spread of attractive old buildings and some of the best markets in the north,

Lampang (ลำปาง) should be more popular than it is with travellers. But if foreigners have yet to be seduced by Lampang's charms, plenty of Thais from around the kingdom are drawn here. Arriving in their wake are an increasing number of hip cafes and restaurants with tasty food, as well as some stylish accommodation options, making Lampang a great stop for visitors seeking a less touristy, more undiscovered destination in the north.

◉ Sights

Th Talad Gao
STREET
(ถนนตลาดเก่า) Lampang's multicultural history can be seen along this riverside street, which is lined with old homes, temples and shophouses showcasing Thai, English, Chinese and Burmese architectural styles. It's also where the town's weekly market, Walking Street (p251), is held.

Wat Phra Kaew Don Tao
BUDDHIST TEMPLE
(วัดพระแก้วดอนเต้า; off Th Phra Kaew; 20B; ⊙daylight hours) The main *chedi* here, which was undergoing renovations at the time of research, shows Hariphunchai influence, while the adjacent *mon·dòp* (the small square-sided building with a spire) was built in 1909. The *mon·dòp* is decorated with glass mosaic in typical Burmese style and contains a Mandalay-style Buddha image. From 1436 to 1468 Wat Phra Kaew Don Tao was among four wát in Northern Thailand to have housed the Emerald Buddha (now in Bangkok's Wat Phra Kaew).

A display of Lanna artefacts can be viewed in the wát's **Lanna Museum** (พิพิธภัณฑ์ล้านนา; Wat Phra Kaew Don Tao; entry by donation; ⊙daylight hours).

Dhanabadee Ceramic Museum
MUSEUM
(พิพิธภัณฑ์เซรามิคธนบดี; off Soi 1, Th Phrabat; incl guided tour 100B; ⊙9am-5pm) Dhanabadee claims to be the first producer of the emblematic 'chicken bowls' used across Thailand. In 2013 the company opened its doors to visitors and began running guided tours that span the history of the chicken bowl in Thailand and explain the various steps involved in making them. English-language tours are given every hour on the hour from 9am to 4pm. The museum is located about 500m south of Th Phahonyothin/AH2.

Baan Sao Nak
MUSEUM
(บ้านเสานัก; 85 Th Radwattana; 50B; ⊙10am-5pm) A huge Lanna-style house built in 1895 and supported by 116 square teak pillars, Baan Sao Nak was once owned by a local *kun·yĭng* (a title equivalent to 'Lady' in England). It now serves as a local museum. The entire house is furnished with mildly interesting antiques from Thailand and Myanmar, but the structure itself and its manicured garden are the highlights.

Wat Pongsanuk Tai
BUDDHIST TEMPLE
(วัดปงสนุกใต้; Th Pongsnook; ⊙daylight hours) Despite having lost much of its character in a renovation, the *mon·dòp* at Wat Pongsanuk Tai is still one of the few remaining local examples of original Lanna-style temple architecture, which emphasised open-sided wooden buildings.

To get an idea of what it was like previously, look at the carved wooden gateway at the entrance to the north stairway. A couple of informal museums on the temple grounds display local artefacts, but there are few captions in English.

Wat Si Rong Meuang
BUDDHIST TEMPLE
(วัดศรีรองเมือง; Th Thakhrao Noi; ⊙daylight hours) Wat Si Rong Meuang was built in the late 19th century by artisans from Myanmar. The temple building was constructed in the 'layered' style from Myanmar, with tin roofs gabled by intricate woodcarvings.

Phum Lakhon Museum
MUSEUM
(พิพิธภัณฑ์เมืองของชาวลำปาง; cnr Th Chatchai & Th Thakhrao Noi; ⊙8.30am-4.30pm Mon-Fri) **FREE** A brief but engaging museum that employs multimedia displays to tell the story of the history, people and culture of Lampang.

> ## HORSE CARTS
> Lampang is the only town in Thailand where horse carts are still found, though they're now mostly used by tourists. You can't miss the brightly coloured carts that drip with plastic flowers and are handled by Stetson-wearing drivers. A 30-minute tour (300B) goes along Mae Wang, while a one-hour tour (400B) stops at Wat Phra Kaew Don Tao and Wat Si Rong Meuang.
>
> Horse carts can be found waiting on Th Suandawg, across from the Pin Hotel, and at another stall on Th Boonyawat, just east of the market, from around 5am to 9pm.

NORTHERN THAILAND

Lampang

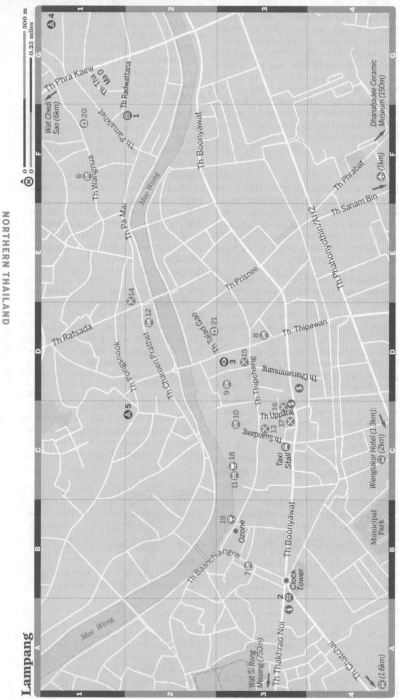

Th Phra Kaew

Th Tha Ma O

Th Radwattana

Th Panakhiet

Wat Chedi Sao (6km)

Dhanabadee Ceramic Museum (150m)

Th Boonyawat

Mae Wang

Th Wangnua

Th Pa Mai

Th Phirabat

Th Saman Bin (1km)

Th Phahonyothin/AH-2

Th Prisnee

Th Ratsada

Th Pongsnook

Th Chaoen Prathet

Th Talad Gao

Th Thipawan

Th Thipchang

Th Charuenmuang

Th Thipchang

Th Suandawg

Th Upparaj

Th Upparaj

Taxi Stall

Wienglakor Hotel (1.3km); (2km)

Municipal Park

Mae Wang

Ozone

Th Baanchiangrai

Th Boonyawat

Clock Tower

Th Thakhrao Noi

Wat Si Rong Meuang (750m)

Th Chaichai

(1.6km)

Lampang

🛏 Sleeping

★ Hug Lampang   HOTEL $

(☑054 224999; www.huglampangboutiquehotel1.com; 59-61 Th Thipawan; r 590-790B; ❈ 🛜) A former bank that's been converted into a stylish, spacious boutique hotel, the Hug is your best bet for midrange comfort at budget prices in Lampang's downtown. Opt for the more expensive rooms, which boast a sofa, a vast balcony and huge windows that let in heaps of light. Free bicycle use is available and there's a cafe downstairs.

Old Town Boutique Hostel   BOUTIQUE HOTEL $

(☑054 017019; Th Talad Gao; r incl breakfast 400-600B; ❈ 🛜) The location is perfect and the seven rooms here are spread across a well-maintained, traditional wooden house and a new annexe out back in the garden. The rooms in the house are the best: nicely decorated and comfortable, but only three have their own bathrooms. There's free bicycle use. Not much English is spoken.

★ Auangkham Resort   GUESTHOUSE $$

(☑054 221305; www.auangkhamlampang.com; 51 Th Wangnua; r incl breakfast 1100-1350B; ❈ 🛜)

Not a resort at all, but rather an exceptionally well-run, boutique-style guesthouse. The 14 rooms feel bright, big and airy, and all have balconies overlooking an attractive garden. The friendly service complements the peaceful vibe, and there are bonus perks such as free use of bicycles and the location steps from Friday's Cultural Street market (p251).

★ Riverside Guest House   GUESTHOUSE $$

(☑054 227005; www.theriverside-lampang.com; 286 Th Talad Gao; r incl breakfast 700-1200B, f 2400B; ❈ 🛜) This leafy compound of refurbished wooden houses is one of the more pleasant places to stay in Lampang. The eight rooms couldn't be any nearer the river, shaded tables for chatting and eating abound, and tours can be arranged. Try to score one of the two upstairs rooms in the main structure that feature vast balconies overlooking the Mae Wang.

Flat White Cafe & Poshtel   HOSTEL $$

(☑061 794 7962; www.facebook.com/flatwhitecafexposhtel; 344/4 Th Baanchiangrai; r/f 990/1600B; ❈ 🛜) The six shiny white rooms upstairs are spotless, spacious and light, with good beds and bathrooms. The shiny white minimalist cafe downstairs attracts Lampang's hipsters.

Karpenter   HOTEL $$

(☑093 226 6059; www.karpenterlampang.com; Th Nah Guam; r incl breakfast 1500B; ❈ 🛜) 'Post-modern barn' is the self-professed theme at this design-conscious, minimalist-chic outpost. The eight rooms are lofty and decked out in exposed wood, concrete and steel, with the comfy beds raised off the floor on platforms Chinese-style. It's a bit of a hike from 'downtown' Lampang.

Villa Rassada   HOTEL $$

(☑054 018547; www.facebook.com/VillaRassada; 35 Th Charoen Prathet; r incl breakfast 790-1190B; ❈ 🛜) Cross the Mae Wang to this contemporary-feeling hotel with attractive and spacious rooms. All come with decent bathrooms, safety boxes and balconies – some have river views.

Prink   GUESTHOUSE $$

(☑080 993 5651; 262-264 Th Talad Gao; r 600-800B; ❈ 🛜) One of Th Talad Gao's noblest historic buildings has been turned into this relaxed guesthouse. The six rooms, located above a cool cafe and ice-cream shop, share bathrooms and a fun retro design theme, although some lack windows and feel somewhat claustrophobic. Avoid this by requesting one of the more expensive balcony rooms. There's no Roman-script sign.

Wienglakor Hotel HOTEL $$$
(☑ 097 924 4345, 054 316430; www.lampang wienglakor.com; 138/35 Th Phahonyothin/AH2; incl breakfast r 1600-3200B, ste 3500B; ❄ 🛜) If you're going upscale, this is Lampang's best choice. The lobby is tastefully decorated in a teak and Northern Thai–temple theme, a design that continues into the rooms. Deluxe rooms feature sitting areas and walk-in closets, and the hotel's attractive outdoor dining area with carp pond is a classy touch. It's 1.5km west of Lampang's centre, at the junction with Th Duangrat.

🍴 Eating & Drinking

Lampang's nightlife scene consists of a few riverside bars mostly clustered at the western end of Th Thipchang.

⭐ **Phat Thai Yay Fong** THAI $
(Th Boonyawat; mains 40-120B; ⊙ 5-8pm Mon-Sat) How do Northern Thais take their *pàt tai*? With minced pork and pork rinds, of course. This very popular stall serves rice and noodle dishes and is located just east of Wat Suan Dok. There's no Roman-script sign.

Mae Hae THAI $
(1017 Th Upparaj; mains 30-50B; ⊙ 11am-7.30pm) Boost your Lampang foodie street cred by eating at this long-standing Northern Thai–style shophouse restaurant. There's no

---

DON'T MISS

WAT PHRA THAT LAMPANG LUANG

This ancient Buddhist temple compound (วัดพระธาตุลำปางหลวง; off Rte 1034; ⊙ daylight hours) has several interesting religious structures, including what is arguably the most beautiful wooden Lanna temple in Northern Thailand, the open-sided Wihan Luang. Dating back to 1476 and thought to be the oldest standing wooden structure in the country, the impressive *wí·hăhn* (sanctuary) features a triple-tiered wooden roof supported by immense teak pillars and early-19th-century *Jataka* murals (showing stories of the Buddha's previous lives) painted on wooden panels around the inside upper perimeter.

A huge, gilded *mon·dòp* (the small square-sided building with a spire) in the back of the *wí·hăhn* contains a Buddha image cast in 1563.

The small and simple Wihan Ton Kaew, to the north of the main *wí·hăhn*, was built in 1476, while the tall Lanna-style *chedi* (stupa) behind the main *wí·hăhn*, raised in 1449 and restored in 1496, is 45m high.

Wihan Nam Taem, to the north of the *chedi*, was built in the early 16th century and, amazingly, still contains traces of the original murals, making them among the oldest in the country.

South of the main *chedi*, Wihan Phra Phut dates back to the 13th century and is the oldest structure in the compound.

Unfortunately, only men are allowed to see a camera obscura image of the *wí·hăhn* and *chedi* in the Haw Phra Phutthabaht, a small white building behind the *chedi*. The image is projected (upside down) onto a white cloth and clearly depicts the colours of the structures outside.

The lintel over the entrance to the compound features an impressive dragon relief, once common in Northern Thai temples but rarely seen today. This gate allegedly dates to the 15th century.

In the arboretum outside the southern gate of the *wát* there are now three museums displaying Buddha figures and various artefacts.

Wat Phra That Lampang Luang is 18km southwest of Lampang in Ko Kha. To get here by public transport from Lampang, flag a blue eastbound *sŏrng·tăa·ou* (passenger pick-up truck; 20B) on Th Boonyawat. From the Ko Kha *sŏrng·tăa·ou* stop, it's a 3km chartered motorcycle taxi ride to the temple (60B). Alternatively, you can charter a *sŏrng·tăa·ou* from Lampang for 400B, or taxis will take you here and back for around the same price.

If you're driving or cycling from Lampang, head south on Th Phahonyothin/AH2 and take the Ko Kha exit, then follow the road over a bridge and bear right. Follow the signs and continue for 3km over another bridge until you see the temple on the left.

menu, so simply point to the dishes – soup, curry, dip or salad – that take your fancy. Look for the light-blue building; there's no Roman-script sign.

Evening Market
MARKET $

(Th Ratsada; mains 40-150B; ⏱4-8pm) Self-caterers or those interested in local eats will want to check out Lampang's evening market, where steaming baskets of sticky rice and dozens of sides to dip it in are on daily display.

Aroy One Baht
THAI $

(cnr Th Suandawg & Th Thipchang; mains 25-110B; ⏱4-11pm; 🖳) On some nights it can seem like everybody in Lampang is here – expect to wait for a table on the upstairs terrace. The wait is understandable, however, as the food is tasty and embarrassingly cheap, while the setting in the wooden house is atmospheric and fun.

Long Jim
AMERICAN $$

(Th Charuenmuang; mains 170-480B; ⏱5-9pm Tue-Sun; 🖳🍴) Long Jim serves top-notch New York–style pizza, as well as calzone, pasta dishes, salads and soups, all overseen by an authentic American and his Thai wife. The locals love it.

★MAHAMITr
CAFE

(278 Th Talad Gao; ⏱8am-6pm; 🖳) Relocated to a peaceful riverside location, with indoor and outside seating, this sophisticated cafe takes its coffee seriously and uses only Northern Thai beans. It's set back from the road.

The Riverside
BAR

(328 Th Thipchang; ⏱11am-midnight; 🖳) This expansive wooden bar with a large terrace right by the side of the Mae Wang has live music most nights. There's also a thick menu of local and Western classics.

🛍 Shopping

Walking Street
MARKET

(Th Talad Gao; ⏱4-10pm Sat & Sun) Lampang has its own Walking Street market along charming Th Talad Gao. On Saturday and Sunday evenings, the usual traffic is replaced by souvenir, handicraft and food stalls.

Cultural Street
MARKET

(Th Wangnua; ⏱5-8pm Fri) The Cultural Street market, less touristy but similar to the Walking Street market, is held across the river every Friday evening.

OFF THE BEATEN TRACK

WAT LAI HIN

If you're visiting Wat Phra That Lampang Luang and you've got your own transport, consider a visit to beautiful Wat Lai Hin (วัดไหล่หิน; off Rte 1034; ⏱daylight hours), near Ko Kha. Built by artists from Kengtung (also known as Kyaingtong and Chiang Tung), Myanmar, the tiny temple is one of the most characteristically Lanna temples around. It was a significant influence on the design of the Dhara Dhevi hotel in Chiang Mai, not to mention a film location for the 2001 Thai historical blockbuster *Suriyothai*.

There's an interesting folk museum on the grounds that the monks can unlock for you.

If you're coming from Ko Kha, the temple is located about 6km down a road that turns off 1km before reaching Wat Phra That Lampang Luang.

ℹ Information

Several banks with ATMs, including **Krung Thai Bank** (Th Boonyawat; ⏱8.30am-4.30pm Mon-Fri) and **Siam Commercial Bank** (Th Boonyawat; ⏱8.30am-4.30pm Mon-Fri), can be found along Th Boonyawat.

ℹ Getting There & Away

Lampang Airport (📞054 821505; off Th Phahonyothin/AH2) is about 1.5km south of the centre of town, at the eastern end of Th Phahonyothin/AH2. At the time of research, **Bangkok Airways** (📞054 821522, nationwide 1771; www.bangkokair.com; Lampang Airport; ⏱6.30am-6.30pm), with three daily flights to/from Bangkok's Suvarnabhumi International Airport (from 1899B, 1½ hours), and **Nok Air** (📞094 494 3440, nationwide 1318; www.nokair.com; Lampang Airport; ⏱8am-6.30pm), with three daily flights to/from Bangkok's Don Mueang International Airport (from 1599B, 1½ hours), were the only airlines operating out of Lampang. Taxis from the airport to downtown cost 50B per person, or 100B for the whole vehicle.

The **Lampang Bus and Minivan Station** (📞054 218219; cnr Th Phahonyothin/AH2 & Th Chantarasurin) is nearly 2km south of the centre of town; frequent *sŏrng·tăa·ou* (passenger pickup trucks; 20B, 15 minutes, 3am to 9pm) run between the station and town. Minibuses head to Chiang Mai (87B, 1½ hours, frequent from 6am to 4pm) and Phrae (90B, two hours, frequent from 6am to 5.20pm).

Lampang's historic **train station** (☐ 054 217024, nationwide 1690; www.railway.co.th; Th Phahonyothin/AH2), dating back to 1916, is about 2.5km from the centre of town, a fair hike from most accommodation. A túk-túk between here and the centre of town should run to around 80B.

ℹ Getting Around

Getting around central Lampang is possible on foot. **Tourism Authority of Thailand** (TAT; ☐ 054 237229, nationwide 1672; Th Thakhrao Noi; ⊙ 9am-4pm Mon-Fri) has free bicycle hire from 8.30am to 4.30pm; bring your passport. For destinations outside of town, there is a **taxi stall** (☐ 054 217233; Th Suandawg; ⊙ 6.30am-5pm) near the Pin Hotel or *sŏrng·tăa·ou* can be hired near the market.

Bicycles and motorcycles are available for hire at **Ozone** (395 Th Thipchang; bicycle per day 60B, motorcycle per day 250-500B; ⊙ 8am-8pm).

Cars can be hired from **Eddy Rent A Car** (☐ 095 641 7080; www.eddy-rentacar.com; Lampang Airport; ⊙ 7am-7pm), at Lampang Airport.

SUKHOTHAI PROVINCE

Most people are drawn to Sukhothai Province (จังหวัดสุโขทัย) by the ruins of the eponymous former kingdom, one of Thailand's most historically significant and impressive destinations.

The Sukhothai (Rising of Happiness) Kingdom flourished from the mid-13th century to the late 14th century. This period is often viewed as the golden age of Thai civilisation, and the religious art and architecture of the era are considered to be the most classic of Thai styles. The remains of the kingdom, today known as *meuang gòw* (old city), feature around 45 sq km of partially rebuilt ruins, making up one of the most-visited ancient sites in Thailand.

Also worth visiting are the province's other ruins, those of the former Si Satchanalai-Chaliang kingdoms.

TRANSPORT FROM LAMPANG

Bus

DESTINATION	FARE (B)	DURATION (HR)	FREQUENCY
Bangkok	457-711	9	frequent 8.15am-10.20pm
Chiang Mai	71-143	2	frequent 12.10am-11pm
Chiang Rai	150-193	4	frequent 6.30am-3pm
Mae Sai	236-367	6	10.15am, 11am & noon
Mae Sot	243-378	4	10.15am, 12.45pm & 2.50pm
Nan	158-203	4	5 departures 9.20am-midnight
Phayao	95-122	3	7am, 9.45am & noon
Phitsanulok	169-259	4½	hourly 6.20am-8.45pm
Phrae	83-165	2	5 departures 9.20am-midnight
Sukhothai	169-218	3½	8 departures 6.30am-8pm

Train

DESTINATION	FARE (B)	DURATION (HR)	FREQUENCY
Bangkok	216-1572	12	5 departures 5.25am-9.10pm
Chiang Mai	23-50	3	5 departures 6.30am-6pm
Phitsanulok	48-1222	5	5 departures 12.47am-11.53pm

Sukhothai

♪ 055 / POP 37,000

The market town of Sukhothai (สุโขทัย; often known as New Sukhothai) is located 12km east of the Sukhothai Historical Park on the Mae Nam Yom. While not particularly interesting, its relaxed atmosphere, good transport links and excellent-value accommodation make it a pleasant base from which to explore the old-city ruins.

History

Sukhothai is typically regarded as the first capital of Siam, although this is not entirely accurate. The area was previously the site of a Khmer empire until 1238, when two Thai rulers, Pho Khun Pha Muang and Pho Khun Bang Klang Hao, decided to unite and form a new Thai kingdom.

Sukhothai's dynasty lasted 200 years and spanned nine kings. The most famous was King Ramkhamhaeng, who reigned from 1275 to 1317 and is credited with developing the Thai script – his inscriptions are also considered the first Thai literature. Ramkhamhaeng eventually expanded his kingdom to include an area even larger than that of present-day Thailand. But a few kings later, in 1438, Sukhothai was absorbed by Ayuthaya.

◉ Sights

★ **Sukhothai Historical Park**   HISTORIC SITE
(อุทยานประวัติศาสตร์สุโขทัย; ♪ 055 697527; central, northern & western zones 100B, plus bicycle 10B; ☉ central zone 6.30am-7.30pm, to 9pm Sat, northern & western zones 6.30am-7.30pm) The Sukhothai Historical Park ruins are one of Thailand's most impressive World Heritage sites. The park includes the remains of 21 historical sites and four large ponds within the old walls, with an additional 70 sites within a 5km radius. The ruins are divided into five zones; the central, northern and western zones each have a separate 100B admission fee. Note that motorbikes and cars are no longer allowed inside the park.

The architecture of Sukhothai temples is most typified by the classic lotus-bud *chedi,* featuring a conical spire topping a square-sided structure on a three-tiered base. Some sites exhibit other rich architectural forms introduced and modified during the period, such as bell-shaped Sinhalese and double-tiered Srivijaya *chedi.*

Despite the popularity of the park, it's quite expansive and solitary exploration is usually possible. Some of the most impressive ruins are outside the city walls, so a bicycle is essential to fully appreciate everything. Electric buggies (two to four people, without/with driver 200/400B per hour) can also be hired to get around the park.

◉ Central Zone

The historical park's **main zone** (โซนกลาง; 100B, plus bicycle 10B; ☉ 6.30am-7.30pm Sun-Fri, to 9pm Sat) is home to what are arguably some of the park's most impressive ruins. On Saturday night much of the central zone is illuminated and remains open until 9pm.

Wat Mahathat   HISTORIC SITE
(วัดมหาธาตุ; central zone, Sukhothai Historical Park; 100B, plus bicycle 10B; ☉ 6.30am-7.30pm Sun-Fri, to 9pm Sat) Completed in the 13th century, the largest *wát* in Sukhothai is surrounded by brick walls (206m long and 200m wide) and a moat that is believed to represent the outer wall of the universe and the cosmic ocean.

The *chedi* spires feature the famous lotus-bud motif, and some of the original stately Buddha figures still sit among the ruined columns of the old *wí·hǎhn.* There are 198 *chedi* within the monastery walls – a lot to explore in what is believed to be the former spiritual and administrative centre of the old capital.

Wat Si Sawai   HISTORIC SITE
(วัดศรีสวาย; central zone, Sukhothai Historical Park; 100B, plus bicycle 10B; ☉ 6.30am-7.30pm Sun-Fri, to 9pm Sat) Just south of Wat Mahathat, this Buddhist shrine (dating from the 12th and 13th centuries) features three Khmer-style towers and a picturesque moat. It was originally built by the Khmers as a Hindu temple.

Wat Sa Si   HISTORIC SITE
(วัดสระศรี, Sacred Pond Monastery; central zone, Sukhothai Historical Park; 100B, plus bicycle 10B; ☉ 6.30am-7.30pm Sun-Fri, to 9pm Sat) Wat Sa Si sits on an island west of the bronze monument of King Ramkhamhaeng (the third Sukhothai king). It's a simple, classic Sukhothai-style *wát* containing a large Buddha, one *chedi* and the columns of the ruined *wí·hǎhn.*

Ramkhamhaeng National Museum   MUSEUM
(พิพิธภัณฑสถานแห่งชาติรามคำแหง; Sukhothai Historical Park; 150B; ☉ 9am-4pm) Near the

NORTHERN THAILAND SUKHOTHAI

Sukhothai Historical Park

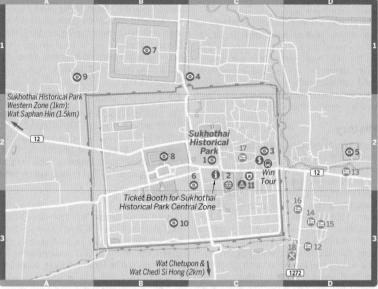

Sukhothai Historical Park

entrance to the central zone, this museum is a decent starting point for exploring the historical-park ruins. A replica of the famous Ramkhamhaeng inscription, said to be the earliest example of Thai writing, is kept here among an impressive collection of Sukhothai artefacts. Admission to the museum is not included in the ticket to the central zone.

Wat Trapang Thong BUDDHIST TEMPLE
(วัดตระพังทอง; off Rte 12; ⊙ daylight hours) Next to the Ramkhamhaeng National Museum, this small, still-inhabited wát with fine stucco reliefs is reached by a footbridge across the large lotus-filled pond that surrounds

it. This reservoir, allegedly the original site of Thailand's Loi Krathong festival, supplies the Sukhothai community with most of its water.

◎ Northern Zone

The **northern zone** (โซนเหนือ; 100B, plus bicycle 10B; ⊙ 6.30am-7.30pm), 500m north of the old city walls, is easily reached by bicycle.

Wat Si Chum HISTORIC SITE
(วัดศรีชุม; northern zone, Sukhothai Historical Park; 100B, plus bicycle 10B; ⊙ 6.30am-7.30pm) This wát contains an impressive *mon·dòp*

(small, square, spired building) with a 15m brick-and-stucco seated Buddha. This Buddha's elegant, tapered fingers are much photographed. Archaeologists theorise that this image is the 'Phra Atchana' mentioned in the famous Ramkhamhaeng inscription (p253). A passage in the *mon·dòp* wall that leads to the top has been blocked so that it's no longer possible to view the *Jataka* inscriptions that line the tunnel ceiling.

Wat Phra Phai Luang   HISTORIC SITE

(วัดพระพายหลวง; northern zone, Sukhothai Historical Park; 100B, plus bicycle 10B; ⊙6.30am-7.30pm) This somewhat isolated wát features three 12th-century Khmer-style towers, bigger than those at Wat Si Sawai in the central zone. This may have been the centre of Sukhothai when it was ruled by the Khmers of Angkor prior to the 13th century.

◉ Western Zone

The **western zone** (โซนตะวันตก; 100B, plus bicycle 10B; ⊙6.30am-7.30pm), at its furthest extent 2km west of the old city walls, is the most expansive. In addition to Wat Saphan Hin (p255), several mostly featureless ruins can be found here. A bicycle is necessary to explore this zone.

Wat Saphan Hin   HISTORIC SITE

(วัดสะพานหิน; western zone, Sukthothai Historical Park; 100B, plus bicycle 10B; ⊙6.30am-7.30pm) This wát is located on the crest of a hill that rises about 200m above the plain. Its name means 'stone bridge' – a reference to the slate path and staircase that lead up to the temple, which are still in place.

All that remains of the original temple are a few *chedi* and the ruined *wí·hǎhn,* consisting of two rows of laterite columns flanking a 12.5m-high standing Buddha image on a brick terrace. The site is 3km west of the former city wall and has good views of the Sukhothai ruins to the southeast and the mountains to the north and south.

◉ Outside The Centre

A few worthwhile destinations lie outside the more popular paid zones.

Sangkhalok Museum   MUSEUM

(พิพิธภัณฑ์สังคโลก; Rte 1293; adult/child 100/50B; ⊙8am-5pm) This small but comprehensive museum is an excellent introduction to ancient Sukhothai's most famous product and export, its ceramics. The ground floor displays an impressive collection of original Thai pottery found in the area, plus some pieces traded from Vietnam, Myanmar and China. The 2nd floor features examples of non-utilitarian pottery made as art, including some beautiful and rare ceramic Buddha statues. The museum is about 2.5km east of the centre of New Sukhothai; a túk-túk here is about 100B.

Wat Chetupon   HISTORIC SITE

(วัดเชตุพน; off Rte 1272, southern zone, Sukhothai Historical Park; ⊙24hr) Located 1.4km south of the old city walls, this temple once held a four-sided *mon·dòp* (a *chedi*-like spire) featuring the four classic poses of the Buddha (sitting, reclining, standing and walking). The graceful lines of the walking Buddha can still be made out today.

Wat Chedi Si Hong   HISTORIC SITE

(วัดเจดีย์สี่ห้อง; off Rte 1272, southern zone, Sukhothai Historical Park; ⊙24hr) Directly across from Wat Chetupon, the main *chedi* here has retained much of its original stucco relief work, which shows still vivid depictions of elephants, lions and humans.

Wat Chang Lom   HISTORIC SITE

(วัดช้างล้อม; off Rte 12, eastern zone, Sukhothai Historical Park; ⊙24hr) Wat Chang Lom (Elephant Circled Monastery) is about 1km east of the main park entrance. A large bell-shaped *chedi* is supported by 36 elephants sculpted into its base.

☘ Activities & Tours

Cycling Sukhothai   CYCLING

(☏055 612519, 085 083 1864; www.cyclingsukhothai.com; off Th Jarodvithithong; half-/full day 800/990B, sunset tour 450B; ▣) A resident of Sukhothai for 20-odd years, Belgian cycling enthusiast Ronny Hanquart offers themed bike tours, such as the Historical Park Tour, which also includes stops at lesser-seen wát and villages.

The office is about 1.2km west of the Mae Nam Yom, off Th Jarodvithithong in New Sukhothai; free transport can be arranged. There are trailers and special seats for kids.

Sukhothai Bicycle Tour   CYCLING

(☏086 931 6242; www.sukhothaibicycletour.com; 34/1 Th Jarodvithithong; half-day 750B, full-day 1050-1150B) A local Thai outfit that gets overwhelmingly positive feedback for their various bicycle tours.

New Sukhothai

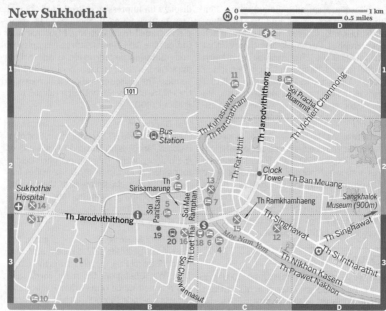

New Sukhothai

🔾 Activities, Courses & Tours
1	Cycling Sukhothai	A3
2	Sukhothai Bicycle Tour	C1

🛏 Sleeping
3	4T Guesthouse	B2
4	Ban Thai	C3
5	Blue House	B2
6	Foresto	C3
7	J&J Guest House	C2
8	Ruean Thai Hotel	C1
9	Rueangsrisiri	B2
10	Sabaidee House	A3
11	Sila Resort	C1
	TR Room & Bungalow	(see 6)

⊗ Eating
12	Dream Café	C3
13	Fueang Fah	C2
14	Jayhae	A2
15	Night Market	C3
16	Poo Restaurant	B3
17	Tapui	A3

🍷 Drinking & Nightlife
18	Chopper Bar	C3

🔵 Transport
19	Prasert Motorcycle Services	B3
20	Sŏrng·tăa·ou to Sukhothai Historical Park	B3

🎇 Festivals & Events

Loi Krathong   CULTURAL
(◷Nov) Sukhothai Historical Park is one of the most popular destinations to celebrate this holiday spanning five days in November. In addition to magical floating lights, there are fireworks, folk-dance performances and a light-and-sound production.

🛏 Sleeping

New Sukhothai has some of the best-value budget accommodation in Northern Thailand. Clean, cheerful hotels and guesthouses abound, with many places offering attractive bungalows, free pick-up from the bus station and free use of bicycles.

There's an increasing number of options near the park, many of them upscale. Prices tend to go up during the Loi Krathong festival.

🛏 New Sukhothai

Ban Thai   GUESTHOUSE $
(✆055 610163; banthai_guesthouse@yahoo.com; 38 Th Prawet Nakhon; r & bungalows 350-800B; ❄🛜) New Sukhothai's longest-running guesthouse, Ban Thai is a relaxed, friendly spot. The cheapest rooms are plain and

fan-only but the cute and compact bungalows set around an attractive garden are a decent deal.

Rueangsrisiri
GUESTHOUSE $

(📞087 314 6113; anuntachai18@gmail.com; dm 120-180B, r 250-650B; ❄️📶) Rueangsrisiri has 53 rooms spread across two blocks just steps away from the bus station. The dorms come with small lockers and clean shared bathrooms. Private rooms are quite big – the cheapest are fan-only. It's well set up for travellers.

4T Guesthouse
HOTEL $

(📞055 614679; fourthouse@yahoo.com; 122 Soi Mae Ramphan; r 300-600B; ❄️📶🏊) An expansive budget 'resort' of 22 rooms and bungalows. The cheapest are fan-only and compact, with hard beds. But the bungalows are a reasonable size and come with balconies. There's also a small, shallow pool.

Foresto
HOTEL $$

(📞095 125 9689; www.forestosukhothai.com; 16/1-3 Th Prawet Nakhon; r 1250-1600B; ❄️📶🏊) Wind through a semisecluded garden to find 15 spacious and stylish rooms, all with decent bathrooms. Choose from the vast rooms in the main structure or the newer rooms that resemble glass cubes and come with big windows. The pool is a bonus.

Sabaidee House
HOTEL $$

(📞055 616303; www.sabaideehouse.com; 81/7 Th Jarodvithithong; r incl breakfast 500-800B; ❄️📶🏊) This cheery guesthouse in a semi-rural setting has seven attractive bungalows set in a shady garden, and four less-impressive rooms that share bathrooms in the main structure. There's also a pool and a restaurant. It's tucked down a quiet lane off Th Jarodvithithong, about 200m before the intersection with Rte 101; look for the sign.

Sila Resort
HOTEL $$

(📞055 620344; www.silaresortsukhothai.com; 3/49 Th Kuhasuwan; incl breakfast r 400-600B, bungalows 750-1500B; ❄️📶) This cheerful compound has flowering trees, a gingerbread Thai villa, wood bungalows, statues, resort-like A-frames and a restaurant. The rooms are comfortable, modern and well kept but not spacious. It's a fair hike from the centre of New Sukhothai.

J&J Guest House
GUESTHOUSE $$

(📞055 620095; www.jjguest-house.com; 12 Th Kuhasuwan; bungalows 700B; ❄️📶) Located in a manicured garden by the river, the eight stone-floored bungalows here are a little dated but still comfortable, cool and relatively spacious. The vibe is friendly and motorbikes can be rented.

Blue House
HOTEL $$

(📞055 614863; www.sukhothaibluehouse.word-press.com; off Th Sirisamarung; r 650-1000B; ❄️📶) This big azure villa in a fine location has 18 rather characterless rooms, all equipped with en-suite bathrooms, air-con, TVs, refrigerators and hot showers.

TR Room & Bungalow
GUESTHOUSE $$

(📞055 611663; www.sukhothaibudgetguest house.com; 27/5 Th Prawet Nakhon; r/bungalows 600/800B; ❄️📶) The rooms here are a little dark, but nicely furnished with decent beds and are a good deal for the price. The five wooden bungalows out back offer more space and come with balconies.

★ Ruean Thai Hotel
HOTEL $$$

(📞055 612444; www.rueanthaihotel.com; 181/20 Soi Pracha Ruammit; r incl breakfast 1480-2180B, ste 4000-4600B; ❄️📶🏊) At first glance, you might mistake this eye-catching complex for a Buddhist temple or a traditional Thai house. The upper-level rooms follow a distinct Thai theme, while the poolside rooms are slightly more modern; there's a concrete building with simple air-con rooms out back. Service is both friendly and flawless, and the whole place boasts a resort-like feel. Call for free pick-up from the bus station.

🛏 Sukhothai Historical Park

★ Thai Thai Sukhothai Guesthouse
HOTEL $$

(📞055 697022; www.thaithaisukhothai.com; off Rte 1272; incl breakfast r 1000-1250B, bungalows 1400B; ❄️📶🏊) This place isn't a guesthouse but is instead a very comfortable hotel that gets rave reviews. The bungalows with their big balconies are especially enticing, but all the rooms are tastefully decorated, spacious and up to date. The service is as good as it gets in Sukhothai and there's a decent-sized pool.

★ Orchid Hibiscus Guest House
HOTEL $$

(📞055 633284; www.orchidhibiscus-guesthouse. com; 407/2 Rte 1272; r/bungalows incl breakfast 900/1500B; ❄️📶🏊) This collection of rooms and bungalows is spread across two compounds; both have pools and are surrounded by a relaxing, manicured garden packed

WORTH A TRIP

ELEPHANT RETIREMENT HOME

Located 8km from the village of Baan Tuek in Sukhothai Province, the worthwhile **Boon Lott's Elephant Sanctuary** (www.blesele.org; per person per night incl meals & transfers 6000B) allows guests to observe 12 rescued and former working pachyderms in their natural environment. It welcomes overnight and multiday visitors, with guests involved in all aspects of sanctuary life, including walking elephants to grazing grounds, and planting vegetation. Three teak guesthouses each sleep two people; book ahead.

with plants and flowers. Rooms are spacious, spotless and fun, featuring colourful design details and accents, plus four-poster beds. It's on Rte 1272, about 500m off Rte 12; the turn-off is between the Km 48 and Km 49 markers.

Wake Up @ Muang Kao　　　GUESTHOUSE **$$**
(☎062 419 6924; www.facebook.com/WakeUpAtMuangKaoBoutiqueHotel; 1/1 Rte 12; r 1000B; ❄️🛜) If there's a homestay equivalent to a flashpackers, Wake Up has nailed it. The five rooms here are spacious and tasteful, come decked out with local touches and are looked after by a friendly local couple. A breath of fresh air in old Sukhothai.

Legendha　　　HOTEL **$$$**
(☎055 697214; www.legendhasukhothai.com; Rte 12; incl breakfast r 3400-3900B; villa 8000B; ❄️🛜🏊) Water, greenery and traditional structures come together at this lauded resort, culminating in the feel of a Northern Thai village. Other perks include the service-minded staff, a pool and a location relatively close to the historical park. An ongoing renovation is leaving the rooms looking better than ever.

Tharaburi Resort　　　HOTEL **$$$**
(☎055 697132; www.tharaburiresort.com; 321/3 Rte 1272; incl breakfast r 3600-4200B; ste 5000B; ❄️🛜🏊) This boutique has a sumptuous air and features three traditional-feeling structures divided up into 13 rooms and suites placed around a lotus pond. Rooms are themed (Thai, Moroccan, Japanese, Chinese), employing faux antiques and silks,

while the suites feel like a small home. A stylish, if somewhat overpriced, choice.

Le Charme Sukhothai　　　HOTEL **$$$**
(☎055 633333; www.lecharmesukhothai.com; 9/9 Rte 1272; r & bungalows 2500-4500B; ❄️🛜🏊) It may not look like much from a distance, but a closer peek at this place reveals an inviting cluster of bright bungalows linked by an elevated wooden walkway, with lush gardens and lotus ponds. Rooms are simple but large and tastefully decorated, with balconies looking out over all the water. There's also an on-site spa.

🍴 Eating & Drinking

Sukhothai's signature dish is gŏo·ay dĕe·o sù·kŏh·tai (Sukhothai-style noodles), which features a slightly sweet broth with different preparations of pork, ground peanuts and thinly sliced green beans. Most places to eat are in New Sukhothai, including a small but decent **night market** (Th Ramkhamhaeng; mains 30-60B; ⏱6-10pm), but a string of food stalls and simple tourist-oriented restaurants can be found along the road to the historical park.

★ Jayhae　　　THAI **$**
(off Th Jarodvithithong; dishes 40-120B; ⏱7am-4pm; 🛜) You haven't been to Sukhothai if you haven't tried the noodles at Jayhae, an extremely popular restaurant that serves Sukhothai-style noodles, pàt tai and tasty coffee drinks. It's located about 1.3km west of Mae Nam Yom.

Tapui　　　THAI **$**
(off Th Jarodvithithong; dishes 40-80B; ⏱7.30am-4pm) Consisting of little more than a brick floor with a tin roof over it, Tapui claims to be the first shop in Sukhothai to have sold the city's namesake dish, gŏo·ay dĕe·o sù·kŏh·tai (Sukhothai-style noodles). It's located about 1.3km west of the Mae Nam Yom; there's no Roman-script sign or English menu but there are pictures to guide your choice.

Poo Restaurant　　　MULTICUISINE **$**
(24/3 Th Jarodvithithong; mains 50-250B; ⏱9am-11pm; 🛜) Named after its original owner (if you were wondering), Poo is a traveller-friendly spot that serves everything from tasty Sukhothai noodles to Thai and Western classics. Portions are big. It's also fine for an evening drink: it does cocktails and has a small selection of Belgian beers.

Sukhothai Kitchen THAI $$

(Rte 1272; mains 95-280B; ⊙10am-10pm; 🛜)
This big and breezy place is set around a garden with the inevitable lotus pond. The menu spans Thai and Northern Thai dishes, with a few Western options. It's more upmarket than the restaurants close to the Sukhothai Historical Park.

Dream Café THAI $$

(86/1 Th Singhawat; mains 120-350B; ⊙5-11pm; 🖊) Having a meal at Dream Café is like dining in an antique shop. Eclectic but tasteful furnishings and knick-knackery abound, staff members are competent and friendly and, most importantly, the food is good. Try one of the well-executed *yam* (Thai-style 'salads').

Fueang Fah THAI $$

(107/2 Th Kuhasuwan; dishes 60-350B; ⊙10am-10pm; 🛜) Pretend you're a local in the know and have a meal at this long-standing riverside restaurant. The speciality here is freshwater fish dishes, such as the tasty 'fried fish', the first item on the barely comprehensible English-language menu. There's no Roman-script sign; it's just after the bridge on Th Kuhasuwan.

Chopper Bar BAR

(Th Prawet Nakhon; ⊙5pm-midnight; 🛜) Travellers and locals congregate at this 2nd-floor bar with a vague cowboy theme for drinks, food (the menu is thoughtfully divided into spicy and nonspicy sections) and live music. Take advantage of Sukhothai's cool evenings on the rooftop terrace. The bar is owned by Sukhothai's finest locksmith, just in case you get locked out.

ℹ Information

There are banks with ATMs and exchange facilities scattered all around the central part of New Sukhothai, particularly in the area west of the Mae Nam Yom, and several in the old city as well.

Kasikorn Bank (Th Jarodvithithong; ⊙8.30am-4.30pm Mon-Sat) This bank has an ATM that accepts international cards.

Siam Commercial Bank (Rte 12; ⊙8.30am-4.30pm Mon-Fri) This bank is close to the Sukhothai Historical Park.

Police Station (📞055 611010, 24hr emergency 191; Th Singhawat; ⊙24hr) In New Sukhothai.

Sukhothai Hospital (📞055 610280; Th Jarodvithithong) Located just west of New Sukhothai.

Tourism Authority of Thailand (TAT; 📞055 616228, nationwide 1672; www.tourismthailand.org; Th Jarodvithithong; ⊙8.30am-4.30pm) About 750m west of the bridge in New Sukhothai, this office has a pretty good selection of maps and brochures and a few English-speaking staff.

Tourist Police (📞1155; Rte 12; ⊙24hr) A tourist-police outpost close to the Sukhothai Historical Park.

ℹ Getting There & Away

Sukhothai Airport (off Rte 1195) is located 27km north of town. **Bangkok Airways** (📞055 647224, nationwide 1771; www.bangkokair.com; Sukhothai Airport; ⊙7am-6pm) is the only airline operating here, with two daily flights to/from Bangkok's Suvarnabhumi International Airport (from 1690B, 1¼ hours). **Eddy Rent A Car** (📞055 647220; Sukhothai Airport; ⊙7am-7pm) operates a minivan service between the airport and New Sukhothai or Sukhothai Historical Park. Alternatively, **AirAsia** (📞094 719 3645, nationwide 02 515 9999; www.airasia.

WORTH A TRIP

FARMER FOR A DAY

Sukhothai's **Organic Agriculture Project** (📞055 647290; off Rte 1195; half-day incl lunch 900B; ⊙8am-5pm Thu-Tue) 🖊 allows visitors to take part in traditional Thai farm activities. The compound is also home to a restaurant serving dishes made from the farm's organic produce (mains 50B to 120B, open 8am to 5pm Thursday to Tuesday).

Taking place at Sukhothai Airport's organic farm, the half-day begins by donning the outfit of a Thai rice farmer and riding an *ee đaan* (a traditional utility vehicle) to gather duck eggs. This is followed by riding a buffalo, checking into an orchid farm, witnessing the stages of rice production and, ultimately, planting or gathering rice. The session ends with an informal cooking lesson asiland meal using organic produce from the farm. Book in advance for an English-speaking guide.

The project is located on the same road as Sukhothai's airport, 27km from New Sukhothai off Rte 1195, and is not accessible by public transport. If you don't have your own wheels, you can arrange a ride with the minivan service Eddy Rent A Car.

com; Phitsanulok Airport; ⊘7am-6.30pm) and **Nok Air** (☑ 055 301051, nationwide 1318; www. nokair.co.th; Phitsanulok Airport; ⊘6am-7pm) offer minivan transfers to/from both old and New Sukhothai via the airport in Phitsanulok, less than an hour away.

Sukhothai's **bus station** (☑ 055 614529; Rte 101) is almost 1km northwest of the centre of New Sukhothai; a motorcycle taxi between here and central New Sukhothai should cost around 50B, or you can hop on any *sŏrng·tăa·ou* (passenger pick-up truck) bound for Sukhothai Historical Park – they stop at the bus station on their way out of town (30B, 10 minutes, frequent from 6am to 5.30pm).

Alternatively, if you're staying near the historical park, **Win Tour** (☑ 099 135 5645; Rte 12; ⊘6am-9.50pm) has an office where you can board buses to Bangkok (338B to 395B, six hours, 8.20am, 12.20pm and 9.50pm) and Chiang Mai (225B to 290B, five hours, 6.40am, 9.50am, 12.10pm and 2pm).

ⓘ Getting Around

A *săhm·lór* (three-wheeled pedicab) ride within New Sukhothai should cost no more than 40B to 50B.

Relatively frequent **sŏrng·tăa·ou** (Th Jarodvithithong) run between New Sukhothai and Sukhothai Historical Park (30B, 30 minutes, 6am to 5.30pm), leaving from a stop on Th Jarodvithithong. Motorcycle taxis run between the town or bus station and the historical park for 120B.

The best way to get around the historical park is by bicycle; bikes can be hired at shops outside the park entrance for 30B for five hours (6am to 6pm).

Motorbikes (from 200B for 24 hours) can be hired at many guesthouses in New Sukhothai, and at **Prasert Motorcycle Services** (215/2 Th Jarodvithithong; ⊘7am-5pm).

TRANSPORT FROM SUKHOTHAI
Bus

DESTINATION	FARE (B)	DURATION (HR)	FREQUENCY
Bangkok	255-382	6-7	every 30min 7.50am-10.40pm
Chiang Mai	211-390	5-6	frequent 6.20am-2am
Chiang Rai	256	9	6.40am & 9am
Kamphaeng Phet	74	1½	every 30min 7.50am-10.40pm
Khon Kaen	310-410	7	7 departures 10.30am-midnight
Lampang	220	3	frequent 6.20am-2am
Mae Sot	153-191	3	2am & 1.15pm
Mukdahan	550	10	7.50pm & 9.30pm
Phitsanulok	52	1	every 30min 7.50am-10.40pm
Sawankhalok	28	1	hourly 6.40am-5pm
Si Satchanalai	49	1½	hourly 6.40am-5pm

Minivan

DESTINATION	FARE (B)	DURATION (HR)	FREQUENCY
Kamphaeng Phet	60	2	frequent *sŏrng·tăa·ou* 9am-4pm
Mae Sot	153	3	4 minivan departures 9.15am-2.15pm
Phitsanulok	42	1	every hour 7.30am-5pm
Sukhothai Historical Park	30	30 mins	frequent *sŏrng·tăa·ou* 6am-5.30pm

Si Satchanalai-Chaliang Historical Park

Set among peaceful hills, the 13th- to 15th-century ruins of the old cities of Si Satchanalai and Chaliang lie 50km north of Sukhothai. Less visited than the Sukhothai ruins, Si Satchanalai-Chaliang Historical Park (อุทยานประวัติศาสตร์ศรีสัชนาลัย-เชลียง; off Rte 101; 100B, combined ticket with Wat Chao Chan & Si Satchanalai Centre for Study & Preservation of Sangkalok Kilns 250B; ☉8.30am-4.30pm) covers roughly 720 hectares and is surrounded by a 12m-wide moat. Chaliang, 1km southeast, is an older city site (dating to the 11th century), though its two temples date to the 14th century.

The nearby towns of Ban Hat Siaw and Sawankhalok are the main centres for the area.

◎ Sights

A combined admission fee of 250B allows entry to Si Satchanalai, Wat Chao Chan (at Chaliang) and the Si Satchanalai Centre for Study & Preservation of Sangkalok Kilns.

Wat Chang Lom   HISTORIC SITE
(วัดช้างล้อม; Si Satchanalai-Chaliang Historical Park; 100B, combined entry with Wat Chao Chan & Si Satchanalai Centre for Study & Preservation of Sangkalok Kilns 250B; ☉8am-4.30pm) This fine temple, marking the centre of the old city of Si Satchanalai, has elephants surrounding a bell-shaped *chedi* that is somewhat better preserved than its counterpart in Sukhothai. An inscription states that the temple was built by King Ramkhamhaeng between 1285 and 1291.

Wat Khao Phanom Phloeng   HISTORIC SITE
(วัดเขาพนมเพลิง; Si Satchanalai-Chaliang Historical Park; 100B, combined entry with Wat Chao Chan & Si Satchanalai Centre for Study & Preservation of Sangkalok Kilns 250B; ☉8am-4.30pm) On the hill overlooking Wat Chang Lom are the remains of Wat Khao Phanom Phloeng, including a *chedi*, a large seated Buddha and stone columns that once supported the roof of the *wí·hǎhn*. From here you can make out the general design of the once-great city. The slightly higher hill west of Phanom Phloeng is capped by a large Sukhothai-style *chedi* – all that remains of Wat Khao Suwan Khiri.

Wat Chedi Jet Thaew   HISTORIC SITE
(วัดเจดีย์เจ็ดแถว; Si Satchanalai-Chaliang Historical Park; 100B, combined entry with Wat Chao Chan & Si Satchanalai Centre for Study & Preservation of Sangkalok Kilns 250B; ☉8am-4.30pm) Next to Wat Chang Lom, these ruins contain seven rows of *chedi*, the largest of which is a copy of one at Wat Mahathat in Sukhothai. An interesting brick-and-plaster *wí·hǎhn* features barred windows designed to look like lathed wood (an ancient Indian technique used all over Southeast Asia).

Wat Nang Phaya   HISTORIC SITE
(วัดนางพญา; Si Satchanalai-Chaliang Historical Park; 100B, combined entry with Wat Chao Chan & Si Satchanalai Centre for Study & Preservation of Sangkalok Kilns 250B; ☉8am-4.30pm) South of Wat Chedi Jet Thaew, this *chedi* is Sinhalese in style and was built in the 15th or 16th century, a bit later than the other monuments at Si Satchanalai. Stucco reliefs on the large laterite *wí·hǎhn* in front of the *chedi* – now sheltered by a tin roof – date from the Ayuthaya period, when Si Satchanalai was known as Sawankhalok. Goldsmiths in the district still craft a design known as *nahng pá·yah*, modelled after these reliefs.

Wat Phra Si Ratana Mahathat   HISTORIC SITE
(วัดพระศรีรัตนมหาธาตุ; Si Satchanalai-Chaliang Historical Park; 20B; ☉8am-4.30pm) These ruins consist of a large laterite *chedi* (dating to 1448–88) between two *wí·hǎhn*. One of the *wí·hǎhn* holds a large seated Sukhothai Buddha image, a smaller standing image and a bas-relief of the famous walking Buddha, exemplary of the flowing, boneless Sukhothai style. The other *wí·hǎhn* contains some less distinguished images.

Wat Chao Chan   HISTORIC SITE
(วัดเจ้าจันทร์; Si Satchanalai-Chaliang Historical Park; 100B, combined entry with Si Satchanalai & Si Satchanalai Centre for Study & Preservation of Sangkalok Kilns 250B; ☉8am-4.30pm) The central attraction here is a large Khmer-style tower similar to later towers built in Lopburi and probably constructed during the reign of Khmer King Jayavarman VII (1181–1217). The tower has been restored and is in fairly good shape. The roofless *wí·hǎhn* on the right contains the laterite outlines of a large standing Buddha that has all but melted away from exposure and weathering. Admission isn't always collected here.

Si Satchanalai Centre for Study & Preservation of Sangkalok Kilns   MUSEUM
(ศูนย์ศึกษาและอนุรักษ์เตาสังคโลก; 100B, combined ticket with Si Satchanalai sites & Wat Chao Chan 250B; ☉8am-4.30pm) Located 5km south

Si Satchanalai-Chaliang Historical Park

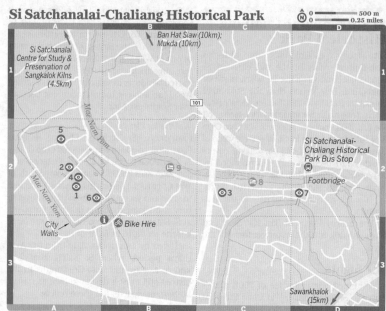

Si Satchanalai-Chaliang Historical Park

of the Si Satchanalai ruins, this centre has large excavated kilns and many intact pottery samples. The exhibits are interesting despite the lack of English labels.

Sawanworanayok National Museum　MUSEUM
(พิพิธภัณฑสถานแห่งชาติสวรรควรนายก; 69 Th Phracharat; 50B; ⏱9am-4pm Wed-Sun) In Sawankhalok town, near Wat Sawankhalam on the western riverbank, this museum houses an impressive collection of 12th- to 15th-century artefacts. The ground floor focuses on the area's ceramic legacy, while the 2nd floor features several beautiful bronze and stone Sukhothai-era Buddha statues.

🛏 Sleeping & Eating

Accommodation near any of the historical sites is mostly limited to basic homestays and hotels. Alternatives include Sawankhalok,

15km to the south, or Ban Hat Siaw, about 9km north of the park. There are some basic stalls and restaurants near the park.

Swankaburi Boutique Hotel　HOTEL $$
(✉087 312 6767; swankaburi@windowslive.com; 15/31 Th Si Satchanalai, Sawankhalok; incl breakfast r 600-900B, ste 1600B; ❄🛜) It's a welcome surprise to find this well set up hotel in a small town like Sawankhalok. Standard rooms are a little tight, but the deluxe ones offer far more space. All are decked out in woods, tiles and attractive local touches. There's free bicycle use for guests. It's located at the northern end of Sawankhalok.

Mukda Resort　HOTEL $$
(✉055 671024; Rte 101, Ban Hat Siaw; r incl breakfast 400-950B; ❄🛜) Mukda Resort has tidy, comfortable rooms relatively close to Si Satchanalai-Chaliang Historical Park, the cheapest of which are fan-cooled. It's at the

northern end of Ban Hat Siaw, at the turn-off to Uttaradit.

Sisatchanalai Heritage
HOTEL $$

(☑095 162 3545, 055 615423; www.sisatchanalai
heritage.com; Chaliang; incl breakfast r 1500B,
bungalows 1000B; ❋🛜) This riverside com-
pound – complete with restaurant and cof-
fee shop – inside Si Satchanalai-Chaliang
Historical Park features 10 neat and com-
pact bungalows and three big family rooms.
There's free bicycle use for guests.

Papong Homestay
GUESTHOUSE $$

(☑055 631557, 087 313 4782; off Rte 1201,
Chaliang; r incl breakfast 600B; ❋🛜) A locally
run outfit near Si Satchanalai-Chaliang Historical Park, with five clean and comfortable
rooms that include private bathrooms.

Sukhothai
Heritage Resort
RESORT $$$

(☑055 647564; www.facebook.com/sukhothai
heritageresort; 999 Mu 2; incl breakfast r 2700-
3700B, ste 5600-8000B; ❋🛜🏊) Approxi-
mately 32km from Si Satchanalai-Chaliang
Historical Park near Sukhothai Airport is
this upscale yet rural and isolated resort.
Seemingly a continuation of the historical
park, the low-lying brick and peak-roofed
structures are interspersed by green fields
and calming lotus-filled ponds, culminating
in a temple-like environment. The rooms
take you back to the contemporary world
with large flat-screen TVs and modern
furniture.

Puu-Yaa House
MULTICUISINE $

(off Th Si Satchanalai; mains 39-399B; ⊘9am-
8.30pm Tue-Sun; 🛜) This hole-in-the-wall
restaurant serves a mix of Thai and Western
food, including rice and noodle dishes, piz-
za, pasta and burgers. Find it to the side of
Sawankhalok's market.

ℹ Information

Information Centre (Si Satchanalai-Chaliang
Historical Park; ⊘8am-4.30pm) This infor-
mation centre at the Si Satchanalai-Chaliang
Historical Park distributes free maps and has
a small exhibit on the history and attractions
here.

ℹ Getting There & Around

Bike hire (Si Satchanalai-Chaliang Historical
Park; per day 30B; ⊘8am-5pm) is available
from the food stalls near the park's Information
centre, or at the bus stop where the bus from
Sawankhalok will drop you.

In Sawankhalok, săhm-lór (three-wheeled ped-
icabs) congregate by the market; trips around
town cost 30B to 40B.

BUS
Si Satchanalai-Chaliang Historical Park is off Rte
101 between Sawankhalok and Ban Hat Siaw.
From New Sukhothai, take a Si Satchanalai bus
(49B, 1½ hours, hourly 6.40am to 5pm) or one of
the two buses to Chiang Rai at 6.40am and 9am
(49B) and ask to get off at meuang gòw (old city).

From Sawankhalok, **buses** (Rte 1180) depart
from the bus-station office in the south of town
from 7.20am to 3pm (15B, every 1½ hours),
heading for the **Si Satchanalai-Chaliang His-
torical Park Bus Stop** (Rte 101), Sukhothai and
Phitsanulok.

Buses to Bangkok (☑055 642037; Rte 1180)
from Sawankhalok leave from another office
close to the centre of town (364B, 8.30am,
9.30am, 10.30am, 9pm and 9.30pm, six hours).

TRAIN
Sawankhalok's original **train station** is one
of the local sights. King Rama VI built a 60km
railway spur from Ban Dara (a small town on the
main northern trunk) to Sawankhalok just so
that he could visit the ruins. There's now a daily
special express from Bangkok to Sawankhalok
(512B, seven hours, 3.50am) that arrives in
Sawankhalok at 10.50am. The train heads back
to Bangkok at 6.01pm, arriving in the city at
4am. There is also a daily train to Phitsanulok
(50B, 3½ hours, 3.59pm).

PHITSANULOK PROVINCE

Phitsanulok Province (จังหวัดพิษณุโลก) is
home to visit-worthy natural attractions and
a pleasant provincial capital with plenty of
food and accommodation options. Howev-
er, most visitors regard the province more
as a base for visiting the historical ruins in
neighbouring provinces than a destination
in itself.

Phitsanulok
☑ 055 / POP 67,000

Phitsanulok (พิษณุโลก) sees relatively few
independent travellers but a fair number of
package tourists. The frenetic and friendly
city also boasts some interesting sights and
museums, chief of which is Wat Phra Si
Ratana Mahathat (p264), which contains
one of the country's most revered Buddha
images.

Those willing to forge their own path can also use Phitsanulok as a base to visit the nearby national parks of Thung Salaeng Luang (p266) and Phu Hin Rong Kla (p269), the latter the former strategic headquarters of the Communist Party of Thailand.

◉ Sights

★ Sergeant Major Thawee Folk Museum MUSEUM
(พิพิธภัณฑ์พื้นบ้านจ่าทวี; Th Wisut Kasat; adult/child 50/25B; ☺8.30am-4.30pm) This fascinating museum displays a remarkable collection of tools, textiles and photographs from Phitsanulok Province, as well as many knick-knacks from previous decades, all accumulated by the eponymous Sergeant Major Thawee. It's spread throughout five traditional-style Thai buildings and the displays are accompanied by informative English descriptions. Those interested in cooking will find much of interest in the display of a traditional Thai kitchen and the various traps used to catch game.

★ Wat Phra Si Ratana Mahathat BUDDHIST TEMPLE
(วัดพระศรีรัตนมหาธาตุ; Th Phutta Bucha; ☺temple 6am-9pm, museum 9am-5.30pm Wed-Sun) FREE The main *wí·hăhn* at this temple, known by locals as Wat Yai, appears small from the outside, but houses the Phra Phuttha Chinnarat, one of Thailand's most revered and copied Buddha images. This famous statue is probably second in importance only to the Emerald Buddha in Bangkok's Wat Phra Kaew.

The story goes that construction of this *wát* was commissioned under the reign of King Li Thai in 1357. When it was completed, the king wanted it to contain three high-quality bronze images, so he sent for well-known sculptors from Si Satchanalai, Chiang Saen and Hariphunchai (Lamphun), as well as five Brahman priests. The first two castings worked well, but the third required three attempts before it was decreed the best of all. Legend has it that a white-robed sage appeared from nowhere to assist in the final casting, then disappeared. This last image was named the Chinnarat (Victorious King) Buddha and it became the centrepiece in the *wí·hăhn*. The other two images, Phra Chinnasi and Phra Si Satsada, were later moved to the royal temple of Wat Bowonniwet in Bangkok.

The image was cast in the late Sukhothai style, but what makes it strikingly unique is the flame-like halo around the head and torso that turns up at the bottom to become dragon-serpent heads on either side of the image. The head of this Buddha is a little wider than that of the Sukhothai standard, giving the statue a very solid feel.

Another sanctuary to one side has been converted into a free museum, displaying antique Buddha images, ceramics and other historic artefacts.

Despite the holiness of the temple, endless loud broadcasts asking for donations, Thai musicians, a strip of vendors hawking everything from herbs to lottery tickets, several ATM machines and hundreds of visitors all contribute to a relentlessly hectic atmosphere. Come early (ideally before 7am) if you're looking for quiet contemplation or simply wish to take photos, and regardless of the time be sure to dress appropriately – no shorts or sleeveless tops.

Wat Ratburana BUDDHIST TEMPLE
(วัดราชบูรณะ; Th Phutta Bucha; ☺ daylight hours) FREE Across the street from Wat Phra Si Ratana Mahathat, Wat Ratburana draws fewer visitors but in some ways is more interesting than its famous neighbour. In addition to a *wí·hăhn* with a 700-year-old gold Buddha, there's a *bòht* (chapel), with beautiful murals thought to date back to the mid-19th century, and two wooden *hŏr đrai* (manuscript libraries).

The temple is also home to a few quirky attractions that offer a fascinating insight into the practices of Thai Buddhism. The most apparent of these is a large wooden boat decked with garlands that originally served to transport King Rama V on an official visit to Phitsanulok. Today the boat is believed to grant wishes to those who make an offering and crawl under its entire length three or nine times. Next to the *wí·hăhn* is a sacred tree with ladders on either side that visitors climb up, leave an offering, then ring a bell and descend, again repeating the action a total of three or nine times. And directly adjacent to the tree is an immense gong that, when rubbed the right way, creates a unique ringing sound.

Near each of these attractions you'll find somebody stationed who, in addition to selling the coins, incense and flowers used in offerings, will instruct visitors in exactly how to conduct each particular ritual, including

Phitsanulok

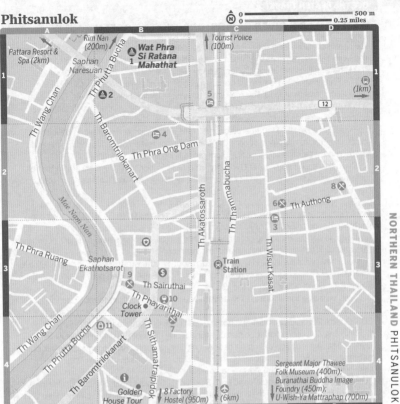

Phitsanulok

how many times to pass, what to offer and what prayer to say.

Buranathai Buddha Image Foundry

WORKSHOP

(โรงหล่อพระบูรณะไทย; 26/43 Th Wisut Kasat; 20B; ☉8am-5pm) **FREE** Almost across the street from Sergeant Major Thawee Folk Museum, and also belonging to Sergeant Major Thawee, is the Buranathai Buddha Image Foundry, where bronze Buddha images of all sizes are cast. Visitors are welcome to watch the process, and there are photo exhibits demonstrating the lost-wax method of metal casting. Some of the larger images take a year or more to complete. There is a small gift shop where you can purchase bronze images.

WATERFALLS & RIVER RAPIDS: DRIVING THE GREEN ROUTE

Rte 12, which runs along the scenic, rapid-studded Lam Nam Khek between Phitsanulok and Lom Sak, is known as the Green Route. Off this road are waterfalls, resorts and the Phu Hin Rong Kla and Thung Salaeng Luang National Parks.

The Phitsanulok TAT office distributes a good map of the attractions found along this 130km stretch of road. You may want to bypass the first two waterfalls, Nam Tok Sakhunothayan (at the Km 33 marker) and Kaeng Song (at the Km 45 marker), which on weekends can be overwhelmed with visitors. The third, Kaeng Sopha (at the Km 72 marker), is a larger area of small falls and rapids where you can walk from rock formation to rock formation – there are more or fewer rocks depending on rainfall. There's now a rather excessive 500B entrance fee to Kaeng Sopha.

When there's enough water (typically from September to November) any of the resorts along this section of Rte 12 can organise white-water rafting trips on the Lam Nam Khek.

Further east along the road is the 1262-sq-km Thung Salaeng Luang National Park (อุทยานแห่งชาติทุ่งแสลงหลวง; ☑ 055 268019, accommodation 02 562 0760; www.dnp. go.th; Rte 12; adult/child 500/300B; ⊗8am-5pm), one of Thailand's largest and most important wildlife sanctuaries. The entrance is at the Km 80 marker, where the park headquarters has information on walks and accommodation.

If you have your own wheels, you can turn south at the Km 100 marker onto Rte 2196 and head for Khao Kho (Khow Khor), another mountain lair used by the Communist Party of Thailand (CPT) during the 1970s.

If you've made the side trip to Khao Kho you can choose either to return to the Phitsanulok–Lom Sak highway, or take Rte 2258, off Rte 2196, until it terminates at Rte 203. On Rte 203 you can continue north to Lom Sak or south to Phetchabun.

Resort-style accommodation can be found along most of the Green Route, with budget accommodation clumping near Kaeng Song, around Km 45, and at the various national parks. Several restaurants are located on the banks of the Lam Nam Khek, most taking full advantage of the views and breezes.

Buses between Phitsanulok and Lom Sak cost 100B, and run from 5.50am to 6pm. For more freedom it's best to do this route with your own wheels; cars can be hired via several companies at Phitsanulok's airport (p268).

🛏 Sleeping

Karma Home Hostel
HOSTEL $

(☑ 088 814 1268; www.facebook.com/karmahome hostel; Soi Lang Wat Mai Apaiyaram; dm 200-250B, r 420B; ❄🛜) There are two open-plan dorms at this cosy hostel, as well as one private room, topped by a hammock-strewn rooftop terrace. Run by an English-Thai couple, the hostel has a traveller vibe, with nightly outings to bars and restaurants and bikes for hire.

Nap Corner Hostel
HOSTEL $

(☑ 091 389 4361; www.facebook.com/napcorner hostel; 77 Th Akatossaroth; dm 300B, r 500B; ❄🛜) The compact dorms at this friendly hostel have bathrooms and small lockers. The beds are hard – a theme of Phitsanulok hostels – and the location close to the railway and main roads means it can get a little noisy. There's free bike use for guests.

8 Factory Hostel
GUESTHOUSE $$

(☑ 098 265 9658; www.facebook.com/the8 factory; 174/11 Th Sithamatraipidok; r incl breakfast 688-988B; ❄🛜) It's not really a hostel – there are no dorm beds – but it does have decent-sized, comfortable rooms decked out in stripped wood and some industrial-chic touches. There's an American-themed downstairs cafe and restaurant and free bikes for guests. It's located south of the train station, a little away from downtown.

Ayara Grand Palace
HOTEL $$

(☑ 055 909999; www.ayaragrandpalacehotel.com; Th Authong; r incl breakfast 1000-2400B; ❄🛜🏊) The '90s-era pastels, fake fireplaces and relentless flower theme of this hotel give it an undeniably cheesy feel. But it's an efficient place and the rooms are big and well equipped with safety boxes and decent beds. The most expensive rooms are vast. There's also a small pool and a restaurant.

★**Pattara Resort & Spa** HOTEL $$$
(☑055 282966; www.pattararesort.com; 349/40 Th Chaiyanupap; incl breakfast r 3800-4500B, villa 7500-9000B; ❄️🛜🏊) This resort about 2km west of the city centre is Phitsanulok's classiest place to stay. Rooms feel vast and have huge bathrooms and wide balconies looking out over lotus ponds and a pool. Better yet, go for one of the two pool villas with private pools, or the two floating villas built over the lotus pond. There's also a spa and gym.

✗ Eating & Drinking

Rim Nan THAI $
(5/4 Th Phutta Bucha; mains 35-50B; ⏰7am-4pm) Just north of Wat Phra Si Ratana Mahathat, plant-filled, semi-open-air Rim Nan is the most attractive of a few similar restaurants along Th Phutta Bucha that offer gŏoay·dĕe·o hôy kăh, literally 'legs hanging' noodles. They're named for the low benches you eat at here, underneath which your legs swing free. There's no Roman-script sign.

Night Market MARKET $
(Th Phra Ong Dam; mains 30-60B; ⏰5pm-midnight) Lining either side of Th Phra Ong Dam north of Th Authong, this market has the usual selection of Thai street foods.

★**Ban Mai** THAI $$
(93/30 Th Authong; mains 80-200B; ⏰11am-10pm) Dinner at this local favourite is what a meal at your grandparents' place might be like: opinionated conversation, frumpy furniture and an overfed cat that appears to rule the dining room. Standout dishes include gaang pèt bèt yâhng (grilled duck curry) and yam dà krái (herbal lemongrass salad). There's no Roman-script sign; look for the yellow compound across from Ayara Grand Palace hotel.

Cafe Veggie INTERNATIONAL $$
(Th Phayarithai; mains 165-250B; ⏰11.30am-9pm; 🛜) Despite the name, this isn't really a vegetarian restaurant. But you can build your own salad and there is a veggie burger. Most of the dishes on the menu fall into the category of Western comfort food – fish and chips, steaks and pasta – but they're all tasty.

Paknang MULTICUISINE $$
(Th Sairuthai; mains 60-500B; ⏰10am-11pm) This corner of old Phitsanulok is the town's Chinese neighbourhood and this long-standing restaurant offers up decent Thai-Chinese-style dishes. The herbal-infused soups are especially good and there's a lot of fish on the big menu. Most dishes cost between 100B and 180B.

In Town BAR
(Th Phayarithai; ⏰6pm-midnight; 🛜) Set in a converted shophouse, with exposed brick walls and a wooden counter to sit at, this is perhaps Phitsanulok's most sophisticated bar. There's an extensive range of foreign brews in the refrigerator, some on tap, and proper cocktails are served.

U-Wish-Ya Mattraphap BAR
(www.facebook.com/Uwishya; 36/110 Th Chan Wetchakit; ⏰5pm-midnight; 🛜) A biker bar as perceived through Thai lens – which means it's a heck of a lot friendlier. There's gentle live music most nights and a menu of Thai-style bar bites.

🛍 Shopping

Night Bazaar MARKET
(Th Phutta Bucha; ⏰7pm-midnight) Phitsanulok's night bazaar is worth a visit if you need some cheap clothes or a foot massage. It's also good for eats.

The southernmost restaurant along the strip specialises in pàk bûng loy fáh (literally 'floating-in-the-sky morning glory vine'), in which the cook fires up a batch of the eponymous vegetable in a wok and then flings it through the air to a waiting server who catches it on a plate.

ℹ Information

Several banks in town offer foreign-exchange services and ATMs. There are also several ATMs inside the Wat Phra Si Ratana Mahathat compound.

Golden House Tour (☑055 259973; 55/37-38 Th Baromtrilokanart; ⏰7am-7pm Mon-Sat) This experienced travel agency can book airline tickets and arrange transport in and around Phitsanulok, including vans to Phu Hin Rong Kla National Park.

Krung Thai Bank (Th Naresuan; ⏰8.30am-4.30pm Mon-Fri) Has an ATM.

Police Station (☑24hr emergency 191; Th Baromtrilokanart) Police station in Phitsanulok.

Tourism Authority of Thailand (TAT; ☑055 252742, nationwide 1672; tatphlok@tat.or.th; 209/7-8 Th Baromtrilokanart; ⏰8.30am-4.30pm) This tourist office has helpful staff who hand out free maps of the town and a walking-tour sheet. The office also oversees the provinces of Sukhothai, Phichit and Phetchabun.

Tourist Police (☑nationwide 1155; Th Akatossaroth) Tourist police office in Phitsanulok.

ⓘ Getting There & Away

Phitsanulok Airport (☎ 055 301002) is about 5km south of town; taxis run to/from town for 150B. AirAsia (p259), Nok Air (p260) and **Thai Lion Air** (☎ call centre 02 529 9999; www.lionairthai.com; Phitsanulok Airport; ☻7am-7pm) operate daily flights to/from Bangkok's Don Mueang International Airport (from 695B, 55 minutes).

The city's **bus station** (☎ 055 212090; Rte 12) is 2km east of town on Hwy 12; túk-túk and motorcycle taxis to/from town cost 60B. Transport options out of Phitsanulok are good as it's a junction for several bus and minivan routes.

Phitsanulok's **train station** (☎ 055 258005, nationwide 1690; www.railway.co.th; Th Akatossaroth) is within walking distance of accommodation and offers a left-luggage service. The station is a significant train terminal and virtually every northbound and southbound train through the area stops here.

ⓘ Getting Around

Rides on the town's Darth Vaderesque săhm·lór (three-wheel pedicabs) start at 60B. Outside the train station there's a sign indicating prices for different destinations around town. Phitsanulok also has a small fleet of **taxis** (☎ 055 338888), and a few motorcycle taxis can be found at the bus and train stations.

Car hire at Phitsanulok's airport, with **Avis** (☎ 089 969 8672, nationwide 02 251 1130; www.avisthailand.com; Phitsanulok Airport; ☻7am-9pm), **Budget** (☎ 055 301020, nationwide 02 203 9222; www.budget.co.th; Phitsanulok Airport; ☻7am-6pm), **Eddy Rent A Car** (☎ 081 534 1535; www.eddy-rentacar.com; Phitsanulok Airport; ☻ 5am-5pm) or **Thai Rent A Car** (☎ 055 301058, nationwide 1647; www.thairent-acar.com; Phitsanulok Airport; ☻7am-8.30pm), costs from around 900B per day.

TRANSPORT FROM PHITSANULOK
Buses & Minivans

In addition to these bus routes, there are also minivans to Bangkok (280B, 4½ hours, hourly from 6.30am to 6.30pm), Mae Sot (196B, four hours, four departures from 8am to 3pm) and Sukhothai Historical Park (50B, 1½ hours, frequent services from 5.20am to 6pm).

DESTINATION	FARE (B)	DURATION (HR)	FREQUENCY
Bangkok	288-382	5-6	hourly 8.45am-11pm
Chiang Khong	298	10	9am
Chiang Mai	220-337	6	frequent 6am-12.40pm
Chiang Rai	258-332	7-8	6 departures 5.30am-1pm
Kamphaeng Phet	80	2	9 departures 5am-6pm
Lampang	259	4	frequent 6am-12.40pm
Lom Sak (for Green Route)	100	1-2	hourly 5.50am-6.15pm
Mae Sai	291-374	7	5.30am, 8am & 1pm
Nakhon Thai (for Phu Hin Rong Kla National Park)	75	2	hourly 5am-6pm
Nan	193	6	7.30am, 11.30am, 2.30pm & 5.30pm
Phrae	122-157	4	9 departures 6am-5.30pm
Sukhothai	42	1	hourly 5.30am-6pm

Train

DESTINATION	FARE (B)	DURATION (HR)	FREQUENCY
Bangkok	69-1354	5-7	10 daily
Chiang Mai	65-1135	7-9	6 daily
Lampang	98-1022	5	5 daily

Phu Hin Rong Kla National Park

Phu Hin Rong Kla was formerly an important remote base for the CPT, the Communist Party of Thailand. Today it's a national park, and while there isn't a huge amount to see from the CPT era, the park's natural attractions – waterfalls, hiking trails and unusual rock formations – act as worthwhile compensation.

History

Between 1967 and 1982, the mountain that is known as Phu Hin Rong Kla served as the strategic headquarters for the Communist Party of Thailand (CPT) and its tactical arm, the People's Liberation Army of Thailand (PLAT). The remote, easily defended summit was perfect for an insurgent army. China's Yunnan Province is only 300km away and it was here that CPT cadres received their training in revolutionary tactics. (This was until the 1979 split between the Chinese and Vietnamese communists, when the CPT sided with Vietnam.)

For nearly 20 years the area around Phu Hin Rong Kla served as a battlefield for Thai troops and the communists. In 1972 the Thai government launched an unsuccessful major offensive against the PLAT. The CPT camp at Phu Hin Rong Kla became especially active after the Thai military killed hundreds of students in Bangkok during the October 1976 student-worker uprising. Many students subsequently fled here to join the CPT, setting up a hospital and a school of political and military tactics. By 1978 the PLAT ranks here had swelled to 4000. In 1980 and 1981 the Thai armed forces tried again and were able to recapture some parts of CPT territory. But the decisive blow to the CPT came in 1982, when the government declared an amnesty for all the students who had joined the communists after 1976. The departure of most of the students broke the spine of the movement, which had become dependent on their membership. A final military push in late 1982 resulted in the surrender of the PLAT, and Phu Hin Rong Kla was declared a national park in 1984.

◉ Sights

Phu Hin Rong Kla National Park (อุทยาน แห่งชาติภูหินร่องกล้า; ☑ 055 233527; www.dnp. go.th; adult/child 500/300B; ⊘ 8.30am-5pm) covers about 307 sq km of mountains and forest, much of it covered by rocks and wildflowers. The elevation at park headquarters is about 1000m, so the area is refreshingly cool even in the hot season. The main attractions aren't too far from the main road through the park and include the remains of a rustic meeting hall and the school of political and military tactics. The buildings in the park are made out of wood and bamboo and have no plumbing or electricity – a testament to how primitive the living conditions were.

There is a modest **museum** at the park headquarters that displays a few battered relics from the CPT days, although there's little English explanation. At the end of the road into the park is a small White Hmong village.

Within the park there are waterfalls, hiking trails and scenic views, as well as some interesting rock formations – jutting boulders called Lan Hin Pum and an area of deep rocky crevices where People's Liberation Army of Thailand (PLAT) troops would hide during air raids, called Lan Hin Taek. Ask at the visitor centre for maps.

Phu Hin Rong Kla can get quite crowded on weekends and holidays; for a more peaceful experience try to visit midweek.

Pha Chu Thong   HISTORIC SITE
(ผาชูธง, Flag Raising Cliff; Phu Hin Rong Kla National Park) An 800m trail leads to Pha Chu Thong (sometimes also called Red Flag Cliff), where the Communist Party of Thailand would raise the red flag to announce a military victory. Also in this area is an air-raid shelter, a lookout and the remains of the main CPT headquarters – the most inaccessible point in the territory before a road was constructed by the Thai government.

⏨ Sleeping & Eating

Accommodation in Phu Hin Rong Kla National Park is limited to that run by **Thailand's Royal Forest Department** (☑ 02 562 0760; www.dnp.go.th; 3-person tent 225B, bungalows 800-3000B), and must be booked online or via phone. Golden House Tour (p267), near the TAT office in Phitsanulok, can help book accommodation at the park. There's a sole restaurant and coffee shop near the park visitor centre.

❶ Getting There & Away

Phu Hin Rong Kla National Park's headquarters is about 125km from Phitsanulok. To get here, first take an early bus to Nakhon Thai (75B, two hours, hourly from 5am to 6pm). From there, near the market, you can charter a *sŏrng·tăa·ou* (passenger pick-up truck) to the park (700B). For a day trip from Phitsanulok, Golden House Tour (p267) charges 1800B for a car and driver; petrol is extra. It's a delightful trip if you're on a motorcycle as there's not much traffic along the way, but a strong engine is necessary to conquer the hills to Phu Hin Rong Kla.

KAMPHAENG PHET

☑ 055 / POP 29,000

Kamphaeng Phet (กำแพงเพชร), located halfway between Bangkok and Chiang Mai, is one of Thailand's more pleasant provincial capitals. It doesn't see many tourists, despite being one of Thailand's most historic towns.

The city's name translates as 'Diamond Wall', a reference to the apparent strength of this formerly walled city's protective barrier. This level of security was necessary, as the city helped to protect the Sukhothai and, later, Ayuthaya kingdoms against attacks from Myanmar or Lanna. Parts of the wall can still be seen today, as can the impressive ruins of several religious structures. The modern city still has many traditional wooden houses and stretches along a shallow section of the Mae Nam Ping.

⊙ Sights

A Unesco World Heritage Site, the **Kamphaeng Phet Historical Park** (อุทยาน ประวัติศาสตร์กำแพงเพชร; 100B, with walled city 150B; ⊙6am-6pm) features the ruins of structures dating back to the 14th century, roughly the same time as the better-known kingdom of Sukhothai. Kamphaeng Phet's Buddhist monuments continued to be built up until the Ayuthaya period, nearly 200 years later, and thus possess elements of both Sukhothai and Ayuthaya styles, resulting in a school of Buddhist art quite unlike anywhere else in Thailand.

The park consists of two distinct sections.

⊙ Walled City

Just north of modern Kamphaeng Phet, a **walled zone** (100B, with Kamphaeng Phet Historical Park 150B; ⊙6am-6pm) is the origin of the city's name, and was formerly inhabited by *gamavasi* (living in the community) monks. It's a long walk or an approximately 40B motorcycle taxi ride from the centre of town.

Wat Phra Kaew HISTORIC SITE
(วัดพระแก้ว; Kamphaeng Phet Historical Park; 100B; ⊙6am-6pm) This former temple dominates Kamphaeng Phet's walled city and is adjacent to what is believed to have been the royal palace (now in ruins). There's an immense reclining Buddha and several smaller, weather-corroded Buddha statues that have assumed slender, porous forms, reminding some visitors of the sculptures of Alberto Giacometti.

Wat Phra That HISTORIC SITE
(วัดพระธาตุ; Kamphaeng Phet Historical Park; 100B; ⊙6am-6pm) The ruins of this temple are distinguished by a large round-based brick and laterite Kamphaeng Phet–style *chedi* surrounded by columns.

⊙ Outside Town

The majority of Kamphaeng Phet's ruins are found in the expansive zone located about 1.5km north of the city walls. The area was previously home to *aranyavasi* (living in forests) monks and (in addition to Wat Phra Si Iriyabot and Wat Chang Rob) contains more than 40 other former compounds, including an additional six currently being excavated, although most are not much more than flat-brick foundations with the occasional weather-worn Buddha image. There is an excellent visitor centre (p273) at the entrance where bicycle hire (30B to 50B per day) can be arranged. A motorcycle taxi from central Kamphaeng Phet to the entrance costs about 80B.

Wat Phra Si Iriyabot HISTORIC SITE
(วัดพระสี่อิริยาบถ; Kamphaeng Phet Historical Park; 100B; ⊙6am-6pm) The highlight here is a towering *mon·dòp* (the small square building with a spire in a *wát*) that contains the shattered remains of standing, sitting, walking and reclining Buddha images, all sculpted in the classic Sukhothai style.

Wat Chang Rob HISTORIC SITE
(วัดช้างรอบ; Kamphaeng Phet Historical Park; 100B; ⊙6am-6pm) Meaning 'Elephant-Encircled Temple', this ruin is just that – a temple buttressed with 68 stucco-covered elephants.

⊙ Other Sights

Kamphaeng Phet National Museum MUSEUM
(พิพิธภัณฑสถานแห่งชาติกำแพงเพชร; Th Pindamri; 100B; ⊙9am-4pm Wed-Sun) Kamphaeng Phet's

Kamphaeng Phet

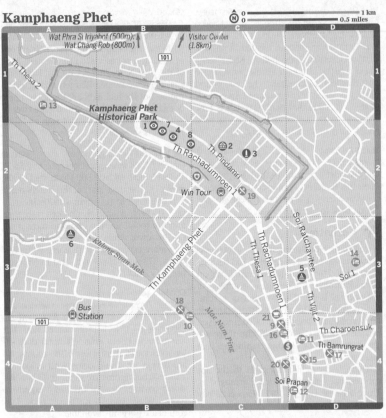

Kamphaeng Phet

visit-worthy museum is home to an impressive collection of artefacts from the Kamphaeng Phet area, including an immense Shiva statue that is the largest bronze Hindu sculpture in the country.

The image was formerly located at the nearby Shiva Shrine (ศาลพระอิศวร; off Th Pindamri) **FREE** until a German missionary stole the idol's hands and head in 1886 (they were later returned).

Wat Phra Borommathat
BUDDHIST TEMPLE

(วัดพระบรมธาตุ; off Rte 1078; ⊙ daylight hours) Across the Mae Nam Ping are the ruins of Wat Phra Borommathat, located in an area that was settled long before Kamphaeng Phet's heyday, although visible remains are post-classical Sukhothai. The compound has a few small *chedi* and one larger *chedi* of the late Sukhothai period, which is now crowned with a Burmese-style umbrella added early in the 20th century.

Wat Khu Yang
BUDDHIST TEMPLE

(วัดคูยาง; Soi 1, Soi Ratchavithee; ⊙ daylight hours) Located just north of central Kamphaeng Phet, this Buddhist temple contains a handsome wooden *hŏr đrai* (manuscript library) dating back to the 19th century.

🏃 Activities

Phra Ruang Hot Springs
HOT SPRINGS

(บ่อน้ำพุร้อนพระร่วง; Ban Lan Hin; 30B; ⊙ 8am-6pm) Along the road to Sukhothai, 20km from Kamphaeng Phet, this complex of hot springs is the Thai version of a rural health retreat. The reputedly therapeutic hot waters have been channelled into seven private bathing rooms (50B) and there are also several places offering traditional Thai massage.

There is no public transport to the hot springs, but transport can be arranged at Three J Guest House (p272). Expect to pay 600B for the return trip.

🛏 Sleeping

Three J Guest House
GUESTHOUSE $

(☏ 055 713129, 081 887 4189; www.threejguesthouse.com; 79 Soi 1, Soi Ratchavitee; r 300-900B; ❋ 🛜) The cheapest rooms at this long-standing guesthouse are fan-cooled and share a clean bathroom, while the more expensive ones have air-con. All are set around a plant-and-rock-filled garden. Bicycles (50B per day) and motorcycles (200B per day) are available for hire. The helpful owner also offers a homestay on his lakeside farm 34km west of Kamphaeng Phet.

Kor Chokchai Hotel
HOTEL $

(☏ 055 711247; 19-43 Soi 8, Th Rachadaumnoen 1; r 280-360B; ❋ 🛜) At this old-school Thai hotel – the air-con units are museum pieces – the rooms are dated, with tired wooden furniture and spongy foam mattresses. But they're clean, the location is ideal and the price is right. The cheapest rooms are fan-cooled. There's no Roman-script sign.

Grand View Resort
HOTEL $

(☏ 055 798104; 34/4 Mu 2, Nakhon Chum; incl breakfast r & bungalows 290-890B; ❋ 🛜) Also known as the Grand River Resort, this is one of a handful of 'resorts' on the western bank of the Mae Nam Ping set up for Thai tourists. There's a range of largely characterless rooms, but the highlight are the six compact bungalows that float on rafts on the river itself. There's no Roman-script sign and little English is spoken.

★ Navarat Heritage Hotel
HOTEL $$

(☏ 055 711219; www.navaratheritage.com; 2 Soi 21, Th Tesa 1; incl breakfast r 900-1400B; ste 13,000B; ❋ 🛜) The 'heritage' part of this hotel's name is a reference to its original 1970s incarnation. It's been extensively updated since then and the rooms are the best and most modern in town, while the service is efficient. The more expensive rooms come with river views. There's a small gym and free bicycle use for guests.

Chakungrao Riverview
HOTEL $$

(☏ 055 714900; www.chakungraoriverview.com; 149 Th Thesa 1; incl breakfast r 850-1100B, ste 3500B; ❋ 🛜) It feels rather dated now, but Kamphaeng Phet's grandest hotel does offer river views from most of its rooms. All are decent sized and come with balconies, although bathrooms are small and plain. It's worth paying extra for the more expensive rooms, which come with better beds. Discounts are normally available.

Scenic Riverside Resort
HOTEL $$$

(☏ 055 722009; www.scenicriversideresort.com; 325/16 Th Thesa 2; bungalows incl breakfast 1500-3700B; ❋ 🛜 ⚊) Picture a Greek fishing village in which the buildings' interior design has been overseen by a pre-teen Thai girl and you'll start to get an idea of this wacky but fun resort. The seven dome-shaped, white-washed, stone-floored villas are decked out with stuffed dolls and other kitsch, but are spacious and share a small pool and a pleasant riverside location.

🍴 Eating & Drinking

For cheap Thai eats, there's a big and busy night market (Th Thesa 1; mains 30-60B; ⊙ 4-10pm) close to the river. There's also a smaller night market (Th Rachadumnoen 1; mains 30-60B; ⊙ 4-9pm) by the town's football field.

★ Bamee Chakangrao
THAI $

(cnr Soi 9 & Th Rachadumnoen 1; mains 30-90B; ⊙ 9am-3pm) Thin wheat-and-egg noodles *(bà·mèe)* are a speciality of Kamphaeng Phet, and this famous and friendly restaurant is one of the best places to try them. The noodles are made fresh every day behind the restaurant, and pork satay is also available. There's no Roman-script sign; look for the green banners on the corner.

Burger Co   MULTICUISINE $$
(141 Th Thesa 1; mains 70-299B; ◎11am-10pm; 🛜) The burgers are good at this Thai–South African venture, but so are the steaks, pasta and many of the Thai dishes, all served in a neat and clean environment. It's popular with both locals and visitors.

Kitti   MULTICUISINE $$
(cnr Th Vijit 2 & Th Bamrungrat; mains 50-380B; ◎10am-2pm & 4-9pm) Kitti excels at Chinese-style dining, much of it seafood-oriented (fish is priced by weight). Try the unusual but delicious fried chicken with cashew nuts, which comes with pork crackling and pickled veggies. There's no Roman-script sign.

Mae Ping Riverside   THAI $$
(50/1 Mu 2, Nakhon Chum; mains 80-350B; ◎5-10pm) Decent eats – fish is a speciality – draught beer and live music can be found here on the western bank of the Mae Nam Ping. There are a few other similar riverside places along this strip. Some English is spoken; there's no Roman-script sign.

Elizabeth Coffee   CAFE
(cnr Th Thesa 1 & Soi 9; ◎10.30am-9pm; 🛜) This cool and bright cafe with an outdoor terrace makes for a good retreat from the heat. There's coffee, tea, smoothies and juices, as well as rice and noodle dishes and a few Western offerings.

ℹ️ Information

Most of the major banks, such as **Bangkok Bank** (Th Charoensuk; ◎8.30am-4.30pm Mon-Sat), have branches with ATMs along the main streets near the river and on Th Charoensuk.

Police Station (📞24hr emergency 191; Rte 101; ◎24hr) Kamphaeng Phet's main police station.

Visitor Centre (Kamphaeng Phet Historical Park; 100B; ◎8am-4pm) This excellent visitor centre is at the entrance to the Kamphaeng Phet Historical Park. Bicycle hire (30B to 50B per day) can be arranged here.

ℹ️ Getting There & Away

Kamphaeng Phet's **bus station** (📞055 799103; Rte 101) is about 1km west of the Mae Nam Ping. Motorcycles (50B) and *sŏrng·tăa·ou* (passenger pick-up trucks; 20B, frequent between 7.30am and 3pm) run between the station and town. If coming from Sukhothai or Phitsanulok, get off in the old city or at the roundabout on Th Thesa 1 to save yourself the trouble of having to get a *sŏrng·tăa·ou* back into town.

Alternatively, if you're bound for Bangkok (281B to 395B, five hours, frequent between 9.30am and 11pm) you can circumvent the bus station altogether by buying tickets and boarding a bus at **Win Tour** (📞055 713971; Th Kamphaeng Phet; ◎8am-11pm), near the roundabout in Kamphaeng Phet.

ℹ️ Getting Around

There are very few motorcycle taxis or túk-túks in Kamphaeng Phet. As such, it's wise to consider hiring a bicycle or motorbike – Three J Guest House (p272) has both (per day bicycle/motorcycle 50/200B).

NORTHERN THAILAND KAMPHAENG PHET

BUSES FROM KAMPHAENG PHET

In addition to these bus services, there are minivans to Mae Sot (140B, three hours, hourly from 9am to 4pm) and Sukhothai (65B, one hour, 9am to 4pm) and *sŏrng·tăa·ou* (passenger pickup trucks) to Sukhothai (65B, two hours, three departures from 8am to noon).

DESTINATION	FARE (B)	DURATION (HR)	FREQUENCY
Bangkok	281-395	5	frequent 9.30am-11pm
Chiang Mai	216	5	hourly 9am-11pm
Chiang Rai	371-433	7	12.30pm & 6pm
Lampang	205-239	4	1.30pm & 5.30pm
Mae Hong Son	851	11	10pm
Mae Sot	162	3	3am & 4am
Phayao	212-326	6	12.30pm & 6pm
Phitsanulok	80	2½	hourly 7am-6pm
Sukhothai	74	1	hourly 7am-4pm

TAK PROVINCE

Tak (จังหวัดตาก) is a vast, mountainous province whose proximity to Myanmar has resulted in a complex history and unique cultural mix.

Perhaps due its relative isolation, much of Tak still remains quite wild. The linked Um Phang Wildlife Sanctuary, Thung Yai Naresuan National Park, Huay Kha Kaeng Wildlife Sanctuary and Khlong Lan and Mae Wong National Parks together form one of Thailand's largest wildlife corridors and one of the biggest intact natural forests in Southeast Asia.

But with the Mae Sot–Myawaddy border now the busiest land crossing between Thailand and Myanmar, and Mae Sot itself designated as a special economic zone, Tak is less isolated than it was and the increase in international trade is sure to lead to more visitors.

Mae Sot

📞 055 / POP 40,750

Mae Sot (แม่สอด) is among the most culturally diverse cities in Thailand, mainly because of its relatively remote location on the Thai–Myanmar border, and the multicultural vibe ensures that many visitors stay longer than they'd anticipated. Walk the town's streets and you'll encounter a fascinating ethnic mix of men from Myanmar in their *longyi* (sarongs), Hmong and Karen women in traditional hill-tribe dress, bearded Muslims, Thai army rangers and foreign NGO workers. Burmese and Karen are spoken as much as Thai, shop signs along the streets are in Thai, Burmese and Chinese, and much of the temple architecture is from Myanmar.

Mae Sot has also become the most important jade and gem centre along the Thai–Myanmar border, with much of the trade controlled by Chinese and Muslim immigrants from Myanmar, while the nearby border crossing with Myawaddy in Myanmar is now the busiest land crossing between the two countries.

⦿ Sights & Activities

Border Market   MARKET
(ตลาดริมน้ำเมย; Rte 12/AH1; ☺7am-7pm) Alongside Mae Nam Moei on the Thai side of the border is an expansive market that sells a mixture of workaday goods from Myanmar, black-market clothes, cheap Chinese electronics and food, among other things. It's

located 5km west of Mae Sot; catch one of the *sŏrng·tăa·ou* (20B, frequent from 6am to 6pm) bound for the border from a spot on Th Chid Lom.

Highland Farm Gibbon
Sanctuary   VOLUNTEERING
(☑081 727 1364; www.gibbonathighlandfarm.org) This sanctuary gives a permanent home to orphaned, abandoned and mistreated gibbons; volunteers are asked for a one-month commitment and to help with daily farm chores. The sanctuary is also home to macaque monkeys. Get in contact in advance to arrange a volunteer stint.

Yoga For Life   YOGA
(☑083 092 2772; Irawadee Resort, 758/1 Th Intharakhiri; class 250B; ☺1hr classes 9.30am, 5pm & 6.15pm Mon-Sat) Daily yoga instruction, held at Irawadee Resort (p276). Courses are also available.

Herbal Sauna   BATHHOUSE
(Wat Mani, Th Intharakhiri; 20B; ☺noon-6pm) Wat Mani has separate herbal sauna facilities for men and women. The sauna is towards the back of the monastery grounds, past the monks' *gù·dì* (living quarters).

🍽 Courses

★ Cookery Course   COOKING
(☑055 546584; www.borderlinecollective.org; Borderline Shop, 674/14 Th Intharakhiri; 1000B; ☺9am-noon & 3-6pm Tue-Sun) The courses here include instruction in four vegetarian Shan, Burmese or Karen dishes, a trip to the market, a cookbook and the chance to share the results in the adjoining cafe. Course costs decrease with bigger groups. They're held at Borderline Shop (p277).

🛏 Sleeping

Many places in Mae Sot are in the budget range and cater to NGO workers and foreign volunteers who stay for months at a time.

Phan Nu House   GUESTHOUSE $
(☑081 886 2950; phannuhouse@gmail.com; 563/3 Th Intharakhiri; r 250-500B; ❄🛜) Phan Nu is a decent budget option, with 20 rooms spread over two buildings set back from the road. The more expensive rooms share communal balconies, the cheapest are fan-cooled. Rooms are sizeable and clean and come with OK beds, desks and fridges. It's a popular choice with foreign volunteer workers.

Around Tak & Mae Sot

⊛ Ban Thai Guest House HOTEL $$

(☏ 055 531590; banthai_mth@hotmail.com; 740 Th Intharakhiri; r 350-1200B; ❄ ✿) Ban Thai is a secluded and peaceful compound of seven converted Thai houses that feature spacious, stylish, suite-like rooms with big bathrooms, Thai-style furniture and textiles. There are also a couple of cheap fan-cooled rooms in the main structure. It's a popular choice with NGO workers and repeat visitors, so book ahead.

Picturebook Guesthouse HOTEL $$

(☏ 090 459 6990; www.picturebookthailand.org; 125/4-6 Soi 19, Th Intharakhiri; r incl breakfast 600-800B; ❄ ✿) Located in an attractive garden, the 10 compact rooms here come with smooth concrete walls, artsy details and custom wood furniture. Staff are friendly and keen to help, and are part of a not-for-profit training programme. You'll find the guesthouse tucked away in unmarked Soi 19,

directly behind the J2 hotel, about 1km east of Mae Sot's centre.

Baan Rabiangmai HOTEL $$

(☏ 055 532144; baanrabiangmaimaesot@gmail.com; 3/21 Th Don Kaew; r incl breakfast 800-1500B; ❄ ✿) Baan Rabiangmai is the sort of comfortable, efficient, no-fuss hotel every town should have. Its 19 modern rooms come equipped with a kitchenette, a sitting area and a small balcony. Bicycles can be rented for 30B per day.

J2 HOTEL $$

(☏ 055 536161; www.facebook.com/j2maesot; 149/8 Th Intharakhiri; incl breakfast r 890-1200, ste 2000-2200B; ❄ @ ✿) The well set-up J2 has efficient staff and 47 spacious and up-to-date, if not very stylish, rooms, some with balconies. Beds are comfortable and bathrooms are decent-sized. It's located about 1km east of the centre of Mae Sot.

Mae Sot

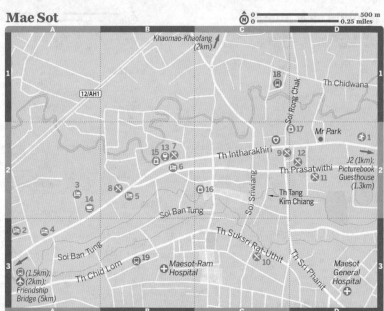

Mae Sot

Irawadee Resort   HOTEL **$$**

(📱055 535430; www.irawadee.com; 758/1 Th Intharakhiri; incl breakfast r/ste 1200/2100B; ❄️🛜) The Irawadee has gaudy, fun and comfortable modern rooms decked out in a vague Thai Lanna theme, with beds raised off the floor on platforms in the traditional Chinese-style. The rooms aren't huge but the bathrooms are spacious, with open-air showers.

🍴 Eating & Drinking

Mae Sot is a culinary crossroads with a buffet of cuisines not seen elsewhere in Thailand. For a fun breakfast head to the area south of the Nurulislam Mosque, where Muslim restaurants serve sweet tea, roti and *nanbya* (tandoor-style bread). Try Burmese dishes such as *mohinga* (Myanmar's unofficial national dish) or Burmese-style curries at the vibrant municipal market (p277). The **night market** (Th Prasatwithi; mains 30-60B;

⊘ 6-11pm) features mostly Thai-Chinese-style dishes.

Borderline Teashop
BURMESE $

(www.borderlinecollective.org; Borderline Shop, 674/14 Th Intharakhiri; mains 20-70B; ⊘7.30am-9pm Tue-Sun; 🛜🍴) This cosy cafe is set in a pleasant shaded garden and offers a small but tasty Burmese-inspired menu of vegetarian dishes, including salads, noodle dishes and sweets. If you like your meal, consider enrolling in the cookery course (p274) here.

Lucky Garden Tea Shop
BURMESE $

(Th Suksri Rat-Uthit; mains 20-85B; ⊘5am-8pm) Come here for the authentic Burmese teashop experience if you're not crossing the border to Myanmar. Biryanis, Burmese curries and salads and lots of sweet tea are the order of the day.

Phat Thai Mae Sot
THAI $

(Th Prasatwithi; mains 40-60B; ⊘noon-9pm) This cosy place serves *pàt tai* with a local twist: toppings of pork rind and barbecued pork. There's no English-language sign; look for the rustic, semi-open-air wood building with a metal roof supported by a tree.

Casa Mia
MULTICUISINE $

(Th Intharakhiri; mains 35-250B; ⊘7.30am-9.30pm; 🍴) This rustic restaurant has a huge range of homemade Italian pasta dishes, including veggie options, all very reasonably priced. It also offers pizza, Western breakfasts, Thai and Burmese selections and some decent desserts as well.

★ Khaomao-Khaofang
THAI $$

(www.khaomaokhaofang.com; 382 Rte 105; mains 100-790B; ⊘11am-3pm & 5-10pm; 🍴) Like dining in a gentrified jungle, Khaomao-Khaofang replaces chandeliers with hanging vines, and interior design with orchids and waterfalls. It's the most atmospheric place to eat in town and the northern Thai food is fine: try one of the several delicious *yam* (Thai-style spicy salads). The fish dishes are also recommended. The restaurant is about 2km north of Mae Sot's centre.

Bai Fern
MULTICUISINE $$

(660 Th Intharakhiri; mains 59-490B; ⊘8am-10pm; 🛜🍴) Unpretentious and friendly, Bai Fern is also surprisingly good. The Western food – breakfasts, steaks, pasta and pizza – is especially reliable, but this is also a fine place to sample Burmese cuisine (tell the staff if this is what you want to eat and they'll make some suggestions that aren't on the menu),

while there are plenty of Thai and vegetarian options, too.

Krua Canadian
INTERNATIONAL $$

(www.facebook.com/KruaCanadianRestaurant; 3 Th Sri Phanit; dishes 70-550B; ⊘8am-2pm & 5-9pm; 🛜🍴) Dave, the eponymous Canadian owner and long-term Mae Sot resident, dishes up some of the finest *fa·ràng* (foreigner) food in town: the Mexican entries on the varied menu are especially popular. Servings are large. Dave is also a reliable source of local information and the restaurant is something of a hang-out for the local expat and NGO crowd.

Border Booze
BAR

(Th Intharakhiri; ⊘6pm-midnight Mon-Sat; 🛜) This amenable bar is probably the most foreigner-friendly place to drink in Mae Sot, with beers, shots, cocktails, a mellow music selection and a laid-back vibe. Food is served from the next-door restaurant.

Braverly
CAFE

(www.braverly.com; 738 Th Intharakhiri; ⊘8.30am-5pm Tue-Thu, to 8pm Fri & Sat; 🛜) Stylish for Mae Sot, Braverly is light and bright and serves bagels, paninis, salads and local coffee. There are sofas and swing seats to perch on. The cafe is the outlet of an organisation that trains ethnic minority women from the area around the Thai–Myanmar border in hospitality.

🛍 Shopping

Mae Sot is the most important jade and gem centre along the Thai–Myanmar border. Check out the hustle and bustle among the glittering treasures in the gem shops along Th Prasatwithi, just east of the morning market. If you are buying, exercise caution unless you know your precious stones.

★ Municipal Market
MARKET

(off Th Prasatwithi; ⊘6am-6pm) Mae Sot's municipal market is among the largest and most vibrant we've encountered anywhere in Thailand. There's heaps of exotic stuff from Myanmar, including books, sticks of *thanaka* (the source of the yellow powder that you'll see on many Burmese faces: it's a natural sunscreen), bags of pickled tea leaves and velvet thong flip-flops (known as 'slippers' in Myanmar) from Mandalay.

Borderline Shop
ARTS & CRAFTS

(www.borderlinecollective.org; 674/14 Th Intharakhiri; ⊘9am-7pm Tue-Sun) This long-running shop sells arts and crafts made by refugee and ethnic-minority women; the profits go back into a women's collective and a child-assistance foundation. The upstairs art gallery hosts local painters, and the house is also home to a tea garden (p277) and cookery course (p274).

Walking Street   MARKET
(Soi Rong Chak; ⊙5-9pm Sat) Every Saturday evening the small street by the police station is closed to traffic, and in its place are vendors selling handicrafts, clothes and food.

ℹ Information

Several centrally located banks have ATMs and exchange facilities. You can also find moneychangers in the municipal market.

Immigration (☑055 563000; Rte 12/AH1; ⊙8.30am-4.30pm) Located next to the Friendship Bridge, this office can process visa extensions.

Maesot General Hospital (☑055 531229; 175/16 Th Sri Phanit; ⊙24hr) Mae Sot's main hospital.

Police Station (☑emergency 191; Th Intharakhiri; ⊙24hr) Mae Sot's main police station.

Tourist Police (☑emergency 1155; Rte 12/AH1; ⊙24hr) Tourist-police post located near the Friendship Bridge.

ℹ Getting There & Away

Tiny **Mae Sot Airport** (☑055 563620; Rte 12/AH1) is about 2km west of town. At the time of research, **Nok Air** (☑055 563883, nationwide 1318; www.nokair.co.th; Mae Sot Airport, Rte 12/AH1; ⊙9am-5.30pm), with five daily flights to/from Bangkok's Don Mueang International Airport (from 2029B, 75 minutes), was the only airline operating out of Mae Sot.

Almost all long-distance *sŏrng·tăa·ou* (passenger pick-up trucks), minivans and buses leave from Mae Sot's **bus station** (☑055 563435; Rte 12/AH1), located next to the airport. A motorcycle taxi to/from here should cost about 60B.

ℹ Getting Around

Most of central Mae Sot can be navigated on foot. Motorcycle taxis and *săhm·lór* (three-wheeled pedicabs) charge 40B for trips within the centre of town. **Taxi Mae Sot** (☑055 030357, 098 101 9345; www.facebook.com/taximaesot) runs taxis between the airport and town for 100B.

TRANSPORT FROM MAE SOT
Bus

DESINATION	FARE (B)	DURATION (HR)	FREQUENCY
Bangkok	290-616	7-8	12 departures 8am-9.45pm
Chiang Mai	315-490	5-6	6.15am & 10am
Chiang Rai	407	9	7am
Lampang	243-378	4	6.15am, 7am & 10am
Mae Sai	700	12	7am
Phitsanulok	196	4	6 departures 7am-2.40pm
Sukhothai	153	3	6 departures 7am-2.40pm

Minivan & Sŏrng·tăa·ou

Minivans to Kamphaeng Phet (off Th Chidwana) leave from a small market in the centre of Mae Sot. *Sŏrng·tăa·ou* to Mae Sariang also stop here after starting their journey from the bus station.

DESTINATION	FARE (B)	DURATION (HR)	FREQUENCY
Kamphaeng Phet	140	3	hourly minivans 8am-4pm
Mae Sariang	200	6	hourly *sŏrng·tăa·ou* 5.45am-noon
Um Phang	140	4	hourly *sŏrng·tăa·ou* 6am-1pm

MAE SOT TO MAE SARIANG

Route 105 runs north along the Myanmar border from Mae Sot all the way to Mae Sariang (226km) in Mae Hong Son Province. The winding, paved road passes through the small communities of Mae Ramat, Mae Salit, Ban Tha Song Yang and Ban Sop Ngao (Mae Ngao). The thick forest in these parts still has a few stands of teak, and the Karen villages continue to use the occasional work elephant.

Nam Tok Mae Kasa, between the Km 13 and Km 14 markers, is an attractive waterfall fronting a cave. There's also a hot spring in the nearby village of Mae Kasa.

In Mae Ramat, don't miss Wat Don Kaew, behind the district office, which houses a large Mandalay-style marble Buddha.

At Km 58, after a series of roadblocks, you'll pass Mae La, home to the largest camp for refugees from Myanmar in Thailand. An estimated 50,000 refugees – most ethnic Karen – live here.

There are extensive limestone caverns at Tham Mae Usu, at Km 94 near Ban Tha Song Yang (not to be confused with the village of the same name further north). From the highway it's a 2km walk to Tham Mae Usu; note that it's closed in the rainy season, when the river running through the cave seals off the mouth.

At the northern end of Tak Province, you'll reach Ban Tha Song Yang, a Karen village attractively set at the edge of limestone cliffs by Mae Nam Moei. This is the last significant settlement in Tak before you begin climbing uphill and into the dense jungle and mountains of Mae Ngao National Park, in Mae Hong Son Province.

Ban Sop Ngao, little more than a roadside village that is home to the park headquarters, is the first town you'll come to in Mae Hong Son. From there it's another 40km to Mae Sariang, where there's ample food and accommodation.

Sŏrng·tăa·ou (passenger pick-up trucks) to Mae Sariang depart from Mae Sot's bus station (200B, six hours, hourly 5.45am to noon).

Sŏrng·tăa·ou to the Friendship Bridge (Th Chid Lom) run frequently between 6am and 6pm (20B, 15 minutes).

Thai Rent A Car (☑ 099 060 0500, nationwide 02 737 8888; www.thairentacar.com; Mae Sot Airport, Rte 12/AH1; ☺ 9.30am-6.30pm) has cars for hire at Mae Sot Airport, and motorbikes can be hired in town at places such as **Mr Park** (☑ 055 533900; 304-304/1 Th Intharakhiri; per 24hr 200-250B; ☺ 8am-5pm).

Um Phang

Sitting at the junction of Mae Nam Klong and Huay Um Phang, Um Phang (อุ้มผาง) is a remote village populated by a mix of Thais and Karen. Outside Um Phang are a number of Karen villages, some of which are quite traditional, and elephants can still be seen, especially in Palatha, a Karen village 25km south of Um Phang. *Yaeng* (elephant saddles) and other tack used for elephant wrangling can be seen on the verandas of the houses in this village.

But most visitors come to Um Phang to experience Nam Tok Thilawsu (p279), Thailand's largest waterfall, and the nature reserve that contains it, Um Phang Wildlife Sanctuary (p280), a popular destination for rafting and hiking.

⊙ Sights

★ **Nam Tok Thilawsu**   WATERFALL
(น้ำตกทีลอซู) Located in the Um Phang Wildlife Sanctuary (p280), this waterfall is Thailand's largest, measuring an estimated 200m high and up to 400m wide during the rainy season. Thais, particularly fanatical about such things, consider Nam Tok Thilawsu to be the most beautiful waterfall in the country. There's a shallow cave behind the falls and several levels of pools suitable for swimming.

The easy 2km path between the sanctuary headquarters and falls has been transformed into a self-guided nature tour. Surrounding the falls on both sides of the river are some of Thailand's thickest stands of natural forest, and the hiking in the vicinity of Nam Tok Thilawsu can be superb. The forest here is said to contain more than 1300 varieties of palm; giant bamboo and strangler figs are also commonplace.

The best time to visit is from November to February (after the rainy season) when the 200m to 400m limestone cliffs alongside

Mae Nam Klong are streaming with water and Nam Tok Thilawsu is at its wettest. In recent years, the access road to the sanctuary headquarters has been closed for part of the rainy season (June to September) to ease environmental damage. It's still possible to visit the waterfall at this time, but only by a three-hour raft trip, followed by a 30 minute 4WD trip to the sanctuary headquarters.

You can camp (30B) at the sanctuary headquarters, although you'll have to bring your own tent, and it's best to book ahead from November to January. This is also the only time of year the sanctuary's basic restaurant is guaranteed to be open.

The vast majority of people visit the falls as part of an organised tour. A one-day tour from Um Phang starts at 2500B per person (minimum two people). It is possible to go independently, but no private transport is allowed into the sanctuary. If you've got your own wheels, take the turn-off to Rte 1167 just north of Um Phang. After 12km, turn left at the police checkpoint onto Rte 1288. Continue 6km until you reach the sanctuary checkpoint, where you pay the entry fee (200B). At this point you must park your vehicle and hire a *sŏrng·tăa·ou* (2000B) to take you the 25km to the sanctuary headquarters. Alternatively, you can take a Poeng Kloengbound *sŏrng·tăa·ou* to the sanctuary checkpoint (30B, hourly from 6.30am to 3.30pm).

Um Phang
Wildlife Sanctuary   WILDLIFE RESERVE
(เขตรักษาพันธุ์สัตว์ป่าอุ้มผาง; ☑ 055 577318, 088 427 5272; 200B; ☺8am-4.30pm) The Nam Tok Thilawsu falls (p279) are near the headquarters of the Um Phang Wildlife Sanctuary, which is about 50km from Um Phang, towards Sangkhlaburi in Kanchanaburi Province. The wildlife sanctuary links with the Thung Yai Naresuan National Park and Huay Kha Kaeng Wildlife Sanctuary (another Unesco World Heritage site), as well as Khlong Lan and Mae Wong National Parks to form one of Thailand's largest wildlife corridors and one of the largest intact natural forests in Southeast Asia.

Tham Ta Khu Bi   CAVE
(ถ้ำตะโก๊ะบิ) From Ban Mae Klong Mai, just a few kilometres north of Um Phang via the highway to Mae Sot, Rte 1167 heads southwest along the Thai–Myanmar border. Along the way is the cave system of Tham Ta Khu Bi, which in Karen allegedly means 'Flat Mango'. There are no guides here, so be sure to bring your own torch (flashlight).

🏃 Activities

Most guesthouses and all tour companies in Um Phang can arrange combination trekking and rafting trips in the area. Um Phang, though, is dominated by Thai tourists, so not

---

ℹ GETTING TO MYANMAR: MAE SOT TO MYAWADDY

The 420m Friendship Bridge links Mae Sot and Myawaddy, in Myanmar's Kayin State. Note that Myanmar time is 30 minutes behind Thailand time.

Getting to the border *Sŏrng·tăa·ou* make frequent trips between Mae Sot and the Friendship Bridge from 6am to 6pm (20B), leaving from close to Mae Sot's municipal market.

At the border Immigration procedures are taken care of at the Thai immigration booth (☑ 055 563004; Rte 12/AH1; ☺5.30am-8.30pm) at the Friendship Bridge. There is a separate line for foreigners, so don't queue up with the locals. Cross to the Myanmar immigration booth (☑ 95 0585 0100; Bayint Naung Rd; ☺5am-8pm Myanmar time), where, if you have a Myanmar visa, you'll be allowed to stay or proceed to other destinations. You can enter and exit Myanmar here with an e-visa. If you don't have a visa, you must pay a fee of 500B for a temporary ID card at the Myanmar immigration booth, which allows you to stay in Myawaddy until 8pm the same day; your passport will be kept at the border.

Moving on ATMs, banks and moneychangers can be found just south of the bridge on the Myanmar side. Shared white vans and taxis bound for Mawlamyine (K10,000, four to five hours, frequent from 6am to 4pm) and Hpa-an (K10,000, six hours, 6am to 4pm) wait 100m south of the bridge. Buses to Yangon (K12,000, 10 to 12 hours, 9am and 5pm) depart from an office on the main road about 250m south of the bridge.

Um Phang

Boonchuay Tour (1.2km); Baan Farang (3km)

Um Phang

Activities, Courses & Tours
1 Napha Tour B1
Trekker Hill ....(see 5)

Sleeping
2 Garden Huts...A2
3 K & K Guest House.............................B2
4 Se Heng Chai Resort.....................A2
5 Trekker Hill...B1
6 Tu Ka Su Cottage A2
7 Umphangburi Resort.......................A2

Eating
8 Evening Market......................................B2
9 Udom & Joy Restaurant...................B2

Drinking & Nightlife
Ban Kru Sun ....(see 3)
10 Sawasdee Umphang.........................A2

Information
11 Hospital B1

Transport
12 Sŏrng·tăa·ou to Mae Sot.....................A1
13 Sŏrng·tăa·ou to Poeng Kloeng B1

many guides speak English or have experience in dealing with foreign visitors.

A typical three-day, two-night trip involves both rafting and hiking. The majority involve trips to Nam Tok Thilawsu and beyond, and longer or shorter trips may also be arranged.

Rafting trips range from one-day excursions along Mae Klong, from Um Phang to Nam Tok Thilawsu, to three-day trips from Palatha to Nam Tok Thi Lo Re, another impressive waterfall. The best time for rafting is between November and February.

Another area for rafting is Um Phang Khi, northeast of Um Phang. Officially there are 47 sets of rapids (some rafting companies claim 67) rated at Class III (moderate) and Class IV (difficult) during the height of the rainy season. The rafting season for Um Phang Khi is short – August to October only – as at other times of the year the water level isn't high enough.

Costs are all-inclusive and start at about 4000B per person (minimum two people) for a three-day rafting and trekking excursion.

Trekker Hill TREKKING, RAFTING
(☑ 055 561090, 081 280 0842; Soi 2, Th Pravatpriwan) This recommended, long-running outfit has the greatest number of English-speaking guides in Um Phang and offers a variety of treks running from one to three days.

Boonchuay Tour TREKKING, RAFTING
(☑ 055 561020, 081 379 2591; off Rte 1090) Mr Boonchuay speaks reasonable English and offers a variety of treks and rafting trips. His guides have experience in dealing with foreign trekkers. Call ahead.

Napha Tour RAFTING, TREKKING
(☑ 082 146 0681, 055 561287; napatour_2@yahoo.com; Soi 2, Th Pravatpriwan) Napha has an emphasis on rafting and offers a variety of trips and English-speaking guides.

Sleeping

Many places in Um Phang cater to large groups of Thai visitors. Um Phang can get busy during peak season, October to March, especially at weekends.

K & K Guest House GUESTHOUSE $
(☑ 087 846 1087; micky.s55@hotmail.co.th; Th Sukhumwattana; r 500B; ❄🛜) Right in the middle of the hustle and bustle of 'downtown' Um Phang is this modern shophouse with five spacious and clean rooms with decent beds. There are an additional three bungalows in the garden behind. Upper-floor rooms have little balconies and fine views. The friendly owner speaks some English.

Se Heng Chai Resort HOTEL $
(☑ 055 561605; Rte 1090; r 500B; ❄🛜) Just west of town, this 'resort' has 13 clean, modern rooms in a well-kept two-storey building. There's no English-language sign, but it's the tallest building on the hill.

NORTHERN THAILAND UM PHANG

BORDER VILLAGES

Rte 1288, which leads to the checkpoint for Um Phang Wildlife Sanctuary, continues for more than 70km, terminating in **Poeng Kloeng** (บ้านเปิงเคลิ่ง), a Karen, Burmese, Talaku and Thai trading village on the frontier with Myanmar .

Poeng Kloeng is a nondescript border village where the main occupations appear to be selling black-market cigarettes from Myanmar and the production of betel nut and durian, but the real reason to make the schlep here is to visit the neighbouring village of **Letongkhu** (เลตองคุ).

It's located 12km south of Poeng Kloeng along a rough uphill track, and, according to what little anthropological information is available, the villagers belong to the Lagu or Talaku sect, said to represent a form of Buddhism mixed with shamanism and animism. Each village has a spiritual leader called a *pu chaik* (whom the Thais call *reu·sĕe* – 'rishi' or 'sage') who wears his hair long – usually tied in a topknot – and dresses in white, yellow or brown robes, depending on the subsect.

If visiting Letongkhu, take care not to enter any village structures without permission or invitation. Likewise, do not take photographs without permission. Overnight stays are not generally permitted.

Five daily *sŏrng·tăa·ou* (passenger pick-up trucks) depart from Um Phang to Poeng Kloeng (100B, 2½ hours) between 6.30am and 3.30pm.

There's no regular transport to Letongkhu, but if you're not willing to walk from Poeng Kloeng or organise a guided visit to the village, a 4WD will do the return trip from Um Phang for about 5000B.

Trekker Hill
HOTEL **$**

(☏ 081 280 0842, 055 561090; Soi 2, Th Pravatpriwan; r 300B; 🛜) This place has six fan-cooled, mattress-on-the-floor huts on a steep hillside. It's rustic but you do get hot water and wi-fi in the communal area. The rafting and trekking trips here come recommended.

Umphangburi Resort
RESORT **$$**

(☏ 055 561576; www.umphangburiresort.com; off Rte 1090; r incl breakfast 700-1200B; ❄🛜) There are 19 well-maintained bungalows at this riverside resort; all are modern, bright and comfortable, and rafting trips can be arranged in high season (November to December). Some English is spoken.

Tu Ka Su Cottage
HOTEL **$$**

(☏ 055 561295; www.tukasu.com; off Rte 1090; r 600-1800B; ❄🛜) This is the most comfortable and best-run accommodation in Um Phang. The attractive collection of brick-and-stone cottages is surrounded by flowers and exotic fruit gardens. Rooms are a little plain for the price but come equipped with air-con, TV, fridge and bright bathrooms. It's popular, so book ahead.

Garden Huts
HOTEL **$$**

(☏ 087 073 7509, 055 561093; Rte 1090; r incl breakfast 350-900B; ❄🛜) Operated by a sweet elderly lady with limited English, this collection of decent-sized budget bungalows of varying degrees of comfort is set in a lovingly tended riverside garden. There are some pleasant sitting areas to lounge in. Most of the rooms are fan-cooled and beds are hard, the way the Thais like them.

🍴 Eating & Drinking

On Friday and Saturday evenings from November to February there's a small but good **evening market** (Soi 9, Th Pravatpriwan; mains 30-60B; ⊙ 3-9pm Fri & Sat Nov-Feb).

Udom & Joy Restaurant
THAI **$**

(Th Sukhumwattana; dishes 35-40B; ⊙ 6am-6pm) Simple rice and noodle dishes, including a decent *kà·nŏm jeen* (rice noodles topped with curry). The owners speak some English.

Ban Kru Sun
CAFE

(Th Sukhumwattana; ⊙ 8am-11pm; 🛜) Owned by a Thai musician, this place multitasks: during the day, it's a coffee and souvenir shop selling local products; at night, it serves rice and noodle dishes, as well as a few pasta options. There's a small, shady garden out back.

Sawasdee Umphang
BAR

(Rte 1090; ⊙ 6pm-midnight) Um Phang's only genuine bar is also a barber shop and a tattoo parlour. If you don't need a haircut or new ink, sit out front with a beer or cocktail and listen to the gentle live music.

ℹ️ Information

There are banks and a number of ATMs in Um Phang.

Hospital (off Th Ratpattana; ⏰24hr) Um Phang's hospital.

Police Station (☑emergency 191; Th Sukhumwattana; ⏰24hr) Um Phang's police station.

ℹ️ Getting There & Away

Sŏrng·tăa·ou to Mae So (Th Pravatpriwan) t depart from a stop at the northern end of Th Pravatpriwan (140B, four to five hours, hourly from 6.30am to 12.30pm).

Sŏrng·tăa·ou to Poeng Kloeng (Th Ratpattana) depart from a stop near the hospital (100B, 2½ hours, five daily between 6.30am and 3.30pm).

MAE HONG SON PROVINCE

Accessible only by steep, endlessly curving mountain roads, or via a flight to the provincial capital, Mae Hong Son (จังหวัด แม่ฮ่องสอน) is arguably Thailand's most remote province. It's thickly forested and mountainous, and, far from the influence of sea winds, the air is often misty, with ground fog in the winter and smoke from slash-and-burn agriculture during the hot season. Mae Hong Son's location along the border with Myanmar ensures that it is a crossroads for ethnic minorities (mostly Karen, with some Hmong, Lisu and Lahu), as well as Shan and Burmese immigrants.

These days, Mae Hong Son's natural splendours – waterfalls and caves especially – mean the province is firmly on the tourist trail. But the vast majority of visitors don't make it much further than Pai, leaving plenty of space for those who do venture into the less-visited areas.

Pai

📱 053 / POP 3000

First-time visitors to Pai (ปาย) might wonder if they've strayed into a northern version of a Thai island getaway, only without the beaches. Guesthouses appear to outnumber private residences in the 'downtown' area, a travel agency or restaurant is never more than a few steps away and the nights buzz with the sound of music and partying.

But Pai's popularity has yet to diminish its nearly picture-perfect setting in a mountain valley that offers natural adventures aplenty. And the town's temples and fun afternoon market are a reminder that Pai has not forgotten its transnational status as a town with roots in Myanmar's Shan State, or that it is a crossroads for the ethnic minorities who live in the nearby hills. There's heaps of quiet accommodation tucked away, lots of activities to keep visitors entertained and a relaxed vibe that prevents some people from ever leaving.

👁️ Sights

Most of Pai's sights are found outside the city centre, making hiring a motorcycle a necessity.

Wat Phra That Mae Yen　BUDDHIST TEMPLE
(วัดพระธาตุแม่เย็น; ⏰daylight hours) This temple sits atop a hill and has terrific views overlooking the valley. To get here, walk 1km east from the main intersection in town to get to the stairs that lead to the top (there are 353 steps). Or, if you've got your own wheels, take the 400m sealed road that follows a different route.

Pai Canyon　NATURE RESERVE
(กองแลนป่าย; Rte 1095; ⏰daylight hours) Pai Canyon is located 8km from Pai along the road to Chiang Mai. A paved stairway here culminates in an elevated lookout over high rock cliffs and the Pai valley. It is best climbed in the early morning when it's not too hot, or at sunset for the views.

Tha Pai Hot Springs　HOT SPRINGS
(บ่อน้ำร้อนท่าป่าย; adult/child 300/150B; ⏰7am-6pm) Across Mae Nam Pai and 7km southeast of town via a paved road is this well-kept local park. Through it flows a scenic stream, which mixes with the hot springs in places to make pleasant bathing areas. The water is also diverted to a couple of nearby spas.

Wat Nam Hoo　BUDDHIST TEMPLE
(วัดน้ำฮู; Ban Nam Hoo; ⏰daylight hours) **FREE**
Wat Nam Hoo is about 2km west of Pai and houses a sacred Buddha image said to have once emitted holy water from its head. The place is popular with visiting Thais and there's a small market on the grounds.

Ban Santichon　VILLAGE
(บ้านสันติชล) The cheesy photo ops in traditional Chinese clothing, piped-in music, tea tastings, pony rides, tacky recreation of the Great Wall of China and mountaintop viewpoint (จุดชมวิว บ้านสันติชล; Ban Santichon;

Mae Hong Son Province

0 ————— 50 km
0 ————— 25 miles

20B; ⏱4.30am-6pm) can make Ban Santichon seem like a Chinese-themed Disneyland. And the number of Chinese visitors often outnumbers the 1000 or so descendants of migrants from China's Yunnan Province who live here. But the Yunnanese food on offer is great. It's located about 4km west of Pai.

🏃 Activities

Rafting & Kayaking

Rafting along Mae Nam Pai during the wet season (approximately June to October) is a popular activity. Trips run from Pai to Mae Hong Son, which, depending on the amount of water, can traverse rapids from Class I to Class V. Rates are all-inclusive (rafting equipment, camping gear, dry bags, insurance and food) and run to around 1800B per person for a one-day trip and to around 3400B per person for two days.

Pai Adventures   RAFTING

(✆062 293 5978, 053 699326; www.paiadventures.com; 138 Th Chaisongkhram; ⏱10.30am-10pm) The one- or two-day white-water rafting trips (from June to October) offered by this recommended outfit can be combined with hiking and other activities. They video your descent down the rapids and will send the

results to you for free. There's also a jungle-survival course (available upon request).

Thai Adventure Rafting   RAFTING

(✆053 699111; www.thairafting.com; Th Chaisongkhram; ⏱10am-9pm) This experienced, French-run outfit leads one- and two-day rafting excursions. Rafters visit a waterfall, a fossil reef and hot springs en route, with one night spent at the company's permanent riverside camp. They also offer combined rafting/trekking trips.

Trekking

Guided treks start from 1000B per person per day in groups of two or more, and prices are all-inclusive. Most treks focus on the Lisu, Lahu and Karen villages in and around neighbouring Soppong (Pangmapha). Treks can be booked through most guesthouses or any travel agency.

Duang Trekking   TREKKING

(✆084 741 8648, 065 421 1418; lungteng1@gmail.com; Th Chaisongkhram; ⏱7am-9pm) A long-established local agency for trekking, white-water and bamboo rafting, kayaking and day tours. Treks start at 1000B per day per person (minimum group of two people), while kayaking and white-water rafting trips begin at 1800B per day per person (also with a minimum of two people).

Massage, Spas & Yoga

There are plenty of traditional Thai massage places charging from around 150B an hour. Reiki, crystal healing, acupuncture, reflexology and other non-indigenous methods of healing are also available, as is yoga; keep your eyes open for signs or refer to the monthly *Pai Events Planner*. In addition to these, a few local businesses, all of which are located approximately 1.5km northwest of Tha Pai Hot Springs (p283), have taken advantage of the area's thermal waters.

Bodhi Tree Yoga   YOGA

(✆084 251 8060; www.bodhitreeyogapai.com; off Th Raddamrong; class 250B; ⏱classes 9am & 5pm) Located in a fine old teak house on a quiet lane, Bodhi Tree offers 90-minute classes in Ashtanga, Bhakti, Hatha, Yin and Yang and more. The teachers here get good feedback.

Pai Traditional
Thai Massage   HEALTH & WELLBEING

(PTTM; ✆083 577 0498; 68/3 Soi 1, Th Wiang Tai; massage per 1/1½/2hr 200/300/400B, sauna per visit 100B, 3-day massage course 3500B; ⏱9am-9pm) This long-standing, locally owned outfit offers very good northern Thai massage, as well as a sauna (November to February only) where you can steam yourself in medicinal herbs. Three-day massage courses begin every Monday and Friday and run three hours per day.

Pai Hotsprings Spa Resort   SPA
(☑ 053 065748; www.paihotspringsresort.com; 84-84/1 Mu 2, Ban Mae Hi; thermal water soak 100B, 1hr massage 350B) A resort-style hotel that also offers massage (from 8am to 5pm) and thermal water soaks (from 7am to 7pm).

🥾 Courses

The curriculum of courses available in Pai ranges from circus arts and drumming to yoga in all its forms. Keep an eye on the flyers in every cafe, or check the *Pai Events Planner* (PEP) or the *Pai Explorer* (www.facebook.com/PaiExplorer) to see what's on when you're in town.

Xhale Yoga Pai   HEALTH & WELLBEING
(☑ 089 758 3635; www.xhaleyogapai.com; 5 days from 14,500B) Need some time out? Sign up for a five-night yoga retreat (Monday to Saturday) in the foothills outside Pai. Courses suit beginners to intermediates and include accommodation, standout meals, yoga and meditation classes, plus an excursion to a nearby hot spring. Instructor Bhud is all smiles, laughter and sunshine, and the vibe is welcoming and non-competitive.

Savoei (A Taste of Pai)   COOKING
(☑ 085 620 9918; Th Chaisongkhram; 700-750B; ⏱ 9.30am-1.30pm & 4-8pm) The half-day classes here involve a visit to the fresh market and instruction in four dishes.

Pai Cookery School   COOKING
(☑ 081 706 3799; www.facebook.com/paicookery school; Th Wanchalerm; 600-750B; ⏱ 11am-1.30pm & 2-6.30pm) With more than 20 years of experience, this outfit offers a variety of daily cooking courses covering three to five dishes. The afternoon course involves a trip to the market for ingredients. Contact them a day in advance. They may be moving in 2020; call or check the Facebook page.

Sitjemam Muay Thai   MARTIAL ARTS
(☑ 083 321 2230; www.sitjemammuaythai.com; Ban Mae Na Toeng; day/week 700/2000B; ⏱ lessons 8-10am & 4-6pm) Located about 5km north of Pai, this rustic *moo·ay tai* (muay thai) training camp has been around a while and will teach beginners.

🛏 Sleeping

Pai is reportedly home to more than 500 hotels, hostels, guesthouses and resorts, and new places continue to spring up. Despite the hotel glut, accommodation can be nearly impossible to come by during the height of the Thai tourist season (December and January). Book ahead.

🛏 In Town

Pai's popularity, particularly among domestic tourists, has resulted in a glut of midrange and upscale places. But there are still some cheap rooms close to the centre of town.

★ Common Grounds Pai   HOSTEL $
(☑ 062 034 8509; www.commongroundspai.com; off Th Chaisongkhram; dm/r 295/895B; ❄ 🛜) The best and most social hostel in Pai, Common Grounds offers well-maintained, comfy, six-bed dorms with lockers and their own bathrooms. The split-level private rooms come with decent beds, big windows and smooth cement walls. There's a large communal bar area and the hostel organises nightly events around Pai. It's located riverside, just off the main strip.

Pai Country Hut   HOTEL $
(☑ 087 779 6541; www.paicountryhut.com; Ban Mae Hi; bungalows 500-700B; 🛜) The bamboo bungalows here are basic, but they're tidy and most have en-suite bathrooms and inviting hammocks on their small verandas. While it's not exactly riverside, it's the most appealing of several similar budget places close to the water.

Juno Hostel   HOSTEL $
(☑ 095 342 5332; junohostel@gmail.com; Th Khetkelang; dm 200B; ❄ 🛜) Like many new hostels, Juno is a shrine to smooth cement walls and floors. There are only dorms here and they have comfy beds and big lockers. All share clean bathrooms. There's a small communal area downstairs.

Giant Guest House   GUESTHOUSE $
(☑ 085 681 2440; Th Wiang Tai; bungalows 250-400B; 🛜) An old-school backpacker crash pad, Giant has ramshackle and fan-cooled bamboo bungalows stationed around a large riverside garden, as well as a few better-maintained cement rooms. The cheapest share bathrooms and are mattress-on-the-floor simple. If you're looking for the authentic Pai hippy vibe, this is your place.

Pai

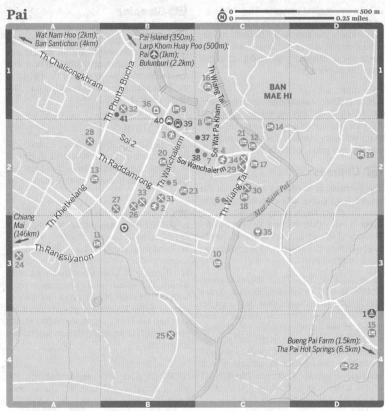

Tayai's Guest House   GUESTHOUSE $
(📞 053 699579; off Th Raddamrong; r & bungalows
400-700B; ❄️ 🛜) This place, a quiet, leafy compound just off the main drag, has simple but
clean fan and air-con rooms and bungalows.
Most have little terraces and the beds are reasonable. It's run by a friendly elderly couple.

Pai River Villa   HOTEL $$
(📞 053 699796; pairivervillaresort@gmail.com; 7
Th Wiang Tai; bungalows incl breakfast 800-1500B;
❄️🛜) The 10 air-con bungalows here are
spacious and stylish, with decent bathrooms
and wide balconies that encourage lazy riv-
erside relaxing and mountain viewing, while
the four fan-cooled bungalows are a much
tighter fit. The setting is peaceful.

Breeze of Pai Guesthouse   HOTEL $$
(📞 081 998 4597; www.facebook.com/BreezeOfPai;
Soi Wat Pa Kham; r & bungalows 700-1000B; ❄️🛜)
This well-groomed compound near the river features nine plain and parquet-floored
rooms and six spacious and simple A-frame

bungalows. They're set in an attractive garden. It's close to the action, without the
noise pollution.

Heart of Pai Resort   HOTEL $$
(📞 053 699984; www.heartofpai.com; Th Rang-
siyanon; r 700-800B; ❄️🛜) The characterless
but sizeable and well-maintained rooms
here have comfy beds, modern bathrooms
and big balconies. All are set in a seclud-
ed compound of pale-yellow buildings and
skinny palm trees. It's a 10-minute walk
from the main strip, and is quiet at night.

Palm House   GUESTHOUSE $$
(📞 098 786 8520; www.facebook.com/palmhouse.
pai; Th Wanchalerm; r 400-800B; ❄️🛜) Palm
House has nine fan-cooled or air-con rooms
in a two-storey compound on a quiet lane.
The rooms are plain – with white walls and
tiled floors – but are reasonably sized and
come with balconies. The cheaper fan rooms
are smaller. Staff, when around, are friendly
and helpful.

Pai

Hotel des Artists　　　　　　　HOTEL $$$

(☏053 699539; www.hotelartists.com; 99 Th Chai-songkhram; r incl breakfast 4400-5200B; ❈🔊) This traditional former Shan mansion has been turned into one of the most charming boutiques in town. The 14 slightly crowded rooms mingle pan-Asian and Western design elements in a tasteful, attractive package. Beds are on an elevated platform and all rooms have balconies. The more expensive riverside rooms are larger and offer the best views.

Pai Vimaan Resort　　　　　　　HOTEL $$$

(☏053 699403; www.paivimaan.com; 73 Th Wiang Tai; incl breakfast r 2500B, bungalows 5000B; ❈🔊) The highlights here are the five riverside tented bungalows. Huge and equipped with air-con, jacuzzi, big TVs and other modern amenities, this is superior glamping. But the big, bright rooms are fine, too, with wide terraces and river views. It's close to the action and set in manicured grounds that slope towards the river.

Rim Pai Cottage　　　　　　　HOTEL $$$

(☏053 699133; www.rimpaicottage.com; 99/1 Th Chaisongkhram; bungalows 2200-3300B; ❈🔊🏊) The tastefully decorated bungalows (which include breakfast from October to February) are spread out along a secluded and beautifully wooded section of Mae Nam Pai. There are countless cosy riverside corners to relax in and a palpable village-like feel about the whole place. Opt for one of the original wooden bungalows as the newer concrete ones have less charm.

Pai Village Boutique Resort & Farm　　　　　HOTEL $$$

(☏053 698152; www.paivillage.com; 88 Th Wiang Tai; bungalows incl breakfast 3000-6500B; ❈🔊🏊) This well-maintained, efficient place offers a luxury version of the basic backpacker bamboo bungalow. The 38 wooden huts are small but plush, with safety boxes and terraces with cushions for lounging. They're set close to each other in an attractive garden. A pool and new wing were under construction at the time of research.

🛏 **Outside Town**

If you've got your own wheels, you'll find many options outside the centre of Pai. Most are targeted at domestic rather than foreign tourists, which means they fall in the midrange and top-end price ranges, and

WATERFALLS AROUND PAI

There are a few waterfalls around Pai that are worth visiting, particularly after the rainy season (October to early December). The closest and the most popular, Nam Tok Mo Paeng (น้ำตก หมอแปง), has a couple of pools that are suitable for swimming. The waterfall is about 8km from Pai along the road that also leads to Wat Nam Hoo – a long walk indeed, but suitable for a bike ride or a short motorcycle trip. Roughly the same distance in the opposite direction is Nam Tok Pembok (น้ำตกแพมบก), just off the road to Chiang Mai. The most remote is Nam Tok Mae Yen (น้ำตกแม่ เย็น), a couple of hours' walk down the rough road east of Pai.

typically take the form of air-con-equipped bungalow compounds.

Spicypai Backpackers
HOTEL $

(☑ 088 294 2004; Mae Yen; dm 180B; 🛜) The large, semi-open-air dorms feature beds that are plastic mattresses on bamboo frames, and the whole ramshackle place could be lifted from a *Survivor* episode. Communal areas include hammocks slung under shade and a firepit, continuing the rustic theme, as does the location down a dirt track surrounded by rice fields. It's 750m east of Mae Nam Pai, just off the road to Tha Pai Hot Springs.

★ Bulunburi
HOTEL $$

(☑ 053 698302; Ban Pong; bungalows incl breakfast 750-3000B; 🕸🛜🏊) Set in a tiny, secluded valley of rice fields and streams, the seductively bucolic location of this place is as much a reason to stay as the attractive accommodation. The 11 bungalows, which range from tight fan-cooled rooms to huge two-bedroom houses, aren't flash but they're well equipped and comfortable. Book ahead; some people stay here for months.

Bulunburi is about 2.5km from the centre of town along the road to Mae Hong Son; look for the turn-off about 1km from Pai.

Sipsongpanna
HOTEL $$

(☑ 053 698259; www.facebook.com/paisipsong panna; Wiang Nua; bungalows incl breakfast 1000-1500B; 🕸🛜) The four adobe-style riverside bungalows here are rustic and quirky, with a mix of bright colours, beds on elevated

platforms and sliding-glass doors opening to wide balconies. If you prefer to keep it old-school, there are also three older wooden bungalows. The hotel's about 2.5km from the town centre, off the road to Mae Hong Son; look for the well-posted turn-off about 1km from Pai.

Pairadise
HOTEL $$

(☑ 053 698065; www.pairadise.com; Ban Mae Hi; r & bungalows 600-1500B; 🕸🛜🏊) This neat resort looks over the Pai Valley from atop a ridge just outside town. The bungalows are spacious and include gold-leaf lotus murals, decent bathrooms and terraces with hammocks. All surround a spring-fed pond that's suitable for swimming. There are also some cheaper fan-cooled rooms. It's 750m east of Mae Nam Pai; look for the sign just after the bridge.

Bueng Pai Farm
GUESTHOUSE $$

(☑ 089 265 4768; www.paifarm.com; Ban Mae Hi; bungalows 1000-2000B; 🛜🏊) In a rural setting about 2.5km southeast of Pai, the 12 spacious, fan-cooled, wood and bamboo bungalows here are attractively positioned around a vast pond stocked with freshwater fish. There's a campfire during the winter months, and a pool, communal kitchen and fishing equipment are available year-round. It's located off the road that leads to Tha Pai Hot Springs; look for the sign.

Pai Phu Fah
HOTEL $$

(☑ 081 906 2718; www.paiphufah.com; Ban Mae Hi; r & bungalows 300-800B; 🕸🛜) This collection of old A-frame bungalows and some newer ones, all with thatched roofs, is set on the edge of a photogenic rice field. The older ones are a bit tatty and dark, with springy beds. The newest offer more space and are better-kept though still plain. The location is about 650m east of Mae Nam Pai, along the road to Tha Pai Hot Springs.

★ Pai Island
RESORT $$$

(☑ 053 699999; www.paiislandresort.com; incl breakfast bungalows 6000-8000B, villas 18,000-28,000B; 🕸🛜🏊) This stylish and popular resort intertwines Pacific Island and African themes. Accommodation takes the form of 10 free-standing, private-feeling luxury bungalows and villas with sparkling white interiors, located on islands connected by bridges. All are equipped with jacuzzis and expansive semi-outdoor bathrooms. The service is probably the best in Pai.

It's located about 700m north of town, along the road that leads to Mae Hong Son.

★ **Puripai Villa**   HOTEL **$$$**
(☑ 053 065175; www.puripaivilla.com; incl breakfast r 3200B, villa 6500-12,000B; ✱ 🞧 ☰) This architecturally striking hotel feels like it should be in a city, rather than on a hillside overlooking the Pai Valley. Rooms are design-conscious, swish and spacious, with balconies that offer some of the best views in the area. The multiroom villas provide even more space, and include kitchens, living rooms and their own private pools.

The hotel is about 3km from the centre of town off the road to Mae Hong Son; look for the well-posted turn-off just after the airport runway, about 1.3km from Pai.

Phu Pai   HOTEL **$$$**
(☑ 053 065111; www.phupairesort.com; Mae Na Theung; incl breakfast bungalows 2150-2550B, ste 3550B; ✱ 🞧 ☰) This self-professed 'art resort' is an attractive, remote-feeling gathering of 40 locally styled, luxury bungalows. Views are the focus here, with most bungalows edging onto rice fields, and an infinity pool framing the Pai Valley.

The hotel is about 4km from the centre of town off the road to Mae Hong Son; look for the well-posted turn-off just after the airport runway, about 1.3km from Pai.

Pai Treehouse   HOTEL **$$$**
(☑ 081 911 3640; www.paitreehouse.com; Mae Hi; incl breakfast bungalows 1000-2500B, ste 3000-5500B; ✱ 🞧) If you can't score one of the six cute, compact treehouse rooms here (they're popular), there are several other attractive and much bigger bungalows, many near the river. On the vast grounds you'll also find elephants and floating decks on Mae Nam Pai. The atmosphere is family friendly. The resort is 6km east of Pai, just before Tha Pai Hot Springs.

Pripta Boutique Resort   HOTEL **$$$**
(☑ 053 065750; www.facebook.com/PriptaBoutique-Resort; 90 Mu 3, Mae Hi; bungalows incl breakfast 2000B; ✱ 🞧) This hillside compound features 12 chic thatched-roof bungalows perched at the edge of the Pai Valley. Rooms are huge, with tall ceilings, and feature vast balconies with outdoor tubs using water supplied by the nearby hot springs. It's about 7km south of Pai, between Tha Pai Hot Springs and Rte 1095.

✕ Eating & Drinking

Pai has an impressive number of restaurants, but many places appear to just be duplicates of their neighbours. Nevertheless, there's some good food to be found, including a notable increase in the number of quality vegetarian/vegan eateries.

Vendors set up along Th Chaisongkhram and Th Rangsiyanon every evening, selling all manner of food from stalls and refurbished VW vans. There are more during high season (November to February).

★ **Larp Khom Huay Poo**   THAI **$**
(Ban Huay Pu; mains 50-100B; ⊙ 8am-8pm; 🞧) Escape the wheatgrass-and-tofu crowd at this unabashedly carnivorous local eatery. The house special is 'larp moo kua', northern-style *lâhp* (minced pork fried with herbs and spices). Accompanied by sticky rice, bitter herbs and an ice-cold beer, it's one of the best meals in Pai. The soups and bamboo worms are fine, too. Located 1km north of town, on the road to Mae Hong Son.

They'll adjust the spice levels on request.

★ **Om Garden Cafe**   INTERNATIONAL **$**
(off Th Raddamrong; mains 60-140B; ⊙ 8.30am-5pm Wed-Mon; 🞧 ▱) Meat-free takes on international dishes, fresh-pressed juices, a pleasant shaded garden, a noticeboard advertising yoga classes, the odd hippy: basically everything you'd expect at a place called Om Garden, except that the food is actually good. It's not exclusively veggie: dishes range from Middle Eastern meze to breakfast burritos, salads and pasta. There are also pastries and fine coffee.

★ **Maya Burger Queen**   AMERICAN **$**
(www.facebook.com/MayaBurgerQueen; Th Wiang Tai; mains 80-165B; ⊙ 1-10pm; 🞧 ▱) Burgers are a big deal in Pai and our arduous research has concluded that Maya does the best job. Everything is homemade, from the soft, slightly sweet buns to the rich garlic mayo that accompanies the thick-cut fries.

YUNNANESE RESTAURANTS

Several open-air restaurants in Ban Santichon, 4km west of Pai, serve the traditional dishes of the town's Yunnanese residents. Choices include *màntŏ* (steamed buns), served here with pork leg stewed with Chinese herbs, hand-pulled noodles and several dishes using unique local crops and exotic ingredients such as black chicken. Mains cost 40B to 250B and most places are open from 7am till 8pm.

PAI'S BAR SCENE

As a general guide to downtown Pai's drinking scene, most of the open-air and VW-van-based cocktail bars are found along Th Chaisongkhram; Th Wiang Tai is where you'll find Pai's highest concentration of drinking dens. Th Rangsiyanon is home to guesthouse-style restaurant-bars, while a few open-air bars/clubs can be found at the eastern end of Th Raddamrong, just across the bridge.

There are no less than six veggie-burger options, too.

Na's Kitchen
THAI **$**

(Th Raddamrong; mains 60-200B; ⊙5-10pm) The slightly eccentric Na – who doesn't always open her restaurant daily – cooks her Thai and Northern Thai dishes with love and serves them up in a no-frills, semi-open-air restaurant that's laid-back yet busy with both locals and visitors.

Charlie & Lek Restaurant
THAI **$**

(Th Rangsiyanon; mains 55-125B; ⊙11am-9.30pm; 🕿🍴) Foreigner-friendly, and none the worse for it, Charlie & Lek serves Thai classics as well as a few Northern Thai specialities in a no-fuss atmosphere that draws the crowds. There are veggie options, too.

Chew Xin Jai
VEGAN **$**

(off Th Rangsiyanon; mains 49-139B; ⊙8am-7pm; 🕿🍴) Chew Xin Jai stands out from Pai's ever-increasing number of vegan/veggie eating spots by virtue of its Chinese take on vegetarian cuisine, with Taiwanese fried rice, dumplings, spring rolls and a faux duck soup. There's no Roman-script sign; look for the Chinese-style building adorned with three Chinese characters.

Cafecito
TEX-MEX **$**

(www.facebook.com/cafecitopai; mains 70-190B; ⊙9am-5pm; 🕿🍴) Cafecito serves tasty Tex-Mex staples – fish tacos, burritos and quesadillas – as well as Mexican breakfasts, all overseen by an American. This is Pai, so there are veggie options too, and it also doubles as a pleasant cafe. It's located about 600m south of Th Rangsiyanon, on the unmarked street adjacent to Pai's police station.

Good Life
INTERNATIONAL **$**

(Th Wiang Tai; mains 50-220B; ⊙8am-10pm; 🕿🍴) Kefir, kombucha, beet juice and wheatgrass are indicators of the vibe of this eclectic and popular cafe. But coffee, herbal teas, soft drinks and alcohol are also available, as is a thick menu of Thai and international dishes, many of which are meat-free. There are free meditation sessions at 11am Monday to Wednesday.

Baan Benjarong
THAI **$**

(179 Th Rangsiyanon; dishes 90-170B; ⊙11am-1pm & 5-8pm) Emulate local families and come to this classy home-based restaurant at the southern end of town on the edge of the fields. Dishes such as stewed salted crabs in coconut milk and a salad of banana flower, shrimp and chicken are some of the better Thai food offerings in town.

Nong Beer
THAI **$**

(cnr Th Khetkalang & Th Chaisongkhram; mains 40-250B; ⊙9am-10pm; 🕿🍴) A long-standing restaurant that's well used to foreigners, Nong's is a reliable go-to option for cheap and authentic Thai eats, ranging from *kôw soy* (curried noodles) to curries ladled over rice. There's a reasonable number of meat-free dishes.

Evening Market
THAI **$**

(Th Raddamrong; mains 30-60B; ⊙3-7pm) For take-home, local-style eats, try the market that unfolds here every day from about 3pm to sunset.

Pai Siam Bistro
INTERNATIONAL **$$**

(Th Chaisongkhram; mains 70-395B; ⊙9am-11.30pm; 🕿🍴) Bright and stylish, with sofas for lounging, this relocated place has Mediterranean-influenced specials, Thai tapas and some decent cakes and pastries. It also offers cocktails and a range of wine.

Witching Well
INTERNATIONAL **$$**

(www.witchingwellrestaurant.com; 97 Th Wiang Tai; mains 165-580B; ⊙10.30am-10pm; 🕿🍴) There's a big wine list at this upmarket, brick-walled, cement-floored, European-style bistro. The menu is what you'd expect: well-presented Mediterranean dishes, tapas and steaks. Service is good and the sophisticated breakfasts are recommended.

Don't Cry
BAR

(Th Raddamrong; ⊙4pm-late) Located just across the river from central Pai, Don't Cry touts itself as the kind of reggae bar you used to get on Ko Pha-Ngan. In fact, when it's swinging (don't bother showing up till after 11pm), it's more like a grungy semi-open-air club. Packed most nights with a young backpacker crowd, it stays open until the last punter staggers home.

🛍 Shopping

Walking Street   MARKET
(Th Chaisongkhram & Th Rangsiyanon; ⊙6-10pm)
Every evening, a walking street forms in the centre of town, with vendors selling food, clothes, souvenirs and knick-knacks. It's far busier during high season (November to February).

ℹ Information

Several exchange booths, banks and ATMs can be found along Th Rangsiyanon and Th Chaisongkhram.

The *Pai Events Planner* (PEP) is a free monthly newsletter that covers cultural events, travel destinations and some restaurant and bar openings; you can find it at various places around town.

Police Station (☑ 053 699191, 24hr emergency 191; Th Rangsiyanon; ⊙24hr) Pai's principal police station.

ℹ Getting There & Away

Pai's **minivan station** (Th Chaisongkhram) handles all public transport to and from town. It is wise to book tickets a day in advance.

TO	FARE (B)	DURATION (HR)	FREQUENCY
Chiang Mai	150	3-4	hourly 7am-5pm
Mae Hong Son	150	3-4	8.30am
Soppong (Pangmapha)	100	1½	8.30am

Aya Service (☑ 053 699888; www.ayaservice.com; 22/1 Th Chaisongkhram; motorcycles per 24hr 140-200B; ⊙7am-10pm) also runs aircon minivan buses to Chiang Mai (150B, three hours, hourly 7am to 5.30pm).

ℹ Getting Around

Most of Pai is accessible on foot. Motorcycle taxis wait at the **stand** (Th Chaisongkhram) next to the minivan station. It costs 50B to Ban Santichon village and 100B to Nam Tok Mo Paeng waterfall.

There are many places around town that rent out motorbikes (from 100B per day), including **Duan-Den** (☑ 053 699966; 20/1 Th Chaisongkhram; motorcycles per 24hr 100-150B; ⊙7.30am-9pm), as well as bicycles (from 50B per day).

Soppong

Sleepy Soppong (สบป่อง; sometimes known as Pangmapha, which is actually the name of the entire district) is a small market town an hour or so northwest of Pai and about 70km from Mae Hong Son. There's not much to see in Soppong itself, but the surrounding area is defined by dense forests, rushing rivers and dramatic limestone outcrops and is *the* place in Northern Thailand for caving. The most accessible cave in the area is Tham Lot (p291), but there are many others waiting to be explored. There are also several Shan, Lisu, Karen and Lahu villages in the area that can be visited on hikes.

⊙ Sights & Activities

The best source of information on caving and trekking in the area is the owner of Cave Lodge (p292). Experienced local guides and recommended kayaking, hiking and caving trips in the area can be arranged here. It's located near Tham Lot, the most accessible cave in the area, 9km from Soppong.

★Tham Lot   CAVE
(ถ้ำลอด; from 150B; ⊙8am-5.30pm) About 9km northeast of Soppong is Tham Lot (pronounced *tâm lôrt* and also known as *tâm nám lôrt*), a large limestone cave with impressive stalagmites, coffin caves (p293) and a wide stream running through it for 600m. Along with Tham Nam Lang further west, it's one of the largest known caves in Thailand, with a total length of 1600m.

Visitors are not permitted to tour the caves alone. At the entrance, you must hire a gas lantern and guide for 150B (one guide leads up to three people) to take you through the caverns. Bamboo rafts (up to three people, one way 300B) from the entrance to the exit take in the Column Cavern, Doll Cave and Coffin Cave. If going one way, you can walk back from outside the cave (20 minutes), but only during the dry season (approximately November to May). In the dry season it may also be possible to wade to the Doll Cave and then take a raft through to the exit (200B). Try to be at the exit at sunset, when hundreds of thousands of swifts pour into Tham Lot and cling to their bedtime stalagmites.

The three side chambers – Column Cavern, Doll Cave and Coffin Cave – can be reached by ladders. It can get crowded on the ladders so watch your step. It takes around 1½ hours to explore the whole complex. During parts of the rainy season (August to October) only one cave is open because of water levels.

A **Nature Education Centre** (ศูนย์ศึกษา ธรรมชาติและสัตว์ป่าถ้ำน้ำลอด; ⊘ 8am-5.30pm) has basic displays on the area, as well as exhibits of pottery remains found in the cave.

🛏 Sleeping & Eating

There are a few simple restaurants, as well as food stalls, in Soppong. Most are closed by 8pm. Some guesthouses have attached restaurants. There's also a row of **outdoor restaurants** (mains 30-70B; ⊘ 9am-6pm) outside the Tham Lot park entrance offering simple Thai fare.

Lemonhill Garden
GUESTHOUSE $

(✆ 064 828 6107; gunnerchiangmai55@gmail.com; Rte 1095; r & bungalows 300-500B, f 1000B; ❄🛜) Centrally located in Soppong, Lemonhill Garden has a spread of faded and worn accommodation that backs onto the Nam Lang. Some rooms are in better condition than others, so take a look first. Only the family room has air-con.

★ Cave Lodge
GUESTHOUSE $$

(✆ 053 617203; www.cavelodge.com; Tham Lot Village; r & bungalows 300-2000B; 🛜) This is one of the more legendary places to stay in Northern Thailand (and was probably the first guesthouse in Mae Hong Son Province). It's run by John Spies, an expert on the area, with rooms and bungalows ranging from basic options with shared bathrooms to still rustic but comfortable ones with more space. All perch on a hillside overlooking Nam Lang.

★ Little Eden Guesthouse
HOTEL $$

(✆ 053 617053; www.littleeden-guesthouse.com; Rte 1095; r & bungalows 400-1600B; ❄🛜🏊) The five fan-cooled A-frame bungalows around a small pool are compact but well maintained, while the four air-con rooms in the newer building are spacious and attractive. But it's the beautiful two-storey 'houses' that make this place special. Perfect for families or a group of friends, they are stylishly decorated with living rooms, interesting nooks and crannies, and terraces with hammocks.

There is an attached restaurant and trekking and rafting trips can be arranged.

Soppong River Inn
HOTEL $$

(✆ 082 998 5345; www.soppong.com; Rte 1095; r & bungalows 500-1400B; ❄🛜) This place has modern rooms in a couple of rambling structures and a handful of individually decorated, high-roofed bungalows, some fan-cooled and some with air-con, all set in a jungly riverside garden with winding paths.

The owner is pleasant and there's an attached restaurant. It's at the western edge of town, within walking distance of the minivan stop.

Baan Cafe Nature Resort
HOTEL $$

(✆ 053 617081; khunjui@yahoo.com; Rte 1095; r 600B, bungalows 1200B; 🛜) Located near the bridge, about 750m west of Soppong's minivan stop, this place combines spotless, fan-cooled rooms and modern bungalows in a park-like setting by Nam Lang. The good-value bungalows include fireplaces and balconies looking over the river.

ℹ Information

There are a couple of ATMs in the centre of Soppong close to the 7-Eleven.

ℹ Getting There & Around

All transport in and out of Soppong is by minivan. They arrive at and depart from a **stop** (Rte 1095) near the town's market, roughly opposite the petrol station.

Motorcycle taxis stationed in front of the 7-Eleven in Soppong will take passengers to Tham Lot or the Cave Lodge for 70B per person; private pick-up trucks will take you and up to five other people for 300B.

Motorcycles can be hired from Pasine Motorbike Hire, at the western edge of town, for 250B per day. **Pasine Motorbike Hire** (✆ 053 617185; Rte 1095; ⊘ 7am-6pm)

MINIVANS FROM SOPPONG

DESTINATION	FARE (B)	DURATION (HR)	FREQUENCY
Chiang Mai	250	5	hourly 8am-6.30pm
Mae Hong Son	100	1½	hourly 10.30am-6.30pm
Pai	100	1	hourly 8am-6.30pm

PANGMAPHA CAVES

The 900-sq-km area of Pangmapha district is famous for its high concentration of cave systems, where more than 200 have been found. Apart from Tham Lot, one of its most famous is Tham Nam Lang, which is 20km northwest of Soppong near Ban Nam Khong. It's 8.5km long and thought to be one of the largest caves in the world in terms of volume.

Many of the caves are essentially underground river systems, some of which boast waterfalls, lakes and sandy 'beaches'. *Cryptotora thamicola*, an eyeless, waterfall-climbing troglobitic fish that forms its own genus, is found in only two caves in the world, both of which are in Pangmapha. Other caves contain little or no life, due to an abundance of noxious gases or very little oxygen.

More than 85 of the district's 200 limestone caverns are known to contain ancient teak coffins carved from solid teak logs. Up to 9m long, the coffins are typically suspended on wooden scaffolds inside the caves. The coffins have been carbon-dated and shown to be between 1200 and 2200 years old. It is not known who made them or why they were placed in the caves, but as most caves have fewer than 10 coffins it's thought that only select individuals were accorded such an elaborate burial. .

The easiest coffins to visit are in the coffin cave (ถ้ำผีแมน; Rte 1095; adult/child 20/10B; ⊙8.30am-5pm) just past Pangmapha Hospital, 2km west of Soppong, and the coffin caves in Tham Lot (p291), 9km northeast of Soppong. Several caves that scientists are currently investigating are off limits to the public, but John Spies at Cave Lodge may know which caves are possible to explore. His book, *Wild Times*, is also a great informal guide to the area's caves.

Mae La-Na

Set in a picturesque mountain valley located 6km off Rte 1095, Mae La-Na (แม่ละนา), a tiny, remote Shan village, feels like it's been cut off from the rest of the world. The village is home to an established homestay programme, while there are several caves to explore in the surrounding area. There are no banks or ATMs in Mae La-Na so it's best to bring cash.

◉ Sights & Activities

The most famous local attraction is Tham Mae La-Na, a 12km-long cavern with a stream running through it. Although local guides are willing to take people inside, in reality the cave lacks the appropriate infrastructure to support visitors, who run a serious risk of permanently damaging delicate cave formations and disturbing the habitat of sensitive cave fish. A better bet is to check out nearby Tham Pakarang (Coral Cave) and Tham Phet (Diamond Cave), both of which feature good wall formations. Guides (200B) can be arranged at the main village shop and petrol station. Some of the caves may not be accessible during the rainy season.

Mae La-Na is a good base for some inspiring walks. Some of Mae Hong Son's most beautiful scenery is within a day's ramble,

and there are several Red and Black Lahu villages nearby. It's also possible to walk a 15km half-loop all the way from Mae La-Na to Tham Lot. Khun Ampha, the owner of Maelana Garden Home, can provide a basic map.

🛏 Sleeping & Eating

There are no restaurants or stalls in Mae La-Na. You'll dine at your homestay (p293) or at Maelana Garden Home (p293).

Maelana Garden Home GUESTHOUSE $
(☑081 706 6021; r/bungalows 300/400B; ☜) At the edge of town, this attractive farm-like compound combines basic, fan-cooled rooms in two wooden houses and a few A-frame bamboo bungalows. Authentic Shan meals can be prepared for 100B per person. Call ahead – transport can be arranged from Rte 1095 (150B) or Soppong (400B) – or ask for the owner, Khun Ampha, at the village shop/petrol station, and she'll pick you up.

Homestay Programme HOMESTAY $
(Ban Mae La-Na; per person per night 100B) Two dozen homes in Mae La-Na have collaborated to form a homestay programme; fees go back into a community fund. Meals can be prepared for 100B per person. Enquire at the sporadically staffed wooden office at

the entrance to town or at any home with a 'homestay' sign.

ℹ️ Getting There & Away

The Mae La-Na junction is 13km west of Soppong, but no public transport reaches the village. A motorcycle taxi here from Soppong costs 200B.

Mae Hong Son

♪ 053 / POP 7000

Surrounded by forested mountains and with a remote and pretty setting by a tranquil lake, Mae Hong Son (แม่ฮ่องสอน) fits many travellers' preconceived notions of how a Northern Thai town should look. A palpable influence from Myanmar and a frontier-settlement feel don't clash with this image and, best of all, there's hardly a túk-túk or tout to be seen. This doesn't mean Mae Hong Son is uncharted territory – tour groups have been coming here for years – but the city is far more laid-back than Pai, while its potential as a base for activities, from boat trips to trekking, ensures that your visit can be quite unlike anyone else's.

History

Mae Hong Son has been isolated from Thailand geographically, culturally and politically for most of its relatively short existence. The city was founded as an elephant-training outpost in the early 19th century, and remained little more than this until 1856, when fighting in Myanmar caused thousands of Shan to pour into the area. In the years that followed, Mae Hong Son prospered as a centre for logging and remained an independent kingdom until 1900, when King Rama V incorporated the region into the Thai kingdom.

◎ Sights

With their bright colours, whitewashed stupas and glittering zinc fretwork, Mae Hong Son's Burmese- and Shan-style temples will have you scratching your head wondering which country you're in.

★ Wat Phra That Doi Kong Mu

BUDDHIST TEMPLE

(วัดพระธาตุดอยกองมู; ⊘ daylight hours) Climb the hill west of town, Doi Kong Mu (1500m), to visit this temple compound, also known as Wat Plai Doi. Two Shan *chedi*, erected in 1860 and 1874, enshrine the ashes of monks from Myanmar's Shan State. Around the back of the wát you can see a tall, slender, standing Buddha and catch views west of the ridge. There's also a cafe and a small tourist market.

The view of the sea of fog that collects in the valley each morning is impressive; at other times you get wonderful views of the town and surrounding valleys.

On Th Pha Doong Muay Do is a long stairway leading to the top of Wat Phra That Doi Kong Mu (it's easier than it might appear); otherwise a motorcycle taxi costs 120B return.

Wat Jong Klang

BUDDHIST TEMPLE

(วัดจองกลาง; Th Chamnansatit; ⊘ daylight hours) Wat Jong Klang houses century-old glass *Jataka* paintings and a **museum** (พิพิธภัณฑ์ วัดจองกลาง; Wat Jong Klang, Th Chamnansatit; entry by donation; ⊘ 8am-6pm) with 150-year-old wooden dolls from Myanmar that depict some of the agonies of the wheel of life. The temple is lit at night and is reflected in Nong Jong Kham – a popular photo op for visitors. Wat Jong Klang has several areas that women are forbidden to enter – not unusual for Burmese-Shan Buddhist temples.

Wat Hua Wiang

BUDDHIST TEMPLE

(วัดหัวเวียง; Th Phanich Wattana; ⊘ daylight hours) This wát, just west of Mae Hong Son's morning market, is recognised for its *bòht* (chapel), boasting an elaborate tiered wooden roof and a revered bronze Buddha statue from Mandalay (Myanmar).

Wat Jong Kham

BUDDHIST TEMPLE

(วัดจองคำ; Th Chamnansatit; ⊘ daylight hours) Next door to Wat Jong Klang, this temple was built nearly 200 years ago by Thai Yai (Shan) people, who make up about half of the population of Mae Hong Son Province.

Wat Phra Non

BUDDHIST TEMPLE

(วัดพระนอน; Th Pha Doong Muay Do; ⊘ daylight hours) Wat Phra Non is home to the largest reclining Buddha in town.

Wat Kam Kor

BUDDHIST TEMPLE

(วัดก้ำก่อ; Th Pha Doong Muay Do; ⊘ daylight hours) This Burmese-style temple is known for its unique covered walkway.

🏃 Activities

Trekking

Mae Hong Son's location at the edge of mountainous forest makes it an excellent base for hikes into the countryside. Trekking here is not quite the large-scale industry it is elsewhere, and visitors willing to get their boots muddy can expect to find relatively untouched nature and isolated villages.

Multiday hikes in groups of two people range from 1000B to 3000B per person per day. Like elsewhere in Thailand, the per-day rates drop significantly with a larger group and a longer trek.

★**Nature Walks**   TREKKING
(☑089 552 6899; www.naturewalksthai-myanmar.com) Treks with Nature Walks might cost more than elsewhere, but Chan, a Mae Hong Son native, is probably the best guide in town. Hikes range from day-long nature walks to multiday journeys across the province. Chan can also arrange custom nature-based tours, such as the orchid-viewing tours he conducts from March to May.

★**Nam Rin Tour**   HIKING
(☑053 614454; rutsiri506@gmail.com; Th Khunlumprapas; ☺8am-9pm) The sardonic Mr Dam advertises 'bad sleep, bad jokes', but his treks get good feedback. They start at 1500B per day per person (minimum two people). Mr Dam has an admirable policy of refusing to take people to the long-necked Kayan villages, or on any elephant-themed tours. As he rightly says, the elephants don't want to hang out with humans.

Friend Tour   TREKKING
(☑053 611647, 086 180 7031; 21 Th Pradit Jong Kham; ☺8am-6.30pm) With over 20 years' experience, this reputable outfit offers trekking and bamboo rafting excursions, as well as day tours. Here you can also rent a motorbike (150B to 300B per day) and arrange car hire (from 1100B per day).

Boat Trips

Long-tail boat trips on the nearby Mae Nam Pai are popular, and guesthouses and trekking agencies can arrange river excursions. The most common boat trip sets off from Tha Pong Daeng, 4km southwest of Mae Hong Son. Boats travel 15km downstream to the 'long-neck' village of Huay Pu Keng (750B, one hour) or all the way to the border outpost of Ban Nam Phiang Din (900B, 1½ hours), 20km from the pier, before returning.

NORTHERN THAILAND MAE HONG SON

MOTORCYCLING TOUR: MAE HONG SON LOOP

Start Chiang Mai

End Chiang Mai

Length 600km; four days

One of the most popular motorcycle riding tours in Northern Thailand is the circuitous route that begins in Chiang Mai and passes through the length of Mae Hong Son Province before looping back to the city.

The Mae Hong Son loop really begins 34km north of Chiang Mai when you turn onto Rte 1095 and lean into the first of its 1864 bends. It's slow going and you'll start climbing almost immediately. However, the good thing about this route is that there is ample potential for overnight stops – many of the towns with good accommodation and food are less than 70km apart – giving riders the chance to reclaim the blood flow to their bottoms. Many of the overnight stops, too, are home to sights that are worth seeing, thus allowing for some cultural exploration alongside the hard riding. Pai, 130km from Chiang Mai, is the most popular overnight stop, thanks to its many accommodation and eating options, but Soppong, another 40km up the road, offers the chance to visit Tham Lot (p291), one of the largest caves in Thailand. Mae Hong Son, 65km from Soppong, has a fascinating mix of ethnic minorities and cultural influences from across the nearby border with Myanmar.

Upon reaching Khun Yuam, 70km south of Mae Hong Son, you can opt to take Rte 1263 to Mae Chaem, before continuing back to Chiang Mai via Doi Inthanon, the country's highest peak, or you can continue south to Mae Sariang and follow Rte 108 all the way back to Chiang Mai via Hot, although the distances between towns here are greater and best done on a more powerful and more comfortable motorcycle.

An excellent driving companion is Golden Triangle Rider's *Mae Hong Son Loop Guide Map*, available at most bookshops in Chiang Mai. The map shows accurate distances between locations along the loop, as well as potential side trips and other helpful information.

Mae Hong Son

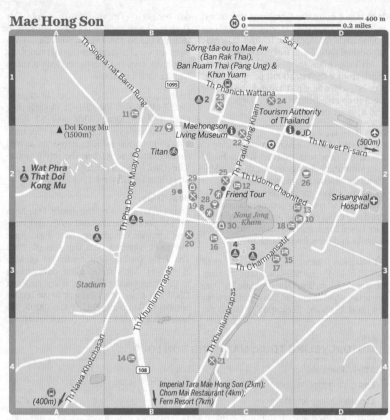

Boats can accommodate a maximum of eight passengers.

Bamboo rafting on the Mae Nam Pai is also popular. Most trekking agencies and guesthouses offer one-day combined trekking and rafting trips for around 1250B.

Spas

Phu Klon Country Club   SPA

(ภูโคลน คันทรีคลับ; ☏ 053 282579; www.phuklon. co.th; mud treatments 80-700B, massage per hr 250-450B; ☺ 8am-6.30pm) This self-professed country club is touted as Thailand's only mud treatment spa. Phu Klon is 16km north of Mae Hong Son in Mok Champae. If you haven't got your own wheels, you can take the daily Ban Ruam Thai- or Mae Aw-bound *sŏrng·tăa·ou* (passenger pick-up truck; 25B), but this means you might have to find your own way back.

Discovered by a team of geologists in 1995, the mud here is pasteurised and blended with herbs before being employed

in various treatments. There's thermal mineral water for soaking, and massage is also available.

Pha Bong Hot Springs   HOT SPRINGS

(บ่อน้ำร้อนผาบ่อง; ☏ 053 686033; Ban Pha Bong; private bath/bathing room 50/400B; ☺ 8am-sunset) Eleven kilometres south of Mae Hong Son in the Shan village of Pha Bong is this public park with hot springs. You can take a private bath or rent a room, and there's also massage (per hour 150B). The springs can be reached by any southbound minivan.

👉 Tours

Rosegarden Tours   TOURS

(☏ 053 611681; www.rosegarden-tours.com; 86/4 Th Khunlumprapas; tours from 700B; ☺ 8.30am-9pm) The English- and French-speaking guides at this long-standing agency focus on cultural and sightseeing tours, but can also arrange bamboo rafting and treks.

Mae Hong Son

Tour Merng Tai   TOURS
(☑ 086 311 5631, 053 611979; www.tourmerng
tai.com) This outfit mostly does day tours
around Mae Hong Son but can also arrange
bamboo rafting, treks and cycling tours.

✦ Festivals & Events

Jong Para Festival   RELIGIOUS
(☉ around Oct) An important local event, this
festival is held towards the end of the Buddhist Rains Retreat around October – it's
three days before the full moon of the 11th
lunar month, so it varies from year to year.

The festival begins with local Shan
bringing offerings to monks in the temples
in a procession marked by the carrying of
models of castles on poles. Folk theatre and
dance, some of it unique to northwest Thailand, is performed on wát grounds.

Loi Krathong   CULTURAL
(☉ Nov) During this national holiday in
November – usually celebrated by floating
grà·tong (small lotus floats) on the nearest pond, lake or river – Mae Hong Son
residents launch balloons called *grà·tong
sù·wăn* (heaven *grà·tong*) from Wat Phra
That Doi Kong Mu (p294).

Poi Sang Long Festival   RELIGIOUS
(☉ Mar) Wat Jong Klang and Wat Jong Kham
are the focal points of this March festival,
where young Shan boys are ordained as novice monks in a ceremony known as *bòoat
lôok gâaou*. As part of the Shan custom, the
boys are dressed in ornate costumes (rather
than simple white robes) and wear flower
headdresses and facial make-up.

🛏 Sleeping

There's a fair range of accommodation here,
although Mae Hong Son lacks genuine hostels. Outside of the high season (November
to February), prices are normally discounted
by up to a third.

🛏 In Town

Friend House   GUESTHOUSE $
(☑ 053 620119; 20 Th Pradit Jong Kham; r 150-
500B; 🌀) A long-standing budget option,
Friend House has simple but spotless fan-
cooled, mattress-on-the-floor rooms. The
more expensive ones are larger and come
with private bathrooms. The riverside location is a bonus; the small garden has views
across to Wat Jong Klang.

Sarm Mork Guest House   GUESTHOUSE $
(☑ 082 192 2488, 053 612122; sarmmork@hotmail.
com; Th Chamnansatit; r 500-600B; ❉🌀) Three
cute green bungalows and two spacious
rooms are set in this tranquil location east
of the lake: all are well kept and come with
air-con, TVs and fridges. The place is run by
a friendly family.

Boondee House   GUESTHOUSE $$
(☑ 088 435 9258; boondeehouse@gmail.com; 6
Th Pha Doong Muay Do; r 800-1000B; ❉🌀) The

DON'T MISS

MAE HONG SON SHORT TREK

Don't have the time for a trek in Mae Hong Son? A taste of the area's natural beauty can be had by tackling the **Mae Sakut Nature Trail** (20B; ⊘8am-5pm), part of Nam Tok Mae Surin National Park. In a relatively easy 5km loop, you'll encounter bamboo forests, teak woods, waterfalls, wildflower fields (in season) and viewpoints.

The trailhead is about 7km north of Mae Hong Son town, along the same road that leads to Fern Resort; proceed about 200m past the resort to the road-block where you're expected to park your vehicle and pay the entry fee.

17 spacious rooms here are spread across two buildings. With white walls and tiled floors, the rooms don't have much in the way of decoration, but they do have decent beds, desks, TVs and fridges. There are also communal areas throughout, the staff are helpful and it's located on a quiet residential street just five minutes' walk from the lake.

Jongkham Place GUESTHOUSE $$
(☑053 614294; 4/2 Th Udom Chaonited; r 700-1500B; ❄🛜) This exceedingly tidy, fami-ly-run place by the lake has three rooms, four attractive wooden bungalows and two penthouse-like suites. All come with air-con. Not much English is spoken but the family is friendly.

Palm House GUESTHOUSE $$
(☑085 969 0989, 053 614022; pondxxxx@gmail.com; 22/1 Th Chamnansatit; r 600-800B; ❄🛜) The 22 rooms are split between those in a stylish new block, with exposed brick walls and modern fittings, and others in the plainer and more dated original building. All rooms are a reasonable size. The helpful owner speaks English and can arrange transport.

Mountain Inn & Resort HOTEL $$
(☑053 611802; www.mhsmountaininn.com; 112/2 Th Khunlumprapas; incl breakfast r 1200-1500B, ste 4500B; ❄🛜⊠) Clean and cosy, if some-what old-fashioned, rooms with wooden floors and decorative Thai touches are the standard here. The rooms surround a pretty courtyard garden with a proper pool, small pond, benches and parasols. Superior rooms come with a terrace overlooking the pool.

It's popular with tour groups and visiting Thai officials.

Romtai House GUESTHOUSE $$
(☑053 612437; www.maehongson-romtai.com; Th Chamnansatit; r & bungalows 500-1000B; ❄🛜) Hidden behind both the lakeside temples and a bland-looking reception area, this place has a variety of accommodation rang-ing from plain but spacious and clean rooms to more attractive bungalows looking over a lush garden with fish ponds. Bicycles can be hired.

Piya Guesthouse HOTEL $$
(☑053 611260; piyaguesthouse@hotmail.com; 1/1 Th Khunlumprapas; bungalows 700B; ❄🛜⊠) Steps from Mae Hong Son's central lake is this neat compound of bungalows ringing a garden and a small but inviting pool. Rooms are well equipped and comfortable, although the bathrooms can be a bit musty.

🛏 Outside Town

★**Sang Tong Huts** HOTEL $$
(☑053 611680; www.sangtonghuts.org; off Th Maka Santi; bungalows 1200-1600B, f 2400B; 🛜⊠) This clutch of ecofriendly, fan-cooled, TV-free, bamboo and wood bungalows is set in an expansive forested garden just outside town and has loads of character. All the huts are individually designed and decorated – some come with stairs to the bathrooms – and they're spaced out from each other for privacy. It's a mellow and popular spot, so book ahead.

Sang Tong Huts is about 1km northeast of Th Khunlumprapas, just off Th Maka Santi – if going towards Pai, turn left at the intersection before the town's northernmost stoplight and follow the signs.

★**Fern Resort** RESORT $$$
(☑053 686110; www.fernresort.info; off Rte 108; bungalows incl breakfast 2000-2500B; ❄🛜⊠) This veteran resort is one of the more pleas-ant places to stay in northern Thailand. The 37 wooden bungalows are spaced out for pri-vacy among tiered rice paddies and streams and are simple but comfortable. There are no TVs, but two swimming pools, a pétan-que court and the nearby nature trails at the adjacent Mae Surin National Park will keep you busy.

The resort is 7km south of town, but free pick-up is available from the airport and bus terminal, and three daily shuttles run to/

from Mae Hong Son, stopping at the Fern Restaurant (p300).

Imperial Tara
Mae Hong Son Resort   HOTEL $$$
(☑053 684444-9; www.imperialhotels.com; Rte 108; r incl breakfast 2200-4500B; ❄️🔌📶🏊) The 104 rooms in this upmarket hotel all have wooden floors and balconies and are tastefully decorated. French windows that open onto terraces make a pleasant change from the standard business-hotel layout. Facilities include a big swimming pool, a small fitness centre and a sauna. It's located about 2km south of town.

✖️ Eating & Drinking

Mae Hong Son is home to several tourist-oriented restaurants and stalls, but to experience the town's unique and delicious Shan-style food, it's necessary to stick to less-formal establishments such as the town's morning market and **night market** (Th Phanich Wattana; mains 30-60B; ⏱4-8pm).

★**Little Good Things**   MULTICUISINE $
(www.facebook.com/littlegoodthings; off Th Khun-lumprapas, mains 40-100B; ⏱9am-3pm Wed Sun; 📶🔌) This small and tempting vegan cafe-restaurant offers breakfast options and light, Thai-influenced meals, all of which are meat-free, made with love, wholesome, embarrassingly cheap and, most importantly, delicious. It sometimes shuts down for a month in the rainy season (June to September).

★**Morning Market**   THAI $
(off Th Phanich Wattana; mains 20-50B; ⏱6am-9am) Mae Hong Son's morning market is a fun place to have breakfast. Several vendors at the northern end of the market sell unusual fare such as *tòo·a poo ùn*, a noodle dish from Myanmar supplemented with thick split-pea porridge and deep-fried 'Burmese tofu'.

Other vendors along the same strip sell a local version of *kà·nŏm jeen nám ngée·o* (thin rice noodles served with a pork- and

LOCAL KNOWLEDGE

LONG-NECKED KAYAN VILLAGES

These villages are Mae Hong Son's most touted – and most controversial – tourist attraction. The 'long-necked' moniker originates from the habit of some Kayan women (sometimes also referred to as Padaung, a Shan term) of wearing heavy brass coils around their necks. The coils depress the collarbone and rib cage, which makes their necks look unnaturally stretched. A common myth claims that if the coils are removed, a woman's neck will fall over and she will suffocate. In fact the women attach and remove the coils at will (visit at night and the women won't be wearing them) and there is no evidence that this practice impairs their health at all.

Nobody knows for sure how the coil custom got started. One theory is that it was meant to make the women unattractive to men from other tribes; another story says it was so tigers wouldn't carry the women off by their throats. Most likely it is nothing more than a fashion accessory. Until relatively recently, the custom was largely dying out, but money from tourism, and undoubtedly the influence of local authorities eager to cash in on the Kayan, have reinvigorated it.

Regardless of the origin, the villages are now on every group tour's itinerary, and have become a significant tourist draw for Mae Hong Son. The villages are often derided as human zoos, and there are certainly elements of this, but we find them more like bizarre rural markets, with the women earning much of their money by selling souvenirs and drinks. The Kayan we've talked to claim to be happy with their current situation, but the stateless position they share with all refugees from Myanmar is nothing to be envied, and these formerly independent farmers are now reliant on aid and tourists to survive.

These days, the most commonly visited 'long-necked' community is based at Huay Pu Keng, which is included on long-tail boat tours departing from Tha Pong Daeng. There are also a handful of Kayan families in Kayan Tayar, near the Shan village of Ban Nai Soi, 35km northwest of Mae Hong Son.

Any of the Kayan settlements outside Mae Hong Son can be visited independently if you have transportation, or any travel agency in Mae Hong Son can arrange a tour. All visitors pay a 200B entry fee to each village. Those who arrive by boat pay an extra 20B per person.

THAM PLA NATIONAL PARK

The most touted attraction of the Tham Pla National Park (อุทยานแห่งชาติถ้ำปลา; Rte 1095; adult/child 100/50B; ⏰8am-6pm) is Tham Pla (Fish Cave), a water-filled cavern where hundreds of soro brook carp thrive. A 450m path leads from the park entrance to a suspension bridge that crosses a stream and continues to the cave. The park is 16km north of Mae Hong Son and can be reached by hopping on any northbound minivan. Guesthouses will arrange transport for 1000B.

A statue of a Hindu sage called Nara, said to protect the holy fish from danger, stands near the cave. The fish grow up to 1m in length and are found only in the provinces of Mae Hong Son, Ranong, Chiang Mai, Rayong, Chanthaburi and Kanchanaburi. They eat vegetables and insects, although the locals believe them to be vegetarian and feed them only fruit and vegetables, which can be purchased at the park entrance.

It's all a bit underwhelming, unless you especially enjoy seeing carp cavorting, but the park grounds are a bucolic, shaded place to hang out. Food and picnic tables are available.

tomato-based broth), often topped with *kàhng pòrng*, a Shan snack of battered and deep-fried vegetables.

Salween River Restaurant & Bar   INTERNATIONAL $

(23 Th Pradit Jong Kham; mains 70-280B; ⏰8am-10pm; 🛜🍴) Salween is an old-school traveller's hang-out, with a menu ranging from burgers to Burmese, beers and cocktails and a few shelves of paperbacks. But unlike most similar places, Salween offers tasty food and as a consequence is enduringly popular: you can tell how busy Mae Hong Son is by whether Salween's dining room is full.

Chom Mai Restaurant   THAI $

(off Rte 108; mains 50-290B; ⏰8.30am-3.30pm; 🛜🍴) The English-language menu here is limited, but don't miss the deliciously rich *kôw soy* (northern-style curry noodle soup) or *kôw mòk gài* (the Thai version of biryani). Chom Mai is located about 4km south of Mae Hong Son, along the road that leads to Tha Pong Daeng – there's no Roman-script sign, but look for the Doi Chaang coffee sign.

Maesribua   THAI $

(cnr Th Pradit Jong Kham & Th Singha-nat Barm Rung; mains 30-60B; ⏰8am-1pm) Like the Shan grandma you never had, Auntie Bua prepares a generous spread of local-style curries, soups and dips on a daily basis. There's a small English-language menu here, or you can simply point and choose what looks tasty.

Fern Restaurant   THAI $$

(Th Khunlumprapas; mains 65-290B; ⏰10.30am-10pm; 🛜🍴) Fern is Mae Hong Son's most upscale restaurant, with tablecloths, professional service, and gentle lounge music

some nights. The food is decent: the big menu covers both Thai and local Shan-style dishes, including a tasty sour and spicy soup. There are quite a few meat-free options, too.

77 Wine & Coffee House   MULTICUISINE $$

(Th Khunlumprapas; mains 60-490B; ⏰7.30am-10.30pm; 🛜) The coffee is good, and there's a selection of wine (and foreign beers), but the food is the bigger draw at this bright place with a quiet garden. The large menu of Thai and Western classics is livened up with some Japanese dishes, while the breakfasts are a good way to start the day.

Coffee Morning   CAFE

(📋053 612234; 78 Th Singha-nat Barm Rung; ⏰7.30am-5.30pm; 🛜) The ground floor of this traditional wooden house houses a cafe-bookshop that makes perhaps the most atmospheric pit stop in Mae Hong Son. Lounge in a leather chair and read a book while enjoying coffee, tea, smoothies or cakes.

Sunflower   BAR

(Th Pradit Jong Kham; ⏰8am-10pm; 🛜) Technically a restaurant (mains 80B to 260B), Sunflower takes its design inspiration from Fred Flintstone's house – with a low stone roof supported by pillars – but its terrace and location right by the lake make it ideal for a sundowner or evening drinks. There's live lounge music some nights, a tacky artificial waterfall and the food is fine, too.

Crossroads   BAR

(61 Th Khunlumprapas; ⏰8am-midnight; 🛜) This ramshackle bar is a crossroads in every sense, from its location at one of Mae Hong Son's main intersections to a clientele that ranges from wet-behind-the-ears backpack-

ers to hardened locals. There's a menu of Thai and Western standards and a pool table upstairs.

Shopping

A few well-stocked souvenir shops can be found near the southern end of Th Khunlumprapas.

Manerplaw/Ethnic Echoes ARTS & CRAFTS
(Th Khunlumprapas; ⏲7.30am-10pm Oct-Feb, from 5pm Mar-Sep) These linked shops specialise in authentic hill-peoples' clothing, as well as other locally produced traditional items.

Walking Street MARKET
(Th Pradit Jong Kham; ⏲5-10pm Oct-Feb) In the evenings from October to February the roads around Nong Jong Kham become a lively Walking Street market, with handicrafts and food vendors.

Information

There are banks at the southern end of Th Khunlumprapas with ATMs and exchange facilities, as well as elsewhere in town.

Maehongson Living Museum (27 Th Singha-nat Barm Rung; ⏲8.30am-4.30pm; wi-fi) An attractive wooden building – formerly Mae Hong Son's bus depot – has been turned into a museum on local culture, food and architecture, although the bulk of information is in Thai. However, there are a few maps and brochures in English and there's free wi-fi.

Srisangwal Hospital (☎053 611378; Th Singha-nat Barm Rung) Mae Hong Son's main hospital.

Tourism Authority of Thailand (TAT; ☎053 612982, nationwide 1672; www.tourismthailand.org/Mae-Hong-Son; Th Ni-wet Pi-sarn; ⏲8.30am-4.30pm) Basic tourist brochures and maps can be picked up here.

Tourist Police (☎053 611812, nationwide 1155; Th Singha-nat Barm Rung; ⏲8.30am-4.30pm) Tourist police outpost in Mae Hong Son.

Getting There & Away

Mae Hong Son's tiny **airport** (off Th Phanich Wattana) has daily flights to Chiang Mai. **Sombat Tour** (☎053 684222; Mae Hong Son Bus & Minivan Terminal, off Th Nawa Khotchasan), has daily big, sleek buses to Bangkok, and there are a couple of old evening buses to Chiang Mai; otherwise all transport in and out of town is by minivan or *sǒrng·tǎa·ou* (passenger pick-up truck).

Getting Around

The centre of Mae Hong Son is easily covered on foot. A few motorcycle taxis can be found near the entrance to the morning market and also at the bus station, and charge 20B to 40B for trips within town. There are also a handful of túk-túk around the same places that charge from 50B per trip within town.

Most of Mae Hong Son's attractions are outside town, so renting a motorcycle or bicycle is a wise move. There are a number of places arouind town, such as **Titan** (Th Khunlumprapas; per day 100B; ⏲10am-7pm), offering bicycle hire. Other places, including **Friend Tour** (☎053 611647, 086 180 7031; 21 Th Pradit Jong Kham; per day motorbike 150-300B, car from 1100B; ⏲8am-6.30pm) and **JD** (☎084 372 6967; Th Ni-wet Pi-sarn; per day 150-250B; ⏲8am-6pm), have motorbike hire.

Mae Aw (Ban Rak Thai)

Located almost on the border with Myanmar's Kayin State and set around a reservoir, isolated Mae Aw (แม่ออ; also known as Ban Rak Thai) was established by Yunnanese KMT fighters who fled from communist rule in 1949. Decades later, the town's population and architecture remain very Chinese,

BUS & MINIVAN FROM MAE HONG SON

Mae Hong Son's **bus and minivan terminal** (off Th Nawa Khotchasan) is 1km south of the city; a túk-túk or motorcycle ride to/from here costs 60B.

DESTINATION	FARE (B)	DURATION (HR)	FREQUENCY
Bangkok (bus)	851-1134	15	4pm & 4.30pm
Chiang Mai (bus)	350	8-9	8pm & 9pm
Chiang Mai (minivan)	250	6	hourly 7am-5pm
Khun Yuam (minivan)	100	1½	8am & 2pm
Mae Sariang (minivan)	200	3½	8am & 2pm
Pai (minivan)	150	2½	hourly 7am-5pm
Soppong (minivan)	100	1½	hourly 7am-5pm

with many residents speaking Mandarin or Yunnanese. The main industries are tourism and tea – Mae Aw is surrounded by tea plantations – and there are numerous places to taste the local brew, as well as several restaurants serving Yunnanese cuisine.

Near Mae Aw is the tiny Shan village of **Ban Ruam Thai** (บ้านรวมไทย), fringed by a reservoir surrounded by pine trees.

🎆 Festivals & Events

Tea-Tasting Festival   CULTURAL
(Mae Aw; ☺Feb) Mae Aw's tea-tasting festival celebrates the village's fame as a supplier of fine oolong, jasmine and green tea, all grown on the plantations around the village. Tea tastings and trips to the plantations are on offer, as is Yunnanese-style food, music and general revelry.

🛏 Sleeping & Eating

Mae Aw and Ban Ruam Thai are easily approached as day trips from Mae Hong Son, but if you like what you see, each of the villages has a spread of basic accommodation.

Ping Ping Guest House   GUESTHOUSE $
(☏084 481 9707; Mae Aw; r 300-600B; 🛜) Ping Ping is one of a number of places that ring Mae Aw's reservoir and which offer basic digs in adobe-style bungalows. Rooms are fan-cooled and no-frills. There's an English sign, but no English is spoken.

Pala Coffee & Guest House   GUESTHOUSE $$
(☏083 571 6668; www.facebook.com/Pala-Coffee-Pang-ung; Ban Ruam Thai; r incl breakfast 1000-2000B; 🛜) Ban Ruam Thai's first guesthouse, Pala consists of several simple and spartan brick bungalows and some newer and more comfortable (but still plain) rooms with smooth cement walls. All are overpriced, but they are positioned on a slope surrounded by coffee plants, tea plants, fruit trees and giant bamboo and the views are great. There's an attached coffee shop and restaurant.

★ Gee Lee Restaurant   CHINESE $$
(Mae Aw; mains 80-600B; ☺8am-7pm; 🛜🖉) This long-standing restaurant serves delicious and authentic Yunnanese-style Chinese dishes. There's a small English-language menu to choose from. Stewed pork leg and stir-fried local veggies are the specialities. There's no Roman-script sign, but it's the low, white building with a red roof at the corner of the lake, close to the centre of the village.

❶ Information

There are no banks that take foreign ATM cards in Mae Aw or Ban Ruam Thai. Bring cash.

❶ Getting There & Away

There are four daily *sŏrng·tăa·ou* (passenger pick-up trucks) that head towards Mae Aw from Mae Hong Son, all of which depart from a **stop** (Th Phanich Wattana) opposite Mae Hong Son's market. Two head to Ban Ruam Thai (80B, one hour, 9.30am and 3.30pm), while two terminate in Mae Aw (80B, one hour, 10am and noon). The last two depart only when full, which can sometimes be a couple of hours after the scheduled departure time. Any tour agency or guesthouse in Mae Hong Son will arrange a vehicle for around 1500B. Heading back to Mae Hong Son, *sŏrng·tăa·ou* leave Ban Ruam Thai at 10am, and Mae Aw at 7.30am and 1pm.

Alternatively, the route also makes a brilliant motorcycle ride – just make sure you have enough petrol, as the only station is in Ban Na Pa Paek, at the end of a very long climb.

Khun Yuam

☑053 / POP 7000
Once a busy trading post – the border with Myanmar's Kayin State is only 35km away – Khun Yuam (ขุนยวม) was a key Japanese army base during WWII. Now it's a small and somnolent hillside town located between Mae Sariang and Mae Hong Son. As such, it makes a pleasant break from more-visited destinations – you are likely to be the only foreigner in town – while there are a few notable sights in the surrounding area, as well as Hmong, Karen and little-seen Lawa villages.

◉ Sights

Thai-Japan Friendship Memorial Hall   MUSEUM
(อนุสรณ์สถานมิตรภาพไทย-ญี่ปุ่น; Rte 108; adult/child 100/50B; ☺8.30am-4.30pm) At the northern end of town is the Thai-Japan Friendship Memorial Hall, which details Khun Yuam's role as a Japanese base during WWII. It's an impressive museum for such a small town. After watching a brief film (with English subtitles) on the history of Khun Yuam, you'll find displays and artefacts on the Japanese presence in Khun Yuam, as well as local history and culture.

Some of the Japanese soldiers stayed in Khun Yuam and married local women; the last Japanese soldier who settled in the area died in 2000.

ROAD TRIP: MAE HONG SON TO MAE AW

Start Mae Hong Son

End Mae Aw

Length 43km; two hours

A worthwhile day trip from the provincial capital of Mae Hong Son is to Mae Aw, an atmospheric Chinese outpost right at the Myanmar border, 43km north of Mae Hong Son.

The road to Mae Aw is a beautiful route that passes through tidy riverside Shan villages such as Mok Champae before suddenly climbing through impressive mountain scenery. Stops can be made at Pha Sua Waterfall, about 5km up the mountain, and Pang Tong Summer Palace, a rarely used royal compound a few kilometres past the waterfall.

For an interesting detour, at Ban Na Pa Paek take a left and continue 6km to the tiny Shan village of Ban Ruam Thai. There are several basic places to stay and eat here, and the road ends 500m further at Pang Ung, a peaceful mountain reservoir surrounded by pines that is immensely popular among Thai day trippers in search of a domestic Switzerland.

From Ban Na Pa Paek it's 6km further to Mae Aw, which is largely populated by the descendants of Yunnanese soldiers from the nationalist armies who fled China after the communist takeover in 1949. You're as likely to hear the Yunnanese dialect here as Thai (many of the locals also speak Mandarin). Local restaurants, too, serve their version of Yunnan cuisine rather than Thai dishes. Tea is the main industry here – there are tea plantations all around – and Mae Aw is a good place to sample or buy some of it.

Beyond Mae Aw, a brief paved road runs from the village to a border crossing with Myanmar's Kayin State. Only locals can cross in either direction here. If you decide to abandon your motorbike or car for a little leg-stretching, be careful where you go, as you could inadvertently cross the border. The area also sees a lot of smuggling, so ask in Mae Aw about where it is safe to do some hiking.

Ban Mae U Khaw   VILLAGE

(บ้านแม่อูคอ) On the slopes of Doi Mae U Khaw, 25km from Khun Yuam via Rte 1263, is the Hmong village of Ban Mae U Khaw. During late November the area blooms with scenic Mexican sunflowers, known locally as *dòrk boo·a đorng*. This event is very popular among Thais and accommodation in town gets booked out at this time of year.

Wat To Phae   BUDDHIST TEMPLE

(วัดต่อแพ; ☉ daylight hours) About 6km to the west of Khun Yuam, the atmospheric Wat To Phae sits alongside a rural stream and boasts a Mon-style *chedi* and an immaculate Burmese-style *wí·hǎhn*. Inside the main wooden building there's an exquisite 150-year-old *kalaga* (embroidered and sequined tapestry) from Myanmar. It's kept behind curtains but you can open them.

Nam Tok Mae Surin   WATERFALL

(น้ำตกแม่สุรินทร์; off Rte 1263; 200B) The 100m-high Nam Tok Mae Surin, located in the mountainous Mae Surin National Park, is reportedly Thailand's highest waterfall. It's at its most impressive during the rainy season (June to September). The park is about 32km northeast of Khun Yuam and you'll need private transport to get here.

🛏 Sleeping & Eating

There are modest rice and noodle shops at the northern end of town close to the 7-Eleven, as well as along the east side of Rte 108, towards the southern end of town. Most are closed by 8pm.

Ban Farang   HOTEL $

(☎ 053 622086; www.facebook.com/banfarang; 499 Th Ratburana; incl breakfast r & bungalows 400-1000B; ❄ 🛜) Ban Farang is off the main road towards the northern end of town (look for the signs near the minivan stop), with exceedingly tidy bungalows set on a wooded hillside. The cheaper fan rooms are plain and dark but have a terrace, while the more expensive ones come with air-con, fridge and TV.

Mitkhoonyoum Hotel   HOTEL $$

(☎ 053 691057; www.mitkhoonyoum.com; Rte 108; r 500-1000B, bungalow 1500B; ❄ 🛜) On the main road through town, this long-standing place has simple, fan-cooled rooms, as well as more sizeable and comfortable wood-panelled air-con rooms and bungalows. All are spick and span, if a little dark, and come with OK bathrooms. The owner speaks English and bicycles can be hired (100B per day).

ⓘ Information

There are a couple of banks with ATMs along the main strip.

ⓘ Getting There & Away

All transport to/from Khun Yuam is by minivan or *sŏrng·tăa·ou* (passenger pick-up truck). Minivans depart from a **stop** (Rte 108) at a forecourt in the north of town close to a school. *Sŏrng·tăa·ou* to Mae Hong Son (80B, two hours, 7am and 7.30am) leave from a **stop** (Rte 108) opposite the police station.

TO	FARE (B)	DURATION (HR)	FREQUENCY
Chiang Mai	300	5-6	5 departures 6am-6pm
Mae Hong Son	100	1½	8.30am
Mae Sariang	150	2	5 departures 6am-6pm

LIVE LIKE A LOCAL

The residents of Muang Pon, a picturesque and traditional Shan village just south of Khun Yuam, have collaborated in the Muang Pon Homestay Programme (☑ 087 181 2286; per night incl breakfast & dinner 400B) for more than a decade. Approximately 15 households are involved, and the fee includes breakfast and dinner, and involvement in daily activities such as making traditional handicrafts, cooking local-style sweets, taking part in agriculture and sightseeing.

The locals are keen to open their homes and share their knowledge, but it must be noted that the level of English speaking among the villagers is low.

Muang Pon is about 10km south of Khun Yuam; any minivan bound for Mae Sariang or Chiang Mai can drop you off here.

Mae Sariang

☑ 053 / POP 21,000

Mae Sariang (แม่สะเรียง) has gained a low-key buzz thanks to its attractive riverside setting and its potential as a base for sustainable tourism and hiking and rafting opportunities. There are several settlements of hill peoples in the greater area, particularly around Mae La Noi, 30km north of the Mae Sariang, while the area south of town is largely mountainous jungle encompassing both Salawin and Mae Ngao National Parks.

Mae Sariang itself is a laid-back, friendly town that sees relatively few visitors. Those who do stop here often end up staying longer than they intended.

⊙ Sights

Phra That Jom Thong   BUDDHIST TEMPLE
(พระธาตุจอมทอง; off Rte 105; ☉ daylight hours) This giant, golden hilltop Buddha statue offers great views over Mae Sariang and the surrounding countryside. It's located about 3km south of town, just off the road that leads to Mae Sot.

Wat Jong Sung
& Wat Si Bunruang   BUDDHIST TEMPLE
(วัดจองสูง/วัดศรีบุญเรือง; off Th Wiang Mai; ☉ daylight hours) These two adjacent Burmese-Shan temples are located just off Mae Sariang's main street. Built in 1896, Wat Jong Sung is the more interesting of the two and has slender, Shan-style *chedi* (stupas) and wooden monastic buildings.

🏃 Activities & Tours

The area surrounding Mae Sariang is probably one of the best in Northern Thailand for trekking, nature tours and other outdoor pursuits. It's so good that some tour operators based in Chiang Mai bring people here. There are a couple of Mae Sariang tour outfits that can arrange worthwhile excursions and some guesthouses can also organise hiking and rafting trips. Prices for treks range from 2000B to 5000B per day, per person, for groups of at least two people. Bamboo rafting trips run from around 6000B per day, per person, for a group of at least two people.

Dragon Sabaii Tours   TREKKING
(☑ 085 548 0884; www.thailandhilltribeholidays. com) ✐ This outfit mostly runs tours out of Chiang Mai, but can organise treks from Mae Sariang as well. They emphasise

Mae Sariang

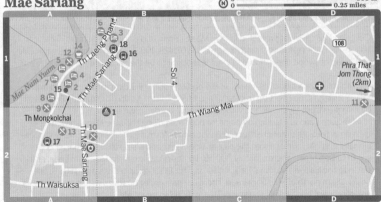

Mae Sariang

⊙ Sights
1 Wat Jong Sung & Wat Si
  Bunruang..B2

⊕ Activities, Courses & Tours
Northwest Tour ....(see 4)

⌷ Sleeping
2 Above The Sea...A1
3 Chok Wasana..B1
4 Northwest Guest House.........................A1
5 PS@Riverview Guesthouse....................A1
6 River Bank Guest House B1
7 Riverhouse Hotel....................................A1
8 Riverhouse Resort A1

⊗ Eating
9 Coriander in Redwood A2
10 Intira Restaurant....................................A2
11 Muu Thup..D1
12 Sawaddee Restaurant & Bar................A1
13 Sunday Market..A2

⊙ Drinking & Nightlife
14 Barnana Cafe...A1

⊕ Transport
15 Mr Beum Bike Rental Shop A1
16 Sombat Tour B1
17 Sŏrng·tăa·ou to Mae Sam Laep A2
18 Sŏrng·tăa·ou to Mae Sot.......................B1

ecotourism and cultural tourism. Potential activities range from non-intrusive tours of hill-tribe villages to homestays, 'volunteerism', and cooking and farming with hill tribes, all of which are designed to directly benefit local communities.

Mae Sariang Tours 1980 TREKKING, RAFTING
(☎088 404 8402; maesariang.man@gmail.com) Mae Sariang Man, as the owner of this company prefers to be known, is an experienced trekker who leads environmentally conscious and community-based treks and rafting trips in the jungles and national parks surrounding his native city, in Sop Moei and even into Myanmar. He has no office in town; call or visit his Facebook page (search 'Mae Sariang Tours 1980') to arrange excursions.

Northwest Tour TREKKING
(☎086 420 4907; Northwest Guest House, 81 Th Laeng Phanit) This outfit can arrange treks to

Karen villages and natural environments in Mae Sariang and Sop Moei Districts.

⌷ Sleeping

PS@Riverview Guesthouse GUESTHOUSE $
(☎053 681049; www.facebook.com/psRiverview; 79 Th Laeng Phanit; r 250-450B; ❈☎) This guesthouse is the cheapest Mae Sariang digs with river views, with 11 rooms that are simple but reasonably sized and with hot-water bathrooms. Only the most expensive have air-con. The owner is affable and there's a small communal area for riverside beers.

Northwest Guest House GUESTHOUSE $
(☎086 420 4907; patiat_1@hotmail.com; 81 Th Laeng Phanit; r 200-500B; ☺Oct-Mar; ❈☎) The cheapest rooms in this cosy wooden house are fan-cooled, share bathrooms and are mattress-on-the-floor basic. The more expensive rooms offer some space and natural light and come with air-con and a private bathroom. There's free bicycle use for guests

WORTH A TRIP

SALAWIN NATIONAL PARK & MAE SAM LAEP

Covering 722 sq km of protected land in Mae Sariang and Sop Moei districts, **Salawin National Park** (อุทยานแห่งชาติสาละวิน; ☎053 071429; 100B) is heavily forested with teak and Asian redwood and is home to what is thought to be the second-largest teak tree in Thailand.

Within the park's bounds, nearly at the end of a 50km winding mountain road from Mae Sariang, is the riverside trading village of **Mae Sam Laep** (แม่สามแลบ). Populated by refugees from Myanmar, the village has a raw, border-town feel.

Mae Sam Laep is a launching point for boat trips along the Mae Nam Salawin. These trips pass through untouched jungle, unusual rock formations along the river and occasionally enter Myanmar. From the pier at Mae Sam Laep it's possible to charter boats south to Sop Moei (approximately 2000B, 1½ hours), 25km from Mae Sam Laep, and north to the Salawin National Park station at Tha Ta Fang (approximately 1500B, one hour), 18km north of Mae Sam Laep. There are passenger boats as well, but departures are infrequent and, unless you speak Thai, difficult to negotiate.

Sŏrng·tăa·ou (passenger pick-up trucks) from Mae Sariang to Mae Sam Laep (100B, two hours, five departures from 7am to noon) depart from a stop on Th Laeng Phanit near the morning market.

and treks and tours can be arranged here. The guesthouse shuts down from April to September.

★Riverhouse Hotel HOTEL $$
(☎053 682323; www.riverhousehotelgroup.com; 77 Th Laeng Phanit; r incl breakfast 900-1100B; ❄📶) The combination of teak and stylish decor – not to mention the riverside location – makes this boutique hotel the best spot in town. Rooms have air-con, huge balconies overlooking the river, as well as floor-to-ceiling windows. Guests here can use the pool at the Riverhouse Resort (p306), just south on Th Laeng Phanit and run by the same folks.

Chok Wasana GUESTHOUSE $$
(☎053 682132; www.chok-wasana.com; 104 Th Laeng Phanit; r incl breakfast 800-1000B; ❄📶) If you don't require river views, consider one of the six well-kept rooms in this residential-like compound. They're spacious and come equipped with TVs and large refrigerators.

Above The Sea HOTEL $$
(☎091 859 5264, 053 682264; www.abovethesea maesariang.com; Th Laeng Phanit; r incl breakfast 1200-1500B; ❄📶🏊) This place has nine decent-sized, comfortable rooms on two levels decked out in an industrial-chic-artsy style, including one large 'family room' with a basic kitchenette.

Downstairs rooms are poolside, upstairs ones share a wide communal balcony. There's also a bar/restaurant and motorbikes can be hired.

River Bank Guest House GUESTHOUSE $$
(☎053 682787; riverbankmaesariang@gmail.com; Th Laeng Phanit; r 600-800B, f 1500B; ❄📶) Rooms in this attractive riverfront house are decked out in hardwood and have terraces. It's worth shelling out 200B more for the rooms on the upper floors, which get loads of natural light. The stylish and inviting communal riverside balcony is a highlight.

Riverhouse Resort HOTEL $$$
(☎053 683066; www.riverhousehotelgroup.com; Th Laeng Phanit; r incl breakfast 1800-2800B; ❄@📶🏊) Located close to the Riverhouse Hotel, and efficiently run by the same people, this place backs onto the river and has a pool. The wood-floored rooms are comfortable, if a little plain for the price, but the more expensive ones come with bathtubs and safety boxes. Free bicycles for guests.

Eating & Drinking

Th Laeng Phanit, north of the junction with Th Mongkolchai, is home to a small strip of riverside bars.

★Muu Thup THAI $
(Th Wiang Mai; mains 35-175B; ⏲8am-6pm) An authentic – and utterly delicious – northern Thai–style grilled-meat shack. You can't go wrong with the eponymous *mŏo đúp* (pork that's been grilled then tenderised with a mallet). There's no Roman-script sign, but look for the crowd of salivating locals standing around a smoking grill.

TRANSPORT FROM MAE SARIANG

DESTINATION	FARE (B)	DURATION (HR)	FREQUENCY
Bangkok	581-904	12	4 departures 4-7.30pm
Chiang Mai	200	4-5	10 departures 7am-10pm
Khun Yuam	150	3	5 departures 10am-6pm
Mae Hong Son	150	3-4	7am & 2pm

Sunday Market   THAI $
(Th Wiang Mai; mains 30-60B; ⊘3-8pm Sun) If
you're in Mae Sariang on a Sunday, don't
miss this tiny but worthwhile market, where
you'll find an impressive selection of local-style dishes.

Sawaddee Restaurant & Bar   THAI $
(Th Laeng Phanit; mains 50-180B; ⊘6pm-mid-
night; 🛜🍴) Like a beachside bar, Sawaddee
is a great place to recline with a beer and
watch the water (in this case the Mae Nam
Yuam). There's a lengthy menu with lots
of options for vegetarians. The owners are
good sources of information for fun destinations and activities in the area.

Intira Restaurant   THAI $
(Th Wiang Mai; mains 80-250B; ⊘8am-9pm; 🍴)
Deservedly popular, the Intira offers tasty
and reliable Thai and northern Thai dishes,
including some that use unusual ingredients
such as locally grown shiitake mushrooms
and fish from Mae Nam Moei. There are
also a few veggie options. Some English is
spoken.

Coriander in Redwood   THAI $$
(Th Laeng Phanit; mains 100-470B; ⊘11am-10pm;
🛜) The city's poshest restaurant, this attractive and breezy wooden structure makes a
big deal of its steaks, but the Thai dishes,
such as the various *nám prík* (chilli-based
dips) are fine, too. There's also ice cream and
iced coffee drinks for an afternoon cooler.

Barnana Cafe   CAFE
(Th Laeng Phanit; ⊘7am-6pm; 🧒) A family-
friendly cafe – paints for the kids – with

sofas and comfy leather seats that offer good
river views. It does coffee and smoothies as
well as breakfasts, a few pasta dishes and
Thai bites.

ℹ Information

Mae Sariang has several banks with ATMs and
exchange facilities, mostly along the western
end of Th Wiang Mai.

Hospital (☏053 681032; 74 Th Wiang Mai;
⊘24hr) Mae Sariang's main hospital.

Police Station (☏emergency 191; Th Mae
Sariang; ⊘24hr) Mae Sariang's principal police
station.

ℹ Getting There & Away

Apart from buses to Bangkok, handled by
Sombat Tour (☏053 681532; Th Mae Sariang;
⊘7am-7.30pm), all transport in and out of Mae
Sariang is by minivan or *sŏrng·tăa·ou* (passenger
pick-up truck). Minivans leave from a **terminal**
(off Rte 108) at a forecourt a couple of kilometres north of town just off Rte 108.

Yellow *sŏrng·tăa·ou* to **Mae Sam Laep** (Th
Laeng Phanit) (100B, two hours, five departures
7am to noon) depart from a stop on Th Laeng
Phanit, while *sŏrng·tăa·ou* to **Mae Sot** (Th Mae
Sariang) (200B, six hours, hourly 6.30am to
noon) depart from a covered stop across the
street from Sombat Tour.

ℹ Getting Around

Motorcycles (200B per day) and bicycles (50B
to 100B per day) are available for hire at the **Mr
Beum Bike Rental Shop** (☏084 485 2525;
Th Mongkolchai; ⊘6am-6pm) and at a few
guesthouses.

AT A GLANCE

POPULATION
1.7 million

HEIGHT OF DOI INTHANON
2565 m above sea level (Thailand's highest mountain; p364)

BEST HIDDEN TEMPLE
Wat Pha Lat (p324)

BEST MARKET
Talat Warorot (p320)

BEST HIKING TRAIL
Monk's Trail (p327)

WHEN TO GO
Nov–Jan During cool season, temperatures are mild and rain is scarce.

Mar–Jun Mercury regularly climbs above 35°C. March and April are Chiang Mai's smoky season when the air quality drops.

May–Oct Monsoon rains usually peak in August and September.

Wat Chedi Luang (p315), Chiang Mai
SEAN PAVONE/SHUTTERSTOCK ©

Chiang Mai Province

Thailand's northern capital is an overnight train ride and light-years away from the bustle of Bangkok. Wrestled from Burmese control by the kingdom of Siam, the former capital of the Lanna people is a captivating collection of glimmering monasteries, manic markets, modern shopping centres, and quiet residential streets that wouldn't look amiss in a remote village.

It's more country retreat than mega-metropolis, but this beguiling city still lures everyone from backpacking teenagers to young families, round-the-world retirees and an expanding contingent of tourists from China. Historic monasteries and cooking courses are highlights. Get out into the surrounding Chiang Mai Province to find a jumble of forested hills, great for rafting, hiking, mountain biking and other adrenalin-charged activities. Most visitors will leave the city at least once to interact with elephants, dip into hot springs, and wander experimental farms and botanic gardens.

INCLUDES

CHIANG MAI

☑ 053 / POP 201,000

The former seat of the Lanna kingdom is a blissfully calm and laid-back place to relax and recharge your batteries. Participate in a vast array of activities, or just stroll around the backstreets, and discover a city that is firmly Thai in its atmosphere and attitude.

A sprawling modern city has grown up around ancient Chiang Mai (เชียงใหม่), ringed by a tangle of superhighways. Despite this, the historic centre of Chiang Mai still feels overwhelmingly residential, more like a sleepy country town than a bustling capital. If you drive in a straight line in any direction, you'll soon find yourself in the lush green countryside and pristine rainforests dotted with churning waterfalls, serene wát and peaceful country villages – as well as a host of markets and elephant sanctuaries.

History

King Phaya Mengrai (also spelt Mangrai) is credited for founding the kingdom of Lanna in the 13th century from his seat at Chiang Saen, but his first attempt at building a new capital on the banks of Mae Ping at Wiang Kum Kam lasted only a few years: the city was eventually abandoned due to flooding.

In 1296 King Mengrai relocated his capital to a more picturesque spot between the river and Doi Suthep mountain and named the promising city Nopburi Si Nakhon Ping Chiang Mai (shortened to Chiang Mai, meaning 'New Walled City'). In the 14th and 15th centuries, the Lanna kingdom expanded as far south as Kamphaeng Phet and as far north as Luang Prabang in Laos, but it fell to Burmese invaders in 1556, starting an occupation that lasted 200 years.

After the fall of Ayuthaya in 1767 to the Burmese, the defeated Thai army regrouped under Phraya Taksin in present-day Bangkok and began a campaign to push out the occupying Burmese forces. Chao Kavila (also spelt Kawila), a chieftain from nearby Lampang principality, helped 'liberate' northern Thailand from Burmese control, and was appointed king of the northern states, placing Chiang Mai under the authority of the kingdom of Siam.

Under Kavila, Chiang Mai became an important trading centre, aided by its abundant supplies of teak, and monumental brick walls were built around the inner city. Many of the later Burmese-style temples were built by wealthy teak merchants who emigrated from Burma during this period. In their wake came missionaries and British teak concessionaires who built colonial-style villas around the old city.

The demise of the semi-autonomous Lanna state was only a matter of time. Bangkok designated Chiang Mai as an administrative unit in 1892 in the face of expanding colonial rule in neighbouring Burma and Laos, and the Lanna princess Dara Rasmee was sent to Bangkok to become one of the official consorts of King Rama V, cementing the ties between the two royal families.

The completion of the northern railway to Chiang Mai in 1922 finally linked the north with central Thailand and in 1933 Chiang Mai officially became a province of Siam. Even so, Chiang Mai remained relatively undeveloped until 2001, when prime minister and Chiang Mai native Thaksin Shinawatra sought to modernise the city by expanding the airport and building superhighways.

A high-speed rail link to Bangkok that will reduce travel time to 3½ hours is largely still in planning stages, but construction on an initial section began in 2017.

◉ Sights

Chiang Mai overflows with temples, markets and museums, but don't overlook the sights outside the old city, both inside and outside the fringing highways.

◉ Old City

Within the old city, temples dominate the skyline, orange-robed monks weave in and out of the tourist crowds and the atmosphere is more like a country town than a heaving modern city. However, the residential feel of the old city is changing as government offices move out, residents sell up and developers move in.

Suan Buak Hat   PARK

(สวนสาธารณะหนองบวกหาด; Map p312 Th Bamrungburi; ⊙5am-9pm; ⏰) The old city's only public park is a delightful spot to unwind, particularly as the afternoon sun slides towards the horizon. In the mornings and evenings locals gather for Tai Chi, yoga, jogging on running tracks, playground time, feeding the fish and ducks in the ponds, or just hiring reed mats (15B) to sit and relax.

Wát & Religious Sites

The highlight of any visit to the old city is exploring the temples that burst out on

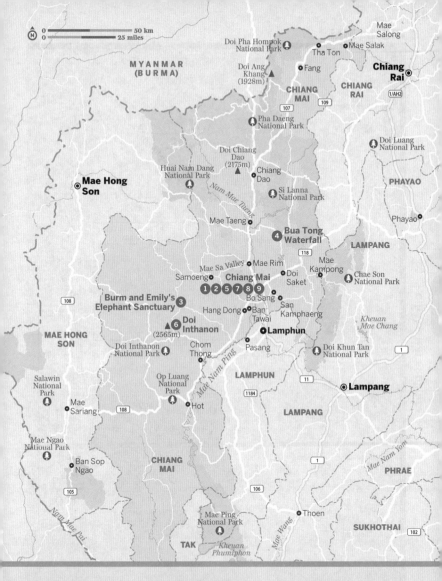

Chiang Mai Province Highlights

1 Monk's Trail (p327) Hiking alongside monks en route to Wat Pha Lat and Wat Phra That Doi Suthep.

2 Talat Warorot (p320) Plunging into Chiang Mai's timeless commercial beehive.

3 Ethical elephant visits (p361) Observing these wonderful creatures.

4 Sticky Waterfall (p360) Day-tripping to forest paradise and walking up a waterfall.

5 Kao Soi Fueng Fah (p343) Searching for your favourite *kôw soy*.

6 Doi Inthanon (p364) Driving to Thailand's highest peak and trekking in the forest.

7 Cooking classes (p331) Learning how to make the perfect green curry.

8 Monk Chat (p315) Meeting monks and discovering what motivates Chiang Mai's men in orange.

9 Sunday Walking Street (p352) Joining the human shopping parade.

Chiang Mai

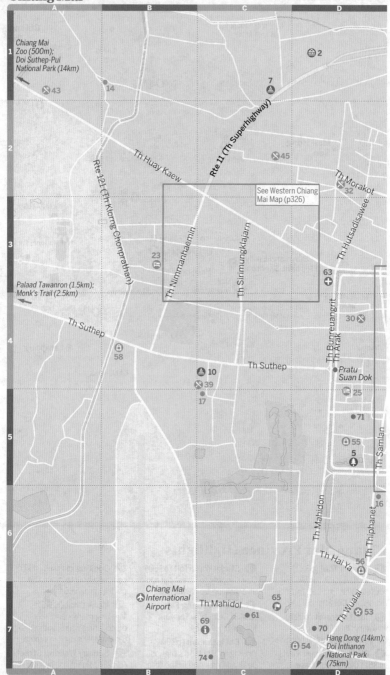

CHIANG MAI PROVINCE

Chiang Mai
Zoo (500m);
Doi Suthep-Pui
National Park (14km)

43

14

2

7

Th Huay Kaew

Rte 11 (Th Superhighway)

45

Th Morakot

32

See Western Chiang
Mai Map (p326)

Rte 121 (Th Klong Chonprathan)

Th Nimmanhaemin

Th Srimungklajarn

Th Hutsadisawee

23

63

Palaad Tawanron (1.5km);
Monk's Trail (2.5km)

Th Suthep

30

58

Th Bunreuangrit

Th Arak

Th Suthep

10

39

Pratu
Suan Dok

25

17

71

Th Samlan

55

5

16

Th Mahidol

Th Thiphanet

Th Hai Ya

56

Chiang Mai
International
Airport

Th Mahidol

65

53

Th Wualai

61

69

70

54

74

Hang Dong (14km);
Doi Inthanon
National Park
(75km)

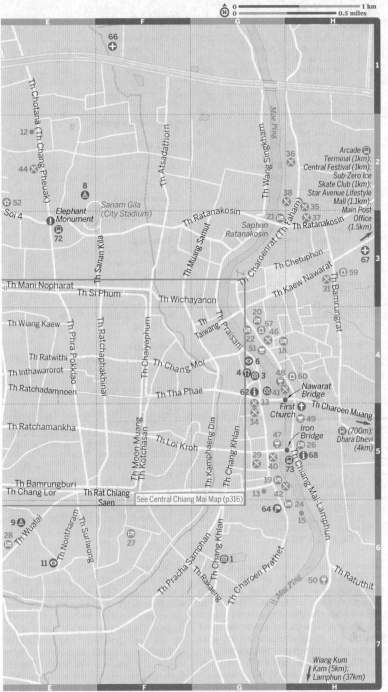

0 — 1 km
0 — 0.5 miles

66

Th Chotana (Th Chang Pheuak)

12

44

52
Soi 4

8

Elephant Monument

72

Sanam Gila (City Stadium)

Th Atsadathorn

Th Sanan Kila

Th Muang Samut

Th Ratanakosin

36

Mae Ping

Th Wang Singkham

38

21

35
37
Th Ratanakosin

Saphan Ratanakosin

Th Charoenrat (Th Faham)

Arcade
Terminal (1km);
Central Festival (1km);
Sub-Zero Ice
Skate Club (1km);
Star Avenue Lifestyle
Mall (1.1km);
Main Post
Office
(1.5km)

67

Th Chetuphon

Th Kaew Nawarat

Th Bamrungrat

59

31

Th Mani Nopharat

Th Si Phum

Th Wichayanon

Th Wiang Kaew

Th Phra Pokklao

Th Ratchaphakhinai

Th Ratwithi

Th Inthawarorot

Th Ratchadamnoen

Th Chaiyaphum

Th Chang Moi

Th
Taiwang

Th Prasani

Th Tha Phae

20

57

22

51

6

4

3

62

33

34

48

46

18

41

60

First
Church

Nawarat
Bridge

Th Charoen Muang

Dhara Dhevi
(700m);
(4km)

Th Ratchamankha

Th Moon Muang

Th Kotchasan

Th Loi Kroh

Th Kamphaeng Din

Th Chang Khlan

Iron
Bridge

49

47

26

68

73

29

40

19

13

42

Th Chiang Mai-Lamphun

Th Bamrungburi

Th Chang Lor

Th Rat Chiang
Saen

See Central Chiang Mai Map (p316)

64

24

15

9

28

Th Wualai

Th Nontharam

Th Suriwong

27

11

1

Th Pracha Samphan

Th Rakaeng

Th Chang Khlan

Th Charoen Prathet

Mae Ping

50

Th Ratuthit

Wiang Kum
Kam (5km);
Lamphun (37km)

Chiang Mai

almost every street corner, attracting hordes of pilgrims, tourists and local worshippers. For a calmer experience, visit late in the afternoon, when the tourist crowds are replaced by monks attending evening prayers. Visitors are welcome but follow the standard rules of Buddhist etiquette: stay quiet during prayers, keep your feet pointed away from Buddha images and monks, and dress modestly (covering shoulders and knees).

★ **Wat Phra Singh**   BUDDHIST TEMPLE
(วัดพระสิงห์; Map p316; Th Singharat; ☉5am-8.30pm) Chiang Mai's most revered temple, Wat Phra Singh is dominated by an enormous, mosaic-inlaid *wí·hăhn* (sanctuary). Its prosperity is plain to see from the lavish monastic buildings and immaculately trimmed grounds, dotted with coffee stands and massage pavilions. Pilgrims flock here to venerate the famous Buddha

image known as Phra Singh (Lion Buddha), housed in Wihan Lai Kham, a small chapel immediately south of the *chedi* (stupa) to the rear of the temple grounds.

This elegant idol is said to have come to Thailand from Sri Lanka and was enshrined in 1367. The chapel is similarly striking, with gilded *naga* (serpent) gables and sumptuous *lai·krahm* (gold-pattern stencilling) inside.

Despite Phra Singh's exalted status, very little is known about the Phra Singh image, which has more in common with images from northern Thailand than with Buddha statues from Sri Lanka. Adding to the mystery, there are two nearly identical images elsewhere in Thailand, one in the Bangkok National Museum and one in Wat Phra Mahathat Woramahawihan in Nakhon Si Thammarat. Regardless of its provenance, the statue has become a focal point for celebrations during the Songkran festival.

As you wander the monastery grounds, note the raised temple library, housed in a dainty teak and stucco pavilion known as Ho Trai, decorated with bas-relief angels in the style of Wat Chet Yot. The temple's main *chedi*, rising over a classic Lanna-style octagonal base, was constructed by King Pa Yo in 1345; it's often wrapped in bolts of orange cloth by devotees.

★ Wat Chedi Luang   BUDDHIST TEMPLE
(วัดเจดีย์หลวง; Map p316; Th Phra Pokklao; adult/child 40/20B; ⊙5am-10.30pm) Wat Chedi Luang isn't as grand as Wat Phra Singh, but its towering, ruined Lanna-style *chedi* (built in 1441) is much taller and the sprawling compound around the stupa is powerfully atmospheric. The famed Phra Kaew (Emerald Buddha), now held in Bangkok's Wat Phra Kaew, resided in the eastern niche until 1475; today, you can view a jade replica.

This was possibly the largest structure in ancient Chiang Mai, but the top of the *chedi* was destroyed by either a 16th-century earthquake or by cannon fire during the recapture of Chiang Mai from the Burmese in 1775 (nobody knows for sure). Like most of the ancient monuments in Chiang Mai, Chedi Luang was in ruins when the city began its modern renaissance, but a restoration project by Unesco and the Japanese government in the 1990s stabilised the monument and prevented further degradation.

As you wander around the *chedi* you can easily spot the restoration work on the four *naga* stairways in each of the cardinal directions. The base of the stupa has five elephant sculptures on the southern face – four are reproductions, but the elephant on the far right is the original brick and stucco. The restorers stopped short of finishing the spire, as nobody could agree what it looked like.

In the main *wí·hăhn* is a revered standing Buddha statue, known as Phra Chao Attarot, flanked by two disciples. There are more chapels and statues in teak pavilions at the rear of the compound, including a huge reclining Buddha and a handsome Chinese-influenced seated Buddha barely contained by his robes. The daily Monk Chat under a tree in the grounds always draws a crowd of interested travellers.

If you enter the compound via the main entrance on Th Phra Pokklao, you'll pass Wat Chedi Luang's other claim to fame, the Làk Meuang (หลักเมือง, City Pillar; ⊙daylight hours).

★ Wat Phan Tao   BUDDHIST TEMPLE
(วัดพันเตา; Map p316; Th Phra Pokklao; donations appreciated; ⊙daylight hours) Without doubt the most atmospheric *wát* in the old city, this teak marvel sits in the shadow of Wat

CHIANG MAI PROVINCE CHIANG MAI

MONK CHAT

If you're curious about Buddhism, many Chiang Mai temples offer popular Monk Chat sessions, where novice monks get to practise their English and tourists get to find out about the inner workings of monastery life. It's a fascinating opportunity to discover a little more about the rituals and customs that most Thai men undertake for at least a small portion of their lives. Remember to dress modestly as a sign of respect: cover your shoulders and knees. Because of ritual taboos, women should take care not to touch the monks or their belongings, or to pass anything directly to them.

Wat Suan Dok (p327) Dedicated room for Monk Chats from 4pm to 7pm Monday to Friday.

Wat Srisuphan (p323) Holds chats from 5.30pm to 7.15pm on Tuesday, Thursday and Saturday, with meditation sessions following.

Wat Chedi Luang Has a table under a shady tree where monks chat from 8am to 5pm daily.

Central Chiang Mai

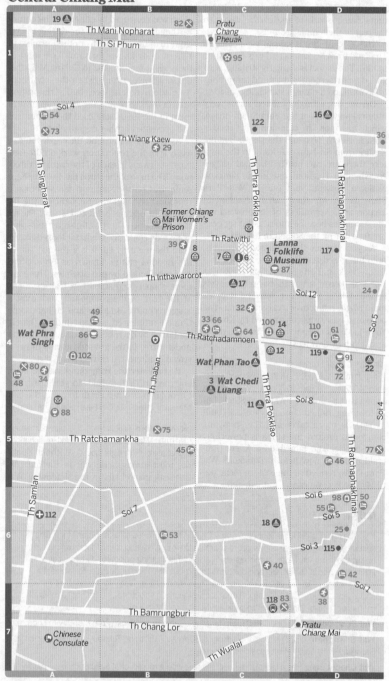

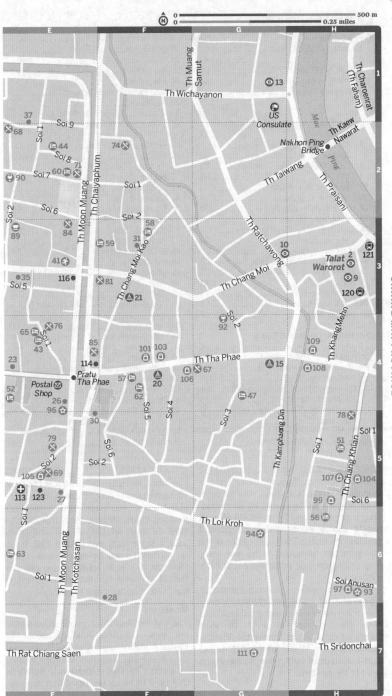

Central Chiang Mai

Chedi Luang (p315). Set in a compound full of fluttering orange flags, the monastery is a monument to the teak trade, with an enormous prayer hall supported by 28 gargantuan teak pillars and lined with dark teak panels, enshrining a particularly graceful gold Buddha image. The juxtaposition of the orange monks' robes against this dark backdrop during evening prayers is particularly sublime.

Above the facade is a striking image of a peacock over a dog, representing the astrological year of the former royal resident's birth. The monastery is one of the focal points for celebrations during the Visakha Bucha festival in May or June, when monks light hundreds of butter lamps around the pond in the grounds.

Wat Chiang Man   BUDDHIST TEMPLE

(วัดเชียงมั่น; Map p316; Th Ratchaphakhinai; donations appreciated; ◎ daylight hours) Chiang Mai's oldest temple was established by the city's founder, Phaya Mengrai, sometime around 1296. In front of the *ubosot* (ordination hall), a stone slab, engraved in 1581, bears the earliest-known reference to the city's founding. The main *wí·hăhn* also contains the oldest-known Buddha image created by the Lanna kingdom, cast in 1465.

Museums

The old city has three excellent historical museums – the Lanna Folklife Museum, the Chiang Mai City Arts & Cultural Centre and the Chiang Mai Historical Centre – located in a series of Thai-colonial-style buildings that used to house the city administration.

You can buy a single ticket covering all three, valid for a week, for 180/80B (adult/child).

⭐ **Lanna Folklife Museum**   MUSEUM
(พิพิธภัณฑ์พื้นถิ่นล้านนา; Map p316; ☏ 053 217793; www.cmocity.com; Th Phra Pokklao; adult/child 90/40B, combo ticket adult/child 180/80B; ⏱ 8.30am-5pm Tue-Sun) Set inside the former Provincial Court, dating from 1935, this imaginative museum re-creates Lanna village life in a series of life-size dioramas that explain everything from *lai-krahm* pottery stencilling and *fon lep* (a mystical Lanna dance featuring long metal fingernails) to the intricate symbolism of different elements of Lanna-style monasteries.

Chiang Mai Historical Centre   MUSEUM
(หอประวัติศาสตร์เมืองเชียงใหม่; Map p316; ☏ 053 217793; www.cmocity.com; Th Ratwithi;

adult/child 90/40B, combo ticket adult/child 180/80B; ⏱ 8.30am-5pm Tue-Sun) Housed in an airy Lanna-style building behind the Chiang Mai City Arts & Cultural Centre, this museum covers the history of Chiang Mai Province, with displays on the founding of the capital, Burmese occupation and the modern era of trade and unification with Bangkok.

Chiang Mai City Arts & Cultural Centre   MUSEUM
(หอศิลปวัฒนธรรมเชียงใหม่; Map p316; ☏ 053 217793; www.cmocity.com; Th Phra Pokklao; adult/child 90/40B, combo ticket adult/child 180/80B; ⏱ 8.30am-5pm Tue-Sun) Set in the former Provincial Hall, dating from 1927, this museum provides an excellent primer on Chiang Mai history. Dioramas, photos, artefacts and audiovisual displays walk

visitors through the key battles and victories in Chiang Mai's story, from the first settlements to the arrival of the railway. Upstairs there's a charming re-creation of a wooden Lanna village.

Lanna Architecture Center MUSEUM
(ศูนย์สถาปัตยกรรมล้านนา; Map p316; www.lanna-arch.net; 117 Th Ratchadamnoen; ⊙9am-5pm Tue-Sat, 1-8pm Sun) FREE Formerly owned by prince Jao Maha In, this handsome mansion built in a hybrid Lanna and European style between 1889 and 1893 houses a small education centre with some interesting models showing the changing face of Lanna architecture through the centuries.

Treasury Pavilion Coin Museum MUSEUM
(ศาลาธนารักษ์; Map p316; Treasury Pavilion, 52 Th Ratchadamnoen; ⊙8.30am-4pm Mon-Fri) FREE It's worth ducking into this government museum to see the bizarre shapes that Thai money has taken over the years, from hammered coins to silver balls and ingots.

◉ East of the Old City & Riverside

Beyond Pratu Tha Phae is Chiang Mai's traditional commercial quarter, with sprawling bazaars and old-fashioned shophouses running down to the riverbank.

★Talat Warorot MARKET
(ตลาดวโรรส; Map p316; cnr Th Chang Moi & Th Praisani; ⊙6am-5pm) Chiang Mai's oldest public market, Warorot (also spelt Waroros) is a great place to connect with the city's Thai soul. Alongside souvenir vendors you'll find numerous stalls selling items for ordinary Thai households: woks, toys, fishing nets, pickled tea leaves, wigs, sticky-rice steamers, Thai-style sausages, *kâab mŏo* (pork rinds), live catfish and tiny statues for spirit houses.

It's easy to spend half a day wandering the covered walkways, watching locals browsing, and haggling for goods that actually have a practical use back home.

You'll know you've arrived at the market when traffic comes to a standstill and carts

---

WÁT TO SEE AROUND TOWN

If you still have a taste for more Thai religious architecture, there are dozens more historic wát scattered around the old city and the surrounding streets. Here are some good places to start your explorations.

Wat Inthakhin Saduemuang (วัดอินทขิลสะดือเมือง; Map p316; Th Inthawararot; donations accepted; ⊙5am-9pm) Marooned in the middle of Th Inthawararot, this was the original location of the *làk meuˑang* (city pillar), and the gilded teak *wíˑhǎhn* (sanctuary) is one of the most perfectly proportioned buildings in the city.

Wat Phan On (วัดพันอั้น; Map p316; Th Ratchadamnoen; donations appreciated; ⊙6am-5pm) Set with gilded Buddhas in alcoves decorated with *lai krahm* (gold-pattern stencilling), the gold *chedi* (stupa) at this prosperous wát is visited by scores of devotees after dark. The courtyard becomes a food court during the Sunday Walking Street (p352) market.

Wat Jet Lin (วัดเจ็ดลิน หรือ วัดหนองจลิน; Map p316; Th Phra Pokklao; donations appreciated; ⊙4am-6pm) This friendly wát was used for the coronation of Lanna kings in the 16th century; today you can see a collection of giant gongs, a big old *mon·dòp*-style *chedi* and a large gilded Buddha with particularly graceful proportions.

Wat Lok Moli (วัดโลกโมฬี; Map p316; 298/1 Th Mani Nopharat; donations appreciated; ⊙6am-6pm) An elegant wooden complex dotted with terracotta sculptures. The *wíˑhǎhn* is topped by a dramatic sweeping three-tiered roof and the tall, barrel-shaped *chedi* still has some of its original stucco.

Wat Ou Sai Kham (วัดอู่ทรายคำ; Map p316; Th Chang Moi Kao; donations appreciated; ⊙7am-6pm) This friendly neighbourhood wát has an impressive collection of jade Buddhas and jade and nephrite boulders in its main *wíˑhǎhn*.

Wat Mahawan (วัดมหาวัน; Map p316; Th Tha Phae; donations appreciated; ⊙6am-6pm) A handsome, whitewashed wát that shows the obvious influence of the Burmese teak traders who used to worship here. The *chedi* and Burmese-style gateways are decorated with a stucco menagerie of angels and mythical beasts.

TEAK-ERA CHIANG MAI

Chiang Mai was never colonised by European powers, but the city has many of the hallmarks of European influence, dating back to the time when teak concessionaires from Britain and the US built fortunes on the timber being hauled from surrounding forests.

One of the most striking colonial relics is the weatherboard **First Church** (คริสตจักร ที่ ๑ เชียงใหม่; Map p312; Th Chiang Mai-Lamphun), just south of Nawarat Bridge on the east bank, founded by the Laos Mission from North Carolina in 1868. Just south of here, the Iron Bridge was built as a homage to an older, demolished Nawarat Bridge, whose steel beams were fabricated by engineers from Cleveland in England. Local folklore states that the famous Memorial Bridge in Pai is not a WWII relic but a 1970s fake, built using reclaimed beams from Chiang Mai's Nawarmat Bridge.

If you head in the other direction along the west bank, you'll pass the colonial-style former **Main Post Office**, which now houses a small **philatelic museum** (พิพิธภัณฑ์ ตราไปรษณียากร; Map p312; Th Praisani; ⊙9am-4pm Tue-Sun) FREE. Similar Thai-colonial administrative buildings spread out around the junction of Th Ratwithi and Th Phra Pokklao in the old city, where the former **Provincial Hall**, now the Chiang Mai City Arts & Cultural Centre (p319), and **Provincial Courthouse**, now the Lanna Folklife Museum (p319), show the clear influence of the British 'gentlemen foresters' who controlled 60% of Chiang Mai's teak industry in the 19th and 20th centuries.

Many of the teak concessionaires' mansions have fallen into disrepair, but the colonial style of architecture was adopted by the Lanna royal family. One of the most impressive surviving teak-era mansions is the Lanna Architecture Center (p320), formerly owned by prince Jao Maha In, built between 1889 and 1893; it displays some interesting models showing the changing face of Lanna architecture through the centuries. The former British Consulate, now the Service 1921 (p344) restaurant at the Anantara Resort, the central building at 137 Pillars (p339), and the Dara Pirom Palace (p358) in Mae Rim are also fine examples of this hybrid style.

laden with merchandise weave between the cars. The location by the river is no coincidence; historically, most of the farm produce sold in Chiang Mai was delivered here by boat along Mae Ping.

Immediately adjacent to Talat Warorot is Talat Ton Lam Yai, the city's main flower market, and to the south are more bazaars, full of 'wet and dry' foodstuffs, fabric vendors, Chinese goldsmiths and apparel stalls. The northern end of the bazaar area is thronged by fruit vendors selling bushels of lychees, longans, mangosteens and rambutans. Sǎhm·lór (three-wheel pedicabs, now rarely seen in the city) wait to shuttle shoppers home with their produce.

Talat Ton Lam Yai　　　　　　MARKET
(ตลาดต้นลำไย; Map p312; Th Praisani; ⊙24hr) Adjacent to Talat Warorot, Talat Ton Lam Yai morphs from a covered household market into an animated flower market (gàht dòrk mái), flanking the river on Th Praisani. Florists here are almost architects, assembling blooms and banana leaves into fantastically elaborate sculptures for festivals and home shrines.

The smell of jasmine floats along the passageways, and drivers stop outside day and night to purchase strings of miniature roses and jasmine blossoms to sweeten their cabs. Though the market is open 24/7, the bulk of its trade takes place after dark, away from the wilting daytime heat, and goes into overdrive for festivals such as Loi Krathong and the annual Flower Festival.

During the day Talat Ton Lam Yai also features fresh and wet market sections as well as indoor stalls in a multistorey building filled with Buddhist decorations, toys, dried goods and clothing.

**Maiiam Contemporary
Art Museum**　　　　　　MUSEUM
(☑052 081737; www.maiiam.com; 122 Mu 7, Tonpao, San Kamphaeng; adult/student/child under 12yr 150/100B/free; ⊙10am-6pm Wed-Mon; P) Located on the 'handicraft highway' between Chiang Mai and San Kamphaeng, this museum showcases the only standalone collection of Thai and Southeast Asian contemporary art in the country. The small but innovative museum is housed in a converted warehouse and brings a sense of urban sophistication to Chiang Mai's rather rural

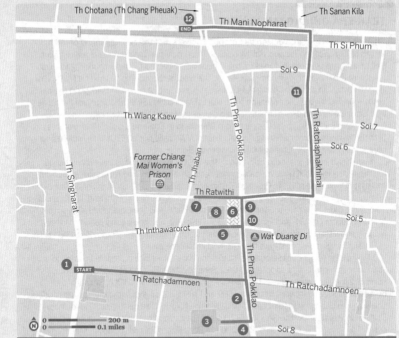

City Walk
Old City Temple Tour

START WAT PHRA SINGH
END TALAT PRATU CHANG PHEUAK
LENGTH 2.5KM; FIVE HOURS

No visit to Chiang Mai is complete without a temple tour. Start with the best, **1 Wat Phra Singh** (p314), home to the city's most revered Buddha image, the Lion Buddha, then stroll down Th Ratchadamnoen and turn right onto Th Phra Pokklao. In swift succession, you'll get to the gorgeous teak *wí·hǎhn* of **2 Wat Phan Tao** (p315), which deserves a good wander, and the looming mass of **3 Wat Chedi Luang** (p315), the largest and grandest Lanna *chedi* in the city. Perform a ceremonial circumambulation clockwise around the stupa, then duck into the **4 Làk Meuang** (p315; Buddhist rules dictate that only men enter) to view the revered city pillar.

Follow Th Phra Pokklao north to the junction with Th Inthawarorot, where you'll see the postcard-perfect *wí·hǎhn* of **5 Wat Inthakhin Saduemuang** (p320), which enshrined the city pillar in medieval times,

perched surreally in the middle of the road. Walk another block north on Th Phra Pokklao to the **6 Anusawari Sam Kasat** (อนุสาวรีย์สามกษัตริย์; Map p316; Th Phra Pokklao), and pay your respects to the three Lanna kings who founded Chiang Mai. You are now in the perfect location to take in Chiang Mai's trinity of excellent city museums, the airy, Lanna-style **7 Chiang Mai Historical Centre** (p319), the large **8 Chiang Mai City Arts & Cultural Centre** (p319) in a 1927 colonial building, and the **9 Lanna Folklife Museum** (p319), which is arguably the best museum in town (all accessible on a combination ticket). If you're hungry or just want to relax over blended Thai tea or ice coffee, the **10 Café de Museum** (p348) is your spot.

Continue north along Th Ratchaphakhinai to reach atmospheric and ancient **11 Wat Chiang Man** (p318), the oldest *wát* in a city awash with ancient temples. To finish, walk on to the moat and enjoy the Cowboy Hat Lady's fabulous *kôw kǎh mǒo* (slow-cooked pork leg with rice) at **12 Talat Pratu Chang Pheuak** (p342).

setting. It also contains a restaurant and small gift shop.

Featuring the private collection of one family along with temporary exhibitions, the Maiiam shows a different side to Thai art than the readily reproduced traditional woodcarvings, temple paintings and historic handicrafts.

Talat Muang Mai
MARKET

(ตลาดเมืองใหม่; Map p316; Th Praisani; ⏰24hr) Chiang Mai's main wholesale fruit market is a riot of activity every morning, when enormous cargoes of mangoes, durians, rambutans, longans, watermelons, Malay apples, passionfruit and just about any other tropical fruit that are in season are unloaded from trucks along the east bank and sold on to juice-stand owners and market traders.

Chinatown
AREA

(ไชน่าทาวน์; Map p316; Th Chang Moi) The area dominated by the Warorot and Ton Lam Yai markets doubles as the city's small Chinatown, marked by a flamboyant **Chinese welcome gate** (ประตูต้อนรับจีน; Map p316; Th Chang Moi) across Th Chang Moi. Dotted around the bazaar area are several small Confucian temples, a handful of Chinese apothecaries and lots of Chinese jewellery shops, decorated in brilliant red, a symbol of good fortune.

However, the area has lost some of its prominence with the construction of the vast Samakkee Charity Foundation temple.

South of the flower market on Th Praisani is the **Pung Tao Gong Ancestral Temple** (ศาลเจ้าปุงเถ่ากง; Map p312; Th Praisani; ⏰6am-6pm) FREE. A small parade winds through the streets for Chinese New Year.

Wat Bupparam
BUDDHIST TEMPLE

(วัดบุปผาราม; Map p316; Th Tha Phae; 20B; ⏰5am-8pm) This highly ornate temple shows the clear influence of the Burmese teak merchants who immigrated to Chiang Mai during the 19th century. The eye-catching dharma hall has a *mon·dòp* (library) downstairs and a large prayer room above, but the most striking feature is the gorgeous, wonky *wí·hăhn*, built from teak inlaid with mirror mosaics in the classic Lanna style.

The *chedi* at the rear of the compound is in the Burmese Mon style, with four stucco *singha* (lions) around the base.

Art in Paradise
MUSEUM

(พิพิธภัณฑ์อาร์ตอินพาราไดซ์; Map p312; http://chiangmai-artinparadise.com; 199/9 Th Chang Khlan; adult/child 400/200B; ⏰9am-8.30pm (last entry 7pm); 🅿) Just a whole lot of fun, this museum has a range of 3D optical-illusion art displays, from cliff faces and movie sets to a levitation room and a magic carpet ride where you can get in the scene, snap photos and just be silly. Kids in particular will enjoy it but adults often love it, too.

◉ South of the Old City

The main highway running southwest from the old city, Th Wualai is famous for its **silver shops** and the entire street reverberates to the sound of smiths hammering intricate religious designs and ornamental patterns into bowls, jewellery boxes and decorative plaques made from silver, or, more often, aluminium. This is also the location for the Saturday Walking Street market (p352).

Wat Srisuphan
BUDDHIST TEMPLE

(วัดศรีสุพรรณ; Map p312; Soi 2, Th Wualai; ⏰6am-6pm) It should come as no surprise that the silversmiths along Th Wualai have decorated their patron monastery with the same fine artisanship shown in their shops. The 'silver' *ubosot* is covered with silver, nickel and aluminium panels, embossed with elaborate repoussé-work designs. The effect is like a giant jewellery box, particularly after dark, when the monastery is illuminated by coloured lights.

Wat Srisuphan was founded in 1502, but little remains of the original *wát* except for some teak pillars and roof beams in the main *wí·hăhn*. The murals inside show an interesting mix of Taoist, Zen and Theravada Buddhist elements. Note the gold and silver Ganesha statue beneath a silver *cha-tra* (umbrella) by the *ubosot,* a sign of the crossover between Hinduism and Buddhism in Thailand.

Because this is an active ordination hall, only men may enter the *ubosot*. While guests can enter the main temple building free of charge, there is a 50B fee to enter the area near the *ubosot* to see it up close.

Weave Artisan Society
CULTURAL CENTRE

(สานสังคมช่างฝีมือ; Map p312; ☎080 071 3218; https://weaveartisansociety.com; 12/8 Soi 3, Th Wualai; ⏰9am-6pm) A brand new culture centre, gallery, coffee shop, bookstore and immersive theatre space south of the old city, where you can attend a performance or just sip on some local coffee and admire the

LOCAL KNOWLEDGE

CHIANG MAI FOR CHILDREN

Chiang Mai is very popular with families, both for its easygoing vibe and for the massive range of activities on offer. As a sensible first step, pick a hotel with a pool and plan out your days to avoid overload; chartering a *rót daang* (literally 'red truck', operating as shared taxi) or túk-túk will give you the independence to come and go as you please. **Suan Buak Hat** (p310) has the most convenient playground in the old city. At meal times you can find familiar Western food in the old city and shopping centres.

Set aside one day for an elephant experience – ChangChill (ช้างหนาว; ☑064 340 6776; http://changchill.com; 45/2 Mu 19, Baan Pratumuang; full day adult/child 2500/1800B; ⊙10am-3pm) 🌿 and **Burm and Emily's Elephant Sanctuary** (p361) are leading the pack ethically – and another day for a scamper up the **Sticky Waterfall** (p360). Kids six and up will adore ziplining with **Flight of the Gibbon** (p328). Wát trips are popular with kids and the compounds are calm and mostly traffic free; **Phra That Doi Suthep** (p325), **Pha Lat** (p324), **Suan Dok** (p327), **Umong Suan Phutthatham** (p325), **Chedi Luang** (p315) and **Phra Singh** (p314) have the most going on to keep small sightseers entertained. The three old-city **museums** (p318) have plenty of modern, kid-friendly displays, and zoo-style wildlife encounters are possible at the Chiang Mai Zoo (สวนสัตว์เชียงใหม่; ☑053 221179; www.chiangmaizoo.com; 100 Th Huay Kaew; adult/child 150/70B, combined zoo & aquarium ticket 520/260B; ⊙8am-4.30pm; 🚻) and Chiang Mai Night Safari (เชียงใหม่ไนท์ซาฟารี; ☑053 999000; www.chiangmainightsafari.com; Rte 121; tours adult/child 800/400B; ⊙11am-10pm; 🚻).

For days when the temperature rises to unbearable levels, all the big shopping centres have icy air-con, multiscreen cinemas and kids' activities; Central Festival has the Sub-Zero ice-rink (☑053 288868; www.subzeroiceskate.com; 3rd fl, Central Festival; per 90min weekday/weekend 250/300B; ⊙11am-10pm Mon-Fri, from 10am Sat & Sun), complete with 'walkers' for first-time skaters. Grand Canyon Water Park (☑061 796 3999; http://grandcanyonwaterpark.velaeasy.com; 202 Mu 3, Namprae; adult/child 550/400B; ⊙9am-7pm) is another great escape, especially for older kids who like adrenalin-charged water fun.

displayed local artworks. Check the website for upcoming events, which include things like bamboo building, weaving and natural dye workshops.

Wiang Kum Kam HISTORIC SITE
(เวียงกุมกาม; Rte 3029; tours by horse cart/tram 300/400B; ⊙8am-5pm) The first attempt at founding a city on the banks of Mae Ping, Wiang Kum Kam served as the Lanna capital for 10 years from 1286, but the city was abandoned in the 16th century due to flooding. Today, the excavated ruins are scattered around the winding lanes of a sleepy village 5km south of Chiang Mai.

The centuries haven't been kind to Wiang Kum Kam, but the brick plinths and ruined *chedi* give a powerful impression of its former magnificence.

The landmark monument of the ruins is Wat Chedi Liam, with a soaring stucco *chedi* divided into dozens of niches for Buddha statues, an architectural nod to India's famous Mahabodhi Temple. In fact, this spire was created as part of a rather fanciful restoration by a Burmese trader in 1908. Over 1300 inscribed stone slabs, bricks, bells

and *chedi* have been excavated at the site and some pieces are displayed at the visitors centre. The most important archaeological discovery was a four-piece stone slab, now housed at the Chiang Mai National Museum, inscribed with one of the earliest known examples of Thai script.

Most people explore the ruins by horse cart or tram, starting from the visitors centre on Rte 3029; if you come with your own transport via Th Chiang Mai–Lamphun (Rte 106), follow the signed road past a small roundabout with a fountain and turn left at the T-junction to reach Wat Chedi Liam.

⊙ West of the Old City

Modern Chiang Mai has sprawled west from the old city towards Doi Suthep and the Chiang Mai University, but there are a few historic sites dotted around the streets. The main attraction here is the Nimmanhaemin area with its trendy restaurants and shops.

★ **Wat Pha Lat** BUDDHIST TEMPLE
(วัดผาลาด) A hidden jungle temple tucked into the mountain along the way to Wat

Phra That Doi Suthep. Old stone structures, intricate carvings, *naga*-flanked stairways and Buddhist statues dot the serene grounds, and a walkway over a sheetrock waterfall affords postcard-pretty views of Chiang Mai. The temple was seldom visited before 2018, but word of its beauty spread among travellers and expats, and the Monk's Trail (a jungle path from the city to the temple) is now an open secret.

As the story of the temple goes, in 1355 a white elephant belonging to King Kuena took a break to rest on the future site of Wat Pha Lat before dying at the future site of Wat Phra That Doi Suthep. The king ordered temples constructed on both sites, and the hidden jungle temple became a rest stop for monks making the pilgrimage to the larger, more opulent temple. After the road was constructed in 1935, Wat Pha Lat became a monks' residence and meditation site.

Note that there are no food stalls or shops here, which for many visitors is preferable.

★ Wat Phra That Doi Suthep
BUDDHIST TEMPLE

(วัดพระธาตุดอยสุเทพ; Th Huay Kaew, Doi Suthep; 30B; ⊙5am-9pm) Overlooking the city from its mountain throne, Wat Phra That Doi Suthep is one of northern Thailand's most sacred temples, and its founding legend is learned by every schoolkid in Chiang Mai. The wát is a beautiful example of northern Thai architecture, reached via a 306-step staircase flanked by *naga* (mythical sea serpents). The climb is intended to help devotees accrue Buddhist merit.

The monastery was established in 1383 by King Keu Naone to enshrine a piece of bone said to be from the shoulder of the historical Buddha. The bone shard was brought to Lanna by a wandering monk from Sukhothai and it broke into two pieces at the base of the mountain, with one piece being enshrined at Wat Suan Dok (p327). The second fragment was mounted onto a sacred white elephant that wandered the jungle until it died, in the process selecting the spot where the monastery was later founded.

The terrace at the top of the steps is dotted with breadfruit trees, small shrines, rock gardens and monuments, including a statue of the white elephant that carried the Buddha relic to its current resting place. Before entering the inner courtyard, children pay their respects to a lizard-like guardian dragon statue known as 'Mom'.

Steps lead up to the inner terrace, where a walkway circumnavigates the gleaming golden *chedi* enshrining the relic. The crowning five-tiered umbrella marks the city's independence from Burma and its union with Thailand. Pilgrims queue to leave lotus blossoms and other offerings at the shrines surrounding the *chedi,* which are studded with Buddha statues in an amazing variety of poses and materials.

Within the monastery compound, the Doi Suthep Vipassana Meditation Center (p333) conducts a variety of religious outreach programs for visitors.

Rót daang (literally 'red trucks') run to the bottom of the steps to the temple from several points in Chiang Mai, including from in front of the zoo (per person 40B) and in front of Wat Phra Singh (per person 50B), but they only leave when they have enough passengers and prices may very depending on the driver's mood. Travellers can also work out a private ride with a *rót daang,* taxi or using the Grab Car mobile application. Many people cycle up on mountain-biking tours from Chiang Mai, and you can also walk from the university.

Bhubing Palace
GARDENS

(พระตำหนักภูพิงค์, Phra Tamnak Bhu Bing; ☑053 223065; www.bhubingpalace.org; Th Huay Kaew, Doi Suthep; 50B; ⊙8.30-11.30am & 1-3.30pm) The serene grounds of the royal family's winter palace are open to the public (when the royals aren't visiting). The unusually strict dress code requires bottoms below mid-calf and shoulders covered – no scarves. The mountain's cool climate allows the royal gardeners to raise 'exotic' species such as roses, attracting lots of Thai sightseers.

Climb up to the reservoir that is sometimes brought to life by fountains that dance to the king's own musical compositions.

Wat Umong Suan Phutthatham
BUDDHIST TEMPLE

(วัดอุโมงค์; Soi Wat Umong, Th Khlong Chonprathan; 20B; ⊙daylight hours) Not to be confused with the small Wat Umong in the old city, this historic forest wát is famed for its sylvan setting and its ancient *chedi,* above a brick platform wormholed with passageways, built around 1380 for the 'mad' monk Therachan. Keep an eye out for the Sri Lankan–style stupa, and as you wander the arched tunnels, look for traces of the original murals and several venerated Buddha images.

Western Chiang Mai

Western Chiang Mai

The scrub forest around the platform is scattered with centuries' worth of broken Buddha images. The attendant monks raise cows, deer, chickens and, curiously, English bull terriers, and in the grounds is a pretty artificial lake, surrounded by gù·đì (monks' quarters). Check out the emaciated black-stone Buddha in the Burmese style, behind the *chedi*.

Wat Phra That Doi Kham BUDDHIST TEMPLE
(วัดพระธาตุดอยคำ; Mae Hia; donations appreciated; ⊙6am-6pm) Reached via a steep *naga* stairway through the forest, this handsome *wát* looms above the city from the hillside

above Royal Park Rajapruek. With its gilded *chedi*, super-sized Buddha statues and panoramic city views it's an attractive and quieter alternative to Wat Phra That Doi Suthep. The easiest way to get here is by rented motorcycle or chartered *rót daang;* follow the signs for Royal Park Rajapruek from Rte 121 and go right at the roundabout before the entrance.

Royal Park Rajapruek   GARDENS
(ลานมหกรรมพืชสวนโลก;www.royalparkrajapruek.
org; Rte 121, Mae Hia; adult/child 200/150B; ☺8am-6pm) This sprawling formal park has 23 themed gardens donated by international governments, along with nine Thai gardens and six 'corporate' gardens. It sounds a bit stuffy on paper, but the complex is actually lush, green and peaceful, with a vast wát-shaped central pavilion full of slightly over-the-top displays honouring the Thai royal family.

Wat Suan Dok   BUDDHIST TEMPLE
(วัดสวนดอก; Map p312; Th Suthep; donations accepted, hall admission 20B; ☺daylight hours) Built on a former flower garden in 1373, this important monastery enshrines one half of a sacred Buddha relic; the other half was transported by white elephant to Wat Phra That Doi Suthep. The main *chedi* is a gilded, bell-shaped structure that rises above a sea of white memorial *chedi* honouring the Thai royal family, with the ridge of Doi Suthep soaring behind.

The hangar-like main *wí·hǎhn* contains a huge standing Buddha statue that almost touches the ceiling. Take some time to wander the memorial garden of whitewashed *chedi* in front of the monastery, which contain the ashes of generations of Lanna royalty.

Mahachulalongkorn Buddhist University is located on the same grounds and foreigners often join the popular Monk Chat (p315) and English-language meditation retreats.

◉ North of the Old City

From Pratu Chang Pheuak (White Elephant Gate), it's a short walk north to the Elephant Monument (อนุสาวรีย์ช้าง; Map p312; Th Chotana), whose twin elephant statues in stucco pavilions are said to have been erected by King Chao Kavila in 1800.

Chiang Mai National Museum   MUSEUM
(พิพิธภัณฑสถานแห่งชาติเชียงใหม่; Map p312; ☑053 217665; Rte 11/Th Superhighway; 100B; ☺9am-4pm Wed-Sun) Operated by the Fine Arts Department, this museum is the primary caretaker of Lanna artefacts and northern Thai history, covering everything from the region's geographical background and cultural history, to ancient royal kingdoms and Lanna fine art.

Bags must be left in the free lockers by the ticket desk. To make your trip here more worthwhile, combine this with a visit to Wat Chet Yot and the Chinese cemetery.

Wat Chet Yot   BUDDHIST TEMPLE
(วัดเจ็ดยอด; Map p312; Rte 11/Th Superhighway; donations appreciated; ☺8.30am-5pm) This wát was established by King Tilokarat in 1455 as part of an effort to prevent a predicted decline in Buddhism. It still has much of its original stucco intact and is topped by *jèt yôrt* (seven spires) representing the seven weeks Buddha spent in Bodhgaya in India after his enlightenment. Though the sanctuary is thought to be a replica of Bodhgaya's Mahabodhi Temple, scholars believe that the plans were copied from a clay votive tablet showing the temple in distorted perspective.

The main structure was completed in 1476, a year before the eighth World Buddhist Council, and its historic *wí·hǎhn* is decorated with time-worn stucco bas-reliefs of *deva* (angelic Buddhist spirits). Dotted around the compound are more chapels and *chedi*, as well as lots of mature ficus trees propped up with wooden stakes by devotees seeking merit.

Wat Ku Tao   BUDDHIST TEMPLE
(วัดกู่เต้า; Map p312; Soi 6, Th Chotana/Th Chang Pheuak; donations appreciated; ☺6am-6pm) Behind the Muang Chiang Mai sports stadium, photogenic, 1631 Wat Ku Tao incorporates many Burmese and Confucian elements. The distinctive *chedi* is said to resemble a stack of watermelons, hence the name (*tao* means 'melon' in the northern Thai dialect). Contained inside are the ashes of Tharawadi Min, son of the Burmese king Bayinnaung, who ruled over Lanna from 1578 to 1597.

🏃 Activities

Adventure Activities

⭐ **Monk's Trail**   HIKING
This dreamy, increasingly popular jungle hike to Wat Pha Lat (p324) takes about 45 minutes, starting from behind Chiang Mai

University and snaking up through the forest before reaching the temple. Monks are regularly seen hiking in sandals, but close-toed shoes are a better choice for the loose rocks and steep parts. Bring mosquito repellent and dress appropriately for visiting the temple.

To get to the start of the path, go to the end of the university perimeter wall on Th Suthep and then follow the signposted road on the right towards Palaad Tawanron (☑053 216039; https://palaadtawanron.com; off Th Suthep; mains 160-380B; ⊙11am-midnight) to reach the back entrance to the zoo; bear left at this fork and you'll reach the TV tower and a brown sign showing the start of the trail.

From Wat Pha Lat you can either take a *sǒrng·tǎa·ou* back to the city (60B) or continue on the trail, following the river (and the power lines) all the way to Wat Phra That Doi Suthep (p325), which takes an additional 75 minutes.

★ Green Trails   ADVENTURE
(☑053 141356; www.green-trails.com; 111/70 Th Mahidol; treks for 2 people from 2900B) 🍃 A very reliable, eco and socially responsible outfit that can arrange trekking trips to Doi Inthanon, overnight trips to Ban Mae Kampong, responsible elephant encounters and much more. Overnight trips to Akha, Lisu and Palong villages in Chiang Dao and to Hmong villages in Mae Rim are particularly rewarding.

Trailhead   CYCLING
(Map p316; ☑095 538 0202; www.trailhead.co.th; 48-50 Soi 1, Th Pra Pokklao; half-/full-day cycling tours from 1199/1999B; ⊙7.30am-8pm) Runs popular mountain biking tours and city cycling tours in and around Chiang Mai. Also on offer: a boat-and-bicycle tour to the Sticky Waterfall (p360), and a variety of multiday adventures to Doi Suthep-Pui (p335), Chiang Dao and beyond.

Siam River Adventures   RAFTING
(Map p316; ☑089 515 1917; www.siamrivers.com; 17 Th Ratwithi; per day from 1800B; ⊙8.30am-8pm) In operation since 2000, this outfit running white-water rafting and kayaking trips has a good reputation for safety and professionalism. The guides have specialist rescue training and additional staff are located at dangerous parts of the river with throw ropes. Trips can be combined with elephant encounters and overnight village stays.

Chiang Mai Rock Climbing
Adventures   ADVENTURE
(CMRCA; Map p316; ☑053 207102; www.thailandclimbing.com; 55/3 Th Ratchaphakhinai; climbing course from 3995B, climbing gym day pass 250B; ⊙8am-8pm) With a very experienced and passionate owner, CMRCA developed and maintains all of the climbs at the limestone crag Crazy Horse Buttress, with bolted sport routes in the French 5a to 8b+ range. As well as climbing and caving courses for all levels, it runs a shuttle bus to the crag daily at 8am (395B return; book one day before).

The outfitter has also developed 50 new routes up a limestone crag in Lampang, and runs semi-regular buses to the area. You can rent all the gear you need here, either piece by piece, or as a 'full set' for two climbers (1875B).

Flight of the Gibbon   ZIPLINING
(Map p316; ☑053 010660; www.flightofthegibbon.com; 29/4-5 Th Kotchasan; day tours 4199B; ⊙8am-5.30pm) This adventure outfit started the zipline craze, with nearly 5km of wire strung up like spiderwebs in the gibbon-populated forest canopy near Ban Mae Kampong, an hour's drive east from Chiang Mai. The day tour includes an optional village visit, waterfall walk and lunch cooked by the community. There are also multiday, multiactivity tours that can include a night at a village homestay.

In 2019 a 25-year-old tourist plunged from the zipline to his death. The operation closed temporarily for an investigation, after which no information was released. The tours have since resumed.

Elephant interactions

Chiang Mai is one of Thailand's most famous destinations for elephant encounters, with more elephant camps opening by the day it seems, though many still offer packages of non-bareback elephant rides, bathing, circus-like sideshows, and buffalo cart rides or bamboo rafting on the nearest river. Better camps offer observation in place of exploitation: visitors observe the elephant herds and prepare food for them, but avoid activities that are harmful to the animals' welfare.

Thai Elephant
Care Center   ELEPHANT INTERACTION
(☑053 206247; www.thaielephantcarecenter.com; Mae Sa; entrance 250B, half-/full-day program 2000/3000B) This small centre at Mae Sa,

CHIANG MAI PROVINCE CHIANG MAI

ⓘ ELEPHANT INTERACTIONS: THE ETHICS

Elephants have been used as beasts of burden in Thailand for thousands of years, hauling logs from the teak forests and transporting the carriages of Thai royalty. The elephant-headed deities Erawan and Ganesha are revered by Buddhists and Hindus alike, and even the outline of Thailand resembles an elephant's head, with its trunk extending down into the isthmus.

With the nationwide ban on logging in 1989, thousands of working elephants suddenly found themselves out of a job, and herders and mahouts (elephant drivers) looked for new ways to generate revenue from their animals. So were born Chiang Mai's elephant camps, where former logging herds learned to entertain visiting tourists with circus-style displays and rides through the forest. In recent years, though, a growing awareness of animal welfare issues is shining a new spotlight on this industry and its practices.

Elephant rides are particularly problematic, with just one of the many issues including the fact that the *howdahs* (carriages) used to carry tourists place severe strain on elephants' spines and can cause debilitating damage over time. Circus-like performances also put elephants at risk of injury, many camps keep their elephants chained and segregated, and traditional *ankus* and similar types of metal hooks are used to control the animals. Government regulations offer little to no oversight, as they still classify elephants as modes of transport, and many animals show clear signs of psychological damage, which has manifested itself in attacks on humans.

There are alternatives. Ideally, activist groups state, elephants should be left unchained and allowed to form their own social groups in sprawling compounds (although there is rarely enough land for this). In place of rides, visitors can watch as elephants interact with each other and behave as they normally would without any human interference. Although assisting with elephant bathing was for a long time considered a viable alternative to rides, in 2018 animal rights groups condemned the practice. The problem, they say, is that anytime elephants are forced to interact with the public, the elephants must be trained and tightly controlled (calling for the use of chains, hooks and rods). Furthermore, elephants are perfectly happy to bathe themselves, which more responsible camps allow visitors to observe from a distance.

Increasingly, you can contribute to elephant conservation without the uncomfortable feeling that you are contributing to the problem. The reality is that most elephants cannot be returned to the wild and tourist dollars are often the only way to finance their ongoing care. The scientific community stresses that the best camps should have a dedicated veterinary station where the animals can be treated for injuries and medical conditions. If rides are offered, bareback riding, where the rider sits on the elephants' shoulders, is less harmful than rides in wooden *howdahs*, though many animal welfare experts insist that rides should be avoided altogether because elephants undergo brutal abuse to 'learn' how to accept riders. Groups such as the ACEWG (Asian Captive Elephant Working Group) and Asian Elephant Projects are working with communities and elephant tourism operators to help them transition to ethical and sustainable programs. The end goal is of course to provide better lives for the elephants.

about 25km northwest of Chiang Mai, was set up to provide care for elderly elephants retired from logging camps and elephant shows. There are no rides, and visitors feed the old-timers with ground grass, herb balls and bananas, help out at bath time, and visit the cemetery for elephants who have died of old age.

Elephant Nature Park ELEPHANT INTERACTION
(Map p316; ☏ 053 272850, 053 818754; www.elephantnaturepark.org; 1 Th Ratchamankha; 1-/2-day tours 2500/5800B) ✍ One of the first

sanctuaries for rescued elephants in Chiang Mai, Elephant Nature Park has led the movement to abandon rides and shows and put elephant welfare at the top of the agenda, under the guidance of founder Saengdeuan (Lek) Chailert. Visits are focused on interaction – the day is spent wandering with mahouts and their charges, helping feed elephants. As is the case with all of the better elephant camps, some 80 elephants here have been rescued from logging camps and tourist shows. The most rewarding experience is seeing the interaction between the elephants, with baby elephants having trunk tug-of-wars and older elephants taking care of blind and disabled members of the herd. The main park is in the Mae Taeng valley, 60km from Chiang Mai, and the property is also home to rescued dogs, cats, cows, horses, ducks and chickens. Day trips include a vegetarian buffet lunch. Longer volunteering packages are also available.

Elephant Retirement Park
ELEPHANT INTERACTION

(Map p316; ☑ 081 671 9110; www.elephantretirementpark.com; Soi 5, 5 Th Kotchasan; half-/full-day tours 1700/2600B) An ethical operator at Mae Taeng offering walking, feeding and bathing encounters with elephants, but no rides; the herd are allowed to maintain their own family units. For guests who prefer even less interaction, there is also an 'elephant observation lunch'. The experience lasts six hours, includes pick-up from the city, a guide and food, all for 2000B.

Massage & Wellness

⭐ **Zira Spa**
SPA

(Map p316; ☑ 053 222288; www.ziraspa.com; 8/1 Th Ratwithi; treatments 700-6200B; ⊙ 10am-10pm) In the centre of Chiang Mai, Zira Spa offers some of the best spa treatments and massages in the region, all for a decent price. You need to book in advance for the larger spa packages, but same-day service is available for one or two of the 30-, 60- or 90-minute treatments.

Fah Lanna
SPA

(Map p326; ☑ 053 416191; www.fahlanna.com; 4/1 Soi 15, Th Nimmanhaemin; 30/60min Thai massage 350/700B, packages 2800-5500B; ⊙ 10am-10pm) New in the trendy Nimman neighbourhood, Fah Lanna is a bamboo and stucco wellness sanctuary defined by natural colours and crafts produced by artisans across northern Thailand. There are 11 treatment rooms and one suite, where treatments range from traditional Thai massage (they really get in there!) to packages that include reflexology, exfoliation, steam baths and body scrubs.

There's a sister spa (Map p316; 57/1 Th Wiang Kaew; 1hr traditional Thai massages 700B; ⊙ 10am-10pm) in the old city.

Wild Rose Yoga Studio
YOGA

(Map p316; ☑ 089 950 9377; www.wildroseyoga.org; Soi 4, 15/2 Th Phra Pokklao; per class 250-300B; ⊙ daily drop-in classes; check online schedule) Follow the scent of incense and path of flower petals to Wild Rose Yoga Studio near Pratu Chiang Mai. As one of the most established studios in town, Wild Rose attracts returning students and teachers year after year with advanced daily yoga classes and various workshops in a picturesque teak Thai house.

Lila Thai Massage
MASSAGE

(Map p316; ☑ 053 327043; Th Phra Pokklao; standard/herbal body scrub from 250/600B; ⊙ 10am-10pm) Established by the former director of the Chiang Mai women's prison, Lila Thai offers post-release employment for graduates

---

❶ AVOIDING THE SMOKY SEASON

Chiang Mai's annual smoky season, caused by crop burning and exhaust fumes, has become increasingly long and hazardous. In the past, the season lasted from March to April, and the levels of pollution were tolerable for all but the most sensitive people. By 2019, though, the smog was beginning to creep in as early as January, lasting until mid-May. In March and April, the air quality index reached never-before-seen levels, indicating an all-time high of dangerous particulates. Assuming this trend continues, we strongly advise visitors to avoid travel to Chiang Mai in March and April.

If you do wind up in the city during this time, know that views of nearby mountains and buildings are obscured by a yellow haze. A bonfire smell permeates the air, and after being outside you'll smell like it, too. A gritty film appears on surfaces and dust clouds are visible in the area. Sensitive people may experience itchy eyes, a burning throat, coughing fits, sinus problems, bronchial inflammation, laboured breathing and asthma attacks.

The only thing that clears the air is rain, and lately the region's weather has become increasingly unpredictable. If you find yourself in the area during the worst of the smoky season, stay indoors during the hottest part of the day, and consider wearing a face mask with a filter grade of at least N95. You can monitor the city's real-time Air Quality Index (AQI) levels at http://aqicn.org/city/chiang-mai, and there's also a helpful smartphone app called Air4Thai.

ℹ️ CHIANG MAI'S PACKAGED HIKES

Thousands of visitors trek into the hills of northern Thailand each year hoping to see fantastic mountain scenery, interact with traditional hill-tribe communities and meet elephants. A huge industry has grown up to cater to this demand, but the experience is very commercial and may not live up to everyone's notion of adventure.

The standard package involves a one-hour minibus ride to Mae Taeng or Mae Wang, a brief hike to an elephant camp, bamboo rafting and, for multiday tours, an overnight stay in or near a hill-tribe village. Many budget guesthouses pressure their guests to take these trips because of the commissions paid, and may ask guests to stay elsewhere if they decline. Note that they also arrange elephant rides, though these are not recommended as rides can be detrimental to the health of the animals.

While these packages are undeniably popular, they may visit elephant camps that have a questionable record on elephant welfare. Hill-tribe trips can also disappoint, as many of the villages now house a mix of tribal people and Chinese and Burmese migrants and have abandoned many aspects of the traditional way of life. Rafting can also be a tame drift on a creek, rather than an adrenalin-charged rush over white water.

If you crave real adventure, you'll have to be a bit more hands-on about organising things yourself. To get deep into the jungle, rent a motorcycle and explore the national parks north and south of Chiang Mai; Chiang Dao is an excellent place to base yourself for jungle exploration. To see elephants in natural conditions, spend a day at Elephant Nature Park (p329), then raft real white water with Siam River Adventures (p328). To encounter traditional hill-tribe culture, you'll need to travel to more remote areas than you can reach on a day trip from Chiang Mai; your best bet is to travel to Tha Ton and book a multiday trek from there.

from the prison's massage training program. There are seven branches across the city, including a **Th Ratchadamnoen branch** (Map p316; ☑ 053 327243; Th Ratchadamnoen; standard/ oil massage from 250/550B; ⊗ 10am-10pm).

Oasis Spa MASSAGE
(Map p316; ☑ 053 920111; www.oasisspa.net; 4 Th Samlan; massages from 1200B) If you just want to be indulged, Oasis offers an upmarket take on the traditional Thai massage experience, with scrubs, wraps, massage and Ayurvedic treatments in a tranquil garden full of Lanna-style pavilions.

Vocational Training Centre of the Chiang Mai Women's Correctional Institution MASSAGE
(Map p316; ☑ 053 122340; 100 Th Ratwithi; foot or traditional massage from 200B; ⊗ 8am-4.30pm, from 9am Sat & Sun) Offers fantastic massages performed by female inmates participating in the prison's job-training rehabilitation program. The cafe next door is a nice spot for a post-massage brew.

Volunteering

Burma Study Centre VOLUNTEERING
(Map p326; www.burmastudy.org; 302/2 Soi 13, Th Nimmanhaemin; ⊗ 11.30am-8pm Mon-Fri, to 6pm Sat) This nonprofit community centre conducts classes in English for Burmese migrants living in Thailand. Many of the students are young, low-wage workers whose education has been disrupted by political instability in Myanmar or dislocation from their home communities. It also maintains an outreach to educate the international community about Burmese-related issues through its lending library, book discussions and film screenings.

🍴 Courses

Chiang Mai offers several opportunities to learn arts and crafts (particularly weaving) from local artisans and craftspeople. Thai Tribal Crafts Fair Trade (p350) offers daily weaving classes with an expert, and Weave Artisan Society (p323) holds sporadic workshops in things like bamboo building, weaving and natural dyes.

Cooking

⭐ **Small House Chiang Mai Thai Cooking School** COOKING
(Map p312; ☑ 095 674 4550; www.chiangmaithai cooking.com; 19/14 Th Thiphanet; group classes per person 1500B, day-long private classes from 3500B) Arm offers delightful and intimate Thai cooking classes in a dwelling outside Chiang Mai. Courses include transport and a visit to a local market, and they span northern Thai

DON'T MISS

RIVER CRUISES

Before the construction of the roads and railways, Mae Ping was the main route of transit for goods coming into Chiang Mai. The markets along the riverbank are where the Lanna kingdom came to trade with the rest of Thailand and, via the Silk Route, with the rest of Asia. The river was used to transport everything from fruit and vegetables to the giant trunks of teak trees, but trade on the river slowly died after the arrival of the railways in 1922.

Mae Ping still traces a lazy passage through the middle of Chiang Mai, but few vessels ply its waters today, with the exception of tour boats, which provide an excellent vantage point from which to view the city. Mae Ping River Cruise (p333) offers trips starting from Wat Chaimongkhon, south of the centre on Th Charoen Prathet, as well as longer cruises to Wiang Kum Kam (p324) and dinner cruises. Riverside Bar & Restaurant (p344) also runs popular, nightly dinner cruises.

If you don't mind paddling yourself, Chiang Mai Mountain Biking & Kayaking (p356) offers guided kayak tours along Mae Ping, visiting forested stretches north of the city.

dishes. The small two- to four-person classes feel more local than touristy.

Asia Scenic Thai Cooking   COOKING
(Map p316; ☑053 418657; www.asiascenic.com; 31 Soi 5, Th Ratchadamnoen; half-day courses 800-1000B, full-day courses 1000-1200B; ⊗half-day courses 9am-2pm & 5-9pm, full-day courses 9am-3pm) On Khun Gayray's cooking courses you can study in town or at a peaceful out-of-town farm. Courses cover soups, curries, stir-fries, salads and desserts, so you'll be able to make a three-course meal after a single day.

Chiang Mai Thai Cookery School   COOKING
(Map p316; ☑053 206388; www.thaicookery school.com; 47/2 Th Moon Muang; courses from 1450B) One of Chiang Mai's first cooking schools, run by TV chef Sompon Nabnian and his team. Classes are held in a rural setting outside of Chiang Mai, and there's a special evening masterclass led by the founder, with northern Thai delicacies.

Thai Farm Cooking School   COOKING
(Map p316; ☑081 288 5989; www.thaifarmcooking. com; 38 Soi 9, Th Moon Muang; courses 1500B) Cooking classes at a beautiful and serene organic farm, 17km outside Chiang Mai; return transport from the city is included.

Massage
Lanna Thai Massage School   HEALTH & WELLBEING
(Map p316; ☑053 232547; http://lannathaimas sageschool.net; 37 Th Chang Moi Kao; 10-day course private/group 14,300/8300B) Close to Wat Chomphu, this reputable school is recognised by the Thai Ministry of Education and Public Health; training includes the

preparation of herbal treatments using fresh ingredients.

Thai Massage School of Chiang Mai   HEALTH & WELLBEING
(TMC; ☑053 854330; www.tmcschool.com; 203/6 Th Chiang Mai-Mae Jo; basic courses from 8500B) Northeast of town, this well-known school offers a government-licensed massage curriculum. There are three foundation levels and an intensive teacher-training program.

Chetawan Thai Traditional Massage School   HEALTH & WELLBEING
(Map p312; ☑053 410360; www.watpomassage. com; 7/1-2 Soi Samud Lanna, Th Pracha Uthit; general courses 12,000B; ⊗8am-6pm) Bangkok's respected Wat Pho massage school established this Chiang Mai branch outside of town near Rajabhat University.

Yoga & Meditation
Wat Suan Dok Meditation Retreat   HEALTH & WELLBEING
(Map p312; ☑084 609 1357; www.monkchat.net; Wat Suan Dok, Th Suthep; 1-/2-day retreats donation-based/800B; ⊗Mon-Fri) The Buddhist university affiliated with Wat Suan Dok (p327) conducts one-, two- and four-day meditation retreats at a centre about 40 minutes away. Register in advance for more information.

Northern Insight Meditation Centre   HEALTH & WELLBEING
(☑053 278620; Wat Ram Poeng, Th Suthep Muang; by donation) The intensive course of 26 days or longer at Wat Ram Poeng, 4km south of Chiang Mai, is best suited to serious meditation students; days start at 4am and meals are taken in silence.

Doi Suthep Vipassana
Meditation Center   HEALTH & WELLBEING
(☑ 053 295012; www.fivethousandyears.org; Wat Phra That Doi Suthep, Th Huay Kaew; by donation) Set within the grounds of Wat Phra That Doi Suthep (p325), this centre offers meditation training retreats for all levels, lasting from four to 21 days.

Moo·ay tai (Thai Boxing)

Santai Muay Thai   MARTIAL ARTS
(☑ 082 528 6059; www.muay-thai-santai.com; 79 Mu 9, San Kamphaeng; per week/month from 4000/13,000B) Run by former prize fighters, with a focus on reaching competition standard. The gym is east of town.

Lanna Muay Thai   MARTIAL ARTS
(Map p312; ☑ 053 892102; 161 Soi Chang Khian, Th Huay Kaew; per day/week/month from 400/2200/8000B) Offers instruction to foreigners and Thais. The gym is famous for having trained the title-winning, transgender boxer Parinya Kiatbusaba.

Language

Payap University   LANGUAGE
(☑ 053 851478; http://ic.payap.ac.th; Kaew Nawarat Campus, Th Kaew Nawarat; language courses 8000B) This private university founded by the Church of Christ of Thailand offers intensive Thai-language courses in 60-hour modules.

American University Alumni   LANGUAGE
(AUA; Map p316; ☑ 053 214120; www.learnthai inchiangmai.com; 24 Th Ratchadamnoen; group courses 5300B) Conducts 60-hour Thai courses, with two hours of classes daily, Monday to Friday. Private instruction is also available.

🖝 Tours

⭐ Chiang Mai on Three Wheels   TOURS
(☑ 053 141356; www.chiangmaionthreewheels. com; 111/70 Th Mahidol; 4hr tours for 2 people 1700B) 🛈 There are few better ways to tour Chiang Mai than by slow, quiet, culturally immersive sǎhm·lór (three-wheel pedicabs; also spelt sǎamláw). This organisation helps promote this dying industry by connecting tourists with the often non-English-speaking drivers and pairs you with an English-speaking guide. Profits go entirely to the drivers and to support their industry.

Mae Ping River Cruise   BOATING
(Map p312; ☑ 053 274822; www.maepingriver cruise.com; Wat Chaimongkhon, 133 Th Charoen Prathet; 2hr cruise from 550B; ⊙9am-5pm) Mae Ping River Cruise offers trips starting from Wat Chaimongkhon, south of the centre on Th Charoen Prathet, as well as longer cruises to Wiang Kum Kam (1000B) and dinner cruises (per person 750B). There's a small, open-air cafe with coffee and ice cream at the start point.

Chiang Mai Street Food Tours   FOOD & DRINK
(☑ 085 033 8161; www.chiangmaistreetfoodtours. com; tours per adult/child 950/600B) These foodie trips through the city's morning and night markets are a great introduction to northern Thai cuisine.

Click and Travel   CYCLING
(☑ 053 281553; www.chiangmaicycling.com; 158/40-41 Soi Mu Ban Wiang Phing 5; half-/full-/multiday tours from 990/1500/5350B; ⊙9am-6pm; 🚸) Click and Travel offers family-friendly pedal-powered tours with a cultural focus, visiting temples and attractions in and outside the city centre. Children's bikes and bike trailers of a few different sorts are on offer.

🎉 Festivals & Events

Songkran   NEW YEAR
(⊙mid-Apr) The traditional Thai New Year (13 to 15 April) is celebrated in Chiang Mai with an infectious enthusiasm that's made it one of the best places in the country to be for the occasion. Thousands of revellers line all sides of the moat to throw water on passers-by and each other, while more restrained Songkran rituals are held at Wat Phra Singh.

Loi Krathong   RELIGIOUS
(⊙Oct/Nov) Also known as Yi Peng, this lunar holiday is celebrated along Mae Ping with the launching of small lotus-shaped boats honouring the spirit of the river, and the release of thousands of illuminated lanterns into the night sky.

Jai Thep   MUSIC
(https://jaithepfestival.com; Jan/Feb) Increasingly popular with travellers, this arts and music festival is held in January or February in venues around Chiang Mai. Offerings also include workshops and other styles of performances (theatre, dance, fire spinning, circus acts etc).

Flower Festival   CULTURAL
(⊙early Feb) A riot of blooms, held over a three-day period. There are flower displays, cultural performances and beauty pageants,

CHIANG MAI PROVINCE CHIANG MAI

plus a floral parade from Saphan Nawarat to Suan Buak Hat.

Chiang Mai Chinese New Year   NEW YEAR

(☉ Feb) The city's Chinese inhabitants herald the New Year in February with Chinese festival food, lion dances and the like.

Poy Sang Long (Poy Luang)   RELIGIOUS

(☉ usually Apr) This three-day ordination ceremony originated in Myanmar with the Shan people, and takes places in several wát around the city. It involves dressing boys from ages 7 to 14 in make-up and garish costumes representing Buddha's early life as a pampered prince.

Chiang Mai Red Cross & Winter Fair   CULTURAL

(☉ Dec-Jan) This 10-day festival feels a bit like a country fair, with cultural performances and food hawkers doing a lively trade in northern Thai cuisine, all in the name of raising funds for charities. The main venue is the Chiang Mai City Arts & Cultural Centre.

Inthakhin Festival   RELIGIOUS

(☉ mid-May) Held at Wat Chedi Luang, this religious festival propitiates the city's guardian deity, who resides in the city pillar, ensuring that the monsoon will arrive on time.

🛏 Sleeping

🛏 Old City

There are literally hundreds of places to stay in the old city. Go for the quieter ones dotted around the tiny lanes linking the main streets.

Hostel by Bed   HOSTEL $

(Map p316; ☎ 053 217215; www.hostelbybed.com; Th Singharat; incl breakfast dm 450-700B; d from 1250B; @ 🛜) Although you can find a room in Chiang Mai for the same price as these dorm beds, you get a lot of flashy facilities for your baht here, including a good breakfast, a chic kitchen, high cleanliness standards and a big bed with a curtain. Common areas inspire meeting people and it's in a decent location near cheap street food.

The private rooms are OK value too if you want privacy alongside a convivial atmosphere.

Diva Guesthouse   GUESTHOUSE $

(Map p316; ☎ 053 273851; www.divaguesthouse. com; 84/13 Th Ratchaphakhinai; dm 130-190B, s/d from 330/380B; ✳ @ 🛜) An energetic, vaguely bohemian spot on busy Th Ratchaphakhinai, Diva offers the full backpacker deal – dorm beds, budget boxrooms, adventure tours, net access, ambient tunes, and fried rice and *sà·đé* (grilled meat with peanut sauce) in the downstairs cafe. Accommodation ranges from dorms to family rooms and comes with either fan or air-con.

Banjai Garden   GUESTHOUSE $

(Map p316; ☎ 085 716 1635; www.banjai-garden. com; 43 Soi 3, Th Phra Pokklao; d with fan 450B, with air-con 550-1200B; ✳ 🛜) Set in an orderly wooden house, Banjai Garden has a calm air and a pleasant garden for hanging out. Take your pick from simple but clean and great-value fan rooms or better air-con rooms. Staying here feels a little like staying in a Thai home.

60 Blue House   GUESTHOUSE $

(Map p316; ☎ 086 919 2777; www.60bluehouse. com; 32-33 Th Ratchaphakhinai; dm 250B, s/d from 350/400B; ✳ 🛜) This appealing, clean and colourful hostel has one eight-bed dorm and clean private rooms with shared bathroom. Owner Khun Tao is a mine of local information, so guests always know where to go and what to do. A great bargain for high standards.

Gap's House   GUESTHOUSE $

(Map p316; ☎ 053 278140; www.gaps-house.com; 3 Soi 4, Th Ratchadamnoen; s/d incl breakfast from 420/550B; ✳ 🛜) The overgrown garden at this old backpacker favourite is a veritable jungle, providing plenty of privacy in the relaxing communal spaces. Modest budget rooms are set in old-fashioned wooden houses. The owner offers cooking courses.

Julie Guesthouse   HOSTEL $

(Map p316; ☎ 053 274355; www.julieguesthouse. com; 7 Soi 5, Th Phra Pokklao; dm 200-250B, d with/without bathroom from 360/300B; 🛜) Julie is perennially popular, though this is as much about budget as facilities. For not much more than the price of a fruit smoothie you can get a basic dorm bed, and tiny boxrooms cost only a little more. In the evenings travellers congregate on the covered roof terrace.

★ Sri Pat Guest House   HOTEL $$

(Map p316; ☎ 053 218716; http://sri-pat-guest -house.hotelschiangmai.net; 16 Soi 7, Th Moon Muang; d from 1500B; ✳ 🛜 ☟) A standout flashpacker guesthouse with all the trim-

SACRED PEAKS

Often bearing a crown of clouds, sultry **Doi Suthep** (1676m) and **Doi Pui** (1685m) are two of northern Thailand's most sacred peaks. A dense cloak of jungle envelops the twin summits, which soar dramatically on the fringes of Chiang Mai. A 265-sq-km area on the slopes of the mountains, encompassing both summits, is preserved as **Doi Suthep-Pui National Park** (อุทยานแห่งชาติดอยสุเทพ – ปุย; ☎053 210244; Th Huay Kaew; adult/child 200/100B, 2-person camping incl/not incl tent 255/60B, bungalows 400-2500B; ⏲8.30am-4.30pm). It attracts hordes of nature-lovers, and legions of pilgrims who come to worship at Wat Phra That Doi Suthep (p325).

As you climb, lowland rainforest gives way to cloud forest, full of mosses and ferns, providing a haven for more than 300 bird species and 2000 species of ferns and flowering plants. The park is also a renowned destination for mountain biking, and several Chiang Mai–based agencies run technical mountain-biking tours along trails that were once used as hunting and trade routes by hill-tribe villagers.

The park accommodation makes a comfortable base from which to explore and a trail runs for 2km from the campground to the summit of Doi Suthep, though the only view is of eerie mists swirling between the trees.

As with other national parks in the area, Doi Suthep is blessed with many thundering waterfalls, including **Nam Tok Monthathon**, about 2.5km off the paved road, which surges into a series of pools that hold water year-round. Swimming is best during or just after the monsoon, but you'll have to pay the national park fee to visit. Closer to the start of the road to Doi Suthep, **Nam Tok Wang Bua Bahn** is free, and full of frolicking locals, although this is more a series of rapids than a proper cascade.

Above the Bhubing Palace (p325) are a couple of Hmong villages. **Ban Doi Pui** is off the main road and is basically a tourist market at altitude; it's more interesting to continue to **Ban Kun Chang Kian**, a coffee-producing village about 500m down a dirt track just past the Doi Pui campground (ask the park staff for directions). *Rót daang* (literally 'red trucks', operating as shared taxis) run from the Wat Phra That Doi Suthep parking lot to both Ban Doi Pui (60B) and Ban Kun Chang Kian (200B return).

The entrance to the park is 16km northwest of central Chiang Mai. Shared *rót daang* leave from Chiang Mai University (Th Huay Kaew entrance) to various points within the national park. One-way fares start at 50B to Wat Phra That Doi Suthep and 80B to Bhubing Palace. You can also charter a *rót daang* for a half-day of exploring for around 600B.

mings: wi-fi, pool, wood-decked communal areas, scattered Buddha carvings and smart tiled rooms with flat-screen TVs and little Thai details. You get plenty of personality for your baht and staff members are cheerful and friendly.

Awana House HOTEL **$$**
(Map p316; ☎053 419005; www.awanahouse.com; 7 Soi 1, Th Ratchadamnoen; d with fan 495B, with air-con 700-1000B; ❄@📶🏊) The pick of the guesthouses around the medieval city gate of Pratu Tha Phae has rooms for every budget – all kept spotless – and a mini swimming pool under cover on the ground-floor terrace. Rooms get more comfortable and better decorated as you move up the price scale and there's a rooftop chill-out area with views across old Chiang Mai.

Staff are delightful and go the extra mile for children, so it's a big hit with families; book ahead.

Good Morning Chiang Mai Tropical Inn HOTEL **$$**
(Map p316; ☎053 272113; www.goodmorningchiangmai.com; 29/5 Soi 6, Th Ratchamankha; d incl breakfast 1300-2000B; ❄📶🏊) A relaxing pool, superior breakfasts and a tranquil location south of Wat Phra Singh all score points for this comfortable guesthouse in a vaguely Spanish-style villa. Rooms full of natural timber come with crisp linen and vast, tasteful bathrooms. Excellent value.

Baan Hanibah BOUTIQUE HOTEL **$$**
(Map p316; ☎053 287524; 6 Soi 8, Th Moon Muang; s/d from 1000/1600B; ❄📶) Protected by a garden of fragrant frangipani trees, Baan Hanibah is a relaxed boutique escape on a quiet lane in the heart of the old city. Behind an ornate gateway, in a converted teak house, you'll find small, quite stylish rooms with floaty drapes and Thai trim.

❶ NAVIGATING CHIANG MAI

When travelling in and beyond the old city, directions are often given in relationship to the old city's four cardinal gates.

Pratu Tha Phae (east) Head east from here along Th Tha Phae to reach the riverside, Talat Warorot and the Night Bazaar.

Pratu Chang Pheuak (north) Head north from here along Th Chotana (Th Chang Pheuak) to reach the Chang Pheuak Bus Terminal and Rte 107 to northern Chiang Mai Province.

Pratu Suan Dok (west) Head west from here along Th Suthep to reach Chiang Mai University, Doi Suthep, and the entertainment district of Th Nimmanhaemin.

Pratu Chiang Mai (south) Head southwest from here along Th Wualai for the Saturday Walking Street market and Rte 108 to southern Chiang Mai Province.

Thapae Gate Lodge Guesthouse
GUESTHOUSE $$

(Map p316; ☎095 135 9433; https://thapae-gatelodge.thailandhotels.site; 38/7 Soi 2, Th Moon Muang; d from 800B; ❄️🛜) An upgrade of a typical Thai house, with simple but good-value backpacker rooms, some quite large and/or with balconies. It was purchased and remodelled by new owners in 2017. Delicious breakfasts are worth the extra 100B.

★ Tamarind Village
HOTEL $$$

(Map p316; ☎053 418 8969; www.tamarindvillage.com; 50/1 Th Ratchadamnoen; d incl breakfast from 5200B, ste 8200-10,700B; ❄️🛜🏊) This refined, atmospheric Lanna-style property sprawls across the grounds of an old tamarind orchard in a prime location off Th Ratchadamnoen. Walkways covered by tiled pavilions lead to secluded and beautiful spaces, and tall mature trees cast gentle shade around the huge pool and gardens. Design-magazine-worthy rooms are full of gorgeous tribal fabrics and artefacts. There's a babysitting service for children aged one year or older.

The Ruen Tamarind restaurant (p343) serves beautifully presented Thai dishes, and there's an opulent spa offering the full range of treatments.

U Chang Mai
BOUTIQUE HOTEL $$$

(Map p316; ☎053 327000; www.uhotelsresorts.com/uchiangmai; 70 Th Ratchadamnoen; d from 6000B; ❄️🛜🏊) Tucked efficiently into the heart of the old city, this graceful boutique hotel stands out for its excellent service and stellar location. The apartment-style accommodation surrounds a 19th-century former governor's mansion housing the spa, library and reception, and two plunge pools are tightly squeezed between buildings. The onsite restaurant serves good Thai food.

BED Phrasingh Hotel
BOUTIQUE HOTEL $$$

(Map p316; ☎053 271009; www.bed.co.th; Soi 1, Th Samlan; d from 2250B; ❄️🛜🏊) This is our favourite of the near-identical, towering black, sleekly modern hotels in this small chain now in four locations in Chiang Mai. Hidden behind vines on a small lane only a few minutes' walk from some of the city's most splendid, glittering sights and local food, it's insanely popular so book ahead.

Baan Huen Phen
BOUTIQUE HOTEL $$$

(Map p316; ☎053 281100; www.baanhuenphen.com; 117/1 Th Ratchamankha; d incl breakfast 2000-5500B, ste 5500B; ❄️🛜🏊) Near the northern Thai restaurant of the same name, this upgraded Thai house has large, comfy rooms with immaculate bathrooms, and sit-on balconies out front. There's a small but lovely swimming pool and lots of Hang Dong crafts and antiques in the communal areas downstairs.

Vieng Mantra
HOTEL $$$

(Map p316; ☎053 326640; www.viengmantra.com; 9 Soi 1, Th Ratchadamnoen; d incl breakfast 2500-3200B; ❄️@🛜🏊) A proper hotel tucked into winding Soi 1, Vieng Mantra creates a little oasis with its courtyard pool and landscaped gardens. Rooms range from simple standards to swanky deluxe-plus accommodation with circular divans and plump silk cushions. Balconies have built-in seats with a view over the electric-blue pool.

Tri Yaan Na Ros
BOUTIQUE HOTEL $$$

(Map p312; ☎053 273174; www.triyaannaros.com; 156 Th Wualai; d incl breakfast 2300-2500B; ❄️🛜🏊) South of the main tourist bustle on Th Wualai, and tucked away behind a restaurant, this charming boutique hotel features elegant period decor – perhaps the best re-creation of a traditional Thai home in Chiang Mai. Rooms come with four-poster beds, flowing drapes, oodles of dark timber and antique Buddhas. There's also a peaceful courtyard pool.

Buri Gallery
GUESTHOUSE $$$

(Map p316; ☎053 416500; www.burigallery.com; 102 Th Ratchadamnoen; d incl breakfast 1700-3500B; ❄️🛜🏊) Seconds from Wat Phra Singh, Buri Gallery is a perfect base for exploring the old city. Rooms, set around a lovely pool that's ideal for families, are tucked away behind the coffeeshop and garden in a series of converted teak buildings. Although pricey, the villas have bits and bobs of Lanna art and the best have balconies where you can sit and enjoy the sunset.

Villa Duang Champa
HOTEL $$$

(Map p316; ☎053 327199; www.villaduangchampa.today; 82 Th Ratchadamnoen; d incl breakfast 2380-2980B; ❄️🛜) In a prime piece of real estate for the Sunday Walking Street (p352) market, the airy rooms here have polished-concrete floors, antique wooden French doors, eclectic furniture, lots of colonial charm and small nooks that catch the sun. The staff are exceptionally friendly and helpful, which only brightens the space more.

Rachamankha
HOTEL $$$

(Map p312; ☎053 904111; www.rachamankha.com; 6 Soi 9, Th Rachamankha; incl breakfast d 12,387-14,022B; ste 29,891B; ❄️@🛜🏊) Entering Rachamankha is like walking into an ancient monastery or a medieval village. Interlinked courtyards lead past perfectly manicured gardens to shady terracotta-tiled pavilions boasting statues and ancient artwork. The rooms continue the opulent theme with one-of-a-kind antiques and four-poster beds.

🛏️ East of the Old City

While it isn't as quaint as the old city, Th Tha Phae is just as convenient for sightseeing and nightlife and is even closer to the Night Bazaar.

★ Purple Monkey
HOSTEL $

(Map p316; ☎099 150 5534; https://purple monkey-chiang-mai.business.site; 56/6 Th Chaiyaphum; incl breakfast dm 150B, d with fan/air-con 400/480B; ❄️🛜) This sister hostel to the wildly popular namesake in Pai opened just outside the eastern edge of Chiang Mai's old city in 2019. Rooms in the five-storey hostel

are adequate and clean, but the social atmosphere and events (including pub crawls and rooftop parties) are the real draw for backpackers. Great location near markets and bars.

Natlen Boutique Guesthouse
GUESTHOUSE $$

(Map p316; ☎053 233179; www.natlenboutique guesthouse.com; 2/4 Soi Wat Chompu, Th Chang Moi; d 1000-2400B; ❄️🛜🏊) Quirky rooms are spread over several colourful houses at this low-key guesthouse just outside the city walls. Our favourite feature is the pale-blue pool with its bubbling whirlpools. It's a five-minute walk to Tha Phae Gate, and there are lots of interesting wát in the surrounding alleyways.

Thapae Boutique House
HOTEL $$

(Map p316; ☎053 284295; www.thapae boutiquehouse.com; 4 Soi 5, Th Tha Phae; d/ste from 1000/2350B; ❄️🛜) This friendly, ageing hotel has enough murals, Thai textiles and wooden trim to justify the boutique tag, and the location is handy for both the old city and the Night Bazaar. Rooms are a little past their prime but have some character.

★ Banthai Village
HOTEL $$$

(Map p316; ☎053 252789; www.banthaivillage. com; 19 Soi 3, Th Tha Phae; d incl breakfast 3600-4800B, ste 5600-7800B; ❄️@🛜🏊) True to its name, Banthai does indeed resemble a country village transported to the modern city. The hotel sprawls over a series of wooden buildings with broad balconies, surrounding an idyllic pool and gardens overflowing with birds-of-paradise flowers. Rooms do the heritage thing, but subtly, with low wooden beds, dark-wood furniture, and scattered cushions and triangular Thai pillows.

Thanatee Boutique Hotel
BOUTIQUE HOTEL $$$

(Map p312; ☎053 274500; www.thannatee boutiquehotel.com; 2/3-7 Th Rajchiangsan; d incl breakfast 1620-1750B; ❄️🛜🏊) In a quiet residential setting southeast of the old city, this four-storey oasis will please travellers looking for luxury at an affordable price. Rooms are small and dim and bathrooms are cramped, but the dark wood, lovely Thai art and fabulous design choices throughout the hotel more than compensate, and the koi pond is a stunner. There's free airport pick-up and drop-off.

COUNTRYSIDE RESORTS

For those who find downtown Chiang Mai too hectic, there are many scenic country resorts just beyond the superhighways where you can surround yourself with misty mountains, green fields and tropical forests. The following are less than two hours' drive from Chiang Mai.

Proud Phu Fah (☑ 053 879389; www.proudphufah.com; Rte 1096, Km 17; d incl breakfast 5500-15,000B; ❄ @ ⊚ ▣) Designer chic in the jungle, this elegant country resort offers atmospheric accommodation on the Mae Sa–Samoeng loop.

Tharnthong Lodges (☑ 081 961538; www.tharnthonglodge.com; d 1200-4000B; ⊚) An eclectic chalet-style jungle resort close to Mae Kampong, with trickling brooks, scattered statues and rabbits leaping around the lawns.

Four Seasons Chiang Mai (p359) Ultra-upmarket but beautifully executed, with lodges scattered through rainforests and rice fields tilled by local farmers, close to Mae Rim.

Dhara Dhevi (☑ 053 888888; www.dharadhevi.com; 51/4 Th Chiang Mai–San Kamphaeng, off Rte 1006; d from 12,500B; ❄ @ ⊚ ▣) Chiang Mai's most elegant address, this lavish resort conjures a medieval Lanna village, right down to the farmers toiling on rice terraces between the villas. It's 5km east of the city.

Kaomai Lanna Resort (☑ 053 481201; www.kaomailanna.com; Rte 108, San Pa Thong; d incl breakfast 1800-8000B; ❄ ⊚ ▣) This resort is set in a series of converted tobacco-curing sheds, redeveloped as swish hotel rooms. The resort can arrange tours to nearby handicraft villages and the cafe is delightful.

Chai Lai Orchid (☑ 086 923 0867; www.chailaiorchid.com; 202 Mu 9, Tambon Mae Win, Mae Wang; d 1500-1800B; ❄ ⊚) This collection of comfortable jungle huts is planted in the middle of the forest, reached via a suspended footbridge across Mae Wang.

Panviman Chiang Mai (☑ 053 879 5405; www.panvimanresortchiangmai.com; 197/2 Mu 1, Tambol Pongyeang; d incl breakfast from 8000B; ❄ ⊚ ▣) On the Mae Sa–Samoeng loop, a mountaintop stay with opulent villas, a tasty Thai restaurant and amenities galore.

Mo Rooms
HOTEL $$$

(Map p316; ☑ 053 280789; www.morooms. com; 263/1-2 Th Tha Phae; d incl breakfast 2800-3900B; ❄ @ ⊚ ▣) Mo Rooms is designer in the urban mould, all exposed concrete and sculptural timbers juxtaposed with natural materials. Each of the Chinese-zodiac-themed rooms was decorated by a different Thai artist, ensuring some unique visions in interior decor – our top picks are 'Monkey' with its woven pod bed and 'Horse' with its surreal bed-tree.

There's a pebble-lined pool out the back and an Asian-fusion restaurant up the front. Prices plummet to around 1500B in low season.

Le Meridien Chiang Mai
HOTEL $$$

(Map p316; ☑ 053 253666; www.lemeridien chiangmai.com; 108 Th Chang Khlan; d from 4800B; ❄ @ ⊚ ▣) This corporate hotel delivers a sleek modern package on the doorstep of the Night Bazaar. Cool, silent corridors open onto spacious, contemporary rooms with bathrooms linked to the bedrooms by glass walls to bring in natural light. The infinity pool with mountain views is a big draw, and cheaper walk-in rates are sometimes available.

DusitD2 Chiang Mai
HOTEL $$$

(Map p316; ☑ 053 999999; www.dusit.com; 100 Th Chang Khlan; d from 3550B; ❄ @ ⊚ ▣) DusitD2 is a slice of modern minimalism in the chaos at the Night Bazaar. The dominant orange colour scheme spills over from the lobby into the designer rooms, and hotel facilities run to a pool and a fitness room with city views.

🛏 Riverside

The neighbourhoods on either bank of the riverside are less touristy, but are handy for the night market and the riverside eateries on the east bank.

Hollanda Montri
GUESTHOUSE $

(Map p312; ☑ 053 242450; www.hollandamontri. com; 365 Th Charoenrat/Th Faham; d with fan/air-con from 550/750B; ❄ ⊚) A good-value alternative to the old-city backpacker places, within walking distance of the riverside restaurants and a half-hour walk to the old city walls. Rooms are super basic and the riverbank location is lovely and quiet. Bike and motorcycle hire can be arranged.

Riverside House   GUESTHOUSE $$

(Map p312; ☑053 241860; www.riversidehouse chiangmai.com; 101 Th Chiang Mai-Lamphun; d incl breakfast 1000-1300B; ❋@ ⬤ ⬤) Plain yet spotless and rather large rooms are spread across three blocks; you pay top baht for the central block, by the pool and away from the traffic noise, but all the rooms are good for the money. It's great value and a fine choice for families. Note that, despite the name and location, only a few rooms offer river views.

★Hotel des Artists
Ping Silhouette   BOUTIQUE HOTEL $$$

(Map p312; ☑053 249999; www.hotelartists. com; 181 Th Charoenrat/Th Faham; d incl breakfast from 3720B; ❋ ⬤ ⬤) An elegant, minimalist boutique hotel channeling the Chinese and European roots of its neighbourhood with chinoiserie details throughout, including two Tang Dynasty–style horse statues perched beside a rectangular koi pond. The on-site cafe mimics a Chinese merchant shophouse, while the accommodation is plush and modern with high ceilings and relaxing terraces. The saltwater pool is divine.

★Baan Orapin   B&B $$$

(Map p312; ☑053 243677; www.baanorapin.com; 150 Th Charoenrat/Th Faham; d incl breakfast 1800-4000B; ❋ ⬤ ⬤) Set within the historic Wat Ket district, Baan Orapin has been a family affair since the owner's relatives first occupied the stately teak house and surrounding gardens in 1914. Today, two elegant villas situated in the front and rear of the property contain 15 guest rooms full of graceful furniture and fabrics.

Na Nirand   BOUTIQUE HOTEL $$$

(Map p312; ☑053 280988; www.nanirand.com; 1/1 Soi 9, Th Charoen Prathet; d from 7500B; ❋ ⬤ ⬤) A magnificent, giant, century-old rain tree anchors this romantic boutique property perched at the edge of Mae Ping. A restored teak house contains the spa and a small library, while posh villas flank a relaxing swimming pool and are defined by ornate woodcarvings, Lanna textiles and rattan furnishings made by local artisans. Bathrooms are huge, with freestanding tubs and rain showers.

The resort restaurant, **TIME Riverfront Cuisine & Bar**, serves tasty fusion dishes and offers a pretty setting right on the river, beside the magnificent rain tree.

137 Pillars   BOUTIQUE HOTEL $$$

(Map p312; ☑02 079 7137, 053 247788; https: //137pillarschiangmai.com; 2 Soi 1, Th Nawatgate; d from 20,000B; ❋ ⬤ ⬤) This elegant resort is built around Baan Borneo, an old teak house once managed by Louis Leonowens, Rajah Brook and others as a timber trading centre. Rooms continue with the colonial luxury theme with lots of teak, period tiles and spacious bathrooms. The grounds contain several towering trees, a chic pool, two restaurants and a small museum.

Anantara Resort & Spa   DESIGN HOTEL $$$

(Map p312; ☑053 253333; www.anantara.com/en/ chiang-mai; 123 Th Charoen Prathet; d incl breakfast from 10,000B; ❋@ ⬤ ⬤) Where James Bond would stay if he came to Chiang Mai, the Anantara sprawls across the grounds of the handsome former British Consulate, and it offers a perfect blend of cutting-edge modern design and period elegance. Rooms are simply gorgeous – natural timber in varied tones, floor-to-ceiling windows, flatscreens, balconies with divans – and all overlook the Zen-inspired grounds and river.

The old consulate now houses the Service 1921 restaurant (p344) and there's a serene garden pool and a pond where staff place floating lanterns at night.

🛏 West of the Old City

Staying west of the old city puts you close to Chiang Mai University and trendy Th Nimmanhaemin's bars and restaurants.

Lab Poshtel   HOSTEL $

(Map p326; ☑063 361 4426; https://thelabposh tel.com; 64 Th Sirimungklajarn; dm 490B, d incl breakfast 1090B; ❋ ⬤) A laboratory-themed boutique hostel that takes this theme very seriously. The bright, stylish common space is somewhat creepily decorated with things like beakers, lab coats, mounted insects and anatomy charts. But the vibe is otherwise cosy, and the attached cafe, lifestyle shop and quaint outdoor bar are all fabulous.

Bunk Boutique   HOSTEL $

(Map p326; ☑091 859 9656; bunkboutique@hot mail.com; 8/7 Th Ratchaphuek; dm 250-500B, d 900-1200B; ❋ ⬤) Bunk Boutique offers comfortable accommodation in four-bed dorms in a large apartment block behind Th Huay Kaew. Blonde-wood bunks have curtains for privacy and everyone gets a locker. You can rent a dorm as a private room if there's space.

Baan Say-La   GUESTHOUSE $$
(Map p326; ☑ 053 894229; www.baansaylaguesthouse.com; 4 Soi 5, Th Nimmanhaemin; d with fan/air-con 600/900B; ❈ ☎) Set in a Nimmanhaemin shophouse, this boutique guesthouse has stylish rooms in a mixture of styles – modernist, heritage, flowery colonial – and the owners keep the place looking immaculately clean and prim. Prices are as low as you'll find this close to the action.

Hotel Noir   BOUTIQUE HOTEL $$$
(Map p326; ☑ 064 351 7007; www.hotelnoir.co.th; 5/8 Th Nimmanahaemin; d from 1800B; ❈ ☎) The prime Nimman location, tranquil and leafy courtyard and friendly service are the big selling points at this quaint little boutique hotel. Rooms are minimally adorned but perfectly comfortable, with nice views of the block. Vintage bicycles are available for city touring.

Kantary Hills   HOTEL $$$
(Map p312; ☑ 053 222111; www.kantarycollection.com; Soi 12, Th Nimmanhaemin; d 3800-7200B, apt per month from 50,000B; ❈ ☎ ⊠) Immaculately turned-out Kantary Hills offers stylish apartment-style rooms with kitchens in a vast, self-contained complex set back a bit from the Nimmanhaemin action. It's a favourite with the business and diplomatic set. The bland studios are overpriced but the one- and two-bedroom choices are quite luxurious.

Artel Nimman   BOUTIQUE HOTEL $$$
(Map p326; ☑ 053 213143; www.facebook.com/theartelnimman; Soi 13, Th Nimmanhaemin; d from 1700B; ❈ ☎) We're suckers for hotels with slides, so the Artel delivers in spades. The modernist building is all round windows, polished concrete, geometric forms and juxtaposed materials, and the rooms are cool, calm, creative spaces. It's built mostly with upcycled materials and is as friendly as can be.

Yesterday Hotel   BOUTIQUE HOTEL $$$
(Map p326; ☑ 053 213809; www.yesterday.co.th; 24 Th Nimmanhaemin; d from 3200B; ❈ ☎) In the heart of the action on Th Nimmanhaemin, Yesterday offers a quick trip back to the near past. Communal spaces are decorated

with vintage prints, old phonographs, Bakelite phones and flashback tube TVs, and the rooms have a more subtle mid-century mood.

✕ Eating

The city's fabulous night markets (p342), which sprawl around the main city gates and several other locations, offer the best food. The Chinese-influenced love for pork is exemplified by the northern Thai speciality of *sâi òo·a* (pork sausage). A good-quality *sâi òo·a* should be zesty and spicy with subtle flavours of lemongrass, ginger and turmeric. Sample them at any food market.

✕ Old City

★**SP Chicken**   THAI $
(Map p316; 9/1 Soi 1, Th Samlan; mains 40-170B; ◷10am-5pm) Chiang Mai's best chicken emerges daily from the grills at this tiny cafe near Wat Phra Singh. The menu runs to salads and soups, but most people just pick a half (90B) or whole (170B) chicken, and dip the moist meat into the spicy, tangy sauces provided.

★**Lert Ros**   THAI $
(Map p316; Soi 1, Th Ratchadamnoen; mains 30-160B; ◷noon-9pm) As you enter this local hole in the wall, you'll pass the main course: delicious whole tilapia fish, grilled on coals and served with a fiery Isan-style dipping sauce. Eaten with sticky rice, this is one of the great meals of Chiang Mai. The menu also includes fermented pork grilled in banana leaves, curries and *sôm·đam* (spicy green papaya salad).

★**Talat Pratu Chiang Mai**   MARKET $
(Map p316; Th Bamrungburi; mains from 40B; ◷4am-noon & 6pm-midnight) In the early morning, this market is Chiang Mai's larder, selling foodstuffs and ready-made dishes. If you want to make merit to the monks, come early and find the woman who sells pre-assembled food donations (20B); she'll explain the ritual to you. Things quiet down by lunchtime, but the burners are reignited for a popular night market that sets up along the road.

Blue Diamond   VEGETARIAN $
(Map p316; ☑ 053 217120; 35/1 Soi 9, Th Moon Muang; mains 65-260B; ◷7am-9pm Mon-Sat; ☑) Tucked into a leafy compound with a waterfall and koi pond, Blue Diamond offers an

KÔW SOY SAMPLER

Chiang Mai's unofficial city dish is *kôw soy*, wheat-and-egg noodles in a curry broth, served with pickled vegetables and sliced shallots, and garnished with deep-fried crispy noodles. The dish is thought to have its origins with the Yunnanese traders who came to Chiang Mai along the Silk Road, and the vendors along **Halal Street** (Soi 1, Th Charoen Prathet) near the Night Bazaar still serve some of the best in town. For our baht, Kao Soi Fueng Fah (p343) has the edge over other vendors, with its particularly flavourful bowls, but the more simple and salty broth at Khao Soi Islam Noodles (p343) is more popular with locals.

Another great place to try *kôw soy* is around **Wat Faham** on Th Charoenrat (also known as Th Faham), north of the Th Ratanakosin bridge on the eastern bank of Mae Ping. Our top pick is Khao Soi Lam Duan Fah Ham (p344), a modest-looking place that is packed to the rafters at lunchtime with hordes of locals slurping down bowls of deliciously rich *kôw soy*. Nearby **Khao Soi Samoe Jai** (Map p312; 391 Th Charoenrat/Th Faham; mains 40-70B; ⊘ 8am-5pm) also cooks up a tasty soup.

adventurous menu of delicious breakfasts, sandwiches, salads, curries, stir-fries and curious fusion dishes such as *đôm yam* (Thai-style sour soup) with macaroni. There's also a lovely, attached store featuring fresh produce, prepackaged spice and herb mixes, freshly baked treats, and organic soaps and oils.

Huen Phen THAI $
(Map p316; ☑ 053 277103; 112 Th Ratchamankha; mains lunch 30-100B, dinner 80-200B; ⊘ 8.30am-4pm & 5-10pm) Huen Phen restaurant serves a comprehensive, and usually quite delicious, selection of northern Thai food in an antique bric-a-brac and plant-filled house that feels more like a garden. It's phenomenally popular, so come early or face a long wait for a table. We loved the Burmese-style pork curry.

Bird's Nest Cafe MEDITERRANEAN $
(Map p312; ☑ 095 914 0265; https://facebook. com/birdsnestcafe; 11 Soi 3, Th Singharat; mains 100-180B; ⊘ 8.30am-4.30pm Wed-Mon; ☑) A tranquil little cafe serving Thai and Mediterranean food and spread over two stories of a lovely teak house on a quiet block in the old city. The shakshuka and potato hash breakfasts are particularly good, and the organic local produce and homemade bread, yogurt, salad dressings and cookies all pair perfectly with the cosy environment.

Vegans will be pleased to know there's a set, three-course breakfast menu designed specifically for them.

Goodsouls Kitchen VEGAN $
(Map p316; ☑ 088 819 9669; 52/2 Th Singharat; mains 100-180B; ⊘ 7am-10pm; ☑) Serving food

that's good for the stomach and soul, Goodsouls Kitchen whips up vegan Thai, Western and fusion fare. Though some dishes are pricey for Chiang Mai (such as 120B for potato wedges), others are reasonable and the variety makes it a popular spot for vegans and meat eaters alike. The mushroom burger is a real crowd pleaser.

Good Morning Chiang Mai INTERNATIONAL $
(Map p316; 29/5 Soi 6, Th Ratchamankha; breakfast & mains 80-150B; ⊘ 8am-8pm) A favourite among expats, this guesthouse cafe near Wat Phra Jao Mengrai serves big, international breakfasts, from pancake towers to continental spreads and *đôm yam*–flavoured pasta. You can eat inside, in the cafe covered with movie memorabilia, or in the garden by the pool.

Dada Kafe VEGETARIAN $
(Map p316; Th Ratchamankha; mains 75-180B; ⊘ 9.30am-9.30pm Mon-Sat; ☑) A lovely little restaurant that does a busy trade in vitamin-rich, tasty vegetarian health food and smoothies. Wholesome ingredients such as pollen and wheatgrass are whisked into fruit shakes and the food menu includes veggie burgers, omelettes, salads, sandwiches and curries with brown rice.

★ **Ginger & Kafe @ The House** THAI $$
(Map p316; ☑ 053 287681; www.thehousebyginger cm.com; 199 Th Moon Muang; mains 160-390B; ⊘ 10am-11pm) Dining at the restaurant in The House boutique feels like eating in a posh Thai mansion, with antique furniture, comfy sofas and fine china. The Thai food is delicious and lavishly presented, with wonderful dishes including items like Massaman

MARKET MEALS

Everyone knows that the best food in Chiang Mai is served on the street, and the city's night markets are fragrant, frenetic and fabulous. Every evening from around 5pm, hawker stalls set up in key locations around the old city, alongside smoothie stalls and beer and soft-drink vendors. Each stall has a speciality: you'll find everything from grilled river fish and *pàt gà prow* (chicken or meat fried with chilli and holy basil) to Western-style steaks, grilled prawns, and 'Tornado potato' (a whole potato, corkscrew-sliced and deep-fried).

The city's day markets are also thronged by food stalls and wholesale vendors, who prepare *gàp kôw* (pre-made stews and curries served with rice) and other takeaway meals for busy city workers. And, of course, the Saturday and Sunday Walking Street markets (p352) are mobbed by food hawkers. Here's a guide to Chiang Mai's best market eats:

Talat Pratu Chiang Mai (p340) This heaving market sells foodstuffs and ready-made packed lunches by day and night-market treats after dark. It's mobbed nightly, particularly during Th Wualai's Saturday Walking Street.

Talat Pratu Chang Pheuak (Map p316; Th Mani Nopharat; mains from 30B; ⊙5-11pm) Sprawling west from the city's northern gate, this is one of Chiang Mai's most popular night markets, serving all the usual suspects, alongside the city's finest *kôw kǎh mǒo* (slow-cooked pork leg with rice), prepared with a flourish by the 'Cowboy Hat Lady' – you can't miss her stall.

Talat Somphet (Map p316; Soi 6, Th Moon Muang; mains from 30B; ⊙8am-7pm) A small local food market north of Pratu Tha Phae that transforms into a night market after hours. Many of the cooking schools do their market tours here.

Talat Ton Phayom (Map p312; Th Suthep; ⊙8am-6pm) This local market off Th Suthep is a popular stop for visiting Thais who come to pick up authentic northern foodstuffs such as *kàap mǒo* (pork rinds).

Talat Warorot (p320) The grandmother of Chiang Mai markets has northern Thai food stalls (mains from 30B) tucked in all sorts of corners.

Talat Thanin (Siri Wattana; Map p312; off Th Chotana/Th Chang Pheuak; mains from 30B; ⊙5am-7pm) North of the old city off Th Chotana (Th Chang Pheuak), this public market specialises in takeaway meals, with vendors serving fish stews, curries, stir-fries and spicy condiments from huge pans, vats and platters.

Talat Na Mor (Map p312; Malin Plaza, Th Huay Kaew; mains from 40B; ⊙5-10pm) A cheerful night market for the college set, with low prices and lots of choice; the student restaurants nearby on Th Huay Kaew are also worth investigating.

curry with slow-cooked beef in lime-coconut cream. There's also a lovely fashion shop and a swanky cocktail lounge under the same ownership next door.

Fahtara Coffee
THAI **$$**

(Map p316; ☏053 416191; www.fahtara.coffee; 57/1 Th Wiang Kaew; mains 250-450B; ⊙8am-9pm; 🛜) Tucked into the dreamy Fah Lanna (p330) spa complex in the old city, this ambient Thai cafe can do no wrong. The excellent coffee is grown by hill-tribe communities, and the fruit shakes, hearty breakfasts, healthy salads and Thai dishes are all delicious and gorgeously presented. Outdoors, a garden patio is adorned in brightly colored pillows, parasols and a giant, decorative water wheel.

Overstand Coffee Shop
CAFE **$$**

(Map p316; ☏085 711 2762; www.facebook.com/OverstandCoffee; Soi 2, 19/3 Th Ratchamankha; mains 100-220B; ⊙8am-3.30pm; 🛜🥬) Western breakfasts done right, killer local coffee and a bit of attitude. Overstand is a longstanding favourite for Chiang Mai expats due to its high-quality ingredients and range of dishes. While there's plenty of bacon and eggs, the cafe also does several vegetarian, vegan and gluten-free options. The walls feature local artists. There's another location at Soi 5, 29 Nimmanhaemin.

Mit Mai
CHINESE **$$**

(Map p316; Th Ratchamankha; mains 60-900B; ⊙10am-10pm) If you didn't make it to northern Thailand's mountaintop Chinese outposts, this decades-old restaurant is the place to go for Yunnanese specialities. Just about anything flash-fried is tasty, and you can't go wrong with the air-dried Yunnanese ham. There's no Roman-script sign, but it's adjacent to Wat Pha Khao.

Girasole   ITALIAN $$

(Map p316; ☑ 053 276388; Kad Klang Wiang, Th Ratchadamnoen; mains 120-450B; ⊙ 11am-11pm) In the tidy little Kad Klang Wiang arcade, Girasole makes a convincing claim to offer the city's best pizzas, prepared using real pepperoni and other hard-to-find ingredients. There are several spaces for eating, both inside and outside, and the menu runs to superior pasta dishes and *secondi piatti,* plus tasty gelato for dessert.

Ruen Tamarind   THAI $$$

(Map p316; 50/1 Th Ratchadamnoen; mains 250-580B; ⊙ 7-10am & 11am-11pm; ☑) For a sophisticated dinner, the restaurant at Tamarind Village (p336) hotel serves superior northern Thai food in sleek surrounds overlooking the pool. Dishes such as *yum tawai gài* (spicy chicken salad with tamarind dressing) are presented as works of art, and musicians serenade diners.

✖ East of the Old City

In the early morning, vendors sell *nám đow·hôo* (soy milk) and baton-shaped *you-tiao* (Chinese-style doughnuts) from stalls in Chiang Mai's small Chinatown (p323). For the very best *sâi òo·a* (pork sausage) seek out the stall known as **Dom Rong** inside the dried-goods hall at Talat Warorot (p320).

Asa   VEGAN $

(Asa Kitchen; Map p316; ☑ 087 304 3220; www. facebook.com/asakitchenandstudio; 217 Th Tha Phae; mains from 125B; ⊙ 9.30am-7pm; ☑) This shophouse eatery serves nutrient-packed vegan dishes ranging from herbal Burmese and Thai-style salads to creamy curries and rice bowls topped with colourful veggies. Meaning 'to volunteer' in Thai, Asa is more than just a cafe. Upstairs you'll find regular drop-in yoga classes, plus the restaurant organises various workshops and volunteer opportunities.

Khao Soi Islam Noodles   THAI $

(Map p312; Soi 1, Th Charoen Prathet; mains from 50B; ⊙ 7.30am-5pm) The locals' favourite for *kôw soy* (wheat-and-egg noodles in curry broth), although we found it less flavourful

and more salty than other options on this street. Portions are large, however.

Hideout   BREAKFAST $

(Map p316; Th Sithiwongse; breakfast 55-160B; ⊙ 8am-5pm Tue-Sun; ☑) Hidden but found by expats looking for Western breakfast and coffee a cut above the rest, this place takes great care to serve perfectly cooked eggs, bacon fried to order, house-made muesli and yogurt, creative sandwiches on fresh bread and excellent banana bread.

Thanom Phochana   THAI $

(Map p316; Th Chayaphum; mains 60-80B; ⊙ 11am-1pm & 5-8pm Mon-Fri) Thanom Phochana has all the atmosphere of a hospital cafeteria, but central Thai eats here are as good as any in Bangkok. There's no English sign – look for the 'Please Dress Politely' sign (a policy they do enforce) – nor is there a menu; just point to what looks tasty.

Kao Soi Fueng Fah   THAI $

(Map p312; Soi 1, Th Charoen Phrathet; mains 40-60B; ⊙ 7.30am-9pm) The most flavourful of the Muslim-run *kôw soy* (wheat-and-egg noodles in a curry broth) joints along Halal St, with the choice of beef or chicken with your noodles.

Swan   BURMESE $

(Map p316; 48 Th Chaiyaphum; mains 70-150B; ⊙ 11am-11pm) This quaint restaurant just east of the old city offers a trip across the border, with a menu of tasty Burmese dishes such as tea leaf and pennywort salads, and *gaang hang lay* (dry, sour pork curry with tamarind and peanuts). The leafy courtyard provides an escape from moat traffic.

✖ Riverside

The east side of Mae Ping is a good hunting ground for upscale choices.

★ Laap Kao Cham Chaa   THAI $

(Map p312; Th Ratanakosin; mains 50-200B; ⊙ noon-9pm Mon-Sat) Popularised by the late, great Anthony Bourdain, this low-key street stall beneath a rain tree (after which it is named) is now a staple for authentic northern Thai food. Plop down in a plastic chair, grab a Singha and feast on heaping plates of pounded-pomelo salad, Thai-style beef or pork *lâhp* (raw or cooked) and crab paste.

Feeling even more adventurous? There's always the roasted pork tongue or the fried frog with garlic. No English menu.

★ **Khao Soi Lam Duan Fah Ham** THAI $
(Map p312; 352/22 Th Charoenrat/Th Faham;
mains from 40B; ⊙9am-4pm) North of the Th
Ratanakosin bridge on the east bank, Th
Faham is known as Chiang Mai's *kôw soy*
(wheat-and-egg noodles in curry broth)
ghetto. Khao Soi Lam Duan Fah Ham is the
pick of the bunch, serving delicious bowls of
kôw soy to eager crowds of punters.

★ **Woo** CAFE $$
(Map p312; ☑052 003717; www.woochiangmai.
com; 80 Th Charoenrat/Th Faham; mains 150-
500B; ⊙10am-10pm; 🛜) A riverside, three-in-
one stop for delicious meals, contemporary
art and perhaps a bit of shopping. The styl-
ish, modern cafe specialises in Thai food,
salads and freshly baked goods, but the
menu is enormous and also includes every
imaginable beverage. Edgy art adorns the
walls, and regular exhibitions feature a ro-
tating crop of Thai artists.

**Riverside Bar &
Restaurant** INTERNATIONAL $$
(Map p312; ☑053 243239; www.theriverside
chiangmai.com; Th Charoenrat/Th Faham; mains
100-370B; dinner cruise adult/child 180/90B;
⊙10am-1am) Almost everyone ends up at
Riverside at some point in their Chiang Mai
stay. Set in an old teak house, it feels like
a countryside reimagining of a Hard Rock
Cafe, and bands play nightly until late. Stake
out a claim on the riverside terrace or the
upstairs balcony to catch the evening breeze
on Mae Ping.

The restaurant also runs a popular dinner
cruise along Mae Ping that leaves the dock
at 8pm each night. Over an enchanting,
75-minute ride, the boat drifts past ancient
temples and centuries-old homes along the
riverbank. Reserve well in advance.

Service 1921 SOUTHEAST ASIAN $$
(Map p312; ☑053 253333; 123 Th Charoen Prathet;
mains 180-600B; ⊙noon-11pm; 🍴) The pan-
Asian restaurant at the Anantara Resort &
Spa (p339) is straight out of a spy movie,
with waitstaff in 1920s garb, menus deliv-
ered in 'top secret' envelopes and interior
decor resembling the offices of MI6. It's ap-
propriate, considering that the gorgeous
teak villa housing the restaurant used to be
the British Consulate. Ask to see the secret
room behind the false bookcase.

River Market THAI $$
(Map p312; ☑053 234493; https://therivermar
ket.com; Th Charoen Prathet; mains 155-500B;
⊙11am-11pm) Trading on its location rather
than its kitchen, River Market nevertheless scores romantic dinner points for the
nighttime views across the illuminated Iron
Bridge. The menu covers all the usual Thai
bases.

Oxygen Dining Room INTERNATIONAL $$$
(Map p312; ☑053 931999; X2 Chiang Mai Riverside,
369/1 Th Charoenrat; lunch tasting menu 990B,
dinner tasting menu from 1990B; ⊙7-10.30am,
11.30am-2.30pm & 6.30-10.30pm) Adventurous
palates will be pleased with the imaginative
tasting menus dreamed up by chefs here,
who bring their French training to South-
east Asian dishes. Think *lâhp* croquettes
and *khao soi gai* with sheets of noodles en-
casing chicken and bathed in coconut foam.
The all-glass dining room affords lovely
views of Mae Ping and the mountains.

Save some room for the mango sticky rice.

🍴 West of the Old City

Th Nimmanhaemin and the surrounding
soi excel in international cuisine, but restau-
rants and cafes appear and vanish overnight.

Kinlum Kindee THAI $
(Map p326; ☑064 614 0817; www.facebook.com/
Kinlumkindee; 25 Soi 9, Th Nimmanhaemin; mains
60-120B; ⊙11am-9.30pm) 🍴 Meaning 'eat
delicious, eat well', Kinlum Kindee aims
to elevate northern Thai cuisine by using
high-quality, sustainable ingredients from
local producers. The brand has a food line
sold in markets and online, but at the res-
taurant you'll find the specialities, such as
sâi òo·a and *nám prík nùm,* featured in
dishes to share.

Tong Tem Toh THAI $
(Map p326; ☑053 894701; www.facebook.com/
TongTemToh; 11 Soi 13, Th Nimmanhaemin; mains
57-177B; ⊙7am-9pm) Set in an unpretentious
garden of a teak house, this highly popu-
lar restaurant serves deliciously authentic
northern Thai cuisine. The menu roams be-
yond the usual to specialities such as *nám
prík ong* (chilli paste with vegetables for
dipping), *gaang hang lay* (Burmese-style
pork curry with peanut and tamarind) plus
a few more adventurous dishes using snake-
head fish and ant eggs.

Tikky Cafe THAI $
(Map p312; ☑098 796 2182; www.facebook.
com/tikkycafe; 20 Th Taeparak; mains 50-80B;
⊙9.30am-8pm) In a new, quiet location

northeast of Nimman since 2019, Tikky Cafe is worth the extra effort. The colourful cafe specialises in delicious fruit drinks that make perfect sense with a healthy Thai salad, noodle or rice dish (you set the spice level). Woven tablecloths and a koi pond lend some tranquility, while a full bar keeps things interesting.

Nong Bee's Burmese Restaurant and Library
BURMESE $

(Map p326; 28 Soi 1, Th Nimmanhaemin; mains 30-60B; ⊙10am-9pm) The name may be a bit misleading, as this street food stall is in no way connected with a library. But the tea leaf and pennywort salads are delicious, and the price is impossibly low. Northern Thai food is also on offer, with specialities such as fried noodles with minced pork and fried rice with seafood.

Free Bird Cafe
VEGAN $

(Map p326; ☑099 351 4404; www.facebook.com/FreeBirdCafe; Soi 9, 14 Sirimungklajarn; mains from 95B; ⊙9am-9pm Tue-Sat, to 5pm Sun; ☑) 🌿 Chiang Mai's original 'cafe with a cause', Free Bird Cafe supports community art and language classes for refugees from Myanmar. The vegan restaurant is known for tangy Shan salads along with a solid all-day breakfast menu. You'll also find secondhand clothing for sale as well as zero-waste goods ranging from reusable food containers to bulk shampoos, soaps and more.

Somtum Der
THAI $

(Somtum Der Chiang Mai; Map p326; ☑090 325 1181; www.facebook.com/SomtumDerChiangmai; One Nimman, Soi 1; mains 65-150B; ⊙11am-10pm, from 10am Sat & Sun) Get ready to feel the heat at Somtum Der, a fun and friendly eatery serving authentic Isan dishes including several kinds of *sôm·đam* (spicy green papaya salad), flavourful soups, deep-fried chicken and marinated grilled pork, all eaten with sticky rice. Make sure to order several dishes to share, family-style!

Cosy and casual, the restaurant has received Michelin recognition for its Bangkok and New York branches yet still offers dishes starting at 65B.

Neau-Toon Rod Yiam
THAI $

(Map p326; Soi 11, Th Nimmanhaemin; mains 60-100B; ⊙9.30am-8pm, to 6pm Sat & Sun) Build your own soup at this yummy corner-shop cheapie. Choose between rice or several types of noodles, spice level, then meat,

ranging from basic chicken to beef entrails. It also makes a decent *kôw soy* and hotpot.

Anchan Noodle
THAI $

(Map p326; ☑084 949 2828; www.facebook.com/anchannoodle; Soi 9, Th Sirimungklajarn; mains 40-70B; ⊙8am-4pm) No, your eyes aren't playing tricks on you, those really are blue noodles. Naturally coloured by dark-blue butterfly pea blossoms, and known as *anchan* in Thai, these bowls of noodle soup are otherwise similar to the typical *gŏo·ay đěe·o* you'll find throughout the country. And along with the blue noodles you can also get a yummy blue-hued latte.

Imm Aim Vegetarian and Bike Cafe
VEGETARIAN $

(Map p312; ☑092 798 2436; 10 Th Santhitham; mains 45-90B; ⊙10am-9pm; ☑) 🌿 This vegetarian place was originally opened as a sister restaurant to Pun Pun. Although it is now independent, the manager still sometimes buys vegetables from the Pun Pun farm. The pad Thai and fresh spring rolls are especially tasty, and should be accompanied with ginger tea. There's also an organic chocolate-making operation on-site.

Pun Pun
VEGETARIAN $

(Map p312; www.punpunthailand.org; Wat Suan Dok, Th Suthep; mains 40-90B; ⊙8am-4pm; ☑) 🌿 Tucked away at the back of Wat Suan Dok, this studenty cafe is a great place to sample Thai vegetarian food prepared using little-known herbs and vegetables and lots of healthy whole grains grown on its concept farm, which doubles as an education centre for sustainable living.

Smoothie Blues
INTERNATIONAL $

(Map p326; 32/8 Th Nimmanhaemin; mains 95-200B; ⊙7.30am-8pm) This expat favourite is a top spot for breakfast – pancakes, sandwiches, granola, an array of egg dishes from egg-white-only omelettes to decadent Benedicts, you know the drill – plus, of course, smoothies and fresh juices.

Larder Cafe & Bar
CAFE $$

(Map p326; ☑052 001594; 3/9 Th Suk Kasame; mains 130-270B; ⊙8.30am-3pm; ☑) In hip Nimman, there are a lot of bright, healthy little cafes serving muesli bowls and salads and good coffee. The Larder is one of the best, though, and in addition to all the usual suspects, it also serves uncommon items such as breakfast hot dogs, open-face pumpkin sandwiches and the occasional steak and egg special. There are lots of gluten-free, vegetarian and vegan options, too.

Italics
ITALIAN $$

(Map p326; ☑ 053 216219; www.theakyra.com/chiang-mai; 22/2 Soi 9, Th Nimmanhaemin; pizzas 260-550B; ⊙ 7am-11pm; ❈ 🛜) Yes, the modern black decor and gigantic, golden candelabra-style chandeliers are interesting, pastas and mains innovative and cocktails addictive – but it's the perfect pizzas that make Italics a top choice in Chiang Mai. We are still dreaming of the Akyra, with mozzarella, mushrooms, salami, bacon, blue cheese and truffle paste.

Ginger Farm Kitchen
THAI $$

(Map p326; ☑ 089 433 7493; www.facebook.com/gingerfarmkitchen; One Nimman, Th Nimmanhaemin; mains 115-175B; ⊙ 10am-11pm) Part of the One Nimman shopping plaza, this quaint Thai eatery and its attached organics shop put fresh, local creations front and centre, with produce flowing in from Ginger Farm (จินเจอร์ฟาร์ม; ☑ 052 004473; 34/1 Mu 12, Hang Khawe Soi 9, Saraphi; ⊙ 10am-7pm Mon-Fri, 9am-8pm Sat & Sun; 🛗). Beloved dishes include fried sea bass with mixed herbs, fried pineapple with grilled river prawns and pomelo salad with crab paste. Sister restaurant Ginger & Kafe (p341) is also wonderful.

L'Elephant
FRENCH $$$

(Map p326; ☑ 097 970 8947; http://lelephant chiangmai.com; 7 Soi 11, Th Sirimungklajarn; set lunch/dinner from 550/670B; ⊙ 11.30am-4pm & 5.30-10pm Tue-Sun) When you simply can't stomach any more Thai street food, saunter into this elegant oasis and feast on melt-in-your-mouth beef carpaccio, hearty ox tongue stew and tender (and crunchy!) duck confit. Service is friendly and on the ball, and the charming rooms, corridors and garden are tastefully adorned in fine art and antiques. The tasting menus offer superb value.

✖ Elsewhere

Out-of-town spots are favourites for Thais celebrating a special occassion.

★ Huean Jai Yong
THAI $

(64 Mu 4, Th San Kamphaeng; mains 30-80B; ⊙ 10am-4pm Tue-Sun) Northern Thai food enthusiasts shouldn't miss this out-of-town gem, where authentic, hard-to-find dishes beloved by the people of Myanmar's Shan State (and their Lanna ancestors) are served in traditional ways – and with the customary

amount of spice. Try the tilapia or raw pork *lâhp*, and a spicy soup with either (whole) frog or sun-dried fish and ant eggs.

Wash all the goodness down with fresh fruit juice.

Nic's Restaurant & Playground
THAI $$

(☑ 087 007 3769; www.nics.asia; Th Ratchapruek; mains 150-400B; ⊙ 11.30am-10pm Tue-Sun; 🖉 🛗) This family-friendly restaurant has the perfect combination of Western and Thai dishes, plus an imaginative bamboo playground for children to play, climb and bounce. It has a good selection of vegetarian and vegan options, wine and beer, and even gluten-free desserts. Nic's is a very popular place for birthday parties, offering a variety of activities, decorations and entertainers when booked in advance.

David's Kitchen
FRENCH $$$

(Map p312; ☑ 091 068 1744; https://davidskitchen.co.th; 113 Th Bamrungrat; 4-course set menu 1450B; mains 460-2600B; ⊙ 6-10pm Mon-Sat) A perennial favourite among well-heeled travellers, expat-owned David's Kitchen offers a bright, elegant atmosphere and level of service unparalleled in Chiang Mai. And the food is, well, pretty good. Dishes like prawn ravioli in lobster sauce are rousing and flavourful, while items on the long-standing set menu are well executed but unremarkable.

The attached wine and tapas bar Piccolo and its candlelit veranda are a good bet for live music after dinner. Best of all, every wine in the cellar can be ordered by the glass.

🍷 Drinking & Nightlife

Chiang Mai has three primary areas for watering holes: the old city, the riverside and Th Nimmanhaemin. Almost everyone ends up at either Riverside (p344) or Good View) on the east bank of Mae Ping at some point in their stay.

Bars & Clubs

★ Good View
BAR

(Map p312; www.goodview.co.th; 13 Th Charoenrat/Th Faham; ⊙ 10am-1am) Good View attracts plenty of locals, with a big menu of Thai standards, Japanese dishes and Western options (mains 100B to 400B), and a nightly program of house bands with rotating line-ups (meaning the drummer starts playing guitar and the bass player moves behind the piano).

CHIANG MAI'S COFFEE BUZZ

If you closed your eyes and started randomly walking in central Chiang Mai, chances are high you'd walk into a cafe – there are that many. While global chains are present, most places are local, selling coffee sourced from the hill tribes and forest communities around the city. The high-quality arabica beans grown here were introduced as a replacement crop for opium. Some cafes have started taking coffee culture even further by roasting their own beans and brewing cups that would fit right in in Melbourne or San Francisco. Here are our picks for the most snob-worthy coffees in Chiang Mai:

Graph (Map p316; 086 567 3330; www.graphdream.com; 25/1 Soi 1, Th Ratwithi; coffee 80-220B; 9am-5pm;) It's famous for its Nitrobrews, and its employees are involved in every step of the process, 'tree to cup'. Also an old city location and another at One Nimman.

Akha Ama Cafe (Map p316; www.akhaama.com; 175/1 Th Ratchadamnoen; 8am-5.30pm;) A cute local coffee shop founded by an enterprising Akha who was the first in his village to graduate from college.

Ristr8to (Map p326; 053 215278; www.ristr8to.com; Th Nimmanhaemin; espresso drinks from 88B; 7am-6pm) Inspired by Australian coffee culture with roasting skills learned in the US; drinks come with a caffeine rating and are often topped with award-winning latte art. There are two branches in the Nimmanhaemin area.

Khagee (Map p312; Soi 1, Chiang Mai-Lamphun; espresso drinks 75B; 10am-5pm Wed-Sun;) A Japanese-style place that's insanely popular. Pair basic but near-perfect brews with its fresh breads and pastries.

Wawee Coffee (Map p316; www.waweecoffee.com; Th Ratchadamnoen, Kad Klang Wiang; drinks from 50B; 8am-9pm Mon-Sat, to 11pm Sun;) It's hard to go more than a few blocks in Chiang Mai without stumbling across an air-conditioned Wawee Coffee branch. If you're in a bind, this will do.

Cru Wine Bar
WINE BAR

(Map p316; 089 552 2822; www.facebook.com/CRUwinebarcm; 2nd fl, 8-10 Th Samlan; glasses 150-300B; 6pm-midnight Tue-Sun) Chiang Mai's only wine bar is up a hidden stairway with just a tiny sign pointing the way, but those who uncover it are in for a treat. The cosy space is adorned in dark wood and fairy lights, and the well-chosen, rotating international wine offerings pair well with a small menu of delicious tapas.

Hotel Yayee
ROOFTOP BAR

(Map p326; 099 269 5885; 17/5 Soi Sai Naam Peung; 5-11.30pm) Overlooking Doi Suthep and the Nimmanhaemin neighbourhood, Hotel Yayee's 5th-floor rooftop bar is a delightful spot to take in the sunset as you sip a speciality cocktail. Owned by a popular Thai actor, the fern-filled bar is one of Chiang Mai's best rooftop options.

Rise Rooftop
ROOFTOP BAR

(Map p326; Soi 9, 22/2 Th Nimmanhaemin; 3pm-1am) This chic rooftop bar is great for cocktails and chillin' by the infinity pool, which is encased in translucent glass and glows brightly after dark thanks to coloured lighting. On Sundays the bar throws pool parties from 11am until late, with live bands from 7pm.

Bus Bar
BAR

(Map p312; 084 173 3113; 79/1 Th Loi Kroh; 7pm-midnight) Ensconced to the west of the Iron Bridge, this fun outdoor bar features a red, double-decker public bus that visitors can hang out in while they drink mojitos or share whisky buckets and listen to live music. There are also some yummy Thai food stands and candlelit tables.

We Didn't Land on the Moon Since 1987
BAR

(Map p316; 085 499 6245; www.facebook.com/wedidntlandonthemoonsince1987chiangmai; Soi 2, Th Tha Pae; 5pm-midnight Wed-Sat) This tiny haunt tucked down a quiet soi feels more like hanging out at your artsy friend's studio than a bar. While drinks are standard (Singha, SangSom and mojitos), the eclectic crowd will make throwing back a couple of beers here stand out during your time in Chiang Mai.

Parallel Universe of the Lunar 2 on the Hidden Moon
BAR

(Map p326; ☑ 092 706 0736; www.facebook.com/puol2ohm; 5th fl, One Nimman, 1 Th Nimmanhaemin; ⊙ 5-11.30pm) Parallel Universe provides a trendy spot to test out craft beers. The intimate bar serves 10 local and international microbrews on tap along with various bottles. But the rooftop location and views are just as big a draw as the brews.

Namton's House
CRAFT BEER

(Map p312; Th Chiang Mai-Lamphun; ⊙ 3-11.30pm Thu-Tue) Come here for Chiang Mai's biggest selection of Thai craft beers, plus local concoctions like lychee honey mead and a good bunch of international choices. Expect friendly service, chilled-out garden seating and occasional live music. There's a small bar menu for basic eats too.

Warmup Cafe
CLUB

(Map p326; ☑ 053 400677; www.facebook.com/warmupcafe1999; 40 Th Nimmanhaemin; ⊙ 7pm-1am) A Nimmanhaemin survivor, cavernous Warmup has been rocking since 1999, attracting a young, trendy and beautiful crowd as the evening wears on. Hip-hop spins in the main room, electronic beats reverberate in the lounge, and rock bands squeal out solos in the garden.

Cafes & Teahouses

Vieng Joom On Teahouse
TEAHOUSE

(Map p312; ☑ 053 303113; https://vjoteahouse.com; 53 Th Charoenrat/Th Faham; tea from 120B; ⊙ 10am-7pm; ☎) A dainty pink house on Mae Ping serving every conceivable cup of tea: fruity teas, flowery teas, blended tea, ice tea, Chinese tea and of course high tea, which comes with layered trays of desserts, fruit, sandwiches and other goodies. There's both indoor and riverfront seating. Full meals are also available to go with whichever tea your heart desires, and a small shop in front sells boxed tea (among other things).

Khun Kae's Juice Bar
JUICE BAR

(Map p316; ☑ 081 022 9292; Soi 7, Th Moon Muang; drinks from 40B; ⊙ 9am-7.30pm) Our vote for Chiang Mai's best juice shack. Tonnes of fresh fruit, heaps of delicious combinations, generous serves and all this for prices that are almost comically low.

Café de Museum
CAFE

(Map p316; Lanna Folklife Museum, Th Ratwithi; coffee from 80B; ⊙ 9am-6pm; ☎) The perfect spot to refuel after touring the old-city

museums, with a full range of stimulating hot, cold and blended brews. You can sit indoors in comfortable air-conditioning or outside on the terrace in front of the Lanna Folklife Museum (p319).

Raming Tea House
CAFE

(Map p316; Th Tha Phae; drinks 50-120B; ⊙ 8.30am-6pm; ☎) This elegant Victorian-era cafe within the Siam Celadon (p351) shop serves Thai mountain teas alongside tasty Thai and Western food. It's a beautiful setting for a cuppa and a snack. Afternoon-tea spreads with snacks and desserts start at 190B.

☆ Entertainment

Live performance

Apart from the dedicated music venues, the Riverside (p344) and Good View (p346) bars host bands nightly.

★ Old Chiang Mai Cultural Centre
DANCE

(ศูนย์วัฒนธรรมเชียงใหม่; Map p312; ☑ 053 202993; https://oldchiangmai.com; 185/3 Th Wualai; per person from 570B; ⊙ 7-10pm) For an interactive immersion in all things Lanna, this first-of-its-kind Khantoke dinner-theatre experience remains unparalleled in Thailand. Guests stretch out on floor mats to feast on northern Thai dishes served family-style on rattan trays, while musicians strum, blow and beat traditional instruments as costumed performers dance, chant and twirl the occasional sword.

The 'long nails' dance is a perennial crowd favourite, as is the fire finale. The tasty food is all-you-can-eat, but note that beverages of any kind cost extra (and are exorbitantly priced). It's possible to purchase a ticket with refillable water or herbal drinks included.

★ North Gate Jazz Co-Op
LIVE MUSIC

(Map p316; www.facebook.com/northgate.jazzcoop; 95/1-2 Th Si Phum; ⊙ 7pm-midnight) This compact jazz club tends to pack in as many musicians as it does patrons, with local and visiting instrumentalists offering nightly sets and experimental jam sessions that tend to go long. The performances are so inspired that a crowd regularly gathers at tables set up on the sidewalk; arrive early to get a good spot.

Chiang Mai Cabaret Show
CABARET

(Map p316; Anusarn Night Bazaar, Th Chang Khlan; per person incl a beer 290B; ⊙ 9.30-11.30pm)

Chiang Mai's most eye-catching show is this nightly so-called 'ladyboy cabaret' in which cross-dresser and transgender performers wear carnival-style costumes, dance provocatively and lip-sync to high-energy, mostly American pop music. There's some truly hilarious audience interaction, but somehow the spectacle manages to remain appropriate for a general audience. Arrive early for a good seat.

Sangdee Gallery LIVE MUSIC
(Map p326; ☑ 053 894955; www.sangdeeart.com; 5 Soi 5, Th Sirimungklajarn; ⊙ 2pm-midnight Tue-Sat) Part gallery, part music club, bar and cafe, Sangdee is beloved by the art set, who gather here for live music, DJ sets and art shows.

Moo·ay Tai (Thai boxing)
Chiang Mai has three popular *moo·ay tai* (Thai boxing; also spelt *muay Thai*) stadiums – **Thapae Boxing Stadium** (Map p316; ☑ 089 434 5553; Th Moon Muang; tickets 500-1500B; ⊙ 9pm-midnight Mon-Sat), **Loi Kroh Boxing Stadium** (Map p316; ☑ 063 242 4614; Th Loi Kroh; tickets 400-600B; ⊙ 9am-midnight Tue & Fri) and **Chiangmai Boxing Stadium** (Map p312; ☑ 081 594 4151; 177 Soi 4, Th Chotana/Th Chang Pheuak; tickets from 600B; ⊙ 8.30-11.30pm) – that showcase a mixture of Thai and international fighters. Chiang Mai Stadium stages professional fights but purists may find the scene at the other two a bit contrived, particularly compared to the real deal down south.

Cinemas
All the big shopping centres have flashy multiplex cinemas, screening the latest Thai and Hollywood blockbusters, with tickets from 100B up to 350B for deluxe seats with waitress service. Try the Maya Lifestyle Shopping Center (p352), Central Airport Plaza (p354), **Central Festival** (www.central.co.th; Rte 11, Faham; ⊙ 11am-9.30pm Mon-Thu, 11am-10pm Fri, 10am-10pm Sat & Sun), or the less flashy but cheaper **Kad Suan Kaew Shopping Centre** (Map p326; www.kadsuankaew.co.th; Th Huay Kaew; ⊙ 10am-9pm).

🔒 Shopping

Chiang Mai is Thailand's handicraft centre, and an incredible volume and variety of crafts are produced and sold here, from handwoven hill-tribe textiles to woodcarving, basketry and reproduction antiques (frequently sold without that disclaimer).

The Saturday and Sunday Walking Street markets (p352) are Chiang Mai's most entertaining shopping experiences.

🔒 Old City

HQ Paper Maker ARTS & CRAFTS
(Map p316; ☑ 053 814717; www.hqpapermaker.com; 3/31 Th Samlan; ⊙ 8am-6pm) This intriguing shop sells reams of handmade mulberry paper *(săh)*, in a remarkable range of colours and patterns, including gorgeous marbled sheets that resemble the end leaves of bound 19th-century books. Ask about its low-key, three-hour paper-making course for 800B per person (minimum of two people).

Mengrai Kilns CERAMICS
(Map p312; www.mengraikilns.com; 79/2 Th Arak; ⊙ 8am-5pm) In the southwestern corner of the old city, Mengrai Kilns keeps the tradition of Thai handmade pottery alive, with cookware, dining sets, ornaments and Western-style nativity scenes.

Chaitawat Bikeshop SPORTS & OUTDOORS
(Map p316; 75/4 Th Ratchaphakhinai; ⊙ 10am-6pm Mon-Sat) Well-stocked bike shop with parts for all the big foreign brands.

Lost Book BOOKS
(Map p316; Th Ratchamankha; ⊙ 8am-8pm) A popular secondhand bookstore open for more than 27 years, packed with English-language novels, guidebooks and maps.

Herb Basics COSMETICS
(Map p316; www.herbbasicschiangmai.com; Th Phra Pokklao; ⊙ 9am-7pm Mon-Fri, to 6pm Sat, 10am-10pm Sun) A great stop for fragrant

CHIANG MAI PROVINCE **CHIANG MAI**

DON'T MISS

BASKET ALLEY

Woven bamboo, banana fibre and reed hats are the must-have souvenir from Southeast Asia, and you'll find them in all of Chiang Mai's street markets. However, Thais use basketry for an incredible range of purposes, from pillows and footstools to fish traps and lampshades. You'll find all sorts of basketry bits and bobs in the specialist basket shops lined up along Th Chang Moi, just east of the city walls. Basketry dinner trays and rice boxes make fantastic souvenirs that won't make a big dent in your baggage weight allowance.

NIGHT SHOPPING

At times, it can feel like the whole of Chiang Mai is an engine built to sell souvenirs, and nowhere is this feeling stronger than in the Chiang Mai Night Bazaar (Map p316; Th Chang Khlan; ☺6pm-midnight), between the river and the old city walls. As the afternoon wears on, hundreds of hawkers fill the pavement on both sides of the street, selling silk boxer shorts, 'I Love Chiang Mai' T-shirts, miniature wooden spirit houses, hill-tribe silver, dried mango, carved soaps, wooden elephants, wire models of túk-túk, Buddha paintings, fabrics, teddy-bear dioramas and selfie sticks. This slightly frenetic shopping experience is the modern legacy of the Yunnanese trading caravans that stopped here along the ancient Silk Road, and you'll still need to haggle hard today.

Within the Night Bazaar are two large covered markets, signposted as Night Bazaar (Map p316; Th Chang Khlan; ☺7pm-midnight) and Kalare Night Bazaar (Map p316; Th Chang Khlan; ☺7pm-midnight), selling more of the same, with an emphasis on wooden carvings, paintings and other handicrafts. The Kalare Night Bazaar is the more raucous of the two, with a blues bar on a raised podium in the centre.

South of Th Loi Kroh on Th Chang Khlan is the less claustrophobic Anusarn Night Bazaar (Map p316; Th Chang Khlan; ☺5-10pm), a semi-covered market filled with tables of vendors selling hill-tribe trinkets, wooden elephants, carved soap flowers and other cottage-industry goods. It's also good for dried mango and other local preserves, and beloved for its nightly Chiang Mai Cabaret (p348) featuring cross-dresser and transgender performers. Fringing the market are numerous massage and fish-nibbling-your-feet places.

For food, there are abundant fast-food joints, some excellent *kôw soy* canteens along Halal St (Soi 1, Th Charoen Prathet) and some touristy seafood places inside the Anusarn Food Centre (Map p312; Anusarn Night Bazaar, Th Chang Khlan; mains 60-350B; ☺5-10pm). There's also a noisy open-air night market (Map p316; Th Chang Khlan; mains from 40B; ☺6-11pm) just north of Halal St, serving a good range of hawker favourites.

Túk-túk and *rót daang* loiter around the junction of Th Loi Kroh and Th Chang Khlan to transport you and your purchases home for a slightly elevated fare.

herbal balms, scrubs, creams, soaps and shampoos, all made in Chiang Mai with natural ingredients. There are several Herb Basics stores in Chiang Mai, including a branch (Map p316; www.herbbasicschiangmai. com; Th Tha Phae; ☺9am-8pm Mon-Fri, 9am-6pm Sat, 2-10pm Sun) on Th Tha Phae and a small shop at the airport.

🏠 East of the Old City

Elephant Parade ARTS & CRAFTS
(Map p312; ☑053 111849; www.elephantparade. com; Th Charoenrat/Th Faham; ☺10am-8pm; 🚻) In venues around Chiang Mai, you may notice life-sized, decorated baby elephant sculptures created by artists and celebrities through the social enterprise Elephant Parade. The organisation runs this store to educate visitors about the plight of elephants, with large and small statues available for purchase. Children and artsy adults will appreciate the station for painting your own.

John Gallery ART
(Map p316; Th Tha Phae; ☺9am-9pm) Opened in 1980, this place is a warren of paintings

on cotton, cards and rocks, often inscribed with feel-good or creative quotes. John also hawks dusty hill-tribe embroidery and art, 'witch doctor' recipe books and other oddities. Everything is overpriced but so much soul has gone into this unusual place it's worth spending a few baht here.

Head upstairs for views of the crumbling *chedi* out back.

Sop Moei Arts CLOTHING
(Map p312; www.sopmoeiarts.com; 150/10 Th Charoenrat/Th Faham; ☺9am-10pm, to 5pm Sat) 🖉 High-end hill-tribe crafts, from off-the-loom textiles to baskets, are sold at this economic-development shop, which provides assistance for Karen villagers in Mae Hong Son Province.

Thai Tribal Crafts Fair Trade CLOTHING
(Map p312; ☑053 241043; www.ttcrafts.co.th; 208 Th Bamrungrat; ☺9am-5pm Mon-Sat) 🖉 Baskets and ornate needlework from the provinces are the offerings at this missionary-backed, fair-trade shop near the McCormick Hospital. It also runs a hill-tribe weaving class

every weekday from 9am to noon and 1pm to 4pm (1200B). There's no morning class on Monday.

Siam Celadon
CERAMICS

(Map p316; www.siamceladon.com; 158 Th Tha Phae; ⊙8.30am-6pm) This long-established company sells fine cracked-glazed celadon ceramics in a lovely fretwork-covered teak building from the time of the British teak concessionaires. After browsing, stop for a cuppa at the attached Raming Tea House (p348).

Suriwong Book Centre
BOOKS

(Map p316; 54 Th Sridonchai; ⊙10am-7pm) A Chiang Mai institution, with a well-organised and well-stocked bookshop upstairs, and a magazine shop downstairs packed with international mags from *Elle* to *Wallpaper*.

Nakorn Kasem
ARTS & CRAFTS

(Map p316; ☑053 275063; 231-3 Th Tha Phae; ⊙8am-8pm Mon-Sat) One of a string of ma-and-pa antique shops selling ceramics, statues, carvings and bronzes of hard-to-determine age and authenticity. Pick something because you like it, rather than as an investment in an heirloom.

Praewphun Thai Silk
CLOTHING

(Map p316; ☑053 275349; 83-85 Th Tha Phae; ⊙8.30am-5pm) This shop, open since the 1960s, sells silks of all ilks, made into clothing and sold loose by the metre.

Kesorn Arts
ARTS & CRAFTS

(Map p316; 154-156 Th Tha Phae; ⊙9.30am-6pm) The collector's best friend, this cluttered shop has been trading old bric-a-brac from the hills for years. It specialises mainly in textiles, lacquerware and jewellery.

Vila Cini
FASHION & ACCESSORIES

(Map p312; www.vilacini.com; 30-34 Th Charoenrat/Th Faham; ⊙8.30am-9pm) Set in an atmospheric teak house with marble floors, Vila Cini sells high-end, handmade silks, decorative items and cotton textiles that are reminiscent of the Jim Thompson brand.

⌂ West of the Old City

★Studio Naenna
CLOTHING

(www.studio-naenna.com; 138/8 Soi Chang Khian; ⊙9am-5pm Mon-Fri) ⬦ The colours of the mountains have been woven into the naturally dyed silks and cottons here, part of a project to preserve traditional weaving and embroidery. You can see the whole production process at this workshop. The goods are also available for purchase at the Nimmanhacmin store, Adorn with Studio Naenna (open 10am to 7pm).

Baan Kang Wat
ARTS & CRAFTS

(www.facebook.com/Baankangwat; 123/1 Mu 5 Muang, Th Baan Ram Poeng, Suthep; ⊙10am-6pm Tue-Sat, from 7am Sun) Though a little out of the way, Baan Kang Wat is worth the trip simply to coo over the cute architecture and picturesque ambience. The open-air artists enclave is home to several small art and handicraft shops and studios, intimate cafes, a community garden and plenty of potted succulents.

Along the same road as Baan Kang Wat you'll find several other clusters of shops and cafe hubs to check out – bring your camera!

One Nimman
SHOPPING CENTRE

(Map p326; ☑052 080900; www.onenimman.com; 1 Th Nimmanhaemin, Suthep; ⊙11am-11pm; ⓦ) Featuring upmarket Chiang Mai clothing, cafes and art, eclectic Nimman also houses an open-air food hall, regular pop-up markets, and even free salsa and yoga classes. The collection of grand brick, concrete and wood buildings looks like it would fit into a European capital rather than northern Thailand but somehow still manages to work.

Opened at the end of 2017, One Nimman has quickly become a key reference point in the trendy Nimmanhaemin neighbourhood. Spend time wandering the 2nd-level gifts and souvenirs department store, then head back down to the main level to discover local shops such as Monsoon Tea, Graph Cafe and Outfit of the Day.

SHOPPING FOR A CAUSE

Chiang Mai is often described as Thailand's conscience, with dozens of nongovernmental organisations working to alleviate the plight of impoverished villagers in the surrounding mountains. You can do your bit by shopping at the craft emporiums set up to provide a sustainable living for neglected people. Here are some good places to start:

➡ Studio Naenna

➡ Doi Tung (p352)

➡ Sop Moei Arts

➡ Thai Tribal Crafts Fair Trade

DON'T MISS

WEEKEND 'WALKING STREET' MARKETS

As Bangkok has the Chatuchak Weekend Market, so Chiang Mai has its weekend 'walking streets' – carnival-like street markets that close off main thoroughfares in the city on Saturday and Sunday for a riot of souvenir shopping, street performances and hawker food.

As the sun starts to dip on Saturday afternoon, the Saturday Walking Street (ถนน เดินวันเสาร์; Map p312; Th Wualai; ⊙4-11pm Sat) takes over Th Wualai, running southwest from Pratu Chiang Mai. There is barely space to move as locals and tourists from across the world haggle vigorously for carved soaps, novelty dog collars, woodcarvings, Buddha paintings, hill-tribe trinkets, Thai musical instruments, T-shirts, paper lanterns and umbrellas, silver jewellery, herbal remedies, you name it.

An eclectic soundtrack is provided by wandering street performers – blind guitar players, husband-and-wife crooners, precocious school children with headset microphones – and food vendors fill every courtyard and alleyway. There are additional street-food offerings at nearby Talat Pratu Chiang Mai (p340). To escape the crowds, duck into Wat Srisuphan (p323), whose silver *ubosot* (chapel) is illuminated in rainbow colours after dark.

On Sunday afternoon, the whole shebang moves across the city to Th Ratchadamnoen for the equally boisterous Sunday Walking Street (ถนนเดินวันอาทิตย์; Map p316; Th Ratchadamnoen; ⊙6-11pm Sun), which feels even more animated because of the energetic food markets that open up in *wát* courtyards along the route. If you went to Th Wualai on Saturday, you'll recognise many of the same sellers and buskers that you spotted the night before. The markets are a major source of income for local families and many traders spend the whole week handmaking merchandise to sell on Saturday and Sunday.

Doi Tung
FASHION & ACCESSORIES

(Map p326; www.doitung.org; Th Nimmanhaemin; ⊙10am-7pm) 🖉 Part of a development project for rural communities in Chiang Rai Province, this very chic emporium is full of handmade scarves, tablecloths, clothing and men's ties made from graceful and very touchable textiles in understated, modern colours. Expect to pay around 3500B for a tablecloth.

Maya Lifestyle Shopping Center
SHOPPING CENTRE

(Map p326; www.mayashoppingcenter.com; Th Huay Kaew; ⊙11am-10pm, from 10am Sat & Sun) Chiang Mai's flashiest shopping centre hides behind a geometric facade, with all the big international brands, a whole floor of electronics, a good supermarket, a multiscreen cinema, and excellent eating options on the 4th floor.

Shinawatra Thai Silk
CLOTHING

(Map p326; www.shinawatrathaisilk.co.th; 18 Th Huay Kaew; ⊙9am-6pm) This venerable family-owned silk shop was already a household name before the owners' nephew, Thaksin Shinawatra, became (now exiled) prime minister. The range here is a little more dowdy and middle-aged than at the competition, but it's good for scarves, shirts, ties and the like.

There's also a showroom in San Kamphaeng that offers an opportunity to learn about how Thai silk is made.

Srisanpanmai
FASHION & ACCESSORIES

(Map p326; ☑053 217243; 6 Soi 1, Th Nimmanhaemin; ⊙10am-6.30pm) The display cases here are like a library of Lanna textiles, with reams of silk and cotton shawls, scarves and hill-tribe costumes. You're guaranteed to find something to surprise the folks at home.

ℹ Information

EMBASSIES & CONSULATES

Canadian Consulate (☑053 850147; 151 Superhighway, Tambon Tahsala; ⊙9am-noon Mon-Fri)

Chinese Consulate (Map p316; ☑053 280380; http://chiangmai.china-consulate.org; 111 Th Chang Lor, Tambon Haiya; ⊙9-11.30am & 3-4pm Mon-Fri)

French Consulate (Map p312; ☑053 281466; 138 Th Charoen Prathet; ⊙10am-noon Mon & Wed-Fri)

Indian Consulate (☑053 441618; Sanpakwan; ⊙9am-noon Mon-Fri)

Japanese Consulate (Map p312; ☑053 203367; Ste 104-107, Airport Business Park, 90 Th Mahidol; ⊙8.30am-noon & 1-5.15pm Mon-Fri)

UK Visa Application Centre (Map p326; 6th fl, 191 Siripanich Bldg, Th Huay Kaew; ⊙8.30am-2.30pm Mon-Fri) While there is no UK consulate in Chiang Mai (the nearest is in Bangkok), other nationals can apply for UK visas here.

US Consulate (Map p316; ☑053 107700; https://th.usembassy.gov; 387 Th Wichayanon; ⊙7.30am-4.30pm Mon-Fri) Has murals on the outside walls honouring Thai and US friendship.

IMMIGRATION

Chiang Mai Immigration Office (Map p312; ☑053 201755; www.chiangmaiimm.com; 71 Th Sanambin; ⊙8.30am-4.30pm Mon-Fri) Chiang Mai's foreign-services office, where visa extensions and other such things are handled.

INTERNET ACCESS

Almost all hotels, guesthouses, restaurants and cafes in Chiang Mai have free wi-fi access. The city has excellent mobile-phone data coverage, but roaming charges for Thailand can be crippling.

MEDIA

➡ The weekly English-language *Chiangmai Mail* is a useful source of local news.

➡ Look out for the free tourist magazines *Citylife, Chang Puak* and *Chiang Mai Mag;* all have interesting articles as well as maps and blanket advertising.

MEDICAL SERVICES

There are English-speaking pharmacies along Th Ratchamankha and Th Moon Muang.

Centre of Thai Traditional & Complementary Medicine (Map p316; ☑053 934899; ttcmmedcmu@gmail.com; 55 Th Samlan; ⊙8am-8pm) Run by the Faculty of Medicine; offers Western medical check-ups, Thai herbal therapies and Chinese traditional medicine.

Chiang Mai Ram Hospital (Map p312; ☑053 920300; www.chiangmairam.com; 8 Th Bunreuangrit) The most modern hospital in town.

Lanna Hospital (Map p312; ☑052 134777; www.lanna-hospital.com; Rte 11/Th Superhighway) Modern well-equipped hospital.

McCormick Hospital (Map p312; ☑053 921777; www.mccormick.in.th; 133 Th Kaew Nawarat) Former missionary hospital; good for minor treatments.

Mungkala Traditional Medicine Clinic (Map p316; ☑053 278494; 21-27 Th Ratchamankha; ⊙9am-12.30pm & 2-7pm Mon-Sat) This is a government-licensed clinic using acupuncture, massage and Chinese herbal remedies.

MONEY

All of the big Thai banks have branches and ATMs throughout Chiang Mai and most operate small exchange booths with ATMs in the old city.

POST

Main Post Office (☑053 241070; Mae Khao Mu Soi 4; ⊙8.30am-4.30pm Mon-Fri, 9am-noon Sat & Sun) Other convenient branches on **Th Samlan** (Map p316; Th Samlan; ⊙8.30am-4.30pm Mon-Fri, 9am-noon Sat), **Th Praisani** (Map p312; Th Praisani; ⊙8.30am-5pm Mon-Fri, 9am-4pm Sat), **Th Phra Pokklao** (Map p316; Th Phra Pokklao; ⊙9am-4pm Mon-Sat), and at the airport and university.

Postal shop (Map p316; Th Ratchadamnoen; ⊙8am-8pm Mon-Fri, to 4pm Sat) Charges Thailand Post rates; staff specialise in wrapping awkwardly shaped packages to send home.

SAFE TRAVEL

Compared to Bangkok, Chiang Mai is a safe haven for tourists. But keep in mind:

➡ During rush hour, traffic can snarl. Take care when crossing busy roads, as motorcyclists and *rót daang* ('red trucks', operating as shared taxis) drivers rarely give way.

➡ In March and April, smoky, dusty haze becomes a massive problem because of farmers burning off their fields. Don't go at this time.

➡ Outbreaks of dengue fever are common in the monsoon; protect yourself from mosquitoes, especially in the daytime.

➡ In 2019, a tourist died on the zipline at Flight of the Gibbon, and a number have drowned after cliff-jumping at Grand Canyon Water Park.

Police Station (Map p316; ☑053 276040, 24hr emergency 191; 169 Th Ratchadamnoen)

Tourist Police (☑053 212147, 24hr emergency 1155; 196 Soi Sriwichai; ⊙6am-midnight) Volunteer staff speak a variety of languages.

TOURIST INFORMATION

Chiang Mai Municipal Tourist Information Centre (Map p312; ☑053 252557; Th Tha Phae; ⊙8.30am-noon & 1-4.30pm Mon-Fri) City-run centre near the Night Bazaar.

Tourism Authority of Thailand (TAT; Map p312; ☑053 248604; www.tourismthailand.org; Th Chiang Mai-Lamphun; ⊙8am-5pm) English-speaking staff provide maps and advice on travel across Thailand.

Tourist Assistance Centre (Map p312; ⊙7am-11pm) Tourist information in Chiang Mai International Airport.

ⓘ Getting There & Away

AIR

Chiang Mai International Airport From Arrivals Exit 9 there is a licensed airport taxi service costing around 150B to 170B to the old town. Cheaper shuttle and minibus services charge 40B. An Uber or Grab Car will cost around 60B.

Domestic and international flights arrive and depart from **Chiang Mai International Airport**

(Map p312; ☎ 053 922000; www.chiangmaiairportonline.com), 3km southwest of the old city.

Schedules vary with the seasons and tourist demand. Tickets to Bangkok start at around 540B. Heading south, expect to pay from 2160B to Phuket and 1080B to Surat Thani. The bulk of the domestic routes are handled by the following airlines:

Air Asia (Map p316; ☎ 080 902 2636, nationwide 02 515 9999; www.airasia.com; 416 Th Tha Phae; ⊙10am-8.30pm)

Bangkok Airways (Map p326; ☎ 053 289338, nationwide 1771; www.bangkokair.com; Room 302, Kantary Terrace, 44/1 Soi 12, Th Nimmanhaemin; ⊙8am-noon & 1-5.30pm Mon-Fri)

Nok Air (☎ 02 088 8955, nationwide 1318; www.nokair.com)

Thai Smile (☎ nationwide 02 118 8888; www.thaismileair.com)

Thai Airways International (THAI; Map p316; ☎ 053 902999; www.thaiairways.com; 240 Th Phra Pokklao; ⊙8am-5pm Mon-Sat)

Direct flights linking Chiang Mai to neighbouring nations are also expanding fast, with regular flights to Kuala Lumpur (Malaysia), Yangon (Myanmar), Hanoi (Vietnam) and destinations around China. **Lao Airlines** (Map p326; ☎ 053 223401; www.laoairlines.com; 2/107 Th Huay Kaew; ⊙8.30am-5pm Mon-Fri, to noon Sat) has direct flights to Luang Prabang, and there are less frequent services to Ho Chi Minh City (Vietnam). To reach Cambodia, you'll have to go via Bangkok.

The airport has luggage storage (7am to 9pm, 200B per day), a post-office branch (8.30am to 8pm), banks, souvenir shops and a tourist assistance centre (p353). If you have time to kill, you could just stroll back down the highway to the large **Central Airport Plaza** (Map p312; www.centralplaza.co.th; Rte 1141/Th Mahidol; ⊙11am-9pm Mon-Fri, from 10am Sat & Sun).

SM Travel (Map p316; ☎ 053 281045; www.yourtripthailand.com; 87-95 Th Ratchadamnoen; ⊙8am-6pm) in the old city is a good place to book flights and tours.

BUS

Chiang Mai has two bus stations, and *sŏrng·tăa·ou* run from fixed stops to towns close to Chiang Mai.

Chang Pheuak Bus Terminal

Just north of the old city on Th Chotana (Th Chang Pheuak), the **Chang Pheuak Bus Terminal** (Map p312; Th Chang Pheuak) is the main departure point for journeys to the north of Chiang Mai Province. Government buses leave regularly to the following destinations:

Chiang Dao 40B, 1½ hours, every 30 minutes

Hot 50B, two hours, every 20 minutes

Samoeng 90B, two hours, six daily

Tha Ton 92B, four hours, seven daily

Local blue *sŏrng·tăa·ou* run to Lamphun (30B, 1½ hours, frequent) and yellow ones head for Mae Rim (30B, 30 minutes, frequent). Air-con minibuses to Chiang Dao (150B, two hours, hourly) leave from Soi Sanam Gila, behind the bus terminal.

Arcade Bus Terminal

About 3km northeast of the city centre, near the junction of Th Kaew Nawarat and Rte 11, Chiang Mai's **main long-distance station** (Th Kaew Nawarat) handles all services, except for buses to northern Chiang Mai Province. This is the place to come to travel on to Bangkok or any other major city in Thailand. A chartered *rót daang* ('red trucks', operating as shared taxis) from the centre to the bus stand will cost about 60B; a túk-túk will cost 80B to 100B. There are also two bus routes between the bus terminals and town: B1 makes stops at Chiang Mai's train station and Tha Phae Gate (15B, hourly 6am to 6pm), and B2 makes stops at Tha Phae Gate and Chiang Mai International Airport (15B, hourly 6am to 6pm).

There are two terminal buildings, with ticket booths for dozens of private and government bus companies. Nominally, **Building 2** is for towns north of Chiang Mai and **Building 3** is for towns south of Chiang Mai, but in practice buses leave from both terminals to most destinations. There is also a third depot behind Building 2 used exclusively by the private bus company **Nakornchai Air** (www.nca.co.th; Arcade Bus Terminal, Th Kaew Nawarat), which has luxury buses to Bangkok and almost everywhere else in Thailand.

Facilities for travellers are a little lacklustre; there's a parade of local-style restaurants beside the two terminal buildings, and a left-luggage office (8am to 8.30pm, 30B per item). If you have time to burn, head over to the **Star Avenue Lifestyle Mall** (Arcade Bus Terminal; ⊙24hr) by Building 3, which has air-conditioned coffee shops and restaurants.

There is a regular international bus service linking Chiang Mai to Luang Prabang, via Bokeo, Luang Namtha and Udom Xai. You can also travel by bus across to Nong Khai and on to Vientiane.

SŎRNG·TĂA·OU

There are several stops for *sŏrng·tăa·ou* (passenger pick-up trucks) running to towns close to Chiang Mai. Fares are around 30B and services run frequently throughout the day.

Talat Warorot Sŏrng·tăa·ou Stop (Map p316; Th Praisani) White and yellow *sŏrng·tăa·ou* run northeast to Doi Saket, blue head south to Lamphun and green run to the north of Chiang Mai.

Saphan Lek Sŏrng·tăa·ou Stop (Map p312; Th Chiang Mai-Lamphun) Blue *sŏrng·tăa·ou* serve Lamphun.

TRANSPORT FROM CHIANG MAI

DESTINATION	AIR	BUS	MINIVAN	TRAIN
Bangkok	from 540B, 70min, frequent	488-759B, 10hr, frequent	N/A	231-1653B, 10-12hr, 5 daily
Chiang Khong	N/A	202-451B, 6½hr, 1 daily	N/A	N/A
Chiang Rai	N/A	166-288B, 4hr, frequent	N/A	N/A
Hanoi (Vietnam)	from 1320B, 90min, 2 daily	N/A	N/A	N/A
Ho Chi Min City	from 1500B, 2hr, 4 weekly	N/A	N/A	N/A
Khon Kaen	from 1020B, 70min, 2 daily	535B, 12hr, 5 daily	N/A	N/A
Khorat (Nakhon Ratchasima)	N/A	540-662B, 12hr, 11 daily	N/A	N/A
Lampang	N/A	66-143B, 1½hr, hourly	83B, 1hr, hourly	N/A
Luang Prabang (Laos)	from 3030B, 1hr, 4 weekly	1200B, 20hr, 9am (Mon, Wed, Fri, Sat, Sun)	N/A	N/A
Mae Hong Son	from 1170B, 40min, 3 daily	N/A	250B, 5hr, 3 daily	N/A
Nan	N/A	197-254B, 6hr, 6 daily	N/A	N/A
Nong Khai	N/A	890B, 12hr, 1 daily	N/A	N/A
Pai	from 1170B, 45min, 2 daily	N/A	150B, 3hr, hourly	N/A
Phuket	from 2160B, 2hr, 8 daily	1646B, 22hr, 1 daily	N/A	N/A
Sukhothai	N/A	225-290B, 5-6hr, hourly	N/A	N/A
Ubon Ratchathani	N/A	802B, 15hr, 5 daily	N/A	N/A
Udon Thani	from 1170B, 1hr, 3 daily	594-832B, 11hr, 4 daily	N/A	N/A
Vientiane (Laos)	N/A	890B, 10hr, 1 daily	N/A	N/A

Pratu Chiang Mai Sŏrng·tăa·ou Stop (Map p316; Th Bamrungburi) Yellow sŏrng·tăa·ou serve locations southwest of Chiang Mai.

Sŏrng·tăa·ou to San Kamphaeng (Map p316; Th Khang Mehn) White sŏrng·tăa·ou that heads east of the city.

TRAIN

Run by the State Railway of Thailand, **Chiang Mai Train Station** (053 245363, nationwide 1690; Th Charoen Muang) is about 2.5km east of the old city. Trains run five times daily on the main line between Bangkok and Chiang Mai. The government has promised more investment in the railways in future, including the creation of a new high-speed rail link between Chiang Mai

and Bangkok. The train station has an ATM, a left-luggage room (6am to 6pm, 50B per item) and an advance-booking counter (you'll need your passport to book a ticket).

There are four classes of trains running between Chiang Mai and Bangkok's Hualamphong station: rapid, sprinter, express and special express. Most comfortable are the overnight special express services leaving Chiang Mai at 5pm and 6pm, arriving in Bangkok at 6.15am and 6.50am. In the opposite direction, trains leave Hualamphong at 6.10pm and 7.35pm. However, schedules change regularly, so see the State Railway of Thailand website (www.thairailways.com) for the latest information.

BUS SERVICES FROM CHIANG MAI'S ARCADE TERMINAL

DESTINATION	FARE (B)	DURATION (HR)	FREQUENCY
Bangkok	488-759	10	frequent
Chiang Khong	202-451	6½	1 daily
Chiang Rai	166-288	4	frequent
Khon Kaen	535	12	5 daily
Khorat (Nakhon Ratchasima)	540-662	12	11 daily
Lampang	66-143	1½	hourly
Lampang (minivan)	83	1	hourly
Lamphun	30	1	hourly
Luang Prabang (Laos)	1200	20	9am (Mon, Wed, Fri, Sat, Sun)
Mae Hong Son (minivan)	250	5	3 daily
Mae Sai	205-234	5	7 daily
Mae Sariang	104-187	4-5	6 daily
Mae Sot	290	6	3 daily
Nan	197-254	6	6 daily
Nong Khai	890	12	1 daily
Pai (minivan)	150	3	hourly
Phayao	142-249	3	hourly
Phitsanulok	210-320	5-6	frequent
Phrae	133-266	4	4 daily
Phuket	1646	22	1 daily
Sukhothai	225-290	5-6	hourly
Ubon Ratchathani	802	15	5 daily
Udon Thani	594-832	11	4 daily
Vientiane (Laos)	890	10	1 daily

At the time of research, fares to Bangkok were as follows:

3rd class (bench seat) 231B to 271B

2nd class (reclining seat) 391B to 641B

2nd-class sleeper berth (fan-cooled) 531B to 581B

2nd-class sleeper berth (air-con) 751B to 1041B

1st-class sleeper berth (air-con) 1253B to 1653B

ⓘ Getting Around

Both Uber and Grab Car exist in Chiang Mai and although there have been ongoing threats to limit or shut down services, at the time of research both were running strong. Rides within the city average 50B.

BICYCLE

Cycling is a good way to get around Chiang Mai but be cautious on the ring roads circling the old city. Rickety sit-up-and-beg bikes can be rented for around 50B a day or 300B per week from guesthouses and shops around the old city.

Check the bike carefully before you hire – brakes in particular can be iffy.

If you want a superior bike, you can rent good-quality foreign-made road bikes (100B to 400B per day) and mountain bikes (250B to 1000B) from **Chiang Mai Mountain Biking & Kayaking** (Map p312; ☑081 024 7046; www.mountainbikethailand.com; 92/1-2 Th Si Donchai; tours 1250-2700B; ⊙7am-10pm), Trailhead (p328) and **Spice Roads** (Map p316; ☑053 215837; www.spiceroads.com; 1 Soi 7, Th Moon Muang; half-/full-/multi-day tours from 1200/4000/26,000B). Spare parts for foreign bikes are available at Chaitawat Bikeshop (p349).

BUS

Launched in 2018, the **RTC City Bus** (☑052 060001; http://rtccitybus.com; per ride 20B; ⊙6am-late) is now the most affordable and convenient way to get around the city of Chiang Mai. The spacious, air-conditioned buses transport passengers along nine routes, which can be monitored in real time via a mobile app, CM Transit. The app displays stops, routes and the real-time locations of buses, which also offer free wi-fi.

Passengers pay either in coins (20B per ride), or with a rechargeable Rabbit Card upon boarding. The cards are available at RTC counters at the airport, in malls and sometimes from the bus driver, and the value can be topped up at convenience stores and fast-food restaurants. Another good option for travellers is the Tourist Card, which costs 180B for an unlimited day or 400B for three unlimited days.

Be sure to raise your arm as the bus approaches so that the driver knows to stop.

CAR & PICK-UP TRUCK

Cars and pick-up trucks can be hired from rental agencies throughout the city, particularly along Th Moon Muang, but stick to companies that offer full insurance (liability) coverage and breakdown cover, and check the terms so you're clear on what is and isn't included. Most companies ask for a cash deposit of 5000B to 10,000B.

Standard rental rates for small 1.5L cars start at around 1000B per day; prices include unlimited kilometres but not petrol. Well-regarded agencies include the following:

Budget Car Rental (Map p312; ☑ 053 202871; www.budget.co.th; 201/2 Th Mahidol) Across from Central Airport Plaza.

North Wheels (☑ 053 874478; www.north-wheels.com; 70/4-8 Th Chaiyaphum; ◷8am-6pm) Offers hotel pick-up and delivery, 24-hour emergency road service and comprehensive insurance.

Thai Rent a Car (Map p312; ☑ 053 904188; www.thairentacar.com; Chiang Mai International Airport; ◷7am-8pm)

MOTORCYCLE

Renting a motorcycle or scooter is an extremely popular option in Chiang Mai. Agencies and guesthouses rent out everything from 100cc automatic scooters (from 150B per day) to larger Honda Dream bikes (from 350B) and full-sized road and off-road bikes up to 650cc (700B to 2000B). Smaller bikes are fine for city touring but if you plan to attempt any of the mountain roads around Chiang Mai, pick a machine with an engine size of 200cc or more.

Mr Mechanic (Map p316; ☑053 214708; www.mr-mechanic1994.com; 4 Soi 5, Th Moon Muang; scooter/motorcycle/car per day from 250/600/800B; ◷8am-6pm) and **Cat Motors** (Map p312; ☑090 729 9090; https://catmotors.net; 197/1 Th Ratchamanka; per day/week/month from 200/1200/3000B; ◷8am-6pm) are probably the best operators in town in terms of insurance and support, with well-maintained fleets and comprehensive insurance. There are two other branches of Mr Mechanic at **33 Th Ratchaphakhinai** (Map p316; ☑053 214708; www.mr-mechanic1994.com; 33 Th Ratchaphakhinai; scooter/motorcycle/car per day from 250/600/800B; ◷8am-6pm) and **135/1 Th Ratchaphakhinai** (Map p316; ☑053 214708; www.mr-mechanic1994.com; 135/1 Th Ratchaphakhinai; scooter/motorcycle/car per day from 250/600/800B; ◷8am-6pm).

Toon's Bikes (Map p316; ☑053 207124; www.chiangmai-motorcycle-rental.com; 17 Th Ratchamankha; per day 200-2500B) rents well-maintained 125cc to 300cc motorbikes, and also gives touring advice and repairs motorcycles; rates are negotiable in low season.

By law, you must wear a helmet, and police frequently set up checkpoints to enforce this. You should also carry photo ID and an International Driving Permit (IDP) to present at police checkposts. If you show a foreign driver's licence but can't present an IDP, you'll be fined 500B and receive a ticket that allows you to drive for just three days without getting fined again.

Saving a few baht by renting without proper insurance could cost you dearly; stick to companies offering breakdown cover and full insurance. Most policies have a 1500B excess in case of accident and a 10,000B excess if the motorbike is stolen; use the chain and padlock!

Most bike-hire places will ask for your passport as a security deposit. While there are rarely any problems with this, better agencies will accept a cash deposit of 3000B to 10,000B as an alternative. This cannot be paid by credit card.

For tips on touring the countryside around Chiang Mai, check out the advice at Golden Triangle Riders (www.gt-rider.com).

CHIANG MAI PROVINCE CHIANG MAI

ⓘ **DRIVING INSURANCE**

When renting a motorcycle, scooter or car in Chiang Mai, check the insurance small print carefully. Some companies hire out vehicles with only the most basic compulsory insurance, which gives limited cover if you harm somebody else in an accident, but provides no medical cover for you and no cover for damage to the vehicle you are hiring or to any other vehicle you might collide with. If your vehicle is stolen, you could be fully liable. Play it smart and use a company that offers full insurance and breakdown cover, with the level of cover clearly spelt out in the contract.

ⓘ **TÚK-TÚK VS SÖRNG-TĂA·OU**

Túk-túk are more expensive and their drivers are likely to rip you off, but they do offer a direct service and most drivers speak English. Sŏrng·tăa·ou drivers are cheaper and less inclined to rip off passengers (because many Thais use them too), but English can be a problem and routes are not always direct. Riding in a sŏrng·tăa·ou is an excellent way to meet local Thais.

LOCAL TRANSPORT

Rót daang (literally 'red trucks') operate as shared taxis, and they roam the streets picking up passengers who are heading in the direction they are travelling. sThere are no fixed routes so the easiest thing to do is to ask if the driver will take you where you want to go. Journeys start from 30B for a short trip of a few blocks and 40B for a longer trip (eg from the old city to Th Nimmanhaemin).

Drivers are also happy to hire out the whole vehicle for charter trips for a higher price, including day trips out into the countryside. If the vehicle is parked by the roadside instead of moving along the street, the driver is normally looking for a charter fare. Either way, there's little hassle involved; indeed, many rót daang are family businesses, with husbands driving and wives sitting alongside dealing with the money and route planning.

Túk-túk work only on a charter basis and are more expensive than rót daang, but they offer that energising wind-through-your-hair feeling and are faster in traffic. Rates start at 60B for short trips and creep up to 100B at night, although you'll probably have to bargain hard for these rates. Some drivers can be pushy and may try to steer you towards attractions that pay commissions. Chiang Mai still has a few sǎhm·lór (three-wheeled pedicabs), which offer short transfers around Talat Warorot for 20B or so.

TAXI

It is very rare to see a metered taxi to flag down in Chiang Mai, but you can call for a pick-up from **Cnx Taxi Chiang Mai** (☑ 095 675 0676; www.cnxtaxichiangmai.com) – fares within Chiang Mai are unlikely to top 200B.

NORTHERN CHIANG MAI PROVINCE

North of Chiang Mai, the land rucks up into forested mountains on either side of Mae Nam Ping as northern Thailand merges into southeastern Myanmar. With a chartered rót daang ('red trucks', operating as shared taxis) or rented motorcycle (with sufficient horsepower) you can roam high into the hills, visiting national parks, spectacular viewpoints, Royal Project farms and hill-tribe villages. The website www.gt-rider.com has trip reports posted by motorcyclists who have made sorties through this region.

Mae Rim

☑ 053 / POP 7480

The nearest town north of Chiang Mai, sleepy Mae Rim (แม่ริม) is an easy 30km ride from the city along Rte 107. Here you can visit the former palace of princess Dara Rasmee, and kick back at the Huay Teung Thao reservoir.

◉ Sights

Elephant Poopoopaper Park MUSEUM
(☑ 053 299565; www.poopoopaperpark.com; 87 Mu 10, Th Maeram; 50B; ☺ 9am-5.30pm; ⊕) ⦿
At this crafty, eco-friendly little park to the north of Chiang Mai, visitors are walked through the fascinating art of converting elephant dung fibers into paper. The chemical-free process involves no trees and employs ethnic minorities from hill-tribe villages, and paper sales adhere to fair-trade principles. Waste is re-pulped for integration into new sheets or rolls of paper.

Guests can create their own products during the tour, including bookmarks, fans, greeting cards or even beaded jewellery. There's also a lovely on-site cafe and picnic area.

Dara Pirom Palace MUSEUM
(พระตำหนักดาราภิรมย์; 20B; ☺ 9am-5pm Tue-Sat)
Dara Rasmee, the last princess of the Lanna kingdom, lived out her days in this handsome 19th-century residence, built in classic Thai-colonial style, with tall ceilings, elegant fretwork vents and timbered verandas. Rooms full of heirlooms, photos and personal effects recall the princess's life and times.

The palace lies in the grounds of the Mae Rim police compound on the west side of Rte 107; turn right after the police station and follow the signs past the runway for the police helicopter.

Huay Teung Thao Reservoir LAKE
(อ่างเก็บน้ำห้วยตึงเฒ่า; 50B; ☺ 7am-7pm) For Thais, a reservoir is not just a water store,

it's a place for some serious R&R. At this expansive body of water just west of Mae Rim, families gather to swim or hang by the shore and picnic over the water in elevated bamboo huts. It's like a day at the beach.

There are several informal restaurants surrounding the lake, many of which sell adventurous northern Thai dishes such as fried frog and 'dancing shrimp'.

To get here, follow Rte 107 and turn southwest onto Rte 121, then turn right across the bridge by the Khuang Phra Chao Lanna shrine.

🛏 Sleeping & Eating

⭐ **Four Seasons Chiang Mai** RESORT **$$$**
(☑ 053 298181; www.fourseasons.com; 502 Mu 1, Th Mae Rim–Samoeng Kao, off Rte 1096; d from 21,900B; ❄@🛜🌊) Chiang Mai's lavish Four Seasons resort is a sprawl of vaulted pavilions and self-contained residences scattered through the rainforest near Mae Rim, with landscaped gardens and rice terraces tended by farmers in traditional garb. Rooms offer the design-magazine experience, all flowing fabrics and antique arts. There's also an excellent Thai restaurant (mains 310-590B, tasting menu from 2200B; ⏱ 7-10.30am & noon-10pm), an award-winning spa and a tennis court, among other five-star flourishes.

Huay Teung Thao Restaurant THAI **$**
(☑ 080 135 2045; Huay Teung Thao; mains 80-180B; ⏱ 7am-6pm) One of several informal restaurants at the lake serving spicy salads, grilled or fried meat and some adventurous dishes, such as fried frog with garlic and *goong ten,* otherwise known as 'dancing shrimp'. The name refers to the way tiny freshwater shrimp continue moving when mixed into chili, fish sauce and lime, and they're still alive even as they enter the mouth. Visitors often order from the restaurants, then bring the food into overwater bamboo gazebos to feast.

ℹ Getting There & Away

Mae Rim is easily accessible by bus or *sŏrng·tăa·ou* (30B, 30 minutes, frequent) from Chiang Mai's Chang Pheuak Bus Terminal.

Chiang Dao

☑ 053 / POP 15,000

In a lush jungle setting in the shadow of a mighty limestone mountain, Chiang Dao (เชียงดาว) is where domestic travellers come to escape the heat of the plains. It gets cooler still as you leave the village and climb towards the summit of Doi Chiang Dao (2175m). The forest is a popular stop for birdwatchers and trekkers, and at the base of the mountain is a highly venerated wát

CHIANG MAI PROVINCE CHIANG DAO

OFF THE BEATEN TRACK

MON CHAM

For a glimpse at one of the province's destinations that's become increasingly popular with Thai tourists, hop on a motorbike or charter a *rót daang* (literally 'red trucks') to the mountaintop agricultural wonderland of **Mon Cham** (ม่อนแจ่ม; Nong Hoi Mai) **FREE**. Attractions include a busy market, informal restaurants, bountiful gardens and cliffside bamboo pavilions, all made possible for the local Hmong community thanks to the Nong Hoi Royal Project. The project has helped residents capitalise on high-income, sustainable crops such as strawberries, cabbage, herbs and lavender, and the multicoloured crop terraces provide some truly spectacular views.

When you're done feasting on local produce, sipping local fruit liqueurs and taking selfies in the **flower garden** (adult/child 20/10B), consider renting a traditional **Formula Hmong** (Mon Cham; 1-/2-person ride 50/80B; ⏱ 7am-6pm) and racing a friend down the hill. Then relax over some coffee and maybe a Thai soup at **Rai Phor Doi Coffee** (Mon Cham; coffee 50-70B; mains 60-100B; ⏱ 6am-10pm), or dip into a mineral bath at **Onsen @ Moncham** (☑ 053 111606; www.onsenmoncham.com; 293 Mu 2, Tambon Pong; 2-person day pass from 2200B; ⏱ 8am-10pm).

If you're still not quite ready to return to the city, settle into one of the area's many platform camping accommodation options or bungalows, most of which cost round 2000B per night. One good choice is **Phu Fasai** (Mon Cham; d from 2000B), a laid-back retreat set in a traditional Hmong village that overlooks an enchanting valley.

WORTH A TRIP

CLIMBING THE STICKY WATERFALL

Ever walked up a waterfall? An increasingly popular day trip from Chiang Mai to Si Lanna National Park's **Nam Tok Bua Tong (Sticky Waterfall)** (น้ำตกบัวตอง; Si Lanna National Park; ☉ 6am-6pm) allows visitors (with no magic powers or even climbing skills) to do just that. The secret lies not in the cartoonish-looking, mysteriously clingy rocks, but in the calcium-rich spring above that feeds the three-tiered, 100m waterfall. That water leaves mineral deposits on the rocks, preventing slippery stuff (like algae) from growing.

After you climb the scenic, forest-flanked chutes, why not have a picnic at the top? You can also hike to the spring; the start point is the sign at the top for Namphu Chet Si.

Plenty of locals and travellers arrive at the falls via motorbike, but be aware that the 60km trip can take up to two hours. Other options include chartering a *rót daang* for around 1000B, or visiting with a guided tour. Most tour operators in the city offer the trip, sometimes in combo with Wat Phra That Doi Suthep (p325), and prices can vary based on group size. If you're driving, take Rte 1001 east and look for the sign for the waterfall. Make a right, and it's about 3km to the parking lot.

marking the entrance to one of Thailand's deepest limestone caverns.

Buses to Chiang Dao stop in the modern village on the eastern side of Rte 107, but most travellers head to the nearby village of Ban Tham on the western side of the highway, where all the accommodation and the famous cave temple can be found.

☉ Sights

Doi Chiang Dao
Wildlife Sanctuary　　　NATURE RESERVE
(ดอยเชียงดาว, Doi Luang; 200B; ☉ Nov-Mar) Doi Chiang Dao rises dramatically above the plain, wrapped in a thick coat of tropical forest. This jungle wonderland is one of Thailand's top spots for birdwatching, with more than 300 resident bird species, and is one of the best places in the world to see giant nuthatches and Hume's pheasants. It's a steep full-day hike to the summit, which offers spectacular views over the massifs. Guides typically charge between 1000B and 2000B per person; an overnight stay costs 500B.

If you just want a taste of the marvellous scenery, take a right at the junction just before the cluster of lodges at Ban Tham and follow the gorgeously scenic, winding mountain road that climbs to the ridge through the forest. This is a challenging route and you'll need transport with sufficient power to handle the gradients.

Pha Daeng National Park　　NATIONAL PARK
(อุทยานแห่งชาติผาแดง; ☏ 053 046370; www.dnp.go.th; adult/child 100/50B, camping per person 30B, vehicle 50B) North of Chiang Dao and reached by following Rte 1178, Pha Daeng National Park offers lush, jungle

scenery and stunning birdlife. Flanking the Myanmar border, the park is pockmarked by deep cave systems and has the usual full hand of scenic viewpoints, summit hikes and spurting waterfalls. Bungalow accommodation (600B to 2500B) is available at the park headquarters.

The most popular attractions within the park are Nam Tok Sri Sangwan (the waterfall just off the main road near the park headquarters) and Pong Arng Hot Springs (open daily from 8am to 6pm). The waterfall is like a mini version of the popular Sticky Waterfall (p360), and its 20m, three-tiered limestone cascade makes for a scenic spot to relax or picnic. About 3km south, the hot springs feature two natural bathing ponds that fluctuate between 58°C and 64°C.

Wat Tham Pha Plong　　BUDDHIST TEMPLE
(สำนักสงฆ์ถ้ำผาปล่อง; Ban Tham; donations appreciated; ☉ daylight hours) This beautiful and serene forest *wát* lies on the edge of the Chiang Dao massif. A steep *naga* stairway climbs through the forest to the rocky crevice where the revered meditation master Luang Pu Sim once practised. You'll feel far, far away from the tourist crowd here. Continue on the road about a kilometre past the Chiang Dao lodges to reach the parking lot for the temple.

Wat Tham Chiang Dao　　CAVE
(ถ้ำเชียงดาว, Chiang Dao Cave; 40B; ☉ 7am-5pm) Set in pretty grounds that teem with jungle butterflies, this forest *wát* sits at the entrance to Chiang Dao Cave, a chilly warren of passageways that extend more than 10km beneath the limestone massif of Doi Chiang Dao. For Buddhists, the cave is a meditation

retreat, a sort of extension of the wát itself, and the twisting tunnels overflow with stalactites and stalagmites.

The chambers at the start of the network of tunnels – known as Tham Sua Dao and Tham Phra Non – are illuminated by electric lights, but the most interesting section of the cave system is unlit and you'll need to hire a guide (200B) with a gas lantern to explore, providing a living for a local villager in the process (they are actually volunteers so a 50B tip is appropriate and expected). The tour wriggles through narrow passageways to other large chambers – Tham Mah (735m), Tham Kaew (474m) and Tham Nam (660m) – and your guide will point out bat colonies and limestone features that have been named for their resemblance to animals. At the end of the illuminated section, you'll reach a small but highly revered sleeping Buddha in a small antechamber.

Local legend says that the cave was the home of a *reu·sĕe* (ascetic, holy man) who convinced the spirits to create several magic wonders inside the caverns: a stream flowing from the pedestal of a solid-gold Buddha, a storehouse of divine textiles, and a city of *naga* (mythical serpents). These miraculous features are said to be much deeper inside the mountain, beyond the last of the illuminated caverns.

Sleeping & Eating

Chiang Dao Hut
GUESTHOUSE $

(☏053 456625; http://chiangdaohut.com; 303 Moo 5; bungalows from 315B; ☏) This cute collection of rooms and bungalows is set in a glade that drops down to a stream. Cheaper accommodation has shared bathrooms with hot water, and the atmosphere is appropriately laid-back and unhurried. Tasty meals are on offer in the open-air restaurant, Hut Kitchen, across the street.

Chiang Dao Nest 2
BOUTIQUE HOTEL $$

(☏089 545 9302; www.chiangdaonest.com; Ban Tham; bungalows 995-3500B; ✳☏) Bamboo bungalows sit in a serene garden with views of the jungle-clad mountains. You'll feel like family here within minutes, and don't miss the world-class Thai cuisine in its chic patio restaurant overlooking flowers and greenery. There's also on-site massage service.

Chiang Dao Nest
GUESTHOUSE $$

(☏053 456242; www.chiangdaonest.com; bungalows 995-3500B; @☏✳) The guesthouse that put Chiang Dao on the map is a charming country retreat, with comfortable, bamboo-weave bungalows scattered around a gorgeous tropical garden with plenty of shady gazebos where you can kick back with a book. There's a lovely, forest-flanked swimming pool with mountain views, and a pavilion with a ping-pong table.

BURM AND EMILY'S ELEPHANT SANCTUARY

At the community-based Burm and Emily's Elephant Sanctuary (BEES; ☏086 197 2519; http://bees-elesanctuary.org; 188/1 Tambon Chang Keung, Mae Cham; day visit from 1000B, overnight stay from 1500B; ◷8am-5pm), an elephant retirement and small animal rescue sanctuary, humans work for the elephants (not the other way around). Just three elephants reside here, along with plenty of rescued cats, dogs and injured wildlife, which the sanctuary works to rehabilitate and release. Travellers and volunteers report high satisfaction in learning about Asian elephants here, as well as observing them, preparing food for them, cleaning the areas they inhabit and helping care for other rescued animals.

Most visitors stay for a week, though shorter programs with overnight stays on Monday or Thursday or sequences of three nights (Monday to Thursday or Tuesday to Friday) are also possible. Thai-style accommodation is basic, with private or shared rooms containing floor mattresses, mosquito nets and fans. Bathrooms are all shared, with Western toilets. Day visits are also an option, but guests must transport themselves.

There is of course no riding, bathing or interacting with elephants whatsoever, which animal welfare groups consider harmful and dangerous for everyone involved. For those visitors who stay for multiple nights, additional activities include teaching English to school children, tree-planting, cooking classes, temple visits, river tubing and visiting a local weaving village. The sanctuary is located 2½ hours southwest of Chiang Mai, and offers rides to and from the city.

WORTH A TRIP

STEAMY HOT SPRINGS

About 10km west of Fang at Ban Meuang Chom, near the agricultural station, the seren **Doi Pha Hompok National Park** (อุทยานแห่งชาติดอยผ้าห่มปก, Doi Fang/Mae Fang National Park; ☑084 483 4689, 052 080801; www.dnp.go.th; adult/child 300/150B, car/motorcycle/bike 30/20/10B, camping per person 30B, bungalows 1000-2000B; ⊙7am-7pm) is part national park and part public spa, with a gorgeous hot-springs complex (*bor náam hórn* in northern Thai) set in a forest. Find everything from private mineral bathhouses (adult/child 50/20B) to a public pool (20/10B) and a sauna (30/10B); masseurs complete the package. To get here, turn off Rte 107 onto Rte 5054 and follow the signs.

The springs are wonderfully peaceful and the setting is sublime, with steam vents blasting up from a meadow crossed by boardwalks and dotted with almost boiling hot springs. The exception is at weekends, when *sŏrng·tăa·ou* (passenger pick-up trucks) full of Thai picnickers head out from Fang to boil eggs and bathe in the springs. Accommodation is in simple but comfortable bungalows and there's a campsite with equipment for rent.

Beyond the hot-springs complex, the rest of the park is a ruckus of forested mountains, with lots of hiking trails and forest campsites. The most popular destination is the 2285m summit of Doi Pha Hompok, Thailand's second-highest peak. Most trekkers camp below the summit and leave early to reach the top at sunrise for an epic view over the surrounding countryside. At the top of the mountain, average temperatures are a mere 2°C during winter and 14°C during summer.

Malee's Nature Lovers Bungalows
GUESTHOUSE $$

(☑081 961 8387; www.maleenature.com; camping per person 200B, bungalows 900-2200B; 🛜🏊) Run by the orchid-obsessed and outrageously friendly Malee, this green-fingered spot on the road to Tham Pha Plong has simple, clean cottages with hot showers in an orchid-filled garden. The cheapest share bathrooms, while posher cabins have en suites. One is set high off the ground for birdwatchers to enjoy the canopy activity.

★ Chiang Dao Nest
INTERNATIONAL $$

(☑053 456242; www.chiangdaonest.com; mains 315-695B; ⊙8am-3.30pm & 6-9.30pm; 🖉) The undisputed culinary highlight of the area, Chiang Dao Nest is worth the trip from Chiang Mai all by itself. Discover imported ales, fine wines and sophisticated modern European dishes you wouldn't expect to find in the jungle, such as salmon fillet wrapped in filo pastry with green tapenade. For equally outrageous Thai fare, head to Nest 2 (p361) down the road. On Thursday nights from November to Februrary, the Nest throws a delicious all-you-can-eat BBQ.

🛍 Shopping

Tuesday Market
MARKET

(⊙7am-noon Tue) Chiang Dao's Tuesday Market has vendors selling hill-tribe handicrafts. Note that during the rainy season fewer people tend to show up.

ℹ Getting There & Away

Chiang Dao is 72km north of Chiang Mai along Rte 107. Buses travel to Chiang Mai (40B, 1½ hours, every 30 minutes) and Tha Ton (63B, 2½ hours, five daily). There are also air-conditioned minivans to Chiang Mai (150B, two hours, hourly).

ℹ Getting Around

It's a 100B motorcycle taxi or 150B *sŏrng·tăa·ou* ride from the bus stand in Chiang Dao village to the guesthouses near the cave temple. Some of the lodges rent out mountain bikes (from 150B per day) and motorbikes (from 350B). Alternatively, you can hire a *sŏrng·tăa·ou* for around 1000B to visit Pha Daeng National Park, for 1500B to go to hill-tribe villages and for 2500B to drive around Doi Chiang Dao Wildlife Sanctuary for the day.

SOUTHERN CHIANG MAI PROVINCE

To the south of Chiang Mai is the Ping Valley, a fertile agricultural plain that runs out to densely forested hills. Southwest is Thailand's highest peak, Doi Inthanon (2565m).

San Kamphaeng & Bo Sang
POP 33,000

About 14km southeast of Chiang Mai along Rte 1006, the town of San Kamphaeng (สันกำแพง) was once famous as a production centre for cotton, silk and other handicrafts, but many of the small factories have relocated and those remaining seem a little down on their luck. *Sŏrng·tăa·ou* and *rót daang* drivers in Chiang Mai push trips to San Kamphaeng quite heavily, steering tourists towards factories and workshops that pay a commission.

The most engaging option is the 'umbrella village' of Bo Sang (บ่อสร้าง), just west of San Kamphaeng, with a string of souvenir shops, showrooms and workshops, most devoted to the production of paper and bamboo umbrellas and parasols. However, prices aren't especially cheap and you'll find similar items in Chiang Mai's night market.

🏃 Activities

San Kamphaeng Hot Springs　　HOT SPRINGS
(📞053 037101; adult/child 100/50B; ⏱7am-6pm) About 36km east of Chiang Mai, these hot springs are a delight. Set in a meandering country garden are public and private bathhouses, massage pavilions and a hot lazy river where you can soak away the tiredness.

Locals flock here at weekends to picnic and boil eggs in the hot vents, which emerge from the ground at a scorching 100°C. During the week, however, things are calm and peaceful, apart from the whoosh of steam roaring out of the steam vents. If you want the full-immersion experience, a dip in the public mineral pool costs 100/50B (adult/child), while a private bathhouse costs 65B for 15 minutes. Simple but comfortable rooms (from 750B, with free use of the pool) are available and there's a campsite (300B per person) and several restaurants.

For a posher stay, the clean and comfortable bungalows at **Roong Aroon Hot Spring Resort** (📞053 101981; d from 1600B; ❄) have access to its own set of hot springs. It's a few kilometres beyond the main springs.

✪ Festivals & Events

Bo Sang Umbrella Festival　　　　ART
(Bo Sang; ⏱late Jan) In late January the surprisingly untouristy Bo Sang Umbrella Festival *(têt·sà·gahn rôm)* features a colourful umbrella procession along the main street.

ⓘ Getting There & Away

White *sŏrng·tăa·ou* to San Kamphaeng town (15B, 30 minutes) leave Chiang Mai frequently during the day from the lane south of Talat Warorot market; white *sŏrng·tăa·ou* to Bo Sang (20B, 25 minutes) leave from the riverside on Th Praisani.

Hang Dong

📋 053 / POP 83,300

About 15km south of Chiang Mai on Rte 108, the village of Hang Dong (หางดง) built its fortune on the production and sale of furniture, woodcarving, antiques (both real and imitation) and handicrafts. Hang Dong's 'furniture highway' – Th Thakhilek – runs east from Rte 108 towards Ban Tawai; look for the turn-off just south of the market. Lined up along the road are dozens of antique and handicraft dealers, selling everything from elaborate antique Chinese wedding beds (with astronomical price tags) to gigantic Buddhist woodcarvings, Burmese lacquer boxes and cheaper and more portable Thai knick-knacks.

✕ Eating

Pankled Coffee Corner　　　　THAI $
(📞053 433779; Soi 9, Tambon Khun Khong; mains 50-120B; ⏱8.30am-5.30pm) Located in Ban Tawai, the Pankled Coffee Corner is a favourite of locals in the Hang Dong area. A perfect place to have lunch after perusing the local craft stores, this restaurant and cafe offers northern and southern Thai dishes, and is well known for having excellent *pàt tai*.

🛍 Shopping

Good places to browse include: **De Siam** (📞053 441545; www.desiam-antiques.com; Th Thakhilek, Ban Tawai; ⏱8.30am-5.30pm) for extravagant antique beds and cabinets; **Mandala** (📞081 490 9251; Th Thakhilek, Ban Tawai; ⏱9am-5pm Mon-Sat) for Japanese heirlooms; **Siripat Antique** (📞053 433246; Th Thakhilek, Ban Tawai) for reproduction antiques and enormous woodcarvings; **Chilli Antiques & Arts** (📞087 919 8750; 125 Th Thakhilek, Ban Tawai; ⏱9am-5pm) for top-notch Thai and Burmese Buddhas; **World Port Services** (📞053 434200; www.legendscollection.com; Th Thakhilek, Ban Tawai; ⏱8am-5pm Mon-Sat) for portable handicrafts and Burmese lacquerware; and **Crossroads Asia** (📞092 984 4105; www.crossroadsasia.com; 214/7 Th Thakhilek, Ban Tawai; ⏱9am-5pm) for ethnic art and textiles spanning 26 countries.

Ban Tawai Tourism Village ARTS & CRAFTS
(www.ban-tawai.com; ⊙8am-5pm) About 2km east of Hang Dong, Ban Tawai is a sprawling, pedestrian-friendly tourist market, with hundreds of small shops selling handicrafts and knick-knacks to spruce up your interiors back home. This vast enterprise was kicked off by local woodcarvers, who are famous for their artistry and prodigious output.

Today, carvings are produced on an industrial scale by numerous workshops. It's all very commercial, but you'll find the same kinds of handicrafts and souvenirs that you see in Chiang Mai's Walking Street markets, spread out across covered 'zones'. Signs saying 'antiques made to order' should make you question the origins of anything purporting to be old.

ⓘ Getting There & Away

It is possible to reach Hang Dong by *sŏrng·tăa·ou* from Pratu Chiang Mai (30B, 20 minutes) but it's easier to come with a chartered *rót daang* (1000B to 1500B for three hours) so you can also visit nearby Ban Tawai.

Doi Inthanon National Park

Thailand's highest peak, Doi Inthanon (ดอย อินทนนท์) soars to 2565m above sea level, an impressive altitude for the kingdom. Surrounding this granite massif is a 482-sq-km **national park** (อุทยานแห่งชาติดอยอินทนนท์; ☑053 286729; http://nps.dnp.go.th; adult/child 300/150B, car/motorcycle 30/20B; ⊙4am-6pm), dotted with hiking trails and waterfalls and enveloped in an impenetrable curtain of jungle. When the heat of Chiang Mai gets too much, locals decamp to Doi Inthanon, especially during the New Year holiday when there's the rarely seen phenomenon of frost at the summit.

◉ Sights

Waterfalls

During the wet season, the highlands collect rain like a sponge, sending it surging down towards the plains in raging torrents over eight dramatic waterfalls. Although swimming is discouraged because of the risk of flash floods, the falls are wonderfully scenic and spectacular after rain.

The most accessible cascade is **Nam Tok Mae Klang**, near the Km 8 marker, close to the turn-off from Rte 108 (take the signposted road just before the national park

entrance), but the falls can get crowded with picnickers and coach tours at weekends. Reached via a side road near the Km 21 marker and tucked into a forested basin, **Nam Tok Wachirathan** has a huge frothy mane that plummets 50m and after heavy rain it can be as loud as an AC/DC concert. There's an enticing collection of food vendors by the parking lot. Near the Km 30 marker, **Nam Tok Siriphum** is a delicate ribbon of silver when viewed from nearby Ban Khun Klang village.

Villages

Also in the park are a few hill-tribe villages surrounded by rice terraces, which are rather picturesque. Most villagers now work at farms and flower nurseries on the lower slopes. Near the national park headquarters, the Hmong village of **Ban Khun Klang** is worth visiting for its views of the Siriphum waterfall.

🏃 Activities

Most visitors charge straight to the stupas and the summit. The only easy access into the forest is via the slippery Ang Ka Nature Trail (a 360m-long boardwalk) into the cloud forest, near the Km 48 marker. A more ambitious jungle walk is the Kew Mae Pan Nature Trail near the Km 42 marker.

At the summit of Doi Inthanon (2565m), the forest is dank and chilly, and often partly obscured by swirls of mist due to the condensation of warm humid air from lower down the mountain. It's otherworldly, and at times a little spooky. Do as Thai visitors do and bring a jacket and an umbrella or rain poncho in case of sudden showers.

The summit itself is reached via a 50m trail near the radar station, just beyond Doi Inthanon's twin *chedi*. At the end is a 'Highest Point in Thailand' sign, and a shrine to one of the last Lanna kings (Inthawichayanon). Don't expect a rewarding view; you'll see more from the terraces of the two *chedi*. The tiny cafe by the boardwalk is frequented by laughing thrushes and other exotic birdlife.

Ang Ka Nature Trail HIKING
Ideal for those with limited time or small children, or anybody looking for an easy stroll through nature, this 360m boardwalk leads through the cloud forest near the summit of Doi Inthanon. The wooden trail snakes over a peat bog and past old, fern- and moss-covered

trees and red rhododendron, all regularly shrouded in fog. Look out for the green-tailed sunbird. This 'coat-wearing forest', as the locals call it, is open year-round, with no guide necessary. There's parking across the street from the trailhead.

Kew Mae Pan Nature Trail   WALKING
(200B; ⊙Nov-Jun) The Kew Mae Pan Nature Trail, near the Km 42 marker, snakes for nearly 3km, passing a string of viewpoints and a pretty waterfall; a guide is compulsory (covered by the admission fee) and should be arranged at the park headquarters. The views are best in the cool dry season from November to February.

Sleeping & Eating

Park accommodation is available in comfortable bungalows located next to the national park information centre at Ban Khun Klang village, near the Km 31 marker; the best ones overlook the water. Camping is also possible (with your own equipment) at Nam Tok Mae Pan. There are restaurants at the hotels and a large food hall on the climb up the highway where most tour buses stop.

One of the best options if you want to stay near the park entrance is a homestay in the rice-paddy-encircled Karen village of Ban Mae Klang Luang. Perched over the rice terraces, the clean, polished wood cabins at **Mae Klang Luang View** (☑086 189 4075; bungalows 1000B) are our favourite, although there are plenty of other options with prices hovering around 500B.

There are some okay places to stay at the bottom of the mountain about 40km from the summit, near the junction of Rte 1009 and Rte 108; the nicest is **Nok Chan Mee Na** (☑088 762 3627; nokchanmeena184@gmail.com; 184 Ban Luang, Chom Thong; d incl breakfast from 500B; ※ 🖥 ✉), which is tucked into a village and perched over a rice paddy. Further on, only about 29km from Chiang Mai proper, is the stunning and tranquil boutique resort, Kaomai Lanna (p338).

ⓘ Getting There & Away

Most visitors come with private transport or on a tour from Chiang Mai; if coming by motorcycle from Chiang Mai, allow for 2½ hours each way.

To reach the park via public transport, you first need to take a bus from Chiang Mai to Chom Thong (60B) on Rte 108. There are occasional public *sŏrng·tăa·ou* into the park from the highway junction, but these will only take you to the summit and back. Considering the risk of getting marooned, it makes more sense to charter a *rót daang* for the round-trip (about 1000B).

Mae Kampong

☑053 / POP 360

About 50km northeast of Chiang Mai, hidden away in the emerald jungles above Rte 1317, the pocket-sized village of Mae Kampong has become an offbeat retreat for travellers looking to escape the commercialism of Chiang Mai and rediscover the village way of life. Most visitors are introduced to the area on zipline tours with Flight of the Gibbon (p328), but it's worth coming under your own steam to explore the village and the surrounding jungle.

Perched at an altitude of about 1300m, Mae Kampong (แม่กำปง) is locally famous as a centre for the production of *mêeang* (pickled tea leaves), and local coffee is sold at many small coffee shops dotted along the road through the village. The steep road continues through the forest into **Chae Son National Park** (อุทยานแห่งชาติแจ้ซ้อน; ☑054 380000, 089 851 3355; adult/child 200/100B), where you'll find waterfalls, hot springs and cottages in the woods.

Sleeping

The Community Ecotourism Committee provides local **homestays** (☑089 559 4797; Mae Kampong; per person from 560B). You can find a room just by asking at houses displaying a 'homestay' sign; Green Trails (p328) or Flight of the Gibbon (p328) in Chiang Mai can arrange overnight trips by minibus.

An alternative overnight stop is Tharnthong Lodges (p338) just few kilometres downhill from Mae Kampong.

ⓘ Getting There & Away

There is no public transport from Chiang Mai, but the village is easy to reach with a decent-sized motorcycle or by chartered *rót daang* – just follow Rte 1317 from the city past Mae On to Ban Huai Kaew, and follow the signed road.

POPULATION
22 million

**NUMBER OF
NATIONAL PARKS**
26

BEST TEMPLE
Wat Phu Thok (p396)

BEST SHRINE
Sala Kaew Ku (p381)

BEST ISAN FOOD
Ting Song Tam
(p376)

WHEN TO GO
Nov–Feb During the
cool season, temper-
atures are pleasantly
warm.

Mar–May Tempera-
tures soar to the high
30s. Travelling can
be exhausting, but
wonderful festivals
happen now.

Jun–Oct Isan is at
its most beautiful
during the rainy
season. It generally
only rains a little in
the afternoon.

Phu Thok viewpoint (p374), Chiang Khan
ADCHARIN CHITTHAMMACHUK/SHUTTERSTOCK ©

Northeastern Thailand

The northeast is Thailand's forgotten backyard. Isan (อีสาน), as it's usually called, offers a glimpse of the Thailand of old: rice fields along the horizon, water buffalo wade in muddy ponds, silk weavers work looms under their homes, and pedal-rickshaw riders pull passengers down city streets. If you have a penchant for authentic experiences, you'll surely be satisfied here.

Spend a little time in the region and you'll discover as many differences as similarities to the rest of Thailand. The language, food and culture are more Lao than Thai, with hearty helpings of Khmer and Vietnamese thrown in. And spend time here you should, because it's home to some of Thailand's best historic sites, national parks and festivals. Thailand's tourist trail is at its bumpiest here (English is rarely spoken), but the fantastic attractions and daily interactions could end up being highlights of your trip.

Northeastern Thailand Highlights

❶ Prasat Phanom Rung (p424) Climbing an extinct volcano to Thailand's most impressive Khmer ruins.

❷ Khao Yai National Park (p417) Spotting elephants, gibbons and deer in Thailand's oldest national park.

❸ Nong Khai (p380) Chillin' along the Mekong River in Isan's long-time traveller hotspot.

❹ Pha Taem National Park (p438) Walking a cliff-face trail in search of 1000-year-old rock paintings.

❺ Phu Kradueng National Park (p380) Climbing the high-altitude plateau of this monkey-filled national park.

❻ Phimai (p414) Marvelling at Thailand's largest Khmer ruin, the inspiration for Cambodia's Angkor Wat.

❼ Chiang Khan (p374) Sleeping in a converted wooden shophouse at this charming riverside town.

❽ Prasat Ta Meuan (p435) Side-stepping the crowds at Phanom Rung for the quieter ruins of this Khmer complex.

❾ That Phanom (p402) Gawping at Isan's iconic, 53m-tall, golden-trimmed Buddhist stupa.

❿ Nakhon Phanom (p398) Biking beside the Mekong in the region's most cycle-friendly town.

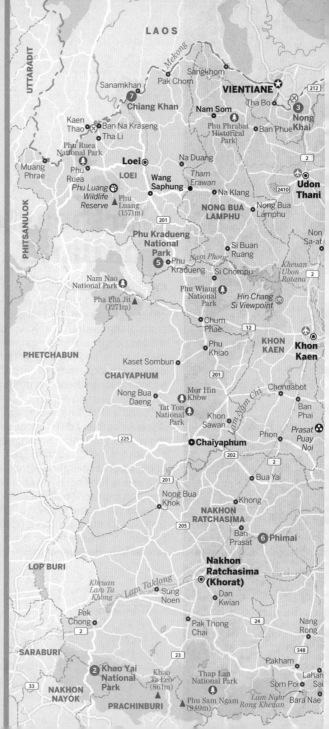

History

The early social history of the Isan region remains a mystery. Ancient rock paintings are widespread, and while they could be up to 10,000 years old, dating is not possible. It appears that the Ban Chiang culture, and closely related ones around them, began making bronze tools about 2000 BCE, well before the Bronze Age began in China.

Dvaravati kingdoms, about which very little is known, held sway here from somewhere between the 7th and 10th centuries, and traces of the culture can be found at Phu Phrabat in Udon Thani and Muang Sema in Nakhon Ratchasima.

The Khmer arrived in the 9th century and occupied most of the region for more than 400 years, though for much of this time it was in partnership with rather than dominion over local leaders. Hundreds of their iconic temples remain over most of Isan, most notably at Phimai in Nakhon Ratchasima and Phanom Rung in Buriram. After the Khmer empire waned, Isan was under the thumb of Lan Xang and Siam kings, but remained largely autonomous.

As the French staked out the borders of colonial Laos, Thailand was forced to define its own northeastern boundaries. Slowly but surely, for better and worse, Isan fell under the mantle of broader Thailand. It was for a long time Thailand's poorest region and the Thai government, with considerable help (and most of the money) coming from the US, only began serious development here in the 1960s as a way to counter the communist threat. There was also a dedicated program to make Isan more 'Thai' in the interests of national solidarity. The result was an improved economy and increased opportunity, but the per capita income here remains only one-third the national average.

Language & Culture

Isan is a melting pot of Thai, Lao and Khmer influences. The Isan language, still a more common first tongue than Thai, is a dialect of Lao. In fact, there are probably more people of Lao heritage in Isan than in Laos. Many villages in the far south still maintain Khmer as their primary language.

The people of Isan are known by other Thais for their friendliness, work ethic and sense of humour: flip through radio stations and you'll hear DJs laughing at their own jokes. Respect and hospitality towards guests is a cornerstone of Isan life, and most villagers, plus plenty of city folk, still pride themselves on taking care of others before themselves. Isan people are far less conservative than most Thais, but short shorts and spaghetti-strap tops will earn more stares than in other places in Thailand because of the scarcity of tourists here.

Though this is by far Thailand's poorest region, historically, surveys show that the people of the northeast are generally the happiest because of their strong sense of community and close family ties. In the villages it's often hard to tell who is rich or poor because big homes and fancy clothes garner little respect. Modern culture, however, is changing this in the minds of many young people. Additionally, the massive influx of Western men marrying local women has brought changes too, and these days many Isan village women and their families work hard towards the goal of landing a foreign husband.

LOEI PROVINCE

Loei (จังหวัดเลย), meaning 'to the extreme', is a diverse, beautiful province mostly untouched by mass tourism, despite all it has to offer. This isn't the wildest place in Thailand, but the region's national parks and nature reserves are excellent. And if you have the luck to arrive at the right time, you can balance the hush of nature with the hubbub of Dan Sai's incredible Phi Ta Khon Festival.

The terrain here is mountainous and temperatures fluctuate from one extreme to the other: it's hotter than elsewhere in Thailand during the hot season and it's also one of the few provinces in Thailand where temperatures drop below 0°C.

The majority of the people are Tai Loei, thought to have migrated from Luang Prabang via Chiang Mai. They're proud of their distinct culture and you'll notice unique offerings at many temples and hear the Tai Loei dialect often.

Loei

📞 042 / POP 22,700

Loei (เลย) is a relatively small provincial capital and easy to get around. It doesn't have anything that will wow tourists, and most foreigners visit just briefly while on their way to the province's national parks and small towns. However, good accommodation options – not to mention craft beer! – make

Loei Province

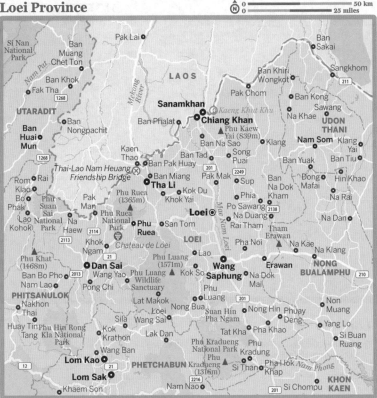

```
N    0                    50 km
     0                    25 miles
```

Sí Nan National Park
Ban Muang Chet Ton
Pak Lai
LAOS
Ban Khiri Wongkot
Ban Sakai
Sangkhom
Nam Pat
Ban Khok
Fak Tha
1268
UTARADIT
Ban Huai Mun
1268
Ban Nongpachit
Mekong River
Sanamkhan
Pak Chom
Ban Phalat
Chiang Khan
Kaeng Khut Khu
Ban Kong
Sawang
Na Khae
UDON THANI
Nam Som
Klang Yai
211
Kaen Thao
Thai-Lao Nam Heuang Friendship Bridge
Ban Pak Huay
Ban Miang
Ban Tad
Pak Mak
201
Song Puai
Ban Yuak
Ban Tiu
Klang
Ban Na Sao
Phu Kaew Yai (839m)
2249
Tha Li
Kok Du
Sup
Ban Na Dok Kham
Dong Mafai
Hin Khao
Na Rai
Rom Rai
Klao
Bo
Phak
Lao National Park
Phu Suan Sai
Pak Man
Phu Ruea (1365m)
Khok Yai
Phia
Po Sawang
2138
Na Duang
Na Dan
Kohok
Na Haew
Phu Ruea National Park
Phu Ruea
San Tom
Loei
Rai Tham
Tham Erawan
2114
LOEI
Pha Noi
Na Kae
Na Klang
2113
Khok Ngam
Chateau de Loei
Lao
Phu Luang (1571m)
Phu Khat (1468m)
Dan Sai
Wang Yao
Phu Luang Wildlife Sanctuary
Kok So
Wang Saphung
Erawan
NONG BUALAMPHU
210
Ban Bo Pho
2013
Pong Chi
Na Dok Mai
Nam Lao
PHITSANULOK
Nakhon Thai
Lat Makok
Nong Bua
Phu Luang
201
Non Muang
Huay Tin Phu Hin Rong Tang Kla National Park
Sila Wang Sai
Loei Pha Ngam
Suan Hin
Nong Hin
Phuay Deng
Yang Lo
Kok Krathon
Lak Dan
Tat Kha
Pha Khao
Si Buan Ruang
Wang Ban
Phu Kradueng National Park
Phu Kradung
Lom Kao
21
PHETCHABUN
Phu Kradueng (1316m)
Si Than
Pha Hok
Nam Phong
Lom Sak
12
2216
Nam Nao
Si Chompu
KHON KAEN
Khaem Son
201

longer stays pleasant if you want to use it as a base for your Loei Province exploration.

◎ Sights & Activities

Phu Bo Bit Forest Park   VIEWPOINT
(วนอุทยานภูบ่อบิด; Rte 2138; ⊙5am-7.30pm) If you want to harden up your legs for Loei's national parks, Phu Bo Bit gives you about 1400 steep steps to practise on, and rewards your effort with great 360-degree views of the town and surrounding mountains. The climb, which passes a Buddha cave, can be done in an hour and a half return.

The park is about 3km from the town centre along Rte 2138. You can get a túk-túk there and back for about 250B, including wait time. Many locals come up here at sunset and stay till after dark to see the lights of Loei. Lighting along the steps is supposedly turned off at 8pm, but locals advised us that sometimes it's switched off early, so plan to be down by 7.30pm.

Museum of Art & Culture Loei   MUSEUM
(ศูนย์วัฒนธรรมจังหวัดเลย; ☑042 835223; Rte 201; ⊙8.30am-4.30pm) FREE This little museum, also known as 'Maloei Museum', is 5km north of town at Rajabhat University. The first gallery has an animatronic dinosaur (fossilised footprints have been found nearby) and the second has a few displays about the culture of the Tai Loei people, including the Phi Ta Khon (p378) festival. Check in at the office down below and they'll open the museum for you.

Loei Palace Hotel
Swimming Pool   SWIMMING
(Th Charoen Rat; 90B) Non-guests can use the pool at Loei's top hotel.

☞ Tours

Sugar Guesthouse (p372) and freelance guide **Poppy** (☑088 698 3995; bornto be_travel@hotmail.com) both lead reasonably priced day trips to **Suan Hin Pha Ngam**

Loei

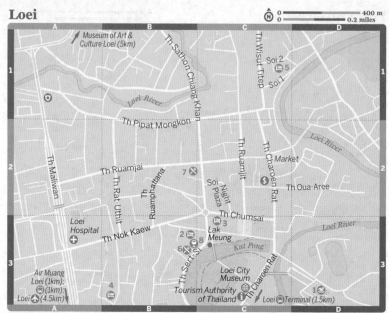

Loei

🟢 Activities, Courses & Tours

🛏 Sleeping

🍴 Eating

🍷 Drinking & Nightlife

(สวนหินผางาม; ☎ 094 514 9231; tour per person 50B, tractor ride per person 20B; ☉ visitors centre 8am-5.30pm, last departure to the mountain 4.30pm) and elsewhere in Loei Province.

🛏 Sleeping

★ Sugar Guesthouse
GUESTHOUSE $

(☎ 089 711 1975; sugarguesthouse@gmail.com; Soi 2, Th Wisut Titep; s with fan 200-270B, d with air-con 380B; 🅿 ❄ @ 🛜) This guesthouse has simple, spotless rooms (the fan rooms share a bathroom), and the friendly owner Pat speaks good English. There's bike and motorcycle hire and tours to sites around the province.

Baan Sabai
HOTEL $

(☎ 042 811132; baansabai.loei@gmail.com; off Th Nok Kaew; tw/d 350/400B; 🅿 ❄ 🛜) Lovely little

hotel with terracotta roof tiles and spotless guest rooms with air-con, TV and small balconies. No English spoken, and no English sign, but it represents good value.

King Hotel
HOTEL $$

(☎ 042 811225; kinghotel.loei@hotmail.com; Th Chumsai; d incl breakfast 600-800B; 🅿 ❄ 🛜) Fit for a king? No; though a thorough modernisation of this old classic has given the rooms a simple but attractive style and made it a pleasant place to stay. The rooms surround a courtyard and it's quiet here, despite the city-centre location. You can get rooms for a bargain 450B if you forgo breakfast.

Loei Village
HOTEL $$

(☎ 042 833599; www.loeivillages.com; Soi 3, Th Nok Kaew; d incl breakfast 990-1500B; 🅿 ❄ 🛜)

Starting with a cool welcome drink as you walk in, the focus is on service at this stylish hotel. The decor is smart, and little extras such as free minibar snacks and a good buffet breakfast make this one of the city's top choices. There are also free bikes for guests' use. Staff are especially helpful. The price is still a bit steep, though.

Loei Palace Hotel HOTEL $$$
(☑042 815668; www.mosaic-collection.com/loeipalace; Th Charoen Rat; incl breakfast d 1600-3000B, ste 3500-5000B; P✳@🛜🏊) Loei's ageing flagship hotel is an old-fashioned hulk of a building but it backs onto a pleasant park and retains a certain charm with spacious rooms decked out in wooden furniture. Discounts can bring rooms down to around half price. There's a pool, a gym and bikes for rent (half-/full-day 50/100B).

✖ Eating & Drinking

★**Khao Tom Raeng Ngan** THAI $
(☑042 033050; Th Sert-Si; mains 60-120B, fish 250-380B; ⊗5pm-3am; 🛜) As busy as the street it sits on, this large open-fronted place serves not only the rice soup (*kôw đôm*) it's named after, but dozens of other dishes too. The service is quick and friendly, and the food won't disappoint. There's an English menu, and you can order a cold beer (from 75B) with your meal.

Phuloei Coffee CAFE $
(Th Ruamjai; coffee from 45B, mains 60-150B; ⊗8am-8.30pm; 🛜) This pleasant, friendly cafe serves excellent locally grown coffee and delicious baked goods, and has a full Thai menu (in English).

Noi Tam Suea @ Loei THAI $
(Th Sert-Si; mains 35-40B; ⊗9am-8pm; 🛜) This popular restaurant has all the expected Isan foods including *plah pŏw* (grilled fish) and duck *lâhp,* plus several less common options including *sôm·dam* made with *dôrng dêng* noodles, a super-thick version of the typical *kà·nŏm jeen* noodles. It's an English-free zone.

★**Outlaw Brewing** CRAFT BEER
(☑096 695 8784; Th Sert-Si; beer 120-160B; ⊗7pm-midnight Tue-Sun; 🛜) Loei is the unexpected home of one of Thailand's most serious brewmasters. Stop by this little spot for some of his own craft brews, infused with exotic local ingredients such as pomelo and durian, or try some of their bottled craft beers from elsewhere.

ⓘ Information

Krung Thai Bank (Th Oua-Aree; ⊗9am-5pm) The only bank in the city centre that's open extended hours.

Loei Hospital (☑042 862123; Th Maliwan) The top hospital in Loei.

Tourism Authority of Thailand (TAT; ☑042 812812; tatloei@tat.or.th; Th Charoen Rat; ⊗8.30am-4.30pm) Provides a good map of the province and has helpful staff, though not much English is spoken.

Tourist Police (☑042 867364, nationwide 1155; Th Pipat Mongkon)

ⓘ Getting There & Away

AIR

Nok Air (☑088 874 0883, nationwide 02 900 9955; www.nokair.com; Loei Airport; ⊗6am-4pm) and **Air Asia** (☑042 844629, nationwide 02 515 9999; www.airasia.com; Loei Airport; ⊗9am-5pm) both connect Loei to Bangkok's Don Mueang Airport. Together there are three daily flights, with prices starting at around 900B.

A taxi into town from the **airport** (☑042 811520), 5km south of town, runs to 150B. A túk-túk from the bus station to the airport is 100B.

NORTHEASTERN THAILAND LOEI

ⓘ GETTING TO LAOS: NA KRASENG TO KAEN THAO

Foreigners can get Lao visas at the seldom-used Thai–Lao Nam Heuang Friendship Bridge in Amphoe Tha Li, 60km northwest of Loei.

Getting to the border An international bus runs daily from Loei to Luang Prabang in Laos (700B, 10 hours) via Sainyabuli (500B, seven hours). Buses leave Loei at 8am. There's no other public transport to the Thai border here.

At the border The border is open from 8am to 6pm and it's never busy.

Moving on If you somehow get to the border on your own, rather than using the international bus, you can take a túk-túk (50B) between the two border posts, but you'll find very little onward transport from Kaen Thao.

BUS

Loei's **bus terminal** (☑ 042 833586; Th Maliwan) is south of town. **Air Muang Loei** (☑ 042 832042; Loei bus terminal) has good VIP service to Bangkok. Note that *sŏrng·tăa·ou* (passenger pick-up trucks) to Chiang Khan take you to near the city centre, while buses leave you pretty far away.

TO	FARE (B)	TIME (HR)	FREQUENCY
Bangkok	360-655	9-10	hourly 6am-10.35pm
Chiang Khan	34	1	9 departures 6.30am-11.45pm
Chiang Khan (sŏrng tăa ou)	35	1½	every 30min 5.30am-7.45pm
Chiang Mai	436-570	10	3.30pm, 8.30pm, 9.30pm, 11.30pm
Dan Sai	60-134	1½-2	10.30am, noon, 2.20pm, 3.30pm, 8.30pm, 9.30pm, 11.30pm
Khon Kaen	125	4	every 30min 3.45am-6.10pm
Nakhorn Ratchasima	252-342	7	hourly 5.30am-4.30pm
Nong Khai	140	7-8	6am
Pak Chom (sŏrng tăa ou)	60	2½	hourly 6am-5pm
Phitsanulok	202-266	5	10am, noon, 2.20pm, 3.30pm, 8.30pm, 9.30pm, 11.30pm
Udon Thani	90-115	2½-3	every 30min 4am-5pm

ⓘ Getting Around

Sŏrng·tăa·ou (10B) run from the bus station into the centre of town, or you can take a túk-túk for 50B to 60B. It's an easy 1.5km walk, though; turn left out of the back of the station, right past Cafe Mona, then right again at the end of the

lane. At the big market at the end of the road, turn left onto Th Charoen Rat, from where you can branch left onto Th Sert-Si.

Loei also has a few taxis. They park at the bus station and airport, and do not use their meters. Sugar Guesthouse (p372) hire bikes (50B per day) and motorcycles (250B per day).

Chiang Khan

☑ 042 / POP 6100

What was once a sleepy, little-known Mekong-side town full of traditional timber shophouses became a trendy destination for Thais and is now full of gift shops, cute cafes and places for taking selfies. That said, Chiang Khan (เชียงคาน) is far from spoiled and is still a charming place to visit. The photogenic views of the river and the Lao mountains beyond are still there, as are the old buildings, and things remain peaceful in the daytime before the evening shopping stampede begins. Every evening Th Chai Khong turns into a busy Walking Street market with buskers, artists and street-food vendors. Chiang Khan is less busy in the hot and rainy seasons (April to September).

◉ Sights

Chiang Khan Vernacular House Learning Centre HISTORIC BUILDING
(แหล่งเรียนรู้บ้านถิ่นเชียงคาน; Soi 19; ⊙ daylight hours) FREE This modest but fascinating set-up showcases informative displays (in English as well as Thai) that discuss the different kinds of traditional wooden houses found in Chiang Khan, and is located underneath one such 120-year-old family home.

Phu Thok VIEWPOINT
(ภูทอก) In the cool season, people head from Chiang Khan to nearby Phu Thok mountain for sunrise and 'sea of fog' views. If you don't have your own vehicle, ask your hotel to arrange a ride. Túk-túk charge 100B per person and then you have to ride a *sŏrng·tăa·ou* (25B per person) to the top.

Kaeng Khut Khu NATURAL FEATURE
(แก่งคุดคู้) With the mountains making an attractive backdrop, this famous bend in the Mekong, and its small set of rapids, is a popular stop for visitors. You can also take shared boat trips around here (100B per person). It's 5km downstream from town; túk-túk drivers charge 100B per person there and back.

Chiang Khan

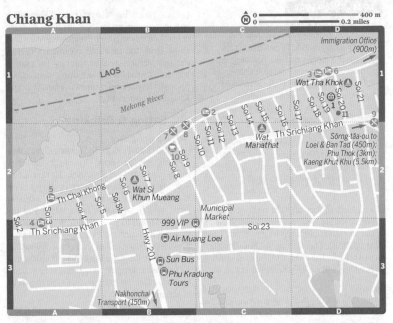

Chiang Khan

The surrounding park has a bevy of vendors selling *má·prów gâew* coconut candy, a local speciality. (It's sold in town too.) This is also a good place to try *gûng-paa* (crispy fried shrimp), which looks a little like frisbees, and *gûng đên* (dancing shrimp), little bowls of live shrimp.

🏃 Activities

Many guesthouses arrange boat trips to Kaeng Khut Khu or further afield, and the mountain scenery makes them highly recommended, especially at sunset. Rates swing with petrol prices, but the typical one-hour trip costs around 800B for up to 15 people.

If you make you own way to Kaeng Khut Khu, you can take shared boat trips around there for 100B per person.

🎉 Festivals & Events

Phi Kon Nam   CULTURAL
(Ban Na Sao; ⊙ May or Jun) The little-known Phi Kon Nam festival in Ban Na Sao, 7km south of Chiang Khan, is part of the village's rain-inducing Bun Bâng Fai (rocket festival (p436)), and coincides with Visakha Bucha. Locals believe that the souls of their departed cows and buffaloes wander around the village so, to show respect, the villagers don wild bovine-inspired masks and colourful costumes to commune with them.

🛏 Sleeping

Chiang Khan Guesthouse   GUESTHOUSE **$**
(☏ 086 325 7958; guesthouse.ck@gmail.com; 282 Th Chai Khong; d with fan/air-con 200/500B; ❄ 🛜) This basic, traditional-style place is

MORNING ALMS

Buying a tray of food to *dàk baht* (give food to the monks on their morning alms round) has become big business in Chiang Khan, particularly with visitors from Bangkok. We suggest giving it a pass since it runs counter to the local tradition of putting only sticky rice in the monks' bowls – other food should be taken to the temple and donated there. The Dos and Don'ts signs along Th Chai Khong include this request, along with no littering or making loud noises.

all creaking timber and tin roofing, and it's the inescapable wear-and-tear that makes it so cheap (fan-cooled, river-view room 1 is a steal at 200B). The communal 2nd-floor terrace overlooks the river and the ever-smiling owner Ong will make you feel at home.

Garage　　　　　　　BOUTIQUE HOTEL **$**
(☑ 081 565 4330; Th Srichiang Khan; s/d/tr/q 500/600/700/800B; ✳☏) A quirky guesthouse for the hipster tourist, this funky little place has a gritty, urban-warehouse vibe, a car-garage theme and five individualised rooms, including one with a double bed inside a converted VW camper van! Owner Jo speaks English, and runs a home-brew bar around the corner.

Buppa Boutique Hotel　　　GUESTHOUSE **$$**
(☑ 089 694 3336, 042 821705; 340 Th Chai Khong; d 1000-1200B; ✳☏) The owners of this three-room spot have mixed historic touches from the family's 1925 home with modern stylings, and the results are impressive. More than any other place we've seen in Chiang Khan, it exudes a back-in-the-day vibe. Two of the rooms have river views. There's no breakfast, but you can have tea and coffee in the comfortable living area.

**Old Chiangkhan
Boutique Hotel**　　　　BOUTIQUE HOTEL **$$$**
(☑ 088 340 3999; Soi 20, Th Chai Khong; d incl breakfast 1600-1800B; ℙ✳☏) This stately old Thai-style home, built in 1852, has been modified and converted into a hotel. It has tastefully decorated rooms, all with double beds, around a courtyard. The more expensive rooms have Mekong views.

Norn-Nab-Dao　　　　　　HOTEL **$$$**
(☑ 086 792 0215; Soi 3; incl breakfast d & tw 1700-2200B, q 2900B; ℙ✳☏) This hotel isn't all

timber, but it has charm nonetheless. The cutely painted rooms lie around an airy central courtyard, and there are great river views from the four end rooms. It's one of the best choices within the city for people who don't need luxury, but don't want to put up with the particular quirks of most Chiang Khan accommodation.

🍴 Eating & Drinking

⭐ **Ting Song Tam**　　　　　　THAI **$**
(☑ 088 029 8251; Soi 21, Th Srichiang Khan; mains 30-100B; ☺ 8.30am-6pm) One of our favourite restaurants in Loei Province. There's a full Isan menu but its speciality is *đôrng đêng* noodles (a super-thick version of *kà·nŏm jeen*), which are made fresh when you order. Add them to your *sôm·đam* (50B) or eat with chilli sauce and vegetables, a Chiang Khan speciality called *kôw pûn rórn* that pairs well with *gài yâhng* (grilled chicken).

There's no English sign, but it's the restaurant with the washing machines at the front of the dining area.

⭐ **Rabiang Rim Khong**　　　　THAI **$**
(Soi 10, Th Chai Khong; mains 60-250B; ☺ 10.30am-9.30pm) This place has been popular with locals since long before the tourism boom. The prices have risen a bit since those good old days and the building has changed, but the quality has not dropped.

Jer Loei　　　　　　　　　　THAI **$**
(เจอเลย; 379 Th Chai Khong; mains 80-150B; ☺ 5pm-midnight; ☏) From the decor to the music, this is a full-on Thai 'indy' place, and the seating is close enough to the river to catch a sunset view. The small menu is big on Thai-style salads and Isan *đôm sâep* soups.

⭐ **Husband & Wife**　　　　　　CAFE
(Soi 8, Th Chai Khong; coffee from 40B, meals 50B; ☺ 7am-9pm; ☏) The most pleasant of a number of cutesy cafes that dot Th Chai Khong, this plant-filled, wooden-shuttered, road-side perch serves excellent coffee as well as teas, smoothies and a handful of tasty Thai dishes (rice, noodles, soups). The welcome is friendly and there are three simple but smart guest rooms upstairs (1000B, with shared bathroom 600B).

ℹ Information

Immigration Office (☑ 042 821911; Soi 26, Th Chai Khong; ☺ 8.30am-noon & 1-4.30pm Mon-Fri) For visa extensions.

ℹ Getting There & Away

AIR

Air Asia and Nok Air have fly-and-ride service to Bangkok's Don Mueang Airport via Loei Airport. Air Asia's meeting point is the Old Chiangkhan Boutique Hotel and **Nok Air** (Triple Z Hostel; ☑ 097 319 9097; Soi 20) uses Triple Z Hostel.

BUS

Sŏrng·tăa·ou (passenger pick-up trucks) to Loei (35B, 1½ hours) depart about every 30 minutes from a stop on Th Srichiang Khan (at Soi 26). They drive west along Soi 23 before turning south onto Hwy 201 and will pick up passengers on the way. Buses to Loei (34B, one hour, hourly 6.30am to 3.30pm) leave from the **Nakhonchai Transport** (☑ 042 821905; Hwy 201) terminal. They continue to Khorat (283B, seven hours).

No transport runs direct to Nong Khai. The quickest way there is via Loei and Udon Thani, but for the scenic river route take a Loei-bound *sŏrng·tăa·ou* south to Ban Tad (20B, 30 minutes), where you can catch the 6am bus from Loei to Nong Khai or one of the Loei–Pak Chom *sŏrng·tăa·ou*.

Four companies, with buses departing from their own offices, make the run to Bangkok (10 to 11 hours) in the morning and early evening: **Air Muang Loei** (☑ 082 642 1629; Soi 23, Th Srichiang Khan), **999 VIP** (☑ 089 893 2898; Soi 9), **Phu Kradung Tours** (☑ 089 842 1524; petrol station, Hwy 201) and **Sun Bus** (Hwy 201). Tickets range from 419B to 652B; 999 VIP and Sun Bus have the best deluxe service.

ℹ Getting Around

Most hotels have free bikes for their guests, but if yours is an exception they can be hired around town for 50B per day. Soi 9 is the hub of motorcycle rental (250B per day), with three companies based there.

Pak Chom

☑ 042

Around 70km east of Chiang Khan along the Mekong is the dusty town – just an overgrown village, really – of Pak Chom (ปากชม). It's a regional market centre with no attractions other than the spectacular river views that far exceed those of its better-known sibling. And because of the beauty, there are some outstanding resorts that make this a place worth visiting if you're looking for rustic relaxation and natural charm.

🍴 Sleeping & Eating

Despite its remoteness – actually, in large part because of it – there's excellent accommodation around Pak Chom for all budgets.

There are several restaurants in town, but most people eat at their resort.

★ Mekong Riverside
Resort & Camping   RESORT $$

(☑ 082 272 7472; www.mekongriverside.com; Hwy 211; d incl breakfast from 1350B, camping 150B per person; P ❄ 🛜) This delightful spot, nestled up against a postcard-worthy view of the Mekong, is popular with travellers. Owner Khun Ben and her husband Mike are founts of knowledge on the local area and can give good tips on activities and places to go. The four rooms are simple but tastefully designed and comfortable. Reservations are highly recommended.

Camping is also available, but you need to bring your own gear. An evening boat cruise is par for the course, and the resort's restaurant does excellent meals (mains 80B to 400B), including international food.

Rim Nam Kong
Homestay & Camping   HOMESTAY $$

(☑ 099 125 0461; Hwy 211; d incl breakfast 600-900B, camping per person with own/hired tent 150/200B; P ❄ 🛜) Charming, friendly and attractively decorated, it's like a little bit of Chiang Khan plopped down in the countryside. Excellent English is spoken, and the family are great hosts. All rooms have private bathrooms, though the one with the best river view requires a walk outdoors. It's 1km west of town; staff will pick you up at the bus station.

ℹ Getting There & Away

Pak Chom's bus stop is at the market, 500m east of the junction. Large *sŏrng·tăa·ou* depart to Loei (60B, 2½ hours) hourly from 5.50am to noon and then once more at 4pm. There's no public transport between Pak Chom and Chiang Khan. Instead, take the Loei-bound *sŏrng·tăa·ou* to Ban Tad (45B, 1½ hours) and change to another for Chiang Khan (20B, 30 minutes). To Nong Khai (80B, four hours) there are non-air-con buses at 5am, 10am and 3pm.

Dan Sai

☑ 042

For 362 days a year, Dan Sai (ด่านซ้าย) is an innocuous little town where life revolves around a small market and a dusty main street. For the remaining three days, however, it's the site of one of the country's liveliest and loudest festivals, Phi Ta Khon. At its normal peaceful self, the town won't appeal to everyone, but for people who appreciate slow travel and want a good look at local life, Dan Sai delivers in spades.

⊙ Sights

Phi Ta Khon Museum   MUSEUM
(พิพิธภัณฑ์ผีตาโขน; Th Kaew Asa; ⊙8.30am-4.30pm) FREE Wat Phon Chai, the temple behind the big white gate, plays a major role in the Phi Ta Khon festivities, so it's an appropriate home for this museum, also known as the Dansai Folk Museum. It has a collection of costumes worn during the celebrations and a display showing how the masks are made. There are few English captions, but the masks are great to see nonetheless. From the Dan Sai bus stop on the main highway, walk up the side road towards Dan Sai and the museum is on your right after 200m.

★☆ Festivals & Events

Phi Ta Khon Festival   CULTURAL
Combining a Buddhist festival (called Phra Wet) with Bun Bâng Fai (the rocket festival; p436), this festival produces a curious cross between the drunken revelry of Carnival and the spooky imagery of Halloween.

The origins of the festival are shrouded in ambiguity, but some aspects appear to be related to tribal Tai (possibly Tai Dam) spirit cults. The dates for the festival (usually June) are divined by Jao Phaw Kuan, a local spirit medium who channels the information from the town's guardian deity. On the first day of the festival Jao Phaw Kuan performs a sacrifice to invite Phra Upakud (an enlightened monk with supernatural powers who chose to transform himself into a block of white marble to live eternally under water) to come to town. Locals then don wild costumes and masks for two days of dancing that's fuelled by lôw kŏw (rice whisky) and is full of sexual innuendo, before launching the rockets and heading to the temple to listen to sermons on the third day. The Phi Ta Khon Museum is dedicated to this unique event.

🛏 Sleeping & Eating

Homestay   HOMESTAY $
(☑088 491 4319, 042 892339; dm/tw & d 200/550B; Ⓟ) Several villages near Dan Sai have been running a successful homestay program for many years and the families dote on fa·ràng (Westerner) guests. When not at work (most of the hosts who speak English are teachers), they'll take you out to share typical daily activities. Everything can be arranged at Kawinthip Hattakham.

Baan Chan Bhu   HOTEL $
(☑042 891072, 081 561 7530; Rte 2013; d 600B; ❄🛜) Rooms are plain but kept very clean. Nothing special, but this small two-storey place is above average for Dan Sai. If nobody is here when you arrive, check upstairs. It's on the main highway, 500m from the Dan Sai bus stop, towards Phitsanulok.

PhuNaCome Resort   RESORT $$$
(☑042 892005; www.phunacomeresort.com; Rte 2013; d incl breakfast 4200-6500B; Ⓟ❄@🛜⊛) 🌿 This luxury resort makes the most of its country location, and the kitchen uses the organic rice and veggies grown on the grounds. (The resort makes its own low-impact soaps and detergents, too.) Standard hotel rooms and some cool wood-and-thatch Isan-inspired cottages line a row of ponds. Both are plush and lovely with nice views.

The lobby has a library, a massage service and a restaurant with Thai and Western food (for guests only), and free bikes are available. The pool is saltwater, in keeping with the resort's chemical-free policy. Off the main highway, the resort is 2.5km back towards Loei, just off the main highway.

★ Baan Doen Cake & Coffee   CAFE $
(Rte 2013; coffee from 45B, smoothies 55B, burgers 69-99B; ⊙9am-5.30pm; 🛜) This funky streetside cafe does great coffee and spectacularly good fresh-fruit smoothies, as well as homemade cookies and cakes and a couple of types of gourmet burgers. It's 100m back up the highway towards Loei.

Dan Sai Night Market   MARKET $
(Th Kaew Asa; ⊙4-9.30pm) Across from Dan Sai's municipal market, just past Kawinthip Hattakham craft shop, you'll find a few food carts selling Thai and Isan food, including the local version of sôm·đam, which doesn't use any fish sauce.

🛍 Shopping

★ Kawinthip Hattakham   GIFTS & SOUVENIRS
(กวินทิพย์หัตถกรรม; ☑042 892339, 086 862 4812; 197/1 Th Kaew Asa; ⊙8am-7pm) This shop selling Phi Ta Khon masks and other festival-related artefacts makes for a fun browse and is great for unusal souvenirs.

ISAN CUISINE

Isan's culinary creations are a blend of Lao and Thai cooking styles that make use of local ingredients. The holy trinity of northeastern cuisine – *gài yâhng* (grilled marinated chicken), *sôm·đam* (spicy papaya salad) and *kôw nĕe·o* (sticky rice) – is integral to the culture. Also crucial are chillies – a fistful of potent peppers find their way into most dishes. Outsiders, including most other Thais, are rarely fans of *plah ráh*, an earthy fermented fish sauce, but Isan people consider it almost essential for good cooking. If your *sôm·đam* doesn't have this, it's not original real-deal *sôm·đam*.

Fish dominates Isan menus, with *plah dùk* (catfish), *plah chôrn* (striped snake-head) and *plah boo* (sand goby) among the most popular, although fish-farmed tilapia (*plah nin*) is now the most common. Insects traditionally comprised a large part of the typical family's diet and are still very common as snacks. Silk weavers eat the boiled silkworm larva as they work and virtually every night market has an insect vendor. Purple lights shining out in the countryside are for catching giant water bugs *(maang dah)*, which make a fragrant chilli paste *(prík maang dah)*.

Along with the *gài yâhng*, *sôm·đam*, *kôw nĕe·o* and insects already mentioned, trying the following dishes will provide a well-rounded introduction to Isan food.

lâhp Thailand's famous 'minced-meat salad', as it's usually called, is actually an Isan dish and, when eaten here, it's one of the spiciest foods in Thailand. Sometimes the meat (it can be made with almost anything as a base, including mushrooms) is raw, but this is not recommended due to bacteria and parasites.

nám đòk Essentially the same as *lâhp*, but with the meat sliced and grilled rather than diced and boiled.

đôm sâap The Isan version of *đôm yam* (spicy and sour soup). Usually full of innards, tendons, the soft parts of an animal left over after making *lâhp*.

súp nòr mái Sometimes translated as 'bamboo shoot salad', *súp* is really more of a dipping sauce. It's usually less spicy than most other Isan foods.

gaang òrm This prototypical Isan curry is heavy on herbs and only mildly spicy. Like all Isan curries, there's no coconut milk.

gaang hèt Another common northeastern dish, this 'mushroom curry' often has tamarind to make it a little sour. The mix is generally seasonal, depending on what mushrooms have just been picked in the forest.

sâi gròrk ee·săhn 'Isan sausage' uses fermented pork for a sour taste. Sticky rice, garlic and salt also go inside the skin.

plah pŏw Grilled fish coated in salt (to keep it moist) with its stomach stuffed with pandanus leaves and lemongrass.

It also has bike hire (100B per day), Loei-grown coffee and manages the homestay program. It's about 500m further down the same street as the Phi Ta Khon Museum, but on the left.

ℹ️ Information

Bangkok Bank (Rte 2013; ☺10.30am-7pm) Inside Tesco-Lotus, this is Dan Sai's only bank open evenings and weekends.

ℹ️ Getting There & Away

The number of buses to Dan Sai has decreased over the years, though it's still fairly easy to get a bus here from Loei. Two bus companies stop at the Dan Sai bus stop near the junction of Th Kaew Asa and Rte 2013. Of the seven daily buses between Loei (60B to 134B, 1½ to two hours) and Phitsanulok (64B to 90B, three hours), most going east toward Loei pass through during the night, though there are a couple that pass through in the afternoon.

Two minivans (80B, 1½ hours, 11am and 3pm) to Lomsak park across from the 7-Eleven near the municipal market, where you can easily catch a connection west to Phitsanulok or east to Khon Kaen; the scheduled times are highly subject to change. There are also four buses to Bangkok (342B, nine hours, 8am, 12.30pm, 8.30pm and 10pm) via Lomsak starting across the road from the PT gas station on Rte 2013 west of the junction.

Phu Kradueng National Park

Phu Kradueng National Park (อุทยานแห่ง ชาติภูกระดึง; ☑ 042 810833; 400B; ⊙ trail to summit 7am-2pm Oct-May) is one of the most popular national parks in Thailand, and spending the night atop its eponymous peak is something of a rite of passage for many students in the region. The park covers a high-altitude plateau cut through with trails and peppered with cliffs and waterfalls. Rising to 1316m, Thailand's second national park is always cool at its highest reaches (average year-round temperature is 20°C), where its flora is a mix of pine forest and savannah. Various forest animals, including elephants, Asian jackals, Asiatic black bears, sambar deer, serows, macaques and white-handed gibbons, inhabit the 348-sq-km park.

The park can get very crowded during school holidays (March to May and especially New Year) and it's closed from June to September.

Climbing Phu Kradueng

There's a small visitors centre at the base of the mountain, where you should register before you start climbing, and a few shops and restaurants, but almost everything else is up top. The main trail scaling Phu Kradueng is 5.5km in length and takes about three to four hours to climb. It's strenuous (you'll climb 1200m in height), but not too challenging (except when it's wet) since there are steps at most of the steep parts. The hike is quite scenic and there are rest stops with food vendors about every 1km. Once on top, it's another 3km to the main visitors centre and all the accommodation. You can hire porters to carry your gear balanced on bamboo poles for 30B per kg. For safety reasons, you are not allowed to start your hike up the mountain after 2pm.

Hiking around the Top

The trail that passes six waterfalls in a forested valley is the most beautiful destination, even after November, when the water has largely dried up. There are also many clifftop viewpoints, some ideal for sunrise and sunset, scattered around the mountain.

🛏 Sleeping & Eating

Restaurants at the top stay open late into the night, as long as there are customers.

There are also restaurants and shops at the bottom.

Phu Kradueng National Park Campsite CAMPGROUND $
(☑ 042 810833; per person with own tent 30B, tent hire 200B) Atop the mountain there's space for 5000 people to camp. Sleeping bags (30B), mats (20B) and pillows (10B) can also be rented. Showers are cold, but facilities are good.

Phu Kradueng National Park Bungalows BUNGALOW $
(☑ 042 810833; http://nps.dnp.go.th/reservation.php; bungalows 900-3600B) Phu Kradueng National Park has a variety of large bungalows sleeping six to 12 people.

❶ Information

Register at the **lower visitors centre** (☑ 042 810833; ⊙ 7am-5pm) before you start your climb, then at the **upper visitors centre** (⊙ 6am-7pm) to arrange your accommodation.

❶ Getting There & Away

Buses between Loei (53B, 1½ hours, every 30 minutes) and Khon Kaen (91B, 2½ hours) stop in Phu Kradueng town where *sŏrng·tăa·ou* (30B per person, charters 300B) or motorbike taxis (100B) take people to the base of the mountain, 10km away.

The **park entrance** (400B; ⊙ Oct-May) is about 500m before the lower visitors centre and this is where you pay your entrance fee.

NONG KHAI PROVINCE

Occupying a narrow sweep along the banks of the Mekong, Nong Khai Province (จังหวัด หนองคาย) is a beautiful region. Being on the travel route to/from Vientiane, Laos, just a short hop across the river via the Friendship Bridge, it's also one of northeastern Thailand's most popular destinations. The surreal Sala Kaew Ku sculpture park is a must-see on any jaunt through the region, while the towns and temples along the Mekong west of the capital encourage travellers to slow down.

Nong Khai

☑ 042 / POP 47,600

Sitting on the banks of the Mekong, just across from Vientiane in Laos, Nong Khai (หนองคาย) has been a hit with travellers for years. Its popularity is about more than just

Around Nong Khai

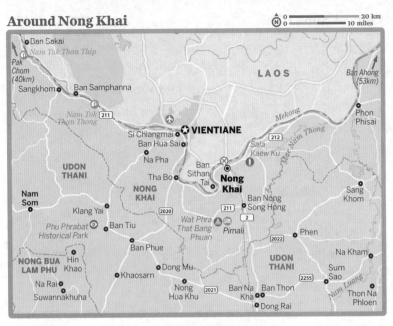

its proximity to Vientiane and its bounty of banana pancakes, though. Seduced by its dreamy pink sunsets and sluggish pace of life, many visitors who mean to stay one night end up bedding down for many more.

History

For most of its modern existence, this territory fell within the boundaries of the Vientiane (Wiang Chan) kingdom, which itself vacillated between independence and tribute to Lan Xang and Siam. In 1827 Rama III gave a Thai lord, Thao Suwothamma, the rights to establish Meuang Nong Khai at the present city site, which he chose because the surrounding swamps (nong) would aid in the city's defence.

When western Laos was partitioned off from Thailand by the French in 1893, the French demanded that Thailand have no soldiers within 25km of the river, and so the soldiers and administrators moved south and created Udon Thani, leaving Nong Khai's fortunes to fade.

One hundred and one years later, the opening of the US$30 million, 1174m-long Saphan Mittaphap Thai-Lao (Thai-Lao Friendship Bridge) marked a new era of development for Nong Khai as a regional trade and transport centre, though it remains a small town at heart.

◉ Sights

★ **Sala Kaew Ku** SCULPTURE
(ศาลาแก้วกู่, Wat Khaek; 40B; ☉7am-6pm) One of Thailand's most enigmatic attractions, Sala Kaew Ku can't fail to impress. Built over 20 years by Luang Pu Boun Leua Sourirat, a mystic who died in 1996, the park features a wonderful smorgasbord of bizarre cement statues of Buddha, Shiva, Vishnu and other deities. The main shrine building is packed with hundreds of smaller sculptures of various description and provenance, photos of Luang Pu at various stages throughout his life, and his corpse under a glass dome ringed by flashing lights.

As he told his own story, Luang Pu tumbled into a hole as a child and met an ascetic named Kaewkoo who introduced him to the manifold mysteries of the underworld and set him on course to become a Brahmanic-yogi-priest-shaman. Shaking up his own unique blend of Hindu and Buddhist philosophy, Luang Pu developed a large following on both sides of the Mekong in this region. In fact, his original project was on the Lao side of the river, where he had been living until the 1975 communist takeover in Laos.

Some of the sculptures are quite amusing. If you're travelling with kids, they'll

Central Nong Khai

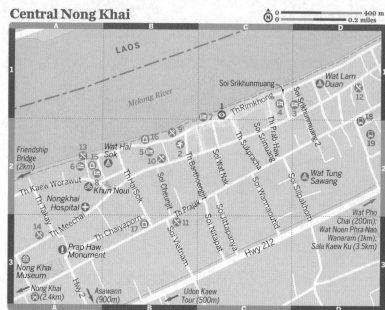

Central Nong Khai

enjoy the serene elephant wading through a pack of anthropomorphic dogs (which teaches people to not be bothered by gossip). The tallest sculpture, a Buddha seated on a coiled *naga* (serpent deity) with a spectacular seven-headed hood, is 25m high. Also not to be missed is the Wheel of Life, which you enter through a giant 'mouth'. An explanation is available on the back side of the handy map of the sculpture park provided by Mut Mee Garden Guesthouse.

All buses headed east of Nong Khai pass the road leading to Sala Kaew Ku (10B). It's about a five-minute walk from the highway. Chartered túk-túk will probably cost 250B return with a one-hour wait. You can reach it by bike in about 30 minutes; the Mut Mee map shows the scenic route.

Wat Pho Chai   BUDDHIST TEMPLE
(วัดโพธิ์ชัย; Th Phochai; ☉daylight hours, ubosot 6am-6.30pm) FREE Luang Po Phra Sai, a large Lan Xang–era Buddha image awash with

gold, bronze and precious stones, sits at the hub of Nong Khai's holiest temple. The head of the image is pure gold, the body is bronze and the *ùt·sà·nít* (flame-shaped head ornament) is set with rubies. Due to the great number of miracles attributed to it, this royal temple is a mandatory stop for most visiting Thais.

Phra That Klang Nam   BUDDHIST STUPA

(พระธาตุกลางน้ำ) FREE The 'Stupa in the Middle of the River' (sometimes called Phra That Nong Khai) is a ruined Lao-style *chedi* submerged in the middle of the river and can only be seen in the dry season when the water is low: the river rises and falls about 13m annually. It was gobbled up by the meandering Mekong in the middle of the 18th century and it toppled over in 1847.

Despite the destruction, it's still holy and when it's exposed, people attach coloured fabrics to it. Phra That La Nong (พระธาตุ หล้าหนอง; Th Rimkhong) FREE, a modern *chedi* inspired by the original, glows brightly at night from the adjacent shore.

Wat Noen Phra
Nao Wanaram   BUDDHIST TEMPLE

(วัดเนินพระเนาวนาราม; Hwy 212; ⊙daylight hours) FREE This forest *wát* on the south side of town is a respected *vipassana* (insight meditation) centre on pleasant, tree-shaded grounds. Most of the extremely ornate temple architecture, covered with stencil and mosaic, stands in contrast with the usual ascetic tone of forest monasteries. There are many Vietnamese graves here, and some of the statuary would fit right in at Sala Kaew Ku (p381).

Tha Sadet Market   MARKET

(ตลาดท่าเสด็จ; Th Rimkhong; ⊙8.30am-6pm) This is the most popular destination in town. Almost everyone loves a stroll through this covered market despite it being a giant tourist trap. It offers the usual mix of clothes, electronic equipment, food and assorted bric-a-brac, most of it imported from Laos and China, but there are also a few shops selling quirky and quality stuff.

🏃 Activities

Pantrix Yoga   HEALTH & WELLBEING

(www.pantrix.net; Soi Mutmee; per week 9900B) Pantrix offers week- and month-long yoga courses (they are not live-in) for serious students by experienced teachers. There's also a free daily yoga session from 2pm to 3pm.

It's in the lane leading to Mut Mee Garden Guesthouse, who can point you in the right direction.

Healthy Garden   MASSAGE

(☑042 423323; Th Banthoengjit; Thai/foot massage per hr 170/200B; ⊙8am-8pm) For the most effective treatment in Nong Khai, this place has foot massage and traditional Thai massage in air-conditioned rooms.

⭐ Festivals & Events

Songkran   CULTURAL

(⊙mid-Apr) During Songkran the priceless image of Luang Po Phra Sai from Wat Pho Chai is paraded around town.

Rocket Festival   CULTURAL

(⊙late May/early Jun) Nong Khai's rocket festival (p436) *(bun bâng fai)* begins on Visakha Bucha day.

Chinese Dragon Festival   CULTURAL

(⊙usually Nov) Nong Khai's version of the Chinese Dragon Festival is a particularly fun event held over 10 days with dragon dancing, acrobatics, Chinese opera and lots of firecrackers.

Anusahwaree Prap
Haw Festival   STREET CARNIVAL

(⊙5-15 Mar) The Anusahwaree Prap Haw Festival boasts the city's biggest street fair.

🛏 Sleeping

Catering to the steady flow of backpackers, Nong Khai's budget lodging selection is the best in Isan, and there are many good midrangers too.

⭐ Mut Mee Garden
Guesthouse   GUESTHOUSE $

(☑042 460717; www.mutmee.com; Soi Mutmee; d 220-1200B; ❋🛜) Nong Khai's budget classic has a riverfront garden so relaxing it's intoxicating, and most nights it's packed with travellers. Mut Mee caters to many budgets, with a huge variety of rooms (the cheapest with shared bathroom, the most expensive with an awesome balcony) clustered around the thatched-roof garden lounge, where owner Julian freely shares his wealth of knowledge about the area.

E-San Guesthouse   GUESTHOUSE $

(☑086 242 1860; 538 Soi Srikhunmuang; d with fan & shared bathroom 300B, with air-con 500B; 🅿❋🛜) Just off the river in a small, beautifully restored wooden house ringed by a

OFF THE BEATEN TRACK

COUNTRYSIDE RETREAT

Pimali (📞042 089725; www.pimali.org; d incl breakfast 2200B; 🅿 ❄ 🛜) is a non-profit organisation providing training for poor local youths (mostly orphans) in the hospitality industry. Its students manage four plush, fully stocked bungalows overlooking rice paddies, and a white-linen restaurant serving Thai, Isan and European food. It's deep in the countryside, 20km from Nong Khai; a one-way transfer costs 300B.

long veranda, this is an atmospheric place for backpackers to stay. The air-con rooms in a new building are fine, though they lack the character of the original house. Bikes are free. There are two other wooden guesthouses on the same street.

Khiangkhong Guesthouse HOTEL $
(📞042 422870; Th Rimkhong; d with fan/air-con 400/500B; 🅿 ❄ 🛜) Catch a refreshing breeze and snag some river views from the 3rd-floor terrace (and some of the rooms) at this family-run concrete tower that falls between guesthouse and hotel. Bicycles are free.

Siri Guesthouse HOTEL $
(📞042 420299; Soi Hai Sok; d/tw 500/600B; 🅿 ❄ 🛜) Reliable best sums up this hotel, which for many serves as a backup when its famous neighbour Mut Mee Garden Guesthouse (p383) is full. The rooms lack character, but have verandas and there's a small garden lounge.

Ban Sai Thong GUESTHOUSE $$
(📞081 975 6451; Soi Srikhunmuang 2, Th Rimkhong; d incl breakfast 600B; 🅿 ❄ 🛜) Though it's a modern building, the all-wood construction and large tiled roof give this nine-room hotel a bit of a historic atmosphere. The rooms are spacious and have verandas with sitting areas in front. Bikes are free.

Na Rim Khong River View BOUTIQUE HOTEL $$$
(📞042 412077; www.narimkhongriverview.com; Th Rimkhong; d incl breakfast 2500B; ❄ 🛜) This new boutique hotel may be overpriced, but it does have super-stylish rooms with bags of space and a natty finish. Every room has a river view, a private balcony and its own different piece of artwork on the wall above the bed.

🍴 Eating

Mae Ut VIETNAMESE $
(637 Th Meechai; mains 50-100B; ⊘ 9.30am-4pm) This little place, serving just four items, including fried spring rolls, *khâo gee·ab þahk mŏr* (fresh noodles with pork), and a Vietnamese take on a pancake-pizza, is essentially grandma's kitchen, and it's fascinating to watch the food being made to order on large banana leaves. No English sign, and English is limited, but the welcome is friendly.

Khao Soi THAI $
(949 Th Meechai; mains 40-50B; ⊘ 8am-3pm) If you're missing the flavours of northern Thailand, this descriptively named hole-in-the-wall will satisfy your cravings. For the uninitiated, *khao soi* (curry noodle soup) is northern Thailand's most famous dish. Friendly owner.

Darika Bakery THAI $
(Sweet Cake & Coffee; Th Meechai; mains 40-150B; ⊘ 5.30am-3pm; 🍴) It's hard to categorise this place, run by a sweet old lady who makes standard Thai dishes and also many international favourites such as baked cakes and banana pancakes. Enjoy the homely atmosphere for breakfast or lunch, or just a coffee (instant, brewed or traditional Thai).

Dee Dee Pohchanah THAI $
(1155/9 Th Prajak; mains 50-150B; ⊘ 11am-1am; 🛜) How good is Dee Dee? Just look at the dinner-time crowds. But don't be put off by them: despite having a full house every night, this open-air place is a well-oiled machine and you won't be waiting long.

Saap Lah THAI $
(Th Meechai; mains 25-150B; ⊘ 8.30am-7.30pm) For excellent *gài yâhng* (grilled chicken), *sôm·đam* (spicy green papaya salad) and other Isan foods, follow your nose to this no-frills, open-fronted restaurant.

Nagarina THAI $$
(📞081 975 0516; Th Rimkhong; mains 50-480B; ⊘ 10am-9pm) Docked down below Mut Mee Garden Guesthouse (p383), this floating restaurant specialises in Thai and Isan fish dishes, and though the prices are a bit high, the quality is good. There's a one-hour sunset cruise most nights (80B; at least 10 guests needed before the cruise will go ahead) around 5pm or 5.30pm; order food at least 30 minutes before departure.

Daeng Namnuang
VIETNAMESE $$

(Th Rimkhong; mains 70-270B; ⊘6am-8.30pm; P🛜) This massive river restaurant has grown into a Nong Khai institution, and hordes of out-of-towners head home with car boots and carry-on bags stuffed with their *năam neu·ang* (DIY pork spring rolls).

🍷 Drinking & Nightlife

There are several small bars along the river between Mut Mee Garden Guesthouse and Tha Sadet Market that cater to travellers and expats. For something truly Thai, follow the Mekong-hugging Th Rimkhong east past Tha Sadet Market and you'll pass a bevy of restaurants and bars, some earthy, some fashionable, churning out dinner and drinks.

🛍 Shopping

Nong Khai Walking Street Market
MARKET

(⊘4-10pm Sat) This weekly street festival featuring music, handmade items and food takes over the promenade every Saturday night. It's smaller, but far more pleasant than the similar Walking Street markets in Chiang Mai.

Village Weaver Handicrafts
ARTS & CRAFTS

(☑042 422651; 1020 Th Prajak; ⊘8am-7pm) 🖋 This place sells high-quality, handwoven fabrics and clothing (ready-made or made to order) that help fund development projects around Nong Khai. The *mát·mèe* cotton is particularly good here.

Hornbill Books
BOOKS

(Soi Mutmee; ⊘10am-7pm Mon-Sat) Buys, sells and trades books in English, French and other languages.

ℹ Information

There are banks with extended opening hours at **Asawann** (Hwy 2; ⊘10am-9pm) shopping centre.

Immigration (☑042 990935; Hwy 2; ⊘8.30am-noon & 1-4.30pm Mon-Fri) One kilometre south of the Friendship Bridge. Offers Thai visa extensions.

Nongkhai Hospital (☑042 413456; Th Meechai; ⊘24hr) Has a 24-hour casualty department.

ℹ Getting There & Away

AIR

The nearest airport is 55km south in Udon Thani. **Udon Kaew Tour** (☑042 411530; Th Pranang Cholpratan, Hwy 212; ⊘8.30am-5.30pm) travel agency runs minivans (200B per person) to/from the airport. Coming into town it will drop you at your hotel or the bridge; going back you need to get yourself to its office. It's best to buy tickets in advance.

BUS

Nong Khai bus terminal (☑042 421246) is located just off Th Prajak, about 1.5km from the main pack of riverside guesthouses. Although there's only one direct bus to Nakhon Phanom, you can also get there in stages via Bueng Kan or Udon Thani.

There are also vans departing from the border/bridge (they park next to the 7-Eleven) to Udon Thani (50B, hourly, 7am to 7pm); some go to the old bus station and some go to Central Shopping Mall.

Nakhonchai Air (☑042 420285) has the best-quality bus service between Nong Khai and Bangkok (536-714B, nine hours, 10am, 7.45pm and 8.30pm).

TO	FARE (B)	TIME (HR)	FREQUENCY
Bangkok	329-714	10-11	frequent in late afternoon & early evening, hourly during the day
Bangkok (Suvarnabhumi International Airport)	464	10	8pm
Bueng Kan (van)	150	2½	every 45min 6am-5.50pm
Chiang Mai	750-820	12	7pm
Kanchanaburi	495	12	7pm
Khon Kaen	120-155	3½-4	hourly 7am-6pm
Loei	140	7-8	7.30am
Nakhon Phanom	200	7-8	11am
Nakhon Ratchasima	257-409	6	hourly 6am-8.45pm
Sangkhom	60	2½	11am, 3pm
Udon Thani (van)	50	1	frequent 5.30am -7pm

ⓘ GETTING TO LAOS: NONG KHAI TO VIENTIANE

Getting to the border If you already have your Lao visa, the easiest way to Vientiane is the direct bus from Nong Khai's bus terminal (55B, 1½ hours, six daily 7.30am to 6pm). There's also a bus to Vang Vieng (270B, six hours, 9.40am). There's a 5B surcharge for tickets to Laos on weekends, holidays and the 7.30am and 6pm weekday services.

If you plan to get your visa at the border (6am to 10pm), take a túk-túk there – expect to pay 100B from the bus station or 60B from the town centre. Unless you're travelling in a large group, there's no good reason to use a visa service agency, so don't let a driver take you to one.

You can also go to Laos by train (there are immigration booths at both stations), though it doesn't go through to Vientiane, so this is not recommended. The 15-minute ride (20B to 30B, 7.30am and 2.45pm) drops you in Thanaleng (aka Dongphasay) station just over the bridge, leaving you at the mercy of túk-túk drivers who charge extortionate prices.

At the border After getting stamped out of Thailand, you can take the buses (15B to 20B) that carry passengers across the bridge to the hassle-free, but sometimes busy, Lao immigration checkpoint, where 30-day visas are available.

Moving on It's about 20km to Vientiane. Plenty of buses, túk-túk and taxis will be waiting for you, and it's easy to find fellow travellers to share the costs.

TRAIN

For Bangkok, one daytime express train (2nd-/3rd-class seat 498/253B, 9½ hours, 7.45am) and three evening express trains (10 hours, 11 hours and 11½ hours respectively, 6.30pm, 6.50pm and 7.40pm) leave from **Nong Khai train station** (☏ 042 411637, nationwide 1690), which is 2km west of the city centre. Only the latest of the evening trains has sleeper accommodation (1st-/2nd-class sleeper from 1357/898B).

The daytime train and the two later evening trains go via Udon Thani (30 minutes), Khon Kaen (two hours) and Ayuthaya (eight hours). The earlier evening train goes via Udon Thani, Khon Kaen, Nakhon Ratchasima (four hours), Pak Chong (six hours) and Ayuthaya.

ⓘ Getting Around

Nong Khai is a great place for cycling due to the limited traffic and the nearby countryside. Many guesthouses let you use their bikes for free. If you need to hire one, **Khun Noui** (☏ 081 975 4863; Th Kaew Worawut; ◷ 8am-4pm), who sets up on the roadside across from the entrance to Mut Mee (p383), has reliable bikes (50B per day) and motorcycles (200B); if he's not there, any of the túk-túk drivers parked nearby will give him a call and he'll be right over.

You can find metered taxis at the bus station and the bridge. Generally, people agree on a price rather than use the meter. A túk-túk between the Mut Mee area and the bus station or the bridge will cost about 60B and 100B respectively for two people.

Sangkhom

☐ 042 / POP 3500

The little town of Sangkhom (สังคม), facing the Lao island of Don Klang Khong, makes a great rest stop for those following the Mekong between Nong Khai and Loei. There are no notable attractions in town, other than the river views, but there are some beautiful spots in the surrounding area.

◉ Sights

Wat Pha Tak Sua   BUDDHIST TEMPLE
(วัดผาตากเสื้อ; off Rte 211; ◷ 6am-6pm) **FREE**
The forest wát peering down on the town lies just 2km away as the crow flies, but it's 19km to drive. Once a very serious meditation temple, it's now highly commercialised, with crowds coming up for the amazing Mekong views, which can be seen from a glass-bottomed 'sky walk'. In the cold season you might see the valley filled with fog early in the morning. An overgrown footpath once used by the monks every morning to collect alms (they're now driven to town) begins east of town just before the Km 81 pillar. Follow Soi 5 past the last house, then veer right by the mango and papaya trees.

Nam Tok Than Thip   WATERFALL
(น้ำตกธารทิพย์; ◷ daylight hours) **FREE** Three-tiered Nam Tok Than Thip waterfall, 13km west of Sangkhom (2km off Rte 211), is the largest waterfall in the area. The lower level drops 30m and the second level, easily

reached via stairs, falls 100m. The 70m top drop is barely visible through the lush forest.

🛏 Sleeping

Bouy Guesthouse GUESTHOUSE **$**
(📞091 050 7426, 042 441065; toy_bgh@hotmail.com; Rte 211; d with fan/air-con 250/500B; 🅿✳@🛜) As the ever-smiling owners will tell you, Sangkhom's veteran lodge has just a few 'simple huts', but they're popular for good reason. The thatch-built fan-cooled ones come with hammocks and wooden decks, and the riverside location just west of town is wonderfully relaxing. The air-con bungalows in front lack charm and a view, but are priced fairly. Bike/motorbike hire costs 50/200B per day.

Sangkhom River View HOTEL **$$**
(📞042 441088; Rte 211; d 600-1500B; 🅿✳🛜) This attractive set-up, featuring wooden walkways and decorative stonework, will satisfy those who demand a certain level of comfort. Many rooms have river views, and the restaurant is good. It's 1.5km east of the town centre.

Tantawan THAI **$**
(Sunflower Restaurant; Rte 211; mains 40-250B; ⏰8am-9pm; 🛜) The first choice for many visitors to Sangkhom because of the good food and big views. It offers all the expected Thai and Isan dishes (the Mekong River fish *lâhp* is recommended) plus a page of pastas.

ℹ Getting There & Away

There are two rickety fan-cooled buses a day from Nong Khai (60B, 2½ hours, 11am and 3pm). A third bus (7.30am) doesn't always run. Returning to Nong Khai, buses leave at 6.30am and 11.30am. There's no bus stop in town; wave buses down when they pass.

UDON THANI PROVINCE

The province of Udon Thani (จังหวัดอุดรธานี) is dominated by its flashy, congested and rather nondescript capital. It's the World Heritage–listed Ban Chiang, amazing Red Lotus Sea and mysterious Phu Phrabat that make it a fascinating destination.

Udon Thani

📞042 / POP 153,000
Udon Thani (อุดรธานี) is a big, brash city with one of the largest expat populations in Thailand. The city boomed on the back of

the Vietnam War as the site of a large US airbase, and it subsequently became the region's primary transport hub and commercial centre. The town itself doesn't have any must-see attractions, but there are some tremendously interesting spots around it.

👁 Sights

Nong Prajak Park PARK
(สวนสาธารณะหนองประจักษ์) Udon's most popular park starts to rev up as the afternoon winds down. It's home to colourful attractions such as a giant Ban Chiang–style pot and a huge floating rubber duck that has become an Udon icon. A lot of action takes place along Th Thesa on the sunset-watching side of the lake where there are many restaurants, paint-your-own-pottery shops, and streetside **masseurs** (Th Thesa; per hr 180B; ⏰8am-10pm). There's a bike-hire (p392) shop on the northeast shore.

Udon Thani Thai-Chinese Cultural Centre CULTURAL CENTRE
(ศูนย์วัฒนธรรมไทย-จีน; Th Nittayo; ⏰9am-7pm) **FREE** This cultural centre features a gorgeous garden, a tea shop and the **Moral Museum**, which has excellent displays about the history of the Chinese community in Udon Thani, Chinese culture and Confucius. A small Chinese orchestra plays on Mondays and Tuesdays from 4pm to 7pm.

Udon Thani Museum MUSEUM
(พิพิธภัณฑ์เมืองอุดรธานี; Th Phosri; ⏰8.30am-4.30pm Tue-Sun) **FREE** Filling a 1920s colonial-style building that used to be a girls' school, this museum has a fairly interesting catch-all collection ranging from geology to handicrafts. Some captions are in English, but the multi-media installations are in Thai only.

Sanjao Pu-Ya TEMPLE
(ศาลเจ้าปู่ย่า; Th Nittayo; ⏰daylight hours) **FREE** This large Chinese temple on the southern shore of Nong Bua lake attests to the wealth of the local Thai-Chinese community. At its heart, the Pu-Ya Shrine houses small images of the Chinese gods Pu (Grandpa) and Ya (Grandma).

🎊 Festivals & Events

Thung Si Meuang Fair CULTURAL
(⏰Dec) For the first 15 days of December, Udon celebrates the Thung Si Meuang Fair, with Isan cultural performances and all the usual shopping and eating. The Pu and Ya

Udon Thani

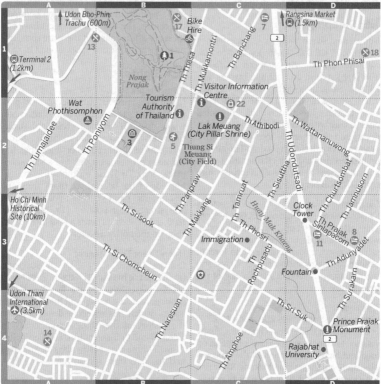

Udon Thani

statues from Sanjao Pu-Ya (p387) spend the first 10 days in a temporary temple in Thung Si Meuang park. The transfers on 1 and 10

December are grand processions accompanied by a 99m-long dragon.

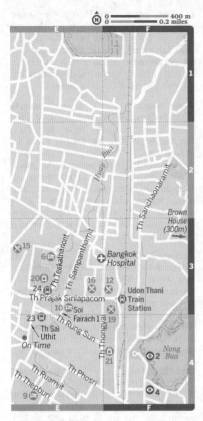

Pakdee House HOTEL **$**

(📞 080 461 9600; Th Thepburi; d 450B; 🅿 ❄ 🛜)
A clean, well-run place that's the clear pick
of the pack of several other similarly priced
hotels in this area. And though it's not exactly central, one of its best features is the
neighbourhood full of university students
and local restaurants.

Oldie & Sleepy Hostel HOSTEL **$**

(📞 088 697 9406; oldie.sleepy.hostel@gmail.com;
Th Adunyadet; dm incl breakfast with fan/air-con
220/250B; ❄ 🛜) The rooms are simple, as
you'd expect at this price, but the whole
package combines to make a fantastic place
to stay. Pear and Thong's hospitality, and chill
nights hanging out in the eclectic, jazz-in-
fused lounge lead some guests to extend
their stays. There's a kitchen and free-flow-
ing travel advice. Free bikes too.

★ Jamjuree Home GUESTHOUSE **$$**

(📞 042 241727, 087 951 7940; 10/9 Th Banchang; d
incl breakfast 950-1290B; 🅿 ❄ @ 🛜) The 'home'
part of the name is literally true as your
hosts live on the ground floor of this fantas-
tic four-room guesthouse. Rooms are mod-
ern and cosy and solid contenders for the
cleanest in all of Isan. The two largest have
kitchenettes. Though it's not the most tour-
ist-friendly location, there are many good
restaurants around and it's only a 10-minute
walk to Nong Prajak lake (p387). Free bikes
are available.

Brown House HOTEL **$$**

(📞 042 322888; www.brownhousehotel.com;
234/5 Moo 1, Rim Nhong Bua 6; incl breakfast d &
tw 1300-1700B; tr 1600B; 🅿 ❄ @ 🛜 ❄) Technically in the city, but with an aura of deep
countryside, this splendid hotel is centred
on an infinity pool looking out over a lotus-filled lake. Though isolated, it sends its
own túk-túk into town a few times a day for
its guests. Rooms are large and comfy with
subtle decoration.

Centara HOTEL **$$$**

(📞 042 343555; www.centarahotelsresorts.com;
Th Teekathanont, off Th Prajak Sinlapacom; d & tw
from 1880, incl breakfast from 2400B; 🅿 ❄ @
🛜 ❄) This large, full-service hotel makes a
good impression with an attractive lobby
and attentive staff. The quality continues
in the rooms, which are stationed around a
cavernous inner atrium that is eerily quiet
and strangely attractive, almost like a set
from a sci-fi movie.

🛏 Sleeping

★ Udon Backpackers HOSTEL **$**

(📞 086 858 4969; Soi Fairach 1; dm 320B, d 350B;
❄ 🛜) This super-central, urban-industrial
backpackers hostel, with concrete floors
and exposed-brick interior, has a great at-
mosphere, helpful owners and bunks with
privacy curtains, reading lamps and power
points. There are a few fan-cooled double
rooms, but it's mostly dorms. Bikes are free
for guests, and the cafe is a cool hangout.

Whereder Poshtel HOSTEL **$**

(📞 088 214 2555; www.whereder.com; 212-214 Th
Prajak Sinlapacom; dm/d 450/1200B; ❄ 🛜) A
warehouse-style, metal-cage lift takes guests
up from the chilled-out, split-level, ground-
floor cafe to the super-smart dorms (privacy
curtains, reading lamps, charging sockets)
and the equally slick but slightly overpriced
private doubles before settling at the top-floor
communal Netflix lounge. It's pricy for a hos-
tel, but hey, it's posh; a hostel for grown-ups.

✖ Eating

Udonites take their night markets very seriously. The three adjoining markets in front of the train station, Centre Point, Preecha and UD Bazaar, offer an impressive spread of food. Also, the sheer number of expats means there's a lot of Western food available in town.

★ **UD Bazaar**   MARKET **$**
(Th Prajak Sinlapacom; ⊘ 11am-11pm) The largest of Udon Thani's many night markets is also the one offering the most varied cuisine. There's a stage for live music as well. A few shops serve lunch, but most get going about 4pm.

Centre Point Night Market   MARKET **$**
(⊘ 4-10pm) About half the food for sale in this night market is Isan fare, including grilled fish and roasted insects.

Preecha Night Market   MARKET **$**
(⊘ 4-10pm) The stalls at this night market are mostly cook-to-order shops with low prices. One woman serves the local speciality *kôw pee·ak,* a soup of thick rice noodles served with pork that is normally only sold during the daytime. It's similar to *gŏo·ay jáp yoo·an,* but with a different noodle.

★ **Samuay & Sons**   THAI **$$**
(Th Phon Phisai; mains 79-280B; ⊘ 11am-2.30pm & 5-9.30pm Tue-Sun; 🛜) This small chef-driven, open-kitchen place is Isan's version of a trendy Soho bistro. It does some Thai and Isan standards like panang curry and om curry with algae, but sets itself apart with fusion dishes and modern twists on old recipes such as tapioca shrimp balls and coconut milk duck confit with mango jam.

Phetkasem   THAI **$$**
(Th Adunyadet; mains 78-358B; ⊘ 6pm-midnight; ℗🛜) A garden restaurant where groups of friends come to eat, drink and eat some more. The menu covers the usual Thai and Isan options plus some less common ones like *plah nêung búay* (steamed fish in Chinese plum sauce) and *lâhp mah·mâh,* a fun version of this classic Isan dish using instant noodles instead of the usual meat.

Grey Cabin   INTERNATIONAL **$$**
(Th Sinchaithani; mains 80-285B; ⊘ 10am-9.30pm; ℗🛜) There are many restaurants serving *fa·ràng* food in the Central Plaza/Soi Farang area, but we far prefer this small mother-and-daughter operation 2km south of Nong Prajak lake. The varied options, all fresh and delicious, include maple mustard-glazed salmon, chicken pesto pasta, apple and brie salad, an artery-clogging three-cheese grilled cheese, seafood ramen and Thai mushroom salad.

Rabiang Phatchanee   THAI **$$**
(Th Suphakit Janya; mains 60-300B; ⊘ 10am-11pm; ✳🛜) On the lake's east shore, this sprawling restaurant offers all the usual Thai dishes, but also many you've probably never tried, such as fish-stomach salad, and fried duck with crab in gravy. Eat outdoors on the deck or in air-conditioned dining rooms. Note that some menu prices are 'per 100g' (ขีดละ).

Good Everything   INTERNATIONAL **$$$**
(Th Poniyom; mains 190-690B; ⊘ 10am-10pm; ℗🛜🖉) This white cottage and surrounding garden feels transported from the English countryside. It features fresh and healthy cuisine, such as salmon with spinach, roasted pumpkin soup, and *fa·ràng*-style salads, plus quality coffees and teas. It's one of Udon's most expensive restaurants, but the many regulars consider it money well spent.

🍷 Drinking & Nightlife

Udon Thani's busiest nightlife area fronts the train station. Many of the bars here are sleazy, but far from all. Nearby Phetkasem is a chill alternative. Also, the three night markets offer a range of diversions besides dining. You can shop for clothes, sing karaoke, play snooker, get a tattoo, have your fortune told and listen to live bands.

🛍 Shopping

Central Plaza   SHOPPING CENTRE
(Th Prajak Sinlapacom; ⊘ 10.30am-9pm Mon-Fri, from 10am Sat & Sun) Udon's biggest shopping centre, with a large basement food court and a branch of the English-language bookstore **Asia Books.**

ℹ **PATTAYA OF THE NORTHEAST**

Udon has the largest and most in-your-face sex-tourism scene in Isan, and the Th Sampanthamit area (sometimes called 'Soi Falang', meaning 'foreigners' street') is rather sleazy at night – even in the day you'll have to endure people relentlessly touting 'massages'. That said, there are several foreigner-focused businesses here that are not a part of this scene.

RED LOTUS SEA

You'll see pictures of the Red Lotus Sea (ทะเลบัวแดง, Nong Han; Kumphawapi District – really, it's a pink water-lily lake – all over Udon as it's now one of Isan's top attractions, but few Westerners make it here. You need to hire a boat (300B to 500B for up to 10 people) to go out into the middle of the lake to see the bloom, and the earlier the better as the flowers start to close up around 10.30am and are completely shut by noon.

The season depends on Mother Nature, but it generally starts in late October and lasts to the end of February; January is often, but not always, the peak time.

The main access point is Nong Han, the lake's actual name, is 40km southeast of Udon city in Ban Dieam; there are so many road signs for it that it's impossible for drivers not to find it. There's no public transport, but half-day trips (499B per person) depart from McDonald's at UD Town (p391) at 6.30am. Confirm details at your hotel or call Udon Thani's Tourism Authority of Thailand office for information as details change year to year.

UD Town SHOPPING CENTRE

(Th Thongyai; ⊙8am-11pm) UD Town is an open-air shopping precinct that also stages events from time to time.

Udon City Walking Street MARKET

(Th Athibodi & Th Panpraw; ⊙5-10pm Fri & Sat) With just a handful of the hundreds of vendors selling handmade items, Udon's Walking Street doesn't rise to the level of the markets in Chiang Mai and Khon Kaen that inspired it, but it's fun and has good food.

ⓘ Information

The free *Udon Thani Map* (www.udonmap.com) and its companion magazine, the *Udon Thani Guide,* are mostly geared towards expats, but are helpful for travellers, too. They're available free at hotels, the airport and *fa-ràng*-focused businesses.

Immigration (📞042 249982; Th Phosri; ⊙8.30am-noon & 1-4.30pm Mon-Fri) Does visa extensions.

Tourism Authority of Thailand (TAT; 📞042 240616; tatudon@tat.or.th; Th Thesa; ⊙8.30am-4.30pm) Not much English spoken.

Visitor Information Centre (📞085 010 3837; ⊙8am-5pm Sun-Thu, to 6pm Fri & Sat; 📶) Has information for all of Udon Thani Province.

Bangkok Hospital (📞042 343111; Th Thongyai; ⊙24hr) The best medical facility in Udon Thani.

Tourist Police (📞042 211291; Th Naresuan)

ⓘ Getting There & Away

AIR

Thai Smile (📞042 246697, nationwide 1181; www.thaismileair.com; Udon Thani Airport; ⊙7.30am-7pm) connects Udon Thani to Bangkok through Suvarnabhumi International

Airport, while **Air Asia** (📞nationwide 02 515 9999; www.airasia.com; Udon Thani Airport; ⊙7am-9pm), **Thai Lion Air** (📞025 299999; www.lionairthai.com; Udon Thani Airport; ⊙6am-8pm) and **Nok Air** (📞nationwide 02 900 9955; www.nokair.com; Udon Thani Airport; ⊙6.15am-7.30pm) use Don Mueang Airport. Each flies four or five times daily and prices start around 900B one way. There are also daily direct flights to Chiang Mai (Nok Air), Hat Yai (Thai Lion Air), Phuket (Air Asia) and Pattaya (Air Asia). Buy tickets online or at **On Time** (📞042 247792; ontimethailand@gmail. com; Th Sai Uthit; ⊙8am-5pm Mon-Sat, 9am-3pm Sun), one of several travel agencies near Bus Terminal 1.

Some hotels pick up guests at the airport for free; otherwise shuttle vans to the city centre cost 80B per person; tickets are sold at the 'Limousine Service' counter.

Despite the name, there are no international flights at **Udon Thani International Airport** (📞042 244426).

BUS

Most buses and minivans use Udon's slightly chaotic **Bus Terminal 1** (📞042 221916; Th Sai Uthit) in the heart of town. **Nakhonchai Air** (📞1624; Th Sai Uthit) has the best VIP service to Bangkok. For Nong Khai, note that some minivans departing here go to the bus station, while others go to the border bridge. Also, most Nong Khai vehicles stop to pick up passengers at **Rangsina Market** north of downtown on their way out of Udon. Rangsina Market is also where you catch transport for Phu Phrabat Historical Park. For the buses to Laos, you must already have a Lao visa to buy a ticket, and there's a 5B surcharge for the 6pm weekday departure and for all buses on weekends and holidays.

Almost next door to Bus Terminal 1 is the **Central Plaza Van Station** (Th Prajak Sinlapacom), with minivans to Nong Khai (55B, one hour, every 30 minutes 6am to 8pm), Bueng Kan (200B, 3½ hours, every 30 minutes 5am to 7pm) and Roi Et (209B, four hours, every 30 minutes 5am to 5.40pm) via Khon Kaen (90B, two hours), and buses to Chiang Mai (594B, 12 hours, 10.45pm, 5.45pm, 6.45pm, 8.45pm), Nakhon Phanom (221B, three hours, 5.15am, 5.30am, 10pm) and Roi Et (139B to 150B, 4½ hours, every 30 minutes 6am to 5pm) via Khon Kaen (76B to 80B, 2½ hours).

Bus Terminal 2 (☑ 042 214914) on the western ring road has few buses, mostly for western cities such as Loei (90B to 115B, 2½ to three hours, every 30 minutes 4.50am to 5.50pm), Phitsanulok (311B to 493B, seven hours, every two hours 7.30am to 8.50pm) and Chiang Mai (760B, 12 hours, 7.15am, 2.30pm, 7.15pm, 8.30pm).

TRAIN
There are six daily trains between Bangkok (seat 95B to 457B, 1st-class sleeper upper/lower 1117/1317B, 9½ to 11 hours) and **Udon Thani train station** (☑ 042 222061), three departing in the early evening (7.05pm, 7.38pm and 8.20pm) and three during the day (5.55am, 8.16am and 1.40pm). Five trains head north to Nong Khai (11B to 48B, one hour, 3.13am, 5.44am, 7.07am, 11.21am and 4.58pm).

❶ Getting Around

Sŏrng·tǎa·ou (10B) run regular routes across town. Route 6 (white) is handy since it runs up and down Th Udondutsadi (with a convenient detour to the Th Prajak-Surakarn junction), past Rangsina Market and out to Bus Terminal 2. There are also two city buses (20B); City Bus 21 follows Th Udondutsadi from the university all the way north to Rangsina Market; City Bus 20 tracks Th Phosri, connecting the two bus ter-minals and the airport in the process. The *Udon Thani Map* (www.udonmap.com) shows all bus and *sŏrng·tǎa·ou* routes.

You can rarely flag a **taxi** (☑ 042 244554, 042 343239) down on the street, but they park at Bus Terminal 1, Central Plaza and the airport. Drivers don't use meters. Túk-túk (called 'skylab' here) are seemingly everywhere. The cost from Central Plaza to Nong Prajak Park is usually 60B.

Lek Car Rental (☑ 086 059 3028; www.lekcarrentaludonthani.com) is a reputable local company, and there are many smaller ones around Central Plaza. **Avis** (☑ 089 969 8678; www.avisthailand.com; Udon Thani International Airport; ⊙7am-9pm), **Thai Rent a Car** (☑ 082 668 5057; www.thairentacar.com; Udon Thani International Airport; ⊙ 6.30am-9pm) and the other big-name car-hire companies have branches at the airport.

Bike hire (1-/2-/3-seater per hr 20/40/50B; ⊙10am-8pm Mon-Fri, from 8am Sat & Sun) is available on the northeast shore of the lake in Nong Prajak Park.

Ban Na Kha
☑ 042 / POP 6360

Ban Na Kha (บ้านนาข่า), 16km north of Udon city, is an excellent fabric-shopping destination. The village also has two temples worth a peek.

◎ Sights

Wat Na Kha Taewee   BUDDHIST TEMPLE
(วัดนาคาเทวี; ⊙daylight hours) **FREE** Wat Na Kha Taewwat pee was established by a wandering monk who found a hole from which bellowed the sound and smoke of a *naga*. He plugged the hole with a rock and

BUSES & MINIVANS FROM BUS TERMINAL 1

DESTINATION	FARE (B)	DURATION (HR)	FREQUENCY
Bangkok	423-658	8-10	every 30min
Bueng Kan	208	4	hourly 4.10am-4.10pm
Khon Kaen	76-120	2½	frequent 5am-4.50pm
Khon Kaen (minivan)	80	2	frequent 6am-8pm
Nakhon Phanom	147-200	4	every 45min 4.30am-4.20pm
Nong Khai (minivan)	50	1	every 30min 6am-8pm
Pattaya	441-636	11	hourly 4.30am-9pm
Suvarnabhumi Airport	392	8	9pm
Vang Vieng (Laos)	320	7	8.30am
Vientiane (Laos)	80	2	8 departures 8am-6pm

decided to settle here. The hole, sandwiched between the *ubosot* and the stupa, is now an important local shrine. Pottery and human skeletons unearthed during various construction projects at the temple are on display under the giant Buddha.

Wat Tung Toomkam　　　BUDDHIST TEMPLE
(วัดทุ่งตูมคำ; ☉ daylight hours) FREE This small shady temple 700m southeast of the village features some curious Buddhist art, including many Buddhas covered with coins.

🛍 Shopping

Covered Market　　　MARKET
(☉ 7am-6pm) Dozens of shops sell a great variety of silk and cotton, both raw fabric and finished clothes. Much of it is hand-woven in this district, but other styles from elsewhere in Thailand and Laos are available. Many of the smaller shops only open on weekends and holidays.

Mae Bah Pah Fai　　　ARTS & CRAFTS
(☎ 042 206104; ☉ 8am-5.30pm) Across from Wat Na Kha Taewee temple entrance, this shop has as good a fabric selection as any in the village: the *mát·mèe* in particular is exquisite. A piece of century-old *kít* cloth hangs on display in the back.

ⓘ Getting There & Away

Sŏrng·tăa·ou 3 (15B, 30 minutes) runs along Th Udondutsadi in Udon Thani city and up to Ban Na Kha, as does the much less frequent White Bus. Minivans headed between Udon Thani and Nong Khai will also drop you here, but you have to pay the full 50B fare.

Ban Chiang

☎ 042 / POP 5050

Now one of Southeast Asia's most important archaeological finds, Ban Chiang (บ้านเชียง) was brought to the world's attention accidentally in 1966 when a sociology student from Harvard tripped while walking through the area and found the rim of a buried pot right under his nose. Looking around he noticed many more and speculated that this might be a burial site. He was right. Serious excavations began soon after and a treasure trove of artefacts and dozens of human skeletons were unearthed. The museum is one of Thailand's best and one excavation site was left open.

Ban Chiang was declared a Unesco World Heritage site in 1992.

OFF THE BEATEN TRACK

UDON THANI'S 'MONKEY VILLAGE'

Like a mini Lopburi, the otherwise ordinary rural market town of **Kumphawapi** (กุมภวาปี), 50km southeast of Udon Thani, has a troop of monkeys living alongside its human residents. They call the city-centre park home, but frequently wander beyond it to lounge on buildings. Buses (30B to 35B, one hour) depart Udon Thani's Bus Terminal 1 every 30 minutes.

◉ Sights

Despite being an important tourist destination, Ban Chiang village remains a very traditional place so simply strolling around town can be rewarding.

Ban Chiang National Museum　　　MUSEUM
(พิพิธภัณฑสถานแห่งชาติบ้านเชียง; incl burial site 150B; ☉ 9am-4pm Wed-Sun) This excellent museum, developed with some assistance from the Smithsonian Institution, exhibits a wealth of pottery from all Ban Chiang periods, plus myriad spearheads, sickles, fish hooks, ladles, neck rings and other metal objects. The displays (with English labels) offer excellent insight into the region's distant past, though note that dates shown have all been revised to more recent ones by archaeologists based on new information, and the museum has chosen not to fix them.

Wat Pho Si Nai Burial Site　　　ARCHAEOLOGICAL SITE
(หลุมขุดค้นทางโบราณคดีวัดโพธิ์ศรีใน; Included with museum ticket, Mon free; ☉ 8.30am-6pm) A 700m walk east of the Ban Chiang National Museum turn left out of the museum and keep going, this is the largest of the burial grounds excavated in the town and the only one kept open for tourism. It has a cluster of 52 individual bodies, most from the late period (300 BCE to CE 200), buried with pottery. Due to flooding, the whole site is now a replica, with the skeletons made of resin – the real ones are in the museum.

Sor Hong Daeng Ban Chiang Weaving Group　　　ARTS CENTRE
(กลุ่มทอผ้าฝ้ายย้อมครามบ้านเชียง ส.หงษ์แดง; ☎ 086 221 2268; ☉ 9am-5pm) FREE This women's weaving group mostly makes indigo-dyed cotton fabric, including *mát·mèe*.

OFF THE BEATEN TRACK

PHU PHRABAT HISTORICAL PARK

No one really knows the history of this mysterious, mystical place peppered with bizarre rock spires, whale-sized boulders and improbably balanced rocks. **Phu Phrabat Historical Park** (อุทยานประวัติศาสตรภูพระบาท; ☎042 219837; 100B; ⏲8.30am-4.30pm) is one of Isan's most compelling sights and experiences. In prehistoric times many of the rock formations were modified to form various religious functions. Buddhist sema stones from the Dvaravati era, presumably about 1000 to 1200 years ago, are plentiful, and the ground under some rocky overhangs has been painstakingly carved into smooth platforms. The Khmer later added some Hindu elements to the site. In addition, prehistoric paintings on several rock overhangs, best seen at side-by-side Tham Wua and Tham Khon, show this was probably regarded as a holy site perhaps 3000 years ago.

The park's highlight is **Hor Nang Usa**, an overturned-boot-shaped outcrop with a shrine built into it. Nearby is **Bo Nang Usa**, a man-made reservoir carved 5m deep into solid rock. Many of these rock formations are signposted with names that allude to the local legend of Princess Nang Usa and Prince Tao Baros – you can read the tale online at www.timsthailand.com/nang-usa-story.

A climb beyond the rock formations to **Pha Sa Dej** cliff ends with vast views of the farms and forest beyond. A web of trails meanders past the many sites and you can see them all in a leisurely two hours, but it's worth spending several more. The remote northern trail loop has fewer sites along it. South of the entrance is **Wat Phra Phutthabaht Bua Bok**, with its namesake Lao-style chedi covering a Buddha footprint. It also has rocks like those in the park, though not as big or interesting.

Sleeping & Eating

There's nowhere to stay at the park. The nearest accommodation is in Ban Phue. There's a simple noodle and rice shop at the site and a good Isan restaurant in Ban Tiu, the village at the base of the hill (50m to your right as you face the park entrance).

How to get there

The park is 65km from both Udon Thani and Nong Khai and can be visited as a day trip from either city.

Sŏrng·tăa·ou from Nong Khai's bus station to Ban Phue (60B, 1½ hours, 7.30am, 8am, 8.30am) travel via Tha Bo. Vehicles from Udon Thani's Rangsina Market continue past Ban Phue to Ban Tiu (sŏrng·tăa·ou/minivans 35/100B, two/1½ hours, hourly starting at 6am), the village at the base of the hill leading up to the park, from where a motorcycle taxi costs 100B return for the final 5km climb.

Túk-túk from Ban Phue to Ban Tiu cost around 350B return and motorcycle taxis about half as much. It's much cheaper to catch a passing sŏrng·tăa·ou (15B). The last vehicle from Ban Phue back to Nong Khai leaves at 4pm and the last to Udon a little after 5pm.

Visitors are welcome. It's an 800m walk from the museum; turn left out of the museum, take the first right, then left at the end and it's on your left.

Sleeping & Eating

You won't have trouble finding a room; there are three or four decent homestay options near the museum, mostly in traditional wooden homes. Not much English spoken, but the welcome is friendly.

Boon Rung Homestay HOMESTAY **$**
(☎081 739 9273, 083 666 4671; d 600B; ❄📶) The best of three or four homestays within shouting distance of the museum, Boon Rung is a traditional-style, stilted wooden home with the family on the 1st floor and three spacious guest rooms below. Rooms open onto a large veranda, and the plant-filled garden contains a cute little cafe called **Puan Coffee**. It's in the lane directly opposite the museum.

Krua Fah Nao THAI **$**

(mains 50B; ⊘8am-4pm) The 'Cold Sky Kitchen', diagonally opposite the museum entrance, does Thai standards quite well and has an English menu.

ⓘ Getting There & Away

From Udon Thani, take a bus bound for Sakon Nakhon or Nakhon Phanom and get off at Ban Nong Mek (35B, 45 minutes, every 30 minutes), from where túk-túk charge 200B to take one or two people to Ban Chiang (8km away) and back.

BUENG KAN PROVINCE

Bueng Kan

☑ 042 / POP 4850

Little Bueng Kan (บึงกาฬ) city is a workaday town and, not surprisingly, most travellers only stop long enough to catch connecting transport to Wat Phu Thok. The only thing that qualifies as an attraction is the Thai-Lao Market (ตลาดไทย-ลาว; Soi Buengkan; ⊘4am-1pm Tue & Fri). You can also join hundreds of locals in a late-afternoon stroll along the riverfront promenade; on Friday and Saturday evenings it hosts a Walking Street Market.

🛏 Sleeping & Eating

There's a handful of restaurants and cafes along the riverfront road, close to the immigration office.

Rachawadee Hotel HOTEL **$**

(☑042 492119; www.rachavadeehotel.com; Th Bungkan; d 450B; P✳🛜) Basic but clean and good for the price, this L-shaped hotel has the best budget rooms in town. It's two blocks back from the riverfront promenade, at the north-western end of town (to your left as you face the river), so it's quiet but convenient. There are some wonky old bikes available free for guests. No English sign.

The One HOTEL **$$**

(☑042 492234; www.theonehotel-bk.com; Hwy 212; d incl breakfast from 790B; P✳@🛜❄) Out on the highway, 100m from the bus station (turn left out of the station to reach it), Bueng Kan's top hotel won't wow you, but it offers excellent value and service for the price. The pool is like a mini water park, with slides and such for kids and there's also a fitness room, free bikes for guests and a restaurant.

ⓘ Information

Bangkok Bank (Hwy 212; ⊘10.30am-7pm) There are loads of ATMs around town, but this is the only bank in Bueng Kan open evenings and weekends. It's inside the Tesco-Lotus, next to The One hotel.

Bueng Kan Immigration (☑042 491832; Th Bungkan; ⊘8.30am-4.30pm Mon-Fri) Does visa extensions; arrive before 3pm. It's on a street corner facing the river. Walk into town from the main crossroads near The One hotel, and it'll eventually be on your right. If you're going to Laos, you don't need to stop here.

ⓘ Getting There & Away

Bueng Kan functions as the transport hub for the province and its oversized bus station (☑042 491302; Hwy 212) is out on the highway east of town. Although there's only one direct bus to Nakhon Phanom, you can also make the trip in stages.

TO	FARE (B)	TIME (HR)	FREQUENCY
Bangkok	511-874	13	6.30am & 7am, 12 departures 4.30-6.15pm
Nakhon Phanom	130	4	2pm
Nong Khai	120	2½-3	3pm
Nong Khai (minivan)	150	2½	every 40min 6am-6pm
Udon Thani	208	4	hourly 5am-3pm
Udon Thani (minivan)	200	3½	every 40min 6am-6pm

ⓘ Getting Around

There are no taxis or formal car hire in Bueng Kan and túk-túk are pretty much only available at the bus station (50B to the city centre) so it's a good thing 'downtown' Bueng Kan is small enough to tackle on foot. The riverfront is about 1km from the main highway.

Phu Wua Wildlife Sanctuary

The 186-sq-km Phu Wua Wildlife Sanctuary (เขตรักษาพันธุ์สัตว์ป่าภูวัว; ☑081 260 1845; 100B) (เขตรักษาพันธุ์สัตว์ป่าภูวัว) is one of Isan's biggest and best wildlife reserves. With lots of exposed bedrock and some tall hills, it has a rugged beauty. The forest has several large waterfalls only active during or just after the

BUENG KAN'S WONDROUS ROCK-MOUNTAIN TEMPLE

With its network of rickety staircases and walkways built in, on and around a giant sandstone outcrop, **Wat Phu Thok** (วัดภูทอก; ☺ 6am-5pm, closed 10-16 Apr) is one of the region's wonders. The precarious paths lead past shrines and *gù·dì* (monk's huts) that are scattered around the mountain on cliffs and in caves and provide fabulous views over the surrounding countryside. A final scramble up roots and rocks takes you to the forest on the summit, which is considered the 7th level.

If you hustle and take all the shortcuts you can be up and down in about an hour, but we advise against it: this is a climb that should be savoured. The quiet isolation entices monks and *mâa chee* (nuns) from all over Thailand to come and meditate here, so remember to be quiet and respectful as you explore.

Monastery founder Luang Pu Juan died in a plane crash in 1980, along with several other highly revered forest monks who were flying to Bangkok for Queen Sirikit's birthday celebration. A marble *chedi* containing Luang Pu Juan's belongings, some bone relics and fantastic exterior sculptures sits below the mountain amid a lovely garden.

Túk-túk in Bueng Kan ask 1000B (this is negotiable) for the return journey to Wat Phu Thok, including a few hours of waiting time. It's cheaper to take a bus from Bueng Kan to Siwilai (20B to 30B, 45 minutes), where túk-túk drivers will do the trip for 400B. If you catch an early bus to Bueng Kan, Wat Phu Thok can be visited as a day trip from Nong Khai, although there's no need to backtrack since you could also just catch one of the vans or buses running from Bueng Kan to Udon Thani.

If you're driving or cycling, continue past Bueng Kan for 27km until you reach Chaiyaphon, then turn right at Rte 3024, the road signed for Chet Si and several other waterfalls. After 17.5km make a right and continue 4km further. (These are in the Phu Wua Wildlife Sanctuary (p395) and make worthy detours, as much for the weird rocky landscape as for the cascades. There's only water from mid-May through December.)

rainy season (July to September mainly) and more than 40 elephants. Visitors may encounter the elephants (chances are best near Ban Kham Pia village in the rainy season) and even occasionally see them outside the park, but there has been a growing number of fatalities caused by them, so it's not recommended to go hiking through the park on your own. There are also monkeys, barking deer and a fair number of bird species.

◉ Sights & Activities

The biggest waterfalls, Nam Tok Chet Si ('Seven Colours Waterfall') and Nam Tok Tham Phra ('Monk Cave Waterfall'), are both east of Rte 3024, near Wat Phu Thok. Tham Phra waterfall is reached by a boat (8am to 4pm, per person 30B), and foreigners pay the inflated entry fee of 200B.

Hiking

While the various waterfalls signposted from surrounding roads can be visited independently by motorbike, in the park proper you can only drive up to the visitors centre – after that it's hiking trails only. The authorities sometimes let you hike the trails on your own (though sometimes they don't). Either

way, we don't recommend it, as trails are unmade and go through thick forest in places, and the risk of encountering aggressive or startled wild elephants should not be dismissed. You can in theory use a park guide, but this needs to be arranged beforehand with a letter of permission from the Department of National Parks, Wildlife and Plant Conservation in Bangkok, and none of the park staff speak much English.

Bunloed, the owner of Bunloed's Huts, is a recommended guide (around 400/600/800B per half-day/full day/overnight). He's a wealth of knowledge, and understands the potential dangers of wildlife. Bunloed will also give you advice (and maps) on exploring the villages in the surrounding countryside, either by foot, bicycle or motorbike.

⛏ Sleeping & Eating

There's no accommodation inside the park, but the nearest village, Ban Kham Pia, is 3km from the visitors centre and has a fabulous homestay, Bunloed's Huts. There's also accommodation in the nearby town of Bung Khla on a gorgeous stretch of the Mekong; Mon Prasit Resort is the best value. Bueng Kan can also serve as a base for a Phu Wua visit, but if you're hiking it's better to stay close by.

Food is available in any of the gateway towns and some of the surrounding villages, but not in the reserve itself, except for a few food vendors at Nam Tok Chet Si and Nam Tok Tam Phra in the rainy season.

⭐ **Bunloed's Huts** HOMESTAY **$**
(☎ 087 861 0601; www.bunloedhuts.jimdo.com; Ban Kham Pia; s in bungalow 260-300B, d in bungalow 320-360B, s/d with shared bathroom 200/260B, s/d in tent 80/100B, meals 60-100B; **P** 🛜) Bunloed and Angelina (he's Thai, she's French) welcome guests to this charming cluster of self-built huts they call home on the edge of peaceful Ban Kham Pia village, near Phu Wua Wildlife Sanctuary. This is not only the best place from which to explore Phu Wua, it's also a fabulously friendly homestay offering a rare window into traditional Isan village life.

Bunloed built this place himself in order to establish a homestay in his home village. He designed and built the bamboo guest huts, the mud-walled, open kitchen and dining area, and the mud-brick family home. He also planted all the tropical trees and plants that scatter the garden – orchids, pineapples, coconut palms, mangoes, mangosteens, rambutans; all grown organically. He can act as your park guide (around 400/600/800B per half-day/full day/overnight), or simply give you advice on how to explore the area on your own. There are bikes and motorbikes you can use, tasty Isan meals are available, and the owners can introduce you to the *mát·mèe* weavers and rice farmers of the village. In fact, the homestay is surrounded by rice paddies, most of which are owned by Bunloed's brothers and sisters.

This is a rare opportunity to experience traditional Isan life with a family who can speak English (and French) and who understand the needs and expectations of both foreign travellers and local villagers. Accommodation is basic but comfortable; you fall asleep to the magical sounds of the forest, to be woken by the cry of the village cockerels. It's the sort of place you visit for a day or two, then don't want to leave.

If you're coming by bus, Bunloed will pick you up from Ban Don Chik village on the highway, but it's only a 3km walk. There's no sign for the homestay, but it's the first place to the left of the school at the far end of the village.

Mon Prasit Resort HOTEL **$**
(☎ 042 499147; Bung Khla; d with fan 300B, with air-con 350-600B, bungalows 600B; **P** ❄️ 🛜) Right on the Mekong, and with the forested 'snake mountains' butting up against the river on the opposite shore (in Lao), Bung Khla is all about the location. The rooms at this simple hotel are clean, though small; it's well worth upgrading to one of the six riverside wooden bungalows, where you can soak up the magical views from your private veranda.

Coming from the highway into the village, once you hit the river turn left, then follow the road around to the other side of a small tributary and you'll soon reach the resort.

ℹ Getting There & Away

Unless you're visiting while staying at Bunloed's Huts in Ban Kham Pia, you'll need your own transportation to visit Phu Wua, and formal motorcycle rental isn't available at either Bung Khla or Bueng Kan.

The easiest way to get to Ban Kham Pia is the daily bus between Nong Khai (100B, 3½ to four hours) and Nakhon Phanom (130B, three to four hours), which will drop you at Ban Don Chik, 3km away. Bunloed will pick you up from there, or you can just walk. There are also hourly Bueng Kan–Ban Phaeng minivans (from 5.30am to

NORTHEASTERN THAILAND PHU WUA WILDLIFE SANCTUARY

ℹ **GETTING TO LAOS: BUENG KAN TO PAKSAN**

Although it's very rarely done by travellers, you can cross the Mekong from Bueng Kan to Paksan, but only if you already have your Lao visa.

Getting to the border The pier is 2.5km northwest of town and immigration formalities are done there. A túk-túk from the city centre costs 60B to 70B.

At the border Boats (per person 60B) cross the river frequently between 8.30am and 4pm on weekdays and infrequently on weekends, leaving when they have about 20 passengers. You can go any time you want if you pay the full 1200B.

Moving on Túk-túk wait on the Lao shore, though the highway and a few hotels are an easy walk from the landing.

3.30pm), which go past Bung Khla and Ban Don Chik (50B). Coming the other way, start with a minivan from Nakhon Phanom to Ban Phaeng (80B, two hours, 12.30pm, 1.30pm, 2.30pm and 4pm), then switch to a minivan to Ban Don Chik or Bung Khla (50B, 45 minutes).

NAKHON PHANOM PROVINCE

Lao and Vietnamese influences are strong in Nakhon Phanom (จังหวัดนครพนม), a province bordered by the Mekong and full of highly revered temples. For the most part it's a region of subtleties rather than can't-miss attractions, but there are plenty of fine river views and interesting historic sites, and the colossal Wat Phra That Phanom is one of the icons of Isan culture.

Nakhon Phanom

042 / POP 22,710

Nakhon Phanom (นครพนม) means 'City of Mountains', but the undulating sugarloaf peaks all lie across the river in Laos, so you'll be admiring rather than climbing them. The views are fantastic, though, especially during a hazy sunrise.

Nakhon Phanom's temples have a distinctive style. This was once an important town in the Lan Xang Empire and, after that, Thai kings sent their best artisans to create new buildings. Later a vivid French influence crossed the Mekong and jumped into the mix.

◉ Sights

Mekong Walking Street   MARKET
(ถนนคนเดินแม่น้ำโขง; Th Sunthon Wijit; ⊙4-9.30pm Fri-Sun) This street market has little in the way of arts and crafts, but there's plenty of souvenirs and, of course, lots of food. The historic buildings give it a nice atmosphere too.

**Former Governor's
Residence Museum**   MUSEUM
(จวนผู้ว่าราชการจังหวัดนครพนม (หลังเก่า); Th Sunthon Wijit; adult/child 50/20B; ⊙9am-5pm Wed-Sun) Museum Juan, as it's also known, is on the riverfront and fills a beautiful restored 1925 mansion with photos of old Nakhon Phanom, many labelled in English. Out the back are detailed displays on the illuminated boat procession Lai Reua Fai, and cooking

utensils in the old kitchen. Bai-Tong, the gift shop's owner and artist, speaks excellent English and is a great source of local advice.

Ho Chi Minh House   MUSEUM
(บ้านโฮจิมินห์; ☑042 522430; Ban Na Chok; donations appreciated; ⊙daylight hours) FREE
The best of the three Ho Chi Minh–related attractions in Ban Na Chok village (p400), this is a replica of the simple wooden house where 'Uncle Ho' sometimes stayed in 1928 and 1929 while planning his resistance movement in Vietnam. A few of the furnishings are believed to be originals. It's a private affair located within a lush, flower- and fruit-tree-filled garden in the back of a family home, and they're very proud of it.

Wat Okat   BUDDHIST TEMPLE
(วัดโอกาส; Th Sunthon Wijit; ⊙daylight hours)
FREE Predating the town, Wak Okat is home to Phra Tiow and Phra Tiam, two sacred wooden Buddha images covered in gold that sit on the highest pedestal in the wí·hăhn (sanctuary). The current Tiam (on the right) is a replica because the original was stolen in 2010. The amazing modern murals showing the story of Phra Tiow and Phra Tiam floating across the Mekong from Laos are among our favourites – see if you can find the backpackers.

🏃 Activities

Nakhon Phanom is extremely cycle-friendly, with reasonably quiet roads and a dedicated, tree-shaded cycle path along the riverfront (heading north is more pleasant than south). It's also possible to cycle out to Ban Na Chok (p400), a rural village with three Ho Chi Minh tourist sights. Many hotels in town rent bikes, usually for around 50B per day.

**Maekhong Paradise
Sunset Dinner Cruise**   BOATING
(☑089 780 7179; Th Sunthon Wijit; adult/child 200/100B) The larger of the city's two cruise boats, this is a two-hour dinner cruise with a full menu of Thai and Isan food available. It departs at 6pm.

Thesaban Sunset Cruise   BOATING
(☑086 230 5560; Th Sunthon Wijit; per person 50B) The city runs this hour-long Mekong River cruise on creaky old Thesaban, which docks across from the Indochina Market. Departure is around 5pm. Snacks and drinks are available.

Nakhon Phanom

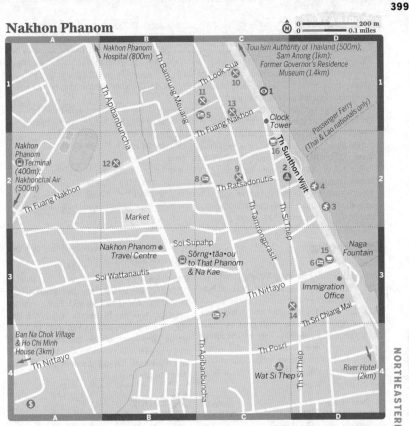

Nakhon Phanom

🎇 Festivals & Events

Lai Reua Fai   CULTURAL
(🕑 late Oct/early Nov) Nakhon Phanom is famous for this illuminated boat procession. A modern twist on the ancient tradition of sending rafts loaded with food, flowers and candles down the Mekong as offerings for

the *naga*, today's giant bamboo rafts hold up to 20,000 handmade lanterns, and some designers add animation to the scenes.

Boat races, music competitions and other festivities run for a week, but the boats are launched on the night of the full moon, which is Ork Phansaa, the end of Buddhist Lent.

WORTH A TRIP

UNCLE HO'S VILLAGE

After the lovely views, Nakhon Phanom is best known for its Ho Chi Minh connection. The village of Ban Na Chok, about 3km west of Nakhon Phanom, is one of a dozen places where 'Uncle Ho' stayed in Thailand between 1928 and 1930 while planning his resistance movement against the French in Vietnam.

The village remains mostly ethnically Vietnamese today and there are now three Ho Chi Minh tourist sites. The faithful replica of the house (p398) where he stayed is the best, the memorial (อนุสรณ์สถานประธานโฮจิมินห์; Ban Na Chok; ☺8am-5pm) FREE is aimed at tour buses and the museum (พิพิธภัณฑ์ประธานโฮจิมินห์; Ban Na Chok; ☺7am-4pm) FREE is the least visited but most educational.

Túk-túk drivers usually ask for 200B for the return trip, but it's easy to cycle out here: follow Th Nittayo west for about 3km, then turn left immediately after the temple that's after the big 'Ho Chi Minh's House' sign. After passing under the village's entrance archway, the museum is down the second lane on the right (signposted). The house and the memorial are two lanes further on.

🛏 Sleeping

Windsor Hotel
HOTEL **$**

(☏042 511946; 272 Bamrung Meuang; s with fan 300B; d & tw 450B; P ✳ 🗟) The best of Nakhon Phanom's city-centre cheapies, it's clear that decades ago this was a top-level address. Today, it has a fresh coat of paint and it's kept meticulously clean which, along with the large rooms (with TV and mini-fridge), makes it decent value. Mountain views are available at the top. English sign, but no English spoken.

SP Residence
HOTEL **$$**

(☏042 513505; Th Nittayo; d 590-800B; P ✳ @ 🗟) Plain but modern, the rooms here are less institutional than the exterior and hallways would lead you to believe, and it's set back from the road, keeping it quiet. Staff are very friendly, and there are bikes available (free for the first hour). No English signage; look for the spearmint-green building.

777 Hometel
HOTEL **$$**

(Tong Jed Hometel; ☏042 514777; Th Tamrongprasit; d incl breakfast 600-800B; P ✳ @ 🗟) Don't let the boxy exterior put you off – inside are some fairly stylish rooms. It's well managed, priced right and has some of the friendliest staff in town. Bike rental available too.

Landmark Nakhon Phanom Hotel
HOTEL **$$**

(☏042 530890; Th Nittayo; d & tw incl breakfast 950-1250B; ste 2800B; ✳ 🗟) Relatively new, this stylish little hotel has a great location (reflected in the prices) and elegant, well-furnished rooms. The back rooms (950B) have no natural light, though, so upgrade to one of the front rooms with a balcony (1250B)

or, if you can afford it, one of the fabulous river-view suites.

River Hotel
HOTEL **$$**

(☏042 522999; www.therivernakhonphanom.com; Th Sunthon Wijit; d/tw from 990/790B; P ✳ 🗟) Arguably Nakhon Phanom's best hotel, this place is on the riverfront, but unfortunately about 2km south of the centre. It's stylish and modern, has plush rooms, solid service and big views. It's just a shame it isn't a bit closer to the action.

🍴 Eating

Aunt Kaew's Noodles
NOODLES **$**

(ก๋วยเตี๋ยวป้าแก้ว; Th Ratsadonutis; noodles 50B; ☺8am-3pm Mon-Sat) The auntie who rules this simple, open-fronted noodle house – wildly popular with the locals – knocks up delicious bowls of glass noodles mixed with thick slices of beef and crunchy bean sprouts. There's a complimentary cup of iced tea and a warm welcome.

Little Home
THAI **$**

(Th Tamrongprasit; mains 60-80B, coffee from 40B; ☺11am-7pm; ✳ 🗟) Modern, big-windowed cafe-cum-restaurant with good coffee and a decent selection of Thai dishes plus a few Western choices (macaroni, spaghetti etc).

Sam Anong
THAI **$**

(Th Samut Bunhan; mains 40-250B; ☺8am-8pm; ✳ 🗟) This no-frills place is a great choice for down-home Isan food with what must be a contender for best *gài yâhng* (grilled chicken) in Nakhon Phanom. And as a bonus, you can choose regular or black sticky rice. Following the riverfront, it's the third road on the left after the Tourism Authority of Thailand office, then almost immediately on the left.

Phornthep Naem Nueang VIETNAMESE $
(Th Si Thep; mains 40-200B; ☺6am-4pm) Classic, chaotic place with a full selection of Vietnamese dishes including the titular *năam neu·ang* (assemble-it-yourself pork spring rolls). Come in the morning for *khài gràtá* (a mini-skillet of eggs topped with sausages). There's no English sign, but it's located directly across from the old movie theatre next to Srithep Hotel.

Night Market THAI $
(Th Fuang Nakhon; ☺4-10pm) Nakhon Phanom's night market is large and diverse (Thai, Isan, Vietnamese, international) but has few places to sit.

Ohio THAI $$
(Th Fuang Nakhon; mains 69-169B, seafood 150-300B; ☺5pm-4am; ☜) This popular restaurant has gone through many incarnations during its 25 years – the current is colourful and classy and it feels more Bangkok than Nakhon Phanom – but it has always turned out good food. Though the menu is mostly Thai, with fish featuring prominently, there are some Isan and Western dishes too. Also good for late-evening craft beer and cocktails.

Champasak SEAFOOD $$
(☑042 514541; Th Sunthon Wijit; mains 40-400B; ☺10am-10pm; ❄☜) Champasak specialises in Mekong river fish. The owner, the daughter of Mekong fisherfolk, knows her fish and takes pride in her selection. The shop has both air-con and open-area sections. The picture menu helps you get through the sketchy English descriptions of the standard Thai, Isan and Vietnamese fare. No English sign; look for the large, gaudy orange-painted building.

🍸 Drinking & Nightlife

After dinner, head to one of the laid-back, attractive riverside bars that fill historic shophouses on Th Sunthon Wijit, north of the clock tower.

Cafe Le Landmark CAFE
(Th Nittayo; coffee from 50B, tea & smoothies 80B; ☺6am-10pm) This sweet little cafe attached to Landmark Nakhon Phanom Hotel does good coffee, tea and smoothies as well as croissants and, bizarrely, 16 different types of toast, from strawberry jam to shredded

pork and salad cream. It's great for a cooling blast of air-con, but there's also pleasant seating outside on the covered terrace.

P Cafe CAFE
(Th Si Thep; espresso 40B; ☺7.30am-7.30pm; ☜) Come here for coffee, tea, Italian sodas, smoothies and as much style as you are going to find in Nakhon Phanom. Old photos, big chairs and a piano make this a lovely and relaxing spot. No proper food, though they do have cookies, cakes and the like.

ℹ️ Information

Bangkok Bank (Tesco-Lotus, Th Nittayo; ☺10.30am-7pm) The nearest bank with evening and weekend hours in the city centre.
Immigration Office (☑042 532644; www.nakhonphanom-imm.com; Th Sunthon Wijit; ☺8.30am-noon & 1-4.30pm Mon-Fri) For visa extensions.
Tourism Authority of Thailand (TAT; ☑042 513490; tatphnom@tat.or.th; Th Sunthon Wijit; ☺8.30am-4.30pm) Covers Nakhon Phanom, Sakon Nakhon and Mukdahan provinces.
Nakhon Phanom Hospital (☑042 511422; www.nkphospital.go.th; Th Apibanbuncha) The city's best medical facility.

ℹ️ Getting There & Away

AIR

Nakhon Phanom's airport is located 20km west of town. **Air Asia** (☑042 531571, nationwide 02 515 9999; www.airasia.com; Nakhon Phanom Airport; ☺8am-5pm) flies several times daily to/from Bangkok's Don Mueang Airport. **Nok Air** stopped flying here for a while, but was due to resume its flights between here and Bangkok at time of research. **Nakhon Phanom Travel Centre** (☑042 520999; Th Apibanbuncha; ☺8.30am-6pm Mon-Sat) sells tickets. For a taxi from the airport into town, expect to pay 150B to 200B.

BUS

Nakhon Phanom's **bus terminal** (☑042 513444; Th Fuang Nakhon) is a short walk west of the town centre. From here buses head to Nong Khai (200B, seven to eight hours, 11am), Udon Thani (147B to 200B, four hours, every 45 minutes from 7.15am to 5pm), Khon Kaen (212B, five hours, 13 daily from 5.50am to 9.30pm) and Ubon Ratchathani (155B to 200B, 4½ hours, 7am, 8.30am and 2pm). **Nakhonchai Air** (☑042 191299) runs luxury bus services from the bus terminal.

Most people use minivans for Ubon Ratchathani (182B, four hours, hourly from 5.45am to 4pm) and Mukdahan (80B, 2½ hours, frequent from 5.30am to 6pm), all of which stop in That Phanom (40B, one hour). There are frequent buses to

ⓘ GETTING TO LAOS: NAKHON PHANOM TO THA KHAEK

Getting to the border Passenger ferries cross the Mekong to Tha Khaek in Laos, but they're for Thai and Lao travellers only. All other travellers must use the Third Thai–Lao Friendship Bridge, north of the city. The easiest way to cross is to take the bus directly to Tha Khaek from Nakhon Phanom's bus station (70/75B weekdays/weekends, eight departures from 8am to 5pm).

At the border The Thai border is open from 6am to 10pm. All immigration formalities, including getting Lao visas, are handled at the bridge. Things get pretty chaotic when droves of Vietnamese workers are passing through.

Moving on The bus tends to wait a long time at the bridge, so total travel time to Tha Khaek can be more than two hours.

Bangkok (554B to 862B, 11 to 12 hours) between 4.30pm and 7.30pm plus two in the morning (7.30am and 7.45am), and three to Chiang Mai (737B, 14 to 15 hours, 9am, 3pm and 5pm).

Sŏrng·tăa·ou to That Phanom (50B, 1½ hours, frequent 7am to 5pm) park next to Kasikornbank in the town centre.

ⓘ Getting Around

Túk-túk drivers expect 40B for one or two people from the bus station to most places in town, and 200B for the return trip to Ban Na Chok (p400). Nakhon Phanom also has a **taxi** (☑ 080 903 7222) service; drivers park at the bus station and they don't use meters.

Sŏrng·tăa·ou to Na Kae depart from next to Kasikornbank and pass the turn-off to Ho Chi Minh's House (15B, 10 minutes), leaving you with a 1km walk.

Avis (☑ 062 597 3611, nationwide 02 2511131; www.avisthailand.com; Nakhon Phanom Airport; ⊙ 8am-7.30pm), **Budget** (☑ 042 531592, nationwide 02 203 9222; www.budget.co.th; Nakhon Phanom Airport; ⊙ 8am-6pm) and **Thai Rent a Car** (☑ 042 530681, nationwide 1647; www.thairentacar.com; Nakhon Phanom Airport; ⊙ 9am-7pm) offer car hire at Nakhon Phanom's airport and River Hotel (p400) also does car hire. The price of a car alone is about 1200B per day and a driver will cost 500B. River Hotel and 777 Hometel (p400) have motorcycle hire for 250B per day.

Nakhon Phanom's sparse traffic and riverside bike trail, which takes you all the way north to the bridge, makes it a great place for cycling. Most hotels have free bikes for their guests, but if yours doesn't you can rent from another one such as 777 Hometel.

That Phanom

☑ 042 / POP 11,680

Towering over the small, peaceful town of That Phanom (ธาตุพนม), the spire of the colossal *chedi* at Wat Phra That Phanom is one of the region's most emblematic symbols and one of the great pillars of Isan identity. Some historic buildings in the Mekong-hugging half of town can round out a pleasant visit.

◉ Sights

★Wat Phra
That Phanom   BUDDHIST TEMPLE

(วัดพระธาตุพนม; Th Chayangkun; ⊙ 5am-9pm) FREE This temple is a potent and beautiful place – even if you're feeling templed out, you'll likely be impressed. At its hub is a stupa *(tâht)*, more impressive than any in present-day Laos and highly revered by Buddhists from both countries. It's 53.6m high, and a 16kg real-gold umbrella laden with precious gems adds 4m more to the top. The stupa is lit up spectacularly at night, and a visit in the evening is extra-special, with prayer chants and gongs reverberating around the complex.

The local legend tells that the Lord Buddha travelled to Thailand and directed that one of his breast-bone relics be enshrined in a *chedi* to be built on this very site; and so it was in 535 BCE, eight years after his death. Historians, on the other hand, assume the first construction was around the 9th century AD, and modifications have been routine since then. In 1690 it was raised to 47m and the current design went up in 1941, but it toppled during heavy rains in 1975 and was rebuilt in 1978. There's a replica (พระ ธาตุองค์เดิมจำลอง) FREE of how the original, short stupa may have looked in a pond in front of the temple. And you'll find replicas of both the present and the previous designs all over Isan.

Behind the surrounding cloister is a shady little park with more statuary and a museum (พิพิธภัณฑ์รัตนโมลีศรีโคตรบูรณ์;

⊙8.30am-4pm) **FREE**. To the north is what was once the largest gong in Thailand, and to the south is a market with food and handicrafts for all the Thai tourists visiting.

Tai-Lao Open-Border Market   MARKET
(ตลาดนัดไทยลาว; Th Rimkhong; ⊙5am-2pm Mon & Thu) This busy market running along the river takes place every Monday and Thursday. It's mostly the same fresh food and household goods found in other Thai markets, but some Lao traders come over to sell herbs, roots, mushrooms, bats and other forest products.

✦✦ Festivals & Events

That Phanom Festival   CULTURAL
(⊙late Jan/early Feb) Visitors descend from all over Thailand and Laos to make merit and pay respect to the *tâht*. The streets fill with market stalls, many top *mŏr lam* troupes perform and the town hardly sleeps for nine days. On the morning of Ork Phansaa (the end of Buddhist Lent), Phu Tai dancers perform their 'peacock dance' in front of Wat Phra That Phanom.

🛏 Sleeping

During the That Phanom Festival, rates soar and rooms are booked out well in advance.

★Baan Ing Oon Guesthouse   HOTEL $
(☑042 540111; baaningoonguesthouse2@gmail.com; Th Phanom Phanarak; d incl breakfast 490-790B; P❄❀) This place, a block off the river, offers cleanliness, comfort and finesse for a very fair price. The building is new, but has the classic French-Indochina style (the building next door is a genuine original) and a pleasant vibe. The family who run it speak little English, but are very friendly and helpful. Guests can use bikes for free.

Kritsada Rimkhong Hotel   HOTEL $
(☑083 005 8621; Th Rimkhong; d incl breakfast 500-600B; P❄@❀) There is a mix of rooms here, some older than others, and none particularly inspiring. But it's all about the pair of 2nd-storey river-view rooms; grab one if you can. If the friendly English-speaking owner is around when you call, he'll pick you up at the bus station for free. Free bikes for guests.

That Phanom Riverview Hotel   HOTEL $$
(☑042 541555; www.thatphanomriverviewhotel.com; Th Rimkhong; d & tw incl breakfast 850-1300B; P❄@❀) Rooms at That Phanom's

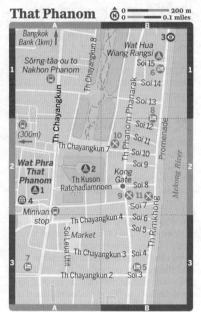

That Phanom

⊚ Top Sights
1 Wat Phra That Phanom A2

⊚ Sights
2 Replica Stupa A2
3 Tai-Lao Open-Border Market B1
4 That Phanom Museum A2

🛏 Sleeping
5 Baan Ing Oon Guesthouse B3
6 Kritsada Rimkhong Hotel B1
7 That Phanom Place A3
8 That Phanom Riverview Hotel B1

✕ Eating
9 Dao Thong B2
   Krua Kritsada Rimkhong .... (see 6)
10 Night Market B2
11 Pugtukhong B2

biggest and best lodge are pretty plain for the price, but being large and bright helps compensate, and the service and amenities are what you'd expect. Note that despite the name, most rooms have little or no view. There are free bicycles for guests' use.

That Phanom Place   HOTEL $$
(☑042 532148; thatphanomplace@gmail.com; Th Chayangkun; d/tw incl breakfast 790/890B;

P ❄ 🛜) There's a lot to like about this friendly place set back from the road behind its namesake restaurant. You get a quality room – designed to catch a breeze – at a fair price and grade A service, often in English. If only it were by the river instead of 500m away along the highway. Free bikes for guests.

🍴 Eating & Drinking

The restaurants along the river are good places to lounge with a beer or *lôw kŏw* (local whiskey) at night. There are also some locals bars by the junction of Th Chayangkun and Th Chayangkun 2 south of the *tâht*.

Dao Thong　　　　　　　VIETNAMESE $
(Th Phanom Phanarak; 40-150B; ⊘7.30am-8.30pm; ❄🛜) That Phanom's largest restaurant is set up for tour groups, but the food is excellent (mostly Vietnamese; some Isan) and the menu is in English. Leo, one half of the young couple that run the place, speaks good English, so if you can catch him when it's quiet you'll have a good meal here.

It doesn't have an English sign, but the attached Cafe Higherland (coffee from 30B) does.

Pugtukhong　　　　　　　　　THAI $
(📱091 057 0351; Th Rimkhong; mains 40-150B; ⊘10am-late; 🛜) Khun Maew, who speaks English and is a good source of local info, serves heaping plates of delicious Thai and Isan standards with a river view. Also good for a late-night beer or two.

Krua Kritsada Rimkhong　　　THAI $
(Th Rimkhong; mains 40-200B; ⊘8am-10pm; P🛜) The food here, with an emphasis on Mekong River delicacies, is consistently delicious, and it's usually quieter than most of the town's many other riverside restaurants, although there is a seldom-used karaoke machine.

Night Market　　　　　　　MARKET $
(⊘3.30-9.30pm) Isan food predominates at That Phanom's night market, but there's also Thai and Vietnamese. It's all served for takeaway.

ℹ️ Information

There are several regular banks in the centre of town. For weekends and evenings, there's a **Bangkok Bank** (⊘10.30am-7pm) north of town in the Tesco-Lotus shopping centre on Th Chayangkun.

ℹ️ Getting There & Away

From That Phanom's new **bus station** (Rte 2030), inconveniently located west of town (a túk-túk to the river should cost 30B to 40B), there are buses to Ubon Ratchathani (162B, 4½ hours, seven daily), Udon Thani (160B to 180B, five hours, four daily) and Bangkok (473B to 818B, 11 to 12 hours, 7.20am, 8am, and 11 between 5pm and 7pm), and minivans to Nakhon Phanom (40B, one hour, frequent 6am to 6pm) and Ubon Ratchathani (145B, four hours, hourly 6.30am to 5pm) via Mukdahan (40B, one hour).

Most people, however, don't use the bus station since the minivans also stop just south of the *tâht* on **Th Chayangkun** (Th Chanyangkhun), and for Nakhon Phanom you can take one of the **sŏrng-tăa-ou** (Th Chayangkun) (50B, 1½ hours, frequent 7am to 4pm) that depart from the highway 300m north of the *tâht*.

ℹ️ Getting Around

You can walk everywhere in That Phanom, but a bike is great for riding along the river. Most hotels have them available for guests.

MUKDAHAN PROVINCE

Mukdahan (จังหวัดมุกดาหาร) is an often overlooked province. Its capital city is a low-key hard sell, but there's some beautiful scenery and historic temples along the Mekong River.

Mukdahan

📞042 / POP 34,290
On the banks of the Mekong, directly opposite the Lao city of Savannakhet, Mukdahan (มุกดาหาร) – just plain *múk* to locals – sees few visitors despite being the home of the Thai–Lao Friendship Bridge 2 connecting Thailand to Laos and Vietnam by road. It's not a hugely exciting place, but there's enough of interest to fill a relaxing day, and the vibe is friendly.

◉ Sights

Hor Kaew Mukdahan　　　　　MUSEUM
(หอแก้วมุกดาหาร; Th Samut Sakdarak; 50B; ⊘8am-6pm) This eye-catching 65m-tall tower was built for the 50th anniversary of King Rama IX's ascension to the throne. The nine-sided base has a good museum with displays (labelled in English) on the eight ethnic groups of the province. There are great views and a few more historical displays in 'The 360° of Pleasure in Mukdahan by the Mekong' room, up at the 50m level.

The ball on the top holds a locally revered Buddha image believed to be made of solid silver.

Indochina Market
MARKET

(ตลาดอินโดจีน, Talat Indojin; Th Samran Chaikhongtai; ⏱8am-5pm) Among Thais, Mukdahan is most famous for this riverside market, which stretches along and under the promenade. Most Thai tour groups on their way to Laos and Vietnam make a shopping stop for cheap food, clothing and assorted trinkets – much of it from China and Vietnam – plus silk and cotton fabrics made in Isan. A massive renovation project, with little sign of completion, has meant the market has had to trade from temporary street-side stalls for more than two years.

Wat Pa Silawiwek
BUDDHIST TEMPLE

(วัดป่าศิลาวิเวก; Th Damrongmukda; ⏱daylight hours) **FREE** It's the resident monkeys rather than anything religious or artistic that make this forest temple on the edge of town worth a visit. They reside in the far back of the temple and are most active in the early morning.

Phu Manorom
VIEWPOINT

(ภูมโนรมย์; ⏱4am-7pm) **FREE** You can get an impressive view of Laos and the Mekong from this mountain south of the city. The temple here has a small garden and an 84m-tall Buddha image is under construction. It's a popular place for photo ops, and while it's promoted as a sunrise-watching spot, odds are it will just be you and the monks at that time.

🎏 Festivals & Events

Mukdahan Thai Tribal Festival
CULTURAL

(Red Cross Fair; ⏱9-17 Jan) Besides the usual activities, the Mukdahan Thai Tribal Festival, held in the field fronting the provincial hall (săh·lah glahng), features dancing and other cultural activities from Mukdahan's eight ethnic groups.

🛌 Sleeping

Huanum Hotel
HOTEL $

(☑042 611137; Th Samut Sakdarak; d/tw with fan & cold-water shared bathroom 200/350B; ste d/tw 350/450B; P✳🛜) This Mukdahan classic is a friendly, reliable, clean old-timer that's long been the first choice of backpackers.

Riverview Maekhong Hotel
HOTEL $

(☑087 945 4949; Th Samran Chaikhongtai; d 450-750B; P✳🛜) This quiet place has a great

Mukdahan
ⓃN 0 ▭▭ 200 m
0 ▭▭ 0.1 miles

Mukdahan

👁 Sights
1 Hor Jao Mae Song Nang Pi Nong	B1
2 Indochina Market	B2
3 Wat Pa Silawiwek	A2
4 Wat Yod Kaeo Sivichai	B2

🛌 Sleeping
5 Hotel de Ladda	B3
6 Huanum Hotel	B1
7 Riverfront Hotel	B2
8 Riverview Maekhong Hotel	B3

🍴 Eating
9 Goodmook*	B1
10 Mukdahan Night Market	A1
11 Saigon Kitchen	B1

ⓘ Information
12 Mukdahan International Hospital	B3

ⓘ Transport
13 Air Asia	A1
14 LA Bicycle	B2
15 Ploy Travel	A2
16 Ying Mongkhol Motor	B3

waterfront location, and the spacious layout means the river breezes are fully taken advantage of. However, the rooms are a little faded these days, and some parts of the guesthouse smell musty. Still, if you can snag a river-view room you won't care. There's also a terrace overlooking the river and a riverfront bar-restaurant.

Riverfront Hotel
HOTEL $$

(☑042 633348; www.riverfrontmukdahan.com; Th Samran Chaikhongtai; d & tw incl breakfast from 850B, with river view from 1250B; P❄@◈) Managed by a charming elderly woman who speaks good English, this place near the market is tastefully decorated, with plenty of timber finishings and furnishings and cool-tile flooring. Most of the cheapest rooms have partial river views from small balconies, but other rooms really make the most of the riverfront location.

Hotel de Ladda
HOTEL $$$

(☑042 611499; www.hoteldeladda.com; Th Samran Chaikhongtai; d incl breakfast from 2400B; P❄◈⊠) The best address in Mukdahan offers large, plush rooms with European-inspired style right up against the Mekong. Every room has a river view and a balcony. There's also a riverside swimming pool in a small landscaped garden, a fitness centre and a spa.

🍴 Eating

⭐ Bao Pradit
THAI $

(Th Samran Chaikhongtai; mains 30-300B; ◷11am-10pm; P◈) It's a bit of a trek south of the centre, but this is a real Isan restaurant with dishes such as *gôry kài mót daang* (raw meat 'salad' with red-ant eggs) and *gang wǎi* (rattan curry). Though the English menu is mysterious (Bao Pradit doesn't really serve python), it's rare that a restaurant of this sort has any English.

In the evenings there's live Thai folk music *(pleng pêua chee·wít)*. There's no English sign, but the entrance is across from a tall lime-green building.

Mukdahan Night Market
MARKET $

(Th Song Nang Sathit; ◷4-9pm) Mukdahan's night market is the most buzzing place in town for evening food. It has all the Thai and Isan classics, but it's the Vietnamese vendors that set it apart. A few sell *bǎhn dah* (they'll tell you it's 'Vietnamese pizza'), which combines soft noodles, pork, spring onions and an optional egg served on a crispy cracker.

There are lots of takeaway treats (barbecued skewers, grilled fish, servings of fresh fruit), but many stalls serving soups, noodles

---

BUSES FROM MUKDAHAN

Mukdahan's **bus terminal** (☑042 611207; Rte 212), which has a nice little coffee shop, is on Rte 212, 2km west of town. Yellow *sŏrng·tǎa·ou* (10B, 6.30am to 5pm) run north along Th Samut Sakdarak and west along Th Phithak Phanomkhet and end up at the station. Túk-túk from the bus station cost 50B to the city centre. *Sŏrng·tǎa·ou* to Don Tan, for going to Phu Pha Thoep National Park, depart from in front of Pornpetch Market.

DESTINATION	FARE (B)	DURATION (HR)	FREQUENCY
Bangkok	477-778	10-11	hourly in the morning, frequent 5-8pm
Khon Kaen	161-214	4½	hourly 3.30am-4pm
Khon Kaen (minivan)	240	4½	every 45min 4am-6pm
Nakhon Phanom (minivan)	80	2½	frequent 5.30am-6pm
Nakhon Ratchasima	272	7	hourly 5.45am-6.30pm
That Phanom (minivan)	40	1	frequent 5.30am-6pm
Ubon Ratchathani	100-140	2½	hourly 11am-3.45pm
Ubon Ratchathani (minivan)	125	2½	every 30min 6am-5pm
Udon Thani	175-200	5	hourly 8.45am-3.30pm
Udon Thani (minivan)	180	5	hourly 6.30am-5.30pm
Yasothon	103	2	5.45am, 6.45am, 8.45am, 10.30am, noon, 4pm
Yasothon (minivan)	84	2	every 30min 5.30am-6.10pm

ⓘ GETTING TO LAOS: MUKDAHAN TO SAVANNAKHET

Getting to the border Thai and Lao citizens can use the boats that cross the Mekong from Mukdahan's city centre, while everyone else must use the bridge. The easiest way to cross is with the direct buses to Savannakhet (45B to 50B, hourly 7.30am to 7pm) from Mukdahan's bus station. There's a 5B fee during weekends, holidays and non-business hours.

At the border The border is open from 6am to 10pm. The crossing to Savannakhet can take from one to two hours, depending on the length of the immigration queues. There's time enough at the border to get a Lao visa.

Moving on From Savannakhet there are buses to various points in Laos, as well as Vietnam.

---

and the like also lay out small tables and stools so you can enjoy a no-frills al-fresco meal.

Saigon Kitchen   VIETNAMESE $
(68/1 Th Phitak Santirat; mains 40-150B; ⊙8am-8.30pm) It's nothing flash, but for some this is Mukdahan's best Vietnamese restaurant, with standout spring rolls (the skin's so thin it's translucent) as well as soups, noodle dishes, savoury pancakes and 'Vietnamese pizza'. No English sign, and no English spoken, but there is an English menu with photos.

Goodmook*   INTERNATIONAL $$
(☑042 612091; Th Song Nang Sathit; mains 80-400B; ⊙9am-5pm Tue-Sun; ✸🛜) This delightful place has a cool, retro theme and a mix of Thai and international food (expensive but good), art on the walls, chill music and good coffee. It's a great place to drop in and meet other travellers, both Thai and Western.

ⓘ Information

Krung Thai Bank (Th Song Nang Sathit; ⊙10am-6pm Mon-Fri) In the city centre; stays open late on weekdays, but for weekend banking you'll need to hit up one of the shopping malls along the highway north of the bus station.

Mukdahan Immigration Office (☑042 674072; ⊙8.30am-noon & 1-4.30pm Mon-Fri) For visa extensions. It's north of town by the bridge, in a hard-to-find spot south of the large border gate.

Mukdahan International Hospital (☑042 611222; www.mukinter.com/en; Th Samut Sakdarak; ⊙24hr) Good private hospital.

ⓘ Getting There & Away

If you're driving to Ubon Ratchathani, Rte 212 will zip you there in about three hours, but if you can spare a whole day, take the Mekong-hugging back roads through a gorgeous stretch of rural Thailand.

AIR

Mukdahan does not have an airport, but **Air Asia** (☑nationwide 02 515 9999; www.airasia.com; Mukdahan Grand Hotel, Th Song Nang Sathit) and Nok Air (p373) have daily fly-and-ride services using both Nakhon Phanom and Ubon Ratchathani airports. Air Asia departs from and drops at Hotel Mukdahan Grand, while Nok Air uses nearby Ploy Palace Hotel. Also at Ploy Palace Hotel, **Ploy Travel** (☑042 614599; Ploy Palace Hotel, Soi Ploy 1; ⊙8am-5pm) sells tickets and arranges van transport to Ubon's airport for other flights.

ⓘ Getting Around

Mukdahan is a decent place for a bike ride. Not the town itself, so much, but following the Mekong River north along various little roads takes you past historic temples, scenic rapids and deep countryside. Also, there's a proper bike path leading most of the way to Phu Pha Thoep National Park, south of the city. **LA Bicycle** (Th Samut Sakdarak; per day 100B; ⊙8am-5pm) rents second-hand mountain bikes.

Ying Mongkhon Motor (☑086 428 1338, 042 613993; Th Samut Sakdarak; motorcycle hire per day from 200B; ⊙8am-5pm Mon-Fri, to 4.30pm Sat), which has signs at many hotels using the name Tony Rental, hires motorcycles.

Rides with **Taxi Mukdahan** (☑042 613666; ⊙6am-midnight) have a 60B flagfall plus the meter, although sometimes the price is just negotiated.

Phu Pha Thoep National Park

Despite only covering 48 sq km, hilly Phu Pha Thoep National Park (อุทยานแห่งชาติ ภูผาเทิบ; ☑089 619 7741, 094 289 2383; 200B, car/motorcycle 30/20B) as a host of beautiful attractions – most famously, large mushroom-shaped rock formations. The main rock group sits right behind the visitors centre, and wildflowers bloom there from October through December. Besides the weird rocks there are several clifftop viewpoints and Nam Tok Phu Tham Phra, a scenic waterfall (May to November only) with a grotto atop it holding hundreds of small Buddha images. It only takes a few hours and about 4km on the well-marked trails to see all these sights. Tham Fa Mue Daeng, a cave with ancient hand paintings, is an 8km drive from the main park area and then a 1.5km walk.

🛏 Sleeping & Eating

For accommodation, there's camping (per person with own tent 30B, 4-person tent hire 300B) and a three-bedroom bungalow (☑ 094 289 2383; http://nps.dnp.go.th/reservation.php; bungalow 1800B) right by the visitors centre.

There's an Isan restaurant at the visitors centre serving *gài yâhng* (grilled marinated chicken), *sôm·đam* (spicy papaya salad) and *plah pŏw* (grilled fish). Typically last order is 6pm, but go no later than 5pm to be safe. There are also a couple of shops with instant noodles and snacks.

ℹ Information

The **visitors centre** (☑ 094 289 2383; ⊙ 8.30am-4pm) has helpful staff. Hire rangers for visiting Tham Fa Mue Daeng here.

ℹ Getting There & Away

The park is 15km south of Mukdahan via Rte 2034. A bike path alongside the highway makes riding there reasonably safe and easy.

Sŏrng·tăa·ou (20B, 30 minutes, every 30 to 45 minutes) to Don Tan, departing from Pornpetch Market, 300m north of Hor Kaew Mukdahan, pass the turn-off to the park, from where it's a 1.3km-walk to the visitors centre, or you can ask drivers to detour off the route and take you; they'll probably do it for 100B. Buses to Ubon Ratchathani from the Mukdahan bus station also pass the same junction. Be back at the junction by 4.30pm to guarantee finding a bus or *sŏrng·tăa·ou* back to town.

NAKHON RATCHASIMA PROVINCE

If you had just a single day to experience Thailand, Khorat (จังหวัดนครราชสีมา) – the original and still most commonly used name for Nakhon Ratchasima (นครราชสีมา), Thailand's largest province – would be a great place to spend it. Most visitors are here to jump into the jungle at Khao Yai, Thailand's oldest national park. Its large size and easy access make it one of the best wildlife-watching sites in Thailand.

While Khao Yai is the soaring pinnacle of the province's tourist industry, history aficionados can soak up an evocative glimpse of the Angkor era's heyday at the beautifully restored ruins at Phimai.

Khorat city offers little in terms of tourist sights, but is a pleasant place to stay, with a solid selection of hotels and restaurants making it a good base for your Isan sojourn.

Nakhon Ratchasima (Khorat)

☑ 044 / POP 166,000

Nakhorn Ratchasima (นครราชสีมา) is a big, busy city with little in the way of sights, but one that for many travellers serves as the gateway to Isan. Khorat, as most people call the city, has a strong sense of regional identity (people call themselves *kon koh·râht* instead of *kon ee·săhn*) and is at its best in its quieter nooks, such as inside the eastern side of the historic moat, where local life goes on in a fairly traditional way and you are more likely to run into a metre-long monitor lizard than another traveller.

⊙ Sights

Maha Viravong National Museum   MUSEUM
(พิพิธภัณฑสถานแห่งชาติมหาวีรวงศ์; Th Rajadamnern; 50B; ⊙ 9am-4pm Wed-Sun) Though the collection at this seldom-visited museum is very small, it's very good. There's prehistoric pottery (don't miss sneaking a peek at what's stored in the back), Khmer bronze statues and a variety of Buddha images spanning the Dvaravati to Rattanakosin eras.

Wat Salaloi   BUDDHIST TEMPLE
(วัดศาลาลอย; Soi 1, Th Thaosura; ⊙ daylight hours) The city's most interesting temple was said to be founded by local heroine Thao Suranari and her husband in 1827. Half of her ashes are interred in a small stupa (the other half are at her monument) and there are also singing troupes on hire to perform for her spirit here. A small statue of the heroine sits praying in the pond in front of the temple's award-winning *bòht* (ordination hall).

Built in 1967, the *bòht* resembles a Chinese junk and holds a large gleaming-white Buddha Image in 'calming the ocean' posture. It, and other buildings, are decorated with Dan Kwian (a nearby village) pottery. Elsewhere around the grounds are a variety of spirit shrines that have little to do with Buddhism.

Thao Suranari Monument SHRINE
(อนุสาวรีย์ท้าวสุรนารี; Th Rajadamnern; ⊙24hr)
FREE Thao Suranari, wife of the assistant governor during Rama III's reign, is something of a Wonder Woman in these parts. Ya Mo (Grandma Mo), as she's affectionately called, became a hero in 1826 by organising a successful prisoner revolt after Chao Anou of Vientiane had conquered Khorat during his rebellion against Siam. One version of the legend says she convinced the women to seduce the Lao soldiers (another says she got them drunk) and then the Thai men launched a surprise attack, saving the city.

Wat Phayap BUDDHIST TEMPLE
(วัดพายัพ; Th Pholsaen; ⊙daylight hours, cave shrine 8am-5pm) FREE When the abbot of Wat Phayap learned that blasting for a quarry in Saraburi Province was destroying a beautiful cave, he rescued pieces of it and plastered the stalactites, stalagmites and other incredible rocks all over a room below his residence, creating a shrine like no other.

The walls and, very unusually, roof of the beautiful new *bòht* next to the cave shrine are made of polished granite.

Chumphon Gate GATE
(ประตูชุมพล; Th Chumphon) The city's only original gate left standing. It was a part of the city walls erected in 1656 by French technicians on the orders of King Narai (Ayuthaya). A replica section of the wall sits in the northeast corner of the moat.

This is the gate troops assembled at before heading out to battle.

🎆 Festivals & Events

Candle Parade CULTURAL
(⊙Jul) During Khao Phansaa, the beginning of Buddhist Lent, Khorat has a large candle parade.

Thao Suranari Festival CULTURAL
(⊙23 Mar–3 Apr) Khorat explodes into life during the Thao Suranari Festival, when the city celebrates the namesake heroine. It features parades, theatre, shopping and other events along Th Rajadamnern.

🛏 Sleeping

Sansabai House HOTEL $
(☎044 255144; www.sansabai-korat.com; Th Suranaree; d with fan 300B, with air-con 450-1000B; P✱🕸) Long the best budget sleep in Khorat, this clean, quiet and friendly place has spacious rooms with good mattresses, mini-fridges and little balconies. If you can live without air-con, the fan-cooled rooms are particularly good value. It has a small restaurant-cafe (7am to 8pm) out back.

Rom Yen Garden Place HOTEL $$
(☎044 260116; www.romyenhotel.com; Th Jomsurangyat; d from 990B; P✱🕸📶☰) With a very modern, welcoming feel, this stylish hotel is a great addition to Khorat's accommodation roster. The comfy, attractive rooms are good value and there's a pool, a fitness centre and a large deck in front. It's set back off the road, so noise isn't much of an issue. Add 200B per person for the with-breakfast rate.

Thai Inter Hotel HOTEL $$
(☎044 247700; Th Yommarat; d incl breakfast 650B; P✱@📶) This little hotel patches together an odd mix of styles. The lobby is homely, the rooms are comfy, if small, and the furniture's a little worn, but it has a good location near decent restaurants, cafes and bars.

Fortune Rajpruek Hotel HOTEL $$$
(☎044 079900; www.fortunehotelgroup.com; Th Mittaphap; tw/d incl breakfast from 1400/1600B; P✱@📶☰) Refurbished and rebranded in 2017, this veteran hotel feels newer than it is. Rooms are spacious and comfortable, there's a pool and a gym, and the location is central.

LOCAL KNOWLEDGE

KHORAT SPECIALITIES

Two local dishes to seek out are **sôm·dam koh·râht** (the same ingredients as the mild Central Thai version of *sôm·dam* but with the addition of Isanstyle fermented fish sauce) and **pàt mèe koh·râht**, which is similar to *pàt tai*, but boasts more flavour, has chilli pepper, and is made with a local style of soft rice noodles (*mèe koh·râht*). Pàt mèe koh·râht is widely available in Nakhon Ratchasima Province but very rare elsewhere.

Nakhon Ratchasima (Khorat)

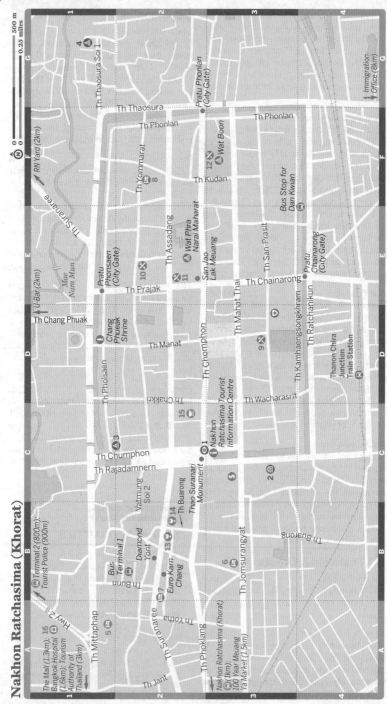

Nakhon Ratchasima (Khorat)

✗ Eating

Khorat is a decent food city, for both Thai and *fa·ràng* food. The best night markets are far from the centre but worth the trip for foodies. There are also good food courts inside the city's huge, modern shopping malls; Terminal 21 (p412) is the closest to the centre.

RN Yard
MARKET $

(Th Suranari; ⊙4-10pm; 🛜) With both variety (Thai, Isan and more) and quality, many locals consider this Khorat's best night market. Most customers are here for takeaway, but there's a two-level seating area in the back. Night Baan Koh (NBK) across the road is a poor man's Chiang Mai Walking Street. It's just north of the The Imperial hotel.

Wat Boon Night Bazaar
MARKET $

(Th Chomphon; ⊙5-9.30pm) This is the largest night market inside the old town. All the usual Thai and Isan dishes are available for takeaway.

Third World Cafe
AMERICAN $

(Th Assadang; burgers 120-150B, sides 80B, coffee 50B; ⊙noon-10pm Mon-Sat; 🛜) This hipster burger joint is young and friendly and does a range of juicy burgers, including crispy fried chicken and pulled pork, each cooked on a grill outside the cafe. There are side dishes too, although the burgers come with their own small portion of fries. The unlimited refills of coffee are a nice touch.

★ Daya's Cafe
THAI $$

(256/17 Yommarat Rd; coffee 35-50B, mains 80-300B, burgers 110-300B; ⊙8am-7pm Fri-Wed; ✻) One of a number of funky little cafes on this stretch of Th Yommarat, Daya's is a friendly place that serves good strong coffee, but it's the delicious handmade burgers and exquisitely presented contemporary Thai dishes that really make this place stand out.

Chez Andy
INTERNATIONAL $$$

(📞044 289556; Th Manat; mains 350-950B; ⊙11am-11pm; 🅿🛜) Not your ordinary *fa·ràng* hangout in Isan, this Swiss-owned spot is a proper restaurant, not just a bar that also serves food. Run by a chef, it aims high and usually succeeds. The European-focused menu includes fondue, braised lamb shank, pizza, paprika schnitzel, and green curry, and there's informal al-fresco seating.

🍷 Drinking & Nightlife

★ Yellow Pumpkin
CAFE

(Soi Samranjit; coffee 55-65B, cake slices 95B; ⊙10am-7pm Fri-Wed; 🛜) Hidden deep in a tiny soi east of the Thao Suranari Monument (take the second soi on your right as you walk along Th Assadang), this is where in-the-know locals come for quality coffee, matcha lattes and sumptuous slices of carrot cake.

Some Might Say
CRAFT BEER

(201/1 Th Suranaree; beers 140-190B; ⊙6pm-midnight Tue-Sun) The most popular of a handful of craft-beer joints that have started to spring up in town. Speciality brews include Coconut IPA and Lemongrass Kölsch.

Tiger is Coming
BAR

(173 Th Suranaree; beers 80-450B, mains 150-250B; ⊙6pm-midnight) This buzzing bar on the corner of Th Suranee and Th Buarong opens out onto the pavement come evening and stocks hundreds of bottled beers from around the world, most of which cost around 200B. It also does cocktails and has a fairly extensive Thai menu.

Shopping

Terminal 21   SHOPPING CENTRE
(www.terminal21.co.th/korat;   Th   Mittaphap;
⊙10am-10pm) This is one of the Isan region's
largest and glossiest shopping malls. Each
floor follows a theme such as Paris and Tokyo. Besides shopping and eating, there's a
movie theatre (some movies are shown in
English or with subtitles), an ice skating
rink, and a 110m-tall observation tower.

Information

Immigration Office (☎ 044 212997; Division
4, 323 Moo 9, Ban Nong Bua Sala; ⊙8.30am-
noon & 1-4pm Mon-Fri) Located 8km south of
the city, just off Hwy 224.

**Nakhon Ratchasima Tourist Information
Centre** (Th Rajadamnern; ⊙9am-5pm) The
city-run, sometimes unstaffed, booth is by the
Thao Suranari Monument.

Tourism Authority of Thailand (TAT; ☎ 044
213666; tatsima@tat.or.th; 2102-2104 Th Mittaphap; ⊙8.30am-4.30pm) Khorat's branch of
TAT is inconveniently located 3km or 4km west
of the centre, next to the Sima Thani Hotel.
Staff speak very little English.

Bangkok Hospital (☎ 044 429999; www.
bangkokhospital.com; Th Mittaphap) 24-hour
casualty department and many English-
speaking doctors.

Police Station (☎ 044 242010; Th San-Prasit;
⊙24hr)

Tourist Police (☎ 044 370356; Hwy 2)

Getting There & Away

BUS

Khorat has two bus terminals. **Terminal 1** (Bor
Kör Sör Nèung; ☎ 044 242899; Th Burin) in the
city centre serves Bangkok (191B, 3½ to four
hours, frequent) and most towns within the province, including Pak Chong (56B to 72B, 1½ to
two hours, frequent 5.30am to 6.30pm) and Pak
Thong Chai (21B, one hour, frequent). Minivans
to Pak Chong (66B, 1½ hour, frequent 6.30am
to 8pm) also leave from this terminal. Buses to
most other destinations, plus more Bangkok
buses and minivans, use the much larger **Terminal 2** (Bor Kör Sör Sörng; ☎ 044 256007; Hwy

BUSES & MINIVANS FROM TERMINAL 2

DESTINATION	FARE (B)	DURATION (HR)	FREQUENCY
Aranya Prathet (border with Cambodia)	157	4	5.30am, 9am, noon, 3pm, 4pm
Ayuthaya (minivan)	132	3½-4	6am, 7am, 8am, 5pm, 6pm
Bangkok	148-508	4	frequent
Bangkok (minivan)	171	4	frequent 6.30am-7.30pm
Chiang Mai	526-613	13	7 departures 3am-8.30pm
Khon Kaen	146-220	3½-4	frequent
Khon Kaen (minivan)	126	3-3½	every 40min 6.40am-6.30pm
Krabi	924	16	4.50pm
Loei	252-342	7	hourly 5am-midnight
Lopburi	164	4-4½	6am, 8am, 10.45am, 1.30pm
Lopburi (minivan)	148	3½-4	every 40min 4.50am-6.30pm
Nang Rong	119	2	half-hourly 4.50am-8.10pm
Nang Rong (minivan)	64	2	every 30min 4.30am-8.10pm
Nong Khai	257-409	6	11 departures, mostly in the afternoon
Mukdahan	297	7-8	6.15am, 8.30am, 12.30pm, 2.30pm, 6.30pm
Phimai	50	1	every 30min 5am-10pm
Phimai (minivan)	50	1	hourly 10am-5.30pm
Surin	115-218	4	every 30min
Trat	324	8-9	1am, 3am, 8.30am, 10.30am, 11.45am, 9pm
Ubon Ratchathani	248-386	7-8	hourly
Udon Thani	178-300	5½	frequent
Vientiane (must have Lao visa)	900	6	noon

2), north of the centre. For **Dan Kwian** (14B, 30 minutes), frequent buses leave from inside the old city, east of Pratu Chainarong.

Many trains pass through **Khorat train station** (📞 044 242044), and though less frequent than buses, they offer a much more comfortable, safer and cheaper option. There's no need to book tickets in advance (though you may want to for overnight trains to Bangkok); just buy tickets at the station.

Destinations include Bangkok via Ayuthaya (50B to 425B, four to six hours, five daytime trains, five overnight), Ubon Ratchathani (58B to 453B, five to six hours, 11 trains day and night), Pak Chong for Khao Yai National Park (18-251B, 1½ hours, six daily 8.22am to 6.47pm), Khon Kaen (37B, three hours, 6.20am, 8.29am and 3.55pm) and Udon Thani (56B, five hours, 6.20am and 3.55pm).

Khorat's smaller **Thanon Chira Junction train station** (Jira Train Station; 📞 044 242363) is closer to the old city, so it may be more convenient to get off there.

❶ Getting Around

There are fixed *sŏrng·tăa·ou* (8B) routes through the city, but even locals find it hard to figure them out because of their dizzying array of numbers and colours. Most pass the junction of Th Suranaree and Th Rajadamnern, so if you want to go somewhere, just head there and ask around. Heading west on Th Suranaree, yellow *sŏrng·tăa·ou* 1, with white and green stripes, will take you past the train station, the tourism office and The Mall; the white 1 with yellow and green strips also passes the train station. Heading north on Th Rajadamnern, the white 6 with red and yellow stripes passes The Mall more directly. Also going north on Th Rajadamnern, the white and blue 7 with no stripes, the white 10 with red and yellow stripes and the white 15 with purple stripes all go to Bus Terminal 2. The white and blue 7 also passes in front of Thanon Chira Junction train station.

Túk-túk cost between 50B and 80B to most places in town. Motorcycle taxis and *săhm·lór*, both of which are common, always cost less. Metered **taxis** (📞 095 602 3636; ⏰ 24hr) pretty much only park at Bus Terminal 2 and **The Mall** (www.themall.co.th; Th Mittaphap; ⏰ 10am-10pm), so you'll need to call. There's almost no chance of getting drivers to use the meter.

Motorcycles can be hired at **Euro Karn Chang** (📞 088 355 9393; 241 Th Suranaree; ⏰ 8am-5pm Mon-Sat) and **Diamond Yont** (📞 081 878 7367; 100 Th Suranaree; ⏰ 8.30am-4pm Mon-Sat, shorter hours Sun) from 250B per day for use within Nakhon Ratchasima Province.

Korat Car Rental (📞 081 877 3198; www.koratcarrental.com) rents cars with and without drivers.

Ban Prasat

📞 044 / POP 1590

About 3000 years ago a primitive agricultural civilisation, closely related to Ban Chiang, put down roots at Ban Prasat (บ้านปราสาท), near the banks of Mae Nam Than Prasat. It survived around 1500 years, planting rice, domesticating animals, fashioning coloured pottery, weaving cloth and forging metal tools. The secrets of this early civilisation were revealed during extensive archaeological digs completed in 1991; some of the excavation pits have been left open as tourist attractions, and a museum houses some of the discoveries.

South of the museum, one family still does silk weaving and they welcome visitors to come by for a look.

◉ Sights

Ban Prasat
Excavation Pits   ARCHAEOLOGICAL SITE
(แหล่งโบราณคดีบ้านปราสาท; ⏰ daylight hours)
FREE Three excavation pits with replica skeletons (the originals were damaged over time) and pottery left in situ from the 1991 excavations are on display in the village.

Ban Prasat Museum   MUSEUM
(พิพิธภัณฑ์บ้านปราสาท; ⏰ 8am-4.30pm) **FREE**
This small but good museum houses some of the artefacts found around Ban Prasat. It also explains what village life was like in those days and in the village today.

🛏 Sleeping & Eating

The homestay program includes dinner; for lunch there are a couple of *gŏo·ay đĕe·o* carts in town, including one across the road from the museum. A **night market** (⏰ 3-6pm Fri) takes over the bridge on Friday nights.

Ban Prasat Homestay   HOMESTAY $
(📞 081 725 0791, 044 213666; per person incl dinner 250B) Many families (some speak a little English) are part of an award-winning homestay program where villagers put up visitors in their homes and show them daily activities such as basketry and farming. Participating homes have signs outside, though ideally reservations should be made in advance (you may have to get a Thai speaker to reserve for you).

ⓘ Getting There & Away

Ban Prasat is 45km northeast of Khorat and 1.5km off Hwy 2. Buses (35B, one hour) heading to points north will drop you at the junction. A motorcycle taxi will zip you around to all the sites for 60B per person, but note that often only one driver is working.

Muang Sema Historical Site

Little is known about the ancient city of Muang Sema (โบราณสถานเมืองเสมา), roughly halfway between Nakhon Ratchasima (Khorat) and Pak Chong, though it was clearly important in its day. It began as a Dvaravati outpost in the 7th or 8th century BCE, during which it is presumed to have been the capital city of a small kingdom. Later, probably in the 10th century, it was occupied by the Khmer, although Mahayana Buddhism continued alongside Hinduism. Many artefacts found here are on display at the Phimai National Museum.

Other than one evocative reclining Buddha, it's mostly ruined foundations and a pair of moats. While Muang Sema isn't spectacular, what you get here is a sense of being off the beaten track. Beyond the temple, there's no tourist infrastructure other than a few explanatory signs, and you'll most likely have the place to yourself.

◉ Sights

**Wat Dhammachakra
Semaram**   BUDDHIST TEMPLE
(วัดธรรมจักรเสนาราม; ⊘ daylight hours) FREE
Locally known as Wat Phra Norn ('Temple of the Reclining Buddha'), this temple is significant for housing a 1300-year-old, 13.3m-long reclining Buddha carved from sandstone blocks by the Dvaravati. It's the oldest reclining Buddha sculpture in Thailand.

Bo Eka   RUINS
(บ่ออีกา) FREE Right in the centre of the main moat, this is the most significant of Muang Sema's ruins, after Wat Dhammachakra Semaram. Labelled as Monument 1 on the site's signs, it was from the Khmer era and would surely have been a typical *prang* (Khmer-style stupa), though now all that sits atop the pedestal is a *yoni,* the base for shiva lingas, and a *somasutra,* the channel in

which holy water flowed out of the sanctuary after washing the main religious image.

The road leading to it starts just 500m from Wat Dhammachakra Semaram.

🛏 Sleeping & Eating

There's no lodging at the historic site, but there are hotels and guesthouses in Sung Noen and out on the highway.

There are snacks sold at the temple. The nearest village, Ban Hin Tang, has a few rice and noodle shops; and Sung Noen has many restaurants.

ⓘ Getting There & Away

Muang Sema is 37km from Khorat. Minivans between Khorat and Pak Chong will stop along the highway, 8km away, from where you can hire a motorcycle taxi to take you around the site for about 150B, though it may take a while to find one. A few buses (22B, 45 minutes) from Terminal 1 and local trains (6B to 63B, 30 minutes, five per day) run from Khorat to Sung Noen city, 4.5km away from the sites, where finding a motorcycle taxi is usually easier.

Phimai

☐ 044 / POP 9770
The unassuming little town of Phimai (พิมาย) has one of Thailand's finest surviving Khmer temple complexes right at its heart. The architectural inspiration for Cambodia's Angkor Wat, Prasat Phimai once stood on an ancient highway linking the Khmer capital of Angkor with the northern reaches of the realm.

Being located smack in the centre of this small and pleasant town, Phimai is not just one of the most impressive ancient monuments in Thailand, it's also one of the most accessible. It's an easy day trip out of Nakhon Ratchasima (Khorat), but if you prefer the quiet life, you could always make Khorat a day trip out of Phimai instead.

◉ Sights

★**Phimai Historical Park**   HISTORIC SITE
(อุทยานประวัติศาสตร์พิมาย; ☐ 044 471568; Th Ananthajinda; 100B; ⊘ 7am-6pm, visitors centre 8.30am-4.30pm) Prasat Phimai is one of the most impressive Khmer ruins in Thailand, both in its grand scale and its intricate details. Though built as a Mahayana Buddhist temple, its carvings feature many Hindu deities, and many design elements – most

Phimai

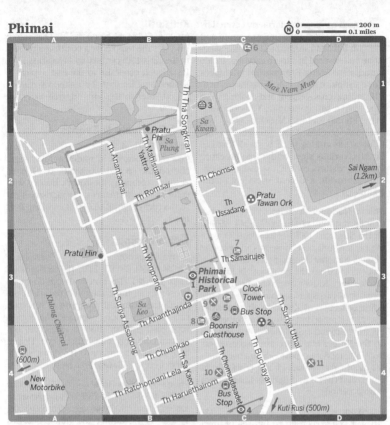

N 0 —————————— 200 m
   0 —————————— 0.1 miles

Phimai

◉ Top Sights
1 Phimai Historical Park B3

◉ Sights
2 Meru Bhramathat.................................C3
3 Phimai National Museum.....................C1
4 Pratu Chai C4

🛏 Sleeping
5 Benya Guesthouse..............................C3
6 Moon River Resort Phimai C1

🛏 Sleeping (cont.)
7 Phimai Paradise Hotel...........................C3
8 Phimai Paradise House.........................C3

✕ Eating
9 Barai Coffee...C3
10 Mee Gaan..C4
11 Talat Jae Jae......................................D4

---

notably the **main shrine**'s distinctive *prang* tower – were later used at Angkor Wat. There has been a temple at this naturally fortified site since at least the 8th century, though most of the existing buildings were erected in the late 11th century by Khmer King Jayavarman VI.

You enter over a cruciform **naga bridge**, which symbolically represents the passage from earth to heaven, and then through the **southern gate** of the outer wall, which stretches 565m by 1030m. The orientation to the south (though not due south) is unusual since most Khmer temples face east. It's often written that Phimai was built facing south to align with the capital, though historians reject this theory since it doesn't face Angkor directly.

A raised passageway, formerly covered by a tiled roof, leads to the inner sanctum and the 28m-tall main shrine built of white sandstone and covered in superb carvings. Inside the adjacent **Prang Brahmathat** is a replica stone sculpture of Angkor King Jayavarman VII, sitting cross-legged and looking very much like a sitting Buddha. The original is in the Phimai National Museum.

Knowledgeable local students sometimes act as guides, but few speak English. Luckily, various signs and a free brochure from the visitors centre just inside the entrance provide a decent overview of the complex.

Phimai National Museum MUSEUM
(พิพิธภัณฑสถานแห่งชาติพิมาย; ☎044 471167; Th Tha Songkran; 100B; ☉9am-4pm) One of the biggest and best museums in Isan, the Phimai National Museum is well worth a visit. Situated on the banks of Sa Kwan, a 12th-century Khmer reservoir, the museum consists of two spacious buildings housing a fine collection of Khmer sculptures from not just Phimai but also many other ruins from around Isan. Though the focus is on the Khmer era, there are also artefacts from Muang Sema (p414), distinctive trumpet-mouthed and black Phimai pottery from Ban Prasat (p413) and Buddha images from various periods.

Sai Ngam PARK
(ไทรงาม; ☉daylight hours) A bit east of town is Thailand's largest and oldest banyan tree, a 350-plus-year-old giant spread over an island. The extensive system of interlocking branches and gnarled trunks makes the 'Beautiful Banyan' look like a small forest.

Pratu Chai GATE
(ประตูชัย, Victory Gate) This south gate is the most intact and noteworthy of Phimai's three surviving 13th-century city gates (the east gate is in ruins), built by King Jayavarman VII, because it served the road to Angkor. The city wall was atop the mounded dirt ridge beside it.

Meru Bhramathat RUINS
(เมรุพรหมทัต; Th Buchayan) **FREE** Meru Bhramathat is a toppled brick stupa dating back to the late Ayuthaya period (18th century). Its name is derived from a folk tale that refers to it as the cremation site of King Bhramathat.

Kuti Rusi RUINS
(กุฏิฤๅษี; ☉daylight hours) **FREE** This minor ruin was the temple for a health centre built in the early 13th century by Jayavarman VII. It's aligned generally to the east, typical of Khmer temples, but for unknown reasons it's off-kilter to the same degree as Prasat Phimai.

★ Festivals & Events

Phimai Festival CULTURAL
(☉mid-Nov) Staged in mid-November (usually on the second weekend), the Phimai Festival celebrates the town's history with cultural performances, sound-and-light shows (tickets 200B to 600B) and long-boat races.

⌣ Sleeping

Benya Guesthouse GUESTHOUSE $
(☎044 471541, 081 976 2471; Th Ananthajinda; d 399B; P❋🖘) This immaculate little guesthouse has an unbeatable location right opposite the historical park and is run by a super-friendly young woman who speaks very good English. Rooms are small, but neat and tidy and come with air-con, TV and little en-suite bathrooms. It's down a side street next to 7-Eleven. Free bicycles.

Phimai Paradise Hotel HOTEL $
(☎086 468 8402, 044 287565; www.phimaiparadisehotel.com; Th Samairujee; d/tr 550/800B; P❋@🖘🏊) Nothing too fancy, but this hotel close to one side of the historical park has for many years offered the best rooms in town, and the swimming pool is a nice bonus. There are bicycles for hire for 100B per day. Breakfast is 170B.

Moon River Resort Phimai GUESTHOUSE $$
(☎061 4236 939; www.moon-river-resort-phimai.com; Soi 2, Ban Sai Ngam Patana; d 600-800B; P❋🖘) This Thai-German-run guesthouse is in an almost rural location on the north bank of the river (where you can swim) and features simple but good wooden and concrete cabins. They're surrounded by greenery and connected by a cool boardwalk. It's just outside town off the road to Khorat, 1km from the historical park entrance. Guests can hire bikes and motorcycles.

✕ Eating

The string of vendors next to Sai Ngam (Phimai's much-revered banyan tree), open for breakfast and lunch, serve Thai and Isan basics, including *pàt pàt mèe pímai,* which is the same as *pàt mèe koh·râht* except it is spicier and uses a slightly different noodle. Some restaurants in town have it on their menus too.

Talat Jae Jae MARKET $
(ตลาดจอแจ; Th Suriya Uthai; ⊙5-8am) This small morning street market is a good place to look for some breakfast.

Barai Coffee CAFE $
(☑085 611 5841; Th Ananthajinda; sandwiches 20-30B, waffles 30-40B, coffee from 40B, smoothies 70B; ⊙8.30am-5pm; ❄🖨) Just in front of the historical park entrance, this is a convenient stop for a brewed coffee and a blast of air-conditioning. They also do smoothies, sandwiches and waffles and have some back-garden seating.

Mee Gaan THAI $$
(☑061 414 5585; cnr Th Chomsudasadet & Th Haruethairom; mains 65-250B, fish dishes 400-650B; ⊙9am-9pm; ❄🖨) This friendly newcomer has a cafe vibe but with restaurant-quality food and is the best place in town for a meal. The speciality is the delicious *pad mee mee gaan* (65B), its own take on *pàt mèe koh·râht,* but it also does rice dishes, Thai curries, seafood, and all-day breakfasts. There's cold beer, good coffee and the cakes aren't half bad either.

❶ Getting There & Away

Buses (50B, one hour) and minivans (50B, one hour) to Phimai leave Nakhon Ratchasima's Bus Terminal 2 about every 30 minutes throughout the day. All buses heading in and out of town pass official stops near **Pratu Chai** (Th Haruethairom) and the **clock tower** (Th Buchayan) and will also stop anywhere along the road north of town, such as the museum. Minivans only use Phimai's inconvenient **bus station**. If you're heading somewhere north of Phimai, take the bus to Tala Khae (13B, 15 minutes) and catch a connection there; you may have to wait a while.

❶ Getting Around

Phimai is small enough to stroll around, but to travel further, hire a bike from **Boonsiri Guesthouse** (☑044 471159; Th Chomsudasadet; per half-/full day 40/80B) or **Phimai Paradise House** (☑044 471918, 086 468 8402; www.phimaiparadisehotel.com; Th Chomsudasadet; incl breakfast tw 500B, d 600-800B; 🅿❄@🖨) (per day 100B), or a motorcycle from **New Motorbike** (☑044 481880; Th Ananthajinda; per day 300B; ⊙8am-5pm Mon-Sat).

Khao Yai National Park

Up there on the podium with some of the world's greatest parks, Khao Yai (อุทยานแห่งชาติเขาใหญ่; ☑086 092 6529; 400B, car/motorcycle 50/30B; ⊙entrance 6am-6pm) is Thailand's oldest and most visited national park. Covering 2168 sq km, Khao Yai incorporates one of the largest intact monsoon forests remaining in mainland Asia, which is why it was named a Unesco World Heritage site (as part of the Dong Phayayen–Khao Yai Forest Complex). But despite its size, it's one of the easiest national parks in Thailand for independent travellers to visit.

◉ Sights & Activities

The park spans five forest types, each teeming with wildlife. There are good hiking trails and some fantastic waterfalls that put on thundering shows in the rainy season.

Visiting independently is quite easy as the English-speaking staff at the visitors centre are very helpful, motorcycles and bicycles can be hired, and visitors with cars are usually happy to pick up pedestrians; though tours are reasonably priced and easy to arrange.

The greater Pak Chong region surrounding the park boundaries is a very popular escape for Bangkokians, and for many of them the national park is beside the point. The area is full of enough sweetcorn stands, shopping malls and go-kart tracks that families can stay busy all weekend without even thinking about nature. There are, however, some non-tourist-trap attractions outside the park that are also worth a visit.

In the Park

⭐**Nam Tok Haew Narok** WATERFALL
(น้ำตกเหวนรก; ⊙7am-5pm) Nam Tok Haew Narok ('Hell Gorge Waterfall') is in the far south of Khao Yai National Park, 23km from the visitors centre. Its three levels combine to form a 150m drop, making it the park's biggest. It's pretty easy to walk the 800m paved path to the top of the 50m first level, but then it's a 199-step descent to the viewpoint. The second and third levels aren't accessible.

Nam Tok Haew Suwat WATERFALL
(น้ำตกเหวสุวัต; ⊙7am-5pm) The park's loveliest waterfall, 25m-high Nam Tok Haew Suwat scooped a starring role in Danny Boyle's film *The Beach.* It has water year-round

Khao Yai National Park

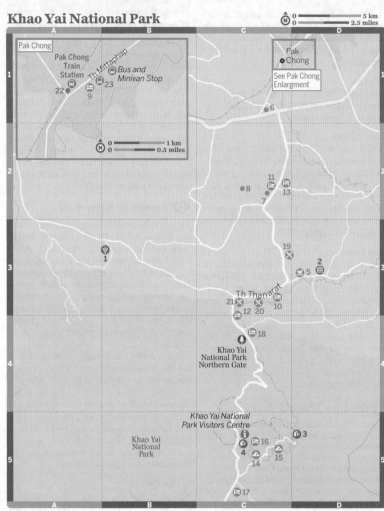

(though very little in the hot season) and you can walk down to the bottom, but swimming isn't allowed. Though accessible by car, Haew Suwat can also be reached by a couple of walking trails.

Nam Tok Kong Kaew   WATERFALL
(น้ำตกกองแก้ว) Little Nam Tok Kong Kaew sits just 150m from the Khao Yai National Park visitors centre.

Pha Diew Dai Viewpoint   VIEWPOINT
(จุดชมวิวผาเดียวดาย) Up over 1100m, this is the most impressive of Khao Yai National Park's viewpoints. And it's rarely crowded.

It's part of an easy 500m boardwalk nature trail starting 14km from the visitors centre.

Outside the Park

Ban Tha Chang Spring   SWIMMING
(Tambon Mu Si; ⏰24hr) **FREE** These crystal-clear spring-fed lagoons are a hugely popular spot for swimming. Easy to reach, they are visible from the road; heading towards Pak Chong, turn right at the sign for Belle Villa then bear left.

Khao Yai Art Museum   GALLERY
(เขาใหญ่ อาร์ต มิวเซียม; ☎044 756060; ⏰10am-5.30pm) **FREE** This excellent private gallery

Khao Yai National Park

has three rooms of modern art from some of Thailand's top artists, including Anupong Chantorn and Lampu Kansanoh, and a sculpture garden. It's 3km east of Th Thanarat; heading towards Pak Chong, turn right at the sign for Belle Villa then bear left, go past the swimmers at Ban Tha Chang spring, then follow the signs.

GranMonte   WINERY
(กราน·มอนเต้; ☏044 009543; www.granmonte. com; tour incl tasting per person 450B; ⊘ tours weekdays 10am, 11.30am, 1.30pm, 3pm & 4pm, weekends 11am, 1.30pm & 3pm) The top-tier winery closest to the Khao Yai National Park entrance, which is 16km away, is home to Thailand's first female oneologist, Nikki Lohitnavy. It's

scenically set, offers tours (book in advance), a gourmet gift shop, luxury lodging and a classy restaurant. It lies along the Muak Lek–Khao Yai road, the direct route from Bangkok to Khao Yai (exit at Km 144).

Hiking Trails

There are five hiking trails through the forest that visitors can walk on their own. All other forest hiking requires a guide. Park rangers can be hired as guides (500B to 1000B per group depending on the time) through the visitors centre. They can also lead you on longer off-trail treks, but only if they speak English or you speak Thai, so deep forest exploration is best done with a private guide arranged through local tour companies (p420) or hotels.

No matter where you hike, you should wear boots and long trousers. During the rainy season leeches are a problem. Mosquito repellent helps keep them away, but the leech socks sold in the visitors centre work much better.

Trail 1 (1.2km) The Kong Kaew Waterfall Nature Trail is a paved loop starting at the suspension bridge behind the visitors centre. It's not difficult, but it does have some steep spots.

Trail 2 (3km) This easy trail connects Haew Suwat (p417) and Pa Kluai Mai waterfalls. Crocodiles are often seen in the river a short way past the latter falls. This trail was closed at the time of research, so check in at the visitors centre before hitting the trailhead.

Trail 3 (3.3km) This mildly challenging walk to the Nong Phak Chi observation tower (p420) starts at a small parking area by the Km 33 pillar. This is one of Khao Yai's best wildlife-watching and birdwatching areas. It's used by many tour groups. Combine it with Trail 5 to walk back to the visitors centre.

Trail 4 (2.7km) An easy, relatively little-travelled trail to a viewpoint of the Sai Sorn Reservoir.

Trail 5 (5km) Starting not too far south of the visitors centre, this is a good wildlife-watching trail that ends at the Nong Phak Chi observation tower. It makes a good combination with Trail 3.

Trail 6 (8km) The longest marked trail in the park goes from the visitors centre to Haew Suwat waterfall. It used to be open to independent trekking, but it's not well-trodden so many people got lost; some were even forced to sleep in the forest overnight. Now guides are required. Overall it's not too difficult, though there are a few rough spots and big hills.

Wildlife Watching

Both the size and variety of habitats make Khao Yai one of the best wildlife-watching spots in Thailand. Rising to 1351m at the summit of Khao Rom, the park's terrain covers five vegetation zones: evergreen rainforest (100m to 400m), semi-evergreen rainforest (400m to 900m), mixed decid-uous forest (northern slopes at 400m to 600m), hill evergreen forest (over 1000m) and savanna-secondary-growth forest in ar-eas where agriculture and logging occurred before the area was protected.

Around 200 elephants tramp the park's boundaries. Other mammals include tigers, leopards, bears, gaur, barking deer, otters, various gibbons, macaques and some rather large pythons. Khao Yai's bird list boasts 392 species, and one of Thailand's largest popu-lations of hornbills lives here, including the great hornbill (*nók gòk* or *nók gah·hang*).

There are several **viewpoints** and **salt licks** (sometimes attracting elephants in the late afternoon and early morning) along the roads through the park. The best chance for seeing elephants is during a **night safari** (☑086 092 6529; per vehicle up to 10 people 500B; ⊙7pm & 8pm), where you also stand a good chance of seeing porcupines and jackals. You'll probably hear gibbons in the morning, but seeing them will require some walking – Trail 1 (p419) is a good place to try. You'll have to be very lucky (like lottery-winner lucky) to see a tiger. You will, however, surely see sam-bar deer, which congregate around the visitors centre and the Lam Tha Khong Campground in the morning and afternoon, and macaques, which roam park roads all day.

The **Nong Phak Chi observation tower** overlooks a little lake and a salt lick, and is one of the best wildlife-spotting sites in the park. The shortest way (900m) to the tower is a wide, easy path starting 1.8km north of the visitors centre, but two park hiking trails (p419) also go there.

👉 Tours

Most hotels and resorts around Khao Yai arrange park tours. This is the ideal way to visit because a good guide will show you creatures you probably won't see on your own.

Three established companies – **Green-leaf Guesthouse & Tour** (☑089 424 8809; www.greenleaftour.com; Km 7.5, Th Thanarat; full-day tour 1500B), **Khao Yai Garden Lodge** (☑044 936352, 094 191 9176; www.khaoyaigarden-lodge.net; Km 7, Th Thanarat; d incl breakfast 950B; 🅿️❄️@🛜🏊) and **Bobby's Apartments & Jungle Tours** (☑086 262 7006; www.bob-bysjungletourkhaoyai.com; off Th Mittaphap, Pak Chong) – have pretty much cornered the budget group-tour market, and they have long earned praise for their tours, though the lodging is mostly aimed at backpackers and is not right for everyone. The typical trip is for one and a half days and costs around 1500B per person, though many people opt to do just the full-day portion. Lunch, snacks, wa-ter and 'leech socks' are always included, and free pick-up in Pak Chong town might be. The full-day program includes a morn-ing walk in the forest looking for wildlife, a visit to a waterfall and a drive around park roads looking for elephants. The half-day portion stays outside the park to visit a cave, swim in a spring and watch a million or so wrinkle-lipped bats disgorge from a moun-tain-top cave.

Khao Yai & Beyond (☑089 946 1906; www.khaoyaiandbeyond.com) is a small company whose speciality is remote overnight trips with camping in the forest; all camping equipment is provided. One noted **bird-watching** guide is Tony, who owns **Khao Yai Nature Life & Tours** (☑096 565 5926; www.khaoyainaturelifetours.com).

The park offers one-hour night safaris, us-ing spotlights to look for animals.

🛏️ Sleeping

There are dozens of places to stay on and near Th Thanarat (Rte 2090), the road lead-ing to the park, and plenty too in the not-so-pleasant gateway town of Pak Chong. Most places can provide transport to/from Pak Chong, and the popular budget places will provide this for free if you are doing a tour with them. Most offer weekday and low-season (April to October) discounts of up to 40%.

The best setting for sleeping is, of course, in the park itself. There are campsites and a variety of rooms and bungalows around the park; none have air-con, but some have TVs and refrigerators. There's a 30% discount Monday to Thursday. Note that you must book from the annoying national-park web-site (http://nps.dnp.go.th/reservation.php; requires advanced payment) or in person at the park; phone reservations aren't allowed. Lodging is often fully booked except for low-season weekdays. Tent rental is almost always available.

In the Park

Khao Yai National Park – Pa Kluai Mai Campground
CAMPGROUND $

(☎086 092 6529; http://nps.dnp.go.th/reservation.php; Khao Yai National Park; per person with own tent 30B, camping gear rental 285B (tent 225B, sleeping bag 30B, roll mat 20B, pillow 10B); ℗) Smaller and with more forest, this campground is 2km up the road from the Lam Tha Khong Campground and is the better of the two for nature lovers. However, backpackers should note that there's limited late-afternoon traffic passing by.

Khao Yai National Park – Lam Tha Khong Campground
CAMPGROUND $

(☎086 092 6529; http://nps.dnp.go.th/reservation.php; Khao Yai National Park; per person with own tent 30B, camping gear rental 285B (tent 225B, sleeping bag 30B, roll mat 20B, pillow 10B); ℗) The larger and more modern of Khao Yai's two campgrounds is 6km from the visitors centre on the road to Nam Tok Haew Suwat (p417). It can be jam-packed and noisy when full of Thai students, which is most weekends and school breaks.

Khao Yai National Park – Zone 4
BUNGALOW $$

(Thanarat; ☎086 092 6529; http://nps.dnp.go.th/reservation.php; Khao Yai National Park; d 800B, bungalows 3000-3500B; ℗) This place is larger and less wooded than Zone 2, but the big mountain view makes it just as pleasant. There are a lot of birds (and potentially wildlife) around plus an observation tower. There are both bungalows (two and three bedrooms for four to six people) and some simple rooms; the four-person rooms have shared facilities. It's 5km south of the visitors centre, just off the main road.

Khao Yai National Park – Zone 3
ROOMS $$

(Suratsawadee; ☎086 092 6529; http://nps.dnp.go.th/reservation.php; Khao Yai National Park; tw 800B; ℗) Down below a large 'youth camp' dormitory, which is potentially noisy though often empty, this zone has aging but still comfortable rooms with large front porches. There's no food available here. It's 1.5km from the visitors centre.

★ Khao Yai National Park – Zone 2
BUNGALOW $$$

(Thio That; ☎086 092 6529; http://nps.dnp.go.th/reservation.php; Khao Yai National Park; bungalows 2000-2400B; ℗) The smallest zone, Thio That is a pleasant place on a shady hillside 2.5km from the visitors centre. There are five two-bedroom, two-bathroom bungalows with beds for either six or eight people. There's no restaurant. It's along a seldom-travelled dead-end road, so don't stay here if you don't have your own vehicle.

Khao Yai National Park – Zone 1
BUNGALOW $$$

(Kong Kaew; ☎086 092 6529; http://nps.dnp.go.th/reservation.php; Khao Yai National Park; bungalows 2400-9000B; ℗) This is a shady, somewhat cramped area behind the visitors centre. It has large bungalows meant for groups.

Outside the Park

Greenleaf Guesthouse
GUESTHOUSE $

(☎089 424 8809; www.greenleaftour.com; Km 7.5, Th Thanarat; d 300B) Kao Yai's budget-tour specialist also has a simple but pleasant little guesthouse with fan-cooled rooms off a leafy back garden, and a roadside restaurant out front. It doesn't rent bikes or motorbikes, but the sŏrng·tăa·ou that shuttle between Pak Chong and the park gate pass by.

San Khao Yai Guesthouse
BUNGALOW $$

(☎086 245 7882; www.sankhaoyaitour.com; Th Thanarat; bungalows 800B; ℗✱🛜) These colourful cottages just 100m from the park entrance are basic but very clean and a step up from most other budget lodging in the area. There's no better place to be if you want to stay outside the park but get an early start on your wildlife-watching. It also rents out motorcycles (per day 500B; deposit 20,000B or passport), arranges tours and serves food and beer.

★ Hotel des Artists
HOTEL $$$

(☎044 297444; hoteldesartists@gmail.com; Km 22, Th Thanarat; d incl breakfast from 2800B; ℗✱@🛜🏊) This tasteful hotel goes for French-colonial chic rather than the typical nature theme, though with its mountain views out the back you won't forget where you are. The rooms are gorgeous, though small, and open out beside an unusual, slimline swimming pool.

Balios HOTEL $$$

(☑ 044 365971; www.balioskhaoyai.com; Km 17, Th Thanarat; d incl breakfast 2700-4600B; P ❄ @ ☏ ☸) Khao Yai's original luxury lodge has kept up with the times and has an attractive, vaguely Italian theme. All of the rooms have patios overlooking either the pool or the attractive gardens and are tastefully designed.

🛏 In Pak Chong

At Home Hostel HOSTEL $

(☑ 081 490 6601; Pak Chong; dm 280-300B, d 600-750B; ❄ ☏) This friendly hostel is run by helpful staff who speak excellent English, and is the best of a handful of hostels in Pak Chong. It rents motorbikes (per day 300B), but it's a long slog to the park from here. The hostel is down the lane diagonally opposite the 7-Eleven near from where the *sŏrng·tǎa·ou* leave to get to the park.

From the train station, walk straight ahead, turn left at the main road and take the second right.

✘ Eating

The park itself has restaurants at all busy locations, including the visitors centre, campgrounds and some waterfalls, but they all close early, so plan ahead. The last service at the visitors centre is 6pm and elsewhere the times aren't fixed. Outside the park there are many restaurants along Th Thanarat, including a surprising number serving Italian food.

Yaek Kut Kha Night Market MARKET $

(แยกกุดคั้ก; Km 20, Th Thanarat; ☯ 3.30-7.30pm) A bustling night market serving take-home food to the local community. A few street carts in this area are open during the morning hours, too.

Roma Sausage INTERNATIONAL $$

(Km 18, Th Thanarat; mains 80-850B; ☯ 10.30am-9.30pm Sun-Tue & Thu, to 11pm Fri & Sat; P ☏) This casual alfresco spot on one of the busiest stretches of Th Thanarat manages to succeed at both Thai (yellow curry with mackerel and crispy tofu *lâhp*) and European (smoked chicken wings, duck confit and ultra-thin pizzas) food.

Khrua Khao Yai THAI $$

(Km 13.5, Th Thanarat; mains 100-270B; ☯ 9am-8pm, to 9pm if busy; P ☏ ✎) This open-air hut is hugely popular with visiting Bangkokians because of both the quality of the food and the emphasis on healthy eating, with choices such as mushroom *dôm yam* and stir-fried sunflower sprouts. The English-language menu is limited, so if you don't see what you want it's worth asking if it's available.

ℹ Information

Khao Yai National Park Visitors Centre
(☑ 086 092 6529; Khao Yai National Park; ☯ 6am-9pm, staffed from 8am) The staff here are friendly and knowledgeable and many speak good English. There are displays giving a quick overview of the park's ecology, and there's also a little **cafe** through the back with decking overlooking the river.

ℹ Getting There & Away

Sŏrng·tǎa·ou (Th Mittaphap, Pak Chong) travel the 30km from Pak Chong down Th Thanarat to the park's northern gate (40B, one hour) every 30 minutes from 6am to 5pm. They start their journey from near the 7-Eleven by the deer statue. It's another 14km to the visitors centre, but park guards are used to talking drivers into hauling people up there if there's a big group. Alternatively, rent a motorcycle from San Khao Yai Guesthouse (p421) beside the gate. The last *sŏrng·tǎa·ou* from the park gate back to Pak Chong departs around 3pm.

Pak Chong does not have a bus station: all departures are from the centre of town along the main road. Frequent minivans (66B, 1½ hours) and occasional 2nd-class buses (56B, two hours) to Khorat use a **bus stop** (Th Mittaphap, Pak Chong) about 500m northeast of the deer statue near *dà·làht kàak* market between 5am and 6pm. Minivans to Bangkok (160B, three hours, every 30 minutes) depart from both sides of the road near the deer statue. First-class buses to both Bangkok (133B, three hours) and Khorat (72B, 1½ hours) stop at **Ratchasima Tour** (☑ 044 312131; Th Mittaphap, Pak Chong) across the highway from the deer statue; the last departure to Bangkok is 8pm. You can also catch minivans (departing from Khorat) to Ayuthaya (100B, 2½ hours) and Lopburi (80B, two hours) directly across the street from *dà·làht kàak* market (wait at the benches in the traffic island), if they have empty seats when they pass through, which they usually do.

You can also get to Pak Chong easily by **train** (☑ 044 311534) from Bangkok (86B to 292B, four to 4½ hours, every two hours) and Khorat (18B to 251B, 1½ hours, every two hours), as well as other destinations in Isan. Trains are less frequent than buses/minivans, but much more comfortable, far cheaper and a lot safer. There's no need to book tickets in advance; just buy one at the station and hop on the next train. Note that express trains are much more expensive than ordinary trains as they don't have a third class, which is the best-value ticket to get.

Ayuthaya has no direct bus service and not many minivans, so the train (23B to 363B, two to three hours, 10 daily) is definitely the best option.

If you are driving from Bangkok, there's a second, seldom-used southern entrance in Prachinburi Province.

ⓘ Getting Around

The sights and the services are quite spread out, so you limit yourself by visiting without a vehicle, but not as much as you might think since it's really quite easy to catch a lift in the park during the day. However, getting a ride is never a sure thing so you shouldn't come without wheels if you aren't willing to walk.

Motorcycle is a good way to visit the park and they can be hired from San Khao Yai Guesthouse (p421) (per day 500B, deposit 20,000B or passport) near the park gate, or from several shops on the main thoroughfare through Pak Chong, including Thai Yen, which is across from the road to the train station.

Bicycles are available for rent in the park visitors centre for 50/200B per hour/day. But remember, the park name means 'Big Mountain' and there are a lot of ups and downs between destinations.

BURIRAM PROVINCE

The city of Buriram (บุรีรัมย์) is a friendly place, but lacks much of interest to tourists. The southern reaches of the province, on the other hand, have some of Thailand's must-see Khmer relics. The countryside is peppered with dozens of ancient ruins, the crowning glory of which is Phanom Rung, a beautifully restored complex climbing to the summit of an extinct volcano. The most spectacular Angkor monument in Thailand, Phanom Rung is well worth the journey and should impress even those who've already experienced Angkor Wat in Cambodia.

Nang Rong

📞 044 / POP 21,260

The workaday town of Nang Rong (นางรอง) is the most convenient base for visiting Phanom Rung Historical Park. A full range of services and a good selection of hotels make it a friendly and comfortable stay.

🛏 Sleeping

P California Inter Hostel GUESTHOUSE **$**
(📞 081 808 3347; www.pcalifornianangrong.webs. com; Th Sangkakrit; d with fan 250-350B, with air-

con 450-650B; 🅿 ✴ 🛜) This great place on the eastern side of town offers bright, nicely decorated rooms and a shady central yard that makes a pleasant spot for breakfast (100B). English-speaking owner Khun Wicha has a wealth of knowledge about the area, can give you a map of the surrounding countryside and advise you on the best way to explore.

Bicycles are free. Motorbikes are for rent (per day 250B). It's 2.5km from the bus station; turn left out of the station, right onto the highway, and keep going until you see the sign on your right. A motorcycle taxi/taxi costs 50/60B, but they'll pick you up if you call ahead.

Nang Rong Hotel HOTEL **$**
(📞 044 631014; Th Phradit Pana; d 450B; ✴ 🛜) This new budget hotel has rooms that are plain but smart and clean, and unlike other options, it's smack bang in the middle of town. Free bicycles, too. It's 2km from the bus station; turn right out of the station, left at the end, and keep on walking, past the lakes, until you see it on your right.

Socool Grand Hotel HOTEL **$$$**
(📞 044 632333; www.socoolgrand.com; Th Sapakitkoson; d incl breakfast 1500-2500B; 🅿 ✴ 🛜 ❄) Most certainly cool, this boutique-like hotel with attractive black-and-white decor and funky wicker furniture, is top of the heap in Nang Rong. Rooms are spacious, bright and comfortable and there's a large pool-fitness complex in front. It's 1.5km from the bus station; turn left out of the station, right onto the highway, then look for the sign on the left.

Nang Rong Night Market MARKET **$**
(Sankhakrit; ⏰ 5-10pm Fri & Sat) This surprisingly large night market has plenty of Thai street food on offer. It's mostly grab-and-go takeaways, but a couple of stalls have tables and chairs for a no-frills evening meal. It's 400m west of P California Inter Hostel (left as you exit the hostel), and one block behind Nang Rong Hotel.

ⓘ Getting There & Away

Nang Rong's **bus station** (📞 044 631517) is on the western side of town and sees buses to/from all big cities in southern Isan including Surin (80B to 100B, two hours, every 30 minutes), Ubon Ratchathani (144B to 265B, six to seven hours, 12 daily), Khorat (60B to 95B, two hours, hourly) and Pak Chong (125B, three hours, hourly), plus Bangkok (231B to 300B, six to seven hours, hourly).

ℹ Getting Around

P California Inter Hostel (p423) rents motorcycles (per day 250B) and gives you a map of the local area. It also runs Phanom Rung tours (half-day per car 700B). Baan Bong Pha Om, which is closer to the main ruins, also rents motorbikes (per day 250B). Nang Rong **taxis** (☑ 093 551 4175, 092 478 0529) park at the bus station; a return trip to Phanom Rung should run to about 1000B and it costs 200B to add Muang Tam.

Phanom Rung Historical Park

The most spectacular Khmer monument in Thailand, Prasat Phanom Rung (พนมรุ้ง) or 'Big Mountain Temple' sits on the summit of a spent volcano 200m above the paddy fields. The dramatic entrance and beautiful design make it a must-visit attraction for anyone in the area.

About 8km down below is the wonderful but often overlooked Prasat Muang Tam or 'Lower City Temple', which is also part of the historical park. It's smaller and less complete, but the peaceful setting – you'll often have it to yourself – and unique design make many people prefer it over its more famous neighbour.

◉ Sights

★ Prasat Phanom Rung   RUINS
(ปราสาทเขาพนมรุ้ง; ☑ 044 666251; 100B, combined ticket with Prasat Muang Tam 150B; ⊙ 6am-6pm) Prasat Phanom Rung has a knock-you-dead location. Crowning the summit of a spent volcano, this sanctuary sits 200m above the paddy fields below. To the southeast you can see Cambodia's Dongrek Mountains, and it's in this direction that the capital of the Angkor empire once lay. The temple was erected as a Hindu monument to Shiva between the 10th and 13th centuries, the bulk of it during the reign of King Suriyavarman II (r CE 1113–50).

Below the main sanctuary, above the long row of gift shops, an information centre (ศูนย์ข้อมูลพนมรุ้ง; ⊙ 8.30am-4.30pm) FREE houses artefacts found at the site and displays about both the construction and the restoration, which took 17 years. You can pick up a free informative brochure or arrange a Thai-speaking guide (price is negotiable) here. Those who don't want to climb can use an upper car park (per car 50B), but the brochure usually isn't available there,

and you'll miss out on the fabulous promenade leading up to the main gate.

In fact, the promenade is one of the most remarkable aspects of Phanom Rung. It begins on a slope 400m east of the main tower with three earthen terraces. Next comes a cruciform base for what may have been a wooden pavilion. To the right of this is the Phlab Phla, assumed to be where royalty bathed and changed clothes before entering the temple complex. You then step down to a 160m-long processional walkway flanked by sandstone pillars with early Angkor-style lotus-bud tops. This walkway ends at the first and largest of three naga bridges, flanked by 16 five-headed *naga* (mythical serpent) in the classic Angkor style. As at all Khmer temples, these symbolic 'bridges' represent the passing from the earthly realm to the heavenly.

At the top, the magnificent east gallery leads into the main sanctuary. The main tower has a gallery on each of its four sides, and excellent sculptures of Shiva and Vaishnava deities can be seen in the lintels and pediments over the doorways and in various other key points on the exterior. On the eastern portico of the mandapa (hall in front of the main tower) is a Nataraja (Dancing Shiva) and the well-known Narai Bandhomsindhu lintel, which represent the destruction and rebirth of the universe respectively, while on the southern entrance are the remains of Shiva and Uma riding their bull mount, Nandi. The central cell of the main tower contains a Shiva lingam, and in front of it is an evocative Nandi statue.

★ Prasat Muang Tam   RUINS
(ปราสาทเมืองต่ำ; ☑ 044 666251; 100B, combined ticket with Prasat Phanom Rung 150B; ⊙ 6am-6pm) In the little village of Khok Meuang, the restored Khmer temple of Prasat Muang Tam is an ideal bolt-on to any visit to Phanom Rung, which is only 8km to the northwest. Dating back to the late 10th or early 11th century, this is generally considered Isan's third most interesting temple complex in terms of size, atmosphere and the quality of restoration work, but because so few people visit (you might have it all to yourself) it is some people's favourite.

The whole complex, built as a shrine to Shiva, has an unusual layout. Most significantly, the five towers (the main one could not be rebuilt) are grouped three in front and two in back rather than the expected quincunx cross shape. Also, Muang Tam

Around Phanom Rung

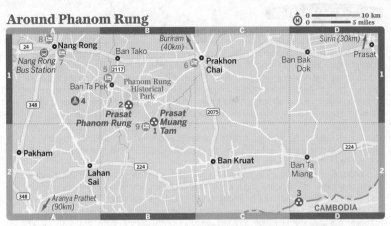

is the only Khmer temple to have four L-shaped ponds at each corner.

Begin your visit across the road in the small information centre (⊘8am-4.30pm), next to Baray Muang Tam (a 510m-by-1090m Khmer-era reservoir), which has good displays about the site.

Motorcycle/car taxis will add Muang Tam onto a trip to Phanom Rung for another 100/200B.

✨ Festivals & Events

Phanom Rung Festival   CULTURAL
(⊘Apr) Phanom Rung faces east, and four times a year the sun can be seen through all 15 sanctuary doorways. The correct solar alignment happens during sunrise from 3 to 5 April and 8 to 10 September and sunset from 5 to 7 March and 5 to 7 October (some years are one day earlier). The park extends its hours during these events, and locals celebrate the Phanom Rung Festival around the April alignment with ancient Brahman ceremonies and modern sound-and-light shows.

🛏 Sleeping

The best of the very limited accommodation in the immediate area of the temple complex is Thanyaporn Homestay (p426), a great budget guesthouse very near Prasat Muang Tam (though 8km downhill from Phanom Rung). Staying at the wonderful Baan Bong Pha Om in the village of Ban Ta Pek is another option, as they rent motorbikes. Most people, though, spend the night in Nang Rong, the nearest town, where you can also rent motorbikes.

Around Phanom Rung

★ **Baan Bong Pha Om**   GUESTHOUSE $
(☏084 236 5060, 095 620 5932; Ban Ta Pek; d incl breakfast 490-1000B; P❄🛜) Bringing artistic flair and fantastic value to the rice fields of rural Buriram, this family-run place is fun, attractive and utterly relaxing. Many of the 14 creative rooms are up on stilts, with balconies and open-air showers. Some are in converted shipping containers, while the best – the House rooms (690B) and the Big Room (1000B) – are borderline luxurious and worth the extra baht.

The charmingly cluttered, open-sided cafe-bar area is a wonderful place to chill

OTHER KHMER RUINS AROUND PHANOM RUNG

For those with an insatiable appetite for Khmer ruins, the area around Phanom Rung offers a smorgasbord of lesser-known sites that, taken together, create a picture of the crucial role this region once played in the Khmer empire. Most people find these places of only minor interest, but driving through this rice-growing region offers an unvarnished look at village life and will surely make for an enlightening trip. All of the following sites, restored to some degree by the Fine Arts Department, are free of charge and open during daylight hours.

Kuti Reusi Nong Bua Rai sits right below Phanom Rung to the east, and the similar but more atmospheric Kuti Reusi Khok Meuang is just northwest of Prasat Muang Tam across the road from Baray Muang Tam.

Little of Prasat Khao Plaibat is left standing, but the adventure of finding it, along with cool views of Phanom Rung and the Dangrek Mountains on the Cambodian border, makes it worth seeking out. The seldom-used trail starts at Wat Khao Plaibat, 3km from Prasat Muang Tam. Pass the gate (even though there's a 'monk zone, no entry' sign in Thai on the gate, we have been assured that it's okay to use this path to visit the ruin) behind the giant Buddha image, veer right at the gùdì (monks' quarters) and slip through the barbed-wire fence. From here take the path to the right, and then a quick left up the hill and follow the strips of orange cloth tied to trees. The walk up the hill should take less than 30 minutes if you don't get lost along the way, though it's likely you will. Just keep aiming for the top of the hill and you'll eventually get there.

Prasat Khok Ngio, 3km before Pakham, has a small, dirty museum with old pots, human bones and Buddha images unearthed at and near the temple.

Prasat Thong (aka Khok Prasat), near the market in the middle of Ban Kruat town, is small and the three towers have lost their tops, but it's worth a stop if you're passing through.

The sandstone used to build these ancient structures came from the widely scattered Lan Hin Dtat Ban Kruat (Ban Kruat quarry), which is best seen at Wat Lan Hin Dtat, southwest of Ban Kruat town. Several cutting sites can be seen along a 1km-long surfaced path that starts east of the parking lot. The biggest cutting site is 100m down a side branch of this path: from the parking lot take the trail to the right after the Buddha statue and it's just past the last gùdì.

Also near Ban Kruat are Tao Nai Chian and the larger Tao Sawai, two kilns that supplied pottery to much of the Khmer empire between the 9th and 13th centuries. Today they're little more than piles of dirt and brick with protective roofs over them.

You can easily add Surin Province's Prasat Ta Meuan (p435) to your trip around this region. It's 55km from Phanom Rung.

with a cold beer or a smooth cup of drip coffee, and the reggae-loving owner will happily set the mood with a few choice tunes. This also makes an ideal base for exploring Phanom Rung; it's closer to the ruins than Nang Rong, and it rents motorbikes too (per day 250B).

To get here, take any Khorat–Surin bus and ask to get off at the intersection at Ban Tako, from where you can get a motorcycle taxi to Ban Ta Pek village. The guesthouse, which is signposted from the village, is 700m west of the village crossroads. If you call ahead, though, they'll pick you up from the Ban Tako intersection.

Thanyaporn Homestay GUESTHOUSE $
(☑087 431 3741; d incl breakfast 500-800B; P❈☜) This modern and cosy guesthouse is just 500m southwest of Prasat Muang Tam ruins (turn right out of the complex, right again, and it's soon on your left), and staying here lets you enjoy village life without needing to rough it. There's no English name on the sign; look for the orange building on the corner that says 'Homestay & Guesthouse'.

Whilst you'll be able to walk from here to the ruins at Muang Tam, you'll be 8km downhill from Phanom Rung, though finding a lift shouldn't be too difficult.

Hotel de l'Amour HOTEL $$$
(☎ 044 651555; www.hotel-delamour.com; Rte 24, Prakhon Chai; incl breakfast r 3445-3700B, ste 8240B; P ✳ @ 🛜 ☲) A surprising find for this remote region, this is a proper four-star hotel in the small town of Prakhon Chai. Every square centimetre is beautiful and you're taken care of by properly trained, albeit timid, staff. Though the plush rooms are overpriced, especially considering the meagre breakfast, it has no competition in this class.

It's also possible to visit without your own transport as the hotel is on the main Bangkok–Surin highway, and once you're there it can organise private tours by car of Phanom Rung and Muang Tam (per car 1900B). It also rents motorbikes (per day 400B).

❶ Getting There & Around

There's no public transport to Phanom Rung or Muang Tam. The best budget option is hiring a motorcycle (per day 250B) from either P California Inter Hostel (p423) in Nang Rong or Baan Bong Pha Om (p425) in the village of Ban Ta Pek. There are no longer motorcycle taxis in Ban Ta Pek. You can go by motorcycle taxi (600B return) or car with driver (1000B) from Nang Rong. It costs 100/200B for the motorcycle/car to add Muang Tam.

P California Inter Hostel's standard half-day tour of Phanom Rung and Muang Tam (per car 700B) is good value if you're in a group. You can also add on extras such as Wat Khao Angkhan and a silk-weaving village.

Alternatively, you can take a bus from Nang Rong (or any Khorat–Surin bus) to the busy Ban Tako (20B to 30B, 20 minutes, every 30 minutes) junction 14km east of Nang Rong, where motorcycle taxis usually charge 300B to Phanom Rung, including waiting time, but they sometimes demand more from non-Thai speakers. Buses from further afield (Pak Chong, Surin etc) also stop here, so if you are only visiting on a day trip you don't need to go into Nang Rong first.

UBON RATCHATHANI PROVINCE

Little-visited Ubon Ratchathani (จังหวัด อุบลราชธานี) is one of Thailand's most interesting provinces. The capital city has plenty of history and charm, as does the laid-back riverside village of Khong Jiam and the fascinating national parks that surround it. The scenery along the Mekong River is often as bizarre as it is gorgeous and Pha Taem Na-tional Park has so much to see that it warrants a couple of days. Even more remote is the jungle-clad intersection of Thailand, Laos and Cambodia, now known as the 'Emerald Triangle' (inspired by northern Thailand's 'Golden Triangle') due to the magnificent jungle landscape of Phu Chong Nayoi National Park.

Ubon Ratchathani

☎ 045 / POP 86,800

Few cities in Isan reward aimless wandering as richly as Ubon Ratchathani (อุบลราชธานี). Survive the usual knot of choked access roads, and the 'Royal City of the Lotus' will reveal an altogether more attractive face. Racked up against Mae Nam Mun, Thailand's second-longest river, the historic heart of the city, south of Th Kheuan Thani, has a sluggish character rarely found in the region's big conurbations. And throughout the city there are many interesting temples beckoning culture-loving travellers.

Ubon grew prosperous as a US airbase during the Vietnam War and is now a financial, educational and agricultural market centre. It's not a busy tourist destination, but the nearby Thai–Lao border crossing at Chong Mek generates a small but steady stream of travellers who by and large enjoy their visit.

◉ Sights

Temples

Wat Thung Si Meuang BUDDHIST TEMPLE
(วัดทุ่งศรีเมือง; Th Luang; ⊙ daylight hours) FREE
Built during the reign of Rama III (1824–51), Wat Thung Si Meuang has a classic *hŏr đrai* (Tripitaka hall) in excellent shape. Like many *hŏr đrai,* it rests on stilts in the middle of a pond to protect the precious scriptures (written on palm-leaf paper) from termites. It's kept open so you can look inside. The original murals in the little *bòht* beside the *hŏr đrai* show life in that era and are in remarkably good condition.

Wat Ban Na Meuang BUDDHIST TEMPLE
(วัดบ้านนาเมือง; ⊙ daylight hours) FREE This temple, also known as Wat Sa Prasan Suk, stands out from other temples in many ways. Most famously, the *bòht* sits on a boat: a ceramic-encrusted replica of the late King Rama IX's royal barge *Suphannahong,* complete with crew. The *wí·hăhn* also has a boat-shaped base, this one resembling the

Ubon Ratchathani

second-most-important royal barge, *Anantanagaraj*; and it's surrounded by an actual pond.

These were not just artistic endeavours: the water represents our desires and the boats represent staying above them. The commissioner of these creations, Luang Pu Boon Mi, died in 2001 and there's a memorial to him under the large Buddha, though his relics are in the *săh·lah* alongside the boat *bòht*. To reach all of these you pass under an immense statue of Airavata (Erawan in Thai), Hindu god Indra's three-headed elephant mount.

The temple is north of the airport. *Sŏrng·tăa·ou* 8 passes near, but you need to tell the driver you're going here or he won't make the turn down the little road.

Wat Si Pradu BUDDHIST TEMPLE
(วัดศรีประดู่; Th Buraphanok; ⊙daylight hours) **FREE** This temple's lovely, modern *bòht* has a soaring wing-shaped design that creates a

striking scene inside. The delightful murals cover many subjects including the *Jataka* (past life stories of the Buddha) and feature many brightly coloured creatures from the mythical Himmapan forest.

A neighbourhood women's group does various handicrafts in a couple of buildings on the grounds.

Wat Phra That Nong Bua BUDDHIST TEMPLE
(วัดพระธาตุหนองบัว; Th Thammawithi; ⊙daylight hours, chedi 7am-7pm) **FREE** This spectacular, gleaming gold-and-white *chedi* is sure to dazzle. It loosely resembles the Mahabodhi stupa in Bodhgaya, India (where the Buddha reached enlightenment), and inside is another beautiful golden *chedi*. The latter was built in 1956 in honour of the 2500th anniversary of Buddhism, and the 55m-tall exterior went up over it 12 years later.

The temple is on the outskirts of town, reached by *sŏrng·tăa·ou* 10.

Ubon Ratchathani

Wat Sri Ubon Rattanaram BUDDHIST TEMPLE
(วัดศรีอุบลรัตนาราม; Th Uparat; ⊙daylight hours)
FREE The *bòht* at this important temple was
built to resemble Bangkok's Wat Benchama-
bophit (p89), but it's the 7cm-tall topaz
Buddha inside that most Thais come to see.
Phra Kaew Butsarakham, as it's known, was
reportedly brought here from Vientiane at
Ubon's founding and is one of the city's holiest possessions. It sits behind glass high up
the back wall, all but out of sight. The image
directly in front of the largest Buddha is a
copy and actual-sized replicas are for sale.

Wat Jaeng BUDDHIST TEMPLE
(วัดแจ้ง; Th Nakhonban; ⊙daylight hours) **FREE**
Founded around the same time as the city,
Wat Jaeng has an adorable Lan Xang–style
bòht (built in 1887) with large *naga* eave
brackets on the sides, crocodiles along the
stairs and Airavata with two mythical lions
atop the carved wooden facade. A travelling market fills up the grounds every
Wednesday.

Other Sights

**Ubon Ratchathani
National Museum** MUSEUM
(พิพิธภัณฑสถานแห่งชาติอุบลราชธานี; Th Kheuan
Thani; 100B; ⊙9am-4pm Wed-Sun) Occupying the former city hall (built in 1918), this
is a very informative museum with plenty
on show, from Dvaravati-era Buddhas and
2000-year-old Dong Son bronze drums to
Ubon textiles and clever little animal traps.
The museum's most prized possession is a
9th-century Khmer Ardhanarisvara, a com-
posite statue combining Shiva and his con-
sort Uma into one being. It's one of just two
ever found in Thailand.

**Wat Sri Ubon
Rattanaram Museum** MUSEUM
(พิพิธภัณฑ์วัดศรีอุบลรัตนาราม; Th Uparat; ⊙9am-
4pm Wed-Sun) **FREE** The temple has turned
a beautiful old wooden *săh·lah* (hall) into
a museum of religious items. The highlight
is the collection of 18th-century *đôô prá
đraiþìdòk,* cabinets used for storing sacred
palm-leaf texts.

Thung Si Meuang PARK
(ทุ่งศรีเมือง) The centrepiece of this city-
centre park is a huge concrete Candle
Parade statue (ต้นเทียนเฉลิมพระเกียรติ ทุ่ง
ศรีเมือง). The City Pillar Shrine (ศาลเจ้า
หลักเมือง, San Lak Meuang) is to the south.

Hat Wat Tai BEACH
(หาดวัดใต้) **FREE** Locals flock to this island
beach in Mae Nam Mun during the hot, dry
months from February to May when the

sand rises out of the receding river. A cool makeshift bamboo bridge connects it to the northern shore and bamboo-raft restaurants set up shop on the water.

🏃 Activities

Ubonvej Thai Massage
MASSAGE
(☎045 260345; 113 Th Thepyothi; 1/2hr massage from 200/280B; ⊗9.30am-10pm) The front door declares boldly 'No Sex', but step inside this classy place and this would never be in doubt. There are many different kinds of massage to choose from besides just the standard Thai, and some English is spoken.

Legacy Gym
MARTIAL ARTS
(☎045 264708, 089 627 8423; www.legacy gymthailand.com; Th Srisangthong; half-/full-day sessions 400/700B, training with accommodation per month from 12,500B) This gym, 3km northeast of town, is run by Ole Laursen, a Filipino-Danish former professional *moo·ay tai* (Thai boxing) fighter now living in Ubon. It's well set up for Westerners and offers accommodation and training packages. Women and men train here (although there's no 'women-only' session) and it's suitable for both serious fighters and those just wanting to train in fitness.

🎆 Festivals & Events

Candle Parade
CULTURAL
(Kabuan Hae Tian; ⊗usually Jul) Ubon's famous Candle Parade began during the reign of Rama V, when the appointed governor decided the rocket festival (p436) was too dangerous. The original simple designs have since grown (with the help of internal frames) to gigantic, elaborately carved

wax sculptures. The parade is part of Khao Phansaa (the start of Buddhist Lent).

Prize-winning candles go on display along Th Srinarong next to Wat Thung Si Meuang for three days after the parade, and most of them will be parked at the city's temples (Wat Si Pradu (p428) and Wat Phra That Nong Bua (p428) are two of the better places to look) until the next June when the wax is melted down to construct a new one. The festival is very popular with Thai tourists and the city's hotels are booked out long in advance.

Lai Reua Fai
CULTURAL
(⊗late Oct/early Nov) Ubon has a modest Lai Reua Fai (illuminated boat procession) during Ork Phansaa (the end of Buddhist Lent).

🛌 Sleeping

28 Rachabutr Hostel
HOSTEL $
(☎089 144 3789; 28 Th Ratchabut; dm 180-230B, r with fan 280-380B, with air-con 430B; ❄️🛜) Friendly and welcoming, with a great location, this home-turned-hostel, run by a charming elderly woman, is very backpacker-friendly. Rooms are simple (the dorms have just thin mattresses on the floor), and it's shared bathrooms only, but the whole place has character, with bric-a-brac furniture and creaky wooden floorboards. Some rooms have partial river views. Also rents motorbikes (200B).

Phadaeng Hotel
HOTEL $
(☎045 254600; thephadaen@gmail.com; Th Phadaeng; d/tw 500/600B; 🅿️❄️@🛜) One of the best-value hotels in Ubon, Phadaeng has well-maintained rooms (they look almost brand new) with good furnishings including

---

WORTH A TRIP

HILLTOP TEMPLE
....

The peaceful Buddhist temple, **Wat Khao Angkhan** (วัดเขาอังคาร; ⊗daylight hours) **FREE**, sits in a forest atop an extinct volcano and has an ancient past, as evidenced by the 8th- or 9th-century Dvaravati sandstone boundary markers. But it's the modern constructions that make it worth a visit. The *bòht* (ordination hall) and several other flamboyant buildings were erected in 1982 in an unusual nouveau-Khmer style that sort of harks back to the age of empire. Inside the *bòht*, the Jataka murals, painted by Burmese artists, have English captions.

The temple also hosts a Chinese-style pagoda and a 29m reclining Buddha, and offers beautiful views of the surrounding mountains.

The temple is about 20km from either Nang Rong or Phanom Rung, but there's no public transport. However, the route is pretty well signposted, and easy to reach on rented motorbike from either Nang Rong or Ban Ta Pek.

ⓘ GETTING TO CAMBODIA: CHONG CHOM TO O SMACH
....

Getting to the border Because of the casino, there are plenty of public minibuses (45B, 1½ hours, frequent from 5.30am to 6.30pm) from Surin's bus terminal to the border at Chong Chom.

At the border The Cambodian border is open from 7am to 10pm and visas are available on the spot. There's a 5B fee at Thai immigration on weekends and early mornings//late afternoons.

Moving on There are two buses from O Smach to the City Angkor Hotel in Siem Reap (350B, three hours, 8am and 5pm). Chartering a 'taxi' (drivers wait at the border looking for passengers) for the drive to Siem Reap should cost 2000B or less, and you can wait for others to share the costs, though this is generally only possible in the morning.

---

large TVs and desks. It's a good location just minutes from Thung Si Meuang park, and the large parking area separates it from street noise. The hotel is livened up with copies of classic paintings. Bike hire costs 50B per day.

★ **Outside Inn**   GUESTHOUSE **$$**
(🗋 088 581 2069; www.theoutsideinnubon.com; 11 Th Suriyat; d incl breakfast 650-799B; 🅿 ❋ @ 🗟) A nice little garden lounge area sets the relaxed, communal vibe here. The rooms are large, comfy and fitted with tastefully designed reclaimed-timber furnishings. Owners Brent and Tun are great hosts, cook some good food (p432), and have lots of advice on what to see and do in the area.

It's a long walk to the town's main attractions, but there are bikes (free for guests; 50B per day for others) and motorcycles (per day 250B), and *sŏrng·tăa·ou* 10 can deliver you from the bus station.

T3 House   HOTEL **$$**
(🗋 045 244911; t3house.ubon@gmail.com; Soi Saphasit 1, Th Saphasit; d 600-700B; 🅿 ❋ 🗟) A solid option at this price, with a modern, stylish look and quality all around including rain showers, fast internet and excellent mattresses. It's tucked down a small soi so it's quite quiet. Breakfast isn't included in the price, but the lobby has a small cafe.

Sunee Grand Hotel   HOTEL **$$$**
(🗋 045 352900; www.suneegrandhotel.com; Th Chayangkun; d incl breakfast from 1800B; 🅿 ❋ @ 🗟 ❄) Although it's not truly 'grand', this is Ubon's best hotel. From the stylish light fixtures to the at-a-snap service, it will meet expectations. There's a piano in the lobby, airport pick-up and a spa, and the adjacent shopping mall has a cinema and a kid-sized rooftop water park. It routinely discounts down to 1400B for a standard room.

✖ Eating

★ **Rung Roj**   THAI **$**
(Th Nakhonban; mains 60-140B; ⊘ 10am-8.30pm Mon-Sat) An Ubon institution serving excellent food, using family recipes and only fresh ingredients. Many people swear by the ox-tongue stew. From the outside it looks more like a well-to-do house than a restaurant, and inside it has 1950s and '60s classic rock-and-roll music and decor to match.

Porntip Gai Yang Wat Jaeng   THAI **$**
(Th Saphasit; mains 40-130B; ⊘ 8am-6pm) It looks like a tornado has whipped through this no-frills spot, but the chefs cook up a storm of their own. This is considered by many to be Ubon's premier purveyor of *gài yâhng* (grilled chicken), *sôm·đam* (spicy green-papaya salad), sausages and other classic Isan foods. Eat in the fan-cooled shack out front, or with air-con out back.

Night Market   MARKET **$**
(Th Kheuan Thani; ⊘ 4.30-11pm) Though it's smaller than you'd expect, Ubon's city-centre night market makes an excellent dining destination, especially when paired with the weekend Walking Street Market (p432). Vendors sell Thai, Isan and Vietnamese food.

Jam   BARBECUE **$**
(Th Saphasit; small/large 89/119B; ⊘ 3.30-11pm) *Mu kratha* (หมูกระทะ) or 'pork pan' is very popular in Thailand. It's a combination of Korean barbeque and Chinese hotpot where you cook your own food on a table-top barbeque (pork on the hot plate, veggies in the broth). The small set at this buzzing outdoor restaurant is enough for one or two people. No English sign.

NORTHEASTERN THAILAND UBON RATCHATHANI

> **ⓘ GETTING TO LAOS: UBON RATCHATHANI TO PAKSE**
>
> **Getting to the border** Almost every traveller uses the direct Ubon Ratchathani–Pakse buses (200B, three hours, 9.30am and 2.30pm), which wait long enough for you to buy Lao visas at the border. Otherwise, Chong Mek's little bus terminal serves minivans to/ from Ubon Ratchathani (120B, two hours, every 30 minutes) via Khong Jiam and Phibun Mangsahan, and buses for Bangkok (484B to 638B, 12 hours, five daily). It's 600m from the bus station to the border; motorcycle taxis charge 20B.
>
> **At the border** The border is open from 6am to 8pm and the crossing, involving walking though an underground tunnel, is largely hassle-free. Although it seems like a scam, there is a legitimate overtime fee on the Laos side after 4pm weekdays and all day on weekends and holidays. The real scam is that the officials ask for 100B even though the actual price is 10,000 Lao kip (about 40B). Just tell them you want a receipt and you'll pay the correct price. They sometimes ask for this at other times, but they're usually not too insistent.
>
> **Moving on** Pakse is about an hour away in one of the frequent minivans (20,000K, 45 minutes) or *sŏrng·tăa·ou* that park in a dusty/muddy parking area about 500m from the Lao immigration office.

Chiokee

THAI $

(307-317 Th Keuan Thani; mains 30-200B; ⊙6am-2.30pm) A steady stream of old-timers linger over *congee* (rice porridge), tea and newspapers at this classic breakfast spot. Although it's less popular during the rest of the day, the menu has all your Thai favourites so it makes a nice lunch spot too.

Sam Chai Cafe

THAI $

(Th Phadaeng; mains 35-70B, coffee 15B; ⊙5.30am-1.30pm) Not really a cafe, this bustling breakfast stop serves *kôw dôm* (rice soup), *gŏo·ay dĕe·o* (noodle soup), *kài gà·tá* (pan egg with sausage) and traditional Thai coffee. The service is lightning-fast, and it's a great local experience. No English sign, but there's a clear, well-translated English menu.

Outside Inn

MEXICAN $

(11 Th Suriyat; mains 50-225B; ⊙11am-2.30pm & 5-9pm; P 🛜 🍴) This guesthouse (p431) restaurant sets itself apart with good Mexican meals (way above average for Thailand), but the Thai food is delicious, too. The menu also features sandwiches and a full roster of cocktails.

🍷 Drinking & Nightlife

★ LIFE Roaster

CAFE

(Th Suriyat; ⊙7am-6pm Thu-Tue) Local coffee enthusiast Nut has his own plantation up in Chiang Mai and he roasts his own beans in this funky and charming wooden coffee house to produce what is probably the best coffee in town. There's no food, but it does

some bakery treats, and the adjacent noodle joint is decent.

Ubon Tap Taste House

CRAFT BEER

(Th Phichitrangsan; ⊙5pm-midnight) The craft beers are all imported from abroad rather than brewed locally, but this modern, family-run bar has up to 14 taps on the go at a time, and plenty more bottled beers in the fridge.

Wrong Way

BAR

(Th Phadaeng; ⊙4pm-midnight Mon-Sat, from 6pm Sun) This friendly, laid-back cafe-bar has an open-fronted facade and a cosy atmosphere for a quiet street-side drink.

🛍 Shopping

Punchard

ARTS & CRAFTS

(☑089 719 9570; www.punchard.net; Th Phadaeng; ⊙9am-6.30pm Thu-Tue) Though pricey, this is the best all-round handicrafts shop in Ubon. It specialises in silks and homewares; many of its products merge old methods and modern designs.

Khampun

ARTS & CRAFTS

(☑045 424121; Th Phadaeng; ⊙9am-6pm) Ubon's most famous silk specialist makes some exquisite fabrics, often with original patterns not found elsewhere. For two days before the Candle Parade (p430), the owner hosts a mini cultural festival at his gorgeous home-workshop just outside town.

Walking Street Market

MARKET

(Th Srinarong; ⊙6-10.30pm Fri-Sun) This fun, youthful market takes over Th Srinarong and part of Thung Si Meuang (p429) park on weekends.

(p429)

Rawang Thang
ARTS & CRAFTS

(Th Kheuan Thani; ⊙8.30am-7pm) Specialising in locally themed cotton goods, this cute little shop sells fun and funky shirts, pillows, soft toys, postcards, picture frames and assorted bric-a-brac, most made and designed by the friendly husband-and-wife owners.

Camp Fai Ubon
TEXTILES

(Th Thepyothi; ⊙8.30am-5pm) You'll find a good assortment of affordable, stylish, contemporary Thai clothing, plus bags and fabric (much of it coloured with natural dyes) at this shop, which is signed as Peaceland. It also has a branch at the airport.

ℹ Information

There are plenty of ATMs dotted around the centre. The shopping mall attached to Sunee Grand Hotel (p431) also has banks.

Tourism Authority of Thailand (TAT; ☑045 243770; tatubon@tat.or.th; 264/1 Th Kheuan Thani; ⊙8.30am-4.30pm) Has helpful staff and a free city map.

Tourist Assistance Centre (☑086 361 4291; Ubon Ratchathani Bus Terminal) Run by the Ministry of Tourism and Sport, it has branches at the bus station, the train station and the airport.

Ubon Ratchathani Immigration (☑045 312133; Rajabhat University; ⊙8.30am-noon & 1-4.30pm) Inside Rajabhat University campus.

Ubonrak Thonburi Hospital (☑045 429100; Th Phalorangrit) The best private hospital in Ubon, it has a 24-hour casualty department.

Tourist Police (☑045 251451; Hwy 217) The tourist police office is well out of the city on the road to Phibun Mangsahan.

ℹ Getting There & Away

AIR

Together **Air Asia** (☑045 255762, nationwide 02 515 9999; www.airasia.com; Ubon Ratchathani Airport; ⊙7am-7pm), **Nok Air** (☑nationwide 02 900 9955; www.nokair.com; Ubon Ratchathani Airport; ⊙7am-7pm) and **Thai Lion Air** (☑nationwide 02 529 9999; www.lionairthai.com; Ubon Ratchathani Airport; ⊙6am-7pm) fly to/from Bangkok's Don Mueang Airport (one hour) a dozen times daily, with prices well under 1000B usually available. **Thai Smile** (☑087 776 2266, nationwide 1181; www.thaismileair.com; Ubon Ratchathani Airport; ⊙7am-7.30pm) has daily flights to/from Bangkok's Suvarnabhumi International Airport (one hour) for a little bit more. Nok Air also flies to Chiang Mai.

Sakda Travel World (☑045 254333; www.sakdatour.com; Th Phalorangrit; ⊙8.30am-6pm Mon-Sat) sells plane tickets, hires out cars and leads tours.

BUSES FROM UBON RATCHATHANI

DESTINATION	FARE (B)	DURATION (HR)	FREQUENCY
Bangkok	414-556	10	hourly 4am-midnight, frequent 4-8pm
Chiang Mai	707-790	12-14	7.30am, 12.45pm, 1.45pm, 2.45pm, 3.45pm, 5.45pm, 6.30pm
Chong Mek (Lao border)	120	2	every 30min 5am-6pm
Khon Kaen	176-244	4½-5	every 30min 5.30am-5.40pm
Khong Jiam	40	1½	every 30min 5am-6pm
Mukdahan	130	2½	5.45am, 7.30am, 8.40am, 11.30am, 1pm
Mukdahan (minivan)	111	2½	every 30min 6am-5.30pm
Nakhon Ratchasima (Khorat)	248-386	7-8	hourly 5am-8pm
Nang Rong	144-265	5-6	hourly 5am-8pm
Pakse (Laos)	200	3	9.30am & 2.30pm
Rayong	515-801	13	7am, 7.15am, 5pm, 6pm, 7.30pm, 7.45pm, 8pm, 8.15pm
Surin	130-202	3½	hourly 5am-8pm
Udon Thani	284-332	7	every 30min 5.30am-5.40pm
Yasothon	66-99	2	hourly 5.30am-5.30pm
Yasothon (minivan)	80	2	hourly 5.30am-5.30pm

SURIN'S 'ELEPHANT VILLAGE'

Around 50km from the workaday city of Surin, the little Kui village of Ban Ta Klang (บ้านตากลาง), aka Elephant Village, is where people and pachyderms live side by side. It's well known locally, but it's a bit of a mixed bag. Its most famous attraction, mostly for Thai tourists, is Elephant World (Elephant Study Centre; ☑ 044 145050; 100B; ⊙ 10-11am & 2-3pm), the only elephant camp in Isan, and is focused on a circus-like elephant show where these great creatures are trained to perform humiliating tricks for a goading audience. You'll also see lots of elephants chained up as you walk around the village. On the other hand, the modern ethical elephant-encounter programs nearby, where the elephants are well cared for and there is no riding or tricks, are among the best in Thailand.

The veteran Surin Project (☑ 084 482 1210; www.surinproject.org; Ban Ta Klang; full-board per person per week 13,000B) ✎ and the newer Elephant Lover Home (☑ 081 618 5232; www.elephantnaturepark.org; Khun Chai Thong; full-board per person per week 15,000B) ✎, both supported by Chiang Mai's renowned Elephant Nature Park (p754), are not elephant rescue sanctuaries; rather, they provide employment for local *mahouts* (elephant trainers) so their elephants don't need to do tricks, give rides or spend their days chained up (p753). Both programs are essentially the same, with a mix of walking and swimming with the elephants, working alongside the mahouts to care for them, and various cultural activities. And, unlike the typical Thai elephant program, here you are staying in a village.

They offer week-long full-board programs which should be booked in advance (www.elephantnaturepark.org). Shorter visits are possible when space is available; call the projects directly about this. The minimum age is 16.prasa

Ban Ta Klang has a few simple but decent restaurants, open for breakfast, lunch and dinner, plus a couple of air-con-cooled coffee shops, all on the road outside Elephant World.

How to get there

Sŏrng·tăa·ou run to Ban Ta Klang from Surin's bus terminal (50B, two hours, hourly 6am to 4pm), which has frequent buses to Nang Rong (2 hours), Nakhon Ratchasima (Khorat; 4 hours), Ubon Ratchathani (3½ hours) and Bangkok (7-8 hours). Note, you may be transferred to a second *sŏrng·tăa·ou* halfway there in Chom Phra. The last *sŏrng·tăa·ou* back to Surin leaves at 4pm.

The *sŏrng·tăa·ou* stop is right outside Elephant World, which is the only place well signposted in English. Surin Project is 100m further on, on the corner beside the first turning on the left. Elephant Lover Home is 9km north in Khun Chai Thong village.

BUS

Ubon's **bus terminal** (☑ 045 316085; Hwy 231) is north of town; take *sŏrng·tăa·ou* 2, 3 or 10 to the city centre. The best service to Bangkok is with **Nakhonchai Air** (☑ 045 955999), which has its own station across the road from the main bus station, but also sells tickets and picks up passengers at the main station.

The early-morning **sŏrng·tăa·ou** from Ubon Ratchathani to Phibun Mangsahan (40B, 1½ hours, 6am, 7am, 8am) park in front of Ban Du Market.

TRAIN

Ubon's **train station** (☑ 045 321004; Th Sathani) is in Warin Chamrap, south of the river; take *sŏrng·tăa·ou* 2. There are eight daily trains between Ubon and Bangkok (3rd/2nd/sleeper from 205/331/631B, 8½ to 12 hours), with sleepers departing at 7pm (10 hours), 7.30pm (11 hours) and 8.30pm (11 hours). All these trains also stop in Si Saket, Surin and Khorat.

ℹ Getting Around

Numbered *sŏrng·tăa·ou* (10B) run throughout town. No 2 is the handiest of the lot, running between the train station and the bus station, via the centre of town, past the TAT tourist office.

A túk-túk trip within the centre should cost about 50B. Metered taxis (flagfall 40B) park at the bus and train stations and the airport and aren't too hard to find driving around town. Drivers usually use their meters.

Phadaeng Hotel (p430) and Outside Inn (p431) hire bikes for 50B per day.

Ubon's airport is home to large car-hire companies including **Avis** (☑ 090 197 2262, nationwide 02 251 1131; www.avisthailand.com; Ubon Ratchathani Airport; ⊙ 7am-9.30pm), **Budget** (☑ 081 261 4360, nationwide 02 203

9222; www.budget.co.th; Ubon Ratchathani Airport; ◷7am-8pm), **Hertz** (☑ 092 509 1441, nationwide 02 266 4666; www.hertzthailand. com; Ubon Ratchathani Airport; ◷8am-8pm), **Sixt** (☑ 092 223 1296, nationwide 1798; www. sixtthailand.com; Ubon Ratchathani Airport; ◷7am-8pm) and **Thai Rent a Car** (☑ 092 284 0220, nationwide 1647; www.thairentacar. com; Ubon Ratchathani Airport; ◷7am-8pm) and several local companies including **Chow Watana** (☑ 045 242202; Ubon Ratchathani Airport; ◷7.30am-7.30pm). Outside Inn can arrange cars with drivers for a good price, and is also a reliable place for motorcycle hire (per day 250B), with discounts for long-term rentals.

Ban Pa-Ao

♪ 045 / POP 1400

Ban Pa-Ao (บ้านปะอาว) village is famous for producing brass and bronze items using a unique lost-wax casting method involving long strands of wax. You can see ancient products using the same method in many museums, including at Ban Chiang, and this is the last place in Thailand that still does it.

Ban Pa-Ao is also a silk-weaving village and there's a silk centre at the entrance to the village with a silk shop (the quality of the *mát·mèe* here is excellent) and a few looms. As a bonus, Wat Burapa Pa-Ao Nuea has a wonderful museum within its grounds holding various historical artefacts and local handicrafts.

◉ Sights

Ban Pa-Ao Brassware Centre WORKSHOP
(ศูนย์ทองเหลืองบ้านปะอาว, Soon Thorng Leuang Ban Pa-Ao; ☑ 094 505 6292; ◷8am-4.30pm) FREE Come here to see Ban Pa-Ao's famous brass artists using a unique lost-wax casting method. Workers here create bells, bowls and more on-site, although not every step is done daily, so what you'll see is a bit up to luck. A sign with photos and English text explains the entire process. The centre is on the far side of the village, on the edge of the forest.

Wat Burapa Pa-Ao Nuea Museum MUSEUM
(พิพิธภัณฑ์วัดบูรพาปะอาวเหนือ; ◷8am-5pm) FREE A surprising find in such a far-flung village, this gorgeous museum in Wat Burapa Pa-Ao Nuea holds various historical artefacts (in particular pottery, ancient coins and Dong Son bronze drums) and local handicrafts. It's kept locked, so you'll need to get the key from a monk at the temple.

Ban Pa-Ao Silk Centre SHOWROOM
(ศูนย์ทอผ้าไหมบ้านปะอาว; ☑082 153 7364; ◷8am-4.30pm) FREE Also called the 'Native Exhibition Centre', this silk centre has some excellent cloth on sale, much of it naturally dyed, and a few looms, although most of the weaving is done at home. It's on your left as you enter the village.

🛏 Sleeping

Ban Pa-Ao Village Homestay HOMESTAY $
(☑ 081 076 1249, 085 613 4713; per person incl 3 meals 350B, without meals 200B) The village homestay program is intended for Thai tour groups, but anyone can do it if at least one person in your group speaks Thai, since no hosts can speak English. Book at least two days in advance.

❶ Getting There & Away

Ban Pa-Ao is 3.5km off Hwy 23, and around 14km from Ubon Ratchathani. Minivans from Ubon to Maha Chana Chai pass the turn-off (30B, 20 minutes, every 30 minutes 6.30am to 5.30pm), and a motorcycle taxi from the highway costs 20B each way.

> **WORTH A TRIP**
>
> ### PRASAT TA MEUAN
>
> The most atmospheric of Surin's Khmer ruins is a series of three sites in the forest on the Cambodian border known collectively as **Prasat Ta Meuan** (ปราสาทตาเมือน; ◷9am-3pm). They line the ancient Khmer road linking Angkor Wat to Phimai. The first site, Prasat Ta Meuan proper, was built in the Jayavarman VII period (CE 1181–1210) as part of a rest stop for travellers. It's a fairly small monument with a two-door, five-window sanctuary constructed completely of laterite blocks. One sandstone lintel, of a meditating Buddha, remains.
>
> The sites begin 10.3km south of Ban Ta Miang (on Rte 224, 23km east of Ban Kruat) via a winding road used more by cows than cars. You need your own transport to get here, and a visit is just as convenient from Phanom Rung (p424) as from Surin city. Note the closing time: because of its proximity to the border, the times were chosen for security reasons, though there's no actual risk here as long as you don't wander into the forest.

LOCAL KNOWLEDGE

ROCKET FESTIVALS

Thailand's Isan region erupts into festival mode in the hot season, culminating in the riotous rocket festival celebrations held in the 6th lunar month (May and June). The festivals aren't just a chance to get drunk, dance bawdily in the street and tempt fate by firing huge homemade rockets into the sky, they're a reminder to Phaya Taen, a pre-Buddhist god, that it's time for him to send rain.

Legends behind the festival vary from place to place, but most involve a conflict between Phaya Khan Khak, the 'Toad King' (some versions say this is one of the Buddha's pre-enlightenment lives), and Phaya Taen, who either withheld or forgot to send the rains for many years resulting in widespread death down on earth. After they stopped fighting, Phaya Taen promised to always send the rains every year.

While just about every Isan village will launch at least one rocket, many places make it into a huge event. Without a doubt the most raucous and famous is the Yasothon Rocket Festival (Bun Bâng Fai; ⊙ 2nd weekend in May), which is heavily promoted by the Tourism Authority of Thailand.

Most big rocket festivals fall on weekends with parades taking place on Saturday and the rocket launches on Sunday. Far from spontaneous, they take months of planning. Individual villages put in many hours organising the costumes and music, training the dancers and building floats for the parade – as well as building the rockets themselves.

The floats are big and elaborate and usually feature gold paint and a *naga* head on the rocket itself. Dozens, or even hundreds, of dancers and musicians follow each float down the road past a judging booth. The winning village gains glory rather than gold, but *sà·nùk* (fun), not victory, is the real aim.

The rockets themselves were traditionally made of bamboo shafts stuffed with gunpowder, but nowadays PVC pipe is the vessel of choice. The largest can reach 3m in length and hold 120kg of gunpowder. Add to that the large amount of alcohol being consumed and you have a saucy recipe for danger. Accidents, some fatal, do happen. If you go, keep your wits about you and don't necessarily take your safety cues from the locals.

Khong Jiam

☑ 045 / POP 6500

Khong Jiam (โขงเจียม), often spelled Khong Chiam, sits on a picturesque peninsula at the confluence of the reddish-brown Mekong and bluish Mun rivers. It's known as Mae Nam Song Si (Two-Colour River) because of the contrasting colours at the junction. The multicoloured merger is usually visible from the shore, but it's best seen from a boat. When the rivers are high (June to October) the blending waters create small whirlpools and a strange bubbling that resembles boiling lava, though the colour divide is less distinct at this time.

◉ Sights

Wat Tham Khuha Sawan   BUDDHIST TEMPLE
(วัดถ้ำคูหาสวรรค์; Rte 2222; ⊙ daylight hours)
FREE The views from this busy temple above the town (best seen from atop the bell tower) are alone worth the walk up from Khong Jiam, but it also has a beautiful nine-pointed *chedi,* an all-white *bòht* (ordination hall), an

orchid garden (blooming in the cold season), one of the biggest gongs in Thailand, and the body of late abbot Luang Pu Kam covered in gold leaf on display in a glass case on a flamboyant altar.

You can drive here, or walk up the *naga* staircase at the end of town.

☞ Tours

River Tours   BOATING
(☑ 089 283 9825, 090 234 5511; per boat 600B; ⊙ 8am-5pm) Half-hour tours on a shaded 12-person boat are de rigueur in Khong Jiam. They'll also do longer trips to Kaeng Tana National Park (per boat 800B; 1½ hours return including time walking around the park) and Pha Taem National Park (per boat 2000B; two hours return, but you cannot leave the boat; p438).

⌴ Sleeping & Eating

Khong Jiam doesn't get many *fa·ràng* (Westerner) visitors, but it's popular with Thais, so there's an abundance of lodging. In the high season, booking ahead on weekends is wise.

There's a food market near the bus and minivan stand, at one end of the main strip which leads down to the river. Small restaurants and cute cafes are strung out along the main strip. There are also several eateries along the riverfront, including one or two floating on the Mekong. You pay a premium for the views, but it's worth it.

Khongchiam Place HOTEL $
(☑ 045 351046; Th Phookhamchai; d 400B; P ✴ ☏) Rooms at this striking yellow hotel overlook a front lawn and are small and simple but very clean, offering good value overall. It's one block south of the main road.

Ban Pak Mongkhon GUESTHOUSE $
(☑ 045 351352; Th Kaewpradit; d/f from 400/700B; P ✴ ☏) From the simple fan rooms to the four cute, Thai-style wooden cottages (600B), this guesthouse on the main road through town, and also known as Mongkhon Resort, has something for most tastes. The friendly, clued-in owners and free bikes for guests are bonuses. Booking ahead is recommended.

Baansuan Rimnam Resort RESORT $$
(☑ 085 493 3521; Th Rimmoon; d incl breakfast from 800B; P ✴ ☏) This quiet spot sits in a small patch of teak forest along Mae Nam Mun. The air-con log-cabin-type bungalows match the forest location perfectly and command views of the river. The location makes it highly recommended. Heading towards the river on the main village road, turn right after the last row of restaurants/cafes to pick up signs to the resort.

Tohsang Khongjiam Resort HOTEL $$$
(☑ 045 351174; www.tohsang.com; d incl breakfast from 4500B; P ✴ @ ☏ ☲) This place oozes understated class and capitalises on its prime location right on the banks of Mae Nam Mun. While its upmarket nature seems a little incongruous for this stretch of rural Thailand, it's not flashy and blends in well with the rustic surrounds. The ambience is totally restful. The open-air restaurant has spectacular views. There's a spa, and bikes and kayaks are available. It's 3.5km from town, on the opposite bank of the river.

❶ Getting There & Away

All transport to town stops at the highway junction. **Minivans** go every 30 minutes all day long to Ubon Ratchathani (80B, 1½ hours), Phibun Mangsahan (40B, 30 minutes) and Chong Mek (40B, 30 minutes) at the Lao border. There are also **buses to Bangkok** (526B, 10 hours, 7.30am and 4.30pm).

❶ Getting Around

Baan Steak (☑ 081 299 8980; per day 300B; ☉ 6am-9pm) restaurant has motorcycles for 300B per day. Some hotels, including Ban Pak Mongkhon and Tohsang, can also arrange a car with driver.

Kaeng Tana National Park

Along the road to Khong Jiam you can cross the Pak Mun Dam to Kaeng Tana National Park (อุทยานแห่งชาติแก่งตะนะ; ☑ 045 252722; 200B). After circling thickly forested Don Tana (Tana Island), linked to the mainland by two long suspension bridges, Mae Nam Mun roils through the park's beautiful namesake rapids (which are underwater in the rainy season) and passes below some short but photogenic cliffs. Towards the end of the dry season large naturally eroded holes in the rock emerge.

There are several good short walks from the visitors centre: the 1.5km clifftop trail to Lan Pha Phueng viewpoint is especially serene. You can also walk 500m through the forest to the first suspension bridge and cross over it onto the island. Nam Tok Tad Ton is a wide and lovely waterfall in the far south of the park, just 300m off the main road.

🛏 Sleeping & Eating

There are bungalows (☑ 045 406888; http:// nps.dnp.go.th/reservation.php; bungalows 5/10 people 1000/2000B; P) and camping (per person with own tent 30B, 2-/3-/5-person tent hire 150/250/300B; P) available near the visitors centre.

The simple cook-to-order restaurant by the visitors centre opens early and closes depending on the number of customers. There's also a small shop selling snacks and instant noodles.

❶ Information

Kaeng Tana National Park Visitors Centre (☑ 045 252722; ☉ 8am-4pm) Has general information about the park.

❶ Getting There & Away

By road, the park is 14km from Khong Jiam. There's no public transport, but you can get here easily enough on a rented motorbike from Khong Jiam. Alternatively, boats in Khong Jiam will take you upriver and drop you at the park for a quick look around (round trip 800B, 1½ hours).

Pha Taem National Park

A long cliff named Pha Taem is the centrepiece of the awesome but unheralded Pha Taem National Park (อุทยานแห่งชาติผาแต้ม; ☑ 045 252581; 400B, car/motorcycle 30/20B) which covers 340 sq km along the Mekong River. From the top you get a bird's-eye view across the Mekong into Laos, and down below a fabulous tree-shaded walking trail passes prehistoric rock paintings.

The wilderness north of the cliff holds more ancient art, some magnificent waterfalls (all flowing June to December) and scattered rock fields known as Sao Chaliang, which are oddly eroded mushroom-shaped stone formations.

Many Thais come here for the sunrises. Pha Cha Na Dai cliff, which requires a high-clearance vehicle to reach, serves Thailand's first sunrise view of each day. But Pha Taem cliff is only about one minute behind.

◉ Sights

★ Pha Taem   NATURAL FEATURE
(ผาแต้ม) These ancient rock paintings, which are at least 1000 years old but probably much older, sit on a cliff face down below the visitors centre. A fantastic, tree-shaded walking trail (4km, approximately two hours) cut into the cliff face runs past four groups of paintings before looping back to the visitors centre. Painted subjects include *plah beuk* (giant Mekong catfish), elephants, human hands, geometric designs and fish traps that look much like the huge ones still used today.

The second viewing platform fronts the most impressive batch, but don't miss seeing Group 4, further up the cliff face and only accessible via a highly precarious pathway (take extreme care!).

Nam Tok Saeng Chan   WATERFALL
(น้ำตกแสงจันทร์) One of the most amazing waterfalls you'll ever see, Saeng Chan ('Moonbean') flows through a hole cut naturally into the overhanging rock. There's water from June to December, but it's at its best when rain is actually falling.

Nam Tok Soi Sawan   WATERFALL
(น้ำตกสร้อยสวรรค์) Nam Tok Soi Sawan is a 25m-tall waterfall flowing from June to December. It's a 19km drive from the visitors

centre and then a 500m walk, or you can hike with a ranger (this must be arranged in advance) for about 15 largely shadeless kilometres along the top of the cliff.

What the park calls Thailand's largest flower field blooms from October to January (November and December are best) next to the falls.

🛏 Sleeping & Eating

There are a couple of restaurants across the parking area from the visitors centre. Only one stays open in the rainy season and it usually closes before sunset. You can get instant noodles, snacks and espresso coffee behind the visitors centre in Cliff Cafe, which also has stupendous views. There are also a few restaurants along the road leading to the park.

Pha Taem National Park
Campsite   CAMPGROUND $
(per person with own tent 30B, 4-person tent hire 225B; P) Pha Taem's basic campsite is in a semi-remote spot 2km from the visitors centre. There's a second campsite near the bungalows, but it's inferior and little used.

Pha Taem National Park
Bungalows   BUNGALOW $$
(☑ 045 252581; http://nps.dnp.go.th/reservation.php; bungalows 6-person with fan 1200B, 5-person with air-con 2000B; P) Pha Taem National Park has five bare but comfortable bungalows 2km from the visitors centre. Beautiful Mekong views are just a short walk away.

Pha Taem & Kaeng
Phisamai Riverside   RESORT $$
(☑ 087 249 3173; www.pk-riverside.com; d & bungalows incl breakfast 1000-3000B; P ✳ 🛜) 'PK Riverside' is a mixed bag. Rooms are a bit overpriced and it can be noisy on weekends if it's filled with young Thais drawn by the the many selfie stations spread over the grounds, but the views are wonderful and it's the pick of the 'resorts' along this rough road down below Pha Taem National Park.

❶ Information

Pha Taem National Park Visitors Centre
(☑ 045 252581; ⊘ 5am-6pm) Contains exhibits on the park's ancient paintings and local ecology. This is the spot to pick up a free park map and arrange guides for treks, although it's best to call and reserve in advance if you want to do anything other than a short walk. You

don't need a guide to do the fantastic cliff-face walking trail past the park's rock paintings.

❶ Getting There & Away

Pha Taem is 18km from Khong Jiam along Rte 2112. There's no public transport, but you could come on a rented motorbike or car from Khong Jiam. Túk-túk ask for 600B for the return trip. Return boat trips here from Khong Jiam cost 2000B, but they don't allow you to get off the boat and explore the park.

KHON KAEN PROVINCE

The province of Khon Kaen (จังหวัดขอนแก่น), the gateway to Isan for many people arriving from northern Thailand, serves up an interesting mix of old and new. Farming and textiles still dominate life in the countryside, while things are booming in the increasingly modern capital city.

Khon Kaen

☎ 043 / POP 122,370

As the site of the northeast's largest university and an important hub for all things commercial, Khon Kaen (ขอนแก่น) is youthful, educated and on the move. While it's the kind of city that's more likely to land on a best-places-to-live list than a traveller's itinerary, there are more than enough interesting attractions and good facilities to make a stop rewarding.

⊙ Sights

Bueng Kaen Nakhon   LAKE

(บึงแก่นนคร) This 100-hectare lake is the most pleasant place in town to spend some time, and the paths hugging its shore link quite a few interesting spots. There's bike hire (p445) and pedal-boat hire near the evening Rim Bueng Market (p442), and you can easily walk a complete circuit of the lake (45 minutes).

★**Wat Nong Wang**   BUDDHIST TEMPLE

(วัดหนองแวง; Th Robbung; ⊗daylight hours, stupa 6am-6pm) FREE Down at the south end of the lake, **Phra Mahathat Kaen Nakhon**, the gorgeous nine-storey stupa at the heart of this important temple, makes this Khon Kaen's one must-see attraction. It features enlightening modern murals depicting Isan culture and Khon Kaen's history; various historical displays, including a collection of

rare Buddha images on the 4th floor; and a 9th-floor observation deck. The monks open the door to the upper floors when they are ready, which is roughly 7.30am to 5pm.

★**Walking Street Market**   MARKET

(ถนนคนเดิน; Th Na Sunratchakan; ⊗5-10pm Sat) In the spirit of Chiang Mai's weekend street markets (but not touristy like them), hundreds of vendors take over Th Na Sunratchakan. Many of them sell handbags, T-shirts, postcards, picture frames and other handmade products. Dancers, musicians and other buskers work strategic corners, and the whole place is festooned with Chinese-style lanterns, adding to the festive atmosphere.

Wat Pho Ban Nontan   BUDDHIST TEMPLE

(วัดโพธิ์บ้านโนนทัน; Th Pho Thisan; ⊗daylight hours) FREE Just off the lake, this peaceful tree-filled temple and noted meditation centre pre-dates the city and has a *săh·lah* like no other in Thailand. The ground floor is covered with sculpted trees, animals and village scenes of people acting out old Isan proverbs. There's also a small museum under the *bòht,* and this temple is a great place for a Thai massage.

Sanjao Bueng Tao Gong Ma   TEMPLE

(ศาลเจ้าปึงเถ่ากงม่า; Th Robbung; ⊗6am-6pm) FREE This is Khon Kaen's biggest and most impressive Chinese temple. It's beautiful at night, and you can sometimes see people practising dragon and lion dancing then. There's a large Guan-Im (Chinese Goddess of Mercy) statue in the park across the street.

Khon Kaen National Museum   MUSEUM

(พิพิธภัณฑสถานแห่งชาติขอนแก่น; Th Lang Sunratchakan; 100B; ⊗9am-4pm Wed-Sun) This collection of artefacts spans prehistoric times to the present. Highlights are Ban Chiang–era pottery and a beautiful Dvaravati *bai săir·mah* (temple boundary marker) depicting Princess Pimpa cleaning Lord Buddha's feet with her hair. The household and agricultural displays shed light on what you'll see out in the countryside. Unfortunately, the English labelling is not very good.

Talat Banglamphu-Bobae   MARKET

(ตลาดโบเบ๊/ตลาดบางลำภู; Th Klang Muang; ⊗24hr) Right in the heart of the city, the adjacent Banglamphu and Bobae markets comprise Khon Kaen's largest and most

Khon Kaen

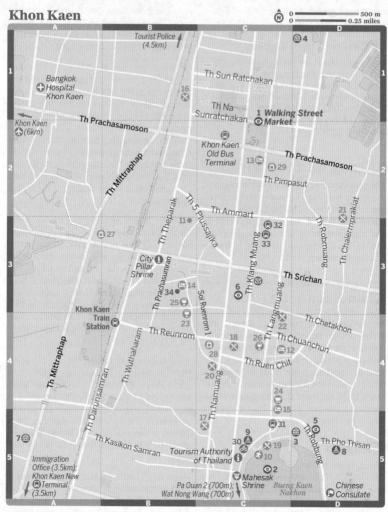

diverse fresh food sources. It's open nonstop, but in the evening most of the action moves out of the stalls and onto Th Namuang.

Wat That   BUDDHIST TEMPLE
(วัดธาตุ; Th Robbung; ⊙ daylight hours, chedi 8am-6pm) **FREE** This old temple has a soaring *bóht* and *chedi*. The latter, dating to 1789 but completely rebuilt in modern times, is surrounded by a cloister featuring many Buddha images, and you can go inside it.

Hong Moon Mung   MUSEUM
(โฮงมูนมังเมืองขอนแก่น; Th Robbung; 90B; ⊙ 9am-5pm Tue-Sat) Inside the amphitheatre at

Bueng Kaen Nakhon lake, this well-executed museum about Khon Kaen provides a good introduction to Isan, with dioramas and displays back to the Jurassic period.

🏃 Activities & Courses

Pedal Boats   BOATING
(Bueng Kaen Nakhon; per hr after 4.30pm 50B, for any length of time before 4.30pm 50B) There are pedal boats for hire on the lakeshore beside Rim Bueng Market.

Centrum Health Massage   MASSAGE
(📞 089 711 8331; veenasspa@gmail.com; Soi Supatheera; courses 3500-15,000B) At Khon Kaen

Khon Kaen

Centrum hotel, Veena teaches Thai massage in English and Thai. There are several different courses; a seven-day course in traditional Thai massage costs 6500B.

☞ Tours

Thai Dream Tours   MEDITATION
(☑089 711 8331; www.thaidreamtours.com; Soi Supatheera) Gregarious owner-guide Veena, who also runs Centrum Health Massage and Khon Kaen Centrum hotel, organises all kinds of tours, but has made her speciality individually tailored meditation tours to forest meditation temples around Isan. A half-day trip for two people costs around 1500B.

Isan Explorer   CULTURAL
(☑085 354 9165; www.isanexplorer.com) Isan Explorer specialises in slow-travel, cultural tours across the entire Isan region. Elephant encounters have a focus on animal welfare (no riding and no chains), and the company also does birdwatching and trekking tours in the mountains west of Khon Kaen.

☆☆ Festivals

The **Silk Fair** and **Phuk Siaw Festival** are held simultaneously over 12 days starting in late November. Centred on the provincial hall *(sǎh·lah glahng)*, the festival celebrates and seeks to preserve the tradition of *pòok sèeo* (friend bonding), a ritual union of friends during which *fâi pòok kǎan* (sacred threads) are tied around one's wrists. Other activities include a parade, Isan music and lots of shopping.

🛏 Sleeping

Slove U House   HOSTEL **$**
(☑094 530 2028; Th Sri Nual; per person 150B; ☎) Up above an excellent coffee shop (p443), this is a closet-sized hostel with small mattresses on the floor and cold-water showers. The real attraction here is the ever-smiling hosts – and the price.

Khon Kaen Centrum   HOTEL **$**
(☑081 574 0507; Soi Supatheera; incl breakfast d 500-750B, tr 750-1250B; P❀☎) What seems like an ordinary small Thai hotel sets itself apart in the details. The rooms are fairly striking in their white-themed decor and have high-quality furnishings. The owner, who lives on-site, is serious about service and cleanliness. And it's quiet because it's built at the back of the block. Guests can rent bikes and motorcycles.

Charoenchit House
HOTEL $

(☏043 227300; www.chousekk.com; Th Chuan-chun; d incl breakfast 500-600B; P✹🛜) A solid budget hotel with a good location just north of the lake. It's clean and the modern, spacious rooms have a fair amount of va-va-voom for the price, making it quite popular. No English spoken, but staff are as helpful as they can be.

Piman Garden
HOTEL $$

(☏043 334111; www.pimangardenhotel.com; Th Klang Muang; d 800-1900B; P✹🛜) Set back off the road around a lovely, tropical garden, Piman offers serenity and privacy despite its city-centre location. Rooms are well pre-sented, and most have balconies or porches. Breakfast costs 120B per person.

Pullman Raja Orchid
HOTEL $$$

(☏043 913333; www.pullmankhonkaen.com; off Th Prachasumran; incl breakfast d 2400-3400B, ste from 4700B; P✹@🛜⛱) A stunning lob-by sets the tone for Khon Kaen's premier hotel. In the heart of the city, it has plenty of razzle-dazzle, including a luxurious spa, pool and gym, a German microbrewery and well-equipped rooms, though it's let down somewhat by its slightly seedy surrounds – there are lots of bars, nightclubs and mas-sage parlours around here.

Insist on a room at the front unless you want to listen to pounding bass drifting out of the nearby nightclubs. And the small in-crease in price from standard to superior is a good investment.

✕ Eating

★ Turm-Rom
THAI $

(Th Chetakhon; mains 49-169B; ⊙5.30pm-1am; 🛜) This superb place combines one of the best kitchens in town with a covered garden to create the perfect place for a night out, rain or shine. The pá·sá plah chôrn (hot and sour curry with snakehead fish) and đam tùa mŏo gròrp (spicy long-bean salad with fried pork) are especially good, but in our many visits we've never had a dud dish.

Also has live music some nights.

★ Somtom Internet
THAI $

(Soi Namuang 19; mains 35-65B; ⊙8am-9.30pm) This popular, no-frills local joint is always busy for good reason – there's no better sôm·đam in Khon Kaen. It also does grilled chicken, sticky rice and fried fish. It's an English-free zone, but it doesn't matter much because everything available is laid out on a table in front, so you can just point.

★ Gai Yang Rabeab
THAI $

(☏043 243413; Th Theparak; mains 45-60B, whole chickens 160B; ⊙9am-3pm) Many Thais be-lieve Khon Kaen Province makes Thailand's best gài yâhng (marinated grilled chicken), and this simple joint, serving an all-Isan menu, gets the most nods as best of the best in the city. If you want the chicken, you have to order a whole one, so come with an emp-ty stomach or bring a friend.

Pa Ouan 2
THAI $

(Th Robbung; mains 40-280B; ⊙9am-8pm; 🛜) This popular Isan restaurant right beside Wat Nong Wang and overlooking the lake from its upstairs terrace has a menu span-ning gài yâhng and duck lâhp as well as 19 kinds of sôm·đam. The English menu is tiny compared to the Thai menu, though, so this restaurant is best visited with a Thai friend for a full culinary experience.

Nan Yuan Noodles
CHINESE $

(Th Namuang; noodles 45-55B, duck mains 120-260B; ⊙11am-9pm; ✹) Popular south-Chi-nese restaurant chain with easy-to-order English photo menu. It does rice, soups and roast duck dishes as well as its signature noodles.

Rim Bueng Market
MARKET $

(ตลาดริมบึง; Th Robbung; snacks 5-50B; ⊙4-9pm) This buzzing little lakeside evening market features a whole stretch of street-food stalls selling everything from barbe-cued skewers and grilled fish to tropical fruits and ready-made portions of mango sticky rice. You can also watch Thai-style sweets such as kà·nŏm being made. The market also contains second-hand clothing and paint-your-own pottery stalls.

Night Market
MARKET $

(Th Reunrom; ⊙5pm-midnight) For cheap but delicious eats, the city's main night market is a good one.

Tawan Thong
VEGAN $

(☏043 330389; Th Ammart; mains 35-45B; ⊙6am-2pm; P🛜♨) Housed in a large, airy dining hall with an open kitchen that's almost as large again, Tawan Thong is an all-veggie health-food buffet with friend-ly staff and cheap, tasty food that's good enough to attract non-vegetarian diners too.

🍷 Drinking & Nightlife

★ Slove U Coffee
CAFE

(📞 095 651 7121; Th Sri Nual; coffee from 40B, matcha latte 75B, smoothies 95B; ⊙ 8am-8pm; 🛜) Khon Kaen's youthful population has spawned many good coffee shops, but this friendly, attractively cluttered, front-terrace cafe is our favourite. It roasts its own beans (grown in Chiang Mai) in a traditional roaster shipped over from Turkey, has a couple of bikes for rent and runs a hostel (p441) upstairs.

Der La Jazz
BAR

(Soi Namuang 25; cocktails 180-280B, lager glass/pitcher 85/260B, craft beer 200-300B; ⊙ 6pm-midnight) Two bars in one, Der La Jazz serves cocktails and ice-cold lager from its main terraced area, where there's live music every night from 9pm, and a choice of around a dozen craft beers from its Monsakod Tap Bar in one corner. There's also an excellent cafe attached.

Yentek
BAR

(Th Langmuang; beer from 80B; ⊙ 5pm-midnight) Housed in a charming old wooden building, Yentek's most endearing feature is in fact its tree-shaded front courtyard, where there's live music from around 8pm most nights. There's a full food menu (in Thai only, though with some photos), but many people just come for an atmospheric place to drink.

U-Bar
CLUB

(Soi Khlong Nam; ⊙ 8pm-2am) U-Bar packs them in with live music, often big-name bands from Bangkok. It's mostly a younger crowd than the numerous other bars around here.

🛍 Shopping

Sueb San
ARTS & CRAFTS

(21/2 Th Klang Muang; ⊙ 8am-6.30pm Mon-Sat) This cute little shop behind a pan-pipe arch stocks natural-dyed fabrics plus some creative handmade notebooks, postcards, bags and other souvenirs, and is run by a charming lady.

Prathammakhant
ARTS & CRAFTS

(📞 043 224080; Th Reunrom; ⊙ 9am-6.30pm Mon-Sat, 9am-5pm Sun) There's an impressively large selection of silk here, both fabric

---

WORTH A TRIP

EPIC KHMER RUIN

The 12th-century Prasat Puay Noi (ปราสาทเปือยน้อย; ⊙ daylight hours) FREE is the largest and most interesting Khmer ruin in northern Isan. About the size of Buriram's Prasat Meuang Tam but far less intact, the east-facing monument comprises a large central sandstone sanctuary surmounted by a partially collapsed prang (Khmer-style stupa) and surrounded by laterite walls with two major gates. There are still some excellent carvings intact, including Shiva riding his bull Nandi on the pediment on the back of the 'library'. It's not accessible by public transport.

---

and finished clothing, plus plenty of other souvenirs.

Ton Tann Green Market
MARKET

(Th Mittraphap; ⊙ 5-10.30pm) Ton Tann is an attractive open space where some vendors sell modern handmade crafts. There's also a fashion zone, an art gallery (หอศิลป์ต้นตาล; Th Mittraphap; ⊙ 4.30-10pm) FREE and many restaurants.

Central Plaza
SHOPPING CENTRE

(Th Srichan; ⊙ 10am-9pm) One of the biggest shopping malls in Isan. Has a branch of the English-language Asia Books.

ℹ Information

EMBASSIES & CONSULATES

Chinese Consulate (Th Robbung; ⊙ 9am-noon Mon-Fri) Tourist visas are available only for Thai citizens and residents.

Lao Consulate (📞 043 393402; Hwy 2; ⊙ 8am-noon & 1-4pm Mon-Fri) Well north of the city, across from Raja City housing estate. Visas require one photo and are ready in about 10 minutes. Payment is by baht only, and at a poor exchange rate, so it's cheaper to pay in dollars at the border.

Vietnamese Consulate (📞 043 242190; Th Chatapadung; ⊙ 9-11.30am & 2-4.30pm Mon-Fri) Visas require one photo and are ready in one hour. It's 400m north of the stoplight on Th Srichan by Khon Kaen Hospital.

EMERGENCIES

Tourist Police (📞 043 465385; 24/222 Th Mittraphap, Tambon Sila, off Hwy 2) Inconveniently located 5km north of the centre.

BUSES FROM KHON KAEN'S NEW BUS TERMINAL

DESTINATION	FARE (B)	DURATION (HR)	FREQUENCY
Bangkok	340-487	7	6.30am-1am (frequent)
Chiang Mai	410-739	12	4.20am-9pm (14 departures)
Khorat	146	3½	3.30am-1am (frequent)
Khorat (minivan)	126	3	every 45min 6.40am-6pm
Nong Khai	120-155	3½-4	hourly 7am-3pm
Phitsanulok	192-247	6	4.20am, 6.20am, 10.30am, 6pm, 7pm
Roi Et	92-107	2	hourly 5.30am-4pm
Surin	205	5	every 2hr 4am-4pm
Suvarnabhumi Airport	317	6½	10.50pm
Ubon Ratchathani	244	4½-5	hourly 5.30am-4pm
Udon Thani	95	2½	every 30min 5.30am-8pm
Udon Thani (minivan)	80	2	5am-7.15pm (frequent)
Vientiane (Laos; must have Lao visa)	180-185	4	8.15am & 3pm

MEDICAL SERVICES

Bangkok Hospital Khon Kaen (☑ 043 042888; www.bangkokhospitalkhonkaen.com; Th Maliwan) The top private hospital in the city. Has a 24-hour casualty department.

MONEY

Khon Kaen's three largest shopping malls, Central Plaza (p443), TukCom and Fairy Plaza, have extended-hours banks.

TOURIST INFORMATION

Immigration (☑ 043 465242; Hwy 2; ⊙ 8.30am-noon & 1-4.30pm Mon-Fri) On the 2nd floor of one of the main buildings at the New Bus Terminal.

Tourism Authority of Thailand (TAT; ☑ 043 227714; tatkhkn@tat.or.th; Th Robbung; ⊙ 8.30am-4.30pm) Distributes maps of the city and can answer questions about surrounding provinces too. Limited English skills, though.

❶ Getting There & Away

AIR

The airport is 6km or 7km northwest of the centre. Flights to **Khon Kaen Airport** (☑ 043 468173) have expanded greatly in the past few years, which helps keep prices to Bangkok low; even on short notice, you can usually find a ticket for under 1000B. **Thai Smile** (☑ nationwide 1181; www.thaismileair.com; Khon Kaen Airport; ⊙ 7am-9pm) has several daily flights using Suvarnabhumi International Airport, while **Air Asia** (☑ 02 515 9999; www.airasia.com; Khon Kaen Airport; ⊙ 5.30am-8.30pm), **Nok Air** (☑ nationwide 02 900 9955; www.nokair.com; Khon Kaen Airport; ⊙ 6am-8pm Apr-Sep, 7am-10pm Oct-Mar) and **Thai Lion Air** (☑ nationwide 02 529 9999; www.lionairthai.com; Khon Kaen Airport; ⊙ 7.30am-6.30pm Mon-Sat, 9am-8pm Sun) each have several daily flights to Don Muang International Airport. Air Asia also operates a daily Chiang Mai and Hat Yai service.

Thai Airways Khon Kaen sales office (☑ 043 227701; www.thaiairways.com; Pullman Raja Orchid; ⊙ 8am-5pm Mon-Fri) sells tickets for Thai Smile's Khon Kaen flights, and also handles Thai Airways flights worldwide.

Several hotels, including the Pullman, send shuttles (100B to 150B per person) to meet flights at Khon Kaen Airport, and you don't need to be staying at the hotels to use them. Taxis at the airport use the meter, but you must pay a 50B airport surcharge.

BUS

Khon Kaen is a busy bus transport hub – you can ride directly to nearly all cities in Isan and many beyond. Now that the **Old Bus Terminal** (☑ 043 237472; Th Prachasamoson) has closed, all services use the **New Bus Terminal** (☑ 043 471562; Th Liang Muang Khon Kaen), also known as Bus Terminal 3, out on the city's ring road. The best service to Bangkok is with **Nakhonchai Air** (☑ 02 939 4999, nationwide 1624; www. nakhonchaiair.com), departing about every 30 minutes throughout the day with six '1st-Class' VIP buses.

Nakhonchai Air still has a sales office at the defunct **Old Air-conditioned Bus Terminal** (Th Klang Muang) (as do a few other companies) and runs an hourly shuttle to the New Bus Terminal for its customers.

While most minivans use the regular bus terminal, they also depart throughout the day from the Old Air-conditioned Bus Terminal to Udon Thani and Khorat, and from **Central Plaza** (Hwy 2) shopping mall to Udon Thani and Roi Et.

TRAIN

For Bangkok, there's one morning express train (2nd/3rd-class 399/227B, 7½ hours, 9.32am) and three evening express trains (1st/2nd-class sleeper from 1198/809B, 8.26pm, 9.12pm and 9.49pm) from **Khon Kaen Train Station** (☑043 221112). For Nakhon Ratchasima, there are three local trains (3rd-class 38B, three hours, 7.50am, 2.30pm and 3.33pm) and one express (2nd/3rd-class 297/188B, two hours, 8.26pm). For Nong Khai, there are two daytime trains: one local (3rd-class 35B, 9.30am, 7½ hours) and one express (2nd/3rd-class 290/185B, two hours, 3.32pm).

ⓘ Getting Around

Sŏrng·tăa·ou (passenger pick-up trucks; 9B) ply regular routes across the city. Some of the handiest (all of which pass the Old Air-conditioned Bus Terminal on Th Klang Muang) are those running line 4, which pass immigration and the Lao consulate; line 8, which go to Wat Nong Wang and also northwest through the university; line 10 (going north), which pass near and sometimes in front of the Vietnamese consulate; and line 21, which go out to the National Museum. There's also the 24-hour **Khon Kaen City Bus** (15B), which starts and finishes at the New Bus Terminal and circles through the city, via Central Plaza and the Old Bus Terminal among other places, with some clearly labelled buses also going all the way to the airport.

For individual rides, túk-túk are the most expensive way to get around (50B to 70B to most places in the centre), but they're the method most people use because it's rare to find **metered taxis** (☑043 465777, 043 342800; flag-fall 30B, call fee 20B) on the street, and when you call for one you sometimes have to wait a while. About the only places in the city you're likely to find a taxi or motorcycle taxi (within town 30B to 40B) parked are the bus stations, airport and Central Plaza, and the taxis parked at the bus station won't use their meters.

There are many car-hire outlets around Tuk-Com. Big names like **Thai Rent a Car** (☑043 468178; www.thairentacar.com; Khon Kaen Airport; ⊗24hr) and **Budget** (☑043 345460; www.budget.com; Khon Kaen Airport; ⊗7am-8pm) have outlets at the airport. **Khun Wanchai** (☑089 984 5503) is a taxi driver who speaks good English and charges around 3000B (including fuel) per day within Khon Kaen Province, and only a little more to go further afield.

Bueng Kaen Nakhon Bike Hire (Th Robbung; per hour 30-50B, per day 100-150B; ⊗noon-8pm) has a variety of bikes available including two- and three-seaters.

Chonnabot

☑043 / POP 4000

The little town of Chonnabot (ชนบท) is at the heart of one of Thailand's most successful silk-weaving regions and is famous for producing top-quality *mát·mèe*. Located 55km southwest of Khon Kaen, it's a major shopping destination and there are many small stores selling fabrics (both silk and cotton) and finished clothes on Th Sriboonruang, aka Silk Rd. The small Sala Mai Thai museum (หอนิทรรศการผ้าไหมไทย, Thai Silk Exhibition Hall; ☑043 286160; ⊗8am-5pm Mon-Fri, 9am-5pm Sat & Sun) FREE outside of town has displays with all the equipment used to make silk fabric, though it's more enjoyable to watch weavers working their looms at their homes. Just wander west or north of Silk Rd and you'll find some.

Chonnabot warrants just a short visit and most people come from Khon Kaen city. There are also some good hotels in Ban Phai along the highway close to Chonnabot.

There are a few simple restaurants and a nice cafe on Th Sriboonruang. There's also an excellent coffee van that's often parked beside the bus shelter where you wait for the *sŏrng·tăa·ou* back to Ban Phai.

ⓘ Getting There & Away

Khon Kaen tour companies run tours to Chonnabot but you can also go by public transport if you're in no rush. Take a bus (35B, one hour, every 30 minutes) or train (8B to 39B, 30 minutes, 7.50am, 9.10am and 1.55pm) to Ban Phai, from where you can get a *sŏrng·tăa·ou* to Chonnabot (13B, 20 minutes, every 30 minutes from 7am to 5pm). The *sŏrng·tăa·ou* leave from Ban Phai bus station, which is about 200m from the train station; turn right out of the train station, take the second left and the bus station is on your right. Two afternoon trains (3.06pm and 6.41pm) return to Khon Kaen from Ban Phai.

Phu Wiang National Park

A geologist looking for uranium discovered a giant patella bone here in 1976, and the palaeontologists who were called to investigate then unearthed a fossilised 15m-long herbivore. It was later named *Phuwiangosaurus sirindhornae,* after Princess Sirindhorn. Dinosaur fever followed (explaining the myriad model dinosaurs in Khon Kaen city), more remains were uncovered and Phu Wiang National Park (อุทยานแห่งชาติ ภูเวียง; ☑043 358073; 200B, car/motorcycle 30/20B) was born.

The park covers a strange horseshoe-shaped mountain that has just a single pass to its interior. Wiang Kao, the district inside the mountain, is a fruit-growing area and is a good place to explore by car if you want to look at traditional village life.

👁 Sights

Most people are here to see the dinosaur fossils left exposed in some excavation sites (แหล่งขุดค้นไดโนเสาร์; ☉8.30am-4.30pm; ♿). The northern section has a new road, making it easy to see the dinosaur footprints (รอยเท้าไดโนเสาร์หินลาดป่าชาด) and Phu Wiang's biggest and best waterfall (น้ำตกตาดฟ้า).

Outside the park is the Phu Wiang Dinosaur Museum (พิพิธภัณฑ์ไดโนเสาร์ภูเวียง; ☑043 438206; adult/child 60/30B; ☉9am-5pm Tue-Sun; ♿) and the photogenic Si Wiang Dinosaur Park (อุทยานไดโนเสาร์ศรีเวียง; ☉daylight hours; ♿) FREE.

🛏 Sleeping & Eating

Phu Wiang is usually visited as a day trip from Khon Kaen, but it doesn't need to be. There are some hotels and village homestays (which must be arranged in advance through a Khon Kaen tour company) outside the park and two rough campsites inside the park. If you're camping, check in at the visitors centre first, and bring your own food.

There's a simple restaurant at the visitors centre that closes in the afternoon. There's more choice outside the park.

Pruksa Garden House HOTEL $
(☑043 291639; http://pruksagardenhouse.com; Phu Wiang–Nong Kae Rd; d incl breakfast 400-900B; 🅿❄🛜) The best hotel in the Phu Wiang National Park area lies away from the mountain in Phu Wiang city. The various sizes of bungalows are all good value and the setting is peaceful.

Chuan Chom Resort HOTEL $
(☑080 450 2502; chuanchomresort@gmail.com; d 600B; 🅿❄🛜) These lime-green bungalows across from the museum are showing their age, but they're still fine for a night if you want to be as close as possible to the national park. The restaurant in front is pretty good.

Tat Fa Campsite CAMPGROUND $
(☑043 358073; per person with own tent 30B, 3-person tent hire 325B; 🅿) The better of Phu Wiang National Park's two campsites is up near Tat Fa Waterfall. Facilities are basic, though the remoteness is a bonus.

❶ Getting There & Away

The park entrance is 90km west of Khon Kaen. Minivans (100B, two hours, six daily from 6am to 6pm) from Khon Kaen's Old Air-conditioned Bus Terminal go all the way to the national park, passing the Phu Wiang Dinosaur Museum on the way.

Nam Nao National Park

One of Thailand's most valuable nature reserves, Nam Nao National Park (อุทยาน แห่งชาติน้ำหนาว; ☑081 962 6236; Hwy 12; 200B, car/motorcycle 30/20B) covers 966 sq km across the Phetchabun Mountains west of Khon Kaen. With an average elevation of 800m, temperatures are fairly cool year-round (*nám nŏw* means 'water that feels cold') and frost can occur in December and January. There are evergreen and deciduous forests mixed with vast bamboo groves.

Nam Nao lies within the Western Isaan Forest Complex, a 6000-sq-km block of eight connected reserves, and wildlife is abundant. Elephant encounters are common enough that there's an electric fence around the campground and bungalows. Lucky visitors might also spot Malayan sun bears, gaur (wild cattle), Asian jackals, barking deer, gibbons and pangolins. There are even a few tigers. More than 200 species of birds, including great hornbill and silver pheasant, fly through the forest, and the exceptional visibility makes this one of Thailand's best bird-watching sites.

⊙ Sights & Activities

There are four marked hiking trails (1km, 3km, 4.5km and 5.8km) branching out from beside the visitors centre through a variety of habitats. You'll need to hire a ranger to walk anywhere else in the park, including the best wildlife-spotting area south of the highway. Spotlighting trips (800B per truck) can be arranged at the visitors centre.

Phu Khor Viewpoint   VIEWPOINT
(จุดชมวิวภูก้อ; Hwy 12, Nam Nao National Park) A gorgeous view at any time, Phu Khor is mostly visited at sunrise. The big mountain on the horizon is Phu Kradueng (p380). Phu Khor is 5km west of the visitors centre, a five-minute climb from the highway. Pickup trucks deliver people to the viewpoint for 50B per person or 600B per truck; reserve a seat at the visitors centre.

Tham Pha Hong Viewpoint   VIEWPOINT
(จุดชมวิวถ้ำผาหงษ์; Hwy 12, Nam Nao National Park) Eleven kilometres west of the visitors centre, this is the nearest place to get a good sunset view. Pickup trucks deliver people to the viewpoint for 70B per person or 840B per truck; reserve a seat at the visitors centre.

Nam Tok Haew Sai   WATERFALL
(น้ำตกเหวทราย; Hwy 12, Nam Nao National Park) Nam Tok Haew Sai, about 900m from the roadside parking area, is a beautiful waterfall dropping about 20m over naturally layered rock. Further down the same trail is smaller Nam Tok Sai Thong. They're really only worth seeing during or just after the rainy season, but the walk is pleasant any time.

⊨ Sleeping & Eating

The accommodation at Nam Nao is above average for Thai national parks. The cheapest bungalows (☑081 962 6236; http://nps. dnp.go.th/reservation.php; 4-12 person bungalows 1000-4000B; Ⓟ) (sleeping from four to 30 people) are pretty old, but the more expensive ones are large, modern and very comfortable. The campsite (☑081 962 6236; per person with own tent 30B, camping set (tent, sleeping bags, pillows & ground mats) for 2 people 250B; Ⓟ) is good too.

There are two very good restaurants (usually open from about 6am to 8pm) serving Thai and Isan food plus a little convenience store for snacks next to the visitors centre. You can order in the afternoon for evening delivery to your room or campsite.

ⓘ Getting There & Away

Take a Phitsanulok-bound bus from Khon Kaen's New Bus Terminal, but don't forget to tell the driver or the ticket collector you want to get off at Nam Nao (175B, 2½ hours). The park entrance is by the main road. The visitors centre and all the accommodation is a further 1.5km into the park.

NORTHEASTERN THAILAND NAM NAO NATIONAL PARK

AT A GLANCE

POPULATION
3,000,000

**DISTANCE FROM
BANGKOK TO KO
SAMET**
168 km

BEST DIVING
Ko Rang (p476)

**BEST SEAFOOD
RESTAURANT**
Pan & David Restau-
rant (p455)

BEST TEMPLE
Sanctuary of Truth
(p456)

WHEN TO GO
Dec–Mar High
season. Crowds and
prices highest on Ko
Chang and Ko Samet.
Weather reliably fine
and dry.

Oct–Nov Tail-end
of wet season;
landscape green and
rates reasonable.

Apr Hot in lead-up
to the monsoon but
most boats still run.
Good time to visit,
especially during
Songkran.

Sanctuary of Truth (p456), Pattaya
AMNAT30/SHUTTERSTOCK ©

Ko Chang & Eastern Seaboard

Two islands – Ko Samet and Ko Chang – are the magnets that draw travellers to the eastern seaboard, though the mainland has plenty of its own attractions, particularly the charismatic, old-world charm of Trat and Chanthaburi and the expat enclave of Pattaya.

Ko Samet, the nearest major island to Bangkok, is a flashpacker favourite. Further down the coast is Ko Chang, Thailand's second-largest island. Spend your days here diving, chilling on the west-coast beaches or hiking through dense jungle – then recover in time to experience the island's vibrant party scene.

Fewer travellers make it to Si Racha or Bang Saen, though their seafood restaurants and the latter's long beach make them worth a stopover. Less serene is the raucous resort of Pattaya, with its hedonistic nightlife and family-friendly attractions.

Ko Chang & Eastern Seaboard Highlights

1 Ko Chang (p474) Snorkelling and jungle trekking on Thailand's second-largest island.

2 Ko Kut (p485) Floating the day away at the marvellous beaches of this southeastern island.

3 Ko Wai (p489) Swimming with the fishes in gin-clear waters at this diminutive favourite near Ko Chang.

4 Ko Samet (p461) Walking between pretty coves on lovely Ko Samet.

5 Chanthaburi (p467) Strolling through the old waterfront community of this historic riverside town.

6 Trat (p470) Kicking back in the old-time atmosphere of this pleasing town's wooden shophouse quarter.

7 Ko Si Chang (p454) Taking a day trip on the ferry from pleasant Si Racha to peaceful Ko Si Chang.

8 Pattaya (p456) Hitting the water parks, ziplines and other family attractions that come as a pleasant surprise in the Pattaya region.

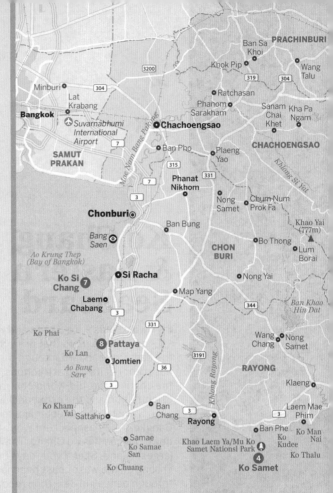

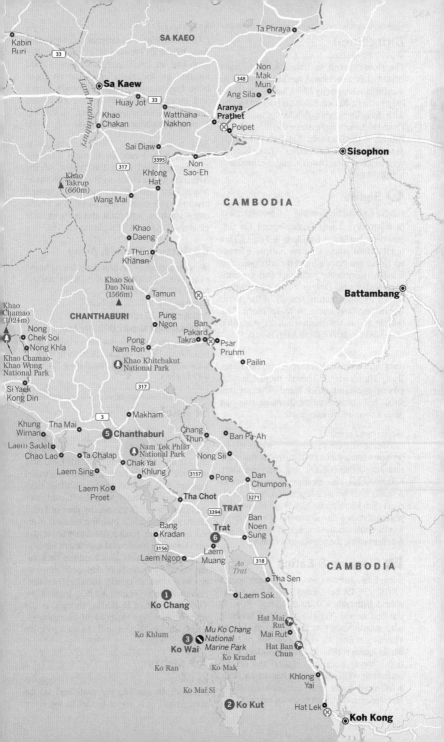

Bang Saen

🎵 038 / POP 45,000

The closest beach to Bangkok, Bang Saen (บางแสน) is a weekend favourite for those wanting to escape city life. A handsome 4km-long palm-lined beachfront is packed tightly with deckchairs beneath a sky of umbrellas. From the beach you can see the high-rises of Pattaya in the southern distance, but it may as well be on another planet – Bang Saen is very much a Thai beach scene. Seafood is a highlight here.

👁 Sights

Nezha Sathaizhu Temple BUDDHIST TEMPLE

(ศาลเจ้าหน่าจาซาไท้จื้อ, Wihahn Tepsatit Pra Giti-chairloem; Ang Sila; ⊙8am-5pm; P) FREE This opulent four-storey Chinese temple is fronted by an enormous heaven-earth pole and filled with intricate paintings and magnificent sculptures. Dragons and bats (which signify fortune) feature heavily in the decor. Locals regularly come to make merit. The temple is on the main road in Ang Sila, about 5km north of Bang Saen beach.

Khao Sam Muk HILL

(เขาสามมุข, Monkey Mountain; ⊙road open 5am-11pm) Hundreds of rhesus monkeys with greedy eyes and quick hands live on this small hill. Avoid feeding them, as this just makes them more aggressive.

Mangrove Forest Conservation Centre NATURE RESERVE

(ศูนย์ศึกษาธรรมชาติและอนุรักษ์ป่าชายเลนเพื่อการท่องเที่ยว; 🎵038 398268; Ang Sila; ⊙8.30am-6.30pm) FREE This expanse of mangroves in Ang Sila is such a well-kept secret, many locals don't even know it's here. A 2km-long wooden walkway runs a circuit around the mangrove forest. Look out for crabs, cockles and mud-fish, and enjoy the sounds and smells.

🛏 Sleeping & Eating

Song Row Guesthouse GUESTHOUSE $

(🎵038 193545; Soi 1, Bang Saen Sai 1; d with/without bathroom 400/300B) Song Row is the first on the left along a street bristling with guesthouses just back from the beach. There's no English sign; look for red and white lozenge tiles. It offers spotless family-run rooms both with shared and private bathrooms. The nicest one has an en suite, a full-sized fridge and a streetside balcony. Hot water and air-con costs an extra 50B.

Alice Hostel HOSTEL $

(🎵096-8489984; www.facebook.com/alices2019; dm/d 350/700B) Fronted by a popular coffee shop and bar, bright-red Alice enjoys a good location on the main beachfront roundabout. Dorms and private rooms are bright and airy, shared bathrooms spotless and there's a well-equipped kitchen. A step up from nearby budget guesthouses.

Andy's Seafood SEAFOOD $$

(Bang Saen Sai 1 near Soi 1; mains 120-350B; ⊙5pm-midnight) This is the busiest of the streetside seafood restaurants across from the beach. Watch the palms wave in the evening breeze as you enjoy whole steamed sea bass, clams stir-fried with chilli and basil, or tasty glass noodles baked with plump prawns.

ℹ Getting There & Away

Minivans and buses leave for the following from either side of Th Sukhumvit, close to the main turnoff into Bang Saen:

Bangkok 80B to 110B, one hour

Pattaya 40B, 30 minutes

Suvarnabhumi Airport 110B, one hour, hourly

Red sŏrng·tăa·ou (passenger pickup trucks) go to Si Racha (15B, 20 minutes, 5.30am to 9pm), while blue ones on Line 1 connect Bang Saen with Ang Sila.

Si Racha

🎵 038 / POP 24,000

Gateway to the lovely little island of Ko Si Chang, Si Racha (ศรีราชา; pronounced 'see-ra-cha') is an unlikely blend of traditional and modern. Colourful fishing boats and squid rigs are still moored here, but these days they share the water with giant container ships anchored off the nearby port of Laem Chabang. Similarly, a building boom is overshadowing the traditional low-rise centre with towering residential apartment blocks.

Sushi restaurants and karaoke bars cater for the hundreds of Japanese employees who work at nearby industrial estates, giving the town centre a Little Tokyo vibe. The real heart of Si Racha, though, is the waterfront, where rickety stilt guesthouses, a peaceful health park and the busy pier are very picturesque.

👁 Sights

Ko Loi ISLAND

(เกาะลอย) Attached to the mainland via an 800m road, this rocky island is the ferry

Si Racha

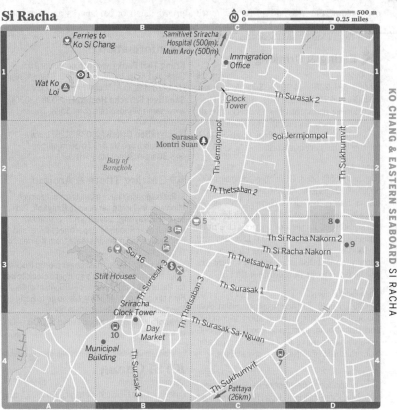

Si Racha

Sights
1 Ko Loi...A1

Sleeping
2 Samchai Resort.....................................B3
3 Seaview Sriracha Hotel B3

Eating
4 My One..B3

Drinking & Nightlife
5 Common Room......................................C3
6 Teab Ta B3

Transport
7 Buses to Bangkok.................................C4
8 Minivans to Bangkok D3
9 Minivans to Pattaya and Rayong.........D3
10 Sörng·tăa·ou to Pattaya & Bang
 Saen...B4

point for Ko Si Chang, and is home to an ornate Thai-Chinese temple and a viewing area for the impressive sunsets.

🛏 Sleeping

Samchai Resort   GUESTHOUSE, HOSTEL $
(☎081 963 1855; Soi 10, Th Jermjompol; d 350-900B; ❈🐾🛜) There's plenty of character at this sprawling pier guesthouse that has a wide range of pretty basic rooms, from functional windowless boxes to air-con sea-view suites.

This is the go-to waterside budget option in Si Racha; cheaper rooms are fan-only. It has a helpful English-speaking owner.

Seaview Sriracha Hotel   HOTEL $$
(☎038 325700; seaview_hotel@hotmail.com; 50-54 Th Jermjompol; d incl breakfast 990-1590B; ❈@🛜) Very central and backing on to the waterfront, this has welcoming staff, large, comfortable rooms with air-con and TV, and a decent restaurant. Rooms at the back

overlooking the sea and piers are much more peaceful than those at the front, which suffer from road noise. There's no lift.

✕ Eating & Drinking

My One VIETNAMESE $
(☎089 693 3270; 14/10 Th Surasak 1; mains 50-160B; ☉9am-9pm) This simple Thai-Vietnamese restaurant has a variety of fresh, healthy dishes, including rice paper rolls and salads. It's not signed in English; look for the coffee cart out front.

Mum Aroi SEAFOOD $$
(☎038 771555; Soi 8, Th Jermjompol; mains 160-550B; ☉10am-11pm; 🐾) Mum Aroi delivers on its name, 'delicious corner'. This is *the* place to enjoy a seafood meal with views of the squid rigs; its tiers of terraces give most diners a shot at a water vista. Live fish and seafood occupy the numerous tanks as you enter and most dishes are sold by weight. It's on the waterfront 1km north of Ko Loi.

Common Room CAFE
(☎089 777 6419; 73 Th Jermjompol; ☉9am-9pm Tue-Sun) The brick interior, spongy couches and bric-a-brac, alongside good strong coffee and cakes make this a soothing pitstop from the heat of Si Racha's busy streets.

Teab Ta CRAFT BEER
(www.facebook.com/teabtasriracha; Soi 16, Th Jermjompol; ☉5pm-midnight Mon-Fri, 4pm-midnight Sat & Sun; 🐾) On the long pier, unassuming Teab Ta has a fabulous selection of craft beer from around the world, including various northern European brewing masterpieces, all at northern European prices. It's a great spot for a sundowner on the deck over the water: a lovely outlook. There's a reasonably priced menu of bar snacks and a modern indie soundtrack.

ℹ Information

Krung Thai Bank (www.ktb.co.th; cnr Th Surasak 1 & Th Jermjompol; ☉8.30am-4.30pm Mon-Fri) Has an ATM and exchange facilities.

Samitivej Sriracha Hospital (☎038 320300; www.samitivejhospitals.com; Soi 8, Th Jermjompol)

Immigration Office (☎038 312571; www.immchonburi.go.th; 3/1 Th Jermjompol; ☉8.30am-4.30pm Mon-Fri)

ℹ Getting There & Around

Si Racha doesn't have a bus terminal as such. Minivans, including services to **Bangkok**, **Pattaya and Rayong**, leave from Th Sukhumvit (Hwy 3) near Robinson department store, and both **buses** and minivans leave from the nearby IT mall, Tuk Com.

White *sŏrng·tăa·ou* (passenger pickup trucks) leave from near Si Racha's southern **clock tower** for Pattaya's Naklua market (40B, 45 minutes, 6am to 6pm); orange *sŏrng·tăa·ou* go to Bang Saen (20B, 20 minutes, 6am to 6pm).

Motorbike taxis zip around town for 30B to 40B.

Ko Si Chang

☎038 / POP 5000

Once a royal beach retreat, Ko Si Chang (เกาะสีชัง) has a fishing-village atmosphere and enough attractions to make it a decent day's excursion from Si Racha, or a fine overnight stop for those who want to chill out. It gets very busy at weekends, when Thais come to eat seafood, snap selfies by the sea and make merit at the local temples.

SI RACHA TRANSPORT CONNECTIONS

DESTINATION	BUS	MINIVAN	TRAIN
Bangkok's Eastern Bus Terminal (Ekamai)	100B, 1½hr, hourly 5am-8pm		
Bangkok Hualamphong			from 30B, 3¼hr, 1 daily Mon-Fri
Bangkok's Northern Bus Terminal (Mo Chit)	110B, 2hr, hourly 5am-7.30pm		
Bangkok Suvarnabhumi International Airport	110B, 1hr, hourly 5.10am-8pm		
Bangkok's Victory Monument		110B, 1½hr, every 30min 5am-8pm	
Pattaya		40B, 30min, frequent	

Hiring a scooter at the pier is a great way to get around, as there's very little four-wheeled traffic here.

◎ Sights & Activities

Several locals run snorkelling trips to nearby Ko Khang Khao (Bat Island), which has a good beach, or you can take a speedboat (400B) there from the main pier.

Kayaks are available (200B per hour) on Hat Tham Phang. You can paddle to Ko Khang Khao in 45 minutes.

Phra Chudadhut Palace   HISTORIC SITE
(พระจุฑาธุชราชฐาน; ⊙9am-5pm; FREE) This former royal palace was used by Rama V (King Chulalongkorn; r 1868–1910) over the summer months, but was abandoned when the French briefly occupied the island in 1893. The main throne hall – a magnificent golden teak structure known as Vimanmek Teak Mansion – was moved to Bangkok in 1910 and is now in Dusit Gardens. What's left are subdued Victorian-style buildings set in garden-like grounds. It's a 15-minute stroll from the ferry. The museum buildings are closed Mondays.

San Chao Pho Khao Yai   BUDDHIST TEMPLE
(ศาลเจ้าพ่อเขาใหญ่) FREE The most imposing sight on the island, this ornate dragon-infested temple dates back to the days when Chinese traders anchored in the sheltered waters. During New Year in February, the island is packed with Chinese tourists. There arc shrine caves, multiple platforms and a good view of the island and sea. It's just north of the main town.

Sichang Healing House   MASSAGE
(☑081 572 7840; off Th Makham Thaew; massages 300-600B; ⊙9am-4pm Thu-Tue) The charming English-speaking owner of this leafy haven offers a reliable range of massages and sells homemade health products. There are also modest bamboo rooms for rent (300B).

🛏 Sleeping & Eating

Rim Talay Resort   CABIN $
(☑089 091 6974; Th Makham Thaew; d 800-1500B) Set behind Pan & David restaurant, this solid series of rooms and bungalows occupies spacious grounds and includes a couple of characterful converted fishing boats in dry dock.

Somewhere Ko Sichang   BOUTIQUE HOTEL $$
(☑038 109400; www.somewherehotel.com; 194/1 Mu 3, Th Thewawong; d incl breakfast 2600-3600B;

P ✳ ⌘) Modern and charming, this place with a pool and sea views occupies a very central but secluded location. The 20 stylish rooms have loads of space and a breezy maritime feel to the decor; most have balconies and sea views. The Verandah restaurant area is handsome and staff eager to please. A relaxing and stylish retreat.

Charlie's Bungalows   GUESTHOUSE $$
(☑061 749 4242; Th Makham Thaew; d 1000-1100B; P ✳ ⌘) Bright, all-white bungalows set around a garden. All come with TVs and DVD players. Friendly and helpful staff. Book ahead at weekends and public holidays.

FlowerBlue   CAFE $
(☑081 305 5544; www.facebook.com/flowerblue.coffee; mains 70-280B; ⊙7am-10pm; 🛜) Popular with the Bangkok set, who appreciates the air-con and fair prices, this trendy cafe is always busy. It does breakfasts, burgers, speciality coffees and more in an attractive space festooned with real plants and other botanical iconography.

★ Pan & David Restaurant   INTERNATIONAL, THAI $$
(☑038 216629; www.ko-sichang.com; 167 Mu 3, Th Makham Thaew; mains 150-450B; ⊙10am-10.30pm Mon, Tue, Thu & Fri, 8.30am-10pm Sat & Sun; 🛜 ☑) Free-range chicken, house-made ice cream, a reasonable wine list, excellent Thai dishes and an Italian touch – you can't go wrong here. Pan & David also specialises in local seafood fresh off the boat – squid, crab, prawns and fish.

❶ Information

The Pan & David website (www.ko-sichang.com) is an excellent source of local information.
Kasikornbank (99/12 Th Atsadang; ⊙8.30am-3.30pm) Has an ATM and exchange facilities. There's also an ATM outside the 7-Eleven before the pier.

❶ Getting There & Around

Boats to Ko Si Chang leave from the Koi Loi pier in Si Racha (one way 50B, 45 minutes, hourly from 7am to 8pm), dodging the plethora of cargo ships unloading in the bay. From Ko Si Chang boats shuttle back hourly from 6am to 7pm.

Motorbike taxis wait at the pier and will take you anywhere for 30B to 50B, and souped-up *săhm·lór* (three-wheel pedicabs; also spelt săamláw) do tours of the main spots for 250B.

Motorbikes are available to rent on the pier (per hour/day/24 hours 80/250/300B).

Pattaya

038 / POP 320,000

Even if you know exactly what to expect of Pattaya, it still comes as an eye-popping sensory explosion. Multicultural, hyper-touristy Pattaya (เมืองพัทยา) offers some excellent and good-value places to stay and eat, and the area is also a family-friendly coastal resort. Nevertheless, the city itself is no tropical paradise; its seedy reputation is totally deserved, with hundreds of beer bars, go-go clubs and massage parlours. Much of the rest is dedicated to mass-market sun-seeking tourism, with a huge retired expat population, and enormous tour groups hurried through town in an almost constant stream. For a relaxing stay in Pattaya, base yourself outside the central area.

The city is built around Ao Pattaya, a wide, crescent-shaped bay that was one of Thailand's first beach resorts in the 1960s when American GIs came for some R & R. Pattaya Neua (North Pattaya) is more upmarket while Pattaya Tai (South Pattaya) remains the nightlife hub.

Sights

Sanctuary of Truth BUDDHIST MONUMENT
(ปราสาทสัจธรรม; ☑ 038 367 2229; www.sanctuaryoftruth.com; Soi Naklua 12; adult/child 450/225B; ☑ 8am-6pm) Made entirely of intricately carved wood (without any metal nails) and commanding a celestial view of the ocean, the Sanctuary of Truth is best described as a visionary environment: part art installation, religious shrine and cultural monument. Constructed in four wings dedicated to Thai, Khmer, Chinese and Indian religious iconography, its architecture and setting is impressive.

Anek Kusala Sala MUSEUM
(อเนกกุศลศาลา/วิหารเซียน, Viharn Sien; ☑ 038 343555; off Th Sukhumvit, Sattahip; 50B; ☑ 8am-5.30pm) A popular stop for tour groups, this museum contains more than 300 impressive pieces of Chinese artwork, mainly bronze and brass statues depicting historical figures as well as Buddhist, Confucian and Taoist deities. Founded by Sa-nga Kulkobkiat, a Thai national who grew up in China, the museum was intended as a friendship-building project between the two countries.

The museum is 16km south of central Pattaya; take a Pattaya–Sattahip sŏrng·tǎa·ou (25B) to the Wat Yangsangwaram turn-off. Hire a passing motorbike to go the final 5km to the museum. Ask the driver to stick around, as a lift back is hard to find. Private transport costs 1500B.

Wat Phra Yai BUDDHIST SITE
(วัดพระใหญ่, Big Buddha) The giant golden Buddha figure of Wat Phra Yai sits atop this forested hill between Jomtien and South Pattaya. The serene Buddha dates back to when Pattaya was a small fishing village. You can walk here from the southern end of Walking St.

Ko Lan ISLAND
(เกาะล้าน) Day trippers head for this small island, 7km offshore from central Pattaya. On weekends, its five beaches entertain thousands of visitors and the aquamarine sea is busy with banana boats and other marine merriment. Take a ferry from Bali Hai pier at the southern end of Walking St. Some go to the main village; others go to Tawaen beach. You can also charter speedboats from along Beach Rd. The last boat back is at 6pm.

Activities

Ramayana Water Park WATER PARK
(☑ 033 005929; www.ramayanawaterpark.com; adult/child 1440/1040B; ☑ 10am-6pm; ☑) This sizeable water park is the pick of the parks for the whole family, with a huge array of slides and pools, as well as bars and buffet restaurants. It's about 20km southeast of Pattaya, with packages that include transport available via the website. Towels and lockers also available.

Flight of the Gibbon ADVENTURE SPORTS
(☑ 053 010660; www.flightofthegibbon.com; tours 3999B) This zipline course extends 3km via 26 platforms through the forest canopy of Khao Kheow Open Zoo, between Pattaya and Bangkok. It's an all-day tour with additional add-on activities, such as a jungle obstacle course and a visit to the neighbouring zoo. Children 1m tall and over can do the zip line independently, while nippers can ride tandem with adults. Free pick-ups from Bangkok or Pattaya.

Sleeping

Accommodation in Pattaya can be pricey by Thai standards but there's a growing number of backpacker hostels along with reasonably priced midrange hotels. Competition means there are good deals to be found at all levels. Rooms around central or South Pattaya tend to be cheaper but closer to the noisy nightlife. North Pattaya and parts of

Pattaya

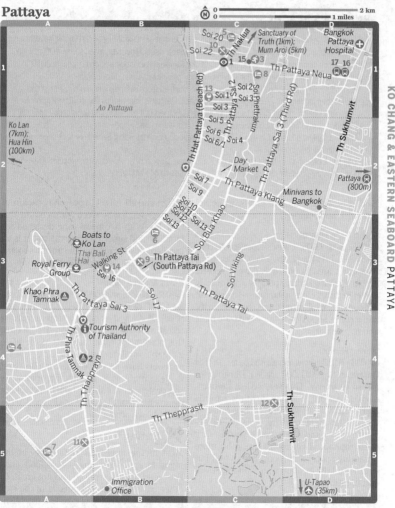

Pattaya

◉ Sights

✈ Activities, Courses & Tours

🛏 Sleeping

✗ Eating

🍸 Drinking & Nightlife

ℹ Transport

PATTAYA'S BEACHES

Pattaya has done a lot to clean up its beach in recent years; smoking and littering have been banned and sand was brought in to widen the beach itself. However, after some 400 million baht was spent on reclaiming the beach, an unseasonal monsoonal storm in early 2019 washed half of it away. A major beach rebuilding project is again underway.

Run-off from the hundreds of boats moored metres from shore make swimming in the centre of town a distinctly unappetising prospect. Better is Jomtien to the south, which has a gay-friendly beach at Hat Dongtan and a more subdued but entertaining and family-friendly beachfront scene all round. To the north, Naklua is also quietly appealing.

Around 20km south of Pattaya, there's a good scene at Bang Sare, a resort area with a long, narrow beach

The best beaches in the area are on Ko Samae San, a tiny island with good snorkelling, and the navy-run Hat Nahng Ram, both 35km south of Pattaya..

Naklua host the signature hotels, while Soi Bua Khao and Jomtien have budget options.

Sleep Cafe Hostel
HOSTEL $

(☏ 063 360 0005; www.sleepcafehostel.com; 78/84 Soi 1, Th Pattaya 2; dm/d 450/1000B; ✳ 🛜) In a quiet area in North Pattaya (opposite Art in Paradise), this spotless and orderly hostel features elegant Japanese-style decor. Air-con and wi-fi throughout, good security, and a coffee shop downstairs. Separate male and female dorms.

Nonze Hostel
HOSTEL $

(☏ 038 711112; www.nonzehostel.com; Th Hat Pattaya; s/tw 600/1300B; ✳ 🛜) Dormitories are so yesterday! This very stylish industrial-chic seafront building features capsule beds – tiny boxes stacked up like building blocks – in singles or twins. They offer plenty of privacy and are sweet if you're not a claustrophobe. Twin rooms give a bit more breathing space. Bathrooms are shared but decent and the location near Walking St will suit nightlife lovers.

Garden Lodge Hotel
HOTEL $$

(☏ 038 429109; www.gardenlodgepattaya. net; cnr Soi 20 & Th Naklua; d/bungalow/ste 1200/1700/3000B; 🅿 ✳ 🛜 🏊) Rooms here are old-fashioned but surrounded by landscaped gardens and a large swimming pool. A favourite among German tourists, it's in the salubrious end of Pattaya and a decent option for families.

⭐ Rabbit Resort
RESORT $$$

(☏ 038 251730; www.rabbitresort.com; Hat Dongtan, Jomtien; d incl breakfast 3000-9000B; 🅿 ✳ @ 🛜 🏊) On a different qualitative planet to most Pattaya accommodation, Rabbit Resort has stunning, stylish and secluded bungalows and villas that showcase Thai design and art, all set in peaceful beachfront greenery hidden between Jomtien and Pattaya Tai. With two pools (one designed for families) and superb service, the resort is an excellent upscale option. The upstairs rooms are particularly luminous and appealing.

Birds & Bees Resort
RESORT $$$

(☏ 038 250556; www.cabbagesandcondoms.com; Soi 4, Th Phra Tamnak; d 2500-11,000B; 🅿 ✳ @ 🛜 🏊) 🍽 As well as being a tropical garden resort with two pools and good-sized rooms, this place helps fund the work of the PDA, a notable rural development charity. Cheaper rooms have no views. The complex itself is delightful, with meandering pathways signposted with quirky, thought-provoking comments about the state of things. There's direct beach access.

🍴 Eating

Most of the numerous restaurants in the nightlife area, including the seafood markets, tend to be overpriced and not great. In other parts of town and outside of the city, however, there are a few excellent establishments; it's worth tracking them down.

Bang Sare, busy at weekends, has a trendy international and Thai dining scene.

Thepprasit Market
MARKET $

(cnr Th Thepprasit & Th Sukhumvit; snacks 30-80B; ⏰ 4-10pm Fri-Sun) As well as intriguing knick-knacks and endless clothes stalls, this thriving weekend night market has a great range of smoothies, noodles and Thai snacks.

⭐ Sketch Book Art Cafe
INTERNATIONAL, THAI $$

(☏ 038 251625; 478/938 Mu 12, Th Tha Phraya; mains 125-325B; ⏰ 8.30am-10pm) This gorgeous leafy art cafe with a warren of rooms offers pleasant respite from the normal Pattaya vibe. It's surrounded by a sprawling garden, and the restaurant's walls are covered in the owner's artwork. Smoothies are lush, the coffee is good and the Thai food fresh. Western dishes easily top 300B. Painting materials are sold if you feel inspired.

Glass House THAI **$$**
(☑ 081 266 6110; www.glasshouse-pattaya.com; Soi Najomtien 10, Hat Jomtien, Sattahip; mains 120-650B; ⊘ 11am-midnight; 🔊) Diners at this partially glassed-in beachfront spot lounge in couches on the candle-lit sand as waiters deliver seafood, pizza and steaks. The quality of the Thai dishes in particular is excellent, and the atmosphere romantic. It's about 9km south of central Pattaya, so requires a special trip unless you're staying at Jomtien.

Five Star J VEGETARIAN **$$**
(www.fivestarj.com; 313/37 Th Pattaya Tai; mains 70-400B; ⊘ 11am-11pm; ☑) This long-running vegetarian and vegan restaurant has a loyal following and is close to the action. It's a tiny place but kept spotless, and has air-con and wi-fi. The food, from noodles and curries to veg pizza and tofu dishes, is consistently good.

La Baguette CAFE, BAKERY **$$**
(☑ 038 421707; www.labaguettepattaya.com; 164/1 Mu 5, Th Naklua; mains 260-340B; ⊘ 8am-midnight; ✳🔊) Just north of the Dolphin Roundabout, this stylish French-style cafe serves excellent salads, crepes, croissants and, of course, baguettes, plus numerous coffee and tea options. The light-filled interior is fine place to sink into an antique sofa. Make a reservation if visiting at the weekend. There's another branch on the way to Jomtien.

🍷 Drinking & Nightlife

Despite the profusion of identikit beer bars, there are still some places for a no-strings-attached drink, several attached to hotels along the beach.

Walking St is a centre of sleaze but its profusion of bars is more fun for those just interested in a night out than are those in the tawdrier red-light zone a block back from the beach. Soi 6 is even more packed with sleazy beer bars.

Hot Tuna BAR
(Walking St; ⊘ 9pm-late) There are a few live-music venues mixed in with the tourist tat on Walking St, but Hot Tuna consistently has the best cover bands. They take requests for classic rock throughout the night and usually deliver flawlessly.

Gulliver's BAR
(www.gulliverbangkok.com; Th Hat Pattaya; ⊘ 3pm-2am; 🔊) The rather grand neocolonial facade and mini Statue of Liberty belie the fairly standard sports bar inside this beach-road spot. Decent beer and service, air-con and an absence of sex workers can make it an attractive option.

ℹ️ Information

EMERGENCY
The tourist police **head office** (☑ emergency 1155; tourist@police.go.th) is beside the Tourism Authority of Thailand office on Th Phra Tamnak. There are police boxes along **Pattaya** and Jomtien beaches.

Bangkok Pattaya Hospital (☑ 038 259999; www.bangkokpattayahospital.com; 301 Mu 6, Th Sukhumvit, Naklua; ⊘ 24hr) For first-class health care.

IMMIGRATION
Immigration Office (☑ 038 252750; www.immigration.go.th; Soi 5, Hat Jomtien; ⊘ 8.30am-noon & 1-4.30pm Mon-Fri)

MONEY
There are banks and ATMs throughout the city.

SAFE TRAVEL
➡ Most problems in Pattaya are alcohol-induced, especially bad driving and fights.
➡ Leave valuables in your room to be on the safe side.
➡ Avoid renting jet skis as scams involving fictional damage are common.

TOURIST INFORMATION
Tourism Authority of Thailand (TAT; ☑ 038 428750; www.tourismthailand.org; 609 Th Phra Tamnak; ⊘ 8.30am-4.30pm) Located at the northwestern edge of Rama IX Park. Helpful staff, brochures and maps.

WEBSITES
Pattaya Mail (www.pattayamail.com) One of the city's English-language weekly newspapers.
Pattaya One (www.pattayaone.news) Offers an intriguing insight into the darker side of the city.
Love Pattaya (https://lovepattayathailand.com) Everything you ever wanted to know about the Pattaya scene.

ℹ️ Getting There & Away

AIR
Pattaya's airport is **U-Tapao** (UTP; ☑ 038 245595; www.utapao.com), 33km south of town.

Make sure taxi drivers know it's this airport you want, or they may assume you're going to Bangkok.

Destinations around Thailand are served from here daily by **Bangkok Airways** (☏ 038 412382; www.bangkokair.com; Fairtex Arcade, Th Pattaya Neua), **Air Asia** (www.airasia.com) and **Lion Air** (https://lionairthai.com).

AirAsia also has international flights, as do a couple of other airlines.

Regular charter flights also operate here.

BOAT

A fast catamaran service across the Gulf of Thailand connects Pattaya and Hua Hin. Despite some problems coping with choppy conditions, the service, run by **Royal Ferry Group** (☏ 038 488999; www.royalferrygroup.com), is now established, charging 1250/1550B for standard/business class for the two-hour crossing, which slashes the overland travel time. At time of writing there was one service daily at 1pm.

Boats to **Ko Lan** leave Pattaya's Bali Hai pier (30B, 45 minutes, 11 daily) at the southern end of Walking St.

BUS & MINIVAN

The main **bus station** (Th Pattaya Neua) has services to Bangkok, including to Bangkok's Suvarnabhumi airport (300B, 1½-two hours, six daily) run by **Bell Travel Service** (☏ 084 427 4608; www.belltravelservice.com; Th Pattaya Neua), which does hotel pick-ups if you prebook.

Roong Reuang Coaches (www.airportpattaya bus.com) runs from Th Tha Phraya in Jomtien, near the corner of Th Thep Prasit, to Suvarnabhumi airport and vice versa for a much cheaper 120B (two hours, hourly 7am to 9pm).

Minivans heading north to Bangkok leave from the corner of Th Sukhumvit and Th Pattaya Klang.

Minivans heading for the Cambodian border leave from the junction of Th Sukhumvit and Th Pattaya Tai.

Downtown travel agents can book minivan services to Ko Chang (550B), Ko Mak (750B) and Ko Kut (800B).

TRAIN

Pattaya Train Station (☏ 038 429285) is off Th Sukhumvit, east of town.

❶ Getting Around

Locally known as 'baht buses', *sŏrng·tăa·ou* (passenger pickup trucks) do a loop along the major roads; just hop on and pay 10B when you get off. If you are going all the way to or from Naklua, you will have to change vehicles at the **Dolphin Roundabout** (วงเวียนโลมา; Th Naklua & Pattaya Neua) in Pattaya Neua. Baht buses also run to the bus station from the Dolphin Roundabout. If you are going further afield, you can charter a baht bus; establish the price beforehand.

Motorbikes can be hired for 200B a day.

Rayong & Ban Phe

☏ 038 / POP 70,000

You're most likely to transit through these towns en route to Ko Samet. Rayong (ระยอง) is a sizeable, sprawling city connected by frequent bus services. The little port of Ban Phe (บ้านเพ), 18km east, has ferry services to Ko Samet and a decent beach.

PATTAYA TRANSPORT CONNECTIONS

DESTINATION	BUS	MINIVAN	TRAIN
Aranya Prathet (for Cambodia)	340B, 5hr, 5 daily	260B, 5hr, hourly 4am-6pm	
Bangkok's Eastern Bus Terminal (Ekamai)	108B, 2hr, every 30min 4.30am-11pm	160B, 2hr, frequent	
Bangkok Hualamphong			from 31B, 4hr, 1 daily Mon-Fri
Bangkok's Northern Bus Terminal (Mo Chit)	117B, 2½hr, every 40min 4.30am-9pm	160B, 2½hr, frequent	
Bangkok's Southern Bus Terminal	119B, 3hr, every 2hr 6am-6.30pm	150B, 2½hr, hourly	
Ko Samet		160B, 1hr, hourly	
Rayong		80B, 1½hr, frequent	
Si Racha		40B, 50min, frequent	from 5B, 30 minutes, 1 daily Mon-Fri

🍴 Sleeping & Eating

Rayong has a wide range of hotel accommodation, though most of it isn't particularly central. Ban Phe is also well stocked with guesthouse rooms for less than 700B. That said, transport links are good enough that there's no real reason to stay in either town.

La Paillote   GUESTHOUSE $

(📞038 651625; www.lapaillotebanphe.com; Ban Phe; d 700-900B; ❀🤖) A decent budget option in Ban Phe, handy for the piers and beach. It offers welcoming staff, simple but comfortable rooms with decent facilities and an on-site outdoor restaurant and bar. There are good family options.

Rayong President Hotel   HOTEL $

(📞038 622771; www.rayongpresidenthotel.com; Soi Klongkhud, off Th Sukhumvit, Rayong; d 600-850B; 🅿❀🤖) Rayong has better hotels than this, but they are all quite a way from the centre; this is one of the few within walking distance of bus station 1. Rooms have been renovated, and offer pretty good value for the price. Rates with breakfast are a bit higher.

From bus station 1, cross to the other side of Th Sukhumvit and walk right. Look for a Siam Commercial Bank on the corner and turn left.

Tamnanpar   THAI $$

(📞038 652884; 167/6 Mu 7, Ban Phe; mains 150-350B; ⊙noon-midnight; 🤖) Though it is heavily visited by coach parties, this impressive rainforest-style resort restaurant is still worth making a detour for. Experience tasty Thai food and check out the appropriately jungly designer bathrooms. There is also a water park on-site (adult/child 200/100B). It's about 750m off the main road between Rayong and Ban Phe.

ℹ Getting There & Away

Rayong has two bus stations: central **bus station 1** and the newer **bus station 2**, 7km northwest of downtown. All long-distance services use bus station 2. *Sŏrng·tăa·ou* (passenger pickup trucks; 15B, 20 minutes) regularly connect the two.

Minivans from Rayong's bus station 2 go to Bangkok's eastern (Ekamai) and northern (Mo Chit) bus terminals (both 160B, 3½ hours, hourly 4.40am to 8pm); these can also drop you off at the AirportLink station one stop away from Suvarnabhumi airport. Frequent minivans also head to Pattaya (100B, two hours), Chanthaburi (150B, two hours) and Trat (200B, three hours).

Regular boats and speedboats connect Ban Phe with Ko Samet. Buses opposite Ban Phe's Nuanthip pier go to/from Bangkok Ekamai (170B, four hours, every two hours, 7am to 6pm).

Ban Phe also has minivan services to Laem Ngop for boats to Ko Chang (250B, three hours, three daily) and Bangkok's Victory Monument (200B, four hours, every 40 minutes). For Pattaya, it's cheaper to go to Rayong and change there.

ℹ Getting Around

From Rayong's central bus station 1, there are frequent *sŏrng·tăa·ou* to Ban Phe (25B, 30 minutes, every 15 minutes). From Ban Phe, catch them outside the main piers.

Ko Samet

Tiny Ko Samet (เกาะเสม็ด) has been attracting backpackers making the relatively short hop from Bangkok for years, but these days you'll find just as many Thais and Chinese tour groups. The sandy shores, cosy coves and aquamarine waters attract ferry-loads of Bangkokians looking to party each weekend, while tour groups pack out the main beach and many resorts. Fire-juggling shows and beach barbecues are nightly events on the northern beaches, but the southern parts of the island are far more secluded and sedate.

Despite being the closest big island to Bangkok, Ko Samet is surprisingly underdeveloped, with a thick jungle interior. Most of the southern coves have only one or two resorts.

◎ Sights & Activities

On some islands you beach-hop, but on Ko Samet you cove-hop. The coastal footpath traverses rocky headlands, cicada-serenaded forests and one stunning bay after another, where the mood becomes successively more mellow the further south you go.

Various activities such as kayaking, parasailing, diving, snorkelling, standup paddleboarding (SUP) and angling are available. You'll see island tours advertised from 400B to 1500B depending on the number of islands visited.

🍴 Sleeping

Though resorts are replacing bungalows, much of Ko Samet's accommodation is simple and old-fashioned. There are a few fan rooms for less than 700B and air-con bungalows with sea views can go for 1000B to 1500B. Beaches south of Hat Sai Kaew have only a handful of places. Look for discounts during low season and on weekdays.

Ko Samet

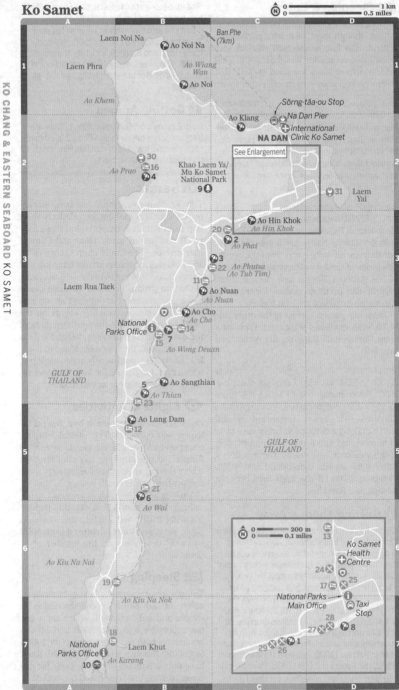

Laem Noi Na

Laem Phra

Ao Noi Na

Ao Wiang Wan

Ban Phe (7km)

Ao Kham

Ao Noi

Ao Klang

Sŏrng·tăa·ou Stop

Na Dan Pier

International Clinic Ko Samet

NA DAN

30
16
4

Ao Prao

Khao Laem Ya/ Mu Ko Samet National Park

9

See Enlargement

Laem Yai

31

Ao Hin Khok

Ao Hin Khok

20
2

Ao Phai

3
22

Ao Phutsa (Ao Tub Tim)

11

Ao Nuan

Ao Nuan

Laem Rua Taek

Ao Cho

Ao Cha

National Parks Office

7
15
14

Ao Wong Deuan

GULF OF THAILAND

5
Ao Sangthian

Ao Thian

23

Ao Lung Dam

12

GULF OF THAILAND

21
6

Ao Wai

Ao Kiu Na Nai

19

Ao Kiu Na Nok

18

National Parks Office

Laem Khut

10

Ao Karang

Enlargement

13

Ko Samet Health Centre

24
25
17

National Parks Main Office

Taxi Stop

28
27
8

29
26
1

Ko Samet

A word on noise: popular beaches Hat Sai Kaew, Ao Hin Khok, Ao Phai and Ao Wong Deuan host loud night-time parties.

🛏 Hat Sai Kaew & Na Dan

In the island's northeastern corner near the ferry pier, and an extension of Na Dan, Hat Sai Kaew is the island's widest, busiest and wildest stretch of sand. Sunbathers, sarong-sellers, speedboats, jet skis and restaurants take up almost every inch of space and the beach can feel totally overrun by package tourists at times. The scene is lively at night, with at least two nightly fire shows.

Mossman House   GUESTHOUSE $
(📞038 644017; Hat Sai Kaew; d 800-1200B; ❄🛜) This sound guesthouse has large, comforta-

ble rooms along a shared veranda and leafy grounds. It's on the main street, just before the national park ticket office; choose a spot at the back for some quiet as the bar opposite stays open late.

Baan Minnie   GUESTHOUSE, APARTMENT $$
(📞086 691 9662; Silver Park Ave, Na Dan; d 1000-1400B, apt from 2000B; 🅿❄🛜) There are several options in these rows of terraced accommodation behind the main strip in Ko Samet's capital village. Rooms have firm, comfortable mattresses and attractive modern decor; some have a patio seating area. There are also 'townhouses', well-kept apartments, some duplex, where you can come and go as you please.

🛏 Ao Hin Khok & Ao Phai

Less frenetic than its northern neighbour Hat Sai Kaew, Ao Hin Khok is a gorgeous bay attracting a younger crowd. Plenty of places to stay, eat and drink.

A short walk west of Ao Hin Khok over a rocky headland, Ao Phai is a pretty bay with some worthy bars and eateries and a backpacker scene.

Silver Sand   RESORT $$
(📞038 644300; www.silversandsamed.com; Ao Phai; d/tr/f incl breakfast 2500/3500/4500B; 🅿❄🛜) An ever-expanding empire, Silver Sand is a miniresort, complete with restaurant, shops and a lively LGBT-friendly bar and nightclub. It can feel a little impersonal but the rooms are decent quality, facilities are great and the place is set on a super strip of beach close to most of the island action.

Samed Pavilion Resort   RESORT $$$
(📞089 097 1112; www.samedpavilionresort.com; 89/1 Moo 4, Ao Phai; d incl breakfast 2550-6000B; 🅿❄@🛜🏊) A step up from those around it, this handsome boutique resort has elegant, spacious rooms in an upstairs-downstairs configuration tightly set around a sociable pool. It's well geared for families, with beach access and seclusion from the main road. Rates are usually best online, but it offers low season and midweek promotions for direct bookings.

🛏 Ao Phutsa & Ao Nuan

Cute, sandy Ao Phutsa (Ao Tub Tim), south of Ao Hin Khok and Ao Phai, strikes a good balance between being relatively accessible but generally not too crowded. Basing yourself

WORTH A TRIP

ISLAND TOURS

Ko Samet, along with nine neighbouring islands, is part of the Khao Laem Ya/Mu Ko Samet National Park. While there is some development on the other islands, most visitors opt for day trips. Ko Kudee has a small, pretty sandy stretch, clear water for decent snorkelling and a nice little hiking trail. Ko Man Nai is home to the Rayong Turtle Conservation Centre, which is a breeding place for endangered sea turtles, and has a small visitor centre.

Agents for boat tours can be found on the popular beaches and have a couple of boat-trip options on offer (from 500B per person).

here lets you enjoy the beach's best moments in the early morning and evening.

★ **Ao Nuan Bungalows**   BUNGALOW $$
(✆ 038 644334, 081 781 4875; Ao Nuan; bungalows with fan 900-1200B, with air-con 1500-3000B; ❄ 🤝) Samet's one remaining bohemian bay is tucked off the main road down a dirt track. Running down a jungle hillside to the sea, these cute wooden bungalows range from simple fan-cooled affairs with shared cold-water bathroom to romantic air-conditioned retreats with elegant deck furniture. There's a bar and simple restaurant; if you need more action, Ao Phutsa is a few minutes' stroll away. You can make reservations by SMS.

Tubtim Resort   RESORT $$
(✆ 038 644025; www.samedtubtim.com; 13/15 Moo 4, Ao Phutsa; d incl breakfast with fan 630-1050B, with air-con 2100-4500B; ☒ ❄ 🤝) This long-running resort on Ao Phutsa (Ao Tub Tim) occupies a secluded stretch of sand and offers a wide range of timber cottages, from budget fan rooms to spacious air-con bungalows. It's a sociable place with nightly barbecues, and has a good beach bar and restaurant. The best cottages are right by the sand, giving a great outlook from bed, desk and deck.

🛏 Ao Wong Deuan & Ao Thian

Ao Wong Deuan ('Crescent Moon Bay') is Samet's second-busiest beach after Hat Sai Kaew, with a range of resorts and more modest guesthouses. It's a wide, flat arc with a shallow gradient that's good for kids. The tracks and burrows of tiny crabs pockmark the white sand. Ferries run between Ao Wong Deuan and Ban Phe on the mainland (140B return), two or three times daily, with increased services at the weekend.

Ao Thian is a delightfully pretty beach punctuated by big boulders that shelter small sandy spots, creating a castaway ambience. It remains one of Samet's most easy-going beaches and is deliciously lonely on weekdays. On weekends, Bangkok university students serenade the stars with all-night guitar sessions. There are a few casual bungalow accommodations. The southern end of the beach is also called Ao Lung Dam.

Apaché   BUNGALOW $
(✆ 081 452 9472; Ao Thian; d 800-1500B; ❄ 🤝) Eclectic, quirky decorations and a cheerfully random colour scheme add character to this superchilled spot at the southern end of a tranquil strip. Bungalows are basic but adequate. The on-site restaurant on stilts is well worthwhile.

Blue Sky   BUNGALOW $
(✆ 089 936 0842; Ao Wong Deuan; d 800-1200B; ❄ 🤝) A rare budget spot on Ao Wong Deuan, Blue Sky has beaten-up bungalows set on a rocky headland at the north end of the beach. It's run by a friendly couple, but it's difficult to make advance bookings.

★ **Viking Holidays Resort**   BUNGALOW $$
(✆ 038 651126; www.vikingholidaysresort.com; 101/4 Moo 3, Ao Thian; d incl breakfast 1500-1800B; ☒ ❄ 🤝 ❄) One of a line of casual bungalow complexes on this tranquil beach, Viking is well run and has pretty, compact, carpeted rooms decorated with strings of seashells. Staff are particularly helpful and friendly, and speak good English. Unlike with many Ko Samet bungalows, you can book online (and pick your bungalow location).

La Lune Beach Resort   HOTEL $$$
(✆ Koh Samet 089 892 9690, reservations Bangkok 02 260 3592; www.lalunebeachresort.com; Ao Wong Deuan; d incl breakfast 3000-7000B; ☒ ❄ 🤝 ❄) This is the new face of Samet: stylish, chic resorts occupying beachfront space in place of cheap huts. The 40 rooms, all with stressed wood underfoot and a soft green-grey and white theme, are set around a central pool in a three-level U-shape that opens onto the beach. Facilities include cable TV, room safes and 24-hour security.

🛏 Ao Wai

Ao Wai is a lovely beach far removed from everything else (though in reality it is only 1.5km from Ao Thian).

Samet Ville Resort RESORT $$
(📞038 651682; www.sametvilleresort.com; Ao Wai; d & cottages 2000-4000B, f 4500-5800B; P 🌊 🛜 🏊) Spread over two bays – Ao Wai and Ao Hin Kleang – this leafy 4.5-hectare resort is secluded and soporific. The rooms, of which there are several types, are all a few steps from the excellent beach. For this price, though, it's looking a bit tired, cramped and insular, with inexperienced staff.

🛏 Ao Prao

On the west coast, Ao Prao is one of the island's prettiest beaches. It's secluded but backed by three high-end resorts, so it still gets quite busy and is popular with Thai day trippers. It's a pleasant spot to enjoy a sunset cocktail.

Lima Coco Resort RESORT $$$
(📞Bangkok 02 129 1140; www.limaresort.co.th; Ao Prao; d incl breakfast 3990-7290B; 🌊 🛜 🏊) West coast Ao Prao has three upmarket resorts; Lima Coco is the most affordable of these, with compact whitewashed rooms in a variety of categories climbing up the hill behind the beach. It's a little down at heel but offers energetic staff, beachside massages and other facilities.

🛏 Ao Pakarang & Ao Kiu

The southernmost tip of the island has an exclusive, discreet feel.

Nimmanoradee Resort RESORT $$
(📞038 644271; www.nimmanoradee.com; Ao Pakarang; d incl breakfast 3000-3800B; P 🌊 🛜) The southernmost resort on the island, Nimmanoradee offers tranquillity, plenty of space and cheerfully coloured octagonal bungalows. There's good swimming here and a pretty little promontory. Kayaks and snorkels are on hand for exploring the area. Staff are friendly, and the very pleasant open-air restaurant serves decent food at fair prices. Rates rise on weekends.

Paradee Resort RESORT $$$
(📞038 644284; www.sameresorts.com/paradee; 76 Moo 4, Ao Kiu; villas incl breakfast 15,000-35,000B, ste from 70,000B; P 🌊 🛜 🏊) Exclusive

and offering the ultimate in privacy, this sleek resort near Ko Samet's southern end is one of the island's most luxurious. Golf carts hum about among discreetly screened thatched villas, most of which have their own Jacuzzi. The lovely beach is effectively private and, across the road, a bar deck lets you appreciate the sunset views from the island's western shore.

✖ Eating

Food and service in Ko Samet are adequate rather than spectacular. Beaches are strung with restaurants and bars that are good for anything from slap-up Thai meals to cold beer. Many hotels and guesthouses have restaurants doing beach barbecues with all manner of seafood at night.

There are cheapie Thai places along the main road in Na Dan, many specialising in seafood.

Banana Bar THAI $
(📞038 644033; Na Dan; mains 80-250B; ⏱11am-11.30pm) Casual and relaxed, this ramshackle yet oddly attractive main street spot is a good choice for well-priced Thai food. It offers smallish portions of Thai curries, salads and Isan (northeastern Thai) dishes.

Funky Monkey INTERNATIONAL $$
(Na Dan; mains 70-450B; ⏱8.30am-11pm; 🛜) At the end of the street near the national-park

---

LOCAL KNOWLEDGE

BEACH ADMISSION FEE

Ko Samet is part of the Khao Laem Ya/Mu Ko Samet National Park (อุทยานแห่งชาติเขาแหลมหญ้า-หมู่เกาะเสม็ด; 📞038 653034; www.dnp.go.th; adult/child 200/100B) and charges all visitors an entrance fee (adult/child 200/100B) upon arrival. If you live and work in Thailand and can prove it, you pay only 40B, the price Thais pay. The fee is collected at the National Parks Main Office (www.dnp.go.th; Hat Sai Kaew; ⏱8.30am-8pm); sŏrng·tăa·ou (passenger pick-up trucks) from the pier will stop at the checkpoint for payment. Hold on to your ticket for later inspections. There's another park office (Ao Wong Deuan; ⏱8.30am-4.30pm) at Ao Wong Deuan, and rangers elsewhere will charge you the fee if you arrive by speedboat. There is a 20B fee when using Na Dan pier.

ⓘ GETTING TO CAMBODIA: BAN PAKARD TO PAILIN

Getting to the border Minivans (☎092 037 6266) depart Chanthaburi at a stop across the river from the River Guest House (p469), where you can book your spot, to Ban Pakard (200B, 1½ hours, 10am and noon). There are also *sŏrng·tăa·ou* (passenger pickup trucks) from the bus station (100B, two hours) that tend to leave early.

At the border This is a far less busy and more pleasant crossing than Poipet further north. You need a passport photo and US$30 for the visa fee. Cambodian e-visas aren't officially accepted here, though some travellers have reported getting through. Demanding US$35 for the visa is standard practice here.

Moving on Hop on a motorbike taxi to Pailin in Cambodia. From there, you can catch frequent shared taxis (US$5 per person, 1½ hours) to scenic Battambang. After that, you can move on to Siem Reap by boat, or Phnom Penh by bus.

post, Funky Monkey is regarded by many as making Ko Samet's best pizza. It certainly does a satisfying line in international comfort food such as English breakfast and burgers, along with staple Thai dishes. It's a good place to meet travellers over a cold beer.

Kitt & Food
SEAFOOD, THAI $$

(☎038 644087; Hat Sai Kaew; mains 100-450B; ◷9am-10.30pm) Better than most of the beachfront restaurants on this popular beach, this is a romantic place for dinner, with tables almost lapped by the waves. Don't plough too deep into the phonebook of a menu – seafood is the speciality here. Various fresh fish (mostly farmed) are arrayed; pick one and decide how you want it done.

Jep's Restaurant
INTERNATIONAL $$

(☎038 644112; Ao Phai; mains 150-450B; ◷7am-11pm) Canopied by arching tree branches decorated with pendant lights, this pretty place right on the sand does a wide range of international food, from Mexican to Italian to crepes, along with the obligatory Thai dishes.

Ploy Talay
SEAFOOD, THAI $$

(☎038 644212; Hat Sai Kaew; mains 110-400B; ◷11am-11pm; 🛜) The busiest of the string of mediocre beach restaurants on Hat Sai Kaew, this packs out for its nightly 8.30pm fire show, which is quite a sight (and smell). You can see it from the beach, but people enjoy their leisurely (service will ensure it) seafood dinners here. The location is better than the quality.

Sea Breeze
SEAFOOD, THAI $$

(Ao Phai; mains 70-280B; ◷11am-11pm) Appropriately named: you can dine on a wide range of seafood right on Ao Phai's pretty beach. It also does barbecued meats and there are some Western dishes on the menu.

🍷 Drinking & Nightlife

On weekends Ko Samet is a boisterous night owl, with tour groups crooning away on karaoke machines and the young ones slurping down beer and buckets to a techno beat. There is usually a crowd on Hat Sai Kaew, Ao Hin Khok, Ao Phai and Ao Wong Deuan.

Audi Bar
BAR

(☎084 418 8213; Na Dan; ◷4pm-4am; 🛜) Sharing an upstairs main-street space with a gym, this bar offers good people-watching from its high vantage point, Samet-standard Day-Glo graffiti and a couple of pool tables. It's notably welcoming and serves as a one-last-drink venue for those straggling back from the beach dance floors.

Talay Bar
BAR

(☎083 887 1588; Hat Sai Kaew; ◷2pm-midnight; 🛜) Cheerily fronted by burning torches and Thai flags, this bar sits at the eastern end of the island's busiest beach, away from the most crowded parts. It's an upbeat, enthusiastic spot, with space to lounge on the sand and kick back with a cocktail or beer bomb from the unfeasibly large (size-wise) menu.

Breeze
BAR

(☎038 644100; www.sametresorts.com; Ao Prao Resort, Ao Prao; ◷7am-10.30pm; 🛜) On the sunset side of the island, this is a lovely seaview restaurant perfect for a sundowner. You will need private transport to reach it, or it's a 2.5km walk from Hat Sai Kaew.

ⓘ Information

The island has plenty of ATMs, including some near the Na Dan pier, outside the 7-Eleven behind Hat Sai Kaew, and at Ao Wong Deuan, Ao Thian and Ao Phutsa, as well as at several resorts.

Tourist Police (⏰24hr 1155) On the main road between Na Dan and Hat Sai Kaew. There's a substation (⏰24hr 1155) at Ao Wong Deuan.

International Clinic Ko Samet (⏰038 644414, emergency 086 094 0566; Na Dan; ⊙8am-8pm, emergencies to midnight) This private English-speaking clinic is near the ferry pier.

Ko Samet Health Centre (⏰081 861 7922, 038 644123; ⊙emergency 24hr) On the main road between Na Dan and Hat Sai Kaew.

ℹ Getting There & Away

Ko Samet is accessed via the mainland piers in Ban Phe. All ferry companies charge the same fares (one way/return from mainland 70/100B, one way from island 50B, 40 minutes, hourly, 8am to 5pm) and dock at **Na Dan** (usage fee 20B), Ko Samet's main pier. The last boat back to the mainland leaves at 6pm.

If you are staying at Ao Wong Deuan or further south, you can catch a ferry or speedboat from the mainland directly to the beach (ferry/speedboat 90/300B, two to three daily departures).

Speedboats (one way 200B to 500B) drop you at the beach of your choice, but usually only leave when they have enough passengers. Otherwise, you can charter one for around 1500B.

Ticket agents at the Ban Phe piers will often try to overcharge on tickets for both ferries and speedboats and will try to pressure you to take a speedboat by saying that there are no slow boats for the next few hours etc. Ticket prices are clearly posted at official windows, so buy tickets there.

From Bangkok, head to Rayong. You'll arrive at bus station 2; there are some minibuses from here to Ban Phe, but it's usually quicker to catch a sŏrng·tǎa·ou (passenger pickup truck) to bus station 1 (25B), then another from there to Ban Phe. There is no Rayong service from Suvarnabhumi airport; either head to Pattaya and change there or head into Bangkok's Ekamai bus station and catch Rayong- or Ban Phe–bound transport from there.

From Ko Samet it's easy to arrange minibus transfers to Bangkok (250B), Suvarnabhumi airport (500B), Ko Chang piers (250B) and elsewhere. Agents in Bangkok (such as on Khao San Rd) sell the same minibus through-ticket to Ko Samet.

ℹ Getting Around

Ko Samet's small size makes it a great place to explore on foot. A network of roads connects most of the island.

Green **sŏrng·tǎa·ou** meet boats at the pier and provide drop-offs at the various beaches (20B to 200B, depending on the beach and number of passengers). Chartering one costs 150B to 700B on the official rate sheet, but you can usually negotiate a discount. Regular taxis also congregate at a **stop** (Hat Sal Kaew) by the national park entrance.

You can rent motorcycles nearly everywhere along the northern half of the island and at main beaches for 100/300B per hour/day (up to 500B per day at more isolated beaches). The road is good, but be careful on steep descents. It's 7km by road from Na Dan ferry pier to the southern tip of the island. For those who prefer four wheels, golf carts can also be hired.

Chanthaburi

⏰039 / POP 126,000

Chanthaburi (จันทบุรี) is an absorbing riverside town where precious stones ranging from sapphires to emeralds are traded every weekend in a bustling street gem market. Nearby, restored waterfront buildings in a charming historic quarter are evidence of how the Chinese, French and Vietnamese have influenced life – and architecture – here.

Vietnamese Christians fled persecution from Cochin China (southern Vietnam) in the 19th century and came to Chanthaburi. The French occupied Chanthaburi from 1893 to 1905 due to a dispute over the border between Siam and Indochina. More Vietnamese arrived in the 1920s and 1940s as they fled French rule, then a third wave followed in 1975 after the Communist takeover of southern Vietnam.

◉ Sights

Chanthaburi is a great walking city. Take some time to wander the historic Chanthaboon quarter and the large King Taksin Park.

★**Chanthaboon Waterfront Community** HISTORIC SITE

(ชุมชนริมน้ำจันทบูร; Th Sukhaphiban) 🏳 Hugging the banks of Mae Nam Chanthaburi, this charismatic area is filled with restored houses and elderly residents who sit around reminiscing about old Chanthaburi. Learning House (ศูนย์เรียนรู้ประจำชุมชนริมน้ำจันทบูร; ⏰081 945 5761; 69 Th Sukhaphiban; ⊙10am-7pm Sat & Sun) FREE displays neighbourhood photos, paintings and architectural designs, including upstairs drawings of intricate ventilation panels that feature Chinese characters and French fleurs-de-lis.

Around 300 years ago, farmers and merchants started trading alongside the river, which provided easy transport links. Later, Chinese and Vietnamese traders and refugees

Chanthaburi

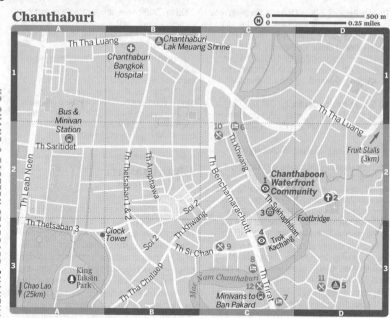

Chanthaburi

◎ Top Sights
1 Chanthaboon Waterfront
Community C2

◎ Sights
2 Cathedral of the Immaculate
Conception D2
3 Chanthaboon Learning House C2
4 Gem Market C3
5 Wat Phai Lom....................................D3

⊨ Sleeping
6 Baan Luang Rajamaitri.........................C2
7 Chernchan Hostel...............................C3
8 River Guest House C3

✕ Eating
9 786 Muslim Restaurant C3
10 Chanthorn...C2
11 Jay Pen Yentafo D3
12 Koff House C3

came to the area. Today the 1km-long street
scene still includes many private homes, but
the art galleries, coffee shops and snack stalls
entice visiting Thais at weekends.

Gem Market   MARKET
(ตลาดพลอย; Th Si Chan & Trok Kachang; ⊙9am-
6pm Fri-Sun) Every weekend, the normally quiet streets near Th Si Chan (or 'Gem
Road') burst into life as gem traders arrive to
bustle and bargain. It's incongruously humble and pedestrian considering the value of
the commodities on offer, as people cluster
around makeshift office tables examining
small piles of unset stones.

**Cathedral of the
Immaculate Conception**   CATHEDRAL
(⊙9am-noon & 1-3pm Mon-Sat, 11am-3pm Sun)
FREE Thailand's largest cathedral, on the

east bank of Mae Nam Chanthaburi, started life as a modest chapel in 1711. Since
then there have been four reconstructions.
The current Gothic-style structure includes
some impressive stained-glass windows and
an upstairs gallery that gives the interior
the feel of a medieval hall. The statue of the
Virgin Mary at the front is bedecked with
more than 200,000 sapphires – a fitting link
between religion and the city's famous gem
trade.

Wat Phai Lom   BUDDHIST TEMPLE
(วัดไผ่ล้อม; ☎086 794 8949; ⊙8am-5pm)
FREE Begun in the early 18th century, this
sizeable complex features a high, ornate
ordination hall with fresco decoration
and another building with an enormous
reclining Buddha.

🛏 Sleeping

River Guest House GUESTHOUSE $
(☏090 936 7499; www.facebook.com/theriver
guesthouse; 3/5-8 Th Si Chan; d 450-700B; tr/f
850/950B; ❄⏾) Right by the river, albeit
next to a noisy bridge, this friendly guesthouse has a range of simple rooms – the best
are those facing the river. Beds are hard but
the riverside seating area compensates. The
cheapest rooms have a shared bathroom;
rooms with hot water and air-con cost a little
more. Bikes and mopeds available for hire.

Chernchan Hostel HOSTEL $$
(☏065 573 8841; www.facebook.com/
chernchan2017; 43/11-13 Th Tirat; dm 450B, d 900-
1500B; ❄⏾) On a quiet lane close to the
river, this boutique hostel has eye-catching
modern design and helpful staff. Dorms and
rooms are compact but comfortable; down-
stairs in the cafe an abundant breakfast is
served (included in room but not dorm
rates). Bike rental available.

⭐**Baan Luang Rajamaitri** HISTORIC HOTEL $$$
(☏088 843 4516; www.baanluangrajamaitri.com;
252 Th Sukhaphiban; r incl breakfast 1690-1990B,
ste 3290-3490B; ❄⏾) 🏠 Community-owned
and named after a local philanthropist, this
expertly restored historic museum-hotel
has wonderfully characterful elegant rooms
in the heart of the riverfront district. Dark
wooden furniture, creaky floorboards and
a great waterside deck make for excellent
atmosphere. The cheapest rooms are small
with a comfortable bunk bed and a little terrace. Quirky antique touches abound.

🍴 Eating & Drinking

Crab noodles and pork with *chamung* leaf
are local specialities. A string of eateries can
be found on Th Sukhaphiban and there are
lots of options around the centr. Across the
other side of the river are some open-air
spots that look across to Chanthaboon.

The most characterful cafes and bars are
along Th Sukhaphiban and have wooden
decks over the river.

786 Muslim Restaurant INDIAN $
(☏081 353 5174; Th Si Chan; mains 50-110B;
⏰9.30am-6pm Tue-Sun) In among all the
Chanthaburi gem dealers, this restaurant
run by Thai Muslims is worth a stop for its
excellent paratha, biryani, curries, meatballs
and chai tea.

WORTH A TRIP

NATIONAL PARKS NEAR CHANTHABURI

Two small national parks are easily reached from Chanthaburi, and make good day trips.
Both are malarial, so take the usual precautions (use mosquito repellent and wear long
sleeves and pants).

Khao Khitchakut National Park (อุทยานแห่งชาติเขาคิชฌกูฏ; ☏039 452074; http://
nps.dnp.go.th; 200B; ⏰8.30am-4.30pm) is 28km northeast of town. Though it's one of
Thailand's smallest national parks (59 sq km), it's bordered by wildlife sanctuaries and
is home to wild elephants. The cascade of Nam Tok Krathing is impressive just after
the rainy season only. Another attraction is a temple atop a hill where, by an enormous
boulder, Buddha is believed to have left a footprint. To get to Khao Khitchakut, take a
sŏrng·tăa·ou (passenger pickup truck) from next to the Chanthaburi post office, near
the northern side of the market (35B, 45 minutes). The *sŏrng·tăa·ou* stops 1km from the
park headquarters on Rte 3249, from which point you will have to walk. Returning transport is scarce, so expect to wait (or hitch, though this is never entirely safe and therefore
we don't recommend it).

Popular Namtok Phlio National Park (อุทยานแห่งชาติน้ำตกพลิ้ว; ☏039 434528;
http://nps.dnp.go.th; 200B; ⏰8am-6pm), off Hwy 3, is 14km southeast of Chanthaburi. A
pleasant short nature trail loops around the waterfalls, which writhe with soro brook
carp; you can bathe here. Also on display are the strikingly mossy Phra Nang Ruar Lom
stupa (c 1876) and Along Khon *chedi* (c 1881). To get to the park, catch a *sŏrng·tăa·ou*
from the northern side of the market in Chanthaburi to the park entrance (50B, 30 minutes). You will get dropped off about 1km from the entrance. Private transport
costs 1500B.

Accommodation is available at both parks; book with the park reservation system (02
562 0760; www.dnp.go.th).

Jay Pen Yentafo
THAI **$**

(☑039 325430; Wat Phai Lom; noodles 100B; ☺9am-3.30pm) Pink-coloured noodle soup combined with crab has given this temple restaurant in the Wat Phai Lom precinct a great reputation with locals.

★Chanthorn
THAI **$$**

(102/5-8 Th Benchamarachutit; mains 100-300B; ☺9am-9pm; ☑) This welcoming family-run restaurant-shop one street west of the waterfront is a great place to try local specialities; the *chamung* leaves with pork and the Chanthaburi crab noodles are particularly good – but everything's really excellent quality. Can close early at dinner time.

Koff House
INTERNATIONAL **$$**

(☑083 649 3395; Tambon Chanthanimit; coffee 55-80B, mains 160-890B; ☺bakery 7.30am-11pm, restaurant 8am-midnight) Part bakery-cafe, part swanky restaurant, riverside Koff is a sophisticated sort of place that contrasts sharply with the old town on the other side of the river. A youthful crowd enjoys the long menu of coffee, tea and breakfasts while lounging on soft couches in the cafe, while a typically older crowd indulges in an international menu over live music next door.

🛈 Information

Chanthaburi Bangkok Hospital (☑039 319888; www.chanthaburihospital.com; Th Tha Luang; ☺24hr) is central and has 24-hour emergency service.

🛈 Getting There & Around

Chanthaburi's **bus station** (Th Saritidet) is west of the river. Minivans also leave from the bus station.

Motorbike taxis charge 20B to 40B for trips around town.

Trat

☑039 / POP 22,000

Trat (ตราด) is a major transit point for Ko Chang and coastal Cambodia, and worth a stop anyway for its underappreciated old-world charm. The guesthouse neighbourhood occupies an atmospheric wooden shophouse district, backing on to the riverfront and bisected by winding sois. It's filled with typical Thai street life: children riding bikes, homemakers running errands and small businesses selling trinkets and necessities.

⊙ Sights

Walk down Th Lak Meuang and you will see that the top floors of shophouses have been converted into nesting sites for birds that produce the edible nests considered a Chinese delicacy. Swiflets' nests were quite rare (and expensive) in the past because they were only harvested from precipitous sea caves by trained, daring climbers. In the 1990s entrepreneurs figured out how to replicate the cave atmosphere in multistorey shophouses and the business has since become a key operation in Trat.

Accessed from Th Thana Charoen is a sweet little canalside walkway with French-style lamps and benches; it's a short but picturesque stroll.

Trat Museum
MUSEUM

(พิพิธภัณฑ์วัดบุปผาราม; Th Santisuk; adult/child/foreigner 5/10/30B; ☺9am-4pm Tue-Fri, 9.30am-4.30pm Sat & Sun) In a beautiful restored timber building on the site of the former city hall, Trat's museum features six rooms of interpretive panels (in English and Thai), models, and displays covering the history of the province from its people, culture and archaeological history to major events such as the Naval Battle of Ko Chang. It's well presented and comprehensive.

CHANTHABURI TRANSPORT CONNECTIONS

DESTINATION	BUS	MINIVAN
Bangkok's Eastern Bus Terminal (Ekamai)	180B, 4hr, 25 daily	200B, frequent
Bangkok's Northern Bus Terminal (Mo Chit)	180B, 4hr, 4 daily	200B, frequent
Nakhon Ratchasima (Khorat)	280B, 4hr, every 2 hours	
Rayong/Ban Phe		150B, 2hr, hourly
Trat		70B, 1hr, frequent

🛏 Sleeping

Trat has many budget hotels in traditional wooden houses on and around Th Thana Charoen. They are characterful places with generally bargain prices.

★ Ban Jai Dee Guest House   GUESTHOUSE $
(☑ 039 520678, 083 589 0839; banjaideehouse@yahoo.com; 6 Th Chaimongkol; s/d without bathroom 250/300B; 🛜) This relaxed traditional wooden house a little way north of the riverside has simple rooms with shared bathrooms (hot-water showers). Paintings and objets d'art made by the artistically inclined owners decorate the beautiful common spaces. There are only seven rooms and an addictively relaxing ambience so it can fill fast. The owners are full of helpful information.

Yotin Guest House   GUESTHOUSE $
(☑ 089 224 7817; Th Thana Charoen; d 300-450B; ❄🛜) Backing a typically venerable building in Trat's lovely old quarter, these are pretty, inviting refurbished rooms with colourful linen and comfortable mattresses. Cheaper rooms are compact and either share a bathroom or have a very tight en suite. The couple who run the place are thoughtful and helpful: it's a very sound base. You can hire bikes here.

Artist's Place   GUESTHOUSE $
(☑ 082 469 1900; pier.112@hotmail.com; 132/1 Th Thana Charoen; d incl breakfast with fan 350B, air-con 800-1100B; 🅿❄🛜) Individually decorated rooms and the pieces of art dotted around the adjoining garden come courtesy of the owner, Mr Phukhao. The triple rooms with loft are super spacious. Cheaper rooms with fans share bathrooms, but are dark and lack the same character. Check in at Pier 112 restaurant (p471) opposite.

★ Rimklong Boutique Hotel   BOUTIQUE HOTEL $$
(☑ 039 523388, 081 861 7181; 194 Th Lak Meuang; d 950-1180B; 🅿❄🛜) Run by helpful Mr Tuu, this hotel offers five compact, sparkling rooms in the heart of the old part of town. Prices are reasonable for the quality, including double doors for noise reduction. Additional rooms are in an annexe a few paces down the soi.

🍴 Eating & Drinking

Trat is all about market eating: head to the day market (Th Tat Mai; ⊘6am-5pm) for *gah-faa bohrahn* (coffee made in the traditional

---

Trat Province

way), the night market (off Th Sukhumvit; dishes 10-100B; ⊘5-9pm), or the indoor market (Soi Sukhumvit; ⊘6am-5pm) for lunchtime noodles. Food stalls line Th Sukhumvit come nightfall.

Cafe Haven   INTERNATIONAL $
(Th Thana Charoen; mains 60-250B; ⊘7.30am-6pm; 🛜) Adjoining Sangjun Guesthouse, Haven is one of the better equipped restaurants in the old guesthouse district, with twisted timber furniture and a large picture menu spanning Thai, seafood, pasta and burgers. A large beer costs 80B.

★ Namchok   THAI $$
(Th Wiwatthana; mains 80-250B; ⊘10am-10pm) This simple open-sided restaurant north of the centre is deservedly a local favourite, with some excellent seafood dishes. There's a helpful English menu, with such intriguing dishes as stir-fried ostrich with black pepper, and fried softshell crab. It's only signposted in Thai: look for the Coke logos and concrete bench seating.

Pier 112   THAI $$
(132/1 Th Thana Charoen; mains 80-200B; ⊘5-10pm; 🛜🍴) In the old town by the river, Pier 112 has a large selection of vegetarian dishes, as well as reliable curries. You can eat outside in a plant-festooned garden. Also here is

Trat

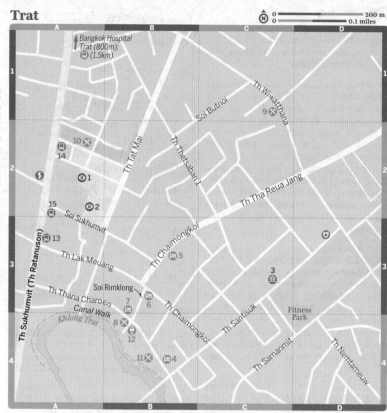

Trat

⊙ Sights
1 Day Market	A2
2 Indoor Market	A2
3 Trat Museum	C3

⊜ Sleeping
4 Artist's Place	B4
5 Ban Jai Dee Guest House	B3
6 Rimklong Boutique Hotel	B3
7 Yotin Guest House	B3

⊗ Eating
8 Cafe Haven	B4
9 Namchok	C1
10 Night Market	A2
11 Pier 112	B4

⊝ Drinking & Nightlife
12 Cafe Oscar	B4

ⓘ Transport
13 Family Tour	A3
14 Sŏrng·tăa·ou to Bus Station & Laem Sok	A2
15 Sŏrng·tăa·ou to Ko Chang ferries	A2

the **Seahouse Cafe** for all-day coffee, beer, breakfast and snacks (from 7am).

Cafe Oscar   BAR
(Th Thana Charoen; ⊙5pm-late) An eclectic crew of locals and expats gather at this cubbyhole corner bar, with wooden furniture and a retro 1970s and '80s soundtrack. It's a great meeting place, and in high season it may open during the day.

ⓘ Information

You'll find the bulk of banks and ATMs on Th Sukhumvit (often called Th Ratanuson), including **Krung Thai Bank** (Th Sukhumvit; ⊙8.30am-4.30pm Mon-Fri).

Police Station (☑ 24hr 1155; cnr Th Santisuk & Th Wiwatthana) A short walk from Trat's centre.

Bangkok Hospital Trat (☑ 039 522555; www.bangkoktrathospital.com; 376 Mu 2, Th Sukhumvit; ☉ 24hr) Located 400m north of the town centre, this hospital offers the best health care in the area.

ℹ Getting There & Away

AIR

Bangkok Airways (☑ 039 525767; www.bangkokair.com; Trat Airport; ☉ 8.30am-6.30pm) operates three daily flights to/from Bangkok Suvarnabhumi International Airport (one hour) to Trat Airport, 35km northwest of the city. A shared taxi or minibus from the airport into town is 500B; to the Ko Chang ferry pier it's 300B.

BOAT
To Ko Chang

The piers that handle boat traffic to/from Ko Chang are located west of Laem Ngop, about 30km southwest of Trat. There are three piers, each used by different boat companies, but the most convenient services are through Koh Chang Ferry (p484), from Tha Thammachat, and Centrepoint Ferry (p484), from Tha Centrepoint.

Sŏrng·tăa·ou (Th Sukhumvit) to Laem Ngop and the piers (50B to 80B per person, 300B for the whole vehicle, 40 minutes) leave from Th Sukhumvit, just past the market. These will pick up from guesthouses in the morning. It should be the same charter price if you want to go directly from Trat's bus station to the pier.

You can catch a bus from Bangkok's Eastern (Ekamai) station all the way to Tha Centrepoint (250B, five hours, three morning departures). This route includes a stop at Suvarnabhumi (airport) bus station as well as Trat's bus station. In the reverse direction, buses have two afternoon departures from Laem Ngop.

To Ko Kut

Ferries to Ko Kut run from the pier at **Laem Sok** (Laem Sok Ferry Pier), 22km southeast of Trat, the nearest bus transfer point. If you prebook, boat operators offer free transport from central Trat or its bus station (but not the airport) to the pier. There's no public transport between Laem Ngop and Laem Sok piers; expect 400B to 500B for a taxi. In high season you can travel directly between Ko Chang and Ko Kut.

To Ko Mak

Speedboats to Ko Mak (450B one way, one hour, six daily) depart from Laem Ngop. The slow boat (200B, three hours) departs at 11am.

BUS & MINIVAN

Trat's **bus station** is 2km out of town, and serves the following destinations:

TO	FARE (B)	TIME (HR)	FREQUENCY
Bangkok Eastern (Ekamai) Bus Terminal	230	4½	hourly 7am-11.30pm
Bangkok Northern & Northeastern (Mo Chit) Bus Terminal	240	5½	2 daily
Bangkok Suvarnabhumi International Airport	240	4-4½	3 daily
Chanthaburi	58	1	6 daily

Minivans run to the following destinations:

TO	FARE (B)	TIME (HR)	FREQUENCY
Bangkok Eastern (Ekamai) Bus Terminal	280	4	every 2hr 8.30am-4.30pm
Bangkok Northern & Northeastern (Mo Chit) Bus Terminal	270	4	every 2hr 8.30am-4.30pm
Chanthaburi	70	50min	frequent 6am-6pm
Hat Lek (for the border with Cambodia)	120	1½	hourly 5am-6pm
Pattaya	300	3½	every 2hr 8am-6pm
Rayong/Ban Phe (for Ko Samet)	200	3½	every 2hr 8am-6pm

A useful minivan operator is **Family Tour** (☑ 081 940 7380; Th Sukhumvit), with services to Bangkok, as well as to Phnom Penh and Siem Reap.

ℹ Getting Around

Motorbike taxis charge 20B to 30B for local hops.

Local *sŏrng·tăa·ou* (passenger pickup trucks) leave from **Th Sukhumvit** (Th Sukhumvit) near the market for the bus station (20B to 60B, depending on the number of passengers). Chartering one to the airport costs 600B.

Motorbikes can be rented for 150B to 200B a day along Th Sukhumvit near the guesthouse area, or from some guesthouses.

Ko Chang

📝 039 / POP 10,000

With steep, jungle-covered peaks, picturesque Ko Chang (Elephant Island; เกาะช้าง) retains its remote and rugged spirit – despite the transformation of parts of it into a package-tour destination. Sweeping bays are sprinkled along the west coast; some have superfine sand, others have pebbles. What the island lacks in sand it makes up for in an unlikely combination: accessible wilderness with a thriving party scene.

Because of its relative remoteness, Ko Chang has been slower to register on the tourist radar than the Gulf and Andaman Coast islands. Today, it's still a slog to get here, but its resorts are busy with package tourists, Cambodia-bound backpackers and island-hopping couples funnelling through to more remote islands in the marine park. Along the populous west coast are sprawling minitowns that have outpaced the island's infrastructure. For a taste of old-school Chang, head to the southeastern villages and mangrove forests of Ban Salak Phet and Ban Salak Kok.

◉ Sights

**Mu Ko Chang
National Marine Park**   NATIONAL PARK
(อุทยานแห่งชาติหมู่เกาะช้าง; 📝 039 510927; www. dnp.go.th; daily entrance adult/child 200/100B) This land and marine national park covers the entire archipelago and protects much of the central part of the island. Conservation efforts are a bit haphazard, but you will be required to pay the park entrance fee when visiting some of the waterfalls (including Khlong Phu, which has a small visitor centre). National Park headquarters (📝039 555080; Ban Than Mayom; ⊗8am-5pm) is on the eastern side of the island near Nam Tok Than Mayom.

Nudity and topless sunbathing are forbidden by law in Mu Ko Chang National Marine Park; this includes all beaches on Ko Chang, Ko Kut, Ko Mak and Ko Wai.

◉ West Coast

The west coast is by far the most developed part of Ko Chang, thanks to its beaches and bays. Public *sŏrng·tăa·ou* make beach-hopping easy and affordable. Some beaches are rocky, so it's worth bringing swim booties for the kids. Most of the time the seas are shallow and gentle but be wary of rips during storms and the wet season (May to October). Head down to Bang Bao pier for dive shops, island-hopping trips, interisland transport, and some decent shopping and seafood restaurants.

Ban Bang Bao   VILLAGE
(บ้านบางเบ้า) At this former fishing community built in the traditional fashion of interconnected piers, the villagers have swapped their nets for renting out portions of their homes to souvenir shops and restaurants. The main enclosed pier is lined with shops but is no worse for that. Most visitors come for the excellent seafood restaurants and shopping.

Hat Khlong Kloi   BEACH
(หาดคลองกลอย) At the eastern end of Ao Bang Bao, Khlong Kloi is a pretty sandy beach that is away from the package tour scene and, though popular, still has a hidden-away feel. There are all the requisite amenities (beer, food, fruit, massage) and a few guesthouses. Truck taxis will drop you off here, or it's a 1km walk from Bang Bao.

Ao Khlong Prao   BEACH
(อ่าวคลองพร้าว; Khlong Prao) Khlong Prao's beach is a pretty sweep of sand pinned between hulking mountainous headlands and bisected by two estuaries. At low tide, beachcombers stroll the rippled sand eyeing the critters left naked by the receding water. Sprawling luxury resorts dominate here and the primary pastime is sunbathing by the pool, as high tide gobbles up much of the beach. A highlight is the canal lined with stilt shophouses and a few seafood restaurants and guesthouses.

Hat Kaibae   BEACH
(หาดไก่แบ้) A companion beach to Khlong Prao, Hat Kaibae is a good spot for families and couples. A slim strip of sand unfurls

around an island-dotted bay that's removed from the worst of the package tourist scene but still has plenty of good bars and restaurants along the main road. There is kayaking to the outlying island of Ko Man Nai and low tide provides hours of beachcombing.

Lonely Beach
BEACH

(หาดท่าน้ำ) The last thing you'll be here is lonely, as this is Ko Chang's backpacker enclave and the liveliest place to be after dark – until at least 5am. Here, vodka buckets are passed around and the speakers get turned up. The beach has pebbles at the southern end and towards Bailan Bay but there's a decent sandy strip to the north. Its original, long-forgotten, name is Hat Tha Nam.

White Sand Beach (Hat Sai Khao)
BEACH

(หาดทรายขาว) The longest, most luxurious stretch of sand on the island, Hat Sai Khao is universally known as White Sand Beach, a developed strip packed with package-tour hotels and serious sunbathers. Head to the north section of the beach to find the more secluded backpacker spot. Along the main road, the village is busy and brash – but comes with all the necessary amenities.

Hat Kai Mook
BEACH

(หาดไข่มุก) Hat Kai Mook means 'Pearl Beach', although the 'pearls' here are really just large pebbles that pack the shore and culminate in fish-friendly headlands. Swimming and sunbathing are out, but there's good snorkelling.

◉ East Coast

The east coast is peaceful and remains undeveloped, filled with undulating hills of coconut and palm trees and low-key fishing villages in the far south. You will need your own transport to explore this charming coast of scenic bays and mangrove forests.

Ban Salak Phet
VILLAGE

(บ้านสลักเพชร) To discover what Ko Chang was like before tourists came, visit Ban Salak Phet, in the far southeastern corner. This sleepy community is full of stilt houses, fishing boats and yawning dogs who stretch out on the roadside; it also provides access to some good treks.

Ao Salak Kok
BAY

(อ่าวสลักคอก) The dense tangle of mangroves here is protected by a group of fisherfolk who recognises its ecological importance. Mangroves are the ocean's nurseries, foster-

ℹ GETTING TO CAMBODIA: HAT LEK TO CHAM YEAM

Getting to the border The closest Thailand–Cambodia crossing from Trat is Hat Lek to the Cambodian town of Cham Yeam, and then on to Ko Kong. Minivans run to Hat Lek (120B, 1½ hours, hourly 5am to 6pm) from Trat's bus station. Agents in Trat sell through-tickets to Sihanoukville, Phnom Penh and Siem Reap by minivan for 600B, but these involve a change of transport at the border.

At the border Attempts to overcharge for the Cambodian visa (officially US$30) at this border are common; officials may quote the e-visa rate (US$37) or demand payment in Thai baht (1200B) at an unfavourable exchange rate. You will need a passport photo. To avoid the hassle, you may decide that getting an e-visa beforehand is worthwhile. Avoid anyone who says you require a 'medical certificate' or other paperwork. The border opens at 7am and closes at 8pm.

ing the next generation of marine species, as well as resident birds and crustaceans, and this bay is now Ko Chang's prime ecotourism site. Villagers operate an award-winning programme to preserve the environment and traditional way of life. They rent kayaks through the Salak Kok Kayak Station (p478) and run an affiliated restaurant.

Nam Tok Than Mayom
WATERFALL

(น้ำตกธารมะยม; park fee 200B; ⏰8am-5pm) A series of three falls along the stream of Khlong Mayom can be reached via the park office near Nam Tha Than Mayom. The view from the top is superb and nearby there are inscribed stones bearing the initials of Rama V, Rama VI and Rama VII.

◉ The Interior

Ko Chang's mountainous interior is predominately protected as a national marine park (p474). The forest is lush and alive with wildlife and threaded by silver-hued waterfalls and trekking routes.

Nam Tok Khlong Plu
WATERFALL

(น้ำตกคลองพลู; Khlong Prao; park fee adult/child 200/100B; ⏰8am-4.30pm) The island's biggest

Ko Chang

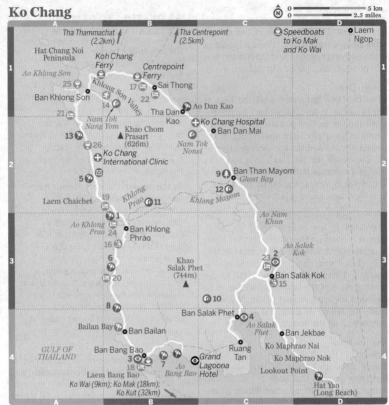

and most impressive waterfall, this is a three-tiered cascade with a pool where you can swim (with fish). It's easily accessible from Khlong Prao: head 1.5km off the main road, pay the national park entrance fee, then head on up a 600m jungle path. The cascade is most stunning just after the rainy season months and more pleasant in the morning before the crowds arrive.

Nam Tok Khiri Phet   WATERFALL
(น้ำตกคีรีเพชร) This small waterfall, 2km from Ban Salak Phet, is a 15-minute walk from the road and rewards you with a small, deep plunge pool. It is usually less crowded than many of the larger falls and is easily reached if you are in the neighbourhood of Ao Salak Phet.

🏃 Activities

Numerous operators offer boat cruises, often with a glass-bottom option and snorkelling stops. Most of these leave from Bang Bao. Typical trips are a three-island half-day tour by speedboat for 800B or a five-island full-day trip by big boat/speedboat for 700/1000B.

Diving & Snorkelling

The dive sites near Ko Chang offer a variety of coral, fish and beginner-friendly shallow waters.

The seamounts off the southern tip of the island within the Mu Ko Chang National Marine Park are reached within a 30-minute cruise. Popular spots include Hin Luk Bat and Hin Rap, rocky, coral-encrusted seamounts with depths of around 18m to 20m. These are havens for schooling fish and some turtles. Near Hin Rap, a 30m gunship was deliberately sunk in 2013, and now lies on its side.

By far the most pristine diving in the area is around Ko Rang, an uninhabited island protected from fishing by its marine park status. Visibility here is much better than near Ko Chang and averages between 10m

Ko Chang

and 20m. Everyone's favourite dive is Hin Gadeng – spectacular rock pinnacles with coral visible to around 28m. On the eastern side of Ko Rang, Hin Kuak Maa (also known as Three Finger Reef) is another top dive spot and is home to a coral-encrusted wall sloping from 2m to 14m and attracting swarms of marine life.

Ko Yak, Ko Tong Lang and Ko Laun are shallow dives perfect for both beginners and advanced divers. These small rocky islands can be circumnavigated and have lots of coral, schooling fish, pufferfish, morays, barracuda, rays and the occasional turtle.

About 7km offshore from Ban Bang Bao there's a popular dive to the wreck of the HTMS Chang, a 100m-long former Thai naval vessel purposely sunk in 2012 to form an artificial reef that now sits 30m beneath the surface.

Reef-fringed Ko Wai (p489) features a good variety of colourful hard and soft corals and is great for snorkelling. It is a popular day-tripping island but has simple overnight accommodation for more alone time with the reef.

The snorkelling on Ko Mak is not as good, but the island offers some decent dives, even if the reefs don't see as many fish as elsewhere.

One-day diving trips typically start at 3000B. Think 15,000B per person for PADI or other certification. Many dive shops remain open during the rainy season (May to October) but visibility and sea conditions are generally poor. The following are recommended dive operators:

BB Divers (☑086 129 2305; www.bbdivers-koh-chang.com; Bang Bao; 2 boat dives 3000B) Based at Bang Bao, this well-run diving outfit has branches in Lonely Beach and Hat Sai Khao, as well as outposts on Ko Kut and Ko Mak (high season only).

Scuba Academy (☑039 611485; www.scubaacademykohchang.com; Bang Bao; snorkelling 800B, 2 tank dives 2500B) The newest dive outfit on Ko Chang has an experienced team of instructors and divemasters and is competitively priced.

Scubadawgs (☑080 038 5166; www.scuba-dawgs.com; Bang Bao; 2 boat dives 3000B) This upbeat outfit based at Bang Bao is

ℹ️ DON'T FEED THE WILDLIFE

On many of the around-the-island boat tours, operators amaze their guests with a stop at a rocky cliff to feed the wild monkeys. It seems innocent enough, but there's an unfortunate consequence: the animals become dependent on this food source and when the boats don't come as often during the low season the young and vulnerable ones are ill-equipped to forage in the forest.

The same goes for the dive or boat trips that feed the fish leftover lunches, or bread. It might be a fantastic way to see a school of brilliantly coloured fish, but the creatures then forsake the coral reefs for an easier meal, and without the daily grooming efforts of the fish the coral is soon overgrown with algae and will eventually suffocate.

helpful and customer focused. It does PADI and RAID certification.

Chang Diving Centre (📞 039 619022; www. changdiving.com; Ban Khlong Prao) Professional diving set-up at Ban Khlong Prao offering a good range of excursions and courses.

Kayaking & SUP

Ko Chang cuts an impressive and heroic profile when viewed from the sea aboard a kayak. The water is generally calm and a few offshore islands provide a paddling destination that is closer than the horizon. Many hotels rent open-top kayaks (from 300B per day) that are convenient for near-shore outings and noncommittal kayakers; some provide them for free. Contact **SEA Kayaking** (📞 092 475 0444; https://southeastasiakayaking. com; Emerald Cove Resort, Khlong Prao; 1-day expedition 4000B) for more serious apparatus.

From Porn's Bungalows (p480) you can kayak across to little Ko Man Nai, where there's a sandy beach. Kayak hire costs 100/400B per hour/day. Standup paddleboarding (SUP) is gaining popularity, particularly in the calm estuary of Khlong Prao. You can rent boards from **SUP Station** (Khlong Prao; per 1/2hr 500/800B; ⏰ 10am-5pm) at Iyasa Resort in Klong Prao (500/800B per one/two hours) and from **SUP Adventure Ko Chang** (📞 064 7251636; Hat Khlong Kloi; per hr 300B) on Hat Khlong Kloi.

Salak Kok Kayak Station   KAYAKING
(Chang Spirit Club; 📞 087 748 9497; Baan Salak Kok; kayak rental per hour 200B) 🏄 On the east

side of the island, explore the mangrove swamps of Ao Salak Kok while supporting an award-winning ecotour programme. Salak Kok Kayak Station rents self-guided kayaks and is a village work project designed to promote tourism without affecting the traditional way of life.

Hiking

Ko Chang isn't just about the beaches. The island has a well-developed trekking scene, with inland routes that lead to lush forests filled with birds, monkeys and flora. A handful of English-speaking guides grew up near the jungle and are happy to share their secrets. Though the inadequate national park map shows a walking trail traversing the island, this is long overgrown: don't try it without a guide.

Tan Trekking   HIKING
(📞 089 645 2019; www.thailandadventureguide. com; hikes 600-1100B) A young hiking guide with good English, Tan offers ascents of Khao Chom Prasart, full-day treks to and around the Khlong Prao waterfall and easier half-day and family-friendly routes.

Mr Raht   HIKING
(📞 086 155 5693; kohchang_trekking@yahoo. com) Leads one-day jungle treks around the southern and eastern parts of the island as well as Friday ascents of Salak Phet. Overnight camping can also be arranged. Treks range from 800B to 1500B.

Cooking Classes

A number of recommended Thai cooking classes are available on Ko Chang. Book at least a day in advance.

Ka-Ti Culinary Cooking School   COOKING
(Khlong Prao; 1500B; ⏰ 11am-3.30pm Mon-Sat) Recommended hands-on cooking (and eating) classes complete with recipe book. If you want to know what the food is like in advance, visit the excellent restaurant (p483).

Koh Chang Thai Cookery School   COOKING
(📞 039 557243; www.kohchangcookery.com; Blue Lagoon Bungalows, Khlong Prao; courses 1800B) Break up your lazy days with cooking classes designed to enhance mind and body at eco-minded Blue Lagoon. Classes are typically four hours and include four courses; book ahead.

Happy Turtle   COOKING
(📞 089 252 9287; 1200B; ⏰ 10am-1pm) Down in Bailan Bay, Happy Turtle runs small-group

cooking classes handy for those staying down south. It also runs drop-in yoga classes, and has bungalows and a restaurant.

Yoga & Wellbeing

Several resorts along the west coast strip offer yoga classes, meditation, spa treatments and other wellness programmes that may be open to nonguests – look out for flyers.

BB Lonely Beach (p481) has drop-in yoga classes (300B) at 10am and 6.30pm Monday to Saturday, as well as a fully equipped gym (200B for casual visits). Spa Koh Chang Resort (p482) also offers morning yoga sessions (450B).

Sima Massage   MASSAGE
(☑ 081 489 5171; Khlong Prao; massages per hour 250-400B; ⊗ 8am-10pm) Sima is regarded by some locals as the best massage on the island – quite an accolade in a place where a massage is easier to find than a 7-Eleven. It's on the main drag through Khlong Prao.

Thai Boxing

Ko Chang Thai Boxing Camp (Ban Bailan; 600B; ⊗ 5pm) offers two-hour daily training sessions with gear included. Beginners welcome.

The Sabay Bar on White Sand Beach has a *moo.ay tai* (muay thai) boxing ring and stadium featuring regular national bouts.

Volunteering

Koh Chang Animal Project   VOLUNTEERING
(☑ 089 042 2347; www.kohchanganimalproject. org; Ban Khlong Son) 🐾 Abused, injured or abandoned animals receive medical care and refuge at this nonprofit centre. With local people it also works on general veterinarian services and spaying and neutering. Volunteers and donations are welcome. Travelling vets and vet nurses often drop by, while nonvets help with numerous odd jobs. It's best to call ahead.

Most *sŏrng·tăa·ou* drivers know how to get here; tell them you are going to 'Ban Lisa' (Lisa's House) in Khlong Son.

🛏 Sleeping

Ko Chang's package-tour industry has distorted accommodation pricing. In general, rates have risen while quality has not, partly because hotels catering to group tours are guaranteed occupancy and don't have to maintain standards to woo repeat visitors or walk-ins. There is also a lot of copy-cat pricing, giving value-oriented visitors little choice.

Backpackers can still find good value hostels with dorm beds and basic huts for 300B or less, especially at Lonely Beach.

🛏 West Coast

On the west coast, Lonely Beach is still the best budget option; Hat Kaibae is the best-value option; and White Sand Beach (Hat Sai Khao) is the most overpriced.

🛏 White Sand Beach

Officially called Hat Sai Khao but universally known as White Sand Beach, the island's prettiest beach is also its most expensive. The northern and southern extremities have some budget and midrange options worth considering if you need proximity to the finest sand. There's a happening backpacker enclave north of KC Grande Resort, accessible only via the beach.

Independent Bo's   GUESTHOUSE $
(☑ 039 551165; White Sand Beach; d 300-800B; 🛜) Quirky and enchanting, this is an old-school bohemian budget place right on the sands. It's a striking sight and experience: a warren of driftwood cabins, common areas and quirky signs, with a communal, hippie feel and the sea at your feet. The fan-only rooms are simple and mostly charming; bathrooms range from extremely basic to modernised. No reservations (and no children).

Like other places along this stretch, Bo's is reached by a walk along the sand, most easily from KC Grande to the south.

Starbeach Bungalows   GUESTHOUSE $
(☑ 089 574 9486; www.starbeach-kohchang. com; White Sand Beach; bungalows 500-750B; 🛜) Right on the prime part of White Sand Beach, this ramshackle-looking spot is a sweet budget place with simple fan-cooled rooms that all look out towards the water. There's a friendly on-site bar and restaurant. No reservations: text or call to see if there's a vacancy. Head towards the beach down the side of the 7-Eleven and turn right.

Rock Sand Resort   GUESTHOUSE $$
(☑ 084 781 0550; www.rocksand-resort.com; White Sand Beach; d incl breakfast with fan/air-con from 800/2700B; 🅿 ❄ 🛜) Touting itself as a flashpacker destination, this is the most upmarket of the knot of budget places at the north end of White Sand Beach, but feels overpriced in high season. The sea-view rooms are, however, decent and share a balcony.

Waves beat against the foundations beneath the restaurant; be prepared to wade here at high tide.

You can only get here on foot along a short stretch of beach (past KC Grande) or the north via the scarily steep road to White Sand Beach Resort.

🛏 Ao Khlong Prao

Ao Khlong Prao is dominated by high-end resorts, with a few budget spots peppered in between. There are a handful of cheapies on the main road that are within walking distance of the beach.

★ Pajamas Hostel
HOSTEL $

(📞 039 510789; www.pajamaskohchang.com; Khlong Prao; dm 480-630B, d/f 2430/4410B; P ✻ 🛜 ☒) A couple of kilometres north of the main Khlong Prao strip and a short walk from the beach, this superb hostel oozes relaxation, with an open-plan lounge and bar overlooking the swimming pool. Modern air-con dorms are upstairs. Private rooms have platform beds, a cool, light feel and your own terrace/balcony. Spotless, and exceedingly well run.

Riverview Hostel
HOSTEL $

(📞 096 765 7669; www.riverviewkohchang.com; Khlong Prao; dm/d 500/900B; ✻ 🛜) In a beautiful riverside house overlooking the canal, not far from the beach, this hostel has spotless mixed and female-only air-conditioned dorms and a very tidy upstairs double room (with shared bathroom).

Tiger Huts
BUNGALOW $

(📞 089 833 1503; Khlong Prao; d 500-1000B; 🛜) These old-school thatch-roof bungalows are pretty basic with fan only but they are absolute beachfront among the palms on one of Ko Chang's quieter beaches. There's a restaurant and bar but it's a laid-back scene.

★ Baan Rim Nam
GUESTHOUSE $$

(📞 087 005 8575; www.iamkohchang.com; Khlong Prao; d 1000-1400B, f 1900B; ✻ 🛜) This marvellously converted fishers house is right over the mangrove-lined river estuary and makes a supremely peaceful place to stay. The five cool, appealing rooms open onto a waterside deck. Free kayaks are provided – the beach is a three-minute paddle away.

Blue Lagoon Bungalows
BUNGALOW $$

(📞 089 515 4617; www.kohchang-bungalows-bluelagoon.com; Ban Khlong Phrao; bungalow with fan 500-1500B, air-con 1100-3700B; P ✻ 🛜) Set beside a scenic estuary, Blue Lagoon has an eclectic bunch of bungalows and rooms arrayed in a rustic manner across a riverside mangrove with a walkway to the beach. There's an eco theme and a welcoming bohemian vibe. There are numerous activities, including yoga and cooking classes (p478).

🛏 Hat Kaibae

Hat Kaibae has some of the island's best variety of accommodation, from boutique hotels to budget huts and midrange bungalows. The trade-off is that the beach is only sandy in parts.

Porn's Bungalows
BUNGALOW $

(📞 080 613 9266; www.pornsbungalows-kohchang.com; Hat Kaibae; d 500-1200B; P 🛜) This is a very chilled spot at the far western end of Kaibae beach, with a popular on-site beachside restaurant (Hat Kaibae; mains 80-220B; ⏲ 9.30am-11pm; 🛜). All of the wooden bungalows are fan-only but the larger beachfront ones have a great outlook, and are a good deal at around 1000B. No reservations are taken, so you might find it full in busy periods. You can rent kayaks here.

Garden Resort
HOTEL $$

(📞 039 557260; www.gardenresortkohchang.com; 98/22 Mu 4, Hat Kaibae; d incl breakfast 2500-2400B; P ✻ @ 🛜 ☒) Just off the main road and yet set back in palm-shaded seclusion, Garden Resort has large, charming bungalows dotted either side of a shady garden pathway that leads to a pleasant pool area. It's a short stroll to a sandy stretch of beach and close to a knot of popular bars.

Green Resort
BUNGALOW $$

(📞 097 110 7094; www.thegreen-kohchang.com; 51/3 Mu 4, Hat Kaibae; d 900-1500B; P ✻ 🛜) Just off the strip in Hat Kaibae, the Green is decidedly downmarket compared with some of its neighbours, though the lime-green bungalows are cheap enough and set around a peaceful lawn.

Chill
RESORT $$$

(📞 039 552555; www.thechillresort.com; Hat Kaibae; d incl breakfast 6500-14,500B; ste from 12,750B; P ✻ @ 🛜 ☒) Cleverly designed, with all ground-floor rooms opening onto one of three fabulous pools, boutique Chill has contemporary, bright rooms with loads of space and bags of facilities. It's right on the beach and has good family-friendly features, a gym, spa, beachfront cafe and very helpful staff.

🛏 Lonely Beach

A backpacker and raver fave, Lonely Beach is one of the cheapest places to sleep on the island, though budget spots smack on the beach are harder to find. Its streets are filled with grungy bars and cheap guesthouses.

★ Paradise Cottage   BUNGALOW $
(📞 081 773 9337; www.paradisecottageresort.com; 104/1 Mu 1, Lonely Beach; d with fan 400-1400B, with air-con 1200-2500B; 🅿✳🛜🏊) Hammock-clad pavilions face the sea or pool, and compact, handsome rooms are scattered around the garden at this well-run and gloriously relaxing retreat. The sea-view rooms have air-con and a marvellous outlook, while the cheapest ones have fans. At low tide a sandbank just beyond the rocks can be reached. It's far enough away from the noisy clubs to ensure sleep.

Little Eden   BUNGALOW $
(📞 084 867 7459; www.littleedenkohchang.com; Soi 3, Lonely Beach; d with fan/air-con 950/1500B; 🅿✳🛜) Up the steep hill on the quiet side of the main road, Little Eden has a series of sweet wooden bungalows, all connected by an intricate lattice of wooden walkways. Rooms are comfortable with a terrace, wooden floors and mosquito nets; expect plenty of chirping noise from forest critters. There are good breakfasts, a pleasant communal area and friendly staff.

BB Lonely Beach   HOSTEL $
(📞 089 504 0543; www.bblonelybeach.com; Lonely Beach; dm 250-350B, d with fan/air-con from 550/1000B; ✳🛜🏊) BB is still the best allround backpacker place in Lonely Beach, with fan or air-con dorms (the air-con dorm comprises private cabins), a few private rooms, a popular cat cafe and a great traveller vibe around the pool. It's a way from the beach but in the thick of the main street action.

Oasis Koh Chang   BUNGALOW $$
(📞 081 721 2547; www.oasis-kohchang.com; 4/28 Mu 1, Lonely Beach; d 750-1400B; 🅿✳🛜) Literally the top place in Lonely Beach (largely due to its hillside location), Oasis has great sea views from its vertigo-inducing 12m-tall tree house that towers above the restaurant. Run by a friendly Dutch couple, it has roomy, midrange stone-and-timber bungalows in four categories. Cheaper rooms are fan-only – the best have sea views.

It's a five-minute walk to the beach.

Warapura Resort   BOUTIQUE HOTEL $$
(📞 039 558123; www.warapuraresort.com; 4/3 Mu 1, Lonely Beach; d incl breakfast 1700-3300B; 🅿✳@🛜🏊) Right by the sea, Warapura has a series of excellent boutique bungalows lightly decorated with rustic furniture and a white-and-turquoise colour scheme. Higher-priced rooms are larger and closer to the sea. There's a sociable bar-restaurant with an exclusive feel. The beach isn't really swimmable here, but the decent pool makes up for it.

🛏 Ban Bang Bao & Around

Despite its touristy veneer, Ban Bang Bao is a charming place to stay. Accommodation options are mainly converted pier houses overlooking the sea, with easy access to departing interisland ferries. The lovely Hat Khlong Kloi is just to the east. Night owls should either hire a motorbike or stay elsewhere, as *sŏrng·tǎa·ou* become rare and expensive after dinnertime.

Cliff Cottage   BUNGALOW $
(📞 080 823 5495; www.cliff-cottage.com; Ban Bang Bao; tent/d/bungalow 560/730/840B; ✳🛜) Partially hidden on a verdant hillside west of the pier are a few dozen simple, comfortable huts overlooking a rocky cove with water on both sides, plus some air-con rooms. Most have sea views and a couple offer spectacular vistas. Accommodation in large prepitched 'glamping' tents is available in high season. Scubadawgs (p477) dive school has a base here.

★ Bang Bao Beach Resort   BUNGALOW $$
(📞 093 327 2788; www.bangbaobeachresort.com; Hat Khlong Koi; d 1500-2300B; ✳) Set along green lawn right on Khlong Koi beach, just east of Bang Bao, this is a marvellous spot. Old and new bungalows are available; both are attractively wooden and air-conditioned. It's a very efficiently run spot with easy access to beach bars and restaurants alongside. Walk along the beach from the canal bridge or drive the long way round.

★ Buddha View   GUESTHOUSE $$
(📞 039 558157; www.thebuddhaview.com; Ban Bang Bao; d 800-1400B; ✳🛜) This swish pier guesthouse has seven thoughtfully designed, all-wood rooms, four of which come with private bathrooms (the shared ones are excellent either way). The restaurant is great: sit at the cutaway tables and dangle your feet over the water and sculptures below.

Chaipura Resort BUNGALOW $$

(☑039 558090; www.chaipura.com; 222 Mu 1, Klong Koi; d/f 2800/3500B; ⓟ❄☎) These elegant northern Thai-style bungalows are beautifully designed with high ceilings, dark-stained timbers finishes and mod cons, all occupying a gardened hillside overlooking a small lake. It's a short stroll to the lovely beach and Bang Bao. Staff are efficient, and the on-site restaurant is good.

🛏 Northern Interior & East Coast

The northern and eastern parts of the island are less developed than the west coast and more isolated. You will likely need your own transport to not feel lonely out here, but you'll be rewarded with a quieter experience.

There are a handful of accommodation options on the east coast at Ao Salak Kok and Ao Dan Kao.

★Mangrove Hideaway GUESTHOUSE $$

(☑080 133 6600; www.themangrovehideaway. com; Ban Salak Phet; d 1930-3640B; ⊙closed Jun & Sep; ❄☎) 🌱 Facing the mangrove forest, this environmentally friendly guesthouse is a fabulous spot. Crisp, attractive rooms face the verdant front garden, while the sumptuous superior suites have gorgeous wooden floors and overlook the dining area and mangroved river estuary. There's an open-air Jacuzzi and massage area upstairs.

Serenity Resort HOTEL $$

(☑088 092 4452; www.serenity-koh-chang. com; Ao Dan Kao; d 3250, 2-/3-bedroom villas 6000/7900B; ⓟ❄☎☀) Not far from the ferries (1.5km from Centrepoint), on the peaceful northeast side of the island, this well-presented resort has serene, cool white rooms right on the beach, where there's a bar and pool. Kayaks and SUPs are on hand.

Spa Koh Chang Resort RESORT $$

(☑083 115 6566; www.thespakohchang.com; Ao Salak Kok; d incl breakfast 2050-3700B; ⓟ❄☎☀) Specialising in health-care packages, including detox, yoga and meditation, this east-coast resort has lush surroundings that almost touch the bay's mangrove forests. Elegantly decorated bungalows scramble up a flower-filled hillside and provide a peaceful getaway. There's no beach access.

Amber Sands HOTEL $$$

(☑039 586177; www.ambersandsbeachresort. com; Ao Dan Kao; d 5100-7650B; ⊙mid-Oct–Aug;

ⓟ❄☎☀) Right on a quiet beach, this is an impeccably run place set around a beautifully kept garden. Rooms have wooden floors, elegant furnishings and are very easy on the eye. The outlook is perfect for relaxation. It feels a world away but is close to the ferries; they'll arrange pick-up for you.

🍴 Eating

Virtually all of the island's accommodation choices have attached restaurants with adequate but not outstanding fare. It's usually worth seeking places outside; though most travellers don't stray too far from their beach base, there's some decent eating to be found along the island's west coast. Bang Bao pier has some excellent seafood restaurants.

Funky Monkey CAFE $

(☑087 180 4828; Hat Kaibae; cakes & ice creams 80-120B; ⊙11am-11pm; ☎) This sweet little cafe, stuffed with old retro couches and artworks, is as much a cocktail bar and teahouse as a place to sit down to a big meal. Locally famous are the ice-cream rolls. There are also decadent cheesecakes and brownies.

Rasta View THAI $

(Ban Bang Bao; mains 80-240B; ⊙9am-midnight; ☎) The green, red and yellow decor, rustic ambience and reggae soundtrack tell the story of this colourful roadside restaurant that has fine views over Bang Bao. The menu is mostly Thai, with good-value curries and noodle dishes.

★Barrio Bonito MEXICAN $$

(☑080 092 8208; Hat Kaibae; mains 250-320B; ⊙5-10pm Jul-late May; ☎🍴) Fab fajitas, burritos, tacos and cocktails are served by a charming French-Mexican couple at this roadside spot in the middle of Kaibae. Offering authentic, delicious, beautifully presented food and stylish surroundings, this is one of the island's finest places for a night out.

★Phu-Talay SEAFOOD $$

(☑039 551300; 4/2 Mu 4, Khlong Prao; mains 90-300B; ⊙10am-10pm) A beautiful place right on the canal, Phu-Talay has a picturesque deck and its own boat (for pickup from nearby accommodation). It specialises in seafood, with standout softshell crab, prawns and other fish dishes, and is far more reasonably priced than many other seafood places.

Dang Seafood SEAFOOD $$

(Lonely Beach; mains 50-300B fish priced by weight; ⊙9am-10.30pm) Lonely Beach's very popular main-street seafood restaurant is set up like a market stall with plastic chairs and tables under a canopy and whole fish displayed on ice and weighed for purchase.

Sleepy Owl
PIZZA $$

(☑088 525 5575; Lonely Beach; mains 80-120B, pizzas 195-350B; ⊙10am-10pm; 🗟) This popular coffeeshop does a range of Thai meals but is best known for its pizzas, which distinguish it from other Thai restaurants in the village. Also a good spot for a late breakfast.

Kung Kra Ta
BARBECUE $$

(☑091 738 7429; Hat Kaibae; all-you-can-eat 229B; ⊙6-11pm) This open-air place packs in locals and tourists alike for its all-you-can-eat hot-pot and grill offer. The quality isn't sky-high but it's a fun way to enjoy a big feed without breaking the bank.

Ka-Ti Culinary
THAI $$

(☑081 903 0408; www.facebook.com/katikhrua thai; Khlong Prao; mains 120-580B; ⊙11am-10pm Mon-Sat, 5-10pm Sun; 🗟) Seafood, a few Isan dishes and the famous homemade curry sauce are the best bets here. There's a children's menu, and Ka-Tï's cooking classes (p478) are recommended.

🍷 Drinking & Nightlife

Parties abound on the beaches and range from a more mature, restrained scene on White Sand Beach, to a younger and more frenetic one on Lonely Beach. Kai Bae has its own mini Walking St with a few bars firing up at night.

★ Shambhala
BAR

(☑098 579 4381; Siam Royal View, Ao Khlong Son; ⊙11am-10pm or later Thu-Tue) Perched at the north end of the island, past the flash marina, this poolside bar has a magnificent outlook across green lawn to a secluded golden sweep of beach. It's the perfect spot for a sundowner cocktail; it also turns out quality Thai and international dishes. Enter via the southernmost 'Marina' entrance to the Siam Royal View complex.

White Elephant
SPORTS BAR

(☑039 612211; www.whiteelephantbar.com; 9/22/6-8, Moo 4, White Sand Beach; ⊙7.30am-2am) White Sand's favourite sports bar among the expat crowd features live music on Fridays, a fortnightly quiz and all the international football you can handle. There's a great range of international beers and a convivial pub-in-the-tropics atmosphere.

Ting Tong
CLUB

(☑091 705 7857; Soi Tian Chai 1, Lonely Beach; ⊙5pm-4am) When you hear the thumping music coming from the back lanes of Lonely Beach, it's usually coming from here. Ting Tong is legendary on the Ko Chang club scene, with regular party nights, imported DJs and live bands. In theory it's open 24 hours, but usually starts slow and goes through till dawn.

ℹ Information

EMERGENCY
Head to the **tourist police station** (☑1155; Khlong Prao) in Khlong Prao for any need.

MEDICAL SERVICES
Bang Bao Health Centre (☑039 558086; Ban Bang Bao; ⊙8.30am-4pm) For the basics. On the pier.

Ko Chang Hospital (☑039 586131; Ban Dan Mai) Public hospital with a good reputation and affordably priced care; south of the ferry terminal.

Ko Chang International Clinic (☑039 551555; www.bangkoktrathospital.com; White Sand Beach; ⊙24hr) Related to the Bangkok Hospital Group; accepts most health insurance and has expensive rates.

MONEY
There are banks with ATMs and exchange facilities along all the west-coast beaches.

POST
Ko Chang Post Office (☑039 551240; White Sand Beach; ⊙9am-5pm) is at the far southern end of White Sand Beach (Hat Sai Khao).

SAFE TRAVEL
➡ Take extreme care when driving from Ban Khlong Son south to White Sand Beach (Hat Sai Khao), as the road is steep and treacherous, with several hairpin turns. There are mudslides and poor conditions during storms. If you rent a motorbike, ride carefully between Hat Kaibae and Lonely Beach, especially in the wet season. Wear protective clothing and a helmet when riding on a motorcycle.

➡ The police conduct regular drug raids on the island's accommodation. If you get caught with narcotics, you could face heavy fines or imprisonment.

➡ Be aware of the cheap minibus tickets from Siem Reap to Ko Chang; these usually involve some sort of time- and money-wasting commission scam.

➡ Ko Chang is considered a low-risk malarial zone, meaning that liberal use of mosquito repellent is probably an adequate precaution.

TOURIST INFORMATION

➡ The free magazine *Koh Chang Guide* (www. koh-chang-guide.com) is widely available on the island and has handy beach maps.

➡ The comprehensive website I Am Koh Chang (www.iamkohchang.com) is a labour of love from an irreverent Brit living on the island. It's jam-packed with opinion and information.

TRAVEL AGENCIES

Nuttakit Tour (☑ 092 647 3009; nuttakittour @gmail.com; Bang Bao), the first agency on the right after entering Bang Bao's pier itself, has helpful English-speaking staff who can arrange tailored boat trips as well as the usual excursions.

❶ Getting There & Away

Whether starting from Bangkok or Cambodia, it is an all-day haul to reach Ko Chang overland. Overnighting in Trat is a pleasant way to break the journey.

Ferries from the mainland (Laem Ngop) leave from either Tha Thammachat, operated by **Koh Chang Ferry** (☑ 039 555188; https:// kohchangferries.com; adult/child/car 1 way 80/30/120B; ☺ 6.30am-7pm), or Tha Centrepoint with **Centrepoint Ferry** (☑ 039 538196; https://kohchangferries.com; Tha Centrepoint; adult 1 way/return 80/150B, child 1 way/return 40/70B, car 1 way/return 100/180B; ☺ hourly 6am-7.30pm, to 7pm May-Oct). Boats from Tha Thammachat arrive at Tha Sapparot, Centrepoint ferries at a pier 3km further south. Koh Chang ferries are faster and a little better.

Travel agents in Ko Chang sell through-tickets including boat and minivan to Siem Reap (650B) and Phnom Penh (900B) in Cambodia, though these require a change of bus at the border.

It is possible to go to and from Ko Chang from Bangkok's Eastern (Ekamai) bus terminal via Chanthaburi and Trat; there are also direct bus and minibus **services** (☑ 083 794 2122; www. bussuvarnabhumikohchang.com) from Bangkok's Suvarnabhumi International Airport.

The closest airport is in Trat. **Ko Chang Minibus** (☑ 087 785 7695; www.kohchangminibus. com) offers a variety of transfer packages from airport to beach.

Bang Bao Boat (☑ 039 558046; www. kohchangbangbaoboat.com; Ban Bang Bao; ☺ Nov-Apr) runs an interisland ferry that connects Ko Chang with Ko Mak and Ko Wai (with a speedboat connection from there to Ko Kut) during the high season. Boats leave from Bang Bao in the southwest of the island.

Speedboats travel between the islands during high season from both Bang Bao and Hat Kaibae.

❶ Getting Around

Shared *sŏrng·tăa·ou* (passenger pickup trucks) meet arriving boats to shuttle passengers to the various beaches:

Khlong Prao 150B

Lonely Beach 200B

White Sand Beach 100B

Hops between neighbouring beaches range from 50B to 200B but prices rise dramatically after

KO CHANG TRANSPORT CONNECTIONS

ORIGIN	DESTINATION	BOAT	BUS
Bangkok's Eastern Bus Terminal (Ekamai)	Tha Thammachat (Laem Ngop)		280B, 6hr, 2 daily
Ko Chang	Bangkok's Suvarnabhumi International Airport		1-way/return 600/900B, 6-7hr, 2-3 daily
Ko Chang	Ko Kut	speedboat 900B, 2½hr, 3 daily; wooden boat plus speedboat 700B, 5hr, 1 daily	
Ko Chang	Ko Mak	speedboat 600B, 1hr, 3 daily; wooden boat 400B, 2hr, 1 daily	
Ko Chang	Ko Wai	speedboat 400B, 30min, 3 daily; wooden boat 300B, 1hr, 1 daily	
Tha Centrepoint (Laem Ngop)	Ko Chang	80B, 40min, hourly 6am-7.30pm	
Tha Thammachat (Laem Ngop)	Ko Chang	80B, 30min, every 45min 6.30am-7pm	

dark, when it can cost 500B to travel from Bang Bao to White Sand.

Motorbikes can be hired from 150B per day. Ko Chang's hilly and winding roads are dangerous; make sure the bike is in good working order.

Hiring a car is an option. **Sawadee Koh Chang Travel** (☑ 086 712 6804; sawadeekohchang@ hotmail.co.th; Hat Kaibae; car per day from 1200B; ⊗ 8.30am-8.30pm) is one of a couple of places on the island to do so.

Ko Kut

☑ 039 / POP 2100

Ko Kut (เกาะกูด), also widely called Ko Kood, is often feted as the perfect Thai island, and it is hard to argue with such an accolade. The supersoft sands are like talcum powder; the water lapping the bays is clear; and there are more coconut palms than people.

Unlike its larger neighbour Ko Chang, here you can escape from any serious nightlife or noise – though there's an infectious little live-music scene in season. Kayaking, snorkelling and visits to waterfalls are the main activities.

◉ Sights & Activities

With its quiet rocky coves and mangrove estuaries, Ko Kut is great for snorkelling and kayaking. Most resorts offer equipment. Standup paddleboards can be rented from View Point Cafe (p486) for 200/800B per hour/day.

A dozen or so dive sites crowd around the island's west coast, and local outfits can also take you to Ko Rang and Ko Mak sites.

Nam Tok Khlong Chao   WATERFALL
(น้ำตกคลองเจ้า) Two waterfalls on the island make good destinations for a short hike. The larger and more popular Nam Tok Khlong Chao is wide and pretty with a massive plunge pool, particularly early in the dry season. It is a quick jungle walk to the base from the end of the road, or you can kayak up Khlong Chao. Further north is Nam Tok Khlong Yai Ki, which is smaller but also has a large pool to cool off in.

Paradise Divers   DIVING
(☑ 087 144 5945; www.kohkood-paradisedivers. com; Ban Khlong Chao; 2 boat dives 3000B, snorkelling 1000B) Ko Kood's original dive outfit runs small-group dive and snorkelling trips to a range of sites, including Ko Rang. PADI certification courses start at 11,000B and Discover Scuba costs 4500B. It's about 700m south of Hat Khlong Chao.

🛏 Sleeping

Each of the southwestern beaches has a handful of options. Hat Khlong Chao hosts some pricey boutique options but also has budget guesthouses tucked behind the main beach road. Families might like the mid-range and budget options on Ao Ngam Kho.

Happy Days   GUESTHOUSE $
(☑ 065 6097835; happydayskohkood@hotmail.com; Ban Khlong Chao; d with fan/air-con 600/1000B) Behind Paradise Divers, this simple nine-room guesthouse is a great budget option, with clean rooms on two floors. There's a cafe-bar, laundry service and discounted dive-stay packages.

Cozy House   GUESTHOUSE $
(☑ 089 094 3650; www.kohkoodcozy.com; Hat Khlong Chao; cottages with fan/air-con 700/1200B, d 1000B, incl breakfast; ❋ 🛜) The go-to place for backpackers, family-run Cozy is a 10-minute walk from delightful Hat Khlong Chao. There are cheap and cheerful fan or air-con bungalows and hotel-quality rooms with TV, air-con and verandas facing the mangroves.

★ **Bann Makok**   HOTEL $$
(☑ 088 203 0699; www.bannmakok.com; 10 Moo 4, Khlong Yai Ki; d incl breakfast 3200-3800B; 🅿 ❋ ◉ 🛜) 🍃 This boutique ecoresort, tucked into the mangroves, uses recycled timbers painted in vintage colours to create a maze of eight rooms that resembles a traditional pier fishing village.

Suan Maprao Ko Kut Resort   BUNGALOW $$
(☑ 086 833 7999; Ao Ngam Kho; d 1500-1800B; 🅿 ❋ 🛜) You'll get a genuine welcome at this place with a garden setting just off the southern beach road. Excellent modern huts are simple and stylish, with timber cladding and smoothed concrete interiors. They sit a short walk back from the beach amid towering coconut palms. It's a lovely spot and is fronted by a decent restaurant.

Dusita Resort   BUNGALOW $$
(☑ 081 707 4546; www.dusitakohkood.net; 45 Moo 2, Ao Ngam Kho; d/tr/f 3090/4390/5390B; 🅿 ❋ 🛜) Justifiably popular with families, whose children can run wild in the huge oceanfront garden, this is a beautifully kept affair with smooth lawns and fancy topiary. For everyone else, well-spaced-out, slightly dated but spacious timber bungalows provide a perfect retreat from the real world. Good online rates.

Ko Mak & Ko Kut

Ko Mak & Ko Kut

◉ Sights
1 Nam Tok Khlong Chao............................D3

◔ Activities, Courses & Tours
2 Koh Mak Divers.......................................B3
3 Smile Ko Mak Cooking School B4

◳ Sleeping
4 Ao Kao White Sand Resort B4
5 Banana Sunset...B4
6 Bann Makok..C3
7 Big Easy..A3
8 Monkey Island A3
9 Seavana A3

✗ Eating & Drinking

★ **Noochy Seafood**　　　　　　　SEAFOOD **$$**
(☏ 086 113 3379; Ao Yai; mains 150-600B;
⊘ 9.30am-9.30pm) The quaint east-coast stilt
fishing village of Ao Yai is home to several
excellent seafood restaurants. Noochy is our
pick for its attentive staff and a great over-
water location at the end of the pier. Choose
from scallops, shrimp, crab, flathead lobster
and squid. Beer available.

You'll need your own transport to get
here, or arrange a taxi to wait for you.

Ra Beang Mai　　　　　　　　　　THAI **$$**
(Hat Khlong Chao; mains 100-380B; ⊘ 9am-9pm
Thu-Tue; ☞) Handy for the cluster of accommodation near Hat Khlong Chao, this family-run restaurant has a covered area as well
as pleasant outdoor seating on rustic wood-
en furniture. Dishes include plump prawn
salads and seafood curries.

View Point Cafe　　　　　　　　　　BAR
(☏ 081 004 4233; Hat Khlong Chao; ⊘ 9am-9pm)
Not as grungy as nearby local bars, View
Point has a fabulous location and a deck
where you can dangle your legs over the

river. There's good espresso coffee, decent food (mains 90B to 150B), a full bar list and standup paddleboards for rent (200/800B per hour/day).

Sunset Bar   BAR
(Hat Khlong Chao; ⊙4pm-late) Across the river from Hat Khlong Chao, Sunset Bar is a favourite with locals and expats at sunset and beyond. It's a rustic place with views over the river and northern tip of the beach, with no-nonsense staff.

☆ Entertainment

Fisherman Hut Music Station   LIVE MUSIC
(☑092 639 1469; off Bang Bao Bay; ⊙7-10pm) This semi-open-air music venue hosts live music from local and visiting bands nightly in season. It's a fine initiative from music-loving locals. It's close to Ao Bang Bao.

❶ Information

There are at least two ATMs on Ko Kut (one near Hat Khlong Chao) but no banks; major resorts can exchange money and accept credit cards, but bring a decent supply of cash anyway.

The **Police Station** (☑1155, 039 525745; ⊙24hr) is near the hospital at Ban Khlong Dam.

The small, inland **Ko Kut Hospital** (☑039 521 852; Ban Khlong Mad; ⊙24hr) can handle minor emergencies.

❶ Getting There & Away

Ko Kut is accessible from the mainland pier of Laem Sok (p473), 22km southeast of Trat, the nearest bus transfer point. Three boat services as well as a speedboat service run from adjacent

piers. Boat services offer free transport from Trat guesthouses and the bus station but not from the airport. In the reverse direction you'll pay 50B.

Speedboats will drop you off at your resort, if possible; regular boats offer free land transfer on your arrival at **Ao Salad Pier** in the north-eastern corner of the island to your destination. Companies include:

Koh Kood Princess (☑086 126 7860; www. kohkoodprincess.com)

Ko Kut Express (☑09 05060020; www. kokutexpress.in.th)

Boonsiri (☑085 921 0111; www.boonsiri ferry.com)

Two firms run speedboats from Ko Chang to Ko Kut (900B, 2½ hours) via Ko Wai and Ko Mak. The cheapest way to do this is to book a through-trip with **Bang Bao Boat** (☑084 567 8765; www.kohchangbangbaoboat.com; Ao Bang Bao) via Ko Mak, with the first section by wooden boat and the second by speedboat (700B).

❶ Getting Around

Ko Kut's roads are steep, which rules out renting a bicycle for island exploration unless you are a champion cyclist. Motorbikes can be rented for 200B to 300B per day.

Ko Mak

☑039 / POP 600

Sweet little Ko Mak (เกาะหมาก) measures just 16 sq km and doesn't have any speeding traffic, wall-to-wall development, noisy beer bars or crowded beaches. Its palm-fringed bays are bathed by gently lapping water and there's a relaxed vibe. Although small, Ko

BOAT SERVICES TO KO KUT

The following depart Laem Sok and dock at Ao Salad pier on Ko Kut.

COMPANY	BOAT	FARE (B)	DURATION (HR)	FREQUENCY
Koh Kood Princess	air-con boat	350	1¾	12.30pm daily
Ko Kut Express	air-con fast ferry	500	1¼	1pm daily
Ko Kut Express	speedboat	600	1	10am & 3pm daily Nov-Apr, returning 10am, 11am & 1pm*
Boonsiri	catamaran	500	1¼-1¾	10.45am (direct) & 2.20pm (via Ko Mak & Ko Chang) daily**

* weekends only and weather permitting in low season. Returns from Ko Kut at 10am and 12.30pm in low season.

**mid-May to mid-October one departure only (1.30pm) and no Ko Mak link; extra boat at 10.45am Fridays. Transport from Bangkok (900B) and Trat Airport (800B) available.

Mak has a decent restaurant and bar scene back from Ao Khao, a couple of dive outfits and boat trips to nearby islands, so there's stuff to do when not on the beach.

Visiting is easier in high season (December to March); during low season (May to September) many boats stop running.

Sights & Activities

The best beach on the island is Ao Pra in the west, but it is mostly taken up by the Mira Montra Resort. For now, swimming and beach strolling are best on the northwestern bay of Ao Suan Yai, a wide arc of sand and looking-glass-clear water.

Offshore is Ko Kham, a resort island that is still popular as a day-trippers' beach; boats heading across from Ko Mak depart 10.30am, 1.30pm and 3pm (300B including island fee and transport). Boats also run from Ao Khao to the island of Rayang Nok (350B, from 10am to 4pm), where there's a fine beach and a resort offering water sports.

Koh Mak Divers
DIVING

(☑ 083 297 7724; www.kohmakdivers.com; 59/4 Wong Si Ri Rd, Ao Khao; 2-dive trips from 2500B) Runs dive trips to the Mu Ko Chang National Marine Park, about 45 minutes away, as well as a range of courses (Discover Scuba 3500B). It has a second shop on the road near Baan Koh Mak.

Smile Ko Mak Cooking School
COOKING

(www.smilekohmak.com; Ban Ao Nid; classes 1200-1300B; ⊙ 10am-2pm & 3-7pm) Leng offers cooking classes in her small kitchen near the Ao Nid pier. You'll prepare and eat four dishes (vegetarians are catered for) and receive a recipe book.

Sleeping & Eating

As well as the numerous beachside restaurants at nearly every guesthouse and resort, there is a string of family-run restaurants on the main road between Monkey Island and Makathanee Resort, including a German bakery and a gelati bar. Another few cluster around the road intersection near Ao Kao Resort and on the road to Ao Din pier.

Banana Sunset
TENTED CAMP

(☑ 087 416 2026; www.bananasunset.com; tents 200B, d bungalow 800-1000B; ☎) This isolated collection of bungalows will please budget travellers – you can climb into a dome tent with fan and mattress set in the garden for just 200B. The bungalows with attached bathrooms are more comfy and still good value.

Monkey Island
BUNGALOW $

(☑ 089 501 6030; www.monkeyislandkohmak.com; Ao Khao; d with/without bathroom 700/500B, with air-con incl breakfast 1200-2000B; ▣ ❄ ☎) A go-to place for budget travellers, Monkey Island has bungalows in three models, which range from very basic to beachfront villa chic. The popular beachfront restaurant does respectable Thai cuisine in a leisurely fashion. Motorbike hire available.

Big Easy
BUNGALOW $$

(☑ 098 575 7427; www.bigeasykohmak.com; Ao Khao; bungalows incl breakfast 2700-3200B; ❄ ☎) At the northern end of Ao Khao on a lovely stretch of beach, Big Easy has seven beautifully constructed timber cottages, well spaced among the palms for maximum privacy. The beachfront deck restaurant is a great meeting place.

Seavana
RESORT $$

(☑ 090 864 5646; www.seavanakohmak.com; Ao Suan Yi; d 3000-5500B; ▣ ❄ ☎ ⊛) Stylish wine-coloured buildings overlook garden, coconut palms and white sand at this top-drawer set-up near the northern pier. The staff are cordial and competent and the range of rooms excellent.

Ao Kao White Sand Resort
BUNGALOW $$$

(☑ 083 152 6564; www.aokaoresort.com; Ao Khao; d incl breakfast 5000B; ▣ ❄ ☎ ⊛) ⊘ In a pretty crook in the bay, Ao Kao White Sand is Ko Mak's top resort. An assortment of stylish concrete bungalows come with fab rooftop terraces offering thatched shade, hammocks and sea views. All have easy beach access. There are lots of amenities, including sports options, pool, yoga and a massage pavilion.

SPEEDBOAT TRANSPORT FROM KO MAK

DESTINATION	FARE (ONE WAY)	DURATION	FREQUENCY
Ko Chang	600B	1hr	3 daily
Ko Kut	400B	45min	3 daily
Ko Wai	400B	30min	3 daily
Laem Ngop (mainland pier)	450B	1hr	6 daily

SPEEDBOAT TRANSPORT FROM KO WAI

DESTINATION	FARE (ONE WAY)	DURATION	FREQUENCY
Ko Chang	400B	30min	3 daily
Ko Kut	700B	1hr	3 daily
Ko Mak	400B	30min	3 daily
Laem Ngop (mainland pier)	450B	50min	3 daily

Ball Cafe
CAFE **$$**

(✆081 925 6591; Ao Khao; mains 60-190B; ◷8.30am-9pm; ☏) Modern coffee shop on the road behind the beach. As well as espresso coffee and various teas, you can indulge in baguettes, breakfast and bakery goods.

Little Red Oven
PIZZA **$$**

(✆062 651 9605; 97 Soi Sodsai; pizza bases from 200B; ◷noon-9pm) Enjoy the island's best woodfired pizza in the large semi-open dining area. Wine by the glass from 150B. It's about 1.5km east of the Ao Kao strip.

ⓘ Information

There's one international **ATM** at the government office (next to the police station) but don't rely on it. Bring cash. Most resorts accept credit cards.

There is a handy information point at **Koh Mak Resort** (✆089 6009597; www.kohmakresort.com; Ao Suan Yai; d incl breakfast 2800-6400B; ⓟ✼☏☲).

Ko Mak has a small **police station** (✆1155) in the centre of the island.

For basic first-aid emergencies and illnesses, **Ko Mak Health Centre** (◷8.30am-4.30pm) is on the cross-island road near Ao Nid Pier.

ⓘ Getting There & Away

Speedboats (450B one way, one hour) from Laem Ngop arrive at the pier on Ao Suan Yai or Ao Nid. The Ko Kut–bound Boonsiri (p487) ferry also stops in here once daily in high season (from mainland 400B). A slow wooden boat (200B) also departs Laem Ngop at 11am.

In low season only one or two boats per day run from the mainland. Guesthouses and hotels will pick you up free of charge.

From Ko Chang, speedboats head to Ko Mak via Ko Wai and on to Ko Kut and back. The Bang Bao ferry (p484) (400B, two hours, one daily) heads to Ko Mak via Ko Wai (300B) and back.

ⓘ Getting Around

Once on the island, you can pedal (40B per hour) or motorbike (200B to 250B per day) your way around. Both can usually be hired through your accommodation.

Ko Wai
✐039

Stunning, tiny Ko Wai (เกาะหวาย) is barely developed but has clear waters, intact glowing coral reefs for snorkelling off the beach and a handsome view across to Ko Chang.

There are no banks or ATMs on the island, so stock up on cash before visiting.

🛏 Sleeping

There are two resorts and three basic bungalow operations on Ko Wai; all close from May to September, when seas are rough and flooding is common. Except at the resorts, generator power is rationed and intermittent.

Ko Wai Paradise
BUNGALOW **$**

(✆081 762 2548; d 400-800B; ◷Oct–mid-May) Simple, rustic wooden bungalows with shared bathroom on a postcard-perfect beach on the western side of the north coast. It's the island's main backpacker scene. You'll share the coral out front with day trippers.

Koh Wai Beach Resort
BUNGALOW **$$**

(✆081 306 4053; www.kohwaibeachresort.com; d incl breakfast 2100-3400B; ◷Oct–mid-May; ✼☏) On the southern side of the island, this upscale collection of bungalows and teak houses with all the mod cons is just a few steps from the beach and accessible only by boat.

ⓘ Getting There & Away

➡ Boat services run to Ko Wai from November to April; outside of this time (when most accommodation is closed anyway) you can ask for the reduced Ko Mak services to stop at Ko Wai.

➡ Speedboats from Laem Ngop will drop you off at the nearest pier to your guesthouse; or you'll have to walk 15 to 30 minutes along a narrow forest trail from the main Pakarang pier.

➡ From Ko Chang, speedboats head to Ko Wai, continuing to Ko Mak and on to Ko Kut and back.

➡ The wooden Bang Bao (p484) ferry (300B, one hour, one daily) heads from Ko Chang to Ko Wai, continuing to Ko Mak (200B) and back.

AT A GLANCE

POPULATION
250,000

LENGTH OF HUA HIN BEACH
4 km (p501)

BEST WILDLIFE EXPERIENCE
Wildlife Friends Foundation (p501)

BEST BUDDHIST STATUE
Wat Huay Mongkol (p501)

BEST THAI RESTAURANT
Jek Pia (p506)

WHEN TO GO
Jan–Mar Best time to learn how to kite-board as the water is usually smooth.

Oct Rainiest month, but stays drier than the rest of the country so no need to stay away.

Nov–Mar Coolest months – see the 'sea of fog' at Kaeng Krachan National Park.

Hat Hua Hin (p501)
8 F/SHUTTERSTOCK

Hua Hin & the Upper Gulf

The upper gulf has long been the favoured playground of the Thai elite due to its proximity to Bangkok. Following in the footsteps of the royal family – every Thai king from Rama IV on has spent his summers at a variety of regal holiday homes here – they have inspired countless domestic tourists to flock to this stretch of coast in pursuit of fun and fine seafood.

A winning combination of outdoor activities and culture is on offer here. Historic sites, national parks and long sandy beaches draw an increasing number of expats for twin delights: unspoiled coastline and the relaxed pace of provincial life. There's not much diving or snorkelling, and the swimming isn't all that great, but kiteboarders will be in paradise – this part of the gulf is by far the best place in Thailand to ride the wind.

Hua Hin & the Upper Gulf Highlights

1 Kuiburi National Park (p510) Spotting wild elephants when lucky.

2 Khao Sam Roi Yot National Park (p510) Making the pilgrimage to see the illuminated cave shrine of Tham Phraya Nakhon.

3 Phetchaburi Exploring the hilltop palace and underground caves while dodging monkeys.

4 Prachuap Khiri Khan (p512) Motorcycling between curvaceous bays and limestone peaks.

5 Kaeng Krachan National Park Escaping into the depths of this national park, spotting tropical birds, swinging gibbons and the sea of fog.

6 Hua Hin (p500) Dining out in Hua Hin, home to countless good Thai restaurants.

7 Ban Krut & Bang Saphan Yai (p517) Stepping off the backpacker trail on your own secluded strip of sand.

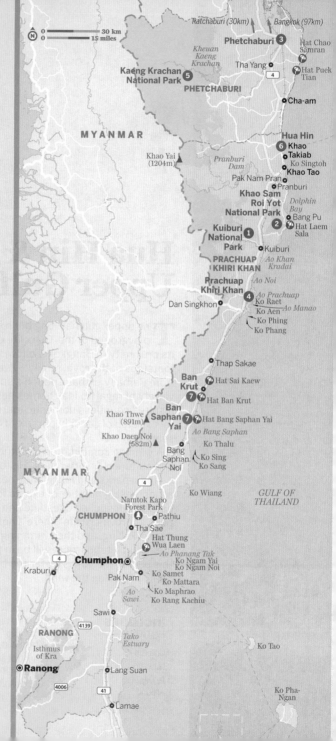

Phetchaburi

☑ 032 / POP 26,000

An easy escape from Bangkok, Phetchaburi (เพชรบุรี) should be on every cultural traveller's itinerary. It has temples, palaces and cave shrines, but best of all, Phetburi, as it's usually called, remains an untouched and largely untouristed provincial town, complete with riverside markets and old teak shophouses. It's a great place for random wandering and makes a convenient stop on your way to the beach.

Phetchaburi is a visible timeline of kingdoms that have migrated across Southeast Asia. During the 11th century, the Khmer empire settled in, although its control was relatively short-lived. As Khmer power diminished, Phetchaburi became a strategic royal fort during the Thai-based Sukhothai and Ayuthaya kingdoms, and in the 17th century, it flourished as a trading post between Myanmar (Burma) and Ayuthaya. Though the great temples of the former capital were destroyed, the town is often referred to as a 'Living Ayuthaya' because the smaller but similar ones live on.

◉ Sights

⭐ **Kaeng Krachan National Park**   NATIONAL PARK
(อุทยานแห่งชาติแก่งกระจาน; ☑ 032 772311; www. thainationalparks.com/kaeng-krachan-national-park; Rte 3432, Visitor Centre; entry 300B, camping fee per night 30B, tent for 2 120B, sleeping bag 30B; ⊙ 8am-4.30pm) Thailand's largest national park is surprisingly close to civilisation but shelters an intense tangle of wilderness that sees relatively few tourists. It's primarily great for butterflies and birds. Occupying an overlapping biozone for birds as the southernmost spot for northern species and the northernmost spot for southern species, it's home to over 400 bird species. The park, except for **Pa La-U Waterfall** (น้ำตกป่าละอู; Kaeng Krachan National Park; ⊙ 8am-4.30pm), a popular day trip from Hua Hin, closes from August to October.

The wildlife-rich Ban Krang area has a nice 2.5km nature trail. Meanwhile, Panoen Thung is a stunning viewpoint up a 4WD-only road; check whether it's open before heading out.

Wake to an eerie symphony of gibbon calls in the early morning mist at campsites at Ban Krang and near Pa La-U Waterfall.

You can reach the headquarters by minivan from Phetchaburi and Bangkok, but be sure to tell the driver you are going to Kaeng Krachan National Park and not just Kaeng Krachan town.

⭐ **Phra Nakhon Khiri Historical Park**   HISTORIC SITE
(อุทยานประวัติศาสตร์พระนครคีรี; ☑ 032 401006; 150B, cable car return 50B; ⊙ park 8.30am-4.30pm, museum 9am-4pm) This national historical park sits regally atop Khao Wang (Palace Hill), surveying the city with subdued opulence. Rama IV built the palace and dozens of surrounding structures in 1859 as a retreat from Bangkok. The hilltop location allowed the king to pursue his interest in astronomy. Parts of the palace, made in a mix of European, Thai and Chinese styles, are now a **museum** furnished with royal belongings.

Rolling cobblestone paths lead from the palace through the forested hill to three summits, each topped by a stupa. The 40m-tall white spire of **Phra That Chom Phet** skewers the sky from the central peak. You can climb up through the interior to its waist. The western peak features **Wat Phra Kaew Noi** (Little Wat Phra Kaew), a small building slightly resembling one from Bangkok's most important temples, and **Phra Prang Daeng** stupa, with a Khmer-influenced design.

TOO MUCH MONKEY BUSINESS

Phetchaburi is full of macaque monkeys who know no shame or fear. Having once just congregated on Khao Wang in Phra Nakhon Khiri Historical Park, they have now spread to the surrounding buildings, and there are additional troops at Tham Khao Luang (p495), Wat Khao Bandai-It (p495) and other forested places. There, they lurk by food stands, or eye-up passing pedestrians as potential mugging victims. These apes love plastic bags – regarding them as a signal that you're carrying food – and beverages, so be wary about displaying them. Keep a tight hold on camera bags, too. It's not just enough to heed the signs and don't feed or tease them, you should be on guard any time they are near. They do bite.

Phetchaburi (Phetburi)

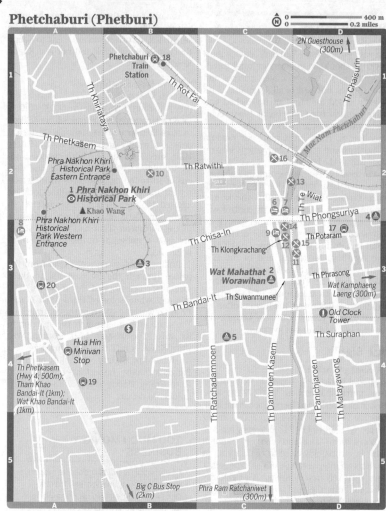

There are two entrances to the site. The **east** (อุทยานประวัติศาสตร์พระนครคีรี ทางเข้าทิศตะวันออก; Th Khiriataya), or front, entrance is across from Th Ratwithi and involves a not-too-strenuous footpath. The **west** (อุทยานประวัติศาสตร์พระนครคีรี ทางเข้าทิศตะวันตก; Th Rim Khao Wang) entrance on the opposite side of the hill has a **cable car** (closed for 10 days each June for regular maintenance and a few other days during the year to change the cable) that glides up and down to the summit. At both, keep a leery eye on the troops of unpredictable monkeys (p493). This place is a popular school-group outing

and you'll be as much of a photo op as the historic buildings.

★ Wat Mahathat Worawihan

BUDDHIST TEMPLE

(วัดมหาธาตุวรวิหาร; Th Damnoen Kasem; ⊘ daylight hours) **FREE** Centrally located, gleaming white Wat Mahathat is one impressive temple. The showpiece is a 42m-tall five-tiered Ayuthaya-style *prang* (corn-cob shaped stupa) decorated in stucco relief, a speciality of Phetchaburi's local artisans you'll see all over town. Inside the *wí·hăhn* (sanctuary) that fronts it are important, though highly damaged, early-20th-century murals.

Phetchaburi (Phetburi)

When leaving or arriving at the temple follow **Thanon Suwanmunee** through the old teak house district, now filled with lottery vendors, for a picture-postcard view of the *prang* from the bridge. There are historical signs in front of some of the notable buildings on this street and Th Klongkrachang.

Tham Khao Luang   CAVE
(ถ้ำเขาหลวง; ◎8am-4pm Mon-Fri, 8am-5pm Sat & Sun) FREE About 4km north of town is Khao Luang Cave, a dramatic stalactite-stuffed cavern that's one of Thailand's most impressive cave shrines, and a favourite of King Rama IV when he was a monk. Accessed via steep stairs, it's lit by a heavenly glow every morning (clouds permitting) when sunbeams filter in through the natural skylight.

Things change throughout the year, but the sun shower generally happens between 9am and noon; earlier is better. And note that you have to be standing in the right spot to see it. From February to April the light illuminates the main Buddha image.

Deeper in the cave there are more chambers and shrines, although the back exit is no longer in use. The story is that Rama IV built the stone gate that separates the main chamber from the others as a security measure for a couple who once lived in the cave.

The cave is located up a steep hill. You'll need to get up part of the way by foot or wheels. Once you reach the temple, you can get a ride in a truck up to the cave and back down the hill for 15B.

Be ready to meet many brazen monkeys (p493), who will be looking for handouts, though they don't go inside the cave.

There are also sometimes guides asking to join you. They're not necessary, and a tip will be expected.

Phra Ram Ratchaniwet   HISTORIC SITE
(พระรามราชนิเวศน์, Ban Peun Palace; ☑032 428506; Th Damnoen Kasem; 100B; ◎8.30am-4pm) Construction of this elegant summer palace, an incredible art-nouveau creation, began in 1910 at the behest of Rama V (who died just after the project was started) and finished in 1916. It was designed by German architects who indulged the royal family's passion for all things European with a Poseidon statue, badminton court, ceramic cherubs lining the double spiral staircase and a state-of-the-art, for the time, adjustable shower in the king's bathroom.

The lack of furnishings and, usually, other visitors makes a visit feel quite odd. It's on a military base and normally no identification is required, but it's best to bring your passport in case things change.

Wat Khao Bandai-It   CAVE
(ถ้ำเขาบันไดอิฐ; Rte 3171; ◎8am-5pm) FREE This hillside monastery, 2km west of town, sprawls through several large caverns converted into simple Buddha shrines and meditation rooms. There are some natural formations and skylights, and one chamber contains quite a few bats, but it's not nearly as beautiful as Tham Khao Luang. It's well lit and the floor is concrete throughout, so the kids who want to guide you aren't necessarily sary but if you do go with them, they expect a tip. When walking up to the cave, be wary of the monkeys (p493).

Wat Yai Suwannaram   BUDDHIST TEMPLE
(วัดใหญ่สุวรรณาราม; Th Phongsuriya; ◎bòht 7am-6pm, săh-lah 8am-5pm) FREE This expansive temple, founded in the late Ayuthaya era, holds quite a bit of history. Foremost are the faded murals inside the beautiful *bòht* (ordination hall), which date back to about 1700,

making them some of the oldest Thai-temple murals still in existence. Mostly they're rows of various deities though the entrance wall vividly shows the demon Mara and his army trying to stop the Buddha from reaching enlightenment.

Wat Phra Phuttaya Saiyat (Wat Phra Non)
BUDDHIST TEMPLE
(วัดพระพุทธไสยาสน์/วัดพระนอน; Th Khiriataya; ⊙ daylight hours) FREE The main attraction at this temple, also known as Wat Phra Non (the Reclining Buddha Temple), is 43m long. It's almost as big as the famous Wat Pho (p69) in Bangkok, but without the crowds.

Wat Yang
BUDDHIST TEMPLE
(วัดยาง; Th Ratchadamnoen; ⊙ daylight hours) FREE This temple west of the city centre has a century-old *hŏr đrai* (sacred manuscript library) on stilts in a pond to protect the contents against termites. It's no longer in use, though it remains in good condition.

Wat Kamphaeng Laeng
BUDDHIST TEMPLE
(วัดกำแพงแลง; Th Phokarang; ⊙ daylight hours) FREE A 13th-century remnant of the time when the Angkor (Khmer) kingdom stretched from present-day Cambodia all the way to the Malay peninsula, this shrine was built of laterite by Khmer King Jayavarman VII, one of the few Khmer kings to make Buddhism the state religion. There's a topless main *prang* with open doorways on all four sides surrounded by four smaller buildings and parts of the laterite wall, all in various states of ruin.

🎎 Festivals & Events

Phra Nakhon Khiri Fair
CULTURAL
(งานพระนครคีรี-เมืองเพชร; ⊙ Feb) Centred on Khao Wang hill, this provincial-style celebration lasts 10 days and usually takes place in February. Phra Nakhon Khiri Historical Park (p493) is festooned with lights, and there are traditional dance performances, craft and food displays, fireworks and a beauty contest.

🛌 Sleeping

★ 2N Guesthouse
GUESTHOUSE $
(📞 085 366 2451; www.2nguesthouse.blogspot.com; 98/3 Mu 2, Tambol Bankoom; incl breakfast d & tw 600B, q 1000B; P 🌀 🛜) In a generally quiet neighbourhood 1.5km north of the city centre, the six rooms here are big and bright, and great for the price. The English-speaking owners are sisters who do everything themselves and are dedicated to pleasing their guests. They have free bicycles and are happy to help with travel planning.

White Monkey Guesthouse
GUESTHOUSE $
(📞 090 325 3885; whitemonkey.guesthouse@gmail.com; 78/7 Th Klongkrachang; dm/tw/d/f incl breakfast 350/600/700/1400B; P 🌀 🛜) Excellent guesthouse with bright, spacious, spick-and-span rooms (the cheapest with shared bathrooms and no air-con) and a great location. There are views of Phra Nakhon Khiri Historical Park and Wat Mahathat Worawihan from the rooftop terrace, and helpful English-speaking staff who can organise trips in the area. Bikes are free.

Sabaidee Resort
GUESTHOUSE $
(📞 086 344 4418; sabai2505@gmail.com; 65-67 Th Klongkrachang; r 350-500B; 🌀 🛜) It doesn't look like much at first but step inside and you'll find good rooms around leafy plants and a shady terrace right on the river. There are modern concrete rooms and bamboo cottages, but only some have private bathrooms. The pleasant owners can arrange Thai cooking classes, and bikes (50B) and scooters (300B) can be hired.

J.J. Home
GUESTHOUSE $
(📞 081 880 9286; www.jjhomephetchaburi.com; 2 Th Chisa-In; r 200-600B; 🌀 🛜) The rooms here are clean and a decent deal, and you get a friendly welcome from the helpful owners. However, there's a lot of street noise and they could do a better job of minor maintenance. The cheapest rooms are quite basic, while more expensive options in a newer building across the road have private bathrooms, air-con and shared balconies.

Sun Hotel
HOTEL $
(📞 032 400000; www.sunhotelthailand.com; Th Rim Khao Wang; r incl breakfast 850-950B; P 🌀 🛜) Sitting opposite the cable car entrance to Phra Nakhon Khiri Historical Park, the Sun Hotel has helpful staff and large, uninspiring rooms that are fine, but should be a little cheaper. There's a pleasant cafe downstairs and bikes are free.

While the location might sound good, it's actually pretty isolated from everything except the historical park.

🍴 Eating

Surrounded by palm-sugar plantations, Phetchaburi is famous for its sweet concoctions, including *kà·nŏm môr gaang* (egg custard) and various 'golden' desserts made from egg yolks and sugar. They're sold in most markets, as is the raw sugar.

Nearby fruit orchards produce refreshingly aromatic *chom·pôo phet* (Phetchaburi rose apple – the fruit that adorns many street signs), pineapples and *nám wáh* bananas.

★ **Talat Taa Rot Tua** MARKET $
(Th Ratwithi; ⊙4-9pm) Big and bustling from the late afternoon, head to this covered night market for all the standard Thai favourites plus Phetchaburi's famous *kà·nŏm jeen tôrt man* (fresh rice noodles with curried deep-fried fishcake). There's lots of seating available.

★ **Rabieng Rimnam** INTERNATIONAL $
(☑098 051 5636; rabieng@gmail.com; 1 Th Chisa-In; mains 45-120B; ⊙8am-midnight; 🅰) This riverside restaurant serves up a real bygone-days atmosphere from an 1897 wooden home perched over the river, and some good food, too – try the sugar palm tree fruit curry with prawn. English-speaking owners Nid and Tom will often join you for a chat about Thailand and share their decades of travel advice.

Kow Chae Mae Awn THAI $
(ข้าวแช่แม่อร; Th Panichjaroen; 20B; ⊙9am-4pm; ✏) Mae Awn sells her famous *kôw châe*

(moist chilled rice) with a choice of fish, shrimp or pickled daikon radish along the walkway at the southeast corner of the Rim Nam Market. She has just a few tables but does a brisk takeaway business.

Pagoda Cafe COFFEE, BAKERY $
(95 Th Klongkrachang; tea & coffee from 35B; ⊙9am-6pm Tue-Sun; ❀🅰) Small cafe that draws lots of students and makes a fine, air-con retreat from the afternoon sun.

Rim Nam Market MARKET $
(Th Panichjaroen; ⊙5-11am) You can pick up a variety of foods for your morning meal here including *kà·nŏm jeen tôrt man* (fresh rice noodles with curried deep-fried fishcake) and fresh fruit. Many of the vendors start shutting down around 8am.

Phetchaburi Walking Street MARKET $
(Th Chaisurin; ⊙4-9pm Sat) Unlike a typical walking street market, almost every vendor here is selling food and you can easily snack yourself full.

JM Cuisine THAI $
(www.jm-cuisine.com; 85 Th Ratwithi; mains 50-100B; ⊙7am-5pm) A cut above your average hole-in-the-wall joint, you can get some really good soups and stir-fries here. It's located a short walk from the Phra Nakhon Khiri east entrance.

PHETCHABURI TRANSPORT CONNECTIONS

DESTINATION	BUS	MINIVAN	TRAIN
Bangkok Hualamphong			34-1933B, 3-3½hr, 12 daily
Bangkok Southern & Northern (Mo Chit) Bus Terminals		100B, 2hr, frequent 3.30am-7.30pm	
Bangkok Thonburi			31-136B, 4hr, 7.16am, 12.56pm
Cha-am	30B, 1hr, hourly 5.40am-4.30pm (from Wat Potaram)	50B, 45min, frequent 5am-6.20pm	8-368B, 40min, 5 daily
Chumphon	328-500B, 6hr, hourly 6.30am-8pm, frequent 8-10pm		58-2102B, 5½-6½hr, 13 daily
Hua Hin	40B, 1½hr, hourly 5.40am-4.30pm (from Wat Potaram)	80B, 1hr, frequent 5am-6.20pm	14-1839B, 1hr, 15 daily
Kaeng Krachan National Park		120B, 1hr, hourly 7.30am-6.30pm	
Prachuap Khiri Khan	150-200B, 2½hr, hourly 6.30am-8pm, frequent 8-10pm	150B, 2½hr, every 40min 5am-6.20pm	31-1460B, 2-3hr, 12 daily

ⓘ Information

There's no formal information source in town, but the guesthouses can provide up-to-date travel tips. The Tourism Authority of Thailand's office in Cha-am handles all of Phetchaburi Province.

Kasikorn Bank (Th Bandai-It; ⊘11am-7pm) at Phetpaiboon Plaza shopping centre is the nearest extended-hours bank to the city centre.

ⓘ Getting There & Away

The train is usually the most convenient and comfortable way to travel, and Phetchaburi's **train station** (🕿 032 425211; Th Rot Fai) is within walking distance of most guesthouses.

There are no longer any buses to Bangkok originating or finishing in Phetchaburi, only minivans. These use the **Wat Tham Kaew Minivan Station** (Th Bandai-It) – *sà·tǎh·nee bor kǒr sǒr wát tâm gâaou* – as do minibuses to Kaeng Krachan National Park.

Minivans (Phetkasem Hwy) to Hua Hin, Cha-am and Prachuap Khiri Khan are 500m south of the minivan station on the side of the road next to Phetcharat Hospital and they also pick up further south in front of the **Big C shopping centre** (Phetkasem Hwy). Some long-distance buses passing through town (going both north and south) will also stop by Big C, but if you want to try it, be prepared for a long wait. For Chumphon and southern cities, there's a small **southern bus stop** (Phetkasem Hwy) 300m south of the hospital. Another option to Hua Hin and Cha-am are the **ordinary buses** that depart from the town centre next to Wat Potaram.

ⓘ Getting Around

Motorcycle taxis go anywhere in the town centre for 20B to 40B. Phetchaburi's four-wheel túk-túk (locally called *rót léng*) cost just a little more. You can also hire them for the day for about 700B to 800B.

All the guesthouses hire out bicycles (50B per day) and motorbikes (150B to 250B). Reserve a motorcycle when you reserve a room because many guesthouses get them from outside sources and you may have to wait awhile to get one if you just ask at the desk.

Cha-am

🕿 032 / POP 35,600

Cheap and cheerful, Cha-am (ชะอำ) is a popular beach getaway for working-class families and Bangkok students. On weekends and public holidays, neon-painted buses (called *chìng·chàp tua*), their sound systems pumping, deliver groups of holidaymakers. It's a very Thai-style beach party, with eating and drinking marathons held around umbrella-shaded beach chairs and tables. The shallow sea is better for strolling and sunbathing than swimming. Entertainment is provided by the banana boats that zip back and forth.

Phetkasem Hwy runs through Cha-am's busy town centre, which is about 1km away from the beach via Th Narathip. This is where you'll find banks, the fresh market, the train station and most bus stops. There are plenty of ATMs and a few extended-hours exchange booths along Th Ruamjit.

Cha-am Forest Park PARK
(วนอุทยานชะอำ; Phetkasem Hwy; ⊘daylight hours) Out on the edge of town, an easy bike ride from the beach, this park is known not for its beauty, but rather its white-handed gibbons. The gibbons usually hang out in the centre of the park (from the entrance go straight over the bridge and turn left) and can pretty much always be seen. Though they have no fear of humans, they're not fully tame – don't get too close.

✲ Festivals & Events

Thailand International Kite Festival ART
(⊘Mar) Most years, but not every, artistic kites from around the world take to the skies over the beach for a long weekend.

Gin Hoy, Do Nok, Tak Meuk FOOD & DRINK
(⊘Sep) You really can do it all at this annual festival held in September. The festival's English name is 'Shellfish Eating, Bird Watching & Squid Catching', a catchy slogan for some of Cha-am's local attractions and traditions. Mainly it's a food festival showcasing a variety of seafood, but there are also birdwatching events at nearby sanctuaries and nightly concerts.

🛏 Sleeping

Cha-am still has cheap, charmless guesthouses in narrow concrete shophouses near the beach – though most are kept clean – but there are increasingly more upmarket options. Avoid staying on seedy Soi Bus Station unless you're not planning to sleep.

Expect significant weekday discounts (30% to 60%) and keep your eyes peeled for guesthouses with 300B fan and 400B aircon deals.

Cha Inn @ Cha-Am HOTEL $$
(🕿 032 471879; www.chainn-chaam.com; 274/34 Th Ruamjit; r incl breakfast 1200-2000B; 🅿 ✳ 🛜)

The owners have creatively and beautifully adapted this old building into a stylish hotel that's refreshingly out of the ordinary for Cha-am. There's a restaurant on the ground floor and an airy lounge up above. And then there are the 17 rooms; large, comfortable and full of the same subtle design found in the public areas.

Pa Ka Ma   GUESTHOUSE **$$**
(☑ 081 986 4060; Soi Cay-ben Tee-wee; r 1000B; ❄ 🛜) Probably the best low-cost guesthouse in Cha-am, and only a little more expensive than the average. It's attractively designed – each room has its own individual style and the rooms at the back have little balconies. The bathrooms are good, though hot water can take a long time to arrive. Not much English is spoken. It's on an unsigned soi between Sois 1 and 2 North. There are a few other good choices nearby if it's full.

Bann Pantai Resort   HOTEL **$$**
(☑ 032 470155; www.bannpantai.com; 2 Th Ruamjit; r incl breakfast 2300-3500B; P ❄ 🛜 ⛱) Rather more upmarket than most hotels in Cha-am, this beautiful, family-friendly place has a huge pool and small fitness centre, and the beach is just across the road. Rooms are big with great beds and terraces in front.

Dream Boutique Hotel   HOTEL **$$**
(☑ 032 470896; tonypresnell@gmail.com; 235/35 Soi Anatachai; d 800-1400B; f 2000B; ❄ 🛜) There's nothing boutique about it, but the misnomer is the only knock on a very well-run, impeccably clean hotel. Rooms aren't fancy, but they're fully kitted out and have balconies, plus guests can lounge on the roof. There's also bike and motorcycle hire.

It lies between Sois 1 and 2 South, which is actually the third soi south of Th Narathip.

Raya Resort   RESORT **$$$**
(☑ 032 472 6412; www.rayaresortchaam.com; 264/2 Th Raumjit; r incl breakfast 5500-25,000B; P ❄ 🛜 ⛱) Raya Resort delivers luxury in the heart of Cha-am, with landscaped greenery and just 12 rooms and four villas ensconced in traditionally inspired wooden houses. The decor and amenities are quite simple – the higher price tag is due to the extra space and privacy, which includes your own small garden area. The minibar is free.

✖ Eating & Drinking

From your deckchair you can wave down vendors selling plastic-wrapped meals, or order from the many nearby beachfront restaurants and they'll deliver.

The top seafood restaurants are found at the far northern end of the beach by the fishing pier, right where your dinner might have been brought ashore.

The main expat enclave, full of cold beer, pool tables, and TV sports, is Soi Bus Station, the first street south of Th Narathip. You can also follow the lead of some Thai visitors and just stay in your beach chair with a bottle, even after the sun goes down.

Chong Heang   THAI **$**
(Th Ruamjit; mains 40-350B; ⊘ 7am-8pm) This blue-and-white restaurant doesn't look inspiring, but the food is well above average. The usual Thai dishes can be found here, including curries, stir-fries and local fish.

Krua Medsai Seafood   THAI **$$**
(off Th Ruamjit; mains 40-450B; ⊘ 10am-10pm; P) Massive Medsai is one of dozens of seafood spots next to Cha-am's fishing port. While some of the smaller restaurants out here have more character, few others can offer this wide a selection or provide a properly translated English menu.

Raya Coffee   CAFE
(☑ 032 472570; 246/2 Th Ruamjit; ⊘ 7am-8pm; 🛜) Right by the beach, Raya Coffee is an air-conditioned haven to beat the heat and indulge in pretty cakes, pastries and iced drinks. Flower arrangements and sage-green paint give the cafe a particularly elegant vibe.

Gravity Sky Bar   ROOFTOP BAR
(☑ 032 708300; www.novotelhuahin.com/hua-hin-restaurants/hua-hin-rooftop-bar/; 854/2 Th Burirom, Novotel Hua Hin Cha Am Beach Resort & Spa; ⊘ 4-11pm; 🛜) Located on the 24th floor of the Novotel, Gravity Sky Bar offers an impressive 360-degree panorama of Hua Hin and the coastline. Graffiti murals by Bangkok street artists, geometric-patterned seats and pop music keep the vibe lighthearted. Don't expect much more than classic cocktails and beer. Happy hour (5pm to 7pm) is buy one, get one free.

❶ Information

The Tourism Authority of Thailand (TAT; ☑ 032 471005; tatphet@tat.or.th; Th Phetkasem; ⊘ 8.30am-4.30pm) office is on Phetkasem Hwy, 500m south of town. Some of the staff speak English well.

CHA-AM TRANSPORT CONNECTIONS

DESTINATION	BUS	MINIVAN	TRAIN
Bangkok Don Mueang International Airport		180B, 4hr, hourly 6.30am-6.30pm	
Bangkok Hualamphong			40-473B, 4-4½hr, 1.40am, 4.55am, 2.33pm
Bangkok Southern & Northern (Mo Chit) Bus Terminals	241B, 4½hr, infrequent	160B, 3½hr, frequent 4.30am-7.30pm	
Bangkok Suvarnabhumi International Airport	294B, 4hr, hourly 6am-6pm		
Bangkok Thonburi			38-87B, 4hr, 6.41am, 12.13pm
Hua Hin	30B, 30min, every half hour 6.30am-5.30pm	50B, 30min, frequent 6am-7.30pm	6-363B, 30min, 5 daily
Kanchanaburi		200B, 3½hr, hourly 6.40am-5.40pm	
Phetchaburi	50B, 1hr, every half hour 6.30am-4.30pm	50B, 45min, frequent 6am-7.30pm	8-368B, 40min, 5 daily

Only Chaam (www.onlychaam.com) is a useful website about visiting Cha-am.

ⓘ Getting There & Away

There's a little **minivan station** (Soi Bus Station) for **Hua Hin-Pran Tour** (☑ 085 933 8840; Th Sasong) at the Soi Bus Station with departures to Bangkok (Southern and Mo Chit terminals) every half-hour from 7am to 5.30pm. All other public road transport stops on **Phetkasem Hwy** (Phetkasem Hwy) at the intersection with **Th Narathip** (Phetkasem Hwy). Mostly it's minivans, since very few buses from Hua Hin or other southern towns stop to pick up passengers in Cha-am. The Airport Hua Hin Bus (p509) from Hua Hin to Bangkok's Suvarnabhumi Airport stops specifically in front of the Government Savings Bank while Shinnakeart Korat, with buses to Bangkok and Nakhon Ratchasima (388B, six hours, six daily), is also here.

The **train station** (☑ 032 471159; Th Narathip) is west of Phetkasem Hwy at the end of Th Narathip and is not served by any express trains. Note that Cha-am is listed in the timetable as 'Ban Cha-am'.

You can hire a taxi (any private car available for hire) along the beach. The fare is 400B to Hua Hin.

ⓘ Getting Around

From the city centre to the beach it's a quick motorcycle (40B) or taxi (100B) ride.

You can hire bicycles (100B per day) and motorcycles (200B to 250B) all along Th Ruamjit.

Hua Hin

☑ 032 / POP 63,100

Thailand's original beach resort is no palm-fringed castaway island and arguably is the better for it. Instead, Hua Hin (หัวหิน) is a refreshing mix of city and sea with lively markets, good golf courses and water parks, excellent accommodation and an ambience that just keeps getting more hip and cosmopolitan. In fact, many visitors never even step foot on the sand.

By the mid-1920s Hua Hin was a full-fledged resort town for the Bangkok-based nobility – even Kings Rama VI and VII built summer palaces here. There's still a lot of money swirling around Hua Hin, but it remains a good budget destination: seafood is plentiful and cheap, there's convenient public transport and it takes a lot less time and effort to get here from Bangkok than to the southern islands.

⊙ Sights

A former fishing village, Hua Hin's old town retains links to its past with an old teak shophouse district bisected by narrow winding sois, fronted by pier houses that hold restaurants and guesthouses, and punctuated with a busy fishing pier still in use today. Along the shore beyond, especially to the north, there are still many historic wooden summer residences, so be sure to keep on eye inland as you roam the beach.

★**Cicada Market** MARKET
(ตลาดจักจั่น; ☎080 650 4334; www.cicada market.com; Soi Hua Thanon 23, Th Phetkasem, South Hua Hin; ⊙4-11pm Fri-Sun) FREE Vastly better than the city-centre Hua Hin Night Market (p508), this popular place 3.5km to the south is a fun mix of food, shopping and performing arts. It's not a high-sell environment; rather it's a very relaxed shopping experience. Many artists come to sell their handmade home decor and clothes, and there's food from Thailand and beyond. Live entertainment hits the stage from 8.30pm and there are buskers all around.

The last green *sŏrng·tăa·ou* back to the city passes about 9pm.

★**Wildlife Friends Foundation Thailand Rescue Centre & Elephant Refuge** ANIMAL SANCTUARY
(มูลนิธิเพื่อนสัตว์ป่า; ☎032 458135; www.wfft.org; full-access tour incl lunch half-/full day 1100/1600B) 🐾 This centre, 45km northwest of Hua Hin, cares for over 700 animals, including bears, tigers, gibbons, macaques, loris and birds. There's also an affiliated elephant-rescue program where the elephants live chain-free. A visit here is great – far better than the elephant and tiger tourist traps featured on many tours out of Hua Hin. The centre offers full-access tours introducing animals and discussing rescue histories. The full-day option includes a meet and-greet with elephants. Drop-in visits are not allowed.

One of the most active groups trying to improve the animal welfare situation in Thailand, the Wildlife Friends Foundation Thailand runs this wildlife rescue centre that adopts and cares for abused, injured and abandoned animals that cannot be released back into the wild.

Hotel transfer from Hua Hin or Cha-am costs 200B per person and there's also a small lodge (per night including meals 4000B) on-site. Those looking for a more in-depth experience can volunteer (p503) at the centre.

Ratchaphakdi Park MONUMENT
(อุทยานราชภักดิ์; Hwy 4; ⊙8am-6pm) FREE Standing 14m high and weighing in at 30 tonnes each, the beautiful bronze statues of Thailand's most revered kings tower over this park with an impressive mountain backdrop. The US$22 million project south of town was built by the military government after the coup in order to inspire loyalty to the monarchy.

Baan Silapin GALLERY
(บ้านศิลปิน; ☎086 162 0162; www.huahinartistvil lage.wordpress.com; Th Hua Hin-Pa Lu-U; ⊙10am-5pm Tue-Sun) FREE Local painter Tawee Kasangam established this artist collective in a shady grove 4km west of town. The galleries and studio spaces showcase the works of over a dozen artists, many of whom opted out of Bangkok's fast-paced art world in favour of Hua Hin's more relaxed atmosphere and scenic landscape of mountains and sea.

Be sure to check out the earthen huts out back, which shelter playful sculptures. Casual art workshops (per hour adult/child 150/100B) are available on weekends and the coffee shop is very relaxing.

★**Wat Huay Mongkol** BUDDHIST TEMPLE
(วัดห้วยมงคล; Tambon Thap Tai; ⊙daylight hours) FREE Colloquially called the big-headed monk, this statue of the revered Luang Phor Thad is a beloved Buddhist pilgrimage site. The southern Thai monk is said to have performed miracles, such as turning seawater into fresh water, inspiring many Thais to travel here to pray. While the 12m figure's head and ears might appear disproportionately large, these features actually represent his enlightenment.

Hat Hua Hin BEACH
(หาดหัวหิน) Hua Hin Beach is a pleasant, but not stunning, stretch of fine white powder lapped by calm grey-green waves. Remarkably shallow, it's made for strolling and sunbathing, not swimming. Watch out for jellyfish, especially in the wet season.

By far the busiest stretch fronts the Hilton and Centara Grand hotels. Restaurants deliver food to people camped out in shaded sunloungers (except on Wednesdays when these are removed to make the beach beautiful for a day) and pony rides are popular.

Hua Hin Train Station HISTORIC SITE
(สถานีรถไฟหัวหิน; Th Liap Thang Rot Fai) Probably the most beautiful train station in Thailand, this red-and-white icon was built in 1926 to replace the original station. It has a Victorian gingerbread design with lots of carved wood pillars and trim. Because Hua Hin owes its prosperity to the train, the station is a major source of pride and you'll find imitations of its design all over town.

Hua Hin

Plearn Wan (1.2km);
Der (1.8km);
Oasis (1.8km);
Seek35 (1.8km);
Seenspace (1.8km)

Gulf of Thailand

Tha Thiap Reua Pramong

Th Naebkehardt

Th Damrongraj (Soi 51)

Th Naebkehardt

Soi 53

Th Naresdamri

Th Chomsin (Soi 55)

Soi Ruampow

Soi 70

Th Sasong

Soi 55/1

Th Dechanuchit

Soi Selekam

Th Phunsuk

Clock Tower

Th Amnuaysin (Soi Hua Hin 74)

Soi Hua Hin 74/2

Soi Hua Hin 59

Th Damnoen Kasem

Soi 63

Train Station

Th Liap Thang Rot Fai

Soi 78

Royal Hua Hin Golf Course

Th Phetkasem

Hat Hua Hin

Soi 88

Soi 88

San Paolo Hospital

Bangkok Hospital Hua Hun (500m)

Soi 88

Hua Hin

🏃 Activities

⭐ Wildlife Friends Foundation Thailand Volunteer Projects   VOLUNTEERING
(📞032 458135; www.wildlifevolunteer.org) 🏝 If you love animals and aren't afraid of a bit of hard work, then consider a stint at the Wildlife Friends Foundation Thailand Rescue Centre (p501), which cares for a menagerie of creatures rescued from animal shows and exploitative owners. Your tasks might include feeding elephants or building an enclosure for macaques.

Volunteers must be at least 18 years old, commit to a minimum of one week and make a compulsory donation (from US$350/10,500B per week) to the centre. Accommodation and three meals per day are included.

Monsoon Valley Vineyard   WINE
(📞081 701 0222; www.monsoonvalley.com; 1 Mu 9 Baan Khork Chang Pattana, Nong Plub; tour 100B, tasting from 240B; ⊙9am-6.30pm Apr-Oct, to 8pm Nov-Mar; 🚗) Monsoon Valley is one of Thailand's few wineries, and it's a good stop for both kids and adults. Vineyard tours and tastings are offered, as well as children's activities like painting and mountain biking. The bistro has a large menu of Thai and international dishes.

The vineyard is located about 45km from Hua Hin, and round-trip shuttles are offered twice daily from Hua Hin Hills Bistro & Wine Cellar at Villa Market (300B).

There is also a 'wine safari' tour combining a full-day visit to the vineyard and Kuiburi National Park (p510) in a 4WD (7000B, two persons).

Velo Thailand   CYCLING
(📞032 900392; www.velothailand.com; 123/50 Th Hua Tanun; full-day tours from 3850B; ⊙8am-6pm Mon-Thu, 8am-7pm Fri-Sun) A local branch of the large Bangkok bike tour company, Velo leads a variety of rides around Hua Hin, including a half-day downhill mountain-biking trip in the hills west of town. High-quality mountain-bike rental is 300B per day with discounts for long-term rentals.

Thai Massage by the Blind   MASSAGE
(📞081 944 2174; The Naebkenhardt; Thai massage 200B; ⊙7am-9pm) Traditional head, foot and body massages by blind masseuses, plus some other treatments like herbal wraps.

KITEBOARDING

Adding to the beauty of Hua Hin's beach are the kiteboarders soaring over the ocean. Hua Hin is Thailand's kiteboarding capital, blessed with strong, gusty winds, shallow water and a long, long beach off which to practise your moves.

From here down to Pranburi, the winds blow from the northeast from October to December, usually with lots of waves, and then from the southeast from January to May, usually with smooth water. Even during the rainy months in between, there are plenty of days when the wind is fine for taking to the waves.

This is also one of the best places in Thailand to *learn* how to kiteboard, with a number of schools in Hua Hin offering lessons. Generally after three days with them you can be out on your own. January to March is the best time, since the sea is less choppy. The schools also cater to more advanced students, and you can qualify as an instructor here.

North Kiteboarding Club (☎083 438 3833; www.nkbclub.com; 113/5 Th Phetkasem, at Soi 67, South Hua Hin; 3-day beginner course 11,000B; ⊗8am-6pm Tue-Sun) Based in Hua Hin, but with outlets in Chumpon and Phuket, this well-established kiteboarding company has a large store and café.

Kiteboarding Asia (☎081 683 1683; www.kiteboardingasia.com; 143/8 Soi 75/1, Th Phetkasem, South Hua Hin; 3-day beginner course 11,000B; ⊗8.30am-7pm) This long-established company operates three beachside shops that rent kiteboarding equipment and offer lessons.

There are two other locations further out from the city centre.

Thai Thai Massage   MASSAGE
(☎084 318 2451; www.thaithaimassagehuahin.com; 20/1 Th Dechanuchit; Thai massage from 250B; ⊗11am-10pm) For something less pricey than posh-hotel luxury spas, but still a cut above the average, the trained and friendly masseuses at this respectable place get excellent feedback.

Hua Hin Golf Centre   GOLF
(☎032 530476; www.huahingolf.com; Th Selakam; ⊗noon-9pm) The friendly staff at this pro shop run by **Hua Hin Golf Tours** (☎032 530 119; www.huahingolf.com; Soi 41; ⊗6am-10pm) can steer you to the most affordable, well-maintained courses (where the monkeys won't try to run off with your balls!). This company organises golf tours and rents sets of quality clubs (500B to 700B per day) to its customers.

🎓 Courses

Thai Cooking Course Hua Hin   COOKING
(☎081 572 3805; www.thai-cookingcourse.com; 19/95 Th Phetkasem, Soi Hua Hin 19; courses 1500B) Aspiring chefs should sign up for the one-day cooking class, which includes a market visit, four dishes and curry paste, and a recipe book to take home. The course runs only if there are a minimum of three people and hotel pick-up is provided.

👉 Tours

Feast Thailand   FOOD
(☎032 510207, 095 461 0557; www.feastthailand.com; 10 Th Naebkehardt, inside Raruk Hua Hin market; from 1350B; ⊗8.30am-4pm Mon-Sat) A small company with highly regarded half-day food tours. You pick your tour – either sample Thai cuisine basics or dive into some less-common foods – and they pick you up at your hotel. Join-in tours are sometimes available.

Hua Hin Bike Tours   CYCLING
(☎081 173 4469; www.huahinbiketours.com; 8/12 Takiab 6; full-day tours from 3250B; ⊗10am-8pm) This husband-and-wife team leads day-long and multiday tours in and around Hua Hin, including a four-day Bangkok to Hua Hin trip. They rent premium bicycles (500B per day, discounts for longer rentals) for independent cyclists and can recommend routes, and also lead the long-distance **Tour de Thailand** (☎081 173 4469; www.tourdethailand.com) charity bike tours across Thailand.

Hua Hin Adventure Tour   ADVENTURE
(☎032 530314; www.huahinadventuretour.com; 69/7 Th Naebkehardt; ⊗9am-6pm Mon-Sat) Hua Hin Adventure Tour offers active excursions, including kayaking trips in Khao Sam Roi Yot National Park and wildlife-watching in Kaeng Krachan National Park.

✨ Festivals

Hua Hin Jazz Festival MUSIC
(☺ Jun; 🎷) In honour of the late King Rama IX's personal interest in the genre, the city that hosts royal getaways also hosts an annual jazz festival featuring Thai and international performers. All events are free. It usually takes place in June.

🛏 Sleeping

This touristy old city has accommodation for all tastes. The best places lie outside the booze-fuelled core. The city's character suddenly becomes more local and less boisterous north of Th Chomsin. Focused on Th Naebkehardt and Soi 51, this is the neighbourhood of choice for Bangkok's trendy youth. Or head south: the beach is fairly quiet and mostly tout-free.

⭐ **King's Home** GUESTHOUSE $
(☎ 089 052 0490; www.huahinkingshome.blogspot.com; off Th Phunsuk; r 750-950B; ❄ 🛜 🏊) Family-run guesthouse with great prices and loads of character – you're greeted at the front door by a crystal chandelier and there's a German shepherd statue on the stairs. The rest of the house, including the six small guest rooms, is also crammed with antiques and kitsch, providing a real homey atmosphere.

Love Sea House GUESTHOUSE $
(☎ 080 079 0922; siamozohlie@hotmail.com; 35 Th Dechanuchit; r 700-900B; ❄ 🛜) Pleasant, family-run guesthouse decked out in a blue-and-white nautical theme. The English-speaking elderly owners keep the good-sized rooms impressively clean. It's very near Hua Hin's party zone, but it's not an appropriate place for those planning to partake in it.

Baan Somboon GUESTHOUSE $
(☎ 032 511538; baansomboon@gmail.com; 13/4 Soi Hua Hin 63, Th Damnoen Kasem; r 700B; ❄ 🛜) With framed photos decorating the walls, polished wooden floors and a compact garden, this place on a very quiet centrally located soi is like staying at your favourite Thai auntie's house. Rooms are small and dated, but it's probably the homiest guesthouse in Hua Hin.

La Maison BOUTIQUE HOTEL $$
(☎ 032 533007; www.lamaison-huahin.com; 172/6 Th Naresdamri; r incl breakfast 3200B; P ❄ 🛜 🏊) You're sure to love boutique hotel La Maison's central, yet quiet location and the swimming pool. The interior spaces are simple and decorated in modern, earthy tones. Continental breakfast is served in the poolside restaurant. There is also a good cafe out front.

Cloud9 Hotel HOTEL $$
(☎ 093 394 4499; www.cloud9hotel.com; 71 Th Naebkehardt; dm 500-600B, r 1820-2520B, f 4200B; ❄ 🛜) Opened in 2019, this newcomer has a great central location, mixed and female-only dorms, and private rooms for couples and families. All are modern yet simple. The rooftop with beanbags is perfect for sundowners on twinkly nights.

Hua Hin Place GUESTHOUSE $$
(☎ 032 516640; www.huahin-place.com; 43/21 Th Naebkehardt; r 600-1000, f 1300B; ❄ 🛜) Straddling a fine line between hotel and guesthouse, this fairly large place still falls into the latter category thanks to the breezy ground-floor lounge – full of a museum's worth of shells, photos and other knick-knacks – where you can chat with the charming owner and other guests.

All rooms are well appointed (the wicker furniture is a nice touch) and most have little balconies with a sliver of a sea view. The 600B air-con rooms are on the side at ground level and rather dark, but are still good value for Hua Hin, making this one of the best budget choices in town.

⭐ **Baan Bayan** HOTEL $$$
(☎ 032 533 5404; www.baanbayan.com; 119 Th Phetkasem, South Hua Hin; r incl breakfast 4500-13,500B; P ❄ 🛜 🏊) Centred on a beautiful teak house built in the early 20th century, Baan Bayan is perfect for travellers seeking a luxury experience without big resort overkill. The hotel is airy, with high-ceilinged rooms and attentive staff, and the location is absolute beachfront. Most of the rooms were added in modern times but share the same historic quality as the three originals.

Laksasubha HOTEL $$$
(☎ 032 514525; www.laksasubhahuahin.com; Th 53/7 Naresdamri; r incl breakfast 3600-14,500B; P ❄ 🛜 🏊) At this fantastic resort, owned by a scion of the royal family, there are 16 much-in-demand villas (with 45 total rooms) on offer. The decor is crisp and subdued and the service is excellent. Everything lies along a meandering garden path leading to the beach and there are lots of activities for kids and adults.

Centara Grand Beach Resort & Villas
HOTEL $$$

(☏032 512021; www.centarahotelsresorts.com; 1 Th Damnoen Kasem; r incl breakfast 10,000-15,000B; P☀@శ☎) The historic Railway Hotel opened in 1922 and was Hua Hin's first hotel. It's been updated and expanded over the decades, but hasn't lost its genteel aura – no other local resort can match the ambience here. The rooms are large, the facilities fantastic and the staff on the ball, plus the vast gardens are full of frangipani and trimmed topiary.

This resort is an especially kid-friendly destination with many scheduled activities. Pop into The Museum coffee shop to see some photos and original equipment from the early years.

✖ Eating

Hua Hin is a fantastic dining destination. The city is famous for its seafood, but few locals eat that in town. They prefer simple restaurants in Ban Takiab south of the city, some of which do 400B buffets.

★ Jek Pia
THAI $

(51/6 Th Dechanuchit; mains 80-200B; ⊙6.30am-12.30pm & 5.30-7.30pm) Once just a coffee shop, this 50-plus-year-old restaurant is one of Hua Hin's top culinary destinations. The late mother of the current owner invited her favourite cooks to come join her and it's now a gourmet food court of sorts, hence the stack of menus you get when you arrive.

It's all delicious, and there's possibly no better mixed seafood *gŏoay đĕeo đôm yam* in Thailand. Last order is 30 minutes before closing.

Pa Jua
STREET FOOD $

(Th Naresdamri, opposite Hilton Hua Hin; mango sticky rice 120B; ⊙9am-4pm) This mango-sticky-rice stand is a local hit, which explains why it's been in business for almost 50 years. You can buy mangoes individually, or in the traditional Thai dessert with sticky rice, coconut cream and sprinkled with crispy yellow mung beans. There are just a few seats; most order takeaway.

Baan Gliwang
THAI $

(☏032 531260; www.baan-gliwang.business.site; Th Naebkehardt; mains 65-285B; ⊙9am-6pm; శ) The palm trees, flower garden, historic wooden beach homes and the sound of the surf make the setting at 'The House Near the Palace' pretty much perfect. For many, it's a place to lounge with coffee and coconut cake, but there's also a small menu of massaman curry, crab fried rice, *kôw châe* (moist chilled rice) and Caesar salad wrap. Note the portions are very small.

Chomsin-Naebkehardt Junction Street Food
STREET FOOD $

(cnr Th Chomsin & Th Naebkehardt; ⊙6am-midnight) These noted street-food spots are a three-for-one deal and though the setting is humble, there's some excellent Thai food here. The action starts early each morning on Th Naebkehardt about 50m south of Chomsin and gradually more street carts start serving both here and across the road at the junction. Both spots sit under roofs for comfortable daytime dining.

At about 5pm the *dtôo rûng lék* (Little Night Market) takes over Soi 55/1 until late. It adds a little Isan (northeastern Thai) food to the mix.

Sôm·dam Tanontok 51
THAI $

(Th Damrongraj/Soi 51; mains 40-190B; ⊙10am-10pm; శ) A standout restaurant in a great dining neighbourhood, this is real Isan food (p379) cooked by a family from Khorat. There's everything you'd expect to find including grilled catfish, *gaang orm* (coconut-milk-less herbal curry) and many versions of *sôm·đam* other than papaya, including cucumber and bamboo shoot. It also does a squid *lâhp*.

There's no English sign; just find the smoky grill.

Velo Cafe
COFFEE $

(☏032 900392; Th Naebkehardt; coffee from 50B; ⊙7.30am-5.30pm Fri-Wed; శ) Coffee shops are everywhere in Hua Hin, but few are as serious as this little one, which roasts its own beans. It also makes very good sandwiches.

★ Koti
CHINESE, THAI $$

(☏095 860 5364; 61/1 Th Dechanuchit; mains 150-500B; ⊙11am-11pm; ✒) This Thai-Chinese restaurant, opened in 1932, is a national culinary luminary. Thais adore the stir-fried oyster with flour and egg, while foreigners frequently aim for the *đôm yam gûng*. Everyone loves the *yam tá-laìr* (spicy seafood salad) and classic green curry. Be prepared to wait for a table.

The Social Salad
INTERNATIONAL $$

(☏081 809 5083; www.thesocialsalad.org; 1/8 Th Chomsin; mains 100-350B; ⊙8am-10pm; శ✒)

🍴 This simple, but nicely decorated place attracts many repeat customers for its 209B make-your-own salads – choose from a long checklist of fresh organic ingredients. Anti-salad folks can opt for Thai dishes and pasta. While most of Thailand is still stuck on plastic straws, this restaurant uses metal ones. Ten percent of proceeds go to tree-planting programmes.

Der THAI $$
(13/14 Soi 35, Seenspace 2nd fl; mains 95-210B; ⊘noon-9pm; 🦽) Located in the beachfront Seenspace mall (p508), Der serves northeastern Isan food the way it should be: spicy and boldly flavoured. A modern set-up is given traditional touches like checkered napkins and dishes served in wicker baskets and banana leaves. Go for the grilled pork neck with tamarind dip and beef brisket *lâhp* salad.

Hua Hin Vegan Cafe THAI $$
(📞 092 536 6241; Th Phetkasem; mains 100-250B; ⊘9.30am-9pm; 🖥🍴) 🍴 Except for the lack of animal products, this modern place has nothing in common with the typical Thai *jae* vegan restaurant: there's wine, garlic, air-con, jazz, organic ingredients and creative cooking. There's lots of Thai – traditional and otherwise (quinoa *lâhp*, for example) – but the menu knows no borders: pulled jackfruit BBQ burgers, pumpkin carbonara and West African peanut soup.

Ratama THAI $$
(12/10 Th Naebkehardt; mains 60-200B; ⊘8am-4.30pm) The menu runs from Thai omelettes to a great panang curry, but Ratama is famous for duck served in many forms, including noodle soup and fried beaks. Try the *sûp̂er đeen gài* (chicken-feet *đôm yam*), and if you ask they'll substitute duck feet.

The English-script sign is very hard to spot, so look for the giant duck statue.

Carlo ITALIAN $$$
(📞 032 511348; www.carlo-huahin.com; 174/1 Th Naresedamri; mains 150-990B; ⊘noon-10.30pm; 🅿🖥🍴) There are loads of Italian places around Hua Hin, but most just turn out cheap pizza and pasta. For a great meal and a nice night out, this white-tablecloth spot on the south side of the tourist zone is Italian through and through: from the chef to the wine list, and the Milanese-style sea bass to the grilled lamb chops.

It's open for lunch, but gets very hot here during the day as there's no air-conditioning – go for dinner instead.

Hagi JAPANESE $$$
(Th Damnoen Kasem; mains 140-2500B; ⊘5-11pm, kitchen to 10pm; 🅿🖥) A lovely open-air spot on the edge of the Centara Grand, Hagi is considered to be the best Japanese in Hua Hin; not that there's much competition. There are teppanyaki tables for people who want to make their meal into a show.

🍸 Drinking & Nightlife

⭐**Vana Nava Sky** ROOFTOP BAR
(📞 032 809999; www.vananavasky.com; 129/129 Th Phetkasem, Holiday Inn; ⊘5pm-midnight Mon-Sat, from 9am Sun; 🖥) Vana Nava Sky is Hua Hin's classiest cocktail joint. Opened in 2018, the 27th-floor stunner features marble floors and lattice iron framing high windows for a steampunk effect. Sip your drink at the bar or on the glass observation deck. Creative cocktails made from infused spirits and fresh ingredients do not disappoint. Dress code is smart casual.

A tapas-style menu of Thai, Japanese and Mediterranean dishes is also available. On Sundays, brunch (888B) includes access to the Holiday Inn's infinity pool.

⭐**Airspace** CAFE
(📞 063 916 0999; www.airspacehuahin.com; 12/399 Soi Ao Hua Dorn; ⊘9am-8pm, restaurant 11am-11pm; 🖥) Gorgeous Airspace, near Khao Takiab, is a great spot to escape the sun or even do some laptop work. Ironwork interspersed with glass, high ceilings and leafy plants set a mood that's comfy or romantic depending on the time of day. Besides caffeine kicks, there is also a menu of all-day breakfast, Thai and international dishes.

McFarland House TEAHOUSE
(📞 032 521234; www.thebarai.com/mcfarlandhouse-must-visit-hua-hin/; 91 Th Khao Takiap, Hyatt Regency; afternoon tea for 2 600B, Sunday brunch from 1499B; ⊘6.30am-10.30pm, afternoon tea 2-4.30pm Mon-Sat, brunch buffet 11.30am-3pm Sun; 🖥) Teatime meets tropical flair at this antique Thai pavilion overlooking the beach. The teak haven, built in the 19th century, is named after its former owner, an American doctor raised in Siam by missionary parents. Now the two-storey pavilion is prime real estate for afternoon tea, Sunday brunch or sunset cocktails.

🛍 Shopping

★ Seenspace MALL
(☑092 350 0035; www.seenspace.com/huahin; 13/14 Soi 35; ☺hours vary) Seenspace is Thailand's first beachfront mall and word is still getting out. A trendy layout of concrete walls and open-air areas comprise food stands and air-conditioned havens, like Isan eatery Der (p507). Most visitors are drawn in by the beach club **Oasis** (☺noon-11pm Mon-Fri, 11am-11pm Sat, to 10pm Sun), with its photogenic beanbags and infinity pool.

There's much more food than shopping at the moment, with the exception being the slick designer store **Seek35** (☑064 962 3635; seek35.seenspace@gmail.com; ☺noon-9pm Mon-Fri, from 11am Sat & Sun). There is also a boutique hotel upstairs.

Plearn Wan MARKET
(เพลินวาน; ☑032 520311; www.plearnwan.com; Th Phetkasem, btwn Soi 38 & Soi 40; ☺10am-8pm) One of Hua Hin's top destinations for Thai travellers, Plearn Wan (Lose Yourself In The Past) is a retro-themed market with small stalls designed to resemble the old shophouses of Thai-Chinese neighbourhoods in Bangkok and Hua Hin. It's full of old photos, vintage furniture and Thais posing for photos.

Hua Hin Night Market MARKET
(Th Dechanuchit; ☺5pm-midnight) An attraction that rivals the beach in popularity, Hua Hin's two-block-long night market is full of tourists every night. There's all the standard knock-off clothes and cheap souvenirs, plus dozens of restaurant hosts waving menus in your face from the middle of the road.

ℹ Information

There are exchange booths open into the evening and ATMs all around the tourist centre, in particular on Th Naresdamri and Th Damnoen Kasen. For full-service banking, head to Th Phetkaksem and for banks open evenings and weekends head to a shopping mall.

Bangkok Hospital Hua Hin (☑032 616800; www.bangkokhospital.com/huahin; Th Phetkasem, at Soi 94, South Hua Hin) An outpost of the well-regarded national hospital chain in south Hua Hin.

Hua Hin Immigration Office (☑032 905111; Th Phetkasem, at Soi 100, South Hua Hin; ☺10am-5pm Mon-Fri, to 12.30pm Sat) In the basement level of Bluport shopping mall. You can extend tourist visas here.

Municipal Tourist Information Office (☑032 511047; cnr Th Phetkasem & Damnoen Kasem; ☺8.30am-4.30pm Mon-Fri) Has a good free map of the city and surrounding area and can answer basic questions.

San Paolo Hospital (☑032 532576; www.sanpaulo.co.th; 222 Th Phetkasem, South Hua Hin) A small private hospital south of town at Soi 86; it's a good option for ordinary illnesses and injuries.

Tourism Authority of Thailand (TAT; ☑032 513854; www.tourismthailand.org/hua-hin; 39/4 Th Phetkasem, at Soi 55; ☺8.30am-4.30pm) Staff here speak English and are quite helpful, though they rarely open on time.

Tourist Police (☑032 533440; Soi Hua Hin 21) Next to the Imperial Hua Hin Beach Resort.

Tuk Tours (☑080 544 2465, 032 514281; www.tuktours.net; 2/1 Th Chomsin; ☺8.30am-8pm) Helpful, no-pressure place that can book activities and transport all around Thailand.

ℹ Getting There & Away

The train is the most pleasant way to get to or leave Hua Hin, but minivan is the most popular. If you prefer to get between Hua Hin and Bangkok as quickly and comfortably as possible, private cars start at 1600B and take as little as three hours. You can also hire a taxi from Bangkok for about the same price, but be prepared to haggle.

AIR

The **airport** (☑032 520180; The Phetkasem) is 6km north of town, but only has charter services and private flights. Past attempts at commercial service have always been short-lived, though there's always talk of new ones.

BOAT

Lomprayah (☑032 532761; www.lomprayah.com; Th Phetkasem; ☺8am-midnight) offers a bus-boat combination from Hua Hin to Ko Tao (1050B, six to nine hours), as well as to Ko Pha-Ngan (1300B, nine to 12 hours) and Ko Samui (1400B, 10 to 13 hours) with departures from its office at 8.45am and 11.30pm.

There's also a **passenger ferry** (☑093 495 9499; www.royalferrygroup.com; Soi Ao Hua Don 3; business 1550B, VIP 7000-14,000B; ☺departs Pattaya/Hua Hin 4pm/1pm) between Hua Hin and Pattaya, allowing you to skip Bangkok.

BUS & MINIVAN

Minivans going north (including to Phetchaburi, Kanchanaburi and many destinations in Bangkok) use the **Hua Hin Minivan Station** (Soi 51), while **minivans** (Th Phetkasem) (and the occasional bus) going south stop in the road next to the clock tower. Services to most places run

HUA HIN TRANSPORT CONNECTIONS

DESTINATION	BUS	MINIVAN	TRAIN
Bangkok Don Mueang International Airport		200B, 4½hr, every 40min	
Bangkok Ekamai (Eastern Bus Station)		200B, 4½hr, hourly	
Bangkok Hualamphong			44-1982B, 3½-4½hr, 12 daily
Bangkok Northern (Mo Chit) Bus Terminal	263B, 4½hr, 9am, noon, 1.30pm, 3pm	180B, 4hr, frequent	
Bangkok Southern Bus Terminal	155B, 4½hr, 3am, 10am, noon daily & 4pm, 9pm Fri & Sat	180B, 4hr, frequent	
Bangkok Suvarnabhumi International Airport	269B, 4½hr, every 90min 6am-6pm		
Bangkok Thonburi			42-96B, 4½hr, 2 daily
Cha-am	20-30B, 30-45min, hourly 6am-4pm	40B, 30min, frequent	6-363B, 30min, 5 daily
Chiang Mai	735-980B, 13hr, 5.30pm, 6pm, 6.15pm		
Chumphon	351B, 5hr, 10am		49-2006B, 4-5hr, 12 daily
Kanchanaburi		220B, 4hr, hourly	
Nakhon Ratchasima (Khorat)	347-518B, 6-7hr, 10am, 6pm, 9pm, 11pm		
Pattaya	389B, 5hr, 11am		
Phetchaburi	40B, 1½hr, hourly 6am-4pm	100B, 1hr, frequent	14-1339B, 1hr, 12 daily
Phuket	637-840B, 10-11hr, 10am, 12.30pm, 7pm, 8.30pm, 9pm, 10.30pm, midnight		
Prachuap Khiri Khan		80B, 1½hr, frequent	19-1403B, 1-1½hr, 11 daily
Pranburi	20B, 30min, every 30min 7am-3pm	30B, 30min, frequent	5-361B, 30min, 3 daily
Ubon Ratchathani	683-868B, 12-13hr, 6pm, 9pm, 11pm		

frequently from about 6am (4am for Bangkok and Phetchaburi) until the early evening.

The quiet little **Hua Hin Bus Station** (Th Phetkasem, at Soi 96, South Hua Hin), south of the city, has a few buses to Bangkok, Chiang Mai, Nakhon Ratchasima (Khorat), Phuket and Ubon Ratchathani, though most services running between Bangkok and the south don't come into town. Tickets should be bought a day in advance.

Buses to Bangkok leaving from the more convenient Southern Bus Terminal can be booked through Hua Hin-Pran Tour (p500) near the night market, though the buses are old. **Airport Hua Hin Bus** (☎ 084 697 3773; www.airport-uahinbus.com; Th Phetkasem, next to Hua Hin Airport) runs from Hua Hin Airport to Bangkok's Suvarnabhumi International Airport and Pattaya. If you use this bus, there's a shuttle to your hotel for 100B, which is cheaper than a túk-túk will charge to take you into town. The green *sŏrng·tăa·ou* don't go quite this far.

Ordinary (fan) buses go to **Pranburi** from Th Sasong near the night market, and to **Cha-am and Phetchaburi** (Th Phetkasem) about hourly all day from Th Phetkasem across from the Esso petrol station.

TRAIN

Hua Hin Train Station (☎ 032 511073; Th Liap Thang Rot Fai) is conveniently located at the western end of Th Damnoen Kasem. Services include Bangkok's Hualamphong and Thonburi stations (42B to 96B, 4½ hours, two daily), Cha-am (6B to 363B, 30 minutes, five daily), Chumphon (49B to 2006B, four to five hours, 12 daily), Phetchaburi (14B to 1339B, one hour, 12 daily), Prachuap Khiri Khan (19B to 1403B, one to 1½ hours, 11 daily) and Pranburi (5B to 361B, 30 minutes, three daily).

ⓘ Getting Around

Green *sŏrng·tăa·ou* (10B) depart from the corner of Th Sasong and Th Dechanuchit, by the night market. They travel from 6am to 9pm along Th Phetkasem south to Khao Takiab (turning east on Th Damnoen Kasem on the way) and north to the airport.

Four-wheeled túk-túk fares in Hua Hin are outrageous and start at a whopping 100B for short trips. Motorcycle taxis are much more reasonable (30B to 50B) for short hops and the drivers generally don't try to rip off foreigners.

Many shops around town hire motorcycles (200B to 250B per day) and a few have bicycles (around 100B per day); try **Lub Sabai Hostel Bike Hire** (📞087 142 4224; huahinlubsabaihotel@gmail.com; 136 Th Chomsin; bike/motorcycle 70/200B; ⊙8am-9pm), **Aeknarin Huahin Car Rental** (📞081 940 0072; www.thaicarrenthuahin.com; Soi 61; per day motorcycle 250B, car from 1500B; ⊙8am-9.30pm) or **Pook Chomsin** (📞092 828 6002; 142/2 Th Chomsin; motorcycle per day 200B; ⊙8am-9pm). Damnoen Kasem, Naebkehardt and Chomsin streets also have several shops each. Hua Hin Bike Tours (p504) and Velo Thailand (p503) rent top-of-the-line bicycles.

There are roadside tables arranging taxis (any vehicle that you can charter, including pickup trucks and túk-túk) all around the city centre. Prices are mostly fixed, but it's worth haggling. Don't agree to anything without knowing exactly what vehicle you are getting. Booking through your hotel or a tour company may cost a little more than doing it yourself, but is more reliable.

Thai Rent A Car (📞083 887 5454; www.thairentacar.com; Th Phetkasem, at Soi 84, South Hua Hin; ⊙8.30am-6.30pm) is a professional Thailand-based car-rental agency with competitive prices, a well-maintained fleet, hotel drop-offs and one-way rentals. The office is next to Villa Market.

Pranburi & Around

📞 032 / POP 24,800

Half an hour south of Hua Hin is the country 'suburb' of Pranburi (ปราณบุรี) district, which serves as a quiet coastal alternative and is home to boutique resorts ideal for escaping the crowds without travelling too far from civilisation.

The core area is the small town of **Pak Nam Pran** (mouth of the Pranburi River), which has the biggest resorts but not much beach. Though tourism is growing, fishing is still the key to the economy: every morning the boats dock in the river, unload their catch and begin the pungent process of sun-drying squid on large racks.

South of Pak Nam Pran there's a sandy shore and the coastal road provides a quick pleasant trip to **Khao Kalok** (Skull Mountain; signed as Thao Kosa Forest Park), a mammoth, oddly eroded headland that shelters the most attractive beach in the area.

⊙ Sights

Pranburi is the gateway to exploring nature's bounty. Nearby mangrove forests are convenient green escapes; 40km away is the birdwatching paradise Khao Sam Roi Yot National Park, and 66km away is the serene Kuiburi National Park, where seeing elephants is almost guaranteed.

Sustainable travel company **Exo Travel** (www.exotravel.com) has a good database of tour operators in Khao Sam Roi Yot and Kuiburi National Parks.

★**Kuiburi National Park** NATIONAL PARK
(อุทยานแห่งชาติกุยบุรี; 📞081 776 2410; Rte 4024; adult/child 200/100B, wildlife-spotting trip per truck 850B; ⊙wildlife trips 2-6pm) Who doesn't want to see herds of wild elephants roaming through the forest or enjoying an evening bath? At Kuiburi National Park's *hôoay lêuk* unit, up near the border with Myanmar and about 65km from Pranburi, it's almost guaranteed. Wildlife-watching drives in the back of pickup trucks go through the forest and reclaimed farm fields where elephants live. They're used to seeing vehicles, so they pay them little mind, making this almost like an African safari experience.

There are also plenty of gaurs (wild cattle) and they're seen fairly often. Most of the spotters don't speak English, but they know some relevant vocabulary. Avoid Saturdays if possible, as the park gets very busy. It's 45 minutes west of Khao Sam Roi Yot National Park; follow the national park signs for 'wildlife watching'. The two make an ideal combo visit.

Khao Sam Roi Yot National Park NATIONAL PARK
(อุทยานแห่งชาติเขาสามร้อยยอด; 📞032 821568; www.thainationalparks.com/khao-sam-roi-yot-national-park; Rte 4020, Bang Pu; entry 200B, per

night camping fee 30B, tent for 2 150B, sleeping bag 30B; ⊙8am-4.30pm) Towering limestone outcrops form a rocky, jigsaw-puzzle landscape at Khao Sam Roi Yot National Park (Three Hundred Mountain Peaks), located about 30km from Pranburi. Most visitors are here to see Tham Phraya Nakhon, one of the most spectacular and, for Thais, famous caves in Thailand. This revered cave shelters the Khuha Kharuehat Pavilion, a royal *săh-lah* built for Rama V in 1890, which is usually bathed in streams of morning light from around 10.30am.

While you're in the park, you can hire a covered boat at Wat Khao Daeng for a one-hour scenic cruise along Khlong Khao Daeng. There are great mountain views and you'll also see birds, macaques, water monitors and mudskippers.

Birders descend on the park during the cool season from November to March to see some of the park's 300 migratory and resident species. At the intersection of the East Asian and Australian migration routes, Khao Sam Roi Yot is home to yellow bitterns, purple swamphens, ruddy-breasted crakes, bronze-winged jacanas, black-headed ibises, great spotted eagles and oriental reed warblers.

Most travellers visit on a day trip from Hua Hin or Prachuap Khiri Khan, both around 50km from the park. There's no public transport, so you'll need to come with your own wheels: hiring a car and driver from either town will cost about 1800B to 2000B including petrol. If you choose to stay overnight, there are bungalows at Khao Daeng, but most people prefer accommodation just outside the park at Hat Sam Roi Yot beach. A taxi from the train station or bus stop in Pranburi to Hat Sam Roi Yot is a fixed 400B.

The fishing village of Bang Pu is the main departure point for visiting Tham Phraya Nakhon. There's no road access to the cave, but you can ride in a boat (200B one way) to Laem Sala Beach (note: it's a shallow, but wet landing), then follow the steep 430m trail and stairway up to the hill. Restaurants at Bang Pu are open from 6am to 6pm.

There's no park gate. Tickets are sold and checked at each of the park's attractions.

Pranburi Forest Park NATURE RESERVE
(วนอุทยานปราณบุรี, Wana-Utthayan Pranburi; ☑032 621608; ⊙6am-6pm) Just north of the Pranburi River is an extensive natural mangrove forest. A 1km-long boardwalk

South of Hua Hin

with interpretive signs, some in English, lets you explore it from the perspective of a mud-dweller, while an observation tower gives you a bird's-eye view. At high tide fisherfolk will take visitors on 40-minute boat trips (500B) along the river and small canals.

You'll see hundreds of crabs, and usually a fair number of birds, mudskippers and water monitors. In some areas you'll hear snapping shrimp. There's quite a bit of variety within this forest – the ecosystem is different enough from the young, replanted mangrove across the river at Sirinart Rajini Mangrove Ecosystem Learning Center (ศูนย์ศึกษาเรียนรู้ระบบนิเวศป่าชายเลนสิรินาถราชินี; Pak Nam Pran; ⊙8am-5pm) FREE that nature lovers will appreciate visiting both.

It's a 14km drive from Pak Nam Pran via Rte 1019, passing very near Hat Sai Noi (หาดทรายน้อย) on the way. A more direct route half this length is shown on many maps, but it's not passable any more.

🛏 Sleeping & Eating

Thongsuk Mini Resort HOTEL **$$**
(☑ 098 423 2661; jamsawang38@gmail.com; r 850B; ℗ ❄ 🛜) Not the cheapest address in Pak Nam Pran, but for about 100B extra than most others, these nine white bungalows are a good budget option. There are free bikes and though the owners speak little English they're very eager to please. It's a two-minute walk from the squid roundabout where the minivans stop.

⭐ La a natu
Bed & Bakery BOUTIQUE HOTEL **$$$**
(☑ 032 689 9413; www.laanatu.com; south of Khao Kalok; incl breakfast & afternoon tea r 5500-16,000B, f 11,000B; ℗ ❄ 🛜 🏊) Turning the humble Thai rice village into a luxury living experience is what La a natu does and it does it with panache. The blissfully remote thatched-roof villas rising on stilts are full Gilligan's Island outside with a touch of luxury inside, and real rice paddies below.

Dolphin Bay Resort RESORT **$$$**
(☑ 032 825190; www.dolphinbayresort.com; Th Liap Chai Tale, Hat Sam Roi Yot; r 1690-2790, f 4590-7690B; ℗ ❄ @ 🛜 🏊) The resort that defined Dolphin Bay as a family-friendly retreat offers a low-key holiday camp ambience with a variety of standard-issue, value-oriented rooms and villas. There are two big pools, a playground and a toy room. The grounds are large enough for kids to roam safely and the beach is right across the road.

Krua Renu THAI **$**
(Th Pak Nam Pran; mains 40-120B; ⊙ 8am-11pm Fri-Mon; ℗) There are both budget and beautiful restaurants along the coastal road, but some of the best food in Pak Nam Pran is in the town at this tall restaurant 200m east of the squid roundabout. Go with the standard *đôm yam* or try the *gaang pàh hâang* (dried jungle curry).

There's no English sign, so look for the brown brick walls and a frangipani tree.

⭐ Chicken and Bee THAI **$$$**
(☑ 092 054 5645; chickenandbee@gmail.com; Sam Roi Yot; mains 100-1000B; ⊙ 10am-6pm Thu-Tue; ℗ 🍽) 🌱 Against the lush greenery of Khao Sam Roi Yot National Park, Chicken and Bee is an organic farm and open-air restaurant where you are sure to feel at home. Spicy seafood pasta, fresh-pressed juices with edible flowers and Thai curry are just a few highlights of its ever-changing nature-loving concept.

Don't forget to go for a stroll around the peaceful gardens and farm area after your meal.

⭐ Boutique Farmers INTERNATIONAL **$$$**
(☑ 081 266 7800; www.theboutiquefarmers.com; Pak Nam Pran; mains 400-550B; ⊙ 5-10pm Fri, 11am-3pm & 5-10pm Sat, 10am-4pm Sun; ℗ 🛜 🍽) 🌱 Chef James Noble is realising his life-long dream of sticking it to the man. His airy cottage-inspired eatery is farm-to-table in its truest sense: biodynamic vegetables and herbs are grown behind the restaurant. Meat and fish are sourced locally from small-scale producers. The menu, spanning many cuisines and influences, changes daily according to what's plucked fresh. Cash payment only.

ℹ Getting There & Away

Pak Nam Pran is about 25km south of Hua Hin. Ordinary buses (30B, 30 minutes, every 30 minutes 7am to 3pm), minivans (30B, 30 minutes, frequent 6am to 7pm) and trains (5B to 361B, 30 minutes, 11.47am, 5.50pm, 8.10pm) will drop you off in Pranburi town, 10km from Pak Nam Pran and taxi drivers charge 200B between the two. There are also minivans (60B, one hour, frequent 5am to 6.40pm) and trains (14B to 62B, one hour, 4.51am, 10.03am, 2.26pm) from Prachuap Khiri Khan.

There's a direct minivan service from Pak Nam Pran (at the squid roundabout on the south side of town) every 30 minutes from early morning to late afternoon to Bangkok's Mo Chit and Southern bus terminals (200B, five hours). These vans also stop in Phetchaburi (140B, two hours), but do not stop in Hua Hin.

ℹ Getting Around

If you want to explore the area, you'll probably want to rent a motorbike as public transport isn't an option. They can be hired from **Luang Utane** (☑ 084 080 4023; Th Pak Nam Pran; ⊙ 7am-6pm) or many hotels for 250B per day. A car and driver can be arranged through any hotel or there's **Cosmo Car** (☑ 080 139 6665; opposite Tesco Lotus) rental in Pranburi town that's reliable and cheap, though limited English is spoken.

Prachuap Khiri Khan

☑ 032 / POP 33,500

A sleepy seaside town, Prachuap Khiri Khan (ประจวบคีรีขันธ์) is a delightfully relaxed place; the antithesis of Hua Hin. The broad bay is a tropical turquoise punctuated by bobbing fishing boats and overlooked by honeycombed limestone mountains – scenery that you usually have to travel to the southern Andaman to find.

In recent years, foreigners have discovered Prachuap's charms and some Bangkokians drive past Hua Hin for their weekends away. But their numbers are still very small compared to better-known destinations, leaving plenty of room on the beaches, at the hilltop temples and in the many excellent seafood restaurants.

◉ Sights

Th Suseuk south of the Municipal Market 1 still has lots of old wooden houses and makes a great walk day and night. It hosts the Suseuk Culture and Fun Street Market with food, crafts, music and more food the first weekend of each month.

Ao Prachuap   BAY
(อ่าวประจวบ) The town's crowning feature is Ao Prachuap (Prachuap Bay), a gracefully curving bay outlined by an oceanfront promenade and punctuated by dramatic headlands at both ends. The sunrise is superb and an evening stroll along the promenade and pier is a peaceful delight.

North of Khao Chong Krajok, over the bridge, the bay stretches peacefully to a toothy mountain, part of Khao Ta Mong Lai Forest Park (วนอุทยานเขาตาม่องล่าย; ☑ 081 378 0026; ☺ daylight hours). The long sandy beach running parallel with the road before the forest park only sees people on weekends and even then not very many, making it a fine place to idle and beachcomb at any time. It's deep enough for swimming, but not very clean.

Khao Chong Krajok   VIEWPOINT
(เขาช่องกระจก) At the northern end of town, Khao Chong Krajok (Mirror Gap Hill, so named for the natural hole that seemingly reflects the sky) provides a cascading view of the coastline and mountains on the Myanmar border about 15km away. You'll need to dodge some fearless monkeys as you climb the 396 steps to the stupa on the summit that was ordered built by King Rama VI.

Wat Ao Noi   BUDDHIST TEMPLE
(วัดอ่าวน้อย; ☺ daylight hours) FREE Leaving Ao Prachuap behind, turn north for 2.5km, passing the fishing village of Ban Ao Noi, where some of the larger boats dock and unload, to this large temple linking two bays: Ao Noi and Ao Khan Kradai. It features a lovely *bòht* constructed entirely of teak without nails, and the murals, mostly telling the Buddha's life story, are composed of framed painted woodcarvings. The pond in front is filled with fish, eager to be fed by merit-makers.

Ao Manao   BEACH
(อ่าวมะนาว; ☺ beach zone 5am-7pm, mountain zone 6am-6pm) On weekends, locals head to Ao Manao, an island-dotted bay ringed by a curving beach within Wing 5 Thai Air Force base – the only beach where locals go swimming as both the water and sand are clean. There are the usual seaside amenities: restaurants, beach chairs, umbrellas and inner tubes, plus some dry-land diversions including quad-bike rides and a petting zoo. It's packed on weekends but can be nearly deserted on weekdays.

You need to register at the base entrance, at the end of Th Salacheep. Normally no passport is necessary, but it's best to bring it in case you're asked. From here it's 2.5km to the beach. Across the bay from the public beach is Khao Lom Muak (เขาล้อมหมวก; ☺ 6am-6pm, museum 9am-3pm Sat & Sun) mountain, with a WWII museum close by.

🏃 Activities

Sunset Cruise   CRUISE
(☑ 097 982 8795; www.samaowtour.com; Th Chai Thaleh; 300B) Sam Aow Princess Tour has a short sunset cruise in Prachuap Bay starting around 5.30pm nightly if there are enough passengers.

🛏 Sleeping

To really enjoy your stay, this is a town where you don't want to be far from the sea. There are no big, fancy resorts here. The closest you can get to luxury are some decent midrange places. On the other hand, there are lots of small homestays and guesthouses in the city centre near the sea. Just turn up and find a room, although on high-season weekends book ahead.

Safehouse Hostel   HOSTEL $
(☑ 087 909 4770; r_jularat@hotmail.com; 28 Soi 6, Th Salacheep; dm 280, r 450-800B; �✿) With fairly frumpy though very tidy rooms, the host Sherry is the real reason this small hostel has become popular. She goes out of her way to please guests and leads good tours to Kuiburi National Park (p510) and elsewhere. There's a communal kitchen.

Prachuap Khiri Khan

Rop Lom (620m)

Prachuap Khiri Khan

◎ Sights
1	Ao Prachuap	B2
2	Khao Chong Krajok	B1

⊕ Activities, Courses & Tours
3	Sunset Cruise	B2

🛏 Sleeping
4	De Boutique Hotel	B4
5	Grandma's House	B4
6	Prachuap Beach Hotel	B4
7	Safehouse Hostel	A4
8	Yutichai Hotel	A3

⊗ Eating
9	Dtom Leuat Mu	B3
	Grandma's House	(see 5)
10	In Town Seafood	B4
11	Krua Chaiwat	B4
12	Municipal Market 1	B3
13	Night Market	A2
14	Pizza Khirikhan	B4
15	Rim Taley Market	B2

⊜ Drinking & Nightlife
	Cro-magnon	(see 4)

⊞ Shopping
	Hachi Coffee & Bike Shop	(see 10)

⊕ Transport
16	Bangkok & Phetchaburi Bus Stop	A3

Grandma's House
BOUTIQUE HOTEL **$**

(☑ 089 526 6896; grandmaprachuap@gmail.com; 238 Th Suseuk; r incl breakfast 690-890B; ❄ 🕾) Up above its popular vintage-themed cafe, these three solid wooden rooms (two small and one large) are decorated with some actual antiques. They share two modern bathrooms. You'll need to endure street noise, but there's normally not too much at night.

Khao Ta Mong Lai
Forest Park Campsite
CAMPGROUND **$**

(☑ 093 014 9919; with tent 100B, 3-person tent hire 300B) There's a shady, seldom-used campground in this park with some of the cleanest facilities in Thailand. There are simple bungalows, but they're intended for large groups. Since it's across the bay from the city centre, you get some great sunsets.

Yutichai Hotel
HOTEL **$**

(☑ 032 611055; yutichai_hotel@hotmail.com; 115 Th Kong Kiat; r with fan 220-350, air-con 500B;

❄ 🕾) A bit of history right near the train station, this old wooden hotel is properly maintained and the price is right. Most rooms (including those with air-con, private bathrooms and hot water) are in a more modern, but still classic, concrete building at the back. Light sleepers will want to stay at the back, or elsewhere.

★ Prachuap Beach Hotel
HOTEL **$$**

(☑ 032 601288; www.prachuapbeach.com; 123 Th Suseuk; d & tw 1000, tr 1200B; 🅿 ❄ 🕾) The best-located, and possibly quietest, hotel in the city is near lots of good restaurants, opens up to the promenade and has great views from upper floors. The 2nd-floor rooms are cheapest, but it's worth paying the extra 100B to be up higher – the 5th floor is the top.

De Boutique Hotel
HOTEL **$$**

(☑ 032 611888; www.deboutiquehotel.com; 141 Th Salacheep; d/tw/f incl breakfast 1800/2500/2690; 🅿 ❄ 🕾) These two bright yellow buildings have comfortable modern rooms with attractive, individual decor, although the fun paintings aren't enough to deserve a 'boutique' label. If you don't mind being two streets away from the sea, it's a very solid choice with a convenient location.

✖ Eating

Restaurants in Prachuap are known for cheap and excellent seafood, while Western options are easy to find. The **Municipal Market 1** (Th Maitri Ngam; ⊙4am-4pm) is the place to get pineapples fresh from the orchards; ask the vendor to cut them for you. There are a pair of small **night markets** (Th Kong Kiat; ⊙4.30pm-2am) in the city centre.

Rim Taley Market   MARKET $
(Th Chai Thaleh; ⊙ 4-8.30pm Mon-Thu, 4-9pm Fri & Sat) The Oceanside Market isn't very large, but it makes an ideal dinner destination because you can eat your food on the promenade or pier. On Friday and Saturday the few dozen regular vendors are joined by about 200 more as the market morphs into **Walking Street**, though there's little in the way of artistic or handmade goods on sale.

Dtom Leuat Mu   THAI $
(Th Salacheep; soup 40B, rice 5B; ⊙ 6am-noon) This actual shack on the corner serves just one dish – the namesake 'pig's blood soup', a piquant broth with many pig parts besides the congealed blood thrown in. This restaurant is constantly busy and some street carts sell snacks, like *kà·nŏm krók* (coconut hotcakes), at the front. It shuts down when it's sold out.

Krua Chaiwat   THAI $
(Th Salacheep; mains 40-240B; ⊙9am-3pm & 4.30-8pm Mon-Sat; 🔊🍴) With good food at low prices, this small restaurant serves a mix of locals and expats. While Thai food is its strength – the *đôm yam* and curries are quite good – there's also steaks and a few fusion foods like the stir-fried spaghetti with salted mackerel.

Grandma's House   CAFE $
(238 Th Suseuk; mains 39-159B, coffee from 35B; ⊙7.30am-6pm Mon-Sat, to 8pm Sun; 🔊) Cool cafe on the ground floor of a renovated century-old wooden house. Run by artists, it's a good spot for breakfast, or a coffee, smoothie or chocolate break.

Rap Lom   SEAFOOD $
(Th Suanson; mains 60-260B; ⊙10am-9pm; 🅿🔊) Popular with the locals, the *pàt pŏng gà·rèe poo* (crab curry) comes with big chunks of sweet crab meat, and the *yam tá·lair* (seafood salad) is spicy and zesty. On the non-oceanic side of things, there's banana blossom salad.

★ Pizza Khirikhan   ITALIAN $$
(☑081 199 0861; 117 Th Susek; mains 120-200B; ⊙4-10pm; 🔊) Bong, Pizza Khirikhan's owner, has put lots of love into his tiki-style restaurant. The former location – a beach hut – has been re-created with palm leaves and wood into a tropical getaway in the heart of town. Bong serves customers and makes the tasty pizzas himself, dreadlocks bobbing to reggae tunes. The service isn't fast, but it's kind and personal.

★ In Town Seafood   THAI $$
(Th Chai Thaleh; mains 50-400B; ⊙3-11pm; 🅿) A go-to place for discerning locals, here you can eat streetside under a utilitarian tent while gazing at the squid boats in the bay. Great range of fresh seafood on display – barracuda, crab and shellfish – so you can point and pick if you don't recognise the names on the menu. Service can be slow.

🍷 Drinking & Nightlife

The beach road is the place to be. There's a small bunch of low-key bars north of the Prachuap Beach Hotel; it's nothing like the loud sleazy bar scene in Hua Hin.

Cro-magnon   CAFE
(☑087 664 9514; mangpor99@hotmail.com; Th Salacheep; ⊙10am-8pm; 🔊) The self-professed espresso studio, Cro-magnon does much more than just coffee: there's also ice-cream sundaes and *kakigōri*, the Japanese shaved-ice dessert. If that doesn't cool you off, the blasting AC sure will.

🛍 Shopping

Hachi Coffee & Bike Shop   VINTAGE
(☑065 434 4694; Th Suseuk; ⊙10.30am-7.30pm Sun-Fri; 🔊) Hachi cafe and secondhand shop is a treasure trove of Hawaiian shirts, vinyl and other quirky items that could make cool souvenirs. Grab a coffee and sit at a wooden counter facing the street. The owner, who named the spot after her daughter, is happy to share travel tips. She also rents bikes for 100B a day.

ℹ️ Information

There are lots of banks and ATMs in the city centre. The nearest banks that are open evenings and weekends are in the Tesco-Lotus shopping mall out on the highway, 3km west of the city centre.

At the foot of the pier, the **tourist office** (📞 032 604143; Th Chai Thaleh; ⏲ 8.30am-noon & 1-4.30pm Mon-Fri) has free city maps and the staff speak English.

ℹ️ Getting There & Away

Most buses do not come into town, they just park along the Phetkasem Hwy (Hwy 4) at an area known as **'sà·tǎh·nee dern rót'** (Phetkasem Hwy), 4km northwest of the city centre. Tickets are sold on the northbound side of the road. To be sure you get a seat, buy your ticket the day before as buses are often full when they pass Prachuap. The exceptions are the four daily

air-conditioned buses to Bangkok's Southern Bus Terminal (200B, 9am, 11am, 1pm, 1am) and Phetchaburi (150B, every hour) that depart from a small **bus stop** on Th Pitak Chat. Minivans form the backbone of Prachuap transportation and they all depart from **kew rót đôo** (Th Prachuap Khiri Khan/Rte 326) minivan station at the junction of Rte 326 and Hwy 4 near the main bus stop. The **train station** (📞 032 611175; Th Maharat) is a 15-minute walk to the main accommodation area.

ℹ️ Getting Around

Prachuap is small enough to get around on foot, but you can hop on a motorcycle taxi to most places for 30B; 60B out to the bus stop and minivan station. Most hotels have motorcycle hire for 200B to 250B per day. A few also do bicycles for 50B.

PRACHUAP KHIRI KHAN TRANSPORT CONNECTIONS

DESTINATION	BUS	MINIVAN	TRAIN
Ban Krut	70B, 1hr, 3 daily (to the town)	70-90B, 1hr, every 30min 5.40am-7pm (to the Hwy)	13-339B, 1hr, 8 daily
Bang Saphan Yai	80B, 1½hr, 10 daily (to the town)	100B, 1½hr, every 30min 5.40am-7pm (8 to the town, all others to the Hwy)	16-347B, 1¼hr, 9 daily
Bangkok Hualamphong			168-455B, 4½-5½hr, 9 daily
Bangkok Northern (Mo Chit) Bus Terminal	240B, 6-7hr, 3.30pm	220B, 5hr, every 45min 1.30am-7.30pm	
Bangkok Southern Bus Terminal	200B, 5hr, 9am, 11am, 1pm, 1am	200B, 5hr, every 45min 3am-7pm	
Bangkok Thonburi			56-130B, 6hr, 4.50am, 10am
Cha-am		120B, 2hr, frequent 5am-6.40pm	24-415B, 2hr, 4 daily
Chumphon	220B, 4hr, hourly 11am-midnight	180B, 3½hr, every 40min 6am-7pm	78-1473B, 2½-3hr, 10 daily
Hua Hin		80B, 1½hr, frequent 5am-6.40pm	19-1363B, 1-1½hr, 11 daily
Phetchaburi	150B, 2½hr, hourly 7.30am-9pm	150B, 2½hr, every 40 min 3am-7pm	31-1460B, 2-2½hr, 11 daily
Phuket	587-913B, 9-10hr, 11am & every 30min 8pm-midnight		
Pranburi		60B, 1hr, frequent 5am-6.40pm	14-392B, 1hr, 3 daily
Ranong		250B, 4½hr, 8am, 10am, 1pm, 3.30pm	

Ban Krut & Bang Saphan Yai

🎣 032 / POP 4200/15,100

While calling Ban Krut (บ้านกรูด) and Bang Saphan Yai (บางสะพานใหญ่) beaches idyllic is a bit of a stretch, they're no slouches in the beauty department. Around 65km and 90km south of Prachuap Khiri Khan, most people don't come here for the scenery, they come because so few others choose to come. There are no high-rises, no late-night bars and no speeding traffic to distract you from a serious regimen of reading, swimming, eating and biking. Ban Krut is getting busier as a getaway for Thai families, but it is still a much more laid-back alternative to Hua Hin. Meanwhile, on Bang Saphan Yai, you'll often be all on your lonesome as you sit or stroll between the coconut trees and the crystalline blue sea that laps the long sandy coastline. There's a November to March high season, though all in all it's a wonderfully meagre one.

⊙ Sights

Ban Krut   BEACH
Ban Krut beach is now a full-on tourist destination with a string of resorts, restaurants and inner-tube rental shops – there's even a 7-Eleven – sitting across the road from the sea. Families park their cars and spend the day eating, drinking and watching their kids splash around. That said, it's still much more subdued than a typical tourist beach as you don't need to go very far south to score a private patch of sand, even on holiday weekends.

Ban Krut is better than Bang Saphan Yai for getting out to explore. The coconut-tree-shaded road to the south, home to scattered farmers and fisherfolk, makes a great bike or motorcycle ride, and to the north **Phra Mahathat Chedi Phakdi Praka** (พระมหาธาตุเจดีย์ภักดีประกาศ; Rte 1029, Hat Ban Krut; ⊙8am-5pm) FREE is a gorgeous modern stupa.

Bang Saphan Yai   BEACH
Bang Saphan Yai is a sit-on-the-beach-all-day kind of place that still clings to that famous beach cliché: Thailand 30 years ago before pool villas and package tourists pushed out all the beach bums. Much of the lodging is right on the beach itself (called Hat Suan Luang) and hawkers are rare.

Islands off the coast, including **Ko Thalu** with its natural rock arch, offer good **snorkelling** and **diving** from March to October, with March and April being the best months. Although they're near Bang Saphan Yai, trips to these islands can also be arranged from Ban Krut.

🛏 Sleeping

Both beaches have accommodation for all budgets, although not a whole lot of options overall. Most places are pretty much empty on weekdays and are only really busy on holiday weekends, when Bangkokians are willing to take the time to drive past Hua Hin. Most hotels and resorts don't, or only slightly, raise their rates on regular weekends.

🛏 Ban Krut

Most accommodation is in the busy core beach area that begins 1km from the tiny and timeless wooden shophouse-filled village. To the north of the temple-topped headland (this beach is called Hat Sai Kaew) and to the south it quickly turns remote and private with only a few scattered resorts in between coconut groves.

Siripong Guesthouse   GUESTHOUSE $
(☎032 695070; Hat Ban Krut; r with fan 250-300B, air-con 500B; ℙ❄☆) The region's cheapest lodging is pretty bare-bones, but the rooms are actually better than the dishevelled exterior would lead you to believe, and it's right at the junction, slightly away from the busiest parts of the beach. The fan rooms have either bucket-dump toilets in the rooms or shared bathrooms.

Some English is spoken and there are discounts for long stays. If nobody is around, pop into the family's grocery store across the road.

Proud Thai Beach Resort   GUESTHOUSE $
(☎089 682 4484; www.proudthairesort.com; Hat Ban Krut; r 800B; ℙ❄☆) Eight wooden bungalows, all with terraces, sit under the shade of trees across the road from the beach. They're old, but well maintained by the English-speaking owner.

Ban Krut Resort   RESORT $$
(☎081 421 1186; www.bankrutresort.com; 212 Tambon Thongchai; r 1000-5400B; ℙ❄☆⛆) The rooms at this guesthouse are simply decorated and have balconies, though the walls are quite thin. It has a small swimming pool,

a private section of chairs on the beach and free bicycles for guest use.

★ Baan Grood Arcadia Resort & Spa
RESORT $$$

(☑ 032 695095; www.bgaresort.com; Ban Krut; incl breakfast r 1400-3700B, ste 3700, f 7000-11,000B; P ✳ ☞ ☲) This resort brings a touch of luxury to laid-back Ban Krut. Thai design features throughout the garden-view rooms and villas, while amenities such as a sparkling pool and big balconies lend the Arcadia a faraway feeling, despite its location right on the main beach road. At the very top end is a two-storey villa with four bedrooms and a private pool.

🛌 Bang Saphan Yai

The beach is 6km south of Bang Saphan Yai town. There's a handful of small flash resorts here and also a row of very basic, budget bungalows with direct beach access to the north of the Why Not Bar. There's some lodging inland, but this kind of defeats the purpose of coming here.

Ploy Bungalows
BUNGALOW $

(☑ 032 817119; Hat Bang Saphan Yai; r 500-700B; P ✳ ☞) A quiet, casual place with brightly painted concrete bungalows. As a bonus to backpackers, all bungalows that are right up on the beach are the 500B fan variety. There are several other places of similar style along this road. There's no food here, so you'll have to walk a bit to eat.

★ The Theatre Villa
HOTEL $$

(☑ 085 442 9150; www.thetheatrevilla.com; Hat Bang Saphan Yai; r incl breakfast 1350-2100B; P ✳ ☞) Quiet even by Bang Saphan standards, this small hotel sits on a great piece of beach and is meticulously cared for. Rooms are bright and very comfortable and come in three varieties: hotel-like rooms at the back, more expensive bungalows in the middle and two sea-view rooms at the front. It's west of the main road.

🍴 Eating & Drinking

In Ban Krut, the restaurants along the beach road are pretty much all about seafood, though there are a few exceptions. Locals eat almost exclusively along the road into town, where there are a few regular restaurants, coffee shops and a mini night market (3pm to 9pm) next to Tesco-Lotus Express. Bang Saphan Yai has a few unexciting

foreigner-focused restaurants scattered amid the accommodation, though there's nothing truly local here.

There are bars in both towns. Ban Krut's cheapest beers are sold informally along the beach across from Siripong Guesthouse – a mix of locals and expats lounge here. Kasama's has a good liquor list.

Bang Saphan Yai has a few popular expat watering holes. Why Not Bar is on the beach and Blue Bar, with a pool table, is up almost at the highway junction. There's often live music at both.

Kasama's Pizza
ITALIAN $$

(☑ 081 139 0220; www.kasamapizza.com; Rte 1029, Hat Ban Krut; mains 50-355B; ☉ 10am-10pm, reduced hours in low season; P ☞) A friendly spot and one of the longest-running restaurants in Ban Krut, Kasama's has substantial sandwiches, all-day breakfasts, pizzas and real chocolate milkshakes. And it delivers, even to the beach. It's located off the access road, behind the 7-Eleven.

ℹ Information

For local information on the areas, check www.bankrutinfo.com and www.bangsaphanguide.com.

Bankrut Tour & Travel (☑ 081 736 3086; www.bankrut.co.th; Hat Ban Krut; ☉ 8am-8pm) This is a friendly and reliable, full-service agency inside Na Nicha Bankrut Resort, just before the beach. Staff arrange day trips, including snorkelling at Ko Thalu, and onward travel, including ferry tickets for the southern islands.

ℹ Getting There & Away

Both towns have train stations. All 11 trains from Bangkok's Hualamphong to the far south stop at **Bang Saphan Yai Train Station** (☑ 032 691552; Soi Bang Saphan) (69B to 1667B, five to seven hours) and seven of these also stop at **Ban Krut Train Station** (☑ 032 695 004). Most of these trains arrive deep into the night. There's also a 7.30am ordinary train from Bangkok's Thonburi station (67B to 316B, 7½ hours). You can also get to both by rail from Prachuap Khiri Khan (16B to 1355B, one hour), Chumphon (20B to 1406B, 1½ to two hours) and Hua Hin (33B to 1469B, two hours).

From Bangkok's southern terminal, buses go to **Bang Saphan Yai** (Soi Bang Saphan) (275B, six hours) about every hour or two between 7.30am and midnight, and first stop in **Ban Krut**. Heading north, these buses will stop in Prachuap Khiri Khan (90B, one hour) and Phetchaburi (193B, 3½ hours), but not Hua Hin. Both bus stops are just a short distance south of the train stations. For a small fee, you can get tickets through your resort or Bankrut Tour & Travel.

Minivans (Rte 3169) from Bang Saphan Yai depart from the highway in front of Sweet Home Bakery in the heart of town. They go to Prachuap Khiri Khan (100B, one hour, eight daily from 6.20am to 4.50pm) and Chumphon (80B, two hours, 8.45am). The Chumphon van normally doesn't pick up in Ban Krut, but Bankrut Tour & Travel (p518) can arrange it with the cost rising to 400B.

Other buses and minivans stop along the highway, about 10km west of both towns, rather than coming into town. Most buses that travel this route stop at Bang Saphan Yai, though few stop at Ban Krut and you risk waiting a long time if you try it there. In both cases, it's about a 100B motorcycle-taxi ride to the town, more to the beach.

There is no minivan service between Ban Krut and Bang Saphan Yai.

ⓘ Getting Around

All but some of the cheapest resorts will pick you up in town and send you back for free, but all charge for going out to the Phetkasem Hwy.

The beach at Bang Saphan Yai is 6km south of the town via Rte 3374 – you can't miss the turnoff as there's a mass of resort signs. Ban Krut is 1km to the beach, though most of the accommodation is spread out far from the junction. Moto-taxis from Bang Saphan Yai to the beach cost 100B; from Ban Krut it's 20B to 30B.

In Ban Krut, Siripong Guesthouse (p517) and Bankrut Tour & Travel (p518) rent motorcycles for 200B per day, as do several other nearby shops around the junction. Several shops at Bang Saphan Yai's beach also hire motorcycles for 250B to 350B. Another option is to hire them in town at **Tae's Restaurant** (☑ 087 919 2910; Soi Bang Saphan; 200-250B; ⊙2pm-2am), just down from the train station for 200B to 250B, though this is a very casual operation and it's recommended you call ahead.

Chumphon

☑ 077 / POP 33,500

A transit town funnelling travellers to and from Ko Tao or southwards to Ranong or Phuket, Chumphon (ชุมพร) is where the south of Thailand starts proper; Muslim headscarves are a common sight here.

While there's not a lot to do in town while you wait for your ferry, it's not an unpleasant place and the surrounding beaches are alternative sun and sand stops far off the backpacker bandwagon. Beautiful Hat Thung

Wua Laen (Fast Running Cow Beach), 15km northeast of town and full of traveller amenities, is the best known and during the week you'll have it mostly to yourself. On weekends it will be rocking.

◉ Sights

Chumphon National Museum MUSEUM
(พิพิธภัณฑสถานแห่งชาติชุมพร; ☑ 077 504105; 100B; ⊙9am-4pm Wed-Sun) It's not one of Thailand's biggest or best national museums, but the prehistoric pottery, axes and jewellery found in Chumphon Province will appeal to history buffs. There are also models of local house styles and photos from Typhoon Gay, which hit Chumphon in November 1989. Unfortunately, it's 3km north of the city centre and staff close early if it rains – best to call ahead before you make the trek.

Chumphon Fresh Market MARKET
(ตลาดสดชุมพร; Th Pracha Uthit; ⊙midnight-3pm) Chumphon's main fresh market spreads far and wide under a giant roof. It's the main source of meat, fruit and veggies for most of the city's restaurants. It's at its busiest very early in the morning.

★ Festivals & Events

Chumphon Marine Festival CULTURAL
(⊙Mar) Normally held in mid-March, this festival takes place at the seaside town of Paknam, 13km southeast of Chumphon city. There are four days of sea-related events, including boat trips, sand sculpture and underwater rubbish pick up.

Chumphon Traditional Boat Race CULTURAL
(⊙Oct) To mark the end of Buddhist Lent (Ork Phansaa), which usually occurs in October, traditional long-tail boats race each other on the Lang Suan River about 60km south of Chumphon. Unlike long-tail boat races everywhere else in Thailand, here the winner must have someone hang on the bow of the boat and snatch a flag.

🛏 Sleeping

As most people overnighting in Chumphon are backpackers, there's a lot of accommodation serving them. Th Tha Taphao is the local Th Khao San, with cheap older guesthouses. Some newer flashier hostels are found east of the train station along Th Krumluang Chumphon. If you prefer sea to

HUA HIN & THE UPPER GULF CHUMPHON

Chumphon

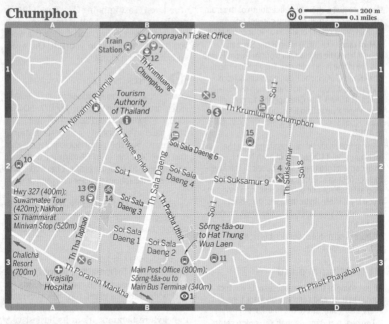

Chumphon

◎ Sights
1 Chumphon Fresh Market B3

🛏 Sleeping
2 Fame Guesthouse B2
3 Salsa Hostel C1

🍴 Eating
4 Kook Noy Kitchen C2
5 Night Market C1
6 Prikhorm A3

🍷 Drinking & Nightlife
7 Aeki's Bar B1
8 Farang Bar A2

ⓘ Information
9 Ocean Shopping Mall C1

ⓘ Transport
10 Bang Saphan Yai Minivan
Stop A2
11 Choke Anan Tour C3
12 KP Ferry Ticket and Services B1
13 Ranong Minivan Stop A2
14 San Tavee New Rest House B2
15 Surat Thani & Prachuap
Khiri Khan Minivan Stop C2

city, there's lodging up at **Hat Thung Wua Laen**, 15km northeast of town.

★ Villa Varich　　　　　　　　　HOTEL $
(☏ 081 543 0344; www.villavarich.com; 56/1 Mu 3, Th Poraminmanka Soi 24; incl breakfast r 700-920, ste 1600B; P ❄ 🛜) Only 4km from Chumphon, but deep in the countryside, Villa Varich is unlike any other Chumphon hotel. The large rooms, half sitting along the jungle-clad Tha Taphao River, are comfortable and attractive, and you'll wake to birdsong. Some balconies have hammocks. Tang and Khom are great hosts.

There's free use of bikes and kayaks, and motorcycles start at 200B. A túk-túk from the train station or bus station at Choke Anan Tour (p523), as well as car transfer from the airport, costs 200B. Booking ahead is recommended.

Salsa Hostel　　　　　　　　　HOSTEL $
(☏ 077 505005; www.salsachumphon.com; 25/42 Th Krumluang Chumphon; dm/d 250/650B; ❄ 🛜) East of the train station near the night market, this is one of the best addresses in Chumphon. It's clean, friendly, not too big and a reliable source of local info in excellent

English. The private rooms are some of the best in town, regardless of the price.

Fame Guesthouse GUESTHOUSE $
(☑077 571077; www.chumphon-kohtao.com; 188/20-21 Th Sala Daeng; r with shared/private bathroom 250/350B; 🛜) A *fa·ràng* depot, Fame does a little bit of everything, from providing clean basic rooms for people overnighting (or just resting during the day) to booking tickets and renting motorbikes. The attached restaurant is a key backpacker hang-out, and offers a wide range of Thai, Indian and Western food.

Chalicha Resort RESORT $$
(☑077 502888; www.chalicha.com; 185 Mu 9 Tumbon Takdad; r 550-1200B, ste 1500B; P❄🛜🏊) At this good-value guesthouse near Chumphon train station even the cheapest rooms are spacious. There are parking spots out front, a comfortable air-conditioned coffee shop and swimming pool, and bicycles are free to use. The only difference between the standard and slightly more expensive superior rooms are the latter have kettles and hairdryers.

Chumphon Cabana
Resort & Diving Centre HOTEL $$
(☑089 724 9319; www.chumphoncabanaresort. com; Hat Thung Wua Laen; r incl breakfast 1000-1500B; P❄🛜🏊) 🏖 Away from the road and on a great piece of beach, this is *the* place to stay at Hat Thung Wua Laen as long as you don't need full-on luxury. The rooms have verandas for lounging and, while an upgrade is in order, they're still plenty comfortable. They can arrange a private transfer from Chumphon for 350B.

They follow a few green practices including growing some of their own food for the Banana Cabana restaurant, which is worth a meal even if you aren't staying here.

✗ Eating & Drinking

Chumphon's main night market (Th Krumluang Chumphon; ⊙4pm-midnight) has a big variety of food options and good people-watching. There's more evening street food at the south end of Th Tha Taphao and south of the train station.

Farang Bar (☑077 501003; 69/36 Th Tha Taphao; beers from 80B, cocktails from 100B; ⊙1pm-midnight; 🛜) is one of the classic watering holes, but for something Thai, head around the corner to a strip of open-air bars and restaurants on Th Tawee Sinka Soi 1.

Aeki's Bar (☑089 185 5485; www.aekis-bar-aek siam-muaythai.business.site; Soi Rot Fai 1; beer from 65B, cocktails from 100B; ⊙3pm-late; 🛜) hosts many travellers waiting for their night train.

★**Kook Noy Kitchen** THAI $
(Th Suksamur; mains 40-400B; ⊙5pm-4am Mon-Sat; 🛜) Just a concrete floor, a corrugated roof and a chaotic kitchen turning out central and southern Thai dishes you know like *dôm yam* with free-range chicken and crab fried rice, plus many you probably don't, including fried ducks beak and river snails.

Pirates Terrace INTERNATIONAL $
(☑083 066 6772; www.piratesterrace.com; Hat Thung Wua Laen; mains 60-400B; ⊙7.30am-10pm; P🛜) Right at the centre of the beach, this is a popular spot for breakfast, a daytime coffee or a drink in the evening. The menu mixes Thai classics with pizza and pasta. They can also book tickets and rent motorbikes for 200B a day.

Prikhorm THAI $$
(32 Th Tha Taphao; mains 85-480B; ⊙11am-11pm; P🛜🚗) This wannabe fancy place has dishes from across the kingdom, from southern *gaang sôm* fish curry to northeastern mushroom *lâhp*, one of many vegetarian dishes.

ℹ Information

Immigration Office (☑077 630282; www. chumphonimmigration.go.th; 23/11 Mu 1 Tombon Kunkrating; ⊙8.30am-noon & 1-4.30pm Mon-Fri) Can do extensions of stays for tourists. It's next to the bus station.

Ocean Shopping Mall (Th Krumluang Chumphon) Has several banks open on weekends and early evenings on weekdays.

Tourism Authority of Thailand (TAT; ☑077 502 7756; tatchumphon@tat.or.th; 111/11-12 Th Tawee Sinka; ⊙8am-5pm) You can probably get all the information you need from your guesthouse, but if not, this office is helpful. And it gives out a good free map of Chumphon.

Virajsilp Hospital (☑077 542555; www. virajsilp.com; Th Poramin Mankha) Privately owned; handles emergencies.

ℹ Getting There & Away

For a transit hub, Chumphon is surprisingly unconsolidated – there's no single bus station and the ferry pier for boats to Ko Tao, Ko Pha-Ngan and Ko Samui are some distance from town. But travel agencies and guesthouses can point you to the right place, and sell tickets for all ferries, flights and many buses.

AIR

Chumphon's airport is nearly 40km from the centre of town. Nok Air has one flight to Bangkok's Don Mueang Airport in the early morning

CHUMPHON TRANSPORT CONNECTIONS

DESTINATION	BOAT	BUS	MINIVAN	TRAIN
Bang Saphan Yai			80B, 2hr, 2pm, 3.30pm	20-1406B, 1½-2hr, 12 daily
Bangkok Hualamphong				82-2224B, 6½-8hr, 11 daily
Bangkok Southern Bus Terminal		358B, 8hr, 14 daily 7.50am-10pm		
Bangkok Thonburi				80-383B, 9½hr, 7.01am
Chiang Mai		235B, 18hr, 6pm		
Hat Yai		355B, 7hr, 8 daily 7am-midnight		79-2205B, 8-10½hr, 7 daily
Hua Hin				49-2006B, 4-5hr, 12 daily
Ko Pha-Ngan (Lomprayah)	1000B, 3¼-3¾hr, 7am, 1pm			
Ko Pha-Ngan (Songserm)	900B, 4½hr, 7am			
Ko Samui (Lomprayah)	1100B, 3¾-4¼hr, 7am, 1pm			
Ko Samui (Songserm)	1000B, 6¼hr, 7am			
Ko Tao (car ferry)	400B, 6hr, 10.30pm or 11pm Mon-Sat			
Ko Tao (Lomprayah)	600B, 1¾hr, 7am, 1pm			
Ko Tao (Songserm)	500B, 2¾hr, 7am			
Ko Tao (Sunday night fishing boat)	450B, 6hr, 10pm Sun			
Nakhon Si Thammarat			300B, 5½hr, every 2hr 8am-2pm	
Phetchaburi		358B, 6hr, 14 daily 7.50am-10pm		58-2102B, 5½-6½hr, 12 daily
Phuket		370-699B, 6-7hr, 5 daily 5.30-11.50am		
Prachuap Khiri Khan		220B, 4hr, hourly 7am-10pm	229B, 3hr, every 45min 6.45am-5.30pm	34-1473B, 2½-3hr, 11 daily
Ranong		110B, 2½hr, 5 daily	350-400B, 2½hr, hourly 7am-6pm	
Surat Thani		166B, 3hr, 11 daily	699B, 3½hr, hourly, 7am-3pm	34-1933B, 2-3hr, 13 daily

and another in the late afternoon, AirAsia also has a morning flight. A ride on the airport shuttle can be organised by most lodgings for 150B per person.

BOAT

There are essentially two options for getting to Ko Tao. **Lomprayah** (📞 city 081 956 5644, pier 077 558214; www.lomprayah.com; Th Krumluang Chumphon; ⊙ 4am-6pm) and **Songserm** (📞 077 506205; www.songserm.com; Pak Nam) have modern ferries sailing during the day. Lomprayah is the best and most popular; Songserm has a reputation for being poorly organised and not providing promised transfers on its bus-boat combo tickets (though this isn't an issue when beginning in Chumphon). These boats also serve Ko Pha-Ngan and Ko Samui.

The other option is to take one of the night boats operated by a variety of companies. From Monday to Saturday there are car ferries that have air-conditioned rooms with beds – essentially a dorm on the sea – while Sunday is a regular wooden fishing boat with mattresses on the floor and only fans, no air-con. **KP Ferry Ticket and Services** (📞 094 221 5896; www. chumphon-nightboat.com; ⊙ 3am-9pm), opposite the train station, can book night boat tickets or transfers to nearby places like Hat Thung Wua Laen.

Boats leave from different piers and transfer costs 50B to 100B. Sometimes tickets are sold that include the transfer, sometimes not – be sure you have a ticket for both the bus and the boat.

BUS

Chumphon's main **bus station** (📞 077 576796; Rte 41) is on the highway, an inconvenient 12km from Chumphon. It's not used much – many ticket offices are unstaffed for much of the day – since the main bus companies have their own stops in town.

Choke Anan Tour (📞 077 511480; www. chokeanantour.com; off Soi 1, Th Pracha Uthit; ⊙ 4.30am-9pm), near the main market, has the most buses to Bangkok (via Phetchaburi and Prachuap Khiri Khan) and Phuket (via Ranong) plus one to Surat Thani. **Minivans to Ranong** (Th Tha Taphao) leave from Th Tha Taphao, while **minivans to Surat Thani and Prachuap Khiri Khan** (Th Krumluang Chumphon) leave

from Chumphon Night Bazaar, 500m down Th Krumluang Chumphon from the train station near Salsa Hostel (p520).

Other services are along Th Nawamin Ruamjai, south of the train station. **Suwannatee Tour** (📞 077 504901; Th Nawamin Ruamjai) is across the river, about 1km away, and runs five buses to Bangkok (including one cheap 2nd-class bus), plus **minivans to Nakhon Si Thammarat** (📞 077 506326; Th Nawamin Ruamjai). **Minivans to Bang Saphan Yai** (Th Nawamin Ruamjai) are at the covered minivan stop that has a yellow sign, 400m south of the **petrol station** (Th Tawee Sinka).

For the few services that do use the station, like buses to Chiang Mai, you can buy tickets at guesthouses and travel agencies. Note that there's no scheduled direct service to Hua Hin; you'll need to change at Prachuap Khiri Khan.

TRAIN

There are frequent services between Bangkok and the far south stopping in **Chumphon** (Th Krumluang Chumphon). Make reservations as far in advance as possible. Second-class sleepers are often available day of departure, but 1st-class rarely is.

ℹ️ Getting Around

Motorcycle taxis (20B to 30B per trip) are seemingly everywhere in town while the more expensive four-wheeled túk-túk are much less common, though there are always some parked at the train station.

Motorcycles can be rented through many guesthouses for 200B to 300B per day. Besides motorcycles, **San Tavee New Rest Home** (📞 089 011 1749; Th Tha Taphao 4; bikes/motorcycles 150/250B) also hires bicycles for 150B.

Yellow sŏrng·tăa·ou (passenger pickup trucks) to Hat Thung Wua Laen (30B, 30 minutes, frequent 5.30am to 6pm) leave from the **Chumphon Fresh Market** (Th Pracha Uthit), then follow Th Sala Daeng north. Little white sŏrng·tăa·ou to the main bus station and immigration (25B, 30 to 45 minutes, frequent 7am to 5pm) depart from **Th Phinit Khadi** next to the City Pillar Shrine. A túk-túk to the bus station will cost upwards of 300B from the city centre. There's also an airport shuttle (150B per person); pick-up can be organised by your guesthouse.

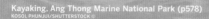

Ko Samui & the Lower Gulf

The Lower Gulf features Thailand's ultimate island trifecta: Ko Samui, Ko Pha-Ngan and Ko Tao, a family of spectacular islands luring millions of tourists every year with their powder-soft sands and emerald waters. Ko Samui is the oldest sibling who made it big, where high-class resorts operate with Swiss efficiency. Ko Pha-Ngan is the slacker middle child with tangled dreadlocks and a penchant for all-night parties. Meanwhile, Ko Tao is the outdoorsy, fun-loving kid with spirit and energy – specialising in world-class diving and snorkelling.

The mainland coast sees few foreign visitors and is far more authentic. Pink dolphins, deserted beaches and waterfalls await in sleepy Ao Khanom, while Thai Muslim heritage can be found in Singha Nakhon and Pattani. Taste the southern flavours of beach-strolling Songkhla and experience the hustle and bustle of real Thai cities in Nakhon Si Thammarat and Surat Thani.

INCLUDES

Ko Samui & the Lower Gulf Highlights

1 Ko Tao (p564) Finding Nemo in this technicolour dive kingdom.

2 Ang Thong Marine National Park (p578) Paddling to hidden bleach-blonde beaches.

3 Ko Pha-Ngan (p546) Stringing up a cotton hammock and toeing the tide along a secluded beach on the east coast.

4 Singha Nakhon (p587) Pulling back jungle vines and thick foliage in search of the forgotten Sultanate of Singora.

5 Ko Samui (p528) Enjoying five-star international cuisine and sipping fancy sunset cocktails.

6 Full Moon Party (p559) Joining the

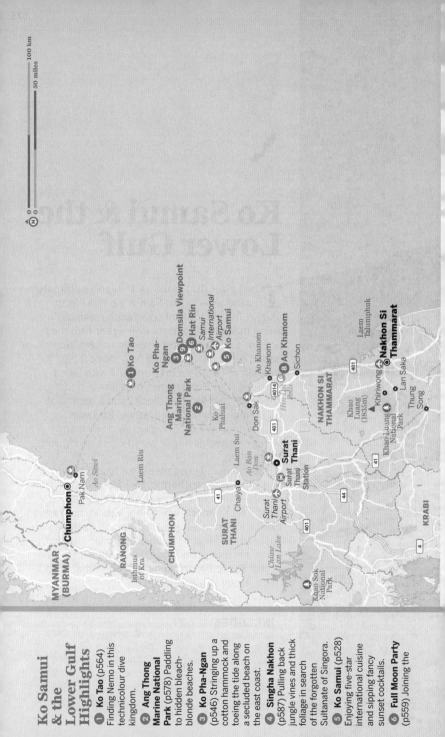

MYANMAR (BURMA)   Chumphon

Isthmus of Kra

RANONG

Pak Nam

Ao Sawi

Laem Riu

CHUMPHON

Chaiya

Laem Sui

Ao Ban Dom

Surat Thani Airport

SURAT THANI

Surat Thani

Surat Thani Station

Chiew Lam Lake

Khao Sok National Park

KRABI

Ko Tao

Ko Pha-Ngan

Ang Thong Marine National Park

Ko Phaluai

Don Sak

Ao Khanom

Khanom

Sichon

Domsila Viewpoint

Hat Rin

Samui International Airport

Ko Samui

Ao Khanom

NAKHON SI THAMMARAT

Hin Lat Falls

Khao Luang (1835m)

Khao Luang National Park

Khiriwong

Thung Song

Lan Saka

Laem Talumphuk

Nakhon Si Thammarat

50 miles
100 km

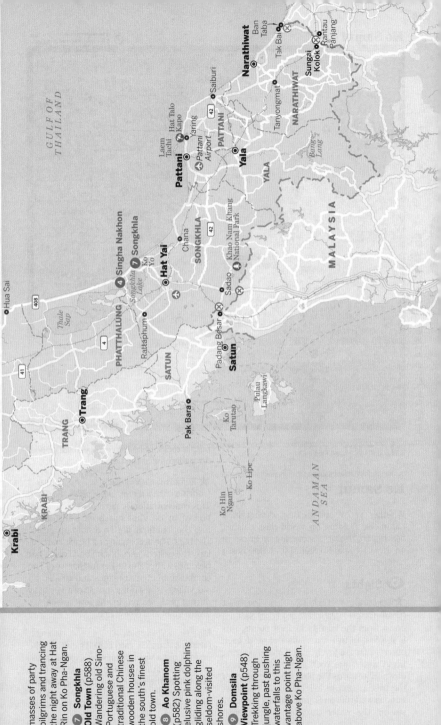

masses of party
pilgrims and trancing
the night away at Hat
Rin on Ko Pha-Ngan.

7 **Songkhla
Old Town** (p588)
Wandering old Sino-
Portuguese and
traditional Chinese
wooden houses in
the south's finest
old town.

8 **Ao Khanom**
(p582) Spotting
elusive pink dolphins
gliding along the
seldom-visited
shores.

9 **Domsila
Viewpoint** (p548)
Trekking through
jungle, past gushing
waterfalls to this
vantage point high
above Ko Pha-Ngan.

GULF OF
THAILAND

ANDAMAN
SEA

MALAYSIA

Krabi

KRABI

Hua Sai

Trang

TRANG

41

408

4

Thale
Sap

PHATTHALUNG

Rattaphum

Pak Bara

Ko
Tarutao

Ko Hin
Ngam

Ko Lipe

Pulau
Langkawi

SATUN

Satun

Padang Besar

Songkhla
Lake

Singha Nakhon **4**

Songkhla **7**

Ko
Yo

Hat Yai 🛈

Chana

SONGKHLA

42

Sadao

Khao Nam Khang
National Park **4**

Laem
Tachi

Hat Thalo

Pattani 🛈

Yaring

Kapo

Pattani
Airport ✈

PATTANI

Pattani

Yala

YALA

Bang
Lang

Saiburi

42

Tanyongmat

Tak Bai

Ban
Taba

Narathiwat 🛈

NARATHIWAT

Tanyongmat

Sungai
Kolok ✕

Rantau
Panjang

Ko Samui

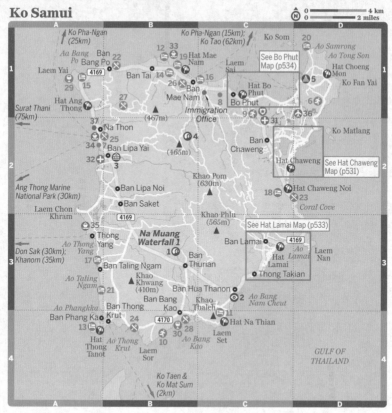

Ko Samui

GULF ISLANDS

Ko Samui

POP 62,500

Whether you're sun-seeking, dozing in a hammock, feasting on world-class cuisine, beach partying or discovering wellness in an exclusive spa, Ko Samui (เกาะสมุย) has it covered.

⊙ Sights

★ Na Muang Waterfall 1   WATERFALL

(น้ำตกหน้าเมือง 1; Map p528; P) **FREE** Spilling down from the island's highest points, this is the first of two waterfalls – close to each other – that are lovely in full spate, pouring frigid water into rock pools as they crash downhill towards the blue sea. The larger of the two, at 18m in height, is the most famous waterfall on Samui. During the rainy season, the water cascades over ethereal purple rocks, to land in a superb, large pool for swimming at the base.

★ Fisherman's Village   VILLAGE

(หมู่บ้านชาวประมงบ่อผุด; Map p534; Bo Phut) This concentration of narrow Chinese shophouses in Bo Phut has been transformed into cool boutique hotels, restaurants, cafes and bars. The accompanying beach, particularly the eastern part, is slim and coarse but becomes whiter and lusher further west. The combination of pretty sands and gussied-up old village is a winner, but it can get busy during peak season. In the low season, it's lovely, quiet and elbow free.

Mae Nam Viewpoint   VIEWPOINT

(จุดชมวิว; Map p528; entry 50B) It's quite a hike on foot, but a scooter can whisk you up most of the way to this viewpoint among the trees just before the **Tan Rua waterfall** (น้ำตกตันเรือ; Map p528). The knockout views of the blue gulf reach all the way to Ko Pha-ngan.

Ko Samui

KO SAMUI & THE LOWER GULF KO SAMUI

Those with scooters can continue on past the switchbacks uphill on the road to Na Thon for even better views, though signs advise to rest brakes on the way down, to avoid overheating.

Wat Plai Laem　　　　BUDDHIST TEMPLE
(วัดปลายแหลม; Map p528; off Chaweng Choengmon Rd; ⊙ daylight hrs) **FREE** The most arresting statue on the island is the thousand-arm Guanyin (Kwan Im), the Buddhist bodhisattva of compassion, displayed with 18 arms in a fan arrangement at this temple completed around 2004. Perched on an island in a lake, the colourful statue rises up next to a temple hall also constructed above the water. To the north is a statue of the jovial Maitreya Buddha (the Buddha to come). The setting is highly picturesque and photogenic.

Ban Hua Thanon　　　　AREA
(บ้านหัวถนน; Map p528; Ban Hua Thanon) This vibrant little village is home to Ko Samui's historic Muslim community, where the headscarf and *pâh sîn* (male sarong) count peaks. You get a genuine glimpse of local life, especially after midday on a Friday, when locals arrive dressed in their colourful 'Friday best' to pray in a huge congregation at the beautiful village mosque. The surrounding alleys are a hive of activity with locals socialising as the waft of delicious halal street food fills the air.

Ko Samui Central Mosque　　　　MOSQUE
(มัสยิดกูรูอีียะห์ซาน; Map p528; Ban Hua Thanon; ⊙ daylight hrs) This photogenic green and gold, domed mosque, built in the Mughal style, sits in the heart of Ko Samui's historic Muslim village. Arrive outside of prayer

KO SAMUI'S BEACHES

Samui is just about small enough to beach-hop without too much difficulty and you'll encounter considerable variety along its sandy lengths. Chaweng is the longest strip, with many different moods, from its rocky and rather subdued north to a crowded and animated central area and the quieter Chaweng Noi. Hat Lamai sees the best swimming in the middle of its beach, but down in the south it's picturesquely studded with huge boulders. Though seas are calmer from July to October, winds from the northeast rake the sands, causing swells from December to April, while rip tides can make swimming in Chaweng and Lamai dangerous, even for strong swimmers.

Mae Nam beach has the best swimming beach on the north coast. On the west coast, the beaches at Taling Ngam and Lipa Noi are pleasant swimming choices. Bo Phut has rather coarse sand and the water is murkier, while in the northeast corner of the island, Ao Thong Sai is lovely. For a total escape, head to Ao Phang Ka in the southwest.

times, enter beneath the five-domed gate and head for the large carpeted hall, where a wide, pastel green *mehrab* (Imam's niche) points towards Mecca (Saudi Arabia). Two Corinthian-style pillars and Arabic inscriptions of 'Allah' and 'Muhammad' decorate the *mehrab*, which houses the mosque's most beautiful feature, a carved dark-wood *mimbar* (pulpit). Visitors must dress modestly. No shorts or revealing clothes, and women should wear a headscarf.

Orthodox Church of
the Ascension   CHURCH
(โบสถ์ออร์โธดอกซ์แห่งสวรรค์; Map p533; ☑081
423 1041; www.churchsamui.com; off Rte 4169;
⊙9am-8pm; P) FREE Ridiculously photogenic, this beautiful, baby blue, Russian orthodox church with gold onion domes (similar to the nearby mosque) sits halfway up a residential hill. Inside the small central hall are a number of intriguing features including a gilded wood stand with Thai motifs for resting the bible, a stunning two-tiered gold chandelier, several bibles with beautiful gilded metal covers and a series of painted frescoes on the walls including one of Christ above the stairwell at the entrance.

Visitors should observe the same rules of modesty as when visiting a temple or mosque.

Magic Alambic Rum Distillery   DISTILLERY
(Map p528; ☑080 092 0035; Ban Bang Kao; tasting shots 100B; ⊙9am-8pm) The only rum distillery in Thailand produces Caribbean agricole-style spirits (distilled from fresh, fermented sugarcane juice) in a variety of all-natural flavours, including a delectable coconut rum obtained from soaking coconut meat in the rum for several months. There's

a video about the production process, a tasting area, an excellent French-Thai restaurant and a shop in beautiful palm-shaded surrounds.

Coconut Museum   MUSEUM
(บ้านมะพร้าว; Map p528; ☑077 421211; www.
samuirenong.com; Na Thon; ⊙12.30-4.30pm Mon-
Sat) FREE This tiny museum is a nod to Ko Samui's history as one of Thailand's premiere coconut supplying islands. As well as the chance to become educated on Samui's coconut heritage, the centre offers tips on how to climb a coconut tree and hosts coconut cooking (350B) and coconut-oil-making (790B) classes. The on-site store also sells a great series of products made by locals using coconuts grown on the island.

🏃 Activities
Adventure Activities

★ 100 Degrees East   DIVING
(Map p534; ☑077 423936; www.100degreeseast.
com; Hat Bang Rak; ⊙9am-6.30pm Dec-Oct) Highly professional and recommended, with a dedicated team, for excellent diving and snorkelling expeditions to Ang Thong Marine National Park, Ko Tao, Sail Rock and other sites.

Blue Stars   KAYAKING
(Map p531; ☑081 894 5032; www.bluestars.info; 82/33 Mu 2, Chaweng Lake Rd; tours adult/child 2600/1700B; ⊙10.30am-9pm) There are many choices for snorkelling and kayak tours to Ang Thong Marine National Park all over Ko Samui, but Blue Stars has the best reputation and the coolest boat in Chaweng. They also have a super friendly team that will do their utmost to give you the best deal.

Hat Chaweng

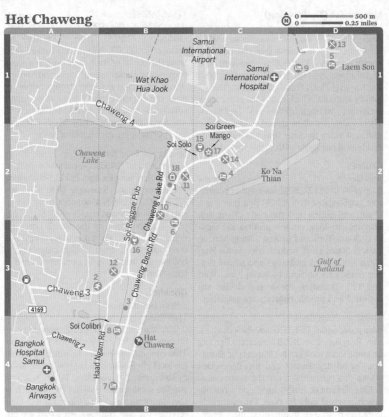

Hat Chaweng

Kiteboarding Asia WATER SPORTS
(Map p528; ☎ 083 643 1627; www.kiteboarding
asia.com; 310/10 Mu 3, Na Thon; 1-/3-day course
4000/11,000B; ⊙ 9am-6pm Apr-Oct) This professional outfit will get you kitesurfing on
flat shallow water within no time at all. The
Na Thon location on the west side is for
April to October winds and there's another
in Hua Thanon in the southeast of the island
for November to March gusts.

Moo·ay Tai (Thai Boxing)

Lamai Muay Thai Camp
MARTIAL ARTS

(Map p533; ☑ 087 082 6970; www.lamaimuaythai camp.com; 82/2 Mu 3, Lamai Beach Rd; day/week training sessions 300/1500B; ⊙ 7am-7pm) The island's best *moo·ay tai* (Thai boxing, also spelt *muay Thai*) training gym (for the seriously serious), which caters for every level, including wet-behind-the-ears beginners. There's also a well-equipped gym for those that just want to come and work out, plus residential packages with meals included.

Cruises

Red Baron
CRUISE

(Map p534; ☑ 083 172 8792; www.redbaron-samui. com; Hat Bang Rak; from 2500B) Red Baron is a traditional sailing junk moored at Bang Rak offering day-long cruises around Ko Samui (9.30am Tue) and to Ang Thong Marine Park (8.30am Thu), brunch trips to Ko Pha-Ngan (10am Wed and Sun) and sunset dinner cruises to Ko Som (4.30pm Mon, Wed and Fri). Transfers, meals and drinks are included and private charters are available.

Chantara Junk Boat
CRUISE

(Map p534; ☑ 087 064 3126; www.junk-chantara. com; Bang Rak; from 3100B per person) Set sail on traditional junk boats Chantara or Simatara, for all day, sunset and private cruises where you can while away the hours snorkelling, fishing or simply laying on a remote beach reached only by boat. Prices include transfers from your hotel, soft drinks, lunch, snacks and the necessary leisure equipment.

Health & Wellness

Samahita Retreat
YOGA

(Map p528; ☑ 077 920090; www.samahitaretreat. com; Laem Sor Beach; ⊙ 7am-9pm) Secreted away along the southern shores, Samahita Retreat has state-of-the-art facilities and a dedicated team of trainers for the growing band of therapeutic holidaymakers, wellness seekers and serious detoxers. Accommodation is in a comfy apartment block up the street, while yoga studios, wellness centres and a health-food restaurant sit calmly along the shore.

Absolute Sanctuary
SPA

(Map p528; ☑ 077 601190; www.absolutesanc tuary.com; Choeng Mon) This award winning sanctuary offers detox, spa, yoga, Pilates, fasting, lifestyle and nutrition packages, as well as residential retreats, all in an alluring Moroccan-inspired setting that is a picture of serenity.

Tamarind Springs
MASSAGE

(Map p533; ☑ 085 926 4626; www.tamarind springs.com; 205/7 Th Takian, off Rte 4169; spa packages from 1500B; ⊙ 9am-8pm) Tucked away from the bustle of the beach, within a silent coconut-palm plantation, Tamarind's collection of villas and massage studios appear to have organically evolved from their jungle surrounds: some have granite boulders built into walls and floors, while others offer private ponds or creative outdoor baths.

Spa at the Four Seasons
SPA

(Map p528; ☑ 077 243000; www.fourseasons.com/ kohsamui/spa; Bang Po; from 2900B; ⊙ 9am-9pm) The luxury Four Seasons (Map p528; villa 22,000-160,000B; P ❋ ☎ ☀) on a rocky peninsula in the northwest corner of Ko Samui has one of the best spas on the island. There is a delightful range of therapies to pamper mind, body and soul, from chakra-balancing to body-wraps and coconut pedicures. Emerge transformed.

Cooking

Samui Institute of Thai Culinary Arts
COOKING

(SITCA; Map p531; ☑ 077 413172; www.sitca.com; Chaweng Beach Rd; courses 1850B) These daily Thai cooking lessons are taught by passionate local chefs who indulge you in the history and heritage of each dish before teaching you the subtleties of cooking curries such as the *Massaman* and *Chu Chee*. Daily 3-hour sessions begin at 11am and 4pm and you can even bring a friend along to eat the finished meal for 250B.

Language Courses

Mind Your Language
LANGUAGE

(Map p528; ☑ 077 962088; www.mindyourlanguage thailand.com; 142/7 Mu 1, Bo Phut) With packages starting from 7900B (15 lessons), this accessible and professional language school in Bo Phut is an excellent choice to begin your journey to speaking fluent Thai. Private tuition starts from 700B per hour.

Koh Samui Tutor & Vocational School
LANGUAGE

(KSTVS; Map p528; ☑ 077 248228, 086 279 1617; www.kstvs.com; Rte 4169) This school offers Thai language classes and courses that come with an education visa that will prolong your stay on Ko Samui. If you want to really immerse yourself in Thai language, check out the detailed website. Classes start from 200B per hour and 600B for a private class.

Hat Lamai

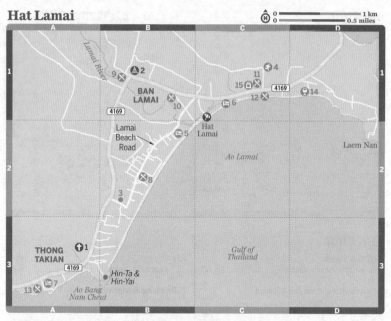

Hat Lamai

◎ Sights
1 Orthodox Church of the Ascension A3
2 Wat Lamai B1

☉ Activities, Courses & Tours
3 Lamai Muay Thai Camp B2
4 Tamarind Springs C1

⬚ Sleeping
5 Amarina Residence B2
6 New Hut C1
7 Rocky's Resort A3
Samui Jasmine Resort .... (see 5)

⊗ Eating
8 Kangaroo B2
9 La Fabrique B1
10 Lamai Day Market B1
11 Pad Thai C1
12 Radiance C1
13 The Dining Room A3

⊕ Drinking & Nightlife
14 Beach Republic D1
Lava Lounge .... (see 8)

⬚ Shopping
15 Island Books C1

Volunteering

**Samui Dog &
Cat Rescue Centre** VOLUNTEERING
(Map p531; ☎081 893 9443, 077 413490; www.
samuidog.org; Soi 3, Chaweng Beach Rd; ⊙9am-
6pm) This organisation has done wonders
to help keep the island's dog population in
check by spaying, neutering and vaccinat-
ing (rabies) many of them. However they
always need donations of time and money,
so animal lovers should contact the centre
and volunteer at their kennel/clinic in Ban
Taling Ngam (not the smaller Hat Chaweng
branch). Check the website for directions.

🛏 Sleeping

🛏 Hat Chaweng

Busy, throbbing, commercial Chaweng is
packed with accommodation, from cheap
backpacker spots to futuristic villas with
swimming pools – often right across the
street from each other. There's little charm,
though: the northern half of the beach is the
biggest party zone and nearby resorts are in
ear-shot of Ark Bar (p541) at the centre of it
all. If you're hoping for early nights, pick a
resort to the south or bring earplugs.

Bo Phut

Bo Phut

Samui Hostel HOSTEL $
(Map p531; ☑ 089 874 3737; Suan Uthit Rd; dm 200-300B, d 850B; ❅@✆) It doesn't look like much from the front, but this neat, tidy, friendly and popular place is very central, with clean fan and air-con dorm rooms and doubles on the nonbeach side of Chaweng Beach Rd. Service is a cut above the rest and there's a sitting room at the front with wooden tables for lounging and chatting.

Pott Guesthouse GUESTHOUSE $
(Map p531; ☑ 084 184 3084; Suan Uthit Rd; r with fan/air-con 300/600B; ❅✆) The big, bright cement rooms all with attached hot-water bathrooms and balcony in this nondescript apartment block are a steal. The Pott's staff is super friendly and helpful and the

location is wonderfully central, making this a great backpacker or solo traveller's choice. Reception is at the adjacent unnamed restaurant also on the main drag.

★ **Jungle Club** BUNGALOW $$
(Map p528; ☑ 081 891 8263; www.jungleclubsamui. com; bungalow 1550-2100B, house 2400-6200B, ste 4600-6500B, villa 4400-11,500B; ℗❅@✆☒) The perilous drive up the steep hill is totally worth it for the incredible views at this popular sleeping choice, which also attracts a large crowd for its excellent restaurant and bar. A relaxed back-to-nature vibe, guests can be found chilling around the stunning horizon pool or catnapping under canopied roofs of an open-air *săh·lah* (hall, often spelt as *sala*).

Ark Bar Beach Resort
RESORT $$

(Map p531; ☑ 077 961333; www.ark-bar.com; Chaweng Beach Rd; d 1530-2520B; ⓟ ❋ ⓡ ⌘) You'll find every type of party animal staying at the clean and well-tended accommodation linked to the popular beach facing Ark Bar (p541). Contemporary, brightly painted rooms with balconies are all within staggering distance of the bar that pumps out music all day and long into the night, so be warned.

Tango Beach Resort
RESORT $$

(Map p531; ☑ 077 300451; www.tangosamui.com; 119 Mu 2, Chaweng Beach Rd; d 1000-1400B, ste 2000-3400B; ❋ ⓡ ⌘) The 2018 renovations have done wonders for the Tango, where a colourful, light lobby gives way to a string of bungalows arranged around a small pool framed by dark wood decking. Close to a busy stretch of beach, with friendly staff and fresh rooms in a modern-Thai style, this is a good-value choice.

Baan Haad Ngam Boutique Resort & Villas
RESORT $$

(Map p531; ☑ 077 332950-7; www.baanhaadngam. com; Chaweng Beach Rd; d 2500-8100B, villa 3500-4500B; ⓟ ❋ @ ⓡ ⌘) Modern and stylish, with a large variety of rooms and villas developed around a landscaped botanical garden where mini waterfalls and streams lead to a small infinity pool overlooking the aqua sea. Located close to the Chaweng action, this is an excellent quiet, private retreat after a night out on the strip.

★ Library
RESORT $$$

(Map p531; ☑ 077 422767; www.thelibrarysamui. comth; 14/1 Mu 2, Chaweng Beach Rd; studios 11,000-13,500B, ste 12,500-29,000B, villas 26,000-63,000B; ⓟ ❋ @ ⓡ ⌘) Rooms are called 'pages' and there is a beautiful on-site library at this boutique resort created by book lovers. The entire complex is a sleek, white mirage accented with black trimmings, slatted curtains and monochromatic wall art set around a huge rectangular pool. This minimalist, modern look is carried into the rooms, which feel light and spacious.

🛏 Hat Lamai & the Southeast

The central, powdery white area of Hat Lamai is packed with sunburned souls lounging on beach chairs, and most of the main resorts are centred around here. Head to the grainier northern or southern extremities and things get much quieter and cheaper.

Head further south and as well as hidden luxury resorts, there are tons of accommodation options with a more local feel, and again prices are cheaper, but your own transport becomes increasingly essential for getting about.

Ananas Samui Hostel
HOSTEL $

(Map p528; ☑ 081 567 6650; www.ananas hostels.com; off Laem Set; dm/tw/tr/bungalow 190/590/790/1200B; ⓟ ❋ ⓡ ⌘) This charming little hostel, set against a jungle-covered mountain backdrop, is run by an extremely sweet elderly lady, and is excellent value for those with their own transport, as it is quite far from any of the main roads and village centres. It's worth considering – given these prices you'll have change to rent a scooter.

New Hut
BUNGALOW $

(Map p533; ☑ 077 230437; www.newhutbungalow. com; Lamai North; huts 300-800B; ❋ ⓡ) Colourful, basic A-frame huts sit right on the beach looking out to the azure waters of the gulf. With a lively restaurant and friendly staff, this has one of the simplest and happiest backpacker vibes in Lamai. The cheaper ones only have fans and shared bathrooms, but when your door opens to these views you probably won't mind.

Amarina Residence
HOTEL $$

(Map p533; ☑ 077 418073; www.amarinaresidence. com; Lamai; studios/d1500/2000B; ❋ ⓡ ⌘) A two-minute walk to the beach, this excellent-value small hotel has two storeys of big, tastefully furnished, tiled rooms encircling the lobby and an incongruous dipping pool.

★ Rocky's Resort
RESORT $$$

(Map p533; ☑ 077 332888; www.rockyresort.com; off Rte 4169; d 3000-5450B, ste 4220-9275B, villas 10,450-15,400B; ⓟ ❋ ⓡ ⌘) With a supremely calm reception area and two swimming pools, Rocky's effortlessly finds the right balance between upmarket ambience and unpretentious, sociable vibe. Ocean views abound, and each room (some with pool) has been furnished with beautiful Thai-inspired furniture that seamlessly incorporates a modern twist. During quieter months prices are a steal.

Samui Jasmine Resort
RESORT $$$

(Map p533; ☑ 077 232446; www.samuijasmine resort.com; 131/8 Mu 3, Lamai; d 3800-4085B, villa 4560B; ⓟ ❋ ⓡ ⌘) Right in the middle of Hat Lamai, the traditionally decorated Samui Jasmine is great value. Go for the

WORTH A TRIP

ISLAND ESCAPES

To experience the castaway life, head for the islands offshore from Ko Samui. You'll flee the crowded east coast by bouncing over the waves on a long-tail fishing boat to Ko Taen (also spelled Ko Tan) and Ko Mat Sum, two sparsely populated islands accessible from the village and bay of Thong Krut on the southwest shore.

The larger of the two islands at 7.5 sq km, Ko Taen has some very good snorkelling and a couple of guesthouses, including Koh Tan Village Bungalows on the main beach, as well as several restaurants. Ko Mat Sum is a much smaller and far less inhabited island, a kilometre or so east of Ko Taen, with a simple guesthouse and a bar.

You'll see signs in Thong Krut advertising boats, or pop into one of the guesthouses or beachfront restaurants – such as Hemingway's on the Beach (p541) – and ask. Trips usually last four to five hours and cost between 1500B and 2500B for up to five people..

lower-priced rooms – most have excellent views of the ocean and the crystal-coloured lap pool. Extremely family friendly, there is a children's pool as well as babysitting and crèche services.

🛏️

BO PHUT & **THE NORTHEAST**

Luxury and boutique resorts line either side of Fisherman's Village and several midrange options can be found along the busy central strip. Aside from the Us hostel there are almost no budget options in this area, so penny-pinchers will have to look further afield or stay in solo travellers' haven, Chaweng. Popular with families, accommodation gets snapped up quickly in Bo Phut during peak season so book in advance.

⭐ **Us Hostel** HOSTEL $

(Map p534; ☑ 098 696 6358; www.ushostel-samui.business.site; off Rte 4169; dm/d 250/800B; P ✳ 🛜 ✖️) Laid-back Us Hostel is a superb backpacker option. A large swimming pool sits surrounded by a series of converted shipping containers that have been stylishly stacked to create a cool, modern hostel with a large open lobby, where excellent coffee and Thai food is served. Rooms are clean and spacious, and the staff are knowledgeable and super friendly.

Eden BUNGALOW $$

(Map p534; ☑077 427645; www.edenbungalows. com; Fisherman's Village; d/bungalow 1500/1900B; ✳🛜✖️) A short walk from the beach, the 10 bungalows and five rooms here are all tucked away in a lovely tangle of garden with a small pool at its centre. Cheaper options are rather shabby but an upgrade gets you a stylish suite with yellow walls and natural wood furniture; for families, there's a 100-sq-m apartment with kitchenette too.

Secret Garden Beach Resort BUNGALOW $$

(Map p534; ☑077 332661; www.secretgarden samui.com; Beach Rd; tw 1800B, bungalow 2100-4360B; ✳🛜✖️) This Dutch-owned establishment has an excellent beach restaurant and bar. Fresh, well-equipped bungalows sit in the eponymous garden and around the pool. There's live music on Sundays when locals, expats and tourists come to chill, but it's fairly subdued the rest of the time.

Hacienda GUESTHOUSE $$

(Map p534; ☑077 960827; www.samui-hacienda. com; Fisherman's Village; d 1860-2350B; ste 3160B; P ✳ 🛜 ✖️) Polished terracotta and rounded archways create a Spanish atmosphere and similar decor filters into the adorable rooms, which sport touches including pebbled bathroom walls and translucent bamboo lamps. Hacienda Suites, the overflow property a few doors along, has smaller, cheaper rooms that are mostly windowless, but still clean and comfortable. The tiny rooftop pool has gorgeous ocean views.

⭐ **Six Senses Samui** RESORT $$$

(Map p528; ☑077 245678; www.sixsenses.com/ resorts/samui; Samrong; villa 13,830-32,600B; P ✳ @ 🛜 ✖️) This hidden bamboo paradise is worth the splurge. Set on 8 hectares along a rugged promontory, Six Senses strikes the perfect balance between opulence and rustic charm. Most of the 66 villas have stunning concrete plunge pools and offer magnificent views of the silent bay below. There's also a world-class spa and two first-class restaurants on-site.

Zazen RESORT $$$

(Map p534; ☑077 425085; www.samuizazen.com; Bo Phut; bungalow 3850-9450B, villa 5100-7290B; P ✳ @ 🛜 ✖️) Welcome to one of the bou- tique-iest boutique resorts on Samui – every inch of this charming getaway has been thoughtfully and creatively designed. Asian minimalism meets modern rococo, with a generous smattering of good taste and handsome looks, as guests relax poolside or on loungers along the very best stretch of the beach. Rooms are stylish in an understated way.

🛏 Mae Nam & the North Coast

Mae Nam has a lot of excellent accommodation choices, especially in the top-end bracket, but budget-seekers can find some good value bungalows, too.

Indy Hostel   HOSTEL $
(Map p528; ☑089 724 6832; www.indyhostel andvilla.com; Mae Nam; dm/s/d 280/350/450B; ❄🐕) We love the eastern vibes in this cute little hostel backing onto the beach in the heart of Mae Nam. Run by warm and friendly staff, this is the perfect choice for backpackers. We're not sure about the tiny communal shower that comes with the cheapest option, so if you can, grab the great double that comes with a bathtub.

Shangri-La   BUNGALOW $
(Map p528; ☑077 425189; Mae Nam beach; bungalows with fan/air-con from 600/1300B; ❄❄🐕) An upmarket backpacker's Shangri-La offering some of the cheapest huts around, including excellent family beachside options. The complex occupies a sublime stretch of the beach and has a pool with great sea views. Grounds are sparsely landscaped but even the basic bungalows are well kept and staff are very pleasant.

Farmer's Boutique Resort   BOUTIQUE HOTEL $$
(Map p528; ☑077 447222; Mae Nam; bungalows 1900-2900B; ❄❄🐕❄) A bamboo-lined entrance leads you into this quiet, family-run boutique collection of spacious traditional Thai-style villas that sit against a green mountain backdrop. The surrounding paddy fields and natural water features really enhance the rural feel. There is a communal pool and a great on-site restaurant (p540). The most expensive villas have the best views and their very own plunge pool.

Belmond Napasai   RESORT $$$
(Map p528; ☑077 429200; www.belmond.com; Bang Po; villa 8000-40,000B; ❄❄@🐕❄) Gorgeously manicured grounds welcome weary travellers as they wander past grazing water buffalo and groundsmen in cream pith

helmets. A generous smattering of villas dot the expansive landscape – all decked out in traditional Thai decor, from intricately carved wood features to vibrant local silks and bamboo interiors. Many offer dreamy views over the blue gulf and private beach.

🛏 Na Thon & the West

Used primarily as an entry point by visitors who quickly head north or across to the east coast, Na Thon has few hotels of merit. Further south down the coast you'll find two of the island's best hotels, offering ravishing views out to the Five Islands and hogging some splendid sunsets.

Chytalay Palace Hotel   HOTEL $$
(Map p528; ☑077 421079; 152 Nathon Mu 3; d 400-850B, tr 1000-1300B; ❄🐕) This quiet hotel on the beachfront road a short walk south from the pier has very good, spacious rooms with a balcony overlooking the sea and some delightful sunsets. The lower-floor rooms have electricity cables partially blocking the view but are cheaper than the newer rooms upstairs. Cheaper doubles are fan only. All rooms have attached showers.

★ Conrad Koh Samui   RESORT $$$
(Map p528; ☑077 915888; www.conradkohsamui. com; villa 18,400-43,850B; ❄❄🐕❄) Sit in your very own private infinity pool, gazing out over an azure sea in one of 81 exceptional, contemporary villas that neatly line the coast at the sumptuous Conrad. Everything here oozes luxury without going overboard. The west coast location means every evening presents a full-on magical sunset. Four restaurants, a wine cellar and a superb spa round off a superb offering.

🛏 The South

Sunset Beach Resort & Spa   RESORT $$
(Map p528; ☑077 428200; www.thesunset beachresort.com; Ban Taling Ngam; r 1850-2600B, villa from 3350B; ❄❄🐕❄) While the west coast views over the Five Islands at sunset, the quiet pebble beach and extra-clean, luxurious rooms and beachfront villas are a draw, it's the smiling, attentive service that elevates this place above others in this area. Free mountain bikes get you around the sleepy surrounding village.

Avani Plus Samui   RESORT $$$
(☑077 485299; www.avanihotels.com; Ao Phang Ka; r 5860-7080B, villa 9900-27,450B; ❄@🐕❄)

Formerly Elements, the Avani Plus occupies a lonely stretch of palm-studded sand with views of the stunning Five Islands. The location is perfect for a meditative retreat or quiet couples' romantic getaway. Chic rooms are arranged in condo-like blocks, while hidden villas dot the path down to the oceanside lounge area.

✖ Eating

✖ Hat Chaweng

With a huge bar-crawling contingent ever present in Chaweng, scores of fast-food options line the main drags and many serve up excellent burgers, kebabs and of course local Thai dishes. Step out of the central strip and several resorts harbour some excellent fine dining options such as the Tree Tops Sky Dining restaurant.

Laem Din Market MARKET $
(Map p531; Chaweng; dishes from 40B; ☻4am-midnight) A busy day market, Laem Din is packed with stalls that sell fresh fruits, vegetables and meats, and stocks local Thai kitchens. Pick up a kilo of sweet green oranges or wander the stalls trying to spot the ingredients in last night's curry. For dinner, check out the adjacent night marketfor tasty southern-style fried chicken and curries.

Chaweng Night Food Market MARKET $
(Map p531; Chaweng Beach Rd; mains from 60B; ☻5-11pm) It's a little bit pricier than other food markets on the island, but there's always a great buzz here in the evenings as groups of revellers sit together clinking beer bottles and tucking into one of the many local or western dishes on offer before hitting Chaweng's lively strip for the night.

Tuk Tuk Backpackers CAFE $
(Map p531; ☑087 268 2575; Chaweng Beach Rd; mains from 120B; ☻10am-2am; ☻) This full-on, no-holds-barred, high-impact, brazen and voluminous saloon-style Western cafe/restaurant/bar on Chaweng Beach Rd does good hangover-cure brekkies, with multiple TV screens, free pool tables and all the other usual trappings. There is also a decent Thai menu on offer.

Khaw Glong THAI $$
(Map p531; ☑089 154 4560; www.khawglong.com; 200/12, Mu 2, Chaweng Beach Road; mains 200B; ☻3-10pm Tue-Sun) This popular Thai restaurant is just off the main drag and serves

excellent local dishes that have diners raving. There is a cosy feel, with dark wood furnishings, touches of traditional decor and superfriendly staff. Arrive early as things do get busy around dinner time.

★ Tree Tops Sky Dining FUSION $$$
(Map p531; ☑077 960333; www.anantara.com; 92/1 Mu 2, Chaweng Choengmon Rd; mains 1000B, set menu from 4550B; ☻6-11pm Sun-Fri, from noon Sat) The most romantic spot in Chaweng. This series of beautiful, interconnected, treetop platforms at the back of the Anantara resort, compete with each other to offer the best views towards the sea (that would be table 7). The menu is so modern dishes have no names, only ingredients, and it's ideal for a special occasion.

Dr Frogs ITALIAN $$$
(Map p528; ☑077 448505; www.drfrogs.com; 103 Mu 3, Rte 4169; mains 400B; ☻7am-midnight; ☻☻) Perched atop a rocky overlook, Dr Frogs combines beautiful ocean vistas with delicious seafood, Thai and Italian favourites. It's a romantic setting but also has a kids playground in the front garden. Live music on Monday, Wednesday, Friday and Saturday at 7.30pm combined with warm and friendly staff make this a winner.

✖ Hat Lamai & the Southeast

Samui's second-most populated beach is slowly catching up on the culinary front with the likes of Hat Chaweng next door. As well as a growing number of dining options suited to tourist tastes around Hat Lamai, the area south is excellent for those wanting to experience a more local flavour by wandering through markets such as Hua Thanon Market (Map p528; Ban Hua Thanon; dishes from 30B; ☻6am-6pm) or grabbing a chair at the uber local Melayu Samui Seafood in the heart of the Muslim village.

Lamai Day Market MARKET $
(Map p533; Lamai; dishes from 30B; ☻6am-8pm) Lamai's market is a hive of activity, selling food necessities and takeaway food. Visit the covered area to pick up fresh fruit or to see vendors shredding coconuts to make coconut milk. Or hunt down the ice-cream seller for homemade coconut ice cream. It's next door to a petrol station.

Pad Thai THAI $
(Map p533; ☑077 458560; www.manathai.com; Rte 4169; mains 140B; ☻12.30-9.30pm; ☻☻) On

the corner of the huge Manathai hotel by the road, this affordable, elegant, semi-alfresco and smart restaurant is a fantastic choice for stir-fry and noodle soup, rounded off with a coconut ice cream.

Melayu Samui Seafood SEAFOOD **$**
(Map p528; ☑ 081 397 4090; Hat Ban Hua Thanon; mains 150B; ⊙ 10am-10pm) This delicious halal joint has a varied and diverse Thai menu, offering fresh seafood bought in the local market at Ban Hua Thanon (p529). The owner is from one of the oldest Muslim families on the island, of ethnic Malay origin and from the south of the mainland, this can be detected in the spicy, sweetness of many dishes here. There are also basic bungalows available for rent on-site.

Kangaroo INTERNATIONAL **$**
(Map p533; ☑ 099 403 1984; 101/4 Mu 3, Lamai Beach Rd; mains from 150B; ⊙ 1-11pm) Colourful, efficient and friendly Kangaroo serves excellent Thai and Western dishes, and a wealth of succulent seafood, including shark steak, barracuda steak and blue crab, as well as more standard chicken curries, sizzling platters, fried-rice dishes and pasta.

La Fabrique BAKERY **$$**
(Map p533; ☑ 089 951 7559; Rte 4169; set breakfast from 160B; ⊙ 6.30am-8pm; 🛜) Ceiling fans chop the air and service is snappy and helpful at this roomy French-style boulangerie/patisserie away from the main drag, near **Wat Lamai** (Map p533; off Rte 4169; ⊙ daylight hrs) FREE on Rte 4169. *The* place for brekkie, select from fresh bread, croissants, gratins, baguettes, meringues, yoghurts, pastries or unusually good set breakfasts that include fresh fruit.

Radiance INTERNATIONAL **$$**
(Map p533; ☑ 077 230985; off Rte 4169; mains 200B; ⊙ 7am-10pm; 🛜✎) This beachside pavilion presents a tranquil and relaxed setting offering a leaner cuisine. Serving a healthy take on traditional Thai, Italian and Mexican cuisine, the menu caters for vegetarians, vegans and even those on raw food diets. Try the amazing raw *tom kha* (coconut green curry soup).

The Dining Room FRENCH **$$$**
(Map p533; ☑ 077 332888; www.rockyresort.com; 438/1 Mu 1, Rocky's Boutique Resort, off Rte 4169; mains 300-950B; ⊙ 10am-11pm) The signature Beef Rossini at this fantastically positioned beachfront restaurant at Rocky's Resort (p535) is cooked to perfection. Combined with the excellent wine menu and delicious views, come day or night, and you can see why this restaurant ticks all the boxes for a romantic fine dining experience.

🍴 Bo Phut & the Northeast

Fisherman's Village has some of the finest beach-side restaurants and places to eat on the island, many serving excellent seafood. There aren't many cheap eats in Bo Phut except for the Friday Night Market, which offers tasty street food. The road leading further north is also worth exploring as there are several restaurants and cafes around Big Buddha Beach, west of Choeng Mon.

Boy Thai Food THAI **$**
(Map p534; ☑ 083 508 6579; Beach Rd (4171); mains 50B; ⊙ 3pm-late) Delicious no frills shack serving up local Thai dishes late into the night when all else is closed along Beach Rd, east of Bo Phut. The fact that it is a little out of the tourist hotspots means you'll normally share your table with locals. The seafood *đôm yam* soup is particularly good.

The Hut THAI **$**
(Map p534; ☑ 077 938029; Fisherman's Village; mains 60-550B; ⊙ 1-10pm; 🛜) Simple, reasonably priced Thai specialities share space with more expensive fresh seafood at this shack where the tables fill up fast, so get here early or late if you don't want to wait. Food is tasty and service is quick even if staff can be a tad surly.

Bootlegger Gourmet Burgers BURGERS **$$**
(Map p534; ☑ 092 559 5085; 30/44 Mu 4, Chaweng Choengmon Rd; burgers from 360B; ⊙ 8am-10.30pm; 🛜) Serving a host of crafts beers to wash down burgers such as the Firestarter, Hot Chick and Gangnam Style, this little gourmet joint has a nice buzz about it and is conveniently located opposite the pier at Bang Rak, making it a great place to grab a bite or pint as you wait for your ferry.

2 Fishes ITALIAN **$$**
(Map p534; ☑ 077 901009; www.2fishessamui.com; 79/5 Mu 1, Fisherman's Village; mains from 250B; ⊙ 5.30pm-late Tue-Sun) This smart Italian restaurant is a breath of fresh air, with a neat personality and a tasty, appetising menu that is laden with seafood options. Portions are not large, but service, overseen by the welcoming and polite owner Leandro, is prompt.

Karma Sutra   INTERNATIONAL $$

(Map p534; ☑088 751 8674; www.karmasutra
samui.com; Fisherman's Village; mains 190-690B;
☺8am-1am; 🛜) A hip, comfy chow spot that
straddles the crossroads heart of Fisherman's Village, dishing up very good international and Thai eats, with outdoor seating by
the people-watching wayside and splendid
ocean views from the first floor.

★ Dining on the Rocks   FUSION $$$

(Map p528; ☑077 245678; www.sixsenses.com/
resorts/samui/dining; Choeng Mon; set menu from
2800B; ☺6pm-midnight; 🛜🚗) At the isolated
Six Senses Samui (p536), the island's ultimate fusion dining experience takes place
on nine cantilevered verandas yawning over
the gulf. After sunset (and wine), guests feel
like they're dining on a barge set adrift on
a starlit sea. Each dish on the set menu is
the brainchild of cooks experimenting with
taste, texture and temperature.

Zazen Restaurant   FUSION $$$

(Map p534; ☑077 425085; Rte 4169; mains 270-
550B, set menu from 1300B; ☺6.30-11pm; 🛜)
This superb romantic dining experience
within the Zazen (p536) resort comes complete with ocean views, dim candle lighting
and soft music. Thai dancers animate things
on Thursday and Sunday nights from 8pm.
Reservations are recommended.

✕ Mae Nam & the North Coast

Mae Nam has lots of eating options, from
beachside, palm-thatch and driftwood spots
serving a mix of Thai, Western and seafood dishes to classier joints tucked along
the tangle of inland roads. Be sure not to
overlook the street food at **Mae Nam Night
Market** (Map p528; Mae Nam; ☺5-11pm Thu) on
Thursday evenings.

Homemade Burgers   BURGERS $

(Map p528; ☑085 788 4162; Rte 4169, Mae Nam;
burgers from 80B; ☺9.30am-10pm; 🚗) This tiny
roadside burger shack does delicious, good
value, homemade, gourmet-style burgers
and sandwiches. All the usual meat fillings
are accompanied by veggie and vegan options. These can be enjoyed with an ice-cold
beer (from 70B) in the cool bamboo-fur-
nished garden at the back.

★ Pepenero   ITALIAN $$

(Map p528; ☑077 963353; www.pepenerosamui.
com; Rte 4169, Mae Nam; mains 280-520B; ☺6-
10pm Mon-Sat; 🛜🚗) Pepenero remains as

popular as ever, and it is easy to see why.
This excellent and elegantly designed Italian restaurant has a beautiful garden dining
area and a terrific menu (including cutting
boards with cheese and cold meats). But
what really keeps customers coming back is
the care and attention given to them by the
sociable and hard-working hosts.

Bang Po Seafood   SEAFOOD $$

(Map p528; ☑077 602208; Rte 4169, Bang Po;
mains 200B; ☺10am-10pm) A meal at Bang
Po Seafood is a test for the taste buds. It's
one of the only restaurants that serves traditional Ko Samui fare: recipes call for ingredients such as raw sea urchin roe, baby
octopus, sea water, coconut and local turmeric, served in a delightfully local setting
that spills onto the beach.

Gaon Korean Restaurant   KOREAN $$

(Map p528; Mae Nam; mains 250-500B;
☺3-11pm Sat-Thu; 🚗🍴) Right in Chinatown
in Mae Nam, this excellent restaurant offers
barbecued meat, grilled fish and steamed
seafood sets, as well as Korean staples
such as delicious *bulgogi* (marinated beef
with mushroom and carrot on a hot plate),
kimchi pancake, Korean ice cream, a kids'
menu and a range of sizzling choices for
vegetarians.

John's Garden Restaurant   THAI $$

(Map p528; ☑077 247694; www.johnsgarden
samui.com; Mae Nam; mains from 130B; ☺1-10pm;
🛜🚗) This picturesque garden restaurant
has seating within intimate little bamboo
and palm huts in the manicured garden.
It's particularly romantic when lantern-lit
at night, so reserve ahead, but pack some
mosquito repellent (which is provided if you
forget). The signature dish on the Thai and
European menu is the excellent Thai-Muslim dish *massaman* chicken.

Farmer's Boutique
Restaurant   INTERNATIONAL $$$

(Map p528; ☑077 447222, 098 655 5314; www.
farmersboutiqueresort.com/restaurant; Mae Nam;
mains 290-890B; ☺7am-10.30pm; ✱🛜) Magi-
cally set in front of a photogenic rice field
with green hills in the distance, fantastic
Farmer's – within the resort (p537) of the
same name – is a choice selection, especially when the candlelight flickers on a starry
night. The mostly European-inspired food is
lovely and well-presented, there's a free pick-
up transport for nearby beaches, and service
is attentive.

✖ Na Thon & the West

The quiet west coast features some great seafood options and one or two restaurants with great views, especially come sunset, but otherwise Na Thon's restaurants don't really stand out. The excellent **Night Food Market** (Map p528; Th Chonwithi, Na Thon Pier; mains 70B; ◷5-10pm) is a fantastic spot to grab a bite before your ferry ride off the island.

Hippocampe French Bakery BAKERY $
(Map p528; cakes/sandwiches 50/100B; ◷6am-6pm Mon-Sat; 🐾) Serving delicious, freshly baked, wholegrain bread, this little french cafe overlooking the popular Th Angthong has a great light lunch menu, scrumptious cakes and excellent coffee.

Phootawan Restaurant THAI $$
(Map p528; 🗹081 978 9241; mains 150B; ◷10am-8pm) Getting up the hill to this restaurant is a struggle on a scooter or in a car, but it's worth the effort for the glorious views over the treetops. The food is nothing to write home about, but at sunset this spot suddenly becomes both romantic and magical.

Lucky INTERNATIONAL $$
(Map p528; 🗹077 420392; Na Thon; dishes 100-420B; ◷8am-9pm Mon-Sat, from noon Sun; 🐾🗹) This restaurant faces the sea and serves tasty, filling Western and Thai food. Time it right and you can find yourself dining to a glorious sunset. It's conveniently close to the pier and Scouse owner Steve is a friendly source of local knowledge.

✖ The South

Ging Pagarang SEAFOOD $
(Map p528; 🗹081 691 2114; Thong Krut; mains 50B; ◷11.30am-8pm) Locals know this is one of the island's best beachside places to sample authentic Samui-style seafood. It's simple and family run, but the food and views are extraordinary. Try the sea algae salad with crab, fried dried octopus or the spectacular fried fish or prawns with lemongrass.

Sweet Sisters Cafe CAFE $
(Map p528; 🗹086 470 8631; Bang Kao; ◷9am-9pm; 🐾) Charming, cosy and with an enticing interior, this roadside cafe down in the quiet south of Ko Samui, just before the turn-off for Ao Bang Kao, is a welcoming place for shots of caffeine, juices and snacks as you explore the beaches, bays and pagodas of the southern shore.

★**Hemingway's on the Beach** THAI $$
(Map p528; 🗹088 452 4433; www.hemingways onthebeach.com; off Rte 4170, Ao Thong Krut; mains 225B; ◷10am-8pm Mon-Sat; 🐾) With appetising Thai dishes, this beachside choice – home to Jaa's Cooking School (1500B per person) – is an excellent reason to escape to the southwest corner of Ko Samui. Tuck into fresh seafood and bask in the views, especially come sundown. Hemingway's also arranges long-tail and speedboat island tours, while massage is at hand for post-meal relaxation.

🍷 Drinking & Nightlife

Island rules mean most bars need to close by 1am, but around Samui's biggest party spot, brash and noisy Hat Chaweng, these rules don't always apply. Lamai and Bo Phut come in second and third respectively, while the rest of the island is generally quiet, with drinking usually focused on resort bars. For sunset cocktails, hit the west coast or parts of the north coast. There's also a growing number of excellent coffee spots turning up across the island.

🍺 Hat Chaweng

★**Warm White** BAR
(Map p531; Chaweng Lake; ◷5pm-2am; 🐾) Where Samui's cool kids hang out. This local bar plays great Thai urban music and serves very reasonably priced beers and cocktails in a hip setting. Pop along in the evening to take a seat in the outdoor patio among the young and beautiful local hipsters, and enjoy a drink knowing you're possibly the only foreigner here.

Green Mango BAR
(Map p531; 🗹077 300672; www.thegreenmango club.com; Soi Green Mango; ◷9pm-2am) This place has an entire soi named after it. Traditionally one of Samui's favourite bar-cum-clubs, the Green Mango is very big, very loud and very *fa·ràng* (Westerner). Blazing lights, expensive drinks and masses of sweaty bodies swaying to dance music throughout the latter part of the evening means this venue ends up on the itinerary of most Chaweng bar crawls.

Ark Bar BAR
(Map p531; 🗹077 961333; www.ark-bar.com; 159/89, Mu 2, Hat Chaweng; ◷7am-2am) Drinks are dispensed from the multicoloured bar to an effusive crowd, guests recline on loungers

on the beach, and the party is on day and night, with fire shows lighting up the sands after sundown and DJs providing house music from the afternoon onwards.

Hat Lamai & the Southeast

Lava Lounge BAR
(Map p533; ☎080 886 5035; Mu 3, Hat Lamai; ⌚4pm-2am) One of the better bars in Hat Lamai, Lava Lounge is a chilled-out spot with an invigorating menu of cocktails (99B to 150B), and a happy hour that runs from 4pm to 9pm. There's also a decent snack menu serving Thai and Western favourites.

Beach Republic BAR
(Map p533; ☎077 458100; www.beachrepublic.com; 176/34 Mu 4, Hat Lamai; ⌚7am-11pm; 📶) Recognised by its yawning thatch-patched awnings, Beach Republic could be the poster child of a made-for-TV, beachside, booze-swilling holiday. There's a wading pool, comfy lounge chairs, an endless cocktail list and even a hotel if you never, ever want to leave the party. The Sunday brunches (11.30am to 3.30pm) here are legendary.

Bo Phut & the Northeast

★**Woobar** BAR
(Map p534; ☎077 915999; www.wkohsamui.com; Bo Phut; ⌚11am-11pm; 📶) With serious wow factor and spectacular panoramas, the W Retreat's signature bar is the best place for sunset cocktails. Get there early to bag the cushion-clad seating pods inside the mesmerising infinity pool that stretches out to an azure horizon, and as the nightly live DJ plays, try to determine where the water ends and the sky begins.

Jack Doyle's Irish Pub IRISH PUB
(Map p534; ☎087 689 9417; Mu 181/6, Rte 4169; ⌚11am-2am; 📶) Serving excellent pizza and showing live sporting events, this Irish pub has a jovial atmosphere and is a great spot to grab a lager and a game of pool with local British expats. There is also a decent food menu that is reasonably priced.

Chez Isa CAFE
(Map p534; ☎082 423 9221; Wat Phra Yai; ⌚9.30am-7pm; 📶) This small, charming and colourful cafe serves no alcohol (as Wat Phra Yai is alongside) and shuts early, but it's a lovely spot to catch the sunset with a mocktail held aloft or relax with a coffee during the day, looking out to sea.

Cafe K.O.B. COFFEE
(King of Bread; Map p534; ☎081 829 9045; ⌚8am-5pm; 📶) Serving excellent coffee and delicious artisan bread and pastries baked on-site, this hip, little coffee shop, decked out in gorgeous dark wood, also has a really good breakfast and lunch menu.

Mae Nam & the North Coast

★**Tree Bridge Coffee** COFFEE
(Map p528; ⌚9am-6pm; 📶) The wander across the rope bridge to the treetop platform isn't for the faint-hearted, but when you get there, you'll hear the gasps long before the spectacular views over the blue gulf and across to Ko Pha-Ngan come into sight. Oh, and the coffee's not bad either. This is the ideal coffee-break spot en route to Tan Rua Waterfall (p528).

About Cafe CAFE
(Map p528; ☎077 938 167; 160/1, Mu 1, Mae Nam; ⌚7.30am-5pm Sat-Mon; 📶) We love this coffee shop in the heart of Mae Nam. Little vintage items create a chic and quirky interior that is small and perfectly formed and looks out to the street. The small staff team can become a tad overwhelmed at times but be patient, the coffee and the breakfasts are well worth the wait.

Beryl Bar BAR
(Map p528; Hat Laem Yai; ⌚6pm-late; 📶) This ramshackle and delightfully remote bar is popular with couples for the tranquillity and divine sunsets. Looking out over an isolated craggy bay, there is a definite end-of-the-world feel about Rasta-themed Beryl. If you're feeling adventurous, north of the bar is a temple cave, with a meditating Buddha. If not, recline on a lounger and take it all in.

Na Thon & the West

Air Bar BAR
(Map p528; ☎077 429100; www.samui.intercontinental.com/air-bar; Intercontinental Samui Baan Taling Ngam Resort, Taling Ngam; ⌚5pm-midnight; 📶) Toast the setting sun as it sinks into the golden gulf from the magnificent outside bar perched above a cliff at this **swanky resort** (Map p528; d 7500-11,500B, ste 11,500B, villa 15,000-21,500B; P❄📶🏊). There's an excellent menu of tapas and snacks if you simply can't pull yourself away and want to make a meal of it. This is pretty much the top romantic choice in Na Thon.

Coffee Island CAFE
(Map p528; ☑ 081 656 3399; Th Chonwithi; ☺ 7am-9pm; 🛜) With delightful views over the sea and across to the pier, this perfectly positioned cafe is an ideal final filling station before boarding a ferry. The coffee is great, as too the menu of breakfast and light lunches. Strong wi-fi also makes it a great candidate for being a first organisational stop for those arriving on the island.

🍴 The South

Buffalo Baby BAR
(Map p528; Ao Bang Kao; ☺ 9am-9pm; 🛜) Way down on the south shore at Ao Bang Kao, this fun beachside bar really comes alive on Saturdays at 5pm when a live DJ and the occasional fire show create a wonderful buzz right on the sand.

☆ Entertainment

Paris Follies Cabaret CABARET
(Map p531; ☑ 087 030 8280; Chaweng Beach Rd; ☺ 8pm-midnight; 🛜) This dazzling and fun cabaret offers one-hour *gà·teu·i* (also spelled *kàthoey*) cabaret featuring cross-dresser and/or transgender performers every night at 8pm, 9pm, 10pm and 11pm and attracts a mixed clientele of both sexes. Admission is free, but you need to buy a drink (from around 300B).

🛍 Shopping

**Fisherman's Village
Night Market** MARKET
(Map p534; Fisherman's Village; ☺ 5-11pm Fri) Every Friday night, this strip of Fisherman's Village close to the parking for The Wharf (Map p534; ☑ 077 425500; Fisherman's Village; ☺ 11am-11pm), transforms into a busy and colourful forest of market stalls, street food, handicrafts, T-shirts and cheap cocktails. Often there is a live-music act offering the perfect soundtrack to wander through grabbing a meat satay stick here and a mango and sticky rice snack there.

Baan Ngurn JEWELLERY
(House of Silver; Map p534; ☑ 085 797 9630; Entrance Rd, Fisherman's Village; ☺ 11am-10pm) This delightful little jewellery shop has a choice array of finely worked silver bracelets, necklaces and earrings. Prices start at around 30B for a pair of earrings to upwards of 8000B, and the owner is usually open to a bit of haggling.

Island Books BOOKS
(Map p533; ☑ 061 193 2132; www.island-books-samui.com; Tapee Bungalows, off Rte 4169; ☺ 11am-7pm) Scouse owner Paul Wotham belongs to a different age; one where people read and loved to wander the isles of a decent bookshop. There may not be many of those around anymore, but if they do find themselves in Ko Samui, they'll love browsing this large selection of – mostly English-language – used books, including an impressive travel section.

Thanon An Thong STREET
(Map p528; Th Anthong, Na Thon) Just a block inland from the pier, this pretty street is lined with wooden shophouses, Chinese lanterns and caged singing birds, with souvenir shops plying goods and gifts you can pick up cheaper and with less pushing and shoving than in Chaweng.

Central Festival SHOPPING CENTRE
(Map p531; ☑ 077 913 000; Chaweng Beach Rd; ☺ 11am-11pm; 🛝) This bright, shiny mall is full of international brand shops, cafes and restaurants. There's a really good dining area that offers street-food-style dishes in an air-conditioned setting, as well as some great facilities to keep children busy including a playground and Thomas the Tank engine train. Its a good place to escape the heat during the day.

ℹ Information

EMERGENCY

Tourist Police (Map p528; ☑ 077 430018) Useful for contacting either for advice or if you are arrested.

INTERNET ACCESS
Wi-fi is free and widespread at all accommodation choices, restaurants and bars.

LEGAL MATTERS
The Thai police tend to leave foreigners alone, but the laws regarding drugs can be rigidly enforced and the penalties for possession of drugs can be severe.

If arrested for any offence, the police will allow you to make one phone call. If arrested, being confrontational will make things worse for you.

Make sure you carry a copy of your passport or ID as the police can ask to see it. While you will see many drivers not wearing one, a helmet is required by law if you are driving a motorbike or scooter.

The Tourist Police can be of great help in any situation regarding the law.

MEDICAL SERVICES

Ko Samui has four private hospitals, located near Chaweng's Tesco Lotus supermarket on the east coast (where most of the tourists tend to gather). The government hospital (Samui Hospital) in Na Thon has seen significant improvements in the past couple of years but the service is still a bit grim because funding is based on the number of Samui's legal residents (which doesn't take into account the many illegal workers).

Bangkok Hospital Samui (Map p531; ☑ 077 429500, emergency 1719; www.bangkokhospitalsamui.com; Rte 4169) Centrally located, internationally accredited hospital in Chaweng. Your best bet for just about any medical problem.

Bandon International Hospital (Map p528; ☑ 077 332706; off Rte 4169; ⏱ 24hr) A private hospital offering international standards of healthcare.

Ko Samui Hospital (Map p528; ☑ 077 913200; www.samuihospital.go.th/weben; Na Thon; ⏱ 24hr) Public, government hospital located in the south of Na Thon.

Samui International Hospital (Map p531; ☑ 077 300394; www.sih.co.th; 90/2 Mu 2, Chaweng Beach Rd; ⏱ 24hr) International hospital in Chaweng. Emergency ambulance service is available 24 hours and credit cards are accepted.

MONEY

ATMs are widely available. Credit cards are accepted in most hotels and restaurants.

POST

In several parts of the island there are privately run post-office branches charging a small commission. You can almost always leave your stamped mail with your accommodation.

SAFE TRAVEL

Roads The repetitive scream of ambulances racing up and down the island's roads is a sure sign the road accident fatality rate on Ko Samui is high. This is largely due to the significant number of (inexperienced) tourists who rent motorcycles and scooters only to find out that the winding roads, sudden tropical rains, frenzied traffic and sand on the roads can be lethal.

Glass on Beaches Look out for glass on less-visited beaches – it's incomprehensible how much broken glass (mainly from discarded beer and soft drink bottles) can lie in the sands. Parts of the beach in Na Thon have a lot of broken glass on them, but you'll also find potentially dangerous shards on lengths of sand such as the sandbar leading to Ko Ma in the northwest of the island. Some of the glass has smooth rounded edges reflecting how long it has been sitting there being polished by the waves, but other glass is very sharp.

Strong Currents The seas of Samui can be rough, even for strong swimmers and drownings do occur, especially in Chaweng and Lamai, which experience strong currents and rip tides. Hotels will usually post warnings of swimming hazards and conditions on a beach board or fly warning flags. If you are caught in a rip tide (a strong surface current heading seaward), it is advised not to fight it and rapidly tire, but instead to swim parallel to the shore to exit the current or float along with it until it dissipates in deeper water and you can paddle to shore.

Dogs Dogs are everywhere on the island – they breed like rabbits and may bite. The Samui Dog & Cat Rescue Centre (p533) has the thankless task of neutering/spaying the huge number of strays, and controlling rabies (largely under control, but check with a health professional if bitten). You may find menacing dogs at temples or sitting around the beaches in packs; exercise caution and don't stroke or approach them.

Persistant Vendors Beach vendors are registered with the government and should all be wearing a numbered jacket. No hawker should cause persistant disturbance – seek assistance if this occurs.

TOURIST INFORMATION

There is no official tourist office on the island. Tourist information is largely provided by hotels and travel agents.

Siam Map Company (www.siammap.com) puts out quarterly booklets including a Spa Guide, Dining Guide and an annual directory, which lists thousands of companies and hotels on the island. Its *Samui Guide Map* is fantastic, free and easily found throughout the island.

VISA EXTENSIONS

The **Immigration Office** (Map p528; ☑ 077 423440; www.suratimmigration.go.th; Soi 1 Mu 1, Mae Nam; ⏱ 8.30am-noon & 1-4.30pm Mon-Fri) is located south of Rte 4169 in Mae Nam, which issues visa extensions.

Don't overlook the option to join a three-month to one-year Thai language course with a school on the island, which would qualify you for a student visa to cover the length of the course.

ⓘ Getting There & Away

AIR

Ko Samui's **airport** (Map p528; www.samuiairportonline.com) is in the northeast of the island just above Chaweng.

Bangkok Airways (www.bangkokair.com) operates flights roughly every 30 minutes between Samui and Bangkok's Suvarnabhumi International Airport (65 minutes). Bangkok Airways also flies direct from Samui to Phuket, Pattaya, Chiang Mai, Singapore, Kuala Lumpur, Hong Kong and other cities in Southeast Asia. Bangkok Airways also flies to Chéngdū and Guǎngzhōu in China. There is a **Bangkok Airways Office** (Map p531; ☑ 077 601300; www.bangkokair.com; ◷ 8am-5.30pm) in Hat Chaweng and another at the airport. The first and last flights of the day are always the cheapest.

During the high season, make your flight reservations far in advance as seats often sell out. If the Samui flights are full, try flying into Surat Thani from Bangkok and taking the short ferry ride to Samui instead. Flights to Surat Thani are always cheaper than a direct flight to the island.

SEA

To reach Samui, the main piers on the mainland are Tha Thong (Tapee), Don Sak and Chumphon. On Samui, the three most used ports are Na Thon, Mae Nam and Bang Rak. High-speed ferry services offer transfers to anywhere on the island via minivan for 150B.

To the Mainland

There are a host of options for boat departures between Samui and the mainland.

High-speed **Lomprayah** (☑ 077 200932; www.lomprayah.com; Tapee Pier) departs from Na Thon (600B; 1hr 40mins; 8am, 12.45pm & 3.15pm) for Tapee Pier; some departures can connect with the train station in Phun Phin (700B) for Surat Thani.

There's also the slower but more comfortable and cheaper **Seatran** (Map p528; ☑ 077 426001; www.seatranferry.com; off Chonwithi Rd; from 250B; ◷ 4am-7pm) car ferry from Bang Rak to Don Sak (400B; 1½ hours) or from Na Thon to Surat Thani via Don Sak (incl coach transfer; 230B; three hours).

Regular **Raja** (Lipa Noi; Map p528; ☑ 092 274 3423-5, 022 768211-2; www.rajaferryport.com; Lipa Noi Pier; adult ferry ticket 130-210B) car ferry (130B; 1½ hours) to Don Sak departs from Lipa Noi. The slow night boat to Samui (300B) leaves from central Surat Thani each night at 10pm, reaching Na Thon around 6am. It returns from Na Thon at 10pm, arriving at around 4am. Watch your bags on this boat.

Lomprayah ferries also depart from **Pralan Pier** (Pralan Pier; Map p528; ☑ 077 950700; www.lomprayah.com; 26/6 Mu 1) in Mae Nam for Chumphon (1100B; 3¾ hours; 8am and 12.30pm). A slightly cheaper alternative to Chumpon is run by Songserm (www.songserm.co.th) from Na Thon Pier (900B; 6½ hours)

To Ko Pha-Ngan & Ko Tao

There are almost a dozen daily departures between Ko Samui and Thong Sala on the west coast of Ko Pha-Ngan, and many of these continue on to

Ko Tao. These leave from the Raja ferry port, Na Thon, Pralan Pier and Bang Rak, taking anywhere from 20 to 90 minutes and costing 150B to 300B to Ko Pha-Ngan, depending on the boat.

To go directly to Hat Rin, the *Haad Rin Queen* goes back and forth between Hat Rin and **Big Buddha Pier** (Map p534; Beach Rd (4171); tickets 200B; ◷ 10.30am-6.30pm) four times a day. The first boat leaves Hat Rin at 9.30am and departs Big Buddha Pier at 10.30am, with double the number of sailings the day after the Full Moon Party and an extra trip laid on at 7.30am the same day.

Also for Hat Rin and the more remote east coast beaches of Ko Pha-Ngan, the small and rickety *Thong Nai Pan Express* runs (infrequently) around noon from Mae Nam on Ko Samui to Hat Rin and then up the east coast, stopping at all the beaches as far as Thong Nai Pan Noi. Prices range from 200B to 400B, depending on the destination. The boat won't run in bad weather.

Bus or Train & Ferry Combos

A bus-ferry combo is more convenient than a train-ferry package for getting to Ko Samui because you don't have to switch transportation in Phun Phin. However, the trains are much more comfortable and spacious – especially at night. If you prefer the train, you can get off at Chumphon and catch the Lomprayah catamaran service the rest of the way.

Several services offer these bus-boat combo tickets, the fastest and most comfortable being the Lomprayah, which has two daily departures from Bangkok to Samui, at 6am and 9pm, and two from Samui to Bangkok, at 8am and 12.30pm (1300B to 1450B; 11 to 12 hours).

ℹ️ Getting Around

Note that once you're in the Ko Samui sticks, you'll see signs everywhere for various bars, restaurants and hotels with distances inscribed. As a rough guide, 300m on these signs normally means about 1km.

Scooter Rentals are widely available and reasonably priced. This is the best option to visit places at your own pace.

Bus *sŏrng·tăa·ou* (pickup minibuses) are the only form of public transport on the island. They are frequent and move between the main hubs.

Taxi As well as local taxis there is the Grab (www.grab.com) option although prices for both can be steep.

Car Cars can be hired all over the island, but stick to the international brands at the airport and drive on the right.

Ko Pha-Ngan

POP 12,500

In the late 1970s, Ko Pha-Ngan (เกาะพะงัน) was a pristine paradise that beckoned the intrepid. Its innocent days may be long gone, but don't let that deter you: this gulf isle offers much more than the Full Moon parties that made it famous.

Choose quieter days in the lunar calendar, or the smaller but still-raucous half-moon party periods, and the island's charms come to the fore. It's easier to get a room, prices are more reasonable and far fewer people are on the island, meaning more solitude and tranquillity. Even Hat Rin – party central when the moon is round – is quiet and relaxing during these periods, and the beaches are kept extremely clean.

The quietest months are April to June, when the island is in low gear – an ideal time to visit for cheap accommodation prices, fewer elbows per square kilometre and safer roads.

👁️ Sights

Beyond Full Moon wild partying, this large island boasts many overlooked, spectacular natural features to explore, including jungle-clad mountains, waterfalls, unspoiled forest and national park land as well as some of the most spectacular, hidden beaches in Thailand.

Remember to change out of your beach clothes when visiting one of the 20-odd wát on Ko Pha-Ngan, each with its own distinctive character, plus don't miss the other

fascinating religious space, a one-hundred-year-old wooden mosque near Ban Khai.

Hat Rin   BEACH
(หาดริ้น, Hat Rin Nok; Map p550; Baan Haad Rin) Also known as Sunrise Beach, aka Full Moon Party Beach, this is actually one of Ko Pha-Ngan's cleanest and most pleasant beaches, because much of the money from the monthly partying admission charge goes towards the (necessary) cleaning of the sands. Its reputation as party central keeps many people away, so it can be surprisingly crowd-free at times.

⭐**Hat Than Sadet**   BEACH
(หาดธารเสด็จ; Map p548; P) This lovely beach of leaning coconut trees has the royal seal of approval, literally. Behind the collection of shacks that line the sands and azure waters are large boulders (signposted) where three Thai kings, Rama V, VII and IX, carved their insignia, affirming their love for this dreamy cove at the mouth of Than Sadet. Consider walking the wooden bridge at the south end beyond the stilted shacks to Hat Thong Reng. The swimming is good at both beaches.

Hat Khuat   BEACH
(หาดขวด, Bottle Beach; Map p548) This lovely, secluded cove has a stretch of soft sand overlooked by green hills and is a superb choice for a relaxing day of swimming and snorkelling. With no proper roads leading to the beach, there is a genuine sense of exclusivity. Most people arrive by water taxi from **Hat Khom** (หาดขอม; Map p548; P) or they pack a bag of water and don a pair of walking shoes and a sun hat to do the Chalok Lam to Bottle Beach Trek (p548) through the jungle.

Wat Samai Kongka   BUDDHIST TEMPLE
(วัดสมัยคงคา; Map p548; ☎ 094 603 3651; ☉ daylight hrs; P) FREE A beautiful green, red and golden gate featuring a dharma wheel greets you at this temple famous for it's terrifying clay model scenes depicting the Buddhist vision of hell. The most terrifying of which shows several sinners being boiled alive in a huge pot decorated with skulls. One of them has a cockerel's head and another is being stabbed in the buttock by the guardian. There are also meditation sessions, so try to seek out the monks who speak English.

Bulao Malayu Mosque   MOSQUE
(มัสยิดบูเลามะลายู; Map p548; Taladkao Rd, Ban Khai; ☉daylight hrs) This quaint, dark, wooden

---

ⓘ BOX JELLYFISH

There are several species of venomous jellyfish in the waters off Ko Pha-Ngan, Ko Samui and Ko Tao, including scyphozoans, hydrozoans and box jellyfish. The most notorious is the box jellyfish, a cnidarian invertebrate whose sting – which contains a potent venom that attacks the nervous system, heart and skin cells – can result in death. Growing up to 3m in length and named after the box-like appearance of its bell, the box jellyfish's sting can be so painful the swimmer can enter a state of shock and drown before reaching the shore. The jellyfish is more prolific in sea waters after heavy rain.

Ko Pha-Ngan and Ko Samui have the highest incidence of fatal and near-fatal box jellyfish stings in the whole of Thailand. Some beaches, such as Hat Rin Nok, are equipped with stations warning of the danger of jellyfish, as well as providing a cylinder containing standard household vinegar, which should be poured onto the area affected by the sting for 30 seconds. Avoid the inclination to rub or scratch the stung area.

---

mosque on stilts, resembling a Chinese house, is reportedly over 100 years old and was originally built using the *waqf* (trust fund) of one of Ko Pha-Ngan's earliest Muslim families. Inside are a colourful array of prayer mats pointing towards an ornate and aged, wood *mimbar*. Rarely used, you'll have the place to yourself.

Chedi Wat Nai   PAGODA
(เจดีย์วัดใน; Map p548; Ban Nok; Ⓟ) This beautiful stone pagoda from the 19th century has carvings of monks, Garudas, demons, elephants, nagas and an intriguing man in a Chinese suit, as well as Ming and Qing dynasty Chinese porcelain pressed into the sides. A standing golden Buddha has been placed in one of the niches, while the bases of two other Buddhas have been claimed, Angkor Wat–style, by two giant bodhi trees wrapped in colourful silks.

Hat Wai Nam   BEACH
(หาดหวายน้ำ; Map p548) A small white-sand beach slung out between Hat Thian and Hat Yao (East) on the more remote east coast. Tiny Hat Wai Nam can be reached on foot from Hat Rin along the path up the mountain, but that's the long way round (you'll need four hours or more), so getting here by long-tail boat is advised. Expect a secluded cove with an almost empty beach and ravishing waters.

Hat Thian   BEACH
(หาดเทียน; Map p548) Hat Thian is a pretty, relatively empty, back-to-nature beach in the southeast of the island, accessible either by boat or on foot trekking from Hat Rin. You can walk here from **Hat Yuan** (หาดยวน; Map p548) in under 10 minutes via the rocky outcrop. The longer trek from Hat Rin (the

mountain path leading here goes from north of Hat Rin) takes just over two hours, but it can be hot so load up on fluids.

Hat Yao (East)   BEACH
(หาดยาว (ตะวันออก); Map p548) This lovely white-sand beach can only be reached on foot or by boat, lending it a gorgeous sense of seclusion. Most arrive by boat, as the walk is a good four- to five-hour hike along the 7km mountain path from Hat Rin, which shouldn't be attempted if it's getting dark.

Hat Sareekantang   BEACH
(หาดสะรีกันตัง, Leela Beach; Map p550) This lovely beach south of Hat Rin, on the southeastern tip of the island, basks in gorgeous sunsets. At the southern end of the beach, you can follow the boardwalk that hugs the rocks around to Lighthouse Bungalows (p552).

Hat Thong Reng   BEACH
(หาดท้องเหรง; Map p548) The smaller, very secluded sibling of Hat Than Sadet, is located by walking over a rickety wooden bridge and beneath the stilts of several shacks (not around the headland) at the southern end of the beach. It is a lovely cove, with good swimming, but the air of hidden paradise is somewhat spoilt by the abandoned shacks and litter piles beyond the sands. Follow the trail of people headed there, and watch your step.

Deang Waterfall   WATERFALL
(น้ำตกแดง; Map p548) Than Sadet has a string of waterfalls down to the beach at Ao Thong Reng, and this is the best. Deang features a sequence of falls, a pool for swimming in and lots of rock-clambering opportunities. You may even find someone slumped in the main flow, cooling off on the rocks in the gush of the water.

Ko Pha-Ngan

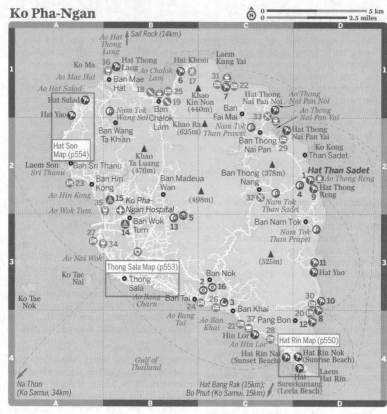

Yang Na Yai Tree LANDMARK

(ต้นยางนาใหญ่; Map p548; Ban Nok) Thrusting 54m into the heavens near Wat Pho (p551), Ko Pha-Ngan's tallest Yang Na Yai (*dipterocarpus alatus*), said to be over 400 years old, is an astonishing sight in the heart of **Ban Nok** (ตำบล บ้านนอก; Map p548; Ban Nok) village. The aesthetically pleasing giant of nature is deemed by Ban Nok villagers to be sacred, which is why there are several small shrines near the foot of the tree and it is often garlanded with colourful ribbons.

Wat Phu Khao Noi BUDDHIST TEMPLE

(วัดภูเขาน้อย; Map p548; Ban Wok Tum; ⊙ daylight hrs; ℗) **FREE** The oldest temple on the island, Wat Phu Khao Noi or 'temple of small mountain', near the hospital in Thong Sala, is believed to have been founded by Buddhist monks in the 15th century and features a historic white pagoda surrounded by eight smaller ones, the base of which is decorated with words attributed to Buddha.

Nam Tok Phaeng WATERFALL

(น้ำตกแพง; Map p548; ℗) Nam Tok Phaeng is protected by a national park and is a pleasant reward after a short but rough hike. After the waterfall (dry out of season), it's a further exhilarating 15-minute climb up a root-choked path (along the Phaeng-Domsila Nature Trail) to the superb **Domsila Viewpoint** (จุดชมวิวโดมศิลา; Map p548). The two- to three-hour trail then loops through the jungle past other waterfalls where the eagle-eyed might spot wild boars, snakes, deer and monkeys.

🏃 Activities

Hiking

⭐ **Chalok Lam to Hat Khuat Trek** HIKING

(Map p548) This moderate 5km trek through light jungle over the ridge of the northern headland is highly rewarding. As you follow the blue and yellow arrows beneath the jungle's canopy, the trail periodically opens up

Ko Pha-Ngan

to stunning vistas over the gulf – the finest are from atop a sheer rock face looking out over jungle-covered hills sliding into the azure waters. The route is tricky in parts, so solid footwear is a must, as too is water and a sun hat.

Do the trail early in the morning or late in the day to avoid the midday sun. The trek takes one to 1½ hours and is well marked, but if you go alone, inform someone of your plans beforehand. Don't attempt the trek in wet weather. Start at either end and use the long-tail shuttle boats in between. There is a brown sign for 'Thansadet Ko Phangan National Park' at the end of the road heading up the hill near the start of the trail at Chalok Lam, and at the other end it starts behind the shacks at the western edge of Hat Khuat (p546; Bottle Beach). From Bottle Beach you can also continue by boat to Thong Nai Pan.

Diving & Water Sports

There's a more laid-back diving scene on Ko Pha-Ngan than on nearby Ko Tao, but there's no shortage of professional, competitively priced dive operations with courses from novice to instructor level.

A drop in Open Water certification prices has also made local rates competitive with Ko Tao. Group sizes tend to be smaller on Ko Pha-Ngan since the island has fewer divers in general. Recommended dive outfits include Haad Yao Divers (p551), Lotus Diving (p551), Chaloklum Diving (p551), and Apnea Koh Pha Ngan (p551) for free-diving.

Like the other islands in the Samui archipelago, Pha-Ngan has several small reefs dispersed around the island. The clear favourite snorkelling spot is Ko Ma, a small island in the northwest connected to Ko Pha-Ngan by a charming sandbar. There are also some rock reefs of interest on the eastern side of the island.

A major perk of diving from Ko Pha-Ngan is the proximity to Sail Rock (Hin Bai), the best dive site in the gulf of Thailand and a veritable beacon for whale sharks. This large pinnacle lies about 14km north of the island. An abundance of corals and large tropical

Hat Rin

N 0 ——————— 400 m
0 ——————— 0.2 miles

Hat Rin

fish can be seen at depths of 10m to 30m, and there's a rocky vertical swim-through called **The Chimney**.

Dive shops on Ko Tao also visit Sail Rock; however, the focus tends to be more on shallow reefs (for newbie divers) and the deep-dive waters at Chumphon Pinnacle. The most popular trips departing from Ko Pha-Ngan are three-site day trips which stop at Chumphon Pinnacle, Sail Rock and one of the other premier sites in the area. These three-stop trips cost around 4000B and include a full lunch. Two-dive trips to Sail Rock cost around 2500B to 3000B.

Sail Rock Divers   DIVING
(Map p548; ☏ 077 374321; www.sailrockdivers
resort.com; 15, Mu 7, Ban Chalok Lam; snorkel-
ling/diving from 1000B/1200B; ☉ 6.30am-8pm)
Equipped with its own lovely 3m-deep pool, bungalow accommodation and restaurant, Sail Rock Divers is a very popular and professional choice.

Apnea Koh Pha Ngan — DIVING

(Map p548; ☑ 092 380 1494; www.apneakoh phangan.com; Chalok Lam; dives from 1600B; ⊗ 8am-7pm) Freediving has taken off on Ko Pha-Ngan and this is the best-known operator on the island, with courses that run around Sail Rock. A one-day intro course costs 4000B (taking you down to a maximum 12m), while the standard two-day course is 7000B (taking you down to a maximum 20m). The instructor-level course is 35,000B. Freediving requires no diving knowledge, just the ability to swim in open water. Don't forget your sunscreen.

Chaloklum Diving — DIVING

(Map p548; ☑ 077 374025; www.chaloklum-diving. com; beach dive 1000B; ⊗ 6am-8pm) One of the longest-established dive shops on the island, these guys (based on the main drag in Ban Chalok Lam) have quality equipment and provide high standards in everything they do, be it scuba diving, freediving, night diving or snorkelling.

Haad Yao Divers — DIVING

(Map p554; ☑ 086 279 3085; www.haadyao divers.com; Hat Yao Rd; snorkelling/diving from 1200/1400B) Established in 1997, this dive operator has garnered a strong reputation by maintaining European standards of safety and customer service. Prices start at 1400B for a beach dive at Hat Yao, but there's a huge selection of courses and options including cheaper snorkelling trips.

Lotus Diving — DIVING

(Map p548; ☑ 077 374142; www.lotusdiving.com; Ban Chalok Lam; ⊗ 7am-6pm) This dive centre is one of the oldest on the island with more than 20 years experience, and consistently gets the thumbs up from divers for their professionalism and friendly approach. It offer services for amateurs who can try a dive in their pool first, through to those wanting to be divemasters.

Wake Up — WATER SPORTS

(Map p548; ☑ 087 283 6755; www.wakeupwake boarding.com; 71/3 Mu 7, Chalok Lam; lessons 1200-3000B; ⊗ Jan-Oct) Jamie passes along his infinite wakeboarding wisdom to eager wannabes at his small water sports school in Chalok Lam. Fifteen minutes of 'air time' will set you back 1200B, which is excellent value considering you get one-on-one instruction. Also kneeboarding, wakeskating, wakesurfing and waterskiing sessions.

Health & Wellness

Wat Pho Sauna — HEALTH & FITNESS

(วัดโพธิ์; Map p548; Wat Pho, Ban Iai; sauna 110B; ⊗ noon-7pm) With a dazzling gateway and extensive temple grounds, Wat Pho, near Ban Nok village, is noted for its herbal saunas (110B) which use a traditional local method that involves heating lemongrass and tamarind leaves on a log fire and is said to have health benefits. They also offer Thai massages for 300B. The sauna is opposite the main temple and all proceeds go to support the temple's upkeep.

Samma Karuna — YOGA

(Map p554; ☑ 077 377049; www.sammakaruna. org; Hin Kong Rd; ⊗ 8am-8pm) Samma Kurana has a serene, landscaped garden, with the sound of running water gently cascading down to a private beach where several open spaces such as the Buddha Hall and Osho Hall sit facing the blue sea. This is where daily sessions (some free) of yoga, tantra, tai chi, reiki and a host of other alternative well-being practices take place.

Cooking

The Phangan Thai Cooking Class — COOKING

(Map p553; ☑ 087 278 8898; 101/13 Mu 1, Thong Sala; classes 1200-1500B) This cooking school is run by the very likeable and laid-back Chef Oy. You start your session by heading to the market and picking out the raw, local ingredients before a seriously fun class learning to master Thai culinary skills in a very homely kitchen.

Courses

C&M Vocational School — LANGUAGE

(Koh Phangan Vocational School; Map p554; ☑ 089 487 6207; http://thaiculture.education; 84/4 Mu 8, Ban Sri Thanu; ⊗ 9am-5pm) Bridging the yawning experiential gulf between yelping at the full Ko Pha-Ngan moon and Thai culture, this large vocational school runs classes and courses in Thai language, cuisine, yoga and massage.

Sleeping

Hat Rin

The thin peninsula of Hat Rin features three separate beaches: beautiful blonde Hat Rin Nok (Sunrise Beach), commonly referred to as just Hat Rin, is the epicentre of Full Moon tomfoolery; Hat Rin Nai (Sunset Beach) is the much less impressive stretch of sand on the far side of the tiny promontory; and Hat Sareekantang (also known as Leela Beach), just south of Hat Rin Nai, is a smaller, lovely white and more private beach. The three beaches are linked by Ban Hat Rin (Hat Rin Town) – an inland collection of restaurants, hotels and bars. It takes only a few minutes to walk from one beach to another.

Hat Rin sees Thailand's greatest accommodation crunch during the Full Moon festivities. At this time, bungalow operations expect you to stay for a minimum number of days (usually five). If you plan to arrive the day of the party (or even the day before), we strongly suggest booking a room in advance, or else you'll probably have to sleep on the beach (which you might end up doing anyway, either intentionally or not).

Some cattle-car-style dorms stack and cram a seemingly impossible number of beds into small rooms, and shared toilets are few. These start at around 200B outside of the Full Moon chaos and escalate to 650B and upwards for party times. Even though these grim options have added a significant number of beds to the town, everything still manages to fill up. Catering to the deluge, new operations constantly spring up.

Full Mooners can also stay on Ko Samui or other beaches on Ko Pha-Ngan and take speedboat shuttles to access the festivities – prices will depend on how far away you're staying but the money you'll save on staying anywhere besides Hat Rin itself will probably make it worth it. With gory and often fatal accidents monthly, driving on Ko Pha-Ngan during the festivities is an absolutely terrible idea. Expect room rates to increase by 20% to 300% during Full Moon.

Same Same Lodge & Restaurant
GUESTHOUSE $

(Map p550; 077 375200; www.same-same.com; Ban Hat Rin; dm 500B, d/tw fan/air-con 550/850B; ❄️🛜) Run by two highly knowledgeable Danish women (Christina and Heidi), this sociable spot offers simple, bright rooms and plenty of party preparation fun for Full Moon beach shenanigans; it's slower going outside of the lunar-lunacy periods. The restaurant and bar are also solid choices serving wood-fired pizza and great beer.

Jungle Gym & Ecolodge
RESORT $

(Map p550; 077 375115; www.junglegymande colodge.com; 110/9 Mu 6, Hat Rin; dm/d 500/1000B; P❄️🛜🏊) As well as clean four-bed dorms with outside terrace and garden-view

doubles, there's lots of outdoor space at this hostel-cum-health-gym, with a fully kitted out workout room and *moo·ay tai* lessons available, as well as a big pool and a bar.

Paradise Bungalows
HOSTEL $

(Map p550; 077 375244; www.paradisehaad rin.com; 130/4 Mu 6, Hat Rin; dm/tw/tr 360/540/720B, bungalow 595-1085B; ❄️🛜🏊) The world-famous Full Moon Party was first hatched on the plot occupied by this hostel – one of the three properties run by Paradise, and staying here puts you right in the heart of the action, though you have to book early. The hotel is right on the beach and the franchise also owns a series of charmless hillside units and two-storey blocks.

Lighthouse Bungalows
BUNGALOW $

(Map p550; 077 375075; Hat Sareekantang; bungalow 480-1350B; ❄️🛜) This remote outpost perched on the rocks south of Hat Rin has simple, good-value fan options and air-con bungalows with sweeping views of the sea; plus there's a cushion-clad restaurant/common area and high-season yoga classes.

Seaview Sunrise
BUNGALOW $$

(Map p550; 077 375160; www.seaviewsunrise. com; 134 Mu 6, Hat Rin Nok; d with fan/air-con 700/800B, bungalow 1500-2000B; P❄️🛜) Budget Full Moon revellers who want to sleep inches from the tide should apply here (but note the minimum five-day policy during the lunar madness). Some of the options back in the jungle are sombre and musty, but the solid beachfront models have bright, polished wooden interiors facing a line of coconut trees and the blue sea.

Sea Breeze Bungalow
BUNGALOW $$

(Map p550; 077 375162; www.seabreeze kohphangan.com; 94/11 Mu 6, Ban Hat Rin; bungalow 1250-6000B; P❄️🛜🏊) Sea Breeze is a pleasant hammocked labyrinth of secluded hillside bungalows of stylish, traditional design that will appeal to any type of traveller. Several, poised high on stilts, deliver stunning views of Hat Rin and the sea. There's a nice range of options here to suit almost any budget and the lovely forested setting adds to the allure. There's also a rooftop restaurant with fantastic views.

Palita Lodge
BUNGALOW $$

(Map p550; 077 375170, 077 375172; www.palita lodge.com; 119 Mu 6, Hat Rin; bungalow 2000-5500B; P❄️🛜🏊) Smack in the heart of the action, family-run Palita is notable for its

Thong Sala

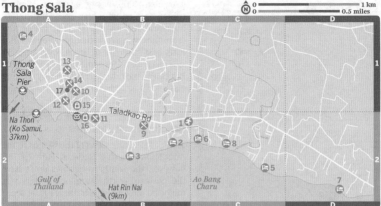

Thong Sala

welcoming service. Spacious concrete bungalows look a bit ramshackle from the outside, but the wooden accents and modern design elements make the interiors much more appealing. It's on a wedge of sand that is great for topping up your tan.

Tommy Resort RESORT $$
(Map p550; ☎ 077 375215; www.tommyresort.net; 90/13 Mu 6, Hat Rin Nok; d 2000B, villas 2650-6000B; ⊞❋🛜🌊) This cool address at the heart of Hat Rin strikes a balance between chic boutique and carefree flashpacker hang-out, with standard rooms, bungalows and pool villas. Wander down to a lovely strip of white sand, past flowering trees, to the resort with an azure pool at the heart of things and helpful, obliging staff.

Delight Resort GUESTHOUSE $$
(Map p550; ☎ 077 375527; www.delightresort.com; Ban Hat Rin; d 1300-1600B, tr 2500B; ❋🛜🌊) Slap bang in the centre of Hat Rin, friendly Delight offers decent lodging in a Thai-style building that comes with subtle designer details (such as peacock murals), sandwiched between an inviting swimming pool and a lazy lagoon peppered with lily pads.

Le Palais Hotel BOUTIQUE HOTEL $$$
(Map p548; ☎ 077 375558; www.lepalaishotel.com; 117/9 Mu 6, Hat Rin; d 9000-25,000B; ⊞❋🛜🌊) Why somebody would recreate Angkor Wat so spectacularly only to call the result Le Palais Hotel is beyond us. The island's most aesthetically stunning hotel boasts large rooms elegantly furnished in regal Khmer-style, two 'seawater' pools by the beach, a great restaurant.

Coast RESORT $$$
(Map p550; ☎ 077 951567; www.thecoastphangan.com; 117/21 Mu 6, Hat Rin Nai; d 4300-13,000B, villa 21,500B; ⊞❋🛜🌊) This dark grey, sharp-angled and stylish resort leads to a slim stretch of beach away from party

Hat Son

N 0 —— 1 km
0 —— 0.5 miles

Ao Hat Salad

Hat Salad

Gulf of Thailand

Three Sixty Bar (2.8km)

Hat Yao

Hat Yao Rd

Hat Son

Hat Chaophao

Hip Kong Rd

Cookies Cafe (350m);
Loyfa Natural Resort (1.3km);
Chills Resort (1.3km);
Chana Masala (2km)

Hat Son

Activities, Courses & Tours
1 C&M Vocational School	A3
2 Haad Yao Divers	B2
3 Samma Karuna	A3

Sleeping
4 Cookies Salad	B1
5 High Life Bungalows	A2
6 Salad Hut	B1
7 Seetanu Bungalows	A3
8 Shiralea Backpackers Resort	B2
9 Tantawan Bungalows	A2

Eating
| 10 Art in Chai Cafe | A3 |
| 11 Pura Vida | B2 |

Drinking & Nightlife
| Bubba's Roastery | (see 11) |
| 12 Secret Beach Bar | A2 |

central. Swanky room interiors feature polished cement and beds topped with white duvets, while an infinity pool overlooks the sea, and the service pulls out all the stops. Hip, cool and minimalist, we like this grown-up hang-out.

Sarikantang Resort & Spa　RESORT $$$
(Map p550; ☑ 077 375055, 086 789 9541; www.sarikantang.com; 129/3 Mu 6, Hat Sareekantang; bun-

galow from 4400B; P ✳ 🗑 ☒) Cream-coloured cabins, framed with teak posts and lintels, are sprinkled among swaying palms and crumbling winged statuettes on one of Hat Rin's best stretches of beach, with a beachside spa at hand for some sunset pampering. Prices also include a complimentary cooking class, kid's club, kayaks, yoga sessions and transfer from Hat Rin pier.

🛏 Southern Beaches

There are fleeting views of the islands in the Ang Thong Marine National Park (p578); however, the southern beaches don't have the postcard-worthy turquoise waters you might be longing for and there's little sense of seclusion. This section starts in Ban Kai and follows the coast towards Thong Sala.

★Infinity Beach Hostel　HOSTEL $
(Map p548; ☑ 062 323 3357; www.infinitybeachclub.com; 17/3 Mu 4 Baan Tai; dm 220B; P ✳ 🗑 ☒) One of the most spectacular settings of any backpacker hostel, the ridiculously good-value spacious dorms, restaurant and bar here at Infinity horseshoe around a large, blue swimming pool metres from a golden beach with swaying palms, thatch-roofed shades and sun loungers. The only downside is the location – halfway between Thong Sala and Hat Rin – otherwise this place is awesome.

Asia Blue - Beach Hostel Hacienda　BUNGALOW $
(Map p553; ☑ 098 032 8649; www.asiabluehostels.com; 100/3 Mu 1, Thong Sala; dm 235B, d 940-1060B, tr 430-1450B; P ✳ 🗑 ☒) With good-looking blue-and-white painted bungalows, rooms in two-storey blocks further down and beachfront air-con dorms, the Hacienda is a spruce and efficient outfit, although the poolside bar can get noisy at night. Dorms are a bit of a squeeze, but there's an open-air gym and dive services on-site.

Coco Garden　BUNGALOW $
(Map p553; ☑ 077 377721, 086 073 1147; www.cocogardens.com; 100/7 Mu 1, Thong Sala; bungalows 500-1350B; P ✳ 🗑) 🌿 One of the best budget hang-outs along the southern coast and superpopular with the backpacker set, fantastic Coco Garden one-ups the nearby resorts. It has well-manicured grounds and 25 neat bungalows plus a funtastic beach bar where hammocks await, and a beachfront restaurant supplies breakfast, lunch and dinner with views.

Boom's Cafe Bungalows
BUNGALOW **$**

(Map p548; ☑ 081 979 3814; www.boomscafe.
com; 32 Mu 4, Ban Khai; bungalow 600-1000B;
❄ 🛜) Staying at Boom's is like visiting the
Thai family you never knew you had. Super-friendly and helpful owners take care
of all their guests and keep things looking
good. No one seems to mind that there's no
swimming pool, since the curling tide rolls
right up to your doorstep.

Baan Manali Resort
BUNGALOW **$$**

(Map p553; ☑ 077 377917; www.baan-manali.com;
210/20 Mu 1 Ao Nai Wok, Thong Sala; bungalow
1150-2200B, tr/f 1700/2000; 🅿 ❄ 🛜 ☀) Quiet,
clean and attractively laid out among the
coconut trees, 14-bungalow Baan Manali is
a convenient, relaxing and well-run choice
with infinity pool and excellent restaurant
overlooking a sheltered cove. Close to Thong
Sala, with a variety of rooms.

V-View Beach Resort
BUNGALOW **$$**

(Map p553; ☑ 089 606 2027; www.v-viewbeach
resort.com; 100/60 Mu 1; d 810-2100B, bungalow
2100-3900B; 🅿 ❄ 🛜 ☀) An effortless air of
seclusion settles over this quiet beach resort,
and although the sea can be a bit swampy,
there are hammocks galore and a fine pool.
Neat, simple, traditional styled bungalows
are kept immaculately clean and the helpful,
owner ensures residents are looked after.

Divine Comedie
RESORT **$$**

(Map p548; ☑ 091 851 8402; www.divinecomedy
hotel.com; 14/8 Mu 1, Ban Tai; d & bungalows 2200-
4300B; 🅿 ❄ 🛜 ☀) A stunning mix of 1920s
Chinese and Mexican hacienda architecture
with a colour palette that shifts from mint to
ochre, this 15-room (10 bungalows and five
bedrooms) boutique oasis not only works,
it's beguiling. Junior suites have rooftop
terraces, while standard rooms have modest
balconies, and the elongated infinity pool
runs to the slim beach. No kids under 12.

B52 Beach Resort
BUNGALOW **$$**

(Map p553; ☑ 077 377927; www.b52resort.com;
31/22 Mu 1, San Chao Road, Thong Sala; bungalow 1150-1910B, villa 1800-3200B, f 2700-3600B;
🅿 ❄ 🛜 ☀) B52's campus of Thai-styled bungalows sports plenty of thatch, polished concrete floors and rustic tropical tree trunks
that lead down to the sea. The staff are super
pleasant and there's a lovely infinity pool.

Milky Bay Resort
RESORT **$$**

(Map p553; ☑ 077 332762; www.milkybaythailand.
com; 103/4 Mu 1, Ban Tai; d/bungalow/studio from

1100/1200/2400B; 🅿 ❄ 🛜 ☀) A delightful pic-
ture in Ban Tai; a tree-bark and wood-chip
covered path leads up to a variety of mini-
malist-chic bungalows with tinted glass hid-
den by the shade of tall bamboo. Facilities
include a covered swimming pool, a sauna,
table tennis and a gym.

Charu Bay Villas
VILLA **$$$**

(Map p553; ☑ 084 242 2299; www.charubayvillas.
com; Ao Bang Charu; villa & studio 1500-10,000B;
🅿 ❄ 🛜) These fully equipped villas on the
bay of Ao Bang Charu, just southeast of
Thong Sala, are good value (especially if
you're a group), and there's a modern garden self-catering seaside studio too, plus a
two-bedroom garden-view villa with rooftop
terrace. The Beachfront Villa is a three-bed
big enough to sleep up to 10, and comes with
a large jacuzzi.

🏖 West Coast Beaches

Now that there are two smooth roads between Thong Sala and Chalok Lam, the west
coast has seen a lot of development. The
atmosphere is a pleasant mix between New
Age yoga and meditation vibes and the east
coast's quiet seclusion, although some of the
beaches along the western shores (particularly towards the south) aren't as picturesque as the other parts of the island.

Shiralea Backpackers Resort
BUNGALOW **$**

(Map p554; ☑ 077 349217; www.shiralea.com;
58/18 Mu 8, Hat Yao; dm 275B, bungalows 645-
1400B; 🅿 ❄ 🛜 ☀) The fresh-faced poolside
bungalows are simple but the air-con dorms
are great. The ambience of this popular
backpacker hang-out, with a cool on-site bar
serving draught beer, is fun and convivial.
It's about 100m away from the beach and is
popular with Contiki student tour groups.

Seetanu Bungalows
BUNGALOW **$$**

(Map p554; ☑ 077 349113; www.seetanu.com;
81/3 Mu 8, Ban Sri Thanu; bungalows 700-4000B;
🅿 ❄ 🛜 ☀) Run by Quentin (who owns the
adjacent Belgian Beer Bar), these 17 bunga-
lows have access to a fine strip of sunset-fac-
ing beach, around a fine pool. From fan
rooms up to three-bed villas, there's lots of
choice, but book ahead.

Salad Hut
BUNGALOW **$$**

(Map p554; ☑ 081 173 4992; 61/3 Mu 8, Hat Salad;
bungalow 2200-4000B; 🅿 ❄ @ 🛜 ☀) Totally
unpretentious, despite sharing a beach with
some distinctly upscale options, this small

clutch of a dozen or so Thai-style bungalows sit a stone's throw from the rolling tide. The pool is rather small but the view of the sun dipping into a golden sea every evening, from your lacquered teak porch or the beach bar, certainly makes up for this.

Loyfa Natural Resort
BUNGALOW $$

(Map p548; ☑ 077 377319, 077 349022; www.loyfanaturalresort.com; 14/1 Mu 8, Ao Sri Thanu; d/bungalow/ste 1250/1800/2200B; P❋☎☒) Loyfa scores high for its friendly and congenial staff, charming gardens, sturdy huts with sweeping ocean views and two pools (one for sunrise, the other for sunset). Modern bungalows tumble down the promontory onto an exclusively private sliver of ash-coloured sand.

Chills Resort
RESORT $$

(Map p548; ☑ 089 875 2100; 14/12 Mu 8, Ao Sri Thanu; d 1000-2500B; P❋☎) Set along a stunning and secluded stretch of stony outcrops north of Ao Hin Kong, Chills' cluster of delightfully simple but modern rooms all have peaceful ocean views letting in plenty of sunlight, sea breezes and sunset views.

Cookies Salad
RESORT $$

(Map p554; ☑ 077 349125, 083 181 7125; www.cookies-phangan.com; Hat Salad; d 870-1900B, apt 900B, bungalow 1200-2500B; P❋☎☒) Relax in a hammock outside your own private Balinese-style bungalow on a steep hill, set around a two-tiered lap pool tiled in various shades of blue. Shaggy thatching and dense foliage give the place a tropical, rustic quality. It's super friendly, popular and books up fast. If you book directly with them there's free transfer from Thong Sala included.

High Life Bungalows
BUNGALOW $$

(Map p554; ☑ 077 349114; www.highlifebungalows.com; 59/2 Mu 8, Hat Yao; bungalow 1300-2750B; P❋☎☒) With dramatic ocean views from the infinity swimming pool, High Life has 25 bungalows of various shapes and sizes, on a palmed outcrop of granite soaring high above the cerulean sea. Staff is polite and responsive.

Tantawan Bungalows
BUNGALOW $$

(Map p554; ☑ 077 349108; www.tantawanbungalow.com; 51/8 Mu 8, Hat Son; bungalow 900-3800B; ❋☎☒) This relaxed, chilled-out 11-bungalow (fan and air-con) teak nest, tucked among jungle foliage, is attractive with fantastic views and a fine pool, but it's a bit of a steep climb with luggage.

★ Kupu Kupu Phangan Beach Villas & Spa by l'Occitane
RESORT $$$

(Map p548; ☑ 077 377384; www.kupuphangan.com; Ao Nai Wok; ste/villa from 5000/5800B; P❋☎☒) This supreme Balinese-style resort is one of the island's most swoon-worthy, with lily ponds, tall palms and a swimming pool straight out of a luxury magazine centrefold. There's also a spa, and each wood villa boasts dipping pools and spacious, elegant interiors. The entire complex sits on the beach near rocky boulders looking out to glorious west-coast sunsets.

🛏 Northern Beaches

Stretching around 8km from Chalok Lam to Thong Nai Pan, the dramatic northern coast is a wild jungle with several stunning and secluded beaches – it's the most scenic coast on the island.

Fantasea Resort
BUNGALOW $

(Map p548; ☑ 089 443 0785; www.fantasea-resort-phangan.info; Chalok Lam; bungalows with fan/air-con from 600/1200B; P❋☎) This friendly place in the extreme north of the island is one of the better of a string of family-run bungalows along the quiet eastern part of Chalok Lam. There is a thin beach out front that is OK for swimming and an elevated, Thai-style restaurant area to chill out in.

Smile Bungalows
BUNGALOW $

(Map p548; ☑ 085 429 4995; www.smilebungalows.com; 74/9 Mu 7, Hat Khuat/Bottle Beach; bungalows 520-920B; ⊙ closed Nov) For real remoteness and seclusion, it's hard to beat this place at the far western corner of Hat Khuat (Bottle Beach). Family-run Smile features an assortment of fan-only, spartan wooden huts climbing up a forested hill.

Bottle Beach II
BUNGALOW $

(Map p548; Hat Khuat; bungalow 850B; ☎) At the far eastern corner of Hat Khuat (Bottle Beach), this double string of very basic, turquoise bungalows is the ideal place to chill out – for as long as you can – as long as you don't need many creature comforts.

Longtail Beach Resort
BUNGALOW $$

(Map p548; ☑ 077 445018; www.longtailbeachresort.com; 2/5 Mu 5, Thong Nai Pan; bungalows with fan/air-con from 1050/1200B; P❋☎☒) Tucked away by the forest at the lovely southern end of Thong Nai Pan (and a long way from Full Moon Ko Pha-Ngan mad-ness), Longtail offers backpackers charming thatch-and-bamboo abodes with plenty of choice for larger groups and families.

Mandalai
BOUTIQUE HOTEL **$$**
(Map p548; ☑077 374316; www.mandalai hotel.com/web2014; 2/3 Mu 7, Chalok Lam; d/ste 1700/2200B; ❄️🛜❄️) This small 'room-on-ly' boutique hotel (with spa) quietly towers over the low-lying form of Chalok Lam, with floor-to-ceiling windows commanding views of tangerine-coloured fishing boats in the bay and a small but inviting pool in the main courtyard, mere metres from the sands.

🛏 East Coast Beaches

Robinson Crusoe, eat your heart out. The east coast is the ultimate hermit hang-out. You'll have to hire a boat (or trek on foot) to get to some of these isolated stretches of sand, and long-tail water taxis are available in several locations including Thong Sala and Hat Rin.

The *Thong Nai Pan Express* boat runs daily at noon from Hat Mae Nam on Ko Samui, stopping at Hat Rin and the east coast beaches as far as Thong Nai Pan Noi. The boat is a casual, rickety fishing-style vessel and won't run in rough weather.

Bamboo Hut
BUNGALOW **$**
(Map p548; ☑098 536 2915; Hat Yuan; bungalows 500-1000B; 🛜) Beautifully lodged up on the bouldery outcrops that overlook Hat Yuan and the jungle, the friendly, hippie-village Bamboo Hut is a favourite for yoga retreats, meditative relaxation and some serious chilling out. The dark wood bungalows are small, with terraces, while the restaurant serves up superb views and reasonable food.

Sanctuary
BUNGALOW **$$**
(Map p548; ☑081 271 3614; www.thesanctuarythai land.com; Hat Thian; dm/bungalow 350/950B, villa 1900-6000B; ❄️🛜) A friendly, forested sanctuary on the deliciously remote and inaccessible (except by boat) Hat Thian. This is a haven for those looking for a yoga and detox retreat. Accommodation, scattered along a tangle of hillside jungle paths, ranges from cheap dorms through to luxury villas, which can all be combined with yoga and detox packages. It's cash only, though.

Pariya Resort & Villas
RESORT **$$**
(Map p548; ☑087 623 6678; www.pariyahaad yuan.com; 153/2 Mu 6, Hat Yuan; villa 1800-3200B;

❄️🛜❄️) The smartest option on the glori-ously soft sands of Hat Yuan, Pariya has a choice of spacious and comfortable villas but they're not cheap. It's remote and quiet, on a beach accessible only by boat, and where electricity is available only via a generator, so getting about isn't easy but then that's not why you would be booking this place.

Mai Pen Rai
BUNGALOW **$$**
(Map p548; ☑093 959 8073; www.thansadet.com; Than Sadet; bungalows 683-1365B; 🛜) By the river at the south end of leisurely Than Sadet, this lovely, secluded retreat elicits sedate smiles. Bungalows – some temptingly right on the edge of the rocks, by the sea – feature desert-island-style thatched, gabled roofs.

🍴 Eating

🍴 Hat Rin

Hat Rin has a large conglomeration of res-taurants and bars on the island, yet many of them are pretty average so it's not worth coming here for the food alone.

Om Ganesh
INDIAN **$**
(Map p550; ☑077 375123; Mu 6, Hat Rin Nai; mains 130B; ⊙9am-11pm; 🛜) Seasoned old-timer Om Ganesh sees a regular flow of customers for its north Indian curries, biryani rice, roti and lassis, with a token spread of Chinese dishes for good measure.

Palita Lodge
SEAFOOD **$$**
(Map p550; ☑077 375170; www.palitalodge.com; 119 Mu 6, Hat Rin; mains 150B) The front restau-rant of the Sunrise Beach bungalows (p552) outfit of the same name offers up tasty Thai seafood and set meals with views overlook-ing a beach that's pretty serene outside of the Full Moon period.

Monna Lisa
ITALIAN **$$**
(Map p550; ☑084 441 5871; www.monnalisathai land.com; 110/7 Mu 6, Hat Rin; mains 230B; ⊙3-11pm; 🛜) Travellers still rave about the pizza here – little wonder given the staff and the stone oven were reportedly brought over from Italy – and the al dente pasta also gets a thumbs-up. It really doesn't get more au-thentic on the island. Run by friendly Ital-ians and has a nice open-air setting.

🍴 Southern Beaches

In recent years Thong Sala has attracted many new excellent restaurants, so spend some time dining here. There are also some well-established cafes that do excellent business and are among the best places on the island for breakfast. There are also some superb restaurants and cafes dotted along the road between Thong Sala and Hat Rin.

On Saturday evenings from 4pm to 10pm, a side street in the eastern part of Thong Sala becomes a fun Walking Street – a bustling pedestrian zone mostly filled with locals hawking their wares.

Fat Cat   CAFE $
(Map p553; ☑087 622 0541; Taladkao Rd, Thong Sala; mains 90-195B; ⊙8.30am-3pm Mon-Sat; 🛜) This small, charming, colourful and busy Portuguese-run cafe does wholesome breakfasts including their very own homemade muesli, and delicious coffee. Fuel up ahead of a day exploring the island.

Nira's   BAKERY $
(Map p553; ☑081 535 5215; Taladkao Rd, Thong Sala; breakfast from 80B; ⊙7am-7pm; 🛜) With lots of busy staff offering outstanding service, a big and bright interconnected two-room interior, scrummy baked goodies, tip-top coffee and hip furniture, Nira's is second to none in Thong Sala, and perhaps the entire island. This is *the* place for breakfast. There's cool, jazzy chill-out music. There's another (small) branch in Hat Rin.

Phantip Food Market   MARKET $
(Map p553; Mu 1, Thong Sala; dishes 60B; ⊙1-11pm) Thong Sala's terrific food market is a must for those looking for doses of culture while nibbling on low-priced street food. Wander the galaxy of stalls and grab a spicy sausage, satay-style kebab, spring roll, Hainanese chicken rice or coconut ice cream. There are even a few vegetarian and Italian options at the back.

Ando Loco   MEXICAN $
(Map p553; ☑085 791 7600; www.andoloco.com; Mu 1, Taladkao Rd, Ban Tai; mains 120B; ⊙2-11pm Thu-Tue) This popular outdoor Mexican hang-out still gets the universal thumbs up. Grab a jumbo margarita, down a 'drunken fajita', line up a quesadilla or two and sink a round of balls on the pool table, with a tequila to liven things up.

Fisherman's Restaurant   SEAFOOD $$
(Map p548; ☑084 454 7240; www.fishermans-phangan.com; 30/6 Mu 1 Ban Tai; mains 250B; ⊙1.30-10pm; 🛜) Sit in a long-tail boat looking out over the sunset and a rocky pier. Lit up at night, this is one of the island's nicest settings, and the food, from the addictive yellow-curry crab to the massive seafood platter to share, is as wonderful as the ambience. Reserve ahead, especially when the island is hopping during party time.

Baraka Phangan   MIDDLE EASTERN $$
(Map p553; ☑094 797 3675; www.facebook.com/barakaphangan; Thong Sala; mains 80-280B; ⊙7-11pm; ❄🛜🍴) If you know your *shakshuka* from your *zatar*, then this airy, spacious, glass-fronted kosher joint near the centre of Thong Sala is the place to be. The hummus with shawarma-style lamb is to die for, and for fitness freaks there's even a protein-rich training menu.

Vintage Burgers   BURGERS $$
(Map p553; ☑099 347 1983; Thong Sala; mains 250B; ⊙5-10pm; 🛜🍴🍺) This great little Portuguese-run gourmet burger bar really hits the nail on the head with six types of superb patties, including veggie, vegan, tuna and kids burger options, complemented by scrumptious salt-and-oregano homemade French fries, served in a sociable vibe.

Fabio's   ITALIAN $$
(Map p548; ☑077 377180; www.facebook.com/fabiocolapietro66; 10/1 Mu 4, Taladkao Rd, Ban Khai; mains 150-400B; ⊙9am-10pm Mon-Sat; ❄🛜) An intimate, authentic and truly delicious Italian place with golden walls, cream linens and bamboo furniture. There are only seven tables, so reserve in advance. House-made delicacies like seafood risotto, pizzas and iced limoncello are as artfully presented as they are fresh and delicious.

🍴 West Coast

★Chana Masala   INDIAN $
(☑081 622 3374; Ban Hin Kong; mains 120B; ⊙11am-10pm Sun-Fri; ❄🛜🍴) Classic Bollywood hits play and wooden faces of Hindu gods Kali and Baghvan peer down at you inside this spacious venue decked out in Indian teak serving the best Indian vegetarian food on the island. If they haven't sold out, go for the excellent-value *thali* (platter), but if they have then the *dosas* (rice crepe) are a great substitute.

Art in Chai Cafe   VEGETARIAN $
(Map p554; mains 90B; ⊙9am-9pm; 🛜🍴) We love the aromatic and fresh Indian chai at this laid-back, hip little cafe that also serves delicious vegetarian Thai dishes. Located

KO PHA-NGAN'S FULL-MOON PARTIES

No one knows exactly when or how these crazy Full Moon Parties (Map p550; Hat Rin; entry fee 100B; ⊙ full moon, dusk-dawn) started – most believe they started in 1988, with accounts of the first party ranging from an Australian backpacker's leaving bash to a group of hippies escaping Samui's 'electric parties'. Today, thousands of bodies converge monthly on the kerosene-soaked sands of Hat Rin (aka Sunrise Beach; p546) for an epic dusk-till-dawn dance-a-thon.

The party really comes alive after 10pm, when the pounding heart of the Full Moon action and Sunrise Beach see crowds swelling to an outrageous 40,000 party-goers during high season, while the low season still sees a respectable 8000 wide-eyed pilgrims. To take a break, refuel or just chill for a bit, head to the excellent Rock (p560) bar at the south end. You'll be knocking into stalls selling buckets of alcohol – vodka, gin, rum and whisky mixed with Coca-Cola and Red Bull – all along the beach, but go easy, you can quickly end up downing more than you think. Try to leave them till late.

Flaming among the thumping bass line and flashing neon are the petrol-drenched fire ropes where dancers are invited to hop over a swinging line of fire (burns are generally the order of the day on that one).

Some critics claim the party is starting to lose its carefree flavour, and becoming too commercial (inevitable really) especially after spats of violence and the fact that the island's authorities now charge 100B entrance fee to partygoers (the money goes towards much-needed beach cleaning and security). One thing is certain, it is no longer dominated by trance music, with DJ stands now also dedicated to urban, dance, afro beats, and drum and bass in a bid to attract a wider, more diverse crowd.

Have your accommodation sorted way up front – if you turn up on the day, you won't find a bed for the night in Hat Rin during peak season, though you can always do an in-and-out from Ko Samui, but beware shuttle prices are hiked up considerably for the night. Ferries will cost between 500B to 1000B each and hiring a long-tail to make the trip will start at around 3000B.

along the busy main road where most of the New Age meditation centres are, it is no surprise the dreadlocked Thai owner has decked out the place to resemble an Indian yoga centre.

Pura Vida CAFE $
(Map p554; ☑ 094 827 7641; Hat Yao Rd; breakfast from 70B; ⊙ 8.30am-5pm Mon-Sat; ☎) This charming and bright Portuguese cafe is an alluring choice as you head up the west coast. Breakfasts are excellent, especially the pancakes and natural yoghurt, or you can go the whole hog with a full brekkie.

Cookies Cafe CAFE $
(Ban Sri Thanu; mains 90B; ⊙ 8.30am-6pm; ☎) This is a good choice to caffeinate on the way up the west coast. For nibbles, there's coconut cookies, dates, oatmeal biscuits and ice cream.

✖ Elsewhere

★ **Chaloklum Food Market** MARKET $
(Map p548; Chaloklum Pier; dishes 40B; ⊙ 4-11pm Sun) Ko Pha-ngan's most authentically local food market is in the far north, where every Sunday in front of the village pier (Map p548; Chalok Lam), a series of red tables and chairs appear beside a stage where locals play live. This is surrounded by stalls serving food you will not see in any of the 'night markets' elsewhere. Be brave and get stuck in. Try the deep-fried fish patty, or the fish in spiced coconut – grilled inside a banana leaf tube.

If it's something sweet you're after, *nám chah* (fresh sugared coconut, wrapped and barbecued in palm leaves) is a delicious, chewy snack. Grab a pile and head for the pier, pull up a reed mat like the locals for 20B, and watch the passing parade.

Crepe's Corner CRÊPES $
(Map p548; Thong Nai Pan; from 70B; ⊙ 11am-10pm) This small and friendly crêpe stall is a hit with adults and kids: choose from a variety of flavours, including Nutella, peanut butter, jam, vanilla custard, coconut custard and a host of savoury choices, too.

Big Bang Art Cafe CAFE $
(Map p548; ☑ 082 813 5376; mains 60-220B; ⊙ 9am-6pm; ☎) Run by energetic Swiss artist

Gil and his Thai wife Na, this relaxing spot before you hit the roundabout for Than Sadet is a lovely place to pitch up for a coffee or a bite to eat as you come through the island's hilly interior.

Bamboo Hut THAI **$$**

(Map p548; Hat Yuan; dishes 100-300B; ⊙8am-10pm; 🛜🍴) Linked to the bungalows on hidden Hat Yuan, you can lounge on a Thai-style cushion or sit at a teak table cooled by the sea breeze bouncing off an infinite blue at this laid-back place. There are plenty of options, from vegetarian specialities and fresh juices for those coming off a fast or cleanse, to classic, very well-prepared Thai dishes.

Cucina Italiana ITALIAN **$$**

(Jenny's; Map p548; ☑081 594 5682; Chalok Lam; pizzas 180-200B; ⊙5pm-midnight Thu-Tue) If it weren't for the sand between your toes and the long-tail boats whizzing by, you might think you had been transported to the Italian countryside. The friendly Italian chef is passionate about his food, and creates everything from the pasta to his tiramisu fresh everyday. The rustic, thin-crust pizzas are out-of-this-world.

🍷 Drinking & Nightlife

Every month, on the night of the full moon, pilgrims pay lunar tribute to the party gods with dancing, wild screaming and glow-in-the-dark body paint. For something mellower, the west coast has several excellent bars, where you can raise a loaded cocktail glass to a blood-orange sunset from a hilltop or over mangrove trees at the water's edge. Thong Sala has a couple of decent bars too and the island's coffee is also excellent, so look out for several cool, hipster caffeine spots scattered around the island.

🍷 Hat Rin

Chillin Beachclub BAR

(Map p550; ☑077 375227; www.phanganbayshore. com; 141 Mu 6, Hat Rin Nok; ⊙4-11pm; 🛜) Listen to laid-back live music and recline on lean-to orange triangle cushions set around candlelit low tables at this chilled space as it sprawls out of the **Bayshore Resort** (d/tr/ste from 4050/7800/9000B; 🅿❄@🛜🌊) onto Hat Rin beach. With the gentle sound of waves lapping at the sands, metres from your feet, you'll find the cocktails taste that much more divine here.

Rock BAR

(Map p550; ☑093 725 7989; 130/4 Mu 6, Hat Rin Nok; ⊙8am-late; 🛜) Offering superb views of the Full Moon party from an elevated terrace – and excellent panoramas at all other times – this bar at the southern end of the Hat Rin beach has super cocktails and a mixed menu of plates at reasonable prices even during the lunar lunacy.

Sunrise BAR

(Map p550; ☑077 375144; www.sunrisephangan. com; 136 Mu 6, Hat Rin Nok; ⊙8am-2am; 🛜) A blue pool looks out onto a delicious spot on the sand where trance beats shake the graffitied walls, with drum 'n bass coming into its own during the Full Moon party. This is a great place to slowly kick off the evening.

Cactus Bar CLUB

(Map p550; 146/9 Mu 6, Hat Rin Nok; 🛜) A restaurant by day and a eardrum bursting bar-cum-club at night famed for its fire shows and young, energetic crowd. If you're in town outside of Full Moon and want to party on the beach, this will be your best bet.

Tommy BAR

(Map p550; ☑077 375215; www.tommyresort.net; Hat Rin; ⊙8am-2am; 🛜) One of Hat Rin's largest venues, Tommy lures the masses with loungers, low tables, black lights, a swimming pool and blaring Full Moon music. Drinks are dispensed from a large ark-like bar and, during the lunar shenanigans (for an extra fee), you can get a great perspective from the VIP balcony.

🍷 Southern Beaches

Bubba's Coffee Bar CAFE

(Map p548; ☑099 164 3478; www.bubbascoffee. com; Mu 1, Ban Tai; ⊙7am-6pm; 🛜) Bubba's serves its famous, locally sourced and roasted coffee alongside an excellent breakfast menu at this sibling of Bubba's Roastery. The atmosphere is easygoing and the interior is hipster coo; it's popular with the island's western expat community.

Hub PUB

(Map p553; ☑088 825 4158; Thong Sala; ⊙8am-11pm; 🛜) With chatty staff and a prime location on the corner straight down from the Thong Sala pier, cavernous wood-floored Hub is the sports bar of choice for those crucial Premier League fixtures, draft beer, cider and excellent pub fare. It also rents out scooters and motorbikes.

Viewpoint Cafe

CAFE

(Map p548; Ban Khai; ⊙8am-midnight; 🛜) If you're heading back from Hat Rin to Thong Sala or Ban Tai, park your scooter and head into this cafe at the Viewpoint Hotel. It serves fruit smoothies, coffee and light snacks from a terrific perch over the gulf. The food is mediocre and so is the service, but you'll be stopping for the views.

🍷 Elsewhere

★ Jam Bar

BAR

(Map p548; Hin Kong; ⊙7pm-2am Sun & Thu) Sit beneath a starry sky at this pop-up stage and bar where it's live DIY music, with anyone welcome to get up and jam. The action is usually kicked off by host Robert, who belts out a few rock classics to get things going.

Bubba's Roastery

COFFEE

(Map p554; 🖉099 0784805; www.bubbascoffee. com; 56/4 Mu 8, Hat Yao; ⊙8am-4pm; 🛜) Coffee connoisseurs will love this sibling of Bubba's Coffee Bar. Sourced from farms in the mountainous north of the country, not only is the coffee excellent – in what is the island's only speciality coffee roastery – but there are also packs available for sale.

Secret Beach Bar

BAR

(Map p554; 🖉084 754 7183; Hat Son; ⊙9am-7pm) There are few better ways to unwind at the end of a Ko Pha-Ngan day than watching the sun slide into an azure sea from this bar on the northwest sands of the island. Grab a table, order a mojito and take in the sunset through the palm fronds. It's worth calling ahead to check it's open during the off season.

Three Sixty Bar

BAR

(Map p548; 🖉086 789 7870; Ban Mae Hat; ⊙8am-midnight; 🛜) High up a road east of Ko Ma, the Three Sixty Bar does what it says on the packet, with splendid, wide-angle panoramic views that mean sunsets are killer. There's also a great Thai food menu.

Amsterdam

BAR

(Map p548; 🖉095 018 4891; Ao Plaay Laem; ⊙noon-1am; 🛜) The rooftop swimming pool staring out to glorious sunsets is the key draw at this popular hillside bar, perched high up on the west coast. Arrive early to avoid the crowds, bring your swimsuit, slip into the warm waters, grab yourself a beer (Chang 70B), and enjoy the crimson Pha-Ngan sun descending into the blue ocean.

🛍 Shopping

Fusion Fashion

CLOTHING

(Map p550; 🖉089 868 1938; 94/17, Hat Rin Nai; ⊙11am-10pm) The Swedish owner of this cute little boutique imports all her wares from India making this one of the few shops worth stopping in along the main drag in Hat Rin. Opened in 2003, the colourful store is littered with attractive and eye-catching lines of boho and colourful gossamer blouses, skirts, hot pants, bags and jewellery.

Phanganer

CLOTHING

(Map p553; 🖉080 534 5075; Taladkao Rd, Thong Sala; ⊙10am-7pm) At the southern end of **Thong Sala's Walking Street** (Map p553; ⊙4-10pm Sat) near the bend towards the sea, this small clothing shop has a cool and colourful selection of some of the island's better offering of shirts, T-shirts, cargo shorts, belts, wallets, and fisherman pants (which you can get on a two for 800B deal).

ℹ Information

EMERGENCY

Ko Pha-Ngan Police Station (Map p548; 🖉077 377114, 191; www.suratthani.police. go.th) About 2km northeast of Thong Sala. Come here to file a report. You might be charged between 110B and 200B to file it but as it will help with any insurance claims, it is money well spent. Plus refusing to pay may lead to complications. If you are arrested, you have the right to an embassy phone call; you don't have to accept the 'interpreter' you are offered. If you have been accused of committing a serious offence, do not sign anything written only in Thai, or write on the document that you do not understand the language and are signing under duress.

LAUNDRY

If you get fluorescent body paint on your clothes during your Full Moon revelry, don't bother sending them to the cleaners – it will never come out. Trust us, we've tried. For your other laundry needs, there are heaps of places that will gladly wash your clothes. Prices hover around 40B per kilo, and express cleanings shouldn't be more than 60B per kilo.

MEDICAL SERVICES

Be wary of private medical services in Ko Pha-Ngan, and expect unstable prices. Clinics will charge between 600B to 3000B entrance fee before treatment. Serious medical issues should be dealt with on nearby Ko Samui, which has superior facilities.

Ko Pha-Ngan Hospital (Map p548; 🖉077 377034; www.kpho.go.th; 6 Mu 4, Ban Wok

Tum; ⏱24hr), about 2.5km north of Thong Sala, is a government hospital that offers 24-hour emergency services.

MONEY

Thong Sala, Ko Pha-Ngan's 'capital', has plenty of banks, currency converters and money transfer offices. Hat Rin also has numerous ATMs and a couple of banks at the pier. There are also ATMs in Hat Yao, Chalok Lum and Thong Nai Pan.

POST

Main Post Office (Map p553; ☑ 077 377118, contact centre 1545; www.thailandpost.co.th; Taladkao Rd, Thong Sala; ⏱8.30am-4.30pm Mon-Fri, 9am-noon Sat)

Hat Rin Post Office (Map p550; ☑ contact centre 1545; www.thailandpost.co.th; Hat Rin; ⏱8.30-4.30pm Mon-Fri, 9am-noon Sat)

SAFE TRAVEL

Some of your fondest holiday memories will be formed on Ko Pha-Ngan; just be mindful of the following situations where things can go pear-shaped.

Drugs There have been instances of locals approaching tourists and attempting to sell them drugs at a low, seemingly enticing, price. Upon refusing the offer, the vendor may drop the price even more. Once purchased, the seller informs the police, which lands said tourist in the local prison to pay a wallet-busting fine. If you're solicited to buy drugs, stand your ground and maintain refusal. This may happen frequently on Ko Pha-Ngan, so be aware and avoid the scenario if you suspect it happening.

Insurance & Drugs Remember your travel insurance does not cover drug-related injuries or treatment. Drug-related freak-outs *do* happen – we've heard firsthand accounts of party-goers slipping into extended periods of delirium. Suan Saranrom (Garden of Joys) Psychiatric Hospital in Surat Thani has to take on extra staff during Full Moon and other party periods to handle the number of *fa·ràng* (Westerners) who freak out on magic mushrooms, acid or other abundantly available hallucinogens.

Women Travellers Female travellers should be particularly careful when partying on the island. We've received numerous reports about drug and alcohol-related rape (and these situations are not limited to Full Moon parties). Women should also take care when accepting rides with local motorcycle taxi drivers. Several complaints have been filed about drivers groping female passengers; there are even reports of severe sexual assaults, and in 2019 a man was arrested for raping a Norwegian woman who accepted a ride from him after attending a Half Moon party.

Motorcycles & Scooters Ko Pha-Ngan has more motorcycle accidents than injuries incurred from Full Moon tomfoolery. Nowadays there's a decent system of paved roads (extended to Than Sadet), but some tracks remain rutted dirt-and-mud paths and the island is also hilly, with some very steep inclines. To combat this, Ko Pha-Ngan has a special ambulance that trawls the island helping injured bikers.

Wild Dogs You will encounter menacing, snarling dogs in some very local, residential areas, around one or two temples and sitting on remoter stretches of beaches in packs; exercise caution, try to avoid going near them, and certainly don't try to stroke or approach them.

Drowning Rip currents and alcohol don't mix well. Drownings are frequent; if swimming, it's advisable to be clear-headed rather than plunging into the sea on a Full Moon bender.

Fake Alcohol This is a common scam during the Full Moon mania at the bucket stalls on the beach and along the road. Buckets may be filled with low-grade moonshine rice whisky, or old bottles filled with home-made alcohol. Apart from obvious health risks, dodgy alcohol is the primary cause of many problems that arise during the Full Moon, from motorcycle accidents to drownings, fights and burns from jumping fire ropes.

Glass on the Beach Beware nasty cuts from broken glass in the sand at Full Moon Party time – be sure to bring good footwear. Also watch out for broken glass on other beaches at all times.

TOURIST INFORMATION

There are no government-run Tourist Authority of Thailand (TAT) offices on Ko Pha-Ngan; instead tourists get their information from local travel agencies, brochures and their accommodation. Most agencies are clustered around Hat Rin and Thong Sala. Agents take a small commission on each sale, but their presence helps to keep prices relatively stable and standardised. Choose an agent you trust if you are spending a lot of money – faulty bookings do happen on Ko Pha-Ngan, especially since the island does not have tourist police. Otherwise ask your hostel to make bookings for you.

Several mini-magazines also offer comprehensive information about the island's accommodation, restaurants, activities and Full Moon parties. Our favourite option is the pocket-sized quarterly Phangan Info (www.phangan.info), also available as a handy app.

Phanganist (www.phanganist.com) is an online resource that's full of insider tips for all things Ko Pha-Ngan.

ⓘ Getting There & Away

Transport via the sea is the only way to arrive on Ko Pha-Ngan. Boats from the mainland, Ko Samui and Ko Tao arrive daily at the piers in Thong

Sala, and there are also boats arriving directly from Ko Samui to Haad Rin Pier.

The **Lomprayah** (Map p553; ☑ 087 887 9791, 07742 3761; www.lomprayah.com; ☺7am-10pm) and **Seatran Discovery** (www.seatrandiscovery. com) services have bus-boat combination packages (Lomprayah from around 1200B, Seatran from 1000B) that depart from the Th Khao San area in Bangkok and pass through Hua Hin and Chumphon. The whole voyage takes between 10 and 17½ hours.

It is also quite hassle-free (unless your train breaks down, which happens a lot) to take the train from Bangkok or Hua Hin to Chumphon and switch to a ferry service. In this case expect to pay 300B for a second-class seat on a train from Bangkok to Chumphon (about 8½ hours); Lomprayah boats from Chumphon to Ko Pha-Ngan take around 3 to 3¾ hours and costs 1000B.

There are almost a dozen daily departures between Thong Sala and Ko Samui. These leave throughout the day from 7am to 6pm, take from 20 to 90 minutes and cost from 150B to 300B depending on the boat.

The *Haad Rin Queen* goes back and forth between **Haad Rin Pier** (Map p550; Hat Rin) and Big Buddha Pier four times a day (the first boat leaves Hat Rin at 9.30am and departs Big Buddha Pier at 10.30am), with double the number of sailings the day after the Full Moon Party and an extra trip laid on at 7.30am the same day. The voyage takes 50 minutes, costs 200B and the last boat leaves Big Buddha Pier at 6.30pm.

The **Thong Nai Pan Express** (Map p550) is a wobbly old fishing boat (not for the taint-hearted) that runs once a day from Mae Nam on Ko Samui to Hat Rin on Ko Pha-Ngan and then up the east coast, stopping at all the beaches as far as the **pier** (Map p548; Hat Thong Nai Pan; from 600B) at Thong Nai Pan Noi. Prices range from 200B to 400B depending on the destination.

Ko Tao-bound Lomprayah ferries (500B to 600B) depart from Thong Sala on Ko Pha-Ngan at 8.30am, 1pm and 6.15pm and arrive at 9.30am, 2.15pm and 7.15pm. The Seatran service (500B, 90 mins) departs from Thong Sala at 8.30am, 1.30pm and 5pm daily. Taxis depart Hat Rin for Thong Sala one hour before the boat departures. The cheaper but slower Songserm (350B) leaves Ko Pha-Ngan at 12.45pm and alights at 2.30pm, before continuing to Chumphon.

There are four daily Lomprayah (700B, 2½ hours) services to Tapee Pier (for Surat Thani), both travelling via Ko Samui. These boats leave from Thong Sala at 7.20am, 12pm, and 2.30pm. Two Seatran boats (550B) also leaves daily from Thong Sala for Donsak (for Surat Thani) at 8am and 10.30am, with a bus connection to Phun Phin train station outside the city (750B). Every night, depending on the weather, a night boat runs from Surat Thani (400B, seven hours), departing at 10pm. Boats in the opposite direction leave Ko Pha-Ngan at 9pm.

Combination boat-bus tickets are available at any travel agency. Simply tell them your desired destination and they will sell you the necessary links in the transport chain. Most travellers will pass through Surat Thani as they swap coasts.

🚌 Getting Around

Bicycle rentals are not such a great idea unless you're fit enough to take on the Tour de France.

Pick-up trucks and *sŏrng·tăa·ou* (pickup minibuses) chug along the island's major roads, and the riding rates double after sunset. Ask your accommodation about free or discount transfers when you leave the island. The trip from Thong Sala to Hat Rin is 100B; further beaches will set you back around 150B to 200B. From Hat Rin, **sŏrng·tăa·ou** (Map p550) bound for Thong Sala depart from west of Hat Rin Nok.

Long-tail boats depart from Thong Sala, Chalok Lam (p559) and Hat Rin, heading to far-flung destinations such as **Hat Khuat** (Map p548; Hat Khuat (Bottle Beach); from 600B) and **Hat Than Sadet** (Map p548; Hat Than Sadet; from 600B). Expect to pay anywhere from 50B each way for a short trip, and up to 300B for a longer journey. You can charter a private boat ride from beach to beach for about 150B per 15 minutes of travel.

The best way to explore Ko Pha-Ngan is by renting a motorcycle/scooter. The going rate ranges from 150B to 300B per day (lower for longer rentals). You'll generally need to hand over your passport as a deposit (you will need it if moving hotel, so plan ahead). You'll see petrol for sale in bottles at 40B a litre, but it's much cheaper at petrol stations.

If you decide to rent a motorcycle/scooter, wear a helmet and ask for one with a plastic visor. While you won't be asked for one when you rent, legally you must have an international driving permit and you may have problems with police checks, or with insurance in the event of an accident – get one before you leave home. If you plan on riding over rough dirt tracks it is imperative that you rent a bike comparable to a Honda MTX125 – gearless scooters cannot make the journey. Avoid driving on the roads during any Full Moon.

Ko Tao

POP 3000

The baby of the Samui–Pha-Ngan–Tao trinity, Ko Tao (เกาะเต่า) may be the smallest in size but there is no identity crisis here. Ko Tao is the gulf's diving mecca. As a result the island is gaining in popularity and going more upscale with each passing year.

This jungle-topped cutie has the busy vibe of Samui mixed with the laid-back calm of Pha-Ngan and, of course, the best and easiest-to-get-to range of diverse dive spots right off its coastline. Cavort with sharks and rays in a playground of tangled neon coral, toast the day with sunset cocktails on a white-sand beach, then get up and do it all over again. The island isn't just about diving of course. Hikers and hermits can re-enact an episode from *Lost* in the dripping coastal jungles. And when you're Robinson Crusoe-ed out, hit the pumpin' bar scene that rages on until dawn.

Sights

★ Ao Tanot
BEACH

(อ่าวโตนด; Map p566; P) With crystal-clear waters and superb snorkelling, pretty Ao Tanot on the east coast also affords excellent rock-jumping opportunities from the huge boulders in the bay. If diving or snorkelling, look out for angelfish, coral trout and bannerfish. There's a sunken catamaran in the bay and several resort and bungalow rentals popular with families operate here if you do want to stay overnight and catch the splendid sunrise.

★ Ko Nang Yuan
ISLAND

(เกาะนางยวน; Map p566; admission 100B; ⊙10am-5pm) These three lovely islands off the northwest coast of Ko Tao are linked together by a sandbar, with superb views from the island's highest points. Boats run from the Lomprayah pier in Mae Hat and visiting them makes for an excellent day trip from Ko Tao.

Hat Laem Thian
BEACH

(หาดแหลมเทียน; Map p566) In the lee of the headland, this secluded and sheltered little white-sand beach in the middle of the east coast, north of Ao Tanot, is a delightful place with excellent snorkelling, fabulous rock jumping and very clear waters. It's quite a hike (1½ hours from Sairee Village) to get here along a dirt track; so in truth it's better to arrive by long-tail boat. There's the shell

of an old resort here, crumbling away and covered in graffiti.

If you do hike, take loads of water, a sun hat, appropriate footwear and sunscreen.

Activities

Diving

If you've never been diving before, Ko Tao is *the* place in Thailand to lose your scuba virginity. The shallow bays scalloping the island are perfect for newbie divers to take their first stab at scuba; the waters are crystal clear, there are loads of neon reefs and the temperatures are bathwater warm. With many sheltered dive sites, waters around Ko Tao can be dived all year round; it's only during the monsoon months that diving may stop for a day or two if the waters are too choppy, but this is actually quite rare.

The best dive sites are found at offshore pinnacles within a 20km radius of the island. The local marine wildlife includes groupers, moray eels, batfish, bannerfish, barracudas, titan triggerfish, angelfish, clownfish (Nemos), stingrays, reef sharks and frequent visits by mighty whale sharks.

Onshore, scores of dive centres are ready to saddle you up with gear and teach you the ropes in a 3½-day Open Water certification course. The intense competition among scuba schools means that certification prices are unbeatably low and standards of service top-notch; dozens of dive shops vie for your baht, so be sure to shop around. The island issues more scuba certifications than anywhere else in the world.

Ocean Republic Diving
DIVING

(Map p568; ☑061 462 7661; www.oceanrepublic diving.com; Mae Hat; basic dive program 3500B; ⊙8.30am-8pm) The only dive school that is Sea Shepard affiliated and that therefore thoroughly encourage, and actively engage in, marine conservation. Providing high-quality, conscientious teaching in small classes (maximum four people) in a relaxed environment, this is one of the friendliest dive schools on the island.

Ban's Diving School
DIVING

(Map p568; ☑077 456466; www.bansdivingresort. com; Hat Sairee; ⊙8am-7pm) A well-oiled diving operation since 1993 at the resort (d 1110-3500B; P ✳ @ 🛜 ≋) of the same name, this is one of Ko Tao's most prolific diver certification schools. Classroom sessions tend to be conducted in large groups, but there's

DIVE SITES AT A GLANCE

In general, divers don't have much of a choice as to which sites they explore. Each dive school chooses a smattering of sites for the day depending on weather and ocean conditions. Deeper dive sites such as Chumphon Pinnacle are usually visited in the morning. Afternoon boats tour the shallower sites such as Japanese Gardens. There are two large sunken vessels off the coast, providing scubaphiles with wreck dives.

Divers hoping to spend some quality time searching for whale sharks at Sail Rock should join one of the dive trips departing daily from Ko Pha-Ngan.

Chumphon Pinnacle (36m maximum depth), 11km northwest of Ko Tao, has a colourful assortment of sea anemones along the four interconnected pinnacles. The site plays host to schools of giant trevally, tuna and large grey reef sharks. Whale sharks are known to pop up once in a while.

Green Rock (Map p566) (25m maximum depth) is an underwater jungle gym featuring caverns, caves and small swim-throughs. Rays, grouper and triggerfish hang around. It's a great place for a night dive.

Japanese Gardens (Map p566) (16m maximum depth), between Ko Tao and Ko Nang Yuan, is a low-stress dive site perfect for beginners and snorkellers. There's plenty of colourful coral, and turtles, stingray and pufferfish often pass by.

Mango Bay (Map p566) (16m maximum depth) might be your first dive site if you are putting on a tank for the first time. Lazy reef fish swim around as newbies practise their skills on the sandy bottom.

Lighthouse Bay (Gluay Teun Bay; Map p566) (14m maximum depth) is a shallow dive site on the northeastern tip of the island with some superb coral and is excellent snorkelling. Look out for yellowtail barracuda, parrotfish and bannerfish.

Sail Rock (40m maximum depth), best accessed from Ko Pha-Ngan, features a massive rock chimney with a vertical swim-through, and large pelagics like barracuda and kingfish. This is one of the top spots in Southeast Asia to see whale sharks; in the past few years they have been seen year-round, so there's no clear season.

Southwest Pinnacle (28m maximum depth) offers divers a small collection of pinnacles that are home to giant groupers and barracuda. Whale sharks are sometimes spotted.

Ao Tanot (p564) (18m maximum depth) is suitable for every level of diver. It's pretty shallow so is a superb snorkelling site. Look out for angelfish, coral trout, bannerfish and the sunken catamaran.

White Rock (Map p566) (29m maximum depth) is home to colourful corals, angelfish, clownfish and territorial triggerfish, and is a popular spot for night divers.

HTMS Sattakut (Map p566) was sunk southeast of Hin Pee Wee in 2011 at a depth of 30m and has become one of the most popular wreck-diving sites.

a reasonable amount of individual attention in the water. A breadth of international instructors means multilingual courses.

Big Blue Diving DIVING
(Map p568; ☑ 077 456050; www.bigbluediving. com; 15/3 Mu 1, Sairee Beach; ☻8am-7pm) If Goldilocks were picking a dive school, she'd probably go for Big Blue – this midsize operation (not too big, not too small) is popular for fostering a sociable vibe while maintaining high standards of service. Divers of every ilk can score accommodation across

the budget ranges, from backpacker dorms up to top-notch family villas at their resort.

Calypso Diving DIVING
(Map p566; ☑ 084 841 5166; www.diving-calypso. com; 40/20 Mu 3, Ao Tanot; dives from 800B; ☻8am-6pm) This easygoing, relaxed but professional and friendly German dive outfit by the beach is an excellent choice with a range of diving courses (from novice to professional level) starting at 800B for a beach dive; also rents snorkelling gear.

Ko Tao

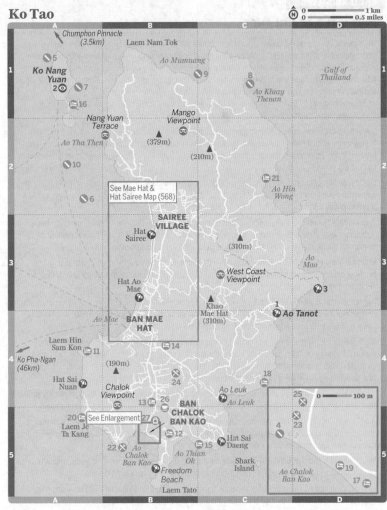

Crystal Dive DIVING

(Map p568; ☑ 077 456106; www.crystaldive.com; 7/1 Mu 2, Mae Hat; courses from 2500B; ☺8am-6pm) This award-winning school (and resort) is one of the largest operators on the island (and around the world), but high-quality instructors and intimate classes keep the school feeling quite personal. Multilingual staff members, air-conditioned classes and two on-site swimming pools sweeten the deal. Crystal also puts considerable energy into marine conservation projects on Ko Tao. Highly recommended. Freediving, videography, underwater photography, night diving, search and recovery offered.

Roctopus Dive DIVING

(Map p568; ☑ 077 456611, 090 863 1836; www. roctopusdive.com; 17 Mu 1, Sairee Village; courses from 1900B; ☺9am-6pm) Centrally located on Sairee Beach, with great staff and high standards, this popular and bubbly dive school is a well-equipped, excellent choice for divers of all abilities. Choose from a half-day Try Dive and Open Water course for novices to speciality and advanced dive courses. It also runs a dedicated speedboat for snorkel trips, cliff-jumping and private charters.

Ko Tao

Snorkelling

Snorkelling is a popular alternative to diving, and orchestrating your own snorkelling adventure here is simple, as the bays on the east coast have small bungalow operations offering equipment rental for between 100B and 200B per day.

Most snorkel enthusiasts opt for the do-it-yourself approach on Ko Tao, which involves swimming out into the offshore bays or hiring a long-tail boat to putter around further out. Guided tours are also available and can be booked at any local travel agency. Tours range from 500B to 800B (usually including gear, lunch and a guideand stop at snorkelling hotspots around the island.

Laem Thian is popular for its small sharks, Shark Island has loads of fish (but ironically no sharks), Ao Hin Wong is known for its crystalline waters, and Lighthouse Bay (p565), in the north, offers a dazzling array of colourful sea anemones. Ao Tanot (p564) is also a popular snorkelling spot.

Dive schools will usually allow snorkellers on their vessels for a comparable price – but it's only worth snorkelling at the shallower sites such as Japanese Gardens (p565).

Freediving

In recent years freediving (exploring the sea using breath-holding techniques rather than scuba gear) has grown massively in popularity, attracting those without any diving experience, as well as scuba divers.

With a large number of fully qualified freedivers on the island, many traditional dive operators now offer freediving. There are, however, a couple of specialist freediving operators worth special mention. Apnea Total (p569) has earned several awards in the freediving world and possesses a special knack for easing newbies into this heart-pounding sport. It's a grade A outfit where the student–teacher ratio of three to one ensures plenty of attention to safety. Also worth a special mention is the highly capable Blue Immersion. Freediving prices are pretty much standardised across the island – a 2½-day SSI beginner course will set you back 6000B.

For those eager to seek out more information on this exciting form of diving, get hold of a copy of the much-celebrated and well-received *One Breath* by Adam Skolnick.

Blue Immersion　　　　　　　　　　DIVING
(Map p568; ☏ 081 188 8488; www.blue-immersion.com; 136 Mu 1, Sairee Beach; courses from 3000B; ☺ noon-8pm) Founded by Akim Ladhari, one of the first people in the world to freedive below 100m, this school is the bees-knees for freedivers of all abilities. There are nine experienced instructors with course prices starting from 3000B for a taster session (up to 10m) right up to 76,000B for a three-month instructor course. There's also a 12-bed dorm (490B) on-site.

Mae Hat & Hat Sairee

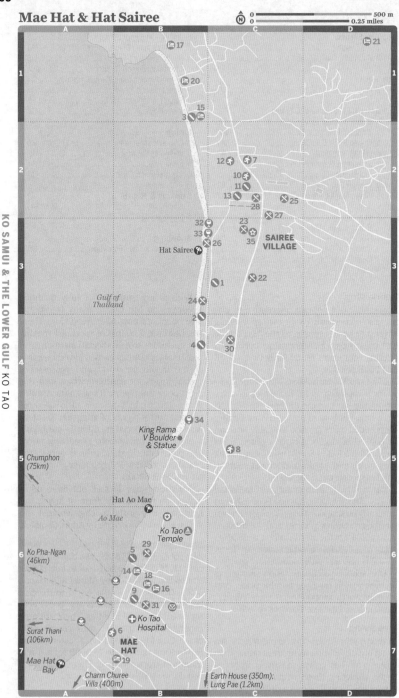

0   500 m
0   0.25 miles

17

21

20

15
3

12   7
10
11
13   25
28
27
32   23
33   35   SAIREE
VILLAGE
Hat Sairee   26

1

22

Gulf of
Thailand   24
2

4
30

Chumphon
(75km)

King Rama   34
V Boulder
& Statue
8

Ko Pha-Ngan
(46km)

Hat Ao Mae

Ao Mae

Ko Tao
Temple

5   29

14   18
9   16

Surat Thani
(106km)

31
Ko Tao
Hospital

6
MAE
HAT
19

Mae Hat
Bay

Charm Churee
Villa (400m)

Earth House (350m);
Lung Pae (1.2km)

Mae Hat & Hat Sairee

Apnea Total DIVING
(Map p568; 081 956 5720, 081 956 5430; www.apneatotal.com; 9/224 Mu 1, Sairee Beach; courses 1000-40,000B; ⊗8.30am-8pm) The capable, outgoing and enthusiastic staff at Apnea Total, which has earned several awards in the free-diving world, possess a special knack for easing newbies into this awe-inspiring sport. The student-teacher ratio of three to one also ensures plenty of attention safety. There are a host of courses for beginners through to those wishing to become free-diving instructors.

Technical Diving & Cave Diving
Well-seasoned divers and wannabe Jacques Cousteaus should contact Tech Dive Thailand (Map p568; 077 456604; www.techdivethailand.com; 14/102 Mu 2, Sairee Beach; ⊗8am-6pm) or one of a handful of other tech diving schools if they want to take their underwater exploration to the next level and try a technical dive. Tech diving goes beyond conventional commercial or recreational diving, exceeding depths of 40m and requires stage decompressions, with a variety of gas mixtures often used in a single dive. You must be a certified tech diver to undertake tech dives; training courses are available at many schools on the island.

The gulf is also excellent for wreck exploration having long been an important trading route. New wrecks are being discovered all the time, from old Chinese pottery wrecks to Japanese *marus* (merchant ships). The HTMS Sattakut (p565) is one of the more accessible and popular, but for a full inventory of sites, check out the website of Tech Dive Thailand, which has a complete online database of dozens of wrecks.

Cave diving has taken Ko Tao by storm, and the most intrepid scuba buffs are lining up to make the half-day trek over to Khao Sok National Park. Beneath the park's main lake lurks an astonishing submarine world filled with hidden grottos, limestone crags and skulking catfish. In certain areas divers can swim near submerged villages that were flooded in order to create a reservoir and dam. Most cave-diving trips depart from Ko Tao on the afternoon boat service and return to the island on the same service the following day.

Underwater Photography & Videography
If your wallet is already full of diving certification cards, consider renting an underwater camera or enrolling in a marine videography course. Many scuba schools hire professional videographers to film Open

ⓘ TAKING THE PLUNGE: CHOOSING A DIVE SCHOOL ON KO TAO

It's no surprise that this underwater playground has become exceptionally popular with beginners. But before you dive in (so to speak) it's important to look around at the various schools available.

When you alight at the pier in Mae Hat, swarms of touts will try to coax you into staying at their dive resort. But there are dozens of dive centres on Ko Tao, so it's best to arrive armed with the names of a few reputable schools and go from there. Give yourself time to make an informed decision. If you're not in a rush, consider relaxing on the island for a couple of days before making any decisions – you will undoubtedly bump into swarms of scubaphiles and instructors who will offer their advice and opinions.

Remember: the success of your diving experience will largely depend on how much you like your instructor. Other factors to consider are the size of your diving group, the condition of your equipment and the condition of the dive sites, to name a few.

For the most part, diving prices are somewhat standardised across the island, so there's no need to spend your time hunting around for the best deal. A PADI (www.padi.com) Open Water Diver (OWD) certification course or an SSI (www.divessi.com) OWD certificate will set you back between 10,000-11,000B. Increasingly popular across the island, a RAID (www.diveraid.com) OWD course is 9,500B. An Advanced Open Water Diver (AOWD) certification course will set you back 10,000B, a rescue course is 10,000B and the Divemaster program costs a cool 30,000-35,000B (which includes the divemaster pack that everyone requires). Fun divers should expect to pay roughly 1000B per dive, or around 7000B for a 10-dive package. These rates include all dive gear, boat, instructors/guides and snacks. Discounts are usually given if you bring your own equipment. Be wary of dive centres that offer too many price cuts – safety is paramount, and a shop giving out unusually good deals is probably cutting too many corners. The market is easy to enter as there are no barriers to access, meaning cheap and poorly run places pop up offering superb deals. Stick to established outfits.

Most dive schools will hook you up with cheap or even free accommodation. Almost all scuba centres offer gratis fan rooms for anyone doing beginner courses. Expect large crowds and booked-out beds throughout December, January, June, July and August, and a monthly glut of wannabe divers after every Full Moon Party on Ko Pha-Ngan.

Water Diver certifications, and if this piques your interest, you could potentially earn some money after completing a video internship. Your dive operator can put you in touch with any of the half-dozen videography crews on the island. An introductory course including camera, diving and instruction is around 5000B and can also be used towards an Advanced PADI certification. Crystal Images (Map p568; ☑ 092 476 4110; www.crystalimageskohtao.com; Mae Hat; ☉6am-5pm) and Oceans Below (Map p568; ☑ 086 060 1863; www.oceansbelow.net; Sairee Village) offer videography courses and internships; each have their own special options.

Hiking

One popular cross-island trek via the West Coast Viewpoint leads up the road just south of the Monsoon Gym, following the road and a dirt trail to a fork in the road named Two Views; turn left to the West Coast Viewpoint, for splendid panoramas over the island's west. You can backtrack to the fork and head left via the reservoir down to Ao Tanot. The whole trip to is around 4.5km and takes around 1½ hours.

Another enjoyable trek follows a coastline trail past several beaches south of Mae Hat and round the cape to Ao Chalok Ban Kao, beginning at Charm Churee Villa and heading south along a concrete path to Hat Sai Nuan, before continuing along a dirt path over the hill to the cape of Laem Je Ta Kang. Before you reach Laem Je Ta Kang, take the turning east to Ao June Juea past Tao Thong 2 Villa and on down to the beach at Ao June Juea; you can continue on to Ao Chalok Ban Kao.

Other Activities

★ Goodtime Adventures ADVENTURE SPORTS (Map p568; ☑ 087 275 3604; www.goodtimethailand.com; 14/2 Mu 1, Sairee Beach; ☉9am-7pm) Dive, hike through the island's jungle interior, swing from rock to rock during a climbing and abseiling session, or unleash your inner daredevil cliff-jumping or throwing yourself into multisport or powerboat handling (15000B). Alternatively, take a shot at a mix of them on the full-day Koh Tao Adventure.

The Goodtime office has its own cafe and and bar along the Sairee sands and also operates a hostel with dorms and doubles.

Monsoon Gym & Fight Club   MARTIAL ARTS
(Map p568; ☑086 271 2212; www.monsoongym. com; 41/4 Mu 1, Sairee Beach; drop-in fight training 300B, 6 sessions 1500B, unlimited monthly 7000B; ☺7am-9pm) This popular club combines *moo·ay tai* programs and air-con dorm accommodation (300B) for students signed up to get to grips with the fighting art. It's an excellent and exhilarating way to spend time in Ko Tao, if diving isn't your scene. The well-equipped concrete gym is right alongside the Thai boxing ring.

Shambhala   YOGA
(Map p568; ☑084 440 6755; www.shambhalayogakohtao.com; 14/2 Mu 1, Sairee Beach; ☺10am-noon & 6-7.30pm Mon-Sat, 10am-noon Sun) Ko Tao's leading yoga centre – making students supple for two decades – is housed in beautiful wooden *săh·lah* on the forested grounds of Blue Wind Resort. Led by experienced teachers, the two-hour classes cost 300B (10 classes 2500B).

🛏 Sleeping

If you are planning to dive while visiting Ko Tao, your scuba operator will probably offer you free or discounted accommodation to sweeten the deal. Some schools have on-site lodging, while others have deals with nearby bungalows. It's important to note that you only receive your scuba-related discount on the days you dive.

🛏 Hat Sairee

Giant Hat Sairee, better known as Sairee Beach is the longest and most developed strip on the island, with a string of dive operations, bungalows, travel agencies, minimarkets and coffee bars backing onto it. The northern end is the prettiest and quietest, while there's more of a party scene towards the south. For most people, this is the choice beach to stay at as it has a great blend of scenery and action, plus the sunsets are superb.

Indie Hostel Koh Tao   HOSTEL $
(Map p568; ☑077 332 524; www.indiekohtao.com; 14/143 Mu 1, Sairee Beach; dm/d 500/1170B; ☀🖥) Go for the smaller dorms at this busy, clean and cheap hostel attracting a good backpacker crowd close to Sairee Beach.

Big Blue Resort   BUNGALOW $
(Map p568; ☑077 456050; www.bigbluediving. com; 15/3 Mu 1, Sairee Beach; dm/d/bungalows from 300/600/800B; ⚟🖥🖥🖥) This scuba-centric resort has a summer-camp vibe – diving classes dominate the daytime, while evenings are spent en masse, grabbing dinner or watching fire twirling. There are basic six-bed fan dorms, air-con bungalows and villas as well as luxury family villas. Some rooms are only available if you are diving with Big Blue (p565).

Palm Leaf Resort   BUNGALOW $$$
(Map p568; ☑077 456731; www.palmleafkohtao. com; 15/2 Mu 1, Sairee Beach; bungalow 2000-4500B; ⚟🖥🖥🖥) These traditional bungalows are set along a quiet, silky northern section of Sairee Beach, away from the crowds. The jungle backdrop adds to the sense of serenity and many of the bungalows open up directly onto the beach adding to the tropical island feel.

Ko Tao Cabana   BUNGALOW $$$
(Map p568; ☑077 456504; www.kohtaocabana. com; 16 Mu 1, Sairee Beach; bungalow 5000-16,700B; ⚟🖥🖥🖥) This prime piece of quiet beachside property offers timber-framed villas and crinkled white adobe huts with woven roofs dotted along the boulder-strewn beach and up the hill, where paths wind through a fern-laden, manicured jungle. The private villas are one of the more upscale options on the island.

🛏 Mae Hat

All ferry arrivals pull into the pier at the busy village of Mae Hat and nearly all the resorts on this beach will have a view and be in earshot of the constant ebb and flow of boat arrivals and departures. As such this isn't the best beach for a tranquil getaway, although it's a good hub if your main goal is diving. Accommodation is spread throughout but the more charming options extend in both directions along the sandy beach, both north and south of the pier.

Moov Inn Garden Hostel   HOSTEL $
(Map p568; ☑086 064 8226; www.moovinnkohtao. com; 25/18 Mu 3, Mae Hat; dm/d 350/415B; 🖥🖥) Located conveniently close to the pier, this cool, little joint has a great, laid-back

atmosphere. Dorms are nice and clean, and every week there's a party of some sort in the bar.

Ko Tao Central Hostel
HOSTEL $

(Map p568; ☑ 077 456925; www.kohtaohostel.com; 9/21 Mu 2, Mae Hat; dm 300B; ❄ ☎) Identified by its London Underground–style logo and decorated with Banksy murals and Tubeline stripes, this clean, central and friendly hostel has good 14-bed dorms, if all you need is a handy bed near the pier. Reception is opposite the Reef Bar; no towel service, so bring your own.

Crystal Dive Resort
BUNGALOW $

(Map p568; ☑ 077 456106; www.crystaldive.com; 7/1 Mu 2, Mae Hat; bungalow/d 400/800B; ❄ ☎ ☁) The bungalow and motel-style accommodation at Crystal is generally reserved for its divers, and prices drop significantly for those taking courses.

Crystal Dive's partner resorts also offer accommodation: the Koh Tao Regal (www.kohtaoregal.com) and the Beach Club (www.thebeachclubkohtao.com).

Ananda Villa
HOTEL $$

(Map p568; ☑ 077 456478; www.anandavilla.com; Mae Hat; d 1650-1800B; bungalows 500-1000B; ❄ ☎) This friendly, two-storey cream-and-white hotel with verandahs and lined with decorative palms and plumeria has a colonial feel, a short walk north of the jetty. The cheapest bungalows are fan only, with hot water.

Captain Nemo Guesthouse
GUESTHOUSE $$

(Map p568; ☑ 092 364 1031; www.captainnemoguesthouse.com; 9/37 Mu 2, Mae Hat; d 950-1750B, f 1500-2300B; ❄ ☎) With five types of rooms, this popular, small choice, a short walk from the pier, is nearly always full so book upfront. The owners are responsive, friendly and helpful, and everything is kept clean.

Charm Churee Villa
RESORT $$$

(Map p566; ☑ 077 456393; www.charmchureevilla.com; 30/1 Mu 2, Jansom Bay, Mae Hat; d 3600-4600, bungalows 5600-39100B; P ❄ ☎ ☁) Tucked under sky-scraping palms on a 48-hectare jungle plot away from the bustle of the pier, the luxuriant villas of Charm Churee are dedicated to the flamboyant spoils of the Far East. Staircases chiselled into the rock face wind their way down a palmed slope revealing teak huts strewn across smoky boulders. The villas' unobstructed views of the swishing waters are beguiling.

🛏 Chalok Ban Ko & the South

Ao Chalok Ban Ko, about 1.7km south of Mae Hat by road, has one of the largest concentrations of accommodation on Ko Tao. This is a slim stretch of sand in a scenic half-circle bay framed by boulders at either end. The milky blue water here is quite shallow and at low tide a sandbar is exposed that's fun to wade out to for prime sunbathing. This is the quietest of the main beaches but there's still a good selection of restaurants, plenty of diving and a mellow but fun nightlife scene.

Dearly Koh Tao Hostel
HOSTEL $$

(Map p566; ☑ 077 332494; www.thedearlykohtaohostel.com; 14/55 Mu 3, Chalok Ban Kao; incl breakfast dm 600-700B, d & tr 2400-3000B; ❄ ☎ ☁) Located on the road that leads inland from Chalok Ban Kao, this hostel has all the right ingredients: clean, comfortable, contemporary (but also traditional) rooms, bubbly and friendly staff, rattan furniture and a rooftop terrace. There's a mix of dorms and private rooms, and a swimming pool.

Ko Tao Resort
RESORT $$

(Map p566; ☑ 077 456133; www.kotaoresort.com; 19/1 Mu 3, Chalok Ban Kao; d & bungalow 1275-4860B; ❄ ☎ ☁) Rooms at this resort are split between 'pool side' and 'paradise zone' – all are well furnished, water-sports equipment is on offer, and there are several bars primed to serve an assortment of fruity cocktails. Views of the milky-blue waters are gorgeous.

Buddha View Dive Resort
BUNGALOW $$

(Map p566; ☑ 077 456074; www.buddhaview-diving.com; 45/1 Mu 3, Chalok Ban Kao; d 400-1600B; P ❄ @ ☎ ☁) Like many large diving operations on the island, Buddha View (Map p566; ☑ 077 456074; www.buddhaview-diving.com; 45/1 Mu 3, Chalok Ban Kao; courses from 2500B; ☺ 7am-6.30pm) offers its divers discounted on-site digs in a super-social atmosphere.

Tao Thong Villa
BUNGALOW $$

(Map p566; ☑ 077 423809; www.facebook.com/taothongvilla2; 33/2 Mu 2, Ao Sai Nuan; bungalow 600-2000B; ❄ ☎) Popular with long-termers seeking peace and quiet, these no-frills bungalows have killer views. Tao Thong straddles two tiny beaches on a craggy cape about halfway between Mae Hat and Chalok Ban Kao.

Chintakiri Resort
RESORT $$

(Map p566; ☑ 077 456391; Chalok Ban Kao; d 2500B; P ❄ ☎ ☁) Perched high over the gulf waters overlooking Chalok Ban Kao, Chinta-kiri is one of Ko Tao's more luxurious prop-erties. Rooms are spread around the inland jungle and feature crisp white walls with lacquered finishing.

New Heaven Resort
BUNGALOW $$

(Map p566; ☑ 077 456045; www.newheavendive school.com; 48 Mu 3, Chalok Ban Kao; bungalow 1500-2500B; ❋ ☞) New Heaven – part of the diving operation of the same name – de-livers colourful huts perched on a hill over impossibly clear waters, air-con sea-view bungalows and glamping air-con tents start-ing from 800B.

★ Jamahkiri Resort & Spa
RESORT $$$

(Map p566; ☑ 077 456400; www.jamahkiri.com; 21/1 Mu 3, Ao Thian Ok; bungalow 10,400-12,400B; P ❋ ☞ ☒) Wooden gargoyle masks and stone fertility goddesses abound amid swirl-ing mosaics and multi-armed statues at this whitewashed estate. Hoots from distant monkeys confirm the jungle theme, as do the thatched roofs and tiki-torched soirees. There are lots of steps, but views are drop-dead gorgeous, the spa is top of the range and the dive centre is excellent.

⌖ East Coast Beaches

The serene eastern coast is, without a doubt, one of the best places in the region to live out your island paradise fantasies. The views are stunning; beaches are silent, yet all of your creature comforts are within 10 minutes.

View Rock
BUNGALOW $

(Map p566; ☑ 077 456548; Hin Wong; bungalows 500-1000B; ☞) View Rock is precisely that: views and rocks; the hodgepodge of wooden huts, resembling a fishing village built into the steep crags, offer stunning views of the bay. Bungalows are simple and modest, but clean enough. Coming down the dirt road into Hin Wong, follow the signs north past Hin Wong Bungalows.

Moondance
Magic View Bungalow
BUNGALOW $$

(Map p566; ☑ 089 909 0083; www.moondance magicviewbungalow.com; Ao Leuk; bungalows with fan/air-con 1250/2500B; ❋ ☞) For those who really want to get away from it all. Stay in quaint, spartan bungalows, high upon the cliffs northeast of Ao Leuk Beach. The 'mag-ic' is the sense of solitude and special views across the gulf. There is no road leading here

so you'll need to come by moped along a dirt track or arrange a pickup.

Montalay Beach Resort
RESORT $$

(Map p566; ☑ 077 456488; www.montalay resort-kohtao.com; Ao Tanote Beach; bungalow 1440-2250B; P ❋ ☞ ☒) Popular with families and set on the quiet Ao Tanote Beach away from the hustle and bustle, the Montalay's simple, little bungalows are spread through a landscaped jungle garden, while the very good restaurant and small swimming pool cascade down to the white sands.

⌖ The Interior

Earth House
BUNGALOW $

(Map p566; ☑ 086 069 9244; www.theearth-house-kohtao.com; 2/35 Mu 3; bungalow 350-600B; ☞) Next to the bar (Map p566; ☑ 089 036 3505; www.theearthhouse-kohtao.com; 2/35 Mu 3; ◐ noon-midnight Mon-Sat) of the same name, the bungalows at this place are a ter-rific escape from the usual. Sure, there's no beach, but the bar is superb and the jungle setting is simply lovely, while the bamboo bungalows (they only sleep one, so single travellers only) are charmingly rustic and clean.

Place
RESORT $$$

(Map p568; ☑ 087 887 5066; www.theplacekohtao. com; villa 8000-9000B; P ❋ ☞) This romantic boutique choice has nine private luxury vil-las nestled in leaf-clad hills with sweeping ocean views. Honeymooners will rejoice: a private plunge pool is standard, and private chef services satisfy those who choose to remain in their nuptial nest instead of ven-turing out.

⌖ Ko Nang Yuan

Photogenic Ko Nang Yuan, just off the northwest coast of Ko Tao, is easily accessi-ble by water taxis that depart from Mae Hat and Sairee (150B each way). There's a 100B tax for all visitors to the island and it can get very busy during peak season.

Ko Nangyuan Dive Resort
BUNGALOW $$

(Map p566; ☑ 081 958 1766; www.nangyuan.com; 46 Mu 1, Ko Nangyuan; bungalow 2500-6000B; ❋ ☞) The rugged collection of wood and aluminium bungalows winds its way across three straw-hat-like conical islands connect-ed by an idyllic beige sandbar. Yes, this is a private-island paradise but note it gets busy with day-trippers. The resort also boasts the best and only restaurant on the island. Prices include round-trip to Ko Tao.

Eating

Hat Sairee

⭐ 995 Roasted Duck
CHINESE $

(Map p568; Sairee Village; mains from 70B; ⊗9am-9pm) You may have to queue a while to get a seat at this glorified shack and wonder what all the fuss is about – it's the excellent roast-duck dishes that start at 70B for a steaming bowl of roasted waterfowl with noodles to 700B for a whole bird, served in a jiffy. You'd be quackers to miss out.

Vegetabowl
VEGETARIAN $

(Map p568; ☑084 692 7749; www.facebook.com/vegetabowl; 9/5 Island Plaza, Sairee Beach; bowls from 120B; ⊗11.30am-8pm; 🖗🖉) Delicious, fresh bowls of vegetarian dishes such as the Mexican, Japanese, Wellness and Power come full of goodness and detox qualities at this fun, colourful, little spot down a side street opposite the 7-Eleven. It's easily one of the finest vegetarian options on Ko Tao, with fast service and friendly staff.

Bang Burgers
BURGERS $

(Map p568; ☑081 136 6576; Sairee Village; burgers from 100B; ⊗10am-10pm; 🖉) You may have to wait in line at this popular burger bar that does a decent trade in Sairee. There's around a half-dozen burgers (cheese, double cheese, red chilli cheese) on the menu, including a vegie choice for meat-free diners.

⭐ Barracuda Restaurant & Bar
FUSION $$

(Map p568; ☑080 146 3267, 077 457049; www.barracudakohtao.com; 9/9 Mu 1, Sairee Village; mains 250B; ⊗4-10.30pm; 🖗) Sociable chef Ed Jones allegedly caters for Thai royalty when they are in town, but you can sample his exquisite cuisine for mere pennies. Locally sourced ingredients are turned into creative, fresh, fusion masterpieces. Try the seafood platter, pan-fried barracuda fillet or vegetarian falafel platter – then wash it down with a passionfruit mojito.

⭐ Cafe Culture
CAFE $$

(Map p568; ☑077 456808; Sairee Beach; mains 160B; ⊗8.30am-9.30pm; 🖗🖉) This delightfully charming all-day cafe starts on the nonbeach side of the tiny walkway along Sairee Beach, crosses over and gently cascades down to the sandy waterfront. Cool, mellow beats play throughout the day as customers enjoy the light lunches and delicious breakfasts.

Shalimar Indian Restaurant
INDIAN $$

(Map p568; ☑089 217 7220; www.facebook.com/shalimarkohtao; 17/59 Mu 1, Sairee Village; thali from 250B; ⊗2-11pm; 🖉) This place is all about the *thalis* (meal platter). The veg option at 250B is super filling and great value for money, but if you're extremely hungry and a meat-eater then don't hold back on the meat version for a mere 20B upgrade. The setting is open and airy with understated Indian decor and an impressive white Arabesque gate at the entrance.

Seashell Restaurant
SEAFOOD $$

(Map p568; Sairee Beach; mains 250B; ⊗7am-10pm; 🖗) The combination of great fresh seafood cooked to perfection, and some of the best sunsets from chairs and tables positioned to maximise this excellent spot on the beach, makes this a fantastic evening dinner spot. Even if you're not eating, it's worth coming here for a cocktail or beer.

Gallery
THAI $$

(Map p568; ☑077 456547; www.thegallerykohtao.com; 10/46 Mu 1, Sairee Village; mains 240B; ⊗noon-10pm; ❄🖗🖉) One of the most pleasant settings in town, the food here is equally special. The signature dish is *hor mok maprao on* (chicken, shrimp and fish curry served in a young coconut) but the white snapper fillet in creamy red curry sauce is also excellent and there's a choice of vegetarian dishes.

If you can't decide, allow the chef to cook a range of starters and mains of their choosing (900B), suited to your spice levels and culinary proclivities.

Su Chili
THAI $$

(Map p568; ☑090 141 1577; Sairee Village; mains180B; ⊗10am-10.30pm; 🖗) Inviting and bustling, Su Chili serves fresh and tasty Thai dishes, with friendly staff always asking how spicy you want your food and somehow getting it right. Try the delicious northern Thai specialities or Penang curries. There's a smattering of Western comfort food for homesick diners.

Mae Hat

Bam Bam
THAI $

(Map p568; mains 70B; ⊗10am-10pm) Everyone 'round here loves Bam Bam. The food is cheap, they'll deliver it to your hostel and when you eat it, it tastes like something a Thai grandma has cooked. The only downside to this open-air shack-on-the-corner is that the well meaning staff can get a little overwhelmed when things get really busy, so be patient.

Pranee's Kitchen
THAI $

(Map p568; Mae Hat; mains 120B; ☺7am-10pm; ☏) An old Mae Hat fave, Pranee's serves scrumptious curries and other Thai treats in an open-air pavilion sprinkled with lounging pillows, wooden tables and TVs. English-language movies are shown nightly at 6pm.

Zest Coffee Lounge
CAFE $

(Map p568; ☑077 456178; Mae Hat; mains 120B; ☺6am-4pm; ☏☒) All brick and wood with a scuffed floor, Zest pulls out all the stops with excellent coffee and brekkies that will cure any hangover. Eggs Benedict gets the morning off on the right foot, while idlers and snackers can nibble on ciabatta sandwiches and delicious seeded, filled bagels.

Cappuccino
CAFE $

(Map p568; ☑077 456870; Mae Hat; mains from 70B; ☺8am-11pm; ☏) With marble tabletops, wall mirrors and good grooves, chirpy Cappuccino's decor is somewhere between New York deli and French brasserie – it's a fine place to prepare for your Ko Tao day over freshly baked croissants and smooth cappuccinos.

This is a Book Cafe
CAFE $

(Map p568; ☑089 041 2020; Mae Hat; snacks 70-180B; ☺7am-9pm; ☏) With lovely white walls, books on shelves, a small scattering of hip furniture and a floral sofa, this charming and very quiet choice is perfect for a coffee, ice cream, baked goodies and a dose of tranquillity.

Whitening
INTERNATIONAL $$

(Map p568; ☑077 456199; www.facebook.com/Whiteningsairee; Mae Hat; mains 200B; ☺1pm-1am; ☏) This starched-white beachy spot is somewhere between a restaurant and a chic seaside bar – foodies will appreciate the tasty twists on indigenous and international dishes, including some excellent pasta. Dine amid dangling white Christmas lights while keeping your bare feet tucked into the sand. And the best part? It's comparatively easy on the wallet.

✖ Chalok Ban Kao & The South

South Beach Cafe
CAFE $

(Map p566; ☑094 369 1979; Chalok Ban Kao; mains 140B; ☺8am-10pm; ☒) We love the coffee art at this fresh, modern joint serving amazing burgers and wholesome breakfasts. It's a handsome addition to Chalok Ban Kao and has a menu that spans panini, salads, pizzas, burgers and even vegan dishes. There are also cheesecakes and glasses of house wine (99B) on offer.

I (Heart) Salad
CAFE $$

(Map p566; ☑087 088 6319; Chalok Ban Kao; mains from 120B; ☺8am-2pm & 4-9pm; ☏☒) This rustic choice offers a healthy array of salads using fresh ingredients, with a good supply of vegetarian and vegan options and sticky desserts to follow. There are also real fruit juices and healthy egg-white-only breakfasts. A great detox spot.

Cape Restaurant
INTERNATIONAL $$$

(Map p566; ☑077 456444; Viewpoint Resort, 27 Mu 3, Chalok Ban Kao; mains 250-1100B; ☺7.30am-10pm) On a beautiful wood deck overlooking Ao Chalok Ban Kao, this is one of the most romantic settings on the island. The food is also the most upscale and holds its own against Ko Samui's best – try the braised pork belly or the whole tuna from the oven. Apart from the Australian beef dishes, prices are reasonable.

✖ Elsewhere

Lung Pae
STEAK $$

(Map p566; ☑086 287 1039; mains from 160B; ☺10am-midnight; ☏) Off the radar of the island's tourist traffic, 'Uncle Pae' sits on a terrace in hilly jungle with views over the blue sea below. The speciality here is steak, which goes well with a generous smattering of pan-Asian appetisers.

🍷 Drinking & Nightlife

As well as a surprising number of banging bars that offer all night dance-a-thons, Ko Tao has a brilliant selection that know how to really take advantage of the island's west coast, sunset-facing orientation. These are mostly found along the main hubs of Mae Hat and Sairee Beach. Into this mix are a number of seriously cool cafes that sprawl out onto the beaches every morning.

KO SAMUI & THE LOWER GULF KO TAO

★ **Lotus Bar** BAR

(Map p568; ☑ 077 456 272; Sairee Beach; ⊙ 8am-2am; 🛜) Lotus is the leading late-night hang-out along the northern end of Sairee, affording front-row seats to some of the most spectacular sunsets on Ko Tao. Muscular fire-twirlers entertain you as you down drinks so large there should be a lifeguard on duty.

Maya Beach Club BAR

(Map p568; ☑ 080 578 2225; www.mayabeachclub kohtao.com; Sairee Beach; ⊙ 10am-8pm; 🛜) Rivalling Fizz for its entrancing sunset visuals and relaxing mood, Maya has nightly DJs and party nights. Make a move for a beach lounger and stay put.

Fishbowl Beach Bar BAR

(Map p568; ☑ 062 046 8996; www.facebook.com/fishbowlbeachbar; Sairee Beach; ⊙ noon-2am; 🛜) This buzzin', hoppin' bar gazes out at sunset onto killer views, with fire shows, live music and DJs kicking things off from 8pm.

Natural High Cafe CAFE

(Map p566; ☑ 077 056 342; ⊙ 10.30am-midnight; 🛜) With a fine elevated open-air terrace and panoramic views over the island's jungle greenery, hammocks for lounging around in, ambient chill-out sounds and coffee served in enamel cups, this cafe is ideal for zoning out. There's even a pool for a slow, lazy swim. It's signposted up a hill on the road to Hat Sai Daeng.

Chopper's Sports Bar SPORTS BAR

(Map p568; ☑ 077 456641; www.choppers-kohtao. com; 14/43 Mu 1, Sairee Village; ⊙ 9am-midnight; 🛜) This raucous venue is frequently rammed as it is a fixture on the Ko Tao pub crawl. Chopper's is a two-storey hang-out with live music, sports on the TVs, billiards, a cinema room and decent pub grub (mains 220B). Happy hour is 5pm to 8pm.

Fizz beachlounge BAR

(Map p568; ☑ 086 278 7319; Sairee Beach; ⊙ noon-1am; 🛜) Come sunset, sink into a green beanbag at the Fizz, order a designer cocktail and let the hypnotic surf and ambient music lull you into uberchill mode at one of Sairee Beach's best bars.

★ **Entertainment**

Queen's Cabaret CABARET

(Map p568; ☑ 087 677 6168; Sairee Village; ⊙ 9pm-midnight; 🛜) Every night is different at this intimate bar where acts range from your standard Abba tributes to steamy topless crooners. If you're male and sitting near the front, you may get 'dragged' into the performance. The show is free but it's expected you'll purchase a (pricey) drink – which is totally worth it. Show starts at 10.15pm.

🛒 **Shopping**

Hammock Cafe Plaeyuan HOMEWARES

(Map p566; ☑ 082 811 4312; www.facebook. com/hammockcafekohtao; 22/5 Mu 3, Ban Ko Tao; ⊙ 9am-6pm Sun-Fri; 🛜) This small French and Thai-run cafe with great coffee on the road to Chalok Ban Kao doubles as a hammock shop, selling a fantastic selection of brightly coloured Mlabri hand-woven hammocks. Prices start at around 1700B for a sitting hammock and reach up to 5000B for the most elaborate. Attractive handmade jewellery is also on sale.

ℹ️ **Information**

EMERGENCY

Police Station (Map p568; ☑ 077 456631) Between Mae Hat and Sairee Beach.

MEDICAL SERVICES

There are several walk-in clinics and mini-hospitals scattered around Mae Hat and Sairee, but all serious medical needs should be dealt with on Ko Samui.

Ko Tao Hospital (Map p568; ☑ 077 456490; ⊙ 24hr) For general medical and dental treatment.

MONEY

There are several banks in Mae Hat, at the far end of town along the island's main inland road. Most dive schools accept credit cards for a 3% handling fee.

There are 24-hour ATMs all over the west coast of the island in Mae Hat and Sairee Village, especially close to the 7-Eleven convenience stores. Be sure to withdraw from these before heading off to the more remote parts. Most will charge a small fee for your withdrawal.

POST

Post Office (Map p568; ☑ 077 456861; www. thailandpost.co.th; Mae Hat; ⊙ 9am-5pm Mon-Fri, 9am-noon Sat) A 10- to 15-minute walk from the pier; at the corner of Ko Tao's main inner-island road and Mae Hat's 'down road'.

SAFE TRAVEL

While hiring a scooter is extremely convenient, this is really not the place to learn how to drive: the roads on Ko Tao are being paved but some remain treacherous. The island is rife with abrupt, steep hills and sudden sand pits along gravel trails, as well as trenches in the road; if driving a scooter, stick to good roads and if you are unsure, turn back. Even if you escape unscathed, scamming bike shops may claim that you damaged your rental and will try to extort some serious cash from you (ensure you check the bike carefully prior to leaving the shop and photograph scratches and dents). Wear a helmet at all times.

TOURIST INFORMATION

There's no government-run TAT office on Ko Tao. Transportation and accommodation bookings can be made at most dive shops or at any of the numerous travel agencies, all of which take a small commission on services rendered.

Koh Tao Complete Guide (www.kohtaocom pleteguide.com) Handy website and an excellent quarterly free guidebook.

Koh Tao Online (www.kohtaoonline.com) An online version of the Koh Tao Info booklet.

Getting There & Away

AIR

Nok Air (www.nokair.com) jets passengers from Bangkok's Don Mueang airport to Chumphon twice daily in each direction. Flights to/from Bangkok can start from as low as 650B if you time your booking right. Upon arriving in Chumphon, it is easy to make the transfer to the catamaran service bound for Ko Tao.

BOAT

Boat services are rarely disrupted by the weather, but you may get some days of cancellations during the monsoon months (September to November), if waves are too high.

Ko Pha-Ngan

The **Lomprayah** (Map p568) catamaran offers a thrice-daily service (500B to 600B), leaving Ko Tao at 6am, 9.30am and 3pm and arriving on Ko Pha-Ngan around 7.10am, 10.45am and 4.10pm. The **Seatran** (Map p568) Discovery Ferry (500B) offers a similar service, at 6.30am and 9am. The **Songserm** (Map p568) express boat (350B) departs daily at 10am and arrives on Ko Pan-Ngan at 12pm. Hotel pick-ups are included in the price.

Ko Samui

The Lomprayah catamaran offers a twice-daily service (600B), leaving Ko Tao at 9.30am and 3pm and arriving at Mae Nam on Ko Samui via Ko Pha-Ngan, around 11.20am and 4.40pm. An earlier boat (700B) at 6am goes to Na Thon on Ko Samui, arriving at 7.50am. The Seatran Discovery Ferry (600B) offers a similar service, with departures at 6.30am, 9am and 3pm. The Songserm express boat (500B) departs daily at 10am and arrives on Samui (again via Ko Pha-Ngan) at 1.15pm. Hotel pick-ups are included.

Surat Thani & the Andaman Coast

Many travellers head to Surat Thani via Ko Pha-Ngan or Ko Samui. Otherwise, board a Surat Thani–bound Lomprayah catamaran (900 to 1000B), then transfer to a bus upon arrival.

Chumphon

Songserm boats leave for Chumphon (500B) at 3pm, arriving at 6pm. Lomprayah catamarans (600B) leave for Chumphon at 10.15am and 2.45pm, arriving at 11.45am and 4.15pm.

BUS

Bus-boat package tickets to/from Bangkok are available from travel agencies all over Bangkok and the south; tickets cost around 1100B and the whole voyage takes just over 10 hours. Buses switch to boats in Chumphon, and Bangkok-bound passengers can choose to disembark in Hua Hin (for the same price as the Ko Tao–Bangkok ticket).

TRAIN

Travellers can plan their own journey by taking a boat to Chumphon, then making their way to Chumphon's town centre to catch a train up to Bangkok (or any town along the upper southern gulf); likewise in the opposite direction. A 2nd-class ticket to Bangkok will cost around 300B and the trip takes around 8½ hours.

From Ko Tao, the high-speed Lomprayah catamaran departs for Chumphon at 10.15am and 2.45pm (600B, 1½ hours), and a Songserm express boat makes the same journey at 3pm (500B) arriving at 6pm. There may be fewer departures if the swells are high.

Getting Around

If you know where you intend to stay, we highly recommend calling ahead to arrange a pickup. Many dive schools offer free pick-ups and transfers as well.

MOTORCYCLE

Renting a motorcycle can be a dangerous endeavour if you're not sticking to the main, well-paved roads. You don't want your diving course to be ruined by a scraped leg or worse.

Daily rental rates begin at 150B for a scooter, with larger bikes starting at 350B. Discounts are available for weekly and monthly rentals. Reconsider renting all-terrrain-vehicles (ATVs) or jet skis – accidents are not uncommon. Most of the bottles of petrol on sale by the wayside are 50B a bottle (on Ko Samui and Ko Pha-Ngan they are 40B).

SŎRNG-TĂA-OU

In Mae Hat *sŏrng·tăa·ou* crowd around the pier as passengers alight. If you're a solo traveller, you will pay 200B to get to Sairee Beach or Chalok Ban Kao. Groups of two or more will pay

100B each. Rides from Sairee to Chalok Ban Kao cost 150B per person, or 300B for solo tourists. These prices are rarely negotiable, and passengers will be expected to wait until their taxi is full unless they want to pay an additional 200B to 300B. Prices double for trips to the east coast, and the drivers will raise the prices when rain makes the roads harder to negotiate.

WATER TAXI

Boat taxis depart from Mae Hat, Chalok Ban Kao and the northern part of Sairee Beach (near Vibe Bar). Boat rides to Ko Nang Yuan will set you back at least 100B. Long-tail boats can be chartered for around 1500B per day, depending on the number of passengers carried.

Ang Thong Marine National Park

The 42 jagged jungle islands of Ang Thong Marine National Park (อุทยานแห่งชาติหมู่เกาะอ่างทอง, Mu Ko Ang Thong Marine National Park; ☑ 077 280222; www.nps.dnp.go.th; adult/child 300/150B), stretch across the cerulean sea like a shattered emerald necklace – each piece a virgin realm featuring sheer limestone cliffs, hidden lagoons and perfect peach-coloured sands. These dream-inducing islets inspired Alex Garland's cult classic novel *The Beach*.

February, March and April are the best months to visit this ethereal preserve of greens and blues; crashing monsoon waves mean that the park is almost always closed during November and December.

◉ Sights

Every tour stops at the park's head office on Ko Wua Talap, the largest island in the archipelago and home to the best viewing point. The naturally occurring stone arches on Ko Samsao and Ko Tai Plao are visible during seasonal tides and in certain weather conditions. Because the sea is quite shallow around the island chain, reaching a maximum depth of 10m, extensive coral reefs have not developed, except in a few protected pockets on the southwest and northeast.

There's a shallow coral reef near Ko Tai Plao and Ko Samsao that has decent but not excellent snorkelling. There are also several novice dives for exploring shallow caves and colourful coral gardens, and spotting banded sea snakes and turtles. Soft powder beaches line Ko Tai Plao, Ko Wuakantang and Ko Hintap.

Viewpoint   VIEWPOINT

(จุดชมวิว; Ko Wua Talap) This viewpoint might just be the most stunning vista in all of Thailand. From the top, visitors will have sweeping views of the jagged islands nearby as they burst through the placid turquoise water in easily anthropomorphised formations. The trek to the lookout is an arduous 450m trail that takes roughly an hour to complete. Hikers should wear sturdy shoes and a sun hat, and bring plenty of water. Walk slowly on the sharp outcrops of limestone. A second trail leads to Tham Bua Bok, a cavern with lotus-shaped stalagmites and stalactites.

Emerald Lake   LAKE

(เกาะแม่เกาะ; Ko Mae Ko) With an ethereal minty tint, the Emerald Lake (also called the Blue Lagoon or Inner Sea) on Ko Mae Ko is a large lake in the middle of the island that spans an impressive 250m by 350m. You can look but you can't touch: the lagoon is strictly off limits to the unclean human body. A dramatic viewpoint can be found at the top of a series of staircases nearby.

☞ Tours

The best way to experience Ang Thong is by taking one of the many guided tours departing Ko Samui and Ko Pha-Ngan. The tours usually include lunch, snorkelling equipment, hotel transfers and (fingers crossed) a knowledgeable guide. If you're staying in luxury accommodation, there's a good chance that your resort has a private boat for providing group tours. Some midrange and budget places also have their own boats, and if not, they can easily set you up with a general tour operator. Dive centres on Ko Samui and Ko Pha-Ngan offer scuba trips to the park, although Ang Thong doesn't offer the world-class diving that can be found around Ko Tao and Ko Pha-Ngan.

Tour companies tend to come and go like the wind. Ask at your accommodation for a list of current operators. The park admission fee should be included in the price of every tour (ask your operator if you are unsure). Private boat charters are also another possibility, although high petrol prices will make the trip quite expensive.

🛏 Sleeping & Eating

Food is generally provided by tours whisking visitors to and from the Marine National Park. A restaurant can be found at the park head office.

Ang Thong Bungalows BUNGALOW **$**
(📞 077 280 222; www.nps.dnp.go.th; Ko Wua Talap; bungalows 600-1500B) These spartan, wooden bungalows on stilts are basic, clean and simple, which is in harmony with the pristine location. There is no hot water and the generator goes off at 11pm every night, but then you wouldn't be staying here if such comforts were important to you. There are 2-/6-/8-berth options and they can be reserved online.

If the bungalows are reserved online, they must be paid for by bank transfer within two days or the reservation is cancelled. The only other option for staying overnight in the national park is to camp on the designated areas. The office can rent you a tent for 250B.

ℹ️ Information

Ang Thong National Park Headquarters
(📞 077 280222; www.nps.dnp.go.th; Ko Wua Talap) There is a visitor centre, restaurant, shop and first aid tent here, as well as basic bungalows and a camping ground.

ℹ️ Getting There & Away

The best way to reach the park is to take a private day tour from Ko Samui or Ko Pha-Ngan (28km and 32km away, respectively). The islands sit between Samui and the main pier at Don Sak; however, there are no commercial ferries that stop along the way.

SURAT THANI PROVINCE

Surat Thani

📞 077 / POP 129,500

Known in Thai as 'City of Good People', Surat Thani (สุราษฎร์ธานี) was once the seat of the ancient Srivijaya empire. Today, this typical Thai town is a busy transport hub moving cargo and people around the country. Travellers rarely linger here as they make their way to the popular islands of Ko Samui, Ko Pha-Ngan and Ko Tao, but it's a great stop if you enjoy real Thai working cities, good southern-style street food and nosing around temples and Chinese shopfronts.

👁 Sights

Most visitors to Surat tend to pass through, going from one coast to the other, but those that hang about can enjoy some real local treats. Highlights include the excellent **Pra Cha Rat Floating Market** (ตลาดน้ำประชารัฐ บางใบไม้; Bang Bai Mai; ⊘8am-5pm Tue-Sun; 🅿) on the banks of the Mae Nam Bang Bai Mai, Wat Sai with its quaint little **museum** (📞 082 239 4695; 192 Th Na Meung; ⊘4pm-8.30pm) **FREE** inside an early 20th-century traditional wooden building, the two giant sitting Buddhas in **Wat Tridhammaram** (วัดไตรธรรมาราม; 11 Th Na Mueng; ⊘daylight hrs) **FREE** and the pretty island **park** (สวนสาธารณะเกาะลำพู; ⊘4am-11pm; 🅿) on Ko Lamphu.

🛏 Sleeping

Staying in central Surat puts you in a bustling Thai city, which is refreshing after the primed-for-tourists gulf islands. Prices are low, but if your only objective is to reach the islands and you're on a very tight budget, head straight for the Night Ferry Pier and board the traditional wooden ferries where you can sleep in spartan conditions as they transport you to your island destination

Port Hostel HOSTEL **$**
(📞 086 595 4444; Th Preedarit; dm 250B; ✳🛜) Close to the Night Ferry (p581) and Night Market (p580) near the historic centre, this friendly hostel has the cheapest beds in town. You get your own spacious pod in a dorm for less than the price of a bunk elsewhere. The showers and toilets are a tad small, but rooms are kept immaculately clean and there are stunning views over the river from the rooftop terrace.

My Place @ Surat Hotel HOTEL **$**
(📞 077 272288; www.myplacesurat.com; 247/5 Th Na Muang; s 229B, d 299-650B; ✳🛜) All smiles and nary a speck of dust, this excellent central hotel offers spacious, clean rooms, bright paint, colourful throw cushions, modern art on the walls, power showers and value for money. It may be budget but it doesn't seem that way and will suit almost anyone. Breakfast is served in the cafe next door.

🍴 Eating & Drinking

Surat Thani is packed with delicious street food. Aside from the night market (p580), every evening stalls appear near the Night Ferry docks. There's also the afternoon **Sunday market** (off Route 401; ⊘4-9pm Sun) close to the TAT office. Food stalls at the downtown bus terminal sell delicious *kôw gài òp* (marinated baked chicken on rice) and if you have the time, eating your way through the excellent Pra Cha Rat Floating Market is a must.

Surat Thani

Surat Thani

★ Night Market
MARKET $

(Sarn Chao Ma; Th Ton Pho; dishes from 35B; ⊘ 6-11pm) A smorgasbord of food, including masses of melt-in-your-mouth marinated meats on sticks, fresh fruit juices, noodle dishes, desserts and a host of other foods that will take some time working out. Primarily a local clientele, this food market feels wonderfully authentic.

Suratthani Vegetarian
VEGETARIAN $

(☎ 084 737 5011; off Karunrat; mains 60B; ⊘ 7am-5.30pm Mon-Sat; 🖥🍃) The calming sound of the Buddha fountain and the restaurant motto 'no money, no problem, eat meal free', sets the tone for this lovely, hidden space of serenity where delicious, wholesome, vegetarian food is cooked to order for the price of street food, and free ginseng tea and filtered water is on tap. They support food for local school children by selling their recycled handicrafts for small donations.

Sweet Kitchen
INTERNATIONAL $

(☎ 062 239 4470; Th Bandon; mains from 80B; ⊘ noon-9.30pm; 🖥🍃) With easy-going music and a charming, unhurried interior, this restaurant also tempts with a fine menu and polite service. Dishes range from excellent seafood chowder and pasta to beef stroganoff and pages of Thai staples, with a decent selection of vegetarian choices, too.

★ Cafeteria Co-working Space
COFFEE

(☎ 077 205206; www.cafeteriathailand.com; 82-86 Th Chomkasen; ⊘ 7am-11.30pm; 🖥) Part cafe, part wine bar, this stylish little spot has an interior decked out in wood, where customers sit on hip retro-style chairs as cool urban tracks play. The coffee is excellent and one wall is covered in an impressive floor-to-ceiling cabinet displaying a fine range of wines and beers. There's also a very good food menu.

ℹ Information

ATMs are widespread in the city centre and there are several banks along Th Na Meuang.

Tourism Authority of Thailand (TAT; ☑ 077 288817; www.tourismthailand.org; 5 Th Talat Mai; ☺8am-5pm) This friendly office southwest of town has useful brochures and maps, and staff speak English.

Tourism Assistance Center (☑ 077 310870; Surat Thani Train Station; ☺7am-9pm) This is an ideal place to get yourself organised if you arrive by train.

Thaksin Hospital (☑ 077 278777; www. thaksinhospital.com; Th Talat Mai; ☺24hr) The most professional of Surat's three hospitals is northeast of the centre of town.

ℹ Getting There & Away

The best way to get in and out of Surat Thani is by bus as the only major transport hub actually in the city is one of the bus stations. The city's train station and airport are several kilometres out of town. The **Night Ferry** and the slower Songserm are the only other modes of transport that arrive and depart from the centre of town.

AIR

Around 18km west of town, **Surat Thani International Airport** (www.suratthaniairport. com; off 41) has daily shuttles to Bangkok on Air Asia (www.airasia.com), Thai Smile (www. thaismileair.com), Thai Lion Air (www.lionairthai. com), Thai Airways (www.thaiairways.com) and Nok Air (www.nokair.com). These are a lot cheaper than flying direct to Samui, however it can be a bit more hassle to get across to the gulf islands from the airport. **Phanthip** (☑ 077 272230; www.phantiptravel.com; Th Talat Mai; ☺8.00am-7pm) and some airlines offer bus and boat shuttles direct from the airport at reasonable prices, which are worth booking in advance.

BOAT

Various ferry companies offer services to the islands that can include a pick up from your accommodation. Try Lomprayah (p545), **Seatran Discovery** (☑ 077 372824; www.seatrandiscovery.com; 17/1 Mu 8, Th Donsak; ☺5am-9pm) or **Songserm** (☑ 02 629 3415; www.songserm. com; Tapee Pier).

Bus-boat Combination Tickets

Travellers can get bus-boat services to Ko Samui and Ko Pha-Ngan directly from Surat Thani town centre, the train station or the airport using companies like Phanthip. These services don't cost any more than if they were booked in Surat Thani and can save you a lot of hassle.

There are also several ferry and speedboat operators that connect Surat Thani to Ko Tao, Ko Pha-Ngan and Ko Samui. Most boats leave from Don Sak pier (about one hour from Surat; bus transfers are included in the ferry ticket). Buses connecting the Seatran service leave from its very own **terminal** (☑ 077 275063; www.seatrandiscovery.com; 19 Th Talad Mai; ☺7am-6pm) in town. The Songserm departs from the heart of Surat town, as do the overnight ferries though these are considerably slower. Most accommodation will be able to arrange any of these tickets for a marginally higher rate than booking with the individual companies.

Night Ferry

From the centre of Surat there are overnight ferries that depart daily at around 10pm to Ko Tao (500B, eight hours), Ko Pha-Ngan (400B, seven hours) and Ko Samui (300B, six hours). These are cargo ships, where a basic mattress and pillow will be laid down on the covered top deck to sleep on, so bring food and water and watch your bags.

BUS & MINIVAN

The most convenient way to travel around the south, frequent buses and minivans depart from the main **Bus Terminal** (Th Tha Thong) in town off Th Talat Mai (the city's main drag): speedy services to Nakhon (120B, 1½ hrs), Phuket (200B, six hours) and Hat Yai (270B, five hours), and regular minibuses to Khanom (100B, 90 minutes, hourly). Buses to the train station leave from **Talat Kaset 1**.

The 'new' **bus terminal** (Bangkok Terminal; ☺5.30am-9pm) (actually quite a few years old now, but still referred to as new by the locals) is 7km south of town on the way to the train station. This hub services traffic to and from Bangkok (500B to 800B, nine to 14 hours).

TRAIN

When arriving by train you'll actually pull into Phun Phin, a nondescript town 15km west of Surat, as that is where **Surat Thani Train Station** (☑ 077 311213, call centre 1690; www.railway. co.th) is situated. From Phun Phin, there are buses to Phuket, Ko Phang-Ngan and Krabi – some via Takua Pa, a junction for Khao Sok National Park. These can be arranged with any of the ticket vendors and small travel agents like **Phantip** (☑ 077 272230; www.phantiptravel.com; Surat Thani Train Station; ☺7am-9pm) near the restaurants north of the station entrance.

DESTINATIONS FROM SURAT THANI

DESTINATION	COST (B)	DURATION
Bangkok	500	9hr
Hat Yai	270	5hr
Khanom	100	90min
Krabi	150	2½hr
Phuket	200	6hr
Trang	180	2hr 10min

If you plan on travelling on the trains during the day, go for the express train. Night travellers should opt for the air-con couchettes. Trains passing through Surat stop in Chumphon and Hua Hin on their way up to the capital, and in the other direction you'll call at Trang, Hat Yai and Sungai Kolok before hopping across the border into Malaysia. Surat Thani train station has a 24-hour left-luggage room that charges 40B a day, and the ticket office is open around the clock. The trip to Bangkok takes more than 8½ hours and costs 608B for sitting and 808B for sleeping, though these sell out a lot quicker.

ℹ Getting Around

Air-conditioned minivans run by Phanthip (p581) to/from Surat Thani airport cost 100B per person and can be booked in advance to drop you off at your hotel.

To travel around town, a *sŏrng·tăa·ou* (pickup minibus) will cost 15B to 30B (it's around 30B to reach Tesco Lotus from the city centre) and Grab taxis (www.grab.com) can be ordered via the app costing around 90B for a short journey.

Fan-cooled orange buses run from Surat Thani train station to the town centre every 10 minutes (15B, 25 minutes), meanwhile taxis charge a cool 200B for a maximum of four people and shared taxis will charge 100B per person. Other taxi rates are posted just north of the train station (near the iron pedestrian bridge).

There is also the option to rent your own scooter from **Motorbike Rentals Surat Thani** (✆ 081 164 6865; ⊙ 8am-7pm) for 250B per day near the City Pillar.

NAKHON SI THAMMARAT PROVINCE

Home to south Thailand's highest peak – Khao Luang (1835m) – and surrounded by the majestic forests of Khao Luang National Park, Nakhon Si Thammarat (นครศรีธรรมราช) Province is best known to travellers for stunning Wat Phra Mahathat Woramahawihaan in the provincial capital of the same name. It's a likeable place with a great night market and museum, especially if pitching up from the gulf islands in search of some genuine Thai flavour.

On the east coast, Ao Khanom is a lovely string of long beaches facing dazzling waters that are home to cavorting pink dolphins. Although a drawcard, the aquatic mammals are also protected, meaning no jet skis allowed, making Ao Khanom a far quieter and more appealing choice – in many ways – than Ko Samui, while offering much of the same: sand, sea and gorgeous sunrises across the gulf.

Ao Khanom

Pretty, placid Ao Khanom (อ่าวขนอม), halfway between Surat Thani and Nakhon Si Thammarat, quietly sits along the blue gulf waters. Overlooked by foreign tourists who flock to the nearby islands, this pristine region is great for those seeking a serene beach setting unmarred by enterprising corporations. The waters are free of jet skis to protect the local pink dolphins, making the region quiet and undisturbed.

The coastal area is long and comprises two beaches: the longer Hat Nadan and the smaller, more remote, Hat Nai Plao. Beyond Hat Nai Plao is quiet Hat Thong Yi at the end of the road. This is well worth a trip for its castaway feel and sits at the start of an excellent ride along a (albeit partially-built) coastal road to Sichon. The area surrounding Khanom town is also home to a number of pristine geological features, including several waterfalls and caves.

◉ Sights

The most unique attraction in Khanom is the pink dolphins living in the sea that surrounds the town – these rare and endangered albino breed of mammals have a stunning pink hue and they number around 50 in these waters. To catch a glimpse of one, you'll have to hire a local long-tail or go on one of the half-day tours offered by several of the resorts (from 1200B for up to six people). There's also a slim chance that you might see one off the coast of either the town's electric plant pier or from the old pier in the fishing village of Thong Niem, about 20km north of Khanom town.

★**Hat Thong Yi**   BEACH
(หาดท้องหยี; P) For a real escape, head as far down the main beach road as you can, till it joins the 4073, and turn left to follow the coast further south past Hat Nai Plao. Keep going as far as you can and the road will end at lovely and often deserted Hat Thong Yi, with its splendid views back down the bay. There's a decent beachside restaurant where you can get a drink and local food.

Samet Chun Waterfall   WATERFALL
(น้ำตกเสม็ดชุน) A large aqua-blue pool is the star attraction here. It sits at the foot of a series of falls, cascading down a hillside creating smaller, equally beautiful, clear pools just begging to be swam in – beware though, the water is very cold. The beautiful jungle setting, lack of tourists and spectacular views add to the sense of a hidden paradise. It's a steep 20-minute walk from the dirt road, but you might get closer if you bring a scooter.

Khao Wang Thong Cave   CAVE
(ถ้ำเขาวังทอง; off Hwy 4014; ⊗9am-4pm; P) Khao Wang Thong is an impressive network of 17 caves and narrow passages that reaches a depth of 150m. Visitors walk past a series of natural limestone formations likened to dinosaurs, pagodas and lotus flowers, as well as impressive stalactites hanging from the roof. The complex is lit up by a string of lights and is also home to bats. Bring a solid pair of shoes and a head torch. Off Hwy 4014 between Khanom and Don Sak.

Khao Dat Fa   MOUNTAIN
(เขาดาดฟ้า; off Rte 4014) For splendid post-card-worthy vistas of the undulating coastline, head to Dat Fa Mountain (732m), about 5km west of the coast along Hwy 4014 (look out for the sign). The area has not been developed for tourism and the hillside is usually deserted, making it easy to stop along the way to snap some photos.

Hin Lat Falls   WATERFALL
(น้ำตกหินลาด; P) The scenic Hin Lat Falls southwest of Hat Nai Plao is the smallest

of the cascades in the area, but the easiest to reach. There are pools for swimming and several huts provide shade.

🏃 Activities

★**Thong Yi Coastal Drive**   SCENIC DRIVE
(Thong Yi; ⊗daylight hrs) Starting near Racha Kiri (p584) resort and ending 10km later at **Moon Coffee and Roti** (📞088 696 6035; Sichon; ⊗8am-8pm; 🛜), this coastal ride dips, climbs and bends its way around the edge of the headland, flanked on either side by jungle-covered mountains and the shimmering azure waters of the gulf. Dotted along the way are platforms where you can take in spectacular views.

The section of the road connecting Hat Thong Yi to Sichon was still being finished at the time of research but it's safe enough to ride with a scooter.

🛏 Sleeping

Khanom's beaches remain low-key and quiet, with many resorts seeing few customers and irregular use, which may mean that some rooms can feel a bit musty. Beachside bungalow are a better option. It's not like Ko Samui: options are spaced far apart so you'll need wheels to get about.

Suchada Villa   BUNGALOW $
(📞075 300213; Hat Naiplau; bungalow 800-1000B; P❄🛜) Right off the main road and a five-minute walk to the beach, Suchada offers a cache of brightly coloured, quite cute but basic bungalows in a tidy little setting.

Hallo Villa   BUNGALOW $$
(📞082 413 3338; www.hallovillakhanom.com; bungalow from 1100B; P❄🛜🛜) Removed from the beachfront, this family run collection of bungalows on stilts is a great choice if you want to stay closer to town. Each bungalow is wonderfully roomy, has an en suite and comes with a small kitchenette, and your own little terrace.

Sea Breeze House   BUNGALOW $$
(📞081 276 1457; www.naiplao.com; 58/2 Mu 8, Hat Nai Plao; d 850-1400B; P❄🛜) With a very secluded location, this lovely Swiss-owned choice has excellent beachfront rooms, including a large suite. If you seek peace and tranquillity, splendid views of the sunrise and the opportunity to witness the famous local pink dolphins swimming past your room, this is an excellent choice, but you'll need wheels to get about.

Khanom Hill Resort
BUNGALOW $$$

(☎081 956 3101; www.khanom.info; 60/1 Mu 8, Hat Naiplau; bungalow 2900-3900B; P❋🐾🖵☲) Travellers love this spot on a small hill leading to a half-circle of dreamy white beach. Choose from modern, concrete villas with thatched roofs, cheaper ones with Thai-style architecture or big family-sized apartments.

Racha Kiri
RESORT $$$

(☎075 300245; www.rachakiri.com; 99 Mu 8; ste 2655-6255B; P❋🐾🖵☲) With spa, pool and elegant rooms, Khanom's upscale retreat is a beautiful campus of rambling villas. The big price tag deters the crowds and the location is serene. Rooms come with terrace.

✗ Eating & Drinking

For cheap eats, head to the area near the Mae Nam Khun Nom river in the north of Khanom town where you'll find a steamy jumble of street-food stands and local shacks offering tasty favourites. There are markets further inland on Wednesday and Sunday; and for slightly more refined dishes try the coastal road, which is dotted with Thai and Western restaurants looking out to sea.

★ Tea Roti Mataba Restaurant
THAI $

(☎080 884 6144; dishes 30B; ⊙7am-11pm) The buzz about this no frills, Muslim-run roti specialist will be apparent from the roadside, where tables and chairs overflowing with locals spill out onto the pavement every evening. The house speciality is sweet, crispy roti or savoury *má·tà·bà* (spiced mincemeat stuffed roti). Both are exceptional and inspired by southern Muslim cuisine. Wash them down with sweetened Indian-style tea.

CC Beach Bar & Bungalows
INTERNATIONAL $$

(☎087 893 8745; www.ccbeachbar.com; 28/1 Mu 6, Khanom Beach; mains 100-300B; ⊙8am-midnight; 🖵) With a splendid perspective onto the bay over the sands, this beach bar and restaurant is a good choice for its mixed menu of Thai and Western food, including hearty English breakfasts, fish and chips, vegetable curry, pizza and fried catfish salad. In the evenings, it doubles as a fun bar attracting a number of the small local expat community.

Le Petit Saint-Tropez
INTERNATIONAL $$

(☎093 727 0063; 52/14 Mu 5; mains from 300B; ⊙8am-9.30pm; 🖵) With an open and breezy setting, this charming restaurant faces out onto the sea and serves a delightful range of French and Thai fare, as well as great pizzas.

ⓘ Information

There are ATMs near both 7-Elevens in the south and north of Khanom town.

The police station is just south of Ban Khanom at the junction leading to Hat Kho Khao.

The **hospital** (☎075 529033; www.khanom. org; 91 Mu 3) is at the junction leading to Hat Kho Khao but is little more than a glorified clinic. The nearest decent hospitals are in either Surat Thani or Nakhon Si Thammarat.

ⓘ Getting There & Away

Minivans from both Surat Thani (100B) and Nakhon Si Thammarat (80B) leave roughly every hour – once they are full – from 5am to 5pm daily and drop passengers off anywhere in Khanom town, which is several kilometres from the beach. Minivans going to both of those towns leave from **Khanom Minivan Station**.

A taxi to/from Don Sak Pier for the gulf islands is 1000B and a motorcycle taxi is around 300B.

ⓘ Getting Around

From Khanom town you can hire motorcycle taxis out to the beaches for about 25B to 100B depending on the distance you're going. If you've booked accommodation in advance your hosts may offer to pick you up in Khanom town for free.

Once at your lodging you'll be stranded unless you hire your own transport or take a tour with your hotel, so the best thing to do is to hire a scooter. There's a rental operator near the minivan station charging around 200B a day or try **14 Khanom** (☎095 069 0670, 083 551 3795; www.the-14-khanom-rent-motorbike-and-car. business.site; ⊙8am-10pm), near the town's southern intersection, where the owner speaks English, French and Thai.

Nakhon Si Thammarat
☎075 / POP 103,200

With one of the most significant temples in the kingdom, the historic city of Nakhon Si Thammarat (นครศรีธรรมราช) – often shortened to 'Nakhon' – is a natural and rewarding stop between Hat Yai and Surat Thani.

Hundreds of years ago, an overland route between the western port of Trang and the eastern port of Nakhon Si Thammarat functioned as a major trade link between Thailand and the rest of the world. This ancient influx of cosmopolitan conceits is still evident today in the local cuisine, and housed in the city's temples and museums.

Wandering through Nakhon, visitors from the north will also notice the increasing visibility of mosques, as Thailand's Muslim community become more apparent in what is the first of several major southern cities where they are well established.

◉ Sights

Your education in Nakhon's culture and history should start at the highly informative National Museum, before heading north for the magnificent Wat Phra Mahathat, which is close to the remains of the historic red-brick city walls near the park and public square of Sanam Na Meuang (สนาม หน้าเมือง; Th Ratchadamnoen). Note also the gold-coloured statues of the 12 animals of the Thai zodiac atop lamp posts along Th Ratchadamnoen, each representing one of the 12 city states that were tributary to the Nakhon Si Thammarat kingdom. Finally, don't miss the Masjid Salah Ud Din (มัสยิด ซอลาฮุดดีน; Th Panead; ⊙ daylight hrs), once visited by Rama IX, in the heart of the city.

★ Wat Phra Mahathat Woramahawihaan
TEMPLE

(Th Si Thamasok; ⊙ 8.30am-4.30pm) 𝐅𝐑𝐄𝐄 The most important wát in southern Thailand, stunning Wat Phra Mahathat Woramahawihaan (simply known as Mahathat) boasts an imposing 77m *chedi* (stupa) crowned by a gold spire piercing the sky. According to legend, Queen Hem Chala and Prince Thanakuman brought relics to Nakhon more than 1000 years ago, and built a small pagoda to house the precious icons. The temple has since grown into a huge site, and today crowds gather daily to purchase the popular Jatukham amulets.

Within the courtyard beneath the towering *chedi* rise up scores of further grey *chedi*. Don't miss the hall enclosing a splendid stairway – all red, green and gold – and the museums featuring antique statues from all eras and corners of Thailand including an 18th-century reclining Buddha. Frequently filled with visiting school kids who apply gold leaf to the temple statuary, the wát is a 10B *sŏrng·tăa·ou* (pickup minibus) ride from the town centre.

★ National Museum
MUSEUM

(พิพิธภัณฑสถานแห่งชาติ นครศรีธรรมราช; ☎ 075 341 075; Th Ratchadamnoen; admission 150B; ⊙ 9am-4pm Wed-Sun; 🅿) If you want to really understand Nakhon, this is the place. A series of interconnected rooms housing stunning artefacts with detailed displays in Thai and English take you chronologically from the Stone Age through to the present era, and culturally from local birth rituals to funeral rites. Standout items include a beautiful, intricately patterned, prehistoric bronze Mahorethuek drum, and the 5th- to 6th-century stone figure of Vishnu found at nearby Ho Phra Narai, the oldest depiction discovered in Nakhon region.

Old City Walls
RUINS

(กำแพงเมืองเก่า จังหวัดนครศรีธรรมราช; Th Ratchadamnoen) The intriguing and well-kept remains of the historic red-brick city walls can be seen in several sections close to one another along Khlong Na Meuang canal near the park and public square of Sanam Na Meuang on either side of Th Ratchadamnoen.

Shadow Puppet Museum
MUSEUM

(บ้านหนังตะลุงสุชาติทรัพย์สิน; Th Si Thamasok Soi 3; ⊙ 9am-4.30pm) 𝐅𝐑𝐄𝐄 There are two styles of local shadow puppets: *năng dà·lung* and *năng yài*. At just under 1m tall, the former feature movable appendages and parts; the latter are nearly life-sized, and lack moving parts. Both are intricately carved from cow hide. Suchart Subsin's puppet house has a small museum where staff can demonstrate the cutting process and put on performances for visitors (50B).

Look out for the shadow puppets from the 18th century upstairs, and others from the WWII era which are smaller than the traditional size and include a biplane.

🛏 Sleeping

As an authentic Thai city, Nakhon has a particular and genuine charm, but accommodation does not feature high on its list of priorities. Lacking the foreign tourist traffic other major cities in Thailand attract, the sleeping options in the city are at best, decent and functional and reminiscent of early Thai accommodation before the tourist trade really took off.

Thai Hotel
HOTEL $

(fax 075 314872; 1375 Th Ratchadamnoen; d with fan/air-con 350/450B; 🅿 ❄ 🛜) The most central sleeping spot in town, not far from the train station, the Thai Hotel is a semi-smart bargain and is perfectly acceptable. Walls may be a bit thin and the wi-fi twitchy, but rooms are clean and a good deal, each with a TV – and the higher floors have good views of the urban bustle – while the staff is lovely.

KHAO LUANG NATIONAL PARK

Known for beautiful hiking trails, cool streams, waterfalls and wildlife, **Khao Luang National Park** (อุทยานแห่งชาติเขาหลวง; ☑ 075 300494; www.dnp.go.th; off Rte 4015; adult/child 400/200B; P), named after the tallest mountain in the south, is a soaring range covered in evergreen forest and inhabited by a plethora of flora and fauna unique to the region. A total of 327 animal species and orchids found nowhere else on earth call it home. Camping is permitted and basic bungalows can be reserved via the website (from 600B). There's also a restaurant at the park's HQ.

Animals that roam Khao Luang include Shy Malayan tapirs, Sumatran serows, pig-tailed macaque, clouded leopards, panthers, tigers, and dusky speckled languars, while bird lovers will enjoy trying to spot black eagles, red jungle fowls, and a number of the impressively beaked hornbills, including the bushy-crested, helmeted and white-crowned.

To reach Khao Luang park, take a *sǒrng·tǎa·ou* for around 40B from Nakhon Si Thammarat to Lan Saka on Rte 4015; drivers will usually take you the extra 10km to the park headquarters (roughly 30km west of Nakhon centre).

V House Nakhon
HOTEL $

(☑ 075 314777; www.vhouse-nakhon.business.site; 1209/30 Yomaraj Road; d 350B; P ✴ 🛜) V House Nakhon sums up the sleeping options in Nakhon city: dated, tired, functional, clean(ish) and cheap. None of the city's accommodation will particularly inspire you and certainly not the 'prison-like' block that is V House. It is however relatively central and staff are friendly and keen to help though they don't speak English.

Twin Lotus Hotel
HOTEL $$

(☑ 075 323777; www.twinlotushotel.net; 6 Th Phattanakan Khukhwang; d/tw 1300-1600B, ste 2700-3150B; P ✴ 🛜 ⛽) The 401-room, 16-storey Twin Lotus is a good choice for those wanting to go a little more upscale in Nakhon; some rooms are a tad dated, but they are spacious. Staff speak English and the hotel has a gym, spa and outdoor pool. Guests are given free transfers to the airport and there's a decent Chinese restaurant on-site.

✗ Eating

Nakhon is a great place to sample cuisine with a distinctive southern twist. The best place to get the cheapest dishes are at the **Night Market** (Rd 4016; dishes 30B; ⊙ 4-9pm) near the river and railway track. This is filled with local Muslims selling delicious *kôw mòk gài* (chicken biryani), *má·dà·bà* (Indian *roti* stuffed with meat or veg) and *roti*. Another good spot is around Th Neramit near the railway station, where food stalls appear every night.

Chaba Restaurant and Cafe
CAFE $

(☑ 098 670 6536; Th Ratchadamnoen; mains 100B; ⊙ 9am-midnight; ✴ 🛜) This cute little cafe with a busy but sweetly decorated interior is conveniently close to the National Museum, making it the ideal spot to refuel. There are a number of comfy armchairs and sofas to relax in, and a menu of light lunches, salads and good coffee.

Hao Coffee
CAFE $

(☑ 075 346563; Rte 4012; mains 30-60B; ⊙ 7am-4pm; 🛜) This charming, well-staffed cafe is always buzzing with talkative locals and decorated with an eclectic array of collectables and knick-knacks, from pith helmets to hunting rifles, ancient ceramics and wall clocks. It's a great place for a scrambled-eggs breakfast, a larger meal or a caffeine fix, either inside or out front.

Krua Talay
THAI $

(☑ 075 346724; 1204/29-30 Th Pak Nakhon; mains 120B; ⊙ 4-10pm) Overseen by an affable matriarch, this restaurant serves the best seafood dishes you will taste in Nakhon in an interior bursting with Buddhist effigies and statues of Ganesha. Pull up a seat in the lovely garden and treat yourself to either the lipsmacking crispy catfish with hot & spicy salad or stir-fried vegetables in oyster sauce.

Pixzel Caffe
CAFE $$

(☑ 086 682 5471; www.facebook.com/pixzelcaffe; 558, Th Ratchadamnoen; pizza from 120B; ⊙ 9am-7pm Thu-Tue; ✴ 🛜) This arty, thin-crust pizza-serving, coffee-connoisseurs hang-out, sits in a gorgeous traditional-style wooden house just across the way from Wat Phra Mahathat (p585). It's a popular and very cosy spot that is ideal for a break after a long morning of temple exploration.

🛍 Shopping

⭐ **Sip Song Naksat** GIFTS & SOUVENIRS
(The Twelve Kingdom; ☑ 075 311680; 895 Th Tachang; ⊙ 8.30am-6pm) Housed in the lower section of a beautiful, historic, wooden house that is open to visitors, this gift shop is the pick of the ones that line Th Tachang as it sells a wide range of authentic, locally produced crafts and textiles including handmade leather shadow puppets and Thai silk garments. There's something to suit all budgets.

ℹ Information

Several banks and ATMs hug Th Ratchadamnoen in the northern end of downtown.

Police Station (☑ 075 341054, 1155; 1019/24 Th Ratchadamnoen)

Post Office (☑ 075 356135; www.thailandpost. co.th; 724/5 Th Ratchadamnoen; ⊙ 8.30am-4.30pm Mon-Fri, 9am-noon Sat & Sun)

Tourism Authority of Thailand (TAT; ☑ 075 346 515, tourist hotline 1627; www.tourismthailand.org; Th Na Meuang; ⊙ 8.30am-4.30pm) Housed in a fine 1926-vintage building in the northern end of the Sanam Na Muang (City Park), this office has some useful brochures, but nobody really speaks English here.

ℹ Getting There & Away

AIR

Carriers Thai Lion Air (www.lionairthai.com), Air Asia (www.airasia.com) and Nok Air (www. nokair.com) fly from Bangkok's Don Mueang International Airport to **Nakhon Si Thammarat Airport** (☑ 075 450545; 🛜), 12km north of the city centre, daily. There are about six daily one-hour flights, with one-way fares around 1500B.

BUS

Ordinary buses to Bangkok leave from the main **bus station** (off Rte 4016) off Rte 4016 in the west of town, a good 25-minute walk from the centre. The journey takes 12 hours and costs 426B to 851B depending on the class of bus. Minibuses also run from the station to Hat Yai (140B, three hours), Surat Thani (120B, 2½ hours) and Khanom (80B, 1½ hours), and buses run to Phuket (350B, six hours).

When looking for minivan stops to leave Nakhon, keep an eye out for small desks along the side of the downtown roads (minivans and waiting passengers may or may not be present nearby). It's best to ask around as each destination has a different departure point. Krabi and Don Sak minivans are grouped together – just make sure you don't get on the wrong one. Stops are scattered around Th Jamroenwithi, Th Wakhit and Th Yommarat.

TRAIN

There are two daily trains to Bangkok (133B to 652B) at 1pm and 3pm (15 hours) stopping at Hua Hin, Chumphon and Surat Thani along the way. There are two trains daily at 6am and 9.58am to Hat Yai (24B), with the 6am one continuing all the way to Sungai Kolok (60B).

ℹ Getting Around

Sŏrng·tăa·ou (pickup minibuses) run north–south along Th Ratchadamnoen and Th Si Thammasok for 10B (a bit more at night). Motorcycle-taxi rides start at 30B and cost up to 50B for longer distances. A motorbike from the centre of town to the bus station is 40B and Grab taxis (www.grab.com) can be ordered via the app costing around 60B for a short journey

SONGKHLA PROVINCE

Songkhla (จังหวัดสงขลา) Province's two main commercial centres, Hat Yai and Songkhla, are less affected by the political turmoil plaguing the cities further south, although some state travel advisories warn against travel here. You won't be tripping over foreign backpackers, but you'll see a fair number of tourists drawn to wandering through local markets, exploring the ruins of ancient Muslim sultanates, savouring Muslim-Thai fusion cuisine, relaxing on breezy beaches and tapping into Hat Yai's fun and eclectic urban vibe.

Songkhla & Singha Nakhon

☑ 074 / POP 163,000
Split by the majestic Songhla Lake, the stories of Songkhla (สงขลา) city and Singha Nakhon (สิงหนคร) are intertwined. The latter founded by Muslim sultans as the Sultanate of Singora in the 17th century was the precursor to Songkhla, the modern provincial capital. Together they represent one of the most fascinating and heritage-conscious towns in the south.

Mainly appreciated by regional and local tourists, the influence of the area's Thai, Chinese and Malay population is apparent everywhere, from the beautiful historic ruins that hark all the way back to the sultanate days, through to the Sino-Portuguese architecture of Songkhla's old town. This cultural fusion is also reflected in the delicious local cuisine that marries the spicy flavours of Thai-Muslim southern cooking with Chinese flavours. Squeezed in between all of this is a vibrant streak of modern, artsy venues that are fast giving Songkhla and Singha Nakhon a reputation as the arts capital of the south.

Sights

For ancient history, head to Singha Nakhon, where remnants of the forgotten Sultanate of Singora include the tomb (สุสานสุลต่าน สุไลมาน; off Hwy 408, Singha Nakhon; ⊙8am-midnight) of its most famous Sultan, Sulaiman Shah, partial ruins of the ancient city walls and more than a dozen forts (ป้อม หัวเขาแดง; Fort Khao Daeng; Rte 4222, Singha Nakhon; P) FREE scattered all over the foothills. Enthusiasts could spend days locating these.

On the Songkhla side, you'll find the best beaches and Songkhla Old Town (Nang Ngam), one of the most beautiful iin the south, where the historic Chinese and Sino-Portuguese buildings have been either beautifully restored or become canvasses for splendid street art. Many buildings have been repurposed as cultural centres, such as the old Rice Mill near the docks. There's also the eclectic architectural mix of historic buildings such as Masjid Asassul (มัสยิด อุสาสนอิสลาม; Th Phattalung; ⊙daylight hrs), which relates the Euro-Indo-Thai influence on the local Muslim community. Wherever you wander, start with a visit to the city's National Museum to contextualise it all.

Tours

Singora Tram Tour   ACTIVITY
(☑074 312025; Th Jana; ⊙9am-3pm) FREE These 90-minute tours in an open-air tram leave from Th Jana close to the National Museum (พิพิธภัณฑสถานแห่งชาติสงขลา; ☑074 311728; 13 Th Wichianchom; admission 150B; ⊙9am-4pm Wed-Sun, closed public holidays). You'll be lucky to get an English narration but you will get a ride through the old part of town past the Songkhla mosque, a Thai temple, Chinese shrine and then out to Hat Samila.

Sleeping & Eating

Sook Som Boon 2 Hotel   HOTEL $
(☑099 472 1648; 14 Th Saiburi; d 550-650B; ❈ 🛜) Well located and close to many of the sights including the Old Time Market (Th Chana; ⊙4-10pm Fri& Sat), this good value hotel has an owner who knows the town well and speaks English. Rooms are clean, if a little musty, and guests are also able to rent bikes here.

★ Ban Nai Nakhon
Boutique Hotel   BOUTIQUE HOTEL $$
(☑095 438 9323; dntche@hotmail.com; 166 Th Nang Ngam; d 1500B; ❈) This beautiful boutique hotel is run by amateur local historian Abdu'r Rahman, hence the lounge resembling a small museum filled with antiquities and curios from either his travels or connected to the history of Songkhla. Inevitably, each room also has that very personal touch, featuring large traditional beds, classic Thai furnishings and one of Rahman's very own mosaics.

★ Songkhla Station   CAFE $
(☑093 771 1181; 10/8 Th Nakhonnok; dishes 70B; ⊙8am-7pm; ❈ 🛜 🔌) Inside a restored historic building, this cafe-cum-restaurant serves a host of traditional Thai dishes from fried chicken wings with sticky rice to sôm·dam (spicy papaya salad) as well as some Western options. The beautifully designed interior is spacious and child-friendly with lots of games and activities to hand.

★ Books and Cafe   COFFEE
(☑094 396 4179; Th Ramvithi; ⊙8.30am-11pm; 🛜) We love this cool little coffee oasis conveniently located metres from Songkhla's old town. It is the ideal spot to take a break after a morning of exploring. Pull up a comfy sofa or armchair surrounded by Thai and English books as mellow tunes play and enjoy the perfect cup of coffee. They also rent bikes for 30B per hour.

Information

Banks and ATMs can be found all over Songkhla town.

Indonesian Consulate (☑074 311544; www.kemlu.go.id/songkhla; 19 Th Sadao; ⊙8.30am-4pm Mon-Fri)

Malaysian Consulate (☑074 311062; www.kln.gov.my/web/tha_songkhla; 4 Th Sukhum; ⊙8.15am-noon & 1-4.15pm Mon-Thu, 8.15am-noon & 2-4.15pm Fri)

Police Station (☑074 321878; www.songkhlapolice.com; Th Laeng Phra Ram)

Post Office (☑074 312982; www.thailandpost.co.th; Th Wichianchom; ⊙8.30am-4pm Mon-Fri & 8.30am-noon Sat)

Getting There & Around

BUS

The main bus terminal is on Songkhla Plaza Alley (off Nakhonnok St) around 1.5km south of the Old Town. Three 2nd-class buses go daily to Bangkok (865B), stopping in Nakhon Si

Thammarat and Surat Thani, among other places. For Hat Yai, buses (21B) and minivans (30B to 40B) take around 40 minutes and leave from the stop on **Th Ramwithi** (Th Ramwithi; ⊙ 6am-8pm). *Sŏrng·tăa·ou* (pickup minibuses) also leave from here for Ko Yo.

A ferry for foot passengers (free), bikes and scooters (3B), and cars (20B) operates across Songkhla Lake, connecting **Singha Nakhon** (Rte 4222; foot/bike/car free/3/20B; ⊙ 5am-10pm) to **Songkhla** (Laem Son On; foot/bike/car free/3/20B).

TRAIN

From Songkhla you'll have to go to Hat Yai to reach most long-distance destinations in the south (trains no longer pass through town).

Hat Yai

☑ 074 / POP 156,601

Welcome to the urban hub of southern Thailand where Western-style shopping malls mingle with wafts of Cantonese street eats and curry from the eclectic range of busy street-food stalls as Old Chinese men sit and watch the world go by on rickety chairs outside junk shops. It's a mix of busy city and laid-back tropics and Hat Yai (หาดใหญ่) has long been a favourite stop for Malaysian men on seedy weekends. You'll notice the town's tourism scene is still predominantly Malaysian mixed with a few Western expats.

Those who get out and explore will be rewarded with some of the best food in the region and the dynamic hustle and bustle of the big smoke of southern Thailand, which is noticeably international in comparison to the other towns in the province.

◉ Sights

★**Hat Yai Municipal Park** PARK
(สวนสาธารณะเทศบาลนครหาดใหญ่; ☑ 074 211898; www.hatyaipark.com; Rte 407; ⊙ 9am-8pm; ℗) Located 7km northeast of Hat Yai, this huge, green oasis of hilly, landscaped gardens is home to several stunning temples, an observatory, and southern Thailand's tallest Golden Buddha (พระพุทธมงคล มหาราช; ☑ 074 211898; www.hatyaipark.com; Hat Yai Municipal Park; ⊙ 9am-8pm; ℗) FREE, a boating lake – complete with artificial waterfall – cafes and food stalls, and a network of cycling routes. Spending a day breathing in the fresh air, exploring the temples, riding the cable car (เคเบิลคาร์ หาดใหญ่; ☑ 074 211898; www.hatyaipark.com; Hat Yai Mu-

nicipal Park; adult/child 200/100B; ⊙ 9am-4pm Mon-Thu & 9-5pm Fri-Sun; ℗) and taking in the spectacular views is a great escape from the often stifling atmosphere of Hat Yai.

★**Khlong Hae Floating Market** MARKET
(ตลาดน้ำคลองแห; Ban Khlong Hae; ⊙ 1-9pm Fri-Sun; ℗) Túk-túk drivers and tour operators all over Hat Yai will offer tours to this vibrant and colourful weekend floating market that straddles the river Mae Nam Toei, 5km north of the city. A row of boats line the banks opposite the nearby wát, but most of the good food and souvenirs are in the network of stalls in front of them. It gets super busy, but is still a wonderful excursion into rural Songkhla Province.

🛏 Sleeping

There is no shortage of accommodation in town. Hat Yai has dozens of business-style hotels in the town centre, within walking distance of the train station, as well as several hostels serving passing backpackers.

Hatyai Dee Hostel HOSTEL $
(☑ 091 049 2737; 194 Nipat Uthit 1; d 250B; ☀ 🛜) This clean, quiet Muslim-run hostel is conveniently close to the train station, has a very good restaurant on-site and can also arrange scooter rentals from 300B. Dorm rooms are clean and spacious, there are no heated showers, but prices are very reasonable all year round.

Hat Yai Backpackers HOSTEL $
(☑ 080 396 4621; 226 Th Niphat Uthit 1; dm 240B; ℗ ☀ 🛜) With four-bed female dorms and eight-bed mixed dorms that are clean and tidy, this cheap hostel is conveniently close to the train station and a decent bet. Staff are helpful for Hat Yai pointers.

Centara HOTEL $$
(☑ 074 352222; www.centarahotelsresorts.com; 3 Th Sanehanusorn; d/apt from 1550/2850B; ste 5550B; ℗ ☀ 🛜 ⛱) The 244-room Centara is a smart choice with pool, excellent rooms, terrific service and some fine views from the upper floors. Evening live jazz in the bar makes it a pleasant watering hole in a town where there are few. The hotel is above the Central Department Store, has a decent spa and gym, and offers airport shuttles.

Red Planet HOTEL $$
(☑ 074 261011; www.redplanethotels.com; 152-156 Th Niphat Uthit 2; d 900-1700B; ℗ ☀ 🛜) Cleanliness, affordability and decent service with

uncluttered, modern and functional rooms are the hallmarks of this hotel. The atmosphere and theme are generically chain charmless and geared towards a business clientele, but the staff is friendly and there is a spa on-site.

Eating & Drinking

The city is the unofficial capital of southern Thailand's cuisine, offering Muslim *roti* and curries, Chinese noodles, duck rice and dim sum, as well as fresh Thai-style seafood from both the gulf and Andaman coasts. Hawker stalls are everywhere, but a particularly good hunting ground is along Th Supasarnrangsan. Meals cost between 25B to 80B.

★ Night Market
MARKET $

(Th Montri 1; ⊙ 5-9.30pm) The night market offers lots of local eats including several stalls selling the famous Hat Yai–style deep-fried chicken and *kà·nŏm jeen* (fresh rice noodles served with curry). There are also a couple of stalls peddling grilled seafood and the southern staple of stuffed *roti*. Pull up a plastic chair and tuck in.

Daothiam
CAFE $

(☑ 074 243268; www.facebook.com/pg/daothiam hadyai; 79/3 Thammanoonvithi Rd; mains from 60B; ⊙ 7am-7pm; 🛜) Serving Hat Yai patrons since 1959, this traditional Chinese cafe has framed banknotes on its walls, friendly staff, a reliable menu of Thai-Chinese dishes and fine breakfasts. The name means 'satellite' and you'll find it opposite the Odean Shopping Mall.

Mata Coffee 9
COFFEE

(☑ 062 280 1717; Th Manasruedee; ⊙ 9am-7pm; 🛜) Mercifully close to the train station, this quiet, air-conditioned oasis is a good place to pause and reorganise yourself after jumping off a long train journey. Away from the chaos and noise of fare-seeking túk-túk and motorcycle-taxi drivers, you can plan your next move sitting on comfortable leather sofas with excellent coffee and strong wi-fi.

Information

EMERGENCY

Tourist Police (1st flr, Hat Yai Plaza 3, Th Niphat Uthit 3; ⊙ 24hr)

SAFE TRAVEL

Hat Yai is seen as safe from the violence witnessed further south; however, it hasn't been ignored in the past. The Lee Gardens Plaza Hotel was bombed in 2012, killing four people in a subsequent fire and injuring 400. Three bombs exploded in Hat Yai in 2014, injuring eight. In previous years pubs, malls, department stores and hotels have been targeted in other bombings, but there have been no major incidents in the city since 2014, with a noticeable upping of security around transport hubs such as the train station and airport.

As the number of international tourists indicate, Hat Yai feels safe to foreigners these days. If you are planning to just pass through there is almost nothing to worry about, even if you do plan to hang about for a while, just keep your wits about you and stay abreast of local news.

TOURIST INFORMATION

Tourism Authority of Thailand (TAT; www.tourismthailand.org/hatyai; 1/1 Soi 2, Th Niphat Uthit 3; ⊙ 8.30am-4.30pm) The staff here are very helpful and also speak English.

Dee Travels Hat Yai (Cathay Tour; ☑ 074 815 400; www.cathaytourthailand.com; 190 Th Niphat Uthit 1; ⊙ 8am-6pm) The pick of the travel agents scattered across the town centre.

VISA EXTENSIONS

Immigration Office (Th Phetkasem) Near the railway bridge, it handles visa extensions.

Getting There & Away

AIR

Hat Yai International Airport (☑ 074 227000; www.airportthai.co.th/en; 🛜) is around 14km southwest of town. Air Asia (www.airasia.com), Nok Air (www.nokair.com) and Thai Lion Air (www.lionairthai.com) have daily flights to and from Bangkok's Don Mueang Airport. **Thai Airways** (☑ 074 233433; www.thaiairways.com; Community Mall, 206-207 Th Prachayindee; ⊙ 8am-5pm Mon-Fri) and Thai Smile (www.thaismileair.com) both fly to Bangkok Suvarnabhumi International Airport.

There's an **airport taxi service** (☑ 099 478 2592; 194 Nipat Uthit 1; 100B per person; ⊙ 7am-5.15pm) to the airport four times daily for 100B (7am, 10.15am, 12.15pm and 5.15pm). A private taxi for this run costs 320B and the same journey will cost around 250B using Grab (www.grab.com).

BUS

Most inter-regional buses and southbound minivans leave from **Hat Yai Bus Station** (73 Th Chotevittayakul) 2km southeast of the town centre and most northbound minivans leave from a **Minivan Terminal** (Rte 4) 5km west of town, about an 80B túk-túk ride from the centre of town. Buses link Hat Yai to almost any location in southern Thailand.

BUSES FROM HAT YAI

The information office at the main bus station is open between 4.30am-9.30pm, and the hub is well organised with each destination assigned its very own booth. Some of the main destinations include:

DESTINATION	FARE (B)	DURATION (HR)
Bangkok	698–1086B	13hr
Krabi	253–507B	5hr
Nakhon Si Thammarat	140B	3hr
Ko Samui	404B	7hr
Phuket	355B	7hr
Songkhla	34B	1½hr
Sungai Kolok	270B	4hr
Surat Thani	240B	5hr
Trang	120B	2hr

Dee Travels Hat Yai can also arrange minivans to many destinations in the south.

TRAIN

Four overnight trains run to/from Bangkok from **Hat Yai Train Station** (☑1690; www.railwaythailand.com; Th Rotfai) each day (259B to 1794B, 16 hours); trains go via Surat Thani (105B). There are also seven trains daily that run along the east coast to Sungai Kolok (92B) and two daily trains running west to Padang Besar (50B) in Malaysia.

There is an advance booking office open from 7am to 5pm where tickets can be bought 90 days in advance. Tickets can also be bought on the phone three days in advance by calling 1690 and online five days in advance at www.railwaythailand.com. There is also a left-luggage office charging 30B to 50B for 24hrs, open from 5am to 6pm.

ⓘ Getting Around

Sŏrng·tăa·ou (pickup minibuses) run along Th Phetkasem (20B per person). Túk-túk and motorcycle taxis around town cost 30B to 60B per person. There are also regular hail and ride taxis as well as Grab taxis (www.grab.com), which can now be ordered via the app costing around 70B for a short journey.

Those wanting to explore the city at their own leisure can rent their own bicycles from **Tyro Bike** (☑092 628 2415; www.facebook.com/ty-robike; Th Rajyindee; ⊗9am-6pm Mon-Sat; 🛜) in the east of the city.

DEEP SOUTH

In the deep southern Thai provinces of Pattani, Yala and Narathiwat the complexion of Thailand makes a pronounced shift. The culture, language, religion and history of this area is distinctly Malay Muslim, with a regional identity rooted in the 16th-century Sultanate of Pattani that once held sway over this section of southern Thailand and parts of northern Malaysia. Most inhabitants of the region speak a dialect of Malay, and are ethnically closer to their Malay cousins over the border.

The tourist potential in this fascinating region is largely unexploited, put on the back foot by a long-simmering insurgency that pits ethnic and religious separatists against the Thai state, with just a small trickle of visitors and consequently a paucity of infrastructure to cater to them. Most of the travelling traffic is crossing the border into, and to a lesser extent, out of Thailand at Sungai Kolok.

Yala

☑073 / POP 63,000

Landlocked Yala (ยะลา) wiggles its way south to the Malaysian border, making it Thailand's southernmost province. Its eponymous capital appears very different from other Thai metropolises and feels distinctly Western, with big boulevards and a well-organised street grid set around a huge circular park. Around three-quarters of the population is Muslim and it is a university town, the educational centre of the Deep South.

◉ Sights

Yala's biggest attraction is Wat Kuhapimuk (วัดคูหาภิมุข, Wat Na Tham or Cave-front Temple; Na Tham, off Rte 409), one of the most important pilgrimage points in southern Thailand.

Further south, Betong is home to the largest mail box in Thailand, first built in 1924.

🛏 Sleeping & Eating

Yala is a pleasant place, but many of the city's cheapest lodgings double as unofficial brothels. There isn't a great selection of places in town but the **Yala Rama** (☑ 073 212815; 15-21 Th Sri Bamrung; r 650B; ❄ ☎) is a good choice.

There are excellent restaurants scattered around the park's perimeter.

ⓘ Information

Betong functions as a legal, but inconvenient, border crossing to Malaysia; contact Yala's **immigration office** (☑ 073 231292; Betong; ☺ 8.30am-4.30pm).

ⓘ Getting There & Away

Yala's bus station is south of the city centre. There are three daily buses to and from Bangkok's southern bus terminal (783B to 1422B, 15 hours).

Four trains a day run between Bangkok and Yala (18 hours). Two trains travel daily between Yala and Sungai Kolok (three to four hours). The train station is just north of the city centre.

Buses to Hat Yai (160B, 2½ hours) stop several times a day on Th Sirirot, outside the Prudential TS Life office.

Minivans to Betong and Sungai Kolok (100B, 2½ hours) depart hourly from opposite the train station.

Pattani

☑ 073 / POP 43,700

Once the heart of a large Muslim sultanate that included the neighbouring provinces of Yala, Narathiwat and parts of northern Malaysia, Pattani (ปัตตานี) Province has never adjusted to Thai rule. Although today's political situation has stunted the area's development, Pattani Town has a 500-year history of trading with the world's most notorious imperial powerhouses. The Portuguese established a trading post here in 1516, the Japanese passed through in 1605, the Dutch in 1609 and the British flexed their colonial muscles in 1612.

Yet despite the city's fascinating past, there's little of interest in Pattani. There are some decent beaches nearby, but the ongoing insurgency has made most of these sandy destinations unsafe for the independent traveller.

🛏 Sleeping & Eating

As with other cities in the region, there is not a great choice for sleeping in Pattani, though a decent option for comfort is the **CS Pattani Hotel** (☑ 073 336090; www.cspattanihotel.com; 299 Mu 4, Th Nong Jik; r from 900B; ❄ @ ☎ ☒).

ⓘ TRAVEL IN THE DEEP SOUTH: SHOULD YOU GO?

At the time of writing many Western governments were advising against all but essential travel to the provinces of Pattani, Yala and Narathiwat, with the attacks and bombings continuing. Despite this, almost everyone in the Deep South is happy to see a *fa·ràng* (Westerner). So few foreigners make it here that those that do are guaranteed a lot of attention from the locals. Nor have tourists or any Westerners ever been targeted by the insurgents. This is a very insular war.

Yet, by nature insurgencies are unpredictable, and bombs kill indiscriminately. Explosive devices planted on parked motorbikes outside shops, schools or in markets, are a common tactic of the separatists and are frequently used in the city centres of Yala, Pattani, Narathiwat and Sungai Kolok.

It's best not to linger on the streets for too long; you could be in the wrong place at the wrong time. Nor is travel in the countryside in the early morning or after dark advisable. This isn't an area to be driving a motorbike in if you can't be identified as a foreigner.

There is another more practical drawback, the insurgency has stifled tourism to such an extent that there is very little infrastructure for visitors and this means travel between the major centres apart, you'll need private transport to get around. There are few hotels and restaurants, and almost no nightlife, while those beautiful beaches have absolutely no facilities, which of course does make it attractive to some. You can also expect to come upon numerous checkpoints scattered all over the provinces and cities, slowing things down considerably. If you do want to travel through the Deep South, research the current situation carefully and take advice from your embassy.

> ⓘ **GETTING TO MALAYSIA: SUNGAI KOLOK TO RANTAU PANJANG**
>
> **Getting to the Border** The Thai border (open 5am to 9pm) is about 1.5km from the centre of Sungai Kolok. Motorbike taxis charge around 30B.
>
> **At the Border** This is a hassle-free border crossing. After completing formalities, walk across the Harmony Bridge to the Malaysian border post.
>
> **Moving On** Shared taxis and buses to Kota Bharu, the capital of Malaysia's Kelantan State, can be caught 200m beyond the Malaysian border post. Shared taxis cost RM$10 per person (75B) or RM$50 (370B) to charter the whole car yourself. The ride takes around 40 minutes. Buses make the hour-long journey for RM$5.10 (38B).
>
> It's possible to continue south by the so-called 'jungle train', but the closest station is at Pasir Mas, located along taxi/bus routes to Kota Bharu.
>
> Tak Bai, also in Narathiwat Province, and Betong, further south in Yala, are also legal crossing points for foreigners, but Sungai Kolok is by far the most convenient place to cross the border.

ⓘ Information

There are several banks along the southeastern end of Th Pipit, near the Th Naklua Yarang intersection.

Police Station (🖉073 348555; 62 Th Pattani Phirom)

Pattani Hospital (🖉073 711010; www.pattanihos.com; 2 Th Nong Jik)

ⓘ Getting There & Around

Minivans and buses depart from Pattani's bus station on the western fringes of town, with frequent daytime departures to Hat Yai (120B, 1½ hours), Narathiwat (120B, 1½ hours) and Sungai Kolok (160B, 2½ hours).

There are two daily buses to and from Bangkok's southern bus terminal (765B to 1250B, 14 hours).

Motorbike taxis charge 30B for hops around town, but they become very scarce after dark.

Sungai Kolok

🖉073 / POP 78,500

It's not the most prepossessing place to enter or exit the 'Land of Smiles', but Sungai Kolok (สุไหงโกลก) is the main gateway between Thailand and Malaysia. As such, it's a scuzzy border town best known for smuggling and sex workers. Less of a target than the other major towns in the region, the unstable situation in the Deep South has nevertheless severely diminished its 'sin city' reputation in recent years, with the Malaysian men who once came here for wild weekends now favouring safer Hat Yai. Few travellers leave Thailand here now; more come in the opposite direction and immediately hop on a train heading north.

🛌 Sleeping

Most hotels here are uniform in quality and price and not of a high standard. Many of the real cheapies won't accept foreigners.

Merlin Hotel HOTEL $
(🖉073 611003; 68 Th Charoenkhet; r 600-700B; ❄🖥) Dated fixtures and furniture, but clean and handy for the train station.

ⓘ Information

There are ATMs and foreign-exchange booths close to the train station. A tourist police office sits at the border.

There is an **immigration office** (🖉073 611231; www.narathiwatimmigration.go.th; 70 Th Charoenkhet; ☺8am-5pm Mon-Fri) opposite the Merlin Hotel with helpful, English-speaking staff.

ⓘ Getting There & Away

The long-distance **bus station** (Th Asia 18, off 4056) is 2km west of the centre on Th Asia 18. There are four buses daily to and from Bangkok's southern bus terminal (707B to 1414B, 17 to 20 hours). Minivans to Hat Yai (270B, four hours) leave from here too.

Minivans heading north to Narathiwat (70B, one hour), Pattani (160B, 2½ hours) and Yala (110B, 2½ hours) depart from opposite the train station, near the **Genting Hotel** (🖉073 613231; 250 Th Asia 18; r 690-790B; ❄@🖥🛉).

Two daily trains (11.30pm and 2.20pm, 18 to 23 hours) connect Sungai Kolok with Bangkok. Trains in the Deep South are often delayed and subject to army and police searches.

ⓘ Getting Around

Motorcycle taxis zoom around town for a flat rate of 30B.

AT A GLANCE

POPULATION
760,000

EXPATS ON PHUKET
115,000

BEST BEACH
Hat Nai Harn (p632)

BEST NIGHT MARKET
Trang Night Market (p686)

BEST BEACH BUNGALOWS
Castaway Resort (p701)

WHEN TO GO

May The start of the five-month-long rainy season. Some resorts close, others slash their prices.

Sep–Oct The Vegetarian Festival is held in Phuket and Trang. Expect pierced-faced worshippers and fantastic food.

Dec Peak tourist season begins and conditions are ideal for diving and snorkelling.

Rock climbing, Thaiwand Wall (p662), Railay
ADIREK.JOB/SHUTTERSTOCK ©

Phuket & the Andaman Coast

The Andaman is Thailand's dream coast: a place that you see on a postcard that makes you want to quit your job and live in flip-flops... forever. And it is stunning. Pure-white beaches of soft sand, a turquoise sea, towering limestone cliffs and jungle-covered isles extend down the Andaman Sea from the border of Myanmar to Malaysia. Phuket is the glitzy show-stealer, but head north and you'll uncover world-class dive sites, little-visited islands, and the waterfalls and caves of Phang-Nga's national parks. To the south, you can lazily island-hop down to the Malaysian border.

The catch? The Andaman Coast is no secret and its beaches are increasingly crowded with backpackers, package tourists, high-end jet-setters and everyone else. Flashy resorts are pushing out the bamboo shacks and Thai-Rasta bars and authenticity hides largely in the backwaters now. But if you're willing to search hard, postcard dreams are still here.

Phuket & the Andaman Coast Highlights

1 Trang Islands (p688) Buzzing across jade-green waters between white-sand beaches.

2 Ko Lipe (p699) Snorkelling over colourful corals and exploring the untouched nearby islands.

3 Phuket (p620) Experiencing the heady mix of luxury lodgings, super spas and street-food treats.

4 Khao Sok National Park (p608) Hiking through a real-life Jurassic Park.

5 Railay (p660) Scaling limestone cliffs above blissful beaches.

6 Ko Phi-Phi

GULF OF THAILAND

Ko Tao

Chong Tao

Ko Pha-Ngan

Thong Sala

Bo Phut
Hat Chaweng
Ko Samui

Chong Pha-Ngan

Chong Samui

Khanom

Sichon

Tha Sala

Phrom Khiri

Nakhon Si Thammarat

Ang Thong Marine National Park

Ko Phaluai

401

4014

Phi Pun

4142

Chawang

4015

Ao Ban Don

Surat Thani

Na Doem

Ban Na San

Wiang Sa

41

Sawi

Ko Kula

Ao Savi

Thung Tako

Laem Riu

Lamae

Chaiya

4112

Tha Chang

Surat Thani Airport

Khian Sa

Chai Buri

4110

La-Un

RANONG

Isthmus of Kra

CHUMPHON

Pha To

4006

SURAT THANI

Khlong Yan

SURAT THANI

Khiriratnikhom

Na Doem

KRABI

Thap Put

Plaiphaya

Tham Wararin

Phang-Nga

4

Ranong

MYANMAR (BURMA)

Kawthoung

Ko Chang

Ranong Airport

Kapoe

Laem Son National Park

Ngan Yong

Chiaw Lan Lake

Ban Takhun

Khao Sok National Park

401

Phanom

PHANG-NGA

Meuang Phang-Nga

Ko Phayam 10

Hat Bang Ben

Ko Kam Noi

Ko Kam Yai

Hat Praphat

4

Khuraburi

Ko Ra

4

Takua Pa

Kapong

4240

Khao Lak/Lam Ru National Park

Thap Lamu

Thai Muang

Takua Thung

4

Surin Islands Marine National Park 7

Surin Islands

Ko Phra Thong

Ko Kho Khao

Hat Bang Sak

Hat Bang Niang
Hat Nang Thong
Hat Khao Lak

ANDAMAN SEA

Ko Tachai

Ko Bon

Similan Islands Marine National Park 7

Similan Islands

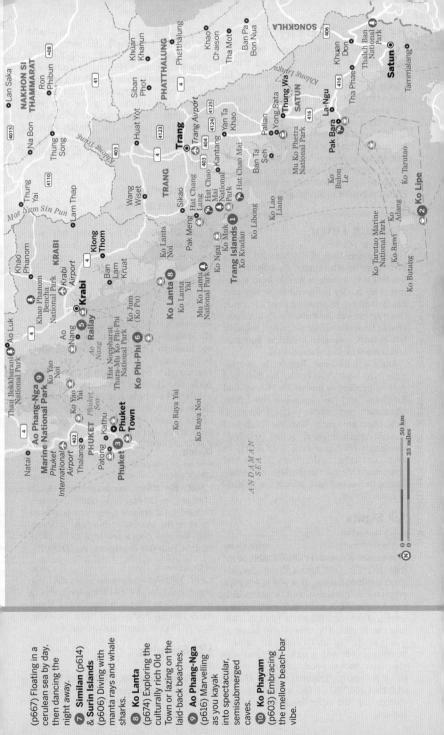

(p667) Floating in a cerulean sea by day, then dancing the night away.

7 Similan (p614) **& Surin Islands** (p606) Diving with manta rays and whale sharks.

8 Ko Lanta (p674) Exploring the culturally rich Old Town or lazing on the laid-back beaches.

9 Ao Phang-Nga (p616) Marvelling as you kayak into spectacular, semisubmerged caves.

10 Ko Phayam (p603) Embracing the mellow beach-bar vibe.

RANONG PROVINCE

Ranong (จังหวัดระนอง) is the Andaman's northernmost province, with lush forests and a smattering of beautiful islands – Ko Chang and Ko Phayam especially – that remain relatively under the radar. However, the province is a whole different package to the white-sand, turquoise-sea paradise that is used to sell the Andamans on tourist brochures. Thailand's least populated and wettest region gets up to eight months of rain a year, so it's soggy, while beaches along the coast are scarce. Most visitors come here to cross the border to Myanmar.

Ranong Town

📞 077 / POP 24,561

On the eastern bank of Mae Nam Pak Chan's turbid, tea-brown estuary, Ranong (ระนอง) lies just a 45-minute boat ride from Myanmar. This border town and busy river port has a thriving population from Myanmar (keep an eye out for women with faces covered in *thanaka* – cosmetic paste), bubbling hot springs, restored historical buildings and some sensational street food.

Once a backwater, Ranong is increasingly busy with cross-border business and visitors heading to nearby Ko Phayam and Ko Chang, and has clearly benefitted from Myanmar's more stable political situation. Now, there are quirky boutique hotels and a style-conscious local scene (relatively speaking). Dive operators specialising in liveaboard trips to the Surin Islands and Myanmar's Mergui Archipelago are establishing themselves here, adding a sprinkling of expat flavour.

👁 Sights

Ngao Waterfall National Park   NATIONAL PARK

(อุทยานแห่งชาติ น้ำตกหงาว; 📞 077 848181; adult/child 100/50B; ⏰ 8.30am-4.30pm) Located 12km south of Ranong, this 668-sq-km park preserves a rainforest and a 300m-high tiered waterfall. A short trail leads up to a section of the waterfall where you can wade into the stream. The area is also home to locally celebrated panda crabs, an unusual freshwater crab with a white body and purple mouth. Both this park and the Pornrang Hot Springs (บ่อน้ำร้อนพรรั้ง; 📞 077 862103; adult/child 100/50B; ⏰ 6am-5.30pm) can be visited with the ticket bought at the hot springs.

Wat Ban Ngao   BUDDHIST TEMPLE

(วัดบ้านหงาว; ⏰ 7am-6pm) This pretty refuge at the base of a hill was originally a resting place for Buddhist pilgrims. A temple was constructed on the site in 1987. You can hike up the concrete steps behind the temple for great views of the valley. There's a pond nearby where enormous protected fish lurk in the dark waters. The temple, around 13km south of Ranong, is close to the Ngao Waterfall National Park; they can be visited together.

🏃 Activities

Spas & Hot Springs

⭐ **Namnong Hot Spa**   SPA

(📞 084 625 3444; 73/3 Th Phetkasem; treatments 400-1000B; ⏰ 11am-8pm) This is a highly recommended mineral bath experience in Ranong Town, classier than the public hot springs opposite. Soak in a private hot tub, then add a salt scrub or a classic Thai massage.

Rakswarin Hot Springs   HOT SPRINGS

(Th Phetkasem; ⏰ 5am-9pm) Located on the southeastern side of town, Ranong's (free) healing waters bubble from a sacred spring hot enough to boil eggs (65°C). The riverside pools have chequered mosaic tiles, showers, towels and sunbeds. Just stretch out and let the heat work its natural magic. One section of the property is run by a private entity (40B; it's cleaner and less crowded.

Diving

Andaman International Dive Center   DIVING

(📞 089 814 1092; www.aidcdive.com; 41/115 Thamuang; ⏰ Oct-Apr) This outfit is mainly focused on extensive excursions (six to 14 days) to the Mergui Archipelago in Myanmar, but also does a few trips to the Surin Islands. Four-day liveaboards are 20,000B.

A-One-Diving   DIVING

(📞 077 832984; www.a-one-diving.com; 256 Th Ruangrat; ⏰ Oct-Apr) A-One-Diving specialises in liveaboards to the Surin Islands and Myanmar's Mergui Archipelago (from 34,900B), plus PADI diving certification courses.

🛏 Sleeping

Tinidee   HOTEL $

(www.tinidee-ranong.com; 41/144 Th Tamuang; r 570B; 🛒) The Tinidee Inn offers clean and quiet rooms in an annexe close to the much larger Tinidee Hotel. Guests who stay at the

Ranong

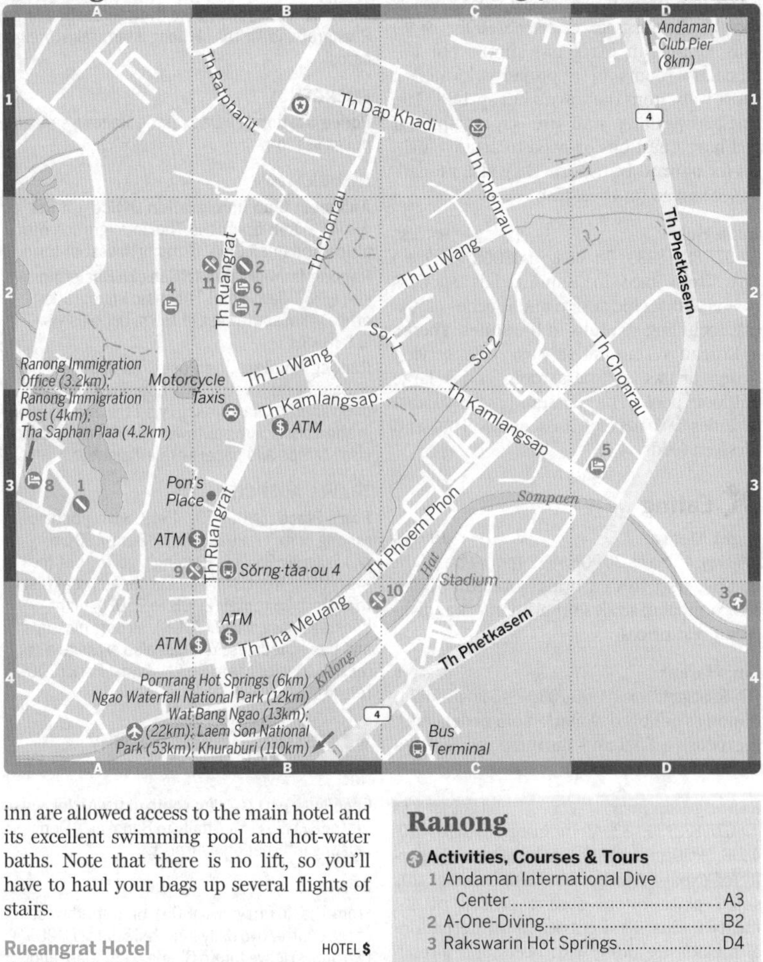

inn are allowed access to the main hotel and its excellent swimming pool and hot-water baths. Note that there is no lift, so you'll have to haul your bags up several flights of stairs.

Rueangrat Hotel HOTEL $
(☎092 279 9919; rueangratranong@gmail.com; 240/10 Th Ruangrat; r 790B; ❄📶) Bright, shiny rooms are set back from the road at this place close to restaurants and shops. All come with fridges, TVs and decent bathrooms. There's free coffee in the lobby area, friendly staff and good wi-fi reception.

Savika Guesthouse GUESTHOUSE $
(☎082 217 5483; savikaranong@gmail.com; 240/14 Th Ruangrat; r 1080B) This friendly, family-run guesthouse, managed by an American-Thai couple, has a perfect location in the thick of Ranong's traveller hub. Rooms are well equipped with fridge, TV and hot-water boiler for tea and coffee. The owners can help arrange boat and bus tickets and are a great resource for scuba divers. The American-style breakfasts are good value.

Ranong

Activities, Courses & Tours
1 Andaman International Dive Center A3
2 A-One-Diving B2
3 Rakswarin Hot Springs D4

Sleeping
4 Galla Hotel A2
5 Madinah Hostel Ranong D3
6 Rueangrat Hotel B2
7 Savika Guesthouse B2
8 Tinidee A3

Eating
9 Day Market B3
10 Night Market B4
11 Ranong Hideaway B2

Madinah Hostel Ranong
HOSTEL $

(☑ 081 416 0825; madinahhostel_ranong@yahoo.com; Th Kamlangsap; dm/r 360/600B; ✱🖥) This family-run place has simple but immaculate rooms in a property located a short walk from the town's hot springs. The English-speaking staff are superhelpful if you have questions or need to arrange tickets for onward transport. They also prepare a nice spread for breakfast.

Galla Hotel
HOTEL $$

(☑ 077 880 8989; Th Mung; r 1800B; ✱🖥🏊) This fresh face in Ranong has spotless rooms with a chic design and touches of luxury, including spa tubs in the suites. There's a Korean restaurant, a cosy cafe serving frozen drinks, a fitness room and a large outdoor pool. The outstanding breakfast includes a variety of East Asian, Thai and Western foods.

✖ Eating

Night Market
MARKET $

(off Hwy 4; mains 30-70B; ⏱ 2-7pm) The night market, next to to a bridge over the Klong Hat Sompaen, sizzles up brilliant Thai dishes at great prices.

Day Market
MARKET $

(Th Ruangrat; mains 40-70B; ⏱ 5am-midnight) Ranong's bubbly day market offers delicious, inexpensive Thai and Burmese meals. It's a wonderfully local scene.

Ranong Hideaway
MULTICUISINE $$

(☑ 077 832730; 323/7 Th Ruangrat; mains 110-480B; ⏱ 10am-11pm; 🖥) A long-time favourite of expats and border businessmen, this small place offers decent pastas, pizzas, meaty mains, Thai curries and international breakfasts, along with beers and foreign liquor.

ℹ Information

ATMs are clustered around the intersection of Th Ruangrat and Th Tha Meuang. Many take foreign cards.

EMERGENCY

Police Station (Th Dap Khadi) Ranong's main police station.

IMMIGRATION

Andaman Club Immigration Office (off Rte 4004; ⏱ 7am-5pm) The Thai immigration office at the Andaman Club, 8km northwest of town.

Ranong Immigration Office (Th Chalermprakiat; ⏱ 8.30am-5pm) The main immigration office, 4km southwest of town, handles visa extensions.

Ranong Immigration Post (Tha Saphan Plaa; ⏱ 8am-5pm) If you're just popping in and out of Myanmar's Kawthoung, visit this small immigration post, 5km southwest of town: it handles visa stamps and paperwork efficiently.

TRAVEL AGENCIES

Pon's Place (☑ 081 597 4549; www.ponplaceranong.com; Th Ruangrat; ⏱ 8am-7.30pm; 🖥) Friendly Pon's is Ranong's go-to spot for everything from wi-fi and European breakfasts to motorbike rental (200B to 250B), flight bookings, visa runs (1300B), airport pick-ups and bus schedules. You can also arrange a car for day trips to Laem Son National Park (2000B return).

ℹ Getting There & Away

AIR

Ranong Airport is 22km south of town. Nok Air (p687) flies twice daily to Bangkok's Don Mueang International Airport.

BOAT

From Tha Ko Phayam (p605), 6km southwest of the centre, two daily long-tail boats (200B, two hours) leave for Ko Chang, at 9.30am and 2pm. In high season, they stop at the west-coast

BUSES FROM RANONG

DESTINATION	FARE (B)	DURATION (HR)	FREQUENCY
Bangkok	510-627	9-10	7.30am, 8.10am, 10.30am, 1.30pm, 3.30pm, 7.30pm, 8pm (VIP) & 8.30pm (VIP)
Chumphon	150	2	hourly 7am-5pm
Hat Yai	380	7	6am, 10am & 8pm
Khao Lak	175	3½	hourly 6.30am-5.45pm
Krabi	210	6	7am, 10am & 2pm
Phang-Nga	180	5	7am, 10am & 2pm
Phuket	245	5-6	hourly 6.30am-5.45pm
Surat Thani	190	4-5	hourly 6am-4pm

beaches, returning at approximately 8.30am and 1pm. During the monsoon, only one long-tail runs, at 2pm, docking at the main pier on the northeast coast. During the November–April high season, two daily speedboats (350B, 30 minutes) travel between Ranong's Tha Ko Phayam and Ko Chang's northeast-coast pier (there's one daily speedboat in low season).

Two daily ferries at 9.30am and 2pm travel from Tha Ko Phayam to Ko Payam (200B, two hours), returning at 8.30am and 3pm. During the November–April high season, speedboats (350B, 35 minutes) make the run almost hourly from 7.30am to 5.30pm, returning to the mainland between 8am and 4.30pm.

Tha Saphan Plaa, 5km southwest of town, has boats to Kawthoung in Myanmar.

BUS

The **bus terminal** (Th Phetkasem) is 1km southeast of the centre. Blue *sŏrng·tăa·ou 2* pass the terminal. From here, minivans head to Surat Thani (200B, 3½ hours, 6am and 2pm) and Chumphon (160B, two hours, hourly from 7am to 5pm).

ℹ️ Getting Around

Motorcycle taxis (Th Ruangrat) can take you almost anywhere in town for 50B, including to Tha Ko Phayam for boats to Ko Chang and Ko Payam, and Tha Saphan Plaa for boats to Kawthoung in Myanmar. The red **sŏrng·tăa·ou 4** (Th Ruangrat) stops near the piers (20B). Pon's Place can help with motorcycle and car rentals and offers shuttle vans to the piers (from its office/the airport 70/200B).

Ko Chang

The little-visited, rustic isle of Ko Chang is a long way (in every respect) from its much more popular Trat Province namesake. The speciality here is no-frills living, and electricity and wi-fi are still scarce. An all-pervading quiet lies over the island, with the hum of modern life replaced by the sound of the sea. Between May and October (low season) it's beyond mellow and many places shut down.

Wide west-coast Ao Yai has gorgeous marbled white-and-black sand in the south, which obscures the otherwise clear sea. White-sand snobs will be happiest on Ao Yai's northern end. A short trail leads south over the bluff to Ao Tadaeng, a boulder-strewn beach and the island's best sunset spot.

Inland is the tiny village capital, cashew orchards and rubber plantations. Dirt trails wind around and across the island and, if you're lucky, you'll spot sea eagles, Andaman kites and hornbills floating above the mangroves.

🤿 Activities

Aladdin Dive Safari DIVING
(☑ 087 274 7601; www.aladdindivesafari.com; Cashew Resort, Ao Yai; 2 dives 5800B; ⊙10am-6pm Nov-May) A relatively flash, long-established liveaboard operation that runs Surin and Similan Islands day trips, Open Water Dive courses (18,700B to 19,800B), and liveaboards to Myanmar's Mergui Archipelago, the Surins, the Similans, Ko Phi-Phi, Hin Daeng and Hin Muang (15,800B to 19,800B).

Om Tao YOGA
(☑ 085 470 9312; www.omtao.net; Ao Yai; classes 300B) This German-run studio has daily yoga (8.30am) from November to April. Classes are by request at other times.

🛏️ Sleeping & Eating

Simple bamboo huts are the norm. Expect a bed, mosquito net, basic bathroom, hammock, small balcony and little else. Most are only open from November to April. Electricity is limited; some places have solar and wind power. Most lodgings are in Ao Yai or tucked away on Ao Tadaeng, immediately south. To really get away from it all, head to the northwest coast.

The only restaurants are inside the resorts.

⭐**Sangsuree Bungalows** BUNGALOW $
(☑ 081 2517726; bungalow.sangsuree@gmail.com; Ao Takien; bungalows 300-500B; 🛜) Ko Chang's northwest coast is dotted with hidden bays, and Sangsuree's seven basic bungalows are positioned just above one of them, commanding fine sea views. Run by a charming husband-and-wife team, this is a classic, old-school Thai island chill-out spot, with communal meals and much lazing around. It's a 10-minute walk to a sandy swimming beach.

⭐**Crocodile Rock** GUESTHOUSE $
(☑ 080 533 4138; tonn1970@yahoo.com; Ao Yai; bungalows 400-700B; ⊙Oct-Apr; 🛜) This place has simple metal-roofed bamboo bungalows with hammocks. Perched on Ao Yai's serene southern headland, Crocodile Rock has superb bay views. The classy kitchen turns out homemade yoghurt, breads, cookies, good espresso, and a variety of veggie and seafood dishes. It's popular, so book ahead.

> ### ℹ️ GETTING TO MYANMAR: RANONG TOWN TO KAWTHOUNG (VICTORIA POINT)
>
> The most hassle-free way to renew your visa is on one of the 'visa trips' (1300B) offered by Ranong travel agencies, including Pon's Place (p600). But it's easy enough to do the legwork yourself.
>
> **Getting to the border** As long as the Thailand–Myanmar border is open, boats to Kawthoung leave from Tha Saphan Plaa (p601), 5km southwest of Ranong. Red *sŏrng·tǎa·ou 4* (pick-up minibuses) go from Ranong to the pier (20B), where long-tail captains lead you to the immigration post, then to their boat (per person oneway/return 100/200B). Confirm whether prices are per person or per ride, and oneway or return. You'll need a photocopy of your passport, which you can get at the pier (5B).
>
> **At the border** At the Kawthoung checkpoint, you must inform the authorities that you're a day visitor if you don't plan on staying overnight – in which case you'll pay a US$10 fee (it must be a crisp bill; long-tail captains can get this from harbour touts for 500B). The only hassle comes from 'helpers' on the Myanmar side, who offer to do everything from carrying your day pack to collecting forms, then ask for tips, but they're generally more friendly than aggravating.
>
> If you're just renewing your Thai visa, the whole process takes two hours. When returning to Thailand, bear in mind that Myanmar's time is 30 minutes behind Thailand's. This has previously caused problems for returning travellers who got through Myanmar immigration before its closing time only to find the Thai Immigration post (p600) closed. It's worth checking Thai immigration closing hours when leaving the country; if you don't get stamped in you'll have to return to Myanmar the next day.
>
> A quicker, easier and much more polished alternative (albeit sterilised and less interesting) is via the Andaman Club (p600). At the terminal, located 8km northwest of Ranong, off Rte 4004, you'll get your passport stamped immediately. A Myanmar-bound speedboat (950B return, 15 minutes each way) leaves hourly from 8.30am to 3.30pm, docking at a flash casino on the island of Pulo in Myanmar. The whole trip takes one hour.
>
> **Moving on** It's possible to stay overnight in one of Kawthoung's overpriced hotels, but you'd probably rather not. If you have a valid Myanmar visa, which you'll have to apply for in advance at the Myanmar embassy in Bangkok (or a third country), you'll be permitted to stay for up to 28 days and can exit anywhere you like. There are daily flights from Kawthoung to Yangon.

Little Italy
BUNGALOW **$**

(☑ 084 851 2760; daniel060863@yahoo.it; Ao Yai; r 400-500B; ☏) Little Italy has just three immaculate bungalows attached to a Thai-Italian restaurant amid the trees at Ao Yai. Two are stilted, split-level concrete-and-wood jobs encircled by wraparound verandas. The third concrete bungalow is on the ground, with a tiled bathroom. Book ahead in high season.

Eden
BUNGALOW **$**

(☑ 080 628 7590, 061 212 9328; Ao Yai; r 300B) These rickety, bare-bones-basic bungalows (forget bathrooms doors) and no-frills shared-shower rooms at the northern end of Ao Yai are kept clean by a friendly family who'll whip you up a sensational massaman curry. It's popular with returnees and there's a social beachside bar-restaurant. The electricity runs between 6pm and 11pm.

ℹ️ Information

There are no ATMs. The nearest ATM is on Ko Phayam, which is not easily accessible, so it's best to bring enough cash for your stay.

Wi-fi has arrived at a few establishments, though connections are weak.

ℹ️ Getting There & Away

From the centre of Ranong, *sŏrng·tǎa·ou* (pick-up minibuses; 20B) and motorcycle taxis (50B) go from Th Ruangrat to Tha Ko Phayam pier near Saphan Plaa, from where two daily long-tail boats (200B, two hours) leave for Ko Chang, at 9.30am and 2pm. In high season, they stop at the west-coast beaches, returning at approximately 8.30am and 1pm. During the monsoon, only one long-tail runs, at 2pm, docking at the main pier on the northeast coast.

During the November–April high season, two daily speedboats (350B, 30 minutes, 8.30am and 10.30am) travel between Ranong's Tha Ko

Phayam and Ko Chang's northeast-coast pier. In low season, one speedboat runs at 1.30pm.

High-season Ko Phayam–Ranong speedboats often drop off and pick up passengers in Ko Chang (350B) on request, though they're unreliable; get your resort to make (and confirm) the booking. You can charter long-tails to Ko Phayam (2000B) through Koh Chang Resort.

Motorcycle taxis meet boats, charging 100B between the northeast-coast pier and Ao Yai.

Ko Phayam

Technically part of Laem Son National Park (อุทยานแห่งชาติแหลมสน; ☎077 861431; www.dnp.go.th; adult/child 200/100B; ☺8am-4.30pm), Ko Phayam is fringed with beautiful soft-white beaches and is becoming increasingly popular as a family destination. If you're coming from Phuket or Ko Phi-Phi, it'll feel refreshingly wild and dozy. The spectacular northwest and southwest coasts are dotted with rustic bungalows, small-scale resorts, breezy sand-side restaurants and barefoot beach bars. Fauna includes wild pigs, monkeys and tremendous birdlife (sea eagles, herons and hornbills).

The island's one village (on the east coast, beside the main pier) caters mostly to tourists. But hit it during a festival (like the February Cashew Festival) and you'll see that the locals still have a firm grip on their island. Narrow motorcycle pathways, concrete roadways and dirt trails run across the island's wooded interior; some are rutted to the point of hazardous – drive slowly.

◉ Sights & Activities

Ko Phayam is dotted with gorgeous blonde sands, but don't expect to have them to yourself between November and April.

The most impressive beaches are Ao Yai (Long Beach), to the southwest, and Ao Khao Kwai (Buffalo Bay) to the northwest. Ao Mea Mai, south of the pier on the east coast, is also nice. Garbage piles up on Ao Yai during the monsoon season.

The east coast is quieter and you're close to the village, but the beaches are not as good. Storms lash the west coast during monsoon season. Ao Khao Kwai is a little more protected and the east coast is even more concealed from the winds.

Ko Phayam's main drawback is that the snorkelling isn't great; high sea temperatures have killed off all the coral. But the Surin Islands are close, and you can hop on liveaboard dive expeditions or speedboat transfers.

Wat Phayam BUDDHIST TEMPLE
(วัดเกาะพยาม; ☺daylight hours) FREE Shrouded in jungle just north of the main pier, on Ko Phayam's east coast, you'll find a majestic golden Buddha here flanked by a three-headed *naga* (serpent).

Moken Village VILLAGE
(หมู่บ้านชาวเลทะเล) A Moken (Sea Gypsy) village is located at the western side of Buffalo Bay. From the end of the road you need to walk through deep sand and cross a river on a hand-pulled rope pontoon. It's also accessible from the northern end of Ao Yai (a 45-minute walk). Signs at the village warn tourists to dress appropriately (no bikinis). It's best to go with Fiona, Australian director of the local NGO All For Villages (p605), which has an office near the main pier.

Most local adults don't want their pictures taken but photographing kids is OK (ask first anyway).

🛏 Sleeping & Eating

Many resorts stay open year-round. It's now more or less standard to have 24-hour power. The west-coast beaches are the most popular places to stay in high season.

There's a smattering of seafood places in the village on the east coast, and a few eateries spread along the west coast. All the resorts have their own restaurants.

🛏 Ao Yai

Frog Beach House HOTEL $
(☎083 542 7559; www.frogbeachhouse.com; Ao Yai; bungalows 500-1400B; 🖥) These well-kept, traditional Thai-style hardwood chalets at the northern end of Ao Yai have wooden floors, outdoor bathrooms, glass-bowl sinks and mosquito nets. They're lined up behind a nice slab of sand beside a small stream.

Bamboo Bungalows BUNGALOW $$
(☎081 273 3437; www.bamboo-bungalows.com; Ao Yai; bungalows 750-2600B; 🖥) These smart, rustic bungalows come with indoor/outdoor bathrooms, some decoration and balconies with hammocks. They are all scattered throughout a leafy garden set just back from the middle of lovely Ao Yai. The beachfront restaurant is pretty good and kayaks and boogie boards can be hired. It has 24-hour electricity in high season.

Ko Phayam

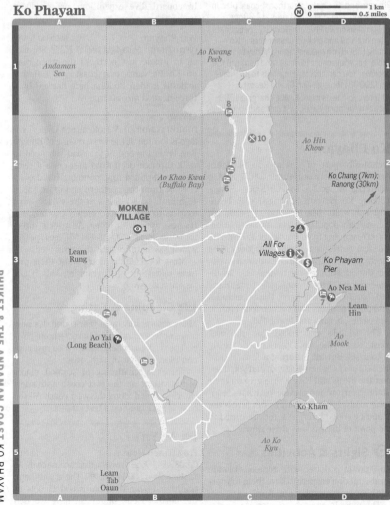

N 0 ——— 1 km
0 ——— 0.5 miles

Ao Kwang Peeb

Andaman Sea

Ao Hin Khow

Ao Khao Kwai (Buffalo Bay)

Ko Chang (7km); Ranong (30km)

MOKEN VILLAGE ⊙1

Leam Rung

All For Villages ⓘ ⊗9

Ko Phayam Pier

Ao Nea Mai

Leam Hin

Ao Mook

Ao Yai (Long Beach)

Ko Kham

Ao Ko Kyu

Leam Tab Oaun

🛏 Ao Khao Kwai

Heaven Beach   BUNGALOW $$
(☑ 082 806 0413; www.ppland-heavenbeach.com; Ao Khao Kwai; r 2000-2500B; 🔊) ∥ A sweet resort on an idyllic slice of beachfront real estate, Heaven Beach has tiled bungalows in shades of pastel that are cutesy, characterful and super-spacious without losing comfort. They feature flower motifs, open-air bathrooms, hot showers, all-day electricity and wide decks with rattan lounges. The resort is family-friendly, with art classes and jewellery-making for both kids and adults.

Mr Gao   BUNGALOW $$
(☑ 086 266 0223; www.mr-gao-phayam.com; Ao Khao Kwai; bungalows 1000-1800B; @ 🔊) These sturdy, varnished wood-and-brick or bamboo bungalows are popular with activity-oriented couples and families and are decent-sized, with mosquito nets, tiled bathrooms and front decks. The owner Mr Gao is a font of knowledge and can offer great day-trip options around the island, kayak rental, snorkelling and multiday trips.

Sun Bungalows & Resort   BUNGALOW $$
(☑ 093 132 3655; www.thesunatranong.com; Ao Khao Kwai; bungalows 1200-3900B; 🌸🔊) At the

Ko Phayam

northern end of Ao Khao Kwai, this friendly resort has some very smart two-storey wooden bungalows, with comfy beds, proper bathrooms and large terraces on the upstairs level. There are also more basic bamboo bungalows and, cheapest of all, rooms in a building at the back. Hornbills are easily spotted here. Kayaks can be rented and boat trips arranged.

Flower Power ITALIAN $$
(☏095 882 5573; www.flowerpowervillage.com; mains 150-300B; ⊙8am-9.30pm; 🛜🅿) For an authentic Italian experience sit down for a meal at Flower Power, where animated hosts Marco and Simona offer an incredible array of dishes, including homemade gnocchi, ravioli and pizza, as well as dishes from Thailand and Myanmar The spaghetti with clams is terrific. Don't miss the authentic Italian desserts and coffee.

🛏 Ao Mea Mai

Sabai Sabai BUNGALOW $
(☏063 142 4507; www.sabai-bungalows.com; Ao Mea Mai; bungalows 400-1000B; 🛜) Five minutes' walk south of the east-coast pier, this long-standing and social travellers' spot has clean, fan-cooled, budget-friendly bungalows. Simple doubles come with sea views, sunken bathrooms and a bit of style. Best is the two-floor, loft-style room with balcony. There's a chilled-out bar, plus hammocks and movie nights. The cheapest bungalows share bathrooms.

Fan's Homemade MULTICUISINE $
(meals 120-200B; ⊙7.30am-5.30pm; 🛜) Owner Fan and her daughters prepare delicious sandwiches, iced coffees, salads, and light meals at this colourful restaurant on the main street in Ko Phayam's village. The incredible fruit shakes must be tried at least once before leaving the island.

ℹ Information

The village has one **ATM**. Some resorts will give cash against your credit card for a 3% fee.
All For Villages (☏061 192 1322; www.allfor villages.org; ⊙hours vary) Provides heath, sanitation and education services to Moken village in Ko Phayam. Stop here for information on visiting the village.

ℹ Getting There & Away

Two daily ferries at 9.30am and 2pm travel from Ranong's **Tha Ko Phayam**, 6km southwest of town, to Ko Phayam (200B, two hours), returning at 8.30am and 3pm. During the November–April high season, speedboats (350B, 35 minutes) make the run almost hourly from 7.30am to 5.30pm, returning to the mainland between 8am and 4.30pm.

High-season speedboats go from Ko Phayam to Ko Chang (350B, 20 minutes) en route to Ranong at 8.30am, 9am, noon, 12.30pm, 3pm and 3.30pm, though they aren't completely reliable.

ℹ Getting Around

Motorcycle taxis from the pier to Ao Khao Kwai/Ao Yai cost 50/70B. Walking distances are long; it's about 45 minutes from the pier to Ao Khao Kwai, the nearest bay. You can rent motorbikes (around 250B) in the village (the best option) or from larger resorts; you'll need one to explore properly.

PHANG-NGA PROVINCE

Jungle-shrouded mountains carved up by thick rivers leading to aqua bays sprinkled with sheer limestone karsts and, below, some of Thailand's finest underwater treasures – this is Phang-Nga (จังหวัดพังงา).

This is national park territory, with four of Thailand's finest conservation areas in fairly close proximity here. Divers can head for the Similan (p614) and Surin Islands (p606), where some of Thailand's most legendary dive sites await (good for snorkellers too), while on terra firma the Khao Sok National Park (p608) is one of the oldest rainforests in the world and home to many rare species, as well as caves and waterfalls. But if you just want to laze on the sand, there are the beaches around Khao Lak (p610) and some still-visited nearby islands.

Phang-Nga is very seasonal. From mid-October to mid-April, visitors flood in for the clear waters, snow-white beaches and colourful reefs. But far fewer arrive during the May-to-October monsoon, leaving you plenty of space.

Khuraburi

🎵 076 / POP 3480

Blink and you'll miss it, but if you keep your eyes wide open, you'll enjoy this soulful, dusty, roadside gateway to the Surin Islands and some of southern Thailand's best community-based tourism opportunities. Khuraburi is a tiny market town spread out along both sides of Hwy 4, relied on by hundreds of squid fisherfolk.

Until the Thai government started cracking down on people smuggling, the surrounding area had an unsavoury reputation as being a key entry point for people being trafficked or smuggled into Thailand from Myanmar.

🏃 Activities & Tours

For tourist information, contact **Tom & Am Tour** (📞 086 272 0588; 298/3 Mu 1, Th Phetkasem; ⏱ 24hr), opposite the bus-station road.

Andaman Discoveries   TOUR
(📞 087 917 7165; www.andamandiscoveries. com; 120/2 Mu 1, Th Phetkasem; 3-day trip per person 6000B; ⏱ 8.30am-5.30pm Mon-Fri) Award-winning, community-based one-day and multiday tours featuring cycling and cultural and handicraft activities, Surin Islands snorkelling trips with *chow lair* (sea gypsies, also spelt *chao leh*), village homestays and Khao Sok National Park ecotours. It also manages community projects that take volunteers, and rents out bicycles for 150B per day. The office is down a small road at the southern end of town.

🛏 Sleeping & Eating

There are only a couple of simple guesthouses in Khuraburi, both close to the bus station on the main road through town.

There's a good **morning market** (Th Phetkasem; mains 20-40B; ⏱ 6-10am) at the northern end of town, and a small **night market** (Th Phetkasem; mains from 30B; ⏱ 3-7.30pm) on the southern outskirts, as well as a few hole-in-the-wall restaurants along the main road (most are shut by 9pm).

Boon Piya Resort   GUESTHOUSE $$
(📞 081 752 5457; 175/1 Th Phetkasem; bungalows 650B; ❄🛜) In a garden compound just

off the main road at Khuraburi's northern end, these spacious, sparkling-clean, modern concrete bungalows with tiled floors, hot-water bathrooms and little balconies are a pleasant surprise. The helpful owner books transport to/from the Surin Islands and Ko Phra Thong.

❶ Getting There & Away

Most buses running between Ranong (110B, two hours) and Phuket (165B, four hours) stop in Khuraburi. Take a Phuket-bound bus to Takua Pa (75B, 1¼ hours), 55km south, to transfer to further destinations including Khao Sok National Park.

The pier for the Surin Islands and Ko Phra Thong is 9km northwest of town. Whoever books your boat to the islands will arrange free pier transfer.

Surin Islands Marine National Park

The five gorgeous isles of the **Surin Islands Marine National Park** (อุทยานแห่งชาติหมู่เกาะสุรินทร์; 📞 076 491378; www.dnp.go.th; adult/child 500/300B; ⏱ mid-Oct–mid-May) sit 60km offshore, 5km from the Thailand–Myanmar marine border. Healthy rainforest, spectacular white-sand beaches in sparkling, sheltered bays, and rocky headlands that jut into the ocean characterise these granite-outcrop islands. Superbly clear water in never-ending shades of jade and turquoise makes for easy marine-life spotting, with underwater visibility of up to 30m outside the monsoon. These shielded waters attract *chow lair* (sea gypsies, also spelt *chao leh*), an ethnic group of Malay origin who live on Ko Surin Tai during the May-to-November monsoon. Here they're known as Moken, from the local word *oken* ('salt water').

Ko Surin Tai (south) and Ko Surin Neua (north) are the two largest islands. Park headquarters, an information office and all visitor facilities are at Ao Chong Khad on southwest Ko Surin Neua.

Khuraburi is the park's jumping-off point.

◎ Sights

Ban Moken   VILLAGE
(Ao Bon, Ko Surin Tai) Ban Moken on east Ko Surin Tai welcomes visitors. After the 2004 Boxing Day tsunami, the Moken (from the sea gypsy ethnic group) resettled in this sheltered bay, where a major ancestral worship ceremony, **Loi Reua**, takes place each

April. The colourfully carved bamboo poles dotted around embody Moken ancestors. This population experienced no casualties during the tsunami, which wiped out the village itself, because they understood nature's signs and evacuated to the hilltop.

The Surin Islands Marine National Park runs two-hour trips from Ko Surin Neua to Ban Moken (150B per person, minimum five people). You'll stroll through the stilted village, where you can ask permission/ guidance for hiking the 800m Chok Madah trail over the jungle-clad hills to an empty beach. Handicrafts for sale help support the local economy and clothing donations are accepted. Please refrain from bringing along alcohol and sweets; alcoholism is a growing problem among Moken.

🏃 Activities

Around park headquarters, you can explore the forest fringes and spot crab-eating macaques and some of the 57 resident bird species, including the beautiful Nicobar pigeon, endemic to the Andaman islands, and the elusive beach thick-knee. Along the coast you're likely to see Brahminy kites and reef herons. Twelve species of bat live here, most noticeably the tree-dwelling fruit bat (flying fox).

Diving & Snorkelling

The park's dive sites include Ko Surin Tai, Ko Torinla (south) and HQ Channel between the two main islands. Richelieu Rock, a seamount 14km southeast, is also technically in the park and happens to be one of the Andaman's premier dive sites (if not the best). Manta rays pay visits and whale sharks are sometimes spotted here during March and April.

There's no dive facility inside the park, so dive trips (four-day liveaboards from 20,000B) must be booked through centres in Khao Lak, Phuket and Ranong. Transfers are usually included. There's a 200B park diving fee per day, plus the national park fee (adult/child 500/300B), which is valid for five days.

Though recent bleaching of hard corals means snorkelling isn't quite as fantastic as it once was, you'll still see plenty of colourful fish and soft corals. The most vibrant soft corals we saw were at Ao Mai Yai, off Ko Surin Neua. There's good snorkelling at Ao Tao (Ko Surin Tai) and Ao Pak Kaad (Ko Surin Tai), where you might spot turtles, off east and south Ko Surin Tai, respectively.

More fish swim off tiny Ko Pajumba, but the coral isn't great. Ao Suthep (Ko Surin Tai), off northern Ko Surin Tai, has hundreds of colourful fish.

The nearest decompression chamber is in Phuket. In the case of an accident, dive operators will contact the chamber's Khao Lak–based SSS Ambulance (p613), which meets boats and rushes injured divers south to Phuket International Hospital.

Half-day snorkelling trips (150B per person, snorkel hire 160B) leave the island headquarters at 9am and 2pm. You'll be mostly in the company of Thais, who generally splash around in life jackets. For more serene snorkelling, charter a long-tail from the national park (3000B per day) or, better yet, directly from the Moken in Ban Moken.

Tour operators in Khuraburi and Khao Lak organise snorkelling day trips to the park (adult/child 3700/2500B).

Greenview Tour   OUTDOORS
(📞081 895 6186; www.toursurinislands.com; 140/89 Mu 3, Khuraburi; ⊙7.30am-9pm) Impressive in safety, service and value, Greenview runs excellent Surin Islands snorkelling day trips (adult/child 3500/2100B) with knowledgeable guides. Rates include transfers, equipment, snacks and a delicious lunch. It also organises multinight stays in the Surins.

🛏 Sleeping & Eating

Ko Surin Neua is the only island it is possible to stay on. The Surin Islands Marine National Park bungalows (📞076 472145; www.dnp.go.th; Ko Surin Neua; campsites per person 80B, with tent hire 300B, r 2000-3000B; ⊙mid-Oct–mid-May; ❄) are good enough, if overpriced for what you get, although it can feel seriously crowded when full (around 300 people). The clientele is mostly Thai, giving the place a lively holiday-camp vibe. You can also camp here (tents can be hired). Book well in advance.

The two park restaurants, where the accommodation is, serve reasonable Thai food.

ℹ Information

Surin Islands Marine National Park Office (Ko Surin Neua; ⊙7.30am-8.30pm mid-Oct– mid-May) Offers information on the islands, and you can book accommodation here.

ℹ Getting There & Away

If you're not visiting on an organised tour, tour-operator speedboats (return 1800B, 1¼ hours one way) leave around 9am, returning between 1pm and 4pm, and honour open tickets. Return whenever you please, but confirm your ticket with the park office in Ko Surin Neua the night before.

Khao Sok National Park

If you've had enough of beach-bumming, venture inland to the wondrous 738-sq-km **Khao Sok National Park** (อุทยานแห่งชาติเขา สก; [☎] 077 395154; www.khaosok.com; Khao Sok; adult/child 300/150B; ⊙ 6am-6pm). Many believe this lowland jungle (Thailand's rainiest spot) dates back 160 million years, making it one of the world's oldest rainforests, and it's interspersed by hidden waterfalls and caves.

Khao Sok's vast terrain makes it one of the last viable habitats for large mammals. During rainy months you may spot bears, boars, gaurs, tapirs, gibbons, deer, marbled cats, wild elephants and perhaps even a tiger. And you'll find more than 300 bird species, 38 bat varieties and one of the world's largest (and smelliest) flowers, the increasingly rare *Rafflesia kerrii*, which, in Thailand, grows only in Khao Sok.

Animal-spotting aside, the best time to visit is the December–April dry season. During the June–October monsoon, trails get slippery and leeches come out in force. The upside is that the waterfalls are in full flow.

◉ Sights & Activities

Kayaking (800B) and tubing (500B; rainy season) are popular activities. We strongly recommend avoiding elephant tours due to animal-welfare concerns.

Chiaw Lan Lake LAKE
(เขื่อนเชี่ยวหลาน; day/overnight trip 1500/2500B) This stunning 165-sq-km lake sits 65km east (an hour's drive) of Khao Sok National Park Headquarters. It was created in 1982 by an enormous shale-clay dam called Ratchaprapha (Kheuan Ratchaprapha or Chiaw Lan). Limestone outcrops protruding from the lake reach up to 960m, over three times higher than Phang-Nga's formations. Most lake visits involve a day or overnight tour (including transfers, boats and guides).

You can charter a boat (2000B per day) from local fisherfolk at the dam's entrance to explore the coves, canals, caves and cul-de-sacs along the lakeshore.

Two caves can be accessed by foot from the southwestern shore. **Tham Nam Thalu**

[FREE] contains striking limestone formations and subterranean streams. Visiting during the rainy season isn't recommended; there have been fatalities. **Tham Si Ru** (Chiaw Lan Lake) [FREE] features four converging passageways used as a hideout by communist insurgents between 1975 and 1982.

Hiking

Khao Sok hiking is excellent. Most guesthouses and agencies arrange hiking tours (full day 1200B to 2000B); just ensure you find a certified guide (they wear official badges). The park headquarters can also line you up with a reliable guide (1200B per day).

The national park headquarters (p609) hands out basic hiking maps. You can hike independently from the headquarters to the waterfall at **Wing Hin** (2.8km). Hikes to the waterfalls at **Bang Hua Rad** (3km), the 11-tiered waterfall at **Sip-Et Chan** (4km), **Than Sawan** (6km), the most impressive and least-visited waterfall, and **Than Kloy** (7km), require a guide.

🛏 Sleeping & Eating

Khao Sok Jungle Hostel HOSTEL $
([☎] 096 142 6539; www.khaosokcentertour.net; dm 250B) This small hostel with just six dorm beds is impeccably run and well maintained. Because it's so small the owner Sunny gives every guest special attention, from pickups and tours to onward travel advice.

Khao Sok Hostel 1 HOSTEL $
([☎] 089 971 8794; nidmorningmist@gmail.com; 53/7 Mu 6, Khao Sok; dm 200B; ❈ 🛜 ⓧ) The dorms at this hostel have beds separated by curtains, offering a little extra privacy. Rooms have air-con, there's a patio deck and access to an off-site swimming pool. A free breakfast spread is included. There are comfortable beds, hot water and small lockers, but no common area.

Jungle Huts BUNGALOW $
([☎] 096 654 4163; www.khaosokjunglehut.com; 242 Mu 6, Khao Sok; r fan/air-con 400/1200B; ❈ 🛜) This popular hang-out contains a collection of decent, individually styled bungalows, all with bathrooms and porches. Choose from plain, stilted bamboo huts, bigger wooden editions, pink-washed concrete bungalows, or rooms along vertiginous walkways.

Art's Riverview Jungle Lodge GUESTHOUSE $$
([☎] 090 167 6818; www.artsriverviewlodge.com; 54/3 Mu 6, Khao Sok; r 1200-2400B; 🛜) In a

monkey-filled jungle bordering a rushing river with a limestone-cliff-framed swimming hole, Art's enjoys Khao Sok's prettiest setting. The stilted brick, shingled and all-wood bungalows are spacious and comfy; they come with balconies and many offer river views. There's a host of family-friendly activities. From the highway junction, travel 1.5km along the main village road, look for the signpost to the hotel and travel another 700m to the lodge.

Nonguests can visit the swimming hole here, which is also popular with locals and monkeys. The breakfast buffet is filling and well made.

★**Elephant Hills**   RESORT $$$
(☑076 381703; www.elephanthills.com; 170 Mu 7, Tambon Klong Sok; 3 days all-inclusive from 20,300B; 🛜🆒) 🍃 Whether you're a family, a honeymooning backpacker couple or a solo traveller, this resort makes everyone smile. Above Mae Nam Sok, at the foot of stunning limestone mountains draped in misty jungle, Khao Sok's only top-end tented camp offers rootsy Serengeti-style luxury. It's real glamping: the luxury tents have wood furnishings, full, big bathrooms, skylights and hammocks on porches.

All-inclusive prices cover meals, guided hikes and canoe trips downriver for a night at its elephant camp, where 12 lovely elephants (rescued from other camps where they were forced to carry tourists around) are treated kindly. You get to feed, bathe and spend quality time with them. It's a special experience. Another option is a night at its floating Rainforest Camp (Chiaw Lan Lake; 3 days all-inclusive from 20,323B) 🍃. Reservations only.

★**Pawn's Restaurant**   THAI $$
(Khao Sok; mains 110-250B; ☉9am-10pm; 🍴) A friendly all-female team runs this humble but deservedly popular open-sided place. It's a great spot for deliciously spiced curries, from searing red-pumpkin-and-veg to beautifully creamy tofu and chicken massaman, as well as huge hearty breakfasts. It's 500m southwest of the national-park headquarters.

Chao Italian Restaurant   ITALIAN $$
(☑087 264 2106; Khao Sok; mains 100-320B; ☉noon-10pm; 🛜) This is the go-to spot for fine, wood-fired pizzas, cooked by a veteran of Italian restaurants on Phuket, as well as pasta, salads and the usual Thai curries,

all served by smiley staff underneath a high thatched roof. It's a couple of minutes' walk south of the Khao Sok National Park headquarters.

ⓘ Information

There are several ATMs along the road leading to the national park headquarters.

Khao Sok National Park Headquarters
(☑077 395154; www.khaosok.com; ☉6am-6pm) Has helpful maps and information. It's about 1.8km northeast off Rte 401 (exit near the Km 109 marker).

ⓘ Getting There & Away

From Surat catch a bus going towards Takua Pa; from the Andaman Coast, take a Surat Thani–bound bus. Buses stop on Rte 401, 1.8km southwest of the visitors centre. If touts don't meet you, you'll have to walk to your chosen guesthouse (50m to 2km). Most minivans will drop you at your accommodation.

There is a daily bus to Bangkok (1000B, 11 hours) at 6pm.

Daily minivan departures include the following:

TO	FARE (B)	TIME (HR)	FREQUENCY
Khao Lak	200	1¼	hourly 8.30am-6.30pm
Ko Lanta	800	5	8.30am
Ko Tao	1000	8	6.30am & 11am
Krabi	350	3	8.30am
Phang-Nga	250	2	8.30am
Surat Thani	200	1	hourly 6.30am-4pm

Ko Phra Thong & Ko Ra

According to legend, pirates buried a golden Buddha beneath the sands at Ko Phra Thong (Golden Buddha Island) many centuries ago. The statue was never found, but the island's modern-day treasures are its endless sandy beaches, mangroves, vast birdlife and rare orchids.

Home to around 300 people, this long, slender, wooded island is as quiet as a night on the open ocean. Fishing (of squid, prawns and jellyfish) remains its main industry; the local delicacy is pungent *gà·bì* (fermented prawn paste). On the southern part of the west coast lies 10km of virgin golden-sand beach kissed by blue sea.

Immediately north is barely inhabited Ko Ra, encircled by golden beaches and mangroves. This small isle is a mountainous jungle slab with impressive wildlife, including over 100 bird species, leopard cats, flying lemurs, wild pigs, monitor lizards, scaly anteaters and slow lorises.

Sleeping & Eating

Mr Chuoi's
BUNGALOW $

(☑087 898 4636, 084 855 9886; www.mrchuoi barandhut.com; Ko Phra Thong; bungalows 500-750B; ☜) Located on the island's northwest coast, Mr Chuoi's has simple, attractive and artsy wood-and-bamboo bungalows with evening electricity. You'll also find a tame deer, a fun bar and a decent restaurant, enlivened by Mr Chuoi himself. Call ahead and he'll arrange transport to Ko Phra Thong.

Horizon
BUNGALOW $$

(☑081 894 7195; www.horizonecoresort.com; Ko Phra Thong; bungalows 1300-1900B) ⬤ This northwest-beach ecolodge has seven roomy wood-and-bamboo bungalows made out of natural local products (from renewable sources wherever possible). They only use fans, and sleep two or four people. Horizon organises hiking tours to neighbouring Ko Ra (1600B, minimum three people) and has the island's only dive school, Blue Guru (☑096 284 8740; www.blue-guru.org; Ko Phra Thong; 2 dives 4500-6500B; ◷ Oct-May), ideally positioned for underwater explorations of the nearby Surin Islands.

Golden Buddha Beach Resort
BUNGALOW $$$

(☑0818922208, 0818952242; www.goldenbuddha resort.com; Ko Phra Thong; bungalows 3500-8500B; ◷ Oct-May; ☜) The area's poshest resort attracts yogis, couples and families keen for a secluded getaway. Accommodation is in uniquely designed, naturalistic-chic, privately-owned wooden houses and big family-sized houses.

Rooms have open-air bathrooms, woodcarved interiors and glimpses of the fabulous 10km beach through surrounding forest and gardens. Everyone congregates at the mosaic-floored clubhouse's restaurant-bar (Ko Phra Thong; mains 220-400B; ◷7.30am-9.30pm; ☑).

ⓘ Getting There & Away

You could theoretically charter a long-tail from the Khuraburi pier to Ko Phra Thong (return 1500B, 90 minutes), but boat operators can be hard to find. For the same price, your accommodation on Ko Phra Thong, or tour operators and guesthouses in Khuraburi, will arrange your transport.

Khao Lak & Around

When people refer to Khao Lak, they're usually talking about a series of beaches hugging Phang-Nga's west coastline 70km north of Phuket. With easy day trips to the Similan and Surin Islands, Khao Sok and Khao Lak/ Lam Ru National Parks, or even Phuket, the area is a base for exploring the northern Andaman.

Southernmost Hat Khao Lak has a handful of resorts and restaurants. From here the highway winds through hills and past the Khao Lak/Lam Ru National Park to the town centre. The beach here, Hat Nang Thong, is walking distance to low-rise hotels, restaurants, bars, shops and tour and dive operators along Hwy 4.

Hat Bang Niang, 2.5km north, is a quieter version of sandy bliss with skinnier beaches.

Hat Pakarang and Hat Bang Sak, 13km north of Hat Khao Lak, make up a sleepy, unbroken sandy stretch surrounded by thick mangroves and rubber-tree plantations. You'll feel like you've really escaped it all..

◉ Sights

Khao Lak/Lam Ru National Park
NATIONAL PARK

(อุทยานแห่งชาติเขาหลัก-ลำรู่; ☑076 485243; www. dnp.go.th; adult/child 200/100B; ◷8am-4.30pm) Immediately south of Hat Khao Lak, this vast 125-sq-km park is a collage of sea cliffs, 1000m-high hills, beaches, estuaries, waterfalls, forested valleys and mangroves. Wildlife includes hornbills, drongos, tapirs, serows, monkeys, Bengal monitor lizards and Asiatic black bears.

The park office and visitors centre, 3km south of Khao Lak proper, off Hwy 4, has little printed information, but there's a scenic open-air restaurant (off Hwy 4, Khao Lak; mains 130-250B; ◷8.30am-7pm) perched on a shady slope overlooking the sea. From here, there's a fairly easy 3km (one-hour) round-trip nature trail south along the cape to often-deserted Hat Lek.

Khao Lak

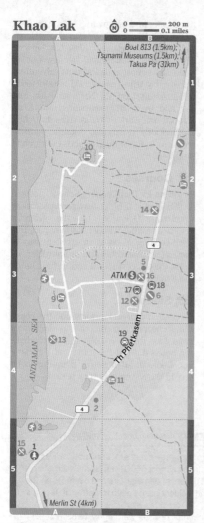

Boat 813 (1.5km);
Tsunami Museums (1.5km);
Takua Pa (31km)

ANDAMAN SEA

Th Phetkasem

Merlin St (4km)

monly considered one of the world's top 10 diving realms. While both the Similan and Surin Islands have experienced vast coral bleaching in recent years, Richelieu Rock (p607), part of the Surin Islands Marine National Park, is still the crème de la crème of the region's dive sites, frequented by whale sharks from March to April. Ko Bon (p614) and Ko Tachai (p614) are rewarding Similan sites due to the traffic of giant manta rays.

Most dive shops welcome snorkellers on selected day dives and liveaboards, and tour operators offer day trips from 3700B. Open Water certification costs between 10,500B and 16,650B, depending on where you dive. Beginners can join one-day Similans Discover Scuba trips for around 6000B. Rates exclude the 700B national park diving fee.

The Similan and Surin dive season runs from mid-October to mid-May, when the national parks are open. Trips in April and May are weather dependent.

★ **Fantastic**   SNORKELLING
(☏076   485998;   www.fantasticsimilan.com;
adult/child 3200/2200B;   ☉mid-Oct–mid-May)

🏃 Activities & Tours

Diving and snorkelling day excursions to the Similan and Surin Islands are immensely popular but, if you can, go for a liveaboard. The islands are around 70km from the mainland (1½ hours by speedboat), so liveaboards allow you a more relaxing trip sans masses of day trippers. Dive shops offer liveaboard package trips from around 19,000B for three days and 35,000B for six days, and day trips for 5000B to 6000B.

Day trips normally involve two dives. On the multiday trips, you'll sink below the sea's surface up to four times daily in what's com-

Fantastic is an over-the-top frolic of a Similans snorkelling tour featuring players from the local cross-dressing cabaret as guides. It's a trip duplicated nowhere else on earth and you get to the prime snorkel sites. Prices include hotel pick-ups from Phuket or Khao Lak. Bookings are essential, online or by phone.

Sea Dragon Dive Center   DIVING
(☑ 076 485420; www.seadragondivecenter.com; 5/51 Mu 7, Khao Lak; 2 dives 6000B; ⊚9am-9pm) Khao Lak's oldest dive centre, superefficient Sea Dragon maintains high standards, running snorkelling day trips (3500B), wreck dives (2600B), Open Water Diver certification (10,500B to 15,000B) and an array of Similan and Surin Islands liveaboards (three-day trips from 10,500B). Look for the small swimming pool outside its office.

Sea Bees   DIVING
(☑ 076 485174; www.sea-bees.com; Th Phetkasem, Khao Lak; 2 dives 2900-4900B; ⊚11am-7pm) This is a well-organised German-run dive operation that offers two-dive Similan day trips, one-day tasters (8500B), Open Water courses (16,650B) and advanced diver courses, plus Similan liveaboards (two-day trips from 17,500B). Snorkellers can join day trips for 2900B.

Khao Lak Land Discovery   ADVENTURE
(☑ 076 485411; www.khaolaklanddiscovery.com; 21/5 Mu 7, Th Phetkasem, Khao Lak; ⊚6am-9.30pm) This multilingual agency, one of Khao Lak's most reliable, runs adventure-activity day trips (adult/child 3000/2450B) to Khao Lak/Lam Ru National Park, and day and overnight excursions into Khao Sok National Park (two-day trip adult/child 7500/6800B). It can also organise snorkelling trips to the Similan Islands (adult/child 3700/2450B).

🍴 Courses

Pa-kin-na-ka Thai Cooking School   COOKING
(☑ 088 760 0767; www.pakinnakacooking school.com) Operated by the friendly, English-speaking Wandee Rathanapan, this small cooking school is an excellent way to learn a few Thai dishes and sample delicious foods. Classes cost 1500B and include lunch and a market tour.

🛏 Sleeping

Three- and four-star resorts line the coast, while cheaper accommodation dominates Khao Lak Town's congested centre. High-end hotels dot Hat Pakarang and Hat Bang Sak. Book ahead if you're planning to be here in the November–April period.

LOCAL KNOWLEDGE

TSUNAMI EARLY WARNING SYSTEM

On 26 December 2004 an earthquake off the Sumatran coast sent enormous waves crashing into Thailand's Andaman Coast, claiming almost 5400 lives (some estimates have it much higher) and causing millions of dollars of damage. Life and business on the islands and coast have bounced back, but the incident hasn't been forgotten. In fact, it's inspired action to prevent a repeat disaster.

In 2005 Thailand officially inaugurated a national disaster warning system, created in response to the country's lack of preparedness for the waves. The Bangkok-based centre anticipates that a tsunami warning can be issued within 15 minutes of the event being detected by existing international systems.

The public will be warned via the nationwide radio network, dozens of TV channels and SMS messages. For non-Thai speakers, there are warning towers along high-risk beachfront areas that will broadcast announcements in various languages, accompanied by flashing lights. There are also now many signs on the islands and along the coast pointing to places to evacuate to inland.

The wave-shaped **Tsunami Memorial Park** (ศูนย์อนุสรณ์สึนามิบ้านน้ำเค็ม; Ban Nam Khem; ⊚24hr) FREE in Ban Nam Khem, a squid-fishing village 26km north of Hat Khao Lak that was nearly wiped out, was built to memorialise those who lost their lives. **Boat 813** (Bang Niang) lies 1km inland from Hat Bang Niang where it was deposited by the wave. **Tsunami museums** (พิพิธภัณฑ์สึนามิ; Hwy 4, Bang Niang; entry to each 100-300B; ⊚9am-9pm) are located near the boat. The moving memorials augment what were, for years, unofficial pilgrimage sites for those who came to pay their respects.

Fasai House
GUESTHOUSE $

(📞076 485867; www.fasaihouse.com; 5/54 Mu 7, Khao Lak; r 950B; ❄@✉) One of Khao Lak's best budget choices, Fasai wins us over with its delightful staff and simple but immaculate, motel-style air-con rooms set in a warm yellow-washed block framing a little pool. It makes a good divers' crash pad. Look for the sign off Hwy 4 towards the northern end of Khao Lak.

Walker's Inn
GUESTHOUSE $

(📞084 840 2689; www.walkersinn.com; 26/61 Mu 7, Th Phetkasem, Khao Lak; dm/r 250/600B; ❄🔊) A long-running backpacker fave, Walker's is looking its age these days. Rooms are old-fashioned and plain, if big, while the dorm is fan-only. But the price is right. The downstairs pub serves hearty breakfasts and Thai and Western classics. It rents motorbikes (200B per day).

Les Fleurs House
GUESTHOUSE $$

(📞076 485166; www.lesfleurskhaolak.com; 5/53 Mu 7, Khao Lak; r 800-1200B; ❄🔊) The bright rooms at this small hotel are spotless and decorated in pastel colours. There's a small garden, and potted plants give it a homey feel. Rooms include air-con, TV and fridge. The friendly, English-speaking host Wandee also offers cooking classes that can last half a day or longer. It's located up a quiet lane, about 100m from Hwy 4.

Nangthong Bay Resort
RESORT $$

(📞076 485088; www.nangthong.com; 13/5 Mu 7, Hat Nang Thong; r 1800-3000B; ❄@🔊✉) The large turquoise pool at this unpretentious, reasonably priced beach resort dominates lush grounds that ramble to the sand. Freestanding big bungalows follow a minimalist black-and-white chic design, with comfy beds, balconies and open-air showers. Cheaper rooms are set back from the beach. Overall it's a worthwhile option for the beachfront location. On the downside, breakfast is disappointing.

The Sands
RESORT $$$

(www.thesandskhaolak.com; Khao Lak; r 6100-12,000B; ❄🔊✉) This large resort has a terrific water park, multiple pools and playgrounds that will thrill the kiddos. Prices include a buffet breakfast. Lots of on-site activities are available, including *moo·ay tai* (Thai boxing) classes. While it's kid-friendly, there's a pool and garden area that is adult-only. The main road in Khao Lak is within walking distance.

✖ Eating

Khao Lak Town and the neighbouring beaches aren't culinary hotspots, but tourists congregate at a few local haunts to rehash the day's diving. Early-morning divers will struggle to find breakfast before 8.30am, so stock up on snacks the night before at the **Nangthong Supermarket** (🕐8.30am-10pm).

Go Pong
THAI $

(Th Phetkasem, Khao Lak; mains 50-140B; 🕐10am-11pm) Get a real taste of local flavours at this terrific streetside diner. Here they stir-fry noodles and sensational spicy rice dishes and simmer aromatic noodle soups that attract a loyal lunch following. Dishes are packed full of flavour.

835 Street Food
STREET FOOD $

(Th Phetkasem, Khao Lak; dishes from 30B; 🕐noon-10pm) Stir-frys, noodle dishes, Thai soups, crêpes and other snacks can be ordered at this collection of street vendors tucked behind a narrow courtyard.

Coconuts
MULTICUISINE $$

(mains 250-360B; 🕐noon-8.30pm) This lovely beachside restaurant has a nice selection of Western and Thai options, including a tempting grilled seafood platter for two, delicious sweet-and-sour snapper, and some pasta dishes. There's a palm shelter where you can get a massage, as well as a perfect strip of sand for walking off your meal. Reclining beach beds are available for the ultimate comfort.

Merlin Street
SEAFOOD $$

(mains 200-400B; 🕐noon-10pm) Several seafood restaurants are located along this strip of road near the Khao Lak Merlin Hotel. As the sun sets, smoke starts to rise from the barbecues and it's up to you to pick which one looks best. Popular grilled items include barracuda, squid, mussels and prawns. European, Thai and Indian dishes also abound.

ℹ Information

ATMs are spread along the coast, along with banks and money changers. There is an **ATM** in the centre of Khao Lak Town.

SSS Ambulance (📞076 209347, emergency 081 081 9000; 🕐24hr) For diving-related emergencies, the SSS Ambulance rushes injured persons down to Phuket International Hospital (p624), and can also be used for car or motorcycle accidents.

ⓘ Getting There & Around

Any bus between Takua Pa (70B, 45 minutes) and Phuket (150B, two hours) will stop at Hat Khao Lak if you ask. Both **northbound** and **southbound** buses stop and pick up on Hwy 4.

Minivans run daily to Ko Samui (850B, eight hours) at 9am. There are also hourly minivans to Krabi (350B, 3½ hours) from 8am to 4pm. They'll pick you up at your accommodation.

Khao Lak Land Discovery (p612) runs shared minibuses to Phuket International Airport (600B, 1¼ hours). Alternatively, you can take a taxi with **Cheaper Than Hotel** (☑ 086 276 6479, 085 786 1378; cheaperkhaolak1@gmail.com; Hwy 4) to Phuket's airport (1000B) and points south. Otherwise, taxis cost 1200B from Khao Lak to the airport. Or tell a Phuket-bound bus driver to drop you at 'the airport'; you'll be let off at an intersection from which motorcycle taxis usually take you to the airport (10 minutes, 100B).

Numerous travel agencies and guesthouses rent motorbikes by the day (200B to 250B).

Similan Islands Marine National Park

Known to divers everywhere, the beautiful 70-sq-km Similan Islands Marine National Park (อุทยานแห่งชาติหมู่เกาะสิมิลัน; ☑ 076 453272; www.similan-islands.com; adult/child 500/300B; ☺ mid-Oct–mid-May) lies 70km offshore from Phang-Nga Province. Its smooth granite islands are as impressive above the bright-aqua water as below, topped with rainforest, edged with blindingly white beaches and fringed by coral reefs. Coral bleaching has killed off many hard corals, but soft corals are intact and the fauna and fish are still there. However, the Similans are now on the tourist trail and many beaches and snorkel sites get packed with day trippers. The islands close in monsoon season to allow natural rejuvenation of the environment.

You can stay on Ko Miang (Island 4) and Ko Similan. The park visitors centre and most facilities are on Ko Miang. The islands have names, but are more commonly known by their numbers. Hat Khao Lak is the park's jumping-off point. The pier and mainland park headquarters are at Thap Lamu, 12km south (Hwy 4, then Rte 4147).

🏃 Activities

Diving & Snorkelling

The Similans offer diving for all levels, at depths from 2m to 30m. There are rock reefs at Ko Hin Pousar (เกาะหินพูซ่า, Island 7) and dive-throughs at Hin Pousar (หินพูซ่า, Elephant Head Rock), with marine life ranging from tiny plume worms and soft corals to schooling fish, manta rays and rare whale sharks. Ko Bon (เกาะบอน) and Ko Tachai (เกาะตาชัย) are two of the better diving and snorkelling areas. There are dive sites at each of the six islands north of Ko Miang. The park's southern section (Islands 1, 2 and 3) is an off-limits turtle-nesting ground.

No facilities for divers exist in the national park, so you'll be taking a dive tour. Dive schools in Hat Khao Lak book various trips – day trips (two dives 5000B) and liveaboards (three-/six-day trips from around 19,000/35,000B) – as do Phuket dive centres (two-dive day trips from 5600B, three-day liveaboards from 18,900B).

Agencies in Khao Lak offer snorkelling-only day trips that visit three or four sites from around 2900B.

Wildlife Watching & Hiking

The forest around Ko Miang's park visitors centre has some walking trails and great wildlife. The fabulous Nicobar pigeon, with its wild mane of grey-green feathers, is common here and is one of the park's 39 bird species. Hairy-legged land crabs and fruit bats (flying foxes) are relatively easy to spot in the forest, as are flying squirrels.

A small beach track, with information panels, leads 400m east from the visitors centre to a tiny snorkelling bay. Detouring from the track, the Viewpoint Trail (Ko Miang/Island 4), reached after about 500m (30 minutes) of steep scrambling, has panoramic vistas from the top. A 500m (20-minute) walk west from the visitors centre leads through forest to a smooth west-facing granite platform, Sunset Point (แหลมซันเซ็ท; Ko Miang/Island 4).

On Ko Similan, there's a 2.5km forest hike to a viewpoint (จุดชมวิวเกาะสิมิลัน; Ko Similan/Island 8), and a shorter, steep scramble off the north-coast beach to Sail Rock (หินเรือ ใบ, Balance Rock; Ko Similan/Island 8); during the day it's clogged with visitors.

🍽 Sleeping & Eating

A restaurant (Ko Miang/Island 4; mains 120-150B, lunch buffet 230B; ☺ 7.30am-8.30pm mid-Oct–mid-May) beside the park office on Ko Miang serves simple Thai food. There's another one on Ko Similan for those staying the night. Bring snacks for the day trip.

Similar Islands Marine National Park

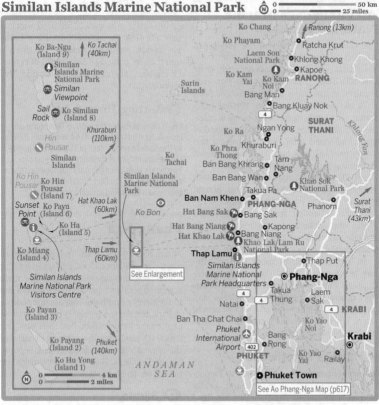

See Enlargement

See Ao Phang-Nga Map (p617)

Similan Islands Marine National Park Accommodation BUNGALOW $$
(☑ 076 453272, in Bangkok 02 562 0760; www.dnp.go.th; Ko Miang/Island 4; r fan/air-con 1000/2000B, campsites with tent hire 570B; ⏰ mid-Oct–mid-May; ❄) On Ko Miang there are 20 bungalows (the best with balconies) and tents to stay in. You are paying for the location: the bungalows are simple. During the day, many tour groups will drop by. Electricity operates from 6pm to 6am. Book ahead online, by phone or through the mainland park headquarters at Thap Lamu. If you are camping, bring repellent: the mosquitoes are ferocious.

❶ Information

Similan Islands Marine National Park Headquarters (☑ 076 453272; www.dnp.go.th; 93 Mu 5, Thap Lamu; ⏰ 8am-5pm) You can book accommodation on the Similan Islands well in advance with this office south of Khao Lak.

Similan Islands Marine National Park Visitors Centre (Ko Miang/Island 4; ⏰ 7.30am-8pm mid-Oct–mid-May) This visitors centre has maps and information about the park's islands.

❶ Getting There & Away

There's no official public transport to the Similans. Theoretically, independent travellers can book return speedboat transfers (2000B, 1½ hours each way) with a Khao Lak day-trip operator, though they discourage independent travel. Most will collect you from Hat Khao Lak, but if you book through the national park you'll have to find your own way to the office in Thap Lamu and wait for a pier transfer.

Dive centres and tour agents in Hat Khao Lak and Phuket book day/overnight tours (from 5000/8500B), dive trips (three-day liveaboards from 18,900B) and multiday trips including park transport, food and lodging, which cost little more than what you'd pay getting to and staying on the islands independently.

Ao Phang-Nga Marine National Park

The classic karst scenery of the 400-sq-km Ao Phang-Nga National Park (อุทยานแห่ง ชาติอ่าวพังงา; ☑ 076 481188; www.dnp.go.th; adult/child 300/100B; ⊙ 8am-4.30pm) was famously featured in the James Bond movie *The Man with the Golden Gun*. Huge vertical cliffs frame 42 islands, some with caves accessible only at low tide. The bay is composed of large and small tidal channels, which run north to south through Thailand's largest remaining primary mangrove forests.

Ao Phang-Nga's marine limestone environment conceals reptiles such as Bengal monitor lizards, two-banded monitors, flying lizards, banded sea snakes, shore pit vipers and Malayan pit vipers. Mammals include serows, crab-eating macaques, white-handed gibbons and dusky langurs.

In high season (November to April) the bay becomes a clogged day-tripper superhighway. But if you visit in the early morning (ideally from the Ko Yao islands) or stay out later, you might just find a slice of beach, sea or limestone karst of your own. The best way to explore is by kayak.

◉ Sights & Activities

You can charter boats to explore Ao Phang-Nga's half-submerged caves and oddly shaped islands from Tha Dan, 9km south of central Phang-Nga. Expect to pay 1500B to 2000B for a half-day tour.

Two- to three-hour tours (1000B per person) head to well-trodden Ko Khao Phing Kan (เกาะเขาพิงกัน, James Bond Island), Ko Panyi (เกาะปันหยี) and elsewhere in the park. Tha Surakul, 13km southwest of Phang-Nga in Takua Thung, has private boats for hire at similar prices to tours. From the national park headquarters, you can hire boats (1400B, maximum four passengers) for three-hour islands tours.

From Phuket Town, John Gray's Seacanoe (p626) is the top choice for Ao Phang-Nga kayakers.

⌂ Sleeping & Eating

Tour operators in Phang-Nga can arrange homestays on Ko Panyi. There's also basic accommodation close to the national park headquarters on the mainland. But most people visit on day tours from either the Ko Yao Islands, Phuket or Phang-Nga.

Ao Phang-Nga National Park Accommodation   BUNGALOW $

(☑ 076 481188, in Bangkok 02 562 0760; www.dnp.go.th; Rte 4144; bungalows 800-1000B; ❄) Simple air-con bungalows sleep two to three in quiet shady grounds 8.5km south of central Phang-Nga. There's a basic waterside Thai restaurant.

❶ Getting There & Away

From central Phang-Nga, drive 7km south on Hwy 4, turn left onto Rte 4144 and travel 2.6km to the park headquarters in Tha Dan. Opposite the headquarters is the jetty where you can hire boats to explore the park. Otherwise take a *sŏrng·tăa·ou* to Tha Dan (30B). If you booked a tour, you'll be picked up from your hotel.

Phang-Nga

☑ 076 / POP 10,800

Phang-Nga (พังงา) is an understated small town with a fabulous location, set in a valley against sublime limestone cliffs. The main reason to set down here is to organise a trip to the nearby Ao Phang-Nga Marine National Park, but the town itself is worth a visit to explore the local market, Buddhist sites and caves. It's also a terrific place to experience the annual Vegetarian Festival (late September or October). Hotels and amenities are mostly on Th Phetkasem.

◉ Sights

Thamtapan Temple   BUDDHIST SITE

(สำนักสงฆ์ถ้ำตาปาน; ⊙ daylight hours) This unusual Buddhist complex (the name means 'Heaven and Hell' temple) has cave shrines, a dragon tunnel and a collection of grotesque figures representing life in hell for sinners. Children may be taken aback by the sometimes brutal depictions that appear better suited for a haunted house. Climb a steep staircase to reach a pavilion affording awesome views of the valley. While the statues here may be shocking for Westerners, this place offers a strong reminder to Thais about the penalties for wrongdoing, and represents a unique opportunity to better understand Thai culture and philosophy.

Phung Chang Cave   CAVE

(ถ้ำพุงช้าง; entry 500B; ⊙ 8.30am-5pm) A dam at the mouth of this cave created an artificial river, which visitors can explore, first by kayak and then bamboo raft as the cave narrows. Headlamps are provided but taking photos is prohibited. The cave, which contains wonderful limestone formations, does require some wading through knee-deep water, so bring appropriate footwear. It's an adventurous tour but not suitable for small children.

☞ Tours

Sayan Tours   BOATING
(📱090 708 3211, 076 430348; www.sayantour.com; 269 Th Phetkasem; half/full day 800/1100B; ⊘7am-9pm) This long-standing Ao Phang-Nga tour company offers day trips to Ko Panyi, Ko Phing Kan and Tham Lod (covered in stalactites), and overnight stays on Ko Panyi (1950B).

⟷ Sleeping & Eating

There's a smattering of guesthouses strung along Th Phetkasem.

Several food stalls along Th Phetkasem sell delicious *kà·nŏm jeen* (thin wheat noodles) with chicken curry, *nám yah* (spicy ground-fish curry) or *nám prík* (spicy sauce). There's also a small **night market** (Th Phetkasem; mains from 30B; ⊘4-9pm).

Thaweesuk Hotel   GUESTHOUSE $
(📱076 412100; www.thaweesuk.com; 79 Th Phetkasem; r incl breakfast with fan/air-con 450/800B; ❋🛜) Thaweesuk is a friendly family-run place in a historic building with a colourful mosaic-floor lobby on north Th Phetkasem. Ground-floor cold-water fan/air-con rooms are simple, compact and clean. Hot-water air-con pads on the 1st floor are rather more stylish, with varnished-wood floors. There's also a four-bed family room. Breakfast is downstairs in the lounge-like lobby.

★ Genesis Garden   INTERNATIONAL $
(📱089 919 3326; 154 Th Phetkasem; dishes 50-150B; ⊘10am-8pm; 🛜) Hidden off the main road, this wallet-friendly cafe with English-speaking staff serves healthy and delicious meals plus one of the best smoothies we've ever had in Thailand. It offers mainly Thai food but it's suited to a Western palate. The *pàt tai* comes in a range of variations, and there's also spaghetti, soups, curries and Italian soda.

❶ Getting There & Away

The nearest airport to Phang-Nga is in Phuket, a 1½-hour drive away.

Phang-Nga's **bus station** (Th Phetkasem) is 4km south of the town centre. Motorcycle taxis charge a flat 50B to/from the station.

Ao Phang-Nga

TO	FARE (B)	TIME (HR)	FREQUENCY
Bangkok (1st class)	533-622	12	8.40am, 3pm, 4.30pm, 5.30pm, 6.30pm & 7.30pm
Bangkok (VIP)	829	12	4pm, 5pm, 7pm & 8pm
Hat Yai	275	6	8.50am, 9.50am, 10.50am, 12.50pm & 1.50pm
Krabi	100	1½	hourly 7.30am-6pm
Phuket	100	1½	hourly 5.30am-5.30pm
Ranong	170	5	10.15am
Surat Thani	150	4	9.30am, 11.30am, 1.30pm & 3.30pm
Trang	175	3½	hourly 8am-4.20pm

Minivans run to Khao Sok National Park (250B, two hours) at 8.30am, 10.30am, noon, 2pm, 3.30pm and 5.30pm. They'll drop you at your accommodation.

Buses for Takua Pa (150B, 1½ hours), where you can connect to Khao Lak, as well as Ranong and Khao Sok National Park, leave at 8am, 10am, 11am, noon, 2pm and 5.20pm.

Ko Yao Islands

With mountainous backbones, unspoilt shorelines, hugely varied birdlife and a population of friendly Muslim fisherfolk, Ko Yao Yai (Big Long Island) and Ko Yao Noi (Little Long Island) are relaxed vantage points for soaking up Ao Phang-Nga's beautiful karst scenery. The islands are part of Ao Phang-Nga National Park (p616), but can be accessed from Phuket and elsewhere easily.

Ko Yao Noi is the main population centre, despite being smaller than its neighbour, with fishing, coconut farming and tourism sustaining its small, year-round population. It's not a classic beach destination: bays on the east coast, where most resorts are, recede to mudflats at low tides. Nevertheless, Hat Pasai (Ko Yao Noi), on the southeast coast, and Hat Paradise (Ko Yao Noi), on the northeast coast, are both gorgeous.

Ko Yao Yai is twice the size of its sibling and wilder. The most accessible beaches here are Hat Lo Pared (Ko Yao Yai), on the southwest coast, and powder-white Hat Laem Haad on the northeast coast.

◉ Sights & Activities

One-day three-island snorkelling tours (2000B) of Ao Phang-Nga are easily arranged through guesthouses or at the piers.

Amazing Bike Tours (p626) runs popular small-group day trips to Ko Yao Noi from Phuket. If you're keen to explore the numerous dirt trails on Ko Yao Noi or Ko Yao Yai independently, most guesthouses rent bikes (250B per day), though they're more readily available on Ko Yao Noi.

🏃 Ko Yao Noi

Kayaks (500B per day) are widely available on Ko Yao Noi, including at Sabai Corner Bungalows.

★ Six Senses Spa   SPA
(☑076 418500; www.sixsenses.com; 56 Mu 5, btwn Hat Khlong Jark & Hat Tha Khao, Ko Yao Noi; treatments 4200-25,000B; ⊙8am-9pm) No lux-ury brand presents back-to-nature elegance like this stilted 'spa village' at Six Senses Hideaway. Therapists are trained in massage and organic-fuelled treatments from China, India and Thailand. The 'Signature Yao Noi Ritual' is a blissful 3½-hour scrub, massage and facial blend.

Island Yoga   YOGA
(☑087 387 9475; www.thailandyogaretreats.com; 4/10 Mu 4, Hat Tha Khao, Ko Yao Noi; classes 600B) This popular yoga school hosts daily drop-in classes at 10am, as well as scheduled classes at 7.30am and 4.30pm. It also has multiday yoga and t'ai chi retreats.

Mountain Shop Adventures   CLIMBING
(☑083 969 2023; www.themountainshop.org; Tha Khao, Ko Yao Noi; half-day 3200B; ⊙9am-7pm) There are over 150 climbs on Ko Yao Noi; Mountain Shop owner Mark has routed most of them himself. Trips range from beginner to advanced and many involve boat travel to remote limestone cliffs. Mark's ramshackle office is just down the road from the Tha Khao pier. Contact him in advance.

🏃 Ko Yao Yai

★ Hat Laem Haad   BEACH
(Ko Yao Yai) Hat Laem Haad is a gorgeous sliver of powder-white sand that extends into a palm-shaped peninsula. A small shack nearby sells drinks and has a toilet and shower block. Try to see it at high tide. Coming from the pier, it's 1.2km from the main road and well signposted.

Elixir Divers   DIVING
(☑087 897 0076; www.elixirdivers.com; 2/3 Mu 3, Ko Yao Yai; 2 dives 2900-3900B; ⊙Oct-Apr) Ko Yao Yai's only dive school is an on-the-ball operator covering a range of PADI courses, two-dive day trips locally and to Ko Phi-Phi, and liveaboards to Hin Daeng, Hin Muang and the Similans (22,900B), plus snorkelling excursions to Ao Phang-Nga, Krabi and Ko Phi-Phi. If you're staying on Ko Yao Noi they can help with transfers.

🛏 Sleeping

Almost all accommodation on Ko Yao Noi is on the east coast. The further north you go, the wilder the roads get and shops and restaurants are very thin on the ground. Ko Yao Yai has fewer sleeping choices, and they're mostly resorts.

🛏 Ko Yao Noi

Pasai Cottage
BUNGALOW $

(☎089 240 8326; www.pasaicottage.blogspot. com; Hat Pasai, Ko Yao Noi; bungalows incl breakfast 800B; 🛜) Simple, fan-only bamboo bungalows run down one side of a garden directly opposite Hat Pasai at this family-run place. It's no frills, but the bathrooms are bearable and all the rooms come with spacious balconies. There's a pleasant communal area/ restaurant (closed May to October), and shops, restaurants and bars are nearby.

Sabai Corner Bungalows
GUESTHOUSE $$

(☎076 597497; www.sabaicornerbungalows.com; Hat Khlong Jark, Ko Yao Noi; bungalows 1000-1900B; 🛜) Pocketed in a rocky headland, these no-fuss bungalows with whizzing fans, mosquito nets and hammocks on terraces are blessed with gorgeous sea views. One oddity is that there are no connecting doors to the bathrooms; you have to go outside to reach them. The good, chilled-out waterside restaurant (mains 95-300B; ⏱8am-10pm; 🛜) is a bubbly place to hang out. There are kayaks for rent.

Suntisook
BUNGALOW $$

(☎089 781 6456, 075 582750; www.facebook.com/ suntisookkoyaonoi; 11/1 Mu 4, Hat Tha Khao, Ko Yao Noi; r 2000-2200B; ❄🛜) Suntisook's comfy and fresh varnished-wood bungalows are sprinkled across an attractive garden just metres from a quiet beach. They're not huge, but all have spacious hammock-laden verandas, fridges and pot plants. It's run efficiently by a helpful English-speaking Thai family, who also have an authentic Thai restaurant (mains 60-150B; ⏱7.30am-9pm; 🛜) and offer kayak hire. It sometimes closes for parts of the low season (May to October).

★ Six Senses Hideaway
RESORT $$$

(☎076 418500; www.sixsenses.com; 56 Mu 5, btwn Hat Khlong Jark & Hat Tha Khao, Ko Yao Noi; villa incl breakfast 35,000-66,000B; ❄🛜⛱) 🌿 This elegant five-star property, with 56 hillside pool villas and an exquisite spa built into an existing rubber plantation, exceeds every expectation. Sunset views of Ao Phang-Nga are jaw-dropping, its clifftop infinity pool is a dream, its lounge bar and white-sand beach are worthy of the frequenting fashionable people, and its commitment to sustainability is unparalleled among global high-end hotels.

🛏 Ko Yao Yai

Thiwson Beach Resort
BUNGALOW $$

(☎081 956 7582; www.thiwsonbeach.com; 58/2 Mu 4, Hat Chonglard, Ko Yao Yai; r incl breakfast 2000-3600B; ❄🛜) Easily the sweetest of Ko Yao Yai's humbler bungalow properties, Thiwson has proper wooden thatch- and tin-topped huts with polished floors, outdoor bathrooms and wide patios overlooking the island's prettiest northeast-coast beach, fronted by an aqua pool. Beachfront bungalows are biggest, but the fan rooms are excellent low-season value.

Koh Yao Yai Village
RESORT $$$

(☎076 363700; www.kohyaovillage.com; 78 Mu 4, Ko Yao Yai; r 4300-10,200B; ❄🛜⛱) This ecofriendly resort is upmarket without being over the top price-wise. It offers big, light, elegantly furnished villas with outdoor bathrooms set high in the trees for spectacular sea views towards Phuket. There's also a tremendous infinity pool, a spa and an onsite restaurant, plus you're handily placed to access Hat Laem Haad.

🍴 Eating

All resorts and guesthouses have restaurants, although some close from May to October. Otherwise, there are a few eateries scattered along Ko Yao Noi's east coast, with less on Ko Yao Yai.

Chaba Café
INTERNATIONAL $

(☎087 887 0625; Hat Khlong Jark, Ko Yao Noi; mains 80-220B; ⏱9am-5pm Mon-Sat; ✍) Rustic-cute Chaba is a haven of pastel-painted prettiness, with driftwood walls, mellow music and a small gallery. Organic-oriented offerings include honey-sweetened juices, coconut-milk-and-avocado shakes, chrysanthemum tea and homebaked paninis, cookies and cakes, plus soups, pastas and Thai dishes. It's just beyond northern Hat Khlong Jark.

Pizzeria La Luna
ITALIAN $$

(☎085 068 9326; btwn Hat Khlong Jark & Hat Tha Khao, Ko Yao Noi; mains 170-320B; ⏱3-10pm; 🛜✍) There's a big range of wood-fired pizzas, including veggie choices, at this laid-back, semi-open-air roadside place, as well as homemade pasta, salads, cakes and antipasto in high season (October to May). It's an equally good place to sip a cocktail, with a proper wooden bar to sit at. The billiards table out back is a nice bonus.

★ **Rice Paddy**   MULTICUISINE $$$

(☎082 331 6581, 076 410233; www.ricepaddy. website; Hat Pasai, Ko Yao Noi; mains 180-890B; ⊙noon-10pm & 6-10pm May-Oct; 🛜🍃) This sweet, German-owned Thai-international kitchen is very special. Flash-fried *sôm·đam* (spicy green papaya salad), fantastic falafel and hummus, spicy, fruit enhanced curries served in clay pots and fresh salads are all delicious. It does excellent veggie dishes, as well as decent cocktails. It's located on a hilltop in the southern part of the island, signposted from the main road.

ℹ️ Information

There are ATMs in Ta Khao, Ko Yao Noi's largest settlement, and a few more dotted along the east coast. There's also an ATM at Phuket's pier **Tha Bang Rong** (Map p622), where boats to Ko Yao Noi and Ko Yao Yai depart from.

There's a handful of ATMs on Ko Yao Yai, but it's wise to take money with you; otherwise you'll have to head back to Tha Bang Rong to cash up.

ℹ️ Getting There & Away

TO/FROM KRABI

From 9am to 5.30pm daily, there are frequent long-tails (150B) between Ko Yao Noi's Tha Khao and Krabi's Tha Len (33km northwest of Krabi Town). *Sŏrng·tăa·ou* (100B) run between Tha Len and Krabi's Th Maharat via Krabi's bus terminal.

TO/FROM PHANG-NGA

From Tha Dan in Phang-Nga there's a 1pm ferry to Ko Yao Noi (200B, 1½ hours), returning at 7.30am.

TO/FROM PHUKET

From Phuket's Tha Bang Rong, there are daily speedboats (300B, 30 minutes) to Ko Yao Noi almost hourly between 7.50am and 5.40pm, plus long-tails (120B, one hour) at 9.15am, 12.30pm and 5pm. Some stop en route at Tha Klong Hia on Ko Yao Yai (300B, 25 minutes). Boats return to Phuket between 6.30am and 4.40pm.

Taxis run from Tha Bang Rong to Phuket's resort areas for 600B to 800B, and *sŏrng·tăa·ou* (40B) leave for Phuket Town twice hourly.

TO/FROM KO PHI-PHI & KO LANTA

Three weekly speedboats run to/from Ko Phi-Phi (600B) and Ko Lanta (600B) from October to April.

TO/FROM AO NANG

From November to April, there's an 11am speedboat from the pier at Hat Noppharat Thara to Ko Yao Noi and Ko Yao Yai (both 650B, 45 minutes). It continues to Phuket's Tha Bang Rong, returning at 3pm.

ℹ️ Getting Around

Frequent shuttle boats run from Ko Yao Noi's Tha Manok to Ko Yao Yai's Tha Klong Hia (50B). On the islands, túk-túk rides cost about 150B, and most guesthouses rent motorbikes (250B to 300B per day). It's 100B for *sŏrng·tăa·ou* transport to the resorts.

PHUKET

POP 525,700

Jade-hued waves concealing rainbows of fish wash white-gold beaches wrapped in Phuketian heritage: Phuket (ภูเก็ต), Thailand's dazzling largest island, is so diverse you may forget to leave.

🏃 Activities

Diving is Phuket's star activity, but you can also go snorkelling, kitesurfing, horse riding, sea kayaking, yachting and surfing, not to mention embarking on a wealth of adrenaline sports.

Diving & Snorkelling

Phuket enjoys an enviable central location relative to the Andaman Sea's top diving destinations. The much-talked-about Similan Islands (p614) lie 100km northwest, while dozens of dive sites orbit Ko Phi-Phi (p667) and Ko Lanta (p674), 40km and 72km southeast. Trips from Phuket to these awesome destinations cost slightly more than from places closer to the sites, as you'll be forking out extra baht for transport costs. Most Phuket operators take divers to the nine decent sites around the island, including **Ko Raya Noi** and **Ko Raya Yai** (Ko Racha Noi and Ko Racha Yai), but these spots rank lower on the wow-o-meter. The reef off the southern tip of Raya Noi is the best among them, with soft corals and pelagic fish species aplenty, though it's usually reserved for experienced divers. Manta and marble rays are frequently glimpsed here and, if you're lucky, you might spot a whale shark.

One-day, two-dive trips to nearby sites start at around 3800B. Nondivers and snorkellers can usually tag along for a significant discount. Open Water Diver certification costs from around 11,000B to 21,000B for three days' instruction. Some schools charge extra for equipment.

From Phuket, you can join a huge range of liveaboard diving expeditions to the Similan Islands and Myanmar's Mergui Archipelago.

Snorkelling isn't wonderful off Phuket proper, though mask, snorkel and fins (200B per day) are available for rent in most resort areas. As with diving, you'll find better snorkelling (with greater visibility and variety of marine life) along the shores of small outlying islands, such as Ko Raya Yai and Ko Raya Noi. Some dive operators also run dedicated snorkel tours.

Like elsewhere in the Andaman Sea, the best diving months are November to April, when the weather is good and seas smooth and clear. Some dive sites may close during the May-to-October monsoon to allow for regeneration, though most dive shops power on (weather permitting) through the low season.

There are recommended dive schools across Phuket, especially in Kata, Karon and Patong.

Surfing

Phuket is an under-the-radar surf destination. With the monsoon's midyear swell, glassy seas fold into barrels. The best waves arrive between June and September, when annual competitions are held on Hat Kata Yai (p641), Phuket's most popular surf spot, and Hat Kalim, just north of Patong. Nautilus Dive & Surf Shop (p642) is based at the south end of Kata Yai near the best break, which tops out at 2m. Hat Nai Harn (p632) gets bigger waves (up to 3m), in front of the yacht club. Both Kata and Nai Harn have vicious undertows that can claim lives.

Hat Kalim is sheltered and has a consistent break that gets up to 3m. This is a hollow wave, and is considered the best break on the island. Kalim also hosts an annual competition. The northernmost stretch of Hat Kamala (p646) has a nice 3m beach break and hosts a surf tournament. Laem Singh (แหลมสิงห์; Map p648; P), 1km north, gets very big and fast waves, plus it's sheltered from wind by a massive headland. Hat Surin gets some of Phuket's most challenging waves.

Hat Nai Yang (p654) has a consistent (if soft) wave that breaks more than 200m offshore. Hat Nai Thon (p654) gets better-shaped waves, with swells up to 3m high a few times per year. In the low season you can rent surfboards (200B to 300B per hour) on most of these beaches; some also offer classes (from 1200B).

Sea Kayaking

Several Phuket-based companies offer canoe tours of spectacular Ao Phang-Nga (p616), a collection of towering karst outcrops

LOCAL KNOWLEDGE

WHICH PHUKET BEACH IS FOR YOU?

Most visitors make a beeline for the west coast's established, social tourist magnets of Hat Kata (p641), Hat Karon (p645) and (seedier) **Hat Patong** (หาด ป่าตอง; Map p638): long sandy swathes lined with resorts, restaurants, bars and every other facility you could dream of. If you'd prefer a more peaceful, secluded vibe, hunt down rocky coves off nondescript coastal roads between the main beaches, or head to Phuket's less touristed northwest coast, where Hat Mai Khao (p654), Hat Nai Yang (p654) and Hat Nai Thon (p654) are protected by Sirinat National Park (p655). For five-star sparkle without the bustle, seek out **Hat Surin** (หาดสุรินทร์) and Ao Bang Thao (p650). In the far south, Rawai has a mellow vibe and beautiful Hat Nai Harn (p632).

rising from the sea northeast of Phuket and close to the mainland. Kayaks can enter semisubmerged caves inaccessible to longtail boats and speedboats. A day paddle (around 4000B per person) includes meals, equipment and boat transfer. John Gray's Seacanoe (p626) is the island's star operator, offering both day trips and all-inclusive, three- or four-day kayaking and camping trips to Ao Phang-Nga and Khao Sok National Park (from 26,750B).

Kitesurfing

One of the world's fastest-growing sports is also among Phuket's big addictions. The best kitesurfing spots are Hat Nai Yang (p654) from May to October and Rawai (p633) from November to March. Reliable outfitters are affiliated with the International Kiteboarding Organisation (www.ikointl.com).

Yachting

Phuket is one of Southeast Asia's main yachting destinations. You'll find all manner of craft anchored along its shores, from 80-year-old wooden sloops to the latest in high-tech motor cruisers.

Marina-style facilities with year-round anchorage are available at several locations. Marinas can advise in advance on the latest port-clearance procedures. Expect to pay

Phuket Province

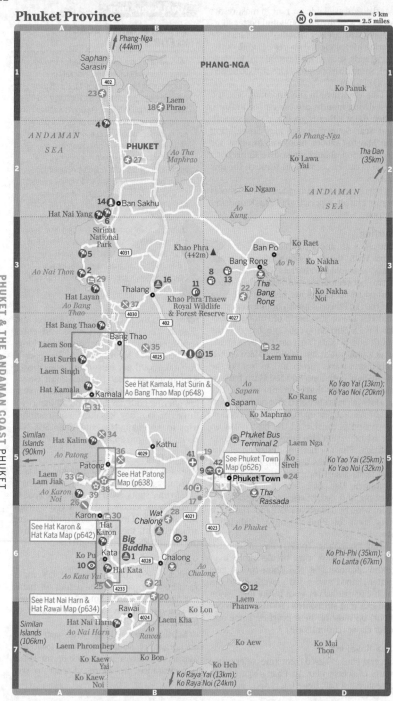

PHANG-NGA

Phang-Nga
(44km)

Saphan
Sarasin

402

23

18 Laem
Phrao

4

ANDAMAN
SEA

PHUKET

27

Ao Tha
Maphrao

Ko Panuk

Tha Dan
(35km)

Ko Lawa
Yai

ANDAMAN
SEA

14 Ban Sakhu

Hat Nai Yang

6

Sirinat
National
Park

5

4031

Ao Nai Thon 2

29

Hat Layan

Ao Bang
Thao

Hat Bang Thao

Laem Son

Hat Surin

Laem Singh

Hat Kamala

Kamala

31

Thalang

Ao
Kung

Khao Phra
(442m)

16

37

4030

4025

Ban Sakhu

Ao Po

Bang Rong

8   13

11

Khao Phra Thaew
Royal Wildlife
& Forest Reserve

402

4027

Ban Po

22

Tha
Bang
Rong

Ko Raet

Ko Nakha
Yai

Ko Nakha
Noi

35

Bang Thao

See Hat Kamala, Hat Surin &
Ao Bang Thao Map (p648)

7 15

32

Laem Yamu

Ao
Sapam

Ko Rang

Sapam

Ko Maphrao

Laem Nga

Ko Yao Yai (13km);
Ko Yao Noi (20km)

Similan
Islands
(90km)

Hat Kalim

34

Ao Patong

36

4029

Patong

See Hat Patong
Map (p638)

Laem
Lam Jiak

33

Ao Karon
Noi

26

39

38

41   19

9

40

17

42

Phuket Bus
Terminal 2

See Phuket Town
Map (p626)

Phuket Town

Ko
Sireh

24

Tha
Rassada

Ko Yao Yai (25km);
Ko Yao Noi (32km)

Karon

30

See Hat Karon &
Hat Kata Map (p642)

Hat
Karon

Ko Pu

Kata

10

Hat Kata

Wat
Chalong

28

3

4021

4023

Ao Phuket

Big
Buddha

1

4028

Chalong

Ao
Chalong

Ko Phi-Phi (35km);
Ko Lanta (67km)

25

4233

21

20

See Hat Nai Harn &
Hat Rawai Map (p634)

Rawai

4024

12

Laem
Phanwa

Similan
Islands
(106km)

Hat Nai Harn

Ao Nai Harn

Laem Phromthep

Ko Kaew
Yai

Ko Kaew
Noi

Laem Kha

Ko Lon

Ko Bon

Ao
Rawai

Ko Aew

Ko Heh

Ko Raya Yai (13km);
Ko Raya Noi (24km)

Ko Mai
Thon

0 ———————— 5 km
0 ———————— 2.5 miles

Phuket Province

from 9000B per day for a high-season, bareboat charter.

Adrenaline Sports

There's no shortage of adrenaline-fuelled activities on Phuket, from bungee jumps to ziplines. Equipment quality and safety levels vary, and there have been serious, even fatal, accidents. Ask for recommendations and don't proceed if you have any doubts.

🍃 Courses

Popular Thai cooking classes are held by Boathouse Cooking Class (p642) in Kata, Blue Elephant Cooking School (p626) in Phuket Town, Phuket Thai Cookery School (Map p622; ☑082 474 6592; www.phuketthaicookery.com; Hat Pleum Suk; 1-day course 2900B; ⊗8am-3pm Thu-Tue) in Ko Sireh and Pum Thai Cooking School (p636) in Patong.

🎊 Festivals & Events

Vegetarian Festival   RELIGIOUS
(⊗late Sep-Oct) Firecrackers pop, the air is thick with smoke and people parade through Phuket Town, some with their cheeks violently pierced with skewers and knives or, more surprisingly, lamps and tree branches. Welcome to the Vegetarian Festival, one of Phuket's most colourful celebrations, where residents of Chinese ancestry

ℹ️ PHUKET TAXIS

Despite crackdowns on Phuket's 'taxi mafia' by the Thai military, taxis remain seriously overpriced across the island. A 15-minute journey from, say, Hat Karon to Hat Patong will set you back 400B. Price boards around the island outline *maximum* journey rates, though drivers rarely budge from them.

To avoid being overcharged, jot down the phone number of a metered taxi and use the same driver throughout your stay. The best way to do this is to take a metered taxi from the airport (the easiest place to find them) when you arrive. Metered taxis are 50m to the left as you exit international airport arrivals. Set rates are 50B for the first 2km, 12B per kilometre for the next 15km and 10B per kilometre thereafter, plus a 100B 'airport tax'. In theory, that's no more than 700B to anywhere on the island from the airport.

The Grab taxi app (www.grab.com) is increasingly popular in Thailand and very handy on Phuket. Taxis booked via Grab use meters and add a small pick-up charge on top, though they aren't always cheaper than taxis hailed on the street. Grab drivers may not understand English, but your accommodation can help with bookings and directions.

adopt a vegetarian diet for 10 days for the purpose of spiritual cleansing.

ℹ️ Information

MEDICAL SERVICES

Most diving emergencies are taken to **Phuket International Hospital** (Siriroj International Hospital; Map p622; ☎ 098 024 9400, 076 361818; www.phuketinternationalhospital.com; 44 Th Chalermprakiat; ⊗24hr), which has a hyperbaric chamber; it's located 3.5km northwest of Phuket Town. **Bangkok Hospital Phuket** (Map p622; ☎ 076 254425; www.phukethospital.com; 2/1 Th Hongyok Uthit; ⊗24hr), 3km north of Phuket Town, is also reliable.

SAFE TRAVEL

➡ Thousands of people are injured or killed every year on Phuket's highways.

➡ Take special care on the roads from Patong to Karon and from Kata to Rawai/Hat Nai Harn: we've had reports of late-night motorcycle muggings and stabbings.

➡ Sunbathing topless is a big no-no in Thailand for women.

➡ Drownings (p57) occur every year off Phuket's beaches; take care.

➡ Drug possession can result in a year or more of prison. Drug smuggling carries considerably higher penalties, including execution.

➡ Jet-ski scams plague Phuket; inspect before hiring.

➡ There have been serious boat accidents; ensure your boat has safety/emergency equipment; if in doubt, find another operator.

TOURIST INFORMATION

You'll find tourist information offices in Phuket Town.

Tourism Authority of Thailand (TAT; Map p626; ☎ 076 211036; www.

tourismthailand.org/Phuket; 191 Th Thalang; ⊗8.30am-4.30pm)

Tourist Information Centre (Map p626; Th Thalang; ⊗9am-10pm)

ℹ️ Getting There & Away

AIR

Phuket International Airport (☎ 076 632 7230; www.phuketairportonline.com) is 30km northwest of Phuket Town.

THAI (Map p626; www.thaiairways.com; 78/1 Th Ranong; ⊗8am-4.30pm) is the national carrier, with flights to/from Bangkok (Suvarnabhumi). AirAsia (p640), Nok Air (p687) and **Bangkok Airways** (Map p626; ☎ 076 225033; www.bangkokair.com; 158/2-3 Th Yaowarat; ⊗8am-5.30pm Mon-Sat) all serve Bangkok, as well as other national destinations, including Chiang Mai, Hat Yai and Ko Samui. Direct international destinations include Dubai, Abu Dhabi, Hong Kong, Kuala Lumpur, Singapore, Beijing, Shanghai, Seoul, Delhi, Mumbai, Melbourne and Sydney.

LAND

Interstate buses (p630) depart from **Phuket Bus Terminal 2** (Map p622; Th Thepkrasattri), 4km north of Phuket Town. Destinations include Bangkok, Chiang Mai, Chiang Rai, Hat Yai, Ko Samui, Ko Pha-Ngan and Surat Thani.

Phuket travel agencies sell tickets (including ferry fares) for shared air-con minivans to destinations across southern Thailand, including Krabi, Ranong, Trang, Surat Thani, Ko Samui, Ko Pha-Ngan and Hat Yai. Prices are usually slightly higher than for buses. Many minivans use **Phuket Bus Terminal 1** (Map p626; Th Phang-Nga) in Phuket Town.

SEA

Phuket's **Tha Rassada** (Map p622; Tha Rassada), 3km southeast of Phuket Town, is the main pier for boats to/from Ko Phi-Phi, Krabi, Ao Nang, Ko Lanta, the Trang Islands, Ko Lipe and even as far as Pulau Langkawi in Malaysia (which has ferry connections to Penang). Additional services to Krabi and Ao Nang via the Ko Yao Islands leave from Tha Bang Rong (p620), 26km north of Tha Rassada.

❶ Getting Around

Local Phuket transport is famously terrible, though things are slowly improving. *Sŏrng·tăa·ou* (passenger pick-up trucks) run between Phuket Town and the west-coast beaches, and the new Phuket Smart Bus means direct beach-to-beach travel is now finally possible. That said, taxis and túk-túk remain heavily overpriced.

BOAT

Chalong Pier (Map p622; Chalong) is mainly used by yachts and dive-operator boats for dive trips.

BUS

The sky-blue **Phuket Smart Bus** (☑ 086 306 1257; www.phuketsmartbus.com) runs between Phuket International Airport and Rawai (two hours) via Ao Bang Thao, Surin, Kamala, Patong, Karon and Kata roughly hourly from 6am to 8.15pm. Fares are 50B to 170B, depending on where you hop off. Three-day unlimited ride passes are available (500B) or you can purchase a prepaid smartcard (300B), which can be bought on board and topped up at designated spots across the island. Don't forget to 'tag off' the card when you get off the bus.

CAR & MOTORCYCLE

Motorbike hire costs around 250B per day and is available everywhere across the island. You can rent cars pretty much anywhere – including at the airport and in Phuket Town – from around 1000B per day.

SŎRNG·TĂA·OU & TÚK-TÚK

Large bus-sized **sŏrng·tăa·ou** (Map p626; Th Ranong) run regularly between Th Ranong in Phuket Town and most of the island's beaches (30B to 40B per person, 30 minutes to 1½ hours), from 7am to 5pm or 6pm. Túk-túk charters are another way to get around.

Phuket Town

☑ 076 / POP 79,300

Long before flip-flops, glossy resorts and selfie sticks, Phuket was an island of rubber trees, tin mines and cash-hungry merchants. Luring entrepreneurs from the Arabian Peninsula, China, India and Portugal, Phuket Town (เมืองภูเก็ต) became a colourful blend of cultural influences.

Today, the Old Town is a testament to Phuket's history, but it's also the island's hipster heart, attracting artists and musicians in particular, which has led to noticeable gentrification. Century-old *hôrng tăa·ou* (shophouses) and homes are being restored, vibrant street art is popping up and it *can* feel like every other building is now a fashionable polished-concrete cafe.

But Phuket Town remains a wonderfully refreshing cultural break from the island's beaches (easily reached by *sŏrng·tăa·ou;* passenger pick-up trucks). Wander down streets lined with distinctive Sino-Portuguese architecture, arty coffee shops, experimental galleries, boutique hotels and incense-cloaked Chinese Taoist shrines, before sampling the island's most authentic Phuketian cuisine and Phuket Town's very local bar scene.

⊙ Sights

Phuket Thaihua Museum MUSEUM
(พิพิธภัณฑ์ภูเก็ตไทยหัว; Map p626; ☑ 076 211224; 28 Th Krabi; 200B; ◎9am-5pm) Founded in 1934 and formerly a Chinese-language school, this flashy museum is filled with photos, videos and English-language exhibits on Phuket's history, from the Chinese migration (many influential Phuketian families are of Chinese origin), the tin-mining era and the Vegetarian Festival (p623) to local cuisine, fashion and literature. The building itself is a stunning combination of Chinese and European architectural styles, including art deco, Palladianism and a Chinese gable roof and stucco, plus a British-iron gate.

Shrine of the Serene Light SHRINE
(ศาลเจ้าแสงธรรม, Saan Jao Sang Tham; Map p626; Th Phang-Nga; ◎8.30am-noon & 1.30-5.30pm) **FREE** A handful of Chinese temples pump colour into Phuket Town, but this restored shrine, tucked away up a 50m alley now adorned with modern murals, is particularly atmospheric, with its Taoist etchings on the walls and the vaulted ceiling stained from incense plumes. The altar is always fresh with flowers and burning candles, and the surrounding Sino-Portuguese buildings have been beautifully repainted. The shrine is said to have been built by a local family in 1889.

Khao Rang VIEWPOINT
(เขารัง, Phuket Hill; Map p622; Ⓟ) For a bird's-eye view of the city, climb (or drive) up Khao

Phuket Town

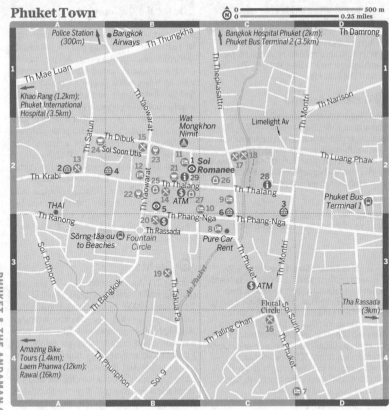

Rang, 2.5km northwest of Phuket Town's centre. An overhanging viewing platform opens up 270-degree panoramas across the town to Chalong Bay, Laem Phanwa and Big Buddha. It's at its most peaceful during the week. There are a few restaurants and cafes up here, as well as monkeys. **Wat Khao Rang** is worth a look along the way. It's about an hour's walk.

Activities

★ **John Gray's Seacanoe**   KAYAKING
(Map p622; ☎ 076 254505; www.johngray-seaca-noe.com; 86 Soi 2/3, Th Yaowarat; adult/child from 3950/1975B) 🦜 John Gray's is the original, the most reputable and by far the most ecologically sensitive kayaking company on Phuket. The 'Hong by Starlight' trip dodges the crowds, involves a sunset dinner and will introduce you to Ao Phang-Nga's famed after-dark bioluminescence. Like any good brand in Thailand, John Gray's 'Seacanoe'

name and itineraries have been frequently copied. It's 3.5km northwest of Phuket Town.

Amazing Bike Tours   CYCLING
(Map p622; ☎ 087 263 2031; www.amazingbike-toursthailand.asia; half-/full-day trip 1900/3200B; ⏰ 9am-8pm) This highly popular adventure outfitter leads small groups on half-day bicycle tours through the villages of northeast Phuket, as well as on terrific full-day trips around Ko Yao Noi and more challenging three-day adventure rides around Khao Sok National Park (14,900B). Prices include bikes, helmets, meals and water.

Courses

Blue Elephant Cooking School   COOKING
(Map p626; ☎ 076 354355; www.blueelephant.com; 96 Th Krabi; half-day class 3296B; ⏰ 9.30am-4.30pm) Master the intricate art of royal Thai cooking in a stunningly restored Sino-Portuguese mansion, with half-day (morning or afternoon) group classes.

Phuket Town

Morning sessions visit the market, while afternoon lessons cover dessert as well. Book ahead.

🛏 Sleeping

Phuket Town is a treasure trove of affordable lodging. The hostel scene has exploded in recent years, and there's now an almost overwhelming number of hostels, guesthouses and boutique hotels dotted around the Old Town. For the best places you'll want to book ahead. There's little top-end accommodation here; go for a characterful boutique hotel instead.

Borbaboom Poshtel　　　　　HOSTEL $
(Map p626; ☑ 096 634 5025; www.facebook.com/borbaboomphuket; 73/1 Th Rassada; dm 300-450B, d 1200B; ❋🛜🛏) With a lively young vibe, helpful English-speaking staff and a small rooftop pool, fresh Borbaboom also appeals for its well-kept, modern six-bunk dorms, the best of which are capsule-style; each bed has a light, a curtain, a shelf, a locker and a plug. Smartish private rooms are painted in blues and have hairdryers, bathrooms and shared terraces.

Neighbors Hostel　　　　　HOSTEL $
(Map p626; ☑ 094 343 3399; 93 Th Phang-Nga; dm 300-340B, d 600-750B; ❋🛜) Housed in a pale-yellow Sino-Portuguese-style build-

ing with a small cafe, this friendly, central, contemporary place has two simple, spotless, eight-bed mixed dorms, plus a six-bed women-only dorm, all with personal lockers, lights, plugs and curtains. The two small private rooms come with slightly more colour and character, and share the same open-brick, polished-concrete bathrooms.

Art-C House　　　　　GUESTHOUSE $
(Map p626; ☑ 082 420 3911; www.facebook.com/artchouse; 288 Th Phuket; d 800B; 🛜) Not many guesthouses have their own climbing wall – cheerful, original Art-C does, along with 13 tidy, good-value private rooms and corridors decorated with the owner's own murals. Only top-floor rooms have external windows. Staff are helpful and welcoming, and there's a downstairs cafe (but no lift). Nonguests can use the climbing wall for 150B per day.

★Casa Blanca Boutique Hotel　　　　　BOUTIQUE HOTEL $$
(Map p626; ☑ 076 219019; www.casablancaphuket.com; 26 Th Phuket; d 2300-2800B; ❋🛜🛏) All whites and pastels, this elegantly revamped Sino-Portuguese beauty gets extra boutique spark from Spanish-themed touches such as patterned tiles and a plant-lined patio. Modern art adorns smart rooms, in soft greens and pale blues. Deluxe rooms have balconies

SINO-PORTUGUESE ARCHITECTURE

Stroll along Ths Thalang, Dibuk, Yaowarat, Ranong, Phang-Nga, Rassada and Krabi for a glimpse of Phuket Town's Sino-Portuguese architectural treasures. The most magnificent examples are the **Standard Chartered Bank** (ธนาคารสแตนดาร์ดชาร์เตอร์ด; Map p626; Th Phang-Nga; ⊘ museum 9am-4.30pm Tue-Sun), Thailand's oldest foreign bank; the THAI office (p624); and the **old post office building**, which now houses the **Phuket Philatelic Museum** (พิพิธภัณฑ์ตราไปรษณียากรภูเก็ต; Map p626; 158 Th Montri; ⊘ 9am-5.30pm Tue-Sat) FREE. Some of the most colourful buildings line **Soi Romanee** (ถนน รมณีย์; Map p626), once home to brothels and gambling and opium dens.

The best-restored residential properties lie along Ths Thalang, Dibuk and Krabi, including **Chinpracha House** (บ้านชินประชา, Baan Chinpracha; Map p626; ☎ 076 211167, 076 211281; 98 Th Krabi; 200B; ⊘ 9am-4.30pm Mon-Sat). The fabulous 1903 **Phra Pitak Chinpracha Mansion** has been refurbished into the upscale restaurant and cooking school **Blue Elephant** (Map p626; ☎ 076 354355; www.blueelephant.com; 96 Th Krabi; mains 350-1000B, tasting menus 1600-2400B; ⊘ 11.30am-2.30pm & 6.30-10pm; 🛜 🍴).

with city panoramas; quieter superior ones overlook the pool. Staff are charming and, in the tile-floored lobby, there's a small cafe.

The two-room suite with lounge suits travelling families.

RomManee BOUTIQUE HOTEL $$
(Map p626; ☎ 089 728 9871; Soi Romanee; d 1200B; ❄🛜) On Phuket Town's prettiest street, this boutique guesthouse certainly has style, with its turquoise-toned Sino-Portuguese exterior, varnished-concrete floors and great little lobby cafe **DouBrew** (Map p626; www.facebook.com/DouBrewCoffee; Soi Romanee; ⊘ 8am-7pm Mon-Sat, to 9pm Sun). The four spacious rooms amount to excellent value and have an arty, contemporary feel: wood floors, colour feature walls and tasteful lighting. Stairs are steep and there's no lift, but the team in charge is welcoming.

There's a less characterful branch, **Rom-Manee Classic** (Map p626; ☎ 092 218 9292; www.facebook.com/TheRomManeeClassic; 4-6 Th Krabi; d 1000-1200B; ❄🛜), a block away.

🍴 Eating

There's great food in Phuket Town, both Thai and international, and meals cost a lot less than at the beach. This is the island's top spot for authentic southern Thai food, especially Phuket's unique Peranakan cuisine, which blends Thai, Chinese and Malay flavours. Restaurants and cafes are dotted all over the Old Town.

★Kopitiam by Wilai THAI $
(Map p626; ☎ 083 606 9776; www.facebook.com/kopitiambywilai; 14 & 18 Th Thalang; mains 95-180B; ⊘ 11am-5pm & 6.30-9pm Mon-Sat; 🛜 ♿) Family-

owned Kopitiam serves fabulous Phuket soul food in an atmospheric old shophouse: Phuketian *pàt tai* with a kick, *chai chae* (chilli-dressed noodle salad) and fantastic *mee sua* (noodles sautéed with egg, greens, prawns, sea bass and squid). Wash it all down with fresh chrysanthemum or passion-fruit juice. There are two branches (one air-con), either side of the **Oldest Herbs Shop** (Map p626; Th Thalang; ⊘ 8am-6pm).

Lock Tien STREET FOOD $
(Map p626; cnr Th Dibuk & Th Yaowarat; meals 35-100B; ⊘ 9am-5pm) Communal tables cluster under whirring fans at fast-and-furious food court Lock Tien, which works up a vast, tempting range of classic Phuket Town dishes. Sample *popiah sod hokkien* (Fujianese fresh spring rolls, stuffed with prawns or veggies), spicy-sour Hokkien-noodle soup, *lobha* (pork cheek and offal) and more at delightfully down-to-earth prices.

Mee Ton Poe NOODLES $
(Map p626; Th Phuket; meals 50-80B; ⊘ 8am-8pm; 🛜) Right on Phuket Town's Clock Tower Circle, amid wooden tables and red-plastic stools, third-generation Mee Ton Poe has been pulling in Phuketians since 1946 with its superb noodle dishes, including *mèe nam tom poe* (Hokkien noodle soup) and the signature *mèe pad hokkien* (fried yellow noodles with pork, shrimp, fish balls and veg in a broth).

★One Chun THAI $$
(Map p626; ☎ 076 355909; 48/1 Th Thepkasattri; mains 100-370B; ⊘ 10am-10pm; 🛜) A sister restaurant to well-established **Raya** (Map p626; ☎ 076 218155; rayarestaurant@gmail.com; 48/1 Th

Dibuk; mains 180-650B; ⊙10am-10pm), though the dishes here are cheaper, which is why Phuketians and visiting Thais crowd it out. There's superb seafood – the coconut-milk crab curry is arguably Phuket Town's best – and great roasted-duck red curry and *pàk miang* (stir-fried spinach-like leaves). The shophouse setting, with 1950s decor, green-painted shutters and patterned-tile floors, fuels the atmosphere.

Tu Kab Khao   THAI $$
(Map p626; ☑076 608888; www.facebook. com/tukabkhao; 8 Th Phang-Nga; mains 160-290B; ⊙11.30am-midnight; ☎) Red lanterns cascade down this inviting 130-year-old Sino-Portuguese building, now reimagined as a packed-out restaurant devoted to Phuketian cooking. With varnished-concrete floors, sofa chairs and a wall made entirely of mirrors, it brings old-world glamour to sampling local specialities and is a particular hit with weekending Bangkokians. Signature dishes – *mŏo hong*, crab-meat curry – are based on the owner's mother's recipes.

★**Suay**   FUSION $$$
(Map p626; ☑087 888 6990; www.suayrestau rant.com; 50/2 Th Takua Pa; mains 400-1000B; ⊙5-11pm) Fabulous fusion and fine wines, courtesy of top Phuket chef-owner Noi Tammasak, are the draw at this converted house just south of the Old Town. Spicy eggplant salads, sweet-basil Shanghai noodles, braised-beef-cheek massaman and grilled-lemongrass lamb chops with papaya salsa are just some of the highlights. A new cocktail bar and Thai-tapas menu were in the works at the time of research.

🍸 Drinking & Nightlife

Phuket Town is where you can party like a local. Bars buzz until late, patronised almost exclusively by Thais and local expats, and the handcrafted-cocktail scene has flourished in recent years. And then there's the booming cafe culture: Phuket Town has some of the island's best coffee shops.

★**Bookhemian**   CAFE
(Map p626; ☑098 090 0657; 61 Th Thalang; ⊙9am-7pm Mon-Fri, to 8.30pm Sat & Sun; ☎) Every town should have a coffee house this cool, with a brick-and-concrete split-level design that makes it both cafe and art exhibition space. Used books (for sale) line the front room, bicycles hang from the wall and a Gabriel García Márquez novel is set into the door handle. There's gourmet coffee (50B to 90B), juices, cakes and all-day breakfasts (120B to 150B).

★**Shelter Coffee**   CAFE
(Map p626; www.facebook.com/thesheltercoffee phuket; 97 Th Dibuk; ⊙8.30am-6pm Thu-Tue; ☎) Some of Phuket's finest coffee (55B to 150B) is crafted at easy-going, experimental, national-award-winning Shelter, whose signature caffeine concoction is a 72-hour cold brew. All the classics are artfully presented, with AeroPress and bean-of-the-day options, and there are Thai herbal teas, soul-soothing hot chocolates, and all-day breakfasts and Thai dishes (90B to 160B). Out the back lies a tucked-away garden.

★**Dibuk House**   COCKTAIL BAR
(Map p626; ☑086 796 4646; www.facebook. com/dibukhouse; 39/2 Th Dibuk; ⊙7pm-2am) The tiled floors and flickering candles of a restyled Sino-Portuguese shophouse mark out Phuket Town's most talked-about cocktail bar. Upping the ante for the local artisan-cocktail scene, it's a sultry, moody place, where waistcoat-clad mixologists artfully prepare potent, avant-garde cocktails (250B to 350B) at the mirror-backed bar. The delicate Wynn de Fleur features gin-infused red-berry tea with aloe, lemon and jasmine.

★**Club No 43**   COCKTAIL BAR
(Map p626; ☑099 305 6333; 43 Th Yaowarat; ⊙6pm-late; ☎) Hendrick's bottles filled with red roses and a red-brick bar lined with antiques set the creative tone at this experimental crafted-cocktails lounge. Thai herbs infuse liquid mixes (300B to 380B) such as the signature *dôm yam*-inspired, spiced-vodka-based 43 Old Town, served in a teapot.

🛍 Shopping

There are boho-chic boutiques scattered throughout the Old Town selling jewellery, women's fashion, fabrics and souvenirs, as well as many whimsical art galleries and antique shops. Phuket Town also hosts several good markets, including the massive **Weekend Market** (Naka Market; Map p622; off Th Chao Fa West; ⊙4-10pm Sat & Sun) and Sunday **Walking St** (Map p626; Th Thalang; ⊙4-10pm Sun).

★**Ranida**   ANTIQUES, FASHION
(Map p626; 119 Th Thalang; ⊙10am-8pm Mon-Sat) An elegant antiques gallery and boutique

featuring antiquated Buddha statues and sculptures, organic textiles, and ambitious, exquisite high-fashion women's clothing inspired by vintage Thai garments and fabrics.

Pink Flamingo FASHION & ACCESSORIES
(Map p626; 39/12 Th Yaowarat; ⊘10am-8pm) In a chicly restored old building with arches over the front door, this self-styled 'tropical concept store' is all about floaty fabrics, bold colours and embroidered handmade dresses, kaftans and accessories from Bali. The upstairs bar-restaurant serves tapas, salads and pastas (105B to 345B) amid gorgeous hand-painted flamingo mural walls.

Ban Boran Textiles TEXTILES
(Map p626; 51 Th Yaowarat; ⊘10.30am-6.30pm Mon-Sat) Shelves at this hole-in-the-wall fashion shop are stocked with quality silk scarves, lacquerware from Myanmar, sarongs, linen shirts, colourful bags and cotton textiles from Chiang Mai, and fabrics sourced from Southeast Asia's tribal communities.

Information

There are numerous ATMs on Ths Phuket, Ranong, Montri and Phang-Nga.

❶ Getting There & Around

AIR

Phuket International Airport is 30km northwest of Phuket Town. THAI (p624) is the national carrier, with flights to/from Bangkok (Suvarnabhumi). Bangkok Airways (p624), AirAsia (p640), and Nok Air (p687) all serve Bangkok, as well as other national destinations, including Chiang Mai, Hat Yai and Ko Samui. Direct international destinations include Dubai, Abu Dhabi, Hong Kong, Kuala Lumpur, Singapore, Beijing, Shanghai, Seoul, Delhi, Mumbai, Melbourne and Sydney.

BUS

Phuket Bus Terminal 1 (p624) is used by minivans and the official, bright-orange **airport bus** (www.airportbusphuket.com), which runs 12 times daily to/from the airport (100B, one hour) via the Heroines Monument; services depart the airport between 8am and 8.30pm and Phuket Town between 6am and 6.30pm. A local bus (30B) and minivans (50B) head to/from Patong between 7am and 5pm.

Interstate buses depart from Phuket Bus Terminal 2 (p624), 4km north of Phuket Town. Pink *sŏrng·tǎa·ou* (passenger pick-up trucks) run between the two bus terminals every 20 minutes (50B); otherwise it's 100B by motorcycle taxi, or 300B in a taxi.

BUSES FROM PHUKET BUS TERMINAL 2

DESTINATION	FARE (B)	DURATION (HR)	FREQUENCY	BUS TYPE
Bangkok	920	12	4pm, 5pm, 5.20pm, 6pm, 6.20pm, 6.30pm & 7pm	VIP
	590-685	12	6.30am, 1.30pm, 3pm, 3.30pm, 4.30pm, 5pm, 5.30pm, 6pm & 6.30pm	air-con
Chiang Mai	1650	24	12.30pm	VIP
Chiang Rai	1750	26	3pm	air-con
Hat Yai	510	7	9.45pm	VIP
	255	7½	hourly 7am-10pm	air-con
Khao Sok	180	4	5am, 6am, 7.30am, 8.30am, 9.30am, 11am, 12.30pm, 1.40pm & 3pm	air-con
Ko Pha-Ngan	550	9½ (bus/boat)	9am	air-con
Ko Samui	450	7½ (bus/boat)	9am	air-con
Krabi	145	3	approx hourly 4.50am-7pm, 8.50pm	air-con
Phang-Nga	80-100	2	approx hourly 4.50am-8.15pm	air-con
Ranong	225	5	5.30am, hourly 7.10am-6.10pm	air-con
Satun	340	8	8.15am, 10.15am, 12.15pm & 8.15pm	air-con
Surat Thani	195-200	5	8am, 10am, 11am, noon & 2pm	air-con
Trang	230	5	approx hourly 4.50am-7pm, 8.50pm	air-con

CAR & MOTORCYCLE

Th Rassada has cheap car-rental agencies including **Pure Car Rent** (Map p626; ☑ 076 211002; www.purecarrent.com; 73 Th Rassada; ☺ 9am-7pm), a good central choice, and others nearby. Cars cost around 1200B per day (including insurance), although you'll get them for more or less the same cost through the big car-hire chains at Phuket International Airport.

You can rent motorcycles on Th Rassada, including at Pure Car Rent, or from many other places around town, for 200B to 250B per day.

MINIVAN

From Phuket Bus Terminal 1 (p624), 500m east of Phuket Town's centre, minivans run to Patong (50B, 7am to 5pm) and destinations across southern Thailand.

TO	FARE (B)	TIME (HR)	FREQUENCY
Hat Yai	370	7	every 2 hours 8am-6pm
Ko Lanta	280	5	hourly 8.30-11.30am, 1.30pm & 3.30pm
Krabi	140	3	18 daily 6.35am-5.55pm
Phang-Nga	100	2	17 daily 5.40am-5.20pm
Surat Thani	200	4-5	hourly 7am-5pm

SŎRNG·TĂA·OU & TÚK-TÚK

Large bus-sized *sŏrng·tăa·ou* (passenger pick-up trucks) run regularly from a stop (p625) near the day market to Phuket's beaches (30B to 40B per person, 30 minutes to 1½ hours) from 7am to 5pm or 6pm. Otherwise you'll have to charter a túk-túk to the beaches, which costs from 400B (Rawai, Kata and Ao Bang Thao), 500B (Patong, Karon and Surin) or 600B (Kamala).

For a ride around town, túk-túk drivers charge 100B to 200B, and motorcycle taxis 50B.

TAXI

Taxis to/from the airport cost 550B. Beware of tales that the only way to reach beaches is by taxi, though it's an option; sample rates are 500B to/from Patong, 600B to/from Kata and 700B to/from Surin.

Laem Phanwa

An elongated jungle-cloaked cape jutting into the sea south of Phuket Town, Laem Phanwa (แหลมพันวา) is an all-natural throwback. Some say this is the very last vestige of Phuket as it once was. The biggest bloom of development is near the harbour at the cape's tip, 12km south of Phuket Town, where you'll find a few high-end resorts and the Phuket Aquarium.

On either side of the harbour, the beaches and coves remain rustic, protected by rocky headlands and mangroves and reached by a leafy, sinuous coastal road. This is very much a place for peace and quiet.

◉ Sights & Activities

Phuket Aquarium AQUARIUM
(สถานแสดงพันธุ์สัตว์น้ำภูเก็ต; Map p622; ☑ 076 391406; www.phuketaquarium.org; 51 Th Sakdidej; adult/child 180/100B; ☺ 8.30am-4.30pm; ℗) Get a glimpse of Thailand's wondrous underwater world at Phuket's popular aquarium, by the harbour on the tip of Laem Phanwa (12km south of Phuket Town). It's not the largest collection of marine life, but there are useful English-language displays and captions. Check out the blacktip reef shark, the tiger-striped catfish (resembling a marine zebra), the electric eel with a shock of up to 600V, and the 80-million-baht multimedia Aqua Dome, launched in 2018.

★**Cool Spa** SPA
(Map p622; ☑ 076 371000; www.coolspaphuket. com; Sri Panwa, 88 Mu 8, Th Sakdidej; treatment from 4500B; ☺ 10am-9pm) One of Phuket's top spas, this is an elegant wonderland of delicate blue tiling, hillside ocean-view pools, six waterfall treatment rooms, and fruit-infused wraps, facials and scrubs. And there's the dreamy setting on the southernmost tip of Laem Phanwa. Treatments mix Thai, Indian, Balinese and Swedish techniques; signature Thai massages are given in classic style on a floor mattress.

✖ Eating & Drinking

There are seafood restaurants along the harbour waterfront where you can watch the fishing boats bobbing by. Further dining options are inside the area's scattered resorts and along its looping coastal road.

★ **Baba Nest** COCKTAIL BAR
(Map p622; ☑ 076 371000; www.babaphuket.com;
Sri Panwa, 88 Mu 8, Th Sakdidej; ☺ 5-9pm; ☎)
Engulfed by beautiful Andaman and island
views and bordered by glittering reflective
pools, the elegant, intimate rooftop Baba
Nest lounge-bar at Sri Panwa (Map p622;
www.sripanwa.com; 88 Mu 8, Th Sakdidej; incl
breakfast ste 13,700-24,000B, 1-room villa 21,300-
31,000B; P✳☎≋) is a truly magical spot
– and one of the island's (and Thailand's)
prime sunset-watching hang-outs, with
smartly prepared classic cocktails (500B to
1000B) and Mexican-inspired tapas (350B).
Book several weeks ahead; reservations require a 2000B minimum spend.

It's on the southernmost tip of Laem
Phanwa, 12km south of Phuket Town.

❶ Getting There & Away

From Th Ranong in Phuket Town, *sŏrng·tăa·ou*
(passenger pick-up trucks) travel southeast to
Laem Phanwa from 8am to 5.30pm (30B); the
last stop is the Phuket Aquarium. Taxis to/from
Phuket Town cost 400B.

Rawai

Rawai (ราไวย์) is a delightful place to stay
or live, which is why this laid-back stretch
of Phuket's south coast is teeming with
retirees, artists and Thai and expat entrepreneurs, catered to by a booming service
sector, countless relaxed, health-focused cafes and plenty of yoga and *moo·ay tai* (Thai
boxing).

The region is defined not just by its
fine salt-white beaches but also by its lush
coastal hills, which rise steeply and tumble into the Andaman Sea, forming Laem
Phromthep, Phuket's beautiful southernmost point. These hills are home to pocket
neighbourhoods and cul-de-sacs knitted together by just a few roads – though more are
being carved into the hills each year and you
can almost envision real-estate money chasing away all the seafood grills and tiki bars.
Let's hope that's several decades away – or
at least one. Even with this growth you can
still experience nature, however, especially
on the beach.

◉ Sights

★ **Hat Nai Harn** BEACH
(หาดในหาน; Map p634) Ask a Phuketian or a local expat for their favourite island beach and
many will choose Hat Nai Harn. A beautifully

curved golden-white crescent with turquoise
water on the west side of Laem Phromthep,
backed by casuarinas and a seafront wát
(temple), it remains one of Rawai's great
swimming and sun-soaking spots (though be
careful of low-season rip tides).

★ **Laem Phromthep** VIEWPOINT
(แหลมพรหมเทพ; Map p634; Rte 4233) Come
here to the island's southernmost point to
see the glittering Andaman Sea wrapped
around Phuket. The cape is crowned by a
mod lighthouse shaped like a concrete crab,
and an evocative, flower-garlanded elephant
shrine, so you'll want to stay a while. At sunset the tour buses descend; if you're craving
privacy, arrive by 4pm, or follow the faint
fisherfolk's trail downhill to watch the sun
drop in peace from the rocky peninsula that
reaches into the ocean.

Chalong Bay Rum DISTILLERY
(ฉลองเบย์รัม ดิสทิลเลอรี; Map p622; ☑ 093 575
1119; www.chalongbayrum.com; 14/2 Mu 2, Soi Palai
2, off Th Chao Fa East; tour 450B; ☺ 11am-10pm,
tours hourly 2-6pm; P) Chalong, 9km north
of Rawai, is home to Phuket's only working
distillery, launched by French couple Marine Lucchini and Thibault Spithakis, who
bonded over booze – rum, in particular.
Upon arrival for the 30-minute tour, you'll
be awarded a mojito concocted from their
delicious product. The distillery also hosts
two-hour cocktail workshops (Monday and
Thursday; 1700B). Book ahead, mostly if
you need directions: it's 3km northeast of
Chalong Circle; turn right (east) at Phuket
Zoo signs, then it's signposted shortly after.

🏃 Activities

Boat Charters BOATING
(Map p634; Hat Rawai) Hat Rawai's waterfront
is a handy place to arrange boat charters
to the islands just offshore (which are pretty popular these days). Destinations include nearby Ko Bon (long-tail/speedboat
1200/2400B) and Coral Island (1800/3500B)
for quiet snorkelling; maximum eight passengers. Prices vary depending on your bargaining skills.

Moo·ay tai
Rawai is the epicentre of Phuket's
ever-growing *moo·ay tai* (Thai boxing, also
spelt *muay Thai*) mania, home to half a doz-
en schools where students (of all genders)
live and train traditional-style in camps with
professional *moo·ay tai* fighters. Popular

NATAI - PHUKET GETAWAY

Officially in Phang-Nga Province, Natai is still close enough to Phuket to be an easy day trip from the island. The broad, white-sand beach here is gorgeous and the main reason to visit is simply to escape the Phuket crowds and find a bit of solitude. There are a few places to stay in the area if you want to spend the night, from midrange hotels to ultra-exclusive luxury resorts. Some of the hotels provide bikes, a great way to explore the area. Natai is located 26km north of Phuket International Airport, just west of the town of Khok Kloi.

Natai is mostly known for its high-end resorts, all eye-wateringly expensive, but sprinkled around the area you'll also find some midrange options. Lantala Residence (☑083 421 0803; Khok Kloi; r from 1600B) is a family-run operation with several bungalows huddled over a pond, each room with hardwood floors, matching dark furniture and a large balcony. The friendly owners provide bicycles for the short bike ride to the beach or to the nearby Tesco supermarket for groceries. Aleenta (☑in Bangkok 02 514 8112; www.aleenta.com; 33 Mu 5, Ban Natai; r incl breakfast from 9400B; ✳ ☞ ⌨) is a boutique hotel with sleek loft-style rooms that spill out into shared infinity pools through floor-to-ceiling windows.

The resorts here pride themselves on their fine dining, and it is superb. A few local places cater to those on a more modest budget. Rabiang Lay Seafood Restaurant (☑061 238 2065; mains 150-400B; ⊙11am-10pm; ☞), for example, is a beachfront property with a relaxed vibe and an extensive menu featuring prawn cakes, seafood salads, steamed fish with lemon sauce, fish and chips and reasonably priced drinks. It's just about perfect for watching the sun set. Cash only.

Taxis to/from Phuket's airport cost 700B. Alternatively, you can rent a car at the airport (from 1000B per day) and drive here yourself.

schools include Kingka Muay Thai (Map p634; ☑076 226495; www.kingkamuaythai.com; 43/42 Mu 7, Soi Sai Yuan, Th Viset; per session/week 600/3000B; ⊙7am-7pm), Sinbi Muay Thai (Map p634; ☑093 690 3322; www.sinbi-muaythai. com; 100/15 Mu 7, Th Sai Yuan; per session/week 400/3000B; ⊙7.30am-6pm Mon-Sat, 9am-6pm Sun) and, in Chalong, Tiger Muay Thai (Map p622; ☑076 367071; www.tigermuaythai.com; 7/35 Mu 5, Soi Taiad, Chalong; per session/week 500/3500B; ⊙7am-7pm Mon-Sat).

Kitesurfing

Rawai is popular with kitesurfers from around November to April. Reliable operators include Kite Zone (Map p622; ☑083 395 2005; www.kitesurfthailand.com; Hat Friendship; 1hr lesson 1600B, 3-day course 10,000-15,000B; ⊙hours vary) and Kiteboarding Asia (Map p622; ☑081 591 4594; www.kiteboardingasia.com; 26/4 Th Viset; 1-/3-day course 4000/11,000B; ⊙9am-6pm Nov-Apr). During the April-to-October monsoon season, many local schools run sessions on Hat Nai Yang in northwest Phuket.

Yoga

Soothing Rawai is home to some of Phuket's most established yoga schools, including Ganesha Yoga Shala (Map p634; ☑089 868 2639; www.ganeshayogaphuket.com; 25/7 Soi Salika, Th Viset; class 350B; ⊙Sun-Fri).

🛏 Sleeping

Good 9 at Home   GUESTHOUSE $
(Map p634; ☑081 834 3898; www.good9athome. com; 62 Mu 6, Soi Wassana, Hat Rawai; d 800B; ✳ ☞) Set beside a pretty patio on a leafy street 300m north of Hat Rawai, these fresh, contemporary-style rooms spiced up with colour accent walls, tiled bathrooms and the odd bit of artwork make for good-value, friendly digs. The lime-green-and-grey house is cosy and spotless, with a little coffee corner and bikes to rent.

Rawai Beach Resort   HOTEL $$
(Map p634; ☑081 311 8189; www.rawaibeachresort. com; 42 Mu 6, Th Viset, Hat Rawai; d 1150-2500B; 🅿 ✳ ☞ ⌨) Just over the road from central Hat Rawai, amid lovely green grounds, this whitewashed, contemporary complex is filled with plain, bright, good-value rooms spread across three houses around a pool. 'Cosy' rooms are perfectly spacious, while 'Suites' are huge, with their own lounges; all have kettles, fridges and balconies. Staff are helpful and there's a small library.

Hat Nai Harn & Hat Rawai

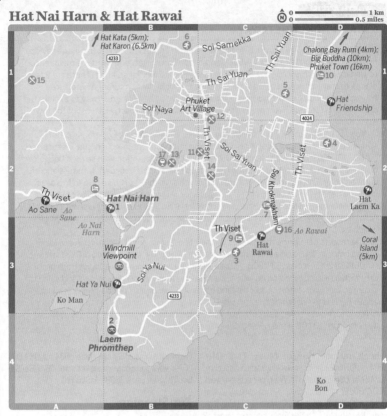

Vijitt RESORT $$$

(Map p634; ☎ 076 363600; www.vijittresort.com; 16 Mu 2, Th Viset, Hat Friendship; villas incl breakfast 6500-30,450B; P✻☎☒) Arguably Rawai's most elegant property, the peaceful Vijitt is strung around a garden sprinkled with frangipani trees. Villas boast limestone floors, large bathtubs, outdoor showers and gorgeous sea views from private terraces (some with their own pools). The stunning, multi-level, black-bottom infinity pool overlooks Hat Friendship.

Families are well looked after with multi-room villas and a kids club.

✗ Eating

Hat Rawai is lined with a dozen locally owned seafood grills sizzling fresh catch along the roadside (mains 90B to 300B) throughout the day. Seating is on plastic chairs or at low tables with blankets on the floor: it doesn't really matter which one you choose. All the fish is fresh, as are the crab, clams, mussels, squid, lobster and tiger prawns.

German Bakery EUROPEAN $

(Map p634; Th Viset; mains 80-200B; ☺7.30am-4.30pm) This fun, friendly, semi-outdoor restaurant does the best pastries in Rawai and remains a deservedly popular breakfast spot. It makes fine brown bread, excellent pineapple pancakes and French toast, plus decent bratwurst and sauerkraut.

Number 1 Thai Food THAI $

(Map p634; 83/40 Mu 2, Th Viset; mains 100-150B; ☺4pm-midnight) Don't let the humble roots fool you. This delightful garden cafe-restaurant run out of the chef's front yard serves some delicious Thai food: searing *pá·naang* curry (clotted with coconut cream), sticky tamarind prawns, spicy fish soup and fresh fish of the day, prepared grilled, steamed or fried.

Hat Nai Harn & Hat Rawai

★ **Natural Efe
Macrobiotic World**   VEGETARIAN $$
(Map p634; ☑ 076 390301; www.macrobiotic
world.com; 14/93-94 Mu 1, Th Viset; mains 140-
300B; ⊙ 9am-9pm; 🛜🍴) This chilled-out
health-food kitchen plates up such organic,
sugar-free vegan delights as tofu sandwich-
es, dried-fruits-and-quinoa salad, lentil soup
and breakfast bowls, at wooden tables set
around an aqua pool in its leafy back court-
yard. There's an all-you-can-eat organic
Saturday and Sunday buffet (300B) in high
season, as well as teas, freshly squeezed juic-
es and health drinks (including hemp milk).

Delish Cafe   CAFE $$
(Map p634; ☑ 076 388149; www.facebook.com/
DelishCafePhuket; 5/30 Th Viset; meals 140-210B;
⊙ 7.30am-5pm Mon-Sat; 🛜) Gorgeous home
made breakfasts involving Chiang Rai coffee
beans and avocados, artisan jams, mues-
li-fruit bowls, stuffed croissants and French
toast with homebaked mango on homebaked bread
are the draw at friendly Aussie-owned Del-
ish, one of Rawai's wonderful cafes. Choose
from seating at the flower-fringed roadside
terrace or in air-conditioning indoors.

Rock Salt   INTERNATIONAL $$$
(Map p634; ☑ 076 380200; www.thenaiharn.
com; 23/3 Mu 1, Th Viset, Hat Nai Harn; mains
500-850B; ⊙ 7.30-10am & 12.30-11pm; 🛜🍴)
Waves lap the rocks below your table at
this wonderfully scenic terrace restaurant
overlooking northern Hat Nai Harn. The
creative Mediterranean-Thai menu has
fun with seasonal, all-organic produce and
global influences, crafting pea-pesto pasta,
Rawai-seafood bouillabaisse and fish of the
day, served steamed or wood-fired. Char-
cuterie, cheeses, breads and yoghurts are

homemade, while the impressive wine list
includes Thai rosés.

It's part of the luxurious **Nai Harn resort**
(Map p634; ☑ 076 380200; www.thenaiharn.com;
23/3 Mu 1, Th Viset, Hat Nai Harn; d incl breakfast
6960-23,250B; 🅿❄🛜🏊), and makes a great
spot for a fancy coffee, cocktail or juice.

🍷 Drinking & Nightlife

Nikita's   BAR
(Map p634; ☑ 076 288703; www.nikitas-phuket.
com; Hat Rawai; ⊙ 9.30am-11pm; 🛜) This
long-running open-air hang-out gazes over
the sea just west of Rawai's pier and offers
reasonably priced beers and cocktails, as
well as coffee, green tea and a good selection
of shakes. A mango margarita, perhaps? If
you're hungry, there are wood-fired pizzas,
international mains and a lot of seafood.

Reggae Bar   BAR
(Map p634; Th Viset; ⊙ noon-late) Spilling out
from an old wooden shed, this creatively
cluttered lounge bobbing to classic roots
tunes is a leathersmiths by day, then later
hosts impromptu jams and erratic concerts,
barbecues and parties, featuring local reggae
bands and, occasionally, some of Thailand's
most legendary Rastas. Leather belts dangle,
art is plastered across walls and graffiti cov-
ers every inch of space. Opening hours vary.

It's on the northern side of Nai Harn Lake.

❶ Getting There & Away

The Phuket Smart Bus (p625) runs between
Rawai pier and Phuket International Airport
(p624; two hours) via Kata, Karon, Patong,
Kamala, Surin and Ao Bang Thao, roughly hourly
from 6am to 8.15pm; rates are 50B to 170B,
depending on where you hop off.

PHUKET & THE ANDAMAN COAST RAWAI

Sŏrng·tǎa·ou (passenger pick-up trucks) run to Rawai (30B) from Phuket Town's Th Ranong between 7am and 5.30pm. Some continue to Hat Nai Harn (40B, 8am to 6pm), but not all, so ask first.

Taxis run between Rawai/Hat Nai Harn and Phuket International Airport (1000B), Patong (700B) and Phuket Town (500B). Taxis from Rawai to Nai Harn cost 200B.

Hat Patong

♫ 076 / POP 20,900

Patong (ป่าตอง) is a free-for-all. It's by far Phuket's most notorious and divisive destination: between the concrete, silicone and moral turpitude, almost anything is available for the right price and, while that's true of other places in Thailand, Patong doesn't try to hide it. Of course, that doesn't mean you're going to like it; some people avoid this part of Phuket entirely.

Gaze out at the wide, white-sand beach and its magnificent crescent bay, however, and you'll understand how the whole thing started. Diving and spa opportunities abound, along with upscale dining, streetside fish grills, extravagant cabaret, Thai boxing, dusty antique shops and – Patong's main draw for many – the chance to party from dusk until dawn.

Meanwhile the sun-scorched visitors in bad knock-off T-shirts, the endless tour groups, the foreign men turning the midlife crisis into a full-scale industry and the overwhelming disregard for managed development make Patong ripe with unintentional comedy.

◎ Sights & Activities

★ Sea Fun Divers   DIVING
(Map p622; ☏ 081 367 4542; www.seafundivers. com; 29 Soi Karon Nui; 2-/3-dive trip 3900/4400B; ☺ 9am-6pm) Based at Le Méridien, just beyond the southern end of Patong, this is an excellent, professional diving operation, with high standards, impeccable service and enthusiastic, well-versed instructors (though it's a little more expensive than other dive operators). Snorkellers can join diving day trips for 2900B. PADI Open Water Diver certification costs 18,400B to 21,400B.

There's another branch in Kata (p641).

Let's Relax   SPA
(Map p638; ☏ 076 366800; www.letsrelaxspa.com; 184/14 Th Pangmuang Sai Kor; massage/treatment 300-4000B; ☺ 10am-midnight) The hushed atrium, infused with eucalyptus, is perfect for mulling over your relaxation strategy at this prize-winning Thailand-wide spa chain. Will it be foot reflexology, then a floral body scrub? A Thai herbal steam bath before a hot-stone massage and a facial? Or the all-in, half-day Day Dream package (4000B)?

There's another branch at the south end of town, plus one in Karon.

Nicky's Handlebar   ADVENTURE
(Map p638; ☏ 084 824 7777; www.nickyhandlebars. com; 41 Th Rat Uthit; 1-/2-day tour incl bike hire from 9000/21,000B; ☺ 7am-1am) The big-beast bikes here are begging to be taken for a spin, but they aren't for amateurs. Nicky has been leading Harley tours around Phuket and Phang-Nga for over a decade. Two-day itineraries tour Phang-Nga and Ranong Provinces. There are Harley rentals for independent explorations (from 4800B per day). You'll need a big-bike licence from home.

Hit the bar (p640) for post-ride refreshments.

Pum Thai Cooking School   COOKING
(Map p638; ☏ 076 346269; www.pumthaifood-chain.co.th; 204/32 Th Rat Uthit; 3/5hr class 1700/3700B; ☺ classes 11am, 4pm & 6pm) This restaurant/cookery school (with other branches in Thailand, as well as France and the UK) holds daily small-group classes. Popular, four-hour 'Little Wok' courses (2400B) include a market tour and a take-home cookbook, or pop in for a 30-minute, one-dish session (500B).

★ Festivals & Events

Phuket Pride Week   LGBT
(www.phuket-pride.org; ☺ Apr) Although Bangkok and Pattaya host big LGBTIQ+ pride celebrations, Phuket Pride is widely considered to be the best in Thailand, possibly even in Southeast Asia. Dates have changed several times since the festival's inception in 1999 (including a complete hiatus for 2018), but it's usually in late April. Revellers, mostly male, descend from all over the world, especially on Patong.

🛏 Sleeping

Patong's extensive accommodation ranges from cheerful guesthouses and party-hard hostels to high-end beachfront resorts. If you can't score a bed in a hostel (there are some good ones, but book ahead), you'll struggle to find a room for under 1000B

BIG BUDDHA

High atop the Nakkerd Hills, northwest of Chalong Circle, and visible from half the island, the 45m-high, Burmese-alabaster **Big Buddha** (พระใหญ่; Map p622; www.mingmongkol-phuket.com; off Rte 4021; ⊙ 6am-7pm; P) FREE sits grandly on Phuket's finest viewpoint. It's a tad touristy, but tinkling bells and flags mean there's an energetic pulse. Pay your respects at the golden shrine, then step up to the glorious plateau, where you can glimpse Kata's perfect bay, Karon's golden sands and, to the southeast, the pebble-sized channel islands of Ao Chalong.

Construction began on Big Buddha in 2007; all in all, the price tag, funded entirely by donations, is around 100 million baht (not that anybody minds).

From Rte 4021, follow signs 1km north of Chalong Circle to wind 5.5km west up a steep country road, passing terraces of banana groves and tangles of jungle. It's also possible to **hike** up to Big Buddha from Karon: a splendid, challenging, 2.5km climb through the jungle, starting from Soi Patak 14 and taking an hour or so. You'll need plenty of water and an early start.

between November and April. Rates drop significantly outside this time period.

★ **Lub*d**   HOSTEL $
(Map p638; ☑ 076 530100; www.lubd.com; 5/5 Th Sawatdirak; ⊙ incl breakfast dm 650B, d 2600-3200B; @ 🕲 ☒) A warehouse-like lobby doubling as a coworking space, a *moo·ay tai* (Thai boxing) ring and a pool/bar area give way to crisp, modern four-bed dorms with individual lockers, shelves, lights and plugs at this buzzy boutique hostel. Private en suite rooms are bright and stylish, especially white-and-blue 'Deluxes' with tiled bathrooms and island-inspired wall art; the best have hammock-strung balconies.

Slumber Party   HOSTEL $
(Map p638; ☑ 076 620414; www.slumberpar-tyhostels.com; off Th Rat Uthit; dm 300-450B; 🕲 🕲) Smartly revamped in 2017, this fun, friendly, party-hard chain hostel fills up fast (book ahead!). Stripped-back, clean en suite dorms sleep four, six or 10 people in tightly packed bunks with curtains, lights, shelves and plugs. But really you're here for the lively travellers' scene: beer pong, happy hour, ladies' night, pub crawls...

Patong Backpacker Hostel   HOSTEL $
(Map p638; ☑ 076 341196; www.patongbackpack-er.thailandhotels.site; 140 Th Thawiwong; dm 350-550B; 🕲 🕲) A great location just across the road from the beach, a communal lounge and welcoming staff are all appealing at this simple, clean budget pick. Dorms sleep four to 10 and come with good mattresses; lockers are at reception. It's very basic, but does the job at fair-enough rates for pricey Patong.

Priew Wan Guesthouse   GUESTHOUSE $$
(Map p638; ☑ 076 344441; www.priewwan.com; 83/9 Th Rat Uthit; d 1200B; 🕲 🕲) This long-running and reliable family-owned, yellow-washed guesthouse is only a 10-minute walk to the northern end of Hat Patong. It's hidden down a mostly residential soi along with a few food stalls. Though a little dated, it has sizeable, decently priced, well-scrubbed rooms with balcony, safe, fridge and TV. There are friendly staff and great low-season (April to October) discounts.

Armoni Patong Beach Hotel   HOTEL $$
(Map p638; ☑ 076 345727; armonihotel8@gmail.com; 92/12 Soi Permpong Pattana 3; d 1170-1800B; 🕲 🕲) At the end of a quietish soi, a few minutes' walk from the beach and Th Bangla, the Armoni has helpful staff and big, bright, clean rooms at competitive prices, though they aren't as exciting as the art-covered lobby suggests. The best include small balconies, but all come with decent beds, modern bathrooms, TVs, fridges and safety boxes.

★ **BYD Lofts**   APARTMENT $$$
(Map p638; ☑ 076 343024; www.bydlofts.com; 5/28 Th Hat Patong; 1-bedroom apt 5400-11,200B; 🕲 🕲 ☒) Spread across four buildings, BYD feels like it's been torn out of an upmarket interior-design magazine. Stylish and comfortable (and only a few minutes' walk from the beach), the apartments are coated in white and come with sharp lines, colourful art and balconies; some have private pools. For everyone else there's a turquoise rooftop pool, plus a smart cafe-lounge.

Hat Patong

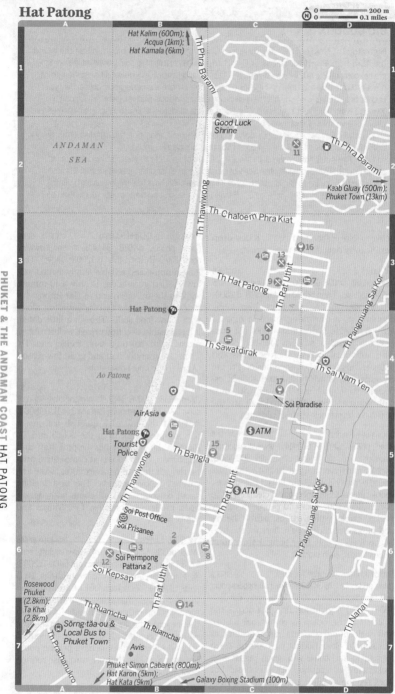

0   200 m
0   0.1 miles

Hat Kalim (600m);
Acqua (1km);
Hat Kamala (6km)

Th Phra Barami

ANDAMAN
SEA

Good Luck
Shrine

Th Phra Barami

Kaab Gluay (500m);
Phuket Town (13km)

Th Chaloem Phra Kiat

Th Thawiwong

4   13

16

Th Hat Patong

9   Th Rat Uthit   7

Hat Patong

5   10

Th Sawatdirak

Th Sai Nam Yen

17

Soi Paradise

Ao Patong

Th Pangmuang Sai Kor

AirAsia

Hat Patong   6

Tourist
Police

$ ATM

Th Bangla   15

$ ATM

Th Rat Uthit

1

Th Thawiwong

Soi Post Office

Soi Prisanee

2

3

Soi Permpong
Pattana 2

8

12

Soi Kepsap

Rosewood
Phuket
(2.8km);
Ta Khai
(2.8km)

Th Ruamchai   14

Th Rat Uthit

Th Nanai

Sörng·tǎa·ou &
Local Bus to
Phuket Town

Th Ruamchai

Th Prachanukro

Avis

Phuket Simon Cabaret (800m);
Hat Karon (5km);
Hat Kata (9km)

Galaxy Boxing Stadium (100m)

Hat Patong

✗ Eating

Patong has masses of restaurants for all budgets. The trick is to avoid the many watered-down Thai and poorly executed international kitchens. The swishest restaurants sit at the north end of town and just beyond around Hat Kalim, which has a night market. Bargain food stalls pop up at night; try **Patong Food Park** (Map p638; Th Rat Uthit; mains 50-200B; ⊙4.30pm-midnight) and the soi (lanes) around Th Bangla.

Chicken Rice Briley   THAI $
(Map p638; Th Rat Uthit, Patong Food Park; mains 50-200B; ⊙6am-9pm) This is one of few places in Patong Food Park (p639) to offer sustenance while the sun shines, and it's almost always busy. Steamed chicken breast is served on rice alongside a bowl of chicken broth with crumbled bits of meat; the chilli sauce is fantastic for dipping. The roasted pork and mango sticky rice are popular.

★ No 9 2nd Restaurant   INTERNATIONAL $$
(Map p638; ☑076 624445; 143 Th Phra Barami; mains 165-800B; ⊙11.30am-11.30pm; ☑) Deceptively simple, with wooden tables and photo-strewn walls, this is one of the best and busiest restaurants in Patong, thanks to its inventive and delicious mix of Thai, Japanese and Western dishes. It's a rare feat for a kitchen to serve real-deal sushi, vegetarian Thai curries and meats such as lamb shank without any dip in quality.

Kaab Gluay   THAI $$
(Map p622; ☑076 346832; 58/3 Th Phra Barami; mains 135-250B; ⊙11am-2am; ☎) At the north end of town, busy, semi-open-air roadside Kaab Gluay is a hit for its authentic, affordable Thai food, with switched-on staff to match the unpretentious dining under a huge roof with ceiling fans. Expect red-curry

prawns, chicken satay, sweet-and-sour fish, deep-fried honeyed chicken, classic noodles and stir-fries, and 30-plus takes on spicy Thai salads.

Orchids   THAI $$
(Map p638; ☑076 340462; 78/3-4 Soi Permpong Pattana 3; mains 85-380B; ⊙10am-11pm) Get fantastic Thai food in a homey, friendly setting with attentive staff. The *larb gai* (minced-chicken salad with chilli, mint and coriander) is delicious, and Orchids serves all your favourite noodle, rice, soup and curry classics, including *dôm yam gûng* (intensely spicy prawn soup). Eat in or take away.

★ Acqua   ITALIAN $$$
(Map p622; ☑076 618127; www.acquarestaurant phuket.com; 324/15 Th Phra Barami, Hat Kalim; mains 400-2000B, 8-course tasting menu 2500-3500B; ⊙5-11pm mid-Jun–late May; ☎☑) At Phuket's top Italian restaurant, amid sleek, monochrome decor, you can dine on homebaked focaccia, deliciously creamy buffalo mozzarella and house-made pumpkin-stuffed cappelletti coated in delicate Gorgonzola sauce. From expertly crafted pizza and pasta to sensational seafood blowouts, Sardinian chef Alessandro Frau's cooking is exquisitely executed and supremely sophisticated. Most of the produce is authentic imported Italian, accompanied by 400-plus wines.

★ Ta Khai   THAI $$$
(Map p622; ☑076 356888; www.rosewoodhotels. com; Rosewood Phuket, Th Muen-Ngern, Hat Tri-Trang; mains 290-900B, tasting menus 950-2200B; ⊙6pm-midnight; ☎☑) ✐ Inspired by traditional fishing-village architecture, with lotus ponds, a glassed-in pavilion and skilled Trang-born chefs, the outstanding, seaside southern Thai restaurant at the **Rosewood**

Phuket (villa incl breakfast 24,000-59,600B; P❄️📶🏊) 🍴 is a standout on Phuket's fine-dining scene. Fresh *sôm·dam* is pounded at your table; green vegetable curries, Phuket-style spring rolls, crabmeat yellow curries and Phuketian *mŏo hong* (pepper-and-garlic-braised pork) are beautifully spiced. Signature cocktails use homegrown herbs. It's 2.5km west of the far southern end of Hat Patong.

⭐**Naughty Nuri's in the Forest**   RIBS $$$
(Map p638; ☑️061 173 0011; www.facebook.com/nnphuket; 112 Th Rat Uthit; mains 250-2000B; ⏱noon-midnight) Meat lovers crowd out an enormous, semi-open, multiroom space with swaying rattan lamps at the hugely popular Phuket outpost of this Bali-born, Australian-Indonesian-owned ribs specialist. Make sure you order the signature barbecue spare ribs (1995B), though the spiced suckling pig is also a huge hit, and the Indonesian-international menu tempts with vegetarian nasi goreng and more.

🍸 **Drinking & Nightlife**

Some visitors may find that Patong's bar scene puts them right off their *pàt tai*, but if you're in the mood for pounding bass, winking neon and short skirts, it's certainly an experience.

Patong is also the centre of Phuket's LGBTIQ+ scene (p636), focused on Soi Paradise and the Royal Paradise Complex.

Th Bangla is beer, club and bar-girl central, featuring spectacular go-go extravaganzas with the usual mix of gyrating ladies and watching men. The techno is loud, the clothes are all but nonexistent and the decor is typically slapstick with plenty of phallic imagery. The atmosphere is more carnival than carnage and you'll find plenty of peers fighting through the throng to the bar.

Zag Club   GAY
(Map p638; www.facebook.com/phuket.zagclub; 123/8-9 Royal Paradise Complex; ⏱8pm-4am) Packed-out Soi Paradise favourite Zag Club hosts fabulous, shimmering LGBTIQ+ cabarets at midnight, 1.30am and at one or two other times. In between, everyone drinks and dances to booming chart-toppers. It's usually Patong's busiest gay bar.

Illuzion   CLUB
(Map p638; www.illuzionphuket.com; 31 Th Bangla; ⏱9pm-late) Still the most popular of Patong's megaclubs, Illuzion is a multilevel mishmash of dance and gymnastics shows, international DJs, reggaeton nights, all-night electronic beats, LED screens and more bars than you could ever count.

Nicky's Handlebar   BAR
(Map p638; ☑️084 824 7777; www.nickyhandlebars.com; 41 Th Rat Uthit; ⏱7am-1am; 📶) This fun biker bar welcomes all, wheels or not. Once a bit of a dive, Nicky's has never looked better. There's a good selection of beers and the menu encompasses Western and Thai cooking, including what the team claims is Thailand's spiciest burger. You can go for a ride here by asking about Harley tours and hire (p636).

Craft Beer Lounge   CRAFT BEER
(Map p638; www.grandmercurephuketpatong.com; Grand Mercure Phuket Patong, Soi Rat Uthit; ⏱10am-11pm) Tapping into one of the world's ongoing booze crazes, this sleekly contemporary boutique beer bar stocks more than 100 international craft labels, mostly from the US, plus local brands. The bartenders also make proper cocktails, including Chalong Bay Rum mojitos. Happy hour runs from 6pm to 8pm. The lounge is tucked into the back of the Grand Mercure's lobby.

☆ **Entertainment**

Phuket Simon Cabaret   CABARET
(Map p622; ☑️087 888 6888; www.phuket-simon-cabaret.com; 8 Th Sirirach; adult 800-1000B, child 600-800B; ⏱shows 6pm, 7.30pm & 9pm) About 500m south of Patong, Simon puts on colourful cabarets that are wildly popular with (and now slightly catered towards) tour groups. The 600-seat theatre is grand, the costumes are feather-and-sequin extravaganzas, and the LGBTIQ+ performers are convincing. The house is usually full – book ahead.

Galaxy Boxing Stadium   SPECTATOR SPORT
(Map p622; www.galaxyboxingstadium.com; Th Phra Metta/Rte 4055; stadium/ringside 1700/2000B; ⏱9pm Tue) This stadium has a packed line-up of competitive *moo·ay tai* (Thai boxing) bouts featuring Thai and foreign fighters.

🛈 **Getting There & Away**

There's an **AirAsia** (Map p638; www.airasia.com; 39 Th Thawiwong; ⏱11am-9.30pm) office in Patong.

The new Phuket Smart Bus (p625) links Patong with Karon, Kata, Rawai, Kamala, Surin,

Ao Bang Thao and Phuket International Airport (approximately hourly 6.41am to 9.18pm, 50B to 170B). In Patong it stops by the beach at the western end of Th Bangla on the way to the airport and outside Jung Ceylon on the way from the airport.

There's also a shared minibus from the airport to Patong (180B, minimum 11 people).

Sŏrng·tăa·ou (Map p638; Th Thawiwong) (passenger pick-up trucks) from Th Ranong in Phuket Town go to the south end of Hat Patong (30B) from 7.30am to 6pm. From here you can walk or hop on motorbike taxis (30B per ride) or túk-túk.

A **local bus** (Map p638; Th Thawiwong) (30B) and minivans (50B) run between Phuket Town's Bus Terminal 1 (p624) and southern Patong from 7am to 5pm.

Taxis to/from the airport cost 800B. After-hours túk-túk (*dúk dúk*) charters from Phuket Town cost 500B.

ⓘ Getting Around

A túk-túk will circle Patong for around 200B per ride.

Numerous places rent motorbikes (250B per day); Nicky's Handlebar (p636) rents Harleys (from 4800B per day). The mandatory helmet law is strictly enforced in Patong, where roadblocks/checkpoints can spring up suddenly. **Avis** (Map p638; 062 604 0361; www.avist-hailand.com; Baumanburi Hotel, 239/1 Th Rat Uthit; 7.30am-9pm) has rental cars at the southern end of Patong. There's a **petrol station** (Map p638; Th Phra Barami; 24hr) at the northern end.

Hat Kata

Classier than nearby Karon and without Patong's seedy hustle, Hat Kata (หาดกะตะ) attracts travellers of all kinds to its lively, beautiful twin beaches. While you won't bag a secluded strip of sand, you'll find lots to do. A prime spot for surfing in the shoulder and monsoon seasons, Kata also has some terrific spas, good food, a highly rated yoga studio and excellent accommodation offerings. Its sandy white-gold beach is carved in two by a rocky outcrop: Hat Kata Yai (หาดกะตะใหญ่; Map p642) lies on the north side; more secluded Hat Kata Noi (หาดกะตะน้อย; Map p642) unfolds to the south. The road between them is home to Phuket's original millionaire's row.

The main Th Kata runs parallel to the beach. There are cheaper restaurants, bars and guesthouses on Th Thai Na, which branches inland just south of where Th

Kata heads up over the hill into scruffier Karon. The southern part of Kata is the most sophisticated.

⊙ Sights & Activities

Both of Kata's beaches offer decent surfing from April to November; one-hour private classes cost 1200B and board rental is 200/800B per hour/day.

Hiring stand-up paddleboarding (SUP) kits or kayaks costs 300/900B per hour/day.

Be careful of rip currents, heed the red flags and don't go past the breakers in the rainy season unless you're a strong, experienced swimmer.

Ko Pu   ISLAND
(เกาะปู; Map p622) The small, uninhabited, jungle-clad islet of Ko Pu glistens across the waves just off Hat Kata Yai (p641), making for gorgeous sunsets.

Sea Fun Divers   DIVING
(Map p622; 076 330124; www.seafundivers. com; Katathani, 14 Th Kata Noi; 2-/3-dive trip 3900/4400B; 9am-6pm) An outstanding and very professional diving operation, albeit slightly more expensive than the competition. Standards are extremely high, service is impeccable and instructors are keen and knowledgeable. PADI Open Water Diver certification costs 18,400B to 21,400B. Snorkellers are welcome to tag along on day trips (2900B).

Rumblefish Adventure   DIVING
(Map p642; 095 441 8665; www.rumblefish adventure.com; 98/79 Beach Centre, Th Kata/Patak West; 2-dive trip 3500-4500B; 9am-7pm) This terrific boutique dive shop offers all the standard courses, day trips and liveaboards from its Beach Centre location in Kata. The PADI Discover Scuba is 4500B; the PADI Open Water Diver certification course costs from 10,900B. There's a small, popular **hostel** (Map p642; 095 441 8665; www. rumblefishadventure.com; 98/79 Beach Centre, Th Kata/Patak West; dm 350B, d 800-950B; ❄🜚) attached: divers get substantial discounts or in some cases free accommodation. Book ahead.

Baray Spa   SPA
(Map p642; 076 330979; www.phuketsawasdee. com; Sawasdee Village, 38 Th Kade Kwan; massage/ treatment 1200-5000B; 10am-10pm) Hidden away in a lush tropical garden full of interwoven canals and gushing waterfalls, this is a quality spa with a sophisticated, romantic

edge. Keep it classic with a traditional Thai massage or spice things up with a full-body coffee scrub, a seaweed bust-firming treatment or a rehydrating facial.

Nautilus Dive & Surf Shop   SURFING, KAYAKING
(Map p642; ☑ 076 330229; www.phuketsurfing. com; 186/1 Th Kata Noi, Hat Kata Yai; class 1200B, board rental per hour/day 200/800B; ⊙ 9am-6pm) Based at southern Hat Kata Yai, Nautilus offers surfboard hire and private one-hour surf lessons, as well as stand-up paddleboarding (SUP) classes and kayak rental (per hour/day 300/900B). It also runs dives to offshore islands and the Ko Phi-Phi area (two-dive day trips 2900B). Check the website for info on local surf breaks.

Boathouse Cooking Class   COOKING
(Map p642; ☑ 076 330015; www.boathouse-phuket. com; 182 Th Koktanod; classes 2570-4450B; ⊙ hours vary) Kata's top fine-dining restaurant, Boathouse (p644), offers fantastic four-course, one-day and two-day Thai cooking classes, taking in a trip to the local market.

🛏 Sleeping

Kata has a good spread of accommodation to suit most styles and budgets. Good hostels and guesthouses cluster near the north end of Kata, where it flows into Karon, while fancier hotels and resorts lie further south, spilling over into Hat Kata Noi.

If you're stuck without shelter, you'll probably find a room at the Beach Centre, a complex of townhouses packed with many guesthouses. From Th Kata, turn inland just south of the intersection with Th Thai Na; it's signposted.

★ Fin Hostel   HOSTEL $
(Map p642; ☑ 088 753 1162; www.finhostelphuket. com; 100/20 Th Kata/Patak West; dm 300-600B, capsules 300-1000B, d 1500-3000B; ☀ 🛜 🏊) Set back from the road, this on-the-ball surf-inspired hostel spreads across two buildings. Dorms (including women-only) are spotless, with comfy mattresses and personal light and plugs; curtained single or double capsules are a step up. Colourful private rooms have beanbags and fridge, and there's a communal area/coworking space plus a small rooftop pool – all walking distance from Kata's beaches.

Kata Beach Homestay   HOSTEL $
(Map p642; ☑ 089 189 9066; www.kata-beach-homestay-th.book.direct; 9 Th Kade Kwan; dm

Hat Karon & Hat Kata

350B, d 600-900B; ☀ 🛜) This welcoming, rather anonymous hostel-guesthouse offers cheap sleeps in an eight-bed dorm with two bathrooms. Clean, compact doubles (some brighter than others), with colourful cushions and walls and either shared or private bathrooms, have a little more character. There's a large communal lounge with free tea and coffee. Enter through the ground-floor travel agency.

OZO Phuket   HOTEL $$
(Map p642; ☑ 076 563600; www.ozohotels.com; Hat Kata; r 3250B; ☀ 🛜 🏊) Opened in 2019, this block of modernity has a large open-air

Hat Karon & Hat Kata

reception and comfortable rooms with Scandinavian simplicity and modern touches like USB ports in walls. There's a quiet garden and pool area with a water slide, gym and kids' play area. It's superbly located a two-minute walk from the beach and is close to Kata's busy nightspots and restaurants.

Sugar Ohana GUESTHOUSE $$
(Map p642; ☑083 696 9697; 88/5 Th Kata/Patak West; d 2500-3000B) From the crisp, fresh, contemporary rooms to the stylish, tile-floored, low-key cafe, this warm little guesthouse on central Kata's main road ticks all the boutiquey 'poshtel' boxes. Bright, spacious, pristine rooms come with desks, slippers, subway tiles, plenty of natural light and, in some case, private balconies.

★**Kata Rocks** DESIGN HOTEL $$$
(Map p642; ☑076 370777; www.katarocks.com; 186/22 Th Koktanod; d 21,400-33,200B; ⓟ☀☎☲) This contemporary all-white beauty, poised on cliffs between Kata's two beaches, is known for its superyacht scene. Villas are minimalist-chic apartments with iPad-controlled sound systems, full kitchens, capsule-coffee machines, private pools and contemporary artwork. Semi-submerged sunbeds dot the pale-turquoise sea-view infinity pool. The innovative Infinite Luxury Spa blends traditional therapies with bang-up-to-date technology, while the sea-vista restaurant (mains 350-1600B; ⊙6.30-10.30am, 11am-5.30pm & 6pm-midnight; ☎☲) is excellent.

Nonguests can book day passes (high/low season 5000/3500B) to use the pool, with fees going towards food, drinks and the spa.

★**Sawasdee Village** RESORT $$$
(Map p642; ☑076 330979; www.phuketsawasdee.com; 38 Th Kade Kwan; d 4000-15,000B; ☀☎☲) This glittery boutique-feeling resort mixes classic Thai style with Moroccan-esque flourishes, immersed in a lush tropical landscape with canals, pools, waterfalls, Buddhist art and the stunning Baray Spa (p641). Ornate bungalows aren't huge but have supercomfy beds, wooden floors, beamed ceilings and lots of character. Villas are two-floor homes with hot tubs and direct access to one of two romantic pools.

✖ Eating

Kata BBQ THAI $
(Map p642; www.facebook.com/katabbq; Hat Kata Yai; meals 80-350B; ⊙8am-10.30pm; ☎) Hot-pink tablecloths, white plastic chairs and a smiling team keep the scene down-to-earth at beachside Kata BBQ, one of several affordable Thai seafood spots tucked into southern Hat Kata Yai. Tasty, simple stir-fried veg noodles, crab with yellow curry, ginger-fried prawns and massaman curries are delivered to a soundtrack of tumbling waves.

★**Istanbul Restaurant** TURKISH $$
(Map p642; ☑091 820 7173; www.istanbulrestaurantphuket.com; 100/87 Th Koktanod; meals 120-320B; ⊙9am-10pm Tue-Sat) This delightful

family-run place is the most popular foreign restaurant in Kata and for good reason. The food is simply splendid, ranging from big Western- or Turkish-style breakfasts to completely authentic and supertasty mains such as *hünkar beğendi* (beef stew on a bed of eggplant puree), kebabs and Turkish *pide*. Then there are the superb soups, salads and delectable desserts. It's 700m inland down Th Koktanod from the junction with Th Kata.

★ **Red Duck** THAI $$
(Map p642; ☑ 084 850 2929; www.facebook.com/redduckrestaurant; 88/3 Th Koktanod; mains 240-380B; ☺ noon-11pm, closed Mon May-Sep; ☎ ☑) Dishes at this hidden-away eatery with a tiny terrace are more expensive than at Kata's other Thai restaurants, but they're delicious, MSG-free and prepared with the freshest of ingredients. The seafood curries and soups are especially fine. Many of the Thai classics can be done in vegan versions, such as beautifully spiced veggie-packed massaman or vegetable *larb*. The service is excellent. It's 600m inland from the southern end of Hat Kata Yai.

Sabai Corner MULTICUISINE $$
(Map p634; ☑ 089 875 5525; www.sabaicorner phuket.com; Soi Laem Mum Nai, off Rte 4233; mains 160-490B; ☺ 10am-10pm; ☎) There's no better Phuket view than the one you'll glimpse from Sabai Corner's wide deck: all the way to Karon in one direction and an endless horizon of blue ocean rippling around the island in the other. The food isn't bad either, from fried rice, grilled fish and searing Thai curries, to salads, pastas and popular wood-fired pizza. From Kata, head 3km south towards Rawai/Hat Nai Harn on Rte 4233, turn downhill right behind Karon Viewpoint and drive 1.5km.

★ **Boathouse** INTERNATIONAL $$$
(Map p642; ☑ 076 330015; www.boathousephuket. com; 182 Th Koktanod; mains 250-1500B; ☺ noon-11pm) It's all very glam at the luxurious, beachside Boathouse, one of Phuket's most respected restaurants. The Thai/Mediterranean food (garlic-grilled tiger prawns, lamb-shank massaman, Australian-beef-tenderloin carpaccio) is fabulous, the wine list famously expansive, the service attentive and the sea views sublime. Special sharing platters are prepared at your table, and there are daily-changing set menus (930B to 1750B).

🍷 Drinking & Nightlife

★ **Art Space Cafe & Gallery** BAR
(Map p642; ☑ 090 156 0677; Th Kade Kwan; ☺ noon-midnight) Hands down the most fabulously quirky bar in Phuket, this trippy, multi-use space bursts with colour and is smothered in uniquely brushed canvases and sculptures celebrating, especially, the feminine form. It's the work of the creative Mr Pan and his tattoo-artist wife, who whip up both cocktails and veggie meals (160B to 400B). There's normally live music at around 8pm.

★ **Ska Bar** BAR
(Map p642; www.skabar-phuket.com; 186/12 Th Koktanod; ☺ 1pm-2am) Tucked into the rocks on the southernmost curl of Hat Kata Yai and seemingly intertwined with the trunk of a grand old banyan tree, laid-back, Rasta-vibe Ska is our choice for seaside sundowners, served by welcoming Thai bartenders. Buoys, paper lanterns and flags dangle from the canopy, and there are often fire shows.

After Beach Bar BAR
(Map p642; ☑ 084 745 9365; Rte 4233; ☺ 11am-10pm) It's impossible to overstate how glorious the 180-degree views are from this stilted, thatched reggae bar clinging to a cliff above Kata: rippling sea, rocky peninsulas and palm-sprinkled hills. Throw in Bob Marley tunes and you have the perfect sunset-watching spot. When the fireball finally drops, fishing-boat lights blanket the horizon. Try the bursting-with-flavour *pàt tai* (dishes 100B to 400B).

ℹ Getting There & Around

Minibuses run from Phuket International Airport to Kata (200B, minimum 11 people).

Stopping in northern Kata, the Phuket Smart Bus (p625) links Kata with Karon, Patong, Rawai, Kamala, Surin, Ao Bang Thao and the airport (roughly hourly from 6.20am to 8.35pm, 50B to 170B).

Sŏrng·tăa·ou (Map p642; cnr Th Kata & Th Pak Bang) (passenger pick-up trucks) run between Kata and Th Ranong in Phuket Town (40B) from around 7am to 5pm.

Taxis (p644) from Kata go to Phuket's airport (1200B), Phuket Town (600B), Patong (500B) and Karon (300B).

Motorbike rentals (250B per day) are widely available. Taxis charge 200B between Kata Yai and Kata Noi.

Hat Karon

Despite Karon's large resorts, it still has more sand space per capita than Patong or Kata and remains popular with families. The further north you go the more beautiful the broad golden beach gets, culminating at the northernmost edge (accessible from a rutted road past the roundabout) where the water is like turquoise glass.

Hat Karon (หาดกะรน) is like the love child of Hat Patong and Hat Kata: chilled-out and starry-eyed but a tad sleazy. Within the inland network of streets and plazas you'll find a jumble of decent local food, more Russian signage than seems reasonable, low-key girly bars and holiday-T-shirt vendors. Towards the more package-touristy north end of the town sits Karon Park, with its artificial lake and mountain backdrop, and the local temple. Southern Karon, meanwhile, blends into more sophisticated Kata.

◉ Sights & Activities

Hat Karon BEACH
(Map p642) This 4km-long west-coast stretch of squeaky-fine sand is popular with families and, while it does get busy, there's always plenty of space to spread out.

During the April-to-October low season, you can take surf lessons (one hour 1200B) and rent surfboards/bodyboards (per hour 250/100B) at its south end.

Big Buddha Hike HIKING
(Map p642; Soi Patak 14) From Karon's Soi Patak 14 (opposite Karon Plaza), a challenging, worthwhile one-hour, 2.5km hike climbs through the lush jungle to the main road just below Big Buddha (p637). Follow the red-and-white signs. Just after the road forks, a dirt path branches off; it's steep initially, but soon you're zig-zagging under shady trees, with ropes to help you up.

Bring water and start early to beat the heat.

Dive Asia DIVING
(Map p642; ☑076 330598; www.diveasia. com; 23/6 Th Karon/Patak West; 2-/3-dive trip 3400/3900B; ⊙10am-9pm) A well-established, long-standing diving outfitter offering a wide range of PADI certification courses (three-day Open Water Diver 9900B) plus day-trip dives to Ko Phi-Phi and liveaboards to the Similan and Surin Islands (from 23,000B).

Sunrise Divers DIVING
(Map p642; ☑084 626 4646, 076 398040; www. sunrise-divers.com; 269/24 Th Patak East; 3-dive trip 3700B, liveaboard per day from 4900B; ⊙10am-6pm daily Nov-Apr, to 4pm Mon-Fri May-Oct) Managed by long-time local blogger Jamie Monk, Phuket's biggest liveaboard agent organises a range of budget to luxury multiday dives to Ko Phi-Phi, the Similan and Surin Islands, Myanmar's Mergui Archipelago and Komodo and Raja Ampat in Indonesia. It also does day-trip dives, including to Ko Phi-Phi and the Similans.

The Spa SPA
(Map p642; ☑076 396139; www.movenpick. com; Mövenpick Resort, 509 Th Karon/Patak West; massage/treatment 1500-2000B; ⊙9am-9pm) Rooms trail off a tree-shaded tropical garden and bowls of frangipanis lie strewn around: this is one of Karon's most ambience-filled spas. Your mind will be revitalised and your body scrubbed with tamarind, wrapped in coconut and given a glow with Dead Sea salts. Get romantic with 2½-hour couples' packages (6700B).

🛏 Sleeping

Doolay Hostel HOSTEL $
(Map p642; ☑062 451 9546; www.doolayhostel. com; 164 Th Karon/Patak West; dm 600B; ❋ 🛜) Bunks are spread across compact four-, six- and eight-bed dorms at this modern, friendly hostel just across the road from the beach. There are good mattresses, lockers, plugs and shelves; one dorm is female-only. There's a bright communal area plus a kitchen, all-day cafe and a 2nd-floor seafront terrace strewn with beanbags. Book ahead.

Chanalai Hillside Resort HOTEL $$
(Map p622; www.chanalai.com; 10 Th Patak; r 2400B; ❋ 🛜 ≋) This high-rise building set around a large pool sports terrific sea views from every angle, though they're best from the smaller rooftop pool. Rooms are clean and modern, and feature glassed-off bathtubs, king-size beds and rain showers. The slightly off-beach location provides quiet nights but is still close to restaurants and amenities. The staff are helpful and attentive. Great low-season discounts.

Karon Sino House HOTEL $$
(Map p642; ☑089 726 4990; www.karonsinohouse. com; 448/1 Th Patak East; d 1600B) Just steps from Wat Suwan Khiri Ket, this modern hotel designed in simple Sino-Portuguese style

emphasises clean, comfy, uncluttered rooms, with fridges and small balconies. Colourful tiles adorn concrete floors and doors are washed in orangey-red. Service hits the balance between friendly and efficient, and there are motorbikes for rent. Though viewless, it's a good-value choice with more character than its neighbours.

Marina Phuket RESORT $$$
(Map p642; ☑ 076 330625; www.marinaphuket.com; 47 Th Karon; d 6500-22,000B; P ✳ 🛜 ⛱) Stilted boardwalks lead through lush, hushed gardens to comfy, secluded sea- and jungle-facing rooms decked out in a classic Thai style. All enjoy breezy terraces, warm-wood decor, teak furniture and silk throws, while villas have hot tubs. There's a big pool fed by waterfalls, along with a spa, courteous service and no fewer than four restaurants.

✖ Eating

There are reliable if not especially exciting Thai and seafood places at the north end of Hat Karon and on the beachfront road near south Hat Karon. For Karon's best culinary finds, head to the main Th Patak East just inland. Hat Kata's restaurants are also within easy reach.

★ Pad Thai Shop THAI $
(Map p642; Th Patak East; mains 50-80B; ⊘ 8am-6pm Sat-Thu) This glorified roadside food shack makes absurdly good *kôw pàt ƀoo* (fried rice with crab), *pàt see·ew* (fried noodles), chicken stew and noodle soup. It also serves up some of the best *pàt tai* we've tasted: spicy and sweet, packed with tofu, egg and peanuts, and plated with spring onions, bean sprouts and lime. Don't miss the house-made chilli sauces.

★ Highway Curry NORTH INDIAN $$
(Map p642; ☑ 083 024 3015; www.highwaycurry.com; 375/2 Th Patak East; mains 180-320B; ⊘ 11am-11pm; 🛜🍴) For a break from Thai flavours, this low-key, orange-walled, Indian-owned restaurant with wooden tables by the roadside rustles up delicately spiced North Indian curries, mopped up with doughy *nan*. There's an impressive vegetarian selection, from samosas and pakora to *aloo jeera, shahi paneer* and *chana masala*. Helpful staff, and takeaway is available.

★ Eat Bar & Grill GRILL $$$
(Map p642; ☑ 085 292 5652; www.eatbargrill.com; 250/1 Th Patak East; mains 200-900B; ⊘ 11am-

10pm Mon-Sat; 🛜) Expect awesome burgers and superb steaks, perhaps the best on Phuket, at this laid-back, busy grill specialist with a wooden bar, concrete walls and limited space (book ahead). The menu includes other dishes (pasta, lamb shank), but beef is the thing: prepared to your taste, stylishly presented and fairly priced, given the quality. There are proper cocktails and coffee.

❶ Getting There & Around

Stopping at Karon Circle and southern Karon/northern Kata, the new Phuket Smart Bus (p625) links Karon with Kata, Patong, Rawai, Kamala, Surin, Ao Bang Thao and Phuket International Airport (p624) (roughly hourly, 6.28am to 8.43pm, 50B to 170B).

Minibuses run from the airport to Karon (200B, minimum 11 people).

Sŏrng·tăa·ou (Map p642; Th Hat Kata/Patak West) (passenger pick-up trucks) run frequently between Hat Karon and Th Ranong in Phuket Town (40B) from 7.30am to 6pm.

Taxis (p646) from Karon go to Phuket airport (1000B), Phuket Town (550B), Patong (400B) and Kata (300B).

Motorbikes are available to rent (250B per day) from tour operators.

Hat Kamala

A chillexd-out hybrid of grittier Karon and glitzier Surin, Kamala (หาดกมลา) is home to a large Muslim population, and lures in a mix of longer-term, low-key visitors, including families, retirees and young couples. The sweeping golden bay is magnificent and serene, with palms and pines mingling on its leafy, rocky northern end, where the water is a rich emerald green and the snorkelling around the rock reef is halfway decent. The entire beach is backed by a paved path and lush rolling hills, though development is creeping in. Flashy resorts are carved into Kamala's southern bluffs, jet skis make an appearance, and the arrival of two glam new beach clubs at the northern end of the bay spells an upmarket swing – but for now at least, most of Kamala remains relatively laid-back by Phuket standards.

◉ Sights & Activities

During the May-to-October monsoon you can hire surfboards (300B per hour) and paddleboards (400B per hour) and take surf classes (1500B) on **Hat Kamala** (หาดกมลา; Map p648).

Tsunami Memorial
MEMORIAL

(อนุสรณ์สถานสึนามิ; Map p648) Kamala was one of Phuket's worst-hit areas during the 2004 Boxing Day tsunami. The 2006 Heart of the Universe Memorial pays tribute to lost loved ones with a moving, wave-inspired metallic oval created by prominent Thai artist Udon Jiraksa. It's set in a small palm-sprinkled park.

Mala Spa
SPA

(Map p622; ☎076 358777; www.keemala.com; 10/88 Mu 6, Th Nakasud; massage 2900-5500B; ☺9am-9pm) ☞ Expert therapists and organic, cruelty-free products are combined to deliver sensational, tradition-meets-innovation treatments at this fabulous spa, set within the fairy-tale-like Keemala resort, 2km inland (south) from Kamala. Massages, facials, body scrubs and wraps, aromatherapy baths and healing therapies happen in oversized, bamboo-laced, nest-inspired huts with outdoor showers. Try the 90-minute detoxifying organic-seaweed-leaf wrap.

🛏 Sleeping

Baan Kamala
HOSTEL, GUESTHOUSE $

(Map p648; ☎076 279053; www.baankamala phuket.com; 74/42 Soi Pajak, Mu 3; dm 450-550B, d 2000B; ✳@☎) A hostel-guesthouse hybrid, welcoming Baan Kamala offers big, light six-bed dorms (with sheets and towels) for backpackers and a collection of individually designed private rooms for flashpackers. The concrete walls of the spacious rooms are livened up with paintings and murals. Beds are comfortable, though bathrooms are a little poky. The communal lounge features a cushion-laden long-tail boat.

Kamala Resotel
BOUTIQUE HOTEL $$

(Map p648; ☎063 464 6409; www.kamala-resotel. com; 68/16 Mu 3; r 1700-2200B; ✳☀) Rising up from a narrow road, this art deco building with curved balconies overflowing with vines is topped with a wonderful rooftop pool that affords stunning views of Kamala. Rooms feature modern furnishings, frost-glass bathrooms and floating beds, although these may be too hard for some tastes. The friendly staff offer a warm welcome and provide a fruit-filled breakfast. Low-season discounts make this a great option.

★ Keemala
RESORT $$$

(Map p622; ☎076 358777; www.keemala.com; 10/88 Mu 6, Th Nakasud; villas incl breakfast 22,200-31,600B; P✳☀☎☀) ☞ Built into a lush hillside 2km inland from Kamala, this soothing, ecoconscious, fantasy-inspired beauty is one of Phuket's most original, sought-after and Instagram-loved resorts, with a splash of Tolkien-esque magic. Stay in cocoon-like, clay-cottage private-pool villas; glammed-up tents with open-air baths; bird's-nest-like hideaways; or tree houses that appear suspended. The excellent Mala Restaurant (Map p622; ☎076 358777; www. keemala.com; 10/88 Mu 6, Th Nakasud; mains 300-800B; ☺7am-10pm; ☎☞) ☞ uses garden-fresh ingredients, and there's the divine Mala Spa.

🍴 Eating & Drinking

Isaan Popeye Thai Food
THAI $

(Map p648; 74/43 Mu 3; mains 80-250B; ☺9.30am-10pm; ☎) One of the few restaurants in Kamala where you'll find locals dining, thanks to the winning combination of authentic and spicy northeastern dishes, fresh seafood and classic stir-fries and noodles, including omelette-wrapped *pàt tai*. This welcoming, straightforward spot also does Western-style breakfasts. It's 500m (a five-minute walk) inland from the beach.

Mam's Restaurant
MULTICUISINE $$

(Map p648; ☎089 032 2009; 32/32 Soi 8, Th Hua Khuan Tai; mains 100-350B; ☺noon-10pm; ☞) There's no beach view, but local expats swear by this quiet, simple place with a handful of tables sprinkled across the patio of a family home. Mam's plates up Thai favourites in flavourful meat, shrimp or veggie versions (including excellent, vegetable-packed massaman curries), plus burgers, pastas, kebabs and even fish and chips. It's 400m east (inland) from the main highway.

Taste Bar & Grill
MULTICUISINE $$$

(Map p648; ☎087 886 6401; www.tastebargrill. com; Th Rim Hat; mains 290-590B; ☺6am-late; ☎☞) Amid colourful boards of chalked-up specials, this elegant terrace restaurant turns out fabulously fresh pizza-oven flat-breads garnished with delectable fusion toppings such as grilled aubergine with Thai basil and melted mozzarella, plus imaginative plates such as tamarind-glazed white snapper or goat's-cheese salad with smoked almonds. Tapas-style bites (99B to 199B) roam from mushroom bruschetta to mango sticky rice.

Hat Kamala, Hat Surin & Ao Bang Thao

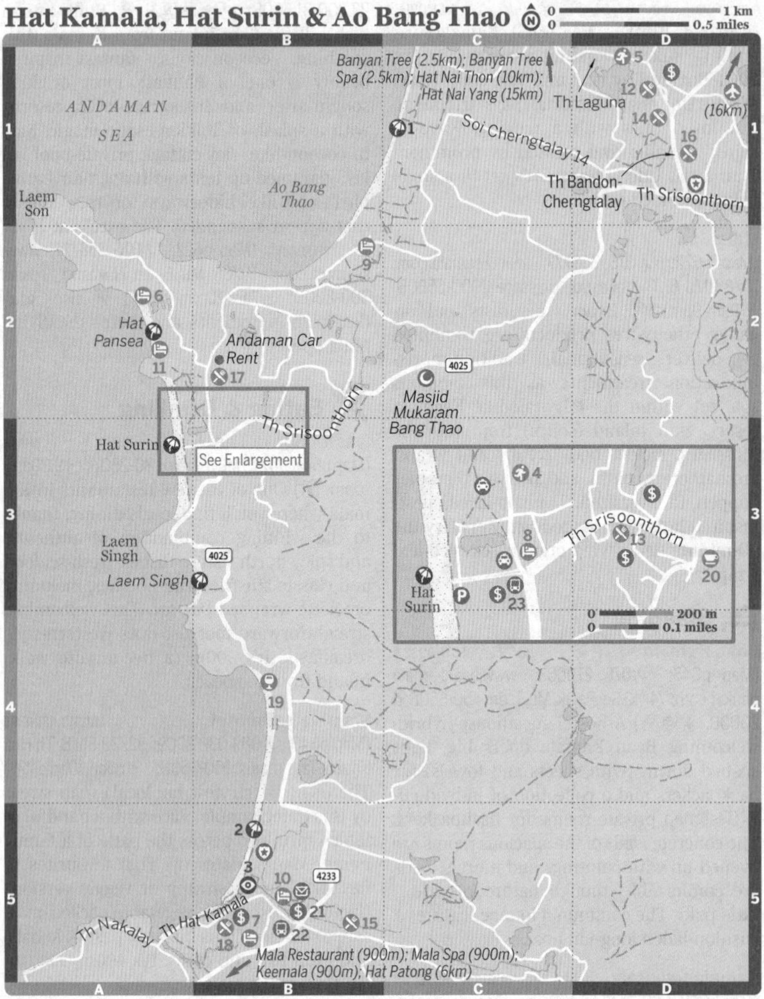

936 Coffee CAFE

(Map p648; ☎081 256 7071; 93/6 Mu 3; ⏰8.30am-10pm; 📶) This hole-in-the-wall cafe on the main drag serves up icy drinks, fresh fruit shakes, light breakfasts, sandwiches and delicious desserts in a fun and friendly atmosphere. The real reason to visit is for the perfectly brewed cups of hot and cold coffees that will satisfy even the snobbiest of coffee snobs. It can get busy so arrive early.

Café del Mar LOUNGE

(Map p648; ☎081 188 1230; www.cafedelmarphuket.com; 118/19 Mu 3; ⏰11am-2am) Ibiza's world-famous, original sunset-gazing brand brings its signature glam-chillout vibe to Phuket with this bold, distressed-concrete beach club on northern Hat Kamala. Hot-orange umbrellas and white-chic daybeds are strung around a gleaming pool; a multi-tiered terrace hosts DJ sessions and Sunday brunches (from 1860B). Cold-meats platters, tiger-prawn pastas and massaman curries mingle on the world-wandering menu (290B to 900B).

ℹ Getting There & Around

Stopping at the Big C supermarket on Kamala's main highway, the Phuket Smart Bus (p625)

Hat Kamala, Hat Surin & Ao Bang Thao

links Kamala with Patong, Karon, Kata, Rawai, Surin, Ao Bang Thao and Phuket International Airport (roughly hourly from 6.46am to 9.16pm, fares 50B to 170B).

Sŏrng·tăa·ou (Map p648; Rte 4233) (passenger pick-up trucks) run between Phuket Town's Th Ranong and Kamala (40B) from 7am to 5pm, and also between Kamala and Hat Surin (20B).

Taxis cost 700B to/from the airport and around 200B to 300B to/from Surin.

Hat Surin

With a wide, blonde beach, water that blends from pale turquoise in the shallows to a deep blue on the horizon, and lush, boulder-strewn headlands, Hat Surin (หาดสุรินทร์) is one of Phuket's most attractive spots. It's very much (though *not* exclusively) an upmarket destination, attracting cashed-up foreigners and Thais, and home to several five-star spa resorts, stunning galleries and fabulous boutiques.

Phuket's crackdown on unlicensed beachfront restaurants and bars has hit Surin particularly hard. All establishments on the sand have been cleared away, with some moving up the road to Ao Bang Thao (p650) and others closing completely. As a consequence, the beach is fairly quiet and there are fewer bars and restaurants here than elsewhere on Phuket's west coast. For some visitors, of course, this is a blessing; others might find it a tad too peaceful.

⊙ Sights & Activities

Sun Spa SPA

(Map p648; ☑ 076 316500; www.twinpalms-phuket. com; Twin Palms, 106/46 Mu 3; massage/treatment 1500-3900B; ⊙ 11am-8.30pm) Pamper yourself with a 'Travellers' Revival' facial, a white-clay body wrap, a Thai-herb bath and/or a signature Surin massage at this luxurious hotel-spa just back from the beach. It also offers mother-to-be massages and a full range of beauty services. The deluxe manicures and pedicures come highly recommended.

⊨ Sleeping

Benyada Lodge HOTEL $$

(Map p648; ☑ 081 889 4173; www.benyadalodge-phuket.com; 106/52 Mu 3; d incl breakfast 2800-4500B; ⊛ @ ⊜) A friendly, reasonably priced option in a neighbourhood dominated by upmarket resorts and just a couple of minutes' walk from Surin beach, Benyada has 29 big, comfortable rooms with modern flair, splashes of colour, fridges and tea/coffee sets. The best rooms come with small balconies and/or four-poster beds.

★ Surin Phuket LUXURY HOTEL $$$

(Map p648; ☑ 076 316400; www.thesurinphuket. com; 118 Mu 3, Hat Pansea; d incl breakfast 11,000-40,000B; ⊠ ⊛ ⊜ ⊠) Almost any establishment fronting a beach this stunning and secluded would be a top pick. But 'cottages' and suites here, hidden beneath hillside foliage and overlooking Hat Pansea, up the ante with earthy, luxurious interiors and a gorgeously abstract six-sided, black-tiled, sea-view pool. There's a Mediterranean-Thai restaurant (mains 320B to 1200B), plus a spa, beachfront yoga and beachfront bar.

It's quite an uphill hike along wooden boardwalks to many of the rooms. Staff are charming.

★ **Amanpuri Resort** LUXURY HOTEL **$$$**
(Map p648; ☑ 076 324333; www.aman.com; Hat Pansea; 1-bedroom villas incl breakfast US$1200-4000; 🅿 ❋ ❖ 🏊) Understated, luxurious and immensely peaceful, celebrity-magnet Amanpuri is one of Phuket's finest, most exclusive hotels. Graceful traditional-design bungalows are all about the location on quiet Hat Pansea, with sea-facing cabanas, warm-wood decor and enormous bathrooms; some have private pools. There's a huge array of activities on offer (yoga, kayaking, surfing), plus a spa, a jet-black pool and superb service.

✖ Eating & Drinking

With all the beachfront bars, clubs and restaurants having closed down or relocated, Surin's dining scene is pretty quiet. Most restaurants lie along the main street, Th Srisoonthorn, in hotels or on the soi just back from the beach. A few street-food stalls congregate in the car park beside the beach.

Blue Lagoon THAI **$**
(Map p648; ☑ 087 923 8235; Th Srisoonthorn; mains 120-200B; ⊙ 9am-11pm) One of a dwindling number of Surin restaurants following the crackdown on beachfront establishments, this friendly, family-run, semi-open-air joint serves up tasty versions of classic Thai dishes, from *sôm·đam* (spicy green papaya salad) to curries and noodle soups, as well as Western breakfasts. With check-cloth tables, swaying lanterns and a roadside terrace, it's more down-to-earth than most Surin eateries.

Surin Chill House INTERNATIONAL **$$**
(Map p648; ☑ 076 636254; 107/3 Mu 3; mains 130-450B; ⊙ 8.30am-4pm & 6-10pm Tue-Sun; 🛜 🍴) Loved for its coffee, cakes and breakfasts (from fruit-salad bowls to omelettes and waffles), this relaxed, polished-concrete, cafe-like space does a bit of everything else too: spicy Thai curries and salads, seafood, fine pizza and some more challenging international mains. All the ingredients are fresh, the team is welcoming and it's very family-friendly.

Phuket Coffee Lab CAFE
(Map p648; ☑ 080 534 5512; www.facebook.com/phuketcoffeelab; 116/4 Mu 3, Th Srisoonthorn; ⊙ 8am-4pm Tue-Sun; 🛜) It's all about the freshly roasted, small-batch, single-origin Thai and international beans at this concrete-floored, industrial-feeling cafe, 700m inland from Hat Surin. Skilled baristas deliver artisan coffees (65B to 120B) and professional training sessions, alongside enticing brunch-style bites (165B to 220B) roaming from smashed-avocado toast to courgette-and-feta omelette.

Beach Bar BAR
(Map p648; ☑ 076 316400; www.thesurinphuket.com; Surin Phuket, 118 Mu 3, Hat Pansea; ⊙ 9am-midnight; 🛜) The low-key, pagoda-like beachfront bar at the swanky Surin Phuket (p649) has a glorious setting, perched on white sands at the southern end of beautiful Hat Pansea. It's a dreamy spot for sunset, when lanterns are lit and the horizon blazes in pinks and oranges. Cocktails (180B to 250B) are cheerfully tropical, and there are pre- and post-dinner happy hours.

❶ Getting There & Around

Phuket Smart Bus (p625) links Surin with Kamala, Patong, Karon, Kata, Rawai, Ao Bang Thao and Phuket International Airport (roughly hourly 6.37am to 9.25pm, fares 50B to 170B).

Sǒrng·tǎa·ou (Map p648; Th Srisoonthorn) (passenger pick-up trucks) run from Phuket Town's Th Ranong to Hat Surin (40B) from 7am to 5pm, continuing to Hat Kamala (20B).

Taxis cluster **outside the Twin Palms hotel** (Map p648; Soi Hat Surin 8) and **near the 7-Eleven** (Map p648; Soi Hat Surin 8), both along Surin's main beach road. To/from Phuket Town, túk-túk (*đúk đúk*) charters cost 500B and taxis 700B. Taxis to/from the airport cost 500B to 700B.

A reliable Surin-based car-hire company is **Andaman Car Rent** (Map p648; ☑ 076 621600; www.andamancarrent.com; 112/12 Mu 3; ⊙ 9am-7pm).

Ao Bang Thao & Cherngtalay

A sweeping 8km of dusty white sand, stunning Hat Bang Thao (หาดบางเทา; Map p648) (หาดบางเทา) is the glue binding together the disparate elements of northwestern Phuket's buzzy Cherngtalay (เชิงทะเล) district, once a tin-mining area.

Bounded by Ao Bang Thao (อ่าวบางเทา), the region's southern end is dotted with midrange resorts and the odd beach club. Further inland you'll find an old fishing village laced with canals, a number of upstart villa subdivisions and some stellar restaurants. Smack in the centre of it all is the somewhat bizarre Laguna Phuket complex, a network of top-end resorts tied together by an artificial lake. At the northern end of the bay, Mother Nature reasserts herself, and a stretch of powder-white sand and tropical blue sea extends into the peaceful bliss you originally had in mind.

Cherngtalay is an increasingly popular expat hang-out and, more than anywhere else on Phuket, this mostly Muslim area is still being remodelled.

◉ Sights & Activities

Thai Carnation   SPA

(Map p648; ☑ 076 325565; 64 Th Laguna; massage or treatment 500-1400B; ⊙11am-10.30pm) Impressively professional yet wonderfully low-key, this fantastic-value spa is a real find, with private massage rooms, well-trained therapists and a local vibe. Ease away tensions with a classic Thai massage, an Indian head massage or an exfoliating Asian-glow scrub. It's 1.5km east (inland) from Hat Bang Thao, near the entrance to the Laguna Phuket complex.

🛏 Sleeping

Ao Bang Thao's Laguna Phuket complex includes seven luxury resorts, an 18-hole golf course and more than 30 restaurants. Frequent shuttle buses make the rounds of the hotels, as do pontoon boats (via the linked lagoons). There are more affordable beachfront resorts and the attractive ChillHub Phuket Hostel (Map p648; ☑ 082 291 1925; www.chillhubhostelphuket.business.site; 69/140-142 Mu 3, Hat Bang Thao; dm 500-600B; ﹡🛜🌀) in southern Ao Bang Thao, along with the fabulous top-end Anantara Phuket Layan (Map p622; ☑ 076 317200; www.anantara.com; 168 Mu 6, Soi 4, Hat Layan; incl breakfast d 10,140-15,780B; one-bedroom villa 11,820-38,450B; 🅿﹡🛜🌀) at the bay's northern end.

🍴 Eating

Cherngtalay has become a foodie hub in recent years. Some of Phuket's finest international restaurants cluster at the entrance to Laguna Phuket or inside its luxury resorts

(book ahead in high season). Cheaper eats abound at the Boat Avenue night market (Map p648; Boat Avenue, 49/14 Th Bandon-Cherngtalay; meals 50-100B; ⊙4pm-late Fri) and the more low-key restaurants at Ao Bang Thao's southern end and along the main road through Cherngtalay.

Gallery Cafe   CAFE **$$**

(Map p622; ☑ 089 103 7000; 122/4 Th Srisoonthorn; meals 140-350B; ⊙8am-8pm; 🛜🌀🍴) This chic-minimalist cafe-restaurant hits the all-day-breakfast spot with spinach-stuffed omelettes, rainbow-coloured smoothie bowls, homebaked breads and bagels, and smashed avo with feta. Coffees arrive on wooden trays with bite-sized cake chunks, and there are mango-passionfruit smoothies. It's a stylish hang-around-all-day lounge, with concrete floors, communal tables, shiplike windows and a sunny terrace.

Pesto   MULTICUISINE **$$**

(Map p648; ☑ 082 423 0184; Th Bandon-Cherngtalay; mains 140-500B; ⊙11.30am-11pm Sun-Fri, 5-11pm Sat; 🛜🌀) Mix a Paris-trained Thai chef with a simple streetside, semi-open-air setting and you get delicious, wallet-friendly Thai and international food. Sweet basil pesto penne and prawn tagliatelle hint at the Mediterranean, or stay local with salmon steak on green-mango salad, *đôm yam gûng* (spicy-sour prawn soup), deep-fried fish of the day and all your favourite curries, including southern Thailand's much-loved massaman.

★Suay   FUSION **$$$**

(Map p622; ☑ 093 339 1890; www.suayrestaurant.com; 177/99 Wana Park, Mu 4, Th Srisoonthorn; mains 350-650B; ⊙4-11pm; 🛜🌀) Launched in 2017 in a sleek glassed-in space, the Cherngtalay branch of star Phuket chef Noi Tammasak's sought-after Suay is a fusion-tastic sensation. Menus feature such creative delights as mushroom carpaccio, lemongrass-grilled lamb chops, Shanghai noodles dressed in sweet-basil pesto and tofu steak doused in *kôw soy* sauce. Don't miss the reimagined mango sticky rice with sesame ice cream.

Vegetarians: you have your own delicious, dedicated menu. The original Suay (p629), in Phuket Town, remains as popular as ever.

★Bampot   INTERNATIONAL **$$$**

(Map p648; ☑ 093 586 9828; www.bampot.co; 19/1 Mu 1, Th Laguna; mains 550-1200B; ⊙6pm-midnight, closed Mon May-Nov; 🛜🌀) Cool-blue booths, an open-plan kitchen and white-brick walls plastered with artwork set the scene for chef Jamie Wakeford's ambitious, contemporary European-inspired cooking – cashew-pesto risotto, crispy-skinned salmon with braised fennel, cauliflower tempura drizzled with truffle mayo. Throw in expertly crafted cocktails (try a gin-based BGT), excellent wines and cheerfully professional service, and Bampot delivers as one of Phuket's top international restaurants.

★ **Project Artisan**　　　MULTICUISINE $$$
(Map p622; ☑ 093 790 9911; www.theprojectartisan.com; 53/17 Mu 6, Rte 4018; meals 200-600B; ⊗8.30am-11pm; ⊗☑☑) Peachy-pink and pineapple-yellow woodcarved doors frame a lantern-lit garden adorned with dreamcatchers at this boho-chic, Bali-inspired, multipurpose creative venue in northern Cherngtalay. Locally sourced breakfasts of just-baked pastries, tropical smoothie bowls, artisan sliders and organic Phang-Nga eggs are followed by live-music sessions, massages at Saparod Spa (900B to 1800B), and cocktails or Thai craft beers at street-food-stall-style Tipsy Bar.

It's popular with well-heeled local expats and, thanks to its kids' menus and massages, families. It also has a takeaway bakery. Find directions on the website.

🛈 Getting There & Around

Making several stops in Ao Bang Thao/Cherngtalay, including at Tesco Lotus on Rte 4025, the Phuket Smart Bus (p625) runs to/from Surin, Kamala, Patong, Karon, Kata, Rawai and Phuket International Airport, roughly hourly between 6.25am and 9.37pm; rates are 50B to 170B.

Sŏrng·tăa·ou (passenger pick-up trucks) run between Phuket Town's Th Ranong and Hat Bang Thao (35B) from 7am to 5pm; túk-túk charters are 450B.

Taxis cost 700B to/from the airport, and around 900B to/from Phuket's southwestern beaches.

Northeastern Phuket

Phuket's lush northeastern hemisphere is laced with waterfalls, temples, singing gibbons and jungle-wreathed hills, its most beautiful sections protected by Khao Phra Thaew Royal Wildlife & Forest Reserve (p654).

Inland from Phuket's golden beaches, untouristed Thalang (ถลาง) unfolds around and just north of the **Heroines Monument**

(อนุสาวรีย์ท้าวเทพกษัตรีท้าวศรีสุนทร; Map p622; Hwy 402), 13km north of Phuket Town. While not exactly in the centre of Phuket, the monument acts as the island's central roundabout where roads heading in all directions intersect. Thalang is an area that people tend to pass through while on their way somewhere else – a shame, because there are some intriguing cultural attractions to be unearthed here, including Wat Phra Thong (p652). That said, most visitors swing through the Thalang area en route to the northeast's two very worthwhile conservation operations: the justifiably popular Phuket Elephant Sanctuary (p653) and the smaller Phuket Gibbon Rehabilitation Project (p654).

👁 Sights & Activities

Wat Phra Thong　　　BUDDHIST TEMPLE
(วัดพระทอง; Map p622; off Hwy 402; ⊗daylight hours; Ⓟ) **FREE** About 7km north of the Heroines Monument (p652), Phuket's tranquil, 250-year-old 'Temple of the Golden Buddha' revolves around a half-buried statue, with only the head and shoulders visible. According to legend, the image simply emerged from the ground, and those who have tried to excavate it have become ill or encountered serious accidents. The temple is particularly revered by Thai-Chinese, who believe the image hails from China. During Chinese New Year, pilgrims descend from Phang-Nga, Takua Pa and Krabi.

Thalang National Museum　　　MUSEUM
(พิพิธภัณฑสถานแห่งชาติถลาง; Map p622; Th Srisoonthorn/Rte 4027; adult/child 200/100B; ⊗9am-4pm; Ⓟ) Thalang's museum chronicles Phuket's history, from prehistoric Andaman inhabitants to the tin-mining era, with Thai and English displays. It traces southern Thailand's varied ethnicities and dialects, and recounts the legend of the 'two heroines' (immortalised on the nearby Heroines Monument, who allegedly drove off an 18th-century Burmese invasion by leading the island's women into battle dressed as men. The museum sits 200m northeast of the Heroines Monument, off Rte 4027, but was closed indefinitely for renovations at the time of research.

🛏 Sleeping & Eating

★ **Point Yamu by Como**　　　RESORT $$$
(Map p622; ☑ 076 360100; www.comohotels.com; 225 Mu 7, Paklok, Laem Yamu; d incl breakfast

PHUKET ELEPHANT SANCTUARY

Phuket's only genuine elephant sanctuary (Map p622; ☑ 088 752 3853; www.phuket elephantsanctuary.org; 100 Mu 2, Paklok, Rte 4027; adult/child 3000/1500B; ⊘ 9.30am-1pm & 2-5.30pm; ⏵) ⬦ is a refuge for aged pachyderms who were mistreated for decades while working in logging and tourism. During the morning tour, you get to feed them, before tagging along a few metres away as they wander the forest, chomp on watermelons, bathe and hang out. It's a rare, environmentally responsible opportunity that visitors rave about.

The sanctuary is a sister project to Chiang Mai's respected Elephant Nature Park and, at the time of research, was home to eight female elephants. If you want to see more of them, it accepts volunteers for one, three or seven days; fees (4500B, 8000B or 16,000B respectively) go directly towards elephant care, and cover vegetarian meals and, if relevant, accommodation.

There's no public access to the sanctuary except via a tour, which must be booked in advance and includes a tasty vegetarian lunch or afternoon tea. The sanctuary picks up visitors from its nearby office; you'll be dropped back there afterwards. Less-interactive afternoon tours involve observing the elephants on a safari-like experience. Beware copycat 'sanctuaries' and taxi drivers on commission who take you elsewhere.

10,600-32,200B; 🅿✳✳) Breeze into the soaring lobby, where white-mosaic pillars frame ponds reflecting encircling palms, and fall in love. This five-star stunner blends Thai influences (monk-robe orange, lobster-trap lamps, Buddhism symbols) into a coolly contemporary, Italian-designed creation. An array of huge rooms (some with private pool) and pool villas come in royal blue or turquoise, intensifying the endless sea and Ao Phang-Nga panoramas.

Laze in the soft-blue pool, the aqua-tiled spa and the private beach club, or join complimentary yoga, Pilates, t'ai chi and bike tours. Two- and three-bedroom villas accommodate families, and there's a babysitting service. There are two fantastic restaurants: one has southern Italian fare (Map p622; mains 430-750B; ⊘ 8am-11pm; ☎🅿), while the other offers refined southern Thai. It's 20km northeast of Phuket Town; you'll never want to leave.

Monkeypod CAFE $$
(Map p622; ☑ 087 909 5252; www.facebook. com/monkeypodcoffeehouse; Rte 4027; mains 140-200B; ⊘ 8.30am-8.30pm Tue-Sun; ☎🅿) A striking minimalist-white creation with floor-to-ceiling windows and a leafy outlook, this contemporary family-run cafe is a welcome surprise close to the Phuket Elephant Sanctuary and Phuket Gibbon Rehabilitation Project. The coffee, smoothies and home-cooked cafe food are all delicious, with reasonably priced salads, pastas, wraps and cakes served alongside Phuketian

classics. It's 6km northeast of the Heroines Monument.

★ Breeze INTERNATIONAL $$$
(Map p622; ☑ 081 271 2320; www.breezecapeyamu. com; 224 Mu 7, Laem Yamu; mains 750-1600B, 5-course tasting menu 2000B; ⊘ noon-10pm Wed-Sun; ☎🅿) Elegant yet understated, one of Phuket's finest restaurants sits in glorious hilltop, sea-surrounded seclusion, 20km northeast of Phuket Town. Blue beanbags overlook the pool and sea from the pillared open-walled dining hall. The divine, inventive European-style dishes are infused with local, often-homegrown produce; menus change regularly. Classic cocktails are given a Thai twist. Book ahead.

ⓘ Getting There & Away

To reach most places in this area you'll need private wheels or a taxi.

Sŏrng·tǎa·ou (passenger pick-up trucks) heading to Hat Surin and Ao Bang Thao from Phuket Town between 7am and 5pm pass by the Heroines Monument (30B). *Sŏrng·tǎa·ou* also run between Phuket Town and Tha Bang Rong (40B) several times daily between 8am and 3.30pm.

Taxis from Phuket Town to the Phuket Elephant Sanctuary cost around 700B. Taxis cost 600B to 900B from Tha Bang Rong to Phuket's west-coast beaches.

Ferries to/from Ko Yao Noi and Ko Yao Yai, some of them continuing to Krabi and/or Ao Nang, use Tha Bang Rong (p620) on Phuket's northeast coast.

Khao Phra Thaew Royal Wildlife & Forest Reserve

Contrary to popular belief, Phuket isn't all sand, sun and sea. Spreading across northeastern Phuket, Khao Phra Thaew Royal Wildlife & Forest Reserve (อุทยานสัตว์ป่าเขา พระแทว; Map p622; off Rte 4027 & Hwy 402; adult/child 200/100B; ⊘ 9am-5pm) 🏊 protects 23 sq km of virgin island rainforest (evergreen monsoon forest), rising to 442m at Khao Phra. It's home to wild boar, monkeys, slow loris, langurs, gibbons, deer, civets, flying foxes, cobras, pythons, squirrels and other smaller creatures, as well as the rare, endemic 3m-to-5m white-backed palm (*langkow* palm), a few scenic waterfalls (best seen during monsoon season) and the Phuket Gibbon Rehabilitation Project.

There is no accommodation inside the park, but it's an easy taxi or car/motorcycle ride away from the rest of Phuket.

On the Bang Pae/Gibbon Project side of the reserve, there's a park canteen serving simple Thai fare (meals 150B), plus a decent lakeside restaurant right next to the park entrance barrier. You could also drop in at Monkeypod (p653) on Rte 4027 for cafe-style food and good coffee.

◎ Sights & Activities

Within the reserve, there are pleasant hill hikes and some photogenic waterfalls, including Nam Tok Ton Sai (น้ำตกโตนไทร; Map p622; off Hwy 402; adult/child 200/100B; ⊘ 9am-5pm) and Nam Tok Bang Pae (น้ำตกบางแป; Map p622; off Rte 4027; adult/child 200/100B; ⊘ 9am-5pm). The falls are most impressive during the June-to-November monsoon, and an 8km walking trail runs between the two (you'll probably need a park guide).

Park rangers *may* guide hikers in the park on request: ask on arrival at park access points (expect to pay around 1500B).

Phuket Gibbon
Rehabilitation Project   WILDLIFE RESERVE
(โครงการคืนชะนีสู่ป่า; Map p622; ☏ 076 260492; www.gibbonproject.org; off Rte 4027; by donation; ⊘ 9am-4.30pm Sun-Fri, to 3pm Sat; P) 🏊 Financed by donations (2100B sponsors a gibbon for a year), this tiny sanctuary adopts gibbons previously kept in captivity in the hope of reintroducing them to the wild. You can meet the gibbons on low-key visits; swing by at around 9am to hear their morning song. You can't get too close to the animals, which may disappoint kids, but the volunteer work here is outstanding. Volunteer opportunities include providing educational information to visitors, cleaning cages, and feeding and tracking released gibbons.

Gibbon poaching is a big problem on Phuket, fuelled in no small part by tourism: captive gibbons are paraded around tourist bars and beaches as photo ops. Phuket's last wild white-handed gibbon was poached in the early 1980s. You can help by not having your photo taken with Phuket's captive gibbons.

❶ Getting There & Away

Khao Phra Thaew can be accessed from both the east and the west. From the Heroines Monument, head 9km northeast on Rte 4027, turn left (west) towards Nam Tok Bang Pae (signposted) and after 1km you'll get to the Phuket Gibbon Rehabilitation Project. Alternatively, head 6km northwest of the Heroines Monument along Hwy 402 then turn east to reach Nam Tok Ton Sai. There's no public transport here.

Northern Beaches

Phuket's northwest coast is one of its sweetest slices: if you're chasing what remains of the island's beach seclusion and tranquillity, where nature and tourism still (just about) manage to coexist, this is it. Within a 15-minute drive of the airport lie some of Phuket's dreamiest and least-developed beaches, with lower tourist traffic than elsewhere and a generally low-key vibe: easy-going Hat Nai Thon (หาดในทอน; Map p622), fun-loving Hat Nai Yang (หาดในยาง; Map p622) and magnificent, 10km-long Hat Mai Khao (หาดไม้ขาว; Map p622); all three are protected by Sirinat National Park (which has its headquarters on Nai Yang).

Kitesurfers flock to Nai Yang from May to October, but otherwise this part of Phuket is fairly quiet in low season.

◎ Sights & Activities

During the May-to-October monsoon, Hat Nai Yang is great for kitesurfing. A number of schools, including Kiteboarding Asia (Map p622; ☏ 081 591 4594; www.kiteboardingasia.com; 116 Mu 1, Hat Nai Yang; 1hr lesson 1300B, 3-day IKO course 11,000B; ⊘ 9am-6pm May-Oct) and Rawai-based Kite Zone (p633), teach budding kitesurfers.

Sirinat National Park
NATIONAL PARK

(อุทยานแห่งชาติสิรินาถ; Map p622; ☑ 076 327152, 076 328226; www.portal.dnp.go.th, 89/1 Mu 1, Hat Nai Yang; adult/child 200/100B; ☺ 6am-6pm) Comprising the exceptional northwestern beaches of Nai Thon (p654), Nai Yang (p654) and Mai Khao (p654), as well as the former Nai Yang National Park and Mai Khao Wildlife Reserve, Sirinat National Park encompasses 22 sq km of coastal land, plus 68 sq km of sea, stretching from the northern reaches of Ao Bang Thao to the northernmost tip of the island. Park headquarters, with accommodation, a basic visitors centre and a restaurant, is at the northern end of Hat Nai Yang. This whole area is relatively peaceful and is conveniently 15 minutes from Phuket International Airport.

Banana Beach
BEACH

(หาดหินกล้วย, Hat Hin Gluai; Map p622; off Rte 4018) Though not quite the secret it once was, this silky little tucked-away beach, 2km south of Hat Nai Thon, makes a refreshingly rustic Phuket escape. From a tiny parking space on the west side of the winding coastal Rte 4018, you clamber down through a jungle of coconut palms to beautifully quiet sands sprinkled with boulders and a single restaurant.

Sea Bees
DIVING

(Map p622; ☑ 076 327006; www.sea-bees.com; Slate, 116 Mu 1, Hat Nai Yang; 2-dive trip 3500B; ☺ hours vary) The Nai Yang outpost of this efficient Phuket-wide operation specialises in half-day, two-dive trips to the watery part of Sirinat National Park; snorkellers can tag along for around half the price. It also offers a range of courses, including a three-day Open Water Diver SSI (16,000B).

Asia Marine
BOATING

(Map p622; ☑ 076 397934; www.asia-marine.net; 141/2 Mu 2, Phuket Yacht Haven Marina, Laem Phrao; ☺ hours vary) One of Phuket's first yacht charters, with a diverse Andaman fleet, Asia Marine has a boat for everyone, from sleek fibreglass catamarans to wooden junks. High-season bareboat charters start at around 9000B per week.

Coqoon Spa
SPA

(Map p622; ☑ 076 327006; www.theslatephuket.com; Slate, 116 Mu 1, Hat Nai Yang; massage or treatment 2200-7000B; ☺ 10am-8pm) Set within the uberstylish Slate resort, this is a fantastic, unique spa where treatment rooms are backed by lush gardens. Therapies include purple-frangipani scrubs, bamboo-charcoal wraps, Anne Semonin facials and detoxes in a suspended 'nest' suite. Book ahead.

Phuket Riding Club
HORSE RIDING

(Map p622; ☑ 081 787 2455; www.phuketridingclub.com; 60/9 Th Thepkasattri, Mu 3, Mai Khao; 1/2hr rides 1200/2200B; ☺ 8am-6.30pm) The perfect opportunity to live out that 'horse riding through the tropics' dream, this long-running outfit offers fun one- or two-hour rides along the beaches and interior of northern Phuket. Book a day ahead.

Soi Dog
VOLUNTEERING

(Gill Daley Foundation; Map p622; ☑ 076 681029; www.soidog.org; 167/9 Mu 4, Soi Mai Khao 10; by donation; ☺ 9am-noon & 1-3.30pm Mon-Fri, 9am-noon Sat, tours 9.30am, 11am, 1.30pm & 2.30pm Mon-Fri, 9.30am & 11am Sat) This nonprofit foundation, 2km inland from Hat Mai Khao, protects hundreds of cats and dogs (many rescued from the illegal dog-meat trade) and focuses on sterilisation, castration, rehoming and animal-welfare awareness. Visits are by in-depth tour. The 'old dogs' enclosure can be upsetting, but it's a happy home. Visitors can play with the animals, or become dog-walking, long-term or animal-transfer volunteers.

🛏 Sleeping

This area mixes top-end resorts with more affordable digs, though if you'd like to stay at one of the cheaper places you'll need to reserve well in advance. Mai Khao is populated mostly by luxury resorts, while Nai Yang has the better budget options; Nai Thon is a bit of both.

Pensiri House
GUESTHOUSE $

(Map p622; ☑ 081 895 9489; www.pensirihouse.com; 112 Mu 5, Hat Nai Yang; d 800-1200B; ❄ 🛜) Just 300m inland from Hat Nai Yang – by the entrance to the glamorous Slate resort (p655) – friendly, efficiently operated Pensiri House is the area's best budget choice. It's popular with long-term travellers volunteering nearby, so book well ahead. Rooms, in a smart new block, are sizeable, contemporary and impeccably kept, with balcony, TV, fridge, safe and plenty of natural light.

The owners also run the nearby beachfront Phen's Restaurant (p656).

⭐ Slate
RESORT $$$

(Map p622; ☑ 076 327006; www.theslatephuket.com; 116 Mu 1, Hat Nai Yang; incl breakfast d 8200-24,300B, villas 44,900-62,000B; 🅿 ❄ 🛜 ⛱) One of Phuket's most original megaresorts takes its design cues from the island's tin-mining history. Mining hardware features in the delicate decor; doors to the sleek contemporary rooms and villas are made of distressed metal. The best rooms have pools and outdoor baths. Culinary offerings include fantastic Thai at Black Ginger, and there's the brilliant Coqoon Spa (p655) plus three pools (one is adults-only).

'Activities range from Pilates and yoga to stand-up paddleboarding (SUP) and kayaking, and bikes are available to borrow. Two-room suites and villas and a kids' club cater to families.

Pullman   RESORT $$$

(Map p622; ☑076 303299; www.pullmanphuket arcadia.com; 22/2 Mu 4, Hat Nai Thon; d 6000-12,000B, villas 29,000-32,000B; P ✴ @ ☎ ☀) With a spectacular setting high on cliffs above northern Hat Nai Thon, this sprawling resort offers stunning sea views from the moment you cross the arched bridge to the lobby. A network of reflection pools extends out above the sea, overlooked by the excellent restaurant Elements (mains 300-1300B; ☉noon-10.30pm; ☎). All 227 rooms and pool villas are spacious, contemporary, neutral-toned and supercomfortable, with balconies.

✕ Eating & Drinking

Hat Nai Yang and Hat Nai Thon have the best selection of reasonably priced restaurants, many of them beachside (though not necessarily *on* the sand), as well as a few cheap-eat food stalls along their beach roads. For anyone wanting to splash out, there are some good top-end restaurants at luxury resorts in the region.

Phen's Restaurant   MULTICUISINE $$

(Map p622; ☑081 895 9489; www.facebook.com/ phensrestaurant; Hat Nai Yang; mains 130-450B; ☉10am-11pm; ☎) Turquoise-on-white tablecloths and attentive staff make Phen's a popular beachside choice. It's one of just a few Phuket spots where you can still dine with sand between your toes. Expect masses of barbecued fresh seafood (lemon-fried crab, red-curry snapper, chilli-smoked shrimp), as well as Phuket favourites such as coconut *pàk miang* (spinach-like veg) and *gaang sôm pla* (southern-style fish curry).

The team also owns the popular guest-house Pensiri House (p655) just inland.

Mr Kobi   THAI $$

(Map p622; Hat Nai Yang; mains 180-300B; ☉10am-11pm) The signs say 'Broken English spoken here perfect', but the ever-popular Mr Kobi speaks English very well. He handles the drinks, while Malee deals with the seafood and Thai faves served in refreshingly unpretentious surroundings decorated with international flags. One wall is dedicated to the story of the 2004 tsunami.

Coconut Tree   THAI $$

(Map p622; Rte 4018, Hat Nai Thon; mains 100-500B; ☉10am-10pm; ☎) This relaxed spot towards the south end of Hat Nai Thon rustles up quality seafood dishes such as stir-fried crab with black pepper, tiger prawns cooked in everything from yellow curry to bitter ginger, and curries, noodles and stir-fries, on a rustic semi-open veranda with pot plants. The Andaman sparkles across the road beyond soaring palms and casuarinas.

Black Ginger   THAI $$$

(Map p622; ☑076 327006; www.theslatephuket. com; Slate, 116 Mu 1, Hat Nai Yang; mains 280-675B; ☉6-11pm; ☎☑) Reached only by hand-pulled barge, this lagoon-side restaurant is a magical spot, with traditional-style wood-walled *săh·lah* (hall) and sparkling fire-lit lanterns. The sophisticated all-Thai menu, with many veggie versions available, has a strong focus on southern Thai classics, like stir-fried *pàk miang,* rich massaman curry and crabmeat curry served on rice noodles. Don't miss the beautiful cashew-nut ice cream. It's inside the top-end tin-mining-inspired Slate resort.

NY Beach Republic   LOUNGE

(Map p622; www.facebook.com/nybeachrepublic; Hat Nai Yang; ☉3pm-1.30am; ☎) As nightlifey as Nai Yang gets, this stylish, palm-studded, sandy-floored lounge bar and restaurant sits just back from the beach, sprinkled with bamboo booths, tall wooden tables, nautical-striped cushions and a snooker table. The bar serves fruity Chalong Bay Rum mojitos (250B) and beer jugs (200B); the Thai menu (150B to 450B) is packed with seafood, soups, noodles and curries.

❶ Getting There & Away

Depending on the beach, taxis cost 300B to 600B to/from Phuket's airport (p624), around 900B to/from Patong and 800B to 1000B to/from Phuket Town.

KRABI PROVINCE

When travellers talk dreamily about the amazing Andaman, they usually mean Krabi (จังหวัดกระบี่), with its trademark karst formations curving along the coast like a giant limestone fortress of adventure, or rising out of the islands and hanging over idyllic white-sand beaches. Rock climbers will find their nirvana in Ton Sai and Railay, partygoers on Ko Phi-Phi, while castaway wannabes should head to Ko Lanta, Ko Jum or any of the other 150-plus islands swimming off this 120km-long shoreline.

Krabi Town

♪ 075 / POP 52,867

The bustling town of Krabi (กระบี่) is majestically situated among impossibly angular limestone karst formations jutting from the mangroves. It's a key transport hub populated with guesthouses and travel agencies and makes a great base for kayaking tours, jungle walks or day trips to nearby emerald pools and hot springs. There's a burgeoning nightlife with some decent bars and no shortage of restaurants so it's easy to while away a few days here.

◉ Sights & Activities

Many companies offer day trips to Khlong Thom, 45km southeast of Krabi on Hwy 4, taking in hot springs and freshwater pools, for around 1200B to 2000B, including transport, guides, lunch and beverages. Bring decent shoes. Various other 'jungle tours' and mangrove and island trips are available.

Wat Tham Seua　　　BUDDHIST TEMPLE
(วัดถ้ำเสือ, Tiger Cave Temple; ⊙daylight hours) This sprawling hill and cave temple complex 9km north of Krabi Town is an easy, worthwhile day trip. At the park entrance you'll come to a gruellingly steep 1260-step staircase leading to a 600m karst peak. After a 30- to 40-minute climb, the fit and fearless are rewarded with golden Buddha statues, a gilded stupa and spectacular views out to sea beyond Ao Nang. Start early and bring water; there are drinking taps at the top.

The best of the rest of the grounds can be found by following a loop trail through a little forest valley behind the ridge where the *bòht* (central sanctuary) is located. Here

you'll find several limestone caves hiding Buddha images, statues and altars.

This is a sacred area of worship: please dress appropriately by covering shoulders to knees and avoiding tight outfits.

Motorcycle taxis from Krabi cost 200B return. A *sŏrng·tăa·ou* (pick-up minibus) from Krabi's Th Utarakit is 70B.

Sea Kayak Krabi　　　KAYAKING
(☑075 680382, 089 724 8579; www.seakayak-krabi.net) Offers a wide variety of recommended sea-kayaking tours, including to Ao Tha Len (half/full day 900/1500B), which has looming sea cliffs; Ko Hong (full day 2200B), famed for its emerald lagoon; and Ban Bho Tho (full day 2200B), which has karsts and sea caves with 2000- to 3000-year-old cave paintings. Rates include guides, transfers, lunch and water.

🛌 Sleeping

★**Pak-Up Hostel**　　　HOSTEL $
(☑075 611955; www.pakuphostel.com; 87 Th Utarakit; dm/r 380/850B; ❄🐱🛜) Still the hostel of choice in Krabi, Pak-Up has contemporary air-con dorms with big wooden bunks built into the wall, each with its own locker. Massive, modern shared bathrooms have hot-water rain showers. The two doubles share bathrooms and women-only dorms are available. The bar gets busy and there's a young, fun-loving vibe here.

Hometel　　　GUESTHOUSE $
(☑075 622301; chaoguai_2504@hotmail.com; 7 Soi 10, Th Maharat; dm 250B, r 650-990B; ❄🛜) There's a friendly welcome in this rickety-looking building. Rooms are small and basic but adequate; ask for one with a window. The four-bed dorm lacks lockers but does have its own bathroom. The downstairs cafe is favoured by locals and does a great *pàt tai*.

Family Tree Hotel　　　BOUTIQUE HOTEL $$
(☑087 499 4544, 075 612562; krabi.familytree@gmail.com; Soi 2, 6 Th Maharat; d 1900-2400B; ❄🛜) This swish family-run boutique hotel has spacious, light and airy rooms. There's a twist to the modern bathrooms – vanity basins are in the bedroom. All rooms have a TV, fridge and complimentary coffee beans for a fresh brew. Downstairs, the **restaurant** (mains 85-350B; ⊙7.30am-5pm; 🛜) is well known for its global coffee selection and delicious homemade pastries.

Krabi Town

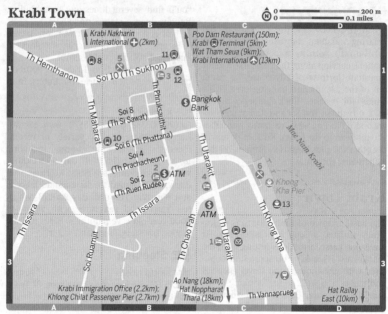

Chan Cha Lay GUESTHOUSE $$
(☑ 075 620952; www.lovechanchalay.com; 55 Th Utarakit; r 400-1400B; ✳@🖥) Rooms at this charming guesthouse are done up in Mediterranean blues and whites with white-pebble and polished-concrete open-air bathrooms. There's a range of cheaper rooms with a shared bathroom, and fan or air-con, which are plain and compact but spotless.

✖ Eating & Drinking

Night Market MARKET $
(Th Khong Kha; mains 30-70B; ⊙4-10pm) Beside Tha Khong Kha, this market is a popular place for an evening meal. Try authentic *sôm·đam* (spicy green papaya salad), wok-fried noodles, *đôm yam gûng* (prawn and lemongrass soup), grilled snapper and all things satay, plus creamy Thai desserts and freshly pressed juices. The English menus are a bonus.

Poo Dam Restaurant SEAFOOD $
(☑ 081 700 6590; Th Utarakit; mains 80-120B; ⊙3-11pm) Favoured by locals and travellers alike, this unpretentious restaurant cooks up a storm of seafood, with fish cooked as you like it – spicy or not. It's opposite the Black Crab statue on the esplanade.

★**May & Mark's** MULTICUISINE $$
(☑ 083 716 2488; 34 Th Sukhon; mains 75-250B; ⊙7am-9pm; 🖥🍴) A classic travellers' meeting spot, May & Mark's is always busy. The homemade sourdough bread is popular and the coffee made from globally sourced freshly ground beans is a winner. Try the fusion experience – pizza topped with spicy Thai curry. It also does popular Thai meals, international salads, sandwiches and mains, plus there's a good vegetarian selection.

★**Booze Bar** BAR
(☑ 095 037 2474; Th Khong Kha; ⊙3pm-1am; 🖥) This welcoming reggae bar has live music every night and really cranks up after 10pm. Prop up at the wooden bar and check out the local portraits hanging on the graffiti-strewn walls. There's also a pool table.

❶ Information

Bangkok Bank (Th Utarakit; ⊙8.30am-3.30pm) Exchanges cash and travellers cheques and has ATMs.

Krabi Immigration Office (☑ 075 611097; 382 Mu 7, Saithai; ⊙8.30am-4.30pm Mon-Fri) Handles visa extensions; 4km southwest of Krabi.

Krabi Nakharin International Hospital (☑ 075 626555; www.krabinakharin.co.th; 1 Th Pisanpob) Located 2km northwest of town.

Krabi Town

😴 Sleeping
1 Chan Cha Lay......................................C3
2 Family Tree Hotel..............................B2
3 Hometel..B1
4 Pak-Up Hostel....................................C2

✖ Eating
Family Tree Restaurant...............(see 2)
5 May & Mark's.....................................B1
6 Night Market......................................C2

🍸 Drinking & Nightlife
7 Booze Bar...C3

ℹ Transport
8 Sŏrng·tăa·ou to Ao Luk........................A1
9 Sŏrng·tăa·ou to Ao Nang & Hat
   Noppharat Thara...............................C3
10 Sŏrng·tăa·ou to Ao Nang & Hat
   Noppharat Thara..............................B2
11 Sŏrng·tăa·ou to Ban Laem Kruat........B1
12 Sŏrng·tăa·ou to Krabi Bus
   Terminal..B1
13 Tha Khong Kha...................................C2

ℹ Getting There & Away

AIR

The airport is 14km northeast of Krabi on Hwy 4. Most domestic carriers fly between Bangkok and Krabi. **Bangkok Air** (www.bangkokair.com) flies daily to Ko Samui and **AirAsia** (www.airasia.com) to Chiang Mai.

Taxis between the airport and Krabi Town cost 350B; motorcycle taxis cost 200B. Agencies and Pak-Up Hostel (p657) can arrange seats on the airport bus (90B). Several international car-rental companies have offices at the airport (vehicle hire from 1100B).

BOAT

Ferries to Ko Phi-Phi and Ko Lanta leave from the **Khlong Chilat Passenger Pier** (Tha Khlong Chilat), 4km southwest of Krabi. Travel agencies selling boat tickets include free transfers.

Hat Railay East Long-tail boats (150B, 45 minutes) leave from Krabi's **Tha Khong Kha** between 7.45am and 6pm. Boat operators wait until they have eight passengers before leaving; otherwise, you can charter the whole boat (1200B). Boats to Hat Railay West leave from Ao Nang.

Ko Jum From November to late April, Ko Lanta boats stop at Ko Jum (450B, one hour), where long-tails shuttle you to shore.

Ko Lanta From November to late April, one daily boat (450B, two hours) leaves at 11.30am. During the rainy season, you can only get to Ko Lanta by frequent air-con minivans (250B to 300B, 2½ hours), running year-round.

Ko Phi-Phi Year-round boats (300B to 350B, 1½ to two hours) leave at 9am, 10.30am, 1.30pm and 3pm, returning at 9am, 10am, 1.30pm and 3.30pm. Ferries don't always run every day between May and October.

Phuket & Ko Yao Islands The quickest route is with direct boats from the pier at Hat Noppharat Thara, 19km southwest of Krabi. *Sŏrng·tăa·ou* (50B) run between Krabi's Tha Khong Kha and the pier at Hat Noppharat Thara; taxis cost 600B. Boats also run several times daily to Ko Yao Noi from Tha Len (150B), 33km northwest of Krabi Town.

BUS

Krabi Bus Terminal (☎ 075 663503; cnr Th Utarakit & Hwy 4) is 4km north of central Krabi at Talat Kao.

MINIVAN

Travel agencies run air-con minivans and VIP buses to popular southern tourist centres, but you'll end up crammed cheek-to-jowl with other backpackers. Most offer combined minivan and boat tickets to Ko Samui (650B, five hours) and Ko Pha-Ngan (750B, seven hours). More (usually cheaper) minivans depart from the bus terminal (p659). Departures from Krabi include the following:

DESTINATION	FARE (B)	TIME (HR)
Hat Yai	240	4
Ko Lanta	250-300	2½
Phuket	140	2-3
Satun	350	4
Surat Thani	180	2½
Trang	240	2

SŎRNG·TĂA·OU

Sŏrng·tăa·ou (pick-up minibuses) run from the bus station to the centre of Krabi Town (25B) and on to Hat Noppharat Thara (60B), Ao Nang (60B) and the Shell Cemetery at Ao Nam Mao (60B) between 6am and 7pm, picking up passengers along the way.

The most convenient places to catch them in Krabi's town centre are Th Utarakit and Th Maharat. From Th Maharat, you can catch *sŏrng·tăa·ou* to **Ao Luk** (Th Maharat) (80B, one hour, 6am to 3pm), **Ao Nang and Hat Noppharat Thara** (Th Maharat). From Th Utarakit, there is also a service to **Ao Nang and Hat Noppharat Thara** (Th Utarakit), as well as to **Ban Laem Kruat** (Th Utarakit). In the opposite direction, Th Utarakit is the best place to pick up a *sŏrng·tăa·ou* to the **bus terminal** (Th Utarakit).

In high season services run until 10pm (though services after 7pm are less frequent and carry a small surcharge).

BUSES FROM KRABI

DESTINATION	FARE (B)	DURATION (HR)	FREQUENCY
Bangkok (VIP bus)	892	12	5pm
Bangkok (air-con bus)	587	12	8am, 8.20am, 4pm & 5pm
Hat Yai	260	4½	hourly 8.30am-7.20pm
Phuket	140	3	every 30min 8.30am-7.20pm
Ranong	250	5	8am & noon
Satun	350	5	11am, 1pm, 2pm & 3pm
Surat Thani	180	2½	hourly 4.30am-4.30pm
Trang	180	2	every 30min 7.30am-5pm

❶ Getting Around

You can explore central Krabi on foot. *Sŏrng·tăa·ou* between the bus terminal and Krabi (25B) stop on Th Utarakit, outside the River View Hotel. Most travel agencies and guesthouses, including Pak-Up Hostel, rent out motorbikes (150B per day).

Railay

Krabi's fairy-tale limestone formations come to a dramatic climax at Railay (อ่าวไร่เลย์; also spelt Rai Leh), the ultimate Andaman gym for rock-climbing fanatics. Monkeys frolic alongside climbers on the gorgeous crags, while down below some of the prettiest beaches in all of Thailand are backed by proper jungle.

Railay is accessible only by boat, just a 15-minute ride from Ao Nang, with its busiest parts sandwiched between scrappy Hat Railay East (not good for swimming) and the high-end resorts and beautiful white sand of Hat Railay West and Hat Tham Phra Nang.

Railay is more crowded than it once was and sees many day trippers and noisy boat traffic. Thankfully, though, it remains much less developed than Ko Phi-Phi.

◉ Sights

Hat Tham Phra Nang
BEACH

(หาดถ้ำพระนาง) A genuine candidate for Thailand's most beautiful beach, Hat Tham Phra Nang is on the southwest side of the headland and has a crescent of pale, golden sand, framed by cave-carved karst cliffs and Ko Kai (Chicken Island) and Ko Poda peeking out of the cerulean sea. There's only one place to stay here – the peninsula's most exclusive resort, Rayavadee (p663).

Tham Phra Nang
CAVE

(ถ้ำพระนาง, Princess Cave; Hat Tham Phra Nang) At the eastern end of Hat Tham Phra Nang is this important shrine for local fisherfolk (Muslim and Buddhist), who make offerings of carved wooden phalluses in the hope that the inhabiting spirit of a drowned Indian princess will provide a good catch. According to legend, a royal barge carrying the princess foundered here during the 3rd century BC. Her spirit took over the cave, granting favours to all who paid their respects.

Sa Phra Nang
LAGOON

(สระพระนาง, Holy Princess Pool) Halfway along the trail linking Hat Railay East to Hat Tham Phra Nang, a sharp 'path' leads up the jungle-cloaked cliff wall to this hidden lagoon. The first section is a steep 10-minute uphill climb (with ropes for assistance). Fork right for the lagoon, reached by sheer downhill climbing. If you fork left, you'll reach a dramatic cliff-side viewpoint; this is a strenuous but manageable, brief hike.

🏃 Activities

You can rent kayaks on Hat Railay West (half/full day 300/500B).

Freebird Paddle
KAYAKING

(☑ 061 953 9913; www.gofreebird.com; Walking St; kayak tour per person day/night 800/1800B; ◷10am-9pm) See what lies beneath in these tours' see-through kayaks and experience bi-oluminescent plankton on the night tours. Also offered are stand-up paddleboarding (SUP) tours (day/night tours 800/1800B).

Rock Climbing

With towering limestone cliffs fringed with lush jungle and perfect white-sand beaches it's no surprise that Railay, along with Ton Sai, is among the world's top climbing spots.

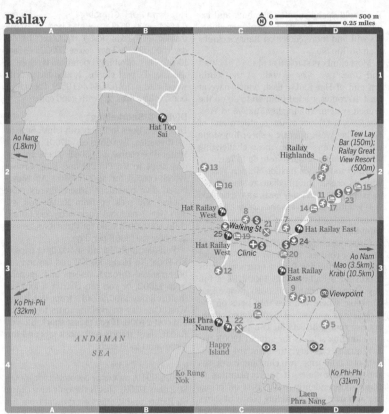

Railay

PHUKET & THE ANDAMAN COAST RAILAY

You could spend months climbing and exploring – many people do. Beginner climbers will find more choice on Railay's climbs than on Ton Sai.

Most climbers start off at **Muay Thai Wall** and **One, Two, Three Wall**, at the southern end of Hat Railay East, which have at least 40 routes graded from 4b to 8b on the French system. The mighty **Thaiwand Wall** (Hat Railay West) sits at the southern end of Hat Railay West, offering a sheer limestone cliff with some of the most challenging climbing routes, graded from 6a to 7c+.

Other top climbs include **Hidden World**, with its classic intermediate routes, **Wee's Present Wall** (Hat Railay West), an overlooked 7c+ winner, and **Diamond Cave**, for beginner and intermediate climbers. There's climbing information at www.railay.com.

Climbing outfits on Railay offer standard prices for courses: 1200B for a half-day and 2000B for a full day. Private instruction runs 3500B for a half-day and 5000B for a full day. Three-day courses (6500B) involve lead climbing, where you clip into bolts on the rock face as you ascend. Experienced climbers can rent gear sets for two people from the climbing schools for around 1200B per day (quality can vary); the standard set consists of a 60m rope, two climbing harnesses and climbing shoes. If you're planning to climb independently, you're best off bringing your own gear, including plenty of slings and quickdraws, chalk (sweaty palms are inevitable in the tropics) and a small selection of nuts and cams as backup for thinly protected routes. Some climbing schools sell a limited range of imported climbing gear.

Real Rocks   CLIMBING
(☑ 080 718 1351; www.realrocksclimbing.com; Hat Railay East; half-/full day 1200/2000B, 3-day course 6500B; ⊘ 8am-10pm) This Thai-American-run operation is efficiently managed and gets good feedback.

Hot Rock   CLIMBING
(☑ 085 641 9842; www.railayadventure.com; Hat Railay East; half/full day 1200/2000B, 3-day course 6500B; ⊘ 9am-8pm) Owned by one of the granddaddies of Railay climbing, Hot Rock has a good reputation.

King Climbers   CLIMBING
(☑ 081 797 8923; www.railay.com; Walking St; half/full day 1200/2000B, 3-day course 6500B; ⊘ 8.30am-9pm Mon-Fri, to 6pm Sat & Sun) One of the biggest, oldest and most reputable climbing schools.

Highland Rock Climbing   CLIMBING
(☑ 084 443 9539; www.highlandrockclimbing thailand.weebly.com; Railay Highlands; half/full day 1000/1800B, 3-day course 6000B; ⊘ 8am-10pm) This climbing operation is close to the island's best climbs. It also has a driftwood-clad cafe (☑ 084 443 9539; Railay Highlands; ⊘ 8am-8pm; ☎) with good coffee.

Diving & Snorkelling

Dive operations in Railay run trips out to local dive sites. Two dives cost 3700B; an Open Water dive course is 14,500B. There are also dive trips to Ko Phi-Phi and King Cruiser Wreck (p669) for 4900B. Most Ao Nang–based dive operators (where there's more choice) will pick up from Railay. You will also pay a national park entry fee (adult/child 400/200B) valid for three days, as well as a dive fee (200B per day).

Full-day, multi-island snorkelling trips to Ko Poda, Ko Hong, Ko Kai and beyond can be arranged through resorts and agencies from 1200B, or you can charter a long-tail (half/full day 1800/2800B) from Hat Railay West. One-day snorkelling tours to Ko Phi-Phi cost 2400B. If you're just snorkelling off Railay, most resorts rent mask sets and fins for around 150B each.

Railay Dive Center   DIVING
(☑ 075 819417; www.railay-divecenter.com; Walking St; 2 dives 3700B) This is the only dive centre on Railay, and it offers everything from fun dives to Open Water courses (14,900B) to dive trips to Koh Phi-Phi, as well as guided snorkelling trips (from 1500B). Prices don't include national park entry fees.

🛏 Sleeping & Eating

Hat Railay West and Hat Tham Phra Nang are home to upmarket resorts, while there are many midrange options around Hat Railay East. For the best budget choices and a buzzing backpacker/climber scene, head to nearby Hat Ton Sai. It's a 10- to 15-minute walk over the headland.

Overnight trips to deserted islands can be arranged with local boat owners, but you'll need your own camping gear and food.

🛏 Hat Railay West

★ **Railei Beach Club**   VILLA $$$
(☑ 086 685 9359; www.raileibeachclub.com; Hat Railay West; house 2900-28,800B; ❈☎) At the northern end of the beach, hidden in forested grounds that stretch back to luscious

limestone cliffs, is this collection of Thai-style homes for six to eight people, rented out on behalf of absent owners. They come with patios, kitchens and amenities, and there are also a few smaller but impeccably stylish dark-wood doubles. Only a few have air-con.

Sand Sea Resort
RESORT $$$

(☑ 075 819463; www.krabisandsea.com; Hat Railay West; bungalows incl breakfast 5000-10,500B; ✳ 🛜 🕸) One of the few resorts on this sublime beach, this place offers comfortable bungalows, quaint cottages and smart, contemporary rooms with every amenity. There are two peaceful, foliage-enclosed pools, one with karst views, making this a reasonable deal for the location.

🛏 Hat Railay East

Blanco Hideout @ Railay
HOSTEL $

(☑ 064 314 3922; www.blancothailand.com; Hat Railay East; dm 500-650B; ✳ 🛜 🕸) Opened in 2018, this is the only hostel in Railay. It sits above a steep stairway and has killer views, with dorms that surround a large, inviting pool – perfect for parties. All dorms have private en suites, and the large bunk beds have decent mattresses. The hostel organises pub crawls and boat parties.

Anyavee Railay Resort
RESORT $$

(☑ 075 819437; www.anyaveerailay.com; Hat Railay East; r 3050-3600B; ✳ 🛜 🕸) This place has consistently been one of the best midrange options on what is a pricey island. The bungalows are roomy, with large balconies, TVs, fridges and safety boxes. All are set around a real jungle garden – expect to see white-faced monkeys passing through – with an attractive pool. It's overlooked by karst cliffs.

Railay Garden View
BUNGALOW $$

(☑ 088 765 0484; www.railaygardenview.com; Hat Railay East; bungalow incl breakfast 1650-2450B; 🛜) A steep set of stairs leads to this collection of tin-roofed, fan-cooled, woven-bamboo and shiny-wood bungalows, stilted between tropical gardens high above the mangroves at the northeastern end of the beach. The bungalows are simple but spacious, the best have fine sea views. Bring mosquito repellent and a torch for after-dark walks. It's in a quiet location.

Rapala Rockwood Resort
BUNGALOW $$

(☑ 080 973 7778; www.rapalarockwood.com; Hat Railay East; bungalow 600-1200B; ✳ 🛜) Hang your hammock on the veranda of simple, fan-cooled, wooden bungalows (favoured by climbers) or modern Thai-inspired concrete, glass and wood bungalows. The most expensive have air-con. The woodland hilltop location means visiting wildlife, breezes, sea panoramas and some steep steps. There's a teensy paddling pool.

★ Railay Great View Resort
RESORT $$$

(☑ 075 819472; www.railaygreatview.com; Hat Railay East; bungalow incl breakfast 6300-7700B; ✳ 🛜 🕸) Follow the path at the far northern end of Hat Railay East to this secluded nature retreat. The thatch-roofed bamboo and wood cottages in this woodland paradise are romantic, tropical-chic with lattice-wood headboards, floor-to-ceiling glass, and large windows in the bathrooms that bring the outside in. It has a small private beach and an infinity pool.

There's a free scheduled long-tail shuttle to Hat Railay East or it's a 20- to 30-minute walk.

Sunrise Tropical Resort
RESORT $$$

(☑ 075 819418; www.sunrisetropical.com; Hat Railay East; bungalows incl breakfast 3900-6300B; ✳ 🛜 🕸) Swish 'chalets' and 'villas' here rival some of the finest on Hat Railay West but are priced for Hat Railay East – so we reckon this is one of the best deals in Railay. Expect soothing, smart decor, hardwood floors, four-poster beds or wooden mattress-platforms, lush bathrooms with aqua-tiled floors and private balconies or patios.

🛏 Hat Tham Phra Nang

★ Rayavadee
HOTEL $$$

(☑ 075 817630; www.rayavadee.com; Hat Tham Phra Nang; incl breakfast pavilion 15,900-51,500B, villa 58,500-138,000B; ✳ 🛜 🕸) Arguably one of Thailand's finest chunks of beachfront property, this exclusive resort sprawls across huge grounds filled with banyan trees, flowers and meandering ponds. The two-storey, mushroom-domed pavilions are packed with antique furniture, locally sourced spa products and every mod con (including butler service). Some have private pools. There's also a top-notch spa, a gym and no less than four restaurants.

The Terrace
ASIAN $$$

(Hat Tham Phra Nang; mains 450-1890B; ⊙ 11am-11pm; 🍴) An upscale pan-Asian menu – of Japanese, Vietnamese, Indian and Thai dishes – is served on a terrace.

Walking Street

Kohinoor INDIAN $$

(📞081 654 8100; Walking St; mains 100-350B; ⊙11am-11pm; 🌐) This highly recommended Indian restaurant on Walking St has an extensive menu. The chef's special is *palak paneer* (spinach and cottage cheese in green curry). It also makes good pizza.

Mangrove Restaurant THAI $$

(Walking St; mains 80-350B; ⊙10am-10pm; 🌐) This humble, heaving, local-style place, set beneath a stilted thatched roof between Railay's east and west beaches, turns out all the Thai favourites, from glass-noodle salad and cashew-nut stir-fry to curries, spicy *sôm·đam* (spicy green papaya salad) and the wonderful egg-grilled sticky rice.

🍷 Drinking & Nightlife

⭐Tew Lay Bar BAR

(Hat Railay East; ⊙11am-midnight; 🌐) Kick back at this chill-out open-air bar decked out with tree platforms, hammocks, lounge cushions and fairy lights. Its superb and isolated waterfront location on a rocky headland offers lazy views of Hat Railay East. It's the perfect place to escape the hustle.

ℹ️ Information

There's lots of local information on www.railay.com.

Clinic (📞084 378 3057; Railay Bay Resort, Hat Railay West; ⊙8am-midnight) Treats minor injuries. For anything serious, head to Krabi or Phuket.

ℹ️ Getting There & Away

Long-tail boats run to Railay from Krabi's Tha Khong Kha and from the seafront at Ao Nang and Ao Nam Mao. To Krabi, **long-tails** (Hat Railay East; ⊙7.45am-6pm) leave from Hat Railay East. Boats in both directions leave between 7.45am and 6pm when they have eight people (150B, 45 minutes). Chartering the boat costs 1200B.

Boats to Hat Railay West from the southeastern end of Ao Nang (15 minutes) cost 100B from 8am to 6pm or 150B from 6pm to midnight. Boats don't leave until eight people show up. Private charters cost 1200B. Services stop as early as 5pm May to October. **Long-tails** (Hat Railay West; ⊙8am-6pm) return to Ao Nang from Hat Railay West on the same schedule.

During exceptionally high seas, boats from Ao Nang and Krabi stop running; you may still be able to get a **long-tail** (Hat Railay East; ⊙8am-6pm) from Hat Railay East to Ao Nam

Mao (100B, 15 minutes), where you can take a *sŏrng·tăa·ou* (pick-up minibus; 50B) to Krabi or Ao Nang.

A year-round ferry runs to Ko Phi-Phi (450B, 1¼ hours). In high season, from October to April, it leaves from Hat Railay West at 9.45am and 2.45pm; long-tails motor over to meet it. In low season it leaves from the **ferry jetty** (Hat Railay East) at Hat Railay East at 9.45am. Boats to Ko Lanta (550B, two hours, 10.45am daily) operate only during the high season. For Phuket (650B, 2¼ hours), there's a year-round ferry at 3.15pm. Some ferries pick up off Hat Railay West.

Ao Nang

Huddled in the shadows of stunning karst scenery, Ao Nang (อ่าวนาง) is a noisy, chaotic strip of bars, restaurants and hotels. There's a never-ending stream of traffic along its beachfront esplanade, while turquoise seas lap the golden strip of sand, though it's not ideal for swimming as oil slicks from the constant putter of long-tail boats pollute the water.

If you're hankering for a snorkel in clearer waters, it's easy to get to the little islands that dot the horizon and divers are close to some prime spots for getting underwater. Above all, Ao Nang is a straightforward and compact – if blandly touristy – destination best served as a jump-off point to Railay beach and the islands further out.

🏃 Activities

Cycling

Take a Tour de Krabi by hooking up with **Krabi Eco Cycle** (📞081 607 4162, 075 656508; www.krabiecocycle.com; 309/5 Mu 5; half-/full-day tour 1500/3000B). The recommended full-day 15.5km pedal takes you through rubber plantations, small villages, hot springs and, finally, a cooler dip at the aptly named Emerald Pool. Lunch is included on all tours except the half-day bike-only tour.

Diving & Snorkelling

Ao Nang has numerous dive schools offering trips to 15 local islands, including Ko Si, Ko Ha, Ko Poda, Yava Bon and Yava Son. Ko Mae Urai is one of the more unique local dives, with two submarine tunnels lined with soft and hard corals. Expect to pay 3200B for two dives.

Other trips run further afield to King Cruiser Wreck (p669) or Ko Phi-Phi, for 3500B to 3900B, and Hin Daeng, Hin Muang and Ko Haa (p682) south of Ko

Lanta for 5300B to 6600B. An Open Water course costs from 14,900B. Most dive companies also arrange snorkelling trips (from 1500B).

You'll also pay a marine park entry fee (400B) valid for three days, and a dive fee (200B per day) on top of dive prices.

🛏 Sleeping

⭐ Glur
GUESTHOUSE, HOSTEL $

(☑ 075 695297, 089 001 3343; www.krabiglur hostel.com; 22/2 Mu 2, Soi Ao Nang; dm 600B, d incl breakfast 1200-1500B; ◉❄@❄❄) Glur is a fabulous combination guesthouse and hostel, designed, built, owned and operated by a talented Thai architect and his wife. This quiet complex incorporates shipping containers, glass, and moulded and polished concrete to create sumptuous rooms with beds on platforms and dorms with curtained-off turquoise bunk beds. There's an open-air kitchen, and it's set in a lovely garden with a small pool.

Family rooms (2400B) have two bedrooms. It's a walkable 1.5km northeast of Ao Nang proper.

Mini House
BOUTIQUE HOTEL $$

(☑ 075 810678; www.minihouseaonang.com; 675 Mu 2; r incl breakfast 1850-2500B; ❄❄) Local-life murals, warm-wood furnishings, an airy reception lounge and a trickling river feature bring a boutiquey edge to this place. All rooms have balconies. It's a quiet retreat located up a lane by a 7-Eleven minimart, about 1km from the beach.

⭐ Ban Sainai
RESORT $$$

(☑ 075 819333; www.bansainairesort.com; 11/1 Mu 2, Soi Ao Nang; bungalow incl breakfast 6000-12,500B; ◉❄❄❄) Away off the main strip (there's a daily shuttle to the beach), Ban Sainai sports cushy, thatched faux-adobe bungalows in burnt orange, sprinkled amid the palms and crushed up so close to the surrounding karst cliffs you can almost kiss them. Rooms are very comfortable, with jacuzzis in the most expensive ones, and come with big balconies. There's a great pool, too.

🍴 Eating & Drinking

Krua Ao Nang Cuisine
SEAFOOD $$

(☑ 075 695260; Soi Sunset; mains 150-400B; ◉10am-10pm) This is one of the best (and most popular) of several seafood restaurants with gorgeous sea vistas in this pedestrian-only alley at the western end of the beach. A model ice boat at the entrance shows off the day's catch (you pay by the kilo for seafood). It's a little more pricey than other options around Ao Nang; you're paying for the view.

Thailandia Bar & Restaurant
THAI $$$

(☑ 089 455 6853; 198 Mu 2; mains 120-500B; ◉2-11pm; ❄) With a tropical safari vibe, tasteful Thai decorations, cushion-covered cane armchairs, live-music shows and mood lighting, you know you'll be paying for the ambience as well as the food. The menu is extensive, with spicy Thai dishes and a recommended massaman curry. It's opposite McDonald's.

Last Fisherman
BAR

(☑ 081 267 5338; 266 Mu 2; ◉10am-midnight) Sit at one of the breezy tables overlooking the beach, or perch at the long-tail-boat-shaped bar, to enjoy your sundowner at this mellow but popular place at the southern end of Ao Nang.

ℹ Information

There are many ATMs and foreign-exchange windows (open approximately 10am to 8pm).

ℹ Getting There & Away

AIR

Krabi's airport is 14km northeast of Krabi Town on Hwy 4. Most domestic carriers fly between Bangkok and Krabi. **Bangkok Air** (www.bangkok air.com) and **AirAsia** (www.airasia.com) have frequent flights to Chiang Mai.

White airport buses (150B) run hourly from 9am to 5pm, stopping outside McDonald's on the Krabi road. Private taxis (600B) and minivans (150B) run to/from the airport.

LAND

Sŏrng·tăa·ou (pick-up minibuses) run to/from Krabi (60B, 30 minutes). The route goes from Krabi's bus terminal via Th Maharat to Krabi's Tha Khong Kha and on to Hat Nopparat Thara, Ao Nang and the Shell Cemetery. From Ao Nang to Hat Nopparat Thara or the Shell Cemetery costs 30B.

Dozens of agencies along the main strip rent out motorcycles (150B to 250B per day). A number of places offer car hire from 1100B per day. **Budget Car Hire** (www.budget.co.th) has a desk at Krabi airport (vehicle rental per day from 1200B).

Daily minivans (often combined boat-minivan tickets) run to destinations across southern Thailand.

DESTINATION	FARE (B)	TIME (HR)
Khao Sok	400	3
Ko Lanta	400	3
Ko Lipe	1000	6
Ko Pha-Ngan	750	5
Ko Samui	650	4
Ko Tao	900	7
Phuket	450	3

SEA

Boats to Hat Railay West (100B to 150B per person, 15 minutes) are run by **Ao Nang Long-Tail Boat Service** (northwestern end of Hat Ao Nang; ⊗ 8am-4pm, to 2pm May-Oct) and **Ao Nang Long-Tail Boat Service Club** (southeastern end of Hat Ao Nang; ⊗ 8am-midnight, to 8pm May-Oct). Boats leave with eight passengers; you can charter the whole boat for the cost of eight people.

Hat Noppharat Thara

Ao Nang's strip of bars, restaurants and hotels flows north into Hat Noppharat Thara (หาดนพรัตน์ธารา) without a break. Once a quiet seaside town, it's now a busy spot, popular with holidaying Thai nationals. The long stretch of sandy beach turns more natural as it curves 4km around the headland, until the sea eventually spills into a busy natural lagoon at the headquarters for the Hat Noppharat Thara-Mu Ko Phi-Phi National Park.

◉ Sights

Hat Noppharat Thara-Mu Ko Phi-Phi National Park NATIONAL PARK
(อุทยานแห่งชาติหาดนพรัตน์ธารา-หมู่เกาะพีพี; ☑ 075 661145; www.dnp.go.th; adult/child Ko Phi-Phi 400/200B, other islands 200/100B) This park protects 397 sq km of Krabi Province coastline and islands, including Ko Phi-Phi, Ao Nam Mao and the **Shell Cemetery** (สุสานหอย, Gastropod Fossil, Su-San Hoi; adult/child 200/100B; ⊗ 8am-6pm).

🛏 Sleeping & Eating

Hat Noppharat Thara-Mu Ko Phi-Phi National Park Accommodation BUNGALOW, CAMPGROUND $$
(☑ 075 661145; www.dnp.go.th; camping per person 30B, bungalows 1000B; ❄) These rustic but well-maintained air-con, 24-hour-electricity bungalows are just over the road from the beach. There's no wi-fi. Note that while you can still camp here, just behind the park HQ, you will need your own tent as they're no longer available for rent. Book ahead online or at the **visitors centre** (☑ 075 661145; www.dnp.go.th; ⊗ 8am-4.30pm).

Sabai Resort BUNGALOW $$
(☑ 075 637791; www.sabairesort.com; 79/2 Mu 3; bungalows 1200-3000B; ❄ ⊛ 🛜 😎) Sabai is the most professionally run of the area's bungalow properties. Tiled-roofed, mint-green, well-kept bungalows come in fan-cooled or air-con versions, with pebbled concrete patios overlooking a palm-shaded pool and flower-filled gardens. There are four-person family-sized rooms as well.

⭐ **Holiday Inn Resort** RESORT $$$
(☑ 075 810888; www.holidayinnresorts.com; 123 Mu 3; 2800-6500B; 🅿 ⊛ 🛜 😎) This is not your typical bland, chain-style Holiday Inn. Set on a sprawling estate with manicured gardens, a breezy restaurant, two pools (and a swim-up bar), it's just across the road from the beach. Rooms are tastefully decorated and come in nine different styles. All have balconies and views, and some have direct pool access. Great deals for families.

⭐ **Krua Thara** SEAFOOD $$
(☑ 075 661166; 82 Mu 5; mains 150-350B; ⊗ 11am-10pm) This cavernous, tin-roofed delight comes highly recommended for its seafood selection. There's no pretension here, just the freshest fish, crab, clams, oysters, lobster, squid and prawns done dozens of ways. The snapper fried in red curry is also one of the best fish dishes we've ever eaten in Thailand (and we've had a few). Service is superefficient and the place gets packed.

If seafood isn't your thing, they do tasty versions of all your other Thai faves.

ℹ Information

Hat Noppharat Thara-Mu Ko Phi-Phi National Park Visitors Centre offers information about the national park. You can also book park accommodation here.

ℹ Getting There & Away

Sŏrng·tǎa·ou (pick-up minibuses) between Krabi (60B) and Ao Nang (30B) stop in Hat Noppharat Thara.

Boats leave from Hat Noppharat Thara's pier for the following destinations:

Ko Phi-Phi The *Ao Nang Princess* runs daily (450B, two hours) from around November to April, and on Wednesday, Friday and Sunday from May to October. Boats leave at 9.30am, returning from Ko Phi-Phi at 3.30pm, via Railay.

Ko Lanta A 10.30am the *Ao Nang Princess* runs to Ko Lanta (550B, 2¾ hours).

Phuket From November to April, the fastest option to Phuket is the **Green Planet** (☑ 075 637488; www.krabigreenplanet.com) speedboat to Tha Bang Rong (1200B, 1¼ hours), via Ko Yao Noi and Ko Yao Yai (both 650B, 45 minutes). The boat leaves Hat Noppharat Thara's pier at 11am, returning from Phuket at 3pm; transport to your Phuket accommodation is included. There's also a 4pm *Ao Nang Princess* boat to Phuket (700B, three hours; reduced services May to October).

Ko Phi-Phi

With their curvy, bleached beaches and stunning jungle interiors, Phi-Phi Don (เกาะ พีพีดอน) and Phi-Phi Leh (เกาะพีพีเล) – collectively known as Ko Phi-Phi – are the darlings of the Andaman Coast. Phi-Phi Don is a hedonistic paradise where visitors cavort by day in azure seas and party all night on soft sand. In contrast, smaller Ko Phi-Phi Leh is undeveloped and hotel-free, its coral reefs and crystal-clear waters overseen by soaring, jagged cliffs, and visited only on day or sunset cruises.

Rampant development has rendered the centre of Ko Phi-Phi Don, as well as the two bays that flank it, a chaotic, noisy mess of hotels, restaurants, bars and shops. If you want tranquillity, head to the stunning white coves of the east coast, or less-developed Hat Yao in the south.

Tread lightly, manage your expectations and Ko Phi-Phi may seduce you as it has so many other travellers. You might, equally, find you can't wait to leave.

◎ Sights

★ **Phi-Phi Viewpoint**   VIEWPOINT
(จุดชมวิวเกาะพีพีดอน; Map p668; Ko Phi-Phi Don; 30B) The strenuous Phi-Phi viewpoint climb is a steep, rewarding 20- to 30-minute hike up hundreds of steps and narrow twisting paths. Follow the signs on the road heading northeast from Ton Sai Village; most people will need to stop for a break (don't forget your water bottle). The views from the top are exquisite. From here, you can head over the hill through the jungle to the peaceful eastern beaches.

🏃 Activities

Phi Phi Pirate Boat   BOATING
(Map p670; ☑092 710 6807; www.phiphipirate.com; per person 1200B; ⊙tours 1pm) Runs a sensational sunset cruise that sees you bobbing around Phi-Phi Leh aboard a double-decker boat to mellow beats, snorkelling and kayaking between Ao Pi Leh's sheer-sided cliffs, and dining on fried rice off Maya Beach. The cruise is led by an enthusiastic, organised team; the price includes national park entry fees.

Diving

Crystalline water and abundant marine life make the perfect recipe for top-notch scuba diving.

Phi-Phi dive prices are fixed across the board. PADI/SSI Open Water certification costs 13,800/12,900B, while standard two-dive trips cost 2500B to 3400B and Discover Scuba costs 3400B. Hin Daeng and Hin Muang, 60km south, are expensive ventures from Ko Phi-Phi (5500B); it's slightly cheaper to link up with a dive crew in Ko Lanta. Rates generally exclude national park fees (adult/child 400/200B), which are valid for three days, and a daily dive fee of 200B.

Princess Divers   DIVING
(Map p670; ☑088 768 0984; www.princessdivers.com; Ton Sai Village, Ko Phi-Phi Don; ⊙9.30am-10pm) This recommended dive outfit speaks multiple languages and uses big boats, rather than long-tails or speedboats. It offers Discover Scuba (3400B) and SSI/PADI Open Water courses (12,900/13,800B).

Blue View Divers   DIVING
(Map p668; ☑094 592 0184; www.blueviewdivers.com; Phi Phi Viewpoint Resort, Ao Lo Dalam, Ko Phi-Phi Don; 2 dives 2500B; ⊙10am-8pm) 🌿 This professional outfit focuses on community involvement, beach clean-ups and environmental conservation, with two-dive trips (2500B), night dives (1900B), shark snorkelling ecotours (1000B), Open Water courses (13,800B) and Discover Scuba (3400B).

Snorkelling

Ko Mai Phai (Bamboo Island; Ko Phi-Phi Don), 6km north of Phi-Phi Don, is a popular shallow snorkelling spot where you may see small sharks. There's good snorkelling along the eastern coast of **Ko Nok** (near Ao Ton

Ko Phi-Phi Don

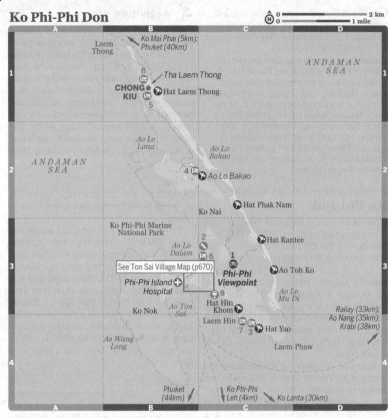

↑N 0 ———————— 2 km
    0 ———————— 1 mile

Ko Phi-Phi Don

◎ Top Sights
1 Phi-Phi Viewpoint...................................C3

✿ Activities, Courses & Tours
2 Blue View Divers.....................................C3

⊜ Sleeping
3 Paradise Pearl Bungalow.......................C4
4 Phi-Phi Island Village.............................B2
5 PP Erawan Palms Resort........................B1
6 Sunflower Boathouse.............................C3

⊗ Eating
Paradise Pearl Bungalow..............(see 3)

◐ Drinking & Nightlife
Apache Beach Club.......................(see 6)
9 Hippie's Bar...C3
Sunflower Bar................................(see 6)

7 Viking Natures Resort............................C4
8 Zeavola..B1

Sai), along the eastern coast of **Ko Nai**, and off **Hat Yao**. Most resorts rent out snorkel, mask and fin sets (per day 200B).

Snorkelling trips run from 600B to 1500B, not including national park fees, depending on whether you travel by long-tail or speedboat. Snorkellers can also tag along with dive trips, and many dive operators also offer specialised snorkelling tours.

🎓 Courses

**Pum Restaurant
& Cooking School**   COOKING
(Map p670; ☑081 521 8904; www.pumthaifood chain.com; 125/40 Mu 7, Ton Sai Village, Ko Phi-Phi Don; classes from 1500B; ⊙classes 11am, 4pm & 6pm) Thai food fans can take highly recommended cooking courses here ranging from two-hour sessions (1500B) to five-

hour 'healthy lifestyle' extravaganzas and, the most expensive, a whole-day class with Pum herself (7500B). You'll learn the secrets behind some of the excellent dishes served in Pum's Ton Sai Village restaurant and go home with a cookbook.

🛌 Sleeping

On Ko Phi-Phi Don, expect serious room shortages and extortionate rates, especially at peak holiday times. Book ahead. Life is much easier in low season (May to October), when prices drop dramatically.

There is no accommodation on Ko Phi-Phi Leh. Nor can you camp here anymore. Your only option is to sleep on a boat offshore, which can be arranged with Maya Bay Sleepaboard (p672).

🛌 Ao Ton Sai & Ao Lo Dalam

The flat, packed-out, hourglass-shaped land between Ao Ton Sai and Ao Lo Dalam is crammed with lodging options. Central Ton Sai is called the 'Tourist Village'.

Ao Lo Dalam is the traditional backpacker beach and there are many functional hostels here but it's clogged with people, long-tail boats, many beach bars and day trippers. After 9pm, it turns into a vast open-air nightclub.

Blanco Beach Bar HOSTEL $
(Map p670; ☑061 231 4101; www.blancothailand. com; Ao Lo Dalam, Ko Phi-Phi Don; dm 500-600B; ❄🛜) This bare-bones but modern party hostel offers cramped four- to 12-bed dorms,

but you aren't here to sleep. Prepare to keep vampire hours, as this fun-loving place stages nightly parties in the supersociable bar. You're just steps away from the night-time madness on the beach.

Rock Backpacker HOSTEL $
(Map p670; ☑081 607 3897; Ton Sai Village, Ko Phi-Phi Don; dm 300B; r fan/air-con 900/2000B; ❄🛜) If you can ignore the rude management you'll find this hostel on the village hill has big dorms lined with bunk beds, small private rooms, an inviting restaurant-bar and a rugged, graffiti-scrawled exterior. It's still one of Ton Sai's cheaper pads and there's a buzzing backpacker scene. Walk-ins only.

Up Hill Cottage BUNGALOW $$
(Map p670; ☑075 601124; www.phiphiuphill cottage.com; 140 Mu 7, Ton Sai Village, Ko Phi-Phi Don; r 2000-2500B; ❄🛜❄) These cream-painted, wood-panelled bungalows come in cute pastels offset by colourful bed runners and snazzily tiled bathrooms. Most enjoy island views (of varying beauty) from private balconies.

There's a small pool. It's at the eastern end of the main street heading north from Ton Sai Village. Beware the hundreds of stairs.

Anita Resort RESORT $$
(Map p670; ☑075 601282; www.phiphianitaresort. com; Ao Lo Dalam, Ko Phi-Phi Don; r incl breakfast 2500-3500B; ❄🛜❄) It's in the party zone (read 'noisy') but, for the money, this

---

KO PHI-PHI DIVE SITES

Leopard sharks and hawksbill turtles are common at Ko Phi-Phi's dive sites. Whale sharks sometimes make cameo appearances around Hin Daeng, Hin Bida and Ko Bida Nok in February and March. November to February has the best visibility. Top dives around Ko Phi-Phi include the following:

DIVE SITE	DEPTH (M)	FEATURES
Anemone Reef (p675)	17-26	Hard coral reef with plentiful anemones and clownfish
Hin Bida Phi-Phi (Ko Phi-Phi Don)	5-30	Submerged pinnacle with hard coral, turtles, leopard sharks and occasional mantas and whale sharks
King Cruiser Wreck (Ko Phi-Phi Don)	12-30	Sunken passenger ferry (1997) with snappers, leopard sharks, barracudas, scorpionfish, lionfish and turtles
Kledkaeo Wreck (Ko Phi-Phi Don)	14-26	Deliberately sunk decommissioned Thai navy ship (2014) with lionfish, snappers, groupers and barracudas
Ko Bida Nok (Ko Phi-Phi Don)	18-22	Karst massif with gorgonians, leopard sharks, barracudas and occasional whale sharks and mantas
Phi-Phi Leh	5-18	Island rim covered in coral and oysters, with moray eels, octopuses, seahorses and swim-throughs

Ton Sai Village

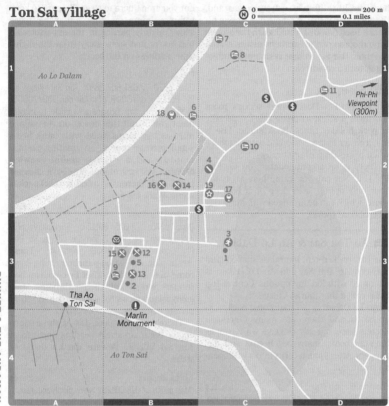

Ton Sai Village

🏂 Activities, Courses & Tours
1 Maya Bay Sleepaboard	C3
2 Phi Phi Pirate Boat	B3
3 Plankton Sunset Cruise	C3
4 Princess Divers	C2
5 Pum Restaurant & Cooking School	B3

🛌 Sleeping
6 Anita Resort	B1
7 Blanco Beach Bar	C1
8 Ibiza House	C1
9 Panmanee Hotel	B3
10 Rock Backpacker	C2
11 Up Hill Cottage	D1

🍴 Eating
12 Aroy Kaffeine	B3
13 Efe	B3
14 Esan Ganeang	B2
15 Local Food Market	B3
16 Only Noodles	B2
Unni's	(see 13)

🍸 Drinking & Nightlife
17 Banana Bar	C2
18 Slinky	B1

✪ Entertainment
19 Kong Siam	C2

resort just back from Ao Lo Dalam is one of the better deals on Ko Phi-Phi. Rooms are big, with good beds and contemporary bathrooms, while the bungalows that surround the pool are tastefully done up with woodcarved-elephant lamps, floor-to-ceiling headboards and private decks.

Panmanee Hotel HOTEL **$$**
(Map p670; ☎ 075 819379; www.panmaneehotel. com; 287 Mu 7, Ton Sai Village, Ko Phi-Phi Don; r incl

breakfast 2200B; ❈ 🛜) Tucked to the side of the food market and away from the noise of the bars (although the nearby mosque's early morning call to prayer may wake you), the rooms here are comfortable without being spectacular and come with decent-sized, contemporary bathrooms. The location close to the pier and different beaches is ideal if you're in exploring mode.

Ibiza House HOSTEL, BUNGALOW $$
(Map p670; ☏ 075 601274, 080 537 1868; www.ibizahouse-phiphiisland.com; Ao Lo Dalam, Ko Phi-Phi Don; dm 450-680B, r incl breakfast 2000B, villas 3200-5000B; ❈🛜❀) Ibiza House is known for its famous (or infamous) pool parties on the beach.The dorms here are stock standard and some don't have windows, but you're really here for the large and perennially popular pool, strategically flanked on two sides by the busy bar. Rooms and villas are big and clean and better value but don't expect an early night.

Sunflower Boathouse GUESTHOUSE $$
(Map p668; ☏ 080 038 3374; sunflowerboathouse@hotmail.com; Ao Lo Dalam, Ko Phi-Phi Don; r 1500-3000B; ❈🛜) Lovingly built, varnished dark-wood rooms with a bit of space and character and sporting colourful bed-throws are spread across a thatch-roofed, ship-like structure, cosied up to the wonderfully chilled-out Sunflower Bar (p673) at the northern end of Ao Lo Dalam. Simple and welcoming.

🏖 Hat Hin Khom

A 15-minute beach or jungle walk east of Ao Ton Sai, this area has a few small white-sand beaches in rocky coves and a few midrange resorts.

★Viking Natures Resort BUNGALOW $$
(Map p668; ☏ 075 819399; www.vikingnaturesresort.com; Hat Hin Khom, Ko Phi-Phi Don; bungalows incl breakfast 1750-4500B; ❈🛜) If it's character you're after, Viking's driftwood-clad, dark-wood, thatch-and-bamboo bungalows are just the ticket. They're decorated with shell curtains, colourful art, stone-cut sinks and hammock-decked lounging spaces that enjoy fabulous views of Phi-Phi Leh, and are set around a steep, jungle garden (which you will sometimes be sharing with monkeys) that runs down to a small but lovely beach.

Splurge on the large wooden lodge rooms that open onto inviting verandas.

🏖 Hat Yao

This lively stretch of pure-white south-coast beach is perfect for swimming, but don't expect it to yourself. There are also midrange resorts here. You can walk here in 30 minutes from Ton Sai via Hat Hin Khom or take long-tails (100B to150B) from Ton Sai pier.

Paradise Pearl Bungalow RESORT $$$
(Map p668; ☏ 075 601248; www.phiphiparadisepearl.com; Hat Yao, Ko Phi-Phi Don; r incl breakfast 3000-5000B; ❈🛜) This sprawling complex of dark wood Thai chalets, decked out with art, is tucked into the rocky headland on the northern curl of lovely Hat Yao. Delightfully old-fashioned beach-facing wooden 'houses' have four-poster beds, lace curtains and tea/coffee stands. The **restaurant** (mains 120-400B; ⏲ 7.30am-10pm; 🛜), typically packed with young couples, rambles to the edge of the sand.

🏖 Ao Lo Bakao

Ao Lo Bakao's fine stretch of northeastern palm-backed sand, ringed by dramatic hills, is one of Phi-Phi's loveliest, with offshore views over aqua bliss to Bamboo and Mosquito Islands. A long-tail charter from Ao Ton Sai costs 1000B.

★Phi-Phi Island Village RESORT $$$
(Map p668; ☏ 075 628900; www.phiphiislandvillage.com; Ao Lo Bakao, Ko Phi-Phi Don; r incl breakfast 9200-26,400B; ❈🛜❀) This whopping resort – 201 wood-and-concrete bungalows mostly set just back from the beach with palms swaying between them – is its own self-contained world, with everything you'd need on-site, including two pools, restaurant, cafe, spa, dive shop and tennis courts. There's no need to wander far and the beach is white-powder bliss.

🏖 Hat Laem Thong

Despite the upmarket resorts here, this northeastern white-sand beach is busy (it's a stop on day tours from Phuket) and has a small, rubbish-strewn *chow lair* (sea gypsies, also spelt *chao leh*) settlement at its northern end. Long-tail charters from Ao Ton Sai cost 1200B; hotels arrange transfers.

★Zeavola BUNGALOW $$$
(Map p668; ☏ 075 627000; www.zeavola.com; Hat Laem Thong, Ko Phi-Phi Don; bungalows incl breakfast 11,800-22,600B; ❈🛜❀) Hibiscus-lined

LOCAL KNOWLEDGE

MAYA BEACH

Ever since Leo (DiCaprio) smoked a spliff in the film rendition of Alex Garland's *The Beach* in 2000, Phi-Phi Leh has become a pilgrimage site. By 2017, the once-perfect castaway beach (อ่าวมาหยา, Maya Bay; Ko Phi-Phi Leh) of Maya Bay (the stunning, remote bay featured in the film) counted up to 5000 people and 2000 boats visiting the beach each day. Sadly, this overwhelming mass tourism devastated Phi-Phi Leh's ecosystem, destroying an estimated 80% of Ao Maya's coral due to irresponsible boat anchoring, uncontrolled footfall, and runoff from rubbish and sunscreen. This finally led to the closure of Maya Bay beach in 2018.

Since its closure, however, the bay has shown signs of recovery. Blacktip reef sharks have returned to the bay and there have been promising results from a coral restoration project. Maya Bay's idyllic beach is not set to re-open until at least 2021. Thai authorities have stated that boat traffic and visitor numbers will be restricted to protect the bay. However, you can still feast your eyes on the gorgeous white sands of Maya Bay from the deck of a boat and, without hordes of people crowding the beach, the view is simply outstanding.

Though you can no longer camp on Maya Beach, Maya Bay Sleepaboard (Map p670; ☑ 090 570 9204; www.mayabaytours.com; Ton Sai Village, Ko Phi-Phi Don; per person 3500B) can arrange for you to spend the night just offshore. Prices include food, sleeping bags and national park entry fees; tours depart at 3pm, returning at 10am the following morning. The same team runs the popular Plankton Sunset Cruise (Map p670; www.mayabaytours.com; Ton Sai Village, Ko Phi-Phi Don; per person 2000B) to Phi-Phi Leh.

pathways here lead to shady teak bungalows with sleek, distinctly Asian indoor-outdoor floorplans. Each comes with floor-to-ceiling windows on three sides, beautiful 1940s fixtures and antique furniture, huge ceramic sinks, indoor/outdoor showers and tea/coffee pods on a private terrace. The finest villas enjoy their own infinity pools and there's a fabulous couples-oriented spa and impeccable service.

PP Erawan Palms Resort RESORT $$$
(Map p668; ☑ 075 627500; www.pperawanpalms.com; Hat Laem Thong, Ko Phi-Phi Don; r incl breakfast 4800-9300B; ❋🛜❄) Step onto the grounds and let the stress fall away as you follow a meandering path through gardens to bright, spacious, and modern yet traditional-feeling 'cottages' and smaller rooms decorated with Thai art and handicrafts. It's in a great location, has an inviting pool bar plus friendly service.

✗ Eating

On Ko Phi-Phi Don, most resorts and bungalows have restaurants and on the east coast you're more or less bound to them. Restaurants in Ao Ton Sai have improved in quality in recent years and there are tonnes of options, whether it's seafood, Thai or international you're after, but don't expect fine dining. There are no restaurants on Ko Phi-Phi Leh.

Esan Ganeang THAI $
(Map p670; Ton Sai Village, Ko Phi-Phi Don; mains 70-150B; ⏰10am-midnight) On an alley jammed with hole-in-the-wall places favoured by the locals, family-run Esan Ganeang has fantastic and authentic dishes from the Isan region in northeast Thailand. Come here for fiery salads and soups, as well as more mild curries and noodle dishes packed with flavour. Be sure to order sticky rice to accompany your meal.

Only Noodles THAI $
(Map p670; Ton Sai Village, Ko Phi-Phi Don; mains 70-150B; ⏰10.30am-10.30pm; 🛜) The name doesn't lie. Come to this popular tucked-away spot for straightforward, flavour-packed *pàt tai,* served with your choice of noodles in meat, seafood or veg format at just two simple street-side tables.

Local Food Market MARKET $
(Map p670; Ton Sai Village, Ko Phi-Phi Don; mains 60-80B; ⏰7am-10pm) Phi-Phi's cheapest, most authentic eats are at this market close to the pier. A handful of enthusiastic local stalls serve scrumptious *pàt tai,* fried rice, *sôm·đam* (spicy green papaya salad) and smoked catfish.

★**Aroy Kaffeine** MULTICUISINE $$
(Map p670; ☑ 095 257 5452; www.facebook.com/AroykaffeinePhiphiIsland; Ton Sai Village, Ko Phi-Phi Don; mains 130-250B; ⏰9am-9pm; 🛜✏) The

artfully presented gluten-free, vegan and vegetarian options at this trendy cafe will have you salivating. Acai, spirulina, chlorella and turmeric are just some of the superfoods sprinkled throughout the menu and on your plate. But all dishes here are tasty – from the curries to the pancakes. There's great service and awesome coffee.

★**Efe** TURKISH $$
(Map p670; ☑095 150 4434; www.facebook.com/eferestaurant; Ton Sai Village, Ko Phi-Phi Don; mains 170-600B; ☺noon-10.30pm; 🛜) The menu at this popular Mediterranean restaurant in the heart of 'the village' has a super selection of kebabs served on sizzling plates. The salads and wraps are tasty and there are fine burgers and pizzas. It's a cosy place, with a few tables inside and a tiny patio, so expect to wait for a table during the dinner rush.

★**Unni's** INTERNATIONAL $$
(Map p670; ☑091 837 5931; www.facebook.com/unnis.phiphi; Ton Sai Village, Ko Phi-Phi Don; mains 140-600B; ☺8am-11pm; 🛜) Swing by this local expat fave for homemade breakfast bagels topped with everything from smoked salmon to meatballs, or specials such as avocado-and-feta toast, served in a bright and pleasant cafe-style atmosphere. Other excellent global treats include massive Greek salads, pastas, burritos, nachos, burgers, tapas and more. Top marks for cocktails, ambience and the menu, even if it's overpriced.

🍸 Drinking & Nightlife

A loud party scene saturates Phi-Phi, although efforts are underway to tone down its rowdy reputation. That might take awhile and, until then, buckets of cheap whisky and Red Bull and sickly sweet cocktails make this the domain of gap-year craziness and bad hangovers.

Be wary of anyone offering you drugs on the beaches: they may be setting you up for a visit from the local police.

★**Hippie's Bar** BAR
(Map p668; ☑085 476 1761; Hat Hin Khom, Ko Phi-Phi Don; ☺7am-midnight; 🛜) This sprawling, laid-back restaurant and bar set right on the beach is a welcome alternative to the mayhem in Ton Sai Village. It has a romantic ambience with candlelit tables, lanterns in the trees, chill reggae music and a nightly fire show.

Apache Beach Club CLUB
(Map p668; ☑081 535 4613; www.facebook.com/apachebeachclub; Ao Lo Dalam, Ko Phi-Phi Don; ☺9pm-late; 🛜) Rivalling Slinky as the best beach dancefloor on Ko Phi-Phi, Apache is perfect if you're after buckets of booze, gyrating bodies, fire shows and loud, throbbing beats.

Banana Bar BAR
(Map p670; ☑087 330 6540; www.facebook.com/BananaBarPhiPhi; Ton Sai Village, Ko Phi-Phi Don; ☺11am-2am; 🛜) The 'alt' bar destination in Ton Sai Village, inland for those seeking to escape the house and techno barrage on the beach, Banana Bar is spread over multiple levels. Climb to the rooftop, or lounge on cushions on the raised decks around the bar. There are solid sounds and it's popular with people who like to roll their own cigarettes. It also does Mexican food.

Slinky CLUB
(Map p670; www.facebook.com/slinkybeachbarofficial; Ao Lo Dalam, Ko Phi-Phi Don; ☺9pm-late; 🛜) Slinky is still the best fire show on Ao Lo Dalam and still the beach dancefloor of the moment. Expect throbbing bass, buckets of liquor (from 350B) and throngs of tourists mingling, flirting and flailing to the music.

Sunflower Bar BAR
(Map p668; ☑080 038 3374; Ao Lo Dalam, Ko Phi-Phi Don; ☺11am-2am; 🛜) This ramshackle driftwood gem is one of Phi-Phi's most chilled-out bars and is excellent for nursing a beer while the sun dips into the sea. Destroyed in the 2004 tsunami, it was rebuilt with reclaimed wood. The long-tail booths are named for the four loved ones the owner lost in the deluge.

☆ Entertainment

Kong Siam LIVE MUSIC
(Map p670; www.facebook.com/Kongsiam-Live-Bar-Phi-Phi; Ton Sai Village, Ko Phi-Phi Don; ☺6pm-1am; 🛜) There's live music nightly at this popular place that draws Thais and *fa·ràng* (Westerners). The talented band plays everything from classic covers to modern tunes.

ℹ Information

ATMs are spread thickly throughout the Tourist Village on Ko Phi-Phi Don, but are nonexistent on the eastern beaches and there are none on Ko Phi-Phi Leh.

TO & FROM KO PHI-PHI DON

DESTINATION	FARE (B)	DURATION (HR)	TO KO PHI-PHI	FROM KO PHI-PHI
Ao Nang	450	1¾	9.30am	3.30pm
Ko Lanta	350-600	1½	8am, 11.30am, 1pm & 4pm	11.30am, 3pm & 3.30pm
Krabi	350	1½-2	9am, 10.30am, 1.30pm & 3.30pm	9am, 11am, 2pm & 3.30pm
Phuket	350	1¼-2	9am, 11am, 1pm, 1.30pm & 3pm	9am, 11am, 2pm, 2.30pm & 3.30pm
Railay	450	1¼	9.45am & 2.45pm	3.30pm

Phi-Phi Island Hospital (Map p668; ☑086 476 9420, 075 622151; Ao Ton Sai, Ko Phi-Phi Don) Emergency care at the west end of Ao Ton Sai. For anything truly serious, get on the first boat to Krabi or, better still, Phuket.

❶ Getting There & Away

Ko Phi-Phi Don can be reached from Ao Nang, Krabi, Phuket, Railay and Ko Lanta. Most boats moor at **Tha Ao Ton Sai** (Map p670; Ton Sai Village, Ko Phi-Phi Don), though a few from Phuket use isolated, northern **Tha Laem Thong** (Map p668; Ko Phi-Phi Don). Ferries operate year-round.

There are also combined boat and minivan tickets to destinations across Thailand, including Bangkok (850B, 11 hours, 3.30pm), Ko Samui (500B, 6½ hours, 10.30am) and Ko Pha-Ngan (600B, seven hours, 10.30am).

You can travel to Ko Phi-Phi Leh on tours, or by long-tail boat (600B to 800B) and speedboat (2500B).

❶ Getting Around

There are no real roads on Ko Phi-Phi Don and while some locals do use motorbikes, foreigners can't hire them. Transport is by foot, or long-tail boats can be chartered at Ao Ton Sai for short hops around both islands.

Long-tails leave Ao Ton Sai pier for Hat Yao (100B to 150B), Hat Rantee (700B), Hat Phak Nam and Ao Lo Bakao (1000B), Laem Thong (1200B) and Viking Cave (on Ko Phi-Phi Leh; 1000B). Chartering a long-tail for three/six hours costs 1500/3000B; a half-day speedboat charter costs 5000B.

Ko Lanta

☑075 / POP 10,830

Once the domain of sea gypsies, Lanta (เกาะลันตาใหญ่) has morphed from a luscious Thai backwater into a getaway for international visitors seduced by its divine miles-long beaches and excellent diving.

Although pockets of low-key tourist developments on the west-coast beaches are slowly spreading and the backpacker party scene isn't hard to find, Lanta manages to retain its natural charm. The ban on motorised water sports means only the ruffling of palm fronds breaks the lazy, beach-day quiet, especially on the more scenic and less developed south coast.

Apart from a ridge-like spine, Lanta is reasonably flat and the 22km pot-holed main road running north to south is easily toured on a motorbike, as are the two roads crossing the jungle-clad interior to stilted sea gypsy villages on the east coast.

Ko Lanta is technically called Ko Lanta Yai. Boats pull into Ban Sala Dan, on the northern tip of the island.

◉ Sights

★ **Ban Si Raya** VILLAGE
(บ้านศรีรายา, Lanta Old Town; Map p680) Located halfway down Lanta's eastern coast, Ban Si Raya was the island's original port and commercial centre, providing a safe harbour for Arab and Chinese trading vessels sailing between Phuket, Penang and Singapore. Known to the locals as Lanta Old Town, here the vibe is very different from the rest of the island, with wooden century-old stilt houses and shopfronts transformed into charming, characterful guesthouses. Pier restaurants offer fresh catch overlooking the sea, and there are some cute bohemian shops dotted around.

Every Saturday afternoon from November to April the main street is transformed into a Walking St filled with food stalls, DJs, live music and traditional Thai dancing.

Tham Khao Maikaeo CAVE
(ถ้ำเขาไม้แก้ว; Map p680; ☑089 288 8954; tours 300B) Monsoon rains pounding away at limestone crevices for millions of years have created this complex of caverns and tunnels.

There are cathedral-size chambers dripping with stalactites and stalagmites, tiny passages you have to squeeze through on hands and knees, and even a subterranean pool. A local family runs hourly treks to the caves (with headlamps). The full trip takes two hours; sensible shoes are essential. It's signposted off the main road from Hat Khlong Tob to the east coast. Phone ahead for times.

🏃 Activities

Diving & Snorkelling

Some of Thailand's top diving spots are within arm's reach of Lanta. The best diving can be found at the undersea pinnacles of Hin Muang and Hin Daeng, two hours away by boat. These lone mid-sea coral outcrops act as important feeding stations for large pelagic fish such as sharks, tuna, barracudas and occasionally whale sharks and manta rays. Hin Daeng is commonly considered to be Thailand's second-best dive site after Richelieu Rock (p607), near the Myanmar border.

The sites around Ko Haa have consistently good visibility, with depths of 18m to 34m, plenty of marine life (including turtles) and a three-chamber cave known as 'the Cathedral'. Lanta dive outfitters run trips up to King Wreck (p669), Anemone Reef and several other Ko Phi-Phi dive sites.

Lanta's dive season is November to April, though some operators run weather-dependent dives during low season. Trips to Hin Daeng and Hin Muang cost from 4000B; Ko Haa dives are 3100B to 4000B. PADI Open Water courses cost 13,700B to 15,900B. Rates generally exclude national park fees (adult/child 400/200B), which are valid for three days, and a daily dive fee of 200B. From mid-October to April, agencies across Lanta offer four-island snorkelling and kayaking tours (1200B to 1900B) to Ko Rok Nok, the Trang Islands and other nearby isles.

Scubafish
DIVING

(Map p680; ☎075 665095; www.scubafish.com; Ao Kantiang; 2 dives 3500B; ⊗8am-8pm) This long-running outfit has an emphasis on education and participation in environmental projects. It runs the Ko Lanta Coral Propagation project and offers coral propagation workshops (5900B) and a three-day certification course (15,900B). Other programmes include Liquid Lense underwater photography courses, shark monitor-

Ko Lanta

ing dives, popular three-day dive packages (9975B), one-day Discover Scuba (5200B) and Open Water certification (15,900B).

Lanta Diver
DIVING

(Map p678; ☎075 668058; www.lantadiver.com; 197/3 Mu 1, Ban Sala Dan; 2 dives 3600B; ⊗8am-9pm high season, 10am-6pm low season) This is a very professional Scandinavian-run operator, based near the pier and with smaller resort concessions. Two-dive day trips to Hin Daeng and Hin Muang run 4000B to 4900B; two-dive Discover Scuba is 4500B and Open Water certification is 14,400B.

Blue Planet Divers
DIVING

(Map p678; ☎075 668165; www.blueplanetdivers. net; 3 Mu 1, Ban Sala Dan; 2 dives 3300B; ⊗8.30am-9pm) This outfit was the first Lanta school to specialise in free-diving instruction (from 2700B). It also has Open Water certification (13,700B), Discover Scuba (4300B) and snorkelling tours (1500B).

Yoga

Drop-in classes (250B to 400B) are offered at Oasis Yoga (Map p678; ☎085 115 4067; www.oasisyoga-lanta.com; Hat Khlong Dao; ⊗Oct-May). Sri Lanta (p678) has classes year-round for 550B.

Volunteering

Lanta Animal Welfare VOLUNTEERING
(Map p678; ☑084 304 4331; www.lantaanimal
welfare.com; 629 Mu 2, Ban Phra Ae; tours by donation; ◷9am-5pm) This long-standing animal
rescue (and veterinary) centre cares for Ko
Lanta's homeless and injured dogs and cats
through feeding, sterilising and re-homing,
and vaccination and local awareness cam-
paigns. Visitors can join hourly 40-minute
facilities tours (every two hours; May to October) and play with kittens. The centre also
welcomes casual dog-walking visitors and
volunteers for longer placements.

🍴 Courses

Time for Lime COOKING
(Map p678; ☑075 684590; www.timeforlime.
net; Hat Khlong Dao; ◷class 4pm) On south
Hat Khlong Dao, this popular beachfront
school-restaurant offers excellent cooking
courses (2000B) and fun cocktail courses
(440B). In high season grab a friend and
take on the 'cooking and cocktail course'
(4000B for two people). Profits finance Lanta Animal Welfare. Book ahead. The on-site
restaurant offers a tasting menu from Monday to Saturday (540B).

🛏 Sleeping

Ko Lanta has masses of long, good-looking
golden beaches, most on the west coast.
You'll experience the island in different in-
carnations depending on where you bed
down. Some resorts close for the May–October low season; others drop rates by 50%.
Reservations are essential in high season.

🛏 Ban Sala Dan

La Chambre HOTEL $$
(Map p678; ☑087 887 5191; www.lachambre.in.th;
Ban Sala Dan; r 800-1200B; 🖤) In the unlikely
event you don't want to wake up near the
beach, try this small hotel just off the road
to the pier at Sala Dan. The rooms are com-
fortable enough, with reasonable beds and
bathrooms, and it's close to most of the dive
shops. The cheapest rooms lack windows.

🛏 Hat Khlong Dao

Lanta Island Resort BUNGALOW $$
(Map p678; ☑075 684124; www.lantaislandresort.
com; 10 Mu 3, Hat Khlong Dao; bungalows 1800-
5500B; 🅿✳@🖤🏊) These unpretentious
bungalows have dated furnishings but are

clean and roomy and dotted around a leafy
garden with shady trees. The beach location
is spot-on and there's a pool as well. The resort's **Island Bar** (◷noon-late; 🖤) is popular
for sundowners and has live music in high
season (November to April).

★**Crown Lanta Resort & Spa** RESORT $$$
(Map p678; ☑075 626999; www.crownlanta.com;
Hat Khlong Dao; d incl breakfast 5800-22,000B;
✳@🖤🏊) In a prime location, the luxurious
Crown Lanta sits back from its own private
strip of white sand past the northern end
of Khlong Dao. Rooms and villas are set
around two pools, two restaurants, a top-
notch spa and, incongruously, a reggae bar.
It's a three-minute stroll to the beach, but if
you can't manage the walk they'll drive you
in a golf buggy.

🛏 Hat Phra Ae

Chill Out House HOSTEL $
(Map p678; ☑082 183 2258; www.chillouthouse
lanta.com; Hat Phra Ae; dm 220B, d 280-320B;
◷Sep-Apr; 🖤) This driftwood treehouse set
back from the beach has three different and
simple dorms, shared bathrooms and rick-
ety doubles with bathrooms. It's backpacker
basic, but you can't beat the laid-back vibe
(or the price): swings at the bar, a communal
iPod dock, and a wonderful chill-out lounge
heavy on hammocks. Everyone is treated
like family.

Thai House Beach Resort BUNGALOW $$
(Map p678; ☑075 684289; www.thaihousebeach
resort.net; Hat Phra Ae; bungalow 900-2500B;
🅿✳🖤) Set just back from the beach are
these pleasant bungalows in a variety of
choices to suit all budgets. Traditional Thai
wooden houses are spacious with air-con,
large fridges and hot showers, while simple bamboo bungalows come with fans and
mosquito nets. In between are functional
and clean concrete bungalows. It's in a great
location. It's just behind the classy Fat Turtle
Beach Bar and Restaurant (p681).

Hutyee Boat BUNGALOW $$
(Map p678; ☑083 633 9723; Hat Phra Ae; bunga-
lows 600-1200B; 🖤) This is a hidden, hippy
paradise of big, basic, fan-only bungalows
on stilts with tiled bathrooms, mini-fridges
and swinging hammocks in a forest of palms
and bamboo. It's a short walk to the beach,
and is run by a friendly Muslim family. The
eccentric patriarch speaks English.

WHERE TO STAY IN KO LANTA

Ban Sala Dan There's decent budget accommodation in characterful Ban Sala Dan. It's also handy for local-flavoured seafood restaurants and boat arrivals/departures, but not on the beach.

Hat Khlong Dao (หาดคลองดาว) Once an outstanding 2km white-sand stretch perfect for swimming, this beach has become so eroded that at high tide there's no sand at all. This is a big issue throughout northern Lanta.

Hat Phra Ae A large travellers' village (with restaurants oriented to Western tastes, beach bars and tour offices) has grown up along sandy Hat Phra Ae, 3km south of Ban Sala Dan. The beach has suffered erosion recently, but there's a nice stretch on its northern flank.

Hat Khlong Khong This is thatched-roof, Rasta-bar bliss and backpacker central, with beach volleyball, moon parties and the occasional well-advertised mushroom shake, 9km south of Ban Sala Dan. It's still fairly low-key, but the parties are more frequent than they used to be. The thinning yet ample stretch of beach goes on forever in either direction, lapped by turquoise shallows.

Hat Khlong Nin (p678) The main road heading south forks 13km south of Ban Sala Dan (after Hat Khlong Tob). The left road leads to the east coast; the right road hugs the coastline for 14km to Ko Lanta's southernmost tip. On the right fork the first beach is the lovely white-sand Hat Khlong Nin, which has lots of small, flashpacker-type guesthouses at its north end. Shop around.

Ao Kantiang (p678) This superb southwestern sweep of sand backed by mountains is also its own self-contained village with minimarts, motorbike rental and restaurants. It's upmarketish and far from everything. Don't expect to move much.

Ao Mai Pai (p679) A lush nearly forgotten cove at the southwestern curve just before the cape, Ao Mai Pai is one of Lanta's finest beaches. It's backed by elegant palm groves, with a rock reef jutting north, a jungle-swathed headland to the south and jade waters in between.

Laem Tanod (แหลมโตนด; Map p679) The wild, jungled, mountainous southern tip of the island has sheer drops and massive views.

Ban Si Raya (p679) There's a handful of guesthouses in Lanta's oft-ignored, wonderfully dated and culturally rich east-coast Old Town, which has its own bohemian groove.

Somewhere Else BUNGALOW **$$**
(Map p678; ☏ 081 536 0858; Hat Phra Ae; bungalow 800-1700B; ⊘ Nov-Apr; 🕾) Choose between basic thatched bamboo huts with terracotta-tiled bathrooms and bigger octagonal polished-concrete bungalows, all of which dot a shady lawn on Long Beach. The popular restaurant has a good selection of Thai staples.

★**Lazy Days** BUNGALOW **$$$**
(Map p678; ☏ 075 656291; www.lantalazydays.com; Hat Phra Ae; bungalows incl breakfast 4400-5200B; ⊘ Oct-Aug; ❄🕾) Lazy days indeed if you can score one of the nine bungalows tucked away here in a secluded spot at the end of Hat Phra Ae. The bamboo bungalows have thatched roofs and balconies; inside they are very comfortable, with great beds, fridges and stylish bathrooms. There's a restaurant.

🛏 Hat Khlong Khong

Isara Lanta BUNGALOW **$**
(Map p678; ☏ 088 823 2184; www.isaralanta.com; Hat Khlong Khong; bungalow 500-1100B; ⊘ Oct-Apr; 🕾) Isara Lanta is a popular little set of neat, pastel-painted, tin-roofed bungalows with woven bamboo flourishes lining a simple flowery path and spreading back behind a rustic blue-and-white-washed restaurant-bar.

Bee Bee Bungalows BUNGALOW **$$**
(Map p678; ☏ 081 537 9932; Hat Khlong Khong; bungalows 700-1000B; 🕾) Bee Bee's is comprised of a dozen creative bamboo cabins managed by superfriendly staff. Each bungalow is unique; a few are stilted in the trees. The on-site restaurant has a library of tattered paperbacks to keep you occupied. Popular with backpackers.

Ko Lanta North

house perfect for families. There are special solo rates with discounts of up to 20%.

Sri Lanta　　　　　　　BOUTIQUE HOTEL **$$$**
(Map p680; ☑ 075 662688; www.srilanta.com; Hat Khlong Nin; r incl breakfast 3400-7400B; P ❀ 🛜 🏊) At the southern end of the beach, this ecospot popular with Asian tourists consists of comfortable suites and wooden villas spread over a wooded hillside. Across the road there's a flower-fringed beachside area with two pools, a restaurant and massage pavilions. It's away from everything so be prepared for quiet nights.

It also hosts year-round yoga classes (550B) and retreats.

🛏 Hat Khlong Nin

Round House　　　　　　　BUNGALOW **$$**
(Map p680; ☑ 086 950 9424; www.lantaround house.com; Hat Khlong Nin; bungalows without/ with bathroom 300-900B/1200-2200B, house 3000B; ❀ 🛜) This is a cute multi-option find on the north end of the beach. Stilted bamboo-and-wood fan bungalows are simply styled (the cheapest share hot-water bathrooms) and sit just behind the breezy beachfront restaurant. Also available is a cool two-person adobe round house, rooms fronted by porches and an air-con beach

🛏 Ao Kantiang

Phra Nang Lanta　　　　　　　HOTEL **$$$**
(Map p680; ☑ 075 665025; www.vacationvillage. co.th; Ao Kantiang; r incl breakfast 4800-9600B; ❀ 🛜 🏊) These 15 gorgeous, Mexican-style, adobe-looking studios are straight off the pages of an interiors magazine, with clean lines, hardwood and whites accented with vibrant colours, lounge cushions and ceramic sinks. Outside, flowers and foliage climb over bamboo lattice sunshades, and the pool and restaurant-bar look over the beautiful beach. There are excellent low-season deals.

🛏 Ao Mai Pai

La Laanta　　　　　　　BOUTIQUE HOTEL **$$**
(Map p680; 📞087 883 9977, 087 883 9966;
www.lalaanta.com; Ao Mai Pai; bungalows incl
breakfast 2800-6200B; ❋❄➹) Operated by
a young English-speaking Thai-Vietnam-
ese couple, this is one of the coolest spots
on Lanta. Thatched bungalows have pol-
ished-concrete floors, platform beds and
decks overlooking a sandy volleyball pitch,
which blends into a rocky beach. The laid-
back **restaurant** (Map p680; mains 120-350B;
⊙8am-9pm; ➹➷) does a tasty Thai menu
with lots of veggie-friendly choices. It's the
last turn before Mu Ko Lanta National Park.

It provides extra beds for children and
there's a kids' swimming pool. There are
steep low-season discounts.

Baan Phu Lae　　　　　　　BUNGALOW **$$**
(Map p680; 📞075 665100, 085 474 0265; www.
baanphulaeresort.com; Ao Mai Pai; bungalows
1800-2400B; ⊙Oct-Apr; ❋➹) Set on secluded
rocks at the northern end of the final beach
before Lanta's southern cape, these cute,
canary-yellow concrete fan and air-con bungalows have thatched roofs, colourful art,
bamboo beds and private porches. Just behind stand stilted, wooden, air-con bungalows. Baan Phu Lae also arranges diving and
snorkelling trips, cooking classes, massages
and transport.

🛏 Laem Tanod

Mu Ko Lanta
National Park
Accommodation　　BUNGALOW, CAMPGROUND **$**
(Map p680; 📞075 660711, in Bangkok 02 561
4292; www.dnp.go.th; Laem Tanod; bungalows
1500-3000B, campsite per person 40B, with tent
hire 300B) Engulfed by craggy outcrops and
the sound of crashing waves, the secluded
grounds of the national park headquarters
are a gloriously serene place to stay, with
simple four- to eight-person bungalows or
tents. There are toilets and running water,
and there's also a shop but you'll need to
bring your own food. You can also get permission for camping on Ko Rok here.

🛏 Ban Si Raya

Sriraya　　　　　　　GUESTHOUSE **$**
(Map p680; 📞075 697045; punpun_3377@hot
mail.com; Ban Si Raya; r with shared bathroom
600B; ➹) Sleep in a simple but beautifully

restored, thick-beamed Chinese shophouse.
The rooms are basic industrial-chic, the balcony juts over the water, and it's quaint and
charming.

★Old Times　　　　　　　GUESTHOUSE **$$**
(Map p680; 📞081 854 6000; www.facebook.com/
theoldtimeslantabnb; Ban Si Raya; r 500-1700B;
❋➹) Tucked into two artfully revamped
100-year-old teak houses facing each other
across the street, this is an excellent choice.
There are impeccably styled rooms of vari-
ous sizes and prices. The best – bright and
decked out with black-and-white photos
– jut out over the sea on the jetty, where
there's a cushioned communal chill-out
area. Charming, romantic and fun.

★Mango House　　　　　　　GUESTHOUSE **$$**
(Map p680; 📞089 867 1067; www.mangohouses.
com; Ban Si Raya; ste 1650-3000B, villa 5800B; ➹)
These century-old Chinese teak pole houses and former opium dens are stilted over
the harbour. The original time-worn wood
floors are intact, the ceilings soar and the
three, house-sized suites are kitted out with
kitchenettes, satellite TVs and ceiling fans.
There are also Old Town–style seafront villas sleeping two to six people. Rates drop by
50% in low season.

🍴 Eating

The best-value places for seafood are the
restaurants along the northern edge of
Ban Sala Dan, which offer fresh fish sold
by weight (including cooking costs) on verandas over the water. There are numerous
Thai and international restaurants scattered
throughout the island, and most resorts
have their own eateries.

★Shanti Shanti Beach House　　　THAI **$**
(📞084 324 6941; Ban Khlong Tob; mains 70-
150B; ⊙noon-10pm; ➹) In an outdoor, drift-
wood-inspired, shabby-chic setting above
the beach, this charming place has it all – a
superb location, cool sea breezes, a decent
wine list, and exquisitely prepared and presented Thai, French and seafood dishes. It's
at the northern end of Khlong Tob.

Phad Thai Rock'n'Roll　　　　　THAI **$**
(Map p680; 📞080 784 8729; www.facebook.com/
phadthairock77; Ao Kantiang; mains 90-150B;
⊙11am-9pm) It's not every day you get your
spiced-to-taste *pàt tai* whipped up streetside by a guitarist. Choose from just six options ('jazz' fried rice, 'blues' fried noodles,

Ko Lanta South

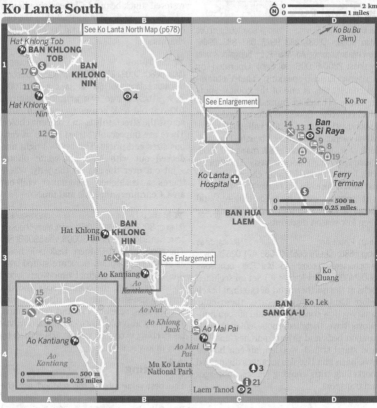

See Ko Lanta North Map (p678)

Ko Bu Bu
(3km)

Ko Por

See Enlargement

*Ban
Si Raya*

Ko Lanta
Hospital

**BAN HUA
LAEM**

Ferry
Terminal

Hat Khlong Tob
**BAN KHLONG
TOB**

**BAN
KHLONG
NIN**

Hat Khlong
Nin

Hat Khlong
Hin

**BAN
KHLONG
HIN**

Ao Kantiang
*Ao
Kantiang*

See Enlargement

Ko
Kluang

Ko Lek

**BAN
SANGKA-U**

Ao Nui
*Ao Khlong
Jaak*

Ao Mai Pai
*Ao Mai
Pai*

Mu Ko Lanta
National Park

Laem Tanod

Ao Kantiang

Ko Lanta South

veg, chicken, pork or seafood), swiftly and artfully prepared in simple contemporary surrounds. It's deservedly popular, and, with about as many tables as dishes, you may have to wait.

Patty's Secret Garden   THAI $$

(Map p678; ☑092 843 5740; www.pattyssecret garden.com; 278 Mu 2, Hat Phra Ae; mains 120-320B; ☺9am-11pm; ☎ 🅿) This casual, family-friendly place set in a pleasant, plant- and flower-filled shaded garden consistently dishes up tasty meals. The menu mixes Thai favourites with Western standards, including a kids' selection, and it's also good for breakfast.

There's also a branch in a lovely seaside setting, Patty's Secret Garden by the Sea, at Hat Khlong Khong.

Beautiful Restaurant   SEAFOOD $$

(Map p680; ☑086 282 1777; Ban Si Raya; mains 80-350B; ☺10am-9pm; ☎) At the northwest end of the Old Town, the tables here are scattered on four piers that extend into the sea. The menu features all the Thai faves but the fish is the draw. Highly recommended.

Drunken Sailors   MULTICUISINE $$

(Map p680; ☑075 665076; www.facebook.com/ drunkensailors; Ao Kantiang; mains 130-200B; ☺9am-3pm & 6-10pm Jul-Apr; ☎🎵) This su- per-relaxed place features beanbags, ham- mocks and low-lying tables spilling out onto a terrace. The global, want-to-eat-it-all menu employs quality ingredients and roams from handmade pasta, baguettes and burgers to top-notch Thai, including perfectly spiced ginger stir-fries and red curries cooked to personal taste. Coffees, cakes and juices are also excellent.

★Fat Turtle Beach
Bar & Restaurant   MULTICUISINE $$$

(Map p678; ☑092 612 0953; www.facebook.com/ FatTurtleLanta; Hat Phra Ae; mains 120-400B; ☺8am-10pm; ☎) A refined beach bar and restaurant set on a wooden platform over- looking rocks towards the southern end of Long Beach, this is the perfect spot for a romantic candlelit dinner. It has a creative menu of both Thai and international dishes (try the creamy risotto). Large portions, re- laxed ambience and majestic views make it well worth the prices.

🍷 Drinking & Nightlife

If you're after heaving clubs, pick another island. If you fancy a more low-key bar scene

with music wafting well into the night, Lan- ta has options on most beaches, and par- ticularly around Hat Phra Ae. Things move around depending on the day, so check out posters island-wide for upcoming events. Low season (May to October) is very mellow.

★Pangea   BAR

(Map p678; www.facebook.com/pangeabeachbar; Hat Phra Ae; ☺11am-midnight) Chill out in the thatch-roofed cabanas or laze back on raised floor cushions at this sandy bar in the heart of Long Beach. As the sun goes down the volume goes up with regular DJ beats and popular beach parties.

★Why Not Bar   BAR

(Map p680; ☑083 644 1333; www.facebook.com/ WhyNotBarKohLanta; Ao Kantiang; ☺11am-1am; ☎) Tap into Ao Kantiang's laid-back scene at this driftwood-clad beachfront hang-out. It keeps things simple but fun with a killer mix of fire twirlers, sturdy cocktails, bubbly bar staff and fantastic nightly live music jams, best enjoyed at low-slung wooden tables on a raised deck.

Rasta Baby   BAR

(Map p680; www.facebook.com/RastaBabyBar; Hat Khlong Nin; ☺9am-late; ☎) It's not hard to lose a few hours chilling at this beachfront reggae Rasta bar. The ambience is set with polished driftwood, floor cushions, salty rope and shells hanging from the ceiling and there's a shop in the front that sells unique handmade clothing. There's live music and fire shows.

🛍 Shopping

Malee Malee   FASHION & ACCESSORIES

(Map p680; ☑084 443 8581; 55/3 Mu 2, Ban Si Raya; ☺9am-9pm) A bohemian wonderland of quirky homemade goods, from silk-screened and hand-painted T-shirts and silk scarves to journals, toys, baby clothes, paintings, jewellery and handbags. Prices are low, it's superfun to browse and a sweet cafe (coffees around 80B) sits on the doorstep.

Hammock House   HOMEWARES

(Map p680; ☑082 262 9566; www.jumboham mock.com; Ban Si Raya; ☺10am-6pm) For unique, quality, colour-bursting hammocks, crafted by rural villagers and threatened Mlabri tribespeople in Northern Thailand, don't miss Hammock House. It some- times closes for part of low season (May to October).

WORTH A TRIP

MU KO LANTA NATIONAL PARK

Established in 1990, this marine national park (อุทยานแห่งชาติหมู่เกาะลันตา; Map p680; ☑ 075 660711, in Bangkok 02 561 4292; www.dnp.go.th; adult/child/motorbike 200/100/20B; ⊙ 8am-6pm) protects 16 islands in the Ko Lanta group, including the southern tip of Ko Lanta Yai. The park is increasingly threatened by the runaway development on west-coast Ko Lanta Yai, though other islands in the group have fared slightly better.

Ko Rok Na (เกาะรอกใน)i is still very beautiful, with a crescent-shaped bay backed by cliffs, fine coral reefs and a sparkling white-sand beach. Camping is permitted on adjacent Ko Rok Nok (เกาะรอกนอก) with permission from the park headquarters. On the eastern side of Ko Lanta Yai, Ko Talabeng has some dramatic limestone caves that you can visit on sea-kayaking tours (1300B). National park fees apply if you visit any of the islands. Ko Rok Nai, Ko Rok Nok and Ko Haa are off limits to visitors from 16 May to 31 October.

The national park headquarters and visitors centre are at Laem Tanod, on the south-ern tip of Ko Lanta Yai, reached by a steep paved road. There are some basic hiking trails, two twin beaches and a gorgeously scenic lighthouse, plus camping facilities and bunga-lows amid wild, natural surroundings.

❶ Information

EMERGENCIES

There are police stations on the **west coast** (Map p678; Hat Phra Ae) and in the **north** (Map p678; ☑ 075 668192; Ban Sala Dan), plus there's a **police outpost** (Map p680; Ao Kantiang) in the south of Lanta.

MEDICAL SERVICES

Ko Lanta Hospital (Map p680; ☑ 075 697017; Ban Si Raya) Located about 1km south of the Ban Si Raya Old Town.

MONEY

ATMs that take foreign cards can be found in the **north** (Map p678; Ban Sala Dan), on the **east coast** (Map p680; Ban Si Raya) and on the **west coast** (Map p680; Hat Khlong Nin). There are also ATMs all along the west coast.

TOURIST INFORMATION

Lanta Pocket Guide (www.lantapocketguide. com) A useful resource.

Mu Ko Lanta National Park Headquarters (Map p680; ☑ 075 660711, in Bangkok 02 561 4292; www.dnp.go.th; Laem Tanod; ⊙ 8am-4pm) Located in the far south of Lanta.

Mu Ko Lanta National Park Visitors Centre (Map p680; ☑ 081 090 1466, 082 816 6885; Laem Tanod; ⊙ 8am-6pm) Also in the far south of Lanta.

❶ Getting There & Away

Transport to Ko Lanta is by boat or air-con mini-van. If arriving independently, you'll need to use the frequent **vehicle ferries** (motorcycle/pedes-trian/car 20/20/200B; ⊙ 6am-10pm) between Ban Hua Hin and Ban Khlong Mak (Ko Lanta Noi) and on to Ko Lanta Yai.

LAND

Minivans are your easiest option from the main-land and they run year-round, but they're par-ticularly packed in this region and traffic jams for vehicle ferries can cause delays. Most minivans offer pickups from resorts. Frequency is reduced in low season.

Minivans to Krabi's airport (350B, 2½ hours) and Krabi Town (350B, three hours) run hourly between 6am and 4pm in both directions. You can connect in Krabi for further destinations, including Khao Lak and Bangkok. Departures from Lanta include the following:

TO	FARE (B)	TIME (HR)	FREQUENCY
Ko Pha-Ngan	1100	8½	8am
Ko Samui	1000	6½	8am
Trang	450	3	8am, 9am, 10.30am & 1pm

SEA

Ban Sala Dan has two piers. The **passenger jet-ty** (Map p678; Ban Sala Dan) is 300m from the main strip of shops; **vehicle ferries** (Map p678; Ban Sala Dan) leave from a jetty 2km east.

From November to April, the high-speed Tiger-line (p688) ferry runs between Phuket (1500B, two hours) and Ban Sala Dan (Ko Lanta) and on to Ko Lipe (1700B, five hours), via Ko Ngai (750B, one hour), Ko Kradan (850B, 1½ hours) and Ko Muk (850B, two hours). The service heads south at 10am, returning from Lipe at 10am the following day and stopping on Ko Lanta around 3pm before continuing north.

Ko Phi-Phi Ferries between Ko Lanta and Ko Phi-Phi run year-round. Boats leave Ko Lanta at 8am and 1pm (350B, 1½ hours), returning from

Ko Phi-Phi at 11.30am and 3pm. There are also high-season speedboats between Lanta and Phi-Phi (700B to 800B, one hour).

Krabi From November to late April, boats leave Ko Lanta for Krabi's Khlong Chilat pier at 8.30am and 11.30pm (450B, two hours) and return from Krabi at 11.30am. During high season, they stop at Ko Jum (400B, one hour).

Phuket There are year-round ferries to Phuket at 8am (800B) – and 1pm in low season – although you normally have to transfer boats at Ko Phi-Phi.

Trang Islands From mid-October to late April, speedboats buzz from Ko Lanta to the Trang Islands, including the Satun Pak Bara Speedboat Club (p688) and Bundhaya Speedboat (p688). Stops include Ko Ngai (650B, 30 minutes), Ko Muk (900B, one hour), Ko Kradan (1150B, 1¼ hours), Ko Bulon Leh (1600B, two hours) and Ko Lipe (1900B, three hours).

Ko Lanta Noi A **vehicle ferry** (Ko Lanta Noi) and a **passenger ferry** (Ko Lanta Noi) link Ko Lanta Noi to Ko Lanta Yai.

❶ Getting Around

Most resorts send vehicles to meet the ferries – a free ride to your resort. In the opposite direction expect to pay 100B to 400B. Alternatively, take a motorcycle taxi from outside 7-Eleven in Ban Sala Dan; fares run from 50B to 400B, depending on distance.

Mun Lanta (089 971 7792, 093 576 2637; www.munlanta.com) offers English-speaking private tours and taxi services in airconditioned 4WDs (half/full-day 1500/2500B).

Motorbikes (250B per day) can be rented everywhere (without insurance), as can bicycles (150B per day). Agencies in Ban Sala Dan rent out small 4WDs (1300B per day).

Ko Jum & Ko Si Boya

Just north of Ko Lanta, Ko Jum (เกาะจำ) and its low-lying neighbour Ko Si Boya (เกาะศรีบอยา) are surprisingly undeveloped; what's there is tucked away in the trees. There's little more to do than wander the long golden-sand beaches on Ko Jum (Ko Si Boya's beach is less impressive) and soak up the rustic beauty. The island is 12km long and there are just three small fishing villages with a total population of around 1500 inhabitants. It's a tropical gem with dense inland jungles, vibrant gardens and a bewitching low-key vibe.

Local people consider only the flatter southern part of Ko Jum to be Ko Jum, although technically it's one island. The northern hilly part is Ko Pu.

🛏 Sleeping & Eating

Most resorts on Koh Jum line the west coast where long golden-sand beaches stretch for miles. Developments have been slow to take off but new resorts are slowly spreading up the northwest coast.

There is a handful of restaurants outside the resorts on Ko Jum, most in the fishing village of Ban Ko Jum. On Ko Si Boya, you'll be eating at Siboya Bungalows (p684).

🛏 Ko Jum

Bodaeng BUNGALOW $
(📱081 494 8760; Hat Yao, Ko Jum; bungalows 200-400B; ⏱Oct-Apr) This place is an old-fashioned hippy vortex with basic bamboo bungalows and a couple of newer wood huts with their own bathrooms, set in the trees behind Hat Yao. There are no fans (sea breezes only) or wi-fi, shared bathrooms have squat toilets and there's limited electricity. But the grinning matriarch owner is a charmer and the location is right by the beach.

Jungle Hill Beach Bungalows BUNGALOW $$
(📱081 968 9457; www.junglehillbungalow.com; Ban Ting Rai; bungalows 500-2500B; 🛜) Perched in a dramatic location on a clifftop, these red-roofed, wooden bungalows with balconies and hammocks tower above a secluded, rocky beach and have fine sea views towards Ko Phi-Phi. Cheaper bungalows are set higher up in a garden favoured by visits from curious (and hungry) monkeys. You pay more for the beachfront bungalows.

Woodland Lodge BUNGALOW $$
(📱081 893 5330; www.woodland-koh-jum.com; Hat Yao, Ko Jum; bungalows 1300-1700B; 🛜) Tasteful, clean, fan-cooled bamboo huts here have proper thatched roofs, polished wood floors and verandas, and are spaciously laid out in a woodland setting. Concrete-and-wood family bungalows sleep three. The friendly British-Thai owners organise boat trips. The on-site Fighting Fish Restaurant (mains 100-300B; ⏱7am-9pm; 🛜) is good value.

★Koh Jum Beach Villas VILLA $$$
(📱086 184 0505; www.kohjumbeachvillas.com; Hat Yao, Ko Jum; villas incl breakfast 13,000-35,000B; 🛜🏊) 🌿 The poshest digs on Ko Jum, these huge, elegant wooden homes with living rooms, kitchens and sea views

sprawl back among frangipani- and bougainvillea-filled gardens from a luscious golden beach. Some have romantic private infinity pools. The resort keeps things as environmentally responsible as possible. It organises snorkelling and trekking tours, Thai cooking classes and has a lovely restaurant (mains 250-900B; ☺ 7.30am-10pm; ☎).

The biggest villas have up to five bedrooms, making them ideal for families.

Koh Jum Lodge
RESORT $$$

(☑ 089 921 1621; www.kohjumlodge.com; Hat Yao, Ko Jum; bungalows incl breakfast 4500-8000B; ☺ Nov-Apr; ☎☒) An ecolodge with style: the 19 spacious cottages here have lots of hardwood and bamboo, gauzy mosquito netting, coconut palms, Thai carvings and silk throws. Then there are the manicured grounds, massage pavilions and a hammock-strewn curve of white sand out front. It strikes that hard-to-get balance of authenticity and comfort. There's a minimum three-night stay in high season.

🛏 Ko Si Boya

Siboya Bungalows
BUNGALOW $

(☑ 081 979 3344; www.siboyabungalows.com; Ko Si Boya; bungalows 350B, house 500-1800B; ☎) Ko Si Boya's beach isn't spectacular, but the mangrove setting is wild and full of life. The simple bamboo bungalows here are set in manicured gardens, some have floor-to-ceiling windows. Private homes are large, stylish and affordable. It's great value, especially if you're looking for hammock-lounging tranquillity. There are family-friendly homes that sleep four people.

🛈 Getting There & Away

From November to May, the boat from Krabi to Ko Lanta will drop you at Ko Jum, for the full fare (450B, one hour, 11.30am); boats return from Lanta at 8.30am. In high season, daily boats run from Ko Jum to Ko Phi-Phi (600B, 1½ hours) at 8.30am, collecting guests from the Hat Yao resorts; boats return from Phi-Phi at 2pm.

There are year-round long-tails to Ko Jum from Ban Laem Kruat, 38km southeast of Krabi at the end of Rte 4036, off Hwy 4. Boats (100B, 30 minutes) leave at 9am, 10am, 11.30am, noon, 1pm, 2.30pm, 4pm, 5.30pm and 6.15pm, and return at 6.30am, 7.15am, 7.40am, 8am, 8.30am, 10.30am, 1.30pm, 2.30pm and 4pm.

If you're arriving on Ko Jum via Laem Kruat, note that boats run to three different piers; Ban Ko Jum and Mu Tu piers are the most convenient. Guesthouses will arrange transfers from the piers if you call in advance, otherwise you're relying on the kindness of strangers.

Daily boats to Ko Si Boya (50B, 15 minutes) run from Laem Kruat hourly between 8am and 5.30pm, returning hourly from 6.15am to 5pm. Call Siboya Bungalows (p684) to arrange transfer from the pier.

Sŏrng·tăa·ou (pick-up minibuses) meet boats at Laem Kruat and go to Krabi (100B), via Krabi's airport and Nua Khlong (where you can connect to Ko Lanta).

🛈 Getting Around

Several places in Ban Ko Jum and some Ko Jum guesthouses rent out bicycles (100B) and motorcycles (250B).

TRANG PROVINCE

South of Krabi, Trang Province (จังหวัดตรัง) has an impressive limestone-covered Andaman coastline with several sublime islands that see marginally fewer visitors than their nearby and better-known counterparts. For the adventurous, there's plenty of big nature to explore in the lush interior, including dozens of scenic waterfalls and limestone caves. And it's nowhere near as popular as Krabi, which means you're more likely to see working rubber plantations here than rows of T-shirt vendors. Transport links are good and during the high season (November to April) you can easily island-hop all the way to Malaysia.

Trang
☑ 075 / POP 60,700

Trang (ตรัง) is a delightful old-school Thai town. While most visitors here are in transit to the offshore tropical island paradises, Trang is far more than just a transport hub. If you're an aficionado of culture, Thai food or markets, stay a day or more and get lost in the wet markets, hawker markets and Chinese coffee shops. At nearly any time of year, there will be some minor festival that oozes local colour. Trang also makes a great base for day trips to caves, waterfalls and jungle trails in the nearby national parks.

Most tourist facilities lie along Th Praram VI, between the clock tower and the train station.

Trang Province

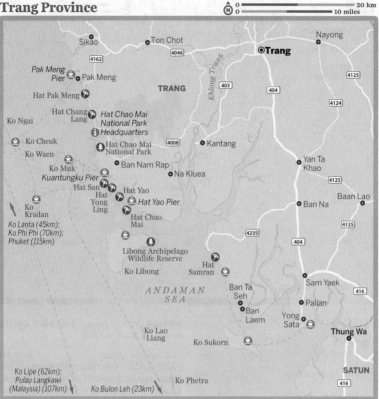

N 0 ___ 20 km
0 ___ 10 miles

Sikao • Ton Chot
4046
Nayong
⊙ Trang
4162
Khlong Trang
Pak Meng  Pak Meng
Pier
403 404
4125
Hat Pak Meng
TRANG
4124
Hat Chang
Lang
Hat Chao Mai
National Park
Headquarters
Ko Ngai
Ko Cheuk
Hat Chao Mai
National Park
4008
Kantang
Yan Ta
Khao
Ko Waen
Ban Nam Rap
4125
Ko Muk
Kuantungku Pier
Na Kluea
Baan Lao
Hat San
Hat
Yong
Ling
Hat Yao
Ban Na
Ko
Kradan
Hat Yao Pier
4125
Ko Lanta (45km);
Ko Phi Phi (70km);
Phuket (115km)
Hat Chao
Mai
4235
404
Libong Archipelago
Wildlife Reserve
Hat
Samran
Sam Yaek
416
Ko Libong
Palian
ANDAMAN
SEA
Ban Ta
Seh
Ban
Laem
Yong
Sata
Thung Wa
Ko Lao
Liang
Ko Sukorn
SATUN
Ko Lipe (62km);
Pulau Langkawi
(Malaysia) (107km)
Ko Bulon Leh (23km)
Ko Phetra
416

PHUKET & THE ANDAMAN COAST TRANG

◉ Sights & Activities

Trang is more a business centre than a tourist town. The lively, colourful wet and dry markets on **Th Ratchadamnoen** (Th Ratchadamnoen; ⏱ hours vary) and **Th Sathani** (Th Sathani; ⏱ hours vary) are worth exploring.

Tour agencies around the train station and Th Praram VI offer boat trips to Hat Chao Mai National Park and the Trang Islands (850B, plus park fees), snorkelling trips to Ko Rok (per person 1700B) and private car trips to local caves and waterfalls (2000B, maximum four people).

Meunram Shrine   TEMPLE
(ศาลเจ้าพ่อหมื่นราม; btwn Th Visetkul & Th Ratsada; ⏱ daylight hours) **FREE** Hazy with incense smoke, the Chinese Meunram Shrine conceals a surprisingly elaborate interior behind a blander facade. It sometimes sponsors southern Thai shadow theatre.

🎎 Festivals & Events

Vegetarian Festival   CULTURAL
(⏱ Oct) As much a Buddhist festival as it is food heaven for veggies – by not eating meat participants gain merit for themselves – this wonderful nine-day festival is celebrated all over town in the first two weeks of October and coincides with Phuket's Vegetarian Festival (p623).

🛏 Sleeping

Yamawa Guesthouse   GUESTHOUSE **$**
(☎ 075 290477; yamawagh@outlook.com; 94 Th Visetkul; r fan/air-con 350/450B; ❄ 🛜) This place has simple, spotless, old-fashioned fan or air-con rooms with fridges that are decent value for the price. It's often overlooked as it's nothing fancy and is a 1km walk from the train station (where most travel agencies are located), but the sweet local owners hand out detailed Trang maps and sound advice, and rent motorbikes (250B per day).

Trang

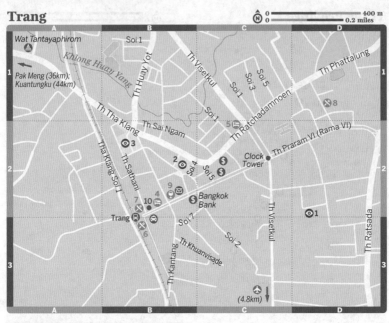

Trang

◎ Sights
1 Meunram Shrine	D2
3 Wet & Dry Market	B2
2 Wet & Dry Market	B2

⌂ Sleeping
4 Mitree House	B2
5 Yamawa Guesthouse	C2

⊗ Eating
6 Kopi	B3
8 Night Market	D1
7 Night Market	B2
Wine Corner Bar & Bistro	(see 6)

◎ Drinking & Nightlife
9 92 Bar & Studio	B2

ⓘ Information
10 Trang Happy Trip & Tour	B2

Mitree House GUESTHOUSE **$$**
(☑ 075 212292; mitreehouse.trang@gmail.com; 6-8
Th Sathani; r 750-1050B; ❋ ♠) In a great loca-
tion near the train station, this guesthouse
has immaculate, modern rooms with com-
fy beds and reasonably sized bathrooms.
The cheapest rooms lack windows; the
more expensive ones upstairs are big and
bright. There are communal areas on both
floors, helpful staff and a simple breakfast is

included in the price. Motorbikes can be
rented for 250B per day.

Rua Rasada Hotel HOTEL **$$$**
(☑ 075 214230; www.ruarasadahotel.com; 188 Th
Phattalung; r incl breakfast 2280-50,780B; ❋ ♠ ▣)
Trang's slickest choice is this hulking mono-
lith handily located opposite the bus station,
a 10-minute (40B) motorbike ride northeast
from the train station. From the outside it
looks like a typical business hotel but the
rooms here are huge and comfortable, while
the pool is massive. You can normally score
40% to 50% discounts in low season.

🍴 Eating & Drinking

Trang has two popular night food markets.

The town is famous for its *mŏo yâhng*
(crispy barbecued pork), spongy cakes, early-morning dim sum breakfasts and *ráhn
go·bǐi* (coffee shops) that serve real filtered
coffee. You can find *mŏo yâhng* in the mornings at some coffee shops or by weight at the
wet market on Th Ratchadamnoen.

★ **Night Market** MARKET **$**
(btwn Th Praram VI & Th Ratchadamnoen; mains from
40B; ⊙ 4-9pm) This highly recommended traditional night market will have you salivating
over curries, fried chicken and fish, deep-fried
tofu, *pàt tai* and an array of Thai desserts. Go

BUSES FROM TRANG

DESTINATION	FARE (B)	DURATION (HR)	FREQUENCY
Hat Yai	120	3	every 30min 5.30am-5.30pm
Krabi	110	2	hourly 5.30am-6.30pm
Phang-Nga	170	4	hourly 5.30am-6.30pm
Phuket	230	5	hourly 5.30am-6.30pm

with an empty stomach and a sense of adventure. There's a second, equally glorious weekend night market (mains from 40B; ⊙6-10pm Thu-Sun) opposite the train station.

Kopi
THAI $

(☑ 075 212516; Th Sathani; mains 25-200B; ⊙7am-5pm; ☎) Open for 60-plus years, this cool, old school Sino-Thai coffee shop has vintage marble-topped tables, helicopter fans and a menu that includes excellent soups, as well as delicious roast duck and crispy pork. Traditional coffee, known locally as *kopi,* is served black and sweetened with condensed milk.

★ Wine Corner Bar & Bistro
MULTICUISINE $$

(☑ 075 290192; 25-31 Th Sathani; mains 120-360B; ⊙5pm-midnight; ☎) An unexpected find in Trang is this decent wine cellar and restaurant (owned by a certified wine specialist), with imported wines stored in a temperature-controlled environment and an impressive Thai and international menu to match. Rustic wooden furniture and wine-barrel tables create a pleasant ambience, and there's live music as well.

92 Bar & Studio
BAR

(www.facebook.com/92BarAndStudio; 93 Th Kantang; ⊙5pm-midnight; ☎) Step inside this slick hole-in-the-wall bar and you might imagine stepping into a trendy pad in Sydney or Soho. The long wooden bar, black leather stools, mood lighting and classy jazz are the backdrop to an impressive menu of craft beers.

ⓘ Information

Bangkok Bank (Th Praram VI; ⊙8.30am-3.30pm) Has an ATM that accepts foreign cards.

Trang Happy Trip & Tour (☑ 075 219757; www.facebook.com/tranghappytrip&tour; 22 Th Sathani; ⊙6.30am-10pm) Knowledgeable and reliable Sai and Jip run this travel agency close to the train station. Jip speaks excellent English and can arrange private cars, rent out motorbikes, book minivan and boat tickets/transfers and one-day tours around the Trang Islands.

ⓘ Getting There & Away

AIR

The airport is 5km south of Trang. **AirAsia** (www.airasia.com) and **Nok Air** (www.nokair.com) fly here daily from Bangkok (Don Mueang).

Minivans to town (90B) meet flights. In the reverse direction, taxis, motorbike taxis or túk-túk (pronounced *đúk đúk*) cost 100B to 120B. Agencies at airport arrivals sell combined taxi-boat tickets to Trang's islands, including Ko Ngai (1000B).

BUS

Buses leave from Trang's **New Bus Terminal** (Th Phattalung), 3.5km northeast of the centre. There are 1st-class air-con buses to Bangkok (583B, 12 hours) at 9.30am, 4.30pm, 5pm and 5.30pm, and more comfortable VIP 24-seat buses at 5pm and 5.30pm (907B). From Bangkok, VIP/air-con buses leave between 6.30pm and 7.30pm.

MINIVAN & SHARED TAXI

Minivans depart from Trang's New Bus Terminal (p687). Agencies sell minivan tickets including in-town pick-ups.

Local transport is by air-con minivan. From the bus station, minivans leave regularly from 7.30am to 4pm for Pak Meng (80B, one hour), Hat Chao Mai (100B, one hour) and Kuantungku (100B, one hour), sometimes stopping in town just east of where Th Tha Klang crosses the railway tracks.

Other departures include the following:

TO	FARE (B)	TIME (HR)	FREQUENCY
Hat Yai	120	2	hourly 6am-6pm
Ko Lanta	250	2½	five daily 9.50am-4.30pm
Krabi	100	2	hourly 7am-5pm
Satun	120	2	every 40min 6am-6pm
Surat Thani	160	3	hourly 7am-5pm

TRAIN

Only two trains run between Bangkok and Trang: the express 83 and the rapid 167, which leave from Bangkok's Hualamphong station at 5.05pm and 6.30pm and arrive in Trang the next morning at 8.05am and 10.30am respectively.

From Trang, trains leave at 1.30pm and 5.25pm, arriving in Bangkok at 5.35am and 8.35am the following morning. Fares range from 245B for 3rd class to 1480B for 1st-class air-con sleeper.

ℹ Getting Around

Túk-túk and motorbike taxis congregate at the **taxi stand** near the train station, charging 40B for local trips. Travel agencies rent out motorbikes (250B per day). Most agencies can also arrange car rental (200B per day), and you can rent them at the airport as well.

A blue 'local bus' runs from the train station to the New Bus Terminal (12B) via Th Sathani.

Trang Beaches & Islands

The scenery around Trang's beaches is dramatic, with limestone karsts rising from steamy palm-studded valleys and swirling seas. Much of it is inside the Hat Chao Mai National Park, which covers a big stretch of the Trang coastline as well as including two of the Trang Islands – Ko Muk and Ko Kradan – and many tiny islets. And it is the Trang Islands that are the real draw here: covered in verdant jungle and lined with pure white sand beaches, they are less developed than other Andaman islands and have far smaller populations.

This is real honeymooners' territory – there's very little nightlife – so don't come here if you want to party all night long. Trang's beaches are also mostly just jumping-off points to the Trang Islands and are rather scruffy.

ℹ Getting There & Away

Boats to the Trang Islands run from three different piers: Hat Yao, Kuantungku and Pak Meng, all an hour's drive from Trang. Regular minivans run to Pak Meng pier (80B, one hour, 7.30am to 5pm) with less frequent services to the other two. If you book your boat ticket with a travel agency in Trang, it will arrange the transfer to the boat.

From October to April, speedboats operated by **Tigerline** (☏081 358 8989, 075 590490; www.tigerlinetravel.com), **Bundhaya Speedboat** (☏075 668043; www.bundhaya

speedboat.com) and **Satun Pak Bara Speedboat Club** (☏085 670 2282; www.spcthailand.com) connect Ko Muk, Ko Kradan and Ko Ngai with each other and Phuket, Ko Phi-Phi, Ko Lanta and Ko Lipe. Speedboats and ferries rarely depart at the scheduled times and usually take longer than predicted to reach their destination. Note that high-season start dates vary from year to year and are also weather-dependent – visit the operators' websites for the latest schedules.

There are regular minivans from Trang to Hat Chao Mai National Park (100B, one hour, 7.30am to 4pm).

THE 50-BAHT SURCHARGE

Ferries and speedboats operated by Tigerline (p688) often stop off at the Trang and Satun Islands, rather than docking. There's a 50B surcharge for long-tail transfers onto/off islands, which you'll be asked for once you're aboard the long-tail; boat operators usually refuse to continue until you pay up. Yes, it's frustrating, but it'll hardly ruin your trip, so keep your cool and your change handy.

Hat Pak Meng & Hat Chang Lang

The limestone karst scenery at Hat Pak Meng (หาดปากเมง) is spectacular and equals that of better-known Railay and Ko Phi-Phi. Otherwise it's little more than a scruffy beach and a transit point for boats heading to and from lovely Ko Ngai. Immediately south, casuarina-backed Hat Chang Lang (หาดฉางหลาง) is a prettier beach, but still can't compare to the ones on the nearby islands. The Hat Chao Mai National Park headquarters is at the southern end of the beach.

Although the Pak Meng pier is closer to the beaches it's actually better to spend the night in Trang, as accommodation and restaurant options are limited, as are transport services along this stretch of road. It's far more convenient (and economical) to organise ferry tickets through Trang travel agencies and hotels as transport to the pier is included in the price.

◉ Sights & Activities

Pak Meng tour agencies organise one-day boat tours to Ko Muk, Ko Cheuk, Ko Ma and Ko Kradan, as well as snorkelling day tours, all including lunch (per person 750B, plus Hat Chao Mai National Park fees).

Hat Chao Mai National Park NATIONAL PARK

(อุทยานแห่งชาติหาดเจ้าไหม; ☑075 203308; www.dnp.go.th; adult/child 200/100B; ⊙9am-4pm) This 231-sq-km park covers the shoreline from Hat Pak Meng to Laem Chao Mai, and encompasses the islands of Ko Muk, Ko Kradan and Ko Cheuk (plus a host of small islets). While touring the coast and islands, you may spot endangered dugongs and rare black-necked storks, as well as more common species such as barking deer, sea otters, macaques, langurs, wild pigs, pangolins, little herons, Pacific reef egrets, white-bellied sea eagles and monitor lizards.

The national park headquarters (☑075 210099; www.dnp.go.th; Hat Chang Lang; ⊙8am-4pm) are at the southern end of Hat Chang Lang, just south of where the beachfront road turns inland.

🍴 Sleeping & Eating

There are a few hotels along Hat Chang Lang, and simple bungalows and a campground (tents can be hired) inside the Hat Chao Mai National Park.

Several basic, no-frills seafood restaurants, popular with Thais on day trips or weekend getaways, can be found in Pak Meng, where Rte 4162 meets the coast.

Hat Chao Mai National Park Accommodation CAMPGROUND, BUNGALOW $

(☑075 203308; www.dnp.go.th; Hat Chang Lang; bungalows 800B, campsites per person 30B, with tent hire 225B; ⊙mid-Oct–mid-May) A basic but well-priced choice if you decide to explore this area are these simple fan-cooled cabins that sleep two to six people. Or you can camp under the casuarinas. There's also a restaurant.

ℹ️ Getting There & Away

Air-con minivans run regularly from Trang's New Bus Terminal (p687) to Hat Pak Meng (80B, one hour) and Hat Chao Mai (100B, one hour) between 7.30am and 4pm. Taxis from Trang cost 1000B.

Boats leave Pak Meng for Ko Ngai at noon daily (350B, one hour), with the reverse journey to Pak Meng leaving at 9am (350B, one hour). Long-tail charters cost 1500B.

The Hat Chao Mai National Park headquarters is 1km off the main road, down a clearly signposted track.

Ko Kradan

Beautiful Ko Kradan (เกาะกระดาน) is simply exquisite, with silky, white-sand beaches, pale turquoise shallows and shady, swaying palms. The handful of resorts nestled under the trees along the slender east-coast beach has dreamy views of Ko Muk, Ko Libong and dramatic limestone karsts rising from the sea. The water is clean, clear and inviting, and there's a small but lush tangle of jungle inland.

Unfortunately, word has spread and this formerly hidden treasure is a popular snorkelling stop on island day trips. In high season expect crowds from late morning to midafternoon, but after the day trippers leave, the island reverts to castaway heaven.

👁 Sights & Activities

Hat Sunset BEACH

(หาดพระอาทิตย์ตก) A short signposted track at the south end of the main beach leads past the Paradise Lost guesthouse and over the ridge to Hat Sunset, a mostly wet and rocky patch of sand facing open seas and flaming-pink sunsets. However, the west side of the island is strewn with plastic and garbage washed in from the sea.

Hat South SNORKELLING

Although some of Kradan's coral structure has been decimated, there's good snorkelling when the wind is calm off the island's south beach, which you can reach in a 10-minute walk along a jungly path from the Paradise Lost guesthouse, signposted at the south end of the main beach.

🍴 Sleeping & Eating

There are no standalone restaurants here, but all the resorts have eateries of varying quality. Italian dishes are popular as a few of the resorts are run by Italians.

★ Kalume BUNGALOW $$

(☑099 195 7340; www.kalumekradan.com; bungalow incl breakfast 2600-2900B; 🛜) The cheapest (but still overpriced) beachfront resort on Ko Kradan, Kalume has a collection of bamboo and wooden bungalows set around a garden. They're basic but cute with mosquito nets, fans, and cold-water showers in the indoor/outdoor bathrooms. Kradan's perfect beach is a mere step away from the beachfront cabanas (perfect for lazing and reading) and Kalume's laid-back restaurant and island bar.

BOATS FROM KO KRADAN

DESTINATION	BOAT COMPANY	FARE (B)	DURATION (HR)	FREQUENCY
Hat Yao (for Trang)	Tigerline	1050	1	11.30am
Ko Lanta	Tigerline	950	1½	10.45am & 1.30pm
	Bundhaya Speedboat/Satun Pak Bara Speedboat Club	1150	1¼	10.45am/10.50am
Ko Lipe	Tigerline	1600	3½	11.30am
	Bundhaya Speedboat/Satun Pak Bara Speedboat Club	1400	2	11.35am/11.40am
Ko Muk	Tigerline	300	15min	11.30am & 2.30pm
	Bundhaya Speedboat/Satun Pak Bara Speedboat Club	300	15min	10.45am/10.50am
Ko Ngai	Tigerline	750	30min	10.45am & 1.30pm
	Bundhaya Speedboat/Satun Pak Bara Speedboat Club	400	45min	10.45am/10.50am

Paradise Lost   BUNGALOW **$$**
(☑ 080 146 7152; dm 300B, bungalows 700-1800B)
One of Kradan's first lodgings, this inland
property is in walking distance of all three of
Kradan's main beaches. There's an airy five-
bed, fan-cooled dorm, but the bungalows are
basic, with the cheapest sharing bathrooms.
The bigger and more expensive bungalows
have their own bathrooms but are still only
functional. It's closed in the low season.

The open-plan **kitchen** (☑ 080 146 7152;
mains 140-350B; ⊘ 8am-9pm) dishes up tasty
food in big portions.

Seven Seas Resort   RESORT **$$$**
(☑ 082 490 2442; www.sevenseasresorts.com;
r incl breakfast 6000-12,000B; ✻ ◈ ⊠) This boutique resort is by far the plushest option on
Kradan. Supersleek rooms draw many Scandinavian visitors with their terrazzo floors,
indoor/outdoor bathrooms blending into
tropical gardens, enormous low-slung beds
and, for some, private cabanas. Hugging the
jet-black infinity pool, the resort's breezy
restaurant (☑ 075 203389; mains 200-1000B;
⊘ 7am-10pm; ◈) serves pricey Thai/interna-
tional dishes. It's in a prime location halfway up Kradan's main beach, with 24-hour
electricity.

ⓘ Getting There & Away

From November to April, daily boats to Kuantungku on the mainland leave at 8.30am and
1pm; tickets include connecting minibuses to
Trang (450B) or Trang's airport (600B). From
Trang, combined minibus-and-boat services
depart for Ko Kradan at 11am and 4pm. You can
charter long-tails to/from Kuantungku (1500B,

45 minutes to one hour), Ko Muk (800B, 30
minutes) and Ko Ngai (1500B, 45 minutes).

From October to April, Bundhaya Speedboat
(p688), Satun Pak Bara Speedboat Club (p688)
and the Phuket-Ko Lipe ferry with Tigerline
(p688) link Ko Kradan with other islands. Speedboats and ferries rarely depart at the scheduled
times and usually take longer than predicted to
reach their destination.

Ko Muk

Motoring towards jungle-clad Ko Muk (เกาะ
มุก) is unforgettable, whether you land
on the eastern sugary white sandbar Hat
Sivalai (หาดศิวาลัย), on humble, local-flavoured Hat Lodung (หาดลอด) or on southwest Hat Farang (หาดฝรั่ง), where jade water
kisses a golden beach.

Ko Muk is an island begging to be explored – on foot, bicycle, motorbike or kayak
– between lazy days spent on the beach. The
principal village by the main pier remains
more real than those on many tourist islands, and you'll be mixing with travellers
who are more likely to relish the calm than
party all night. It's an easy hop to most islands in the province, which means there's a
steady stream of package tourists tramping
Hat Sivalai and day tripping over to Tham
Morakot from Ko Lanta.

◉ Sights & Activities

Between Ko Muk and Ko Ngai are two small
karst islets, Ko Cheuk (เกาะเชือก) and Ko
Waen (เกาะแหวน), both with small sandy
beaches and good snorkelling.

Many resorts rent out bikes (100B to 150B per day) and motorbikes (250B per day) and several rent kayaks (100B to 300B per hour). You can walk through rubber plantations and the island's devout Muslim sea shanty villages (remember to cover up).

Tham Morakot
CAVE

(ถ้ำมรกต, Emerald Cave) A beautiful limestone tunnel leads 80m into a cave on Ko Muk's west coast. No wonder pirates buried treasure here. You have to swim through the tunnel, part of the way in darkness, before exiting at a small white-sand beach surrounded by lofty limestone walls. A piercing shaft of light illuminates it at around noon. National park fees (adult/child 200/100B) apply.

The cave features prominently on most tour itineraries, so it can get ridiculously crowded in high season. It's best to charter a long-tail boat (800B to 1000B) or rent a kayak and zip over at daybreak or late afternoon when you'll have it to yourself, but note that you can't get inside at high tide.

🛏 Sleeping

Hat Sivalai has the poshest digs, while Hat Lodung has cheaper options, though the beach isn't nearly as nice.

The sea is cleaner on crescent-shaped Hat Farang. The beachfront bungalows here are overpriced for what you get but just a short walk inland you'll find good-value digs as more and more resorts are being built minutes from the beach. It's a 10-minute motorbike taxi to/from the pier (50B).

Koh Mook Hostel
HOSTEL $

(☑ 089 724 4456; www.kohmookhostel.com; incl breakfast dm/d 400/1300B; ❄ 🛜) The only hostel in the Trang Islands, this place is run by a friendly Muslim family and consists of three decent-sized and clean dorm rooms (one is female-only) as well as a private double with en suite. The rooms are painted in breezy pastel colours, the attached bakery-cafe serves homemade bread, cakes and pizza, and it's a 10-minute walk from Hat Sivalai.

⭐ Nature Hill @ Koh Mook
BUNGALOW $$

(☑ 089 014 1614; www.naturehillkohmook.com; bungalow 2000B; 🛜) On a tree-clad hill just five minutes' walk from Hat Farang, these gorgeous bungalows are an excellent choice. The rustic designs incorporate distressed timber, polished concrete, recycled glass and indoor/outdoor bathrooms with pebble-floored showers. Bungalows have fans, high ceilings and slatted wooden breezeways to keep rooms cool, and the filmy mosquito netting over pallet beds spells jungle romance.

There are also family bungalows (4000B). The wi-fi is available only in the restaurant.

Koh Mook Garden Beach Resort
BUNGALOW $$

(☑ 081 748 3849; kohmookgarden@gmail.com; Hat Lodung; r 1000-1500B; ❄ 🛜) Endearingly ramshackle and very laid-back, Garden Beach Resort stands out for its family feel and very helpful host. Bungalows, both the older and basic bamboo ones and the newer, more comfortable concrete ones, are scattered around a lush garden, but the beach isn't as nice as others on the island. The attached restaurant serves tasty Thai food.

Sivalai
RESORT $$$

(☑ 089 723 3355; www.komooksivalai.com; Hat Sivalai; bungalows incl breakfast 5500-8500B; ❄ 🛜 ⛱) Straddling an arrow-shaped white-sand peninsula framed by views of karst islands and the mainland, Sivalai wins the award for Ko Muk's most fabulous location. The elegant dark-wood bungalows are sizeable and tasteful; some have wraparound verandas. There are two pools, a handy spa (massages from 700B) and the restaurant sits right at the tip of the peninsula.

Kayak rental is 300B per hour.

🍴 Eating

More restaurants are springing up in the village by the main pier, and there are even a few spread out inland from Hat Farang. Most resorts have restaurants open to everyone.

Ko Yao
THAI $

(☑ 062 485 4591; Hat Farang; mains 80-120B; ⏱ 8am-9pm; 🛜) Perched above the rocks at the southern end of Hat Farang, this cliffside restaurant and bar has dramatic sea views. Mismatched wooden tables and chairs sprawl over a rough plank deck that hugs the rockface. The location is superb and the Thai dishes are usually good but the service can be slow.

Hilltop Restaurant
THAI $$

(☑ 084 847 9133; mains 100-300B; ⏱ 9am-10pm) Recommended as one of the best restaurants on the island, this family-run operation serves all your Thai favourites using organically grown local produce. It's in an atmospheric, jungle-cloaked garden setting about 800m inland from Hat Farang.

ℹ️ Getting There & Away

Boats and long-tails to Ko Muk (120B to 250B, 30 minutes) leave daily from the pier at Kuantungku at noon, 1pm and 4pm from November to April, returning to the mainland at 8am, 9am and 2pm (services peter out in November and April). Minibus-and-boat combo tickets take you to/from Trang (350B, 1½ hours) and Trang's airport (500B, 1½ hours). You can also charter long-tails to/from Kuantungku (800B, 30 minutes).

From October to April, Ko Muk is a stop on the ferry operated by Tigerline (p688), and the **Bundhaya Speedboat** (📞074 750388, 074 750389; www.bundhayaspeedboat.com) and Satun Pak Bara Speedboat Club (p688) services connecting Ko Lanta (950B, one hour), Ko Ngai (350B to 750B, 30 minutes) and Ko Lipe (1400B to 1600B, two hours). Note that speedboats and ferries rarely depart at the scheduled times and usually take longer than predicted to reach their destination.

Long-tail charters from Ko Muk to Ko Kradan (800B, 30 minutes), Ko Ngai (1500B, one hour) and Pak Meng (1500B, 45 minutes to one hour) are easily arranged on the pier or by asking at your accommodation.

Ko Ngai

Encircled by coral and clear waters, densely forested Ko Ngai (เกาะไหง; Ko Hai) rivals stunning Ko Kradan as the south Andaman's poster paradise idyll. The long, blonde wind-swept beach on the eastern coast spills into turquoise water that ends at a reef drop-off (good for snorkelling). It's a romantic place where dewy-eyed couples stroll the beach, and with only a handful of resorts and no indigenous population on the island, it can be very quiet, especially at night.

Ko Ngai is technically part of Krabi Province, but its mainland link is with Pak Meng, 16km northeast. The island is a popular stop on day trips during high season – expect some crowds.

Ko Ngai has a couple of dive centres (dives from 1300B). Resorts rent snorkel sets and fins (300B per day) and sea kayaks (100B per hour), or you can join half-day snorkelling tours of nearby islands (from 600B).

🛏️ Sleeping & Eating

It's mainly upscale resorts here but a couple of budget options have sprung up, and they're all along the main east-coast beach.

Not all resorts remain open year-round – some close for at least a month during low season.

There are no standalone restaurants here. All the resorts have their own eateries.

Sea Camp by Sea Open Diving TENTED CAMP $
(📞065 265 6255; dm 300B, tent 950B; ⊙Oct-Apr; ❄️🐾) A welcome budget option on Ko Ngai, Sea Camp has air-conditioned tents with mosquito netting, shared bathrooms and cold-water showers in a prime location on the gorgeous main beach. The eight-bed dorm (with bunk beds) can't get more basic – the floor is the sandy beach. There's a restaurant and dive shop on-site, and a popular bar (⊙10am-late; 🐾).

Ko Ngai Seafood Bungalows BUNGALOW $$
(📞095 014 1853; kob_1829@hotmail.com; bungalow 1500-1800B; 🐾) Located in the middle of the main beach and boosted by its friendly family-style set-up, these simple, well-kept, stone-floored, fan-cooled bungalows with sea-view porches are the best no-frills beachfront digs on Ko Ngai. The attached seafood-focused **restaurant** (📞081 367 8497; mains 170-300B; ⊙7am-9pm; 🐾) is well worth a visit, too.

Coco Cottage BUNGALOW $$$
(📞089 724 9225; www.coco-cottage.com; bungalows incl breakfast 3300-7900B; ⊙Jul-Aug & Oct–mid-May; ❄️🐾) These cottages are coconut thatched-roof extravaganzas with coconut-wood walls and coconut-shell lanterns, set in a jungle garden just back from the north end of the main beach. Wake up to twinkling Andaman vistas through floor-to-ceiling windows in sea-view bungalows. Other perks include bamboo loungers, massage pavilions and a decent Thai/fusion beachfront **restaurant-bar** (📞089 724 9225; mains 170-260B; ⊙7am-9.30pm; 🐾).

Thanya Resort BUNGALOW $$$
(📞075 206967, 086 950 7355; www.kohngaithanya resort.com; bungalow incl breakfast 5250-6900B; ❄️@🐾🏊) Ko Ngai's Bali-chic choice has dark but spacious teak bungalows with indoor hot showers and outdoor bucket showers (don't knock it until you've tried it). Laze at the gorgeous beachside pool and gaze across the frangipani-filled lawn rolling out towards the sand from your terrace. There's an on-site **dive centre** (📞085 056 3455; 1 dive

KO SUKORN

Little-visited Ko Sukorn (เกาะสุกร) is a natural paradise of tawny beaches, light-green sea, jungle-shrouded black-rock headlands, and stilted shack neighbourhoods home to 2600-odd mainly Muslim residents with rice fields, watermelon plots and rubber plantations unfurling along narrow concrete roads. Spin past fields occupied only by water buffalo, through pastel villages where people are genuinely happy to see you, and sleep soundly through deep, silent nights. Sukorn's stillness is breathtaking, its authenticity a tonic to the jaded, road-weary soul.

With few hills, plenty of shade, expansive panoramas and lots of opportunities to meet islanders, Sukorn is best explored by bicycle. The main beach, dotted with a few low-key resorts, extends along the island's southwestern coast. Cover up away from the beach.

Sleeping

Sukorn has only a few places to stay, most along the pleasant beach on the southwest coast: Yataa Island Resort (☎ 089 647 5550; www.yataaresort.com; Ao Lo Yai Beach; bungalow incl breakfast 1400-6500B; ✳ 🛜 🌊) has pastel-painted, green-roofed concrete air-con bungalows that frame a cool blue pool and have varnished-wood verandas. Staff offer Sukorn maps, guided island tours and bicycle/motorbike rental (100/250B). There's a gorgeous long beach out front, and the restaurant is good value.

At Sukorn Cabana (☎ 089 724 2326; www.sukorncabanaresort.com; bungalow incl breakfast 1200-1800B; ⊘ closed May; ✳ 🛜), sloping landscaped grounds dotted with papaya, frangipani and bougainvillea hold large, clean and well-managed (if a little old) bungalows sporting thatched roofs, fridges, polished-wood interiors and plush verandas.

Eating

There are a few independent eateries, mainly in Ban Saimai close to the pier, but all shut by 8pm. All the resorts have restaurants.

How to get there

The easiest way to get to Sukorn is by private transfers from Trang, arranged through your resort (per person 1900B). The cheapest way is to take a sŏrng·tăa·ou from Trang to Yan Ta Khao (80B, 40 minutes), then transfer to Ban Ta Seh (50B, 45 minutes), from where long-tails to Ban Saimai (50B), Sukorn's main village, leave when full. Trang guesthouses and travel agents arrange sŏrng·tăa·ou-and-boat transfers (250B to 350B) to Ban Saimai via Ban Ta Seh, departing Trang at 11am daily. Otherwise, book a taxi from Trang to Ban Ta Seh (900B). The resorts are a 3km walk or 100B motorcycle-taxi ride from Ban Saimai. You can charter long-tails directly to the beach resorts (400B).

1300-1500B; ⊘ 9am-7pm Nov-Apr), plus a reasonably priced Thai restaurant (☎ 094 583 2888; mains 150-300B; ⊘ 7am-8pm; 🛜). It's at the south end of main beach.

ℹ Getting There & Away

There's a daily boat from Ko Ngai to Pak Meng (350B, one hour) at 9am, returning to Ko Ngai at noon. You can also charter long-tails to and from Pak Meng (1500B), Ko Muk (1500B), Ko Kradan (1800B) and Ko Lanta (2000B); enquire at Ko Ngai Seafood Bungalows (p692). Most resorts arrange transfers to the mainland.

From October to April, Tigerline (p688), Satun Pak Bara Speedboat Club (p688) and Bundhaya Speedboat (p692) stop just off Ko Ngai en route between Phuket and Ko Lipe. Note that boats rarely depart at the scheduled times and

usually take longer than predicted to reach their destination.

The pier is at Koh Ngai Resort, but long-tails (100B) usually drop you at the resort you're staying at.

SATUN PROVINCE

The Andaman's southernmost region, Satun (จังหวัดสตูล) was until recently mostly overlooked, but that's all changed thanks to the dynamic white sands of Ko Lipe – a one-time backpacker secret turned mainstream beach getaway. Beyond Ko Lipe, the rest of the province passes by in the blink of an eye, as visitors rush north to Ko Lanta or south to Pulau Langkawi (Malaysia). Which means, of course, that they miss the untrammelled

BOATS FROM KO NGAI

DESTINATION	BOAT COMPANY	FARE (B)	DURATION (HR)	FREQUENCY
Ko Kradan	Tigerline	750	30min	11.15am & 2.15pm
	Bundhaya Speedboat/Satun Pak Bara Speedboat Club	400	25min	11.10am/11am
Ko Lanta	Tigerline	750	1	11am & 1.45pm
	Bundhaya Speedboat/Satun Pak Bara Speedboat Club	650	30min	11.20am/11.30am
Ko Lipe	Tigerline	1600	4	11.15am
	Bundhaya Speedboat/Satun Pak Bara Speedboat Club	1600	2½	11.10am/11am
Ko Muk	Tigerline	750	1	11.15am & 2.15pm
	Bundhaya Speedboat/Satun Pak Bara Speedboat Club	350	30min	11.10am/11am
Ko Phi-Phi	Tigerline	1200	2½	11am & 1.45pm
	Bundhaya Speedboat/Satun Pak Bara Speedboat Club	1350	2	11.20am/11.30am
Phuket	Tigerline	1800	3½	11am & 1.45pm
	Bundhaya Speedboat/Satun Pak Bara Speedboat Club	1800	3	11.20am/11.30am

beaches and sea caves of Ko Tarutao, the rugged trails and ribbon waterfalls of Ko Adang, the rustic beauty of Ko Bulon Leh and easy-going Satun itself.

Largely Muslim in make-up, Satun has seen little of the political turmoil that plagues the fellow Muslim-majority provinces of neighbouring Yala, Pattani and Narathiwat. Around 60% of inhabitants speak Yawi or Malay as a first language, and the few humble wát in the region are vastly outnumbered by mosques.

Satun

📞 074 / POP 23,800

Lying in a steamy jungle valley surrounded by limestone cliffs and a murky river, isolated Satun (สตูล) is a surprisingly bustling little city: the focal point of a province that's home to over 300,000 people. Few foreign visitors pass through, and most of them are heading to and from Malaysia, or are yachties dropping in for cheap repairs in Satun's acclaimed boat yard. If you do stick around you'll discover that Satun has some intriguing Sino-Portuguese and religious architecture, delicious food, lots of friendly smiles and plenty of authentic charm. The surrounding countryside is lovely and ripe for exploration.

👁 Sights & Activities

Satun National Museum   MUSEUM

(พิพิธภัณฑ์สถานแห่งชาติสตูล, Kuden Mansion; Soi 5, Th Satun Thanee; 50B; ⏰ 9am-4pm Wed-Sun) Housed in a restored 1902 Sino-Portuguese mansion, Satun's excellent little museum was originally constructed as a temporary home for King Rama V during a royal visit. It was subsequently used as a headquarters by the Japanese military in WWII. Now it features informative displays on local history, customs and Muslim life in southern Thailand. There are good English captions.

Monkey Mountain   WALKING

Soak up Satun's refreshing shabby beauty by hiking this jungle mound of limestone teeming with macaques. You can also walk over a bridge here to a stilted fishing village 1km west of town.

🍴 Sleeping & Eating

Quick, cheap Chinese and Muslim restaurants are on Th Burivanich and Th Samanta Prasit. Chinese food stalls specialise in *kôw mŏo daang* (red pork with rice); Muslim restaurants offer roti with southern-style chicken curry and the local version of biryani. There's a decent **night market** (off Th Satun Thanee; mains from 40B; ⏰ 5-9pm).

On's Guesthouse
GUESTHOUSE $

([📞] 081 097 9783; onmarch13@hotmail.com; 17 & 36 Th Burivanich; dm 250B, r 250-600B; [❄][🛜]) On, Satun's dynamic tourism matriarch, has tweaked her long-standing guesthouse so that it is now spread across two buildings opposite each other. The buildings also house her restaurant and bar. The dorm is a massive open space with lockers, while there's a range of private fan and air-con rooms that get bigger and brighter the more you spend. All share bathrooms.

Satun Tanee Hotel
GUESTHOUSE $

([📞] 074 712309, 074 711010; www.satuntaneehotel.com; 90 Th Satun Thanee; r incl breakfast 300-800B; [❄][🛜]) Behind the lime-green-and-orange exterior lie reasonably sized, modern rooms with comfortable beds and wood-panelled floors, plus dingier, cheaper, unrenovated fan-only rooms on the top floor (there's no lift and no breakfast). It's a bit institutional, but you get a warm welcome.

On's Living Room
MULTICUISINE $$

([📞] 081 097 9783; 17 Th Burivanich; mains 70-250B; [🕐] 8am-8pm; [🛜]) On is a legend in tiny Satun. The restaurant and Western-style bar here sits on the ground floor of a converted shophouse (upstairs houses part of On's Guesthouse). The Thai dishes are spicy and there's a good selection of Western fare. It's comfortable, with wood and cane furniture and high bar stools.

ℹ️ Information

Bangkok Bank (Th Burivanich; [🕐] 8.30am-3.30pm Mon-Fri) Has a foreign-exchange desk and an ATM.

Immigration Office ([📞] 074 711080; info@sat-unimmigration.go.th; Th Burivanich; [🕐] 8.30am-4.30pm Mon-Fri) Satun's immigration office sits opposite the clock tower, and handles visa issues and extensions, though it's easier for tourists to exit and re-enter Thailand via the border checkpoint at Tha Tammalang.

Police Station (Th Satun Thanee) Satun's main police station.

ℹ️ Getting There & Away

The nearest airport to Satun is at Hat Yai, a two-hour drive away.

BOAT

From Tha Tammalang (10km south of Satun), there are two ferries daily to Pulau Langkawi (9am and 3.30pm, 350B) in Malaysia. In the reverse direction, ferries leave Pulau Langkawi daily for Satun at 10.30am and 5.15pm (RM36).

Satun

BUS

Buses leave from Satun's **bus terminal**, 2km south of town. **Buses to Trang** (Th Satun Thanee) (120B, two hours, hourly 5am to 4.30pm) also pick up passengers on Th Satun Thanee by the 7-Eleven. Trang buses go via La-Ngu (50B), where you can catch a *sŏrng·tǎa·ou* (pick-up minivan) to Pak Bara (20B) for boats to Ko Lipe and other islands.

TO	FARE (B)	TIME (HR)	FREQUENCY
Bangkok (air-con bus)	736	14	7am, 2.30pm, 3pm & 4.30pm
Bangkok (VIP bus)	1331	14	4pm
Krabi	200	5	8.15am, 10.15am, 12.15pm & 8pm
Phuket	358	8	8.15am, 10.15am, 12.15pm & 8pm

MINIVAN

Minivans run from Satun's bus terminal to Krabi (200B, five hours, 7am and 2pm), Trang (120B, two hours, hourly 5am to 5pm), Hat Yai (100B, two hours, 6am to 5pm) and Hat Yai's airport (300B, 2½ hours, 6am to 5pm). Minivans to Hat Yai (p695) also pick up passengers on Th Satun Thanee by the 7-Eleven.

There are also minivans, though not running every day, to Kuala Perlis in Malaysia (400B). They pick you up from your accommodation. On's Guesthouse (p695) can organise tickets.

ⓘ Getting Around

The centre of Satun is easily walkable, but you can rent bicycles (150B per day) and motorbikes (250B per day) from On's Guesthouse (p695).

Sŏrng·tăa·ou (pick-up minibuses) to the bus station cost 40B per person. Orange *sŏrng·tăa·ou* to **Tha Tammalang** (Th Sulakanukoon) pick up passengers at the 7-Eleven on Th Sulakanukoon. Motorcycle taxis run around town for 50B.

Pak Bara

☏ 074 / POP 3000

Pak Bara (ปากบารา), 60km northwest of Satun, is the main jumping-off point for the dazzling islands of the Ko Tarutao Marine National Park. Facilities are slowly improving as Pak Bara becomes increasingly packed with tourists, although most are in transit to the islands. The peaceful fishing town has forgettable sleeping options, and, aside from great seafood, there's no pressing reason to stick around.

The main road from La-Ngu (Rte 4052) terminates at the pier, which is basically a massive passenger terminal for Lipe- and Tarutao-bound speedboats, with travel agencies, cheap restaurants, ATMs and stalls flogging beach gear. The Ko Tarutao Marine National Park visitors centre is by the pier; here you can book Ko Tarutao and Ko Adang accommodation, buy speedboat tickets and obtain camping permission. Local travel agents arrange one-day tours (2000B) to the park's islands.

ⓘ Information

There are plenty of ATMs close to the pier and you can change money at many travel agencies here.

Ko Tarutao Marine National Park Visitors Centre (☏ 074 783485; Pak Bara Pier; ⊙ 8am-5pm) The helpful visitors centre is to the side of the pier. Here you can book Ko Tarutao and Ko Adang accommodation and speedboat tickets and obtain permission for national park camping.

ⓘ Getting There & Away

BOAT

From mid-October to mid-May, speedboats run by the Satun Pak Bara Speedboat Club (p688) run from Pak Bara's **ferry terminal** to Ao Pante Malacca on Ko Tarutao (450B, 30 minutes), and on to Ko Lipe (650B, 1½ hours) at 11.30am. There are speedboats to Ko Tarutao (450B) at 11.30am from mid-October to mid-May. Speedboats run directly to Ko Lipe at 9.30am, 11.30am, 1.30pm and 3.30pm. Boats return from Ko Lipe at 9.30am, 11.30am, 1.30pm and 4pm. There are fewer trips in low season.

For Ko Bulon Leh (450B, 30 minutes), boats depart at 1pm and buzz on to Ko Lipe. If you miss the Bulon boat, you can charter long-tails from local fisherfolk (2000B, 1½ hours). During low season, services to Ko Lipe are less frequent, but you can always count on the 11.30am boat from Pak Bara (weather permitting), returning at 9.30am.

BUS

From Satun, take an ordinary Trang bus and get off at La-Ngu (50B, 30 minutes), continuing by *sŏrng·tăa·ou* (pick-up minibus) to Pak Bara (20B, 20 minutes). A few minivans also make the run daily (60B). Pick up the buses and minivans outside the 7-Eleven on Th Satun Thanee.

MINIVAN

Air-con minivans run every 45 minutes between 7.30am and 6.30pm from Hat Yai to Pak Bara pier (120B, two hours). Departures from Pak Bara include the following:

TO	FARE (B)	TIME (HR)	FREQUENCY
Hat Yai	150	2	11.30am, 1.30pm & 3.30pm
Hat Yai Airport	250	2	11.30am, 1.30pm & 3.30pm
Ko Lanta	450	3-4	11.30am
Krabi	450	4	11.30am
Phuket	650	6	11.30am
Trang	200	2	11.30am

Ko Tarutao Marine National Park

One of Thailand's most exquisite, unspoilt regions, Ko Tarutao Marine National Park (อุทยานแห่งชาติหมู่เกาะตะรุเตา; ☎074 783485; www.dnp.go.th; adult/child 200/100B; ☺mid-Oct–mid-May) encompasses 51 islands blanketed by well-preserved rainforest teeming with fauna, surrounded by healthy coral reefs and radiant white beaches. Within, you might spot dusky langurs, crab-eating macaques, mouse deer, wild pigs, sea otters, fishing cats, tree pythons, water monitors, Brahminy kites, sea eagles, hornbills, reef egrets and kingfishers.

Ko Lipe has become a high-profile tourist destination and it's where most travellers stay. It's exempt from national park rules governing development because it is home to communities of *chow lair* (sea gypsies, also spelt *chao leh*). The only other islands you can stay on are Ko Tarutao, the biggest island and home to the park headquarters (p699), and Ko Adang.

Rubbish on the islands is a problem. Do your part and tread lightly. Apart from Ko Lipe, the park officially shuts from mid-October to mid-May.

There are no ATMs or foreign-exchange facilities on Ko Tarutao or Ko Adang. Bring cash. There are many ATMs and places to change money on Ko Lipe, as well as at Pak Bara.

Ko Tarutao

Most of the whopping 152 sq km that comprises Ko Tarutao (เกาะตะรุเตา) is covered in jungle, which rises sharply to the park's 713m peak, making this one of Thailand's wildest islands. Mangrove swamps and limestone cliffs circle much of it, while steep trails and rough roads lead through the interior, making this a great place for fit hikers and mountain bikers. Tarutao's beaches are less inviting, thanks to tidal garbage and cloudy water. If you're after idyllic strips of sand and snorkelling, head to Ko Adang or Ko Rawi instead.

Ko Tarutao has a squalid past as a prison island: one of the reasons why it has never been developed.

The island closes officially from mid-May to mid-October.

◉ Sights & Activities

With a navigable river and long paved roads, Tarutao is perfect for independent exploration. You can hire kayaks (200/500B per hour/day) or mountain bikes (50/250B) from park headquarters (p699) and at some of the ranger stations.

Ao Molae   BEACH
(อ่าวเมาะและ) Quiet, wonderfully secluded and with white sands, Ao Molae is the pick of Ko Tarutao's beaches. Behind it is a **ranger station** (☺8am-5pm mid-Oct–mid-May), bungalows and a campsite, all a (very) hilly 4km walk/cycle south of Ao Pante Malacca.

Tham Jara-Khe   CAVE
(ถ้ำจระเข้, Crocodile Cave) The large stream flowing inland from Ao Pante Malacca, on northwest Ko Tarutao, leads to Tham Jara-Khe, once home to deadly saltwater crocodiles. The cave is navigable for 1km at low tide and can be visited on long-tail tours (500B) from Ao Pante Malacca's jetty.

🛏 Sleeping & Eating

There are basic government-run bungalows at Ao Pante Malacca (www.dnp.go.th; Ao Pante Malacca; r 600-1200B; ☺mid-Oct–mid-May) and Ao Molae (www.dnp.go.th; Ao Molae; r 600B; ☺mid-Oct–mid-May). Water is rationed, and electricity runs from 6.30pm to 6am. You can also camp at Ao Molae and Ao Son. Facilities are very basic and monkeys often wander into tents. Shut them tight.

Accommodation can be booked online or, more easily, at the park's visitors centre (p696) in Pak Bara.

There are simple canteens offering Thai food at Ao Pante Malacca (Ao Pante Malacca; mains 80-180B; ☺7.30am-2.30pm & 5-8.30pm) and Ao Molae (Ao Molae; mains 70-140B; ☺7.30am-2.30pm & 5-8.30pm).

PHUKET & THE ANDAMAN COAST

Ko Tarutao Marine National Park & Around

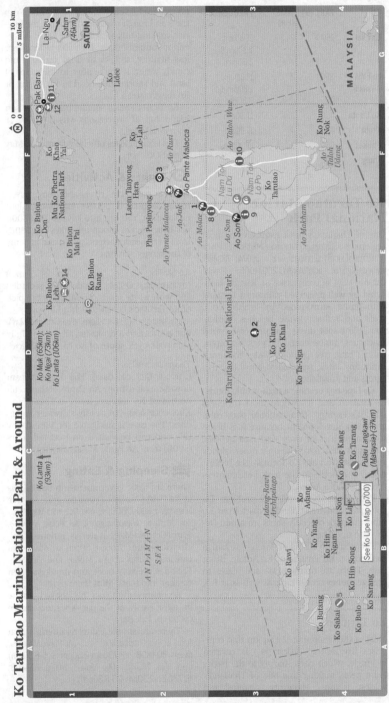

Ko Tarutao Marine National Park & Around

ℹ Information

Ko Tarutao Marine National Park Headquarters (Ao Pante Malacca; ⊗8am-5pm) Hire kayaks and mountain bikes here.

Ko Tarutao kite Centre (Ao Pante Malacca; ⊗8am-5pm) Maps and local information.

There are ranger stations across the island, at Ao Molae (p697) in the northwest, **Ao Son** (⊗8am-5pm mid-Oct–mid-May) on the west coast and **Ao Taloh Waw** (⊗8am-5pm mid-Oct–mid-May) on the east of the island.

ℹ Getting There & Away

From mid-October to mid-May, there's a daily speedboat from Pak Bara to the **ferry terminal** (Ao Pante Malacca) at Ao Pante Malacca on Ko Tarutao (450B, 30 minutes), leaving at 11.30am. A private long-tail boat from Pak Bara for up to eight people is 4500B for a return trip.

If you're staying at Ao Molae, take a shared van from Ao Pante Malacca at 11am or 1pm daily (per person 50B; demand-dependent).

Ko Lipe

Ko Lipe (เกาะหลีเป๊ะ) is blessed with two beautiful, wide white-sand beaches separated by jungle-covered hills and is close to protected coral reefs. However, while once a serene tropical paradise, it's now a poster child for untamed development. Ko Lipe's centre has transformed into an ever-expanding maze of hotels, restaurants, travel agencies and shops. Tourist-inspired growth has led to issues with waste management, noise pollution and energy supplies. The biggest losers have been the 700-strong community of *chow lair* (sea gypsies, also spelt *chao*

leh), whose ancestors were gifted Lipe as a home by King Rama V in 1909, but who sold it in the 1970s.

Despite all the development, Lipe's stunning beauty shines through: gorgeous beaches, sensational dive sites, a jungle interior, a contagiously friendly vibe and a good few inhabitants keen to minimise their environmental impact. It's more chill than party but it's not the remote castaway island it once was.

◎ Sights & Activities

Keep your eyes open for long-tail boats while swimming, especially in low season. People have been run down before. Don't expect boats to see you.

Do not try to swim the narrow strait between Lipe and Adang at any time of year; currents are swift and can be deadly.

Diving

While it would be a stretch to call the diving here world-class most of the year, it's outstanding when the visibility clarifies, somewhat counterintuitively in the early part of the wet season (mid-April to mid-June). There are some fun drift dives and two rockstar dive sites.

Eight Mile Rock is a deep pinnacle that attracts devil rays and (very) rare whale sharks. It's the only site in the area to see pelagics. **Stonehenge** is popular because of its beautiful soft corals, resident seahorses, rare leopard sharks and the reef-top boulders behind its inspired name. **Ko Sarang** is another stunner, with gorgeous soft corals, a

PHUKET & THE ANDAMAN COAST KO TARUTAO MARINE NATIONAL PARK

Ko Lipe

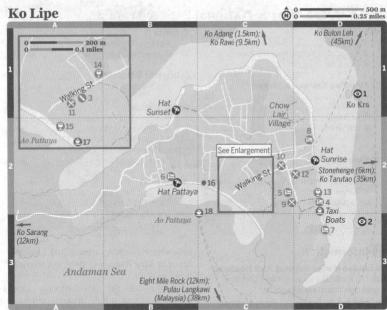

Ko Lipe

ripping current and solar flares of fish that make it many people's favourite Lipe dive spot.

All divers are required to pay a 200B fee to dive in the Ko Tarutao Marine National Park.

Ko Lipe Diving DIVING
(☎ 087 622 6204, 088 397 7749; www.kolipediving.com; Walking St; 1/2 dives 1700/2800B; ⊗8am-10pm) Well-organised, professional dive operator with consistently glowing reviews for its selection of specialist courses and fun

dives focused on diving education. Two-dive Discover Scuba costs 2800B; SSI Open Water certification is 14,500B. The marine national park dive fee (200B) is not included.

Davy Jones' Locker DIVING
(☎ 062 963 4425; www.scubadivekohlipe.com; Hat Pattaya; dives from 3000B) One-dive Discover Scuba sessions cost 2500B; PADI Open Water certification is 14,500B (including free accommodation at Koh Lipe Backpackers Hostel). Prices do not include the marine national park dive fee (200B).

Castaway Divers DIVING
(📞 083 138 7472; www.kohlipedivers.com; Castaway Resort, Hat Sunrise; 1/2 dives 2500/3800B; ⊙ 8am-6pm) Offers a range of specialised courses (night diving, underwater photography) as well as PADI Open Water certification (13,500B), snorkelling trips (700B) and more intimate dives off long-tail boats. Prices do not include the marine national park dive fee (200B).

Snorkelling

There's good coral along the southern coast and around Ko Kra (เกาะกระ) and Ko Usen, the islets opposite Hat Sunrise (be careful with oncoming long-tails though). Most resorts rent out mask-and-snorkel sets and fins (100B to 200B). Travel agents and some dive operators arrange four-point snorkel trips to Ko Adang, Ko Rawi and other coral-fringed islands from 450B per person.

Yoga

Swing by Castaway Resort for beachfront yoga (400B; 7am, 9am and 4.30pm).

🛏 Sleeping

More and more Ko Lipe resorts are staying open year-round. A few humble bamboo bungalows still stand strong, but resorts are colonising, particularly on Hat Pattaya. If you want tranquillity, head to less busy Hat Sunset. Book well ahead during high season and holidays, when prices skyrocket.

⭐ **Chic Lipe** HOSTEL $
(📞 090 767 6763; www.thechiclipe.com; 447 Mu 7; dm without/with bathroom 650/750B, r 1200-2500B; ❄ 🛜) Marketed as a boutique hostel, Chic Lipe has simply outstanding rooms, with polished concrete, distressed timber, and contemporary designs showcasing dorms with large bunk beds, and there are artfully decorated double-bed dorms, and private doubles that shame most hotels. A cosy library, coffee nook, restaurant, bar, fancy reception and wrought-iron chandeliers make this a decidedly chic and upmarket hostel/hotel.

Koh Lipe Backpackers Hostel HOSTEL $
(📞 062 963 4425; www.kohlipebackpackers.com; Hat Pattaya; dm 500B, r 2500-3000B; ❄ 🛜) The only beachfront hostel in Ko Lipe is housed in a contemporary-style concrete block on west Hat Pattaya. Showers are shared, but you get private lockers, wi-fi, the on-site Davy Jones' Locker dive school (divers get a discount) and the beach location is ace.

Upstairs are six simple but comfortable aircon private rooms with en suites.

⭐ **Castaway Resort** HOTEL $$
(📞 081 170 7605, 083 138 7472; www.castaway resorts.com; Hat Sunrise; bungalows 2700-4750B; 🛜) 🌿 Roomy dark-wood bungalows with hammock-laden terraces, cushions everywhere, overhead fans and fabulous, modern-meets-natural bathrooms embody Ko Lipe at its best. This welcoming resort is also one of Lipe's most environmentally friendly. There's a superchilled beachside cafe and bar (📞 089 724 2604; www.facebook.com/cornerbarlipe; Hat Sunrise; ⊙ 3pm-2am; 🛜), daily meditation and yoga classes (400B) and a good dive school (p701).

Wapi Resort BUNGALOW $$
(📞 089 464 5854; www.wapiresortkohlipe.com; Hat Sunrise; bungalows incl breakfast 2800-4800B; ❄ 🛜) These cute French-run bungalows slap-bang in the middle of Hat Sunrise are extremely popular. Beachfront bungalows have modern bathrooms and large verandas, but even the garden bungalows aren't far from the sandy beach. Beds in the family bungalow (6800B) are side by side. Clean, simple and good value.

⭐ **Serendipity** BUNGALOW $$$
(📞 088 395 5158; www.serendipityresort-kohlipe. com; Hat Sunrise; bungalows incl breakfast 6000-14,400B; ❄ 🛜) Serendipity is in an exquisitely designed spot, delightfully isolated by draping itself up above the boulder-strewn southern point of Hat Sunrise and accessed via a wooden boardwalk. Spacious dark-wood thatched bungalows feature private patios offering super views, great beds and stylish bathrooms, while the most expensive have plunge pools.

🍴 Eating & Drinking

There's some great seafood here: the best places are mostly inland. Find cheap eats at the roti stands and small Thai cafes along Walking St. Please take advantage of the waste-reducing water-refill points at many resorts and eateries.

Nee Papaya THAI $
(📞 087 714 5519; mains 80-150B; ⊙ 9am-11pm) Delightful Nee offers an affordable fish grill nightly, all the standard curries (including a dynamite beef *pá·naang*), noodles and stir-fries (beef, chicken, seafood or veggie), along with an array of fiery Isan dishes. She'll tone down the chillis on request, but her food is

best when spiced for the local palate, which is why she attracts many Thai tourists.

Café Tropical
MULTICUISINE $$

(📞083 169 1216; www.tropicalkohlipe.com; Walking St; mains 80-400B; ⊙7am-11pm; 🛜🍴) Colourful and tasty gluten-free, vegan and vegetarian burgers and salads come in large portions here, as do all the beef and chicken dishes. Ingredients are fresh and wholesome, the coffee has almond, rice and soy-milk options, and juices with kale and ginger will kick-start your day.

Barracuda
SEAFOOD $$

(📞089 739 3940; mains 80-250B; ⊙9am-10pm) Every second restaurant on Lipe offers fresh seafood barbecue, but this is the one the locals patronise the most. The other dishes on the menu are also great, especially the salads. The ramshackle, slightly tucked-away setting adds to the sense that you're eating at a place designed for Thais rather than foreigners.

Elephant Coffee House & Bar
INTERNATIONAL $$

(📞089 657 2178; www.facebook.com/Elephant KohLipe; Walking St; mains 120-420B; ⊙7am-1am) The bar is a long-tail, there are secondhand books for sale and black-and-white local-life photos are plastered across the walls. Pop into this coolly contemporary cafe for fabulous all-day breakfasts of thick French toast, excellent coffee and homemade muesli loaded with tropical fruit. Otherwise choose from fresh salads, sandwiches, burgers and pizzas. It's buzzing most evenings with a full crowd and live music.

★ Reggae Bar
BAR

(Hat Pattaya; ⊙4pm-1am) As the sun goes down, flickering candle flames cast a dreamy light over the beach mats and cushions sprawled across the sand at this superchilled reggae bar on Hat Pattaya. Sip cocktails, gaze at the stars or catch an impromptu fire show at one of the best beach bars on the island.

★ Maya Bar
BAR

(www.facebook.com/mayabarkohlipe; Walking St; ⊙5pm-1am) This is the swishest bar on Walking St, with 'love' slogans, hanging mobiles made from found objects, floor cushions on raised wooden platforms, inviting divans, flickering candles, beach-sand floor and

a feature bamboo 'wall'. DJs spin dance/electronic beats after dark and the cocktails (from 200B) work.

❶ Information

Immigration Office (⊙8am-4pm) Immigration has its own official kiosk on Hat Pattaya next to Bundhaya Resort.

❶ Getting There & Away

From mid-October to mid-May, speedboats run from Pak Bara to Ko Lipe (some via Ko Tarutao) at 9.30am, 11.30am, 1.30pm and 3.30pm (650B, 1½ hours). Boats return to Pak Bara at 9.30am, 11.30am, 1.30pm and 4pm. Low-season transport is weather dependent, but there's usually a direct daily boat from Pak Bara to Lipe at 11.30am, returning at 9.30am.

From November to April, the high-speed Tigerline ferry (p688) departs Ko Lipe at 10am for Phuket (2100B, eight hours), via Ko Phi-Phi (1750B, seven hours), Ko Lanta (1700B, five hours), Ko Muk (1400B, 3½ hours), Ko Kradan (1400B, 3½ hours) and Ko Ngai (1600B, 4½ hours).

From mid-October to late April, Bundhaya Speedboat (p692) and Satun Pak Bara Speedboat Club (p688) leave Ko Lipe at 9am for Ko Lanta (1900B, three hours), via Ko Bulon Leh (600B, one hour), Ko Kradan (1400B, two hours), Ko Muk (1400B, two hours) and Ko Ngai (1600B, 2½ hours). Speedboats return from Lanta at 10.30am.

Speedboats and ferries rarely depart at the scheduled times and usually take longer than predicted to reach their destination.

Boats also run from Ko Lipe to Pulau Langkawi (1000B, 1½ hours) in Malaysia from mid-October to late April.

No matter which boat you end up using, you'll have to take a 50B long-tail shuttle to/from the floating **ferry jetty** off Hat Pattaya, and pay a 200B national park fee as well as a 20B 'entrance fee' (as part of a local sharing agreement). Speedboats *may* drop you directly on Hat Pattaya. During low season (May to October), boats mostly dock at Hat Sunrise and there's no long-tail shuttle fee.

❶ Getting Around

There are few experiences as relaxing as pottering between the jungle gems of Ko Rawi, Ko Adang and the surrounding islets. The best way to see the archipelago is to hire a **taxi boat** (Hat Sunrise) with a *chow lair* (sea gypsy) captain from the stand on Hat Sunrise. You can rent kayaks (250B per hour) across the island.

Ko Bulon Leh

Stunning Ko Bulon Leh (เกาะบุโหลนเล), 23km west of Pak Bara, is surrounded by the Andaman's signature clear waters and has its share of faultless alabaster beaches and swaying casuarinas. This gorgeous island is in that perfect phase of being developed enough to offer some facilities, yet still retains a serene, low-key castaway vibe.

An exceptional, salt-white beach extends along the east coast between the island's two main resorts – Bulone Resort and Pansand Resort. In places it narrows, especially where buffered by gnarled mangroves and strewn with thick sun-bleached logs, making it easy to find a secret shady spot with dreamy views.

It's a tiny island, with electricity at the resorts only available in the evenings, and there are no ATMs (the nearest are at Pak Bara; bring cash). It's also a highly seasonal destination, with no tourist facilities during the low season, but its seductive charms lure travellers to return again and again to its sublime tropical shores.

🏃 Activities

Sunbathing, swimming or simply feasting your eyes on Bulon's main beach, a gorgeous ribbon of white sand fringed with calm turquoise water, is reason enough to visit this castaway gem. But Bulon's lush interior is interlaced with tracks and trails that are fun to explore, though the dense, jungle-covered rock that makes up the western half remains inaccessible on foot.

The island's wild beauty is accessible on the northern coast at blue, coral-gravel-laden Ao Panka Yai, which has decent snorkelling. This bay is linked by a small paved path to Ao Panka Noi, a fishing village with beautiful karst views, long-tails docking on a gravel beach and a clutch of good, simple restaurants, on the eastern half of the northern coast. Follow a nearby signposted trail west through remnant jungle and rubber plantations – with your eyes open wide lest you miss one of Bulon's enormous monitor lizards – to wind your way south to Ao Muang (Mango Bay), where there's an authentic *chow lair* (sea gypsies, also spelt *chao leh*) squid-fishing camp.

There's good coral off Laem Son on the northeastern edge of the island and down the eastern coast. You can rent kayaks (per hour 200B) at Bulone Resort and Pansand Resort. Snorkelling is best at low tide.

Resorts can arrange guided snorkelling trips (2000B, four hours, maximum eight people) to other islands in the Ko Bulon group. Tours usually take in the glassy emerald waters of Ko Gai (เกาะไก่) and Ko Ma (เกาะแม่), whose gnarled rocks have been ravaged by wind and time. But the most stunning sight is White Rock: bird-blessed spires shooting out of the open sea. Beneath

---

ℹ️ GETTING TO MALAYSIA

Keep in mind that Malaysia is one hour ahead of Thailand time.

Ko Lipe to Pulau Langkawi From mid-October to mid-April, Tigerline (p688), Bundhaya Speedboat (p692) and Satun Pak Bara Speedboat Club (p688) run daily from Ko Lipe to Pulau Langkawi in Malaysia (1000B, 1½ hours). Departures are at 10.30am, 11am and 4pm. Head to the immigration office in the centre of Hat Pattaya two hours before to get stamped out. In reverse, boats leave Pulau Langkawi for Ko Lipe at 9.30am and 2.30pm (Malaysian time).

Satun to Kuala Perlis or Pulau Langkawi From Tha Tammalang (10km south of Satun) there are two ferries daily to Pulau Langkawi, Malaysia (9am and 3.30pm, 350B). In the reverse direction, ferries leave Pulau Langkawi daily for Satun at 10.30am and 5.15pm. At the time of research there were no speedboats or long-tail boats running from Satun to Pulau Langkawi in Malaysia. It's possible to take a minivan (400B) from Satun to Kuala Perlis in Malaysia via the Wang Prajan/Wang Kelian border crossing, but they don't run every day. On's Guesthouse (p695) in Satun sells tickets.

At the border Citizens of the US, EU, Australia, Canada and several other countries may enter Malaysia for up to 90 days without prior visa arrangements. If you have questions about your eligibility, check with the nearest Malaysian embassy or consulate and apply for a visa in advance.

the surface is a mussel-crusted rock reef teeming with colourful fish.

🛏 Sleeping & Eating

Most places close from mid-April to November. Pansand Resort stays open until the end of May.

It's worth wandering over to Ao Panka Noi for food. There are a few local restaurants and shops in the Muslim village between Ao Panka Noi and Ao Panka Yai. All the resorts have their own restaurants.

Chaolae Homestay   BUNGALOW $

(☑ 086 290 2519, 086 967 0716; Ao Panka Yai; bungalows 700B; ☺ Nov-Apr) Simple bamboo-and-wood bungalows with cold-water showers and squat toilets. It's a blissfully quiet, shady spot, close to the village and run by a welcoming *chow lair* (sea gypsies) family, and steps away from decent snorkelling at Ao Panka Yai. The restaurant is OK but there's no wi-fi.

Pansand Resort   BUNGALOW $$$

(☑ 081 693 3667; www.pansand-resort.com; Main Beach; bungalow incl breakfast 1600-3500B; ☺ mid-Oct–May) Nestled in the towering trees behind a gorgeous ribbon of salt-white sand is a collection of red-roofed, wooden cottages. Furnishings are minimal and dated but the cottages are spacious and set far enough apart to maintain privacy. The beachfront restaurant serves tasty Thai and international dishes. It's the only Bulon resort to stay open until the end of May.

Bulone Resort   HOTEL $$$

(☑ 095 041 6211; www.bulone-resort.com; Main Beach; bungalows incl breakfast 3000-4500B;

☺ Nov-Apr; ❄ 🛜) Perched on Bulon's northeast cape with access to two exquisite white-sand stretches, Bulone Resort steals the island's top location. Cute white-washed-wood bungalows come with queen-sized beds, iron frames and ocean breezes. Huge alpine chalet-style air-con rooms tower behind on stilts, with glorious views. There's a Thai/international *restaurant* (☑ 095 041 6211; www.bulone-resort.com; mains 180-350B; ☺ 7.30-10am & 6-10pm Nov-Apr; 🛜), a coffee corner, and snorkelling trips can be arranged upon request.

Hug Bulon   BAR

(Main Beach; ☺ 10am-late Nov-Apr) A breezy beachfront bar (and restaurant) next to Pansand Resort, this is the place for chilled music and sunset cocktails. The food (both Thai and international) is highly recommended.

❶ Getting There & Away

From mid-October to late April, speedboats to Ko Bulon Leh (450B, 30 minutes) leave from Pak Bara at 1pm daily. Long-tail ship-to-shore transfers cost 50B; ask to be dropped off on the beach closest to your resort. In the reverse direction, **the speedboat** moors in the bay in front of Pansand Resort at 9am. You can charter long-tails to/from Pak Bara (2000B, 1½ hours).

From mid-October to late April, daily speedboats (600B, one hour) run from Ko Bulon Leh to Ko Lipe at 1pm, stopping in front of Pansand Resort. Boats originate in Ko Lanta (1600B, two hours) and make stops at Ko Ngai (1050B, 1½ hours), Ko Muk (900B, one hour) and Ko Kradan (900B, one hour), returning from Lipe at 9am.

Understand Thailand

History

Thai history begins as a story of migrants heading into a frontier land claimed by distant empires for trade, forced labour and patronage. Eventually the country fused a national identity around language, religion and monarchy. The kings resist colonisation from the expansionist Western powers on its border only to cede their absolute grip on the country when challenged from forces within. Since the transition to a constitutional monarchy in 1932, the country has been predominantly ruled by the military with a few democratic interludes.

Ancient History

Little evidence remains of the cultures that existed in Thailand before the middle of the 1st millennium CE. *Homo erectus* fossils in Thailand's northern province of Lampang date back at least 500,000 years, and the country's most important archaeological site is Ban Chiang, outside Udon Thani, which provides evidence of one of the world's oldest agrarian societies. It is believed that the Mekong River Valley and Khorat Plateau were inhabited as far back as 10,000 years ago by farmers and bronze-workers. Cave paintings in Pha Taem National Park near Ubon Ratchathani date back some 3000 years.

Ancient Sites

....

Ayuthaya Historical Park

....

Sukhothai Historical Park

....

Chiang Saen Historical Park

....

Lopburi Khmer ruins

....

Nakhon Si Thammarat National Museum

....

Phimai Historical Park

Early Empires

Starting around the 10th century, the 'Tai' people, considered to be the ancestors of the contemporary Thais, began migrating from southern China into present-day Southeast Asia. These immigrants spoke Tai-Ka-dai, said to be the most significant ethno-linguistic group in Southeast Asia. Some settled in the river valleys of modern-day Thailand, while others chose parts of modern-day Laos and the Shan state of Myanmar.

They settled in villages as farmers, hunters and traders and organised themselves into administrative units known as *meu·ang,* under the rule of a lord, that became the building blocks of the Tai state. Over time, the Tai expanded from the northern mountain valleys into the central plains and northeastern plateau, where there existed several important trading

TIMELINE	4000–2500 BCE	6th–11th centuries	9th–13th centuries
	Prehistoric people develop pottery, rice cultivation and bronze metallurgy in northeastern Thailand.	Dvaravati establish city-states in central Thailand, develop trade routes and Mon culture and practise Theravada Buddhism.	Angkor extends control across parts of Thailand, building Hindu-Buddhist sanctuaries.

centres ruled by various indigenous and 'foreign' empires, including the Mon-Dvaravati, Khmer (Cambodia) and Srivijaya (Malay).

Dvaravati

The Mon dominated parts of Burma (present-day Myanmar), western Thailand and the central plains. In the 6th to 9th centuries, the Dvaravati culture emerged as a distinct Buddhist culture associated with the Mon people. Little is known about this period but it is believed that Nakhon Pathom might have been the centre, and that overland trade routes extended to Burma, Cambodia, Chiang Mai and Laos, as evidenced by findings of distinctive Dvaravati Buddha images, temples and stone inscriptions in the Mon language.

The Dvaravati was one of many Indian-influenced cultures that established themselves in Southeast Asia, but scholars single out the Dvaravati because of its artistic legacy and the trade routes that might have provided an early framework for what would become the core of the modern-day Thai state.

Khmer

The Khmers were Southeast Asia's equivalent of the Roman Empire. This kingdom became famous for its extravagant sculpture and architecture and had a profound effect on the art and religion of the region. Established in the 9th century, the Khmer kingdom built its capital in Angkor (modern-day Cambodia) and expanded westward across present-day central and northeastern Thailand. Administrative centres anchored by Angkor-style temples were built in Lopburi (then known as Lavo), Sukhothai and Phimai (near Nakhon Ratchasima) and linked by road to the capital.

The Khmer's large-scale construction projects were a symbol of imperial power in its frontier lands and examples of the day's most advanced technologies. Khmer elements – Hinduism, Brahmanism, Theravada Buddhism and Mahayana Buddhism – mark this period in Thailand.

Srivijaya

While mainland Thailand was influenced by forces from the north and west, the Malay peninsula was economically and culturally fused to cultures further south. Between the 8th and 13th centuries, the Malay peninsula was under the sway of the confederation of the Srivijaya, which controlled maritime trade between the South China Sea and Indian Ocean. The Srivijaya capital is believed to have been in Palembang on Sumatra.

Of the series of Srivijaya city-states along the Malay peninsula, Tambralinga established its capital near present-day Nakhon Si Thammarat

Top History Reads

....

Thailand: A Short History (David K Wyatt; 2003)

....

A History of Thailand (Chris Baker and Pasuk Phongpaichit; 2009)

....

Chronicle of Thailand: Headlines Since 1946 (edited by Nicholas Grossman; 2010)

HISTORY EARLY EMPIRES

10th century	1240–1438	1283	1292
Approximate arrival of Tai peoples in Thailand.	Approximate dates of Sukhothai kingdom.	Early Thai script invented by King Ramkhamhaeng of Sukhothai.	Chiang Mai becomes the capital of Lanna, the historic northern kingdom.

and adopted Buddhism in the 13th century, while the states further south adopted Islam, creating a religious boundary which persists to this day. Remains of Srivijaya culture can be seen around Chaiya and Nakhon Si Thammarat. Many art forms of the Srivijaya kingdom – such as *nǎng dà·lung* (shadow theatre) and *lá·kon* (classical dance-drama) – also persist today.

Emerging Tai Kingdoms

In the 13th century, the regional empires started to decline and prosperous Tai city-states emerged with localised power and military might. The competing city-states were ultimately united into various kingdoms that began to establish a Thai identity. Scholars recognise Lanna, Sukhothai and Ayuthaya as the unifying kingdoms of the period.

Lanna

The Lanna kingdom, based in northern Thailand, dates its formation to the Upper Mekong River town of Chiang Saen in the middle of the 13th century by King Mengrai. He migrated south to Chiang Mai (meaning 'New City') in 1292, and four years later made it his capital. The king was a skilled diplomat and forged important alliances with potential rivals, such as King Ngam Muang of Phayao and King Ramkhamhaeng of Sukhothai; a bronze statue commemorating this confederation stands in Chiang Mai today. King Mengrai is also credited with successfully repulsing the Mongol invasions in the early 14th century.

The Lanna kingdom is recognised for its royal patronage of the Sinhalese tradition of Theravada Buddhism, now widely practised in Thailand, and of the distinctive northern Thai culture of the region. The Lanna kingdom didn't experience an extensive expansion period, as it was plagued by dynastic intrigues and wars with rival powers.

Sukhothai

During the 13th century, several principalities in the central plains united and wrested control from the dying Khmer empire, making their new capital at Sukhothai (meaning 'Rising of Happiness'). Thais consider Sukhothai the first true Thai kingdom and the period is recognised as an artistic and cultural awakening.

The most revered of the Sukhothai kings was Ramkhamhaeng, who is credited with developing the modern Thai writing system, which is based on Indian, Mon and Khmer scripts. He also established Theravada Buddhism as the official religion.

In its prime, the Sukhothai kingdom extended as far as Nakhon Si Thammarat in the south, the upper Mekong River Valley in Laos, and Bago (Pegu) in southern Burma. For a short period (1448–86) the

Relief carvings at Angkor Wat depict Tai mercenaries serving in Khmer armies. The Khmer called them 'Syam'. The name was transliterated to 'Siam' by the English trader James Lancaster in 1592.

King Naresuan is portrayed as a national hero and has become a cult figure, especially worshipped by the Thai army. His story inspired a high-budget, blockbuster film trilogy, *King Naresuan*, funded in part by the Thai government.

1351–1767	1511	1688	1700
Reign of Ayuthaya and rise of the Siamese.	Portuguese found foreign mission in Ayuthaya, followed by other European nations.	The death of pro-foreign King Narai is followed by the Palace Revolution and the expulsion of the French. As a result, Thailand's ties with the West are near-severed until the 1800s.	Ayuthaya's population is estimated to be one million, making it probably the largest city in the world at the time.

Sukhothai capital was moved to Phitsanulok, but by that time another star was rising in Thailand, the kingdom of Ayuthaya.

Ayuthaya

In the mid-14th century, the Ayuthaya kingdom began to dominate Mae Nam Chao Phraya basin during the twilight of the Khmer period. It survived for 416 years, defining itself as Siam's most important kingdom with an expansive sphere of influence (including much of the former Khmer empire) and a fundamental role in organising the modern Thai state and social structure.

With a strategic island location formed by encircling rivers, Ayuthaya grew wealthy through international trade during the 17th century's age of commerce and fortified itself with superior Portuguese-supplied firearms and mercenaries. The river system connected to the Gulf of Thailand and to the hinterlands as well.

This is the period when Western traders 'discovered' Southeast Asia, and Ayuthaya hosted many foreign settlements. Accounts by foreign visitors mention Ayuthaya's cosmopolitan markets and court. In 1690 Londoner Engelbert Campfer proclaimed, 'Among the Asian nations, the kingdom of Siam is the greatest'.

Ayuthaya adopted Khmer court customs, honorific language and ideas of kingship. The monarch styled himself as a Khmer *devaraja* (divine king) rather than Sukhothai's *dhammaraja* (righteous king); and Ayuthaya continued to pay tribute to the Chinese emperor, who rewarded this ritualistic submission with generous gifts and commercial privileges.

The kingdom functioned according to a strict and complex hierarchy, much of which was defined by King Trailok (r 1448–88). Elaborate lists of official posts with specific titles and ranks were established. Individual social status was measured in numerical units of how much land one possessed. Fines and punishments were proportional to the person's rank. Ayuthaya society consisted of royalty, nobility and commoners.

RAMKHAMHAENG'S STONE INSCRIPTION

In an inscription of 1292, King Ramkhamhaeng gives a picture of his kingdom as idyllic and free of constraints, and of himself as a benevolent patriarch:

'This land of Sukhothai is thriving. There are fish in the water and rice in the fields… if any commoner in the land has a grievance…King Ramkhamhaeng…hears the call; he goes and questions the man, examines the case, and decides it justly for him.'

Translation by AB Griswold and Prasert Na Nagara, *Journal of the Siam Society* (July 1971)

1767	1768	1782	1826
Ayuthaya is sacked by the Burmese.	King Taksin establishes a new capital in Thonburi.	Founding of the Chakri dynasty and Bangkok as the new capital.	Thailand allies with Britain during the first Anglo-Burmese War.

THE INTERNATIONAL KING

In the 1680s many foreign emissaries were invited to Ayuthaya by King Narai, who was keen to acquire and consume foreign material, culture and ideas. His court placed orders for spyglasses, hourglasses, paper, walnut trees, cheese, wine and marble fountains. He joined the French Jesuits to observe the eclipse at his palace in Lopburi and received a gift of a globe from France's King Louis XIV.

Narai's openness to foreign influence was tested as his health failed and rival factions competed for succession. One of his trusted advisers was the Greek adventurer Constantine Phaulkon, who was later accused of conspiring to overthrow the ailing king. Instead, the accusers led a coup, executed Constantine and closed off Siam to the Europeans.

Commoners were further divided into freemen and enslaved people. Freemen were assigned to a royal or noble overseer. For six months of each year they owed labour to the ruling elite, doing personal errands, public works or military service. Despite the clear social hierarchy, social mobility was possible, depending on personal skills, connections (including marriage) and royal favour. These societal divisions are reflected in the feudal elements that persist in Thai society today.

The glories of Ayuthaya were interrupted by the expansionist Burmese. In 1569 the city fell to the great Burmese king, Bayinnaung, but it regained independence under the leadership of King Naresuan. Then, in 1765, Burma's ambitious and newly established Kongbaung dynasty pushed eastward to eliminate Ayuthaya as a political and commercial rival. Burmese troops laid siege to the capital for a year before destroying it in 1767. The city was devastated, its buildings and people wiped out. The surrounding areas were deserted. So chilling was this historic sacking and razing of Ayuthaya that the perception of the Burmese as ruthless aggressors still persists in the minds of many Thais to this day.

Landmarks of the Bangkok Era

....

Wat Arun

....

Wat Phra Kaew & Grand Palace

....

Dusit Palace Park

The Bangkok Era

With Ayuthaya in ruins, the line of succession of the kings was broken and chaos ensued. A former general, Taksin, claimed his right to rule, defeated potential rivals and established his new capital in Thonburi, a settlement downriver from Ayuthaya with better access to trade. King Taksin, the son of a Chinese father and Thai mother, strongly promoted trade with China. After 15 years, the king was deposed in 1782 by the military.

One of the coup organisers, Chao Phraya Chakri, assumed the throne as King Yot Fa (Rama I) and established the Chakri dynasty, which still rules today. The new monarch moved the capital across Mae Nam Chao Phraya to modern-day Bangkok. The first century of Bangkok

1851–68	1855	1868–1910	1874
Reign of King Mongkut (Rama IV) and a period of Western influence.	Bowring Treaty concluded between Siam and Britain, stimulating the Thai economy and granting extraterritorial rights to British subjects in Siam.	Reign of King Chulalongkorn (Rama V) and increased European imperialism in neighbouring countries.	Slavery is abolished.

rule focused on rebuilding the cultural, political and military might of Ayuthaya. The new rulers extended their influence in every direction. Destroying the capital cities of both Laos and Cambodia, Siam contained Burmese aggression and made a vassal of Chiang Mai. Defeated populations were resettled and played an important role in increasing Siam's production of rice, much of which was exported to China.

Unlike the Ayuthaya rulers who identified with the Hindu god Vishnu, the Chakri kings positioned themselves as defenders of Buddhism. They undertook compilations and Thai translations of essential Buddhist texts and constructed many royal temples.

In the meantime, a new social order and market economy was taking shape in the mid-19th century. Siam turned to the West for modern scientific and technological ideas and reforms in education, infrastructure and legal systems. One of the great modernisers, King Mongkut (Rama IV; r 1851–68) never expected to be king. Before his ascension he had spent 27 years in the monastery, founding the Thammayut sect based on the strict disciplines of the Mon monks.

During his reign, Siam concluded treaties with Western powers that integrated the kingdom into the world market system, ceded royal monopolies and granted extraterritorial rights to British subjects.

Mongkut's son, King Chulalongkorn (Rama V), who ruled between 1868 and 1910, was to take much greater steps in replacing the old political order with the model of the nation-state. He abolished slavery and the corvée system (state labour), which had lingered on ineffectively since the Ayuthaya period. Chulalongkorn's reign oversaw the creation of a salaried bureaucracy, a police force and a standing army. His reforms brought uniformity to the legal code, law courts and revenue offices. Siam's agricultural output was improved by advances in irrigation techniques and increasing peasant populations. Schools were established along European lines.

Chulalongkorn relied greatly on foreign advisers, mostly British. Within the royal court, much of the centuries-old protocol was abandoned and replaced by Western forms. The architecture and visual art of state, like the new throne halls, were designed by Italian artists.

Like his father, Chulalongkorn was regarded as a skilful diplomat and is credited for successfully playing European powers off one another to avoid colonisation. In exchange for independence, Thailand ceded territory to French Indochina (Laos in 1893, Cambodia in 1907) and British Burma (three Malayan states in 1909). In 1902, the former Patani kingdom was ceded to the British, who were then in control of Malaysia, but control reverted back to Thailand five years later. Many residents of the Deep South continue to regard Thailand as a colonial power occupying their land.

In 1868 King Mongkut (Rama IV) abolished a husband's right to sell his wife or her children without her permission. The older provision, it was said, treated the woman 'as if she were a water buffalo'.

HISTORY THE BANGKOK ERA

1890	1893	1902	1909
Siam's first railway connects Bangkok with Nakhon Ratchasima.	French blockade Chao Phraya River over disputed Indochina territory, intensifying threat of colonisation.	Siam annexes Yala, Pattani and Narathiwat from the former sultanate of Patani.	Anglo-Siamese Treaty outlines Siam's boundaries.

Defying old traditions, Chulalongkorn followed in his father's footsteps in allowing himself to be seen in public, photographed in peasant garb, and consented to his image being reproduced on coins, stamps and postcards. He was also well travelled and visited Europe, Singapore, Java, Malaya, Burma and India. He collected art and inspiration from these travels and built fanciful palaces as architectural scrapbooks.

Siam was becoming a geographically defined country in a modern sense. By 1902, the country no longer called itself Siam but Prathet Thai (the country of the Thai) or Ratcha-anachak Thai (the kingdom of the Thai). By 1913, all those living within its borders were defined as 'Thai'.

Democracy vs Military

In 1932 a group of young military officers and bureaucrats calling themselves Khana Ratsadon (People's Party) mounted a successful, bloodless coup which marked the end of absolute monarchy and introduced a

THE THAI MONARCHY

The country's last absolute monarch was King Prajadhipok (Rama VII), who accepted the 1932 constitution, abdicated the throne and went into exile. By 1935 the new democratic government reinstated the monarchy, appointing the abdicated king's 10-year-old nephew, Ananda Mahidol (Rama VIII), who was living in Europe at the time. In 1946, after the king came of age, he was shot dead in mysterious circumstances. In 1950, his younger brother was crowned King Bhumibol (Rama IX) and ruled until his death in 2016.

At the beginning of his reign, King Bhumibol was primarily a figurehead of national unity. The military dictator General Sarit (1958–63) supported the expansion of the king's role as a symbol of modern Thailand. An attractive royal couple, King Bhumibol and Queen Sirikit met Elvis and were portrayed in photographs in the same way as the US president John F Kennedy and his wife, Jackie: fashionable models of the postwar generation. Through rural development projects the king became regarded as the champion of the poor. The Royal Project Foundation was created in 1969 and is credited with helping to eradicate opium cultivation among the northern hill peoples. During the 1970s protest movements, the king came to be a mediating voice, calling for peace between the military and the pro-democracy factions. During another political crisis in 1992, the king summoned the leaders of the political factions to the palace in an effort to quell street protests.

During the most recent political crisis of the 2000s, the ageing king's influence had less of a stabilising effect. Pro-royalist, anti-Thaksin supporters wore yellow in honour of the king and pro-democracy, pro-Thaksin supporters viewed the monarchy with suspicion. The king died on 13 October 2016 and is survived by his wife and adult children, including the new king, Maha Vajiralongkorn, who had assumed many royal duties during his father's illness. Princess Sirindhorn, a beloved member of the royal family, carries on her father's philanthropic endeavours.

1913	1916	1917	1932
King Vajiravudh requires all citizens to adopt surnames.	The first Thai university, Chulalongkorn University, is established.	Siam sends troops to join the Allies in WWI.	Bloodless coup ends absolute monarchy.

constitutional monarchy. The leaders of the group were inspired by the democratic ideology they had encountered during their studies in Europe.

In the years after the coup, rival factions (royalists, military, civilians) struggled for the upper hand in the new power regime. Even the People's Party was not unified in its vision of a democratic Thailand, and before general elections were held the military wing of the party seized control of the government. The leader of the civilian wing of the People's Party, Pridi Phanomyong, a French-educated lawyer, was forced into exile in 1933 after introducing a socialist-leaning economic plan that angered the military generals. Thailand's first popular election was held in 1937 for half of the seats in the People's Assembly, the newly instated legislative body. General Phibul Songkhram, one of the military leaders, became prime minister, a position he held from 1938 to 1944 and again from 1948 to 1957.

Phibul's regime coincided with WWII and was characterised by strong nationalistic tendencies of 'nation' and 'Thai-ness'. He collaborated with the Japanese and allowed them to use Thailand as a staging ground for its invasion of other Southeast Asian nations. The Phibul government was hoping the allegiance would restore historical territory lost during France's expansion of Indochina. Thailand intended to declare war on the US and Britain during WWII. But Seni Pramoj, the Thai ambassador in Washington and a member of Seri Thai (the Thai Liberation Movement), refused to deliver the formal declaration of war, thus saving Thailand from bearing the consequences of defeated-nation status. Phibul was forced to resign in 1944 and was tried for war crimes.

For a brief period after the war, democracy flourished: full elections for the People's Assembly were held and the 1946 constitution sought to reduce the role of the military and provide more democratic rights. And it all lasted until the death of King Ananda, the pretext the military used to return to power with Phibul at the helm.

Military Dictatorships

In 1957 Phibul's successor General Sarit Thanarat subjected the country to a true military dictatorship: abolishing the constitution, dissolving the parliament and banning all political parties. In the 1950s, the US partnered with Sarit and subsequent military dictators Thanom Kittikachorn and Praphat Charusathien (who controlled the country from 1964 to 1973), to allow the US military to develop bases in Thailand during the war in Vietnam in exchange for economic incentives.

By 1973, an opposition group of left-wing activists, mainly intellectuals and students, organised political rallies demanding a constitution from the military government. On 14 October that year the military brutally suppressed a large demonstration in Bangkok, killing 77 people and

HISTORY MILITARY DICTATORSHIPS

> Phibul Songkhram officially changed the name of the country in 1939 from 'Siam' to 'Prathet Thai' (or 'Thailand' in English); it was considered an overt nationalistic gesture intended to unite all the Tai-speaking people.

> Thailand has had 20 constitutions, all rewritten following various miltary coups. A draft version of constitution number 20 was approved by popular referendum in 2016. Each new version redefines how much of the legislature will be popularly elected, who is eligible to be prime minister and how the PM will be selected.

1935	1939	1941	1945
King Prajadhipok (Rama VII) becomes the only Thai king to abdicate. The government chooses Prince Mahidol to replace him.	The country's English name is officially changed from Siam to Thailand.	Japanese forces enter Thailand during WWII.	WWII ends; Thailand cedes seized territory from Laos, Cambodia and Malaysia.

LIBERAL COUNTERWEIGHT

Pridi Phanomyong (1900–83) was a French-educated lawyer and a civilian leader in the 1932 revolution and People's Party. His work on democratic reforms in Thailand was based on constitutional measures and attempts to restrict by law military involvement in Thai politics. He supported nationalisation of land and labour, state-led industrialisation and labour protection. In 1934, he founded Thammasat University. He also served as the figurehead of Seri Thai (the resistance movement against WWII Japanese occupation of Thailand) and was Thai prime minister (1946).

Though acknowledged as a senior statesman, Pridi Phanomyong was a controversial figure and a major foe of Phibul Songkhram and the military regimes. He was accused of being a communist by his critics and forced out of the country under suspicion of regicide. Since the thawing of the Cold War, his legacy has been re-examined and recognised for its democratic efforts and the counterbalancing effects it had on military interests. He was named one of Unesco's great personalities of the 20th-century world in 2000.

wounding more than 800. The event is commemorated by a monument on Th Ratchadamnoen Klang in Bangkok, near the Democracy Monument. King Bhumibol stepped in and refused to support further bloodshed, forcing Thanom and Praphat to leave Thailand.

In the following years, the left-oriented student movement grew more radical, creating fears among working-class and middle-class Thais of home-grown communism. In 1976 Thanom returned to Thailand (ostensibly to become a monk) and was received warmly by the royal family. In response, protesters organised demonstrations at Thammasat University against the perceived perpetrator of the 14 October massacre.

Right-wing, anti-communist civilian groups clashed with the students, resulting in bloody violence. In the aftermath, many students and intellectuals were forced underground, and joined armed communist insurgents – known as the People's Liberation Army of Thailand (PLAT) – based in the jungles of northern and southern Thailand.

Military control of the country continued through the 1980s. The government of the 'political soldier', General Prem Tinsulanonda, enjoyed a period of political and economic stability. Prem dismantled the communist insurgency through military action and amnesty programs. But the country's new economic success presented a challenging rival: prominent business leaders who criticised the military's role in government and their now-dated Cold War mentality. Communists, they maintained, should be business partners, not enemies.

1946	1957	1959	1965
King Bhumibol Adulyadej (Rama IX) ascends the throne; Thailand joins the UN.	Sarit Thanarat leads a coup that introduces military rule that lasts until 1973.	The first tourism authority is created.	Thailand hosts US military bases during the Vietnam War.

The Business Era

In 1988 Prime Minister Prem Tinsulanonda was replaced in fair elections by Chatichai Choonhavan, leader of the Chat Thai Party, who created a government dominated by well-connected provincial business people. His government shifted power away from the bureaucrats and set about transforming Thailand into an 'Asian Tiger' economy. But the business of politics was often bought and sold like a commodity and Chatichai was overthrown by the military on grounds of extreme corruption. This coup demarcated an emerging trend in Thai politics: the Bangkok business community and educated classes siding with the military against provincial business-politicians and their money politics.

In 1992, General Suchinda Kraprayoon inserted himself as prime minister. This was met with popular resistance and the ensuing civilian-military clash was dubbed 'Black May'. Led by former Bangkok mayor Chamlong Srimuang, around 200,000 protesters (called the 'mobile phone mob', representing their rising urban affluence) launched a mass demonstration in Bangkok that resulted in three nights of violence with armed soldiers. On the night of 20 May, King Bhumibol called an end to the violence.

After Black May, a new wave of democracy activists advocated for constitutional reforms. For most of the 1990s, the parliament was dominated by the Democrat Party, which represented the urban middle class and business interests. Its major base of support came from the southern Thai population centres, former port towns now dominated by tourism and exports (rubber, tin and fishing). On the other side of the spectrum were the former pro-military politicians based in the central plains and the people of the agrarian northeast in new provincial towns who focused on state-budget distributions. These political lines still exist today.

In 1997, the boom years ended and the Asian economic crisis unfolded. The country's economy was plagued by foreign-debt burdens, a real-estate bubble and a devalued currency. Within months of the crisis, the Thai currency plunged from 25B to 56B per US$1.

The Thai national anthem is played on TV and radio stations at 8am and 6pm. The video that accompanies the TV broadcast shows a multi-ethnic, multi-religious Thailand living in harmony under the national flag.

THAILAND'S PARLIAMENT

Much of the country's political drama involves a long-standing debate about how to structure Thailand's legislative body and, ultimately, who gets greater control. Thailand's constitution has been rewritten 20 times in the last 80-odd years. Each constitution (or suspension of a constitution) results in a reshuffling of popularly elected members versus appointed members. The current parliament has approximately 750 members: 500 elected MPs and a 250-member senate (the upper house) which is appointed by the military.

1968	1973	1976	1979
Thailand is a founding member of the Association of Southeast Asian Nations (ASEAN).	Thai students, workers and farmers demonstrate for the reinstallation of a democratic government.	Violent suppression of the student movement by the military.	After three years of military rule, elections and parliament are restored.

The International Monetary Fund (IMF) stepped in to impose financial and legal reforms and economic liberalisation programs in exchange for more than US$17 billion to stabilise the Thai currency.

Thaksin Shinawatra was the first prime minister in Thai history to complete a four-year term of office. His sister Yingluck managed three years in power before being deposed.

In the aftermath of the crisis, the Democrats returned to power uncontested, but were viewed as ineffective as the economy worsened.

The Thaksin Era

In 2000, the economic slump began to ease. Thaksin Shinawatra, a telecommunications billionaire and former police officer, and his Thai Rak Thai (TRT or 'Thai Loving Thai') party won a majority in the elections of 2001. Self-styled as a CEO-politician, Thaksin swiftly delivered on his campaign promises for rural development, including agrarian debt relief, village capital funds and cheap health care.

Thanks to the 1997 constitutional reforms designed to strengthen the prime minister's position, his was one of Thailand's most stable elected governments. The surging economy and his bold, if strong-arm, leadership won an outright majority in 2005, introducing one-party rule. His popularity among the working class and rural voters was immense.

In 2006 Thaksin was accused of abusing his powers and of conflicts of interest, most notably in his family's sale of their Shin Corporation to the Singaporean government for 73 billion baht (US$1.88 billion), a tax-free gain thanks to legislation he helped craft. Demonstrations in Bangkok called for his ousting and on 19 September 2006, the military staged a bloodless coup that forced Thaksin into exile. General elections were held shortly thereafter, with Thaksin's political allies forming a government led by Samak Sundaravej.

This was an unsatisfactory outcome to the military and the anti-Thaksin group known as People's Alliance for Democracy (PAD), comprised of mainly urban elites nicknamed 'Yellow Shirts' because they wore yellow (the colour associated with the king's birthday). It was popularly believed that Thaksin was consolidating power during his tenure so that he could interrupt royal succession.

In September 2008, Samak Sundaravej was unseated by the Constitutional Court on a technicality: while in office, he hosted a TV cooking show deemed to be a conflict of interest. Concerned that another election would result in a Thaksin win, the Yellow Shirts seized control of Thailand's main airports, Suvarnabhumi and Don Mueang, for a week in November 2008, until the military manoeuvred a silent coup and another favourable court ruling that further weakened Thaksin's political proxies. Through last-minute coalition building, Democrat Abhisit Vejjajiva was elected in a parliamentary vote, becoming Thailand's 27th prime minister.

1980	1988	1991–2	1997
Prem Tinsulanonda's government works to undermine the communist insurgency movement and eventually ends it with a political solution.	Chatichai Choonhavan becomes the first elected PM since 1976.	General Suchinda attempts to seize power; King Bhumibol intervenes to halt civil turmoil surrounding 'Black May' protests.	Asian economic crisis; passage of historic 'people's constitution'.

Thaksin supporters organised their own counter-movement as the United Front for Democracy Against Dictatorship (UDD), better known as the 'Red Shirts'. Supporters hail mostly from the north and northeast, and include anti-coup, pro-democracy activists; anti-royalists; and die-hard Thaksin fans. There is a degree of class struggle, with many working-class Red Shirts expressing bombastic animosity towards the aristocrats.

The Red Shirts' most provocative demonstration came in 2010, when Thailand's Supreme Court ordered the seizure of US$46 billion of Thaksin's assets after finding him guilty of abusing his powers as prime minister. The Red Shirts occupied Bangkok's central shopping district for two months and demanded the dissolution of the government and reinstatement of elections. In May 2010 the military used force to evict the protesters, resulting in bloody clashes where 91 people were killed and shopping centres set ablaze (US$1.5 billion of crackdown-related arson damage was estimated).

Democracy vs Military Again

In 2011, general elections were held and Thaksin's politically allied Puea Thai party won a parliamentary majority, with Thaksin's sister Yingluck Shinawatra elected as prime minister. Yingluck Shinawatra became both the first female prime minister of Thailand and the country's youngest-ever premier. But throughout her time in power, Yingluck faced accusations that she was just the proxy for her older brother Thaksin, who fled the country to avoid corruption charges following the 2006 coup. Accounts of his influence over the Yingluck government circulated in Bangkok, with Thaksin said to be joining cabinet meetings by Skype from his homes in London, Dubai and Hong Kong.

Trouble loomed for Yingluck's administration due to the so-called rice-pledging scheme. Designed to boost the incomes of small farmers, the government would buy their rice at above market rates, stockpile it – forcing global prices up – and then sell it at a handsome profit. But the scheme went disastrously wrong, as India lifted its ban on rice exports and flooded the world market with grains. Thailand, the world's biggest rice exporter until 2012, could only watch as prices sank. The damage to the economy was huge, while millions of baht were alleged to have disappeared into the hands of the politicians and officials overseeing the policy. In May 2014, Yingluck was indicted on charges relating to the scheme; she was found guilty in 2017, but fled the country before she could be arrested.

Equally contentious was Yingluck's misguided attempt to introduce an amnesty bill that would have pardoned various politicians, including Thaksin. This was widely seen as the prelude to the return of Thaksin to

---

The Democrat Party (Phak Prachathipat), founded in 1946, is the longest-surviving political party in Thailand.

The Buddhist clergy has had its share of scandals, but nothing like the 2017 stand-off between the government and Wat Phra Dhammakaya. Followers have barricaded the temple from police intrusion in an effort to protect the abbot who is charged with money laundering and embezzlement.

2001	2004	2006	2008
Telecommunications tycoon Thaksin Shinawatra is elected prime minister.	Indian Ocean tsunami kills over 5000 people in Thailand and damages tourism and fishing industries; Muslim insurgency reignites in the Deep South.	King Bhumibol celebrates 60th year on the throne; Thaksin government overthrown in a coup and prime minister forced into exile.	Cambodia petitions Unesco to list Phra Wihan as a World Heritage Site, reigniting border tensions; Yellow Shirt, pro-royalist activists seize Bangkok's international airports, causing weeklong shutdown.

Thailand. Street demonstrations against the government began in October 2013, led by former deputy prime minister Suthep Thaugsuban and his coalition of anti-government groups known as the People's Democratic Reform Committee. The group called for Yingluck and the government to step down and introduced yet another round of protest encampments and confrontations in Bangkok.

With sporadic violence between Yingluck's supporters and opponents breaking out, Yingluck and nine of her ministers were forced to step down by the Constitutional Court on 7 May 2014, followed by a military-led coup, the 13th time since 1932.

Return to Military Dictatorship

On 22 May 2014, the Thai military under General Prayuth Chan-o-cha overthrew the elected government and brought to an end months of political crisis. Prayuth said the coup was necessary to restore stability.

Prayuth's military government was known as the National Council for Peace and Order (NCPO). The NCPO set about restoring stability by implementing martial law and silencing critics. All media were under orders to refrain from dissent. Internet providers were ordered to block any content that violated the junta's orders. In March 2015 Prayuth told journalists that he would execute those who did not toe the official line – the domestic media now self-censors their stories.

The crackdown extended into the civilian sphere as well. More than 1000 people – opposition politicians, academics, journalists, bloggers and students – have been detained or tried in military courts. In March 2015, the UN's High Commissioner for Human Rights claimed that the military was using martial law to silence opposition and called for 'freedom of expression to ensure genuine debate'.

In preparation for the inevitable transfer of the crown, the military also increased prosecution of the country's strict *lèse-majesté* laws. In August 2015, one man received a 30-year prison sentence for insulting the monarchy on his Facebook page after sharing a news article. BBC

Voting in Thailand is compulsory for all eligible citizens, apart from monks and other religious figures who are barred from participating in elections.

AN EU FOR SOUTHEAST ASIA

By the end of 2015, the ASEAN Economic Community (AEC) united the association's 10 Southeast Asian countries in a liberalised marketplace where goods, services, capital and labour are shared across borders with little or no country-specific impediments. In theory, the AEC will make it easier to buy and sell goods, hire non-nationals and invest within the ASEAN region. Implementation of the AEC goals has been slow due to the disparities between and political interests of each member nation.

2009	2011	2012	2014
Red Shirt, pro-Thaksin activists force the cancellation of the Fourth East Asia Summit in Pattaya. A state of emergency is declared in Bangkok.	Yingluck Shinawatra becomes Thailand's first female prime minister; devastating floods inundate industrial region.	Multiple car bombings across the Deep South in March leave 16 people dead and over 300 injured.	The military stage their 13th coup since 1932, overthrowing Yingluck Shinawatra's Puea Thai government.

MEDIA

Southeast Asian governments are not generally fond of uncensored media, but Thailand often bucked this trend during the 1990s, even ensuring press freedoms in its 1997 constitution, albeit with fairly broad loopholes. This ended with the ascension of Thaksin Shinawatra, a telecommunications billionaire, at the start of the 21st century. With Thaksin as prime minister and his party holding a controlling majority, the press encountered the kind of censorship and legal intimidation not seen since the 1970s era of military dictatorships. The government filed a litany of defamation lawsuits against individuals, publications and media groups that had printed embarrassing revelations about the Thaksin regime.

After the 2006 ousting of Thaksin, the media managed to retain its guarantees of press freedoms in the new constitution, but this was a 'paper promise' that did little to rescue the press from intimidation, lawsuits and physical attacks. Sweeping powers to ensure national security, often invoked against the press, were added to the emergency powers laws that went into effect after the coup.

Following the 2014 coup, there has been a widespread crackdown on both the media and freedom of expression. In its immediate aftermath, 15 TV and radio stations were closed and 100 websites were blocked, while around 1000 people – academics, bloggers, journalists, students and opposition politicians – were detained for various periods. The domestic media now self-censors its stories to avoid getting into trouble, and some websites, like the Thailand section of the Human Rights Watch website, are periodically blocked in Thailand.

There has also been a sharp rise in the number of people prosecuted under the country's Computer Crimes Act, which is increasingly being used by the government to muzzle the media, political opponents and critics of the monarchy. Recent cases include the leader of the popular Future Forward party being charged under the act with relaying false information about the junta via a Facebook post.

Thai was investigated for defamation of the new king after a 2016 profile piece aired online.

While the NCPO was busy silencing critics, it failed to address Thailand's slumping economy. Foreign investment, exports and GDP all contracted after the coup. In 2016 a much-needed infrastructure investment plan was announced to help bolster the economy. Tourism continued to be the economic bright spot, but by 2019 economic growth was at its lowest point since the coup.

Back to Political Deadlock

In March 2019, after five years of delays which saw the constitution amended once again, Thailand held its first general election since the 2014 coup. The junta and its leader, former general Prayuth Chan-o cha, campaigned under the guise of the Palang Pracharath party.

2015	2016	2017	2018
Terrorist bomb explosion at popular Bangkok Erawan shrine kills 20 people.	King Bhumibol Adulyadej (Rama IX) dies; his son succeeds the throne. Military-backed constitution wins popular referendum.	Yingluck Shinawatra, prime minister between 2011 and 2014, flees into exile to avoid appearing in court to hear a judgement on corruption charges.	12 schoolboy footballers and their adult coach are dramatically rescued after two weeks spent trapped in a cave in Chiang Rai Province.

Founded in 2018 by a charismatic Thai-Chinese businessman, the anti-military, centre-left Future Forward party shook up the political establishment by winning the third-most seats in the 2019 election.

Despite attempts to restrict the media coverage of the other parties – and allegations of voting irregularities – Palang Pracharath failed to win a parliamentary majority. Instead, the Pheu Thai party associated with the Shinawatra clan captured the most seats, while the new Future Forward party came third. Under the latest constitution, though, the unelected, 250-member senate (the upper house of parliament) also votes on the appointment of the prime minister, and Prayuth was duly chosen to head a coalition government in June 2019.

Opposing the coalition are Pheu Thai, Future Forward and a number of other anti-military parties. The coalition has struggled to hold together and has only a small parliamentary majority, leaving Thailand once more politically deadlocked.

Anti-Establishment Protests

In February 2020, a court ruling dissolving the Future Forward Party sparked a series of ongoing mass political protests, unlike anything Thailand has experienced. The so-called pro-democracy movement, which has largely been organised by students and youth activists, and calls for a new constitution, monarchy reform and the prime minister to step down.

The government has sought to thwart the thousands-strong gatherings by arresting its leaders, enacting a short-lived protest ban, and even closing transit stations. In March 2021, several demonstrators went on trial charged with, among other things, breaking Thailand's lèse-majesté laws, a crime punishable with up to 15 years in prison.

2019	2019	2020	2020
Thailand holds its first general election since the 2014 coup. Former army general Prayuth Chan-o cha is appointed prime minister of a coalition government.	King Vajiralongkorn, Rama X, is formally crowned in an elaborate three-day ceremony in Bangkok.	A string of student-led mass protests demands government and monarchy reform.	Thailand closes its borders due to COVID-19 and implements mandatory hotel quarantine.

People & Culture

Thailand's cohesive national identity provides a unifying patina for ethnic and regional differences that evolved through historical migrations and geographic kinships with ethnically diverse neighbours.

Ethnic Make-Up

Some 75% of the citizens of Thailand are ethnic Thais, providing a superficial impression of sameness. But subtle regional differences exist. In the central plains (Chao Phraya delta), Siamese Thais united the country through its historic kingdoms and promulgated its culture and language. Today the central Thai dialect is the national standard, and Bangkok exports unified culture through popular media and standardised education.

Above Akha women (p724) at a tea plantation, Chiang Rai Province

The northeast (Isan) has always stood apart from the rest of the country, sharing closer ethnic and cultural ties with Laos. In the northeastern provinces that border Cambodia there is a distinct Khmer influence, as many families migrated across the border during historical tumult. A group of minority people, known as Suay, live near Surin and Khorat (Nakhon Ratchasima), and are traditional elephant mahouts.

In the south, the Thai Pak Tai people's language and culture reflects the region's proximity to predominantly Muslim Malaysia. Their dialect is a little faster than standard Thai and there is more mixing of Muslim folk beliefs into the regional culture.

If you were to redraw Thailand's borders according to ethnicity, northern Thailand would be united with parts of southern China and northern Myanmar. The traditional homeland of the Tai people was believed to be the Yúnnán region of China. There are also many subgroups, including the Shan (an ethnic cousin to the Thais who settled in the highlands of Burma) and the Tai Lü (who settled in Nan and Chiang Rai Province as well as the Vietnam highlands).

After the Thai Chinese – the most numerous ethnic minority in Thailand, with a population of just under 9.5 million – the second-largest group is the Malays (4.6%), most of whom reside in the provinces of the Deep South. The remaining minority groups include smaller percentages of non-Thai-speaking people such as the Vietnamese, Khmer, Mon, Semang (Sakai), Moken (*chow lair,* also spelt *chao leh;* 'people of the sea', or 'sea gypsies'), Htin, Mabri, Khamu and a variety of hill peoples. A small number of Europeans and other non-Asians reside in Bangkok and the provinces.

Thai Chinese

People of Chinese ancestry – second- or third-generation Hakka, Teochew, Hainanese or Cantonese – make up 14% of the population, the world's largest overseas Chinese population. Bangkok and the nearby coastal areas have a large population of immigrants from China who came for economic opportunities in the early to mid-20th century. Historically, wealthy Chinese introduced their daughters to the royal court as consorts, developing royal connections and adding a Chinese bloodline that extends to the royal family.

The mercantile centres of most Thai towns are run by Thai-Chinese families, and many places in the country celebrate Chinese festivals such as the annual Vegetarian Festival.

Spiritual Reading

Being Dharma: The Essence of the Buddha's Teachings (2001; Ajahn Chah)

Thai Folk Wisdom: Contemporary Takes on Traditional Proverbs (2010; Tulaya Pornpiriyakulchai and Jane Vejjajiva)

Sacred Tattoos of Thailand (2011; Joe Cummings)

MIGRANTS & ASYLUM SEEKERS

The United Nations believes that there are an estimated 3.9 million migrant workers, mainly from Myanmar, Laos, Cambodia and Vietnam, living in Thailand. The majority are low-skilled workers from economically depressed or politically unstable areas, with little to no formal education. Most are motivated to move to Thailand by the prospect of higher wages. Often in the country illegally, smuggled in by a broker, they have no labour protections and are virtual modern-day slaves or indentured servants. The fishing industry, garment factories, brothels and construction sites depend heavily on migrant labour.

Thailand has long struggled with immigration and the number of displaced people seeking refuge in the kingdom. With the slowing of the economy and the law-and-order policies of the military junta that ruled from 2014 to 2019, there has been increased deportation of undocumented migrant labourers in recent years. The Thai government has declared that by 2020 there will be no undocumented migrant children living in the kingdom. In 2019, it was estimated that there were somewhere between 250,000 and 300,000 migrant children living in Thailand.

Thai Muslim boy at prayer

Thai Muslims

At around 5% of the population, Muslims are Thailand's largest religious minority, living side by side with the Buddhist majority. Many of Thailand's Muslims reside in the south, but an ever-greater number are scattered through the nation. Most of Thailand's southern Muslims are ethnically Malay and speak Malay or Yawi (a dialect of Malay written in the Arabic script) in addition to Thai. In northern Thailand there are also a substantial number of Chinese Muslims who emigrated from Yúnnán in the late 19th century.

Hill Peoples

Ethnic minorities in the mountainous regions of northern Thailand are known as *chow kŏw* (mountain people). Each minority has its own language, customs, mode of dress and spiritual beliefs.

Most hill peoples are of seminomadic origin, having come from Tibet, Myanmar, China and Laos during the past 200 years or so. Some were forced out of their traditional homeland in neighbouring countries due to conflicts with the national governments. They are 'fourth-world' people, in that they belong neither to the main aligned powers nor to the developing nations. Language and culture constitute the borders of their world. Research by the former Tribal Research Institute in Chiang Mai recognises 10 different hill-dwelling minorities, but there may be up to 20. Hill peoples are increasingly integrating into the Thai mainstream and many of the old ways and traditional customs are disappearing. Due to urban migration, many minority villages now include a variety of ethnicities, as well as Burmese migrants.

Traditional hill-tribe clothing with silver adornments

Akha (I-kaw)

Population: 80,000
Origin: Tibet
Present locations: Thailand, Laos, Myanmar, Yúnnán (China)
Belief system: Animism with an emphasis on ancestor worship; some groups are Christian

> Many NGOs in Chiang Mai and Chiang Rai work with minority communities to provide education, health care and advocacy efforts.

The Akha are among the poorest of Thailand's ethnic minorities and reside mainly in Chiang Mai and Chiang Rai provinces, along mountain ridges or steep slopes 1000m to 1400m in altitude. They're regarded as skilled farmers but are often displaced from arable land by government intervention. Their most famous festival is the Akha Swing Ceremony, which takes place from mid-August to mid-September, when communities take turns on giant swings to celebrate the upcoming harvest.

Akha culture is focused on family ties and they recite their personal genealogies upon first meeting to determine a shared ancestor. Traditional clothing consists of a headdress of beads, feathers and dangling silver ornaments. With many different dialects, the tonal Akha language belongs to the Lolo branch of the Tibeto-Burman family.

Hmong (Mong or Maew)

Population: 151,000
Origin: South China
Present locations: South China, Thailand, Laos, Vietnam
Belief system: Animism

Divided into two subgroups (White Hmong and Blue Hmong), the Hmong are Thailand's second-largest hill people and are especially numerous in Chiang Mai Province, with smaller enclaves in the other northern provinces. They usually live on mountain peaks or plateaus above 1000m. Kinship is patrilineal and polygamy is permitted.

Hmong people wear simple black jackets and indigo or black baggy trousers with striped borders (White Hmong) or indigo skirts (Blue Hmong) and silver jewellery. Sashes may be worn around the waist, and embroidered aprons draped front and back. Most women wear their hair in a bun.

Karen (Yang or Kariang)

Population: 500,000
Origin: Myanmar
Present locations: Thailand, Myanmar
Belief system: Animism, Buddhism, Christianity, depending on the group

The Karen are one of the largest minority groups in Thailand. They tend to live in lowland valleys and practise crop rotation rather than swidden (slash-and-burn) agriculture. Their numbers and proximity to mainstream society have made them the most integrated and financially successful of the hill peoples. Many Karen also live in refugee camps along the Thai–Myanmar border, having been pushed out of their villages in Myanmar by conflict.

There are four distinct Karen groups: the Skaw (White) Karen, Pwo Karen, Pa-O (Black) Karen and Kayah (Red) Karen. Karen homes are built on low stilts or posts, with the roofs swooping quite low. Thickly woven V-neck tunics of various colours are typically worn (though unmarried women wear white). Kinship is matrilineal and marriage is monogamous. Karen languages are tonal and belong to the Sino-Tibetan family.

Lahu (Musoe)

Population: 100,000
Origin: Tibet
Present locations: Southwest China, Thailand, Myanmar
Belief system: Theistic animism; polytheism; some groups are Christian

The Thai term for the Lahu, *moo·seu*, is derived from a Burmese word meaning 'hunter', a reference to their skill in the forest. The Lahu, originating in the Tibetan plateau, tend to live at about 1000m in remote areas of the Chiang Mai, Chiang Rai and Tak provinces. They typically live in

The Lahu people are known for their strict adherence to gender equality, the result of their society's dyadic worldview that emphasises pairs and cooperation.

PEOPLE & CULTURE ETHNIC MAKE-UP

HILL PEOPLES: LIVING STANDARDS & CITIZENSHIP ISSUES

Hill peoples tend to have among the lowest standards of living in Thailand. The Thai government pursued a 30-year policy of relocating hill peoples, often moving villages from fertile agricultural land to infertile land. As a result, viable subsistence systems in which traditional customs were intact were exchanged for market systems where the hill peoples struggled to compete and began to lose their old ways. In most cases the situation is compounded by hill peoples not having Thai citizenship. Without citizenship, they are technically illegal residents in the country of their birth and they don't have the right to own land, educate their children, earn a minimum wage or access health care.

In recent decades some hill peoples have been issued Thai identification cards, which enables them to access national programmes, though in reality extra fees might still prevent access to public schooling and health care. Other minority families have received residency certificates that restrict their travel outside an assigned district, limiting their access to job opportunities in this mobile modern society. Since 2016, around 16,000 people a year have been granted Thai citizenship, as part of an effort to end statelessness by 2024, but that still leaves over 450,000 stateless people in Thailand, according to 2019 figures from Thailand's Ministry of Interior. That is the fourth-highest number for any country in the world, according to the United Nations High Commissioner for Refugees.

Top 'Long-necked' Kayan woman, Mae Hong Son Province (p299)

Bottom Karen villager, Chiang Mai Province

Hmong women working in rice fields, Chiang Mai Province

mixed ethnic villages and are an ethnically diverse group with five main subsets: Red Lahu (the most numerous Lahu group in Thailand), Black Lahu, White Lahu, Yellow Lahu and Lahu Sheleh.

Houses are built of wood, bamboo and grass, and usually stand on short wooden posts. Lahu food is probably the spiciest of all the hill-peoples' cuisines. Traditional dress consists of black-and-red jackets, with narrow skirts worn by women, and bright green or blue-green baggy trousers worn by men. The tonal Lahu language belongs to the Lolo branch of the Tibeto-Burman family.

Lisu (Lisaw)

Population: 55,000
Origin: Tibet
Present locations: Thailand, Yúnnán (China)
Belief system: Animism with ancestor worship and spirit possession

Lisu villages are usually in the mountains at an elevation of about 1000m and occur in eight Thai provinces: Chiang Mai, Chiang Rai, Mae Hong Son, Phayao, Tak, Kamphaeng Phet, Sukhothai and Lampang. Patrilineal clans have pan-tribal jurisdiction, which makes the Lisu unique among hill-peoples groups (most of which have power centred on either a shaman or a village headman).

Homes are built on the ground and consist mostly of bamboo and thatched grass. The women wear long multicoloured tunics over trousers and sometimes black turbans with tassels. Men wear baggy green or blue pants pegged in at the ankles. Closely related to Akha and Lahu, the tonal Lisu language belongs to the Lolo branch of the Tibeto-Burman family.

Mien embroidery

Mien (Yao)

Population: 30,000
Origin: Central China
Present locations: Thailand, south China, Laos, Myanmar, Vietnam
Belief system: Animism with ancestor worship, Taoism, Buddhism and Christianity

The Mien are highly skilled at crafts such as embroidery and silversmithing. They settle near mountain springs at between 1000m and 1200m, with a concentration in Nan, Phayao and Chiang Rai provinces and a few communities elsewhere. Migration into Thailand increased during the American War when the Mien collaborated with the CIA against Pathet Lao; 50,000 Mien refugees were resettled in the US.

The Mien are influenced by Chinese traditions and use Chinese characters to write their language, although a unified script was also developed in the 1980s. Kinship is patrilineal and marriage is polygamous. Houses are built at ground level, out of wood or bamboo thatch. Women wear trousers and black jackets with intricately embroidered patches and red fur-like collars, along with large dark-blue or black turbans. Men wear black tunics and black pants. Mien is a tonal language and belongs to the Hmong-Mien language family.

Lifestyle

Individual lifestyles vary according to family background, income and geography. Bangkok is by far the richest place in Thailand, but affluence is on the rise throughout the nation.

There continues to be a migration from the countryside or small towns to the urban job centres. It was once standard for Thais to send a portion of their pay home to support their parents or dependent children left behind to be raised in the village. This still happens today in some socio-economic strata, but increasingly affluent parents don't need financial help from their adult children. In fact, an important social shift has occurred: parents continue to support their adult children with big-ticket purchases of cars and real estate that their entry-level salaries can't afford. As a result, the older generation often criticises today's youth as having an inflated sense of entitlement.

In the provincial capitals, life is more traditional, relatively speaking. Civil servants – teachers and government employees – make up the backbone of the Thai middle class and largely live in nuclear families in terraced housing estates outside the city centre. The business class lives in the city centre, usually in apartments above shops, making for an easy commute but a fairly urban life.

From a demographic perspective, Thailand, like most of Asia, is age-ing. It is projected that 35% of the Thai population in 2050 will be over 60 years old. Thailand's population growth rate is low, with a current growth rate of only around 0.3% and analysts are now warning of future labour shortages and overextended pension systems. Women are now pursuing careers instead of starting families; unmarried women now comprise 30% of the population.

Thai Culture

Much of Thailand's cultural value system is hinged upon respect for the family, religion and monarchy. Within that system each person knows his or her place, and Thai children are strictly instructed on the impor-tance of group conformity and suppressing confrontational views. In most social situations, establishing harmony often takes a leading role, and Thais take personal pride in making others feel at ease.

Sà·nùk

In general, Thais place high value on *sà·nùk*, which means 'fun'. It is often regarded as a necessary underpinning of anything worth doing. Even work and studying should have an element of *sà·nùk,* otherwise it automatically becomes drudgery. This doesn't mean Thais don't work, but they labour best as a group, so as to avoid loneliness and ensure an element of playfulness. Nothing condemns an activity more than *mâi sà·nùk* (not fun). Thais often mix their job tasks with a healthy dose of socialising, from the back-breaking work of rice farming to the tedium of long-distance bus driving.

Saving Face

Thais believe strongly in the concept of saving face, or avoiding confron-tation and endeavouring not to embarrass themselves or other people (except when it's *sà·nùk* to do so). The ideal face-saver doesn't bring up negative topics in conversation, doesn't express firm convictions or opin-ions, and doesn't claim to have an expertise. Agreement and harmony are considered to be the most important social graces.

While Westerners might think of heated discussion as social sport, Thais regard any instance where voices are raised as rude and potentially volatile. Losing your temper causes a loss of face for everyone, and Thais who have been crossed may react in extreme ways. Minor embarrass-ments, such as tripping or falling, might elicit giggles from a crowd of Thais. In this case they aren't taking delight in your mishap, but helping you save face by laughing it off.

Status & Obligation

All relationships in traditional Thai society – and those in the modern Thai milieu as well – are governed by social rank defined by age, wealth,

The hill-people communities who lived at altitudes of 900m or above were once opium-poppy cul-tivators, but the illicit cash crop was mostly erad-icated through a royally sponsored crop substitution programme and improved infrastructure.

Ritual offerings during Songkran (Thai New Year; p30)

Lifestyle Statistics

Average marriage age for a Thai man/woman: 28/25 years

Minimum daily wage: 325B

Entry-level professional salary: 12,000–15,000B per month

status and personal or political position. The elder position is called *pôo yài* (literally the 'big person') and is used to describe parents, bosses, village heads, public officials etc. The junior position is called *pôo nóy* (little person) and describes anyone who is subservient to the *pôo yài*. Although this tendency towards social ranking is to some degree shared by many societies around the world, the Thai twist lies in the set of mutual obligations linking the elder to the junior.

Pôo nóy are supposed to show obedience and respect towards the elder. Those with junior status are not supposed to question or criticise those with elder status. In the workplace, this means younger staff members are not encouraged to speak during meetings and are expected to do their bosses' bidding.

In return *pôo yài* are obligated to care for or 'sponsor' the *pôo nóy*. It is a paternalistic relationship in which *pôo nóy* can ask for favours involv-

MERIT-MAKING RITUALS

Pilgrimages to famous temples are an important feature of domestic tourism. During these visits, merit-making is an individual ritual rather than a congregational affair. Worshippers buy offerings such as lotus buds, incense and candles, and present these symbolic gifts to the temple's primary Buddha image. Other merit-making activities include offering food to the temple *sangha,* meditating (individually or in groups), listening to monks chanting *suttas* (Buddhist discourse), and attending a *têht* or *dhamma* talk by the abbot or another respected teacher. Though Thailand is increasingly secular, merit-making remains an important cultural activity, often linked to wish fulfilment (finding love or academic success) rather than religious devotion.

Tea plantation, Chiang Rai Province

ing money or job access. *Pôo yài* reaffirm their rank by granting requests when possible; to refuse would risk a loss of face and status.

The protocol defined by the social hierarchy governs almost every aspect of Thai behaviour. Elected or appointed officials occupy one of the highest rungs on the social ladder and often regard themselves as caretakers of the people, a stark contrast to the democratic ideal of being the voice of the people. The complicated personal hierarchy in Thailand often prevents collaboration, especially between those with competing status. This is perhaps why Bangkok has several modern-art museums with somewhat anaemic collections rather than one consolidated powerhouse.

Most foreign visitors will interact with a simplified version of this elder-junior relationship in the form of *pêe* (elder sibling) and *nórng* (younger sibling). All Thais refer to each other using familial names. Even people unrelated by blood quickly establish who's *pêe* and who's *nórng*. This is why one of the first questions Thais ask new acquaintances is 'How old are you?'.

> Thais are fastidious in their personal appearance, often bathing twice or more a day, and are confused that seemingly wealthy foreigners are so unkempt.

Religion

Buddhism

Approximately 94% of Thai people are Theravada Buddhists, a branch of Buddhism that came from Sri Lanka during the Sukhothai period.

The ultimate end of Theravada Buddhism is *nibbana* ('nirvana' in Sanskrit), which literally means the 'blowing out' or extinction of all grasping and thus of all *dukkha* (suffering). Effectively, *nibbana* is also an end to the cycle of rebirths (both moment-to-moment and life-to-life) that is existence. In reality, most Thai Buddhists aim for rebirth in a 'better' existence rather than the supramundane goal of *nibbana*. The concept of rebirth is almost universally accepted in Thailand, even by non-Buddhists.

The idea of reincarnation also provides Thais with a sense of humility and interconnectedness. Observing a creepy-crawly in the bushes, they might feel that perhaps they too were once like that creature, or that a deceased relative now occupies a non-human body. Reflecting Thailand's social stratification, reincarnation is basically a reward or punishment. This is essentially the Buddhist theory of karma, expressed in the Thai proverb *tam dee, dâi dee; tam chôoa, dâi chôoa* (good actions bring good results; bad actions bring bad results). A good person can improve his or her lot in life today and in future lives by making merit (*tam bun*).

The Buddhist hierarchy in Thailand is made up of the Triratana (Triple Gems) – the Buddha, the *dhamma* (teachings) and the *sangha* (Buddhist community). Historically the Thai king has occupied a revered position in Thai Buddhism, often viewed as semi-divine. Thai royal ceremonies remain almost exclusively the domain of Brahman priests, bestowed with the duty of preserving the three pillars of Thai nationhood, namely sovereignty, religion and the monarchy.

Thai Buddhism has no particular Sabbath day, but there are *wan prá* (holy days), which occur every seventh or eighth day depending on phases of the moon. There are also religious holidays, typically marking important events in the Buddha's life.

> The official year in Thailand is calculated from 543 BC, the beginning of the Buddhist Era, so that CE 2018 is BCE 2561, CE 2019 is BCE 2562 etc.

Monks & Nuns

Socially, every Thai male is expected to become a monk (*bhikkhu* in Pali; *prá* or *prá pík·sù* in Thai) for a short period in his life, optimally between the time he finishes school and the time he starts a career or marries. Traditionally, the length of time spent in the wát is three months, during the *pan·săh* (Buddhist lent), which begins in July and coincides with the rainy season. However, nowadays men may spend as little as a week to accrue merit as monks.

Monks are required to shave their heads, eyebrows and any facial hair during their residence in the monastery, as a sign of renouncing worldly concerns. They are also required to live an ascetic life free of luxury and eat one meal per day (sometimes two, depending on the temple traditions). Monks who live in the city usually emphasise study of the Buddhist scriptures, while those who opt for the forest temples tend to emphasise meditation. Fully ordained monks perform funeral and marriage rites, conduct sermons and instruct monastic teachings.

In Thai Buddhism, women who seek a monastic life are given a minor role in the temple that is not equal to full monkhood. A Buddhist nun is known as *mâa chee* (mother priest) and lives as an *atthasīla* (eight-precept) nun, a position traditionally occupied by women who had no

SPIRIT HOUSES

Many homes or inhabited dwellings in Thailand have an associated 'spirit house', built to provide a residence for the plot of land's *prá poom* (guardian spirits). According to animistic beliefs that predate Buddhism, guardian spirits that reside in rivers, trees and other natural features need to be honoured (and placated). The guardian spirit of a particular plot of land is the supernatural equivalent of a mother-in-law, an honoured but sometimes troublesome family member. To keep the spirits happily distracted, Thais erect elaborate dollhouse-like structures where the spirits can 'live' comfortably separated from humans. To further cultivate good relations and good fortune, daily offerings of rice, fruit, flowers and water are made to the spirit house. If the human house is enlarged, the spirit house must also be enlarged, so that the spirits do not feel slighted. Spirit houses must be consecrated by a Brahman priest.

Top Novice monks, Ayuthaya (p168)

Bottom Matsayit Klang mosque, Pattani (p592)

S. TANONGSAK / GETTY IMAGES ©

other place in society. Thai nuns shave their heads, wear white robes and take care of temple chores. Generally speaking, *mâa chee* aren't considered as prestigious as monks and don't have a function in the merit-making rituals of lay people.

Islam

Theravada Buddhism is often called the southern school because it travelled from the Indian subcontinent to Southeast Asia, while Mahayana Buddhism was adopted throughout the northern regions of Asia.

There are close to 3500 mosques in Thailand – over 170 in Bangkok alone. Of these mosques, 99% are associated with the Sunni branch of Islam (in which Islamic leadership is vested in the consensus of the Ummah, or Muslim community), and 1% with the Shi'ite branch (in which religious and political authority is given to descendants of the Prophet Mohammed). As with other parts of Asia, Islam in Thailand is infused with aspects of Sufism.

Islam was introduced to Thailand's southern region between CE 1200 and -1500 through the influence of Indian and Arab traders and scholars.

Arts & Architecture

Thailand possesses an intensely visual culture, in which an appreciation of beauty and aesthetics infuses everything from extravagant temple buildings and humble old-fashioned houses to the high arts conceived for the royal court. Thailand's ancient arts focused on temple architecture and Buddhist sculpture, but in the modern era creativity is expressed through multiple forms, from social commentary in contemporary paintings to sky-piercing towers. Musical traditions range from classical orchestras to country music and teenage dance anthems.

Architecture

The most striking aspect of Thailand's architectural heritage is its frequently magnificent Buddhist temples (wát). One of the most distinctive features of Buddhist temple architecture is the *chedi* (stupa), a monument that pays tribute to the enduring stability of Buddhism. Many

Above Reclining Buddha statue, Wat Pho (p69), Bangkok

contain relics of important kings, the historical Buddha or the remains of notable monks or nuns. Thai temples freely mix different foreign influences, from the corn-shaped stupa inherited from the Khmer empire to the bell-shaped stupa of Sri Lanka.

Thai temples are replete with Hindu-Buddhist iconography. *Naga*, a mythical serpent-like creature who guarded Buddha during meditation, is often depicted in entrance railings and outlining roof gables. On the tip of the temple hall roof is the *chôr fáh*, a golden bird-shaped silhouette suggesting flight.

A venerated Buddhist symbol, the lotus bud is another sacred motif that often decorates the tops of temple gates, veranda columns and the spires of Sukhothai-era *chedi*. Images of the Buddha often depict him meditating on a lotus pedestal. The lotus carries with it a reminder of the tenets of Buddhism. The lotus can bloom even from the mud of a rancid pond, illustrating the capacity for religious perfection in a defiled environment.

Thais began mixing traditional architecture with European forms in the late-19th and early-20th centuries. The port cities, including Bangkok and Phuket, acquired fine examples of Sino-Portuguese architecture –

THAILAND'S ARTISTIC PERIODS

PERIOD	TEMPLE & CHEDI STYLES	BUDDHA STYLES	EXAMPLES
Dvaravati Period (7th–11th centuries)	Rectangular-based *chedi* (stupas) with stepped tiers	Indian-influenced; thick torso, large hair curls, arched eyebrows (like flying birds), protruding eyes, thick lips and flat nose	Phra Pathom Chedi, Nakhon Pathom; Lopburi Museum, Lopburi; Wat Chama Thewi, Lamphun
Srivijaya Period (7th–13th centuries)	Mahayana Buddhist-style temples; Javanese-style *chedi* with elaborate arches	Indian-influenced; heavily ornamented; human-like features and slightly twisted at the waist	Wat Phra Mahathat Woramahawihaan and National Museum, Nakhon Si Thammarat
Khmer Period (9th–11th centuries)	Hindu-Buddhist temples; corn-cob-shaped *prang* (Khmer-styled *chedi*)	Buddha meditating under a canopy of the seven-headed *naga* and atop a lotus pedestal	Phimai Historical Park, Nakhon Ratchasima; Phanom Rung Historical Park, Surin
Chiang Saen–Lanna Period (11th–13th centuries)	Teak temples; square-based *chedi* topped by gilded umbrella; also octagonal-based *chedi*	Burmese influences with plump figure, round, smiling face and foot-pads facing upwards in meditation pose	Wat Phra Singh, Chiang Mai; Chiang Saen National Museum, Chiang Saen
Sukhothai Period (13th–15th centuries)	Khmer-inspired temples; slim-spired *chedi* topped by a lotus bud	Graceful poses, often depicted 'walking', no anatomical human detail	Sukhothai Historical Park, Sukhothai
Ayuthaya Period (14th–18th centuries)	Classical Thai temple with three-tiered roof and gable flourishes; bell-shaped *chedi* with tapering spire	Ayuthaya-era king, wearing a gem-studded crown and royal regalia	Ayuthaya Historical Park, Ayuthaya
Bangkok-Ratanakosin Period (19th century)	Colourful and gilded temple with Western-Thai styles; mosaic-covered *chedi*	Reviving Ayuthaya style	Wat Phra Kaew, Wat Pho and Wat Arun, Bangkok

Traditional temple mural, Wat Pho (p69), Bangkok

buildings of stuccoed brick decorated with an ornate facade – a style that followed the sea traders during the colonial era. It is locally known as 'old Bangkok' or 'Ratanakosin'.

Visual Arts

Much of Thailand's best ancient art is on display inside the country's myriad temples, while Bangkok's many national and commercial museums curate more contemporary collections.

Traditional Painting & Sculpture

Thailand's early artistic output was based almost entirely on religion, with Buddha sculptures and murals communicating a continuous visual language of the belief system.

The country first defined its own artistic style during the Sukhothai era, famous for its graceful and serene Buddha figures. Temple murals are the main form of ancient Thai art. Always instructional in purpose, murals often depict the *Jataka* (stories of the Buddha's past lives) and the Thai version of the Hindu epic *Ramayana*. There are very few surviving examples of pre-20th-century religious painting, due to a lack of durability. The earliest examples are found at Ayuthaya's Wat Ratburana, but Bangkok is home to some of the best surviving examples.

The development of Thai religious art and architecture is broken into different periods, defined by the patronage of the ruling capital. The best examples of a period's characteristics are seen in the variations of the *chedi* (stupa) shape and in the features of the Buddha sculptures, including facial features, the top flourish on the head, the dress and the position of the feet in meditation.

Art Museums & Galleries

National Museum

Bangkok Art & Culture Centre

100 Tonson Gallery

H Gallery

Kathmandu Photo Gallery

Museum of Contemporary Art

Soy Sauce Factory

Bangkok Art & Culture Centre (p87)

Contemporary Art

Adapting traditional themes to the secular canvas began around the turn of the 20th century as Western influence surged in the region. In general, Thai painting favours abstraction over realism and continues to preserve the one-dimensional perspective of traditional mural paintings. There are two major trends in Thai art: the updating of religious themes, and tongue-in-cheek social commentary, with some artists overlapping the two.

Italian-born Corrado Feroci is often credited as the father of modern Thai art. He was invited to Thailand by Rama VI in 1923 and built Bangkok's Democracy Monument and other monuments in the city.

In the 1970s, Thai artists tackled the modernisation of Buddhist themes through abstract expressionism. Leading works include the colourful surrealism of Pichai Nirand and the mystical pen-and-ink drawings of Thawan Duchanee. Internationally known Montien Boonma uses the ingredients of Buddhist merit-making, such as gold leaf, bells and candle wax, to create installation pieces.

Politically motivated artwork defined a parallel movement in Thai contemporary art. In Thailand's rapidly industrialising society, many artists watched as rice fields became factories, forests became asphalt and the spoils went to the politically connected. Manit Sriwanichpoom is best known for his Pink Man on Tour series, in which he depicted artist Sompong Thawee in a pink suit with a pink shopping cart amid Thailand's most iconic attractions. A graduate of the College of Fine Art in Bangkok, outspoken artist and poet Vasan Sitthiket is more blatantly controversial and uses mixed-media installations to condemn exploitation and corruption. His often powerful works have been banned in Thailand and criticised as anti-Thai.

Top Arts Reading

The Thai House (Ruethai Chaichongrak; 2002)

The Arts of Thailand (Steve Van Beek; 1998)

Flavours: Thai Contemporary Art (Steven Pettifor; 2005)

Bangkok Design: Thai Ideas in Textiles and Furniture (Brian Mertens; 2006)

Buddhist Temples of Thailand (Joe Cummings; 2010)

REGIONAL HANDICRAFTS

Thailand has a long tradition of handicrafts, often region- or even village-specific. Thai ceramics include the greenish celadon products, red-earth clay pots of Dan Kwian, and central Thailand's *ben·jà·rong* ('five-colour' style), employing elaborate, multicoloured enamels on white porcelain. Once exclusively manufactured for the royal court, *ben·jà·rong* is based on Chinese patterns, while celadon is of Thai origin.

Northern Thailand has long produced regionally distinctive lacquerware, thanks to the influence of Burmese artisans. Each region in Thailand has its own silk-weaving style. In ancient times woven textiles might have functioned much like business cards do today – demarcating tribal identity and sometimes even marriage status. Today, village weaving traditions continue but have become less geographically specific.

In the 1990s there was a push to move art out of museums and into public spaces. Navin Rawanchaikul started his 'in-the-streets' collaborations in his hometown of Chiang Mai and then moved to Bangkok, where he filled the city's taxis with art installations, a show that literally went on the road. His other works have a way with words, such as the mixed-media piece *We Are the Children of Rice (Wine)* (2002) and his rage against the commercialisation of museums in his epic painting entitled *Super (M)art Bangkok Survivors* (2004).

Up-and-coming artists use a variety of media and take on more introspective topics, like Maitree Siriboon, who uses collage and photography to explore personal identity, sexuality and transformation. Born in 1979, Thai-Japanese artist Yuree Kensaku creates allegorical, sometimes surreal cartoon-like paintings with vivid pop-culture references.

Closely associated with Buddhist statuary, Thai sculpture is considered to be the strongest of the contemporary arts. Influenced by Henry Moore, who taught him, Khien Yimsiri created elegant human and mythical forms from bronze. Manop Suwanpinta moulds the human anatomy into fantastic shapes that often intersect with technology, such as hinged faces that open to reveal inanimate content. Kamin Lertchaiprasert explores the subject of spirituality and daily life in his sculptures. His *Ngern Nung* (Sitting Money) installation, made between 2004 and 2006, included a series of figures made from discarded paper bills from the national bank, embellished with poetic instructions on life and love.

During the political turmoil of the past decade, artists channelled first-person experiences into multimedia installations. Tanks, guns, violence and protest imagery are woven together to express outrage, grief, anxiety and even apathy. In 2012 Vasan Sitthiket created a collection of colourful but chaotic collages in the series descriptively called *Hypocrisy*. Chulayarnnon Siriphol's short film *A Brief History of Memory* (2010) recounts one woman's experience of violent street protests.

In recent years, there's been a growing sense that art is starting to move beyond purely intellectual, political or even artsy circles and into the mainstream. The number of galleries in Bangkok and elsewhere has increased immensely and in 2017, Kamin Lertchaiprasert was asked to create art that would decorate the trains of Bangkok's Skytrain/BTS network. In 2018, Thailand hosted its first biennale, the Bangkok Art Biennale. The next edition is scheduled to take place in 2020.

Music Sources
Deungdutjai (http://deung-dutjai.com) posts Thai pop hits with Thai and translated or transliterated lyrics.

Music

Throughout Thailand you'll encounter a rich diversity of musical genres and styles, from the serene court music that accompanies classical dance-drama to the bass-heavy house music shaking dance clubs across the nation.

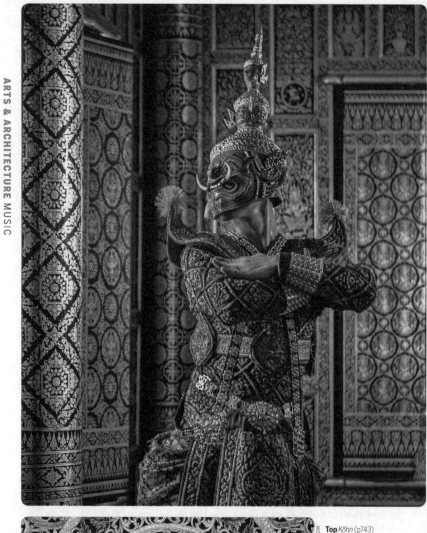

Top *Kŏhn* (p743) performer

Bottom Traditional temple decoration

Traditional Thai weaving (p739)

Classical Music

The classical orchestra is called the *pèe pâht* and was originally developed to accompany classical dance-drama and shadow theatre, but these days can be heard in performances at temple fairs and tourist attractions. The ensemble can include from five to more than 20 players. Prior to a performance the players offer incense and flowers to the *đà·pohn* (or *thon*), a double-headed hand drum that sets the tempo for the entire ensemble.

The standard Thai scale divides the eight-note octave into seven full-tone intervals, with no semitones. Thai scales were first transcribed by the Thai-German composer Peter Feit (also known by his Thai name, Phra Chen Duriyang), who composed Thailand's national anthem in 1932.

Lôok Tûng & Mǒr Lam

The best-selling modern musical genre in Thailand is *lôok tûng* (literally 'children of the fields'), which dates to the 1940s. Roughly analogous to country-and-western music in the US, it appeals to working-class Thais. Traditional subject matter are tales of lost love, tragic early death, and the dire circumstances of struggling farmers. The plaintive singing style ranges from sentimental to anguished, and singers are often backed by Las Vegas–style showgirl dancers.

Mǒr lam is Thailand's blues; it's a folk tradition firmly rooted in northeast Thailand and Laos, based on songs played on the *kaan* (a wind instrument comprised of a double row of bamboo-like reeds fitted into a hardwood soundbox). The oldest style, most likely to be heard at village gatherings, has a simple but insistent bass beat and is often sung in Isan dialect. With songs frequently dwelling on unrequited love and the hardships

Kórng wong yài gongs

of life, *mŏr lam* has jumped the generational fence with an electrified pop interpretation and a seriously silly side.

As economic migrants moved from across the country to Bangkok, the two genres merged with each other as well as with other forms, leading to hybridisation and cross-pollination. Contemporary singers might sing about city woes, factory work or being too fat, often backed up by a dance beat.

Thailand's most famous *lôok tûng* singer was Pumpuang Duangjan, a vocalist who received a royally sponsored cremation and a major shrine at Suphanburi's Wat Thapkradan when she died aged just 30 in 1992. Gravelly voiced Siriporn Ampaipong helped carry the tradition afterwards and is still much loved. The new *lôok tûng* princesses are Yingli Sijumpon from Buriram, and Baitei R Siam, who has crossed over into pop. Pai Pongratorn and Tai Orathai are other stalwarts, while Auu Jeerawat has an acoustic take on the genre.

Thai Rock & Pop

The 1970s ushered in the politically conscious folk-rock of the US and Europe, which the Thais dubbed *pleng pêu·a chee·wít* ('songs for life'). Chiefly identified with the Thai band Caravan, this style defined a major contemporary shift in Thai music, with political and environmental topics replacing the usual love themes. During the authoritarian dictatorships of the '70s many of Caravan's songs were officially banned. Another long-standing example of this style is Carabao, which mixed in rock and heavy metal and spawned a whole generation of imitators.

Thailand's thriving teen-pop industry – sometimes referred to as T-pop – first surfaced in the 1970s and '80s, and centred on artists chosen for their good looks. Thailand's king of pop is Thongchai 'Bird' McIntyre (also known as Pi Bird). His first album hit the shelves in 1986 and he

---

TRADITIONAL INSTRUMENTS

þèe High-pitched woodwind, often heard at Thai-boxing matches.

rá·nâht èhk Bamboo-keyed percussion that resembles a xylophone.

kórng wong yài Tuned gongs arranged in a semicircle.

đà·pohn (thon) A double-headed hand-drum.

pǐn Four-stringed instrument plucked like a guitar.

sor Slender bowed instrument with a coconut-shell soundbox.

klòo·i Wooden flute.

---

has followed up with an album almost every year since. With a nice-guy persona coupled with Elton John's staying power, he is highly popular with Thais in their 30s and 40s. A potential heir-apparent is Chanakan Rattana-udom (Atom), a singer-songwriter who has had a string of sweet hits. The current crop of pop stars have amped up dance beats or are still tugging at the heartstrings. Ballads and booty-shaking always top the charts. And, just like the rest of the world, Thai reality-TV shows turn out a succession of poppy singers all eager for their 15 minutes of fame.

The 1990s gave birth to an alternative pop scene – known as 'indie' – pioneered by the independent record label Bakery Music. During indie's heyday, Modern Dog, composed of four Chulalongkorn University graduates, orchestrated the generation's musical coming of age. Another indie fixture was Loso (from 'low society' as opposed to 'hi-so' or socialites), which updated Carabao's affinity for Thai folk melodies and rhythms. The noughties saw these bands move towards classic-rock status, while Bakery Music was bought by a conglomerate.

The alt scene lives in a variety of forms – lounge pop, garage rock, shoegaze and electronica. The cast of characters changes as underground bands break through and then later break up. In the 2000s, Tattoo Colour, hailing from Khon Kaen, scored several hits from a small indie label. Electro-rock band Futon announced their arrival with a catchy version of The Stooges' 'I Wanna Be Your Dog' in 2003 and then later pursued solo careers. Endorphine was a feel-good noughties band led by sweet-faced Da with almost a decade's worth of hits; Da later went solo.

In more recent years there has been a subtle move away from guitar-based rock and towards electronic music, with outfits like Clokue, Morg, Koichi Shimizu and Gorn Clw making noise and gaining praise. An emerging rap scene has also been gaining popularity and the hip-hop band Thaitanium has been rapping since start of the millennium.

Dance & Theatre

Thailand's high arts have endured decline since the palace transitioned from a cloistered community, although some endangered art forms have been salvaged and revived for a growing tourist community. Folk traditions enjoy broader appeal, but the era of village stage shows is sadly long gone.

Thailand's most famous dance-drama is *kǒhn,* which depicts the *Ramakian,* the Thai version of India's *Ramayana.* The central story revolves around Prince Rama's search for his beloved Princess Sita, who has been abducted by the evil 10-headed demon Ravana and taken to the island of Lanka. Dancers are clothed in elaborate costumes, with some characters masked.

Every region has its own traditional dance style, performed at temple fairs and provincial parades. Occasionally temples also provide shrine

Thailand Playlist

That Song (Modern Dog)

The Sound of Siam: Leftfield Luk Thung, Jazz & Molam in Thailand 1964–1975 (Soundway Records compilation)

Made in Thailand (Carabao)

Best (Pumpuang Duangjan)

I Wanna Be Your Dog (Futon)

Still Resisting (Thaitanium)

dancers, who are commissioned by merit-makers to perform. School-aged children often take traditional Thai dance lessons.

Most often seen at Buddhist festivals, *lí·gair* is a raucous theatrical art form thought to have descended from drama rituals brought to southern Thailand by Arab and Malay traders. It's a colourful mix of folk and classical music, outrageous costumes, melodrama, slapstick comedy, sexual innuendo and up-to-date commentary that's partly improvised.

Puppet theatre also enjoyed royal and common patronage. *Lá·kon lék* (little theatre) used marionettes of varying sizes for court performances similar to *kŏhn*. Two to three puppet masters are required to manipulate the metre-high puppets by means of wires attached to long poles. Stories are drawn from Thai folk tales, particularly *Phra Aphaimani,* and occasionally from the *Ramakian.*

Shadow-puppet theatre – in which two-dimensional figures are manipulated between a cloth screen and a light source at night-time performances – has been a Southeast Asian tradition for perhaps five centuries, originally brought to the Malay Peninsula by Middle Eastern traders. In Thailand it is mostly found in the south. As in Malaysia and Indonesia, shadow puppets in Thailand are carved from dried buffalo or cow hides *(năng).* The capital of shadow puppetry today is Nakhon Si Thammarat, which has regular performances at its festivals. The puppets are popular souvenirs for tourists.

Cinema

There are usually two concurrent streams to Thai cinema: movies that are financially successful and films that are considered cinematically meritorious. Only rarely do they overlap. The proliferation of online streaming of movies has altered the once flourishing Thai cinematic new wave, but it has also given short-film makers access to larger audiences.

Popular Thai cinema ballooned in the 1960s and '70s, especially when the government levied a tax on Hollywood imports, kick-starting a home-grown industry. The majority of films were cheap action flicks that were typically dubbed *năm nôw* ('stinking water'), but the fantastic (even nonsensical) plots and rich colours left a lasting impression on future Thai filmmakers.

Thai cinema graduated into international film circles in the late 1990s and early 2000s, thanks in part to the output of Pratt Institute–educated arthouse director and screenwriter Pen-Ek Ratanaruang and his gritty and engrossing oeuvre of films such as 2003's *Last Life In The Universe.* Apichatpong Weerasethakul (p746), Thailand's leading cinéma-vérité director, has garnered three Cannes accolades, including the Palme d'Or (the festival's highest prize) for his *Uncle Boonmee Who Can Recall His Past Lives* (2010).

Modern life, with its myriad aggravations, represents a recent theme in Thai movies. Nawapol Thamrongrattanarit gained acclaim for his modern-girl-in-the-city screenplay *Bangkok Traffic Love Story* (2009) and followed up with his directorial debut *36* (2012), which uses 36 static camera shots to explore lost love and lost memories. His *Mary is Happy, Mary is Happy* (2013) was a film festival hit that adapted the Twitter feed of a Thai teen into a movie. Anucha Boonyawatana's *The Blue Hour* (2015) blends a coming-out story with magic realism.

Film-fest fare has been bolstered by independent film clubs and online streaming services. Low-budget filmmakers bypass the big studios, the ever-vigilant cinema censors and the skittish, controversy-averse movie theatres by making short films and other DIY projects. Being censored by the film board may seem like the kiss of death, but it often guarantees indie success and cult status. Two political documentaries of 2013

Classic Thai Movies

....

6ixtynin9 (1997)

....

Yam Yasothon (2005)

....

Ruang Rak Noi Nid Mahasan (Last Life in the Universe; 2003)

....

Ten Years Thailand (2018)

....

Mekhong Sipha Kham Deuan Sip-et (Mekong Full Moon Party; 2002)

....

Uncle Boonmee Who Can Recall His Past Lives (2010)

Shadow puppet theatre

challenged the board's sensitivities. Pen-Ek Ratanaruang's historical *Paradoxocracy* had to mute objectionable dialogue, while Nontawat Numbenchapol's *Boundary* was initially banned, though that was lifted after an appeal. The Thai horror *Arbat* was banned in 2015 because it depicted 'improper' conduct by Thai monks, which was considered a slur against Buddhism.

The big studios prefer ghost stories, horror flicks, historic epics, love stories and camp comedies. Elaborate historical movies and epics serve a dual purpose: they can be lucrative and they promote national identity. Criticised as a propaganda tool, the *Legend of King Naresuan* epic focuses on the Ayuthaya-era king who repelled an attempted Burmese invasion. Each chapter (six have been released so far) has been a box-office winner.

In recent years there's been a rise in the number of socially and politically themed films such as Pimpaka Towira's *The Island Funeral* (2016), which follows the journey of a Muslim woman in conflict-plagued Pattani, and Anocha Suwichakornpong's *By the Time it Gets Dark* (2016), which chronicles two students impacted by the 1976 massacre at Thammasat University.

But it is horror that is increasingly becoming the dominant genre of Thai cinema. Movies like *Homestay* (2017) and *Inhuman Kiss* (2019), which was selected as Thailand's entry for the 2019 Oscars, have been box office successes both at home and abroad.

Literature

The written word has a long history in Thailand, dating back to the 11th or 12th century when the first Thai script was fashioned from an older Mon alphabet. The 30,000-line *Phra Aphaimani,* composed by poet Sunthorn Phu in the late 18th century, is Thailand's most famous classical

APICHATPONG WEERASETHAKUL

Bangkok-born independent film director Apichatpong Weerasethakul, winner of the Palme d'Or at the 2010 Cannes Film Festival for his *Uncle Boonmee Who Can Recall His Past Lives*, has made a point of ruffling feathers at home in defence of his art. Joint founder of the Free Thai Cinema Movement, formed to oppose the 2007 draft law devising ratings for films that encouraged censors to demand cuts to his film *Syndromes and a Century*, the enfant terrible of Thai movie-making has said he does not wish his latest feature-length film *Cemetery of Splendour* (2015) to be screened in Thailand, fearing calls for censorship. The film's theme – a group of soldiers receiving treatment in a clinic after suffering from a form of sleeping sickness – has been widely read as a metaphor for Thailand's dysfunctional political culture.

A prolific creator of short films, full-length films and installations, Weerasethakul first came to international attention with his 2002 erotic romance *Blissfully Yours*, which won the Un Certain Regard prize at Cannes in 2002, and *Tropical Malady*, which scooped the Prix du Jury at Cannes two years later, despite an opinion-dividing reception. Weerasethakul favours personal themes and social issues in his films (all produced by his film company, Kick the Machine), conveyed in an often hypnotic, dream-like and sometimes surreal form with a spiritual underlay.

Top Fiction

The Blind Earthworm in the Labyrinth (Veeraporn Nitiprapha; 2019)

The Lioness in Bloom: Modern Thai Fiction about Women (translated by Susan Fulop Kepner; 1996)

Four Reigns (Kukrit Pramoj; 1991)

Bangkok 8 (John Burdett; 2003)

Fieldwork: A Novel (Mischa Berlinski; 2007)

literary work. Like many of its epic predecessors around the world, it tells the story of an exiled prince who must complete an odyssey of love and war before returning to his kingdom in victory.

Of all classical Thai literature, however, *Ramakian* is the most pervasive and influential in Thai culture. The Indian source, *Ramayana*, came to Thailand with the Khmers 900 years ago, first appearing as stone reliefs on Prasat Hin Phimai and other Angkor temples in the northeast. Eventually the Thais developed their own version of the epic, which was first written down during the reign of Rama I (r 1782–1809). This version contained 60,000 stanzas and was a quarter longer than the Sanskrit original.

Although the main themes remained the same, the Thais embroidered the *Ramayana* with more biographical detail on arch-villain Ravana (called Thotsakan, or '10-necked' in the *Ramakian*) and his wife Montho. Hanuman, the monkey god, differs substantially in the Thai version in his flirtatious nature (in the Hindu version he follows a strict vow of chastity). One of the classic *Ramakian* reliefs at Bangkok's Wat Pho depicts Hanuman clasping a maiden's bared breast as if it were an apple.

Modern Thai literature struggles to compete with nonfiction – which is far more widely read – and only a few authors get their work translated into English. Among those that do, short-story writer Prabda Yoon and the novelists Pitchaya Sudbanthad and Veeraporn Nitiprapha are worth checking out.

Environment & Wildlife

Thailand spans a distance of 1650km from its northern tip to its southern tail, a distance that encompasses 16 latitudinal degrees and a variety of ecological zones, making it one of the most environmentally diverse countries in Southeast Asia.

The Land

Thailand's odd shape is often likened to the head of an elephant, with the trunk being the Malay peninsula and the head being the northern mountains. Starting at the crown of the country, northern Thailand is dominated by the Dawna-Tenasserim mountain range, a southeast-trending extension of the Himalayan mountains. Dropping into the central region, the topography mellows into rice-producing plains fed by rivers that are as revered as the national monarchy. Thailand's most exalted river is Chao Phraya, and the river delta is in cultivation for most of the year.

Tracing the contours of Thailand's northern and northeastern border is another imposing watercourse: the Mekong. Rising in the Tibetan Plateau, the Mekong courses through China, Myanmar, Laos, Thailand, Cambodia and Vietnam before reaching the South China Sea. As the artery of Southeast Asia, it is a workhorse river that has been dammed for hydroelectric power, and swells and contracts based on the seasonal rains.

The landscape of Thailand's northeastern border is occupied by the arid Khorat Plateau rising some 300m above the central plain. This is a hardscrabble land where the rains are meagre and the soil is anaemic.

The kingdom's eastern rivers dump their waters into the Gulf of Thailand. The warm, gentle gulf is an ideal cultivation ground for coral reefs. Sliding further south is the Malay peninsula, a long trunk-like landmass. On the western side extends the Andaman Sea, a splendid tropical setting of stunning blue waters and dramatic limestone islands. Onshore, the peninsula is dominated by some final remaining stands of rainforest and ever-expanding rubber and palm-oil plantations.

Flowing through six nations, the Mekong River rivals the Amazon in terms of biodiversity, and shelters endangered and newly discovered species, such as the Khorat big-mouthed frog, which catches prey with its fangs.

Native Animals: A Rich Menagerie

In the northern half of Thailand most indigenous species are classified zoologically as Indo-Chinese, referring to fauna originating from mainland Asia, while those of the south are generally Sundaic, typical of peninsular Malaysia, Sumatra, Borneo and Java.

Thailand is particularly rich in birdlife, with over 1000 recorded resident and migrating species, approximately 10% of the world's bird species. The cool mountains of northern Thailand are populated by montane species and migrants such as flycatchers and thrushes. The arid forests of northeastern Thailand are favourites for hornbills. Marshland birds prefer the wetlands of the central region, while Sundaic species flock to the wetter climate of southern Thailand.

Birds apart, monkeys and apes can be spotted in national parks. Thailand is home to five species of macaque (including the crab-eating macaque and the pig-tailed macaque), four species of the smaller leaf-monkey and three species of gibbon. Monkeys and apes sometimes survive in varying states of domestication with humans.

Other species found in parks and sanctuaries include gaur (Indian bison), banteng (wild cattle), serow (an Asiatic goat-antelope), sambar deer, muntjac (barking deer), mouse deer and tapir.

Thailand has six venomous snakes: the common cobra, king cobra, banded krait, green viper, Malayan viper and Russell's pit viper. The nation's largest snake is the reticulated python, which can reach a whopping 10m.

The oceans are home to hundreds of species of coral, and reefs provide perfect living conditions for fish, crustaceans and tiny invertebrates. Thailand has some of the world's smallest fishes (the 1cm-long dwarf pygmy goby) and the largest cartilaginous fish (the 12m-long whale shark). Deeper waters are home to grouper, barracuda, sharks, manta rays, marlin and tuna. You might also encounter turtles, whales and dolphins.

> The Western Forest Complex in northwestern Thailand comprises approximately 18,000 sq km and 17 protected areas. It is considered a model for natural habitats and supports 500 tigers and other threatened species.

Endangered Species

Thailand's most famous animals are also its most endangered. The Asian elephant, a smaller cousin to the African elephant, once roamed the forests of Indochina in great herds. But the wild elephant faces extinction due to habitat loss and poaching. The population of wild elephants in Thailand is now estimated between 2000 to 3000, according to statistics from the Thai Elephant Conservation Center, with another 2700 so-called domesticated elephants in the country.

Reclusive wild Indochinese tigers stalk parts of Thailand, especially the hinterlands between Thailand and Myanmar, but in ever-decreasing numbers. It is notoriously difficult to obtain an accurate count, but experts estimate that between 150 and 200 wild tigers remain in Thailand. Although tiger hunting and trapping is illegal, poachers continue to kill the cats for the overseas wildlife trade. Thailand, though, has stepped up its tiger conservation efforts and tiger cubs were spotted for the first time in Khao Yai National Park in 2017.

The rare dugong (also referred to as 'sea cows') – a herbivorous marine mammal that can weigh up to 1000kg – was once thought extinct in Thailand. A few small groups of dugong survive around Trang, but they are increasingly threatened by habitat loss and the lethal propellers of tourist boats.

Forests & Flora

Thailand's jungles can be divided into monsoon (with a distinct dry season of three months or more) and rainforest (where rain falls more than nine months each year). The most heavily forested provinces are Chiang Mai and Kanchanaburi.

WILD ELEPHANT ENCOUNTERS

Many of the national parks host wild elephant herds that congregate in the evenings at salt ponds and watering holes. Here are a few parks known for their elephant herds:

Kuiburi National Park (p510), near Prachuap Khiri Khan

Khao Yai National Park (p417), northeast of Bangkok in Nakhon Ratchasima Province

Kaeng Krachan National Park (p493), south of Bangkok in Phetchaburi

ILLEGAL WILDLIFE TRADE

Thailand is a signatory to the UN Convention on International Trade in Endangered Species (Cites), but remains an important transport link and marketplace for the global wildlife trade. Endangered animals and animal parts are poached or smuggled through Thailand en route to China or the US. In 2018, a BBC investigation revealed that endangered animals such as the helmeted hornbill and Siamese crocodile were being sold in Thailand via Facebook.

Although the country's efforts to stop the trade are more impressive than those of its neighbours, corruption and weak laws hinder law enforcement.

Northern Monsoon forests comprise deciduous trees, which are green and lush during the rainy season but dusty and leafless during the dry season. Teak is highly valued, but logging has been banned since 1989.

In southern Thailand, where rainfall is plentiful and distributed evenly throughout the year, forests are classified as rainforests with a few areas of monsoon forest. One remarkable plant found in some southern forests is *Rafflesia kerrii*, with a huge flower 80cm across.

Thailand is home to nearly 75 coastal mangrove species, small salt-tolerant trees that provide an incubator for many coastal fish and animal species. Reforestation programmes of mangrove areas have gained popularity thanks to their protective role during the 2004 Asian tsunami.

Orchids are Thailand's most exquisite native flora. There are over 1100 native species: some ground dwellers, others high up in trees.

Environmental Issues

Coastal & Marine Degradation

Soil erosion is a major coastal problem. Around 30% of Thailand's coastline is at risk, with over five metres of coastline being lost per year in some areas, according to a 2018 Chulalongkorn University study. This is due to coastal development, land subsiding and rising sea levels. Industrial wastewater is also often insufficiently treated in coastal regions.

Coastal degradation, along with rising sea temperatures, puts serious pressure on Thailand's marine environment. But the greatest risk to coral reefs comes from tourism. Untreated waste water from resorts, as well as man-made pollutants such as plastics, have had an alarming impact on reefs in the Andaman Sea in particular.

The overall health of the ocean is further impacted by large-scale fishing. Fisheries continue to experience declining catches as fish stocks plummet.

Deforestation

Natural forest cover constituted about 31.6% of land area in 2018, according to the World Bank, compared to 53.5% in 1961. Depletion of forests coincided with industrialisation, urbanisation and commercial logging. Forest loss has now slowed to about 0.2% per year and total forest cover is up from 27.4% in 1990.

The Thai government created a large number of protected areas, starting in the 1970s, and established an ambitious goal of 40% forest cover by the middle of this century. In 1989 all logging was banned. It is now illegal to sell timber felled in the country, but this law is frequently flouted.

Wildlife experts agree that the greatest danger faced by Thai fauna and flora is habitat loss. Notable species that are extinct in Thailand include the kouprey (a type of wild cattle), Schomburgk's deer and the Javan rhino.

With much of the city around 1.5m above sea level, low-lying Bangkok is sinking at a rate of 2cm per year. Some scientists estimate that the city may face submersion within approximately 15 years due to rising sea levels.

National Marine Parks

Ko Tarutao

Mu Ko Chang

Mu Ko Surin & Similan

AIR POLLUTION

On March 13th 2019, the air quality in Chiang Mai was officially rated the world's worst, beating notoriously polluted cities such as Dhaka in Bangladesh and Ulaanbaatar in Mongolia. Farmers burning waste to clear land in the surrounding area and forest fires caused by extremely dry conditions resulted in Chiang Mai being blanketed in a dangerous haze. Other provinces in the north were also affected.

Air pollution is now a problem across the kingdom. In January 2019, all of Bangkok's public schools closed for two days because of choking smog. It is common to see people in Bangkok wearing face masks as protection. Air pollution in Bangkok is mostly the result of emissions from factories and the nearly 10 million vehicles that clog the capital's roads.

Energy Consumption

Thailand's increasingly affluent society is expected to consume 75% more energy in the forthcoming decades, according to the Oxford Business Group. Thailand is looking to expand oil and gas resources and develop alternative fuel sources, including nuclear. Currently, three quarters of Thailand's energy derives from natural gas. Most of the existing oil and gas fields are in the Gulf of Thailand in an area known as the Pattani Trough.

Thailand also produces biofuels, including ethanols from molasses and cassava, and biodiesel from palm oil. Power generation, agriculture and industrial activity account for the largest proportion of the country's greenhouse gas emissions.

Thailand has a target of generating 6000 MW from solar energy by 2036. The country's first large-scale solar farm in Lopburi started producing power in 2013. There is also great potential for increasing energy-from-waste production.

Flooding

Thailand Stats

Thailand encompasses 514,000 sq km, slightly larger than Spain.

Bangkok sits at N14° latitude, level with Chennai, Manila, Guatemala City and Khartoum.

Seasonal flooding is common in some parts of Thailand due to monsoon rains. But high-level, property-damaging floods have increased in recent years. The record-busting 2011 floods saw 65 of Thailand's 77 provinces declared flood disaster zones; there were 815 deaths and an estimated US$45.7 billion worth of damages, one of the world's costliest natural disasters. More recently, flooding in southern Thailand in early 2017 left 91 people dead and caused an estimated US$4 billion of damage.

Many environmental experts attribute human alteration of natural flood barriers and watercourses and deforestation as contributory factors. The increased incidence of flooding along the Mekong is often linked to upstream infrastructure projects, such as dams, and increasing human populations along the river. Another factor is the potential impact of climate change.

Survival Guide

Responsible Travel

Thailand is a relatively easy country to travel in. But some background knowledge about cultural etiquette and Thai social conventions will make things even easier – both for yourself and for others. And following a few basic guidelines for responsible travel will diminish your footprint as a tourist.

CULTURAL ETIQUETTE

The monarchy and religion (which are interconnected) are treated with extreme deference in Thailand. Thais avoid criticising or disparaging the royal family for fear of offending someone or, worse, being charged with a violation of the country's very strict lèse-majesté laws, which carry a jail sentence.

Buddha images are sacred objects. Thais consider it bad form to pull a silly pose in front of one for a photo, or to clamber upon them (in the case of temple ruins). As part of their ascetic vows, monks are not supposed to touch or be touched by women. If a woman wants to hand something to a monk, the object is placed within reach of the monk or on the monk's 'receiving cloth'.

From a spiritual viewpoint, Thais regard the head as the highest and most sacred part of the body and the feet as the dirtiest and lowest. Many of the taboos associated with the feet have a practical derivation as well. Traditionally Thais ate, slept and entertained on the floor of their homes. So shoes aren't worn inside private homes and temple buildings, both as a sign of respect and for sanitary reasons.

Thais don't touch each others' heads or ruffle hair as a sign of affection. Occasionally you'll see young people touching each others' heads, which is a teasing gesture, maybe even a slight insult, between friends.

Social Conventions & Gestures

The traditional Thai greeting, known as *wâi*, is made with a prayer-like, palms-together gesture. The depth of the bow and the placement of the fingers in relation to the face is dependent on the status of the person receiving the *wâi*. Adults don't *wâi* children, and in most cases service people (when they are doing their jobs) aren't *wâi*-ed, though this is a matter of personal discretion.

In the more traditional parts of the country, it is not proper for members of the opposite sexes to touch one another, either as lovers or as friends. But same-sex touching is quite common and is typically a sign of friendship, not sexual attraction.

Thais hold modesty in personal dress in high regard, though this is changing among the younger generation. Most provincial Thais swim fully clothed. For this reason, sunbathing nude or topless is not acceptable and in some cases is even illegal. Off the beach; wear a cover-up in between the sand and your hotel.

RESPONSIBLE TOURISM

Most forms of tourism have a positive effect on the local economy in Thailand, providing jobs for young workers and business opportunities for entrepreneurs. In addition, many travellers look for opportunities to spend their money where it might be needed, either on charitable causes or activities that preserve traditional ways of life. Thailand has successfully benefitted from this trend by promoting village craft programmes and homestays. It is increasingly easy for foreign tourists to engage with small-scale tourism projects that offer an insight into traditional ways of life.

Overtourism

Thailand was visited by a record 38.3 million people in 2018. Some estimates predict that 60 million people will be visiting Thailand annually by 2030.

Parts of the country are already suffering adversely

ESSENTIAL ETIQUETTE

Do

Stand respectfully for the royal and national anthem They are played on TV and radio stations as well as in public and government places.

Smile a lot It makes everything easier.

Bring a gift if you're invited to a Thai home Fruit, drinks or snacks are acceptable.

Take off your shoes When you enter a home or temple building.

Dress modestly for temple visits Cover to the elbows and ankles and always remove your shoes when entering any building containing a Buddha image.

Sit in the 'mermaid' position inside temples Tuck your feet beside and behind you.

Give and receive politely Extend the right hand out while the left hand gently grips the right elbow when handing an object to another person or receiving something.

Don't

Get a tattoo of the Buddha Nor display one you already have. It is considered sacrilegious.

Criticise the monarchy The monarchy is revered and protected by defamation laws – more so now than ever.

Prop your feet on tables or chairs Feet are considered dirty and people have to sit on chairs.

Step on a dropped bill to prevent it from blowing away Thai money bears a picture of the king. Feet + monarchy = grave offence.

Step over someone or their personal belongings Feet are considered unclean.

Tie your shoes to the outside of your backpack They might accidentally brush against someone: gross.

Touch a Thai person on the head It is considered rude, not chummy.

Touch monks or their belongings Women are expected to step out of the way when passing one on the footpath and should not sit next to them on public transport.

from high visitor volumes, with tourist infrastructure stretched to the limit. There is also a negative impact on the environment, especially on small but busy islands, where maintaining adequate fresh water supplies and disposing of waste is an increasing struggle.

The Thai tourist authorities and government are already taking steps to protect the most environmentally fragile areas. Maya Bay in Ko Phi-Phi has been closed since June 2018, following reports that up to 50% of its coral was dead. It is likely that some of the other most popular destinations on Thailand's islands will be temporarily closed, or restricted, in the future.

Visitors can play their part in reducing the effects of overtourism. One obvious option is to avoid the most-visited destinations. There is much more to Thailand than just Bangkok, Chiang Mai, Phuket or Ko Samui.

Elephant Encounters

Throughout Thai history, elephants have been revered for their strength, endurance and intelligence, working alongside their mahouts harvesting teak, transporting goods through mountainous terrain or fighting ancient wars.

Many of the elephants' traditional roles have either been outsourced to machines or outlawed, leaving the 'domesticated' animals and their mahouts without work. Some mahouts turned to begging on the streets in Bangkok and other tourist centres, but most elephants find work in Thailand's tourism industry. Their jobs vary from circus-like shows and elephant camps giving rides to tourists to 'mahout-training' schools, while sanctuaries and rescue centres provide modest retirement homes to animals that are no longer financially profitable to their owners.

It costs about 30,000B (US$1000) a month to provide a comfortable life for an elephant, an amount equivalent to the salary of Thailand's upper-middle class. Welfare standards within the tourism industry are not standardised or subject to government regulations, so it's up to the conscientious consumer to encourage the industry to ensure safe conditions for elephants.

With more evidence than ever available to support claims by animal welfare experts that elephant rides and shows are harmful to these gentle giants, who are often abused to force them to perform for humans, a small but growing number of sanctuaries offer more sustainable interactions, such as observing retired and rescued elephants.

Lonely Planet does not recommend riding on elephants or viewing elephant performances. We also urge visitors to be wary of organisations that advertise as being a conservation centre but actually offer rides and performances.

Trekking in Ethnic-Minority Areas

Thailand's hill-dwelling minorities remain a strong tourism draw, with large and small businesses organising 'trekking' tours to villages for cultural displays.

Trekkers should realise that hill peoples maintain their own distinct cultural identity and many continue their animistic traditions, which define social taboos and conventions. If you're planning on visiting hillpeoples villages on an organised trek, talk to your guide about acceptable behaviour.

VOLUNTEERING

There are myriad volunteer organisations in Thailand. A regularly updated resource for grassroots-level volunteer opportunities is Volunteer Work Thailand (www.volunteer-workthailand.org). Be aware, though, that so-called 'voluntourism' has become a big business and that not every organisation fulfils its promise of meaningful experiences. It is essential that you do your own thorough research before agreeing to volunteer with any organisation.

Environmental & Animal Welfare Work

A number of NGOs undertake local environmental conservation work, run rescue and sanctuary centres for wild animals that have been kept as pets, or operate veterinary clinics that tend to domestic dogs and cats.

Elephant Nature Park (p329) This elephant sanctuary offers seven-day volunteer programmes at several sister organisations such as Surin Project in the Isan region and Elephant Haven in Kanchanaburi.

Highland Farm Gibbon Sanctuary (p274) Gives a permanent home to orphaned, abandoned and mistreated

gibbons. Volunteers are asked for a one-month commitment and to help with daily farm chores.

Koh Chang Animal Project (p479) Travelling vets and vet nurses often drop by to volunteer here, while non-vets help with numerous odd jobs.

Lanta Animal Welfare (p676) This centre on Ko Lanta invites both casual dog-walking visitors and volunteers for longer placements.

Phuket Elephant Sanctuary (p653) Takes up to six volunteers at a time for weeklong stays.

Samui Dog & Cat Rescue Centre (p533) Volunteers take care of the animals at its kennel/clinic in Ban Taling Ngam.

Soi Dog (p655) This Phuket centre invites visitors to play with the animals, or become a dog-walking or long-term volunteer.

Trash Hero (www.trashhero.org) A rapidly-expanding volunteer outfit that runs weekly clean-ups at 25 official points across Thailand.

Wild Animal Rescue Foundation (WARF; ☑02 712 9715; www.warthai.org) Operates the Phuket Gibbon Rehabilitation Project (where volunteers help with cleaning cages, feeding and tracking released gibbons), as well as several other programmes across the country.

Wildlife Friends Foundation Thailand Rescue Centre and Elephant Refuge (มูลนิธิเพื่อนสัตว์ป่า; ☑032 458135; www.wfft. org; full-access tour incl lunch half-/full day 1100/1600B) 🖉 Volunteers help care for sun bears, macaques, gibbons and elephants at its animal rescue centre in Phetchaburi, 45km northwest of Hua Hin.

Humanitarian & Educational Work

Northern Thailand, especially Chiang Mai and Chiang Rai, has a number of volunteering organisations working with disadvantaged minority groups. Chiang Mai, Mae Sot and Sangkhlaburi have communities of Burmese

---

RESPONSIBLE DIVING

➡ Avoid touching living marine organisms, standing on coral or dragging equipment (such as fins) across reefs. Coral polyps can be damaged by the gentlest contact.

➡ When treading water in shallow reef areas, be careful not to kick up clouds of sand, which can easily smother the delicate reef organisms.

➡ Take great care in underwater caves where your air bubbles can be caught within the roof and leave previously submerged organisms high and dry.

➡ Don't feed the fish or allow your dive operator to dispose of excess food in the water. The fish become dependent on this food source and don't tend to the algae on the coral, causing harm to the reef.

RESPONSIBLE TREKKING

➡ Always ask for permission before taking photos of minority peoples, especially at private moments inside their dwellings. Many traditional belief systems regard photography with suspicion.

➡ Show respect for religious symbols and rituals. Don't touch totems at village entrances or sacred items hanging from trees. Don't participate in ceremonies unless invited.

➡ Avoid encouraging the practice of begging, especially among children. Talk to your guide about donating to a local school instead.

➡ Avoid public nudity and be careful not to undress near an open window where village children might be able to peep in.

➡ Don't flirt with members of the opposite sex unless you plan on marrying them.

➡ Don't drink or do drugs with villagers; altered states sometimes lead to culture clashes.

➡ Smile at villagers even if they stare at you. Ask your guide how to say 'hello' in the local language.

➡ Avoid public displays of affection, which in some traditional systems are viewed as offensive to the spirit world.

➡ Don't interact with the villagers' livestock, even the free-roaming pigs; they are valuable possessions, not entertainment. Also avoid interacting with jungle animals, which in some belief systems are viewed as visiting spirits.

➡ Don't litter.

➡ Adhere to the same feet taboos that apply to Thai culture. Don't step on the threshold of a house, prop your feet up against the fire or wear your shoes inside.

refugees and migrants. There are also many volunteer teaching positions in northeastern Thailand, the country's agricultural heartland.

When looking for a volunteer placement, it is essential to investigate what your chosen organisation does and, more importantly, how it goes about it. If the focus is not primarily on your skills and how these can be applied to help local people, that should ring alarm bells. Any organisation that promises to let you do any kind of work, wherever you like, for as long as you like, is unlikely to be putting the needs of local people first.

For any organisation working with children, child protection is a serious concern, and organisations that do not conduct background checks on volunteers should be regarded with extreme caution.

Volunteering organisations include:

Baan Unrak (p199) A home and school that cares for over 150 orphaned or abandoned children.

Open Mind Projects (☎042 413578; www.openmindprojects.org) Offers volunteer positions in IT, health care, education and community-based ecotourism throughout Thailand.

Starfish Ventures (www.starfish-adventure.com) Places volunteers in building, health care and teaching programmes throughout Thailand.

Directory A–Z

Accessible Travel

Thailand has better facilities for travellers with access needs than any Southeast Asian country, other than Singapore. However, high kerbs, uneven and crowded footpaths and nonstop traffic make Thai cities difficult to navigate for those with a vision or mobility impairment. In Bangkok, many streets must be crossed via pedestrian bridges accessed by steep stairways. In any town or city, wheelchair users who are willing to take the risk and have nerves of steel will find it easier to take to the road. Ramps and other access points for wheelchairs to buildings, pavements and tourist sites are patchy. However, a lack of infrastructure is often made up for by the helpfulness of Thai people.

At Suvarnabhumi Airport in Bangkok facilities for disabled travellers are good. Wheelchairs and electric carts are available, lifts service all levels and accessible toilet facilities are clean and well maintained. The rail link from the airport to the city is well adapted for travellers with access needs, including elevators with Braille buttons and voice announcements, and wheelchair-accessible ticket machines and gates. Most international flights use air-bridges, which isn't always the case for domestic flights at Bangkok's Don Muang Airport or other regional airports around Thailand. It's therefore important to advise your airline at the time of booking if you use a wheelchair or need assistance.

Buses and boats stop barely long enough even for the fully mobile, and long-distance trains and provincial stations are a bit of a lottery for access. In the capital, BTS Skytrain is accessible for wheelchair users, with elevators at all stations except Saphan Taksin. Every MRT metro station has lifts and wheelchair access. Both BTS and MRT staff are extremely helpful.

Note that many taxis in Thailand run on natural gas, with the gas tank located in the boot (trunk), which limits the space available for a wheelchair or mobility aid. Fully wheelchair-accessible taxis are only available in Bangkok and Hua Hin and have to be booked in advance. There are none in Chang Mai. The Bangkok Metropolitan Authority has a handful of vehicles, mainly for locals; call ☎1555 during office hours for availability, or contact Wheelchair Taxi Thailand (www.transport-disabled-bangkok.weebly.com). Most mid-range and top-end hotels have accessible rooms, but standards vary widely, so make sure your needs are met by requesting information and/or photos. Most budget hotels and guesthouses, as well as many boutique hotels, lack accessible facilities, but most will be happy to meet your needs if you are able to be

ACCESSIBLE TRAVEL RESOURCES

Download Lonely Planet's free Accessible Travel guides from https://shop.lonelyplanet.com/categories/accessible-travel.com.

The following tour operators specialise in accessible tours to and accommodation in Thailand, and have their own adapted vehicle(s):

Gehandicapten (☎+31 36 537 6677; http://gehandicapten.com)

Wheelchair Holidays Thailand (☎+66 8 1375-0792; www.wheelchairtours.com)

Wheelchair Thailand Tours (☎http://wheelchair-thailand-tours.weebly.com)

adaptable or have low access needs.

Many Thai towns and cities have at least one modern shopping mall, and this is where to head for hassle-free shopping and eating, as well as an accessible toilet.

Customs Regulations

You do not have to fill in a customs form on arrival unless you have imported goods to declare. In that case you can get the proper form from Thai customs officials at your point of entry. The **Customs Department** (🖉nationwide 02 667 6000; www.customs.go.th) maintains a helpful website with specific information about regulations for travellers. Thailand allows the following items to enter duty-free:

➡ reasonable amount of personal effects (clothing and toiletries)

➡ professional instruments

➡ 200 cigarettes

➡ 1L of wine or spirits Thailand prohibits the import of the following items:

➡ firearms and ammunition (unless registered in advance with the police department)

➡ illegal drugs

➡ pornographic media When leaving Thailand, you must obtain an export licence for any antique reproductions or newly cast Buddha images. Submit two front-view photos of the object(s), a photocopy of your passport, the purchase receipt and the object(s) in question to the **Office of the National Museum** (4 Th Na Phra That, National Museum; ⊗9am-4pm Tue-Fri; 🚢Chang Pier, Maharaj Pier). Allow four days for the application and inspection process to be completed.

Electricity

Thailand uses 220V AC electricity. Power outlets most commonly feature two-prong round or flat sockets.

Type A
120V/60Hz

Type C
220V/50Hz

Embassies & Consulates

Foreign embassies are located in Bangkok; some nations also have consulates in Chiang Mai, Pattaya, Phuket and Songkhla.

Australian Embassy (🖉02 344 6300; www.thailand.embassy. gov.au; 181 Th Witthayu/Wireless Rd, Bangkok; ⊗8.30am-4.30pm Mon-Fri; 🅼Lumphini exit 3) Consulates in Chiang Mai, Ko Samui and Phuket.

Cambodian Embassy (🖉02 957 5851; 518/4 Soi Ramkhamhaeng 39, Th Pracha Uthit, Bangkok; ⊗8.30am-noon & 2-5pm Mon-Fri; 🅼Phra Ram 9 exit 3 & taxi) Consulate in Sa Kaew.

Canadian Embassy (🖉02 646 4300; www.thailand.gc.ca; 15 fl, Abdulrahim Pl, 990 Rama IV, Bangkok; ⊗9am-noon Mon-Fri; 🅼Si Lom exit 2, 🆂Sala Daeng exit 4) Consulate in **Chiang Mai** (🖉053 850147; 151 Superhighway, Tambon Tahsala; ⊗9am-noon Mon-Fri).

French Embassy (🖉02 657 5100; www.ambafrance-th. org; 35 Soi 36/Rue de Brest, Th Charoen Krung, Bangkok; ⊗8.30am-noon Mon-Fri; 🚢Oriental Pier) Consulates in **Chiang Mai** (🖉053 281466; 138 Th Charoen Prathet; ⊗10am-noon Mon & Wed-Fri), Chiang Rai and Pattaya.

German Embassy (🖉02 287 9000; www.bangkok.diplo.de; 9 Th Sathon Tai/South, Bangkok; ⊗8.30-11.30am Mon-Fri; 🅼Lumphini exit 2)

Irish Embassy (🖉02 016 1360; www.dfa.ie/irish-embassy/ thailand; 12th fl, 208 Th Witthayu/Wireless Rd; ⊗9.30am-12.30pm & 2.30-3.30pm Mon-Thu, 9.30am-noon Fri; 🆂Phloen Chit exit 1)

Laotian Embassy (🖉02 539 6667; 502/1-3 Soi Sahakarnpramoon, Th Pracha Uthit/Soi Ramkhamhaeng 39, Bangkok; ⊗8am-noon & 1-4pm Mon-Fri; 🅼Phra Ram 9 exit 3 & taxi)

Climate

Bangkok

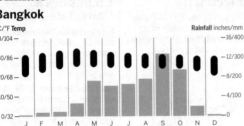

Chiang Mai

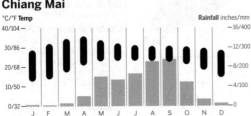

Phuket

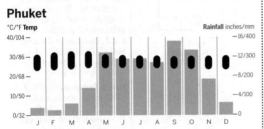

Malaysian Embassy (📞02 629 6800; www.kln.gov.my/web/tha_bangkok/home; 33-35 Th Sathon Tai/South, Bangkok; ⊗8am-4pm Mon-Fri; Ⓜ️Lumphini exit 2) Consulate in Songkhla.

Myanmar Embassy (📞02 233 7250; www.mfa.go.th; 132 Th Sathon Neua/North, Bangkok; ⊗9am-noon & 1-3pm Mon-Fri; Ⓢ️Surasak exit 1/3)

Netherlands Embassy (📞02 309 5200; www.netherlands worldwide.nl/countries/

thailand; 15 Soi Ton Son; ⊗8.30am-noon & 1.30-4.30pm Mon-Thu, 8.30-11.30am Fri; Ⓢ️Chit Lom exit 4)

New Zealand Embassy (📞02 254 2530; www.nzembassy.com/thailand; 87 Th Witthayu/Wireless Rd, 14th fl, M Thai Tower, All Seasons Pl; ⊗8am-noon & 1-2.30pm Mon-Fri; Ⓢ️Phloen Chit exit 5)

UK Embassy (📞02 305 8333; www.gov.uk/government/world/organisations/british-embassy-bangkok; 14 Th

Witthayu/Wireless Rd; ⊗8am-4.30pm Mon-Thu, to 1pm Fri; Ⓢ️Phloen Chit exit 5)

US Embassy (📞02 205 4000; https://th.usembassy.gov; 95 Th Witthayu/Wireless Rd; ⊗8am-4pm Mon-Fri; Ⓢ️Phloen Chit exit 5) Consulate in **Chiang Mai** (📞053 107700; https://th.usembassy.gov; 387 Th Wichayanon; ⊗7.30am-4.30pm Mon-Fri).

Emergency & Important Numbers

Thailand's country code	📞66
Emergency	📞191
International access codes	📞001, 007, 008, 009 (& other promotional codes)
Operator-assisted international calls	📞100
Tourist police	📞1155

Insurance

A travel-insurance policy to cover theft, loss and medical problems is an excellent idea. Be sure that your policy covers ambulances or an emergency flight home. Some policies specifically exclude 'dangerous activities', which can include scuba diving, motorcycling and even trekking.

A locally acquired motorcycle licence is not valid under some policies. You may prefer a policy that pays doctors or hospitals directly rather than you having to pay on the spot and claim later. If you have to claim later, make sure you keep all documentation.

EATING PRICE RANGES

The following price ranges refer to a main dish:

$ less than 150B

$$ 150B–350B

$$$ more than 350B

Internet Access

Wi-fi is almost standard in hotels, guesthouses and cafes. Signal strength deteriorates in the upper floors of a multistorey building; request a room near a router if wi-fi is essential. Cellular data networks continue to expand and increase in capability.

Legal Matters

In general Thai police don't hassle foreigners, especially tourists. They usually go out of their way to avoid having to speak English with a foreigner, especially regarding minor traffic issues. Thai police do, however, rigidly enforce laws against drug possession. Do be aware that some police divisions, especially on the Thai islands, might view foreigners and their legal infractions as a money-making opportunity.

If you are arrested for any offence, the police will allow you the opportunity to make a phone call, either to your embassy or consulate in Thailand if you have one, or to a friend or relative if not. There's a whole set of legal codes governing the length of time and the manner in which you can be detained before being charged or put on trial, but a lot of discretion is left to the police. In the case of foreigners the police are more likely to bend these codes in your favour. However, as with police worldwide, if you don't show respect you will make matters worse.

Thai law does not presume an indicted detainee to be either guilty or innocent but rather a 'suspect', whose guilt or innocence will be decided in court. Trials are usually speedy.

The **tourist police** (☏24hr 1155) can be very helpful in cases of arrest. Although they typically have no jurisdiction over the kinds of cases handled by regular cops, they may be able to

PRACTICALITIES

Newspapers English-language newspapers include the *Bangkok Post* (www.bangkokpost.com), the business-heavy *Nation* (www.nationmultimedia.com) and *KhaoSod English* (www.khaosodenglish.com), the English-language service of a mainstream Thai newspaper. Weeklies such as the *Economist* and *Time* are sold at news stands.

Radio There are more than 400 AM and FM radio stations. Many smaller radio stations and international services are available to stream over the internet.

TV Six VHF TV networks carry Thai programming, plus TrueVision cable with international programming. Digital programming has increased programming.

Smoking Banned in restaurants and bars since 2008, although it still takes place in some bars.

Weights & measures The metric system is used. Gold and silver are weighed in *bàat* (15g).

help with translations or with contacting your embassy. You can call the hotline to lodge complaints or to request assistance with regards to personal safety.

LGBTIQ+ Travellers

Thai culture is relatively tolerant of homosexuality. There is a fairly prominent LGBTIQ+ scene in Bangkok, Pattaya and Phuket, all three of which hold annual pride events. However, public displays of affection – whether heterosexual or homosexual – are frowned upon.

It's worth noting that, perhaps because Thailand is still a relatively conservative place, lesbians generally adhere to rather strict gender roles. Masculine lesbians, called tom (from 'tomboy'), typically have short hair, and wear men's clothing. Femme lesbians refer to themselves as dêe (from 'lady'). Visiting lesbians who don't fit into one of these categories may find themselves met with confusion.

Thailand passed the Gender Equality Act in 2015, the country's first law to provide

protection from unfair gender discrimination. But while transgender and third gender people are quite visible in Thailand, they continue to face discrimination in the workplace and when dealing with branches of the government.

Utopia (www.utopia-asia.com) posts lots of Thailand information for LGBTIQ+ travelers and publishes a LGBTIQ+ guidebook to the kingdom.

Money

Most places in Thailand only accept cash. Foreign credit cards are accepted by some travel agents, and in some upmarket hotels, restaurants, shopping malls and stores.

ATMs

Debit and ATM cards issued by a bank in your home country can be used at ATMs around Thailand to withdraw cash (in Thai baht only) directly from your account back home. ATMs are extremely ubiquitous throughout the country and can be relied on for the bulk of your spending cash. Most

PUBLIC HOLIDAYS

Government offices and banks close their doors on the following public holidays:

1 January New Year's Day

February (date varies) Makha Bucha; Buddhist holy day

6 April Chakri Day; commemorating the founder of the Chakri dynasty, Rama I

13–15 April Songkran Festival

1 May Labour Day

4 May Coronation Day

May (date varies) Royal Ploughing Ceremony

May/June (date varies) Visakha Bucha; Buddhist holy day

3 June Her Majesty the Queen's Birthday

28 July King Maha Vajiralongkorn's Birthday

July/August (date varies) Asanha Bucha; Buddhist holy day

12 August Queen Sirikit's Birthday/Mother's Day

13 October Late King Bhumiphol's Memorial Day

23 October Chulalongkorn Day

5 December Late King Bhumiphol's Birthday /Father's Day

10 December Constitution Day

31 December New Year's Eve

money grubbing as to grab every last baht'. At many hotel restaurants and more upmarket eateries, a 10% service charge will be added to your bill.

Opening Hours

Banks and government offices close for national holidays. Some bars and clubs close during elections and certain religious holidays when alcohol sales are banned. Shopping centres have banks that open late.

Banks 8.30am–4.30pm Monday to Friday; ATMs 24hr

Bars 6pm–midnight or 1am

Clubs 8pm–2am

Government offices 8.30am–4.30pm Monday to Friday; some close for lunch

Restaurants 8am–10pm

Shops 10am–7pm

Photography

Be considerate when taking photographs of locals. Learn how to ask politely in Thai and wait for an embarrassed nod. In some of the regularly visited minority areas, be prepared for the photographed subject to ask for money in exchange for a picture. Some hill peoples will not allow you to point a camera at them.

Post

Thailand has a very efficient postal service (www.thailand post.co.th) and local postage is inexpensive. Typical provincial post offices open from 8.30am to 4.30pm weekdays and 9am to noon on Saturdays. Larger main post offices in provincial capitals may also be open for a half-day on Sunday. You will need to show your passport to send anything.

Most provincial post offices will sell DIY packing boxes.

ATMs allow a maximum of 20,000B in withdrawals per day.

The downside is that Thai ATMs charge a 220B foreign-transaction fee on top of whatever currency conversion and out-of-network fees your home bank charges. Before leaving home, shop around for a bank account that has free international ATM usage and reimburses fees incurred at other institutions' ATMs.

Changing Money

Banks or private money changers offer the best exchange rates. When buying baht, US dollars is the most accepted currency, followed by British pounds, euros and Chinese yuan. Most banks charge a commission and duty for each travellers cheque cashed. Current exchange rates are posted at exchange counters.

Credit & Debit Cards

Credit and debit cards can be used for purchases at some shops, hotels and restaurants. The most commonly accepted cards are Visa and MasterCard. American Express is typically only accepted at high-end hotels and restaurants.

Contact your bank and your credit-card provider before you leave home and notify them of your upcoming trip so that your accounts aren't suspended due to suspicious overseas activity.

Tipping

Tipping is not generally expected in Thailand, though it is appreciated. The exception is loose change from a large restaurant bill – if a meal costs 488B and you pay with a 500B note, some Thais will leave the change. It's a way of saying 'I'm not so

Don't send cash or other valuables through the mail.

Thailand's poste restante service is generally very reliable, though these days few tourists use it. When you receive mail, you must show your passport and fill out some paperwork.

Safe Travel

Border Issues & Hot Spots

Thailand enjoys friendly relations with its neighbours, and most land borders are fully functional passages for goods and people. However, the ongoing violence in the far south has made the crossing at Sungai Kolok into Malaysia potentially dangerous, and most Muslim-majority provinces (Yala, Pattani, Narathiwat and parts of Songkhla) should be avoided by casual visitors.

Check with your government's foreign ministry for current travel warnings.

Drug Possession

Belying Thailand's anything-goes atmosphere are strict punishments for possession and trafficking of drugs, which are not relaxed for foreigners. It is illegal to buy, sell or possess opium, heroin, cocaine, amphetamines, methamphetamine, ecstasy, hallucinogenic mushrooms or marijuana. Possession of drugs can result in one or more years of prison time. Drug smuggling – defined as attempting to cross a border with drugs in your possession – carries considerably higher sanctions, including the death penalty.

Scams

Thais can be so friendly and laid-back that some visitors are lulled into a false sense of security, making them vulnerable to scams of all kinds. Bangkok is a hotspot for long, involved frauds that dupe travellers into thinking they've made a friend and

are getting a bargain, when in fact they are getting ripped off.

All offers of free shopping or sightseeing help from strangers should be ignored. They will invariably take a commission from your purchases.

Theft & Fraud

Exercise diligence when it comes to your personal belongings. Ensure your room is securely locked and carry your most important effects (passport, money, credit cards) on your person. Take care when leaving valuables in hotel safes.

Follow the same practice when you're travelling. A locked bag will not prevent theft on a long-haul bus.

When using a credit card, don't let vendors take your credit card out of your sight and ensure the transaction has been processed only once. If possible, check your transaction immediately through a smartphone app or similar.

Touts & Commissions

In Bangkok, some túk-túk drivers and other new 'friends' often take new arrivals on city tours that almost always end up in high-pressure sales situations at silk, jewelry or handicraft shops.

They also steer customers to certain guesthouses that

pay a commission. Travel agencies are known to talk newly arrived tourists into staying at inconveniently located, overpriced hotels thanks to commissions.

Some travel agencies masquerade as TAT, the government-funded tourist information office.

Shopping

Many bargains await you in Thailand, but don't go shopping in the company of touts, tour guides or friendly strangers. They will inevitably take a commission on anything you buy, driving prices up.

Antiques

Real Thai antiques are increasingly rare. Today, most dealers sell antique reproductions or items from Myanmar. Bangkok and Chiang Mai are the two centres for the antique and reproduction trade.

Real antiques cannot be taken out of Thailand without a permit. No Buddha image, new or old, may be exported without the permission of the **Office of the National Museum** (4 Th Na Phra That, National Museum; ⊙9am-4pm Tue-Fri; ⊠Chang Pier, Maharaj Pier).

GOVERNMENT TRAVEL ADVICE

The following government websites offer travel advisories and information on current hot spots.

Australian Department of Foreign Affairs (www.smartraveller.gov.au)

British Foreign Office (www.gov.uk/foreign-travel-advice)

Canadian Department of Foreign Affairs (www.dfait-maeci.gc.ca)

New Zealand Foreign Affairs & Trade (www.safetravel.govt.nz)

US State Department (www.travel.state.gov/traveladvisories)

BARGAINING

Thais respect a good haggler. Always let the vendor make the first offer, then ask, 'Can you lower the price?' This usually results in a discount. Now it's your turn to make a counter-offer. Always start low, but don't bargain unless you're serious about buying. If you're buying several of an item, you have much more leverage to request and receive a lower price. It helps immeasurably to keep the negotiations relaxed and friendly.

Ceramics

Many kinds of hand-thrown pottery, old and new, are available throughout the kingdom. Bangkok is full of modern ceramic designs, while Chiang Mai sticks to traditional styles. Ko Kret, outside of Bangkok, and Dan Kwian, in Nakhon Ratchasima Province, are two traditional pottery villages.

Clothing

Clothes tend to be inexpensive in Thailand, but readymade items are not usually cut to fit Westerners' body types. Increasingly, larger-sized clothes are available in metropolitan shopping malls or tourist centres. Finding shoes that fit larger feet is also a problem. The custom of returns is not widely accepted in Thailand, so be sure of your purchases before you leave the store. Markets sell cheap everyday items and clothes, while you'll find designer labels from home and abroad in Bangkok.

Thailand has a long sartorial tradition, practiced mainly by Thai-Indian Sikh families. But this industry is blighted with cut-rate operators and commission-paying scams. Be wary of the quickie 24-hour tailor shops; they often use inferior fabric and have poor workmanship. It's best to ask long-time foreign residents for a recommendation and then go for two or three fittings.

Fake Goods

In Bangkok, Chiang Mai and other tourist centres there's a thriving black-market street trade in fake designer goods. No one pretends they're the real thing, at least not the vendors. Technically, it is illegal for these items to be produced and sold, and Thailand has often been pressured by intellectual-property enforcement agencies to close down the trade. More recently, fake goods are being imported from Chinese factories or produced by factories that no longer have an up-to-date copyright license. Police crackdowns occur when the government intervenes or when the vendors don't pay the requisite bribes. Often, the vendors develop more surreptitious means of distribution.

Furniture

Rattan and hardwood furniture items are often good purchases and can be made to order. Chiang Mai is the country's primary furniture producer with many retail outlets in Bangkok. Due to the ban on teak harvesting and the subsequent exhaustion of recycled teak, 70% of export furniture produced in Thailand is made from parawood, a processed wood from rubber trees that can no longer be used for latex production.

Gems & Jewellery

Thailand is a leading exporter of gems and ornaments, rivalled only by India and Sri Lanka. Although rough-stone sources in Thailand have decreased dramatically, stones are now imported from Cambodia, Myanmar, Sri Lanka and other countries to be cut, polished and traded.

Although there are a lot of gem and jewellery stores in Thailand, it has become so difficult to dodge the scammers that the country no longer represents a safe and enjoyable place to buy these goods. Unless you really know your precious stones, it is better just to window shop.

Lacquerware

Chiang Mai is known for gold-on-black lacquerware. Lacquerware furniture and decorative items were traditionally made from bamboo and teak, but these days mango wood might be used as the base. If the item is top quality, only the frame is bamboo and horse or donkey hairs will be wound round it. With lower quality lacquerware, the whole object is made from bamboo. The lacquer is then coated over the framework and allowed to dry. After several days it is sanded down with ash from rice husks, and another coating of lacquer is applied. A high-quality item may have seven layers of lacquer. The piece is then engraved, painted and polished to remove the paint from everywhere except in the engravings. Multicoloured lacquerware is produced by repeated applications.

It can take five or six months to produce a high-quality piece of lacquerware, which may have as many as five colours. Flexibility is one characteristic of good lacquerware: a well-made bowl can have its rim squeezed together until the sides meet without suffering damage. The quality and precision of the engraving is another thing to look for.

Textiles

The northeast is famous for *mát·mèe* cloth, a thick cotton or silk fabric woven from tie-dyed threads, similar to Indonesia's *ikat* fabrics. Surin

Province is renowned for its *mát·mèe* silk, often showcasing colours and geometric patterns inherited from Khmer traditions.

In the north, silks reflect the influence of the Lanna weaving traditions, brought to Chiang Mai and the surrounding mountains by the various Tai peoples.

Fairly nice batik is available in the south in patterns that are more similar to the batik found in Malaysia than in Indonesia.

All the ethnic minorities in the hills of northern Thailand have a tradition of embroidery that has been translated into the modern marketplace as bags and jewellery. Much of what you'll find in the marketplaces has been machine made, but there are many NGO cooperatives that help villagers get their handmade goods to consumers. Chiang Mai and Chiang Rai are filled with handicraft outlets.

Telephone

The telephone country code for Thailand is ☑66 and is used when calling the country from abroad. All Thai telephone numbers are preceded by a '0' If you're dialling domestically (the '0' is omitted when calling from overseas). After the initial '0', the next three numbers represent the provincial area code, which is now integral to the telephone number. If the initial '0' is followed by a '6', an '8' or a '9' then you're dialling a mobile phone.

International Calls

If you want to call an international number from a telephone in Thailand, you must first dial an international access code plus the country code followed by the subscriber number.

In Thailand there are various international access codes charging different rates per minute. The standard direct-dial prefix is ☑001; it is operated by CAT and is

considered to have the best sound quality. It connects to the largest number of countries, but it is also the most expensive. The next best is ☑007, a prefix operated by TOT with reliable quality and slightly cheaper rates. Economy rates are available through different carriers – do an internet search to determine promotional codes.

Domestic Calls

Inside Thailand all telephone numbers include an initial '0' plus the area code and the subscriber number. The only time you drop the initial '0' is when you're calling from outside Thailand.

Mobile Phones

The easiest option for making calls in Thailand is to buy a local SIM card.

Make sure that your mobile phone is unlocked before travelling.

Local SIM cards can be bought at any 7-Eleven or any of the mobile-phone providers' stores. Tourist SIM cards cost as little as 49B. Various talk-and-data packages are available and SIM cards can be topped up with additional funds. Bring your passport when you buy a SIM card, so

the card can be registered to your name.

Thailand is on the GSM network. The main mobile phone providers include AIS (www.ais.co.th), DTAC (www.dtac.co.th) and True Move (http://truemoveh.truecorp.co.th), all of which operate on a 4G network. Coverage and quality of the different carriers varies from year to year based on network upgrades and capacity. Carriers usually sell talk-data packages based on usage amounts.

Time

Thailand is seven hours ahead of GMT/UTC. Times are often expressed according to the 24-hour clock.

Toilets

The Asian-style squat toilet is becoming less common in Thailand. There are still specimens in rural places, provincial bus stations, older homes and modest restaurants, but sit-down toilets are becoming more prevalent and appear wherever foreign tourists can be found.

If you encounter a squat, here's what you should know.

You should straddle the two foot pads and face the door. To flush, use the plastic bowl to scoop water out of the adjacent basin and pour it into the toilet bowl. Some places supply a small pack of toilet paper at the entrance (5B), otherwise bring your own stash or wipe the old-fashioned way with water.

Even in places where sit-down toilets are installed, the septic system may not be designed to take toilet paper. In such cases there will be a waste basket where you're supposed to place used toilet paper and feminine hygiene products. Many toilets also come with a small spray hose – Thailand's version of the bidet.

Tourist Information

The government-operated tourist information and promotion service, **Tourism Authority of Thailand** (TAT; ☑nationwide call centre 1672; www.tourismthailand. org), was founded in 1960 and produces excellent pamphlets on sightseeing. The TAT head office is in Bangkok and there are regional offices throughout the country; check the website for contact information.

Visas

For visitors from 64 countries, visas are not required for stays of up to 30 days.

The **Ministry of Foreign Affairs** (☑02 203 5000; www.mfa.go.th; 443 Th Si Ayuthaya) oversees immigration and visa issues. There are frequent modifications of visa regulations so check the website or the nearest Thai embassy or consulate for application procedures and costs. The best online monitor is Thaivisa (www.thaivisa.com).

Visa Exemptions & Visa On Arrival

Thailand has visa-exemption agreements with 64 countries (including European countries, Australia, New Zealand and the USA). Nationals from these countries can enter Thailand at no charge without pre-arranged documentation. Depending on nationality, these citizens are issued a 14- to 90-day visa exemption. Note that for some nationalities, less time (15 days rather than 30 days) is given if arriving by land rather than air. Check the **Ministry of Foreign Affairs** (☑02 203 5000; www.mfa.go.th; 443 Th Si Ayuthaya) website for more details. Citizens of an additional 19 countries are eligible for visa-on-arrival, which allows for stays of up to 15 days.

Non-Immigrant Visas

Non-immigrant visas are valid for between 90 days and a year and are intended for foreigners entering the country for business, study, retirement and extended family visits. There are multiple-entry visas available in this visa class. If you plan to apply for a Thai work permit, you'll need to possess a non-immigrant visa first.

Tourist Visas

If you plan to stay in Thailand longer than 30 days, you should apply for the 60-day tourist visa from a Thai consulate or embassy before your trip. You can also apply for a six-month multiple entry tourist visa, which allows stays of up to 60 days for each entry. Contact the nearest Thai embassy or consulate to obtain application procedures and determine fees for tourist visas.

Visa Extensions & Renewals

If you decide you want to stay longer than the allotted time, you can extend your visa by applying at any immigration office in Thailand. The usual fee for a visa extension is 1900B. Those issued with a standard stay of 15 or 30 days can extend their stay for 30 days if the extension is handled before the visa expires. The 60-day tourist visa can be extended by up to 30 days at the discretion of Thai immigration authorities.

Another visa-renewal option is to cross a land border. A new 30- or 15-day visa exemption, depending on your nationality, will be issued upon your return. Be aware that the authorities frown upon repeated entries to extend your stay and discretion is up to the visa agent.

If you overstay your visa, the usual penalty is a fine of 500B per day, with a 20,000B limit. Fines can be paid at the airport, or in

---

advance at an immigration office. If you've overstayed only one day, you don't have to pay. Children under 15 travelling with a parent do not have to pay the penalty.

Foreign residents in Thailand should arrange visa extensions at the immigration office closest to their in-country address.

Volunteering

There are many volunteering organisations (p754) in Thailand that provide work and cultural engagement. Volunteer Work Thailand (www.volunteerworkthailand. org) maintains a database of opportunities.

Women Travellers

Women travelers face relatively few problems in Thailand. It is respectful to cover up if you're going deep into

TAXES & REFUNDS

Thailand has a 7% value-added tax (VAT) on many goods and services. Midrange and top-end hotels and restaurants might also add a 10% service tax. The two combined are known as 'plus plus', or '++'.

You can get a refund on VAT paid on shopping, though not on food or hotels, as you leave the country. For how-to info, visit http://vrtweb.rd.go.th.

rural communities, entering temples or going to and from the beach, but on the whole, local women dress in a variety of different styles (particularly in cities).

As in most countries, attacks and rapes do occur. Some women may prefer to avoid traveling around isolated areas alone.

Keep Thai etiquette in mind during social interactions, and women who aren't interested in romantic encounters should not presume that Thai men have merely platonic motives.

Work

Thailand is a huge destination for temporary work stints, especially those involving English teaching. To work legally in the country, you need a non-immigrant visa and a work permit – which legitimate institutions should be able to provide. Ajarn.com (www.ajarn.com) is an excellent resource for background on teaching in Thailand, as well as a resource for jobs.

Transport

GETTING THERE & AWAY

Entering Thailand

Entry procedures for Thailand, by air or land, are straightforward: you'll have to show your passport and boarding pass as well as completed arrival and departure cards. You can be denied entry without proof of an onward ticket and sufficient funds for your projected stay, but in practice this is a formality that is rarely checked.

Air

Air fares during the high season (December to March) can be expensive and seats book up quickly. Departure tax is included in the price of a ticket.

Airports & Airlines

Thai Airways is the national carrier, and Bangkok is the country's primary international and domestic gateway. Thailand's provincial airports support an extensive domestic and growing international network. Airports with international connections include the following:

Suvarnabhumi International Airport (Map p160; ✆02 132 1888; www.airportthai.co.th; Samut Prakan) The country's main air terminal is located in Samut Prakan, 30km east of Bangkok and 110km from Pattaya. The airport's name is pronounced sù·wan·ná·poom.

Don Mueang International Airport (Map p160; ✆02 535 1192; www.airportthai.co.th; Don Mueang) Located 25km north of central Bangkok, Don Mueang was retired from service in 2006, only to reopen later as the city's de facto budget and domestic hub.

Phuket International Airport (Map p615; ✆076 632 7230; www.phuketairportonline. com) International destinations include Hong Kong, Singapore, Dubai, Seoul and Shanghai.

Chiang Mai International Airport (Map p312; ✆053 922000; www.chiangmaiairportonline.com) International destinations include many Asian and Southeast Asian cities.

Chiang Rai International Airport (Mae Fah Luang International Airport; ✆053 798000; www.chiangraiairportthai.com) International destinations include Kunming, China.

Hat Yai International Airport (✆074 227000; www.airportthai.co.th/en; ☎) International destinations include Singapore.

Ko Samui Airport (Map p528; www.samuiairportonline. com) International destinations include Singapore.

Krabi International Airport International destinations include Chongqing in China, Hong Kong, Kuala Lumpur and Singapore.

CLIMATE CHANGE & TRAVEL

Every form of transport that relies on carbon-based fuel generates CO_2, the main cause of human-induced climate change. Modern travel is dependent on aeroplanes, which might use less fuel per kilometre per person than most cars but travel much greater distances. The altitude at which aircraft emit gases (including CO_2) and particles also contributes to their climate change impact. Many websites offer 'carbon calculators' that allow people to estimate the carbon emissions generated by their journey and, for those who wish to do so, to offset the impact of the greenhouse gases emitted with contributions to portfolios of climate-friendly initiatives throughout the world. Lonely Planet offsets the carbon footprint of all staff and author travel.

U-Tapao Airport (UTP; ☎038 245595; www.utapao.com) International destinations include Singapore, Kuala Lumpur and a handful of cities in China and Russia.

Land

Thailand shares land borders with Cambodia, Laos, Malaysia and Myanmar. Land travel between all of these countries can be done at sanctioned border crossings. With improved highways and new bridges, it has become easier to travel from Thailand to China via Laos.

Border Crossings

CAMBODIA

Cambodian tourist visas (US$30) are available at the border. Bring a passport photo and ignore the touts who want to issue a health certificate or other paperwork for additional fees.

Aranya Prathet to Poipet The most direct land route between Bangkok and Siem Reap (for Angkor Wat), connected by direct government bus.

Hat Lek to Krong Koh Kong The coastal crossing for travellers heading to/from Ko Chang/Sihanoukville.

Ban Pakard to Psar Pruhm A back-door route from Ko Chang (via Chanthaburi) to Battambang and Angkor Wat.

Remote crossings include O Smach to Chong Chom (periodically closed due to ongoing tension between Thailand and Cambodia) and Choam to Chong Sa-Ngam; these aren't as convenient as you'll have to hire private transport on the Cambodian side of the border.

LAOS

It is fairly hassle-free to cross into Laos from northern and northeastern Thailand. Lao tourist visas (US$30 to US$42) can be obtained on arrival; applications require a passport photo and it's a good idea to have crisp,

clean bills to pay with. Direct buses that link major towns on both sides of the border make the border towns just a formality stop. Occasionally Lao officials will ask for an overtime fee.

Nong Khai to Vientiane The first Thai–Lao Friendship Bridge to span the Mekong River is one of the main gateways to/from Laos. Nong Khai is easily reached by train or bus from Bangkok, or air, via Udon Thani.

Chiang Khong to Huay Xai The fourth Thai–Lao Friendship Bridge has increased the popularity of this crossing that links northern Thailand with Luang Prabang. Direct buses from Chiang Mai and Chiang Rai to Laos use this crossing.

Mukdahan to Savannakhet The second Thai–Lao Friendship Bridge provides a trilateral link between Thailand, Laos and Vietnam.

Nakhon Phanom to Tha Khaek The third Thai–Lao Friendship Bridge connects northeastern Thailand to southern Laos.

Chong Mek to Vangtao The border is best accessed via direct bus from Ubon Ratchathani (Thailand) and is a good option for transiting to Pakse (Laos).

Remote crossings in northeastern Thailand include Bueng Kan to Paksan (Lao visas must be arranged in advance) and Tha Li to Kaen Thao (requires chartered

transport). In northern Thailand, another remote crossing links Ban Huay Kon, in Nan, and Muang Ngeun.

MALAYSIA

Malaysia, especially the west coast, is easy to reach by bus, train and even boat.

Hat Yai to Butterworth The western spur of the train line originating in Bangkok terminates at Butterworth, the mainland transfer point to Penang.

Hat Yai to Padang Besar Buses and trains originate out of the southern transit town of Hat Yai en route to a variety of Malaysian destinations. Border formalities are handled at Padang Besar.

Sungai Kolok to Rantau Panjang While this border crossing is a possibility, the continued violence in Thailand's Deep South means that we do not recommend it.

Ko Lipe to Langkawi Boats provide a convenient high-season link between these two Andaman islands. There is also boat service to/from the mainland port of Satun (Thailand) to the Malaysian island of Langkawi and the mainland town of Kuala Perlis.

There are a few other minor crossings along this border, but a private vehicle is a necessity.

AIRLINES IN THAILAND

AirAsia (www.airasia.com) From Don Mueang to Buriram, Chiang Mai, Chiang Rai, Hat Yai, Khon Kaen, Krabi, Loei, Nakhon Phanom, Nakhon Si Thammarat, Nan, Narathiwat, Phitsanulok, Phuket, Roi Et, Sakhon Nakhon, Surat Thani, Trang, Ubon Ratchathani and Udon Thani; from Chiang Mai to Hat Yai, Khon Kaen, Krabi, Pattaya, Phuket and Surat Thani; and from Phuket to Chiang Mai, Pattaya and Udon Thani.

Bangkok Airways (⌨nationwide 1771; www.bangkokair. com) From Suvarnabhumi to Chiang Mai, Chiang Rai, Ko Samui, Krabi, Lampang, Pattaya, Phuket, Sukhothai and Trat; and from Chiang Mai to Ko Samui, Mae Hong Son and Phuket.

Nok Air (ww.nokair.com) From Don Mueang to Buriram, Chiang Mai, Chiang Rai, Chumphon, Hat Yai, Khon Kaen, Krabi, Lampang, Loei, Mae Sot, Nakhon Phanom, Nakhon Si Thammarat, Phitsanulok, Phrae, Phuket, Ranong, Roi Et, Sakhon Nakhon, Surat Thani, Trang, Ubon Ratchathani and Udon Thani; from Chiang Mai to Udon Thani.

Orient Thai (⌨nationwide 02 229 4100; www.flyorientthai. com) From Don Mueang to Phuket.

Thai Lion Air (⌨nationwide 02 529 9999; www.lionairthai. com) From Don Mueang to Chiang Mai, Chiang Rai, Hat Yai, Khon Kaen, Krabi, Nakhon Si Thammarat, Phitsanulok, Phuket, Surat Thani, Trang and Ubon Ratchathani; from Hat Yai to Udon Thani.

Thai Smile (⌨nationwide 02 118 8888; www.thaismileair. com) From Suvarnabhumi to Chiang Mai, Chiang Rai, Hat Yai, Phuket, Khon Kaen, Krabi, Narathiwat, Surat Thani, Ubon Ratchathani and Udon Thani; and from Chiang Mai to Phuket.

MYANMAR

There are four border crossings between Thailand and Myanmar.

Mae Sai to Tachileik This is a well-used border-run crossing. It also hosts a busy border market that can be visited on a day trip from Thailand without a pre-arranged visa. For further travel, a pre-arranged visa is required. You can only travel as far as Kyaingtong in Myanmar by land; onward land travel requires a permit, or you can fly to Mandalay or Yangon.

Ranong to Kawthoung This is now a popular visa-renewal point in the southern part of Thailand

and can be used to enter/exit southern Myanmar.

Mae Sot to Myawaddy One of the most accessible land borders for points within Myanmar.

Phu Nam Ron to Htee Khee This crossing is remote and little used. You cannot enter Myanmar at this point with an e-visa but you can exit with one. The Thai government intends to develop this route as a link between Bangkok and Myanmar's Dawei port in the Andaman Sea.

Bus, Bicycle, Car & Motorcycle

Road connections exist to all of Thailand's neighbours,

and these routes can be travelled by bus, shared taxi and private car. In some cases you'll take a bus to the border point, pass through immigration and then pick up another bus or shared taxi on the other side. In other cases, especially when crossing the Malaysian border, the bus will stop for immigration formalities and then continue to its destination across the border.

Taking a private vehicle across an international border requires some paperwork; it's generally not allowed to take a hired vehicle abroad. No special permits are needed for bringing a bicycle into Thailand. It's advisable to bring a well-stocked repair kit.

Train

Thailand's and Malaysia's state railways meet at Butterworth (93km south of the Thailand–Malaysia border), which is a transfer point to Penang (by boat), or to Kuala Lumpur and Singapore (by Malaysian train).

There are several border crossings for which you can take a train to the border and then switch to car transport on the other side. The Thai–Cambodian border crossing of Aranya Prathet to Poipet and the Thai–Lao crossing of Nong Khai to Vientiane are two examples.

Another rail line travels to the Thai east-coast border town of Sungai Kolok, but because of ongoing violence in Thailand's Deep South we don't recommend this route for travellers.

Sea

You can cross into and out of Thailand via public boat between the Andaman Coast and the Malaysian island of Langkawi and between Ranong and the Myanmar port of Kawthoung.

GETTING AROUND

Air

Hopping around the country by air continues to be affordable. Most routes originate from Bangkok (both Don Mueang and Suvarnabhumi International Airports), but Chiang Mai, Chiang Rai, Hat Yai, Ko Samui, Phuket and Udon Thani all have a few routes to other Thai towns.

Boat

The true Thai water transport is the *reu·a hǎhng yow* (long-tail boat), so-called because the propeller is mounted at the end of a long driveshaft extending from the engine. Long-tail boats are a staple of transport on rivers and canals in Bangkok and neighbouring provinces, and between islands.

Between the mainland and small, less-touristed islands, the standard craft is a wooden boat, 8-10m long, with an inboard engine, a wheelhouse and a simple roof to shelter passengers and cargo. To more popular destinations, faster hovercraft (jetfoils) and speedboats are the norm.

Bus & Minivan

The bus network in Thailand is prolific and reliable. The Thai government subsidises the Transport Company (*bò·rí·sàt kǒn sòng*), usually abbreviated to Baw Khaw Saw (BKS). Every city and town in Thailand linked by bus has a BKS station, even if it's just a patch of dirt by the side of the road.

By far the most reliable bus companies in Thailand are the ones that operate out of the BKS stations. In some cases the companies are entirely state owned; in others they are private concessions.

Be aware of bus scams and other common problems. We do not recommend using bus companies that operate directly out of tourist centres, such as Bangkok's Th Khao San, because of repeated instances of theft and commission-seeking stops.

For an increasing number of destinations, minivans are superseding buses. Minivans are run by private companies and because their vehicles are smaller, they can depart from the market (instead of the out-of-town bus stations) and in some cases will deliver passengers directly to their hotel. Just don't sit in the front – that way you can avoid watching the driver's daredevil techniques!

Bus Classes

The cheapest and slowest buses are the *rót tam·má·dah* (ordinary fan buses) that stop in every little town and for every waving hand along the highway. These buses are less common than before, but still exist in rural areas or for very local destinations.

Rót aa (air-con buses) come in a variety of classes, depending on the destination's distance. Short distances are usually covered by the basic 2nd-class bus, which does not have an on-board toilet. For longer routes, buses increase in comfort and amenities, ranging from 1st class to 'VIP' and 'Super VIP'. The last two of these have fewer seats so that each seat reclines further; sometimes these are called *rót norn* (sleeper buses).

Bring a jacket for long-distance bus trips, as air-con keeps the cabin at arctic temperatures. The service on these buses is usually quite good and sometimes includes a video and a beverage, courtesy of the 'cabin crew'.

On overnight journeys the buses usually stop somewhere en route for a midnight meal.

Bus Reservations

You can book air-con BKS buses at any BKS terminal, or even by phone with a payment at a 7-Eleven. Ordinary fan buses cannot be booked in advance. Privately run buses can be booked through most hotels or any travel agency.

Car & Motorcycle

Cars, 4WDs and vans can be hired in most major cities and airports from local companies as well as all the usual international chains. Local companies tend to have cheaper rates, but the quality of their fleets varies Check the tyre tread and general

---

BICYCLE TRAVEL IN THAILAND

For exploring the more rural, less-trafficked corners of Thailand – Ayuthaya Historical Park, Pai, Sukhothai Historical Park – bicycles are a great way to get around. They can usually be hired from guesthouses for as little as 50B per day; you'll pay more for a decent mountain bike.

Elsewhere, lack of infrastructure and dangerous roads mean that cycling isn't generally recommended as a means of transport for the casual tourist. Exceptions are the guided bicycle tours of Bangkok and some other large cities that stick to rural routes.

Yet despite the risks, bicycle touring is an increasingly popular way to see Thailand, and most roads are sealed and have roomy shoulders. A good resource for cycling in the country is Bicycle Thailand (www.bicyclethailand.com).

upkeep of the vehicle before committing.

Motorcycles can be hired in major towns and tourist centres from guesthouses and small mom-and-pop businesses. Hiring a motorcycle in Thailand is relatively easy and a great way to independently tour the countryside. For daily hires most businesses will ask that you leave your passport as a deposit. Before hiring a motorcycle, check the vehicle's condition and ask for a helmet (which is required by law).

Driving Licence

In theory, short-term visitors who wish to drive vehicles (including motorcycles) in Thailand need an international driving permit (IDP). In reality this is rarely enforced, but you will need to show it if stopped by police to avoid a fine.

Fuel & Spare Parts

Modern petrol (gasoline) stations are plentiful. All fuel in Thailand is unleaded; diesel is used by trucks and some passenger cars. Thailand also uses several alternative fuels, including gasohol (a blend of petrol and ethanol that comes in either 91% or 95% octane levels) and compressed natural gas, used by taxis with bi-fuel capabilities. In more rural areas *ben·sin/ nám·man rót yon* (petrol containing benzene) is usually available at small roadside or village stands.

Insurance

Thailand requires a minimum of liability insurance for all registered vehicles on the road. The better hire companies include comprehensive coverage for their vehicles. Always verify that a vehicle is insured for liability before signing a rental contract; you should also ask to see the dated insurance documents. If you have an accident while driving an uninsured vehicle, you're in for some major hassles.

Road Rules & Hazards

Thais drive on the left-hand side of the road – most of the time! Other than that, just about anything goes, in spite of road signs and speed limits.

The main rule to be aware of is that right of way goes to the bigger vehicle – this is not what it says in the Thai traffic laws, but it's the reality. Maximum speed limits are 50km/h on urban roads and 80km/h to 100km/h on most highways – but on any given stretch of highway you'll see various vehicles travelling as slowly as 30km/h and as fast as 150km/h.

Indicators are often used to warn passing drivers about oncoming traffic. A flashing left indicator means it's OK to pass, while a right indicator means that someone's approaching from the other direction. Horns are used to tell other vehicles that the driver plans to pass. When drivers flash their lights, they're telling you not to pass.

In Bangkok traffic is chaotic, roads are poorly signposted and motorcycles and random contraflows mean you can suddenly find yourself facing a wall of cars coming the other way.

Outside of the capital, the principal hazard when driving in Thailand, besides the general disregard for traffic laws, is having to contend with so many different types of vehicles on the same road – trucks, bicycles, túk-túk and motorcycles. This danger is often compounded by the lack of working lights. In village areas the vehicular traffic is lighter but you have to contend with stray chickens, dogs and water buffaloes.

ROAD SAFETY

Thailand's roads are dangerous. In 2018, they were the deadliest in Southeast Asia and the seventh-deadliest in the world, according to the World Health Organization. Several high-profile bus accidents involving foreign tourists have prompted some Western nations to issue travel advisories for highway safety due to disregard for speed limits, reckless driving and long-distance bus drivers' use of stimulants.

Fatal bus crashes make headlines, but nearly 75% of vehicle accidents in Thailand involve motorcycles. Less than half of the motorcyclists in the country wear helmets and many tourists are injured riding motorcycles because they don't know how to handle the vehicles and are unfamiliar with local driving conventions.

If you are a novice motorcyclist, familiarise yourself with the vehicle in an uncongested area of town and stick to the smaller 100cc automatic bikes. Drive slowly, especially when roads are slick or when there is loose gravel. Remember to distribute weight as evenly as possible across the frame of the bike to improve handling. And don't expect that other vehicles will look out for you: motorcycles are low on the traffic ladder.

Hitching

Hitching is never entirely safe in any country and we don't recommend it. Travellers who decide to hitch should understand that they are taking a small but potentially serious risk. Other than at some national parks where there isn't public transport, hitching is rarely seen these days in Thailand, so most passing motorists might not realise the intentions of the foreigner standing on the side of the road with a thumb out. Indeed, Thais don't 'thumb it'; instead, when they want a ride they wave their hand with the palm facing the ground. This is the same gesture used to flag a taxi or bus, which is why some drivers might stop and point to a bus stop if one is nearby.

Local Transport

City Bus & Sŏrng·tăa·ou

Bangkok has the largest city-bus system in the country, while Udon Thani and a few other provincial capitals have some city-bus services. The etiquette for riding public buses is to wait at a bus stop and hail the vehicle by waving your hand palm-side downward. You typically pay the fare once you've taken a seat or, in some cases, when you disembark.

Elsewhere, public transport is provided by sŏrng·tăa·ou ('two rows'; a small pickup truck outfitted with two facing benches for passengers). They sometimes operate on fixed routes, just like buses, but they may also run a shared taxi service where they pick up passengers going in the same general direction. In tourist centres, sŏrng·tăa·ou can be chartered just like a regular taxi, but you'll need to negotiate the fare beforehand. You can usually hail a sŏrng·tăa·ou anywhere along its route and pay the fare when you disembark.

Depending on the region, sŏrng·tăa·ou might also run a fixed route from the centre of town to outlying areas, or even points within the provinces.

SĂHM·LÓR & TÚK-TÚK

Sǎhm·lór (also spelt sǎamláw) are three-wheeled pedicabs that are typically found in small towns where traffic is light and old-fashioned ways persist.

The modern era's version of the human-powered sǎhm·lór is the motorised túk-túk (pronounced đúk dúk). They're small utility vehicles, powered by screaming engines (usually LPG-powered) with a lot of flash and sparkle.

With either form of transport the fare must be established by bargaining before departure. In tourist centres, túk-túk drivers often grossly overcharge foreigners, so have a sense of how much the fare should be before soliciting a ride. Hotel staff are helpful in providing reasonable fare suggestions.

Mass Transit

Bangkok is the only city in Thailand to have an aboveground (BTS) and underground light-rail (MRT) public transport system. Both are being expanded, with new stations and lines set to open in the next few years.

Motorcycle Taxi

Many cities in Thailand have mor·deu·sai ráp jâhng, motorcycle taxis that can be hired for short distances. If you're empty-handed or travelling with a small bag, they can't be beaten for transport in a pinch.

In most cities, you'll find motorcycle taxis clustered near street intersections, as well as at bus and train stations. Usually, the drivers wear numbered orange, yellow or green vests. You'll need to establish the price beforehand.

Taxi

Bangkok has the most formal system of metered taxis, although other cities have growing 'taxi meter' networks. In some cases, fares are set in advance or require negotiation.

App-based taxi hailing initiatives are also available, especially in bigger cities and major tourist destinations.

The most popular app-based service is Grab (www.grab.com), which bought out Uber in Southeast Asia in 2018. Other services include All Thai Taxi (www.allthaitaxi.com).

Train

Thailand's train system connects the four corners of the country and is a scenic, if slow, alternative to buses for the long journey north to Chiang Mai or south to Surat Thani. The train is also ideal for short trips to Ayuthaya and Lopburi from Bangkok, where traffic is a consideration.

The 4500km rail network is operated by the **State Railway of Thailand** (SRT; ☑nationwide 1690; www.railway.co.th) and covers four main lines: northern to Chiang Mai, southern to Sungai Kolok, northeastern to Nong Khai or Ubon Ratchathani, and eastern to Aranya Prathet, on the border with Cambodia. All long-distance trains originate from Bangkok's Hualamphong Train Station.

Train stations have printed timetables in English, though this isn't always the case for smaller stations.

Classes

The SRT operates passenger trains in three classes – 1st, 2nd and 3rd – but each class varies considerably depending on whether you're on an ordinary, rapid or express train. In 2019, SRT announced plans to buy 216 new, modern trains, which are expected to start coming into service from 2021.

1st class Private, two-bunk cabins define the 1st-class carriages, which are available only on rapid, express and special-express trains.

2nd class The seating arrangements in a 2nd-class, nonsleeper carriage are similar to those on a bus, with pairs of padded seats, usually recliners, all facing towards the front of the train. On 2nd-class sleeper cars, pairs of seats face one another and convert into two fold-down berths. The lower berth has more headroom than the upper berth and this is reflected in a higher fare. Children are always assigned a lower berth. Second-class carriages are found only on rapid and express trains. There are air-con and fan 2nd-class carriages.

3rd class A typical 3rd-class carriage consists of two rows of bench seats divided into facing pairs. Each bench seat is designed to seat two or three passengers, but on a crowded rural line nobody seems to care. Express trains do not carry 3rd-class carriages at all. Commuter trains in the Bangkok area are all 3rd class.

Costs

Fares are determined on a base price with surcharges added for distance, class and train type (special express, express, rapid, ordinary). Extra charges are added if the carriage has air-con and for sleeping berths (either upper or lower).

Reservations

Advance bookings can be made from one to 60 days before your intended date of departure. You can make bookings in person from any train station. Train tickets can also be purchased at travel agencies, which usually add a service charge to the ticket price. If you're making an advance reservation from outside the country, contact a licensed travel agent; the SRT previously had an online ticket service, but that has been discontinued.

It is advisable to make advanced bookings for long-distance sleeper trains between Bangkok and Chiang Mai, or from Bangkok to Surat Thani, as seats fill up quickly.

For short-distance trips you should purchase your ticket at least a day in advance for seats (rather than sleepers).

Partial refunds on tickets are available depending on the number of days prior to your departure that you arrange a cancellation. These arrangements can be handled at the train station booking office.

Station Services

All train stations in Thailand have baggage-storage services (or 'cloak rooms'). Most stations have a ticket window that will open between 15 and 30 minutes before train arrivals. There are also newsagents, small snack vendors and some full-service restaurants.

Health

Health risks and the quality of medical facilities vary depending on where and how you travel in Thailand. The majority of cities and popular tourist areas have adequate, sometimes excellent, hospitals. However, travel to remote rural areas can expose you to some health risks and less adequate medical care.

Travellers tend to worry about contracting exotic infectious diseases when visiting the tropics, but these are far less common than problems with pre-existing medical conditions, such as heart disease, and accidental injury (especially as a result of traffic accidents).

Other common illnesses are respiratory infections, diarrhoea and dengue fever. Fortunately most common illnesses can be prevented or are easily treated.

Our advice is a general guide and does not replace the advice of a doctor trained in travel medicine.

BEFORE YOU GO

Health Insurance

Even if you're fit and healthy, don't travel without health insurance – accidents *do* happen. You may require extra cover for adventure activities such as rock climbing or diving, as well as scooter/motorcycle riding. If your health insurance doesn't cover you for medical expenses abroad, ensure you get specific travel insurance. Most hospitals require an upfront guarantee of payment (from yourself or your insurer) prior to admission. Enquire before your trip about payment of medical charges and retain all documentation (medical reports, invoices etc) for claim purposes.

Recommended Vaccinations

The only vaccine required by international regulations is yellow fever. Proof of vaccination will only be required if you have visited a country in the yellow-fever zone in the six days prior to entering Thailand. If you are travelling to Thailand from Africa or South America you should check to see if you require proof of vaccination.

All travellers to Thailand should be vaccinated against hepatitis A, in addition to routine immunisations such as measles and flu. Other vaccinations to consider include typhoid, rabies and Japanese encephalitis.

You should arrange your vaccines six to eight weeks prior to departure through a specialised travel-medicine clinic. The Centers for Disease Control and Prevention (www.cdc.gov) has a traveller's health section that contains recommendations for vaccinations.

Medical Checklist

Recommended items for a personal medical kit include the following, most of which are available in Thailand.

➡ alcohol-based hand gel or wipes

➡ antifungal cream, eg clotrimazole

➡ antibacterial cream, eg muciprocin

➡ antibiotic for skin infections, eg amoxicillin/clavulanate or cephalexin

➡ antibiotics for diarrhoea include norfloxacin, ciprofloxacin or azithromycin for bacterial diarrhoea; for giardiasis or amoebic dysentery take tinidazole

➡ antihistamine – there are many options, eg cetirizine for daytime and promethazine for nighttime

➡ antiseptic, eg Betadine

➡ antispasmodic for stomach cramps, eg Buscopan

➡ contraceptives

➡ decongestant

➡ DEET-based insect repellent

➡ oral rehydration solution for diarrhoea (eg Gastrolyte), diarrhoea 'stopper' (eg loperamide) and anti-nausea medication

➡ first-aid items such as scissors, Elastoplasts, bandages, gauze, thermometer (but not one with mercury), sterile needles and syringes (with a doctor's letter), safety pins and tweezers

➡ ibuprofen or another anti-inflammatory

➡ indigestion medication

➡ laxative

➡ paracetamol

➡ permethrin to impregnate clothing and mosquito nets if at high risk

➡ steroid cream for allergic/itchy rashes, eg 1% to 2% hydrocortisone

➡ sunscreen, sunglasses and hat

➡ throat lozenges

➡ thrush (vaginal yeast infection) treatment, eg clotrimazole pessaries or fluconazole tablet

➡ Ural or equivalent if prone to urinary-tract infections

➡ any other medication for pre-existing conditions Some prescription medications, such as narcotics and psychotropics, may require a permit to be brought into Thailand.

IN THAILAND

Thailand has a robust health-care infrastructure. Bangkok is a major global destination for medical tourism, and is home to several internationally accredited hospitals. Hospitals and health centres can be found across the country, even in small towns and villages.

Availability & Cost of Health Care

Bangkok is considered a centre of medical excellence in Southeast Asia. Private hospitals are more expensive than other medical facilities, but offer a superior standard of care and English-speaking staff. The cost of health care is relatively cheap in Thailand compared to most Western countries.

Infectious Diseases

Cutaneous Larva Migrans

This disease, caused by dog or cat hookworm, is particularly common on the beaches of Thailand. The rash starts as a small lump, and then slowly spreads like a winding line. It is intensely itchy, especially at night. It is easily treated with medications and should not be cut out or frozen.

Dengue Fever

This mosquito-borne disease is increasingly problematic in Thailand, especially in the cities. As there is no vaccine it can only be prevented by avoiding mosquito bites. The mosquito that carries dengue is a daytime biter, so use insect-avoidance measures at all times. Symptoms include high fever, severe headache (especially behind the eyes),

nausea and body aches (dengue was previously known as 'breakbone fever'). Some people develop a rash (which can be very itchy) and experience diarrhoea. Chiang Mai and the southern islands are particularly high-risk areas. There is no specific treatment, just rest and paracetamol – do not take aspirin or ibuprofen as they increase the risk of haemorrhaging. See a doctor to be diagnosed and monitored.

Dengue can progress to the more severe and life-threatening dengue haemorrhagic fever, but this is very uncommon in tourists. The risk of this increases substantially if you have previously been infected with dengue and are then infected with a different serotype.

Hepatitis A

This food- and waterborne virus infects the liver, causing jaundice (yellow skin and eyes), nausea and lethargy. The risk in Bangkok is decreasing, but there is still significant risk in most of the country. There is no specific treatment for hepatitis A. In rare instances it can be fatal for those in older age groups. All travellers to Thailand should be vaccinated against hepatitis A.

Hepatitis B

The only sexually transmitted disease (STD) that can be prevented by vaccination, hepatitis B is spread by body fluids, including sexual contact. In some parts of Thailand up to 20% of the population are carriers of hepatitis B, and usually are unaware of this. The long-term consequences can include liver cancer, cirrhosis and death.

HIV

HIV is now one of the most common causes of death in people under the age of 50 in Thailand. Always practise safe sex, and avoid getting tattoos or using unclean syringes.

Influenza

Present year-round in the tropics, influenza (flu) symptoms include high fever, muscle aches, runny nose, cough and sore throat. Flu is the most common vaccine-preventable disease contracted by travellers and everyone should consider vaccination. There is no specific treatment, just rest and paracetamol. Complications such as bronchitis or middle-ear infection may require antibiotic treatment.

Leptospirosis

Leptospirosis is contracted from exposure to infected surface water – most commonly after river rafting or canyoning. Early symptoms are very similar to flu and include headache and fever. It can vary from a very mild ailment to a fatal disease. Diagnosis is made through blood tests and it is easily treated with doxycycline.

Malaria

There is an enormous amount of misinformation concerning malaria. Malaria is caused by a parasite transmitted by the bite of an infected mosquito. The most important symptom of malaria is fever, but general symptoms such as headache, diarrhoea, cough or chills may also occur – the same symptoms as many other infections. A diagnosis can only be made by taking a blood sample.

Most parts of Thailand visited by tourists, particularly city and resort areas, have minimal to no risk of malaria, and the risk of side effects from taking antimalarial tablets is likely to outweigh the risk of getting the disease itself. If you are travelling to high-risk rural areas, seek medical advice on the right medication and dosage for you.

Measles

This highly contagious viral infection is spread through

RARE BUT BE AWARE

Avian Influenza Most of those infected have had close contact with sick or dead birds.

Filariasis A mosquito-borne disease that is common in the local population; practise mosquito-avoidance measures (p776).

Hepatitis E Transmitted through contaminated food and water and has similar symptoms to hepatitis A. Can be a severe problem in pregnant women. Follow safe eating and drinking guidelines.

Japanese Encephalitis Viral disease transmitted by mosquitoes, typically occurring in rural areas. Vaccination is recommended for travellers spending more than one month outside cities, or for long-term expats.

Meliodosis Contracted by skin contact with soil. Affects up to 30% of the local population in northeastern Thailand. The symptoms are very similar to those experienced by tuberculosis (TB) sufferers. There is no vaccine, but it can be treated with medications.

Strongyloides A parasite transmitted by skin contact with soil; common in the local population. It is characterised by an unusual skin rash – a linear rash on the trunk that comes and goes. An overwhelming infection can follow. It can be treated with medications.

Tuberculosis Medical and aid workers and long-term travellers who have significant contact with the local population should take precautions. Vaccination is recommended for children spending more than three months in Thailand. The main symptoms are fever, cough, weight loss, night sweats and tiredness. Treatment is available with long-term multidrug regimens.

Typhus Murine typhus is spread by the bite of a flea; scrub typhus is spread via a mite. Symptoms include fever, muscle pains and a rash. Can be prevented by following general insect-avoidance measures or taking doxycycline.

coughing and sneezing and remains prevalent in Thailand. Measles starts with a high fever and rash and can be complicated by pneumonia and brain disease. There is no specific treatment. Ensure you are fully vaccinated.

Rabies

This disease, fatal if left untreated, is spread by the bite or lick of an infected animal – most commonly a dog or monkey. You should seek medical advice immediately after any animal bite and

commence post-exposure treatment. Having a pretravel vaccination means the postbite treatment is greatly simplified.

If an animal bites you, gently wash the wound with soap and water, and apply iodine-based antiseptic. If you are not prevaccinated you will need to receive rabies immunoglobulin as soon as possible, followed by five shots of vaccine over 28 days. If prevaccinated you need just two shots of vaccine given three days apart.

STDs

The most common sexually transmitted diseases in Thailand include herpes, warts, syphilis, gonorrhoea and chlamydia. People carrying these diseases often have no signs of infection. Condoms will prevent gonorrhoea and chlamydia, but not warts or herpes. If after a sexual encounter you develop any rash, lumps, discharge or pain when passing urine, seek immediate medical attention. If you have been sexually active during your travels, have an STD check on your return home.

Typhoid

This serious bacterial infection is spread through food and water. It gives a high and slowly progressive fever, severe headache and may be accompanied by a dry cough and stomach pain. It is diagnosed by blood tests and treated with antibiotics. Vaccination is recommended for all travellers spending more than a week in Thailand, or travelling outside of the major cities. Be aware that vaccination is not 100% effective, so you must still be careful with what you eat and drink.

Environmental Hazards

Food

Eating in restaurants is the biggest risk factor for contracting traveller's diarrhoea. Ways to avoid it include eating only freshly cooked food and avoiding food that has been sitting around in buffets. Peel all fruit and cook vegetables. Eat in busy restaurants with a high turnover of customers.

Heat

Most people take at least two weeks to adapt to the hot climate. Avoid dehydration and excessive activity in the heat of the day to prevent swelling of the feet and ankles, as well as muscle cramps caused by excessive sweating.

Heatstroke requires immediate medical treatment. Symptoms come on suddenly and include weakness, nausea, a hot dry body with a body temperature of more than 41°C (105.8°F), dizziness, confusion, loss of coordination, fits and eventually collapse and loss of consciousness.

Insect Bites & Stings

Mosquitoes are present year-round in Thailand, although the mosquito population peaks during the rainy season (May to September), and they can be active day and night. In Thailand, mosquitoes spread four diseases: malaria, dengue fever, Japanese encephalitis and lymphatic filariasis (swelling of the lymph nodes). Malaria and dengue fever are the most common, but the risk of being infected is low if you take precautions. Avoid being bitten by using insect repellent, sleeping under a mosquito net and closing your windows at night.

Bedbugs live in the cracks of furniture and walls and then migrate to the bed at night to feed on humans. You can treat the itch with an antihistamine.

Ticks are contracted when walking in rural areas. They are commonly found behind the ears, on the belly and in armpits. If you've been bitten by a tick and a rash develops at the site of the bite or elsewhere, along with fever or muscle aches, see a doctor. Doxycycline prevents tick-borne diseases.

Leeches are found in humid rainforests. They do not transmit disease, but their bites are often itchy for weeks afterwards and can easily become infected. Apply an iodine-based antiseptic to the bite to help prevent infection.

Bee and wasp stings mainly cause problems for people who are allergic to them. Anyone with a serious allergy should carry an injection of adrenalin (eg an EpiPen) for emergencies. For others, pain is the main problem – apply ice to the sting and take painkillers.

Jellyfish Stings

Box-jellyfish stings are extremely painful and can even be fatal. There are two main types of box jellyfish: multi-tentacled and single-tentacled.

Multi-tentacled box jellyfish are present in Thai waters – these are the most dangerous and a severe envenomation can kill an adult

MOSQUITO AVOIDANCE TIPS

Travellers are advised to prevent mosquito bites by taking these steps:

➡ use a DEET-containing insect repellent on exposed skin

➡ sleep under a mosquito net, ideally impregnated with permethrin

➡ choose accommodation with screens and fans

➡ impregnate clothing with permethrin in high-risk areas

➡ wear long sleeves and trousers in light colours

➡ use mosquito coils

➡ spray your room with insect repellent before going out

within two minutes. They are generally found along sandy beaches near river mouths and mangroves during the warmer months.

There are many types of single-tentacled box jellyfish, some of which can cause severe symptoms known as Irukandji syndrome. The initial sting can seem minor, but severe symptoms such as back pain, nausea, vomiting, sweating, difficulty breathing and a feeling of impending doom can develop between five and 40 minutes later.

There are many other jellyfish in Thailand that cause irritating stings but no serious effects. The only way to prevent these stings is to wear protective clothing.

Parasites

Numerous parasites are common in local populations in Thailand, but most of these are rare in travellers. To avoid parasitic infections, wear shoes and avoid eating raw food, especially fish, pork and vegetables.

Skin Problems

Prickly heat is a common skin rash in the tropics, caused by sweat being trapped under the skin. Treat by taking cool showers and using powders.

Two fungal rashes commonly affect travellers. The first occurs in the groin, armpits and between the toes. It starts as a red patch that slowly spreads and is usually itchy. Treatment involves keeping the skin dry, avoiding chafing and using an antifungal cream such as clotrimazole or Lamisil. The fungus *Tinea versicolor* causes small and light-coloured patches, most commonly on the back, chest and shoulders. Consult a doctor.

Cuts and scratches become easily infected in humid climates. Immediately wash all wounds in clean water and apply antiseptic. If you develop signs of infection, see a doctor. Coral cuts can easily become infected.

FIRST AID FOR SEVERE STINGS

For severe, life-threatening envenomations, experts say the first priority is keeping the person alive. Send someone to call for medical help and start immediate CPR if they are unconscious. If the victim is conscious, douse the stung area liberally with vinegar for 30 seconds.

Vinegar can also reduce irritation from minor stings. It is best to seek medical care quickly in case any other symptoms develop over the next 40 minutes.

Australia and Thailand are now working in close collaboration to identify the species of jellyfish in Thai waters, as well as their ecology – hopefully enabling better prediction and detection of the jellyfish.

Snakes

Though snake bites are rare for travellers, there are more than 85 species of venomous snakes in Thailand. Wear boots and long trousers if walking in an area that may have snakes.

The Thai Red Cross produces antivenin for many of the poisonous snakes in Thailand.

Sunburn

Even on a cloudy day, sunburn can occur rapidly. Use a strong sunscreen (at least factor 30+), making sure to reapply after a swim, and always wear a wide-brimmed hat and sunglasses outdoors. If you become sunburned, stay out of the sun until you have recovered, apply cool compresses and take painkillers for the discomfort. 1% hydrocortisone cream applied twice daily is also helpful.

Travelling with Children

Thailand is relatively safe for children. Consult a doctor who specialises in travel medicine prior to travel to ensure your child is appropriately prepared. A medical kit designed specifically for children includes liquid medicines for children who cannot swallow tables. Azithromycin is an ideal paediatric formula used to treat bacterial

---

diarrhoea, as well as ear, chest and throat infections.

Good resources include Lonely Planet's *Travel with Children* and, for those spending longer away, Jane Wilson-Howarth's *Your Child's Health Abroad*.

Traveller's Diarrhoea

Traveller's diarrhoea is by far the most common problem affecting travellers. In over 80% of cases, traveller's diarrhoea is caused by a bacteria (there are numerous potential culprits) and responds promptly to treatment with antibiotics.

Here we define traveller's diarrhoea as the passage of more than three watery bowel movements within 24 hours, plus at least one other symptom such as vomiting, fever, cramps, nausea or feeling generally unwell.

Make sure you stay well hydrated; rehydration solutions such as Gastrolyte are the best for this. Antibiotics such as norfloxacin, ciprofloxacin or azithromycin will kill the bacteria quickly. Seek medical attention if you do not respond to an appropriate antibiotic.

Loperamide is just a 'stopper' that only treats the symptoms. It can be helpful, for example, if you have to go on a long bus ride. Don't take loperamide if you have a fever, or blood in your stools.

TAP WATER

Although it's deemed potable by the authorities, Thais don't drink the tap water and neither should you. Stick to bottled or filtered water during your stay.

Giardia lamblia is a relatively common microscopic parasite that causes giardiasis. Symptoms include nausea, bloating, excess gas, fatigue and intermittent diarrhoea. 'Eggy' burps are often attributed solely to giardiasis. The treatment of choice is tinidazole, with metronidazole being a second-line option.

Amoebic dysentery is very rare in travellers, but may be misdiagnosed by poor-quality labs. Symptoms are similar to bacterial diarrhoea. You should always seek reliable medical care if you have blood in your diarrhoea. Treatment involves two drugs: tinidazole or metronidazole to kill the parasite in your gut and then a second drug to kill the cysts. If left untreated, complications such as liver abscesses can occur.

Women's Health

➡ There have been outbreaks of the Zika virus in Thailand, although not for a couple of years. Check the International Association for Medical Assistance for Travellers (www.iamat.org) website for updates on the situation.

➡ Sanitary products are readily available in Thailand's urban areas.

➡ Bring adequate supplies of your personal birth-control option, which may not be available.

➡ Heat, humidity and antibiotics can all contribute to thrush, which can be treated with antifungal creams and clotrimazole. A practical alternative is one tablet of fluconazole (Diflucan).

➡ Urinary-tract infections can be precipitated by dehydration or long bus journeys without toilet stops; bring suitable antibiotics for treatment.

Language

Thailand's official language is effectively the dialect spoken and written in central Thailand, which has successfully become the lingua franca of all Thai and non-Thai ethnic groups in the kingdom.

In Thai the meaning of a single syllable may be altered by means of different tones. In standard Thai there are five: low tone, mid tone, falling tone, high tone and rising tone. The range of all five tones is relative to each speaker's vocal range, so there is no fixed 'pitch' intrinsic to the language.

low tone – 'Flat' like the mid tone, but pronounced at the relative bottom of one's vocal range. It is low, level and has no inflection, eg bàht (baht – the Thai currency).

mid tone – Pronounced 'flat', at the relative middle of the speaker's vocal range, eg dee (good). No tone mark is used.

falling tone – Starting high and falling sharply, this tone is similar to the change in pitch in English when you are emphasising a word, or calling someone's name from afar, eg mâi (no/not).

high tone – Usually the most difficult for non-Thai speakers. It's pronounced near the relative top of the vocal range, as level as possible, eg máh (horse).

rising tone – Starting low and gradually rising, sounds like the inflection used by English speakers to imply a question – 'Yes?', eg sǎhm (three).

The Thai government has instituted the Royal Thai General Transcription System (RTGS) as a standard method of writing Thai using the Roman alphabet. It's used in official documents, road signs and on maps. However, local variations crop up on signs, menus etc. Generally, names in this book follow the most common practice.

In our coloured pronunciation guides, the hyphens indicate syllable breaks within words, and some syllables are further divided with a dot to help you pronounce compound vowels, eg mêu·a-rai (when).

The vowel a is pronounced as in 'about', aa as the 'a' in 'bad', ah as the 'a' in 'father', ai as in 'aisle', air as in 'flair' (without the 'r'), eu as the 'er' in 'her' (without the 'r'), ew as in 'new' (with rounded lips), oh as the 'o' in 'toe', or as in 'torn' (without the 'r') and ow as in 'now'.

Most consonants correspond to their English counterparts. The exceptions are b (a hard 'p' sound, almost like a 'b', eg in 'hip-bag'); d (a hard 't' sound, like a sharp 'd', eg in 'mid-tone'); ng (as in 'singing'; In Thai it can occur at the start of a word) and r (as in 'run' but flapped; in everyday speech it's often pronounced like 'l').

BASICS

The social structure of Thai society demands different registers of speech depending on who you're talking to. To make things simple we've chosen the correct form of speech appropriate to the context of each phrase.

When being polite, the speaker ends his or her sentence with kráp (for men) or kâ (for women). It is the gender of the speaker that is being expressed here; it is also the common way to answer 'yes' to a question or show agreement.

The masculine and feminine forms of phrases in this chapter are indicated where relevant with 'm/f'.

WANT MORE?

For in-depth language information and handy phrases, check out Lonely Planet's *Thai Phrasebook*. You'll find it at **shop.lonelyplanet.com**, or you can buy Lonely Planet's iPhone phrasebooks at the Apple App Store.

QUESTION WORDS

What?	อะไร	à-rai
When?	เมื่อไร	mêu·a-rai
Where?	ที่ไหน	têe năi
Who?	ใคร	krai
Why?	ทำไม	tam-mai

Hello.	สวัสดี	sà-wàt-dee
Goodbye.	ลาก่อน	lah gòrn
Yes./No.	ใช่/ไม่	châi/mâi
Please.	ขอ	kŏr
Thank you.	ขอบคุณ	kòrp kun
You're welcome.	ยินดี	yin dee
Excuse me.	ขออภัย	kŏr à-pai
Sorry.	ขอโทษ	kŏr tôht

How are you?
สบายดีไหม — sà-bai dee măi

Fine. And you?
สบายดีครับ/ค่ะ แล้วคุณล่ะ — sà-bai dee kráp/ kâ láa·ou kun lâ (m/f)

What's your name?
คุณชื่ออะไร — kun chêu à-rai

My name is ...
ผม/ดิฉันชื่อ... — pŏm/dì-chăn chêu ... (m/f)

Do you speak English?
คุณพูดภาษาอังกฤษได้ไหม — kun pôot pah-săh ang-grìt dâi măi

I don't understand.
ผม/ดิฉันไม่เข้าใจ — pŏm/dì-chăn mâi kôw jai (m/f)

ACCOMMODATION

Where's a ...?	... อยู่ที่ไหน	... yòo têe năi
campsite	ค่ายพักแรม	kâi pák raam
guesthouse	บ้านพัก	bâhn pák
hotel	โรงแรม	rohng raam
youth hostel	บ้านเยาวชน	bâhn yow-wá-chon

Do you have a ... room?	มีห้อง ... ไหม	mee hôrng ... măi
single	เดี่ยว	dèe·o
double	เตียงคู่	đee·ang kôo
twin	สองเตียง	sŏrng đee·ang

air-con	แอร์	aa
bathroom	ห้องน้ำ	hôrng nám
laundry	ห้องซักผ้า	hôrng sák pâh
mosquito net	มุ้ง	múng
window	หน้าต่าง	nâh đàhng

DIRECTIONS

Where's ...?
... อยู่ที่ไหน — ... yòo têe năi

What's the address?
ที่อยู่คืออะไร — têe yòo keu à-rai

Could you please write it down?
เขียนลงให้ได้ไหม — kĕe·an long hâi dâi măi

Can you show me (on the map)?
ให้ดู (ในแผนที่) ได้ไหม — hâi doo (nai păan têe) dâi măi

Turn left/right.
เลี้ยวซ้าย/ขวา — lée·o sái/kwăh

It's ...	อยู่ ...	yòo ...
behind	ที่หลัง	têe lăng
in front of	ตรงหน้า	đrong nâh
next to	ข้างๆ	kâhng kâhng
straight ahead	ตรงไป	đrong bai

EATING & DRINKING

I'd like (the menu), please.
ขอ (รายการอาหาร) หน่อย — kŏr (rai gahn ah-hăhn) nòy

What would you recommend?
คุณแนะนำอะไรบ้าง — kun náa-nam à-rai bâhng

That was delicious!
อร่อยมาก — à-ròy mâhk

Cheers!
ไชโย — chai-yoh

Please bring the bill.
ขอบิลหน่อย — kŏr bin nòy

I don't eat ...	ผม/ดิฉันไม่กิน ...	pŏm/dì-chăn mâi gin ... (m/f)
eggs	ไข่	kài
fish	ปลา	blah

red meat	เนื้อแดง	néu·a daang
nuts	ถั่ว	tòo·a

Key Words

bar	บาร์	bah
bottle	ขวด	kòo·at
bowl	ชาม	chahm
breakfast	อาหารเช้า	ah-hăhn chów
cafe	ร้านกาแฟ	ráhn gah-faa
chopsticks	ไม้ตะเกียบ	mái đà-gèe·ap
cold	เย็น	yen
cup	ถ้วย	tôo·ay
dessert	ของหวาน	kŏrng wăhn
dinner	อาหารเย็น	ah-hăhn yen
drink list	รายการ	rai gahn
	เครื่องดื่ม	krêu·ang dèum
fork	ส้อม	sôrm
glass	แก้ว	gâa·ou
hot	ร้อน	rórn
knife	มีด	mêet
lunch	อาหาร	ah-hăhn
	กลางวัน	glahng wan
market	ตลาด	đà-làht
menu	รานการ	rai gahn
	อาหาร	ah-hăhn
plate	จาน	jahn
restaurant	ร้านอาหาร	ráhn ah-hăhn
spicy	เผ็ด	pèt
spoon	ช้อน	chórn
vegetarian (person)	คนกินเจ	kon gin jair
with	มี	mee
without	ไม่มี	mâi mee

Meat & Fish

beef	เนื้อ	néu·a
chicken	ไก่	gài
crab	ปู	boo
duck	เป็ด	bèt
fish	ปลา	blah
meat	เนื้อ	néu·a

NUMBERS

1	หนึ่ง	nèung
2	สอง	sŏrng
3	สาม	săhm
4	สี่	sèe
5	ห้า	hâh
6	หก	hòk
7	เจ็ด	jèt
8	แปด	bàat
9	เก้า	gôw
10	สิบ	sìp
11	สิบเอ็ด	sìp-èt
20	ยี่สิบ	yêe-sìp
21	ยี่สิบเอ็ด	yêe-sìp-èt
30	สามสิบ	săhm-sìp
40	สี่สิบ	sèe-sìp
50	ห้าสิบ	hâh-sìp
60	หกสิบ	hòk-sìp
70	เจ็ดสิบ	jèt-sìp
80	แปดสิบ	bàat-sìp
90	เก้าสิบ	gôw-sìp
100	หนึ่งร้อย	nèung róy
1000	หนึ่งพัน	nèung pan
10,000	หนึ่งหมื่น	nèung mèun
100,000	หนึ่งแสน	nèung săan
1,000,000	หนึ่งล้าน	nèung láhn

pork	หมู	mŏo
seafood	อาหารทะเล	ah-hăhn tá-lair
squid	ปลาหมึก	blah mèuk

Fruit & Vegetables

banana	กล้วย	glôo·ay
beans	ถั่ว	tòo·a
coconut	มะพร้าว	má-prów
eggplant	มะเขือ	má-kĕu·a
fruit	ผลไม้	pŏn-lá-mái
guava	ฝรั่ง	fa-ràng
lime	มะนาว	má-now
mango	มะม่วง	má-môo·ang
mangosteen	มังคุด	mang-kút
mushrooms	เห็ด	hèt
nuts	ถั่ว	tòo·a
papaya	มะละกอ	má-lá-gor

potatoes	มันฝรั่ง	man fa·ràng
rambutan	เงาะ	ngó
tamarind	มะขาม	má·kăhm
tomatoes	มะเขือเทศ	má·kĕu·a têt
vegetables	ผัก	pàk
watermelon	แตงโม	đaang moh

Other

chilli	พริก	prík
egg	ไข่	kài
fish sauce	น้ำปลา	nám blah
ice	น้ำแข็ง	nám kăang
noodles	เส้น	sên
oil	น้ำมัน	nám man
pepper	พริกไทย	prík tai
rice	ข้าว	kôw
salad	ผักสด	pàk sòt
salt	เกลือ	gleu·a
soup	น้ำซุป	nám súp
soy sauce	น้ำซีอิ๊ว	nám see·éw
sugar	น้ำตาล	nám đahn
tofu	เต้าหู้	đôw hôo

Drinks

beer	เบียร์	bee·a
coffee	กาแฟ	gah·faa
milk	นมจืด	nom jèut
orange juice	น้ำส้ม	nám sôm
soy milk	น้ำเต้าหู้	nám đôw hôo
sugarcane juice	น้ำอ้อย	nám ôy
tea	ชา	chah
water	น้ำดื่ม	nám dèum

EMERGENCIES

Help!	ช่วยด้วย	chôo·ay dôo·ay
Go away!	ไปให้พ้น	bai hâi pón

Call a doctor!
เรียกหมอหน่อย — rêe·ak mŏr nòy

Call the police!
เรียกตำรวจหน่อย — rêe·ak đam·ròo·at nòy

I'm ill.
ผม/ดิฉันป่วย — pŏm/dì·chăn bòo·ay (m/f)

I'm lost.
ผม/ดิฉัน
หลงทาง — pŏm/dì·chăn
lŏng tahng (m/f)

Where are the toilets?
ห้องน้ำอยู่ที่ไหน — hôrng nám yòo têe năi

SHOPPING & SERVICES

I'd like to buy ...
อยากจะซื้อ ... — yàhk jà séu ...

I'm just looking.
ดูเฉย ๆ — doo chĕu·i chĕu·i

Can I look at it?
ขอดูได้ไหม — kŏr doo dâi măi

How much is it?
เท่าไร — tôw·rai

That's too expensive.
แพงไป — paang bai

Can you lower the price?
ลดราคาได้ไหม — lót rah·kah dâi măi

There's a mistake in the bill.
บิลใบนี้ผิด
นะครับ/ค่ะ — bin bai née pìt ná
kráp/kâ (m/f)

TIME & DATES

What time is it?
กี่โมงแล้ว — gèe mohng láa·ou

morning	เช้า	chów
afternoon	บ่าย	bài
evening	เย็น	yen
yesterday	เมื่อวาน	mêu·a wahn
today	วันนี้	wan née
tomorrow	พรุ่งนี้	prûng née

Monday	วันจันทร์	wan jan
Tuesday	วันอังคาร	wan ang·kahn
Wednesday	วันพุธ	wan pút
Thursday	วันพฤหัสฯ	wan pá·réu·hàt
Friday	วันศุกร	wan sùk
Saturday	วันเสาร์	wan sŏw
Sunday	วันอาทิตย์	wan ah·tít

TRANSPORT

Public Transport

bicycle rickshaw	สามล้อ	săhm lór
boat	เรือ	reu·a
bus	รถเมล์	rót mair
car	รถเก๋ง	rót gĕng
motorcycle	มอร์เตอร์ไซค์	mor-đeu-sai
taxi	รับจ้าง	ráp jâhng
plane	เครื่องบิน	krêu·ang bin
train	รถไฟ	rót fai
túk-túk	ตุ๊ก ๆ	đúk đúk
When's	รถเมล์คัน ...	rót mair kan ...
the ... bus?	มาเมื่อไร	mah mêu·a rai
first	แรก	râak
last	สุดท้าย	sùt tái
next	ต่อไป	đòr bai
A ... ticket, please.	ขอตั๋ว ...	kŏr đŏo·a ...
one-way	เที่ยวเดียว	têe·o dee·o
return	ไปกลับ	bai glàp
I'd like a/an ... seat.	ต้องการที่นั่ง ...	đôrng gahn têe nâng ...
aisle	ติดทางเดิน	đìt tahng deun
window	ติดหน้าต่าง	đìt nâh đàhng
platform	ชานชาลา	chan-chah-lah
ticket window	ช่องขายตั๋ว	chôrng kăi đŏo·a
timetable	ตารางเวลา	đah-rahng wair-lah

What time does it get to (Chiang Mai)?
ถึง (เชียงใหม่) těung (chee·ang mài)
กี่โมง gèe mohng

Does it stop at (Saraburi)?
รถจอดที่ (สระบุรี) rót jòrt têe (sà-rà-bù-ree)
ไหม măi

Please tell me when we get to (Chiang Mai).
เมื่อถึง mêu·a těung
(เชียงใหม่) (chee·ang mài)
กรุณาบอกด้วย gà-rú-nah bòrk dôo·ay

I'd like to get off at (Saraburi).
ขอลงที่(สระบุรี) kŏr long têe (sà-rà-bù-ree)

SIGNS

ทางเข้า	Entrance
ทางออก	Exit
เปิด	Open
ปิด	Closed
ที่ติดต่อสอบถาม	Information
ห้าม	Prohibited
ห้องสุขา	Toilets
ชาย	Men
หญิง	Women

Driving & Cycling

I'd like to hire a ...	อยากจะเช่า ...	yàhk jà chôw ...
car	รถเก๋ง	rót gĕng
motorbike	รถมอร์เตอร์ไซค์	rót mor-đeu-sai
I'd like ...	ต้องการ ...	đôrng gahn ...
my bicycle repaired	ซ่อมรถจักรยาน	sôrm rót jàk-gà-yahn
to hire a bicycle	เช่ารถจักรยาน	chôw rót jàk-gà-yahn

Is this the road to (Ban Bung Wai)?
ทางนี้ไป tahng née bai
(บ้านบุ่งหวาย) ไหม (bâhn bùng wăi) măi

Where's a petrol station?
ปั๊มน้ำมันอยู่ที่ไหน bâm nám man yòo têe năi

Can I park here?
จอดที่นี่ได้ไหม jòrt têe née dâi măi

How long can I park here?
จอดที่นี่ได้นานเท่าไร jòrt têe née dâi nahn tôw-rai

I need a mechanic.
ต้องการช่างรถ đôrng gahn châhng rót

I have a flat tyre.
ยางแบน yahng baan

I've run out of petrol.
หมดน้ำมัน mòt nám man

Do I need a helmet?
ต้องใช้หมวก đôrng chái mòo·ak
กันน๊อกไหม gan nórk măi

GLOSSARY

This glossary includes Thai, Pali (P) and Sanskrit (S) words and terms frequently used in this guidebook. For definitions of food and drink terms, see p780.

ajahn – *(aajaan)* respectful title for 'teacher'; from the Sanskrit term *acarya*

amphoe – *(amphur)* district, the next subdivision down from province

AUA – American University Alumni

bâhn – *(ban)* house or village

baht – *(bàat)* the Thai unit of currency

bàht – a unit of weight equal to 15g; rounded bowl used by monks for receiving alms food

BKS – Baw Khaw Saw (Thai acronym for the Transport Company)

bodhisattva (S) – in Theravada Buddhism, the term used to refer to the previous lives of the Buddha prior to his enlightenment

bòht – central sanctuary in a Thai temple used for the monastic order's official business, such as ordinations; from the Pali term *uposatha (ubohsòt);* see also *wí·hăhn*

bòr nám rórn – hot springs

Brahman – pertaining to Brahmanism, an ancient religious tradition in India and the predecessor of Hinduism; not to be confused with 'Brahmin', the priestly class in India's caste system

BTS – Bangkok Transit System (Skytrain); Thai: *rót fai fáh*

ɓah·đé – batik

CAT – CAT Telecom Public Company Limited

chedi – see *stupa*

chow – folk; people

chow lair – *(chow nám)* sea gypsies

CPT – Communist Party of Thailand

doy – mountain in the Northern Thai dialect; spelt 'Doi' in proper names

đròrk – *(trok)* alley, smaller than a soi

fa·ràng –a Westerner (person of European origin); also guava

gà·teu·i – *(kàthoey)* Thailand's 'third gender', usually cross-dressing or transsexual males; also called ladyboys

gopura (S) – entrance pavilion in traditional Hindu temple architecture, often seen in Angkor-period temple complexes

hàht – beach; spelt 'Hat' in proper names

hŏr đrai – a Tripitaka (Buddhist scripture) hall

hôrng – *(hong)* room; in southern Thailand this refers to semi-submerged island caves

Isan – *(ee·sǎhn)* general term used for northeastern Thailand

jataka (P) – *(chah·dòk)* stories of the Buddha's previous lives

jeen – Chinese

jeen hor – literally 'galloping Chinese', referring to horse-riding Yunnanese traders

kàthoey – see *gà·teu·i*

klorng – canal; spelt 'Khlong' in proper nouns

kŏhn – masked dance–drama based on stories from the Ramakian

kŏw – hill or mountain; spelt 'Khao' in proper names

KMT – Kuomintang

KNU – Karen National Union

ku – small *stupa* that is partially hollow and open

kùtì – monk's dwelling

lăam – cape; spelt 'Laem' in proper names

làk meu·ang – city pillar

lék – little, small (in size); see also *noi*

longyi – Burmese sarong

lôok tûng – Thai country music

lôw kŏw – white whisky, often homemade rice brew

mâa chee – Thai Buddhist nun

mâa nám – river; spelt Mae Nam in proper names

mahathat – *(má·hǎh tâht)* common name for temples containing Buddha relics; from the Sanskrit–Pali term *mahadhatu*

masjid – *(mát·sà·yít)* mosque

mát·mèe – technique of tie-dyeing silk or cotton threads and then weaving them into complex patterns, similar to Indonesian *ikat*; the term also refers to the patterns themselves

meu·ang – city or principality

mon·dòp – small square, spired building in a wát; from Sanskrit *mandapa*

moo·ay tai – *(muay thai)* Thai boxing

mŏr lam – an Isan musical tradition akin to *lôok tûng*

naga (P/S) – *(nâhk)* a mythical serpent-like being with magical powers

ná·kon – city; from the Sanskrit-Pali *nagara;* spelt 'Nakhon' in proper nouns

nám – water

nám đòk – waterfall; spelt 'Nam Tok' in proper nouns

neun – hill; spelt 'Noen' in proper names

nibbana (P/S) – nirvana; in Buddhist teachings, the state of enlightenment; escape from the realm of rebirth; Thai: *níp·pahn*

noi – *(nóy)* little, small (amount); see also *lék*

nôrk – outside, outer; spelt 'Nok' in proper names

ow – bay or gulf; spelt 'Ao' in proper nouns

pâh mát·mèe – *mát·mèe* fabric

pěe – ghost, spirit

pík·sù – a Buddhist monk; from the Sanskrit *bhikshu,* Pali *bhikkhu*

PLAT – People's Liberation Army of Thailand

prá – an honorific term used for monks, nobility and Buddha images; spelt 'Phra' in proper names

prá krêu·ang – amulets of monks, Buddhas or deities worn around the neck for spiritual protection; also called *prá pim*

prá poom – earth spirits or guardians

prang – *(ˈbrahng)* Khmer-style tower on temples

prasat – *(brah·sàht)* small ornate building, used for religious purposes, with a cruciform ground plan and needlelike spire, located on temple grounds; any of a number of different kinds of halls or residences with religious or royal significance

rót aa – blue-and-white air-con bus

rót norn – sleeper bus

săh·lah – open-sided, covered meeting hall or resting place; from Portuguese term *sala*, literally 'room'

săhm·lór – three-wheeled pedicab

samsara (P) – in Buddhist teachings, the realm of rebirth and delusion

sangha – (P) the Buddhist community

satang – *(sà·dahng)* a Thai unit of currency; 100 satang equals 1 baht

serow – Asian mountain goat

sêua môr hôrm – blue cotton farmer's shirt

soi – lane or small street

Songkran – Thai New Year, held in mid-April

sŏrng·tăa·ou – (literally 'two rows') common name for small pick-up trucks with two benches in the back, used as buses/taxis; also spelt '*săwngthăew*'

SRT – State Railway of Thailand

stupa – conical-shaped Buddhist monument used to inter sacred Buddhist objects

tâh – pier, boat landing; spelt 'Tha' in proper nouns

tâht – four-sided, curvilinear Buddha reliquary, common in Northeastern Thailand; spelt 'That' in proper nouns

tâm – cave; spelt 'Tham' in proper nouns

tam bun – to make merit

tambon – see *đam·bon*

TAT – Tourism Authority of Thailand

Thammayut – one of the two sects of Theravada Buddhism in Thailand; founded by King Rama IV while he was still a monk

thanŏn – *(tà·nŏn)* street; spelt 'Thanon' in proper noun and shortened to 'Th'

T-pop – popular teen-music

tràwk – see *đròrk*

trimurti (S) – collocation of the three principal Hindu deities, Brahma, Shiva and Vishnu

Tripitaka (S) – Theravada Buddhist scriptures; (Pali: *Tipitaka*)

túk–túk – *(đúk–đúk)* motorised săhm·lór

vipassana (P) – *(wí·pàt·sà·nah)* Buddhist insight meditation

wâi – palms–together Thai greeting

wan prá – Buddhist holy days, falling on the days of the main phases of the moon (full, new and half) each month

wang – palace

wát – temple–monastery; from the Pali term *avasa* meaning 'monk's dwelling'; spelt 'Wat' in proper nouns

wí·hăhn – *(wihan, viharn)* any large hall in a Thai temple, usually open to laity; from Sanskrit term *vihara*, meaning 'dwelling'

Yawi – traditional language of Malay parts of Java, Sumatra and the Malay Peninsula, widely spoken in the most southern provinces of Thailand; the written form uses the classic Arabic script plus five additional letters

yài – big

Behind the Scenes

SEND US YOUR FEEDBACK

We love to hear from travellers – your comments keep us on our toes and help make our books better. Our well-travelled team reads every word on what you loved or loathed about this book. Although we cannot reply individually to your submissions, we always guarantee that your feedback goes straight to the appropriate authors, in time for the next edition. Each person who sends us information is thanked in the next edition – the most useful submissions are rewarded with a selection of digital PDF chapters.

Visit **lonelyplanet.com/contact** to submit your updates and suggestions or to ask for help. Our award-winning website also features inspirational travel stories, news and discussions.

Note: We may edit, reproduce and incorporate your comments in Lonely Planet products such as guidebooks, websites and digital products, so let us know if you don't want your comments reproduced or your name acknowledged. For a copy of our privacy policy visit lonelyplanet.com/privacy.

OUR READERS

Many thanks to the travelers who used the last edition and wrote to us with helpful hints, useful advice and interesting anecdotes: Amanda Raker, Anke Petra Jellema, Chiara Perrone, Chris Greenlaw, David Elliot, Deirdrei Miller, Don Kanare, Elise van Bussel, Filippo Aroffo, Gwen Gerritsen, Herve Wittebroet, Hugo Steedman, Ian McAlpine, James Ong, Jan Ruigrok, Jens Auff'm Ordt, John Gibbon, Jude Bursten, Ken Joye, Luc Ockers, Maria Alice Pires Rebelo, Michael Falso, Pattama Prangphan, Paul Mayhook, Paul Nordhaus, Peter de Bruyni, Peter Wyeth, Petr Yakovlev, Roger Deacon, Sally Kingsbury, Sarah Petra Hopkins, Simone Willems, Stephan Wijland, Sujiva Dewaraja, Virginia Miller, Megan McCarthy, Moritz Liebald.

WRITER THANKS

David Eimer

Thanks to all the locals and travellers who passed on tips along the way, whether knowingly or unwittingly. Special gratitude to Mr Dam in Mae Hong Son for his insights into the area and bad jokes, as well as to the Burmese guy in Chiang Saen who fixed my bike. Thanks also to the LP office crew for their support.

Anirban Mahapatra

Sincere thanks to my resident Bangkokian friends Dirk, Melva, Xavier, Roque, Francisco, Seonmi, Bruno and my wife Roshni, all of whom chipped in with valuable tips and insights on their favourite places and experiences throughout my research. Thanks to Tanya Parker for allowing me the opportunity to dive deep into the splendid socio-cultural matrix of the metropolis I now call home. Thanks also to all my fellow writers for putting together yet another fabulous update of *Thailand*, and to the amazing people of this country of countless smiles.

Daniel McCrohan

Massive thanks to my good friends Wez and Ketsara Hunter, not only for introducing me to the wonders of rural Isan all those years ago, but for helping me through this project with advice, translations, lifts and wonderful hospitality. Thanks to Wachiraphan Chaimanee and Sunti Chaimanee for help with bus timetables, to Tim Bewer for his invaluable Isan expertise and to Tanya Parker for giving me this opportunity. Love, as always, to Taotao, Dudu and Yoyo.

Tim Bewer

A hearty *kòrp kun kráp* to the many people who answered my incessant questions during this update. And, of course, a special thanks to my wife, Suttawan, for all her assistance.

Paul Harding

Thanks to the many people I met along the way in Thailand. In particular thanks to Steve, Apai and Pete in Pattaya, Chris and Mike in Ko Kut. Thanks to Tanya Parker and the team at LP. And most of all, love and thanks to Hannah and Layla for always patiently being there.

Ashley Harrell

Thanks to my editor Tanya Parker and coauthors for all the hard work on this book, Alana Morgan for the local expertise, Franz Betgem for the wisdom and the company, Kellyn Foxman, Ansley Luce and Erik Lokensgard for the excellent recs, Alexis Stranberg and Josh Buermann for supervising the vicious cur, and Steven Sparapani for watching me eat live shrimp and making an honest woman out of me. I love you.

Tharik Hussain

A huge thanks to my Thai 'brothers', the deeply knowledgeable Muhammad Kanzi and Ismail Waiyaveta - your support was invaluable in navigating the wonderful heritage of southern Thailand. A massive thanks to my ol' East-End mucka now in Chiang Mai, Abdul Wadud, for the time we spent together and all the insight you offered. Thanks also to my editor, Tanya Parker, for her support throughout. Finally, a huge thanks to my beloved wife, Tamara, for her endless support, encouragement and patience.

Michael Kohn

A special thanks to my wife, Baigalmaa Kohn, for coming along on the journey and making every moment enjoyable. Thanks also to all those who passed along tips and advice along the way, especially in Ranong and Ko Phayam. And thanks to the editors, cartographers and co-writers who worked tirelessly on this project.

Olivia Pozzan

Huge thanks to Anthony Ham and Paul Harding – your help was much appreciated. Specific thanks to Pak in Krabi, Mun in Lanta, Jip in Trang, and Alen for sharing good stories and cocktails in Lipe. And, of course, thank you to all the wonderful Thai people I met along the way for your friendly help.

Barbara Woolsey

A big heartfelt thanks to all those who have helped in this research and my long-time ambition to work on a Lonely Planet guide in Thailand (in no particular order): Clair Woolsey, Remy Woolsey, René Frank, Marlene Dow and family, The Toogoods (Ku, David and Cassie, plus Alex and Dylan Holtman), Andrea Schulte-Peevers, Diana Hubbell, Trish Elliott, Debby Harris, Dixie Michie, Brenda Woolsey-Hartford, Bhec Fernandez, Alyssa Gabrielle and Allexa Scarlet Masongsong, Nolan Janssen, and Garth and Gloria Pickard.

ACKNOWLEDGEMENTS

Climate map data adapted from Peel MC, Finlayson BL & McMahon TA (2007) 'Updated World Map of the Köppen-Geiger Climate Classification', *Hydrology and Earth System Sciences*, 11, 1633–44.

Illustration pp74–5 by Michael Weldon.

Cover photograph: Murals in Thailand's National Museum (p76), Bangkok, Walter Bibikow/AWL Images ©.

THIS BOOK

This 18th edition of Lonely Planet's *Thailand* guidebook was researched and written by David Eimer, Anirban Mahapatra, Daniel McCrohan, Tim Bewer, Paul Harding, Ashley Harrell, Tharik Hussain, Michael Kohn, Olivia Pozzan and Barbara Woolsey. The previous edition was written by Anita Isalska, Tim, Celeste Brash, Austin Bush, David, Damian Harper and Andy

Symington. This guidebook was produced by the following:

Destination Editor
Tanya Parker

Senior Product Editors
Daniel Bolger, Kate Chapman, Kathryn Rowan

Cartographers Rachel Imeson, Diana Von Holdt

Product Editors Ronan Abayawickrema, Paul Harding

Book Designers Fergal Condon, Meri Blazevski

Assisting Editors Judith Bamber, Nigel Chin, Michelle Coxall, Laura Crawford, Kate

Daly, Gemma Graham, Gabrielle Innes, Kate Morgan, Lauren O'Connell, Charlotte Orr, Lorna Parkes, Susan Paterson, James Smart, Fionnuala Twomey, Anna Tyler, Brana Vladisavljevic

Assisting Cartographers
Julie Dodkins, Michael Garrett

Cover Researcher Brendan Dempsey-Spencer

Thanks to Hannah Cartmel, Bruce Evans, Victoria Harrison, Karen Henderson, Kate Kiely, Kate Mathews, Catherine Naghten, Claire Rourke

Index

Map Legend

Sights
- Beach
- Bird Sanctuary
- Buddhist
- Castle/Palace
- Christian
- Confucian
- Hindu
- Islamic
- Jain
- Jewish
- Monument
- Museum/Gallery/Historic Building
- Ruin
- Shinto
- Sikh
- Taoist
- Winery/Vineyard
- Zoo/Wildlife Sanctuary
- Other Sight

Activities, Courses & Tours
- Bodysurfing
- Diving
- Canoeing/Kayaking
- Course/Tour
- Sento Hot Baths/Onsen
- Skiing
- Snorkelling
- Surfing
- Swimming/Pool
- Walking
- Windsurfing
- Other Activity

Sleeping
- Sleeping
- Camping
- Hut/Shelter

Eating
- Eating

Drinking & Nightlife
- Drinking & Nightlife
- Cafe

Entertainment
- Entertainment

Shopping
- Shopping

Information
- Bank
- Embassy/Consulate
- Hospital/Medical
- Internet
- Police
- Post Office
- Telephone
- Toilet
- Tourist Information
- Other Information

Geographic
- Beach
- Gate
- Hut/Shelter
- Lighthouse
- Lookout
- Mountain/Volcano
- Oasis
- Park
- Pass
- Picnic Area
- Waterfall

Population
- Capital (National)
- Capital (State/Province)
- City/Large Town
- Town/Village

Transport
- Airport
- Border crossing
- Bus
- Cable car/Funicular
- Cycling
- Ferry
- Metro/MTR/MRT station
- Monorail
- Parking
- Petrol station
- Skytrain/Subway station
- Taxi
- Train station/Railway
- Tram
- Underground station
- Other Transport

Routes
- Tollway
- Freeway
- Primary
- Secondary
- Tertiary
- Lane
- Unsealed road
- Road under construction
- Plaza/Mall
- Steps
- Tunnel
- Pedestrian overpass
- Walking Tour
- Walking Tour detour
- Path/Walking Trail

Boundaries
- International
- State/Province
- Disputed
- Regional/Suburb
- Marine Park
- Cliff
- Wall

Hydrography
- River, Creek
- Intermittent River
- Canal
- Water
- Dry/Salt/Intermittent Lake
- Reef

Areas

- Airport/Runway
- Beach/Desert
- Cemetery (Christian)
- Cemetery (Other)
- Glacier
- Mudflat
- Park/Forest
- Sight (Building)
- Sportsground
- Swamp/Mangrove

Note: Not all symbols displayed above appear on the maps in this book

Paul Harding

As a writer and photographer, Paul has been travelling the globe for the best part of two decades, with an interest in remote and offbeat places, islands and cultures. He's an author and contributor to more than 50 Lonely Planet guides to countries and regions as diverse as India, Belize, Vanuatu, Iran, Indonesia, New Zealand, Iceland, Finland, Philippines, Thailand and – his home patch – Australia.

Ashley Harrell

After a brief stint selling day spa coupons door-to-door in South Florida, Ashley decided she'd rather be a writer. She went to journalism grad school, convinced a newspaper to hire her, and starting covering wildlife, crime and tourism, sometimes all in the same story. Fuelling her zest for storytelling and the unknown, she travelled widely and moved often, from a tiny NYC apartment to a vast California ranch to a jungle cabin in Costa Rica, where she started writing for Lonely Planet.

Tharik Hussain

Born in Sylhet, Bangladesh, but raised in east London, Tharik is a freelance travel writer, author, journalist and occasional broadcaster who specialises in Muslim cultures. Tharik has travelled across the globe in search of forgotten Islamic heritage and written about this for the BBC, Lonely Planet, *Aljazeera* and *Arab News* amongst others. He has a Masters in Islamic Studies and has previously lived in Jeddah, Saudi Arabia. Tharik is a member of the British Guild of Travel Writers.

Michael Kohn

Michael has been working as a travel writer for over a decade. In 2003 he jumped in headfirst with Lonely Planet by taking on the Uzbekistan and Kazakhstan chapters of the *Central Asia* guidebook. Since then he has been exploring some of the remoter corners of Asia and the Middle East for LP, while also reporting the news for international media outlets. His LP titles include Sri Lanka, Tibet, Mongolia, Israel and the Palestinian Territories and Trans-Siberia Railway. Michael's particular area of interest is Mongolia, where he has covered the news for Bloomberg, the BBC and others. During his time in Mongolia he wrote *Lama of the Gobi*, a biography of the 19th century poet-monk Danzanravjaa, and *Dateline Mongolia*, a personal memoir about his time spent working as a reporter in Ulaanbaatar.

Olivia Pozzan

Olivia's travel writing career was born from a life of travel and adventure. Her unusual knack for attracting adventure has seen her caving in Oman, expedition-racing in Morocco, and trekking mountain ranges from the Himalayas to the Alps. Her veterinary career has seen her working on remote cattle stations in the outback, vetting on a camel expedition in the heart of Australia, darting lions in South Africa and working for an Arabian prince in the Middle East. With so much raw material at her fingertips, writing was a natural progression. Her articles and books have been published worldwide. For Lonely Planet, Olivia has covered regions in the Middle East, Italy and Australia. Olivia is passionate about animal welfare and has led volunteer veterinary aid projects to Cambodia. When not travelling to the world's most exotic places, she lives the beach lifestyle on the beautiful Sunshine Coast, where she is a freelance writer and practising veterinarian.

Barbara Woolsey

Barbara Woolsey was born and raised on the Canadian prairies to a Filipino mother and Irish-Scottish father – and that multicultural upbringing has fuelled a life's passion for storytelling across cultures and borders. Barbara's career started in Bangkok working for Thailand's largest English-language newspaper, then travelling around Asia as a TV host for a Bangkok-based channel. Since then, she's voyaged across five continents and almost 50 countries by plane, train and motorbike. Some highlights: a 3000km motorbike journey across India, reporting from wildlife reservations and townships in South Africa, and interviewing gang members in Caracas. In addition to writing for Lonely Planet, Barbara contributes as a journalist to newspapers, magazines, and websites with readerships around the world. She spends most of her time in her adopted home of Berlin, Germany.

t and a sense of
Wheeler needed
Asia overland to

...took several months, and at the end – broke but inspired – they sat at their kitchen table writing and stapling together their first travel guide, *Across Asia on the Cheap*. Within a week they'd sold 1500 copies. Lonely Planet was born.

Today, Lonely Planet has offices in Tennessee, Dublin and Beijing, with a network of over 2000 contributors in every corner of the globe. We share Tony's belief that 'a great guidebook should do three things: inform, educate and amuse'.

OUR WRITERS

David Eimer
David has been a journalist and writer ever since abandoning the idea of a law career in 1990. After spells working in his native London and in Los Angeles, he moved to Beijing in 2005, where he contributed to a variety of newspapers and magazines in the UK. Since then, he has travelled and lived across China and in numerous cities in Southeast Asia, including Bangkok, Phnom Penh and Yangon. He has been covering China, Myanmar and Thailand for Lonely Planet since 2006.

Anirban Mahapatra
Anirban is a travel writer, photographer & filmmaker who has authored multiple editions of Lonely Planet's bestselling *India* guidebook, as well as several regional handbooks. He has written and curated Lonely Planet guidebooks on Bangladesh, Sri Lanka & Bhutan, designed content models and held author workshops for Lonely Planet and made videos and documentaries for international television networks, corporates as well as ministries under the Government of India. When not travelling the world, he lives in Kolkata and Bangkok.

Daniel McCrohan
With a Greek father, a Spanish grandfather, an Irish grandmother and a Chinese wife, Daniel has always looked beyond his English homeland for influence and inspiration. He's been travelling the world, on-and-off, for 25 years, and has been writing Lonely Planet guidebooks (42 and counting) for more than a decade. He specialises in China and India, but has travelled extensively throughout Thailand, forming a special bond over the years with Isan, a region he loves. Follow his adventures on Twitter (@danielmccrohan) or at danielmccrohan.com.

Tim Bewer
While growing up, Tim didn't travel much. He's spent most of his adult life making up for this, and has since visited over 80 countries, including most in Southeast Asia. After university he worked briefly as a legislative assistant before quitting capitol life to backpack around West Africa. It was during this trip that the idea of becoming a freelance travel writer and photographer was hatched, and he's been at it ever since. He lives in Khon Kaen, and blogs at Tim's Thailand (www.timsthailand.com).

OVER MORE
PAGE WRITERS

Published by Lonely Planet Global Limited
CRN 554153
18th edition – Oct 2021
ISBN 978 1 78701 780 1
© Lonely Planet 2021   Photographs © as indicated 2021
10 9 8 7 6 5 4 3 2 1
Printed in China